st

e

em
51),

ue

Management Information Systems
The Manager's View

Third Edition

Management Information Systems

The Manager's View

Robert Schultheis
Mary Sumner
Both of
Southern Illinois University at Edwardsville

Integrated Cases Prepared by
Douglas Bock
Southern Illinois University at Edwardsville

IRWIN

Chicago • Bogotá • Boston • Buenos Aires • Caracas
London • Madrid • Mexico City • Sydney • Toronto

We recognize that certain terms in this book are trademarks, and we have made every effort to print these throughout the text with the capitalization and punctuation used by the holder of the trademark.

WordPerfect® is a registered trademark of WordPerfect Corporation.

Screen shots [®1994] Lotus Development Corporation. Used with permission of Lotus Development Corporation. Lotus 1-2-3 is a registered trademark of Lotus Development Corporation.

Screen shots reprinted with permission from Microsoft Corporation.

dBASE III Plus® and dBase IV® are registered trademarks of Ashton-Tate.

Senior sponsoring editor: Rick Williamson
Editorial coordinator: Christine Wright
Marketing manager: Jim Lewis
Project editor: Waivah Clement
Production supervisor: Ann Cassady
Designer: Randy Scott Design, Aurora, Ill.
Art coordinator: Heather Burbridge
Compositor: The Clarinda Company
Typeface: 10/12 Caledonia
Printer: Von Hoffmann Press, Inc.

Library of Congress Cataloging-in-Publication Data

Schultheis, Robert A.
Management information systems : the manager's view / Robert Schultheis, Mary Sumner : integrated cases prepared by Douglas Bock. — 3rd ed.
p. cm.
Includes bibliographical references and index.
ISBN 0-256-13640-8
1. Management information systems. I. Sumner, Mary. II. Bock, Douglas Brian. III. Title
T58.6.S328 1995
658.4′038—dc20 94–3520

Printed in the United States of America

2 3 4 5 6 7 8 9 0 VH 1 0 9 8 7 6 5

PREFACE

THE APPROACH

Management Information Systems: The Manager's View, third edition, represents a managerial approach to information systems concepts and applications. Managers today have increasing responsibility for determining their information system needs and for designing and implementing information systems that support these needs. This has been evident for some time with the advent of the PC and end-user computing. New technologies, such as powerful desktop computer systems, distributed information systems, telecommuting, notebook and handheld computers, local area networks, and graphical user interfaces, have created new opportunities for managers. Students who are majoring in general management, human resource management, accounting, marketing, production, finance, and management information systems (MIS) should understand how information systems support key business functions, what information resources are available to them, and how both MIS and other professionals are involved in the systems development process.

This book serves the needs of graduate and undergraduate students enrolling in their first MIS course who may not yet have decided to become MIS majors. The book also provides MIS majors with the user-manager's viewpoint of information systems. The book supports introductory information systems courses required by many other programs, such as political science, allied health, and educational administration, as well.

WHY WE WROTE THIS BOOK

Many students who enroll in entry-level management information systems courses are not MIS majors. These students are drawn to an entry-level course for many reasons. Some are required to take the course as part of their majors in the hope that they will then understand how information systems can be used in their disciplines. Most students majoring in a discipline within a school of business are required to take an introductory management information systems course. Others take the course because they wish to complete several MIS courses to make themselves more marketable. Some enroll because they are simply interested in computers and hope that they will find the study of information systems interesting.

For whatever reason, the field of management information systems has remained popular with students who are not MIS majors. Most of these students begin their study of the field by enrolling in the introductory management information systems course at either the undergraduate or graduate level. Nearly all of these students are studying to become managers: business managers, managers of governmental agencies, managers in the music industry, managers in the health industry, managers in the agricultural industry—in fact, managers in a broad array of industries and disciplines.

This book was written to serve these types of students. We felt a text was needed that took a managerial approach to information systems. Thus, we designed the text to do the following:

1. Emphasize how managers can and should be involved with systems planning, development, and implementation.
2. Emphasize what information systems resources are available to managers for decision support.
3. Emphasize how these resources can be used at all levels of decision making and in the major functional management areas.
4. Show how information technology can be used to support business strategy without overwhelming students with technical details.

WHAT'S NEW IN THIS EDITION

This edition incorporates a number of additions and modifications to the second edition. The changes include the following.

Updates for New Technology and Practices

Management information systems is an extremely dynamic area of study. It should be no surprise to find, therefore, that in the three years since the second edition, numerous changes have taken place in computer hardware, software, and information systems theories, practices, and technologies. A thorough revision and updating of the second edition was necessary to incorporate these changes. For example, workflow software, information system reengineering, wireless communications, PCI and PCMCIA bus adapter technology, personal digital assistants and pen-based computing, Pentium, PowerPC, and DEC Alpha chips, flash memory, green machines, desktop video and desktop conferencing, the Internet, asynchronous transmission mode and other high-speed communications protocols, and standard generalized markup language and portable documents are just a few of the new topics that have been added to the third edition. In addition, many topics have received increased space in the text because they have received increased attention in the industry. For example, wireless computing, client/server computing, parallel processing, multiuser operating systems, multimedia systems, EDI and electronic marketing systems, groupware, desktop management and imaging systems, and fax systems are just a few of the topics that received more attention in this edition than in the last.

New concepts are also included in this revision. In Chapters 1 and 21, you will find a discussion of reengineering, and you will learn how companies are reengineering business processes in order to cut bureaucracy and improve their ability to serve customer needs. An entire chapter (Chapter 3) is now devoted to the strategic uses of information technology. This chapter includes a discussion of information partnering, the electronic marketplace, and capabilities-based competition. It also includes an analysis of the risks and impacts of strategic information systems.

The decision support systems chapter (Chapter 14) now includes a description of group decision support systems and electronic meeting systems. The artificial intelligence and expert systems chapter (Chapter 15) includes a new case study on using expert systems support for investment planning.

In Chapter 16, Information Systems Planning, three techniques managers can use to determine their information requirements are described, analyzed, and compared. These are Critical Success Factors, Business Systems Planning, and Ends/Means Analysis.

Chapter 21 closes with a recapitulation of reengineering principles and provides an analysis of how information technology is facilitating changes in organizational structure—particularly through the decentralization of decision making and the flattening of traditional organizational hierarchies.

New Chapters

Two new chapters have been added. These include a chapter on the strategic uses of information systems (Chapter 3), and a chapter on security and ethics of information systems (Chapter 20). Although the second edition included considerable discussion of strategic information systems, we felt that this area was so important that it should receive increased attention. The topics of information systems security and the ethics of information have been added to the third edition because of their growing importance to managers, especially end-user managers.

Additionally, the chapters on the introduction to information systems, office automation, and key issues in information systems have been substantially rewritten and, in some cases, relocated within the text.

More Software-Related Problems

Many more software problems have been added to the Problems section found at the end of each chapter. They include spreadsheet problems, database problems, project management problems, an investment analysis problem, a mapping problem, and forecasting problems.

Free Software

In addition, four software products are provided free to teachers who use this text including:

1. Forecasting software (4KAST).
2. Demonstration diskette of mapping software (MapInfo).
3. Investment analysis software (Value/Screen III).
4. Project scheduling software (FastTrack Schedule).

More Problems and Cases

The number of questions at the end of each chapter has been increased when needed to reflect updated technology and issues. The number of cases found at the end of most chapters has also increased.

New Integrated Cases

A new series of comprehensive, integrated cases, all based on the same firm, has been added, with one case appearing at the end of each part of the text. These cases allow students to integrate what they have learned from the chapters that precede the cases.

Presentation Graphics Case Support

A supplementary presentation graphics product, developed by Leah Pietron of the University of Nebraska, Omaha, is available that supplies a slide show for every end-of-chapter case and integrated case in the text. The slide shows are designed to run independent of the presentation graphics software used to prepare them; that is, they are provided in run time version form. Each slide show displays the main points of each case, discussion questions for each case, and the questions for each case found in the text. The booklet that accompanies the package explains the use of the slide shows and provides miniatures of the slides available in each show.

Classroom Video Support

Ten video tapes are available from the Irwin Information Systems Video Library for use with this text. The videos cover the following topics: Introduction to Information Systems (Chapter 1), Technology (Chapters 4–8), Multimedia Presentations (Chapter 5), Telecommunications (Chapter 7), Finance Systems (Chapter 10), Marketing Systems (Chapter 11), Manufacturing Systems (Chapter 12), Human Resource Management Systems (Chapter 13), Corporate Training Systems (Chapter 13), and Information for the Retail Market (Chapters 11 and 12). The video tapes are all about 10 to 12 minutes in length and can be used to enrich and supplement regular classroom instruction.

WHAT THIS BOOK IS ALL ABOUT

Clearly, the most important activity in which managers engage is decision making. For many managers, decisions must be made in a very competitive environment. This text focuses on how information systems support managerial decision making. Specifically, the text is organized around the three major levels of managerial decision making: operational decisions, tactical decisions, and strategic planning decisions. This organizational theme is followed throughout the text to focus students on the types of decisions that managers must make. The book also emphasizes how information systems help managers provide their organizations with a competitive advantage. This approach recognizes that the design and use of information systems have become part of every manager's job and that information systems planning is no longer the sole province of information systems professionals.

Typical introductory texts in management information systems present the field from the specialist's view. Even many texts that assume a management perspective still present many information systems topics from the traditional, specialist viewpoint. This text overcomes these limitations by providing the following.

A User-Manager Perspective. Many texts cover the system life cycle from the traditional systems analyst perspective instead of from a user-manager perspective. They provide detailed descriptions of the systems analyst's role in requirements definition, design, and implementation rather than explaining how the user-manager should be involved in these cycle activities. In short, many texts lead students through the various stages of the systems life cycle as if they were expected to become professional systems analysts. This book leads students through the cycle expecting them to become functional area managers.

A Managerial Emphasis. Many texts present technical hardware and software concepts in too detailed a manner for students who are not MIS majors. The underlying criterion for selecting the content for this text was "Does the manager need to know it?" Thus, even in the chapters that cover computer hardware, computer software, database management systems, and communications systems, the overriding concern is "What does the manager need to know about these topics?" We believe that students will find these chapters interesting and easy to read. We also believe that students will appreciate that these chapters continuously refer to why managers need to know the technical concepts presented and provide many examples of how managers can use technical information in decision making.

Practical, Management-Oriented Cases. Many texts do not provide enough problems and cases that place students in the role of user-managers and ask them to use information systems skills and concepts. This text provides many problems and cases in which students must assume the role of managers and make decisions about information systems problems. Many of these problems and cases are software supported; that is, they can be used in conjunction with templates or data files contained on the data diskette, forecasting software contained on the data diskette, and demonstration diskettes, which are available from the publisher. In addition to the end-of-chapter cases, the text also includes integrated, comprehensive cases involving experiences at one company following each of the five parts of the text.

Managerial Coverage. Many introductory texts provide a survey of information systems topics. Thus, they really are short systems courses. This text selects information systems topics on the basis of their importance to the manager. Rather than providing a survey course for majors, this text helps managers understand information systems concepts and applications.

The Integration of Information Theory and Practice. Major information management theories important to the manager are covered. These include

1. Hammer's framework for categorizing the impact of information systems (IS)—efficiency, effectiveness, and transformation (Chapter 1).
2. Mintzberg's framework for analyzing the structure of organizations (Chapter 2).
3. Anthony's paradigm of decision making—operational, tactical, and strategic decisions (Chapter 9).
4. Nolan's stage assessment for the analysis of the evolution of information systems (Chapter 9).
5. Keen's theories of decision support systems design (Chapter 14).
6. Buchanan and Linowes's concept of distributed data processing (Chapter 14).
7. Porter's analysis of competitive strategy (Chapters 3 and 16).
8. Porter and Millar's value chain analysis of organizational activities (Chapter 3).
9. Rockart's critical success factors (Chapter 16).
10. Gremillion and Pyburn's framework for evaluating systems development alternatives (Chapter 18).
11. McFarlan's portfolio approach to evaluating the risks of systems development projects (Chapter 18).
12. Schein's theory of organizational learning (Chapter 9).
13. Information partnering and electronic marketplaces (Chapter 3).
14. Group decision support systems and electronic meeting systems (Chapter 14).
15. Reengineering business processes (Chapters 1 and 21).
16. Impact of information technology on organization structure (Chapter 21).

The book presents each theory or framework and then applies it to real information systems issues so students can develop an understanding of how to apply the theories to real-life situations.

New Information Technology. New information technology is presented throughout the text. Students will have opportunities to learn how new technology creates opportunities for an organization by providing a competitive advantage, by identifying new markets, or by improving productivity. To cite a few examples, students learn about local area networks (Chapter 7), manufacturing software tools (Chapter 12), decision support tools (Chapter 14), executive information systems (Chapter 14), expert systems and artificial intelligence (Chapter 15), and computer-assisted software engineering tools (Chapter 17).

Microcomputer Technology. The use of microcomputer systems to support management decision making has become commonplace. As a result, information about the use of microcomputers and microcomputer software is integrated extensively throughout the text. The technology of microcomputers is first presented in Chapters 4 and 5. Microcomputer software used by managers is then presented in Chapters 6 and 7 as part of the database and communications systems chapters, and again in the chapters pertaining to the functional business areas (Chapters 10 through 13).

FEATURES

This text has numerous features of use to both teachers and students.

End-of-Chapter Questions

Each chapter ends with a series of short questions that are designed to measure student understanding of the facts and concepts presented in the chapter. Students will find that reading these questions before they read the chapter will help them focus on the important points developed in the chapter. They also will find that answering the questions after reading a chapter is an effective means of reviewing the content of the chapter. Teachers may use these questions as part of quizzes or examinations.

Following the review questions are a series of more complex questions that usually ask the students to compare or evaluate what they have learned. These questions are useful as discussion questions for a classroom session.

Problems

Like most instructors, we like to provide our students with many practical, hands-on activities. This text provides numerous practical problems and cases at the end of each chapter. A number of the problems are supported by software, in the form of data sets for data-based and forecasting problems and spreadsheet templates for "what if" problems. In many of the chapters, students can choose among problems requiring use of spreadsheet software, database software, mapping software, project management software, and forecasting software.

Chapter Cases

Each chapter (except Chapters 15 and 16) contains two to five cases for students to solve. These cases are primarily targeted to the content presented within the chapter. They require students to analyze organizational situations using the information from the chapter.

Integrated Cases

At the end of each part of the text is a comprehensive case that requires students to integrate what they have learned from the chapters in that part.

Examples and Boxes

Each chapter contains many practical, management-oriented examples and cases. Each chapter also presents current, real-life examples of information systems in boxed sections within the narrative.

Other Student Study Features

Student study skills are enhanced through an introduction to each chapter ("Manager's View"), a chapter summary ("Management Summary"), the highlighting of key terms ("Key Terms for Managers"), and the glossary of terms found at the end of the text.

Text Style

The text is written in a clear, readable writing style with a "you" emphasis to help students relate to the concepts and ideas presented. Although many of the concepts presented are complex, the way in which they are presented is designed to be just the opposite.

HOW THIS BOOK WAS DEVELOPED

This book was developed recognizing that the introductory information systems course often consists of large numbers of students, including majors and nonmajors. The content and sequence of the text and the problems and cases have been tested in our own classes. Our students provided important feedback that we used to revise the content, problems, and cases. However, the text was not based solely on our own perspective. Many faculty members throughout the country, both those who use the text and those who do not, reviewed the revision of the text continuously as it was developed. Their pointed criticisms and suggestions improved the organization, content, and style of the text.

THE INSTRUCTIONAL MATERIALS PACKAGE

The entire instructional package consists of several components.

Text

The text consists of 21 chapters organized into five parts:

Part I—Information Systems
Part II—Computer System Resources
Part III—Common Business Application Areas
Part IV—Planning and Development of Information Systems
Part V—The Management of Information Systems

Each chapter begins with "Manager's View," which describes why current and future managers need to learn the topics in the chapter. Each chapter closes with a management summary, key terms, review questions and discussion questions, practical problems, and cases. A comprehensive case appears at the end of each part.

Data Disk

A data diskette accompanies the Instructor's Manual and provides data sets, spreadsheet templates, and a forecasting program that allows students to make market projections. The data sets are designed to be used by dBASE III PLUS and dBASE IV; however, they can be read by many other microcomputer database management systems. The spreadsheet templates can be read by Lotus 1-2-3, 1-2-3 clones, or by any spreadsheet program that can read 1-2-3 files.

Free Forecasting Software

Also included on the data diskette is 4KAST, a set of shareware forecasting programs developed by Douglas Bock. This software can be used to solve the several forecasting problems, using linear or multiple regression, included in the Problems sections of chapters. This software may be used without charge by students who have purchased the textbook.

Free Investment Analysis Software

A copy of a demonstration diskette for Value/Screen III, the investment analysis tool offered by Value Line, is available to instructors who use this text. The diskette is a full-featured implementation of the original Value/Screen III program. The diskette contains stock data on about 300 companies, however, instead of the 1,700 companies included on the commercial version of the product. The software is used in the Problems section of Chapter 10, Accounting and Financial Information Systems.

Free Mapping Software Demonstration Diskette

A copy of a demonstration diskette for MapInfo, a desktop mapping software product of MapInfo Corporation, is also available to instructors who use this text. The diskette contains a presentation of the uses of desktop mapping software and is used in the Problems section of Chapter 11, Marketing Information Systems.

Free Project Management Software

A copy of a demonstration diskette for FastTrack Schedule for Windows, which produces Gantt charts, is also available to instructors. The diskette is a full implementation of the commercial product with the exception that the student cannot save his or her work. The software is used in the Problems section of Chapter 12, Manufacturing and Production Information Systems.

Instructor's Manual

A companion Instructor's Manual provides the following for each chapter.

Teaching Suggestions. These provide a variety of ideas for presenting each chapter and the integrated cases, including suggestions for introducing topics, overcoming typical student learning problems, using the transparency masters provided in the instructor's manual, and sequencing the topics.

Answers to Chapter Questions, Problems, Cases, and the Integrated Cases.
Suggested answers to end-of-chapter exercises and integrated cases are provided on a chapter-by-chapter basis.

Assignment Schedules. Both 15-week and 10-week suggested schedules are included in the Instructor's Manual.

The text includes several chapters on the functional areas of finance, marketing, production and personnel. These functional areas are used to develop an understanding of information systems at the operational (transaction), tactical (management control), and strategic planning levels. If you prefer to provide instruction directly in operational, tactical, and strategic planning information systems without emphasizing the functional areas, we provide an assignment schedule which allows you to do that.

Transparency Masters

A separate companion document provides transparency masters taken generally from text illustrations may prove useful for class discussion.

Test Bank

A third companion document provides a series of true-false, multiple choice, and short case questions for each chapter along with the suggested answers. There are also one-hour exams of 50 multiple choice questions and a two-hour exams of 100 multiple choice questions.

Computest 3

A computerized testing package, Computest 3, allows you to select test questions, organize the questions in the order you want, and print them for exams.

Case Slide Shows

A supplementary presentation graphics product is available that supplies a slide show for every end-of-chapter case and integrated case in the text. This product is described in more detail under the title, "Presentation Graphics Case Support," earlier in the Preface.

ACKNOWLEDGMENTS

We would like to acknowledge the contributions made by a number of people who helped us in the development and refinement of this text. First, we would like to thank Rick Williamson and Christine Wright, who reviewed our ideas and our work and managed the text development process.

Second, many faculty members in management information systems and computer information systems departments who used the text reviewed our work constantly as we developed and refined it. Additional faculty, who did not use the text, also reviewed our work. Their criticisms and suggestions were extremely valuable. These reviewers were: David Bateman, Saint Mary's University; Roger Bloomquist, University of North Dakota–Grand Forks; Drew S. Cobb, The Johns Hopkins University; Frank G. Duserick, Alfred University; Richard T. Fernald, Midlands Technical College; Virginia R. Gibson, University of Maine–Orono; Thomas Hilton, Utah State University; Albert L. Lederer, Oakland University; John C. Malley, University of Central Arkansas; Judy Mondy, McNeese State University; Michael R. Padbury, Arapahoe Community College; Ann D. Theis, Adrian College; Jack W. Thornton, East Carolina University; Robert W. Van Cleave, University of Minnesota–Minneapolis; and L. Richard Ye, California State University–Northridge.

A special thanks goes to our colleague, Douglas Bock, who prepared the integrated cases that appear at the end of each part of the text and who developed the 4Kast software.

We would also like to thank the students at Southern Illinois University at Edwardsville who tested the text materials and provided us with many ideas for improvement.

Robert A. Schultheis
Mary Sumner

Contents in Brief

Contents

Chapter 13
Human Resource Information Systems, 488

Chapter 14
Decision Support Systems, 522

Management Information Systems
The Manager's View

Part I

Information Systems

As a manager, you will use computer-based information systems throughout your career. Information technology supports every business function, from the purchasing of goods and services to the servicing of products. To be useful, information technology should serve business needs. An on-line diagnostic hotline connected to an appliance maintenance database can provide customers with timely help diagnosing small appliance problems. A frequent flight bonus program can create customer loyalty to an airline. A national rental car reservations information system can provide customers with access to rental information in remote sites.

To be a successful manager, you must be able to identify information systems needs that create a business advantage. That is, you must understand how information technology can provide better products, enhance existing services, and create new business opportunities. Then you will be able to plan and develop information systems that improve market share, counteract rivals, and facilitate linkages with customers and suppliers.

Chapter 1 will start you on the road to being a successful manager by describing the fundamental concepts of information systems in business. You will learn how information systems support three types of business objectives: efficiency, effectiveness, and transformation. You will also learn how information technology provides some organizations with a competitive advantage.

In Chapter 2, you will learn about the systems approach and how it can be useful in problem solving. You will learn about various types of organizational structures and how information systems are used in each. This chapter provides fundamental knowledge that you can apply throughout the text, particularly in analyzing management case studies.

Chapter 3 will describe how organizations are using information technology to gain a competitive advantage. You will learn about the *strategic* uses of information technology, the emerging electronic marketplace, and how information partnerships are being organized to address the needs of customers, buyers, and suppliers.

An Introduction to Information Management

C 1

Chapter Outline

Manager's View

A number of trends affect today's business environment. One of them is the transition from an industrial economy to an information services economy. Beginning with the Industrial Revolution, productivity gains in the U.S. economy were tied to industrial production and manufacturing of goods and services. Since the 1960s, 50 percent of all productivity gains have been attributable to the use of information technology. The ability to capture, store, process, and distribute information is critical to most organizations.

Today the traditional organization is being transformed into the information-based organization, which uses information and information technology to produce significant changes in work patterns. The organization of the past was highly structured and composed of many different functions. In this type of organization, each unit maintained its own information. The organization of the future will have a flexible, changeable structure. Teams consisting of specialists from various functional areas will work together on projects that address new market opportunities. Shared information databases will link individuals to each other.

In the future, managers in the information-based organization will become responsible for using and managing technology. They will use information technology (IT) as a tool to provide effective customer service, analyze marketing opportunities, and manage production and manufacturing operations. IT will become an integral part of business. To understand the information-based company of the future, let's first learn why traditional organizations are evolving into information-based organizations.

THE EVOLUTION OF INFORMATION TECHNOLOGY

Historically, organizations have become hierarchies of complex functions over time. One of the fundamental principles influencing the evolution of industrial organizations was specialization of labor. The division of labor led to the fragmentation of work, with workers in many different areas—marketing, manufacturing, accounting, and so on—performing specialized tasks.

A second factor in the development of modern organizations is the command-and-control structure that can be traced back to early railroad companies, which required predictable, safe control systems. Today's business bureaucracy, with its formalized operating procedures and formal lines of authority, evolved from these early railroad organizations. The standard pyramid, with work broken down by departments—each with its own budget and control system—is still a common organizational form today.

The third factor influencing the performance of modern organizations was the nature of the post–World War II market: It was a seller's market. Given the unrelenting demand for goods and services, customers were willing to buy anything that was available. Customer service was not necessarily a critical success factor.

What Has Changed

In the 1990s, the nature of the market has changed. Customers have power over suppliers that they didn't have before. Part of this customer power comes from access to information. When prospective car buyers can look up dealer invoice cost on a new auto in *Consumer Reports,* they gain new leverage over the dealer.

Secondly, competition has changed. Look at the success of Wal-Mart. Wal-Mart changed the retailing equation by developing new strategies that focused upon customers' needs. By continuously dispatching goods from distribution centers to its stores, a process called *cross-docking,* Wal-Mart made sure that popular retail items were always in stock. Using its own fleet of 2,000 company-owned trucks, Wal-Mart replenishes stores inventories continually. Such increased responsiveness to customer needs is a key factor in competitive success in the 1990s.

The third factor influencing business in the 1990s is technology. Information technology is a factor in Wal-Mart's success. Wal-Mart uses a private satellite communications system to send point-of-sale data directly to its 4,000 vendors so they can meet Wal-Mart's purchasing needs on a more timely basis. Technology also makes it possible for Wal-Mart store managers to exchange information with each other and with management via regular videoconferences.

Information technology provides a means to focus on the customer. By carefully tracking and analyzing customer buying behavior, companies like Wal-Mart can allocate inventory to meet customer needs. They can also use information technology to provide better customer service. Whirlpool has a customer service network that routes customer calls to the same service representative again and again, thus creating a sense of personal service. Otis Elevator uses a service management network to provide on-line technical service for almost 100,000 elevators. When a support call is dispatched to service technicians, the system automatically provides data on the maintenance history of a particular elevator. Many microcomputer vendors give their customers access to bulletin board systems that provide up-to-date technical information on product features.

Finally, information technology is transforming the scope of doing business. Worldwide communications networks enable businesses to operate in global markets and to reach new customers. Information technology also makes it possible to do business 24 hours a day. Individuals on project teams may work in distant locations and interact using electronic communications networks and videoconferencing facilities. For example, programmers in India can work with project leaders in Cincinnati on large software development projects, coordinating their efforts through electronic mail. This chapter and subsequent chapters explain more about how information technology is extending organizational boundaries.

THE REENGINEERING OF WORK

In the 1990s and beyond, there will be winning companies and losing companies—the difference is likely to be the ability to serve customers better with the products and services they want. The ability to serve customers will mean a fundamental shift in the way many companies do business that will involve redesigning basic business processes.

The reason many companies are inefficient today is that no one is in charge of fundamental business processes such as order fulfillment or accounts payable. Companies consist of dozens of fragmented units, and processes are broken down into many different pieces. Information is also fragmented because it is "owned" by each unit involved in the process. The result is that simple processes get bogged down in the fragmentation of work, backlogs occur, and ultimately the customer suffers. For example, a customer who requests a home improvement loan may wait days while the application is moved from desk to desk. At each step, different files may be checked and different databases updated. Figure 1–1 shows the isolated "buckets" of data that can develop to support specific business functions.

We can cite several examples of businesses that improved their performance by reengineering the traditional ways business processes are organized. Hammer and

Figure 1–1
Data maintained by many organizational units

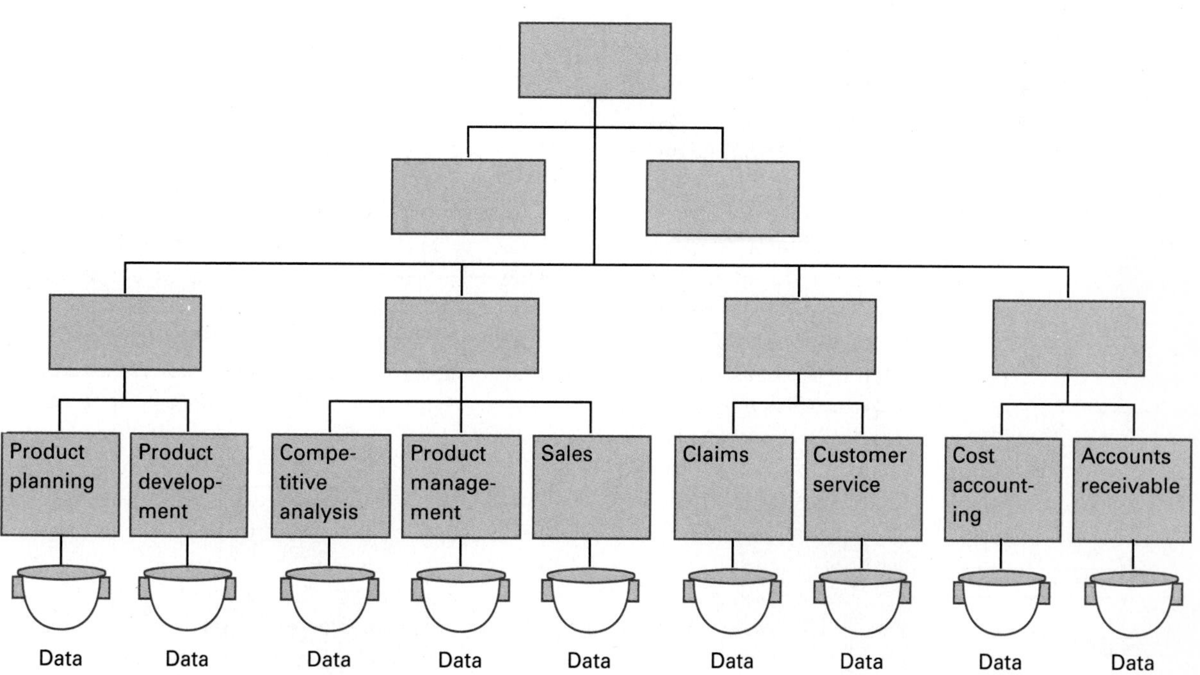

Champy describe a number of reengineering examples in their book, *Re-engineering the Corporation*. In almost every case, information technology is a critical factor in changing business processes.

Ford Motor Company's Accounts Payable System. Ford's widely known revamping of its accounts payable system was motivated by a striking comparison: Ford had 500 people in Accounts Payable, whereas Mazda had only five. What accounted for the difference was that Ford's accounts payable procedure involved multiple departments: Purchasing, Receiving, and Accounts Payable. In the old process, Purchasing sent a purchase order to the vendor and a copy to Accounts Payable. When the vendor shipped the goods, a clerk in Receiving completed a receiving document and sent it to Accounts Payable. When Accounts Payable received the invoice from the vendor, it matched the invoice with the purchase order and the receiving document. If these three documents didn't match, then more people became involved. Time and paperwork complicated the process.

The new process (see Figure 1–2) applies this business rule: "We pay when we receive the goods," instead of "We pay when we receive the invoice." In the new process, the purchase order amount is entered into a database when a purchase order is generated. When the goods arrive, a clerk in receiving checks the terminal to determine if the shipment contents correspond to the outstanding purchase order amount in the database. If the shipment is correct, a check is sent to the vendor. This

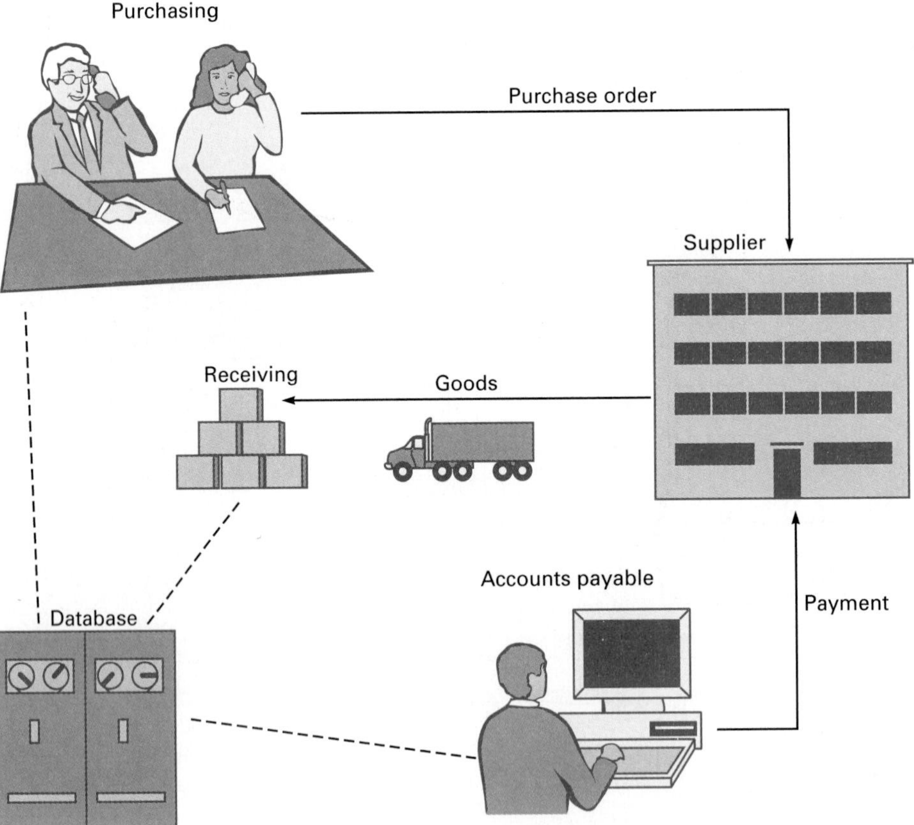

Figure 1–2
The reengineered accounts payable process at Ford

new process circumvents the possibility that the invoice won't match the purchase order or the receiving document, and it focuses upon the critical issue: paying for goods that are received.

Technology is an important part of the new process. The shared Purchasing/Receiving/Accounts Payable database makes it possible to integrate the three functions to accomplish the overall business process, order procurement, successfully.

IBM Credit. A second example of reengineering comes from IBM Credit, a subsidiary of IBM responsible for financing the computers, software, and services that IBM Corporation sells. A customer request for financing in the original system began a multistep credit authorization process involving multiple departments. This process could drag on for as long as two weeks, even though the actual work took only 90 minutes. Too many people—a pricer, a checker, and so on—were involved.

In the old system, an IBM sales representative called in a credit request. Then a credit specialist entered the information into a computer system and checked the borrower's creditworthiness. Next, the credit specialist dispatched the results to the business practices department, which modified the loan contract in response to the customer request and updated a computer file. Then, the credit information was transmitted to a pricer who keyed it into another computer file and determined the interest rate. Finally, information on the credit decision was relayed to a clerical group, which generated a quote letter for the salesperson to give to the customer. This process took from six days to two weeks and sometimes caused customers to seek alternative financing sources.

The redesigned credit issuance process included a newly created position, the "deal structurer," who is equipped with a desktop workstation with various databases needed to make the credit authorization decision from beginning to end. As you can see, information technology was critical to reengineering this process.

Xerox's Product Development Process. The product development process at Xerox was a good candidate for reengineering. Xerox's original product development process was predominantly sequential, which meant that workers on parts of the process had to wait until previous steps were completed. This created numerous bottlenecks and delays.

In the new process, called *concurrent engineering,* (see Figure 1–3), information technology plays a critical role. Using a computer-assisted design and manufacturing (CAD/CAM) system and an integrated database, engineers can develop design specifications for products in half the time.

Wal-Mart's Inventory Management Process. Wal-Mart reengineered the management of its Pampers inventory by letting the vendor, Procter & Gamble, take control. Wal-Mart lets Procter & Gamble know how much stock it moves from its distribution centers into its stores, and Procter & Gamble in turn lets Wal-Mart know how much it needs to reorder. With this reorder information, Procter & Gamble can anticipate Wal-Mart's demand and schedule its production to replenish the Wal-Mart stores continually. Wal-Mart benefits from this program because it can offload its inventory management function to a vendor and receive inventory into its stores even before it pays Procter & Gamble.

Hewlett-Packard's Purchasing Process. A final example shows how technology enabled Hewlett-Packard to integrate a centralized purchasing process with decentralized operations. To improve local operations, Hewlett-Packard gave its divisions autonomy over purchasing. Although decentralized purchasing could have resulted in the loss

Figure 1–3
Product development process

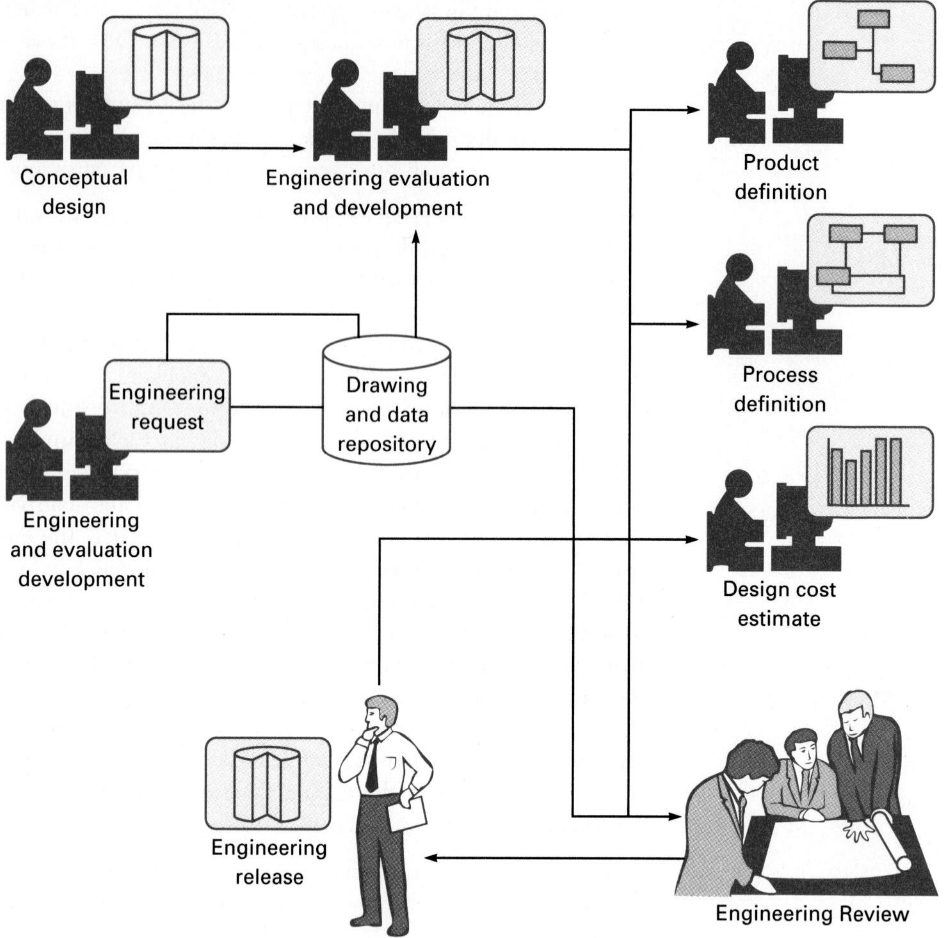

of corporatewide quantity discounts, Hewlett-Packard overcame the problem by creating a standard purchasing database. When a division wanted to order copiers, for example, it could look up the corporate volume discounts and use these prices for its orders. The use of a shared database provided decentralized autonomy along with centralized control.

IMPACT OF TECHNOLOGY

Technology plays an important role in rethinking business processes—it is instrumental in revolutionizing the business environment. Throughout this text you will learn about applications of information technology that enable firms to reengineer their business processes.

Shared **databases** give various units access to the same data. For example, customer databases can be shared by loan officers at autonomous bank branches. Imagine what would happen without a shared database. A prospective loan applicant could obtain a $10 million loan at six different branches, despite a credit limit of $10 million. Using a shared database, loan officers can check on outstanding loans as well as credit history with multiple branches so that customers cannot obtain unauthorized credit.

Notebook Computers. Salesmen with notebook computers can gain access to information at the home office, including electronic mail, price quotes, and promotional information. It is not unusual to see all types of executives carrying notebook computers on airplanes. With linkages to external communications networks, these notebook computers can serve as "offices in a briefcase."

Interactive Videodisk. Using interactive videodisk technology, retailers such as Sears can explain product features and answer consumer questions from the sales floor. Automobile dealers, insurance companies, and other retailers all use videodisk technology to explain product features. Aside from customer service applications, videodisk technology is used extensively in training and education. Students can learn everything from a new procedure in automotive technology to an insurance sales technique using videodisk technology.

Other new technologies will continue to be introduced in the 1990s. Expert systems, decision support tools, high-performance computers, infrared networks, interactive videodisk, distance learning systems, and optical scanning systems all represent new technologies that can transform the nature of work.

A common managerial mistake is to select a new technology and superimpose it on current practices. In this situation, technology drives the application. A manager learns about a new technology such as interactive videodisk and tries to implement it without first defining how it can improve current business processes. The problem with this approach is that the organization may invest in a new technology that really isn't needed.

The manager must learn to let applications drive the use of technology. That is, there must be an underlying *goal* technology can support. If the underlying goal is to distribute training materials to remote dealer sites more efficiently, then interactive videodisk may be an effective technology. If the objective is to provide timely information about the location of railroad freight cars, then freight car scanning technology may provide an effective tool.

THE PURPOSE OF INFORMATION TECHNOLOGY

This section provides a framework for determining the applications of information technology that will help you identify applications that have an impact upon the individual, the functional unit, and the organization as a whole. These applications can be placed into three categories: those designed to improve **efficiency,** those designed to improve **effectiveness,** and those designed to facilitate **transformation.**

Efficiency can be defined as doing things right. An efficient office worker, for example, can update hundreds of documents per hour. An efficient information system can update thousands of employee or student records per minute. Historically, computer-based information processing systems have supported efficiency by automating routine paperwork processing tasks.

Effectiveness can be defined as doing the *right* things. This means doing the things that need to be done to achieve important business results. An effective sales manager, for example, focuses on tasks that pay off in increased sales volumes. Information systems can help managers be more effective. For example, a prospect database housed on a PC may enable a sales manager to identify sales prospects with high potential and direct his staff's attention to contacting those prospects.

The third objective of applying information technology is transformation—using information technology to change the way you do business. This may mean changing the nature of the product or service being delivered or entirely transforming the way business is done in a functional unit or the whole organization. For example, for years Sears maintained extensive databases on customer sales histories and buying preferences that allow the company to target its marketing and promotion strategy to high-potential prospects. Now, Sears is selling access to its customer databases, thus offering a totally different service than its traditional line of business, retailing. An information-based service has in some ways transformed Sears' original line of business.

Next we'll consider how applications that achieve the objectives of efficiency, effectiveness, and transformation affect the individual, the functional unit, and the organization as a whole. Table 1–1 summarizes these objectives.

Impact on the Individual

At the individual level, applications of information technology impact efficiency, effectiveness, and transformation. An individual can use a word processing program, for example, to automate retyping letters. A manager can use a spreadsheet to automate routine budget calculations. These applications are designed to improve efficiency by providing automated tools to support specific tasks.

Other applications improve the effectiveness of the secretary or manager. If a secretary uses a prospect data base to merge prospect data with follow-up letters on sales calls, the combination word processing–database application improves effectiveness because these letters can improve sales—a fundamental objective of the business.

In some ways, transformation is the most challenging outcome of information technology. By using a portable personal computer, a manager can perform "what-if" analyses for investment prospects during sales calls. A prospective customer, for example, may be weighing the advantages and disadvantages of alternative investment options—say, in stocks, bonds, and mutual funds. Sitting in the customer's living room with a PC in hand, the salesperson can compare the anticipated yields on different investment alternatives and give the customer a much better idea of the potential returns on different programs. This capability changes the way the salesperson sells investments. This is an example of transformation. Table 1–2 summarizes applications of information technology that impact the individual.

Table 1–1: A framework for applications of information technology

	Individual	Functional Unit	Organization
Efficiency	Task mechanization	Process automation	Boundary extension
Effectiveness	Work improvement	Functional enhancement	Service enhancement
Transformation	Role expansion	Functional redefinition	Product innovation

Table 1–2: Applications impacting the individual

Efficiency	Task mechanization	Word processing Using a spreadsheet to do a budget plan
Effectiveness	Work improvement	Using a prospect database to generate sales letters
Transformation	Role expansion	Using a portable PC to do "what-if" analyses for investment clients

Impact on the Functional Unit

Applications that automate specific business processes, such as order entry or credit checking, are examples of information technology's impact on the efficiency of the business function. Automated order processing and inventory control systems are other examples of these applications.

An example of an application that improves the effectiveness of the functional unit is using computer-assisted design to improve the quality of the design of shoes, automobiles, or airplanes. Improved designs may lead to better sales.

Finally, information technology can transform the nature of the product or service the functional unit offers. A publishing company may sell business research information on CD-ROM disks. These disks provide access to enormous volumes of business information via PC. Hence, this new technology has produced an altogether new product line. Table 1–3 summarizes applications affecting the functional unit.

Impact on the Organization

The last group of applications of information technology has an impact on the organization as a whole. Linking customers to the order entry system of a supplier can improve efficiency. For example, furniture retailers can use terminals linked to the order entry system of a furniture manufacturer to place orders, check on prices and delivery dates, and manage their own inventories. This system improves the efficiency of placing orders by cutting down on paperwork and enabling retailers to check on available stock before placing orders. The system also gives the furniture manufacturer a competitive advantage because it links customers electronically to the order entry system, making it easier to place orders with this manufacturer than with other suppliers.

The second objective of information technology is effectiveness. The organization can be more effective by providing better service to its customers. General Electric's diagnostic hotline enables customers to call an 800 number to link into a diagnostic database for small electric appliances. Otis Elevator Company has in-car phones so people trapped in an elevator can call emergency service technicians who are dispatched to the problem area immediately.

Information technology can transform the way an organization does business by enabling the organization to introduce new products and services made possible by technology. Holiday Inns introduced videoconferencing facilities so its business clients could arrange electronic meetings with counterparts in other cities. In this way, the hotel chain was able to use a new technology to open up a new business opportunity.

Numerous organizations are using technology to open up new business opportunities. An aggressive market research firm used point-of-sale systems in local grocery chains to record data on customer buying behavior in response to various advertising and promotional strategies. Its advertising impact studies were superior to those of its competitors because it could tie the impact of advertising to an organization's strategy. Table 1–4 summarizes applications that affect strategy.

As you can see, most applications of information technology are directly linked with improving business performance. In many cases, they impact the products and services

Table 1–3: Functional unit applications

Efficiency	Process automation	Order entry Credit checking
Effectiveness	Functional enhancement	Computer-assisted design Computer-assisted manufacturing
Transformation	Functional redefinition	CD-ROM disks for business research

Table 1–4: Organizationwide applications

Efficiency	Boundary extension	On-line order entry linking customers and suppliers
Effectiveness	Service enhancement	On-line diagnostic databases for electrical appliances
Transformation	Product innovation	Holiday Inn's videoconferencing

provided by the business unit. This text will show how information technology also can be used to cut operating costs, add value to products and services, and open up new business opportunities. The next section shows how information technology can provide organizations with a competitive edge.

INFORMATION TECHNOLOGY AND COMPETITIVE STRATEGY

Many applications of information technology can provide organizations with a competitive advantage. Information technology can be used to gain a competitive edge by enabling organizations to offer products and services at lower cost or to provide value-added services.

One competitive strategy information technology supports is *low-cost leadership*—the ability to cut the costs of producing, marketing, and distributing products and services. For example, garment manufacturers who use automated pattern drawers and fabric cutters can reduce labor time by up to 50 percent. Publishers who use computerized word processing and typesetting systems can cut the costs of manual rekeying of text.

The second competitive strategy is *product differentiation*—using information technology to add value to a product or service by providing unique designs, superior product features, better customer service, advanced technology, and access to dealer networks. Digital Equipment Corporation, for example, uses an expert system called XCON to develop custom computer configurations, thereby reducing the time it takes to fill orders and minimizing the chance of errors.

Information technology can also enable organizations to address the needs of a particular market niche more effectively. This competitive strategy is called *market specialization.* For example, a mail-order company can analyze the demographic characteristics of its most frequent mail-order customers and develop products and services that address the needs of its most profitable customers.

Impact of Information Technology on Competitive Forces

In *Competitive Strategy,* Michael Porter identifies five competitive forces that influence the profitability of an industry: the power of buyers, the power of suppliers, the threat of new entrants, the threat of substitute products, and rivalry among existing competitors. Chapter 3 discusses these competitive forces in depth, but the following examples give a brief introduction to how information technology can be used to influence them.

Information technology can help control the first competitive force, the power of buyers, by making it difficult for buyers to switch to other suppliers. Airline companies have introduced frequent flight bonus programs to influence their customers to accumulate mileage points leading to free travel awards and discounted travel accommodations. These frequent flight bonus programs create switching costs because their members perceive the bonus points to be a value-added service.

Firms can compete more effectively if they can control the second competitive force, the power of suppliers. A firm that is linked to the order entry systems of numerous suppliers can gain a competitive edge over these suppliers because it is able to shop for the best price. Design engineers at aerospace manufacturing companies can shop around by querying databases about components offered by several suppliers until they find the best prices for the highest quality components.

Firms can also gain control over their suppliers by checking the quality of incoming goods and services. The automobile industry has electronic links to quality control data on incoming shipments of steel from steel manufacturers. This information enables the automakers to identify faulty raw materials and to negotiate prices with their suppliers.

Established firms in an industry want to create barriers blocking the third competitive force, *new entrants,* from entering the industry. Information technology can create a significant barrier to entry. For example, the on-line **telecommunications** networks tying office information systems of large insurance companies to local insurance agents have cost millions of dollars to construct. Using a terminal linked to the home office, a local insurance agent can update policyholder files, download sales data about various policy options, and obtain training materials. These networks are an excellent example of how information technology can be used to create a significant barrier to entry.

Firms try to control the fourth competitive force, *substitutes,* by deterring customers from finding other products and services to meet their needs. Sometimes information technology can help. A tire company, for example, has built electronic sensors into its new radial tires. These sensors detect low tire pressure and flash a message signaling the problem to the driver. Monitoring tire performance contributes to the longevity of the tire and to the safety of the vehicle. The value-added feature of these tire sensors makes it difficult for customers to find a substitute product.

Firms within an industry can use information technology against the fifth competitive force, their rivals. The railroad industry, for example, has designed telecommunications networks to track freight cars, optimize car utilization, and give customers information about delivery schedules. These on-line systems made it possible for railroads such as Union Pacific and Santa Fe to compete with their major rivals, the trucking companies.

Chapter 3 discusses new information technology that can provide a competitive advantage for your organization at greater length. The next section covers key information planning questions managers need to be able to answer.

IMPLICATIONS OF INFORMATION TECHNOLOGY FOR MANAGERS

Managers today recognize that they can use information systems to improve business performance. To do so, they need access to the right data, the right technology, and the right communications environment. They also need to work with Management Information Systems personnel to design information systems that improve day-to-day operations and establish links with customers, suppliers, and competitors.

Managers should be able to answer the following questions to make effective decisions about information technology and its uses.

What Information Do I Need?

As you have already learned, managers use information systems to keep track of day-to-day business activities, such as sales transactions, inventory updates, and bills to be paid. Information systems that process day-to-day business transactions are often referred to as *operational systems.* Managers also use summary data on sales, inventories, and accounts to be paid to get a better understanding of trends and business opportunities. If store managers see that certain items are constantly out of stock, they can reorder these items on a more timely basis. In contrast, they can reduce or gradually discontinue stock of slow-moving items. Information systems that provide data to better maximize the use of resources to achieve objectives are called *control systems* or *tactical systems*.

Managers use other types of information for planning purposes. External data about market trends and competitive industry statistics can help senior managers chart long-range strategy. Faced with historical data revealing a gradual drop in its market share of sewing machines, its longtime mainstay product, The Singer Company ultimately divested its sewing machine business and embarked upon a diversification program that led to its entry into the furniture and aerospace industries.

The question of "What information do I need?" is further complicated by changing business conditions, industry competition, and internal priorities. Much of the information managers typically receive in the form of daily, weekly, and monthly reports is useless in the face of constantly changing business situations. As a result, managers need the ability to ask questions of existing databases and to generate on-demand reports.

For example, a large passenger elevator company recorded data on service call histories in an on-line database. Using this database, managers were able to focus on recurring elevator maintenance problems that were previously buried in office paperwork. New information on troublesome elevators enabled management to design technical training programs for its staff.

The information systems that help managers answer unexpected questions, often on an ad hoc basis, are called **decision support systems.** In this text, you will use decision support tools such as spreadsheet and database programs to extract valuable information to answer unanticipated questions.

What New Technologies Should We Pursue?

As a manager, you will constantly learn about new technology. Will you want to invest in wireless networks? Computer-assisted design? Desktop conferencing? Notebook computers? Client/server databases? Multimedia computing? These are just a few of the technologies available today. In general, new technology is introduced more rapidly than most organizations can learn to use it effectively. As a manager, you will want to select technologies that support business needs—and you will want these technologies to work.

In viewing technology opportunities, managers must try to imagine how technology can allow them to do things that they are not already doing. Too often, technology is used to automate current practices. Instead, technology should be viewed as a tool to do new things. Most managers have difficulty perceiving the business opportunities technology will support.

One such technology is videoconferencing. Originally, videoconferencing was viewed as a method of cutting travel costs. However, videoconferences could not fill the need to form relationships, to build morale, and to resolve conflicts. That required face-to-face meetings.

Videoconferencing plays a slightly different role in many organizations today. Rather than eliminating travel entirely, videoconferencing provides a mechanism for periodic meetings that would not have been possible otherwise. At McDonnell Douglas, for example, project managers and team members at multiple locations routinely meet via teleconference to monitor the status of ongoing defense contracts. Many of the junior staffers on these project teams would not have been able to travel, but in an electronic meeting they have a chance to voice their ideas. As a result, problems are resolved more quickly.

What Kinds of Information Systems Support Business Needs?

As a manager, you will use information systems that support decisions within functional areas of the business, such as sales and marketing, accounting and finance, and production and manufacturing. These **business information systems** support day-to-day operations, such as credit checking and recording sales transactions. They also help managers determine how to allocate resources effectively. These are tactical decisions. Sales forecasts and budget analyses help managers identify trends affecting the business. A sales forecast indicating rising market share for a particular product line, for example, may influence a sales manager to allocate additional resources—salespeople's time, advertising dollars, and product development—to this product line. Managers also need information for planning purposes that enables them to visualize and evaluate long-term decisions, such as decisions to introduce a new product line or to locate retail outlets in new geographic areas.

In this text, you will learn about business information systems in a number of areas. These systems are described in Chapters 10 through 13. You will learn about financial information systems that support such functions as accounts receivable, billing, and accounts payable; marketing information systems that provide information about sales activity, advertising, and distribution; and human resource information systems that provide personnel and payroll data used to identify candidates with the skills and knowledge needed to fill certain positions. Information systems in manufacturing and production that enable the firm to schedule production, control manufacturing costs, and identify inventory requirements for production are also explained.

How Do We Develop Information Systems Plans?

One of the major questions managers must answer is how information technology can give their businesses a competitive edge. They need to consider whether to put order entry terminals into their customer locations. They need to weigh the feasibility of using computer technology in designing their products. They need to evaluate whether computer-based information systems can provide better information for identifying high-potential target market groups and for depicting the characteristics of high-risk customers.

Technologies such as electronic mail, optical scanners, voice mail, and electronic printing can speed customer orders, facilitate on-time delivery, and provide better information about pricing and special promotions. Managers must evaluate whether these technologies can strengthen their customer relationships and also reduce the cost of excess inventory.

Chapter 16 discusses planning strategies for information technology. These strategies provide managers with methods of setting priorities for information systems projects so they have the greatest impact on business strategy. The planning strategies include methods managers can use to determine their own information needs for planning and control purposes. They also include planning strategies that evaluate the overall information needs of the business.

What Do I Need to Know about the Design of Information Systems?

Systems development refers to the analysis of business needs and the design of an information system to serve these needs. Information systems must be designed to solve business problems. An information system is usually developed to improve service, cut costs, or increase revenues. For example, at one financial services company, the percentage of bad debts was too high. In response to this problem, a customer information system was enhanced to track the characteristics of loan recipients who defaulted on their loans or did not make timely payments. This information was useful in depicting the characteristics of high-risk loan applicants and made it possible for branch managers to disapprove many of these high-risk applicants during the loan application screening process.

Many of the information systems needs occur at the business level. For example, a manufacturing company's plant management needed better information about maintenance problems affecting plant equipment. They wanted to keep track of maintenance so they could better anticipate equipment downtime and to develop preventative maintenance schedules to minimize—or virtually eliminate—equipment downtime. A maintenance tracking information system provided the information they needed to make these decisions.

This system was designed by user-managers within plant operations with technical assistance from MIS professionals. Managers within the plant operations department were responsible for defining their information needs and selecting hardware and software. With the assistance of MIS professionals, they learned how to use database query tools to extract the information they needed to anticipate maintenance problems. In general, the success of an information systems project is closely tied to the sense of participation, responsibility, and accountability the users have for systems design and implementation.

Chapter 17 covers systems development, including how managers can define their information systems requirements using process-modeling and data-modeling approaches and how they can work with information systems designers to transform these requirements into reports and databases.

Which Systems Development Options Should the Manager Choose?

In the traditional data processing environment, programmers wrote software using **procedural languages** such as COBOL. Most of these information systems ran on large mainframe computers. When managers needed changes in reports or databases, they had to go to the MIS department and ask programmers to make necessary modifications and changes in the programs that generated these reports. The entire process of building and modifying information systems took a great deal of time.

Today, a vast array of options is available. Managers can purchase software packages, contract with a software development company, or develop in-house programs. A **software package** is a set of programs designed to automate specific business procedures, such as payroll or accounts receivable. In many cases, it is cheaper and easier to acquire a software package than it is to develop one from scratch.

Traditionally, information systems were built using **third-generation languages** such as COBOL or FORTRAN. With the advent of **fourth-generation languages** and microcomputer-based software packages, managers no longer have to rely upon the information systems department to design and implement the information systems they need. Fourth-generation languages use existing databases and enable users to extract data and reports from them. Many managers use microcomputer-based database query and reporting tools to generate data and reports. In this course, you will use microcomputer databases such as DBASE IV to make queries and to generate reports.

Chapter 18 explains controls and procedures that assure the systems you develop as a user will be reliable. Managers may have extensive knowledge of software tools such as spreadsheets and databases, but they are usually not trained in systems development methods, such as documentation, data security, backup and recovery, and data validation procedures. Effective controls are necessary to assure the integrity of data and the correctness of reports. This text will show you how to assess the potential risk of an application. High-risk applications should be safeguarded with effective controls, whereas low-risk applications may not require many controls.

When Is the Help of MIS Professionals Needed?

With the availability of microcomputer-based software tools, many users are now building their own systems. In many cases, they have acquired hardware, software, operating systems, database management systems, and local area networks. They have also assumed the responsibility for managing these departmental systems.

Some of these local projects should be coordinated with MIS professionals. For example, at one university, department chairs had to wait until the end of each month to get reports on remaining account balances for such budget line items as telephone, commodities, personnel, and contractual services. So they constructed their own expense tracking systems using microcomputer-based spreadsheets. This was a time-consuming process, and each department developed its own unique system. MIS could have helped the department chairs in this situation by recommending communications equipment and mainframe terminal emulation packages to allow departments to query their existing account balances with user-friendly database query and reporting tools. This approach would be far less costly than having the end-users develop their own personal information systems.

You will see a variety of applications within your organization. Some of these applications, such as organizationwide payroll and accounting systems, purchasing systems, and personnel information systems, are the full responsibility of MIS departments. Because these systems provide organizationwide data they require tight security, and they need to be maintained by MIS professionals.

Some information systems require sharing responsibility between the MIS department and the user department. The university budget accounting system described previously is a good example of this type of system. This system was developed by MIS professionals using a large mainframe computer and central accounting data. End-users, however, wanted to have the ability to extract data on account balances. To make queries possible, users needed to acquire the proper hardware and software to link to the central system.

As a manager, you need to assume responsibility for working with MIS professionals in cases in which shared responsibility is the most effective option. Chapter 19 presents the advantages and disadvantages of different ways of organizing information systems activities.

What Are the Responsibilities of MIS Management?

As you have seen, the role of information technology in business is increasing. Large investments in technology, including telecommunications networks, corporate databases, and office automation systems, require central planning and control. The information management function, or MIS function, is responsible for managing the communications network, corporate data, and the development of business information systems.

As a future manager, you need to understand the roles and responsibilities of MIS leadership. One of the most important roles for MIS professionals is technology planning. MIS professionals must forecast technology trends and recognize technology opportunities affecting the business. Holiday Inn executives, for example, recognized the potential competitive impact of offering videoconferencing facilities in their hotels. Gallery of Homes real estate firms recognized the impact of transmitting facsimile copies of home listings so that prospective buyers could view properties from distant locations.

You will learn about new information technologies in the chapters dealing with office automation, decision support systems, and artificial intelligence and expert systems. You will learn about new technologies that improve the productivity of the systems development process as well. Computer-assisted software engineering tools, fourth- and fifth-generation languages, and departmental computing systems all provide new challenges and opportunities to speed the development of business information systems.

In the future, MIS professionals will serve as consultants and facilitators. End-user consultants will help managers build their own information systems, using tools such as ad hoc query and reporting languages. They will also help users make local hardware and software choices with full knowledge of corporatewide computing and networking plans.

THE FUTURE OF INFORMATION TECHNOLOGY

Over 30 years ago, Harold Leavitt and Thomas Whisler, in their article "Management in the 1980's" (*Harvard Business Review,* November-December 1958), predicted that information technology would have a significant impact upon organizational structure. They predicted that computerization would reduce the ranks of middle management, enable top management to take on more creative functions, and provide an opportunity for recentralization.

Today, the organizational impacts of information technology are significant. Three groups of applications that have had a significant impact on organizational structure and management communications—electronic mail systems, group and cooperative work systems, and expert systems—serve as examples.

Electronic Mail Systems. Electronic mail or E-mail has been available for a number of years but today its use is so widespread among managers at all levels that it is having a profound impact on management communications. Electronic mail overcomes the "filtering" of information that often occurs when messages are sent upward through levels of the corporate hierarchy. It provides an opportunity for groups in different functional units to work on collaborative projects. Electronic mail draws together specialists in remote locations and enables managers to obtain timely feedback on project activities and accomplishments. In many ways, electronic mail is contributing to a more flexible organizational structure.

Group and Cooperative Work Systems. A defense contractor had difficulty managing multimillion dollar design and manufacturing projects because of the massive project management problem of organizing hundreds of workers on long-term commitments. When one group missed a project deadline, it was difficult to get needed status and progress reports to middle management in time to realign resources to correct the problem. When a cooperative work system was put in, however, middle-level managers were able to get timely information. This enabled them to anticipate problems, provide resources where they were needed, and adjust schedules accordingly. Senior management estimated that project completion time was cut because of more effective communications and coordination resulting from use of electronic mail and a joint project tracking system. Information systems supporting group and collaborative work provide software for decision making, electronic brainstorming, and meeting support.

Expert Systems. The computers of today work like the human brain. "Neural networks" store information as patterns of connections among millions of tiny processors linked together. Using knowledge bases where expertise is stored about specific areas, computers apply logic to decipher problems of all kinds. This technology provides "expert consultants" to financial planners, insurance underwriters, claims adjusters, and credit authorizers. With the help of such "expert" opinion, managers make decisions with less risk.

Technology is bringing about the transition to the information-based organization (IBO). Today's desktop workstations are as powerful as yesterday's minicomputers. Standard mobile telephones provide access to high-speed telecommunications networks for the transmission of data, voice, image, and text. Computers can translate speech into machine-readable text to transmit video images over long distances and to pay bills electronically.

In the IBO, teams are organized to solve specific business problems and disband when the job is done. In Peter Drucker's view, the company of the 1990s will more closely resemble a networked jazz ensemble than a traditional corporate hierarchy. Members of project-oriented teams will use computer-based networks to support communication, group decision making, and consensus building. (See Figure 1–4.)

In the 1990s and beyond, computers enable organizations to pull people and project resources together using databases and communications networks. Organizations will be able to benefit from both internal expertise and the expertise of expert systems and external consultants. Work will be interesting because individuals with specific types of expertise will be assigned to a variety of different projects. People will be paid and rewarded based upon their individual contributions, without upsetting pay and incentive systems based upon the traditional hierarchy.

Figure 1–4
The networked organization

Management Summary

The evolution of computers shows that Leavitt and Whisler's prediction over 30 years ago that computers would change organizational structure and the nature of managerial work is coming true. Early attempts to manage paperwork used computers to mechanize tasks such as information retrieval. In the 1980s and 1990s, organizations learned that information technology could provide a competitive edge by adding value to products and services. Telephone links to diagnostic databases, vendor hotlines, and dealer networks supported by telecommunications links all provide better service to customers. Computer systems can link buyers and sellers, manufacturers and dealers, and home offices and branch offices.

Today, as most organizations make the transition to becoming information-based organizations, it is essential for managers to understand emerging technologies and their applications. These applications should be focused upon efficiency, effectiveness, and transformation. The key to the 1990s will be using information technology to do things that were altogether impossible before.

As a future manager, you will want to become thoroughly acquainted with the challenges that information technology provides. This text will give you an opportunity to learn about information systems, to use information systems tools, and to become familiar with the systems development process—all from the manager's viewpoint.

Key Terms for Managers

business information systems, **17**
database, **10**
decision support system, **16**
effectiveness, **11**
efficiency, **11**
fourth-generation language, **18**
procedural language, **18**
software package, **18**
systems development, **17**
telecommunications, **15**
third-generation language, **18**
transformation, **11**

Review Questions

1. What problems occur when data are maintained by different organizational units?
2. What did Ford do to reengineer its accounts payable process?
3. How did a central database help Hewlett-Packard reengineer its purchasing process?
4. What is efficiency?
5. What is an example of an application of information technology that supports efficiency of an individual manager?
6. What is *effectiveness?*
7. Give an example of an application of information technology that improves the effectiveness of a functional unit of the business.
8. What is *transformation?*
9. Give an example of an application of information technology that supports transformation of the work of the individual.
10. Give an example of an application of information technology that supports transformation of the work of a functional unit of the business.
11. How does a linkage between an automaker's order-entry system and a steelmaker's quality control system create power of the buyer (the automaker) over the supplier (the steel manufacturer)?

12. How can an automobile manufacturer differentiate its products and services using information technology?

13. What are the advantages of group and cooperative work systems?

Questions for Discussion

1. Why is it important for the manager to assume a role in providing input into information systems design and implementation?

2. Why should the manager become familiar with the capabilities of new information technologies?

3. Why should the manager understand the roles and responsibilities of MIS professionals?

4. What is one of the important responsibilities of MIS management?

5. How are electronic mail systems changing the nature of managerial work?

Problems

1. **Impact of technology.** Using the framework for describing applications of information technology shown below, identify the type of impact of each application (e.g., efficiency, etc.) and the scope of its impact (e.g., individual, etc.).

   a. With the introduction of point-of-sale inventory systems, store managers have timely reports on inventory turnover. When scanners replaced older inventory systems, store managers could use the reports they generated to reduce stock of slow-moving items and to adjust inventory levels to serve customers' needs.
   b. At Windsor University, students register for classes using a touch-tone telephone system from home or work, making it much more convenient for them to enroll in classes and giving the university a competitive edge in obtaining students. With the system, students can key in desired course information, check prerequisites, and enter a Visa or MasterCard number for payment.
   c. A consumer loan company has experienced difficulty reducing the percentage of bad debt expense incurred when customers default on loans. In response to this problem, the firm developed a database of loan applicant information and began to identify the characteristics of customers who were most likely to default on their loans. Now, these high-potential delinquents are screened out during the application review process, which has greatly reduced the bad debt problem.
   d. A textbook publisher has developed an inventory control system linking its branches. If one branch has insufficient stock of a text, the distribution manager can query databases of other branches to determine where sufficient stock exists. In this way, the publisher can rely upon a nationwide inventory of texts to fill orders if necessary.
   e. Information technology can help sales managers align their sales incentive strategies with market trends. One retail bank developed a system to allocate its salespersons' time to pushing new financial services with the highest potential clients. With data on customers' financial holdings, the salespersons could direct their attention to the most potentially profitable prospects.

2. **Reengineering work.** One of the issues of the 1990s is reengineering work, or changing fundamental business processes. Reengineering may mean completely redoing the way things are done to make them simpler, faster, and more effective.

Can you find a reengineering example? Visit a local firm and describe changes that have occurred over the past year that were designed to improve the effectiveness of the business. Explain what changes in business practices have taken place to make this reengineering possible.

Cases

1. **Consolidated Petroleum.** Doug Smith, the manager of the local office of a Big Six accounting firm, has been interested in purchasing a minicomputer to house local customer records. With the assistance of a consultant, Doug conducted a feasibility study to assess the office's needs and to evaluate systems development options, including packages, in-house development, and a service bureau. The system he selected was a minicomputer with database, word processing, and accounts receivable software. It would enable users in the office to query customer records and generate their own reports.

   When Doug submitted his request for the minicomputer system to the corporate review committee at the New York–based home office, he felt that the feasibility study documenting the applications for the system would more than substantiate its need. He was shocked when the corporate review committee flatly refused the request, stating that the proposed minicomputer system was not compatible with the corporate information processing system. In the future, the committee argued, the company was planning to link local information systems with databases at the home office. The minicomputer would not fit into this plan.

   Evaluate the advantages and disadvantages of Doug's arguments. Should Doug insist on his request? What should he do?

2. **National Paper Company.** Managers at National Paper Company are very impatient with the MIS department because the backlog of systems development requests is three and a half years long. Managers need information on sales trends, customer profitability, and product profitability. As a result of their frustration with getting the necessary information with the help of MIS, many user-managers have set up small information systems using personal computers and packaged software.

   Dick Strickland, manager of data processing at National Paper, has become nervous about the burgeoning number of user-developed information systems, and he wants them stopped. His argument is that users do not have enough knowledge of information systems to develop well-designed systems. He is worried about data management issues. He is also concerned about the potential proliferation of incompatible hardware and software and large expenditures on PCs.

   On the other hand, users argue that they understand their own information needs better than the MIS group does. In fact, some users are more knowledgeable than some of the existing MIS professionals in using PC-based tools such as spreadsheets and databases.

   The argument between MIS and the users at National Paper is a familiar one. Try to answer these questions:

   a. Who is right?
   b. Should MIS professionals control the projects being done by the users?
   c. Should users be permitted to acquire the hardware and software they need to accomplish these projects?

Benjamin, Robert; Charles Dickinson; and John Rockart. "Changing Role of the Corporate Information Systems Officer." *MIS Quarterly* 9, no. 3, 1985, pp. 177–88.

Selected References and Readings

Lucas, Henry C., Jr., "Utilizing Information Technology: Guidelines for Managers." *Sloan Management Review,* Fall 1986, pp. 39–47.

McFarlan, F. Warren, and James McKenney. "IS Technology Organization Issues." In *Corporate Information Systems Management,* ed. F. W. McFarlan and J. McKenney. pp. 27–48. Homewood, Ill.: Irwin, 1983.

Marchand, Donald A. "Information Management: Strategies and Tools in Transition." *Information Management Review* 1, no. 1 (1985), pp. 27–34.

Porter, Michael E. "How Competitive Forces Shape Strategy," *Harvard Business Review,* March–April 1979, pp. 137–45.

Porter, Michael E., and Victor E. Millar. "How Information Gives You Competitive Advantage." *Harvard Business Review,* July–August 1985, pp. 149–60.

An Introduction to Concepts of Systems and Organizations

Chapter Outline

Manager's View

When you begin the study of *information* systems, you should become acquainted with a theoretical framework for understanding their use, development, and effect on organizations; that is, you need to have an understanding of systems concepts as a foundation for further study. The word *system* is often misunderstood—some people think you are referring to a computer system when you use the term, but you may hear people talk about financial systems, air-conditioning systems, school systems, and investment systems as well as about *information systems.* A *system* is a collection of people, machines, and methods organized to accomplish a set of specific tasks. Information systems—which are a major topic in this text—have the same components and characteristics as systems in general.

This chapter introduces the concepts of systems, their characteristics, and their interaction with the environment. As a manager, you'll constantly be dealing with systems, and you'll need feedback about their performance. Information is the feedback you need to determine if systems are achieving their objectives, operating with the necessary components, and meeting the necessary standards. Information systems are designed to give managers the information they require as feedback.

In this chapter, you will learn about the systems approach to problem solving. As a manager, you will be dealing with many types of systems and you will be responsible for improving their performance. For example, you'll determine if procedures, personnel, and equipment need to be changed to achieve objectives. Or you'll need to assess the effect of new equipment on current work methods, procedures, and organization. The systems approach to problem solving will help you deal with these kinds of tasks.

Finally, this chapter explains how organizations operate as systems, with unique characteristics, information flows, and decision processes. You will learn about the components of organizations and about different types of organizational structures. You will need to recognize the structures of organizations to understand the decision-making processes that occur within different types of organization.

SYSTEMS CONCEPTS

A **system** is an integrated set of components, or entities, that interact to achieve a particular function or goal. Systems have characteristics such as boundaries, outputs and inputs, methods of converting inputs into outputs, and system *interfaces,* as we will see. Systems are composed of interrelated and interdependent **subsystems.** Examples of systems are all around us—in fact, an excellent example is a college class. The components of the classroom situation, including an instructor, the students, textbooks, and facilities, all interact to make the accomplishment of learning goals possible. (Figure 2–1 depicts a model of a classroom system.)

A business is also a system. A business uses resources such as people, capital, materials, and facilities to achieve the goal of making a profit. Business procedures, such as order handling, marketing research, financial planning, and manufacturing, are the interactions that need to be managed to achieve this objective.

For a more thorough understanding of systems, though, you need to be familiar with concepts like *boundary* and *interface.*

System Boundaries

All systems have a **boundary** that depicts its scope of activities. For example, the activities in a class include lectures, discussion, testing, grading, and preparation of assigned course work. These activities may represent the boundary of the system for which a teacher is responsible. Within the system of the classroom, the teacher is responsible for organizing class time, assigning homework to students, and evaluating student progress. The boundary, then, delineates an area of responsibility. When defining a system, you must establish a boundary.

System boundaries are also established within a business system. A sales manager may be responsible for managing, motivating, and evaluating the performance of a sales organization. The owner of the business, however, faces different boundaries and may develop a financial plan, a marketing strategy, and a long-range business plan.

Systems and Subsystems

Systems may consist of numerous subsystems, each of which has elements, interactions, and objectives. Subsystems perform specialized tasks related to the overall objectives of the total system. For example, an educational system may consist of individual courses that are subsystems. Each course provides specific knowledge that is a part of the overall educational system and contributes to its goals.

Figure 2–1
A classroom system

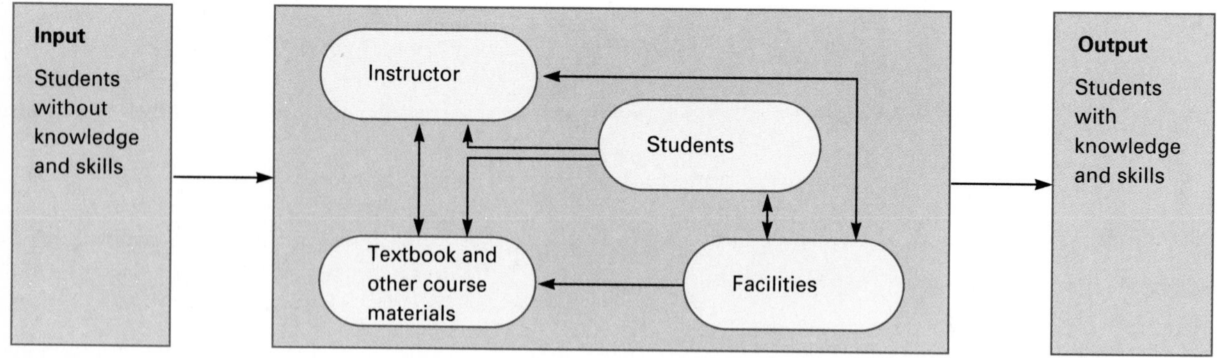

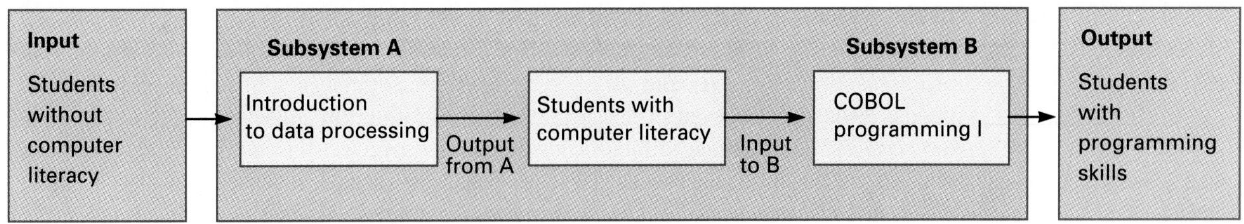

Figure 2–2
Typical subsystems: An example

In a business system, various functions are subsystems. Marketing, finance, and manufacturing, for example, are subsystems. Within the marketing subsystem, the sales order entry and credit-checking functions are subsystems. Each subsystem uses its resources to meet specific objectives. Successful achievement of these goals requires good management of internal resources. For instance, in managing the sales order entry function, the supervisor needs to develop sales order procedures, maintain sales order records, and train sales order personnel.

Outputs and Inputs

The inner workings of a system or subsystem are organized to produce outputs from inputs. In this conversion process, some value or utility should be added to the inputs. For example, a training program should produce trained employees with certain skills, knowledge, or behavior from its inputs—untrained employees.

The outputs of one subsystem usually become inputs into the next. The outputs of a course in introductory data processing concepts, for instance, become inputs into the next course in COBOL programming. (These two subsystems are depicted in Figure 2–2.)

As you'd expect, the outputs of a subsystem have to adhere to certain standards to be acceptable to the next. If students coming out of the introductory data processing course don't understand basic concepts of file organization and file processing, they won't have the prerequisite skills needed for COBOL. If they're not permitted to enter COBOL until they meet certain standards, though, the problem would be alleviated. The more exactly standards are adhered to, the easier it will be to interface the two courses, or subsystems.

An **interface** is a connection at system or subsystem boundaries. An interface serves as a medium to convey the output from one system to the input of another system. An example will help clarify this concept. Two typical business systems that interface with each other are inventory control and purchasing. If inventory levels drop below a certain level, then additional stock of these items should be purchased. Purchasing will need to know what quantity of a particular item to obtain to replenish the stock and information on sales and inventory turnover to learn which items are in greatest demand so these items can be replenished on a timely basis. An inventory control system will provide information on stock to be reordered based upon sales and inventory turnover trends.

However, if the inventory control subsystem triggers erroneous information about the amount of stock to be reordered, then inputs into purchasing will be wrong. This problem can be partially overcome by establishing an economic order quantity, or the quantity of an item that is most economical to buy, for each item in inventory. This quantity, derived from order history and inventory turnover rate, can serve as a standard and prevent reordering too much or too little stock.

Subsystem Interface and Interface Problems

In the previous section we discussed how some interface problems can be alleviated through the development of standards. But you might encounter other types of interface problems. Sometimes the output of one subsystem is not sufficient to accommodate the needs of the next subsystem. For example, the production subsystem may not be able to produce enough stock to meet sales demands during certain peak periods. One way of handling this interface problem is through the use of slack resources. In this situation, excess inventories can be built up on purpose to meet the demand for sufficient inventory at peak times.

Another system interface problem can occur between the authoring subsystem and the editorial subsystem in the development of a textbook. Authors who wait until the last minute to finish their writing may not be able to produce manuscript fast enough to meet production schedules, which involve editing, artwork, layout and design, typesetting, and proofreading tasks. This problem can be avoided in several ways. First, an author may be asked to complete several chapters before production activities begin. This is another example of using slack resources.

Second, an author may be asked to adhere to certain standards for input into the production subsystem. For example, the author may be asked to create and store all text using a word processing package that can be transported to a computer-based typesetting system without rekeying.

Third, an author could hire a library researcher, photo researcher, and typist to provide a support subsystem to expedite the development of manuscript. This is an example of how creating a new subsystem can help solve a system interface problem.

Another situation in which a system interface problem can be solved by designing a new subsystem occurs at a college when it accepts some students with deficiencies in their academic backgrounds. To bridge the gap between high school and college, a remedial subsystem can be created to help students develop prerequisite skills for college work. For instance, students lacking basic writing skills may be required to take a remedial writing class to learn spelling, grammar, punctuation, and composition skills. On successfully completing this class, they may receive permission to enroll in classes in literature.

SYSTEMS AND THEIR ENVIRONMENTS

The system's environment consists of people, organizations, and other systems that supply data to or that receive data from the system. Not surprisingly, the environment is perceived differently by different managers. A sales manager, for example, envisions the system environment to be the company's customers and vendors of the products and services being marketed. But the owner of the business perceives the environment to include the firm's competitors, financial institutions that provide resources for expansion, and government agencies with jurisdiction over company plans and products. Moreover, not only can the environment be perceived differently by different managers, but also various kinds of systems don't always interact with the environment in the same way.

Open and Closed Systems

Open systems operate in an external environment and exchange information and material with that environment. The external environment consists of the activities external to the system boundary with which the system can interact. An *open system* needs to receive feedback to change and to continue to exist in its environment. For example, a marketing system, which is an open system, operates in an environment of competition. If a competitor introduces new technology by providing customers with on-line order entry terminals, the marketing function must adapt to the change in the environment or remain at a competitive disadvantage. One way of accommodating the change in the environment is to offer a similar on-line order entry service. The same type of adjustment is necessary when an airline offers a new service, such as a frequent flier bonus program. Though the new service may temporarily give the air carrier a competitive advantage, the other airlines soon follow suit and offer a similar program.

In contrast, a **closed system** is relatively self-contained; it doesn't exchange information with its environment. Closed systems don't get the feedback they need from the external environment and tend to deteriorate. For instance, if a training program administrator doesn't respond to the needs of the business environment for trained graduates, students may no longer be able to get jobs and may go elsewhere for training. Eventually, the training program may be discontinued.

You might wonder why closed systems exist at all. More often than not, participants in a system become closed to external feedback without fully being aware of it. For example, a university may only offer graduate courses during the daytime hours because it has always scheduled these courses in this way. Without recognizing the growing number of working adults wishing to enroll in evening graduate programs, the university may find registrations dwindling and may even have to discontinue certain courses. If university officials had been more responsive to student needs, however, they might have enjoyed booming enrollments among the population of adult evening students.

System Feedback

A system needs feedback to do its job. Feedback is an indicator of how current performance rates when compared to a set of standards. With effective feedback, continuing adjustments in the activities of a system can be made to assure that the system achieves its goals. Measuring performance against a standard is an effective control mechanism. Employees need feedback to learn how well they are achieving job goals. Students receive grades or other kinds of evaluations from instructors that show whether they are meeting course objectives.

The good thing about feedback is that it usually increases effort. For example, tennis players often perform better when they are keeping score. When salespeople receive positive feedback, it increases their motivation to achieve a sales quota. *Negative feedback* may also serve a useful purpose. Negative feedback is designed to correct or guide activities that are not consistent with achieving the goals of the system. If salespeople are not achieving quotas, they may want to rethink current sales techniques or reorganize their time. Similarly, if students receive low grades, they may need to improve study habits, obtain tutoring, or enroll in courses that better match their abilities or backgrounds.

Product managers also need feedback on how well new products fare in certain markets. They conduct market research studies in test markets to compare new products with established products. They can use feedback from these market tests to redesign a new product or identify target markets for which the product is suitable before its introduction. Products such as shampoos, honey roasted peanuts, and detergents are all market tested in this way. Sometimes a company receives feedback after introducing a new product. When Coca Cola introduced new Coke, negative feedback from its established customer base forced the reintroduction of its original formula as Classic Coke.

Trainers in companies also need feedback about how well their programs are equipping trainees for job tasks. Feedback from supervisors may provide suggestions on what skills trainees need to perform successfully on the job. For example, employees who take a training program to learn how to use Lotus 1–2–3, a popular

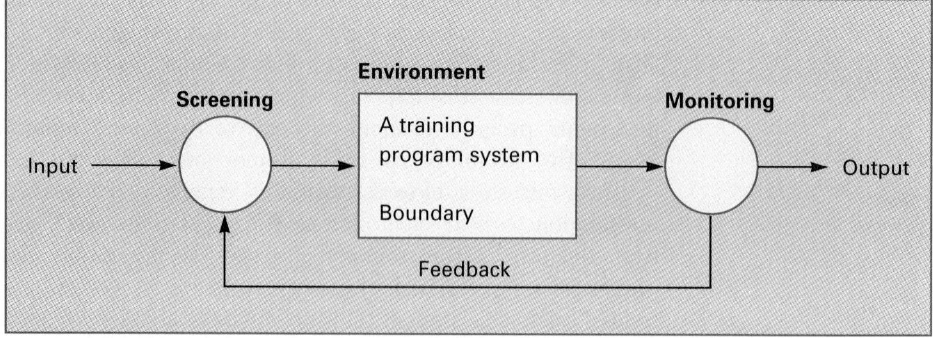

Figure 2–3
A training system and its environment

microcomputer spreadsheet program, may not be taught how to copy formulas from one cell to a range of cells and may experience difficulty performing this procedure on the job. This feedback may be used to build more exercises on the copy command into training classes. Figure 2–3 depicts a training system and its environment. It also shows how feedback from the external environment can be used to modify or improve the system's internal workings.

So far we've emphasized the constructive aspect of feedback. Sometimes the wrong kind of feedback is provided, however. This would be true if students were rewarded for the number of book reports they complete, rather than for the quality of the reports. They may skim books to get just enough information to complete and submit each report without developing comprehension and reading skills—the real objectives of the exercise. Or if employees get the wrong kind of feedback, they may increase their efforts in areas that aren't useful in achieving the objectives of the system. For example, if salespeople are rewarded for the number of sales calls they make instead of the number of sales they close, they will try to fit in as many calls a day as they can rather than spending the time with each customer to make a sale. As a result, the company may lose business and not achieve its objectives.

Such considerations make it clear that feedback mechanisms must be designed for effective control of business functions within an organization. In a business setting, an inventory manager needs to manage the inventory levels of hundreds of items to avoid shortages of items in demand and to prevent excess inventory levels of items that do not turn over frequently. The inventory manager needs feedback to control these inventory levels and determine when to order new stock of certain items. An inventory control system can automatically generate a purchase order for stock replenishment when an item in inventory falls below its reorder point. (The *reorder point* is the inventory level of an item that signals when more stock of that item needs to be reordered.) This is an effective control device, because if inventory levels fall below a safe level, incoming customer orders cannot be filled. However, if excess inventories build up, cash will be tied up unnecessarily.

In short, many information systems provide managers with information they need to allocate their resources to achieve business goals. By having information about current business activities, managers can control production, inventory, and marketing resources and invest these resources in the most profitable ways. Information on planned versus actual sales, for example, can be used to detect slow-moving items and cut production of these items. Fast-moving items should trigger production so the sales function can take advantage of market demand.

System Entropy

Systems can run down if they are not maintained. **Systems entropy** corresponds roughly to chaos or disorder—a state that occurs without maintenance. If employees do not have opportunities to learn new concepts and techniques, the skills they apply to performing job tasks will become out of date. The process of maintaining a system is a process of decreasing entropy or increasing orderliness. Sending automobile mechanics to training classes to learn new diagnostic techniques is an example of decreasing entropy. Orderliness can be achieved through preventive maintenance checks, such as a yearly physical examination for an employee or a routine tune-up for an automobile, and then taking action as a result of these regular checks. These checks provide valuable feedback to help detect faults or problems when none have been anticipated. Diagnostic tools for equipment and machinery help prevent downtime, which may cause delays in production and cost thousands of dollars in lost business.

System Stress and Change

Systems change over time. Some of these changes occur because of identified problems, new business opportunities, and new management directives. Systems may also change as a result of stresses. The achievement levels needed to meet existing goals may change. For example, because of reduced profit margins on sales, a division sales manager may insist on a sales increase of 10 percent instead of 7 percent to achieve the same profits. The tendency is to localize the stress so the pressure for adjusting to new demands is felt primarily by one subsystem, in this case the division sales force.

It is easier to deal with change within one subsystem than within the total system because stress may require rethinking existing work methods and organization. In this case, the sales manager may have to develop more effective procedures to improve the profitability of sales. The sales manager may recommend cutting down calls to smaller customer accounts and substituting telemarketing to service their needs. Salespeople might need to reallocate their time so they can pay special attention to customers who purchase the most profitable product lines and encourage customers who purchase less profitable lines to look at high-margin products. All these procedures require a close analysis of the current system, changes in work procedures, and effective time management.

Another source of system stress occurs if inputs cannot be monitored but the system is expected to produce the same quality of output. Many colleges and universities screen applicants using standardized test scores, high school grades, and references. Some educational institutions, however, have open admissions policies that make it possible for all high school graduates to apply and be admitted. Because admitting candidates without the necessary academic skills for college study places undue stress on the entire educational system, colleges with open admissions policies typically localize this stress by establishing remedial programs and hiring specially trained teachers for these students. Students are expected to pass remedial course work before entering regular college courses.

In a business situation, the same thing happens. New workers participate in training programs before being placed in positions within the firm. During the training period, they learn specific job-related practices so they can become productive in the work environment as soon as possible. After training, they are placed in positions consistent with their skill levels and backgrounds. This orientation and training process helps minimize the stress that might occur if the new employees were placed directly into positions within the firm.

Although it is often easier to deal with stress by changing the activities of a subsystem, it is also important to remember that the subsystem is a part of the whole system and interacts with other subsystems in achieving overall objectives. It may be necessary to consider the entire system in responding to a problem and to modify activities in other subsystems as well.

HOW A SYSTEM WORKS

You can get a better idea of how a system works by considering the activities of a professional baseball team. A professional baseball team consists of components that are organized to achieve its objectives. One of the major objectives of a baseball club is to win games. To achieve this goal, the owner and manager may recruit players, organize training programs, and develop publicity campaigns. When the team needs a good catcher, the manager may acquire a new player by making a trade. All these components—players, management, training, and promotion—interact to enable the ball club to achieve its objectives.

A professional baseball team interacts with its environment, just as other systems do. It accepts feedback from the external environment in order to organize its resources more effectively. It receives feedback from many sources. Sportswriters provide feedback on trades, team strategy, and performance. Fans provide feedback by their support (or lack of it) for the team. The manager and coaches give players specific feedback about their performance. All this feedback provides the manager, coaches, and players with information they need to reallocate resources to meet objectives.

Systems differ in terms of their goals, components, and characteristics. The objective of one ball club may be to win games. To achieve this goal, it may recruit highly paid professionals throughout the season to fill gaps in the lineup. In contrast, the objective of another team may be to make money. Instead of recruiting highly paid athletes, this second team may enlist talented rookies, hoping to fill the ballpark with dedicated fans. Each of these two ball clubs has a different system with different objectives. The measures of success that each club uses to evaluate its performance vary. In the first case, game and player statistics help measure the ability to win games. In the second, box office receipts are a measure of success.

A professional baseball team can exhibit signs of entropy if it is not successfully managed and maintained. New players have to be brought in to fill critical positions and others need to be retrained. Team strategy needs to be constantly formulated to address the competition. All these efforts are designed to maintain the system and to prevent it from becoming noncompetitive in its environment.

SYSTEMS CONCEPTS IN BUSINESS

Now that you have a general picture of how a system works, it will be helpful to look more closely at business systems. The systems approach is a way of analyzing business problems. This approach views the business organization as a system of interrelated parts designed to accomplish goals. Each subsystem is both a self-contained unit and a part of a larger system. Managers must understand the goals of the total system and design the function of subsystems within the total system to make it possible to accomplish these goals.

More specifically, *management* is the practice of organizing resources, including people, materials, procedures, and machines, to achieve objectives. In other words, it entails organizing subsystems to accomplish specific tasks. Using a systems approach, a manager organizes various activities of the business into separate organizational subsystems. The subsystems of the business are connected by resource flows throughout the firm.

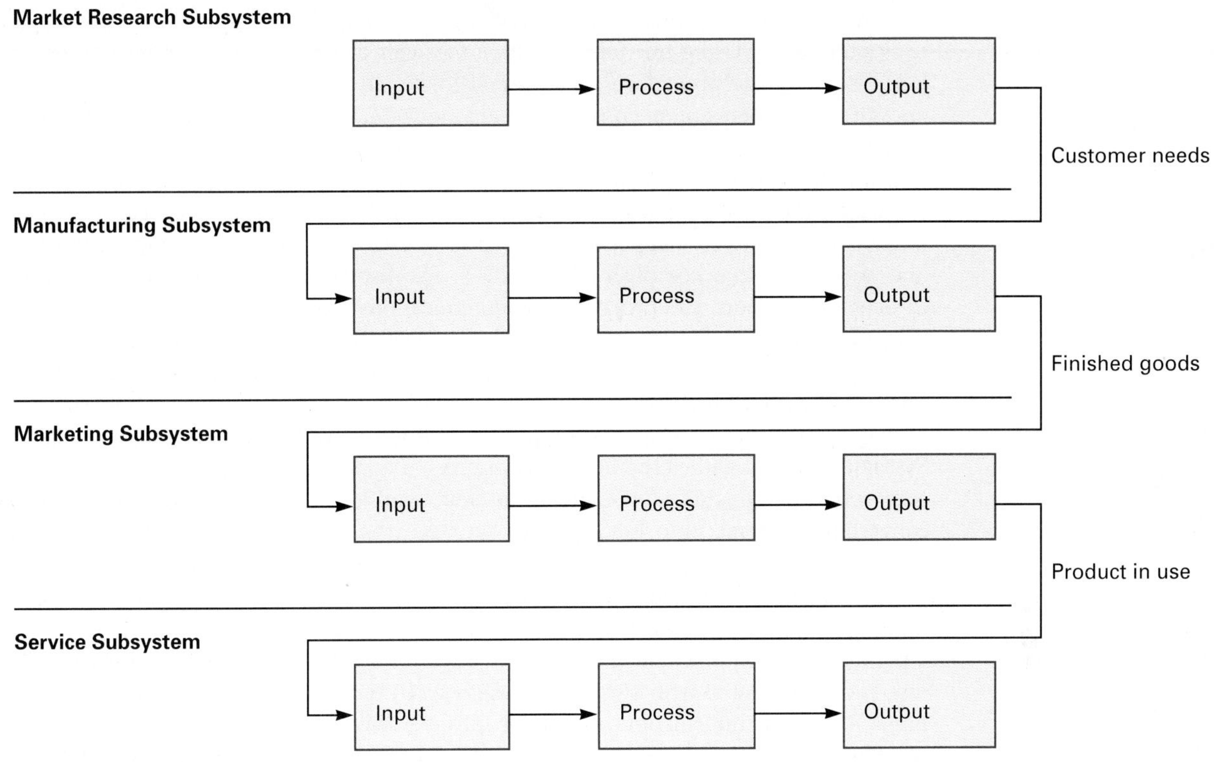

Figure 2–4
The firm's subsystems

To consider an example, the market research subsystem of the business may obtain information from customers about modifications that need to be made in the firm's products and services. This information can be transmitted to the manufacturing subsystem that builds product design changes into its processes. Finally, the finished products are sold to customers through the marketing subsystem. If technical problems occur, the service subsystem may need to provide follow-up support. The interactions among these functional subsystems are depicted in Figure 2–4.

AN INFORMATION SYSTEM AS A SYSTEM

In many ways, *information systems* have the same characteristics as systems in general. The major purpose of an information system is to convert *data* into *information*—**information** is data with meaning. In a business context, an **information system** is a subsystem of the business system of an organization. Each business system has goals, such as increasing profits, expanding market share, and providing service to customers. The information systems of an organization should provide information on the day-to-day activities of a business, such as processing sales orders or checking credit. These systems are called **operational systems.** Information systems also must be designed to provide information that lets management allocate resources effectively to achieve business objectives. These systems are known as **tactical systems.** Finally, information systems must support the strategic plans of the business, and these systems are known as **strategic planning systems.** You'll learn more about these systems in the next chapter. But to sum up our discussion so far, information provides managers with the feedback they need about a system and its operations—feedback they can use for decision making. Using this information, a manager can reallocate resources, redesign jobs, or reorganize procedures to accomplish objectives successfully.

An information system consists of components that interact to achieve the objective of providing information about day-to-day activities that managers can use to control business operations. Information systems can also be designed to provide information to enable managers to allocate resources and establish long-range business plans. An information system contains such elements as hardware, software, personnel, databases, and procedures to accomplish its objectives. The **hardware** consists of the computer devices that support data processing, communications processing, and other computer-related activities. **Software** consists of the instructions that the hardware uses to process information. Software includes both *application software* and *system software.* **Application software** consists of the programs written to support specific business functions, such as order entry, inventory control, and accounts receivable. System software enables the hardware to process application software programs. **System software** consists of the programs that handle such functions as sorting data, converting programs into the machine language the computer can understand, and retrieving data from storage areas.

Information-processing personnel, such as systems designers and programmers, design and write the application programs to support information processing activities. Operations personnel, such as data entry operators and equipment operators, handle day-to-day operations activities. (You'll learn about the roles and the responsibilities of many types of information-processing professionals in Chapter 19.) Finally, all personnel have to follow specific procedures to organize and manage a company's information-processing activities. These procedures include designing and implementing programs, maintaining hardware and software, and managing the operations function. The interactions among these elements constitute the information-processing procedures that are used to generate information needed for decision making. (A general model of an information system is shown in Figure 2–5.)

Subsystems

Operational systems, which are designed to provide information about day-to-day activities, are composed of subsystems that accomplish specialized tasks. A mail-order business, for example, needs a system to process customer orders. The order-processing system actually consists of subsystems set up to handle incoming orders, update inventory levels, and bill customers. Other subsystems are created to purchase new stock, to handle accounts payable transactions, and to apply cash receipts from

Figure 2–5
A model of an information system

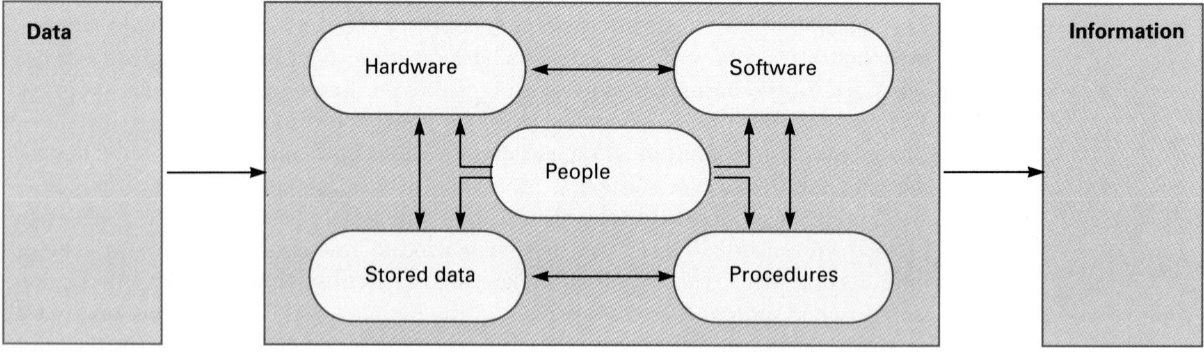

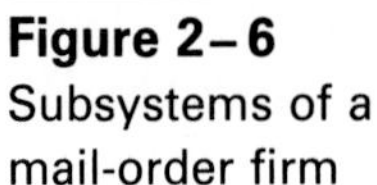

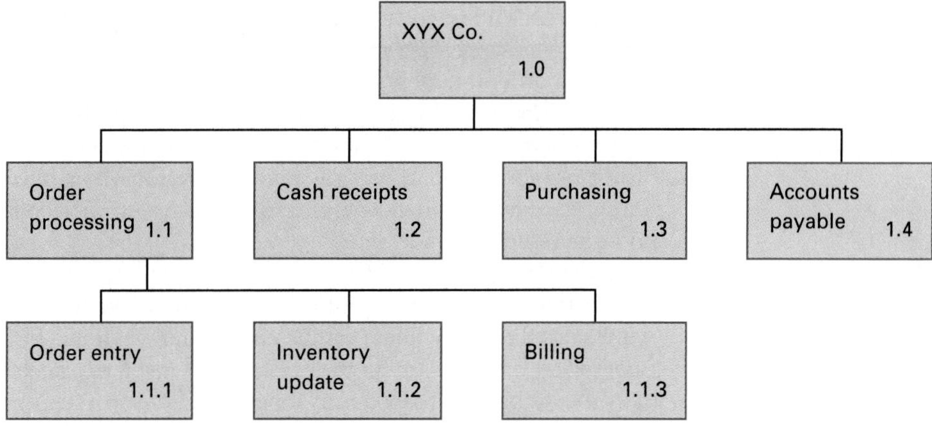

Figure 2–6
Subsystems of a mail-order firm

customers to outstanding accounts receivable balances. Each of these subsystems performs a specialized task that supports the business objectives of increasing sales and providing customer service. You can see how these subsystems are organized in Figure 2–6.

However, if one of these subsystems breaks down, the overall business will feel the effect. For example, if the mail-order company does not maintain sufficient inventories, customers may become frustrated with constant back-orders and shift their business to other mail-order companies.

Outputs and Inputs

An information system, like any other system, receives inputs of data and instructions, processes the data according to these instructions, and produces outputs. This information-processing model can be used to depict any information system. An order entry and inventory update system is shown in Figure 2–7.

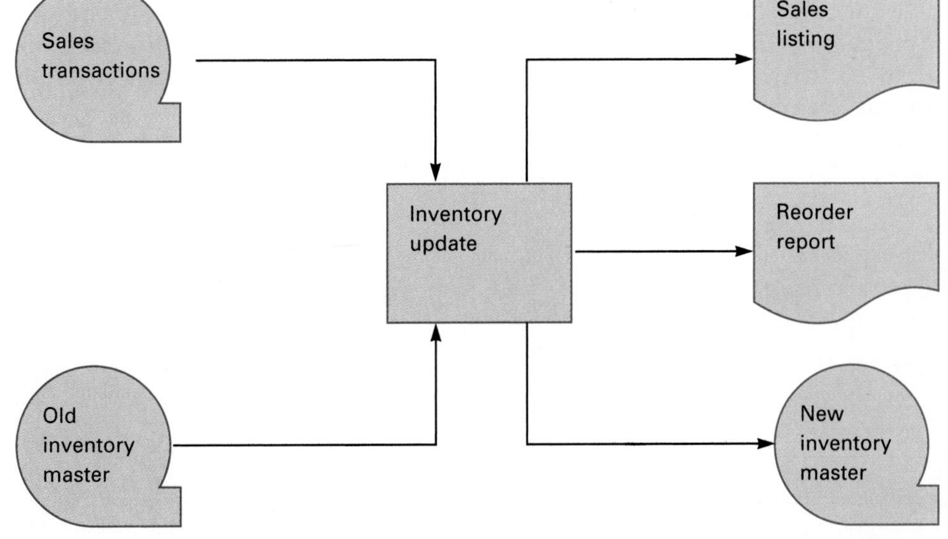

Figure 2–7
An inventory update system

In an inventory update procedure, the inputs are sales order transactions and an old inventory master file. During the update procedure, the item quantities for each item on a sales order transaction are subtracted from the existing inventory level for that item in stock. The new inventory level is then written to the new inventory master file. The outputs of this system are an updated inventory master file, a reorder report, and a sales listing. A reorder report lists any items in inventory that have fallen below their desired inventory level and provides a purchasing manager with feedback about items that need to be reordered.

Hierarchy of Subsystems

The subsystems within an information system can be organized into a hierarchy to represent their functions within the overall system. Each subsystem performs a specialized function. In the order entry and inventory update example, one subsystem may record sales transactions as input, another subsystem may check customer credit, and another may check inventory availability. Other subsystems may update inventory, generate a reorder report, produce information for billing, and so on.

System Feedback

An information system provides **system feedback** to a manager about day-to-day activities and about deviations from planned activity. The manager can use this information to supervise daily operations, such as credit checking and billing, and to reorganize resources to achieve objectives more effectively. In the inventory control example, one of the outputs was a reorder report indicating which inventory items need to be reordered. A purchasing manager could use this report to reorder additional stock on a day-to-day basis. An example of a reorder report is shown in Figure 2–8.

Middle managers might want feedback about which items in inventory are moving rapidly and which items are moving slowly so they can reallocate the investment in inventory to minimize waste and maximize profitability. The information systems providing feedback that can be used to allocate resources effectively, such as inventory and personnel, are called *tactical systems.*

Subsystem Interfaces

As with other systems, there are interfaces between the subsystems of an information system. Again, the outputs of one subsystem become the inputs into the next. For example, the outputs of a sales order entry system become the inputs into an invoicing system. If the outputs of one system are not correct, however, the next subsystem will be affected. If the price of an item is entered incorrectly during order entry, then the charges to the customer may be incorrectly calculated during billing.

Figure 2–8
A reorder report

REORDER REPORT
American Office Supply

DATE: 01/01/95

Item No.	Item Description	Unit	Quantity On Hand	Quantity On Order	Quantity Back Order	Reorder Point	EOQ
5045	3-ring binder	EA	100	0	0	120	40
6565	Pencil sharpener	EA	34	10	0	50	10
7231	Manila folder	BX	0	50	20	50	50

Internal Controls

Good information systems also have internal standards to make sure that data are processed accurately. Input controls, for example, ensure that input data are valid before they are processed. Another type of control is a password security procedure designed to protect against unauthorized access and update of data. All in all, standards make sure the system works properly. Without controls, the data printed out on reports may be inaccurate and managers may not be able to trust the information system to provide valid results. If unauthorized users update data files or if input data are not valid, managers may not even know that the output generated in reports is invalid, and thus they may make decisions using erroneous information.

Effect of the Systems Approach on Information Systems Design

Many of the ideas that are part of the systems approach have implications for the design of information systems. You can learn about the design of an information system by putting yourself in the shoes of an owner of a microcomputer dealership, for example. Systems have objectives, and in this case the owner's objective is to make a profit on the sales of microcomputers, software, and related peripheral equipment.

The Structure of an Enterprise

The entire enterprise has been organized into subsystems, including the marketing subsystem, the service subsystem, and the administrative subsystem. The marketing subsystem promotes and markets microcomputer products and services. When customers have problems with their microcomputers or need preventive maintenance, they use the service subsystem. Finally, the administrative subsystem takes care of billing customers, purchasing equipment and supplies from vendors, paying vendors, and handling accounting activities. The organizational structure of the dealership is depicted in Figure 2–9.

The marketing subsystem of the dealership is managed by a sales manager who recruits salespeople, including experienced veterans and new trainees, to demonstrate and sell the equipment. These salespeople are trained to follow certain procedures, such as giving equipment demonstrations and making follow-up calls. These procedures are an important part of the "system" of selling microcomputer hardware and software. When they are not followed, profitability suffers.

The sales manager needs an information system to provide feedback on how the system is working. On a day-to-day basis, he may receive information about salespeople who have successfully closed sales, about customers who are complaining, and about

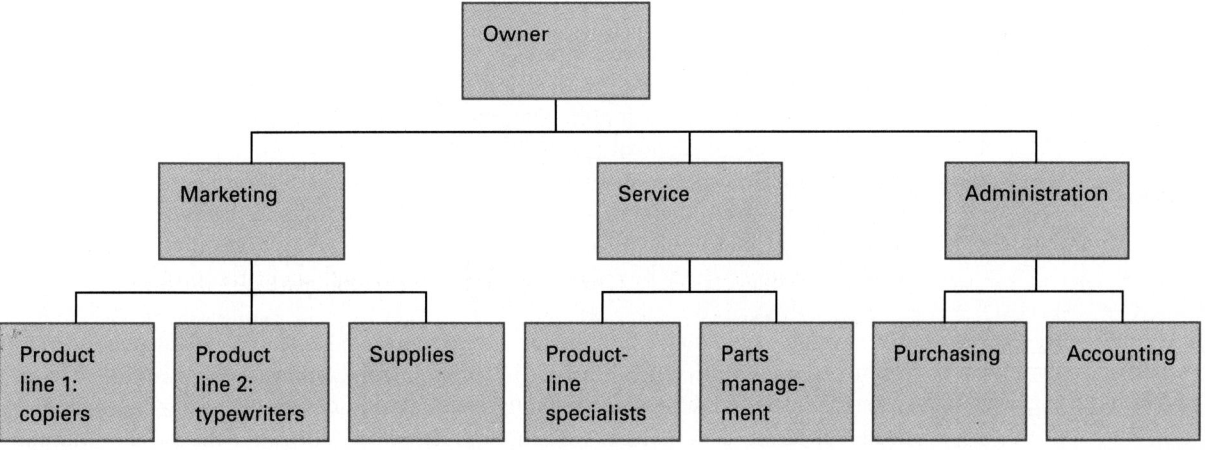

Figure 2–9 Organizational structure of the dealer

technical problems with equipment. This feedback makes it possible to review the procedures and activities of the current system. For example, if a particular model of microcomputer is breaking down too often, the sales manager may encourage the salespeople to push alternative lines of equipment until technical problems are resolved with the manufacturer.

The sales manager also needs to organize personnel resources to achieve the desired objectives. If a certain salesperson is unable to make quota month after month, a more effective training program may be needed. If experienced salespeople seem to be selling more effectively to large accounts, the sales manager may assign them to these accounts.

You can now see that the information the sales manager uses to monitor and control the activities of the marketing system is critical to achieving the objectives of the business. Some of this information may be obtained by word of mouth, and other information may be generated from a computer. A product profitability report, for example, may give the sales manager feedback on the product lines that generate the greatest gross profit. Whether the manager uses informal feedback or computer-generated reports, the information is being used to organize people, procedures, and activities to accomplish objectives.

USING THE SYSTEMS APPROACH IN PROBLEM SOLVING

An owner of a business like the microcomputer dealership must constantly analyze problems and reorganize the resources of the system to deal with these problems effectively. The systems approach is a valuable method of problem solving that takes into account the goals, environment, and internal workings of the system. The systems approach to problem solving involves the following steps:

1. Define the problem.
2. Gather data describing the problem.
3. Identify alternative solutions.
4. Evaluate these alternatives.
5. Select and implement the best alternative.
6. Follow up to determine if the solution is working.

We can understand how the systems approach works by applying it to a problem that the microcomputer dealer might experience.

Define the Problem

The first step in the systems approach to problem solving is to define the problem. Defining the problem is one of the most important parts of the system study, because if the wrong problem is identified, the entire effort to change the system will be off track. At the outset, some of the problems that are identified may be symptoms of the real problem. In order to distinguish between symptoms and problems, it is necessary to gather data describing the problem. Let's say that in this case the owner is concerned about the fact that many of the salespeople are not meeting their quotas. She decides to start a systems study by collecting more information about the problem.

Gather Data Describing the Problem

The owner may study the environment, current standards, management, input resources, and internal procedures to gain an understanding of the problem. The first place the owner might look is the *environment.* The environment of the microcomputer dealer includes its vendors, its customers, its competitors, and the local community. From this investigation, the owner might learn that local competitors are selling comparable microcomputers at prices 10 percent to 15 percent less than the firm can offer.

Next, she might look at the dealership's *standards* to determine if they are valid in the face of the competitive environment. It might turn out that a goal of increasing gross sales by 10 percent for the year is unrealistic when the competition is cutting price.

Another area that could be analyzed is *management.* The owner needs to learn if the sales manager is doing a good job. If the sales manager is not providing salespeople with effective training and feedback regarding their performance, they may feel frustrated.

Input resources are another area that should be analyzed. The owner needs to find out if new sales and technical representatives are being recruited and if these employees are trained to demonstrate computer equipment and software. If new recruits lack knowledge of the technical features of the equipment, for example, they will fail to win new business. If sales materials are not kept up to date, customers may not learn about new product features.

Work methods and procedures also need to be studied. If salespeople are not trained to follow up on new prospects, the company could lose valuable business. If technical support personnel cannot diagnose and solve service problems on a timely basis, customers may be hesitant to purchase more equipment.

One of the major problems identified in this case is that competitors are charging lower prices for comparable products. Many of the difficulties the dealer has identified are symptoms of this fundamental problem. To address it, the owner has to identify and evaluate some alternatives.

Identify Alternative Solutions

Given the fact that competitors have dropped their prices on comparable microcomputers, the owner needs to identify some alternatives responses. These alternatives might include the following:

Alternative 1: Investigate alternative manufacturers of microcomputers to obtain products at a lower cost per unit.

Alternative 2: Decrease the cost of sales by introducing mail-order sales supported by telemarketing. Use salespersons for large accounts only. Cutting the cost of sales efforts would make it possible to reduce machine prices to a more competitive level.

Alternative 3: Differentiate the products being sold by offering on-line diagnostic support services for machine failure, service response time within 5 hours on a 24-hour basis, and annual service checks.

Each of these alternatives supports a slightly different strategy. Finding lower-cost manufactured goods would represent a cost-cutting strategy. The second alternative, using mail-order sales and telemarketing, would also support a low-cost strategy because the cost of mail-order sales would be less than the cost of a large sales staff. Finally, introducing on-line diagnostic support services would provide a "value-added" feature. Upgraded technical support would justify slightly higher equipment costs.

Evaluate These Alternatives

The owner evaluates the extent to which each of these alternatives enables the organization to achieve its objectives. As we saw, the owner's objective was to increase the overall performance of sales personnel. Purchasing lower-cost products from suppliers would enable the owner to cut prices, as suggested in the first alternative, but would create difficulty at the service end if these microcomputer products were less reliable. This might make it more difficult for salespeople to meet their objectives.

Introducing a mail-order program would cut the cost of sales overhead. However, the mail-order program would require creating a database of customer prospects and developing specialized promotional materials. This strategy might free sales representatives to concentrate on direct sales to high-potential accounts while using a less costly strategy to maintain the business of smaller accounts.

The final alternative would offer customers additional levels of service and technical support that add value to the firm's products. Because service is one of the key criteria for microcomputer selection, this strategy might work. However, it is costly and might not satisfy the needs of economy-conscious small businesses that represent a large potential market share.

Select and Implement the Best Alternative

Let's say that the owner decides to develop and implement a mail-order program to reduce the cost of sales overhead to smaller accounts and to enable sales personnel to focus on high-potential accounts. Because this is a new strategy, the owner would have to recruit new customer service representatives or train others for telemarketing. Customer prospect databases would need to be developed and established, as well as a system for shipping merchandise, billing, and authorizing credit transactions.

Follow Up to Determine if the Solution Is Working

The last step in the systems approach to problem solving is follow-up. In the case of the mail-order sales alternative, the owner would need to determine if the system was meeting its goals. If not, changes in management, standards, resources, and procedures would have to be made to achieve these objectives. If either one of the other two alternatives were selected, the owner also would need to follow up to determine if the approach was useful in improving sales effectiveness.

As you can see from this example, the systems approach to problem solving is an important technique for the manager. Every manager needs feedback to determine if the goals of the system are being achieved. One of the most difficult tasks in a systems study is identifying information that can be used to determine how the system is working. This is as true in an organization with a *simple structure* as it is in a more complex organization. The next section discusses the characteristics of organizations with different structures.

SYSTEMS CONCEPTS IN ORGANIZATIONS

The organization is also a system. Henry Mintzberg, in his book *The Structuring of Organizations,* describes five basic parts of organizations and how they function together as a system in which material, information, and decision processes flow. Mintzberg also identified five different types of organizational structures, including the *simple structure,* the *machine bureaucracy,* the *professional bureaucracy,* the *divisionalized form* and the *adhocracy.*

The Five Parts of the Organization

The five parts of the organization are the operating core, the strategic apex, the middle line, the technostructure, and the support staff, as Figure 2–10 shows. The operating core is comprised of the operators that carry out the basic work of the organization. They obtain inputs, transform inputs into outputs, and distribute the outputs. They also provide direct support for these input, transformation, and output functions. You might think of the operating core of an automobile manufacturer as the assembly line workers.

The administrative component of the organization is made up of the strategic apex, the middle line, and the technostructure. The strategic apex is top-level management. Top management is responsible for insuring that the organization serves its mission.

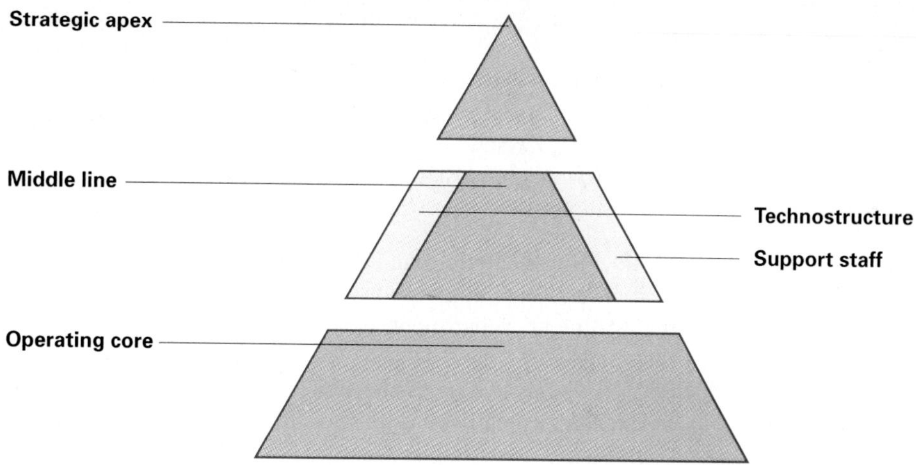

Figure 2–10
The five basic parts of organizations

Top managers are responsible for allocating resources, resolving conflicts, reviewing activities, disseminating information, and serving as spokespersons for the organization in dealing with the external environment. Most importantly, they develop the organization's strategic plans.

The middle line consists of middle-level managers who are below top managers in the chain of command. The middle-line managers are responsible for coordination and control of activities within their functional units. They allocate resources, initiate change, handle conflicts, monitor the environment, establish strategy, and negotiate with outsiders—all to serve the needs of their functional units.

The technostructure consists of analysts who help standardize the work of others within the organization to control outputs and adapt to the environment. Examples of groups in the technostructure are work-study analysts who standardize work processes, planning and budget analysts who standardize outputs, and personnel analysts-trainers who standardize skills used by the organization.

The fifth group in the organization, the support staff, is responsible for supporting the operating core outside the flow of operating work. Support groups include the cafeteria, legal, payroll, public relations, and research and development staffs.

The Organization as a System of Flows

The five parts of the organization are joined together by flows—of authority, work material, information, and decision processes. At the operating level, the parts moving down the assembly line are work flows. Control information flows from the operating level to middle management and serves as feedback. As feedback information passes up through each level of the hierarchy, it becomes more highly aggregated until it reaches the strategic apex. Typically, information about exceptions passes upward through the hierarchy until it reaches a manager who has the formal authority to handle the situation. In addition, commands flow downward from top and middle management to the operating core.

The communications patterns within organizations vary depending upon the structure of the organization. In more traditional organizations, information is filtered as it moves upwards through the hierarchy. In emerging forms of "networked" organizations, informal communication may link members of a project team who represent diverse areas and who work in different locations. By learning about their communications patterns, you can understand how different types of organizations function using feedback from both internal and external sources.

Types of Organizational Structures

In Mintzberg's analysis, the five types of organizations—the simple structure, the machine bureaucracy, the professional bureaucracy, the divisionalized form, and the adhocracy—have unique ways of handling information and communications. As organizations become information-based, information becomes a shared resource that facilitates interaction among specialists in diverse areas. As information technology moves onto the desktop of every manager, it will become a vehicle that supports the transition to the more advanced networked forms of organization.

The Simple Structure. What do an automobile dealership, a middle-sized retail store, a small corporation run by an aggressive entrepreneur, and a brand-new government department have in common? They are all examples of the **simple structure.**

The classic case of the simple structure is the owner-managed entrepreneurship. The chief executive has most of the power and is responsible for formulating strategy and policy. The simple structure has little or no technostructure, few support staffers, and a small management hierarchy. Jobs in the operating core are unspecialized and interchangeable. An example of a simple structure is a family-owned restaurant where the husband is the chef and the wife does the inventory management, purchasing, and accounting. The waiters are the unspecialized operating workers.

In the simple structure, information follows a traditional path through the hierarchy to the single chief executive, the major decision maker. One possible problem is that the leader may become so enmeshed in operating-level information that he or she forgets the strategic direction of the organization.

The Machine Bureaucracy. What do a national post office, a security agency, a steel company, an airline, and an automobile company have in common? They are all **machine bureaucracies.** Characteristics of the machine bureaucracy are a clearly defined hierarchy of authority, centralized power for decision making, and formal communications throughout the organization. At the operating core, you will find standardized procedures and a proliferation of rules and regulations. In the machine bureaucracy, analysts in the technostructure—work analysts, job designers, quality control engineers, and operations researchers—standardize work methods and procedures.

An example of a machine bureaucracy is a fast-food restaurant chain. In each restaurant, food is standardized. Recipes, menus, prices, and specials are fixed. Even the uniforms, interior decor, and external appearance of each restaurant is fixed. Customers depend upon fast-food restaurant chains for consistent food—whether they go to Peoria or Tokyo.

As you have already learned, the machine bureaucracy has a clear chain of command, with clearly defined authority at the top. The information system of the machine bureaucracy aggregates information as it moves up the hierarchy, at the risk of excessive filtering. By the time information hits the strategic apex, bad news may be blocked and good news may be highlighted. Yet, the managers making up the strategic apex are still responsible for making most of the decisions—sometimes without the information they need. This is one of the major issues of the machine bureaucracy.

The Professional Bureaucracy. Universities, general hospitals, school systems, general accounting firms, and social work agencies are still another type of organization, the **professional bureaucracy.** The professional bureaucracy hires professionals who are specialists in their fields and gives them control over their work. Professionals work independently of their colleagues; they work closely with the clients they serve.

Professionals have several tasks: diagnosing a client's need, presenting one or more alternatives, and proceeding with a particular course of action.

You might wonder why professionals join organizations at all. One factor is the market for their skills. Students wishing business training and students seeking a broad liberal arts background represent two distinct markets for a university. Hence a university may group itself into departments, including a marketing department to train students in career skills and a philosophy department to train generalists.

The professional organization is highly decentralized, with most of its power at the operating core. Professional organizations are collegial organizations. Much of the work in policy-setting and organizing activities takes place in committees of the professionals. In this way, the professionals get collective control over the administrative decisions that affect them. In most universities, for example, professors determine their own rules for tenure and promotion. New initiatives, such as the development of new degree programs, are developed by committees of the professionals.

The professional bureaucracy is a democratic form of organization, which means that information flows are widespread and diverse. Much of the feedback comes from the external environment. If the faculty of a business program doesn't receive feedback from potential employers, they may not change programs to prepare graduates with the skills and knowledge they need to succeed in entry-level positions.

The Divisionalized Form. The **divisionalized organization** consists of a group of quasi-autonomous entities coupled together by a central administrative structure. There are divisionalized corporations and universities with multiple campuses. A corporation, for example, may have 15 different divisions—each with its own purchasing, manufacturing, and marketing functions.

The divisionalized structure usually emerges in response to distinct markets. The divisionalized form works well when different products and services are offered to different markets. For example, a multidivisional corporation may have divisions selling copiers, computers, and printing presses to three different markets. In the 1920s, Sloan converted General Motors into a divisionalized firm (e.g., Chevrolet, Cadillac, etc.) but retained central office controls for some functions, including research, engineering, quality control, styling, pricing, and dealer relations. Today, the corporate offices of divisionalized firms provide support services such as financial, legal, personnel services, market research, and research and development.

The key to managing a divisionalized enterprise is a management information system that alerts senior management to deviations in business performance. In this way, the strategic apex can correct fundamental problems of the business, shift resources, and focus on products and markets where business performance is strong. The tendency of the management information system that monitors division performance is to focus on such indicators as profit, sales growth, and return on investment.

The Adhocracy. What do a management consulting firm and an innovative theater project company have in common? They are both examples of an **adhocracy,** the fifth type of organizational structure. The adhocracy combines groups of specialists into small market-based project teams. Each team is a task force designed to conduct a specific project. A high-technology firm, for example, establishes interdisciplinary project teams consisting of highly trained experts. The adhocracy thrives in a rapidly changing environment with strong competition.

The function of management in an adhocracy is different from the other forms of organization. Top managers scan the external environment looking for new projects and sell their services to potential clients. Managers at various levels of the organization

	Simple Structure	Machine Bureaucracy	Professional Bureaucracy	Divisionalized Form	Adhocracy
Key coordinating mechanism	Direct supervision	Work standards	Standardized skills	Standardized outputs	Mutual adjustments
Key part of organization	Strategic apex	Technostructure	Operating core	Middle line	Support staff
Job specialization	Little specialization	Horizontal and vertical specialization	Much horizontal specialization	Some specialization between divisions and headquarters	Much horizontal specialization
Role of strategic apex	Administrative work	Coordinating fine-tuning	External liaison	Performance control	External liaison, project monitoring
Role of operating core	Informal work	Routine, formal work	Standardized skilled work with autonomy	Formalized work at division level	Informal project work
Middle line	Insignificant	Elaborate and differentiated	Controlled by professionals	Division-level managers	Project work
Technostructure	None	Helps to formalize work	Little	Helps headquarters with performance control	Small and blurred
Support staff	Small	Elaborate to reduce uncertainties	Elaborate to support professionals	Split between headquarters and divisions	Blurred, part of projects
Flow of informal communications	Significant	Discouraged	Significant in administration	Some between headquarters and divisions	Significant throughout
Flow of decision making	Top down	Top down	Bottom up	Differentiated between headquarters and divisions	Mixed, all levels
Environment	Simple, dynamic	Simple, stable	Complex, stable	Simple, stable	Complex, dynamic
Power	Chief executive control	Technocratic control	Professional control	Mid-line control	Expert control

Figure 2–11
Characteristics of the five organizational structures

work to coordinate project-related activities. They serve as peers, not as supervisors. Their influence is derived from their expertise and interpersonal skill, not their position power.

The adhocracy works well in organizations developing and marketing diverse, highly technical products in a rapidly changing environment. Sometimes temporary adhocracies are formed to draw together specialists from different organizations to execute single projects. An all-star sports team, an election campaign committee, and a special presidential task force are examples. The matrix-type structure, emphasis on expertise, and project-team orientation make the adhocracy a fashionable form of organizational structure in the 1990s.

Figure 2–11 summarizes the key attributes of the five forms of organization.

Transition to the Information-Based Organization

The transition to the information-based organization is the transition from a traditional bureaucratic organization to a networked organization, or adhocracy. The role of information is different in these two types of organizations. In the traditional organization, information is "owned" by each functional area. Summary information is transmitted up through the hierarchy to senior management. In the adhocracy, information is shared. Teams with representatives from many different functional areas share access to common information resources, such as customer databases, accounting databases, and product development databases.

The role of information is a critical factor in the transition to the networked organization. Access to information is the key to empowering the worker. In Chapter 1, you learned about how deal structurers at IBM Credit used desktop workstations equipped with financial databases to make credit decisions. In another example, insurance application reviewers at Mutual Benefit Life can use desktop workstations to authorize insurance policies because they have access to local and national credit history databases and prior loan records.

Some of the characteristics of the information-based organization are contrasted with the traditional organization in Figure 2–12.

As you can see from this chart, the nature of jobs in the information-based organization changes radically. People like deal structurers, insurance screeners, and product designers have much broader roles. In the information-based organization, people are drawn into process teams to accomplish projects. These teams are assembled and disassembled based upon market needs. Throughout their careers, people may serve on a variety of teams. That is why adaptability and flexibility are so important.

In his article, "The New Society of Organizations," Peter Drucker suggests that as more and more organizations become information based, people must increasingly act as responsible decision makers. "Managers must be prepared to abandon everything they know," Drucker argues, because organizations will be under constant pressure to improve everything they do continuously. Innovation will be key. Change will be constant. In this environment, the ability to capitalize on knowledge, gained from information, will be more critical than remembering the procedures of the past.

As noted in Chapter 1, the organization of the 1990s will more closely resemble a networked jazz ensemble than a traditional corporate hierarchy. The system of information flows will be vastly different from the information flows in the traditional organization. In many respects, information technology facilitates the transition to the

Figure 2–12
Transition to the information-based organization

Organizational Characteristic	Traditional	Information-Based
Job design	Simple tasks	Multidimensional work
Structure	Hierarchical	Flattened
People's roles	Controlled	Empowered
Performance measures	Activity-based	Results-based
Role of managers	Supervisors	Coaches
Work groups	Functional departments	Process teams
Educational implications	Job preparation	Continuous education
People needed	Structured	Adaptive

networked organization. Technologies such as networking and shared databases are enabling factors in the transition to the networked organization. Without these technologies, the transformation would not be possible.

MANAGEMENT SUMMARY

This chapter has introduced systems concepts that provide a foundation for understanding information systems in general and management information systems in particular. Managers have to understand systems, their objectives, their components, and their activities. Information about how a system is working provides them with the feedback they need to allocate resources to achieve their business objectives. Depending on the objectives of a system, its components, standards, and interactions may differ.

We have seen that an information system provides feedback about the activities of the business. Information systems have the same characteristics as other systems, including inputs and outputs, processes that transform inputs into outputs, and methods of system control. In designing an information system, the outputs must be defined, the interactions must be established, and the standards of system control must be organized.

A management information system in particular must be designed to provide information for effective planning and control of business activities. Decision making requires converting data into information. Information is data that have meaning in the decision-making process. An information system must be designed to provide feedback for the business system. This feedback can be used to reorganize, simplify, and improve activities in the business system so that goals are more effectively achieved. In the information-based organization, it is critical for managers to define their information needs and to use information as feedback.

KEY TERMS FOR MANAGERS

adhocracy, **45**
application software, **36**
boundary, **28**
closed system, **31**
data, **35**
divisionalized organization, **45**
hardware, **36**
information, **35**
information system, **35**
interface, **29**
machine bureaucracy, **44**
systems entropy, **33**
open system, **30**
operational systems, **35**
professional bureaucracy, **44**
simple structure, **44**
software, **36**
strategic planning systems, **35**
subsystem, **28**
system, **28**
system feedback, **38**
system software, **36**
tactical systems, **35**

REVIEW QUESTIONS

1. What is a system? Which of the following are systems? Give reasons for your answers.

a. A house.
b. A football team.
c. A textbook.
d. A soccer game.

2. For each of the following systems, identify the subsystems.
   - *a.* An educational system.
   - *b.* A professional baseball team.
   - *c.* A library.
3. What forms of feedback can be used to control the following systems or subsystems?
   - *a.* A student organization.
   - *b.* A retail department store.
   - *c.* An insurance agency.
4. Discuss how interface problems can be solved using an interface subsystem, standards, or slack resources in each of the following examples:
   - *a.* Interfacing a limited supply of concert tickets with great consumer demand.
   - *b.* Interfacing a two-year degree in office management that produces students with good technical skills but inadequate communications skills with a four-year program in business that requires effective speaking and writing skills.
   - *c.* Interfacing components of a microcomputer system.
5. What is the difference between data and information?
6. What information can be used to provide feedback about each of the following?
   - *a.* Employee morale.
   - *b.* New-product success.
   - *c.* Salesperson performance.
7. Classify the following systems as either open systems or closed systems. Give reasons for your answers.
   - *a.* A real estate agency.
   - *b.* A country club.
   - *c.* A symphony orchestra.
   - *d.* A prison.
   - *e.* A dentist's practice.
8. What is the role of top management in an organization with a simple structure?
9. What is one of the main roles of the professional administrator in the professional bureaucracy?
10. What information does headquarters management use in an organization with a divisionalized form?
11. What are some of the advantages of the divisionalized form?
12. What are the characteristics of an adhocracy?

Questions for Discussion

1. Why is feedback useful in controlling the internal workings of a system?
2. Why is a closed system likely to deteriorate?
3. What are some methods of decreasing entropy affecting a newly purchased automobile?

4. Why is the systems approach to problem solving used by many managers?

5. How can standards be used as a method of system control in a graduate program in music at a university?

6. Why is "soft information," which is intangible and speculative, so valuable to managers?

7. Why is the simple structure form of organization often led by a charismatic leader with a high degree of power?

8. What are some of the reasons why professionals who want considerable discretion in performing their work join a professional bureaucratic form of organization?

9. Why does the divisionalized form of organization often evolve from the machine bureaucracy?

10. How might the evolution of the adhocracy be facilitated with the use of information technology?

Problems

1. **New job skills.** Many of the newly hired programmer analysts at Epcon Industries are having problems on the job. Although they have good technical skills, they are falling down on the job because of poor communications skills—particularly writing ability. This is causing the personnel department to think seriously about requiring a prescreening test in basic writing skills, including grammar, punctuation, and spelling.

   The personnel department has also contacted several local universities to express their concern about the problem of communications skills.

   Diagnose this problem from a systems standpoint and suggest some possible solutions.

2. **Town and Country Tennis and Golf Club.** Town and Country Tennis and Golf Club is a rapidly expanding club in suburban Baltimore County. It currently has about 1,200 members but may expand to as many as 3,000 members within the next five years. An 18-hole golf course and eight tennis courts are its major attractions. The club has two restaurants, one of which is casual and one of which is formal, and a bar. It also offers a golf shop and a tennis shop in which sports equipment and clothes are sold. Members can take golf and tennis lessons, enroll in weekly scheduled events, participate in tournaments, and invite guests for certain activities.

   A prospective member needs to obtain three letters of reference from current members of the club. Then the applicant and family are interviewed by a subcommittee of the Board of directors. Once admitted, the member is responsible for paying an entry fee plus monthly dues. When the club does not meet revenue projections, members are assessed an additional fee to cover operating losses.

   A Board of Directors oversees club management, hires staff, and monitors the budget. Subcommittees of the club are responsible for recruiting new members, organizing social events, managing golf and tennis programs, and insuring that members adhere to club rules and regulations.

   With the objective of building membership, the club has recently renovated its facilities, improved several areas of the golf course, and added two tennis courts. Club management is aggressively marketing banquet facilities and special events.

Identify the major systems and subsystems of the club. What are the boundaries of these systems? What are the objectives of each of these subsystems? What elements interact in each of these subsystems?

What methods does the club have to screen input? What types of control mechanisms are in place? Is the club an open system or a closed system? What types of feedback from the environment does the club use?

3. **Amalgamated Paper, Inc.** The MIS department at Amalgamated Paper, Inc., built many data processing systems in the 1960s and 1970s. These systems were written in COBOL, a procedural language, and were maintained by programmer analysts with technical backgrounds. Many of these data processing systems handled the day-to-day paperwork of the company, including order entry, accounts receivable, and inventory control.

   In the mid- to late 1970s, many of the line managers began to be dissatisfied with the computer-generated information they were receiving. They wanted more information on such issues as customer profitability and product profitability. However, the MIS department continued to focus on upgrading hardware, converting old systems to new systems, and resolving technical problems. They were not able to respond to the users' requests for better information.

   As a result, many user-managers started solving their own problems by purchasing their own microcomputers and database programs. By the time the MIS department started to react to this situation, many of the users had developed considerable expertise in managing hardware, software, and data. Although the MIS department wanted to offer mainframe-based tools supporting database query, most of the users had made considerable investments in acquiring and learning how to use microcomputer-based tools and were not interested in MIS support for mainframe-based tools.

   Was the MIS department an open or a closed system? Diagnose the problem described in this situation by using the open versus closed system concept.

4. **A fast food restaurant.** At a popular fast food restaurant, an assembly line is in place to mass-produce hamburgers. The best-selling hamburger has pickles, cheese, ketchup, lettuce, tomato, and onions. Work is highly specialized, and specific workers are responsible for cooking, putting on relishes, wrapping, and distributing the finished hamburgers.

   When a customer requests a plain hamburger or a hamburger with ketchup only, the system breaks down. A special order has to be placed, and the customer may have to wait for 15 minutes or more to get the finished product. This really aggravates some customers.

   How would you change the system to accommodate special orders?

5. **Organizational structures.** Which type of organizational structure would best depict each of the following organizations? Choose from the simple structure, the machine bureaucracy, the professional bureaucracy, the divisionalized form, and the adhocracy.

   a. A community college with an academic campus and a technical program campus.
   b. A consulting firm specializing in network design.
   c. A public accounting firm.

d. An automobile distributorship.
e. A social work agency.
f. A defense contractor in the aerospace industry.
g. A steel company.

Cases

1. **Tip Top Diner.** The Tip Top Diner, a busy restaurant in the downtown area of a major city, is having a problem providing adequate service to customers during the hectic lunch hour period. Often, they have to wait 20 to 30 minutes to get served, and sometimes items on the menu are not available.

   The restaurant is a system. The objectives of the restaurant are to provide good service at low cost and to make a profit of 10 percent of total sales volume. (Much of this profit has been eroded by the hiring of additional part-time workers to handle the busy workload, however.) The components of the restaurant include waitresses, dining facilities, menu items, a kitchen staff, food supplies, kitchen facilities, and a manager. Interactions in the restaurant include ordering, cooking, serving, and collecting cash receipts.

   You have been asked by the manager to study the components, interactions, and other aspects of the restaurant to diagnose its problems and to identify a solution. Develop a plan for conducting a study of the system and explain what activities you would accomplish during each step of your study.

2. **Maine Custom Jewelry, Inc.** Maine Custom Jewelry, Inc., is a large manufacturer and marketer of quality jewelry. Its product line features a variety of costume jewelry in silver with semiprecious stones. Because of its management philosophy, the company will accept orders to custom make almost any jewelry product. This is possible because the jewelry craftsworkers employed by the company perform a job in its entirety. The company does not use production-line techniques. Each jewelry craftsperson is responsible for the complete manufacturing of a given product. Currently, the company employs about 50 jewelry craftsworkers and has been growing at the rate of 20 percent per year over the past three years. Management does not expect this growth rate to continue in the future, but it does predict a steady growth rate of 5 percent over the next decade.

   Maine Custom Jewelry markets a proprietary line of jewelry nationwide. However, these stock products make up only 50 percent of the output from the craftsworkers. The remaining products are produced to special order. When a custom order is received, the specifications for the order are posted along with an expected shipping date. Each craftsworker is then eligible to bid on all or part of an order. Once the bids are evaluated, the company accepts the lowest bid for production. The custom part of the business has shown the greatest growth in recent years. During the last 12 months, there have been an average of 500 orders in process at any one time.

   This growth has posed a problem for Maine Custom Jewelry. In addition, the firm has experienced many difficulties related to providing consistent, on-time delivery. The skilled craftsworkers often fail to meet deadlines. Moreover, management has never had a satisfactory means of ensuring that orders are worked on in a priority sequence. Other problems, such as craftsworkers overcommitting themselves in a given time period or simply losing an order, are also becoming more serious.

Identify and discuss Maine Custom Jewelry's problems from a systems standpoint. In your analysis, discuss the environment, standards, management, input resources, and work methods and procedures. What recommendations would you make for improving the current system?

Selected References and Readings

Boulding, Kenneth. "General Systems Theory—The Skeleton of Science." *Management Science,* April 1956.

Luchsinger, Vincent P., and V. Thomas Dock. "An Anatomy of Systems." In *MIS: A Managerial Perspective.* ed. V. Thomas Dock, Vincent P. Luchsinger, and William R. Cornette. pp. 3–12. Chicago: SRA, 1977.

Mintzberg, Henry. *The Structuring of Organizations.* Englewood Cliffs N.J.: Prentice Hall, 1979.

Von Bertalanffy, Ludwig. *General Systems Theory: Foundations, Development, Applications.* New York: Braziller, 1968.

Strategic Uses of Information Technology

Chapter Outline

Manager's View

As a manager, you will be in a position to assess how information technology can be used to support business activities. Traditionally, data processing applications have supported "back-office" operations, such as transaction processing. With the introduction of information systems such as American Hospital Supply's ASAP system, which electronically linked purchasing personnel with American's order entry system, it became evident that information technology could be used to gain a competitive advantage. American Hospital Supply's ASAP system made it easier for hospitals to order, created access to inventory and delivery information, and provided an electronic interface that eliminated a great deal of costly paperwork. When American Hospital Supply's orders rose dramatically, it was clear that an information system could become a powerful competitive force. This chapter shows how information technology can be used for competitive advantage and how interorganizational systems have transformed the competitive marketplace.

HOW INFORMATION TECHNOLOGY SUPPORTS BUSINESS ACTIVITIES

One of the first challenges to managers is understanding how they can use information technology to support business activities. Porter and Millar's (1985) concept of the **value chain** helps explain what business activities can be analyzed and transformed through the use of information technology. The value chain divides a company's activities into **value activities,** the distinct activities it must perform to do business. In Figure 3–1, you can see these value activities.

Value activities consist of primary activities and support activities. Primary activities include inbound logistics, operations, outbound logistics, marketing, and service. For a manufacturing organization, activities that support inbound logistics include delivery and handling of incoming materials. Operations activities include manufacturing-related functions, such as parts assembly and quality assurance. Outbound logistics activities support order processing and shipping goods and services to customers. Marketing and sales activities include advertising, promotion, and sales force management. The company also organizes activities to support repair and maintenance of its goods and services.

Support activities include the resources that support the primary activities of the business. You can see some of these support activities in Figure 3–2. They provide the organization, human resources, and technologies to deliver primary activities. The firm's organization, which includes activities such as general management, legal work, and accounting, supports the entire value chain.

In Porter's view, the value chain is a system of interdependent linkages. In other words, the way one activity is performed may affect the performance of others. As an example, investments in a more expensive product design and superior materials may reduce after-sale service costs.

To obtain a competitive edge, Porter argues, a firm must be able to perform its value activities at a lower cost than its rivals or in a way that provides its buyers with added value or service.

The value chain of a particular industry works within a larger system of activities called the **value system.** The value system includes the value chains of suppliers, of the firm, of the channels through which the firm distributes its products and services, and

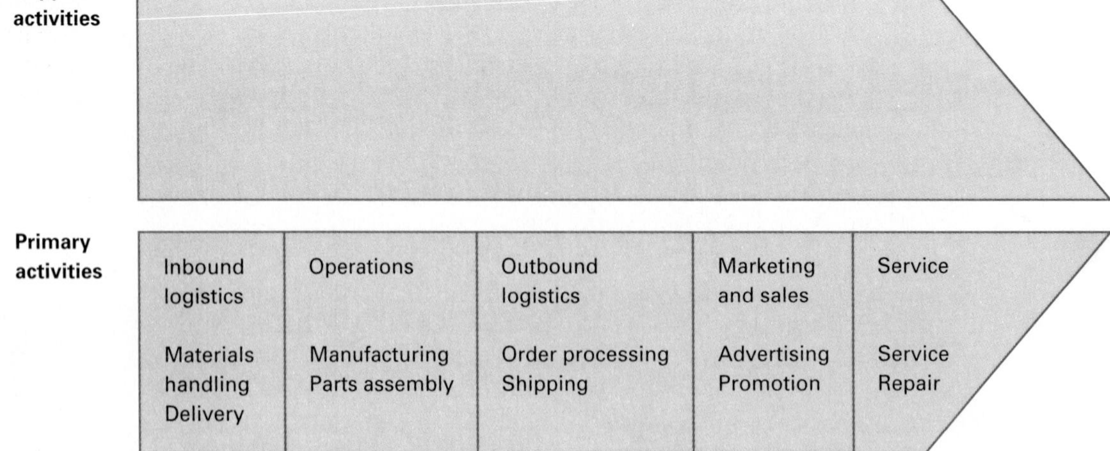

Figure 3–1
Value activities
Source: Adapted from Porter & Millar, 1985.

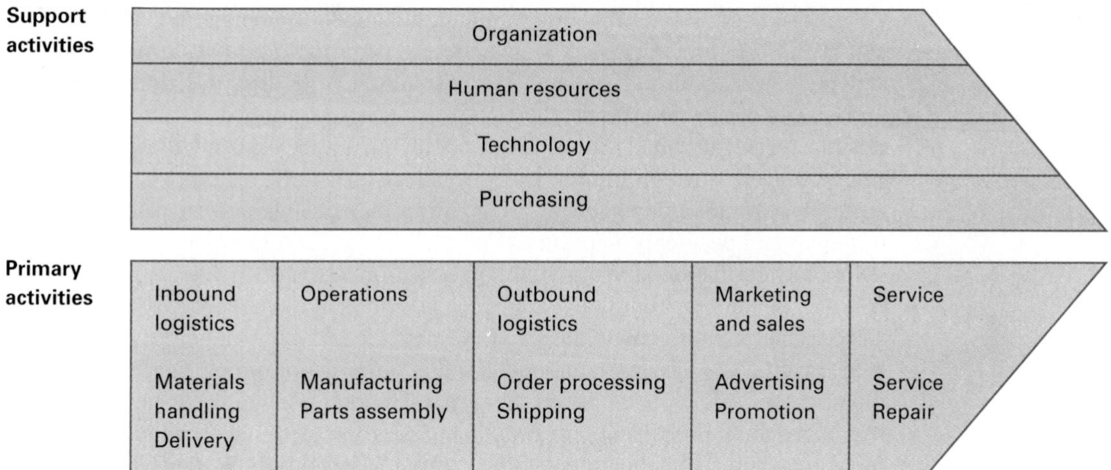

Figure 3–2
Support activities in the value chain

Source: Adapted from Porter & Millar, 1985.

of the ultimate buyer. The value system is depicted in Figure 3–3. According to Porter, the value chain of the firm interacts with the value chain of its suppliers because the suppliers provide the raw materials that are inputs into the firm's own value chain. The distribution activities that are part of the value chain of the firm's suppliers interact with the raw material–handling activities of the firm's value chain. If links between the value activities of the supplier and buyer are coordinated, then both firms can cut costs. For example, an automobile manufacturer obtains raw material from steel manufacturers as a part of its value chain. A link between the automaker and the steelmaker's inventory system can provide information on prices and delivery dates and facilitate ordering and delivery.

The company's products and services sometimes pass through channel value chains on their way to the ultimate buyer. A channel value chain occurs between a supplier and a buyer, for example, a dealer or distributor. In the case of the automobile industry, the dealership provides a channel value chain between the manufacturer and the automobile buyer. Information technology can provide a more effective interface between the buyer and the channel. For example, an automobile buyer may visit a Buick dealership in St. Louis, Missouri, but not be able to locate an automobile with the exact features she wants. Buick dealers use a system called EPIC to enable prospective car buyers to locate automobiles with the features they want in local and regional dealerships. The EPIC system gives the manufacturer a competitive edge by providing instant information about the availability of Buicks and preventing prospective buyers from searching for alternatives.

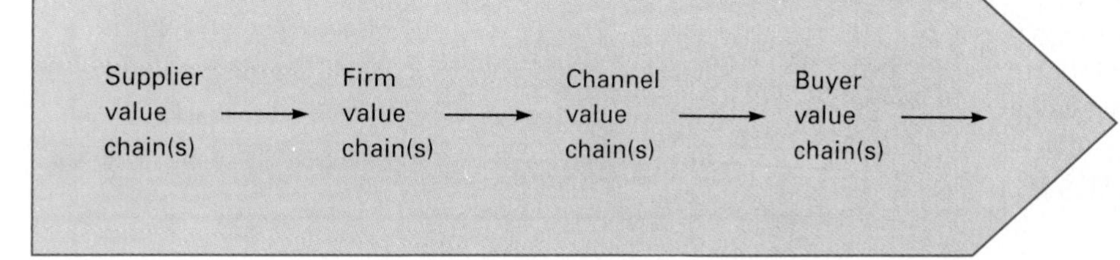

Figure 3–3
The value system

Source: Adapted from Porter & Millar, 1985.

Information systems that link suppliers and buyers, manufacturers and distributors, and distributors and buyers are known as **interorganizational systems (IOSs).** These systems benefit both participants. For example, a large drug distributor places order entry terminals in drugstores, allowing pharmacists to order directly. In this way, the manufacturer gets timely information about buying trends, and the pharmacists get timely delivery on their orders. Large retailers such as Sears and J.C. Penney enable customers to view merchandise using electronic catalogs and to place orders using terminals and personal computers. With technology, these retailers can give customers access to information about a wide range of products and services.

As you can see from these examples, information technology has an effect on the value chain by transforming the way value activities are performed. Each activity in the value chain has a physical component and an information-processing component. The physical component encompasses the physical tasks needed to perform the activity, and the information-processing component includes the steps involved in capturing, manipulating, and channeling the data necessary to carry out the activity. Take Wal-Mart's inventory management activity as an example. The physical task is to stock sufficient inventory to meet customers' needs. The information-processing component must be designed to provide feedback on inventory requirements, based upon sales history data.

The information processing component of each value activity is being increasingly supported by information technology, as you would expect. Examples of how technology supports primary activities are illustrated in Table 3–1.

In the Wal-Mart example, information technology supports inbound logistics. As you learned in Chapter 1, Procter & Gamble supplies Wal-Mart stores with just-in-time inventory of Pampers, reducing both ordering and holding costs. Procter & Gamble has access to sales history and inventory turnover information, and it uses this information to determine inventory requirements for its customer, Wal-Mart. As a result, it fills Wal-Mart's orders automatically.

Information technology also supports operations. Process control systems monitor oil refinement, chemical production, and even assembly of ingredients in the manufacture of paints and cookies. These systems assure quality, timely production and economy in using raw materials.

An insurance salesperson equipped with a laptop computer with a spreadsheet program can simulate the earnings of an insurance portfolio. This is an effective use of technology in marketing insurance plans. In another example, a food company has created a national database of product sales information. Marketing representatives can obtain access to this information via a worldwide network.

Table 3–1
How technology supports value activities

Value Activity	Use of Technology
Inbound logistics	Just-in-time inventory
Operations	Process control systems
Outbound logistics	On-line links to the order-entry systems of suppliers
Marketing and sales	Laptops for direct sales
After-sale service	Electronic dispatch of technical support

A good example of technology support for after-sale service is Otis Elevator's Otisline system. This system automatically dispatches elevator service calls to technicians with the proper training. Remote diagnostics of plant equipment is another way technology can be used to provide a competitive edge. At Xerox Corporation, an on-line database matches service calls with the capabilities of service technicians. Using information about customer service histories, service managers are able to anticipate technical problems, assign qualified service technicians, and make sure that needed parts are available for service calls.

In addition to supporting primary value activities, information technology can be used to support the secondary activities of the value chain, as shown in Table 3–2.

The support activities that are part of the value chain can also be reinforced by the use of information technology. A corporatewide electronic mail system can facilitate interaction among all levels of the management structure and create a more flexible, dynamic organization. Using electronic mail, managers can give their employees timely feedback about project-related activities. Employees can also raise issues that can help their superiors diagnose problems and reallocate resources more effectively.

An on-line personnel information system with a skills database can support the management of human resources. A *database* is a repository of information that can be organized for inquiry and reporting purposes. A skills database is a valuable tool that enables management to identify employees with skills needed for particular assignments on a timely basis. For example, a sales manager can query an employee database for individuals who have college degrees in marketing, the ability to speak German, and a willingness to relocate.

Technology can be a critical part of the support infrastructure. For example, CAD/CAM systems are essential in the aerospace industry. Procurement systems that provide on-line access to suppliers' inventory databases can support purchasing. Using American Hospital Supply's on-line inventory databases, purchasing personnel can check inventory availability of specific items before placing orders using the system.

Examples of how information technology supports activities in the value chain are summarized in Figure 3–4.

Because information technology affects business at every level, more managers are using it to support and control their business activities. As a result, technology is being distributed "to the desktop" and managers at all levels of the organization are using desktop workstations to make decisions about day-to-day activities. Using these desktop workstations, managers can gain access to shared databases and communications networks.

Table 3 – 2
How information technology supports secondary activities

Secondary Activities	**Use of Technology**
Management communications	Electronic mail
Human resources	On-line access to personnel files with a skills database
Technology	Computer-assisted design and manufacturing
Procurement	On-line access to suppliers' inventory files

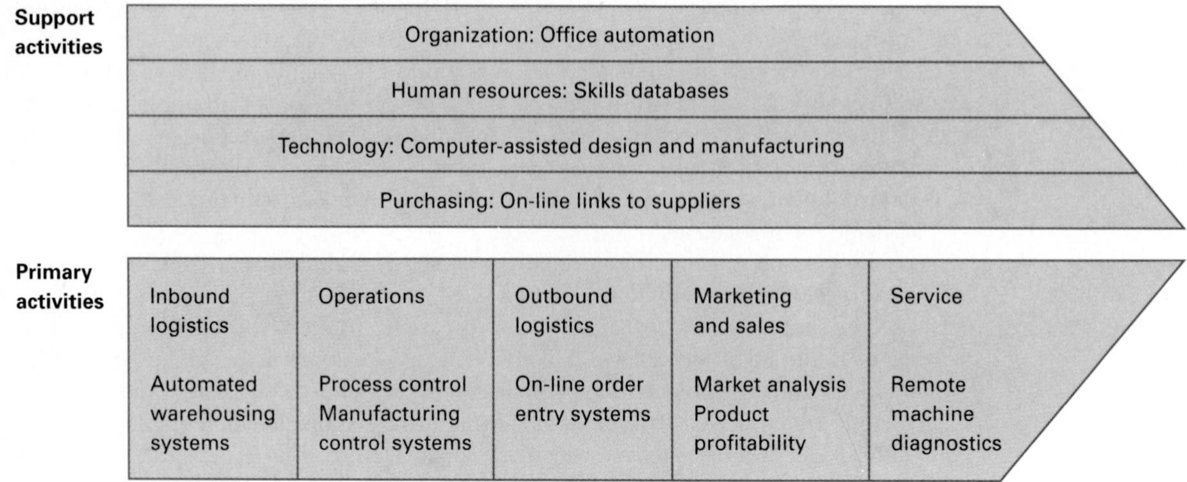

Figure 3–4 Information systems supporting value activities
Source: Adapted from Porter & Millar, 1985.

USING INFORMATION TECHNOLOGY FOR COMPETITIVE ADVANTAGE

New developments in information technology, such as telecommunications, computer-assisted design, and office automation, have created unprecedented opportunities. Managers in most organizations are looking for ways to use new information technology to support business strategy. Gregory Parsons (1983), in his work on information technology and competitive strategy, introduces a three-level framework to help managers assess the current and potential effect of information technology. This framework is shown in Table 3–3.

Industry-Level Effect

Information technology can change the nature of the industry in which the firm competes. The introduction of information technology can affect products and services, markets, and production economics.

Products and Services. First of all, information technology can change the nature of products and services by altering the product development cycle or by increasing the speed of distribution. An example of speeding up the product development cycle comes from the publishing business. If a textbook publisher uses word processing and computer-based typesetting to generate publications, it may be able to reduce the product development life cycle by 30 percent to 40 percent and to cut the costs of document preparation, revision, and distribution by half. A publisher using word processing and typesetting could bring out a revision of a text in 12 months instead of the traditional 24-month product development life cycle, giving it an automatic competitive advantage in the textbook marketplace. Texts produced in this way are more timely and more responsive to market needs.

New information technologies also affect an industry's products and services. A new technology like videoconferencing, for example, affects hotel conference centers. Large hotel chains, such as Holiday Inn and Sheraton, are already setting up videoconferencing centers in various metropolitan hotels so that companies can book on-site electronic

Table 3–3
The three-level effect of information technology

Industry Level
Information technology changes an industry's
Products and services
Production economics
Markets

Firm Level
Information technology affects key competitive forces
Buyers
Suppliers
Substitute products
New entrants
Rivals

Strategy Level
Information technology supports a firm's strategy
Low-cost leadership
Product differentiation
Market specialization

conference rooms. This strategy is designed to address the potential threat of electronic meetings to their traditional hotel business as well as to establish technological leadership in the videoconferencing business.

Production Economics. The second industry-level effect of information technology has to do with production economics. A food marketer with a nationwide network of distribution centers can serve regional markets and also reallocate inventories to serve the national market. For example, if inventories of spaghetti sauce at a Midwestern distribution center are too low to fill local orders, the food marketer can automatically check inventories of spaghetti sauce in other centers and fill the orders from the next most convenient location. A food marketer without a nationwide distribution system like this would have great difficulty satisfying customer orders that could not be handled locally.

Markets. Today, consumers are becoming more computer literate. They are accustomed to banking with automatic teller machines (ATMs) and shopping where point-of-sale scanners are used. Organizations that are not able to offer electronic services to their customers may be at a competitive disadvantage. Table 3–4 summarizes the industry-level effect of competitive systems.

Firm-Level Effect

At the firm level, the competitive forces facing the firm determine the effect of information technology. Five competitive forces influence the profitability of an industry: buyers, suppliers, substitute products, new entrants, and rivals. These competitive forces, shown in Figure 3–5, are described in depth by Michael Porter in his book *Competitive Strategy* (1980). Information technology can be used to address these competitive forces in the following ways.

Table 3–4
Industry-level effects

Type of Impact	How Information Technology Is Used
Products and services	Computer-based word processing and typesetting
Production economics	Nationwide inventory tracking
Markets	ATMs Point-of-sale systems

Buyers. The first competitive force is the power of buyers, a force that can reduce an industry's profits. Information technology can be used to lessen the power that buyers have by introducing switching costs. The American Hospital Supply case we discussed earlier is a good example. When American Hospital Supply gave purchasing agents in hospitals terminals tying them to its order entry system, they introduced switching costs. Once the purchasing agents learned how to use the American Hospital Supply system to check order and delivery status, they could more easily order from American Hospital Supply than from its competitors.

Another way information technology can be used to reduce the impact of buyers is by providing market analysts with the tools they need to analyze buyer profitability. A financial services company, for example, used prior loan data to design an information system depicting the characteristics of potentially delinquent loan applicants. When these characteristics were used to screen out potential bad risks, the firm cut the costs of its delinquent loans dramatically. Decision support tools can be developed to analyze the profitability of specific market groups and to deliver products and services to these groups, raising potential margins and revenues.

Suppliers. The second competitive force is the power of suppliers. Firms can compete more effectively if they are able to control the power of suppliers. The automobile industry, for example, has had to rely on high-priced labor as a major supplier of services. Use of robots to handle assembly-line tasks has partially offset the

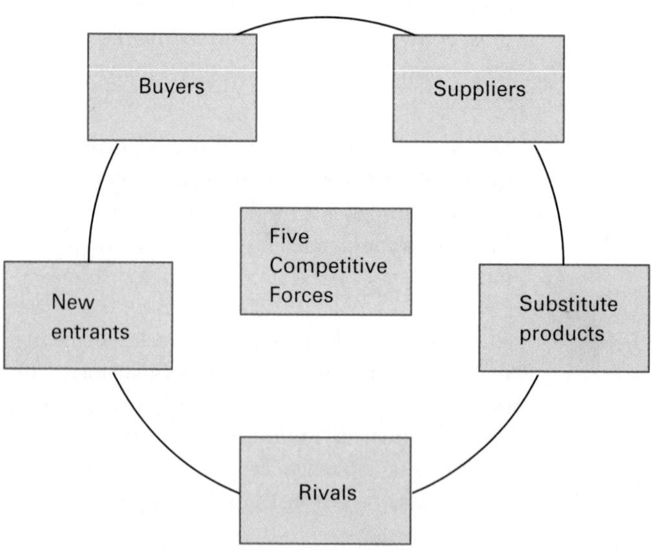

Figure 3–5
Five competitive forces

accelerating costs of unionized labor. Information systems that are designed to track labor efficiency can be tied directly to wage incentive systems and can also provide management with an important advantage in rewarding productivity improvements.

Today, suppliers have to be more cautious because of the sophisticated quality control systems users have designed. Steel producers, for example, must be more quality conscious because the automobile industry has implemented sophisticated quality control systems. The automobile manufacturers use their quality control systems to check incoming shipments from steel manufacturers. In this way, they exercise more control over their suppliers.

The average consumer can gain power over suppliers simply by having access to more information. In the past when consumers purchased automobiles, the dealer had all the information. Now that consumers have access to information about dealer invoice costs, they can negotiate more effectively. This reduces the power of dealers, the suppliers.

Substitute Products. Another competitive strategy is to deter customers from finding substitutes for existing products and services, for example, using margarine for butter. Cost-effective substitutes for products and services can hurt a firm's profits. A firm can attempt to deter its customers from buying substitutes by lowering the cost of its products and services or by improving their perceived performance and value. The Merrill Lynch Cash Management Account (CMA) is an excellent example of this approach. The CMA bundles a brokerage account, a money market account, a Visa card, and a checking account—financial services previously available only as separate products—in one package. As a result, customers find it difficult to substitute for the CMA. With the CMA, Merrill Lynch was able to bring in 450,000 new brokerage accounts and $60 million in annual fees for managing the liquid asset funds. For a number of years, no other brokerage firm was able to come out with a similar product, making a substitute difficult to find. Because it took Merrill Lynch's competitors years to catch up with the CMA-type account, Merrill Lynch was able to create switching costs among its customers and to attain a permanent competitive edge in the marketplace.

How did information technology help Merrill Lynch gain a competitive edge with the CMA account? The sophisticated software behind the CMA was so extensive that it took years for its competitors to catch up and provide similar accounts. As a result, information technology was of strategic value.

New Entrants. The threat of new entrants is a competitive force that established firms in an industry would like to deter or minimize. New entrants can draw profits from firms in an industry. Entry barriers that enable established firms to block the entry of newcomers include reputation, service levels, and distribution channels. Information technology can create entry barriers by preventing new entrants from gaining market share or from entering the industry at all. Leading insurance companies such as Massachusetts Mutual Life Insurance Company have created effective entry barriers by constructing on-line telecommunications networks linking sales agents to home office databases with information about policies and claims. These networks make it possible for local agents to update policies, to receive sales illustrations on new insurance programs, and to obtain local access to training and promotional materials. Without this kind of support for its sales agents, a new entrant would be at a competitive disadvantage. The million-dollar investment in these large-scale telecommunications networks creates a considerable entry barrier to potential new entrants into the insurance business.

The airline industry has created a similar entry barrier with on-line reservations systems. The reservations systems built by American, TWA, and United Airlines in the 1970s cost millions of dollars in development and equipment costs. To win the business of travel agents and business travelers, smaller airlines without reservation systems are forced to list their flights on the reservations systems of the major carriers. These smaller airlines are at an automatic disadvantage because the host carrier has access to information on their flights, their fares, and their bookings. In addition, the smaller airlines may be forced to pay the host airline a percentage of each flight booked on that airline's information system, creating a further disadvantage.

The history of the SABRE system, American Airlines' reservation system, shows how potent a competitive information system can be. SABRE began as a way of assigning seats on airplanes—it listed American flights as well as the flights of other airlines. In the mid-1970s, SABRE was upgraded to generate flight plans, track spare parts, and schedule crews. All these applications supported internal operations. By the late 70s, however, SABRE was enhanced significantly with the addition of new services, including hotel and rental car reservations, to the database.

SABRE has been repeatedly upgraded since its origin in the early 70s. Today, SABRE is a virtual electronic supermarket, a computerized middleman that links suppliers of travel services (e.g., Broadway shows, packaged tours, currency rates) with travel agents and that provides a computerized reservation system for American Airlines, Marriott, Hilton, and Budget Rental Car companies. These enhancements to the original SABRE system provide an even greater barrier to entry.

Rivals. The fifth competitive force that influences the profitability of an industry is rivals. All industries have rivalry among competitors. Competition is valuable because it establishes a market price and enables successful firms to earn profits. Information technology has made it possible for many firms within an industry to deal effectively with rivals. The airline reservations systems have been notorious for their impact on rivals. Frontier Airlines, in testimony before the Civil Aeronautics Board, argued that United's APOLLO reservation system employed an unfair competitive advantage by enabling United to check on prices of Frontier flights and then deliberately lower its prices to meet or to undercut them. In effect, Frontier argued that United had computerized access to confidential information about Frontier's flights, including prices, loading factors, and schedules in competitive markets. In addition, Frontier argued that United flights were preferentially listed on the APOLLO system and that Frontier flights were sometimes dropped without explanation. When Frontier introduced a special fare, such as a $99 one-way fare, United could use its system to send messages to travel agents notifying them that it would match these new fares. United reinforced its strong allegiance to its travel agents by rewarding exclusive APOLLO agents with add-on features such as automatic boarding pass generation.

Firms within an industry can use information technology to compete with rivals in other industries. Firms in the railroad industry have joined to establish communications networks to track freight locations and schedules for their customers, making successful competition against their rivals in the trucking industry possible.

Sometimes, the small players in an industry team up to compete with larger firms in the same industry. Some of the smaller airlines have combined resources to develop airline reservations systems to compete with larger airlines' systems. In another instance, Philadelphia National Bank (PNB) and other smaller banks pooled their resources and formed an ATM network, the Money Access Center (MAC), as a generic

ATM service available to all area banks. The MAC system directly counteracted the ATM network launched earlier by a formidable competitor, Girard, a large Philadelphia-based financial institution.

In considering ways to use information technology for competitive advantage, a firm has to assess the forces affecting its industry position and to develop a strategy that addresses buyers, suppliers, substitute products, new entrants, or rivals. Table 3–5 summarizes the firm-level competitive impacts of information technology.

Rivals

In his book, *Competitive Strategy,* Porter argues that three generic strategies can be used to achieve a competitive edge in an industry: *low-cost leadership, product differentiation,* and *market specialization.* The effective use of information technology can support each of these strategies, as illustrated by the examples given in this section.

Low-Cost Leadership. **Low-cost leadership** refers to the ability to reduce costs or to improve productivity without incurring additional costs. If a commercial bank can process thousands of demand deposit transactions per day at 2 cents per transaction, and one of its competitors processes a similar volume at 4 cents per transaction, the first bank will achieve a competitive advantage in cost leadership. A computer-based information system that cuts the cost of transactions processing will support this low-cost leadership strategy.

A magazine distributor has been able to achieve a position of low-cost leadership by using a computer-based information system to sort and distribute magazines and newspapers to newsstands. Many organizations have introduced office automation systems that mechanize office paperwork and cut administrative costs, supporting a low-cost leadership strategy. Law firms that have introduced word processing, for example, have cut the cost of creating, editing, and distributing documents by as much as one-third.

Inventory control systems that reduce the cost of excess inventories in plants and warehouses support a low-cost leadership strategy. Production control systems that minimize excess raw materials and control the costs of production also support this strategy.

Product Differentiation. **Product differentiation** is achieved by adding value or unique features to a product to improve its image, quality, or service. A good example of product differentiation is giving customers electronic access to an on-line service network. Owners of Gateway Computers have access to a bulletin board system that provides up-to-date information on technical issues and product features. Another form

Table 3–5
Firm-level impacts

Competitive Force Affected	Example of an Information System and Its Competitive Impact
Buyers	American Hospital Supply system introduces switching costs to buyers
Suppliers	Use of robots to do assembly line tasks reduces the cost of the labor supply
Substitute products	Merrill Lynch's CMA provides a "bundled" set of financial services
New entrants	On-line telecommunications networks link insurance agents and home office systems Airline reservations systems

of product differentiation is providing value-added features to existing products or services. Frequent fliers on most airlines today receive frequent flier miles that translate into special discounts and bonuses. Sometimes "value-added" features are embedded in the use of a product. For example, a tire manufacturer has introduced sensors that detect problems and display diagnostic messages about air pressure and tire maintenance that could cut costs and enhance safety.

Sometimes, the ability to provide customers with better information is a source of product differentiation. An innovative travel agency, Rosenbluth Travel, has created a travel supermarket by offering information management services. Rosenbluth can search through its airline reservations system databases and select flights based upon ticket price. By shopping around for the best price, Rosenbluth can offer its clients the best fares. Rosenbluth differentiates its services further by offering its clients access to a back-office expense tracking system that not only controls corporate travel expenses but also provides Rosenbluth with the clout to negotiate preferred rates with the major air carriers based upon the amount of business some of its major clients represent.

A firm can differentiate its products by providing reliable service, quick responses to customer questions, and additional product features. For example, computer-assisted design can create better-quality product designs for shoes, automobiles, and other consumer items. For years, Italian shoemakers and auto designers have designed products that "look better" than their counterparts made elsewhere. Computer-assisted design has helped some American firms win back some of the business lost to Italian manufacturers.

Information technology can also support sales and service levels. A large computer manufacturer provides an 800 number for hotline access to a customer support center, allowing customers to troubleshoot technical problems with specialists. National hotel chains provide access to their reservations systems through 800 numbers. A large beer manufacturer provides its distributors with on-line access to pricing, promotion, and delivery information via an electronic mail network. All these services are examples of product differentiation.

Market Specialization. The third competitive strategy Porter describes is **market specialization,** which is achieved by concentrating on a particular market or product niche. Information systems that support the market specialization strategy provide information about the profitability of specific market segments and enable manufacturers and distributors to design and market products and services addressing the needs of a particular market niche. An example of a service attracting a specific market segment is electronic library access, which would appeal to personal computer owners in academics and business. Table 3–6 summarizes the strategy-level impacts of information technology.

Defining Competitive Strategy

A firm needs to determine what its competitive strategy should be before deciding how to use information technology. This means understanding its competitive position, the competitive forces affecting it, and its overall business strategy. The applications a firm selects should support its competitive strategy and enable it to deal effectively with the competitive forces in its industry. Once the competitive uses of information technology are defined, these plans have to be translated into technology plans.

New Business Opportunities

New information technology is also fostering new business opportunities. Videoconferencing, a technology that makes it possible to hold electronic meetings, could hurt the airline and hotel businesses in the next 5 to 10 years. Holiday Inns has decided to counter this threat by offering videoconferencing facilities for business meetings and in

Table 3 – 6
Strategy-level impacts

Strategy-Level Impact	Use of Information Technology
Low-cost leadership	Office automation Inventory control systems
Product differentiation	Computer-assisted design Hotline to technical support
Market specialization	Electronic library access for PC owners Market profitability analysis

this way has created an entirely new market. Western Union's Easy Link service, which uses a high-speed data communications network to send electronic messages from personal computers and word processors to other electronic devices, takes advantage of the growing market for electronic transmission services.

As you might suspect, information technology has brought many organizations into the information services business itself. Union Pacific Railroad bought the smaller Missouri Pacific Railroad, the designer of an automated freight car tracking system, because of its experience in developing a sophisticated telecommunications network and the software to support it. The information systems developed by Missouri Pacific's information systems department have become one of the most valuable assets in its industry.

Once information technology is in place, companies can market new products and services via existing networks and databases. Sears uses its massive customer databases to market new consumer products. One database, for example, includes information about all customers who have purchased Sears Kenmore appliances, including names, addresses, date of purchase, model, and store of purchase. Telemarketing representatives use this database to contact new appliance owners to offer service maintenance contracts. Marketing personnel also search through the massive sales history databases for the phone numbers of appliance owners who made their purchases over seven years ago and contact these prospects with trade-in offers and equipment upgrades.

Supermarkets with point-of-sale bar-code scanners have become research laboratories for market research firms. One market research firm in Chicago uses two test markets to evaluate the effects of alternative marketing and sales promotional strategies on buyer behavior. Consumers in these test markets are exposed to various marketing programs via radio and television advertising, store coupons, and point-of-purchase specials. Their actual purchases are recorded via point-of-sale systems in regional supermarkets. With the help of these point-of-sale systems, the market research firm can measure the effect of advertising and promotion strategies on actual customer purchases. This innovative use of information technology enables the market research firm to differentiate its services by offering a unique method of assessing the impact of marketing strategies.

Finally, companies with excess computing capacity are able to market information services as a new business opportunity. Sears, for example, markets its know-how in processing credit card accounts to other companies. A. O. Smith, a manufacturer of automotive parts, has used its expertise in building telecommunications networks to win a contract to run a network of automated teller machines for a bank consortium. A number of companies market internally developed software to external companies. For example, a copier distributor has marketed the prospect information system it developed to other distributors throughout the Midwest. This system has a prospect database enabling managers to make queries and generate reports about prospects for different types of products in various sales regions. All these examples illustrate how firms have been able to take advantage of their investment in information technology to create new business opportunities for themselves.

To summarize, the use of information technology has changed the nature of competition and has created new opportunities for using and marketing information services. As a manager, you will have a chance to determine how information technology can be used to support activities that are a part of the value chain (for example, buying and selling) of the business. Using information technology successfully to reduce the cost of value activities or to add value to existing products and services can provide a competitive edge. No matter what industry you find yourself in, you will be relying on information services to a larger extent than has ever been the case before.

INTERORGANIZATIONAL SYSTEMS

Many of the examples of the strategic uses of information technology you have learned about in this chapter involve links between buyers and suppliers. For example, an automobile manufacturer has established a computer-based communications system linking it with its primary suppliers in order to implement a just-in-time inventory system. Just-in-time inventory means that the automobile manufacturer can order parts and components to meet its manufacturing requirements on a day-to-day basis, rather than stockpiling large quantities of excess inventory. This section explains some of the forces behind interorganizational systems (IOS), the participants in IOS, and information-partnering arrangements that have evolved because of IOS.

In general, interorganizational systems have evolved to facilitate the timely exchange of information in a highly competitive marketplace. For example drug stores and pharmacies use McKesson's Economost system to place orders electronically. A store employee orders merchandise in the proper quantities to replenish stocks by using a wand to record inventory items in short supply. Ninety-nine percent of McKesson's order flow arrives electronically.

The evolution of standards such as **UPC (the universal product code), MICR (magnetic character recognition),** and **ATM (automatic teller machines)** has reinforced IOS development. These standards create opportunities to develop information systems based upon common data and interface standards.

Most of the organizations using interorganizational systems are suppliers, customers, manufacturers, vendors, and others who need to use the IOS to exchange information to conduct a primary business process such as order entry, inventory management, electronic funds transfer, or purchasing. In the IOS environment, a new role has emerged, the IOS facilitator.

The **IOS facilitator** provides the information utility or the network that allows the exchange of information among participants. The CIRRUS network, which permits nationwide processing of ATM transactions 24 hours a day, is an IOS facilitator. With CIRRUS, customers have 24-hour, coast-to-coast access to their ATMs. Compuserve's electronic information services are another example. Using Compuserve, a user can gain access to electronic mail networks, electronic databases, and home shopping services. Using the information "superhighways" offered by these IOS facilitators will become an essential element in doing business in the 1990s.

Information Partnering

Information partnering, or forming strategic alliances, is the driving force behind the emerging electronic marketplace. IBM and Sears have teamed up to provide Prodigy, a package of several hundred electronic data services, including home banking, stock market quotations, and airline reservations. American Airlines has joined with Marriott and Budget Rental Car in offering AMRIS, its electronic travel supermarket. Other examples are IVANS (the Insurance Value-Added Network), the Singapore TradeNet, and the Baxter Healthcare System.

IVANS, Insurance Value-Added Network Services, links hundreds of insurance companies' home offices to thousands of independent insurance agents. IVANS makes it possible for independent insurance agents to gain access to information on policies offered by many of the smaller insurance companies. This enables these agents to locate the most competitive prices and policies for their clients and maintains a competitive marketing environment that would not be possible without the multiple providers that have access to the network.

The Singapore TradeNet manages the operations activities of the world's largest shipping port by linking shipping companies, banks, and insurers with relevant government entities, including customs and immigration officials. The TradeNet, which cost the government over $50 million, enables vessels to clear the port in 10 minutes—a striking difference from the two- to four-day interval required before.

The Baxter Healthcare System links a variety of medical supply manufacturers with buyers, including hospital purchasing agents. This system was developed from the original American Hospital Supply order entry system that enabled purchasing agents in hospitals to generate purchase orders electronically. As time went on, the Baxter System added on other hospital suppliers, thereby giving the purchasing agents access to order, inventory, and delivery information from multiple hospital supply organizations.

These information partnerships are representative of the new marketing environment. In most cases, an information facilitator provides the network through which the various participants can interact. An industry trade association initiated the insurance network IVANS because its members were concerned about the loss of market share to direct sales forces representing larger insurers such as Allstate and State Farm. The Singapore TradeNet was a government-sponsored project designed to make the port more competitive. The Baxter Healthcare System evolved from the American Hospital Supply system and grew to accommodate the needs of the medical supply industry.

At times, a company may acquire another company to form an information partnership that will help them both compete more effectively. Union Pacific Railroad acquired Missouri Pacific Railroad to utilize MoPac's sophisticated freight dispatching and tracking system. Strategic alliances such as these are critical to achieving market success.

Increasingly, companies find themselves organizing partnerships to compete with other alliances. Since American joined forces with Marriott and Budget Rental Car, other airlines have teamed up with other hotel and rental car chains. The only downside of an information partnership is the possible transfer of authority to the partners. To participate in an information partnership, a firm must also create and manage a technical capability that supports the alliance. Because electronic communications is an essential element of information partnering, investments in telecommunications planning and design are needed to participate in the electronic marketplace.

The Electronic Marketplace

The emergence of the electronic marketplace is an important trend in the 1990s. Electronic sales channels reduce the costs of locating suppliers, ordering merchandise, and reconciling errors. Customers can save money by ordering just-in-time inventory via electronic market channels. The players in the electronic marketplace include suppliers and buyers, retailers and customers, and manufacturers and dealers. Some examples of players in the electronic marketplace include the following.

Inventory Locator Service, a subsidiary of Ryder System, offers an airline parts inventory database that makes it possible for the airlines to locate suppliers of the parts they need for repair and maintenance. Now planes that used to be grounded for days can fly within hours. This information system links the airlines with airline parts suppliers.

Telaction, an electronic home shopping system introduced by J.C. Penney, simulates shopping at a mall. Customers who view merchandise on a cable TV channel can get more detailed information by using their push-button phones. This system links customers with a retailer.

Comp-U-Card, a system available through Compuserve's Information Service, enables buyers to search through the system's database to obtain the best price on a specific product (e.g., a 19-inch SONY color TV) and lets them call a toll-free number to place an order. This system links customers with multiple suppliers.

Telcot, an electronic market for cotton, enables 12,000 farmers to sell their products. Telcot was established by a cooperative association of cotton farmers in Oklahoma and Texas. The system links sellers (the cotton farmers) with buyers.

MEMA/Transnet, an electronic order system for automotive parts, serves more than 100 manufacturers and over 4,000 customers. MEMA/Transnet was invented by the Motor and Equipment Manufacturers Association, a trade association. The system links manufacturers with automobile dealers and auto parts retailers.

IVANS, the network that links insurance agents, insurance carriers, and other information sources for insurance agents, was created by an industry association of independent insurance agents. As you learned earlier, IVANS links many independent agents with smaller insurance carriers.

SABRE and *APOLLO,* the airline reservations systems of American and United, have not only added the flights of competitive carriers but have also become electronic travel supermarkets for related services, such as hotel and rental car reservations. These information systems link the airlines with travel agents and provide the travel agents with a wide range of travel information.

Med Facts, an electronic market for physicians, lists fees, educational backgrounds, and the specialties of over 1,400 physicians in the Miami area. This system links potential clients with physicians offering the services they need. This kind of information system will become more and more common in many cities in the United States.

As you can tell from these examples, electronic marketplaces include many suppliers' offerings. Although the APOLLO system originally offered only United flights, it was quickly changed to include the flights of competitive carriers. The American Hospital Supply order entry system is now being operated by Baxter Healthcare and includes a wide variety of medical supplies manufactured by multiple suppliers, including Baxter's competitors. In essence, then, electronic markets offer customers access to offerings from competing suppliers. The "competitive" systems designed by American Hospital Supply, United Airlines, and McKesson have all evolved into electronic marketplaces that include many suppliers' goods.

Electronic markets help the buyer because they enable both companies and consumers to search through the databases of competitive products and find the most cost-effective goods and services. The Comp-U-Card system, for example, helps buyers find the cheapest price for consumer goods. In general, the electronic marketplace reduces the costs of shopping around, including locating vendors, comparing products and services, comparing costs, and handling paperwork.

The reduction in transactions costs associated with evaluating, ordering, and purchasing has a related effect. Because it is so easy to order via the electronic marketplace, many companies will inevitably choose to buy rather than to make the products and services they need. What may emerge in this environment is a group of specialized suppliers linked to major firms via the electronic marketplace. A number of components, such as computer parts, and a variety of specialized services, such as specialty printing, will be outsourced to the electronic marketplace because it will be more cost-effective to purchase these goods and services than to manufacture or to create them internally.

In summary, companies will find it important to participate in the electronic marketplace. Strategic alliances between suppliers and vendors, manufacturers and distributors, and retailers and buyers will become commonplace. It is critical for companies that want to participate in the electronic marketplace to build the internal information systems and to design telecommunications networks that will provide access to customers.

STRATEGIC INFORMATION SYSTEMS: THE RISKS

This chapter has given you insight into the competitive impacts of information technology and the benefits of interorganizational systems, but there are risks as well. These risks include shifting the balance of competition, failure to upgrade the capabilities of a strategic system, and litigation.

Shifting the Balance of Competition

Using information systems to link buyers with suppliers can shift the balance of competition. Let us say that a furniture retailer in St. Louis links up to the order entry system of a furniture manufacturer in North Carolina. This link gives a competitive advantage to the supplier, the furniture manufacturer. Why? The electronic link to the supplier's order entry system makes it easier for the furniture retailer to check prices, confirm delivery dates, and place orders with that particular supplier. Eventually, the furniture manufacturer creates switching costs that can cause the furniture retailer to do most of its business with that supplier. This creates an advantage for the supplier (the furniture manufacturer) over the buyer (the furniture retailer).

As time goes on, other furniture manufacturers may develop their own electronic order entry systems. The furniture retailer in St. Louis can now hook up to the order-entry systems of multiple manufacturers, check the cost of goods being offered by various manufacturers, and place an order with the manufacturer that offers the best price. Now the competitive advantage has shifted to the buyer, the furniture retailer.

Although this may seem like an isolated instance, this experience has been duplicated throughout many different industries. Take the airline frequent flight bonus programs, for instance. The first airline to introduce frequent flight bonus points developed a competitive advantage, but soon all the major airlines followed suit and offered similar programs. Thus frequent flight programs raised the investment in information systems that airlines must build to compete in their industry without giving any one airline a competitive advantage over the others. Although the first airline to offer such a program may gain an advantage, this advantage is only temporary.

Exceptions can occur when the innovator maintains its leadership by continually adding features to an already established competitive system. You learned about SABRE earlier in this chapter. SABRE was originally developed in the early 1970s to monitor airline seats. Since then, it has evolved into a computerized middleman linking suppliers of travel services (tours, rental cars, etc.) to travel agents. American has also participated in the joint venture AMRIS, which includes Marriott, Hilton, and Budget Rental Car companies. Information systems that start early and continue to add new services are extremely valuable.

Failure to Upgrade the Capabilities of a Strategic System

Another type of risk occurs if a company makes a one-time move by introducing a competitive information system and then fails to upgrade its capabilities. For example, American Hospital Supply's ASAP system was designed to enable hospitals to link with American's order entry system. However, when ASAP was not enhanced for several years, American's competitors caught up and offered better systems. Eventually, ASAP evolved into the Baxter Healthcare system, which lists the offerings of multiple suppliers.

Litigation

Another risk involves possible litigation. Both United and American Airlines have been the subjects of lawsuits claiming that their reservations systems have created unfair trade practices, such as biased screen displays. Although both United and American have agreed to provide unbiased displays, the litigation on this issue has taken years of effort to resolve.

DO INFORMATION SYSTEMS PROVIDE A COMPETITIVE EDGE?

As you have seen, information technology has created a competitive edge for many organizations. You have also seen that once a competitor introduces an information-based service, such as a frequent flight bonus program, other firms in the industry catch up, eliminating the innovator's original competitive advantage and raising the stakes of participating in an industry. Strategic information systems become a strategic necessity—a part of doing business.

Firms such as American Airlines, American Hospital Supply, and McKesson first designed competitive information systems to establish linkages between themselves and their customers. None of these firms was able to sustain a long-term competitive advantage because of their initial systems. Now that their systems provide linkages between customers and multiple suppliers, they are participants in the electronic marketplace.

In this scenario, what happens to smaller firms that cannot afford to design competitive information systems? In both the airline and pharmaceutical industries, smaller firms that could not afford to develop information systems themselves either had to be absorbed by larger firms or leave the industry. In many industries, including insurance, retailing, and automobile manufacturing, the strategic use of information technology is a necessity for survival. Information technology may not provide a long-term competitive advantage, but it is essential for participation in many industries. The focus today should be not to use information technology for its own sake, but rather to identify competitive uses of technology that reinforce the firm's basic capabilities.

SHIFTING TO CAPABILITIES-BASED COMPETITION

In Chapter 1, you learned that the key building blocks of corporate strategy today are not products and markets, but business processes. In **capabilities-based competition,** competitive success depends upon transforming key processes into capabilities that provide superior value to the customer. A number of rules apply:

1. Set aggressive, customer-oriented goals.
2. Make sure that employees have the skills and resources they need to achieve the chosen capability.

3. Align measurements and rewards—if the goal is to provide more effective customer service, then employees' performance should be measured in terms of their ability to provide effective customer support.
4. Have the CEO provide leadership for the transformation. Without top management support, the transition to a customer-focused, market-driven organization will not happen.
5. Drive the business decision making down to those directly participating in the key business processes, the sales and service staffs.

In Chapter 1, you learned how Wal-Mart was able to overcome K-Mart by introducing new business processes such as cross-docking, the continuous dispatching of good to stores, and management of its own trucking fleet. Wal-Mart's 2,000 company-owned trucks replenish inventory to its stores within 48 hours, whereas its competitors rely upon subcontractors for trucking. In both the cases of cross-docking and trucking fleet management, Wal-Mart uses applications of information technology that support its key business processes. These business processes are designed to make it possible for customers to find the goods they want when they shop at a Wal-Mart store.

To make it possible for store managers to order stock on a timely basis, Wal-Mart provides them with information systems detailing consumer buying trends. Store managers even participate in videoconferences via Wal-Mart's satellite communications system to exchange information about customer trends. Both of these systems are designed to enable Wal-Mart's managers to focus on satisfying customer needs. In so doing, Wal-Mart's store managers have an opportunity to make decisions on stocking levels of inventory items. They are supported by information systems describing buyer behavior and by an inventory management system that virtually guarantees timely deliveries from distributors.

Other organizations have also applied the rules of capabilities-based competition. At Medequip, a medical equipment supplier, on-site service representatives work with selected customer accounts to offer personalized service. Honda provides its dealers with operating policies and procedures for more effective merchandising, selling, floor planning, and service management and reinforces policy with dealer training. By making its dealers more effective, Honda creates a system that brings them the highest ratings for customer satisfaction.

Another example of capabilities-based competition comes from the banking industry. Two banks, Wachovia and Banc One, are today among the nation's fastest growing regional banks. What are the keys to their success? In Wachovia's case, 600 personal bankers provide a total portfolio of banking services, using an integrated customer-information database. Banc One gives its 51 affiliate presidents autonomy over pricing, credit decisions, and management policymaking. In both cases, the key to success is placing decision making with the people responsible for conducting the key business processes: the personal bankers at Wachovia and the affiliate presidents at Banc One.

Technology plays a critical role in capabilities-based competition. The personal bankers at Wachovia, the store managers at Wal-Mart, and the on-site service representatives at Medequip all use information systems and customer databases to make decisions. As you learned in Chapter 1, IBM Credit's deal structurers use information systems to authorize credit decisions, and accounts payable representatives use an integrated database to authorize payments to suppliers. The single most significant factor making it possible to decentralize decision making to the individuals responsible for key business processes is the use of information technology.

As we move into the 1990s and beyond, the strategic uses of information technology must focus upon reinforcing capabilities-based competition. That is, technology must support key business processes like customer service, order follow-up, and inventory control. Although many of these uses of technology may not seem to be innovative, they are rapidly becoming an integral and essential part of doing business. Strategic information systems provide a competitive edge, but they are also becoming a strategic necessity.

Management Summary

As you can see from this chapter, information technology can provide organizations with a competitive edge. You have learned how American Hospital Supply electronically linked its customers to its order entry system, how Merrill Lynch created the CMA, and how American Airlines created an electronic travel supermarket by enhancing its on-line reservation system, SABRE.

While many of these information systems have created a competitive edge, they have transformed the basis of competition within many industries. For example, it is virtually impossible to compete in the airline business today without a computer-based reservation system.

Today, most businesses find themselves in an electronic marketplace. To compete effectively in this environment, organizations like American Airlines and Sears have established information partnerships. Some of the original strategic information systems such as American Hospital Supply's order entry system have been opened up to other suppliers. It is increasingly important for all companies to use technology-based capabilities as an integral part of doing business.

Key Terms for Managers

automatic teller machines (ATM) **68**
capabilities-based competition, **72**
interorganizational systems (IOS), **58**
IOS facilitator, **68**
low-cost leadership, **65**
magnetic character recognition (MICR), **68**
market specialization, **66**
product differentiation, **65**
universal product code (UPC), **68**
value activities, **56**
value chain, **56**
value system, **56**

Review Questions

1. How can information technology be used to affect how textbooks are produced and distributed?

2. What are the five competitive forces that information technology can address at the firm level?

3. How can information technology be used to add value or features to an automobile to prevent consumers from substituting alternative products?

4. How can information technology be used to block new entrants from entering the insurance industry?

5. How can a computer manufacturer use information technology to achieve low-cost leadership?

6. How can a manufacturer of designer shoes differentiate its products by using information technology?

7. Describe the competitive impact of each of these information systems:
   - ***a.*** SABRE.
   - ***b.*** IVANS.
   - ***c.*** Singapore TradeNet.
   - ***d.*** Baxter Healthcare System.
   - ***e.*** Comp-U-Card.
   - ***f.*** Telaction.
   - ***g.*** TELCOT.
8. Explain the role of the IOS (interorganizational systems) facilitator.
9. What changes have occurred with these competitive systems and what are their current roles in the electronic marketplace?
   - ***a.*** SABRE.
   - ***b.*** McKesson's Economost system.
   - ***c.*** American Hospital Supply's ASAP system.
10. How has Wal-Mart used information technology to reinforce capabilities-based competition?

Questions for Discussion

1. How could a financial services company specializing in mortgage loans use information about its customers to gain power over its customers, or buyers?
2. If a furniture dealer gains access to the order entry systems of four different furniture manufacturers and can check prices and delivery dates on each of these systems, how will the balance of power be affected? Will the dealer (buyer) have power over the manufacturer (supplier), or vice versa?
3. How could a national magazine distributor gain a competitive edge by using information technology to pursue a low-cost leadership strategy?
4. How can information technology be used to help a computer manufacturer pursue a product differentiation strategy?

Problems

1. **Information systems for competitive advantage.** The following examples illustrate how companies are using information systems for competitive advantage:
   - ***a.*** Airline companies have developed information systems so that they can offer frequent flight bonus programs to their customers.
   - ***b.*** Digital Equipment Corporation (DEC) has developed an expert system to develop accurate computer configurations for its customers.
   - ***c.*** Walgreen's pharmacies have a prescription information database that enables customers to fill their prescriptions at any Walgreen's pharmacy in the nation.
   - ***d.*** Xerox Corporation has a field service support system that matches information about service calls to the workloads and capabilities of its technical support representatives.
   - ***e.*** Mrs. Fields' Cookies has an electronic mail system that links each store manager to the boss, Mrs. Fields.

   Discuss the major impact of each of these information systems, identifying the level of impact and the type of impact. The impact can be at the industry level (products and services, markets, production economics), at the firm level (buyers, suppliers, substitute products, new entrants, and rivals), and at the strategy level (low-cost leadership, product differentiation, market specialization).

2. **An update on SABRE.** Throughout this chapter, you have learned about SABRE, the American Airlines reservation system. In an article entitled, "Rattling SABRE—New Ways to Compete on Information" (*Harvard Business Review*, May-June 1990), Max Hopper mentions that SABRE has the most sophisticated yield management system ever designed. Its yield management system reviews historical booking patterns to forecast the demand for flights up to a year in advance of their departure. The system monitors bookings at regular intervals, compares American's fares with competitors' fares, and determines the best price to charge for an airline seat to maximize revenue at any given point in time.

   American spent years and millions of dollars developing its yield management information system. Today it markets this software to its competitors. Why do you think American decided to market its yield management system to its competitors?

3. **Competitive advantage versus strategic necessity.** In his article, "Corporate Strategies for Information Technology: A Resource-Based Approach" (*IEEE Computer*, November 1991), Eric Clemons argues that strategic information systems no longer provide a competitive advantage; they become a "strategic necessity." Explain what you think Clemons means. Can you identify any firms that have been innovators in using information technology for competitive advantage, only to find that they lose their edge after their competitors develop the same capabilities?

Cases

1. **State Mutual Life Insurance Company.** State Mutual Life Insurance Company is a well-established company dedicated to providing quality and service to its upper-middle-class insurance customers. It has achieved its position in the insurance industry by offering popular term life and whole life programs. Over 800 insurance agents around the country market State Mutual policies and handle claims.

   In the early 1970s, information systems were developed to automate the paperwork associated with policy creation and maintenance and claims administration. In the late 1970s, most of these early batch systems were upgraded to on-line systems enabling local sales agents to create and maintain policyholder records from local agency locations. This meant that policy information could be updated in hours, rather than in days. By 1980, over 800 sales agents were linked into the on-line network that State Mutual Life had implemented.

   In the early 1980s, State Mutual used its telecommunications network to provide new services to its agents. Agents were able to receive training and promotional materials about new product and service offerings at their local sites. In addition, they could use programs to analyze alternative policy options for their clients. By 1985, State Mutual had designed policy analysis systems for personal computers so that agents could use spreadsheet programs to determine the results of "what if?" questions. State Mutual also began developing PC-based software enabling local agents to create prospect databases that could be used to make queries and generate mailing labels for promotional mailings.

   By 1980, the insurance industry had changed dramatically. New financial services were being designed by competitors, and new insurance products were being introduced daily. The two- to five-year product development cycle for insurance products was reduced to less than a year. To speed up the product development life cycle, State Mutual Life purchased a fourth-generation language and began to use the prototyping approach in systems development. It was able to reduce the lead time for introducing a new product offering by over a year using this approach. Programmers were also charged with developing information systems for new products so that State Mutual could have insurance products "on the shelf" for introduction at convenient times.

During the early 1980s, office automation systems were introduced at corporate headquarters to improve white collar productivity. A number of personal computer–based systems were also developed to provide better information about the profitability of certain buyer groups and the profitability of various policies. Using this information, State Mutual executives planned to develop a target marketing strategy. According to this approach, specific insurance products would be designed and offered to highly profitable customer groups.

Given the information about State Mutual Life Insurance Company's information systems, identify which systems are providing the firm with an advantage in its industry by supporting a particular competitive strategy. Use the framework in this chapter that describes how information systems can be used to support various competitive strategies at the industry, firm, and strategy levels to explain which competitive strategies are being supported by the various information systems projects at State Mutual.

2. **People's Airlines.** The airline industry has been very competitive in using information technology for a competitive edge. Airlines with computer-based information systems have consistently been in the forefront. In this environment it is difficult to understand how a small airline such as People's Airlines could succeed. People's Airlines is a small carrier with a fleet of 737s that provides shuttle service between major Texas cities, such as Dallas/Fort Worth, Houston, San Antonio, and El Paso. It is basically a commuter airline specializing in business travelers' needs. Unlike many of the major airlines, People's advertises itself as a "no-nonsense" airline. It does not have meal service, reserved seating, frequent flight bonus miles, or other add-on's. It offers an economical price and good service to its customers.

   In the era of strategic alliances, People's is in a predicament. While other airlines are teaming up with rental car organizations, hotel/motel chains, and even ticket agencies, People's is still just an airline specializing in a certain market niche. Can People's survive in its industry by remaining a no-nonsense airline or will it need to consider creating the same kinds of strategic alliances its competitors have to stay in business over the long term?

   While no one can forecast the future, use your best judgment to make recommendations to executives at People's Airlines about its future in the electronic marketplace.

Selected References and Readings

Cash, James, and Konsynski. "IS Redraws Competitive Boundaries." *Harvard Business Review,* March–April 1985, pp. 134–42.

Clemons, Eric. "Corporate Strategies for Information Technology: A Resource-Based Approach." *IEEE Computer,* November 1991, pp. 23–35.

Hopper, Max. "Rattling SABRE—New Ways to Compete on Information." *Harvard Business Review,* May–June, 1990, pp. 118–25.

Malone, Thomas; JoAnn Yates; and Robert Benjamin. "The Logic of Electronic Markets." *Harvard Business Review,* May–June 1989, pp. 166–70.

Parsons, Gregory L. "Information Technology: A New Competitive Weapon." *Sloan Management Review,* Fall 1983, pp. 3–13.

Porter, Michael. *Competitive Strategy: Techniques for Analyzing Industries and Competitors.* New York: The Free Press, 1980.

Porter, Michael. "How Competitive Forces Shape Strategy." *Harvard Business Review,* March–April 1979, pp. 137–45.

Stalk, George; Philip Evans; and Lawrence Schulman. "Competing on Capabilities: The New Rules of Corporate Strategy." *Harvard Business Review,* March–April 1992, pp. 57–69.

CASE 1 SOLVING PROBLEMS FOR THE RIVERBEND ELECTRIC COMPANY USING THE SYSTEMS APPROACH

INTEGRATED CASES

BACKGROUND

The Riverbend Electric Company (REC), Inc., was founded by Mr. Stanley Pyszynski in 1938 in a rented workshop in North Alton, Illinois. Mr. Pyszynski achieved early success by acquiring a U.S. Army contract to build small electric motors used in Army Air Corps airplanes. During World War II, Mr. Pyszynski expanded the product line to include electric coils, transformers, voltage regulators, and battery chargers. He easily transferred this product line from military to civilian applications in the booming post–World War II economy.

In 1947 Mr. Pyszynski relocated the firm's corporate headquarters to a factory site on the Riverbend Parkway close to the Mississippi River in North Alton. The 1950s saw the firm grow to over 200 full-time workers. REC kept pace with other firms in the electronics industry by launching into the production of solid-state voltage regulators in 1960.

Today REC is best known as a full-range producer of transformers for all types of appliances and computers. The firm is also a worldwide leader in the production of a complete line of solid-state protective relays for power distribution in the utilities industry. Additionally, REC contracts to assemble special products such as printed wiring boards used in workstations for telecommunications, electrical control, and special military applications.

The corporate headquarters site includes both office and manufacturing facilities. This facility currently houses approximately 800 workers—150 corporate office workers and 650 workers in various manufacturing jobs. In addition to the North Alton plant, the firm includes three other plants located in West Martin, Tennessee; Guadalajara, Mexico; and Calgary, Canada. The Guadalajara plant, which opened in 1985, primarily produces transformers used in appliances. The Calgary plant, which opened last year, completes almost all of the firm's special contract work and also produces a portion of the standard line of solid-state protective relay products. The North Alton plant produces the widest range of electrical and magnetic products because of the availability of special tools and facilities not found at the two foreign plants, whereas the Tennessee plant has manufacturing capabilities that mirror that of the North Alton facility, but on a reduced scale.

Hourly workers at the Riverbend plant are represented by several trade unions, and the Tennessee plant and the plants on foreign soil are nonunion. REC's primary competitors include a large Japanese electronics firm with a limited product line and a German firm that produces a full range of electronic and magnetic components.

CURRENT SITUATION

On this particular Wednesday afternoon, Mr. Delbert St. Onge (Del for short), executive vice president and brother-in-law of the current president of REC, was reviewing a sales report received that morning from Ms. Susan Thornberry, vice president of marketing. Ms. Thornberry had been hired from outside the firm two years previously. Although the firm normally promoted from within, she had been hired because of the lack of an adequate internal candidate. She came with fine credentials and Mr. St. Onge had confidence in her skill and knowledge in the sales arena.

In his 14 years as the executive vice president, Del had never read such a negative report. In it, Ms. Thornberry emphasized clearly that REC was losing market share (see Figure C1–1), and she expected this trend to continue at least for the near future. The only exception was in the special electrical contracts area, which was growing slowly. The report pinned blame for the market share losses on the firm's inability to deliver product orders to customers on time. Even when deliveries were made on time, the production time required to complete an order seemed excessive when compared to the time customers reported that REC's competitors were promising. Although Susan did not directly accuse any specific manager of incom-

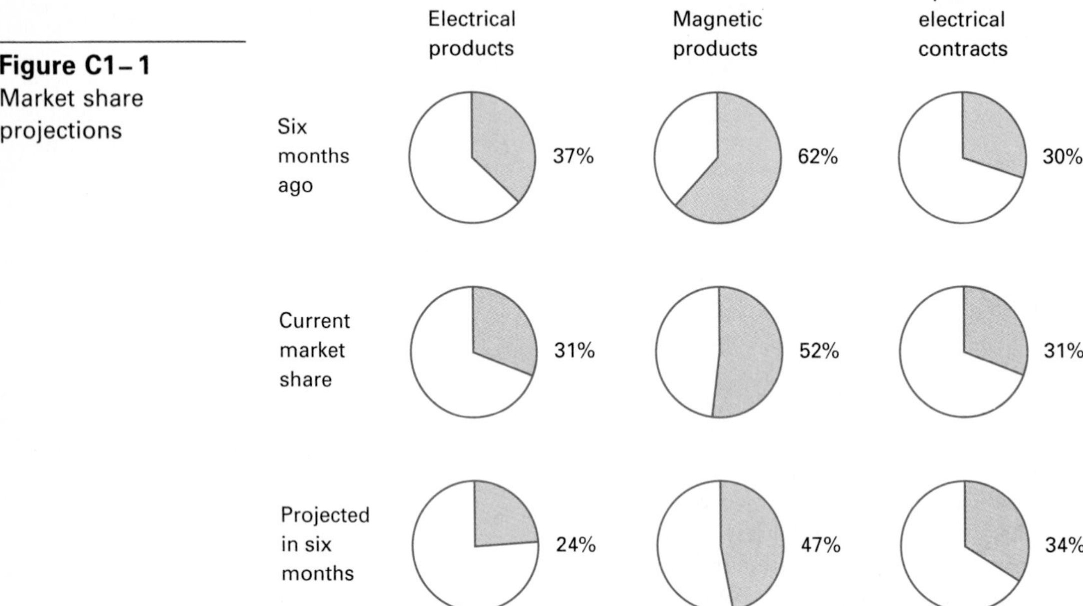

Figure C1–1
Market share projections

petence, the report indirectly cast doubt about the performance of Mr. Marvin Albert, vice president of operations and manufacturing.

Del had been developing doubts about Mr. Albert's abilities for the past year or so himself, even though Marvin had 12 years of experience in the job and 15 years of previous work as an electronics and magnetic engineer. How, Susan asked in the report, could her salespeople be expected to close sales contracts if the manufacturing side of the firm couldn't produce the products required on time? Del decided to meet with Marvin the next day to discuss the situation.

HOW A JOB SHOP WORKS

The North Alton manufacturing facility of REC is organized as a *job shop*, a manufacturing facility where products are manufactured to match specific customer requirements. Some product orders are very unique, for example, a large-scale transformer used in a hydroelectric dam. Other products are fairly standard. In fact, salespeople at REC carry a standard product catalog that lists some 6,400 standard products. Although the large majority of orders (over 90 percent) are for products listed in the catalog, the customer almost always requires some minor change to the standard product's specifications, for example, extra holes in a circuit board or a different kind of connecting plug for a capacitor or transformer.

When an order is taken, the sales department transfers a paper copy of the order to the shop floor manager and his administrative staff (three workers). This manager, who reports to Mr. Albert, coordinates with the engineering staff to create a manufacturing work order. The work order identifies in detail how the product will be manufactured. An individual work order may be for a single product, such as a large-scale capacitor, or for multiple copies of a product, such as 400 small electric motors.

Unlike a *flow shop* where products travel down an assembly line, workers in a job shop manufacture products by moving the work-in-process from one workstation to another on the shop floor until the work order is completed. The work order specifies the actual routing required to complete manufacturing of the product. Figure C1–2 shows an example of a work order, and Figure C1–3 displays the layout of the manufacturing shop floor at REC.

The shop floor manager is responsible for scheduling work, which requires tracking the status of work orders and developing a detailed daily work plan for each workstation on the shop floor. A copy of the actual work order documentation accompanies the product as it is being manufactured and serves as a control document. As the workers at each workstation com-

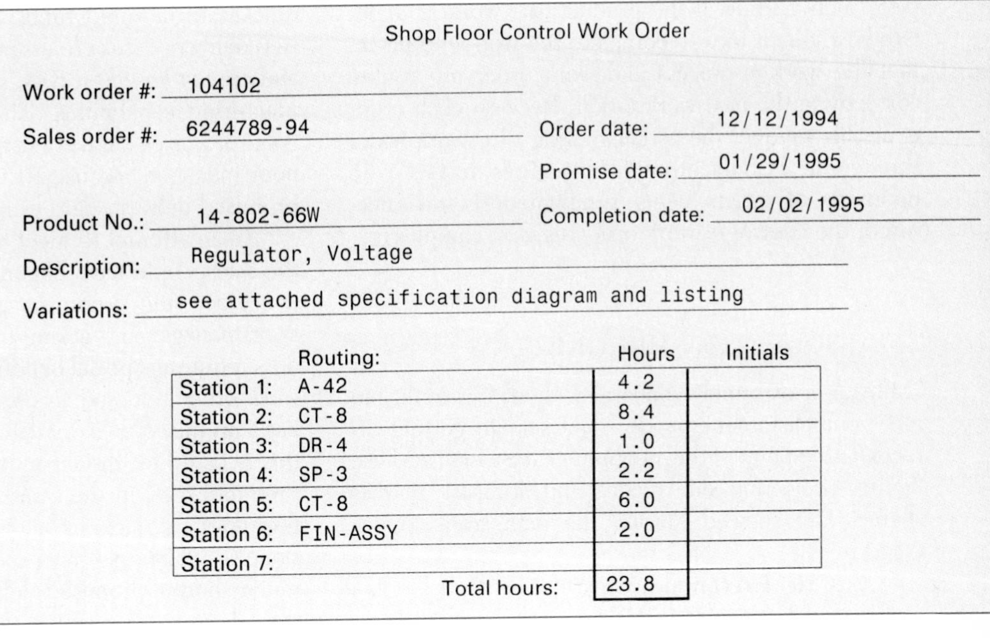

Shop Floor Control Work Order

Work order #: 104102

Sales order #: 6244789-94 Order date: 12/12/1994

Promise date: 01/29/1995

Product No.: 14-802-66W Completion date: 02/02/1995

Description: Regulator, Voltage

Variations: see attached specification diagram and listing

Routing:		Hours	Initials
Station 1:	A-42	4.2	
Station 2:	CT-8	8.4	
Station 3:	DR-4	1.0	
Station 4:	SP-3	2.2	
Station 5:	CT-8	6.0	
Station 6:	FIN-ASSY	2.0	
Station 7:			
	Total hours:	23.8	

Figure C1–2
Sample work order

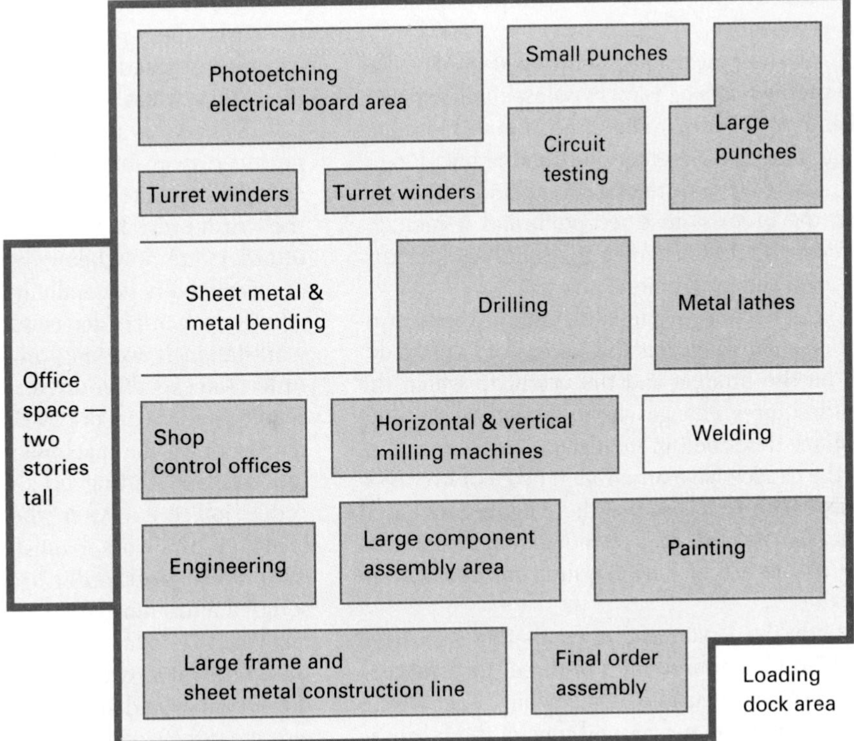

Figure C1–3
North Alton manufacturing shop floor layout

plete their portion of the product, the workers annotate how long it took to complete the work and insure that the work-in-process and work order are routed correctly to the next workstation. Because each order is usually unique, the actual routing of a work order through the manufacturing facility varies. In fact, with hundreds of orders being simultaneously manufactured, the control of work orders is very complex.

THE PRODUCTION MEETING

"Marv, I'm extremely concerned about our ability to meet our customer's needs," Del said in getting directly to the point of the meeting. "Take a look at these figures projecting our recent and forecast market share." Del showed Marvin the data from Figure C1–1.

"Yes, sir. I received a copy of Ms. Thornberry's report, and I reviewed it this morning," replied Marvin. "I've been investigating the situation in order to develop a plan to respond to this report. Actually, I believe we are in pretty good shape."

"Really?" queried Del with a look of disbelief. "Maybe you can give me some advance idea as to your findings." Marvin proceeded to explain the problem from his perspective.

REC receives several dozen orders each day. The standard product catalog used by salespeople provides guidelines as to the turnaround time required for manufacturing a product. Turnaround time is how long it takes the firm to deliver the customer order from the date that the order is first accepted, and it includes order processing time, engineering time, manufacturing time, and shipping time.

REC has been averaging about eight weeks turnaround time per order, but this varies, of course, depending on the product and the extent to which the customer requires changes in the standard product specifications described in the catalog. Most products listed in the catalog have turnaround times of five to six weeks, but Marvin explains that these figures are based on the firm's past performance, not on any real understanding of the actual time required to manufacture each product.

Recently the Japanese firm competing with REC has provided turnaround times in three- to four-week time frames. When customers complain about REC's inability to match the turnaround time of the Japanese firm, the salespeople have responded by promising quicker turnaround times, even though these promised delivery dates are essentially pulled out of thin air and are *not* based on REC's current workload or manufacturing capabilities. The salespeople do not get good promised delivery date estimates from the shop floor manager because REC does not have a reliable promised delivery date estimating system in place.

In an attempt to meet the promised delivery date, the salespeople have begun to bypass the existing order processing system by going directly to the shop floor manager and asking him to label these *rush* orders requiring special handling called *expediting*. Each work order released to the manufacturing shop floor has a promised delivery date annotated on it. Normally this is based on the current date plus the turnaround time indicated in the standard product catalog plus a few days of slack to allow for unforeseen circumstances. Of course, an expedited order must have a much shorter promised delivery date based solely on the salesperson's promise to the customer. The objective is to meet these critical promised delivery dates for the rush orders.

About six months ago, the expediting load became so heavy that the shop floor manager assigned two individuals to serve as full-time expediters for rush orders. These expediters personally track rush orders to "push" them through the shop floor. Recently, the expediters picked up additional expediting responsibilities. Now when a customer calls to complain about late delivery on an outstanding sales order, the salesperson responsible for taking the order automatically calls the expediters and asks them to add this order to their rush order list. Marvin estimates that 20 percent of orders are now being expedited.

Expediters generally go to the actual workstation where the work order is waiting. If the worker at that workstation is working on a job task from a routine order, the expediter directs the worker to halt work on that job and start work on the rush order. This involves tearing down the machine setup for the routine order job task and setting up the machinery for the rush order job task. After the rush order job task is complete, the worker must set up the machinery for the original work order again. Sometimes the actual setup of a machine like a drill press or metal lathe can take one to two hours, so expediting can actually cause the worker at a particular work station to get less work done than would otherwise be the case. Expediting also creates havoc with the shop floor manager's daily detailed work plan, but this cannot be helped.

The current computer system produces a daily work order schedule. The schedule may be slightly inaccurate because the actual status of an individual work order is only updated once the work order is completed. While a work order is in progress, no change for that specific work order is made to the computer database because the workers do not have time to complete the paperwork that would be required to track work orders at this level of detail. Further, having data entry clerks enter the thousands of daily changes that would have to be made to the database would be very time-consuming.

If a customer telephones with a question about the status of an order that is not being expedited, the best the shop floor manager can do is to tell the customer or salesperson that the work is *in-process* and to give the estimated promised delivery date entered into the system at the time that the work order was initiated. For expedited rush orders, the expediters attempt to annotate the daily work order schedule manually to indicate how the rush order is progressing; however, with the increased number of work orders being expedited, this manual tracking system sometimes breaks down.

Actually, Marvin is reasonably pleased with the way that the system is working. He gives Del a graph he has prepared that shows how well expediting has worked in reducing the turnaround time for rush orders (see Figure C1–4). The firm is meeting the promised delivery date for over 90 percent of the rush orders. He believes that one potential solution to the turnaround time problem is to assign three additional expediters to the shop floor. Although he is concerned that the firm's workers seem to be spending too much time in setting up manufacturing machinery, he feels that additional training may be used to reduce how much time workers require to complete machine setups.

PROBLEM SOLVING

Problem-Solving Processes

One of the most important responsibilities you will someday have as a manager is problem solving. Fortunately for us, as the chapters in this section of the textbook indicate, the ability to resolve problems is not inherited. It is an ability that can be learned and im-

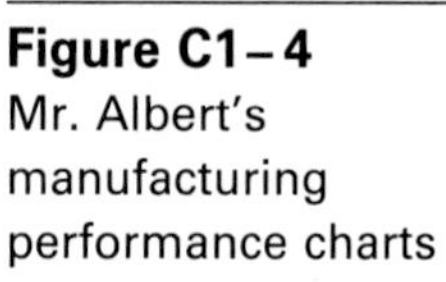

Figure C1–4
Mr. Albert's manufacturing performance charts

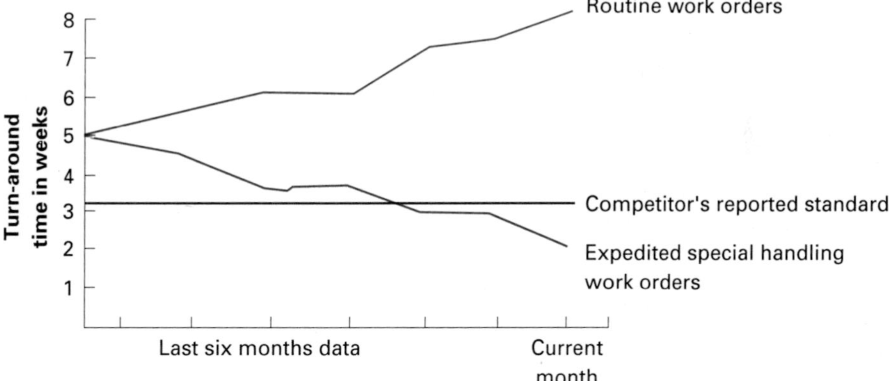

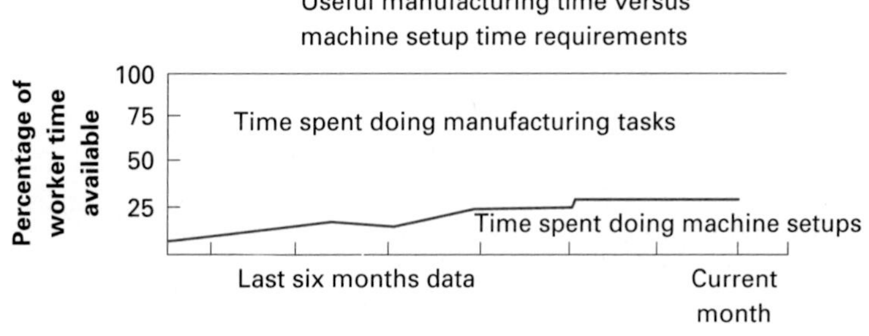

proved on by studying various techniques that aid the problem-solving process.

Figure C1–5 provides a conceptual diagram of the problem-solving process. Quite simply, solving a problem requires taking action that moves you from the *present state* to the *desired state.* The present state is evaluated by using a performance measure to determine the achievement of an established standard or objective. When a problem does *not* exist, the evaluation will reveal the present and desired states to be one and the same; that is, the standard is being met or exceeded.

There are several elements of the problem-solving process to consider. First, you must be skilled at defining the *problem.* Conceptually, this is quite simple. The problem is defined as the failure to be in the desired state. This failing is best recognized when the system under evaluation has a clearly specified *performance standard* or *objective.* For example, production output at a factory work site may be low. This is the present state. The desired state includes high production output. The low output is easier to recognize if a standard for production exists.

In actual practice, defining a particular problem can be difficult. Many of us tend to confuse the problem with *symptoms* of the problem. Symptoms are conditions produced by a problem. Low factory production may be a symptom of poor employee motivation. In turn, poor employee motivation can result from an inadequate benefits package, faulty supervision, inferior work conditions, or a number of other factors. To identify the problem properly, you must gather evidence by working through the cause-effect chain of events. If it appears that a firm is beset by a multitude of problems, you should insure that you are not confusing symptoms with problems. In fact, one or just a few problems can make it appear that a firm is overwhelmed with difficulties.

Once a problem is identified, some managers are quick to implement a plan of action to resolve the situation. When time is of the essence, this approach may be the only one that is satisfactory. However, when time allows, managers should identify *alternative* courses of action. The tendency to skip this step in problem solving must be avoided whenever possible.

Occasionally, managers may find that some alternatives, regardless of how attractive they appear, result in failure. This often happens when *constraints* upon the situation are not factored into the decision-making process. Constraints represent internal or external limits on courses of action. Some examples of constraints affecting employee morale include the lack of a union labor relations contract, nonavailability of replacement personnel, or limits on funds allocated for worker benefits.

Problem-Solving Approaches

Various approaches to problem solving are available. One technique is to analyze the situation based upon a theory or hypothesis that is relevant to it. You will find several integrated cases throughout this book that require such an approach. Another approach involves the use of intuition. When using intuition in problem solving, we primarily rely on past experience. As with other approaches, intuition may require you to make assumptions about the problem situation. By combining

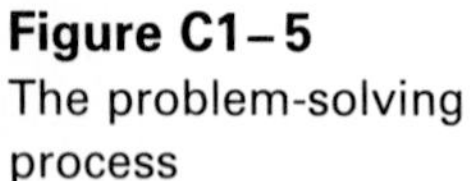

Figure C1–5
The problem-solving process

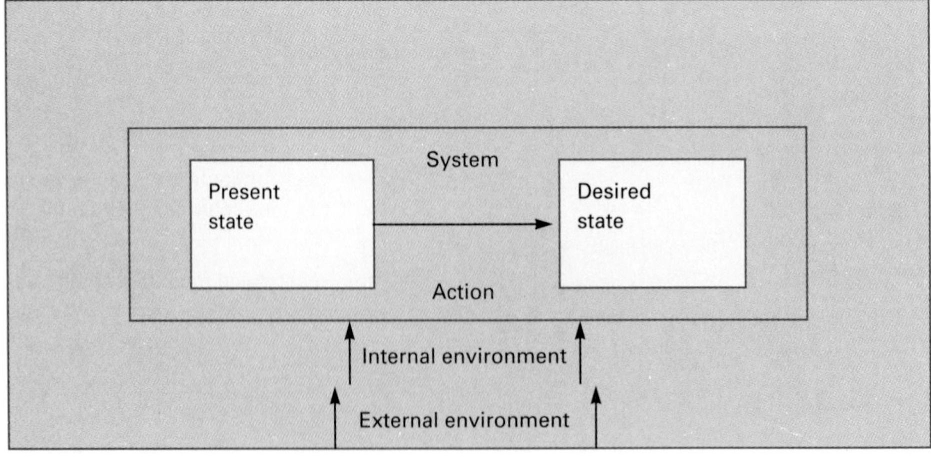

past experience, assumptions, and knowledge of the current situation, you select the best course of action.

One of the more favored techniques for analyzing and solving problems is the *systems approach*. This technique is a multiple-step method that is based on systems theory as described in Chapter 2.

The Systems Approach

We recommend the systems approach as both a method for analyzing this and other cases in the text and for diagnosing problems you may later encounter in operational settings. An advantage of the systems approach is that it enables you to incorporate other techniques. Additionally, the systems approach provides structure to the problem-solving process, reducing the probability of skipping a critical stage of the analysis procedure. In solving the cases in this text, you should combine the systems approach with the application of appropriate theory.

Chapter 2 outlines the steps in the systems approach, which can be summed up as follows:

1. Define the problem based on the performance criteria.
2. Accumulate evidence about the problem.
3. Identify alternative courses of action.
4. Evaluate the alternatives.
5. Select the best alternative.
6. Evaluate the result based on the performance criteria.

Additionally, it is important to understand the system within which the problem seems to lie, which aids in defining the problem. To understand the system you must identify its boundaries, inputs, and outputs. You should also determine if management is adequately monitoring output quality and screening input quality. Another important question to answer is whether or not management has the necessary information technology in place to monitor the overall system's functioning components.

Any assumptions you make during an evaluation—that is, information not available in a case or operational setting—should be clearly stated. It is best to provide your rationale for assumptions to make it clear that your assumptions are reasonable, logical extensions of material evidence uncovered during your investigation.

Case Questions and Exercises

1. Do any of the current corporate officers mentioned in the case have clearly specified performance objectives for the various functional areas within REC? Are these objectives measurable? Is there a standard of performance for the work order processing system and how is it being measured?

2. Analyze the case from a systems perspective. Identify the work order processing system and the various system components. Suggest which component or components are faulty.

3. Using a systems approach to problem solving, analyze the firm's problem in meeting customer turnaround time expectations. At least one of your alternatives should include using computer technology to solve the problem you identify. You should also critique Marvin's suggestion to add three additional expediters.

4. Based on your analysis in questions 1, 2, and 3, write a detailed report analyzing REC's work order situation. If any procedures, personnel, or equipment are required to achieve objectives, determine the impact of new procedures, personnel, or equipment on the system. Clearly specify any assumptions you make.

Part II

Computer System Resources

Part Two is a concise survey of the basic computer resources available to the manager. These resources include computer systems hardware and software, file management and database systems, and communications systems hardware and software. You may have had previous experience with one or more of the topics in this section. If so, this section will serve as a review. Whether you are reviewing the material or reading about it for the first time, it is essential that you have a basic knowledge of these computer resources so that you may learn how to use them to help you manage successfully.

C 4

Computer Hardware

Chapter Outline

Manager's View

Computers have become a common tool on managers' desks. It is almost certain that as a manager you will use a computer system. Many managers rely on computer-generated information to help them make decisions. Furthermore, decisions regarding the acquisition and use of computer systems, especially small computer systems, are increasingly being made at the department level of organizations. As a result, management concerns regarding the acquisition of computer systems have grown and include not only what systems should be acquired but also when, how, and from whom they should be acquired. Because rapid change in computer technology is ongoing, acquisition decisions are always made in a very dynamic environment. To help departmental managers make rational decisions about computer systems in such a complex and dynamic environment, they need a basic understanding of computer systems.

The computer industry, like computer systems themselves, is also undergoing constant change. The major vendors of yesterday may not be the major vendors of tomorrow. Many types of computers produced today are regarded as commodities, and the names of their manufacturers do not carry the weight they did in the past with buyers. Earlier, many computer systems were purchased directly from the manufacturer, who delivered and installed them on the buyer's site. Today, many computers are purchased through the mail or from discount stores and the buyer is expected to assemble them and install some or all of the programs. In this environment, it is particularly important that managers become knowledgeable about computer systems so they can set specifications for the systems they buy and deploy the systems they purchase.

To be an effective computer user, you must not view computer systems as mysterious devices but rather as everyday working tools. Fortunately, computer systems have become much more user friendly. That is, they have become easier to use for people who are not computer experts. In fact, managers have become directly involved in developing computer information systems that serve their needs. Development of computer information systems by users, or "end-user computing," has become an important part of management information systems.

COMPUTER SYSTEMS

Computer systems consist of numerous components, as you will learn in this and the following chapter. One of those components is computer hardware. The term **hardware** refers to computer equipment, the actual machinery used in a computer system. Today, computer system hardware comes in nearly every conceivable shape and size to serve the varying needs of organizations.

Supercomputers

Supercomputers are very large and specialized computer systems. In fact, a supercomputer system is composed of multiple processors that are integrated to work together. Supercomputer systems are usually designed to handle scientific and engineering calculations extremely quickly. Defense agencies and scientific organizations often use these computer systems to process enormous amounts of data extremely rapidly. Because much smaller and much less expensive systems are able to handle common business applications, supercomputers are not likely to be used for these tasks. A supercomputer system with its attachments fills a large room and costs many millions of dollars.

Mainframe Computers

Mainframe computer systems are large computers frequently used in large organizations. In fact, some very large organizations use several mainframe computer systems to handle their activities. Mainframe computer systems usually take up an entire room when all the equipment attached to them is included, and they cost from hundreds of thousands to millions of dollars (see Figure 4–1).

Minicomputer Systems

Another type of computer system is the **minicomputer system,** which small organizations or departments in a large organization may use for all their computing needs. Minicomputer systems have been reduced in size to fit on a desktop or under a desk. The price of minicomputer systems may fall in the $20,000 to $500,000 range. **Superminicomputer systems** are more powerful versions of the minicomputer that have been developed to challenge mainframe systems.

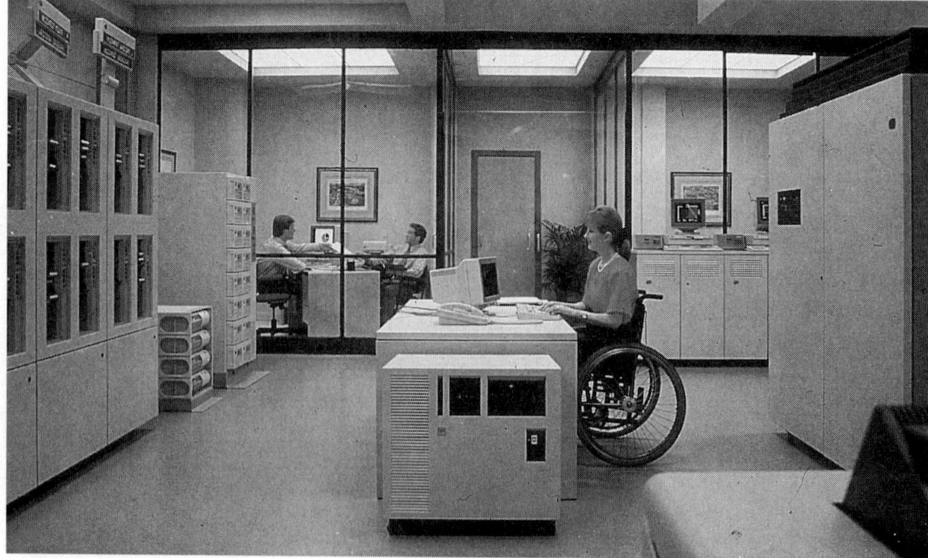

Figure 4–1
A mainframe computer system with computer console and disk drives

Courtesy of the International Business Machines Corporation

Microcomputer Systems

Then there are the very popular **microcomputer systems,** used by small organizations, executives in large organizations, and even by professionals working out of their homes. In the past, IBM set the standards for microcomputer hardware. Many other firms developed microcomputer systems that worked like, or emulated, the IBM-PC, or personal computer. These work-alikes, referred to as IBM-PC *compatibles* (see Figure 4–2), make up one of the two major types of microcomputers sold today in the United States, the other being Apple and Macintosh computer systems. The price of microcomputers varies substantially, ranging from a few hundred to several thousand dollars.

Supermicrocomputer systems are more powerful versions of microcomputers that are frequently used to control and provide resources to other computers in a network. The ability of these systems to handle the volume and complexity of an organization's information processing tasks challenges that of minicomputer systems.

Professional Workstations

Some technical and professional persons need supermicrocomputer systems with high-quality display screens, often called **workstations,** to perform their work. For example, draftsmen may need workstations to create and edit detailed drawings. Computer programmers may need workstations to create and edit complex charts that illustrate the logic of the computer programs they write.

Laptop, Notebook, and Palmtop Systems

The trend for computer systems has been to smaller and smaller sizes (see Figure 4–3). **Desktop** microcomputers (see Figures 4–2 and 4–16a), such as the Apple II computers introduced in the late 1970s, were followed by portable computers in the early '80s, which were followed by **laptop** computers in the late '80s, and then by **notebook** (see Figure 16b) and **palmtop** computers in the early '90s (see Box 4–1).

Regardless of their size and shape or how they are classified, all computer systems are very much alike in that they all contain similar basic components. For example, all computer systems contain a **central processing unit,** or **CPU,** and one or more devices to get data into and out of the CPU. Let's look first at the CPU.

Classifying a computer system as a microcomputer, supermicrocomputer, minicomputer, superminicomputer, mainframe computer, or supercomputer system usually

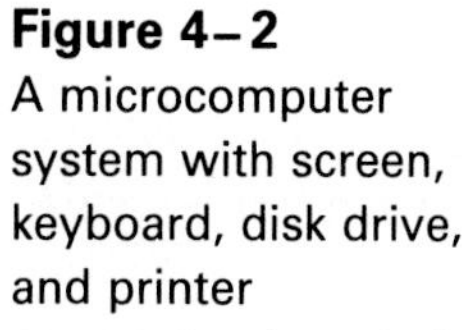

Figure 4–2
A microcomputer system with screen, keyboard, disk drive, and printer
Courtesy of Hewlett-Packard Company

Box 4–1 Personal Digital Assistants

Personal digital assistants, or **PDAs,** are an evolving variety of palmtop computer system. They include pen-based computers, electronic clipboards, pocket organizers, and other special-function devices. The Hewlett-Packard HP 95LX and the Apple Newton are examples. The Newton features a touch screen as an input device rather than a standard keyboard.

Pen-based computers allow you to write or mark on a tabletlike screen with an attached or cordless device that looks like a pen. The handwriting recognition software converts written or marked data into printed text or other output. The pen can also be used as a pointing device, similar to a mouse. In some applications, the tablet screen may display a form to be filled in.

Pen-based computer systems are expected to become popular devices for field personnel, such as meter readers, delivery personnel, salespeople, inventory workers, pipeline workers, and even judges at sporting events and zookeepers. Basically, these devices display a form in which you can record data with ease. For example, Anheuser-Busch is developing a pen-based system that will allow its sales reps to take inventory at customers' stores and record competitor prices. Also, customer information will be stored in the devices so that the sales rep will not forget a customer's birthday, telephone number, or opening or closing times.

Pocket organizers are palmtop devices that provide a small screen and keyboard or an attached pen. The pocket organizer usually provides the user with a calendar, calculator, address book, notepad, and other handy desktop tools.

PDAs are quickly evolving into general purpose devices, allowing users to run their favorite programs, fax messages, control their cellular telephones, and perform other tasks like their bigger brothers, the desktop PCs.

Courtesy of Apple Computer, Inc.

Figure 4–3
The shrinking size of computer systems

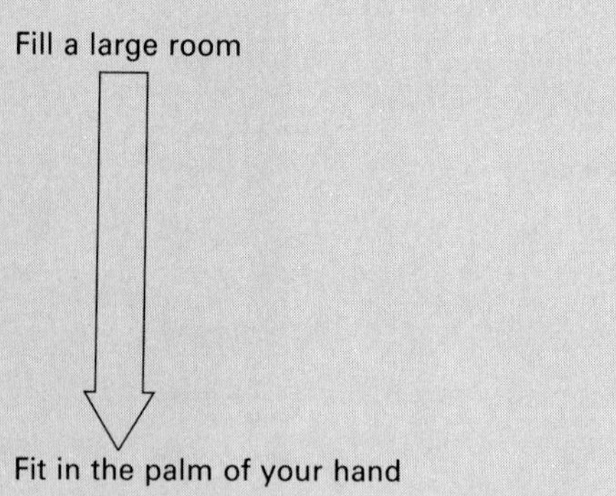

depends on such factors as the amount of memory the system possesses (see the section on memory later in this chapter), the amount of data it can handle at one time (see the discussion of word size later in this chapter), and how many tasks and users it can handle concurrently (see the section on operating systems in the next chapter). Because of advances in technology, the classification system has become fuzzy. That is, it is not hard to find microcomputers today that are as powerful as older minicomputers, or minicomputers with power that was formerly associated with mainframe computers. Nonetheless, these terms provide a convenient way to classify computers, and they remain in common use. As a manager, however, you should be less concerned with how people classify your computer system and more concerned with whether that system fits your needs.

CENTRAL PROCESSING UNIT

The CPU is often referred to as the "brain" of the computer system because it is comprised of the *control unit* and *arithmetic/logic unit* (see Figure 4–4). The control unit obtains instructions from the computer system's memory, interprets them, and notifies the other components in the system to carry them out. The arithmetic/logic unit processes data obtained from memory under the direction of the control unit. The arithmetic/logic unit basically is able to process data in only two ways: (1) arithmetically, such as by adding, subtracting, multiplying, or dividing data; and (2) logically, such as by comparing one group of data with another. Logical processes include comparing one group of data with another to determine whether one group is

1. Equal to the other ($A = B$).
2. Not equal to the other ($A \neq B$).
3. Less than the other ($A < B$).
4. More than the other ($A > B$).
5. Equal to or less than the other ($A \leqq B$).
6. Equal to or more than the other ($A \geqq B$).

Considering how limited the arithmetic/logic unit of a CPU is in terms of what it can do, it is astonishing how many varied and complex tasks a CPU can perform. The fundamental arithmetic processes and six logical comparisons allow the device to process complex mathematical relationships, control space vehicles, draw detailed pictures on a screen, create musical compositions, or simply produce paychecks at the end of the week.

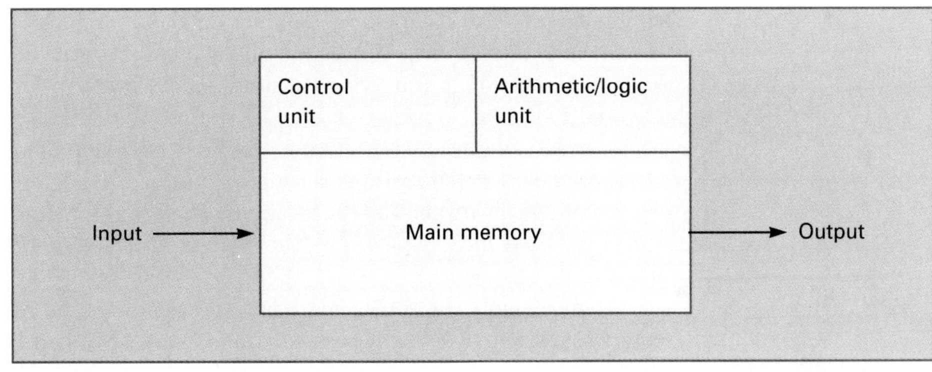

Figure 4–4
A simple model of a CPU and main memory showing the relationship of the control unit, arithmetic/logic unit, and main memory

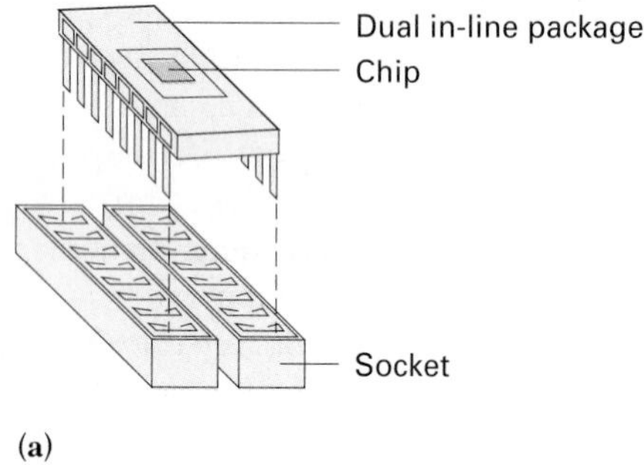

(a)

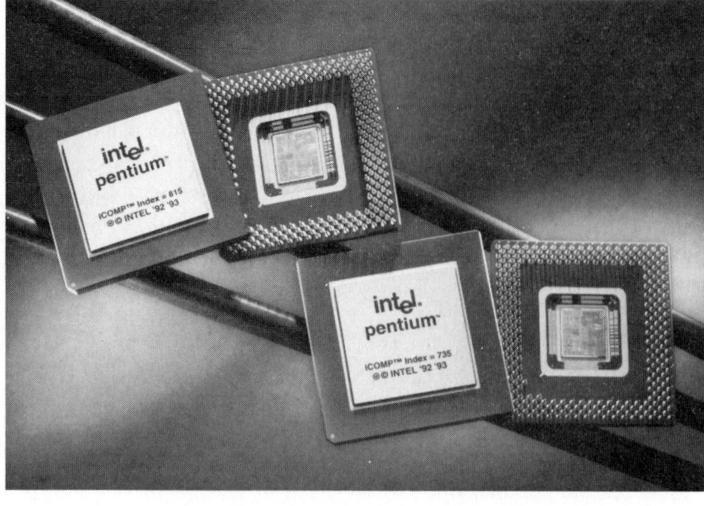

(b)

Figure 4–5 (a) A single microprocessor chip encased in a dual in-line package. The chip can be inserted into a chip socket on the motherboard. **(b)** The Intel Pentium chip.
Courtesy of Intel Corporation; Pentium Chips

On some computers, the circuitry for the control unit and the arithmetic/logic unit has been placed on a single *silicon chip* (see Figure 4–5) called a **microprocessor.** On a microcomputer, the microprocessor chip for the control unit and the arithmetic/logic unit is placed on a board, often called the *motherboard* (see Box 4–2), that comprises the heart of the central processing unit.

MEMORY

The data you wish the computer system to process is stored in *internal memory* or **main memory** along with a set of instructions for processing the data called a **computer program** (see Figure 4–6 on page 96). Chapter 5 will discuss computer programs in detail. Main memory usually must contain (1) part or all of the data you want to work on and (2) part or all of the instructions necessary to process the data.

Main memory has three important characteristics: It is usually volatile, it can be accessed randomly, and it is fast. It is usually volatile because the type of memory commonly used for main memory retains data and programs only as long as the system is on. When the system is turned off, all data and programs stored in main memory are lost. Main memory is also called **random-access memory** or **RAM** because it consists of storage locations in which data can be stored and retrieved directly (see single in-line Memory Modules, Box 4–2). That is, the computer system is able to place or find data at any storage location without having to start at the beginning of main memory and work sequentially through all the locations. To permit the direct access of these memory locations, each location has its own *address.* Main memory is also called *primary storage.*

Main memory, or RAM, is a relatively expensive and fast form of memory for a computer system. That is, it is usually more expensive than other types of memory on the basis of the cost per character of data stored. It is also usually faster than other types

Box 4–2 Inside a Personal Computer

Here are some basic components that you will find inside your computer system:

Expansion slots—These slots let you add expansion boards to your computer system. They might include boards that provide parallel and serial ports, mouse ports, faxes, modems, and video adapters.

Single in-line memory modules (SIMM)—These modules provide the RAM for the system. RAM is where the computer system holds part or all of the programs you use and the data on which you are working.

Motherboard—This is the basic board used in the computer system. It provides the electrical connections between the computer system's components, such as the CPU, ROM, and RAM.

Disk controller board—This board connects the disk drives to the CPU and allows the computer system to save and retrieve data from the drives. It is shown here without the cables that connect to the drives so that the view is not blocked.

Video board—This board allows you to display text, data, and images on your monitor. Your monitor cable connects to this board through the monitor port on the back of your computer system.

Power supply—This component regulates the supply of electricity to the other components of the computer system.

Read-only memory (ROM)—These chips contain the commands your computer needs to get itself going when the power is turned on.

CPU—This is the brain of the computer system.

Math co-processor socket—This is the place where you insert a math co-processor chip, if you need it.

Hard drives—These devices allow you to store large amounts of data.

Floppy drives—These devices allow you to store data to and retrieve data from floppy disks.

Source: *PC Today* 4, No. 4, April 1990, pp. 96–97.

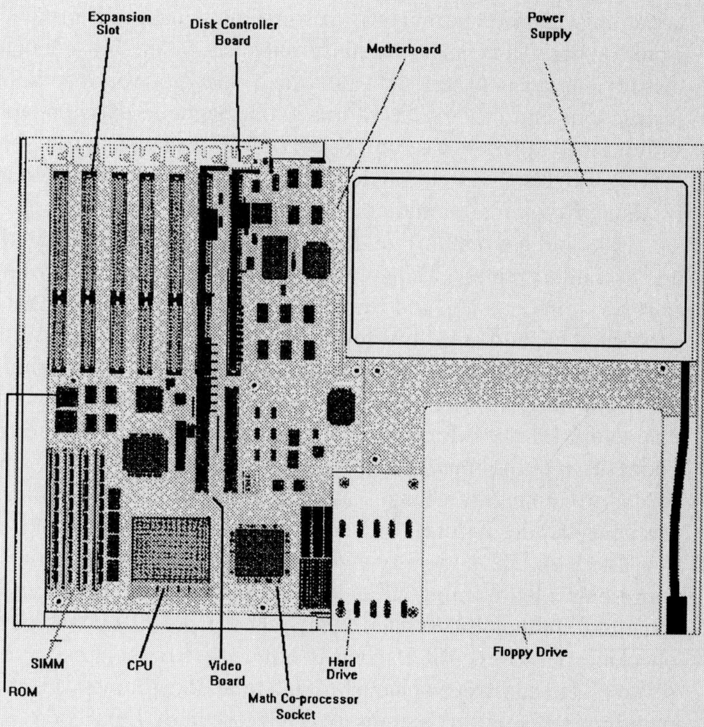

```
1000  OPEN "A", #1, "B:ADLABELS"

1010  WHILE NOT EOF

1020  INPUT #1, LNAME$, FNAME$, MNAME$, ADDRESS$, CITY$, STATE$, ZIP$

1030  LPRINT

1040  LPRINT FNAME$; MNAME$; LNAME$

1050  LPRINT ADDRESS$

1060  LPRINT CITY$; STATE$; ZIP$

1070  LPRINT

1080  LPRINT

1090  WEND

1100  END
```

Figure 4–6
A simple program for printing address labels

of memory. When large amounts of data must be stored, other, less expensive and usually slower forms of memory are used. As a result, most computer systems will have *auxiliary memory,* or **secondary storage,** in addition to main memory, or primary storage. Secondary storage usually takes the form of magnetic disks and tapes. Secondary storage devices permit you to store more data and programs than main memory would allow. Thus, main memory only has to be big enough to store the current instructions and current data on which you are working. You can store your other instructions and other data externally on magnetic disks or tapes. Both disk and tape systems are explained later in this chapter. For now, you can get the idea of a magnetic disk by visualizing an old phonograph record. You can get the idea of a magnetic tape by visualizing a reel of audiotape.

Data and instructions, or the computer program, are stored in both main memory and secondary storage as *bits,* or *binary digits.* In the binary number system there are only two numbers: one and zero. Thus, a binary digit is one that has only two states: on and off. "On" and "off" bits form characters such as letters of the alphabet, numerals, and special characters using a code. Samuel Morse used a similar scheme, combining short and long signals (dots and dashes) to represent letters, numerals, and special characters for the Morse code. To complicate matters, there are several computer codes. Two of the most commonly used codes are *ASCII,* or American Standard Code for Information Interchange, and *EBCDIC,* or Extended Binary Coded Decimal Interchange Code. Figure 4–7 shows how these two codes represent characters.

The EBCDIC code uses eight bits to make up a character. The set of eight bits that represents a letter, numeral, or special character is called a *byte.* The computer system may add another bit to each byte, called a *parity bit,* which the computer uses for checking purposes. ASCII code is often used by personal computer systems. It uses seven bits to construct a character, or a total of eight bits with the parity bit added. IBM mainframe computer systems typically use EBCDIC code. The Digital Equipment Corporation's Vax 9000 mainframe computer system and most microcomputers use ASCII code.

Figure 4–7
ASCII and EBCDIC codes for numerals and letters

Character	EBCDIC	ASCII	Character	EBCDIC	ASCII
0	1111 0000	011 0000	I	1100 1001	100 1001
1	1111 0001	011 0001	J	1101 0001	100 1010
2	1111 0010	011 0010	K	1101 0010	100 1011
3	1111 0011	011 0011	L	1101 0011	100 1100
4	1111 0100	011 0100	M	1101 0100	100 1101
5	1111 0101	011 0101	N	1101 0101	100 1110
6	1111 0110	011 0110	O	1101 0110	100 1111
7	1111 0111	011 0111	P	1101 0111	101 0000
8	1111 1000	011 1000	Q	1101 1000	101 0001
9	1111 1001	011 1001	R	1101 1001	101 0010
A	1100 0001	100 0001	S	1110 0010	101 0011
B	1100 0010	100 0010	T	1110 0011	101 0100
C	1100 0011	100 0011	U	1110 0100	101 0101
D	1100 0100	100 0100	V	1110 0101	101 0110
E	1100 0101	100 0101	W	1110 0110	101 0111
F	1100 0110	100 0110	X	1110 0111	101 1000
G	1100 0111	100 0111	Y	1110 1000	101 1001
H	1100 1000	100 1000	Z	1110 1001	101 1010

The memory capacity of a computer system component is usually measured in terms of the number of bytes, or characters, that it can hold. Usually the measuring unit is 1,024 bytes, or 2^{10} bytes. Because this number is somewhat inconvenient to multiply easily, we usually round off 1,024 bytes to 1,000. Furthermore, we also refer to groups of 1,000 bytes of memory as *KB*s, or **kilobytes** (kilo = 1,000). For example, many computers in the past were sold with an advertised main memory of 640 KB. This means that they really held 640 × 1,024, or 655,360 bytes, of data in main memory. Capacity in bytes is often shortened still further, so that 640 KB becomes 640 K in everyday conversation.

As the amount of memory used in computer systems has grown, the terms **megabytes** (mega = 1 million) or **MBs** and **gigabytes** (giga = 1 billion) or **GBs** of memory have become more common. For example, microcomputer systems today are often sold with main memory capacities of 8 MB, or 8 million bytes. A secondary storage device may store 8 GB, or 8 billion bytes.

Recent software designed for microcomputers often requires megabytes of RAM. It is likely that the RAM required for microcomputer applications will continue to increase. One way to increase RAM in a microcomputer (and other types of computers, for that matter) is to add *memory boards* to the special memory board slots on the motherboard. These memory slots are for *SIMM memory boards*, or single in-line memory modules (see Figure 4–8). A SIMM memory board is small and may contain

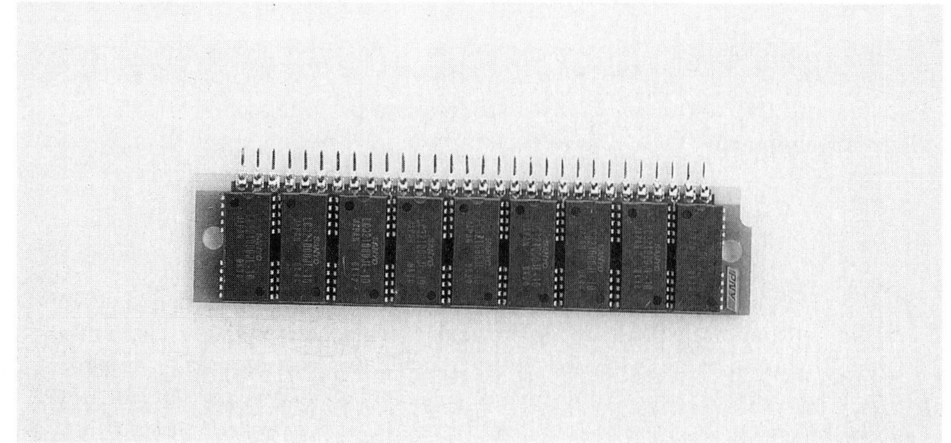

Figure 4–8
A SIMM board
Courtesy of Jameco Electronics Components

256 KB, 1 MB, or 4 MB of RAM. Many microcomputer systems provide eight SIMM memory board slots. If 4 MB SIMM boards are used, the internal memory capacity of those microcomputers becomes 32 MB of RAM.

The internal memory of your computer system also contains **ROM,** or read-only memory (see Box 4–2). ROM usually contains programs that help the computer system start up and operate. However, ROM can only be read; it cannot be written to or altered by the user. Also, ROM is not lost when the power is shut off. That is why ROM is used for these special programs. You cannot alter the programs in ROM, and the programs are not lost when you turn off the power. ROM programs are represented by electronic circuitry in the form of ROM chips and are sometimes called *firmware.* If the ROM programs currently in your computer system need to be changed, the old ROM chips must be removed and new ROM chips containing the new programs inserted in their place.

There are several variations in the types of ROM available. For example, *programmable read-only memory,* or *PROM,* is a form of ROM that allows you or the manufacturer to read a program into it. *EPROM,* or *erasable programmable read-only memory,* allows programs in ROM to be altered with special equipment.

COMPUTER POWER

One measure of the power of a computer is its *word size.* That is, the power of a computer is partly measured by how many bits of data it can transfer between the CPU and main memory at one time. A machine with a 16-bit word size has a 16-bit data path through which the data can be passed. This data path is a set of wires through which data passes between the CPU and its components. The data path is also called the *bus.* In other words, the data path, or word size, is two characters wide (16 bits). Many older personal computers and some minicomputers use a 16-bit data path or word size. Mainframe computers, many minicomputers, and many of the new microcomputers have 32-bit and 64-bit data paths. Think of a 16-bit machine as a highway with two lanes. Only two cars can use the highway at one time. A 32-bit machine is a four-lane highway, allowing four cars to pass concurrently, and a 64-bit machine is an eight-lane highway, on which eight cars can pass at once.

Another way to measure the power of a computer is the speed at which the central processing unit completes its internal processing tasks. The speed at which these tasks

Box 4–3 Breaking the Bus Bottleneck

The bus used in many computers is called the AT bus because it is like the bus used on the venerable IBM PC/AT, an early PC that was very popular. Data runs on that bus at a speed of 8 MHz. Many microprocessor chips, however, run at speeds of 16 to 150 MHz. It doesn't make much sense to have a chip that can process data at 66 MHz if the chip has to slow down when it gets data from main memory, puts data into main memory, or exchanges data with other circuit boards.

To allow computer systems to utilize fully the faster, more powerful microprocessor chips, IBM developed an entirely new bus architecture called MicroChannel Architecture, or the MCA bus. This bus provides a 32-bit data pathway and allows the hardware to complete many tasks at one time. However, the MCA bus will not let you put your old, AT bus expansion cards into the MCA machines. To compete with IBM, a consortium of other computer makers developed a bus standard similar to IBM's microchannel architecture, but one that will accept the old, AT bus expansion cards. This bus structure is called the Extended Industry Standard Architecture, or EISA bus. IBM uses the MCA bus structure in most of its PS/2 line of computer systems. EISA bus machines, at this writing, are primarily used for special purpose computers.

Machines equipped with the Video Electronics Standards Association's (VESA) VL bus architecture allow some circuit boards, such as the boards that control the video screen and hard disks, to run at the same speed as the microprocessor chip. This bus architecture is usually called *local bus* architecture and has been adopted by many large electronics firms and major manufacturers of video circuit boards. At this writing, many of the high-end personal computers being offered use this local bus architecture. However, Intel Corporation, a major manufacturer of computer chips, has developed a different local bus architecture called the Peripheral Component Interconnect, or PCI local bus standard. A major purpose of local bus architectures is to provide for fast processing of video signals because the popular programs for microcomputers, with their nice looking screens, require it. The old AT bus simply does not handle these programs fast enough.

Which bus architecture will become the standard for the 1990s is open to question at this time. However, it is important for the manager to consider the bus architecture of any equipment being acquired. Adopting one bus architecture or the other may have implications for other computer issues, including the kinds of expansion cards, screens, and programs that can be used.

are completed is referred to as a computer system's *clock speed,* and it is measured in millions of clock ticks per second, or *megahertz.* A computer system operating at a clock speed of 66 megahertz completes its internal processing tasks much faster than a computer system operating at a clock speed of 25 megahertz.

Still another measure of computing power is the number of instructions that the CPU can process in a given time period. The unit of measure used here is *millions of instructions per second,* or *MIPS.* A typical range for microcomputer CPUs, for example, is between 20 and 80 MIPS; high-end microcomputers based on Digital Equipment Corporation's Alpha microprocessor may handle up to 400 MIPS.

Although the power of a computer can be and often is expressed in word size, megahertz, and MIPS, these measures are really only rough guidelines. Many other factors contribute to a computer's speed and processing ability. The real power of a computer is *throughput,* or the time it takes to get the job done.

USING MORE THAN ONE PROCESSOR

Most computer systems use more than the central processing unit to do their work. Many computer systems use *coprocessors* to assist the central processor with its work. For example, a coprocessor may be used for math calculations, control of secondary storage devices, and video display units. Large computer systems may use special

Box 4–4 Powerful New Microcomputer Systems and the Instruction Set Wars

A number of new microcomputer systems have recently emerged or will soon emerge that may dominate the 1990s. These systems are very powerful in comparison with popular microcomputer systems in use today. However, remember that the powerful new microcomputers of yesterday, such as those built around Intel's 80386 chip, soon became the standard computing systems for business. Thus, the computer systems described next and the technology on which they are based are likely to become the popular computer systems in the years to come.

One of the differences among these new systems is the *instruction set* they use, or the group of program commands that they understand and can execute. One group of systems are *CISC*, or complex instruction set computing systems. The other group is based on *RISC*, or reduced instruction set computing architecture. RISC systems use a small set of frequently used instructions. CISC systems use a larger set of instructions than RISC systems. For processing that requires only these instructions, RISC systems are very fast. For processing that requires instructions that are not part of the RISC set, RISC systems can be relatively slow.

RISC technology is actually quite old, first introduced by IBM in 1974. Since that time, RISC technology has been used in professional workstations and in other computer systems designed for special uses.

CISC-BASED COMPUTER SYSTEMS

Microcomputer systems based on Intel's *Pentium* microprocessor debuted in 1993. The Pentium chip, sometimes called the 80586 chip, is a 64-bit, 60–150 MHz device that can reach more than 100 MIPS and contains 3.1 million transistors. Compare those statistics to the power of the 8088 Intel chip that powered the first IBM PC: a 16-bit processor that ran at 4.7 MHz and reached only 0.33 MIPS. The Pentium chip, like its Intel predecessors, the 80286, 80386, and 80486, is a *CISC*, or complex instruction set computing processor chip.

Example: Compaq's Deskpro 5/66M Model 510 uses a Pentium chip, runs at 66MHz, has a 510MB hard disk and 32MB of RAM.

Recently, Intel has been increasing the power of its central processing units by doubling and tripling the clock speeds at which they run. Thus, an 80486DX2 is a CPU chip whose clock speed has been doubled; for example, from 33 Mhz to 66 Mhz. An 80486DX3 is a CPU chip

Courtesy of Apple Computer, Inc.

processors to control the input or output of data to secondary storage and printers. These special processors are called *I/O channels.* By offloading special tasks to special processors, the central processor can concentrate on the work it has at hand and become more efficient.

Some computer systems use more than one central processing unit to run several programs simultaneously on a system. A computer system that has more than one processor and uses them to process more than one program simultaneously has *multiprocessing* capability.

Still other computer systems use more than one central processing unit to complete several processing tasks necessary for a single program simultaneously. These computer systems operate their processors in parallel to complete many steps in a program at once, which is called *parallel processing.*

whose clock speed has been tripled; for example, from 33 Mhz to 100 Mhz.

Apple Macintosh computer systems use Motorola's 68040 chip, which, at this writing, runs at only 33 MHz. Like the Pentium, the 68040 chip is a CISC processor.

Example: the Macintosh Quadra 800 uses a Motorola 68040 chip, runs at 33 MHz, and has a 500 MB hard disk and 24 MB of RAM.

RISC-BASED COMPUTER SYSTEMS

IBM introduced a whole line of RISC workstations in the early 1990s based on their RS/6000 processing chip set. This set was comprised of seven to nine separate chips but was still a 32-bit system. Soon thereafter, a consortium comprised of IBM, Apple, and Motorola began development of a microcomputer processing chip that would combine the RS/6000 chip set into a single chip that would run as fast as 80 MHz. This chip is called the PowerPC chip.

Apple intends to introduce a family of computers based on this technology. PowerPC computer systems will be able to run programs designed for IBM RISC systems and also, with some added technology, programs designed for the Motorola 68000 family of CISC chips used in Macintosh computers.

Example: The PowerPC MAC was introduced in early 1994. This family of computers uses a PowerPC chip, runs at 66 MHz, contains 2.8 million transistors, delivers an estimated 100 MIPS, and comes with a large hard drive and 8 MB of RAM. At this writing, a new version of the PowerPC chip, a 64-bit system, has been introduced.

Example: The new models of Digital Equipment Corporation's Alpha AXP PC, introduced in 1994, use an Alpha chip running at 150 MHz and provide 157 MIPS. Models of the Alpha AXP have been unveiled that run over 200 MHz, contain 1.7 million transistors, are able to handle up to 128 MB of RAM, and deliver up to 400 MIPS.

Courtesy of Digital Equipment Corporation

TYPES OF COMPUTER SYSTEM PROCESSING

Events that occur in an organization's day are called transactions. For example, a sale at a store is a transaction. When you enter a sale into a computer terminal connected directly to the store's computer system and the system processes that sale immediately, the computer system processes that transaction using **on-line transaction processing (OLTP).** What this means is that you have entered data into a device that is directly connected, or on-line, to the computer system, and the computer system handled each transaction as it was entered (see Figure 4–9). Because the transactions are processed immediately, these systems may also be called on-line, *real-time,* transaction processing systems.

When transactions are accumulated into a batch for processing at a later time, the computer system is performing **batch processing.** You may or may not be on-line, or

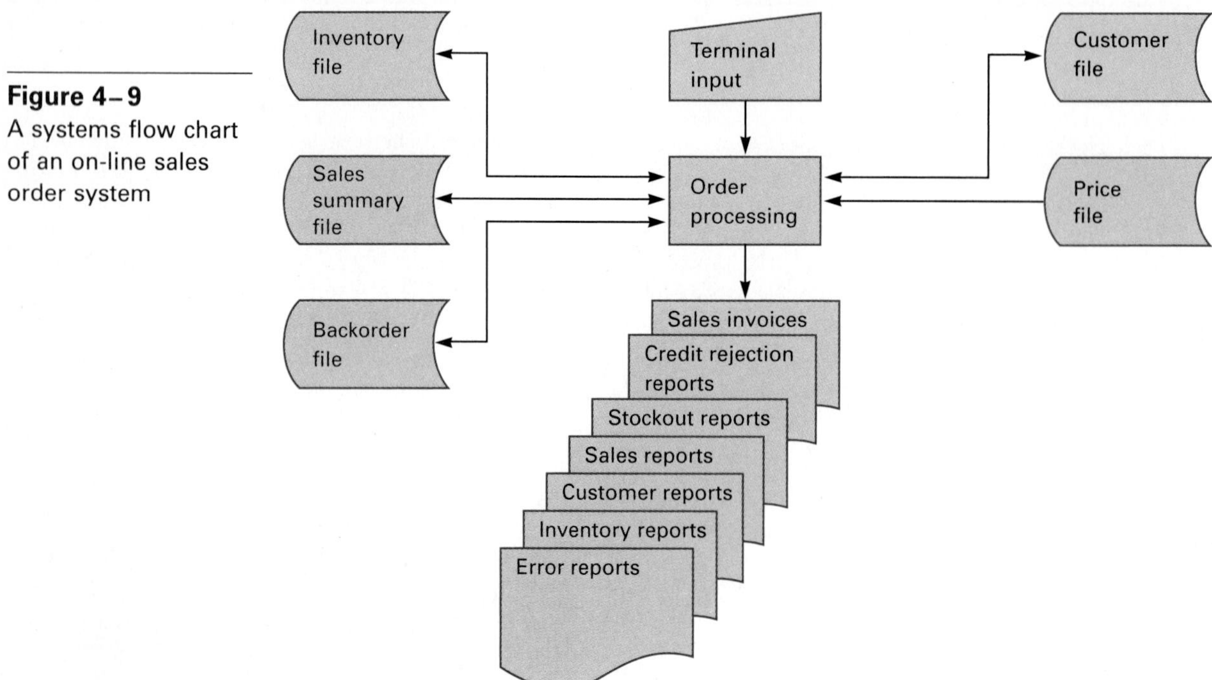

Figure 4–9
A systems flow chart of an on-line sales order system

directly connected to the computer system at the time you enter the data to be processed. The important feature is that the batch of data you enter will be processed later as a group. For example, you may enter many sales transactions during the day into some type of storage device. Later, the entire group of sales transactions is processed in a batch (see Figure 4–10).

On-line transaction processing, or OLTP, has many advantages. In the example described, transaction processing keeps the customer files and sales files current. It also allows you to provide information to the customer immediately if the sales transaction demands it—as would be the case when a customer tries to purchase an airline ticket. There are also many types of transactions that can be handled quite nicely through batch processing methods. For example, the daily hours worked by every employee are usually accumulated each day for processing in a batch at the end of the week. Constant processing of the hours worked for each employee are unnecessary because paychecks are completed only once each pay period. Constant processing would be an inefficient use of employee time and computer resources. Batch processing allows you to delay the processing of some tasks that do not require immediate processing to times when your computer system resources are more available. This is especially true if the delayed tasks require intensive processing and will make heavy demands on the computer system.

SECONDARY STORAGE MEDIA AND DEVICES

Bytes, or characters of data, are composed of bits. Records, such as customer accounts, are made up of bytes. Files, such as customer files, consist of records. Because the number of records within a file can become large, and because the number of files you

Figure 4–10
A systems flow chart of batch processing of sales invoices

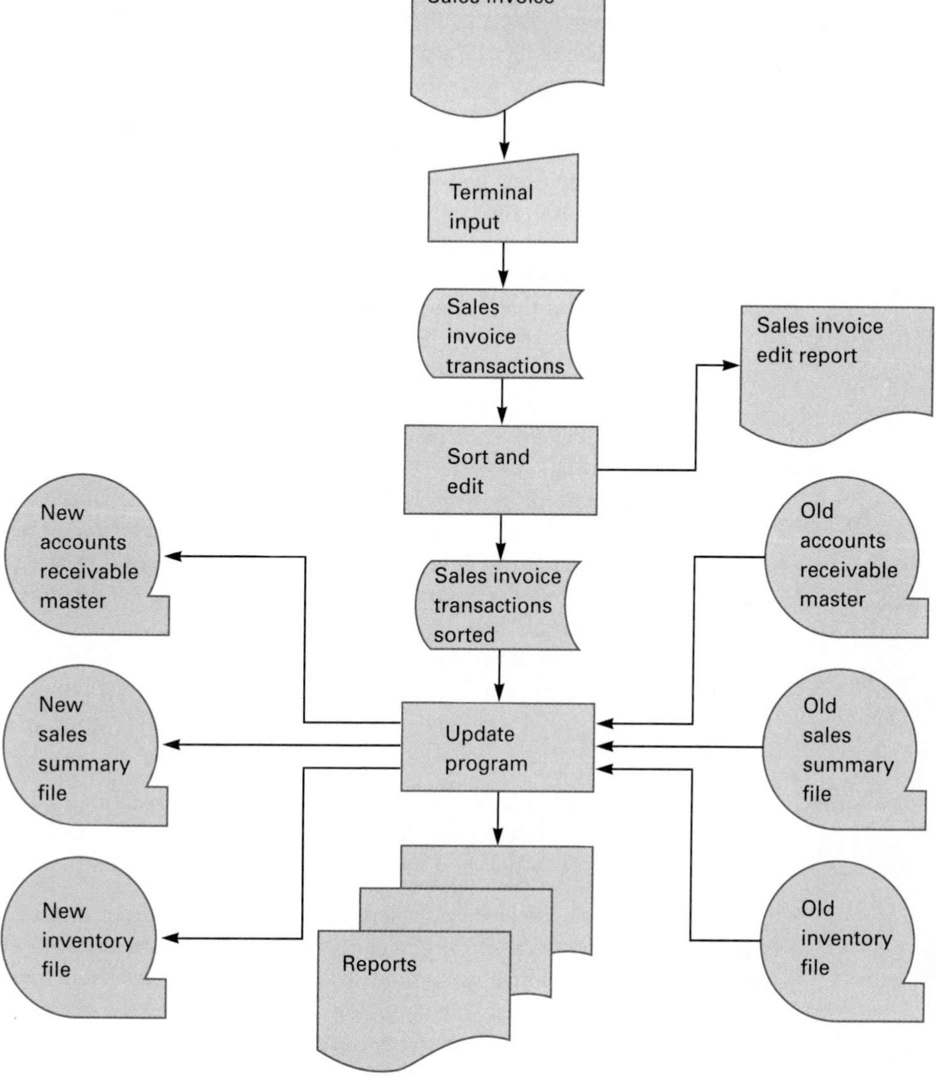

want to work with can also be large, the amount of main memory you have in your computer system may not be large enough to hold all the necessary data.

Secondary storage allows you to store many more bytes, or characters, of both data and programs than main memory does. Two of the most common devices used for secondary storage are **disk drives** and **tape drives.**

Disk drive storage devices are called *direct access storage devices (DASD)* because they permit data to be stored and retrieved directly; it is not necessary to scan all the other data on the medium sequentially. Like main memory, direct access storage devices achieve direct access by dividing the available storage space into discrete locations and giving each location a unique address.

Tape drive storage devices are called *sequential access storage devices (SASD)* because they permit data to be stored and retrieved only sequentially. Thus, if you wished to read record number 1,056 in a file of 3,000 records, the system would have to scan the file starting with record number 1 until it reached the record you wanted, number 1,056.

The ability to access a record directly rather than sequentially is very important. Suppose you needed to view a record of a customer's account rapidly because the customer was standing in front of you waiting. Direct access storage devices would permit you to retrieve and view the customer's record directly. If the storage devices you were using were sequential access devices, however, you would have to scan every record from the beginning of the file to the customer's record. If the customer file was a large one, you—and the customer—might have to wait minutes or hours before the record was found, instead of seconds. However, direct access storage systems typically cost more than sequential access storage systems.

To perform on-line transaction processing, you must be on-line to the computer system and have your data stored on direct access storage devices, or DASD. To perform batch processing, you may or may not need to be on-line to the computer system and may or may not have your data stored on sequential access storage devices, or SASD.

Both disk drives and tape drives use *magnetic storage media.* On magnetic media, bits of data are stored on the media surfaces in the form of magnetic spots. As you might expect, data on these surfaces are easily altered or destroyed through careless handling, heat, static electricity, dust, and a host of other causes. Because of this vulnerability, it is important for any manager to be sure that secondary storage media are handled carefully and that **backup,** or **archive, copies** of the data are created. It would not do to have all your accounts receivable data destroyed because the media on which they were stored were accidentally erased by a careless user.

Disk Storage

Disk drives are of two general types: floppy drives and hard drives. **Floppy drives** use flexible diskettes, or **floppy diskettes,** as storage media (see Figure 4–11). **Hard drives** use polished metal *platters* as storage media (see Figure 4–12).

Floppy Diskettes. Floppy diskettes are made of plastic and store data in magnetic form in concentric circles or tracks. The tracks are divided into pie-shaped sectors, which hold the amount of data that can be transferred from the disk to main memory or back again in one operation. These tracks and sectors are not visible to the eye—they represent magnetic storage patterns on the recording surface. Floppy diskettes come in several sizes. Microcomputers commonly use 5¼-inch and 3½-inch diameter diskettes, although the use of 5¼-inch floppies on microcomputers is waning rapidly. Minicomputers commonly use 5¼-inch or even 8-inch floppy diskettes. Some computer systems may use 2-inch diameter diskettes. Floppy diskettes are single-sided (usable on one side) or double-sided (usable on both sides). Finally, floppy diskettes may store data in single-, double-, or quad-density formats. Density refers to how compactly the data is stored on the diskette. All other things being equal, double-density diskettes will store twice as much data as single-density diskettes, and quad-density diskettes will store four times as much data as single-density diskettes.

The amount of data you are able to store on a floppy diskette for a minicomputer or a microcomputer varies. Some common storage capacities for IBM PCs are 360 KB, 720 KB, 1.2 MB, and 1.44 MB. Common storage capacities for Macintosh computer systems are 800 KB and 1.6 MB. Floppy diskettes vary in cost and are often available for under a dollar. The floppy disk drive (see Figure 4–11b) that allows the computer system to read data from and write data to the floppy diskette may cost less than $100.

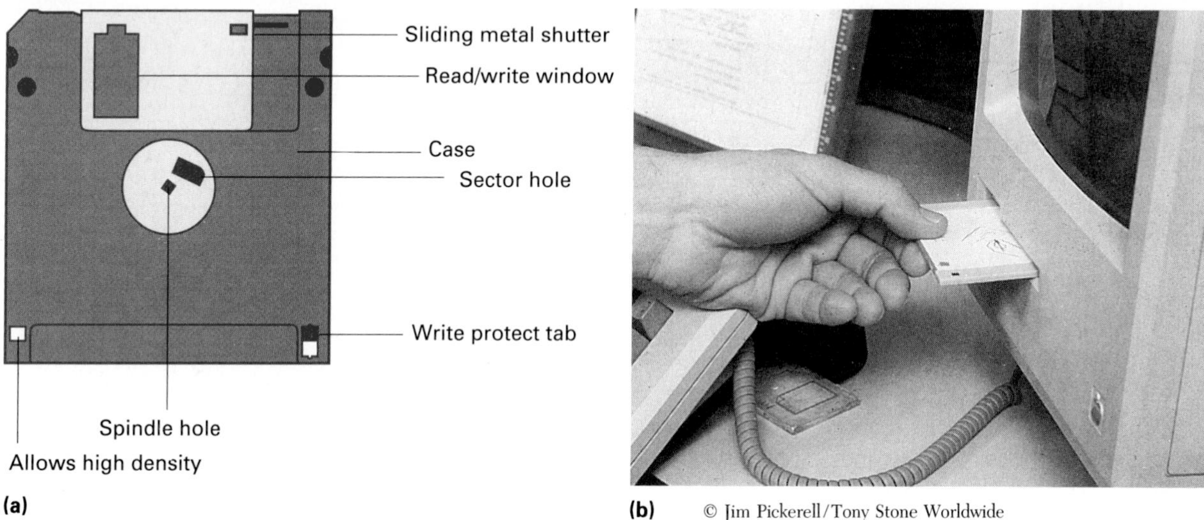

© Jim Pickerell/Tony Stone Worldwide

Figure 4–11
(a) A diskette showing component parts. **(b)** A diskette being inserted into a disk drive.

Hard Disks. Hard disk drives allow you to access data faster and usually hold much more data than floppy disk drives. But, as you might expect, they cost more. One mainframe disk drive unit stores about 1,260 MB of data, and the average time it takes to get data from this unit's hard disks to main memory is 25.3 milliseconds (a millisecond is a thousandth of a second). By comparison, the average time for data to get from a floppy diskette on a microcomputer to main memory is 350 milliseconds, whereas the speed with which the CPU can move data around within main memory is usually measured in nanoseconds (billionths of a second). Thousandths, millionths, and billionths of a second are incredibly small units of time—probably too small for us to imagine. You may think that you will not notice the differences in processing data at these speeds, but if you must process large files of data, you will become a believer.

Hard disk units may use one or more disks, or platters, for storage. Hard disk drives may use removable *disk packs* or disk cartridges that contain one or more platters mounted together in a stack. As with floppy diskettes, each platter has two sides, and the writing surfaces are divided into tracks and sectors (see Figure 4–12). There are also hard disk drives that are mounted on adapter boards, or hard cards, and systems that allow you to use removable hard drives.

Accessing Data. To access data from either a hard disk or a floppy diskette, the disk drive unit goes through three operations. The first operation is to move the read/write heads (see Figure 4–12) to the correct track on which the data are stored. The time this operation takes is called *seek time.* The next operation is to select which read/write head to use. This operation is called *head switching.* The next operation is to allow the data on the track to rotate under the read/write head selected. The time this operation takes is called *rotational delay.* Finally, the read/write head that was selected reads the data and transmits it to main memory. The time it takes for this transmission is called *transfer time.* As you might expect, seek time is by far the longest of these time periods. Because the read/write heads used to read a disk pack move in unison, arrangement of data provides an opportunity for the computer system to reduce seek time to a minimum. If the computer system stores data from one file on the same track on each side of each platter, moving the read/write head to that track allows the system to obtain all

Figure 4–12 (a and b)
Hard disk platters showing tracks, sectors, and cylinders in a disk pack

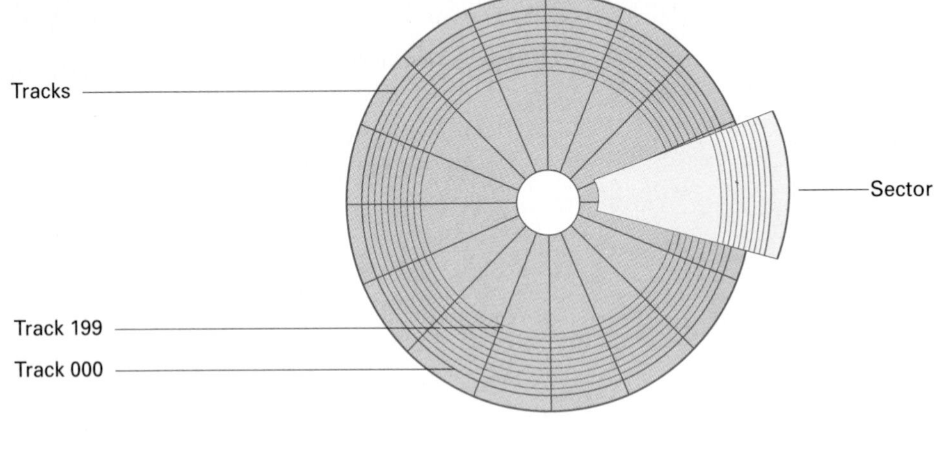

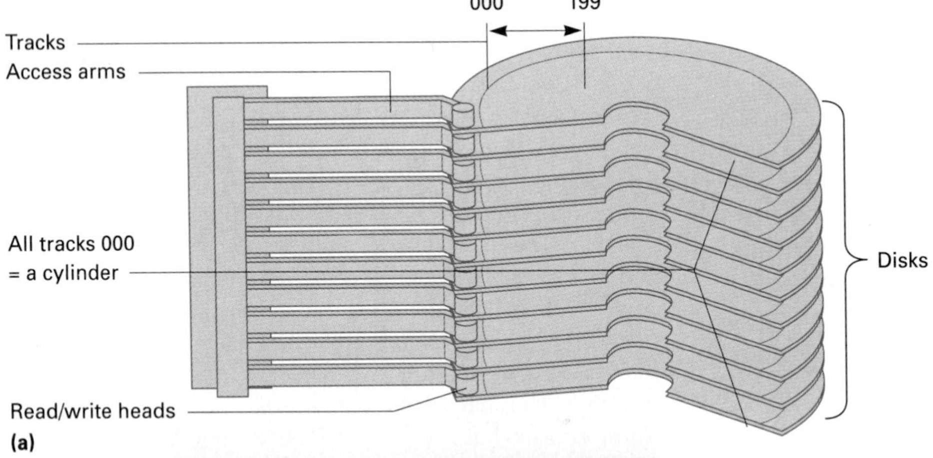

(a)

(b) Courtesy of Seagate Technology

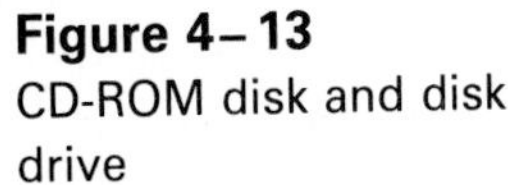

Figure 4–13
CD-ROM disk and disk drive

Courtesy of Toshiba America, Inc.

records in that file with a single movement of the read/write heads. The collection of tracks that can be accessed by a single movement of all the read/write heads is called a *cylinder*, and the method of storing data on the tracks of a cylinder is called the *cylinder method of storage*. On systems that use a single platter or a floppy diskette, the method used to reduce seek time is to store data from one file on contiguous tracks. Though this method reduces read/write head movement, it does not eliminate it.

Another method used to reduce access time is **cache memory.** Cache memory is a small part of a computer system's high-speed memory that is reserved for data that has been recently accessed. Cache memory is based on the idea that a system is likely to use the data it has just accessed more than once. Thus, the data are stored in cache memory when they are first accessed from secondary storage. When the CPU needs more data, it first checks in cache memory. If the CPU finds the data it needs there, it is called a *cache hit*. If it doesn't, it's called a *cache miss*. If the data are in cache, the data are accessed at nanosecond speed. If a cache miss occurs, the CPU has to get the data from secondary storage, which is much slower, usually operating at millisecond speed.

Winchester Drives. On some computers, hard disks are not removable and are called *fixed disks*. Because smaller computers with fixed disks might be placed on factory floors or in otherwise more rigorous environments, the hard disks they use may be sealed in a container with the read/write heads. This prevents dust, dirt, or water from damaging the data on the disks. Sealed hard disks like those just described are usually called *Winchester drives*. The storage capacity of the Winchester drives units available for use with one minicomputer system ranges from 40 MB to 800 MB of secondary storage. The hard disk units available for one microcomputer system range from 120 MB to 600 MB.

Optical Storage

Optical storage systems use **optical disks** that are read by beams of laser light rather than magnetic means. Three types of optical storage systems are commonly available.

CD-ROM Drives. One optical storage system is called **CD-ROM,** or compact disk–read only memory (see Figure 4–13). CD-ROM only lets you read from the optical disk, not write to it. A single, 3½-inch CD-ROM disk used on microcomputer systems typically holds 650 MB of data. Mainframe CD-ROM systems may use 8-inch or 12-inch disks.

CD-ROM storage systems are often used today to store reference materials, such as encyclopedias, directories, the complete annual issues of journals and magazines, census data, and statistical data. For example, Computer Select offers 12 CD-ROM disks to subscribers annually that contain articles and abstracts drawn from over 120 computer, technical, and business periodicals on each monthly disk. The disks also contain hardware and software product specifications, computer company profiles, and a glossary of computer terms. Microsoft Corporation offers Stat Pack, CD-ROM disks that provide government data on business, manufacturing, trade, demographics, economics, politics, and agriculture.

WORM Systems. Another type of optical storage system allows you to write to a disk, but only once, although the disk can be read many times. The latter optical systems are called *WORM,* for *write once, read many* times. The media used for these systems will hold gigabytes, or billions of bytes, of data.

Erasable Optical Disk Systems. *Erasable optical disk systems* permit data to be written to disk many times. Like WORM systems, the media for erasable optical disk systems hold gigabytes of data. For example, one erasable optical disk system holds 650 MB of data and has an average access time of 95 milliseconds. Another system also holds 650 MB of data but has an access time of 36 milliseconds.

Optical disk systems include *jukebox storage systems* that allow you to access multiple CD-ROM, WORM, and erasable optical disks. These systems select and switch optical disks from their stacks in a few seconds, providing you with access to many gigabytes of data. One high-end system available lets you switch between 141 optical disks putting 1.27 **terabytes (TB)** (a thousand gigabytes, or a trillion bytes) on-line for your use. Because of their vast storage capabilities and because optical disk drives can be placed on-line to computer systems, optical memory systems have become an important mass storage technology when large amounts of data must be stored but also kept on-line.

Tape Storage

A second major type of secondary storage media is **magnetic tape.** Magnetic tape is a strip of plastic kept on a reel or in a cassette. Minicomputers and microcomputers, for example, may use magnetic tape cassettes to store backup copies of data and programs on hard disk. Mainframe computers have used magnetic tape reels for secondary storage for many years. Today, however, tape reels are used primarily to back up data stored on hard disks.

Magnetic tape reels used in mainframe systems vary in length and in density, or the amount of data they can hold. Common densities found in existing computer systems are 1,650 and 6,250 bytes of data per inch of tape *(BPI).* A commonly used tape reel contains 2,400 feet of ½ -inch-wide tape that can hold between 100 MB and 200 MB of data. To read data from or record data to the tape, the reel is placed on a *magnetic tape drive* (see Figure 4–14).

This drive may read the tape at rates in excess of 100 inches per second. When this speed is combined with a high data density, it provides a fast transfer rate—in excess of 1 megabyte per second. Furthermore, a tape reel is very inexpensive, typically costing around $20 to $40. Thus, magnetic tape systems store a great deal of data, are relatively fast, and are relatively inexpensive. It should come as no surprise, therefore, that many large organizations choose magnetic tape for backing up or archiving the data they have on their hard disks.

Box 4–5 Comparison of Selected Storage Media

Type	Number of Complete Sets of the Encyclopaedia Brittanica Held	Approximate Cost per Megabyte of Data
CD-ROM	About 7 sets on one disk	$.15 to $1.00
Hard drive	About 1 set on a 100 MB drive	About $1 on average
Floppy drive	About 1/70 of a set held on a single floppy	About $1
Flash memory	About 1/5 of a set on a single card	About $85
Erasable optical drive	About 10 sets on one 1GB disk	About $3
Tape reel	About 2 sets on one reel	About $.22

Source for some of the data: Erica Schroeder. "Speed, Cost Propel CD-ROM into Offices," *PC Week*, February 22, 1993, p. 29.

The tape storage systems used in minicomputer and microcomputer systems often use tape cassettes and cartridges. The tape drive may be installed internally in the computer system or it may be external. Typical minicartridge systems store from 40 to 250 MB of data. Frequently, *QIC* systems, or quarter-inch cartridge systems, store up to 2 GB of data, and *DAT* systems, or digital audiotape cartridges, store up to 8 GB of

Figure 4–14
Mounting a tape reel on a tape drive

Courtesy of Hewlett-Packard Company

data. The tapes may also be stored in jukebox storage systems that hold many tapes. One company offers a jukebox system with 12 tapes that hold 8 GB of data each, providing 96 GB of overall storage. The average access time for this system is between 20 and 30 seconds.

Hierarchical Storage Systems

Hierarchical storage systems combine hard drives, optical drives, and tape drives into a multilayered system for storing large amounts of data. These systems automatically move unused or little-used data from speedy but expensive hard drives to slower but less expensive media based on rules you have formulated. For example, you may decide that you want the system to move data that has not been used for three months from a hard drive to an optical drive. If the data has still not been used after another three months, you may want the system to move it to magnetic tape. After instructing the hierarchical storage system in these rules, the system carries them out automatically.

Other Secondary Storage

Alternate secondary storage devices and media have multiplied during the 1990s. Three new technologies are described here: floptical drives, flash memory, and glass hard drives.

Floptical Drives. *Floptical drives* are drives that store data magnetically, but use optical technology for precision. The degree of precision allows much more data to be stored on a 3½-inch diskette—current models allow 20 MB of data to be stored on a 3½-inch diskette. The same drive reads the .720 and 1.44 densities of the conventional 3½-inch diskette. The drive gives the user a removable, rugged, high-capacity storage medium. Access speeds vary from 65 milliseconds to more than 100 milliseconds.

Flash Memory. *Flash memory* chips are memory chips that, unlike RAM, do not require power to retain their data. Manufacturers offer flash memory chips on cards that can substitute for a small hard drive. The advantage of the flash memory on a card is that it operates at or close to the speed of RAM while simulating a small hard disk. Remember, RAM runs at nanosecond speed, whereas most hard disks run at millisecond speed. However, flash memory cannot be written to at the same speed that it can be read from. Thus, you can store data or programs on the card as if it were a hard disk but read and write to the card at or close to RAM speeds.

Flash memory has not merely been used to substitute for disk storage, however. A number of vendors are using it to substitute for many different types of memory in computer systems, including ROM and even memory for printers. The primary use of flash memory so far has been to provide memory cards for small computer systems (see Box 4–6). For example, Intel Corporation offers a flash memory card that stores 20 MB of data, enough to run many popular programs, for two-pound palmtop computer systems.

Currently, memory stored on flash chips must be erased in blocks. If designers can create the ability to erase data byte by byte, many experts expect that these chips will provide an alternative to current RAM memory chips. In any case, flash memory chips are expected to lead to lighter, more powerful small computer systems.

Glass Drives. As you can see, a great variety of secondary storage memory technologies is available for computer systems. The invention of new types of memory devices never ceases. For example, at this writing, Hewlett-Packard has begun offering a one-ounce, 1.3-inch diameter, removable 21.4 MB hard disk called KittyHawk that uses glass as the storage medium. Hewlett-Packard expects the drive to hold 200 MB by 1995 and to challenge flash memory as a nonvolatile storage medium.

Box 4-6 PCMCIA Technology

As computers have shrunk in size, manufacturers have sought ways to add features to these miniature boxes of technology. Enter PCMCIA technology. PCMCIA is a peripheral standard for small computer systems that was developed by the Personal Computer Memory Card International Association. The standard was developed for credit-card sized add-in boards for very small computer systems.

Currently, PCMCIA slots are being added to palm top computers, personal digital assistants, and notebooks computers to allow users of these Lilliputian devices to add memory cards, faxboards, modems, hard disks, and other peripherals. The cards developed for the slots are thin, lightweight, use little power, and are rugged.

There three types of PCMCIA cards, which are often called PC Cards. All three are 2.1 inches wide by 3.4 inches long, although some cards are longer and stick out of the socket.

Type I Cards: 3.3 mm thick
Type II Cards: 5.0 mm thick
Type III Cards: 10.5 mm thick

The thickest cards (Type III) are thick enough to accommodate small hard disks.

(a) PCMCIA memory card

(b) PCMCIA fax/modem

INPUT AND OUTPUT DEVICES

Each computer system must have a means of **input,** or putting data into the system, and **output,** or getting data out of the system. Input and output devices include keyboards, display screens, printers, disk drives, tape drives, and other devices that are located next to or outside of the CPU. For this reason, these devices are often called **peripherals.**

Input Devices

One of the most common input devices is a **computer terminal.** The typical terminal has a *keyboard* so that data can be typed into the computer and a screen to display what is being typed.

Terminals can be classified according to their intelligence. Some terminals are given little logic or storage capability and are called **dumb terminals.** Dumb terminals rely on the intelligence of the computer to which they are attached to function. They are capable of transmitting data to the computer, but they are not capable of storing and processing the data. *Intelligent,* or **smart terminals,** on the other hand, have a "brain," or CPU, of their own. They can use their own CPU to process data, or they can rely on the intelligence of another computer to which they are attached. Often, intelligent terminals are used to edit data before the data are sent to the main CPU, thus increasing the accuracy of the data transmitted. Microcomputers are increasingly being connected to computer networks and used as intelligent terminals.

Key-to-disk and *key-to-tape* systems usually consist of a terminal of some type with a keyboard that allows the operator to enter data onto a hard disk, floppy diskette, or tape. The data from the disk, diskette, or tape is transferred to the computer system later for processing. These devices are used in batch processing operations. They allow data entry operators to accumulate a great deal of data on magnetic media for processing in a batch mode at some later time. Some key-to-disk devices are really small computers themselves and permit editing of the entered data before it is stored on disk.

The quality of data processing depends on the quality of the data used in the processing. The quality of the data depends, in part, on the accuracy with which it is *keyed in* to the computer system by the computer terminal operator. The terminal, with its keyboard and screen, represent a point at which errors can be introduced into an information system. Thus, careful selection of the computer terminals used for input is important to the quality of the manager's data. A badly designed keyboard, a screen highly susceptible to glare, or a fuzzy, difficult-to-read screen can lead to operator error. Conversely, special colors used to highlight directions and data on a terminal screen reduce operator error.

Entering data using a keyboard also costs money. Operators must be trained and paid to do their work. Furthermore, operators make errors entering data using a keyboard. A number of input devices are available that are specifically designed to reduce the keystrokes used to input data into a computer system. These include *point-of-sale terminals,* which capture transactions at their point of origin or source. For example, a point-of-sale terminal in a store would capture the data about a sale of stock when the customer buys the stock. These data would not have to be reentered into the system again by another employee, thus avoiding rekeying of data and potential rekeying errors.

There are many other ways to reduce or avoid keystrokes. For example, fast food stores often use point-of-sale terminals with special keys to represent each item of food purchased. Another means is through the use of *bar-code readers,* which you have probably seen at the checkout counters of supermarkets. These bar-code readers read special bar codes printed on grocery items when they are manufactured. The special bar codes used follow the *Universal Product Code* adopted by the grocery industry (see Figure 4–15d). Bar-code readers are also used in stock or inventory applications outside the grocery industry. Special bar codes are placed on inventory items or on the shelves that contain the items in warehouses or stores. Then bar-code readers are used to read the bar codes to track inventory levels. These bar-code readers may be located in a hand-held wand or recessed in the sales counter. In automated factories bar codes are placed on items as they move through the production line. Computers use bar-code readers to determine the status of items as they are being produced. By reducing keyed input, monitoring stock is faster and more accurate.

Other input devices that reduce keystrokes are *optical character readers (OCR),* that read optical characters (see Figure 4–15a); *mark-sense readers,* which read optical marks (see Figure 4–15c); and *magnetic-ink character recognition,* or *MICR* readers, which read special characters written in magnetic ink (see Figure 4–15b). OCR, mark-sense, and MICR input devices provide the manager with the means to input data into a computer system with a minimum of keystrokes. Fewer keystrokes mean less cost and less chance for incorrect input. OCR equipment is often used in offices to convert hard

(a) VISA, the band design and the dove design are registered trademarks of VISA International and are reproduced here with permission.

(b) Courtesy of the Data Capture Institute, Inc.

DATA CAPTURE INSTITUTE, INC.
30 TREMONT STREET
P.O. BOX 1625
DUXBURY, MA 02331

ROCKLAND TRUST COMPANY
53-447/113 10

3237

PAY TO THE ORDER OF ____ $____

____ DOLLARS

MEMO____

⑈003237⑈ ⑆011304478⑆ 3⑉797⑉295⑈

Like

Very Much | Somewhat

(c)

(d) Courtesy of the International Business Machines Corporation

Figure 4–15
Four types of data that can be read by optical scanning equipment

copies of documents to magnetic media so they can be edited on word processors. It is also commonly used to convert hard-copy records into records computer systems can use and to convert the records from one computer system to another. In the latter case, the records from one computer system are printed out, scanned by the OCR equipment, and then converted into the format of the new computer system. OCR and mark-sense devices are frequently used in meter-reading for power companies and in scoring examinations, and banks have used MICR devices to process checks for many years. Bar-code devices, optical character and mark devices, and magnetic-ink character devices are examples of optical scanning equipment.

(a1) Courtesy of the International Business Machines Corporation

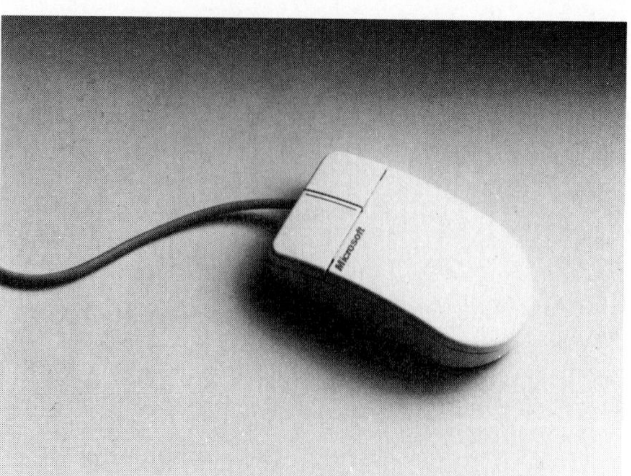

(a2) Courtesy of Microsoft Corporation

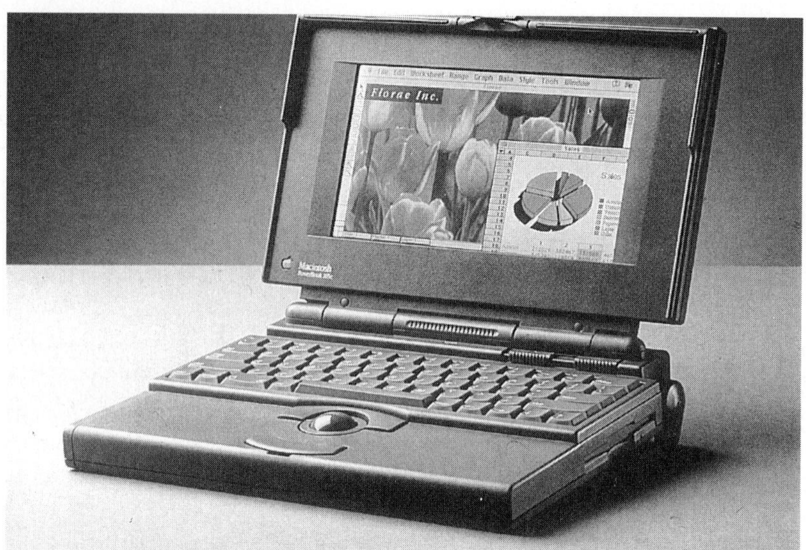

(b) Courtesy of Apple Computer, Inc.

Figure 4–16 (a1, a2, and b) **(a1 and a2)** A mouse on a desktop computer and **(b)** a trackball on a notebook computer

Devices that read bar codes, MICR, text, and images are called **scanners.** Many general purpose scanners are available that, when accompanied by the appropriate programs, allow you to scan text and images and store them on disk where they can be read, edited, and otherwise manipulated. Scanners are available in several sizes from hand scanners that scan about four inches of a page to full-page scanners. Scanners are described in more detail in Chapter 8, "Office Automation."

Other devices provide input for special situations. For example, a **mouse** (see Figure 4–16a), a hand-held device connected to the computer terminal with a wire, allows you to make entries without using the keyboard. The movement of a roller at the base of the mouse sends signals to the terminal that are converted into computer

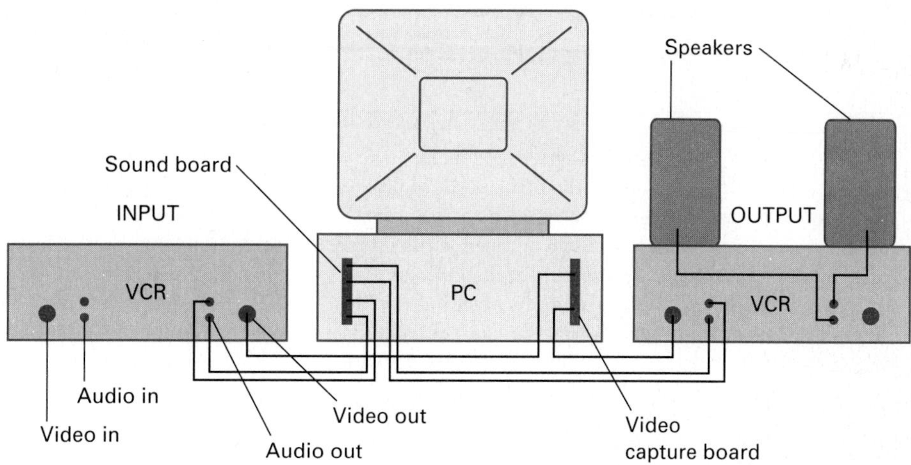

Figure 4–17
Desktop video technology

commands. A variant of the mouse, the **trackball** (see Figure 4–16b) is often used for notebook computers.

Still another input medium that is gaining acceptance is voice input. **Voice recognition technology** consists of a sound board and software that are used to convert the analog waves of sound into digital data that can be stored on disk. In addition to the board, there is usually a microphone to allow input. Voice recognition technology can be especially helpful when it is inconvenient or impossible for the worker to use hands for input. For example, a forklift operator or a factory worker can input data about the quantity of the products they have delivered or worked on without stopping work.

Card and badge readers, which read magnetic data contained on a card or badge, are frequently used to record automatically the in and out times of employees for payroll purposes.

A reemerging input technology that has been applied to very small computer systems is the *light pen.* The light-sensitive pen, or stylus, is connected to a screen or tablet by wire and is used to draw, write, mark, or make selections from a menu. *Touch-screens* are another way to input data. The operator touches menu items or other objects displayed on the screen to enter data or make choices.

Recently, systems that permit you to capture video images from live TV or a VCR tape have become popular. These systems capture video as individual frames, convert them to a format that can be stored on a hard disk or optical disk, and then use graphics software to manipulate the images or sequences of images. **Desktop video technology** allows you to grab frames from a training tape and insert them in an accompanying training document (see Figure 4–17). It also allows you to insert full-motion video, for example, a sequence that shows how to install an adapter board in a slot on a microcomputer motherboard, into a multimedia presentation (see Box 4–7).

Digital cameras have also grown in demand and use. Digital cameras look much like an ordinary camera but they capture the images they take in a format that can be stored on disk. The images can then be manipulated with graphics software. The technology allows you to insert the pictures you take into data files, documents, or presentations. For example, pictures of employees can be inserted into employee files, pictures of products can be inserted into advertising brochures, and pictures of a factory can be inserted into a graphics presentation.

Box 4–7 Multimedia Hardware

Probably one of the most exciting recent technological developments is digital **multimedia** technology. Multimedia technology typically allows you to link data, text, sound, images, live or taped video, and live or taped audio into a presentation or sequence of screens that might be used to introduce a product, show how a product can be used, or show how it can be fixed. Multimedia is a presentation system that may employ one or more of these technologies:[1]

- Waveform audio (digitized audio) that may be used for music, voice, or sound effects.
- MIDI (musical instrument digital interface) music and sound effects generated by synthesizers.
- Drawings and other graphics.
- Digitized photographs.
- Animation.
- Full-motion video with synchronized sound.

To create or show multimedia presentations, your computer system commonly needs several hardware components, including these:

- Lots of RAM (4 MB or more).
- Fast CPU (50 MHZ or more).
- High-resolution color display screen.
- Fast video display board.
- Large hard drive (80 MB or more).
- Mouse or trackball.
- Speakers.
- Headphones.
- Sound board.
- CD-ROM drive.
- Color scanner.
- Video capture/display board for VCR and TV images.

IBM and other computer manufacturers have begun offering computer systems with many of these hardware components "bundled," or sold together, as *multimedia PCs.*

[1] DeVoney, Chris. "Multimedia Authoring Tools: Sound, Video, Interaction!" *Windows Sources,* June 1993, p. 374.

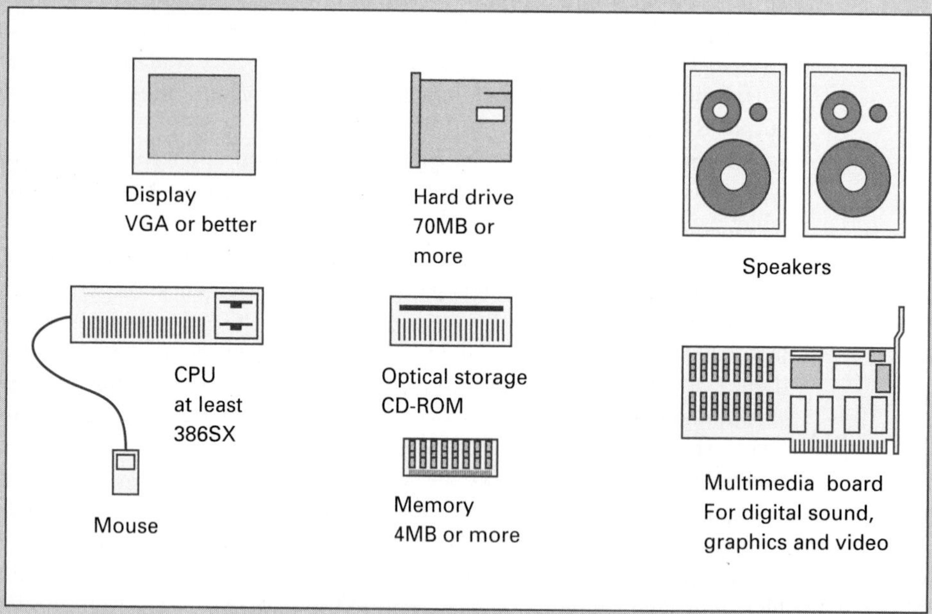

Adapted with permission from *PC World,* March 1990, p. 195.

Output Devices

You have learned that the most common input device is a computer terminal. However, the computer terminal is also the most common output device. The screen of a computer terminal displays data; thus, it is an output device. In fact, many input devices may also serve as output devices.

Display Screens. A computer terminal screen, also called a *CRT* (for cathode ray tube), *VDT* (for *video display terminal*), *monitor,* **display screen** or just plain *screen,* usually looks like a TV screen. Display screens vary in several ways. The displays may be in color or monochrome. Monochrome screens usually are black and white, amber, or green. They also vary in resolution and size. Screen resolution refers to the number of pixels (picture elements) per inch. Size refers to how many columns wide and how many lines long the screen is.

In recent years, color terminals have become standard on desktop microcomputers and for mainframe and minicomputer systems. The screens on color terminals vary in the number of hues they can display. Some screens can represent many colors and many different shades of each color. Color screen resolution is often measured in dot pitch, or the distance between dots of the same color. The lower the dot pitch, the sharper the image.

Special-purpose screens are also available. For example, you can buy a full-page screen (80 columns by 66 lines), a wide screen (120 or 132 columns wide), and even a two-page screen (which presents the pages side by side). Screens are also commonly available for desktop computers in 14-, 15-, and 17-inch sizes.

Liquid crystal display (LCD) screens are often used on notebook and laptop computers because they are flat and lightweight. However, the principal problem with notebook and laptop computers has been the poor quality of the screen images. The LCD technology requires that the screen image be exposed to a lot of light to achieve satisfactory resolution. Recent advances in LCD screen displays have improved the quality of these screens considerably.

Some laptops, portable computers, and mainframe terminals use *glass plasma screens.* This screen provides an orange and black display. Some computer terminals are also *printing terminals.* These terminals are keyboards built into printers, and usually do not have screens. The keyboards can be used for data input, and output from the computer systems is printed on paper.

Still another output device is the ordinary television screen. Using desktop video technology and sound technology, the digital output of a computer system can be converted into the sound and visual signals that are the standard in the television industry. The result is that you can display output with sound using an ordinary TV. This allows you to use a large TV, for example, as a display device for a presentation.

Printers. Many types of printers are available for computer systems. These printers can usually be grouped into two major categories: *impact printers* and *nonimpact printers.* Impact printers bring the paper or other medium into contact with the print element. Nonimpact printers place the print on the medium in other ways.

Two common types of impact printers are line printers and dot-matrix printers. *Line printers* print whole lines of text or numbers at one time. They may be used when large numbers of documents must be printed rapidly, such as invoices, paychecks, or statements of account. Because of the quality of print, line printers are not ordinarily used for text documents, such as reports or letters. Speeds of line printers range from 100 to 4,000 lines per minute. For example, IBM makes a line printer that prints 625 lines per minute and can print documents requiring up to 132 characters on a line.

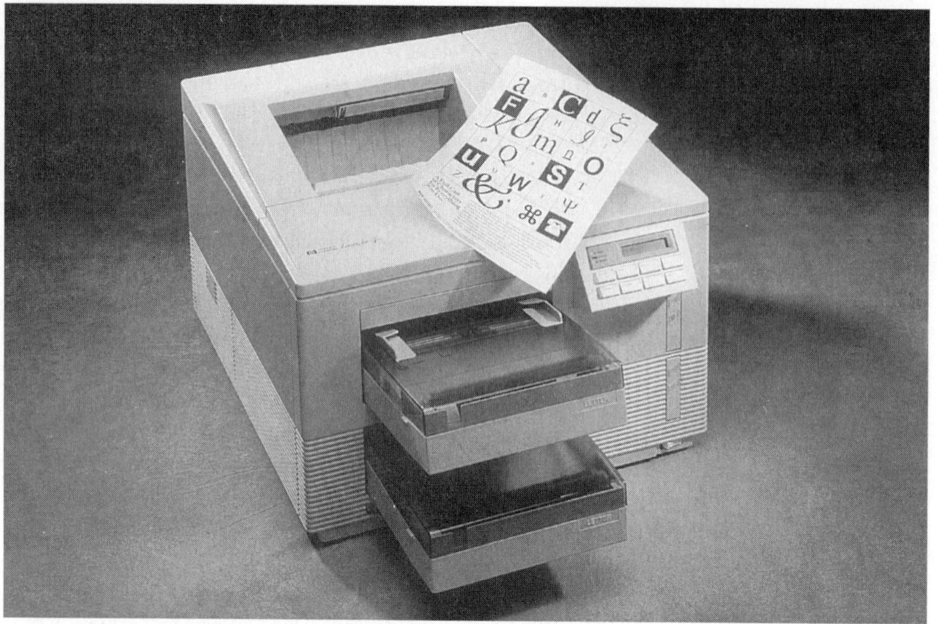

Figure 4–18
A laser printer with printer output
Courtesy of Hewlett-Packard Company

Because nonimpact printers are faster, quieter, and offer better print quality, line printers are not as popular today as they have been in the past.

Another type of impact printer is the **dot matrix printer.** Dot matrix printers form characters by using rods to produce dots on a page. The quality of the end product depends on the number of rods used to form each character. Inexpensive dot matrix printers may use nine pins to form characters in a five-dot by seven-dot or seven-dot by nine-dot rectangle. More expensive dot matrix printers use 24 pins to create very tightly formed characters.

Dot matrix printers are often used to produce rough drafts of documents and documents that will not be sent outside an organization, such as memos. Typical speeds of inexpensive dot matrix printers are 120 to 200 characters per second. Some dot matrix printers will provide what is called *near-letter-quality* output by having the print head make more than one pass on each line of print or for each character. Each time the print head makes a pass, it moves a small increment to the right or left of the first pass. By making several such passes, the dots fill in the spaces of each letter and give the appearance of a letter-quality character.

The advantage of dot matrix printers that offer near letter quality is that they can print rough drafts and in-house documents fast, letter-quality documents at a slower pace, and graphic images. Thus, you are able to obtain all three types of output with a single printer. Dot matrix printers also are relatively inexpensive.

Two common types of nonimpact printers are laser printers and ink-jet printers. **Laser printers** print a whole page at once and are also called *page printers.* Laser printers are often used when drawings, photographs, and graphic images must be reproduced with high quality or in color, or when a large number of pages must be printed and quality and speed are important. Laser printers offer a large number of type styles and allow you to merge multiple print styles, graphics, and other images on a single page (see Figure 4–18).

Laser printers are usually fast. A typical speed for an inexpensive laser printer is eight pages per minute. High-output laser printers produce 600 pages per minute.

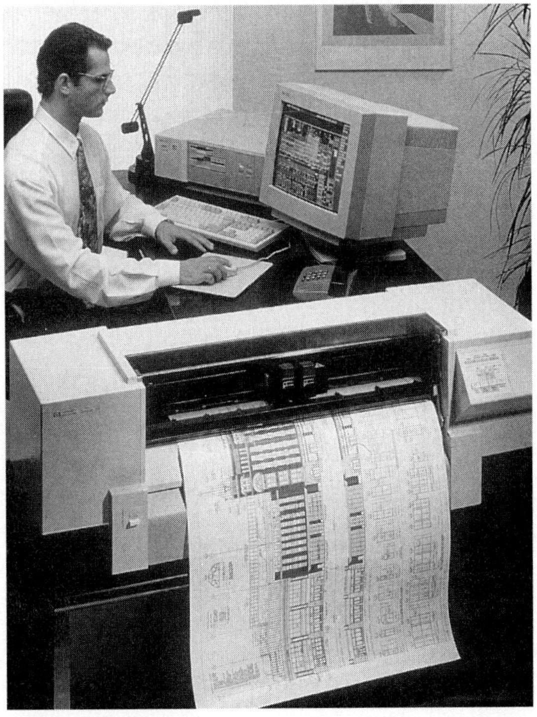

Figure 4–19
A plotter
Courtesy of Hewlett-Packard Company

Laser printers also are not as noisy as the impact printers described below. For example, Xerox Corporation makes a page printer that produces up to 135 pages per minute, can print documents up to 11 inches wide, and is very quiet, as printers go.

Another type of nonimpact printer is the **ink-jet printer.** These printers form characters by spraying ink on the paper. As a result, special types of ink-jet printers can be used to print on surfaces that are not entirely flat, such as packages. Of course, neither ink-jet printers nor laser printers can be used where carbon copies are needed since they are not impact printers; that is, they do not have a print element that strikes the paper. Speeds of ink-jet printers range from slower models that print 90 to 200 characters per second to faster models that print pages per minute.

Other Output Devices. For special purposes, manufacturers have produced special output devices. For example, *plotters* print maps, charts, and graphs (see Figure 4–19).

Another special-purpose output device is a voice synthesizer. Its output is in voice form and is used in a variety of situations such as subway stop warning systems, telephone marketing systems, and voice mail systems. Voice output usually consists of computer-controlled playback of stored speech segments, such as numbers and words.

There are also devices that transfer computer output to microfilm. These devices, called *computer output microfilm,* or *COM,* are used to archive large amounts of records in a form that can be stored relatively inexpensively in reduced size. (Both voice mail and COM will be discussed in more detail in Chapter 8.)

As you can see, there are many specialized input and output devices for computer systems—too many to describe in one chapter. However, for your information, Table 4–1 provides a partial list of these devices.

The capacity of the storage media and the speed with which a computer system can access data from these media and other input devices are important considerations

Table 4–1
Some examples of input and output devices

Input Devices	
Badge reader	Magnetic-ink character reader
Bar-code reader	Microphone
Cartridge drive	Mouse
Cassette drive	Optical character reader
CD-ROM drive	Optical mark reader
Digital camera	Punch card reader
Digitizing tablet	Scanner
Disk drive	Tape drive
Erasable optical drive	Touch screen
Floptical drive	Trackball
Full-page scanner	Video display terminal
Joy stick	Voice recognition device
Keyboard	WORM drive
Light pen	
Output Devices	
Cartridge drive	Line printer
Cassette drive	Magnetic-ink character coder
CD-ROM drive	Plotter
Computer output microfilm	Robot
Daisy-wheel printer	Speech synthesizer
Disk drive	Tape drive
Dot matrix printer	Television screen
Erasable optical drive	Thermal printer
Ink-jet printer	Video display terminal
Laser printer	WORM drive

when you choose a computer system. Storage media and input devices that cannot keep up with the computer system will cause your system to be *input bound.* This may mean that your CPU is idle because it has to wait for data to be transmitted from a slow storage device. In the same way, the speed of output devices is important to the overall performance of a computer system. Output devices that cannot keep up with the CPU will cause the system to become *output bound* unless there is a place for the CPU to place the data that it has already processed. For output devices, that place is usually called a *buffer,* or small amount of memory. The buffer storage may be part of main memory allocated for that task, it may be located in a device positioned between the output device and the CPU, or it may be located in the output device itself. Many printers have buffer storage, for example. A computer system that is input/output bound, or *I/O bound,* is inefficient and wastes valuable resources.

As a manager, you must be certain your equipment has sufficient main memory to handle both your programs and data. You also should be sure that the secondary storage devices you use provide sufficient memory to store the programs and data the computer is not using at the moment. Finally, you should select input and output equipment that fits the jobs your computer system performs.

HARDWARE STANDARDS

The computer hardware you acquire as a manager must fit in with the acquisition scheme of the entire organization. Casual, random, or opportunistic purchasing of equipment can easily lead to many different models, display screen types, bus structures, boards, printers, and other peripherals. Having an array of different hardware types may lead to many problems, including lack of compatibility, expandability, and reliability. To avoid these problems, many organizations attempt to set standards for the computer hardware they acquire.

Compatibility

If an organization does not set standards for computer hardware, each department or each employee may decide to acquire different, incompatible hardware. An expansion board that works in a computer with an EISA bus structure, for example, won't work in a computer system with an MCA bus structure. The output of a Macintosh computer system cannot be used as input to an IBM PS/2 computer system without either additional hardware or software to convert the data from one type to another. Connecting one type of terminal to a mainframe that requires another type of terminal requires additional hardware and software. A computer program developed for one type of hardware may not run on other computer systems, so an organization may need to develop or purchase programs for each type of computer system acquired. The cost of making one system work with another may be higher than the benefit derived from doing so.

Standards for computer hardware affect costs in other ways. For example, maintaining computer system hardware requires expertise with the hardware. If an organization has many different hardware types, it will need people who have expertise with many systems. That may translate into the need for more people, more training, or both. Maintenance may require an inventory of spare parts, but keeping spare parts for many different hardware types may require storing a large number of parts. Purchasing one type of hardware in large quantities offers opportunities for quantity discounts or a lower negotiated price.

Expandability

As an organization's computer needs grow, it may outgrow the capacity of its present computer systems. However, some computer systems can be upgraded to allow increased capacity. Computer systems are also continually changing—the computer industry announces new models, with new features, daily. The ability of a computer system to grow, add capacity, or add new features means that the computer system's life can be extended, and the organization's costs for developing a new system, including system acquisition, start-up costs, and training costs, can be forestalled or reduced. It is important to consider the expandability of hardware when setting standards for an organization to allow future growth and improvement in hardware with minimal cost and disruption to the organization.

Reliability

Purchasing hardware on the cutting edge of technology is appealing to many buyers. The allure of getting the latest technological developments with all the "bells and whistles" shown in the advertising brochures is often great. However, managers should recognize that hardware that is on the cutting edge of technology often has problems that are not described in the advertising brochures. After new products are announced, the trade and computer magazines usually are filled with articles about the various problems users have identified with the hardware that its designers overlooked. Buying computer hardware that has not been tested in the marketplace through use is similar to buying the first car of a new model produced. You can usually expect problems to occur in the early cars produced because testing rarely can duplicate fully the driving conditions of real drivers on real roads.

Standards for the acquisition of hardware should take into account the reliability of the hardware through actual use in the real world. Although organizations may acquire one or two hardware devices for their own testing, it is usually unwise to purchase large amounts of hardware fresh off the designer's drawing boards.

Organizations should develop standards for hardware acquisition to insure that the hardware acquired is compatible, expandable, and reliable. Managers of departments should use those standards to help them in the acquisition process.

OTHER ACQUISITION ISSUES

In addition to hardware standards, managers must face a number of other issues when acquiring hardware.

Timing the Acquisition

Since computer systems became popular in the 1960s, their power has continually increased and the costs of acquiring them have continually decreased. These two trends have not abated. A manager can usually depend on the new models of computer hardware to be more powerful than the old models and the relative costs of those models to be lower. Thus, buyers have a tendency to defer purchasing new or additional computer systems. When buyers finally acquire hardware, they are often upset when later, new models provide more power for lower cost.

However, you must realize that future hardware will continue to provide increased power at lower cost. Your acquisition decision should be based on careful estimates of the costs of the system to you and the benefits it will offer you. If you find that the benefits of acquiring a system will outweigh its costs, then it matters little how much better and less expensive the new models are. If you choose to defer acquisition because newer models are likely to be improved or less expensive, you will wait forever—computer systems will always be less expensive and better in the future. In the meantime, you will lose the difference between the costs and benefits that the current system could offer you.

Renting, Leasing, and Buying

The costs of many minicomputers, supermicrocomputers, and microcomputers have dropped to the point that many organizations do not consider whether they will lease or buy these systems—they simply buy them (see Box 4–8). Mainframe computer systems, superminicomputers, some minicomputers, and even microcomputers, however, still represent substantial investments, even for large organizations. You should determine the costs both of buying and of leasing the computer systems. If you will need the equipment for less than 12 months, you should also price renting it. If the applications you must use computers to perform have been very stable over the years, you might even consider buying used equipment.

The advantages and disadvantages of purchasing or leasing computer equipment are basically the same as those for acquiring any durable good. Rental arrangements usually cost the most on a monthly basis but offer the least risk of obsolescence. Leasing costs, on a monthly basis, are usually less than rental costs but more than outright purchase costs. Purchasing provides the buyer with ownership and a residual value but

Box 4–8 Renting, Leasing, or Buying

Advantages	Disadvantages
Renting	
Short-term commitment	More expensive than leasing
Least risk of obsolescence	Equipment may be used
Requires no capital investment up front	Some equipment vendors do not rent
Leasing	
Lower risk of obsolescence	May be more expensive than purchase
No immediate capital investment	No residual value to owner
May provide purchase option	
Payments may include service	
Less expensive than renting	
Buying	
Residual value to owner	Requires capital investment or borrowing of funds
Usually less expensive than leasing over the long term	Locks buyer into decision
	Owner must obtain or provide maintenance services

tends to lock in the equipment decision because changing equipment will involve trading it in or selling it.

Deciding on the Acquisition

Responsibility for acquiring computer systems may reside in several places in an organization. The decision may be centralized in a data processing or management information systems department. Alternatively, the decision may be centralized in a computer committee in the organization. In such cases, system purchases must be approved first by this department or committee. On the other hand, the decision may be decentralized to the department level. In that case, approval from the department is necessary before acquisition can be completed. In some organizations, individuals may be able to make the decision without regard to other groups within the organization.

In any case, the decision to acquire computer systems for an individual or department usually begins with the manager. That decision may then be forwarded for approval to a department committee, the MIS department, or a computer committee that represents the entire organization. In many large firms, the MIS department provides special services for departments or individuals who wish to acquire computer equipment. The special services are usually provided through an office devoted to the users of computing equipment, such as managers, supervisors, clerical personnel, and other noncomputing specialists. The office helps these buyers plan their acquisitions; select, acquire, and install the systems; and train users.

The issues surrounding how computing resources are organized are discussed in greater detail in later chapters.

Choosing a Hardware Vendor

The selection of a vendor for your hardware may not be an option open to you as a manager. Your organization may already have a relationship with one or more hardware vendors that supply your firm with computing equipment. The special relationship may provide your firm with volume discounts, faster service, special training, installation, or other services.

If you are able to select the vendor to supply the hardware you have selected, the vendor you choose depends to some extent on your knowledge of the systems you are acquiring and the help you will need to purchase, install, and use them. You can buy hardware from many types of vendors, including hardware manufacturers, computer sales and service dealers, and mail-order firms.

Many businesses buy their hardware directly from the manufacturer. Some manufacturers provide a great deal of support for the buyer, including selection advice, installation, and user training. Others provide little or no support and merely ship you boxes of hardware with written installation directions. To help you make your decision, you may ask manufacturers' sales representatives to provide on-site demonstrations of their products or visit a dealer to inspect and use the hardware.

Some vendors provide *hot-line* technical support to customers, sometimes through an 800 phone service that allows them to talk directly to a technician if they have problems installing or using the systems. Other vendors provide help by answering inquiries through the regular mail or through electronic mail systems. Still others provide no technical support at all to the buyer. Clearly, *before* you buy the systems you should find out what level and types of help the vendor will provide *after* you buy the systems.

If you are very knowledgeable about the hardware you want to buy, you may choose to buy from mail-order companies. Ordinarily, their prices are lower than other sources. However, you may find that the hardware or software you have bought is not what you wanted. Some mail-order companies allow you to return your purchases, some allow returns with penalties, and still others allow you to return your purchases with a full refund, under certain conditions. Of course, you should find out the purchase terms before you commit yourself.

Buying from mail-order firms has become popular today because many of them have made the purchase of computer systems much easier than in the past. Mail-order firms now typically preinstall much of the hardware and any programs that come with the computer systems you are buying. When the boxes are shipped, you will probably find all the software that was bundled with the hardware, the expansion cards, and the memory boards already installed. You still have to connect the major parts, such as the CPU, the screen, and the keyboard. However, once that is done, you may be able to turn the computer on and be ready to start using the programs. When you are buying hundreds of machines, this preinstallation of the various hardware components and software saves you an enormous amount of time.

It is important, especially for large purchases, that you find out some details about every vendor you are considering. For example, how many technical support persons do they employ? Where are their nearest service centers? How completely are these service centers stocked with spare parts? How long have the vendors been in business? What other persons or organizations are customers of the vendors? How sound financially are they? Where are their nearest training centers? How often are classes run? What level of training is offered? How comprehensive are their course offerings?

Ordinarily, if you are not knowledgeable about what you need to buy, you should select vendors that provide you with considerable support. For the inexperienced person, obtaining competent, reliable vendors who are helpful both before and after the purchase makes the acquisition and implementation of computer systems much easier. You must realize, however, that providing such support costs money. Support costs may be charged directly to you as line items on an invoice, or they may be reflected in

Box 4–9 The Costs of Information Systems

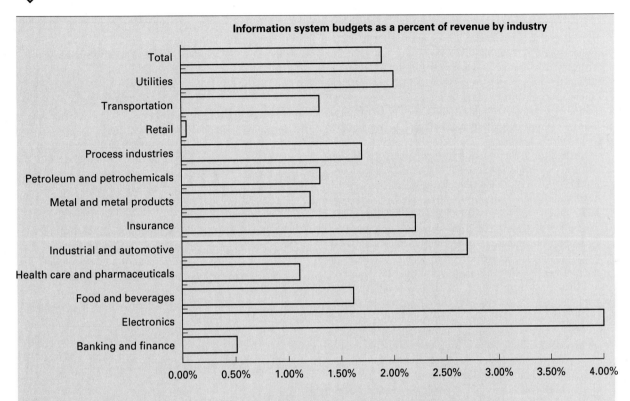

Information system budgets as a percent of revenue by industry

Total
Utilities
Transportation
Retail
Process industries
Petroleum and petrochemicals
Metal and metal products
Insurance
Industrial and automotive
Health care and pharmaceuticals
Food and beverages
Electronics
Banking and finance

0.00% 0.50% 1.00% 1.50% 2.00% 2.50% 3.00% 3.50% 4.00%

How information systems funds are distributed

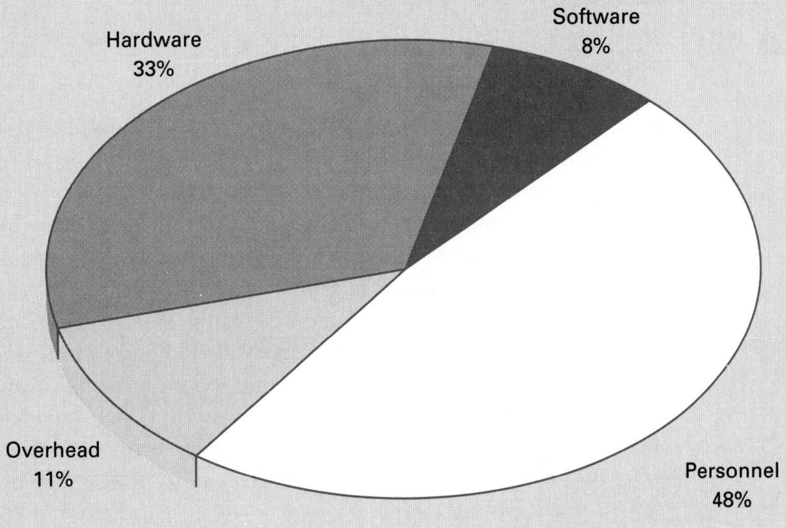

Source: Adapted from "Industry-by-Industry IS Spending," *Datamation*, Suppl. November 21, 1988.

Box 4–10 The Green Machines

"At present, computers are a leading cause of increased demand for electrical power, accounting for an estimated 5 percent of commercial demand . . ."[1] The Environmental Protection Agency estimates that 74 percent of office equipment power usage is gobbled up by PCs. However, a number of microcomputer vendors recently have begun to offer systems that are much less taxing on the environment and on your energy budget. The systems are often advertised as "green" or "Energy Star" computer systems because they conform to the EPA's Energy Star guidelines for low energy consumption. Energy Star systems are much more energy efficient than the standard microcomputer systems on the market today. For example, IBM's "green machine" uses only three-fourths of the power required by conventional systems. Conventional PCs may use from 60 to 150 watts when running. To meet the EPA's Energy Star requirements, however, a PC must use less than 30 watts when it is "idling"—when it is running but not otherwise being used.[2] The EPA estimates that the use of green machines might cut energy costs by $1 billion and CO_2 emissions by the amount of CO_2 produced by 2.5 million cars, and might save $120 per system per year.[3]

A common way for the green systems to reduce power usage is to power down the CPU and the screen automatically during periods of nonusage. While the green machines save energy for our globe and reduce a company's energy bill, they also lengthen the uptime for battery-driven laptops and other nondesktop computer systems. The longer the uptime for such systems, the more acceptable they become to users. Everybody seems to win.

DOING YOUR PART

Brian Nadel offers some other ways that PC users can reduce their load on the environment:[4]

1. Turn off your PC when you will not be using it for some time. Don't leave it running continuously.
2. Set your screen saver to blank instead of using some snappy, high-color, dynamic screen display.
3. View your documents electronically instead of printing them out on hardcopy paper.
4. Use electronic mail instead of interoffice mail.
5. Recycle your printer and copier toner cartridges.
6. Recycle your laptop, notebook, or other computer batteries.
7. Recycle your hardcopies.

[1]Nadel, Brian. "The Green Machine," *PC Magazine*, May 25, 1993, 12, no. 10, p. 112.
[2]Ibid., p. 112.
[3]Quinlan, Tom. "Intel 486 Line Gains SL Power-Saving Features," *InfoWorld*, June 21, 1993, 15, no. 25, p. 27.
[4]Ibid., p. 112.

comparatively higher prices for the systems than those offered by vendors providing little or no support.

Installation, Maintenance, and Training

Acquiring computer systems is only one step in deploying them in your organization. Once delivered, computer systems must be installed and maintained over time. Installation may require substantial modification of your facility. You may need to add additional air conditioning, special wiring, cabling, electrical systems, and/or special security systems. Furthermore, employees are likely to need training in the use of the computer systems. The ease with which computer systems can be installed, the costs and difficulties of maintaining them, and the ease with which they can be used are important management concerns; the original acquisition costs are only one part of the total costs (see Boxes 4–9 and 4–10).

Management Summary

Computers are often classified as supercomputers, mainframe computers, superminicomputers, minicomputers, supermicrocomputers, and microcomputers. These classifications have become fuzzy because the power of computers in one classification may exceed the power of computers in another. However, they are still useful.

All computer systems have a CPU, which consists of a control unit and arithmetic/logic unit. Computer systems also have two types of memory: main, or internal memory, and secondary storage, or external memory. Main memory is composed of RAM, or random-access memory. RAM is volatile, and data stored in RAM can be accessed directly. Computer systems also store programs in ROM, or read-only memory. Common forms of secondary storage include disk drive and tape drive systems.

Computer systems operate under the direction of a program, and they must have parts or all of both the program and the data to be processed in main memory to operate. Computers store programs and data in bytes of code. Each byte is formed by a number of bits, which varies with the code used. The number of bits a computer can transfer between main memory and the control unit and arithmetic/logic unit at one time is called a *word.* The number of instructions a CPU can process in a second is measured in millions of instructions per second (MIPS). Word size, megahertz, and MIPS are measures of computer power. Memory in secondary storage consists of bytes stored on hard disks, diskettes, tapes, or other devices. Input and output devices attached to the computer allow data to enter or exit from the system. Common input and output devices are computer terminals with keyboards, display screens, disk drives, and printers. Many other input and output devices are available for special purposes. The CPU, main memory, and input and output devices are called *computer hardware.*

The acquisition of computer systems generates many organizational issues and provides many concerns for the manager. These issues and concerns include when computer systems should be acquired; whether they should be rented, leased, or purchased; who should decide what systems will be acquired; how the systems should be installed and maintained; and what training for employees should be required.

Managers must also be concerned with developing or following hardware standards to insure hardware compatibility, expansion, upgradability, and reliability. However, computer hardware is only part of a computer system. To make the hardware run—to make it do what you want it to do—the hardware must be told precisely when and how to act. This is the job of computer programs, or software, and computer software is the subject of the next chapter.

Key Terms for Managers

archive copy, **104**
backup copy, **104**
batch processing, **101**
cache memory, **107**
central processing unit (CPU), **91,**
compact disk–read-only memory, (CD-ROM), **107**
computer program, **94**
computer terminal, **111**
desktop, **91**
desktop video technology, **115**
digital cameras, **115**
disk controller board, **94**
disk drives, **104**
display screen, **115**
dot matrix printer, **118**
dumb terminal, **111**
expansion slots, **95**
floppy diskettes, **104**
floppy drives, **95, 104**
gigabytes (GB), **97**
hard drives, **95, 104**
hardware, **90**
ink-jet printer, **119**
input, **111**
kilobytes (KB), **97**
laptop, **91**
laser printer, **118**
magnetic tape, **108**
main memory, **94**
mainframe computer systems, **90**
math co-processor socket, **95**
megabytes (MB), **97**
microcomputer systems, **91**
microprocessor, **94**
minicomputer system, **90**
motherboard, **95**
mouse, **114**

multimedia, **116**
notebook, **91**
on-line transaction processing (OLTP), **101**
optical disks, **107**
output, **111**
output device, **91**
palmtop, **91**
pen-based computer, **92**
peripherals, **111**
personal digital assistant (PDA), **92**
power supply, **95**
random access memory (RAM), **94**
read-only memory (ROM), **95**
scanners, **114**
secondary storage, **96**
single in-line memory modules (SIMM), **95**
smart terminal, **111**
supercomputers, **90**
supermicrocomputer systems, **91**
superminicomputer systems, **90**
tape drives, **103**
terabytes (TB), **108**
trackball, **115**
video board, **95**
voice recognition technology, **115**
workstation, **91**

Review Questions

1. Describe the main parts of a CPU. Explain what each part does.
2. Explain the differences between RAM and ROM.
3. What is a bit? What is a byte? What do 2 MB, 2 GB, and 2 TB mean?
4. Explain what 640 KB of RAM means. How many characters of data can be stored in this much RAM?
5. Explain why word size is important to the processing speed of a computer.
6. Explain why megahertz is important to the processing speed of a computer.
7. Describe two major classifications of printers. Provide one example of each type of printer for each printer classification.
8. What are MIPS and how do MIPS affect the performance of computer systems?
9. What is the difference between on-line transaction processing and batch processing?
10. What is the difference between primary storage and secondary storage? Which is usually faster to access?
11. What is a hard disk? How does a hard disk differ from a floppy diskette in terms of storage capacity? In terms of access speed?
12. Describe the four operations that are necessary to transfer data from a direct access storage device to main memory.
13. Explain what a disk pack is and what a cylinder on a disk pack is. How does the cylinder method of storing data speed up access time?
14. Explain how magnetic tape systems are frequently used in mainframe computer systems.
15. What is flash memory? How does it differ from RAM?
16. Identify major concerns managers should have when they consider acquiring computer systems.
17. What is a RISC system?

18. What is cache memory? How does it increase the speed of data access?

QUESTIONS FOR DISCUSSION

1. What features should managers look for in computer terminals that are used for data entry by data entry clerks? Explain how each of these features will aid management.
2. The business world often uses the terms *supercomputer, mainframe computer, superminicomputer, minicomputer, supermicrocomputer,* and *microcomputer.* What do these computer systems have in common? How might these computer systems differ?
3. Describe options for data input managers might consider that do not require the keyboard entry of data. What advantages do these options have over keyboard entry?
4. Why are hardware standards important to a manager?
5. Describe why it is important to make backup copies of data files stored on magnetic media.
6. How might you describe the power of a central processing unit? What additional characteristics of a complete computer system should be examined when comparing the power of one system to another?
7. What does it mean when a computer system is I/O bound? How might a computer system become I/O bound?
8. What is a multimedia PC? What hardware features are common to multimedia PCs?
9. What is PCMCIA? How might PCMCIA technology be useful to managers?
10. What is a hierarchical storage system? What advantages does it provide?

PROBLEMS

1. **The Jolincraft Corporation.** Jolincraft is a small company that produces cedar furniture for outdoor patios. The company has been in business only one year, but the sales of its products have been growing rapidly because the furniture is relatively inexpensive, strong, and free of maintenance.

   The company is considering the acquisition of a computer system or systems to improve the efficiency of its accounting system. It realizes that it will need to purchase one or more printers for the computer system to produce printed customer invoices, customer statements, periodic financial statements for the firm, purchase orders, paychecks and employee W-2 forms, and other accounting forms and reports.

   a. What factors should the company consider when selecting its printer(s)?
   b. What types of printers might the company consider to accomplish its work?
   c. What type of printer(s) do you recommend for it and why?

2. **Secondary Storage Systems.** Prepare a paper analyzing one of the following secondary storage systems:

   a. Optical disk systems.
   b. Winchester disk systems.
   c. Flash memory cards.

Include in your paper data pertaining to system components, costs, storage capacities, and access times. Use computer magazines as your source of information and use the *Computer Literature Index,* published by Applied Computer Research, Inc., Phoenix, Arizona, as your source of magazine articles.

3. **CISC versus RISC.** Complete a paper that compares one CISC to one RISC system in terms of power (MHz, MIPS, word size, cost, and compatibility). Use articles you find referenced in *Computer Literature Index,* the CD-ROM database Computer Select, or both as your source(s) of information.

4. **System Specifications.** Visit a computer store and examine one of the latest models of microcomputer systems that the store offers. Ask the salesperson to demonstrate the system for you and obtain a list of the system specifications. (The specifications are usually included in one of the brochures describing the system.) Then use computer magazines to obtain at least two reviews of the model you saw demonstrated. Use the *Computer Literature Index* or the *Guide to Business Periodicals* to help you find articles that review the computer system. Prepare a report of your visit and the reviews.

Cases

1. **Toronto Office Supply Company.** Gerald Clark is president of Toronto Office Supply Company in Toronto, Canada. The company began with one store two years ago and has quickly added six branch stores in the Toronto metropolitan area. However, it has not computerized its operations. As a result, costs for record keeping have been escalating. Clark responds to criticism about the lack of computerization by remarking that he has been too involved with the growth of the company to pay attention to this part of the operations. However, costs, mainly the personnel costs needed to maintain records and sluggish office operations, have compelled Clark to face this issue. As a result, he hired Maple Associates, a computer consulting firm, to advise him on the computerization of all seven of his retail outlets.

   After visiting the company and talking with Clark and a variety of managers, sales personnel, and office clerks, a consultant from Maple Associates recommended that Clark purchase and install a number of computer systems, all based on Intel's 80486 chip. She also made recommendations about purchasing computer programs and providing installation, training, and maintenance.

   When Clark discussed the Maple recommendations with his senior staff, however, there was some dissent. Charles Robertson, the company's financial officer, felt that the cost of the computers themselves was too high. He recommended that the company wait a few months for the price of these computer systems to settle down. He pointed out that computer prices have been falling a great deal lately. He didn't see any reason why the company could not wait a few months more to get much better prices for the equipment.

   Sarah Blake, the company's marketing officer, was concerned that the company was purchasing computer systems that were already obsolete. She pointed out that the computer systems Maple Associates recommended were based on the Intel 486 chip, and that Intel had already brought out their next chip, the Pentium.

   a. What is your analysis of Robertson's objection?
   b. What is your analysis of Blake's objection?

2. **Deluxe Deliveries.** Donna Carlino started a packaging and delivery service about three years ago in a small town outside of a major metropolitan area. Her service

offers wrapping, boxing, insurance, delivery, and other services associated with mailing or delivering packages for small businesses and individuals. She operates the store herself for much of the day, relying on part-time help during seasonal peaks and weekends. She believes now is the time for her to automate some of her operations, specifically, accounting and delivery. Output of the system would be primarily accounting reports, delivery schedules, and customer invoices.

Marcus Sykwuz, who runs the only computer store in town, suggested that she purchase a computer system that runs at 90 MHz and provides almost 200 MIPS. The system comes with a very high resolution screen, 16 MB of RAM, and a 500 MB hard drive. He suggested also that she purchase a laser printer for her documents, including the invoices. If you were asked to advise Carlino, would you agree with Sykwuz's recommendations? If not, what would you suggest that Carlino consider in the way of a computer system and peripherals?

3. **Roscoe Manufacturing Company.** The staff of Roscoe Manufacturing Company has been using IBM computer systems that use the MCA bus for several years to write letters, memos, reports, and other documents and to prepare budgets and other financial reports. Because the company has grown and its staff increased, the company wants to buy additional computer systems. Dale Vincent, who is in the accounting area, would like to purchase these computer systems as cheaply as possible. He feels that the company ought to examine a number of IBM PC compatibles that use the EISA bus. He claims that these machines can be purchased for quite a bit less than IBM machines if they are bought through large computer retailers. Rose Delaney, who is in marketing, wants the company to consider buying Macintosh computer systems because she feels that Macintosh computers offer superior graphic, or visual capabilities, permitting her to produce better marketing materials. Shiela Ruggins, who is in engineering, wants the company to consider purchasing a Digital Equipment Corporation VAX minicomputer system so that many people in the engineering department can be attached to the same system. She feels that this would increase communications and reduce paper handling. Chuck Demond, who is in production, wants the company to consider buying the new Breeze computer system offered by WhirlWind Computer Systems. WhirlWind Computer Systems will offer their Breeze computer system commercially in just two months, and Chuck feels that they should wait for the new system to avoid buying existing equipment that will quickly become obsolete. Felix Mannix, who is in personnel, feels that each department should be allowed to buy whatever computer systems it wants. In that way, he feels, each department will acquire the system that best fits its needs.

   You have been placed in charge of acquiring the additional computer resources. What concerns should you have about computing resources at Roscoe, if the recommendations of (a) Mannix or (b) Demond are taken?

4. **Findley Automotive Parts Company.** Findley Automotive Parts Company is a wholesale automotive parts distributor that sells auto parts in a large metropolitan area. The company has one warehouse for its parts, located in the same building as its office, and employs 14 salespeople who spend most of their time in the field calling on retail stores and auto parts shops in a metropolitan area that contains many cities and towns. When salespeople call on customers, the salespeople complete sales order forms for the merchandise the customer wants to buy. The salespeople drop off those sales orders at the office at the end of each day. At the office, four order entry clerks use key-to-tape machines to key in the sales order data dropped off by the salespeople the previous day. On some large orders from

important customers and on rush orders, the salespeople will call the orders in to the order entry clerks directly. The tapes produced by the order entry clerks are mounted on tape drives and read into the computer system on the day following their entry. At the same time, the original orders are sent to the shipping department to be filled.

This system, however, is not working well at Findley. For example, salespeople complain that they have to spend too much time traveling to the office to deliver sales orders. Generally, salespeople end their sales day early to drop off the orders, or they drop them off in the morning of the second day. They feel that their time could be better spent selling. The order entry clerks complain that they often have trouble reading the sales orders completed by salespeople. Conversely, salespeople complain that there are too many errors in filled orders. That is, there are too many orders filled with the wrong amount or type of merchandise. Also, salespeople report that customers are complaining that it takes too long for their orders to be delivered, and they find that too often the goods they ordered are out of stock.

a. What are the features of the current system that might lead to customer complaints of slow deliveries and stockouts?

b. What are the features of the current system that might lead salespeople to complain about order errors?

c. What changes in procedures and what hardware changes might improve the order entry process at Findley? Specifically, what could be done to reduce errors in sales order entry, increase the efficiency of salespeople, and speed up the time needed to deliver orders?

Selected References and Readings

Applied Computer Research. *Computer Literature Index.* A monthly index of computer publications, including those covering mainframe, minicomputer, and microcomputer systems.

Barr, Christopher. "Pen PCs." *PC Magazine,* 11, no. 19 (November 10, 1992), pp. 175–78 ff. Describes the technology of eight pen-based systems.

Coastal Associates Publishing Company. *Computer Shopper.* A monthly magazine containing advertisements for all kinds of computer hardware and programs. It's an excellent source for finding hardware and programs for microcomputers.

Crabb, Don. "The New PCs." *PC Magazine,* 12, no. 11 (June 15, 1993), pp. 110–13 ff. An analysis of the high-end computer systems that were either just out or soon to be out in the summer of 1993.

Datamation. "Industry-by-Industry IS Spending Survey." *Supplement to November 15th Datamation,* November 21, 1988. A report of the spending for information systems by different industries.

Datapro Corporation. *Datapro Reports.* A series of reports pertaining to topics in computer systems, including mainframe, minicomputer, and microcomputer systems.

DeVoney, Chris. "VL-Bus Systems Redefine High Performance." *Windows Sources* 1, no. 2 (March 1993), pp. 311–16 ff. Details the architecture of the VESA bus standard and evaluates several VL-bus computer systems.

DeVoney, Chris. "Multimedia Authoring Tools: Sound, Video, Interaction!" *Windows Sources,* 1, no. 5 (June 1993), pp. 360–61 ff.

Goldsborough, Reid. "PCMCIA Cards: Magic Comes in Small Sizes." *PC Today* 7, no. 9 (September 1993), pp. 64–66. Presents advantages and disadvantages of the cards and also discusses problems in card standards.

Grevstad, Eric. "Downsize without Compromise: Buying a Notebook PC." *Computer Shopper* 13, no. 3, issue 156 (March 1993), pp. 340–46 ff. A description of the features of current notebook PCs, including PCMCIA cards.

Lauriston, Robert. "CD-ROM Shopping?" *Compuserve Magazine* 12, no. 3 (March 1993), pp. 19–22. Describes the features and uses of CD-ROM drives and provides information on bulletin boards for CD-ROM hardware, software, and utilities. Includes a CD-ROM bibliography reference.

Microcomputer Magazines: *VAX Professional* and *Digital Review*, magazines emphasizing Digital Equipment Corporation computers; *Macworld*, a magazine emphasizing Macintosh computer systems; *PC Week*, *PC World*, and *PC Magazine*, magazines that report on IBM and IBM clones; *Byte* and *InfoWorld*, magazines that report on microcomputer systems in general.

Nadel, Brian. "The Green Machine." *PC Magazine* 12, no. 10 (May 25, 1993), pp. 110–12 ff. A review of the features, advantages, and disadvantages of low-power microcomputers.

O'Brien, James. "Debut of Smallest-Ever Hard Drive: HP Says 1.3-Inch Kittyhawk to Hold 200 MB." *Computer Shopper* 12, no. 8, (August 1992), p. 139. Describes the glass media hard disk developed by Hewlett-Packard.

Pallay, Karyn. "Rightsizing: Time Waits for No Technology." *Netware*, May/June 1993, pp. 10 ff. A description of how organizations are choosing the computer platforms for their business needs.

PC Magazine 11, no. 20 (November 20, 1992). The magazine's annual review of printers. In the 1992 issue, the magazine reviewed 100 printers.

Peed Corporation, *PC Today*. Monthly magazine offering information about microcomputer systems and peripherals and a list of low-priced microcomputer hardware and software.

Raymond, John. "Palmtops Put PC Power in Your Pocket" and "Powering Up a Palmtop with Peripherals." *PC Today* 7, no. 6 (June 1993), pp. 30–35. Discuss the details of palmtops and the flashcards and other peripheral devices for them.

Schatz, Willie. "Who's Winning the Supercomputer Race?" *Datamation* 35, no. 14 (July 15, 1989), pp. 18–21. An analysis of the changing environment for supercomputers, including a report on the major manufacturers of supercomputers.

Wallace, Peggy. "Setting Corporate Computing Standards." *InfoWorld* 15, no. 11 (March 15, 1993), pp. 60–61. A description of how several organizations developed corporate standards for computing systems.

Computer Software

Chapter Outline

MANAGER'S VIEW

SYSTEMS SOFTWARE

- Operating Systems
- Communications Software
- Database Management Systems Software
- Other Systems Software
- Microcomputer Operating Systems
- Operating Environments

APPLICATION SOFTWARE

- Word Processing Software
- Spreadsheet Software
- File Management Software
- Personal Information Management Software
- Database Management Software
- Graphics Software
- Presentation Graphics Software
- Multimedia Systems
- Statistical Software
- Project Management Software
- Desktop Publishing Software
- Desktop Organizer Software
- Expert Systems Software
- Security Software
- Compatible and Integrated Software
- Office Automation Software
- Groupware
- Add-on Software
- Industry-Specific Software
- Functionally Specific Software

DEVELOPMENT SOFTWARE

- Programming Languages
- CASE Tools
- Object-Oriented Programming

GENERAL SOFTWARE TRENDS

- Graphical-User Interface
- Windowing
- Data Linking
- Conversion
- Multiplatform Capability
- Ease of Use
- Ease of Installation
- Hardware Demands

SELECTING MICROCOMPUTER SOFTWARE

- Step 1: Identifying Your Application Needs
- Step 2: Seeking the Right Software
- Step 3: Choosing the Software that Best Fits Your Business Needs
- Step 4: Selecting the Hardware
- Step 5: Choosing a Software Vendor

GENERAL FEATURES OF SOFTWARE

- Ease of Use
- Copy Protection
- Version
- Compatibility with Other Software
- Compatibility with Peripherals
- Portability
- Network Capabilities
- Cost
- Memory Requirements
- Site Licensing

MANAGEMENT SUMMARY

KEY TERMS FOR MANAGERS

REVIEW QUESTIONS

QUESTIONS FOR DISCUSSION

PROBLEMS

CASES

SELECTED REFERENCES AND READINGS

Manager's View

So far, you have learned about computer system hardware, or the electronic and electromechanical devices that are part of a computer system. The features, or the "bells and whistles" of computer hardware are very exciting. In fact, the advances that have taken place in computer hardware in the last decade may even be called breathtaking. However, the key issue for the manager is to get the computer system, with all its bells and whistles, working on problems that must be solved. Knowing that some computer terminals offer high-resolution screens or have lots of memory is not the same as knowing how to retrieve the right data from a computer system when you need to make a decision. In other words, the computer system is most useful when it can be applied to what you need done. It is the applications of the computer system that should interest the manager most.

For all their bells and whistles, computer systems are not able to operate without detailed instructions, or programs, called computer **software.** It is the software that makes computer hardware apply itself to your problems and makes the system useful to you. Thus, it is very important for you to have a clear notion of what software is really all about, what software is available to you, and how you can use this software in your work.

You should also know that the United States is a world leader in software development and software products. The creation of software useful to business, science, governments, and homes is one of the tasks done very well in the United States.

Computer system software may be classified into three broad categories: systems software, application software, and development software. Systems software manages the computer system hardware. Application software processes your data in the way you want it processed. Both types of software are essential to a computer system. Development software is used to create software of all types.

This chapter provides the basics about systems, application, and development software. Chapters in Parts 2 and 3 of the book are devoted wholly or partly to specific types of application software and their use in management decision making.

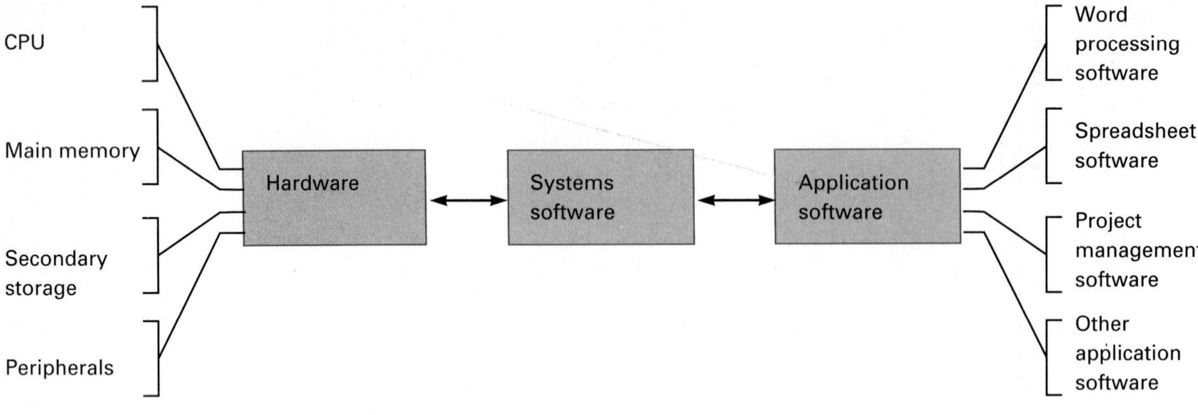

Figure 5–1 The systems software interface

SYSTEMS SOFTWARE

A computer system represents a number of resources that must be managed. These resources include the hardware components of the system: the central processing unit, memory, and peripherals such as secondary storage devices and printers. In many organizations, these resources cost a great deal of money, and their use should be carefully managed. To manage a computer system's hardware components, to coordinate them so that they work together efficiently, and to schedule to make the best use of the computer's time, it is necessary to add a set of instructions that monitors and manages the system. This set of instructions is commonly referred to as **systems software.** By managing a computer system's hardware and available time, systems software acts as the linkage, or *interface,* between the computer system and the application programs the user wants to run (see Figure 5–1).

People who write or maintain systems software are called *systems programmers.* Organizations with large computer systems usually include systems programmers on their staffs to tailor the systems software they use to the special needs of their organizations. Systems programmers are also responsible for optimizing the performance of the organization's computer systems.

Systems software includes many different types of programs, such as operating systems software, communications software, database management software, systems utility software, and language translators (see Figure 5–2).

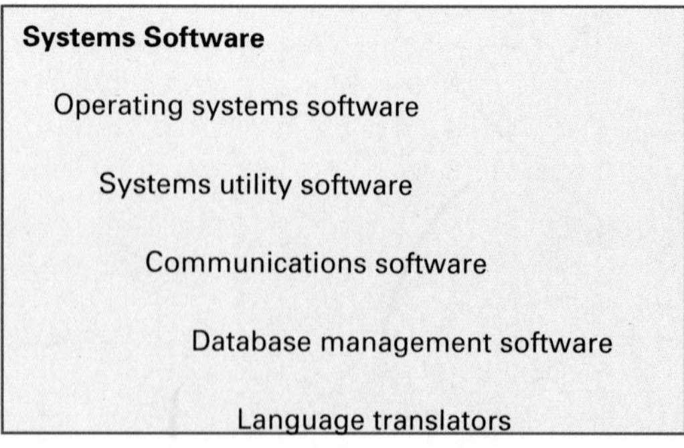

Figure 5–2 Components of systems software

Operating Systems

An **operating system** is a set of programs that manages and controls computer resources, including the CPU, peripherals, main memory, and secondary storage. On large computers, operating systems are often made up of many programs. On small computers, operating systems may consist of only a few programs. In either case, part or all of the operating system must be loaded into main memory for the computer system to function completely.

Operating system programs coordinate hardware through such activities as scheduling jobs to be run, queuing jobs, allocating memory to various job tasks, and communicating to the computer operator the status of the jobs and the computer system. Before operating system programs were developed, these activities had to be accomplished manually by computer operators. Computer operators scheduled jobs to run on the computer, loaded the programs and the data for each job, prepared printers or other devices to receive the output, and otherwise managed the tasks to be accomplished. The problem with this system was that computers operate at billionths of a second and computer operators perform at human rates of speed. While the human operators were setting up the next program and data to be run, the computer sat idle. In fact, studies of the use of computer systems in those days showed that they were idle most of the time. Thus, much computer time was wasted. Operating system software was designed to eliminate these inefficiencies and to manage computer time more effectively. Basically, it accomplishes these objectives by automatically performing the work formerly done by computer operators, or "operating" the computer system much as computer operators once did.

Operating systems typically include supervisory programs, job management programs, and input/output (I/O) management programs (see Figure 5–3). *Supervisory programs* are the heart of the operating system and are primarily responsible for managing computer resources. Those supervisory programs that are used often are usually kept loaded, or *resident,* in main memory. These programs are called *resident programs.* The other supervisory programs and other components of the operating system typically are kept on a direct access storage device, such as a hard disk, so that they may be transferred to main memory quickly when needed. These programs are called *transient programs* (see Figure 5–4).

Job management programs select, initiate, terminate, and otherwise schedule jobs that need to be processed. These programs are designed to maximize the efficiency with which the computer resources are used and the processing is performed. Computer resources include the time a program will take to run, the input and output devices the program will need, and the amount of memory the program will need.

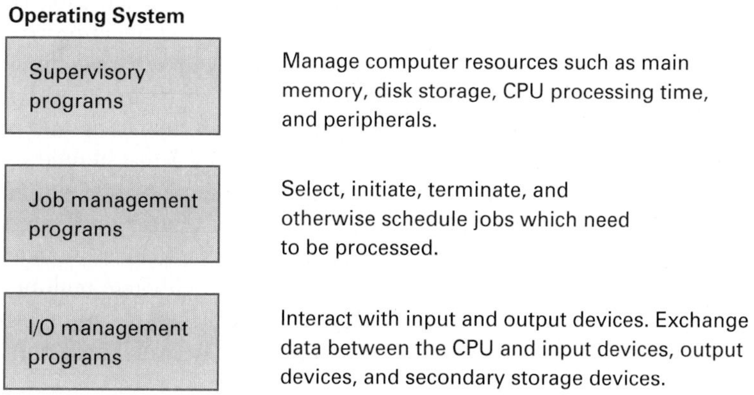

Figure 5–3
Components of an operating system

Operating System

Supervisory programs	Manage computer resources such as main memory, disk storage, CPU processing time, and peripherals.
Job management programs	Select, initiate, terminate, and otherwise schedule jobs which need to be processed.
I/O management programs	Interact with input and output devices. Exchange data between the CPU and input devices, output devices, and secondary storage devices.

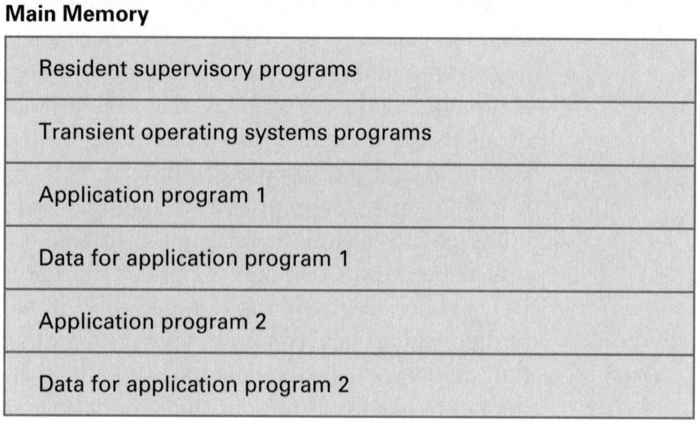

Main Memory

Resident supervisory programs
Transient operating systems programs
Application program 1
Data for application program 1
Application program 2
Data for application program 2

Figure 5–4
A model showing the allocation of main memory when an operating system, more than one application program, and more than one data file are resident

I/O management programs assign input and output resources to programs and manage the transfer of data between main memory and these resources, including disk drives, tape drives, and printers. When data is needed from a disk or data needs to be sent to the printer, the supervisory program turns these duties over to the I/O management programs.

Multiprogramming. One of the important ways operating systems manage computer resources efficiently is to allow multiple programs to run seemingly at the same time through **multiprogramming.** They do this by allowing more than one program and its associated data to reside in main memory at the same time. They divide main memory into partitions, and place each program and its data in separate partitions (see Figure 5–4).

Operating systems that are capable of multiprogramming take advantage of the differences in the speeds of I/O and CPU processing. While the CPU is waiting for data from a hard disk drive to complete one application program, it can complete calculations or other processing for another application program. In fact, because the time it takes to access the data from hard disk is likely to be measured in milliseconds (thousandths of a second) and the processing by the CPU is likely to be measured in nanoseconds (billionths of a second), the CPU has plenty of time to complete processing for several application programs while it waits for data for another application program. By carefully scheduling what the computer system does, control programs can coordinate the running of many application programs so that idle time of the CPU and peripherals is kept to a minimum.

Timesharing. Another way to allow many programs to run is to offer each program a brief amount, or slice, of computer time to process its data. This procedure is called **timesharing** or *timeslicing.* Using timesharing, the system rapidly moves from program to program, performing work. The system moves so quickly that to any one user it appears to be devoted exclusively to his or her program. The difference between multiprogramming and timesharing is that in timesharing, the operating system allots a fixed amount of time to each program. In multiprogramming, the operating system moves from program to program when it encounters a logical stopping point, such as having to wait for data to be read into main memory from secondary storage.

It should be emphasized that although multiprogramming and timesharing operating systems interleave the processing of several programs, they don't actually permit a single CPU to process data from several programs simultaneously; it just seems that way to the user.

Multiprocessing. **Multiprocessing** operating systems permit the simultaneous processing of several application programs by controlling more than one CPU at a time. The operating systems allow two or more CPUs to work together, sharing memory and peripheral devices. Thus, each of the many programs that are being processed may be processed by separate CPUs dedicated to one program. This type of multiprocessing is called *asymmetric multiprocessing.* Another form of multiprocessing also uses multiple CPUs. One CPU acts as the controller of the others and assigns any CPU any application task. The main CPU also controls I/O tasks. This type of multiprocessing is called *symmetric multiprocessing.*

Parallel Processing. Some operating systems use more than one CPU to permit many tasks from *one* program to be completed simultaneously through **parallel processing.** That is, several steps in a program are processed in parallel using multiple CPUs.

Virtual Storage. Operating systems may offer **virtual storage,** or virtual memory, to overcome the size limitations of a computer system's main memory. For example, suppose that the program you wished to use required more main memory than you have in your computer system, or even more main memory than you could possibly have in your computer system. To solve the problem, parts of the program that are not needed immediately are kept in secondary storage until they are required. When these parts are needed, they are read into main memory. The secondary storage device typically used is a hard disk because of its speed in retrieving the parts of the program directly. As a result, you have *virtually* as much main memory capacity as you have in main memory plus the memory capacity that has been allocated on the hard disk. Virtual memory creates the illusion of larger main memory by letting programs and data alternate their usage of main memory.

Communications Software

Communications software is really an extension to the operating system of a computer—it provides the additional logic for the computer system to control a variety of communications equipment so that it can communicate with peripherals, such as display terminals located far from the CPU. Communications software supervises such functions as communicating with remote terminals, monitoring communications equipment and lines, managing traffic on communications lines, logging and analyzing communications traffic, and diagnosing communications problems.

On mainframe computers, communications software is a collection of programs costing many thousands of dollars and involving a host of peripheral equipment. On microcomputers, communications software is designed to permit a microcomputer to "talk" to a mainframe, a minicomputer, or another microcomputer from a remote location, or to connect to a group of microcomputers in a room, floor, or building.

Of particular interest to many managers is software that will allow their office microcomputers to communicate with their organization's mainframes and also let them use their home microcomputers as remote workstations. Communications hardware and software will be presented in depth in Chapter 7.

Database Management Systems Software

Many people regard database management systems software as another extension of the operating system. Database management systems software handles records and files so that many users are able to access data quickly and easily. Database management systems software will be presented in depth in Chapter 6.

Other Systems Software

There are many other types of systems software, only one of which will be mentioned here: system utility software. *System utility programs* are just that—programs that operating systems users find useful. Often, system utility programs are designed to handle repetitive functions such as sorting records in files, finding data and programs on a hard disk, listing the data files and programs stored on hard disks, merging one group of data with another, copying data and programs from one secondary storage device to another, making copies of data and programs, diagnosing system performance, format-

Box 5–1 Powerful Operating Systems for Powerful Microcomputers

Today's powerful microcomputers (see Chapter 4) are being driven by ever more powerful operating systems. Some new and some old operating systems for these new microcomputers include these.

THE NEW

Windows NT

Developed and sold by Microsoft, Windows NT is expected to become as dominant in its arena as MS-DOS and Windows have become in theirs. Windows NT is a 32-bit GUI (graphical-user interface) operating system offering multiuser, multitasking, multiprocessing, and built-in networking capabilities. It is expected to be capable of running on computer systems designed using either CISC or RISC architectures, including computer systems using Digital Equipment Corporation's Alpha chip (see Chapter 4).

Pink

The Pink operating system currently under development by Taligent, Inc., is a product of an alliance between IBM and Apple. The object-oriented GUI operating system is expected to run on a variety of hardware platforms, including computer systems powered by Intel, Motorola, and PowerPC chips. The latter would make the operating system capable of running applications designed for Macintosh's System 7, Microsoft's MS-DOS and Windows, and IBM's OS/2 operating systems.

Chicago

This 32-bit, multitasking operating system is expected to include integrated networking support as well as support for pen-based input and handwriting recognition. Scheduled for release in 1995, Chicago is also expected to replace the combination of DOS and Windows, eliminating the need for DOS entirely. Chicago may include new "plug and play" capability, automatically configuring expansion boards without requiring users to set switches and jumpers. In effect, Chicago is expected to be Windows 4.0.

THE OLD

MS-DOS

This is a single-user, single-tasking operating system for 16- to 32-bit machines from Microsoft. IBM makes a version of this operating system called IBM-DOS. Digital Research, Inc., also makes a version called DR DOS.

OS/2

Sold by IBM, OS/2 has been on the market for some time. Its latest version offers 32-bit processing and multitasking along with a GUI environment called Presentation Manager, but no built-in networking or multiprocessing as of yet.

UNIX

Numerous versions of the UNIX operating system, such as AIX, Xenix, and Ultrix, are offered by several different companies. These versions offer a 32-bit multiuser, multitasking operating system with built-in networking capabilities. The version developed by SunSoft adds multiprocessing capabilities, a GUI environment, and the ability to run on computer systems based on either CISC or RISC architectures.

Macintosh Operating System

This is a single-user, multitasking operating system for 32-bit Macintosh computers.

ting magnetic media so that the media can be used, compressing files, and providing system security.

Microcomputer Operating Systems

As a manager, you may use a computer terminal attached to a mainframe or minicomputer system. In these situations, you may not have much direct contact with the operating system your computer system uses. If you use a microcomputer, however, you almost certainly will make direct, hands-on use of its operating system. Because there is a high probability that you will use a microcomputer in your work, you should know something about typical microcomputer operating systems (see Boxes 5–1 and 5–2).

Single and Multitasking Operating Systems. Many microcomputer operating systems, such as MS-DOS, are *single-user,* **single-tasking operating systems.** They allow only one person to run *one* program at a time. In the past, the term **multitasking operating systems** referred to microcomputer operating systems with multiprogramming capabilities that were limited to a single user, such as the System 7 operating system for Macintosh computers. The term *multitasking* has evolved, however. Micro-

Box 5–2 Solving RAM Cram: Memory Management for DOS

Microcomputers that use DOS operating systems, such as MS-DOS, IBM-DOS, and DR DOS, have been increasingly burdened with memory limitations. DOS divides computer main memory into three main parts: lower, or *conventional memory, upper memory,* and *extended memory.* DOS ends conventional memory at 640 KB. Upper memory is the memory between 640 KB and 1 MB. Extended memory is all memory above 1 MB. The rub is that no matter how much memory you add to your DOS-based computer system, you will still have only 640 KB in conventional memory.

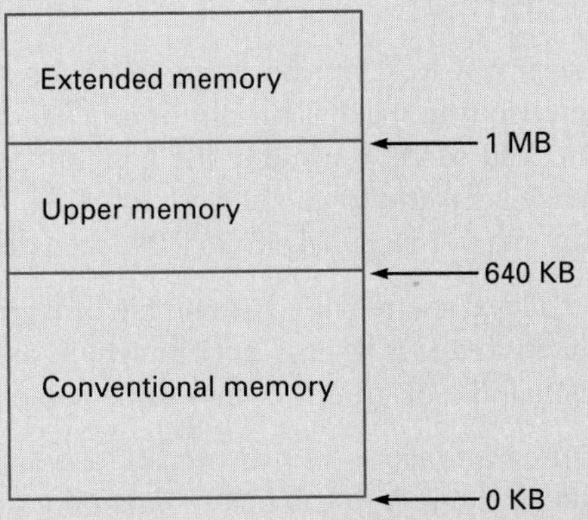

Unfortunately, conventional memory usually holds many programs. For example, it must contain DOS itself. It may also contain a virus protection program, software that allows you to connect to a local area network (See Chapter 7), and software to drive your mouse. When conventional memory gets too crowded, you may not have enough space left to run the programs you want. This state of affairs is called RAM cram.

A number of vendors have developed memory management software to eliminate or reduce RAM cram. The basic approach that these software packages take is to use idle sections of upper memory. Upper memory is ordinarily used to hold specific programs that handle various computer peripherals (for example, the programs that control your video display). These programs are often stored in ROM. ROM, however, is very slow. To increase the speed at which video is handled, the computer system reads the programs in ROM into upper memory. Once that is done, the video programs run at RAM speeds.

However, not all of upper memory is used in most computer systems. Memory management programs take advantage of that fact and place part or all of some programs usually found in conventional memory into the unused space in upper memory. Some programs that may be placed in upper memory are portions of DOS, the mouse program, and local area network programs.

Until recently, DOS did not provide a means to place programs in upper memory, and you had to buy special memory management software from other vendors. Now, however, all three DOS programs—MS-DOS, IBM-DOS, and DR-DOS—provide memory management features.

computer versions of the Unix operating system, for example, now often are characterized as being multitasking and *multiuser* in nature because they permit more than one program to run and more than one person to use the system at one time.

Multitasking microcomputer operating systems may allow you to receive a fax message at the same time you are editing another document or to search a large data file for a specific record while you are entering data into a new record. In multitasking systems, the task that the operating system is working on (searching for a record) while you complete another is called a *background task.* The task that you are working on (entering data into a new record) is called a *foreground task.* When the CPU has no actions to take on foreground tasks, it operates on the background tasks. Given that even the fastest keyboarders type at speeds measured in words per minute, the CPU, which measures its work in nanoseconds, is yawning from lack of work between each key we strike. So, the CPU works on the search task in what appear to it as enormous gulfs of time between the keystrokes of our fast-flying fingers.

Task Switching. Microcomputer operating system software and utility software for microcomputers also can let you load more than one program at a time and switch between these programs. You can have one program running in the foreground and several others suspended in the background. It is important to notice that the programs in the background do not continue to run—their operation is suspended. This process is called **task switching.** These programs typically let you task switch by striking only one or two *hot keys.* Hot keys are simple combinations of one or two keys that allow you to suspend the operation of one program and move to another. For example, the hot keys might be the Alt key and the Ctrl key or the Alt key and the F1 key.

Kernel. On microcomputers, the frequently used portion of the operating system is called the *kernel,* and the kernel is what is loaded into the microcomputer's main memory. The remainder of the operating system and most of the utility programs usually reside on floppy or hard disk storage to be used when needed. Ordinarily the operating system kernel must be on a diskette in the main diskette drive or on the hard drive of the microcomputer when the computer is first turned on. When the microcomputer is turned on, the kernel is *booted,* or loaded into main memory automatically.

Utilities. Some of the most commonly used utilities of a microcomputer operating system include the following.

Disk copy program. This program allows you to copy the entire contents of one diskette to another diskette. Typically you use it to make a *backup* or *archive* copy of a data diskette or an application program. You can also use the disk copy program to transfer data stored from one size or capacity diskette to another, for example, from a 360 KB diskette to a 1.2 MB diskette or from a 5¼-inch diskette to a 3½-inch diskette.

File copy program. A file copy program allows you to copy just one file or a group of files rather than the entire contents of the diskette. It has the same functions as a disk copy utility except that it allows an individual file or groups of files to be copied.

Disk formatting program. This utility program allows you to prepare a new, blank diskette to receive data from the computer system. You can't store data on a diskette until it is *formatted* or initialized. The formatting process writes the sectors on the diskette so that the operating system is able to place data in these locations.

File deletion program. The delete program allows you to delete a file stored on a diskette.

File viewing program. This program allows you to view the contents of a file on the display screen of the microcomputer.

Directory program. This routine allows you to view the file names contained on a diskette. Sometimes the directory program will not only list the files, but also will show you how many kilobytes of memory they occupy, the time and day they were last revised, and how much unused memory is left on the diskette.

Recent versions of microcomputer operating systems seem to be vying with one another to add more and more utilities in an effort to woo buyers. MS-DOS, Version 6.0, for example, added a number of utilities, such as disk compression and memory management (see Boxes 5–3 and 5–4).

Third-Party Software Vendors. Many users are not satisfied with the number, features, or quality of the system utilities their operating systems offer. When this happens, they may purchase system utilities from a software firm other than the one that developed the operating system. In other words, they buy these utilities from a *third-party software vendor.* For example, many microcomputer users feel that the backup utility supplied with MS-DOS is neither as easy to use nor as complete as they would like. So, they purchase a backup utility program (for example, Fastback), or they purchase a bunch of utility programs, including a backup program, bundled into one package (for example, Norton Utilities and PC Tools).

Proprietary Operating Systems. Some operating systems may be used on many brand name microcomputers. For example, MS-DOS may be used on the Zenith, IBM, Compaq, AT&T, Five Star, and many other PCs. Some operating systems are *proprietary* to one brand of microcomputers. For instance, TRS-DOS is a proprietary oper-

Box 5–3 Data Compression

Many computer users fill their hard disks and other secondary storage media very quickly, much like they probably fill their attics. Whether they fill their media with old junk, like their attics, or simply run out of room for better reasons, data compression systems have come to their rescue.

Data compression is a means to reduce the space that data occupy. Some of the means used are eliminating space wasted on inefficient data coding, repetitions of identical patterns of data, and data formatting. For example, compression systems usually look for multibyte repetitions of data, such as a string of zeros in a number, and then use a one- or two-byte "token" to substitute for that data sequence wherever it occurs. The longer these data sequences are and the more frequently they occur, the greater the compression that can be achieved.

The type of data that you have on disk or tape also alters the amount of space you save. Usually you can compress program files very little. You can compress text or document files much more, usually somewhat less than 2 to 1. However, you can compress graphics files a great deal, usually more than 2 to 1. Overall, many experts suggest that you can expect almost to double your hard disk capacity. That means that your 120 MB hard disk can be expanded to hold almost 240 MB of data.

The population of attic fillers must be very large because the demand for disk compression has been very great. For PCs, disk compression is available by buying disk compression hardware, software, or both or by buying an operating system that provides for disk compression. For example, Microsoft added disk compression to its microcomputer operating system, MS-DOS 6.0, and other PC operating systems are likely to follow suit. At this writing, many hard disk manufacturers are considering building data compression into their products.

Box 5–4 Popular GUI Operating Environments

Macintosh's Desktop and Window Manager	Sun Microsystems Inc.'s Open Look
NeXT Inc.'s NeXTStep	Quarter Deck's DESQview/X
Microsoft's Windows	Microsoft's OS/2 with Presentation Manager
Tandy's Deskmate	AT&T's Open Look
Digital Research, Inc.'s GEM3/Desktop	Digital Equipment Corporation's DECwindows
Hewlett-Packard's NewWave Environment	Open Software's Motif

ating system for some Tandy Radio Shack computers and System 7 is a proprietary operating system for the Macintosh computer line. The TRS-DOS operating systems will not work on machines that are made by Macintosh, nor will System 7 work on machines made by Tandy.

Operating Environments

The ease with which you can use an operating system is important to the manager. Clearly, easy-to-use operating systems allow managers and other end-users to save learning and operating time. The operating system features by which the user interacts, or interfaces with the operating system is called the **operating environment.** For example, end-users interact with the MS-DOS and UNIX operating systems by typing keyboard *commands* (the keystroke combinations that make the program do what you want it to) at a *system prompt.* A systems prompt is a character, symbol, or combination of the two that tells you that the system is waiting for you to give it a command.

Command-Line Operating Environments. If you were using the MS-DOS operating system and wanted to find the names of files stored on a diskette, you would place the diskette into drive A and type the command below (DIR) at the systems prompt (A:>):

```
A:>DIR
```

The screen would then display a listing or directory of the files that are on your diskette. For example, the following files might be displayed on your screen:

```
JONES       LET     1290    3-24-91    4:56p
ARNOLD      CON    23089    3-26-91    9:01a
EMPLOYEE    LET     2308    3-26-91   11:02a
```

In response to the command DIR, the operating system has listed the names of each file on the diskette, the size of the files in bytes, and the date and time that the files were created or last changed.

MS-DOS and UNIX are said to provide *command-line operating environments* because you must type commands on a line. You use the keyboard to interface or interact with the operating system.

Graphical-User Interface Environments. Learning, remembering, and using many different keyboard commands can be intimidating. To provide an easier method to "talk" to the operating system, some software firms have developed other operating environments that provide an easier-to-use interface. For example, one type of operating environment uses a **graphical-user interface,** or **GUI** (pronounced gooey) to allow you to interface with the operating system (see Box 5–4). A GUI environment

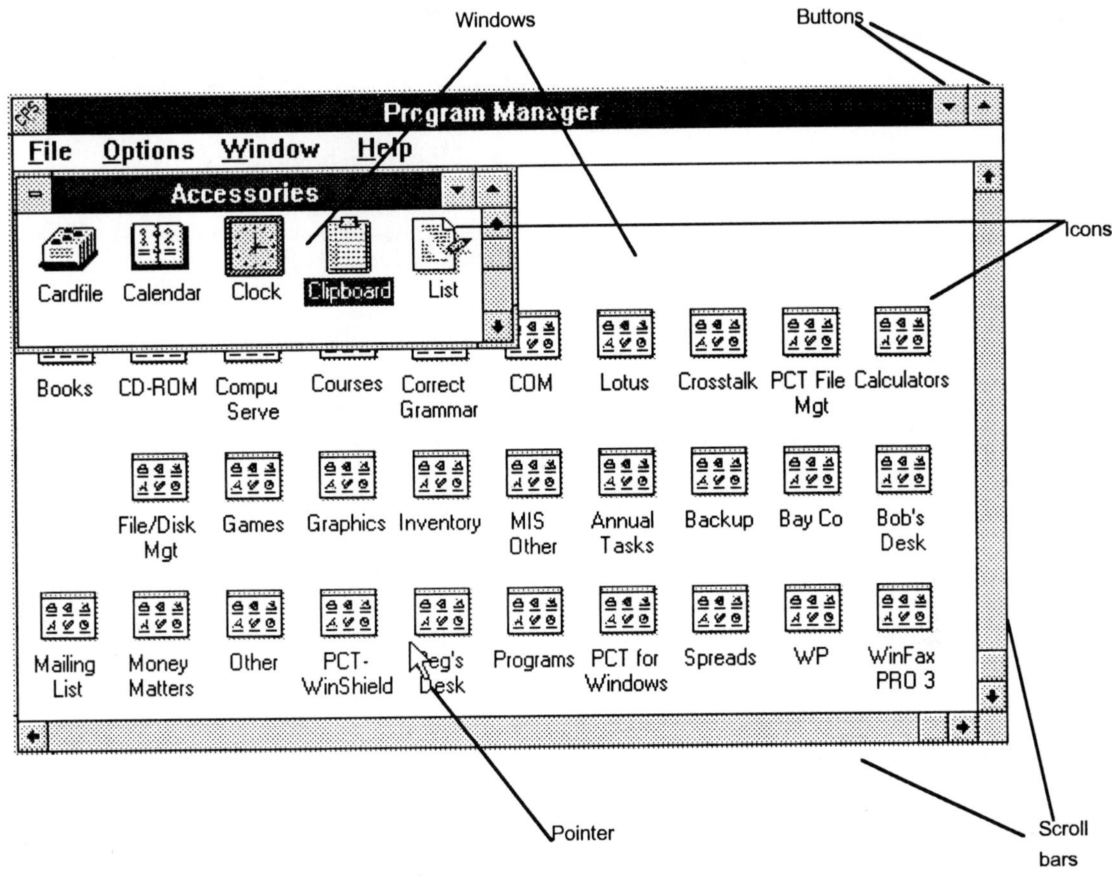

Figure 5–5
Windows, an operating environment that uses a GUI
Courtesy Microsoft Corporation

uses dialog boxes, drop-down menus, buttons, icons, scroll bars, and pointers instead of requiring commands (see Figure 5–5). You may move a pointer around the screen with a mouse to activate programs, data files, or features. Instead of keying in commands, you would "point and shoot"—that is, move a pointer to an icon and click a mouse button. You may also point to icons using a light pen on some systems or you may even use your fingers with a touch-screen system. Pointing at an icon and clicking a mouse button to run a program is a lot simpler for the manager than learning to key in a series of commands. Furthermore, in the near future, voice-synthesizing capabilities may allow you to activate the GUI icons by speaking. Instead of pointing to a screen feature, like an icon, and clicking the mouse, you may simply say the word that represents the icon.

Windowing Environments. Operating environment software may also allow you to run more than one program, view more than one data file at once, or both by splitting your display screen into parts called *windows*. Your display may show a document you are editing using one program in one window and a budget you are creating using another program in another window (see Figure 5–6).

Dynamic Data Exchange. Often users prepare a report on a project using a word processor and a budget for the same project using a spreadsheet. If the user changes an amount in the budget, the information in the document also has to be changed. Making such changes in some systems can be awkward. The user has to close the budget file, exit the spreadsheet program, load the word processing program, load the report doc-

Box 5–5 Microsoft's Windows Strategy

Microsoft's Windows operating environment has been an extremely successful product for microcomputers, and the company plans to extend the operating system to other computer-driven devices such as the TV, VCR, office machines, and even the automobile. The effort is called Windows Everywhere. Some of their plans include these:

MODULAR WINDOWS

The company has developed Modular Windows for entertainment systems, such as home multimedia devices, interactive cable TV devices, or smart cable boxes.

WINDOWS PRINTING SYSTEM

Microsoft has released a hardware/software system that allows two-way communications between your printer and your microcomputer. This allows your printer to notify your PC, for example, that it is out of paper.

MOBILE WINDOWS

The firm is developing an operating system for personal digital assistants, including software that will connect the handheld devices to wireless networks.

OFFICE MACHINES

The firm will soon tackle a form of Windows that will connect fax machine and telephones to computers, again allowing two-way communications between the devices.

STANDALONE WINDOWS

The next versions of Windows (Windows 4.0) is expected to be a standalone version. That is, it is not expected to require any of the versions of DOS, such as PC-DOS, MS-DOS, or DR DOS.

Sources: Paul M. Sherer, "Microsoft Creates Parallel Plans to Bring Windows to Office Equipment, Home Devices." *PC Week* 10, no. 6 (February 15, 1993), p. 22; Stuart Johnston, "Blueprint for Windows 4 Leaves DOS in the Dust," *InfoWorld* 15, no. 11 (March 15, 1993), p. 1.

---

ument, then enter the changes to make the document conform to the revised budget.

Some operating environments, however, have a feature called *dynamic data exchange,* or *DDE,* that automatically links data in one document with another so manual updating is not necessary. In our example, DDE will automatically update the report to conform to the changes made in the budget. Some environments provide this linking process in real time, that is, as you make the changes in the spreadsheet, the changes are also made in the document, provided both the spreadsheet and word processor are loaded in memory.

Desktop Organizers. Operating environment software also may provide a set of desktop organizing programs, including notepad, calendar, card file, clipboard, and calculator (see the Accessories window in Figure 5–5). Using the clipboard utility, you may copy data from a file in one window to a file in another. For example, you may copy the address of a customer from a card file record into a letter to the customer.

APPLICATION SOFTWARE

Application programs perform specific data or text processing functions. For example, word processing and payroll programs are application programs. Programmers who develop application programs are called *application programmers.* To develop programs, application programmers use a programming language or other development software.

Many of the application programs used by organizations that have mainframe or

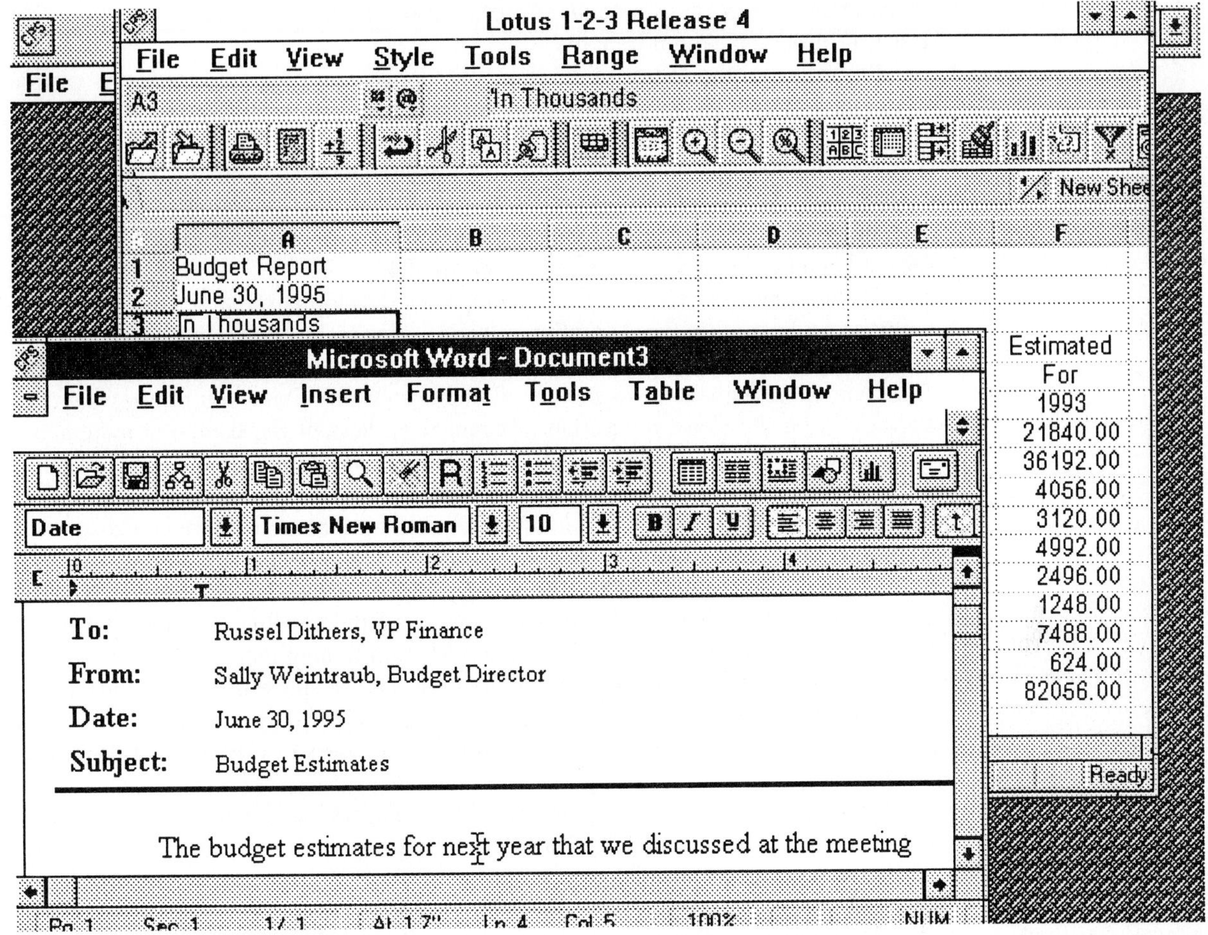

Figure 5–6
A memo being created by one program windowed on top of a budget being developed by another program

Courtesy Lotus Development Corporation (Lotus 1-2-3), and Microsoft Corporation (Microsoft Word for Windows)

minicomputer systems were written and developed by the application programmers employed in the data processing departments of those organizations. That is, the programs were developed *in-house.* In other cases, the software was custom written by consultants or programmers external to the organization. *Custom-written* software is often very expensive, but like software developed in-house, it may be the only way the organization can secure the kind of software it needs to do its work.

Increasingly, the application programs used on mainframes and especially the programs used on minicomputers and microcomputers are produced by professional software development companies. These commercially developed software application programs are purchased "off the shelf" by computer users to satisfy their specific application needs. Commercially developed application software programs are called *canned programs* or *commercial software.*

Two inexpensive sources of application and systems utility programs for microcomputers are *shareware* and *freeware.* Shareware is relatively inexpensive software that often is produced by individuals or "mom and pop" vendors and frequently distributed on the honor system through electronic bulletin boards (see Chapter 7); that is, you can download the software from a bulletin board without a charge. However, if you try the software, like it, and use it, you should pay the small fee to the developers. Prices for shareware software packages frequently range from $15 to $50. There are thousands of shareware programs that can be of great benefit to small businesses and even major corporations. Freeware, or *public domain software,* is similar to shareware except that freeware programs are entirely free.

Regardless of the source of development, application programs are always written to run under a specific operating system. An important feature of any operating system, then, is the quantity and diversity of application programs that have been written for it. The set of application programs written for any one operating system is often referred to as the *library* of application programs available for that operating system, and an operating system with a large number of application programs written for it is said to have a large library of application programs available.

At the same time, many software companies develop *portable software.* Portable software is software (a) that has different versions for many operating systems, (b) that is able to switch between two or more operating systems, or (c) can be easily converted from one operating system to another. Portable software allows you to use what is or appears to be the same application program regardless of the computer system you have. You may use a mainframe computer at times and a minicomputer or microcomputer at other times, or you may switch between different types of microcomputers at your home and office. With portable software you may not have to learn how to operate several word processors simply because you must switch computer systems from time to time. An organization that adopts portable software, such as a word processor that has versions for most or all of its computer systems, saves training time and allows personnel to move easily from one job assignment and location to another.

Like operating systems, application programs may be single-user or multiuser programs. For example, a word processing program may allow only one user to work on a specific document at one time, or it may allow many users to work on that document concurrently.

Commercial application software useful to managers may be grouped into a number of categories. A brief description of the software typically available in some of the most common categories follows.

Word Processing Software

Word processing software is a collection of application programs that permit the user to create, edit, and print text material (see Figure 5–7). Word processing programs range from the very simple to the very complex. Simple programs provide few of the sophisticated editing or text manipulation features of the more complex and expensive programs. But simple programs are usually easy to learn, cost less, and are appropriate for those with infrequent text creation needs. Sophisticated programs are more difficult to learn, provide many features, cost more, and are appropriate for those who perform text editing as a major part of their work.

Word processing software may come with a variety of integrated support programs, such as spelling checkers, grammar checkers, outliners, indexers, table of contents creators, footnote managers, and word finders or a thesaurus (see the drop-down menu of tools in Figure 5–7).

The economic value of word processing software is often measured by the increased productivity of the clerical and secretarial employees who use that software. Though preparing documents the first time is easier and faster with a word processor, the real gains in productivity occur when revisions to the original document must be made. The ability to make revisions quickly, without having to retype the entire document, reduces document preparation costs substantially. Also, the ability to merge customer names and addresses with a form sales letter and print out the finished product on letterhead paper automatically reduces keystroke costs enormously.

At the same time, because the use of microcomputers by managers has become widespread, it is not unusual to witness a manager using a word processor to prepare or

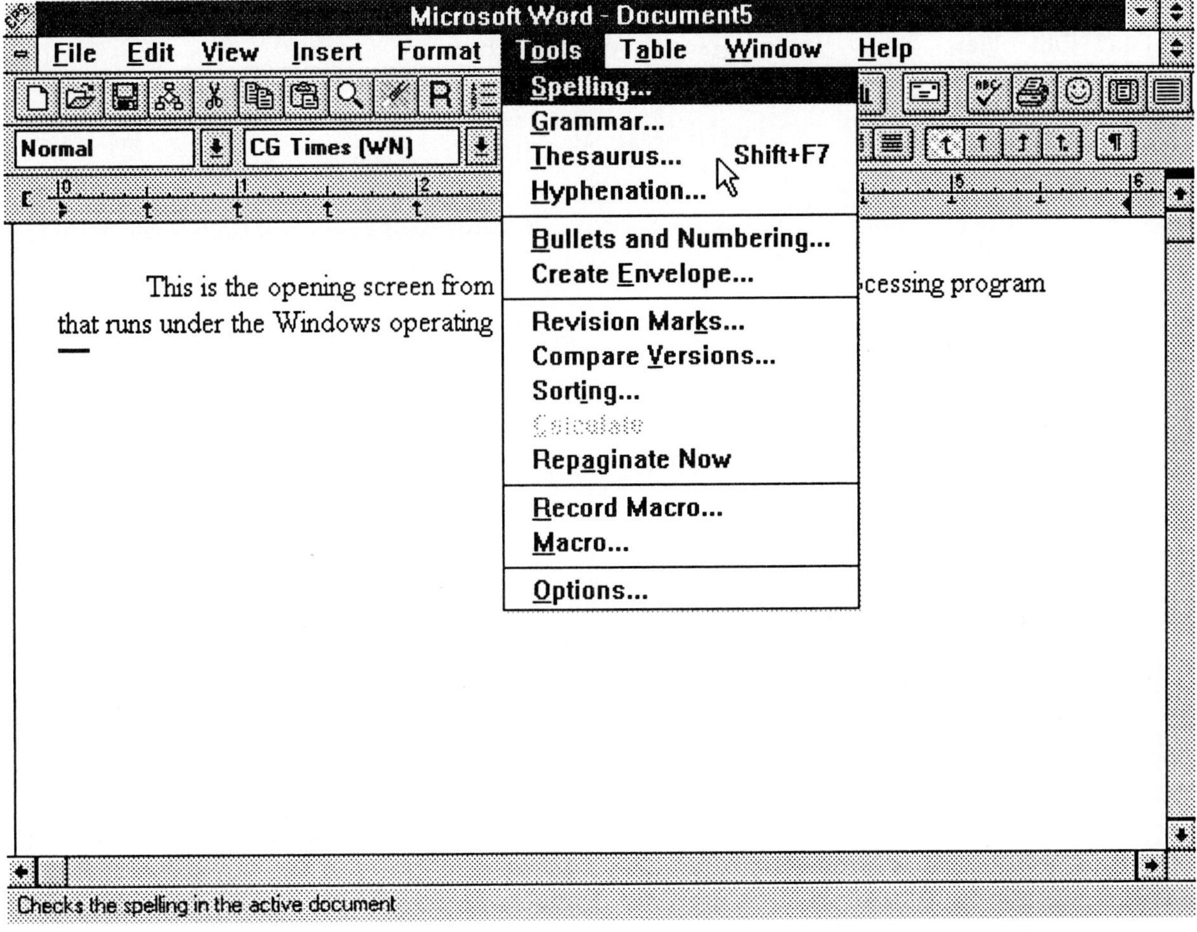

Figure 5–7
The opening screen from Microsoft Word for Windows, a word processing package, showing a drop-down menu that includes access to many integrated support programs such as on-line spell checker, grammar checker, and thesaurus

Courtesy Microsoft Corporation

edit a document—something a secretary would have done in the past. Substituting higher-cost managerial time for lower-cost clerical time to produce or edit documents increases document costs substantially.

Word processing software is also discussed in Chapter 12.

Spreadsheet Software

Spreadsheet software allows the user to prepare budgets, tax analyses, investment portfolio analyses, sales and profit projections, and many other financial documents with ease. Sometimes referred to as an electronic scratch pad, spreadsheets are frequently used to solve financial problems presented in columnar fashion. Often, these problems were completed laboriously with a calculator in the past.

The most powerful use of spreadsheet software involves the ability to enter formulas as well as data so that the user may simulate various solutions to problems, using a "what if" approach. That is, the user may enter a number of different values, such as production costs, and see the effect on the results, such as product profit margins. The formulas entered may vary from a simple column total or percentage to the more

Lotus 1-2-3 Release 4 - [CH8BUDEX.WK1]

File Edit View Style Tools Range Window Help

B16 +B8+B9+B10+B11+B12+B13+B14+B15

New Sheet

	A	B	C	D	E	F	G
1	Budget Report						
2	June 30, 1995						
3	In Thousands						
4		Actual	Actuals	Allocated		Estimated	
5		Payments	Year	Year		For	
6	Budget Item	June	to Date	to Date	Variance	1993	
7	Salaries	3512.34	21074.04	21000.00	-74.04	21840.00	
8	Wages	5814.59	36631.92	34800.00	-1831.92	36192.00	
9	Telephone	655.12	3734.18	3900.00	165.82	4056.00	
10	Equipt. Maint.	500.23	3001.38	3000.00	-1.38	3120.00	
11	Cont. Svces.	378.98	3760.11	4800.00	1039.89	4992.00	
12	Supplies	317.38	1922.59	2400.00	477.41	2496.00	
13	Travel	145.92	1040.62	1200.00	159.38	1248.00	
14	Postage	1289.25	7993.35	7200.00	-793.35	7488.00	
15	Other	62.99	220.47	600.00	379.53	624.00	
16	Totals	9164.46	79378.66	78900.00	-478.66	82056.00	
17							
18							
19							
20							
21							

Fixed 2 Arial MT 12 07/08/93 4:53 PM Ready

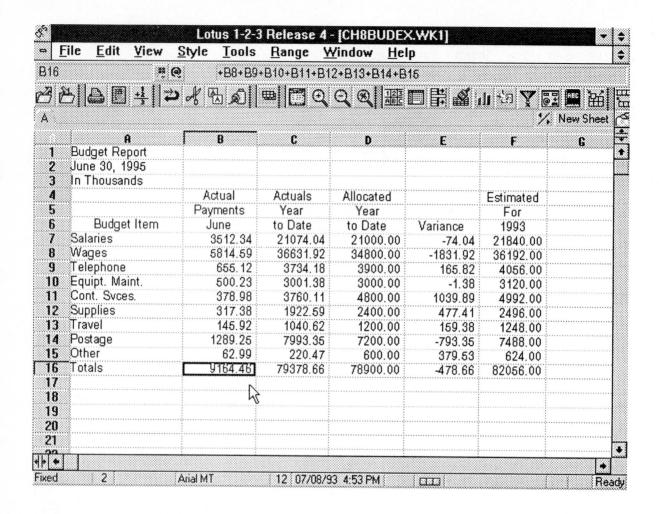

Figure 5–8
Preparing a budget using a spreadsheet

Courtesy Lotus Development Corporation

complicated return on investment or net present value calculation. Because it allows managers to answer "what if" questions pertaining to financial problems, spreadsheet software provides an important managerial decision support tool.

Looking at the simple budget shown in Figure 5–8, the manager can quickly see the effects of increases and decreases in the amounts allocated and spent for salaries, services, or other budget items by merely entering different values on one or more of the lines in the spreadsheet. For example, the manager can easily see the effect on the total budget variance if the allocated amount for phone expenses were increased to $4,000 from $3,900. Of course, the example shown is a simple one; real budget spreadsheets are usually much more complex. However, if the spreadsheet is designed properly, simulating the effects of different values is no more difficult than in our budget example.

The budget shown in the illustration is a simple financial model of a department. Spreadsheets allow the manager to develop financial and quantitative models to help solve many of an organization's problems. One financial model that can be developed on a spreadsheet allows managers to compare the differing costs related to buying, leasing, or renting an asset. Such a model usually compares the net present value of the cash flows resulting from the acquisition of an asset through purchase, lease, rental, and lease/purchase plans.

The design and use of spreadsheet software for financial decision making will be presented in Chapter 10.

File Management Software

File management software replaces the folder and file drawer system many of us were so used to in the past. Typically, file management software allows users to construct forms on the screen similar to the paper forms they had been filing. The users then enter data into the screen version of the form. The end result is that the data on the forms are now filed electronically on some media, such as a diskette, instead of filed in hardcopy form in a folder.

The power of file management software results from the ease with which the data can be searched and sorted and reports prepared. Most file management application programs permit users to search for documents in a variety of ways. The results of these searches can then be displayed in a report automatically. The reports may display sorted lists of selected names, counts of data items, totals of data items, or averages of data items. For example, a salesperson may search a customer file to print out a list of the names and addresses of all customers whose firms have annual sales of $5 million or more or who have certain job titles.

File management software may be used to provide decision support for many decisions that managers must make. It will be covered in more depth in Chapter 6.

Personal Information Management Software

Personal information managers (PIMs) constitute a diverse class of software whose major purpose has not yet been clearly defined by the market. A PIM usually provides some type of file management program as its base. For example, Instant Recall is a PIM that allows you to add, search, or otherwise read and manipulate files you have created while you are also running other applications. However, a PIM might also use an outline program, word processor, project management, or a scheduling program as its base. Some PIMs provide other programs that make them resemble desktop organizing software. For example, Pack Rat is a PIM that provides nine features: a calendar and date list, phone book, phone log, task list, agenda, expense log, index cards (the file management part), disk log, and a global list. Some PIMs are designed to help salespersons manage their sales contacts.

Database Management Software

File management software allows users to prepare reports based on the data found in a single file at one time, such as a customer file, employee file, product file, or equipment file. **Database management software** allows users to prepare reports based on data found in more than one file. Thus, managers may wish to prepare reports that require data about employees in personnel records to be related to data about employees in payroll records. Financial managers may wish to analyze the relationship between data about customers found in customer invoice files and data about products found in inventory files.

Database management software for mainframes, such as IBM's DB2 and Cullinet Corporation's IDMS, may cost hundreds of thousands of dollars. The cost of minicomputer database management software, such as Informix and Oracle, may cost in the thousands of dollars. The cost for microcomputer database management software, such as dBase IV and R:Base, usually is in the hundreds of dollars. As you will soon learn, database management software is an important managerial decision support tool, supporting tactical and strategic planning decisions. Database management software will be presented in more depth in Chapter 6.

Graphics Software

Graphics software usually provides one or more of the following basic components: drawing programs, image manipulation programs, and screen capture programs. Drawing programs allow you to draw your own images to be printed as is or *exported* or added to other documents, such as a text report or a slide show presentation (see presentation graphics software in the next section). The drawing program usually helps you draw by providing a number of drawing tools. Typical tools help you draw and size boxes, circles, lines, and arcs. Other tools help you add shading, color, and text to improve the finished product. Some packages offer tools for common business tasks. For example, a package may draw and arrange the boxes in an organization chart with little help from you and provide the lines to connect the boxes. You might then add the text in each box and the titles to the chart, color or shadow the boxes, or alter the font styles of the text used. Many drawing packages also allow you to edit images created by other software, such as the software used to capture images with a scanner.

Graphics software may also provide *screen capture* programs, or programs that are able to take a "picture" of a computer screen and store it in a computer file. The graphics software then may provide features that allow the user to crop (cut off), rotate, resize, and otherwise manipulate the captured image in the file. Many of the figures in this chapter that show screens from computer software were captured using the screen capture features of graphics software.

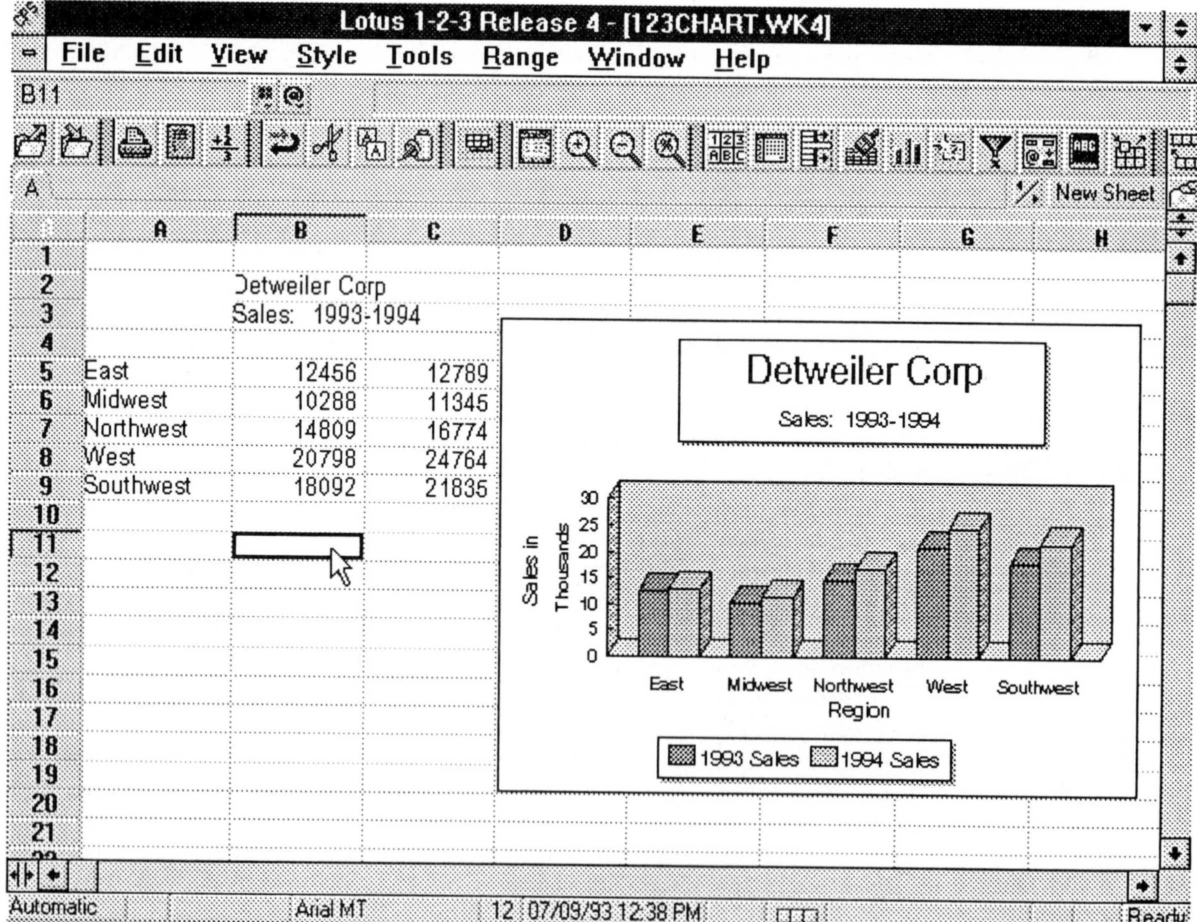

Figure 5–9
Chart produced by a graphics program found in a spreadsheet package
Courtesy Lotus Development Corporation

The information that a manager develops using an application software package may be easier to view and understand if the data are displayed in chart form rather than columnar form. For this reason, commonly used software packages such as word processing, spreadsheet, project management (see the section on project management software in this chapter), and database management include a graphics program. For example, the graphics program in a spreadsheet package may allow the user to display data shown in selected rows and columns in the form of a pie chart, line chart, or bar chart (see Figure 5–9). Also, the program usually lets you overlay one chart on another; for example, you could merge a chart depicting estimated outlays for a year over a chart depicting actual outlays for the year.

Presentation Graphics Software

If the manager wishes to make presentations using graphics output, a **presentation graphics software** program may be used. Presentation graphics software usually provides a *slide show feature* that permits the timed and sequenced display of charts, text, and images on a display screen. Presentation graphics software also provides a variety of special print functions, such as printing to a plotter or printing directly to acetate sheets for transparencies. The software usually permits images to be *imported* from other software, such as drawing and screen capture programs. Importing an image means to convert an image to one of the formats accepted by the program you are using and placing the image in your presentation where you want it to go. Often, presentation graphics software provides libraries of clip art images that you may "cut" and "paste" into a slide to make the slide more attractive and informative. For example, a presentation graphics package might provide libraries of images for business, education, the military, science, and health. The library of business images might contain images of people in business attire, filing cabinets, computers, telephones, offices, and other pictures or scenes commonly found in business environments.

Many presentation graphics packages also include most or all of the drawing and image manipulation features found in graphics software (see Figure 5–10, page 154). Some presentation graphics packages allow you to create slides of text by simply preparing an outline, which is then automatically converted into bullet slides. You can then dress up the bullet slides by adding color, special fonts, clip art, and other features to your presentation. Most presentation graphics software provides a variety of "transition effects" to add interest when you move from slide to slide in your presentation. One transition effect commonly found is fading. If you use that to end one slide and start another, the first slide will gradually fade out on the screen and be replaced by the other.

It is important to recognize that using a presentation graphics software program may require a special display terminal and a special printer that provide the high resolution and colors your software program can deliver.

Multimedia Systems

Multimedia technology is an expansion of the set of tools you have just learned to call presentation graphics software. **Multimedia systems** are a set of hardware (see Box 4–7) and software tools that allow you to present information in many forms, such as data, text, images, live or taped video, and live or taped audio. This information also can be integrated into a presentation. Multimedia systems permit you to merge these presentation types into a collection or a file of screens that users can access in any order they choose.

The most obvious applications of multimedia are in marketing, entertainment, and education. For example, the New England Insurance Company developed a multimedia system that trains their sales representatives about its products and services. This

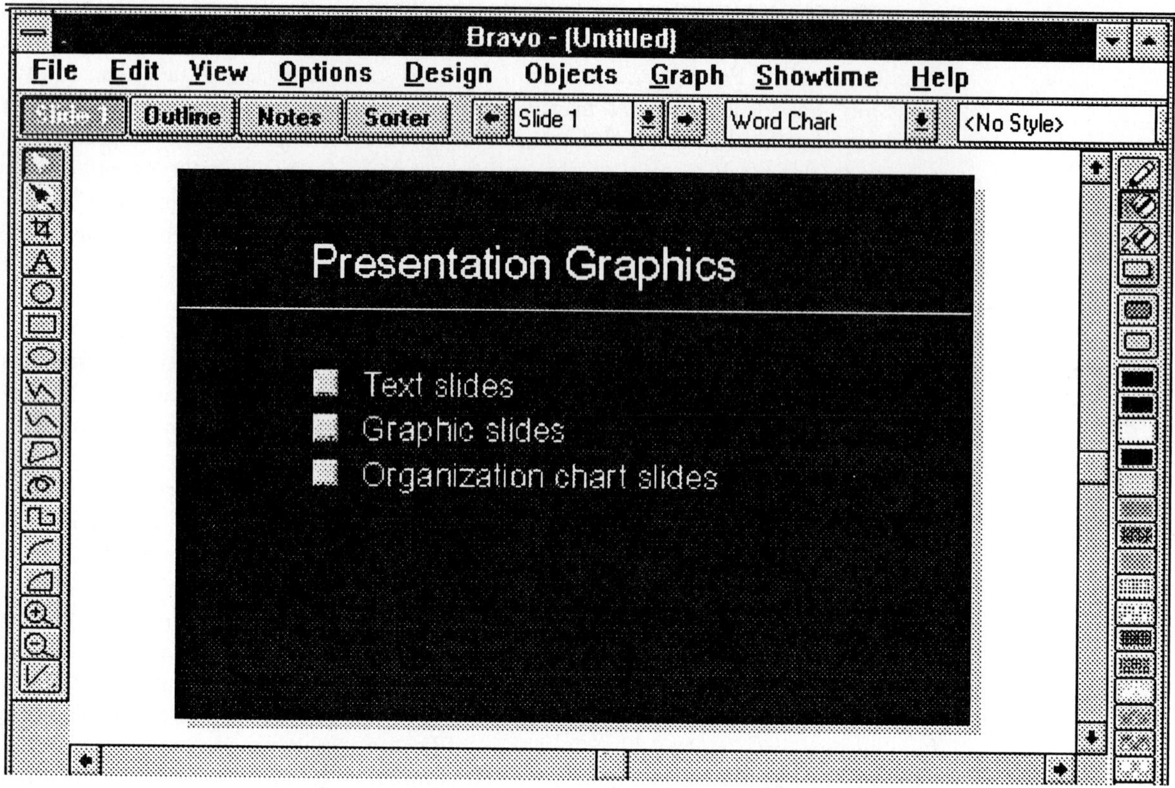

Figure 5–10
A text slide prepared by Bravo, a presentation graphics software package with drawing tools

Courtesy Alpha Software Corporation, 160 Middlesex Turnpike, Burlington, MA 01803

system has reduced training costs for the company. If you buy a copy of the *New Grolier Multimedia Encyclopedia,* you will get all 21 volumes of the encyclopedia on a single CD-ROM disk. Besides the usual text and pictorial entries, the encyclopedia provides animations of the solar system, weather, and the human body. You will be able to listen to famous speeches, music, animal sounds, and bird songs. Many computer games today are in multimedia form, including sound, images, animation, text, and data. Novato, California, uses multimedia kiosks to give tourists and residents an overview of the city, information about job opportunities, and local news. This information is all kept up to date via modem.[1]

Multimedia is often used to prepare *computer-based training,* or CBT, for employee training or education, as the New England Insurance Company did with its sales representative training. Multimedia CBT programs usually are interactive; that is, they require or allow users to respond to questions, menus, or other stimuli and allow for branching in the information presented to the user based on those responses. Thus, how a user is routed through a sequence of screens will depend on how he or she responds to these stimuli. CBT software can be used to develop skills and knowledge in any field. Training software is available for nearly every conceivable topic, including foreign languages, mathematics, chemistry, keyboarding, and human relations.

The software used to develop multimedia applications is a set of tools referred to as *authoring software.* One type of authoring software is called *hypertext.* Hypertext can

[1]Chris DeVoney, "Multimedia Authoring Tools: Sound, Video, Interaction!" *Windows Sources,* June 1993, p. 360.

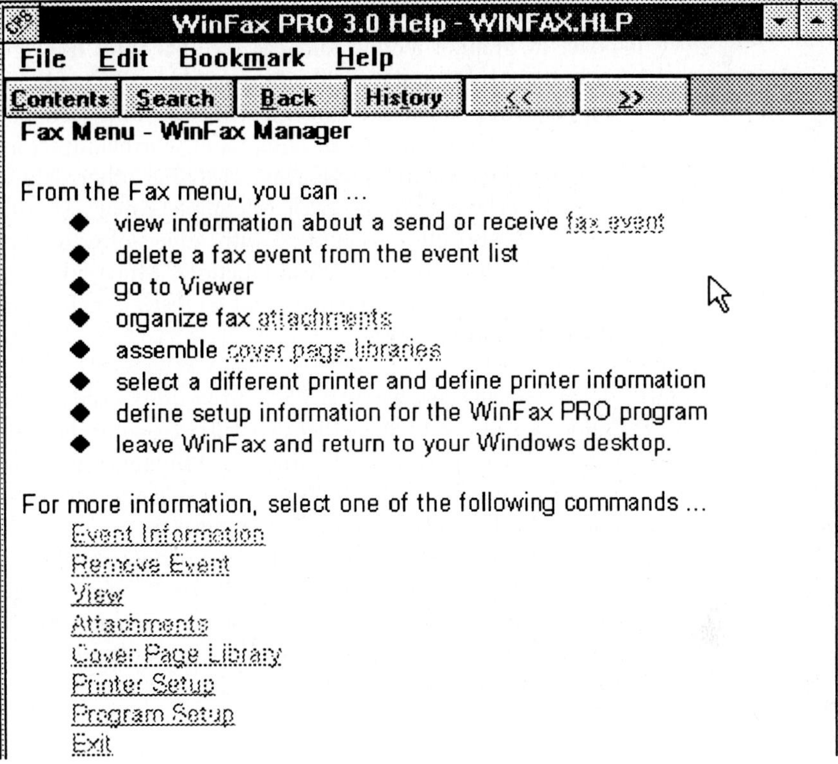

Figure 5–11
A hypertext on-line help menu from Delrina's WinFax PRO™ software. Clicking the mouse on the underlined words will move you to different screens with more text that explains the underlined words

Courtesy Delrina (Canada) Corporation, copyright 1993. Delrina and WinFax PRO are trademarks of Delrina (Canada) Corporation

be used to develop multimedia database applications, such as an encyclopedia. Hypertext stores and presents information on cards, much like a stack of index cards. Users can navigate the database by moving through the cards in sequence, by following a sequencing script of cards developed by others, or by clicking on "hot" words, icons, or buttons that move them to other cards. For example, imagine a user reading cards drawn from a database about politicians. Imagine further that the reader chooses a card about Lincoln. On that card the reader finds the words "Gettysburg address," in bold face to show that they are hot words. Clicking on the words might move the reader to a series of cards describing the situation at Gettysburg when the address was made followed by a card containing a digitized photo of Lincoln. When the reader clicks on an icon of a stereo speaker in one corner of the photo, he or she might hear an actor giving the address.

Hypertext is also frequently used for the on-line help feature of application software and for *tutorial software* (see Figure 5–11). Tutorial software teaches computer users how to do something, such as how to use a particular computer system or software program. Many software programs sold today include hypertext *tutorial software* to help the beginning user learn the commands and features of the programs. In addition, many software companies' primary products are on-line training programs designed to train people to utilize specific software programs. These programs can be invaluable not only because the manager can use them to learn software, but also because he or she can use the software to ease the transition when workers leave, retire, or are promoted.

Statistical Software

Statistical software offers an easy way to treat data statistically and often to display the data in graphic modes, such as pie, bar, and line charts. Like the other software mentioned above, statistical programs are available for all sizes of computers. They offer the manager a means, for example, of comparing yield per acre by seed type, correlating repairs to brand names of equipment, correlating consumer preferences to product features in a market survey, and analyzing other data without the tedium of the numerous calculations necessary to complete many statistical functions. Statistical functions are also often integrated with other software. For instance, many spreadsheet programs offer some statistical functions. Much financial analysis, production management, personnel management, and marketing management software also includes statistical features.

Project Management Software

As a manager you are very likely to be responsible for managing projects within your unit. It is also very likely that you will use one or more project management tools, such as Gantt charts and PERT (program evaluation and reporting technique) charts to help manage projects. These tools help you sequence project events and identify events that are critical to successful project completion.

Project management software not only provides professional-appearing charts as output, but also it allows managers to ask "what if" questions with the sequence of project events and the use of project resources. By experimenting with various sequences of project events, managers can optimize resources, including time, for the completion of projects. Project management software is discussed in more detail in Chapter 12.

Desktop Publishing Software

Photocomposition systems and phototypesetting systems utilize computers to enter text, data, and graphics in a variety of formats suitable for printing. In the past, specialized computer systems and specialized software were required to produce output of printing caliber. Recently, however, a number of companies have developed special text editing and print software that makes it possible to produce documents in formats previously available only with the sophisticated photocomposition systems used by printing organizations. This special software, called **desktop publishing software,** allows you to create documents with multiple font styles and special formats. Many programs permit you to insert images from other files and even draw or "paint" your own illustrations as well as enter text.

Ordinarily, desktop publishing software is designed to be used with a laser printer. Some desktop publishing software is designed to work directly with typesetting machinery.

An advantage of some desktop publishing software is that it allows you to use your current word processing program—which may not have sophisticated formatting features—to enter the original text. On the other hand, many word processing software packages have added many of the features that were formerly only found in desktop publishing software. Photocomposition systems and desktop publishing systems will be discussed in more detail in Chapter 8.

Desktop Organizer Software

Desktop organizer software denotes programs that typically offer a variety of useful features designed to clear your desktop of calculators, memo pads, telephone directories, calendars, and the like. If you are using a microcomputer, desktop organizers usually are loaded completely into RAM, or internal memory, and thus can be called on without exiting the program you are already using. Programs that are placed in RAM for immediate use are called **RAM resident software.** For example, if you were using a spreadsheet to work on a budget, with a few keystrokes or the click of a mouse you could display a window containing a memo pad and write a memo, or display a calculator window to do a computation, or display a telephone directory window to find and dial a telephone number, or display a calendar window to locate a date and check your schedule.

Desktop organizing features are often integrated within mainframe and minicomputer office automation software, electronic mail software, and personal information management software. They have also become commonly integrated with operating environment software, such as OS/2 and Windows (see the accessories window in Figure 5–5).

Expert Systems Software

Expert systems are systems that codify the experience and judgment of experts into (1) a knowledge base and (2) a set of procedures that software can then execute when faced with appropriate problems. For example, a college might codify the experience and judgment of its best academic advisors using expert systems software. The resulting expert system can then be used to help new or less experienced advisors when they work with students. Alternatively, students needing advice may use the expert system directly to find out what expert advisors would advise them to do. The result is that many more students can be served by expert advisors than would be possible without the expert system program and at a lot less cost. You will learn more about expert systems in Chapter 15.

Security Software

Preventing unauthorized access to your firm's data, preventing your data from being corrupted from computer *viruses* (programs that can corrupt your data, destroy your data, or simply annoy you), and preventing users from violating the terms of site licenses are important consideration in today's business world. **Security software** helps you protect your computer systems from a variety of threats. Computer viruses and security software will be presented in detail in Chapter 20, "Security and Ethics in Information Systems."

Compatible and Integrated Software

Commercial software may come "packaged" as standalone packages, compatible packages, or integrated packages. For example, a mainframe COBOL-language processor may be designed for a specific mainframe operating system and sold by itself. A microcomputer spreadsheet may be designed for a specific operating system and also be sold by itself. Packages that are offered independently and are not part of a family of packages that are designed to work together are called *standalone packages.*

Standalone packages may pose problems for the manager. For instance, the manager may have a sales proposal prepared for a customer using a word processor and then prepare a budget using a spreadsheet. If the two packages are standalone packages produced by different software companies, they may not be compatible with each other. That is, it may not be possible for the word processor to read the budget file prepared by the spreadsheet package. As a result, the budget may have to be printed out on paper using the spreadsheet package and then rekeyed into the word processing file to complete the proposal document. Incompatibility of different programs used by managers causes a good deal of frustration and also costs time and money.

Horizontal and Vertically Compatible Software. Because many people need to have data produced by one program and read by other programs, many software companies offer families of *horizontally compatible software.* Horizontally compatible software is a set of software programs that all operate on a specific computer system and are designed to work together. For example, Software Publishing Company offers a series of microcomputer packages for the IBM-PC and PC clones, including Professional Write (a word processor), Professional File (a file management program), and Professional Plan (a spreadsheet), that are all compatible with one another. That is, Professional Write is able to read a Professional Plan spreadsheet document file and Professional Plan is able to read a Professional File data file. In addition, these packages are compatible in that the **menus** (lists of program choices you are shown on a screen), **prompts** (usually helpful hints on the screen about what to do next), and commands are either the same or very similar regardless of the package you are using.

As another example, Microsoft bundles together Miscrosoft Word (a word processor), Excel (a spreadsheet), PowerPoint (a presentation graphics package), and Microsoft Mail (an electronic mail package). The bundled software is called Microsoft Office, and sells for less than the sum of the retail prices of each of the packages if they were purchased separately. The packages are all compatible. For example, you can create outlines in Word and copy them into PowerPoint to prepare a presentation quickly. Left out of the bundle but also compatible with these packages are Microsoft Access (a database management system) and Microsoft Project (a project management package).

You can see that using a family of compatible software packages rather than incompatible standalone packages offers great benefits. Not only can each program you use read files prepared by the other packages, but also you do not have to learn a completely different set of commands for each package. The former reduces the costs and errors that occur because data must be reentered; the latter reduces employee training costs.

However, compatible software packages still have some drawbacks. For example, you may find the spreadsheet package of a compatible family of software appropriate to your needs but find the word processor inappropriate. In addition, compatible programs may require you to move from program to program by quitting one program and then loading the next through a series of save and load commands. On microcomputers without a hard disk, this may require you to take out one diskette and load another. If you have to move from one program to another frequently, this program switching or diskette swapping can become tedious.

A number of software vendors offer *vertically compatible software,* or software that is portable to several different levels of computer systems. As you have already learned, a company might offer word processing software in versions for certain microcomputer, minicomputer, and mainframe computer systems. A document file produced on a micro can then be read by a version of the software that runs on a minicomputer or a mainframe. For example, IBM has developed vertical compatibility among the microcomputer, minicomputer, and mainframe computer versions of its DisplayWrite word processing software.

In 1987, IBM announced a set of procedures and rules for developing computer systems to achieve connectivity, consistency, and portability of software across all levels, or *platforms,* of its computer line—microcomputer through mainframes. This set of procedures, which has become a standard in the IBM world, is called Systems Application Architecture (SAA) and includes a set of specifications for the user interface. Through the SAA standard, IBM plans to develop—and encourage others to develop—software that presents a common user interface regardless of the equipment on which it is running.

code is being written. Machine language is almost never used by programmers today because they can achieve the same level of control over a computer, without the problems, by using assembly language.

Assembly Languages. To relieve the programmer of some of the detail required by machine language and to provide a set of commands that are more readily understandable, higher levels of programming languages were developed. The first of these were *assembly languages.* These languages use mnemonics as symbols for machine operations. For example, "L" may be used as the command for load, "ST" for store, and "A" for add. A program statement in assembly language might look like this:

Symbolic Code	*Meaning*
AR 1,2	Add register 1 to register 2

Symbolic programming commands and statements were much easier to work with than machine language and improved the productivity of programmers.

To be executed by a computer system, the assembly-language instructions first must be translated into machine language by an assembly-language translator program, or *assembler.* The assembly-language program code is called *source code,* and the machine-language code that results from the assembler translation of the source code is called *object code.*

Unfortunately, assembly languages are machine specific; that is, they are limited to use on the machine for which they were developed. This means that a programmer who works with several machines must know the assembly language written for each.

Third-Generation Languages. Although assembly-language instructions were easier to work with than machine language, they were still not very efficient in terms of programmer time. As a result, *third-generation languages* were developed that used commands and programming statements that were even more like English and that required less knowledge of the specific computer system for which the program was being written. Examples of third-generation programming languages include *COBOL (COmmon Business-Oriented Language), FORTRAN (FORmula TRANslator), BASIC (Beginner's All-purpose Symbolic Instruction Code), C,* and *Pascal.*

An example of a coded program statement written in COBOL reads like this:

```
MULTIPLY EMP-HOURS BY EMP-RATE GIVING GROSS-PAY ROUNDED
```

As you can see, the program statement tells the computer system to multiply the employee's hours by the employee's rate of pay and to store the result in a location called gross pay and, by the way, to round the result to the nearest cent.

Like instructions written in any program language, program code written in a third-generation programming language is called source code. The source code must be converted into machine language, or object code, before the program can be run.

Fourth-Generation Languages. Like hardware, computer programming languages have evolved through a number of generations. These generations parallel the levels of user-friendliness of programming languages already discussed. That is, as languages evolved, they were developed at higher levels of user-friendliness. Thus, the later the generation of the language, the more its commands are like English and the less they are machine oriented (see Figure 5–12). As you might expect, the lowest level of languages, machine languages, are classified as *first-generation languages.* They are written in binary representation and require the programmer to have specific knowledge of how the processor works. *Second-generation languages* are assembly languages.

Evolution of Programming Languages

Figure 5–12
Four generations of programming languages

Generation	Language	Characteristics	Degree of User Orientation	Degree of Machine Orientation
First	Machine languages	Commands written in binary representation. Each language can be used only on a specific processor.	↓	↑
Second	Assembly languages	Commands written using simple mnemonics. Each language can be used only on a specific processor.		
Third	High-level languages: COBOL, FORTRAN, BASIC, Pascal, C	Commands can be used on many machines with little change. Requires less knowledge of machine specifics.		
Fourth	FOCUS, RAMIS, SQL	Commands closer to natural English. Requires little or no knowledge of machine specifics.		

Program commands in assembly languages use mnemonics but still require knowledge of how a specific processor works. *Third-generation languages* include COBOL, FORTRAN, BASIC, Pascal, and C. These languages are written at a much more user-friendly level and do not require that the programmer know much about the specifics of the hardware for which the program is being written. **Fourth-generation languages,** or **4GLs,** such as FOCUS by Information Builders, Ramis II by On-Line Software International, RBase by Microrim, and dBASE IV by Ashton Tate are written at a very high level of user-friendliness and require even less knowledge of machine machine specifics. These languages are designed to allow relatively naive computer users to retrieve, manipulate, and analyze data from computer storage.

Third-generation languages required the programmer to spell out in detail each step and the exact order of steps the computer system must take to accomplish a task. Because detailed procedures must be described, these languages are called *procedural languages.* Fourth-generation languages may not require programmers to spell out the steps and sequence a computer system must follow to perform a task—when they don't they are called *nonprocedural languages.* To understand a nonprocedural language, consider the instructions a manager might give to a good administrative assistant when the manager wants to organize a meeting of branch managers. The manager might simply tell the assistant to set up a meeting with branch managers for next week sometime. The assistant would, without further instructions, contact each manager to find matching free times, schedule the use of a room, send reminder memos to each manager, arrange for a person to record the minutes of the session, order coffee or other refreshments if that is the accepted practice, and even prepare a proposed agenda for the manager to review. In short, the manager simply told the assistant what needed to be done. The manager did not tell the assistant how to do it—the steps to take and the sequence of steps to follow to get the job done. Nonprocedural fourth-generation languages allow you to describe what you want the computer system to do for you without requiring you to provide detailed instructions on how to get it done. Nonprocedural fourth-generation languages accept your request and develop the programming code to get the job done.

Although 4GLs are easy to use, they do have some disadvantages. For example, they often produce computer code that is less efficient than code written in lower-level languages. This may mean that the programs written in fourth-generation languages take longer to process your data than if the same programs were written in lower-level languages.

When used by an application programmer, fourth-generation languages improve productivity considerably over third-generation languages such as COBOL. Some people have claimed that programmers using a fourth-generation language have been able to write as much as 5 or 10 times as many lines of code in a day as they would have been able to had they used a third-generation language.

Fourth-generation languages are not defined very well by the information systems profession. Some professionals define fourth-generation languages as easy-to-use languages used primarily to develop applications related to a database. Others define 4GLs broadly to include such software as query and update languages, report generators, application generators, object-oriented programming languages, computer-aided software engineering tools, and natural languages. Often, some of these terms are used interchangeably and certainly some of their definitions overlap.

Recently, a number of software vendors have introduced **graphical fourth-generation languages** designed for application development for GUI environments, including Windows and several versions of Unix GUIs.

Query and Update Languages. Many 4GLs provide end-users with a relatively easy-to-learn *query language* and an update tool. A query language is a set of commands through which end-users can ask questions and retrieve data from computer files. Query languages will be described further in Chapter 6.

Update tools allow the user to add, delete, or change data in records. For example, using a microcomputer-based 4GL, you might retrieve the names of all customers who live in Chicago, Illinois, with these statements:

```
USE CUSTFILE
DISPLAY ALL CUSTNAME FOR CITY = CHICAGO
```

The first statement of code opens a customer file with the name CUSTFILE. The second statement tells the system to display on the screen the names of all customers whose addresses include the city of Chicago.

Report Generators. User-friendly 4GLs also provide easy-to-use *report generators*, or tools that allow the end-user to generate reports quickly and easily from the data processed by the program. Often the end-user can create a report using a report generator without knowing any programming languages at all by making selections from drop-down menus.

Figure 5–13
A conversation with a natural language program

A conversation between a manager at Trend Technology, Inc. (in regular type style) and a computer (in italics) that uses a natural language program might look like this:

How many people do we have working at branch offices in the city?

What do you mean by we?

Trend Technology, Inc.

What do you mean by city?

St. Louis.

Trend Technology, Inc. has 215 people working at branch offices in St. Louis.

Natural Languages. **Natural languages** are languages that are very close to ordinary English. That is, the user enters requests for information in normal, conversational English. The language program then translates that language into commands that the computer system understands and returns the information to the user on a screen or in a printed report (see Figure 5–13).

Graphics Generators. Some 4GLs provide a means to create and edit graphs from the data in reports developed by a report generator.

Application Generators. *Application generators* are 4GL packages that can produce a set of programs for a complete application, such as billing or payroll, largely or wholly without requiring you to write programming code. Developing a complete application means that the generator must be able to create input screens so data can be input to the application. It must be able to create the records and files needed for the application. It must be able to create output reports so reports or other outputs, such as billing invoices and payroll checks, can be produced. It also must be able to create the processing steps to be taken to compute the payroll or to create customer bills. It must create the screens that can be used to delete or update records. Finally, it must be able to coordinate each of these elements into a complete system.

Decision Support Tools. Decision support tools include spreadsheet, statistical, and modeling software packages. These software packages are briefly described later in this chapter and covered in detail in Chapters 10 through 13.

CASE Tools

CASE stands for **computer-aided software engineering.** CASE software products are usually comprised of a bundle of tools to help application developers complete their software development faster and better than when they use standard application development methods. CASE tools might include a fourth-generation language, a program code generator, a library routine developer, a data descriptor, and a data flow diagramming feature. However, CASE tools are not only used to automate the programming process; they are also used to assist developers in application planning, analysis, design, and testing.

Object-Oriented Programming

In a procedural language, the data to be processed and the operations to be used on the data are usually kept separate. In **object-oriented programming (OOP)** languages, the program operations are called *methods* and are joined together with the data. The result is called an *object.* A programmer might join a record with the operation *print.* Merely pointing to the record then will print it out.

The advantage of object-oriented programming is that the objects can be used over and over again in different applications. Thus, programs can be built from libraries of objects that are already available and have already been used and tested instead of developing them from scratch. Application programmers who have a great deal of experience working with procedural languages often find it difficult to switch to object-oriented programming languages. For many the switch represents a major change in the way they approach their work. The payoff, however, could be great. As companies create large libraries of objects, they will find that the time needed to develop new programs should diminish substantially. The library of objects, containing developed and tested code, should help companies reduce the backlog of information systems application requests that most companies have accumulated.

OOP languages have been around since the late 1960s. However, they did not became very popular until GUI applications became popular. OOP languages seem to be especially effective for developing graphical-user interface applications. For example, the OOP language Actor can be used to develop Microsoft Windows applications. Hypertalk is an OOP language that is used in HyperCard, a program that is included with every Macintosh computer system sold, and HyperPAD, a program that runs on MS-DOS computer systems. Some OOP languages come with a library of ready-to-use objects. For example, the OOP language Cause comes bundled with a library of previously constructed objects, including file drawers, file folders, records, and file indexes, which are combined with actions, such as display, report, and compute.

Object-oriented databases are described in some detail in Chapter 6, "File and Database Management Systems."

GENERAL SOFTWARE TRENDS

In general, software is becoming easier to use, more graphical, and loaded with more and more features. Software also requires increasingly more powerful hardware, especially greater amounts of main memory, secondary storage, and fast screens.

Graphical-User Interface

The graphical-user interface has become popular in all types of software, not just operating environment software. Every type of software now has commercial applications that use GUI, including word processing, spreadsheet, project management, and even utility software packages.

Windowing

Many software programs provide some **windowing** capabilities other than those provided by a windowing operating environment. Software offering windowing features provides users who do not have a windowing operating environment some of the same features as users who do. Many word processors, for example, permit you to open, view, and edit more than one document at a time. Many spreadsheets allow you to open, view, and edit several spreadsheet files at one time. Programs that offer windows also usually allow you to copy information from one document or file to another easily.

Data Linking

You have already learned that some operating environments allow you to link data from one program to another. This feature in the Windows operating environment is called *dynamic data exchange,* or DDE. But linking data between files developed by more than one program has also become an important feature of many software packages. For example, many word processors offer data linking to popular spreadsheet software. When these programs are operating under a windowing operating environment, the data links may be made in real time mode—that is, instantly—and are called "hot links." When these programs are running under a single-tasking operating system instead of a windowing operating environment, the data links may update information contained in the spreadsheet only after the user has exited the spreadsheet and reloaded the word processor. These types of data links are called "warm links."

In addition, many spreadsheet programs allow you to link data from one spreadsheet file to another, which allows you to create separate spreadsheet files for individual budget lines and link each line total to a master budget spreadsheet file.

Conversion

File conversion features have become increasingly common on word processors, spreadsheets, databases, and other popular software packages. These conversion features make it easy for users to read, copy, and use files prepared by other programs. For example, many word processors allow you automatically to convert a text file created in another word processor to the format of the word processor you are using, thus making it easy to import files from other word processors. The reverse is also true; it is easy to export files from one word processor to the file format used by other word processors.

Multiplatform Capability

Software vendors are increasingly providing products that are capable of running on more than one hardware platform. For example, Microsoft Corporation provides versions of Excel, a spreadsheet program, that run on computers constructed around Intel's 80X86 chip family and Motorola's 64000 chip family. Apple Computer Corporation is developing versions of its System 7 operating system to run on Intel chip computers and PowerPC chip computers (see Chapter 4) as well as its own Motorola 64000 chip family computer systems. At the same time, Apple is also paying Microsoft to develop a version of Windows NT that will work on the PowerPC while Microsoft is developing Windows NT to run on other hardware platforms (see Box 5–1).

Ease of Use

The graphical-user interface, with its point-and-shoot environment, makes many complex software packages seem easy to operate. Complex programs require a very large number of keyboard commands to make the programs do all that they are able to do. Learning to use all those commands and becoming proficient in them may take employees many months. It is much simpler for an employee to point an arrow at an icon representing a task that must be done and click a mouse.

Ease of Installation

Software has also become easier to install. Ordinarily, when you load a software package on your system for the first time, you must install it, or tell the software what type of screen, printer, and other peripherals your system possesses. Many programs today, however, have the ability to sense many of your system's features and install themselves with little intervention from you.

Hardware Demands

Software that is smarter and uses a graphical-user interface requires more lines of program code. That also means that this software requires more main memory and more secondary storage. Programs that require 512 KB of main memory to run are no longer unusual. The complete code for these same programs may require 15 diskettes and more than 5 MB of hard disk storage space.

Software that uses graphics may require special graphic boards and display screens. The boards and screens may deliver very high density images, but they also cost much more than ordinary screen display systems.

Complex software may require high-speed processors with large word sizes, such as 32-bit processors that operate at 50 MHZ or more, to work well. Many programs may be written only for high-speed and large word-size processors.

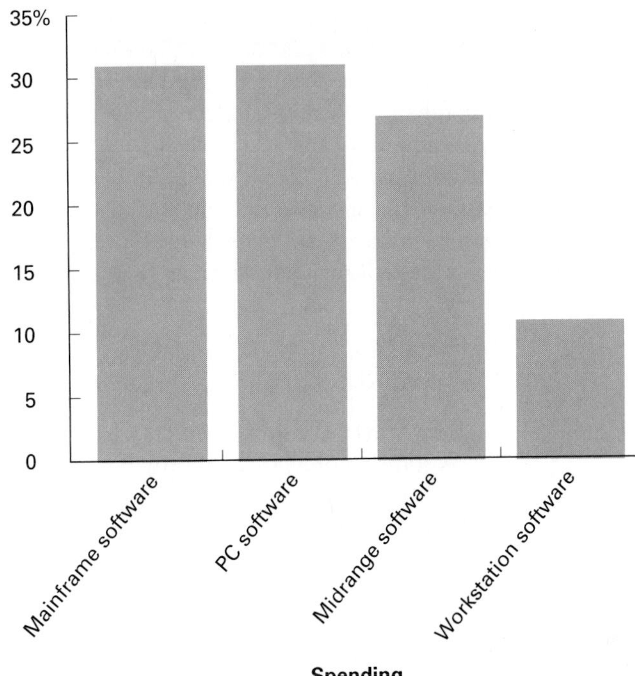

Figure 5–14
Spending for software

Source: Jonathan Littman, "Shopping for Success," *Corporate Computing* 2, no. 2 (February 1993), pp. 148–154 ff.

SELECTING MICROCOMPUTER SOFTWARE

As you can see, the amount and variety of computer hardware and software available to you is bewildering. At the same time, increasing amounts of information systems budgets are being spent on microcomputer software (see Figure 5–14).

Even for the manager who wishes only to select a relatively simple microcomputer system for decision support, the amount and variety of hardware and software may prove overwhelming. Unfortunately, many managers respond to this situation by selecting the microcomputer as their first step in meeting their computer system needs. This approach often proves disastrous because there may not be any software, or at least any appropriate software, that will serve their application needs that runs on the microcomputer system they bought. Thus, they are left with a computer system that does not provide for their application needs at all, or at best, not as well as it should. Here are the steps you should take to select the software you need.

Step 1: Identifying Your Application Needs

Selecting a computer system should not begin with the computer hardware. The starting point should be a clear identification of your business application needs. For example, you might identify sales forecasting as the major application you need to computerize. You should then spell out in some detail the features of a forecasting system you need: the ability to display color graphics, the ability to print displays to transparency acetate, the ability to perform specific statistical functions, the ability to access mainframe data for analysis, and so forth.

Step 2: Seeking the Right Software

Once you have listed your application requirements, you should then identify software that may meet your requirements. Here are some useful steps in identifying software that should improve your chances of a successful hunt.

Determine the Appropriate Associations. Identify the state, regional, national, and international associations that are appropriate to your tasks. For example, identify the state, regional, national, and international marketing associations. Then obtain copies of their publications for the last six months. Usually copies of association publications are readily available in a university library or company library. Examine the publications for software advertisements and articles that pertain to using computers for sales forecasting. If a software developer creates a software package for a specific function or a specific industry, the most likely place for that developer to advertise the software will be in these association journals.

Contact the Authors. Call or write the authors of the articles and ask them for further information about the software they described. These articles are often authored by users of software who describe how they have employed the software in their firm.

Contact Software Companies. Call or write the companies that advertise appropriate software or whose software was described in the journal articles to ask for further information. Many software companies will mail you *demonstration diskettes* of their software so that you can get some idea of what it is all about before buying it. Often, these demonstration diskettes are provided free of charge or at very low cost. Others will provide examination copies of the software so that you can try it out on your hardware before buying it. Still others provide all their software packages on a CD-ROM disk. You can try out each of the software packages on disk. If you like any of them, you call the vendor. The vendor then gives you a code to unlock the software from the CD-ROM disk so you can copy it to your hard disk.

Consult Software Databases. Search software databases for programs that meet your needs. For example, if you were to search the Computer Select CD-ROM database, you would start in the section entitled "Software Product Specifications." You might then enter the search words, "sales forecasting," and browse the products that meet the search criteria. Each product description contains details about the company and the product. You could then contact the companies that make interesting products and ask for more details, for demonstration diskettes, or for examination copies of the actual programs.

Contact Software Search Firms. Call or write *software search firms*. These firms usually advertise in computer magazines. The firms will provide you with reviews of software that meet the requirements you give them. For example, SoftSearch, a division of Synergy Computer Consulting of British Columbia, assists you in identifying those hard-to-find packages that are not found in the computer stores and other common sources.

Search Computer Magazines. Examine computer magazines. These magazines are a useful source of information about software. Many dedicate one issue annually to the review of a major software type. Look for an issue that features the type of software you are interested in. Many magazines also carry the advertisements of wholesale computer distributors who will sell the software you need at substantial discounts from list price.

Some computer magazines are especially well suited for searches. For example, *Computer Shopper* is a monthly magazine that fills its 900-plus pages with articles and advertisements on computer software as well as hardware.

Contact Consultants. Contact consultants who are knowledgeable about computer systems and computer software. Seeking advice from experienced consultants can save you many hours of search time. On the other hand, be aware that the experiences of some consultants can be quite narrow and limited to a few systems. Consultants with limited experience in software may limit their recommendations to the software they know, limiting the options you consider.

Step 3: Choosing the Software that Best Fits Your Business Needs

After identifying potential software packages that may serve your application needs, you should compare the features of each package to the specific features your application requires, which you identified in Step 1. For example, you may need human resource management software that is able to list employees by physical handicap or as members of more than one department.[2] You may need a word processor that is able to import a specific type of image file and merge letters with names and addresses that are part of a specific database.

Once you evaluate software in terms of the specific business features you require, you should evaluate the packages in terms of their general features (see the section "General Features of Software" that follows).

A typical method of comparing software packages in terms of their features is some form of the weighted average method. That is, you list the features that you want in the application and then weight them. Then you rate the quality of those features in each package that you review. Finally, you multiply the weight times the quality for each package, find the average of the results, and choose the package with the highest average.

Reading the evaluations of software packages in computer magazines is very helpful, particularly in identifying features that may be important to your application. However, the overall rating of the software in the article may be misleading in terms of the choice you should make. Often, the writer of an article will weight features that are unimportant or of little importance to you very high, or the reverse. If you use such reviews as your method of selection, you will often choose the wrong software.

Step 4: Selecting the Hardware

Once you have found the software that meets your specific requirements, you should select the computer hardware that uses an operating system that will run that software. In other words, the hardware should be one of the last components of the computer system you should select. In addition to running the software you want to use, you should consider the other hardware selection issues described in this text (see Chapter 4).

Step 5: Choosing a Software Vendor

How you choose a vendor to supply the software you have selected depends to some extent on the knowledge you have of the software you are acquiring and the help you will need to purchase, install, and use the software. Like hardware, you can buy software from many types of vendors, including software companies, computer sales and service dealers, and mail-order firms.

Some vendors provide *hot-line* technical support to customers. Others provide bulletin board service through which you can leave messages for technical experts and view their responses via modem (see Chapter 7). Still others provide no technical support at all to the buyer. Like the hardware you buy, *before* you buy software you should find out what level and types of help the vendor will provide *after* you buy the systems.

If you know a lot about the software you want, you may choose to buy from mail-order companies. Ordinarily, mail-order prices are lower than prices from other sources. However, you may find that the software you buy is not what you wanted. You

---

[2]Suggested by Professor Albert L. Lederer, Oakland University, Rochester, Michigan.

need to find out before you buy what options are available for returning software. When you buy from the company that produces the software, you are often allowed to use the software for 30 days on a trial basis. If you are not happy at the end of the 30 days, you can return the software for a full refund. If you buy from mail-order companies, there may be a small charge to return the software.

As in buying hardware, it is important, especially for large purchases, to investigate every vendor you are seriously considering. How long have the vendors been in business? What has been the history of customer satisfaction with the software the companies produce? How sound, financially, are the vendors? Do they have training centers? How often do they run classes? What level of training do they offer? How comprehensive are their course offerings? What level of technical support do they offer? How do they deliver technical support?

GENERAL FEATURES OF SOFTWARE

In addition to selecting software because it best fits your application needs, some general criteria for selecting software will prove useful.

Ease of Use

A number of factors make software *user-friendly,* or easy to use, including these:

1. The readability and clarity of the documentation, or manual, for the software package.
2. The clarity of the menus and prompts displayed on the screen.
3. The ability of the software package to adapt menus and commands to experienced users. For example, WordStar, a word processing package, provides four help levels, depending on the user's needs. This means that the experienced user can avoid plowing through many of the menus and prompts that the inexperienced user needs to complete a task.
4. The existence of an *on-line help feature* that offers explanations and suggestions for the prompts and commands used in the package.
5. The existence of a tutorial package supporting the software. A tutorial package is another software package designed to train you in the software. A number of companies develop on-line tutorials for popular software. For example, American Training International (ATI) provides tutorials on disk and on a variety of audio and visual media for many popular decision support software packages. Many software companies now include a tutorial diskette as part of the purchase price of their software.

Copy Protection

It is important to make backup copies of all your software in case the original packages become damaged. Some software packages are written in such a way that they cannot be copied easily. These packages are called *copy-protected software.* Other packages can be easily copied using the copy utility of the operating system.

Version

Many software packages are under constant revision. Make sure you are buying the latest version of the software you want. Also, some software vendors offer updated versions of their software to existing users at a substantially reduced charge. Find out about the software company's *update policy* before you buy the software.

Compatibility with Other Software

The importance of buying software that is horizontally and vertically compatible with other software packages you are using has already been described. However, compatibility is also important when you are updating the software you currently use with a new version. That is, the new version of the software should be able to read and use the data files you created with your old version of the software. This feature of software is called *backwards compatibility.* At the very least, the new version should be able to convert the old files to the format of the new version easily.

Compatibility with Peripherals

It is easier to use a software package if it is already set up to use your printer or other peripherals. Many packages, especially word processing packages, have procedures for installing the software on your computer system. The installation procedures may ask you to identify the type and amount of main memory, the type of monitor, the type and number of disk drives, and the type of printer. An easy-to-install package will lead you through the installation process with lots of menus and prompts. For example, the installation procedures may include a screen showing you a menu of what printers the package supports. Installing the software for your printer then merely becomes a matter of selecting a menu item. Some software packages, especially those of more recent vintage, almost install themselves, identifying most elements of the computer system you are using automatically.

At the very least, you should find out if the software package you want to buy will run your printer and other peripherals. For example, some software requires certain types of display screens and certain amounts of main memory. If you can, read the installation section of the software manual before you buy the software to make sure that the software will fit your system.

Portability

If you have more than one type of computer system or platform in your firm, it is important that you can buy versions of the software that will run on all or most of them. As already discussed, software that is portable to many computer platforms reduces learning time and training costs for an organization.

Network Capabilities

Connecting computers to each other has become very important in developing information systems to serve organizations. It is very likely that some applications that you will need will require a computer network. Thus, the ability of software to run on a network of connected computers, in fact to take advantage of the network, is usually an important consideration.

Cost

The cost of the software is always an important consideration. However, you should recognize that often the cost difference between low-end and high-end software is only a few hundred dollars. You should not let a few hundred dollars dissuade you from purchasing a package better suited to your needs, given that you will use the package for many years.

Memory Requirements

Software packages vary in the amount of main memory (RAM) they require. Because memory costs money, you should know if the program you want will fit within the typical memory sizes provided by microcomputer manufacturers—for example, 256 KB, 512 KB, 640 KB, 1 MB, 2 MB, or 4 MB. If the program requires more memory, find out what type of memory is needed and how much more that memory will cost.

Site Licensing

If you plan to use the microcomputer software in more than one machine, you should check on the copyright agreements that the software company provides. Many software companies require that you purchase one copy of the software package for each workstation. Other companies may allow you to pay a flat rate for the use of the software on all or a specified number of stations within your organization or at your location. That is, you will sign a *site licensing agreement* allowing you to pay a flat fee for the software and then use the software on many workstations.

Other criteria for specific types of software packages will be presented in later chapters devoted to database, communications, financial, marketing, production, personnel management, and office information systems.

Management Summary

Computer programs are called software. Three types of software are systems programs, which control and supervise the activities of the computer system, application programs, which process your data, and development software, which are used to create systems and application programs.

Systems software consists of operating systems programs, systems utility programs, communications programs, and database management programs. Operating system programs coordinate the hardware of the system and consist of supervisory programs, job management programs, and I/O management programs. Usually most of the supervisory programs are resident in main memory. Job management programs select, initiate, terminate, and schedule jobs to be processed. I/O management programs assign input and output devices to programs and manage the transfer of data between main memory and I/O resources. Utility programs are programs written to handle repetitive activities and are usually transient programs.

Operating systems may be capable of serving a single-user or multiusers. They may also be capable of running more than one program, seemingly at one time, through multiprogramming or timesharing. Operating systems may also be designed to run many programs concurrently by managing more than one CPU through multiprocessing. Some operating systems permit more than one CPU to perform the tasks needed for one program through parallel processing.

Virtual memory is a method of expanding main memory by using a direct access storage device to store unneeded portions of programs.

Operating environment programs are programs that provide an interface between the user and the systems software. Operating environments may require keyboarding commands, provide multiple windows, or provide both windowing and a graphical-user interface. Operating environments may also provide dynamic data exchange between programs and desktop tools, such as calendars, calculators, and notepads.

Application programs perform specific data, text, and image processing functions and are usually written for a specific operating system. Application programs may be developed in-house, by custom software firms or consultants, or by commercial software firms. Commercial software programs may be stand-alone, horizontally compatible, integrated, or vertically compatible software.

Common application software includes word processing, spreadsheet, file management, personal information management, database management, graphics, presentation graphics, multimedia, statistical, project management, desktop publishing, desktop organizer, security, and expert systems software.

Application software is also available for organizations in specific industries, such as medical clinics, building contractors, and legal firms. Application software is also commonly available to serve functional business areas, such as accounting, finance, marketing, production, and human resources.

Development programs are a group of software used to create systems and application programs. Development programs include first-, second-, third-, and fourth-generation languages. Fourth-generation languages are a diverse group of programs, including query and update languages; report, graphics, and application generators; decision support tools; CASE tools; object-oriented programming languages; and natural languages.

Software is generally becoming easier to use, packed with more features, and more powerful. Software is becoming more user-friendly through improved interfaces, such as graphical-user interfaces, and through easy-to-use installation programs. Software is also providing more features, including windowing, conversion, and data linking. Easier to use and more powerful software comes at the cost of increased hardware requirements (including faster and more powerful CPUs), increased memory (including main memory and secondary storage), and more powerful display screens.

Selecting a computer system should begin with a careful analysis of your application needs. The computer hardware should be chosen on the basis of whether or not it will run the application software that best serves these needs. In addition to fitting your application needs, there are a number of general criteria for selecting software such as ease of use, copy protection, compatibility with other software, compatibility with peripherals, currency, portability, cost, memory requirements, and availability of site licensing.

In this chapter you have learned a little about all kinds of computer software. In the next chapter, you will learn more about two types of software of great importance to managers: file management and database management software. These types of software allow you to store, retrieve, and manipulate large amounts of data that managers often find critical to their decision making.

Key Terms for Managers

CASE, **164**
communications software, **139**
computer aided software engineering, **164**
database management software, **151**
desktop organizer software, **156**
desktop publishing software, **156**
development software, **160**
expert systems, **157**
file management software, **151**
fourth-generation languages (4GLs), **162**
graphical fourth-generation languages, **163**
graphical-user interface (GUI), **144**
graphics software, **152**
groupware, **159**
integrated software, **159**
menus, **158**
multimedia systems, **153**
multiprocessing, **139**
multiprogramming, **138**
multitasking operating systems, **141**
natural languages, **164**
object-oriented programming (OOP), **164**
operating environment, **144**
operating system, **137**
parallel processing, **139**
personal information managers (PIMs), **151**
presentation graphics software, **153**
programming languages, **160**
project management software, **156**
prompts, **158**
RAM resident software, **156**
security software, **157**
single-tasking operating systems, **141**
software, **135**
spreadsheet software, **149**
statistical software, **156**
systems software, **136**
task switching, **142**
timesharing, **138**
virtual storage, **139**
windowing, **165**
word processing software, **148**

Review Questions

1. What are the major components of systems software?
2. What is an operating system? What are the major components of an operating system?
3. List some examples of microcomputer operating system utilities. For each microcomputer operating system utility you list, briefly describe what the utility does.
4. What is a timesharing operating system? How does a timesharing operating system seem to run more than one program at the same time?
5. What is multitasking? How does multitasking compare with task switching?
6. What are foreground and background tasks?
7. What is a transient program? Is the kernel of a microcomputer operating system a resident or transient program?
8. Explain how virtual storage appears to expand the main memory of a computer system.
9. What is an operating environment?
10. What is a command-line operating environment? Name an operating system that uses a command-line operating environment.
11. What is add-on software? Who develops add-on software?
12. List five types of application programs. For each type listed, provide a brief description of what the program type accomplishes.
13. List the four generations of programming languages. What two key characteristics separate each generation from the others?
14. What is the difference between industry-specific and functionally specific software?
15. What is shareware?
16. Explain the difference between source code and object code.
17. What is meant by *booting software?*
18. What is an on-line help feature?
19. Describe the steps you might take in selecting microcomputer software and hardware?
20. List sources of information about software that the manager can use to help in selecting the right software.
21. What does a dynamic data exchange feature provide?
22. What is RAM resident software?
23. What are four types of fourth-generation languages?
24. What is a site-licensing agreement?
25. Explain what canned software is.
26. What does GUI mean? What advantages does GUI provide to the manager?
27. What is portability? What are the advantages of application program portability to the manager?

28. What is a menu? A prompt?

29. What is data linking?

30. What are some characteristics of software vendors you should look for?

Questions for Discussion

1. How is a resident program different from a transient program?

2. How do systems programmers differ from application programmers? In what ways are they alike?

3. What is the difference between multiprogramming and multiprocessing operating systems?

4. What is an application program? How does an application program differ from an operating system?

5. Compare command-line, windowing, and GUI operating environments.

6. Explain the difference between horizontally compatible and vertically compatible software. What advantages might each type of software offer a manager?

7. Compare the advantages and disadvantages of stand-alone, compatible, and integrated software programs.

8. What is meant by *user-friendly software?* What are some features that make software user-friendly?

9. Explain why communications software is considered an extension to the operating system of a computer.

10. What are five general trends in software development today? What implications do these trends have for managers?

Problems

1. Crown Clinic, Ltd. Rob Seavers is an assistant consultant at B & L Associates, a computer consulting firm in Ontario, Canada. The firm is helping Crown Clinic, Ltd., a physical fitness chain, develop information systems. Rob has been asked by his firm to identify sources of commercial software that might contain information useful in the consulting project. What sources of information about software would you suggest?

2. Riggens, Inc. Gwen Bradshaw is an office manager at Riggens, Inc., a marketing research firm. She is considering purchasing a desktop publishing software package to create final reports to clients. Her assistant, Jim Bernstein, has just read a review of 10 desktop publishing packages in *Tech Magazine,* a computer journal. He recommends that Bradshaw purchase the Publishing Company, one of the packages reviewed, because the magazine gave that package the highest rating among all 10 packages. What advice would you give Bradshaw?

3. Bascom and Associates (a). You are a consultant for Bascom and Associates, a managerial consulting firm. You use the following software on your microcomputer: operating system kernel, 70 KB; operating system utilities, 88 KB; a mouse program, 42 KB; and a family of compatible application software. The application software includes a spreadsheet that requires a minimum of 192 KB, a word processor that requires a minimum of 178 KB, a file manager requiring a minimum of 56 KB, and a graphics package requiring a minimum of 148 KB. You also require a minimum of 125 KB to handle portions of your largest data file.

a. What is the minimum amount of RAM you would need, stated in KB, for your microcomputer if you wished to use only one of the compatible application software program at a time?
b. What is the minimum amount of secondary storage space you would need in KB if you wished to have all software available on a disk drive?
c. What type of secondary storage would you recommend for the microcomputer and why?

4. **Bascom and Associates (b).** Another consultant at Bascom and Associates wishes to run a presentation graphics package on her MS-DOS computer system. This computer system provides 640 KB of RAM. The operating system kernel for the system takes 82 KB of RAM. The mouse program takes 44 KB of RAM. A virus protection program takes 36 KB of RAM. Two other system utility programs that must reside in RAM take 42 KB and 28 KB. The presentation graphics package requires 510 KB of RAM and a mouse to run.

   a. Does she have enough RAM for her needs?
   b. What is this condition called?
   c. What are her options if she must run the presentation graphics package and cannot switch or purchase a new computer system?

5. **SuperNet Sports Shop.** The SuperNet Sports Shop has decided that it needs to computerize its office functions, including the preparation, storage, editing, sorting, and printing of documents, budgets, and records. Irene Trevon, the owner, is thinking about purchasing a minicomputer and the following software: WordPrep (a word processor) from DocuPrep, Inc., Multisheet (a spreadsheet package) from HiTech, Inc., and FileRite (a file management package) from FastData, Inc. You are a new employee of SuperNet Sports Shop and the only one with any information systems experience. Irene has asked you to review her pending purchases and make suggestions.

   a. What problems might occur if Irene acquires the programs she is considering?
   b. What criteria for operating system software and for application programs should Irene consider?
   c. What hardware features and components should be considered?

6. **TriTown Furniture Distributors, Inc.** Claude Ramsey is the owner of a small furniture distribution firm. He is considering purchasing a word processing software package for the firm's microcomputer systems to enable him to computerize document preparation, such as form letters, reports, and memos. He is trying to decide between purchasing Quicktype, a simple word processing program, and Secretariat, a complex word processing program.

   What questions would you ask of Claude to help him decide?

7. **Klines, Inc.** Jill Brown manages a team of five people in the advertising department of Klines, Inc., who are developing an advertising program for a new product. What types of application software, described in Chapter 5, might Jill consider to help her and her team in their work? For each type of software you select, briefly describe how the software might be useful.

8. **Microcomputer Utility Programs.** Prepare a report on microcomputer utility programs. The report should include a list of 20 utility programs and a brief description of 10 of these programs. Each description should identify the program's purpose, price, and features. You might start by obtaining issues of microcomputer magazines such as *Byte, PC Magazine, MacUser,* or *Info World.* Examine the advertisements in microcomputer magazines that list and categorize the software offered for sale under "utilities" to develop a list of microcomputer utility programs. Then use microcomputer magazines to find articles describing the utility programs. You might also use a computer database such as *Computer Select* and use "utility programs" as the initial key word search for the database.

Cases

1. **Kriege Construction Company.** Kriege Construction Company (KCC) builds office and retail buildings in a two-province area in Western Canada. KCC is considering automating its procedures for preparing bids for building jobs in response to customer requests for building proposals. The management of KCC has had little first-hand experience with computer systems. They use no computer systems currently, except for some IBM microcomputers that run word processing programs for the company secretaries. As a result, they contacted an information systems consulting firm that is partly owned by a friend of Mr. Kriege, the founder of KCC. The consulting firm, Reade & Owens, dispatched Tom Kaline, a systems analyst, to KCC. After spending some time talking with the management of KCC, examining the forms and procedures used in preparing bids, and learning the algorithms used in computing costs and charges, Kaline developed a list of specific application requirements that were needed for the bidding system. He suggested further that his consulting firm would develop a bid proposal system using Insite, a database management system that his firm has used often for such purposes. Insite runs on Macintosh microcomputer systems. Kaline said both the Macintosh and Insite are very easy to learn to use, and should be just right for managers who have had little experience with computer systems. He felt that his firm could develop the information system in about two months and would like to get started right away on it.

   a. If you were advising KCC, would you let Kaline get started?
   b. What steps might Kaline have taken prior to recommending the Insite software that he didn't?
   c. What problems might result if KCC gives the go-ahead to Kaline's recommendations?

2. **Bradford Lumber Products Corporation.** The Management Information Systems (MIS) Department of Bradford Lumber has been asked by the Human Resource Management (HRM) Department of the corporation to develop an information system to keep track of its employee evaluation program. Bradford Lumber employs over 2,000 people, and the HRM Department needs to insure that each employee is evaluated at the right time, that the people who should be involved in the evaluation are included, and that the information pertaining to the evaluation results is distributed to those who need it and stored for future use. However, Rita Verano, who heads the MIS Department, has responded negatively to Jack Delaney, who heads the HRM Department, about the HRM request. Rita has told Jack that she doesn't think that MIS has enough resources to do the job. She tells Jack that her staff is bogged down developing two major applications for other departments. She feels that she won't be able to get to Jack's application for

probably 18 to 24 months. Furthermore, she tells Jack that developing the system he wants will take many more months of programming and testing. The MIS Department develops all company applications in-house using COBOL, a procedural language.

Jack, of course, is very upset. Recent government rulings and legislation have required a number of reports regarding employee evaluation. He needs the employee evaluation system developed soon so that a variety of laws pertaining to the process are not violated. He is concerned that the company will become vulnerable to legal action if a suitable system is not developed shortly. However, Jack is not the only one at Bradford Lumber who is complaining. Many department personnel are becoming increasingly annoyed at the time it takes the MIS department to address their information systems concerns.

How might Rita speed up the development of applications at Bradford Lumber so that she might address Jack's application and the application needs of other departments sooner and complete them faster, without adding additional, full-time staff?

3. **Manfred Detweiler, Inc.** You are a consultant for Manfred Detweiler, Inc., a small consulting firm. You are assigned to manage and complete projects with client firms in a geographic region. To manage and complete these projects, you often must prepare, or have prepared, project reports, project budgets, and both written and oral presentations to clients regarding the nature and progress of each project. Frequently you have to manage a number of projects at the same time. In addition, you are expected to develop business for the consulting firm by developing new clients, maintaining contact with your old clients, and identifying the problems these clients face. To help you with your work you are assisted by a full-time secretary.

   Develop a report to be submitted to your superior, Mr. Detweiler, for the use of microcomputer systems to improve the operational, tactical, and strategic activities in your office. Your report should include at least these elements:

   a. Identify the applications in this case that you believe should be considered for computerization.
   b. For each application specified in the previous question, identify categories or types of software that would be appropriate to the applications in your office.
   c. Following the steps for selecting software described in the chapter, identify by brand name one commercial software program that would be appropriate to each of the applications you specified for each computer workstation you are recommending. Using magazine ads, specify the approximate cost for each software program. Make certain that each application program will run on the systems software you select in response to the following question.
   d. Using computer magazines, select microcomputers and systems software for the consultant's workstation and the secretary's workstation. Specify the component parts of each microcomputer and also specify the peripherals for the computer systems you are recommending for the workstations. Include estimated prices, taken from the magazine ads, for each component and peripheral for each workstation. Make certain that the software programs you recommended earlier in these case questions will run on the computer systems and the system software you select here.
   e. Append to your report a list of your sources.

4. **Tel-West, Inc.** You are the owner of Tel-West, Inc., a small metals fabricating firm that has made the decision to automate its accounting and production activities. Tel-West had no one on its staff with computer expertise, so you have just hired Carla Wong, who was a system programmer for Canton Fabrics, Inc., in a nearby town. After being on the staff for a week, she comes into your office and is very upbeat. She has just learned that Maray Products Corporation, a wholesale distributor of hunting and fishing equipment, is upgrading its computer system and will be disposing of its old system, an Infotex 1000 mainframe computer. The system is equipped with multiple hard drives, proprietary systems software, several terminals, a tape drive for archiving purposes, and a high-speed printer. Carla feels that she probably can obtain this computer system very inexpensively, and the system should be more than adequate for whatever applications Tel-West may develop. She strongly recommends that Tel-West make a bid for the computer system so that she can get going developing applications for the company.

   a. What problems might you have with her recommendation?
   b. How might she have proceeded to obtain a computer system?
   c. (Optional) Prepare your report for this case using the word processing software available in your college or workplace.

Selected References and Readings

Applied Computer Research. *Computer Literature Index.* A monthly index of computer publications, including those covering mainframe, minicomputer, and microcomputer software.

Bender, Eric. "Desktop Multimedia: You Ain't Seen Nothing Yet." *PC World* 8, no. 3 (March 1990), pp. 191–96. Discusses hardware and software needed for multimedia and presents examples of systems.

Blodgett, Ralph. "Memory Management 101." *Windows Magazine* 5, no. 5 (May 1993), pp. 120–28. A detailed description of memory in a PC and how to manage RAM cram.

Canter, Sheryl. "Statistical Analysis: State of the Art." *PC Magazine* 12, no. 9 (May 11, 1993), pp. 227–30 ff. A review of 14 statistical packages for the PC.

Claiborne, David. "Personal Information Managers," *Windows Magazine* 4, no. 7 (July 1993), pp. 150 ff. A review of five PIMs.

Datapro Corporation. *Datapro Reports.* A series of reports pertaining to computer systems topics, including mainframe, minicomputer, and microcomputer software.

DeVoney, Chris. "Multimedia Authoring Tools." *Windows Sources* 1, no. 5 (June 1993), pp. 360 ff. A major part of this issue of the magazine is devoted to articles on multimedia systems.

Dyson, Esther. "Why Groupware Is Gaining Ground." *Datamation* 36, no. 15 (March 1, 1990), pp. 52–56. A description of the applications for which groupware is useful.

Ezzell, Ben. "Windows NT: The Power Under the Hood." *PC Magazine* 12, no. 11 (June 15, 1993), pp. 173–74 ff. A review of Windows NT. The same issue also reviews OS/2, Unix, and NextStep operating systems.

Goodman, John M. *Memory Management for All of Us.* Carmel, IN: SAMS, a division of Prentice Hall Computer Publishing, 1992. Covers memory and memory management.

Grunin, Lori. "Top Desktop Publishers Go Head to Head." *Windows Sources* 1, no. 6 (July 1993), pp. 207–09 ff. A review of FrameMaker, QuarkXPress, and Ventura Publisher.

Harrel, William. "The Write Choice." *Windows Magazine* 4, no. 7 (July, 1993), pp. 200–201 ff. A review of the major word processors.

Hsu, Jeffrey. "A New Way to Manage and Organize Information." *PC Today* 7, no. 3 (March 1993), pp. 46–49. An overview of hypertext and hypermedia.

Littman, Jonathan. "Shopping for Success." *Corporate Computing* 2, no. 2 (February 1993), pp. 148–54 ff. A discussion of the best ways to buy software.

Randall, Neil. "PIMS Can Change Your Life." *Windows Magazine* 5, no. 5 (May 1993), pp. 286–288 ff. A review of current PIM software.

Remington, Marti. "Buying Software by the Bundle." *PC Today* 7, no. 6 (June 1993), pp. 22–25. A general discussion of bundled and compatible software and their advantages to users and a review of Microsoft Office, Lotus Smartsuite, and CA-Simply Business.

Ricciuti, Mike. "Build Custom Apps at Packaged Prices." *Datamation* 39, no. 11 (June 1, 1993), pp. 71–72. A brief description of the use of CASE tools for IBM's minicomputer series, the AS/400.

Simon, Barry. "Painless Programming." *Windows Sources* 1, no. 6 (July 1993), pp. 305–308 ff. A review of three new visual application development environments, including Visual Basic.

Stevenson, Ted. "The New Synergists." *PC Magazine* 11, no. 15 (September 1992), pp. 311–313 ff. Reviews eight low-cost integrated software packages.

Stetson, Christopher. "GUIs Vie for Best of the Breed." *Windows Magazine* 4, no. 3 (March 1993), pp. 106–112 ff. A review and comparison of Windows, OS/2, NeXTStep, and the X Windows variants (OpenLook, Motif, and DESQView/X) graphical user interfaces.

"Windows NT." *InfoWorld Supplement.* 15, no. 21 (May 24, 1993), pp. S75–S100. A series of articles comparing Windows NT with other leading 32-bit operating systems, such as OS/2, and a variety of Unix versions.

FILE AND DATABASE MANAGEMENT SYSTEMS

CHAPTER OUTLINE

MANAGER'S VIEW

One way to improve managerial decision making is to provide managers with the right information at the right time. Information relevant to the decisions managers must make is essential. They need to know where useful information is stored, how to access it, and how to use it in their decision making.

Much of the information that managers use is stored in a series of computer files or in computerized databases. As a manager, you may use computerized data to complete day-to-day operational tasks, such as using payroll files to prepare the weekly payroll and produce payroll checks. You may use the files to decide if you are allocating your resources appropriately, such as monitoring a sales transaction file for salesperson performance. You may also use the files to assist in long-range planning, such as using the financial accounting files of the organization to identify divisions with high and low profitability. Regardless of the level of management activity for which you are using the information, knowledge of basic file and database concepts improves your ability to locate, access, and use the information available to you for the decisions you must make.

You have learned that data can be stored on many media, such as magnetic tapes, magnetic hard disks, magnetic floppy diskettes, flash memory cards, optical storage media, computer output microfilm, and, of course, paper media such as forms, letters, and reports. There are many advantages to storing data on magnetic instead of paper media. For example, data stored on magnetic media can be stored compactly and easily, and the computer system can edit and check the data more efficiently than people can do so in a manual filing system.

However, the main reason computerized files are so important to the manager is that data in magnetic files can be found and manipulated quickly and easily. Can you imagine searching through 2,000 file folders in an employee file to find those employees who have worked for the firm for more than 10 years? That type of search can be completed in seconds if the data are stored magnetically and searched by a computer program. This is why computer files and databases have changed the decision-making environment for managers. They simply make much more data available at the right time to assist managers in making their decisions.

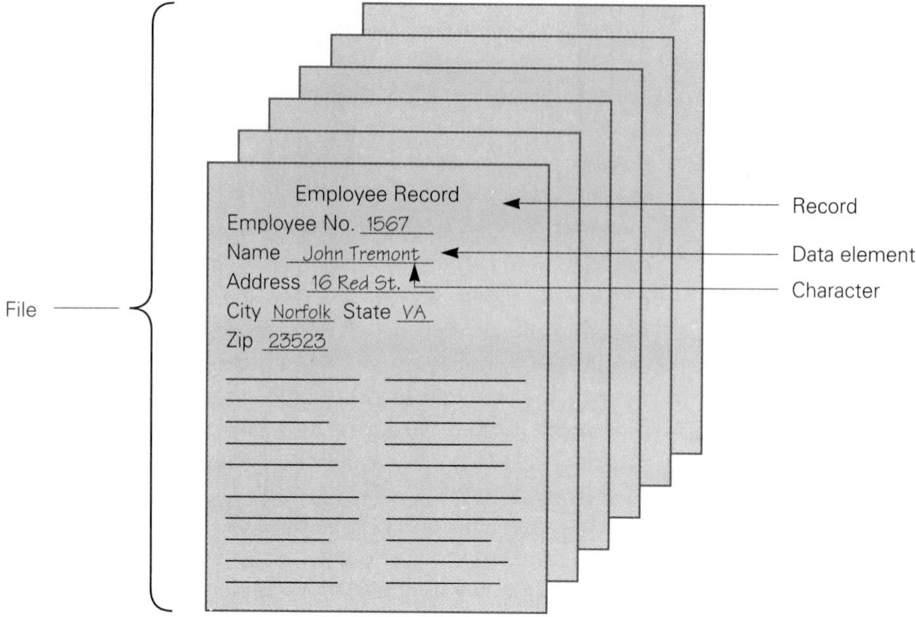

Figure 6–1
Building blocks of a paper-based, manual filing system

FILE CONCEPTS

Data stored in paper-based, manual filing systems are organized into characters, data elements, records, and files (see Figure 6–1). Data stored in a computer-based, electronic filing system are usually stored in their most elementary form: binary digits, or bits. These bits are then organized into characters (or bytes), the bytes into data elements, the data elements into records, and the records into files (see Figure 6–2).

A **data element,** or **field,** is a logical collection of characters. For example, the data element for an employee's last or family name is a collection of characters that make up that name.

A **record** is a collection of logically grouped data elements. For instance, an employee record might contain these data elements: employee number, last or family name, first or given name, middle initial, street address, city, state, ZIP or postal code, date hired, department, job title, and hourly rate of pay (see Figure 6–3). A record is usually a collection of data elements describing an *entity.* For example, last or family name is an attribute of the entity employee.

A **file** is a collection of records of one type. For instance, a set of employee records for a firm is usually called the *employee file.*

In computer files, each type of record and its associated data elements have a definite structure. That is, there is an agreed-upon set of data elements for each record type, and a sequence for those data elements. For example, in the employee record shown in Figure 6–3, it was agreed that the data element employee number would be the first data element.

There is also an agreed-upon set of characteristics for data to be entered into any data element. Two commonly used characteristics of a data element are the maximum number of characters and whether the data to be entered are alphabetic or numeric. Notice in Figure 6–3 that the data element state may not exceed two characters in length. This data element is also restricted to alphabetic characters since no other type of character is required.

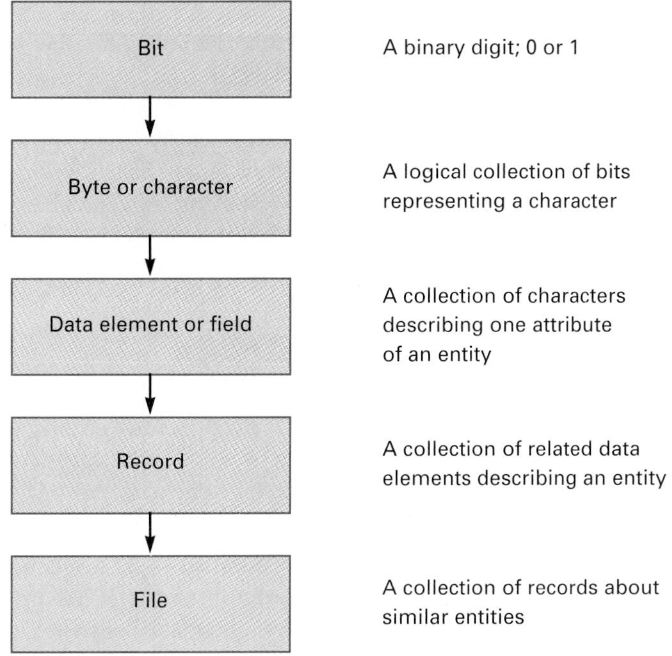
Bit
A binary digit; 0 or 1
Byte or character
A logical collection of bits representing a character
Data element or field
A collection of characters describing one attribute of an entity
Record
A collection of related data elements describing an entity
File
A collection of records about similar entities

Figure 6–2 Building blocks of a computer-based, electronic file system

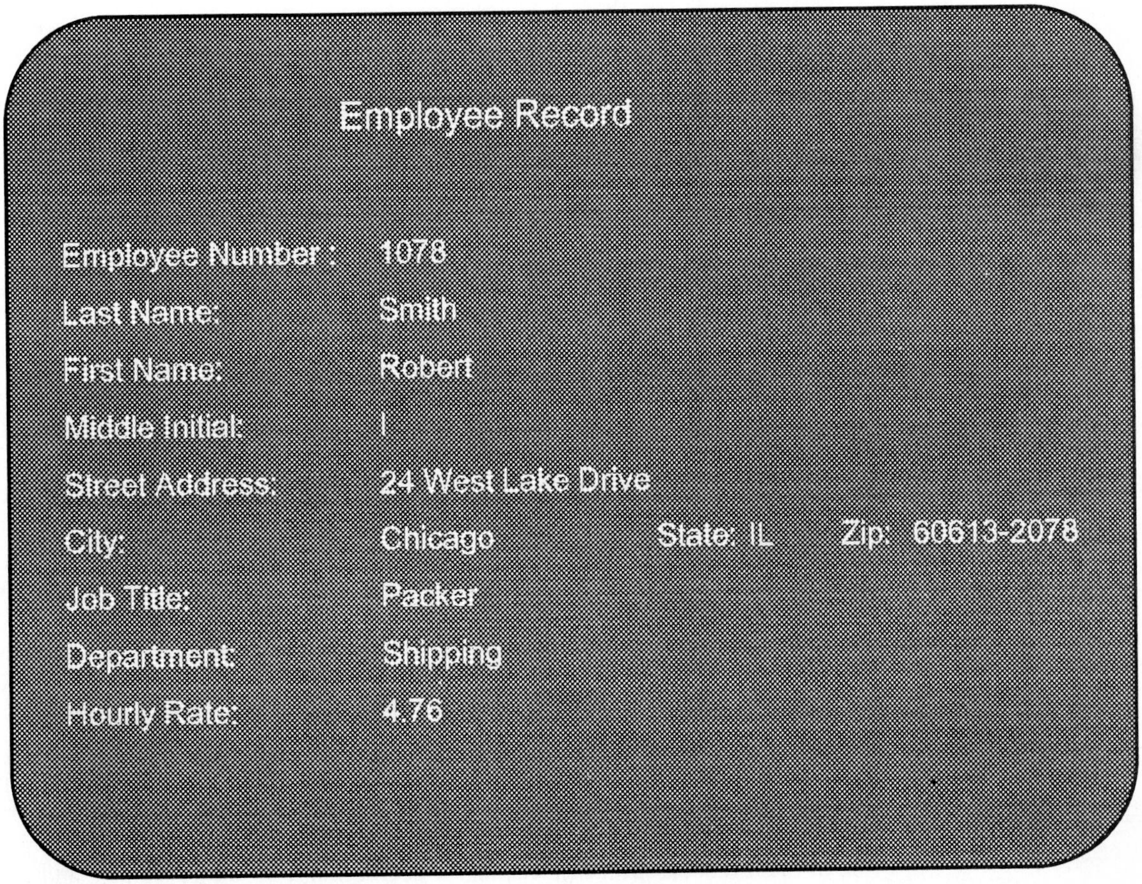

Employee Record

Employee Number:	1078		
Last Name:	Smith		
First Name:	Robert		
Middle Initial:	I		
Street Address:	24 West Lake Drive		
City:	Chicago	State: IL	Zip: 60613-2078
Job Title:	Packer		
Department:	Shipping		
Hourly Rate:	4.76		

Figure 6–3 A display screen showing part of an employee record

In a computer file, each record usually must have a **primary key.** A primary key is a field that is a unique identifier for the record that allows it to be stored and retrieved. For the employee record in Figure 6–3, the data element employee number (1078) was chosen as the primary key. You might wonder why the employee's last or family name (Smith) was not chosen as the primary key. Because there might be many employees with the last or family name *Smith,* this data element would not uniquely identify each employee. The employee number was chosen as the primary key because each employee is given a different number. That way, when you ask a file management system to find the record with a primary key of 1078, you will get only that record.

FILE STRUCTURES

The way you choose to store records on magnetic media is called the *file structure.* Employee records may be stored on magnetic media using several file structures.

Sequential File Structure

One way to store the employee records is *sequentially* by the primary key—in our example, the employee number—on magnetic tape. With **sequential access,** the computer system retrieves an employee record with the employee number 1567 by scanning all the records sequentially between the employee with the first record, 0001, and record 1567. If you were a manager in the personnel department and needed to examine individual employee records throughout the day as various employees visited you for advice, this would not prove to be a very efficient way to store employee records. With more than 1,500 records, you and the employee might fall asleep before the system retrieved the employee's record.

However, sequential access can be fast and inexpensive for storing files that are used only for batch processing operations (see Chapter 4). For example, if a payroll file is only used to produce paychecks in batch processing mode, sequential processing may be satisfactory. Unfortunately, few of an organization's files are used *only* in batch processing operations. After all, employees also visit the payroll office with questions and problems with their paychecks.

Direct File Structure

Another way to store the records is to store them *randomly*—that is, not in any sequential order by primary key. To store records in this way requires that the medium used allows the **direct access** of records. This usually means choosing optical disk, magnetic disk, or floppy diskette as the storage medium. It also means that each record must be given a specific disk address so it can be found directly. One way to specify a disk address for records in a direct access file is to apply a *hashing algorithm* to the primary key. The algorithm might be simply using the last two digits in employee social security numbers for a firm of 80 employees. Or the algorithm might be more complex, such as dividing the primary key by another number. In any event, the result of the algorithm is used as the disk address for the record. By using a hashing algorithm and storing the data on a direct access medium, the computer system is able to retrieve the record with employee number 1567 directly, without having to scan records 0001 through 1566 first and without having you and the employee nod off.

One disadvantage of using hashing for file storage is that several record numbers may generate the same address. When this happens, two or more records may compete for the same storage space on disk. Several methods of handling this problem exist, but all of them require special processing, which may slow down the storage and retrieval of records.

INDEX	
PRIMARY KEY	DISK ADDRESS
3548	845528
3549	853658
3550	861788
3551	869918
3553	886178
3554	894308
3557	918699
3558	926829
3559	934959
3560	943089
3561	951219
3565	983739

Figure 6–4
An index of a file of records organized sequentially—the index allows each record to be accessed directly

Indexed Sequential File Structure

A third way to store records is sequentially on a direct access medium, such as a hard disk with a specific disk address for each record (or in some systems, every block of records). An **index** is then prepared showing the disk address of each record or block of records (see Figure 6–4). This method is called the **indexed sequential access** method, or **ISAM,** and permits both sequential and direct access of records in a file.

The neat thing about storing records in an ISAM format is that you can access these records in more than one way. You can access the records sequentially by starting at the beginning of the file and moving through it one record at a time to find the needed records. For example, if you were doing a sequential search for the record with a primary key of 3559 in the index shown in Figure 6–4, the system would start at the record with the primary key of 3548 and read each record in order until it reached the correct one. However, the system can also access any record directly if you ask for a specific record. In this case, the file management system looks up the record you have asked for in the index, finds the disk address of the block of records where the record is located, and goes directly to that block of records to capture the record for you. In our example, the file management system would look up record 3559 in the index, find that it is located in a block of records starting at disk address 934959, and search only that block of records to find that record.

Another advantage to ISAM files is that more than one index can be created. The records in Figure 6–4 are indexed by the primary key, which might be student number, stock number, customer number, or the like. However, records can be indexed on any field. For example, you might wish to build an index of your records based on the ZIP code field so that you can prepare mass mailings quickly and easily. These other indexes would be called *secondary indexes* and the fields that are indexed would be called *secondary keys.*

On the downside, ISAM files require maintenance of the indexes and records. That is, when records are added, the records must be resorted to restore them to sequential order. Then, the indexes must be updated. These tasks require time and computer system resources.

Accessing Records

The methods you use to store records in a computer file—sequential, direct, and indexed sequential—affect the way you can access those records. Ordinarily, you are interested in accessing records to complete these types of operations:

1. Adding new records to a file.
2. Deleting records from a file.

3. Modifying records in a file.
4. Viewing records from a file on a screen.
5. Creating reports from records in a file.

Suppose that you are a personnel manager and you want to be able to view and modify an employee's record while you confer with the employee. Clearly, a sequential file structure would not be an effective choice because it would require you to arrange your interviews in sequential order by employee number. If you did this, you would still have to wait for the computer system to scan the file sequentially until it locates the record you want, but at least you wouldn't have to start at the beginning of the file for each employee.

Either a direct or an indexed sequential storage method would provide faster record access. If you used a direct storage method, the file program might apply a hashing algorithm to the primary key of the record whose disk address you want to find. The computer system would then go directly to that disk address and display the record on the screen. If you used an indexed sequential storage method, the computer system would consult an index to find the disk address of the record you want, and then go directly to that record without scanning other records.

You should know that indexes also can be used to improve the retrieval of records stored directly. Thus, when records are stored directly using a hashing algorithm the records are stored on a primary key basis. You may wish to build indexes of these records on one or more secondary keys. For example, you may wish to build indexes for several fields in an employee file other than the primary key, employee number. You may wish to build an index using the field *job title*, so that you can list the employees with the same job title quickly or the field *shift*, to retrieve the names of those employees who are working on the day and night shifts easily.

Another advantage of indexes is that they are usually much, much smaller than the actual data files themselves. Therefore, they may be able to be read into main memory in their entirety. This means that searching for the record address can be done at main memory speeds instead of secondary storage speeds.

Sometimes access to records is not based on indexes. Instead, a pointer is imbedded in each record that points to the next record with the same value in a field. In this system, an employee record containing the value "night" in the shift field would also contain a pointer to the next record with the same value in the shift field. When you ask for a list of employees on the night shift, the program finds one record with that value and uses the pointer in that record to find the next record, and so on, until it builds a list of all records with "night" in the shift field. Thus, a list is built by linking each record with the value "night" in the shift field to the other records. This method for retrieving records is called *linked lists.*

File Structures in On-Line, Real-Time Processing

Operations 1 through 4 listed above can be completed directly with either the indexed sequential structure or the direct structure. That is, you can go to the record you want directly and view it, delete it, or modify it immediately. As you learned in Chapter 4, this type of processing is called on-line, real-time processing because any processing occurs immediately. This type of processing is also usually **interactive** as well. For example, if you make an error while modifying the employee record, the computer system will display an *error message* on your terminal. You could then correct your error immediately. Such processing is called *interactive* because you are interacting with the computer system while you are processing the record.

File Structures in Batch Processing

If you do not need to process employee records immediately, then a sequential access file structure might be appropriate. Suppose that you can accumulate a batch of requests for additions, deletions, and modifications to employee records. These requests can then be sorted by employee number and processed in a batch.

Thus, records stored on a sequential medium, such as tape, are *batch processed.* Any other processing using this medium is simply too inefficient. For the manager, this means that use of sequential storage media, such as magnetic tape, precludes the on-line, real-time processing of records. If you were a personnel manager and needed to view individual employee records directly, as opposed to sequentially, the use of magnetic tape for personnel files would not be appropriate for your decision needs. You would need to utilize a storage medium that permits direct access to records (such as hard disk or floppy diskette) and use a filing program that stores records either in a direct access or indexed sequential file structure.

FILE MANAGEMENT SOFTWARE

Many computer files are managed by programs developed in-house. That is, programs to store and process records in a single file—**file management software**—were written by the staff of the management information systems department using COBOL, FORTRAN, or some other computer language. Ready-made file management software may also be purchased from commercial software houses.

Commercially Prepared File Management Software

Simple files can be managed by commercially prepared file management software packages. These packages let end users create a record format on the computer screen, enter data using the record format, and then search, sort, and prepare reports using the records you have created. For example, a file management software package might present you with the menu shown in Figure 6–5.

Creating an equipment file with this software package is very easy. Just move your mouse arrow to the word FILE in the menu bar at the top of the screen and click the left mouse button. This would be called "selecting" FILE. Selecting FILE means that you point and click on the word FILE. When you do, a drop-down menu appears. Now select NEW from the drop-down menu. When you do, the screen clears. Now you only have to type the equipment form, which might look like the one shown in Figure 6–6. When you are done typing the form, you select FILE again and then SAVE to save the file. When you select SAVE, the program will ask you to give the file a name. You name the file EQUIPINV. After you save the form, it can be used for data entry. Each time you want to add an equipment item, you select FILE, then OPEN, and then type in the name of the file, EQUIPINV. When you do, a blank equipment form just like the one you created is displayed on your screen, and you can enter the data for a new record into the form.

After all the equipment records are entered, you can create reports quickly and easily by selecting REPORTS from the menu bar at the top of the screen. For example, suppose you wish to create a report that lists the cost and type of equipment purchased from the vendor Rogers Co. during 1994, by date. The software might display a blank equipment form and you would indicate which data elements you want and in what order you want them on the report. You would do this by merely entering 1 in the date field, 2 in the equipment type field, and 3 in the cost field. Now the program knows that it is to produce a three-column report using the date, equipment type, and cost fields from the records.

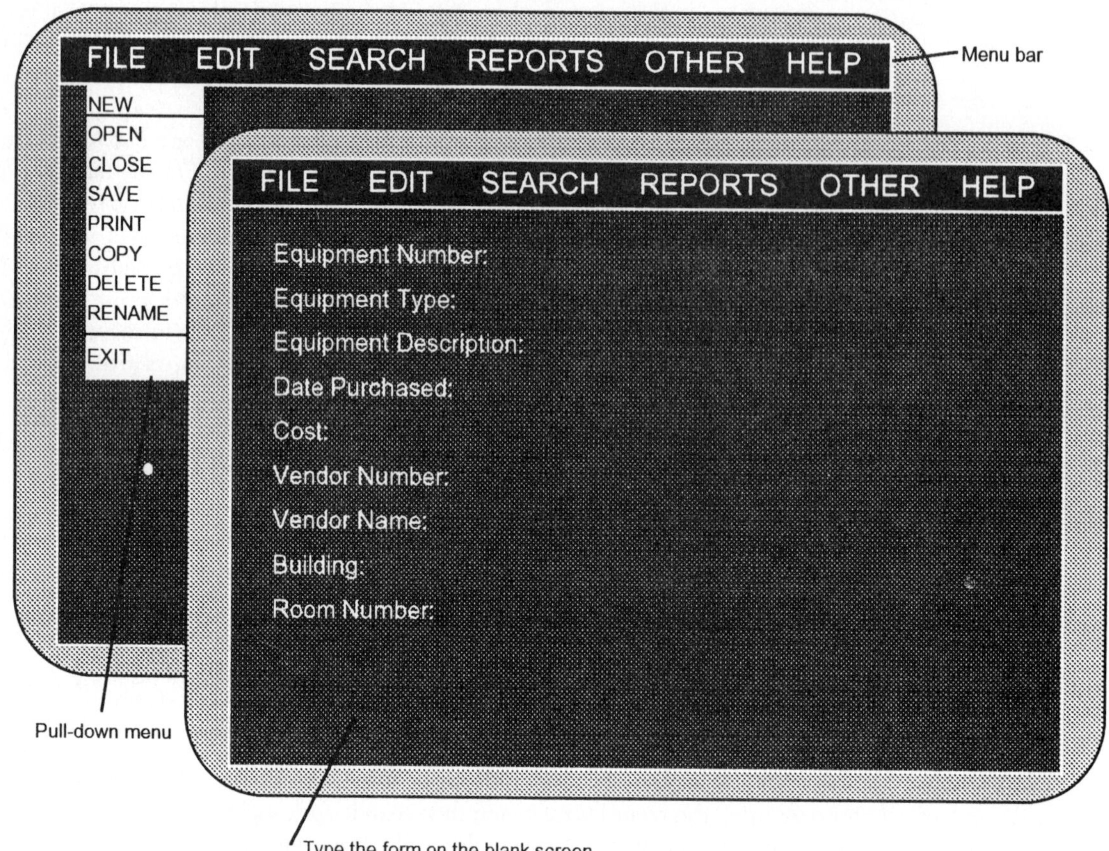

Figure 6–5
Creating an equipment file using a file management program

Next the program might display the blank form again and ask you to identify which records you wish to include in the report. You would merely enter "Rogers Company" into the vendor name field, and "**/ **/ 94" in the date purchased field. The asterisks are called wild cards and they tell the program that you will accept any numbers in the month and day portions of the date, but only 94 in the year portion. The program might then ask you for a title of the report and if you wish any computations by field to be performed. You would then direct the program to count the number of records reported and sum the cost field. The completed report might look like the one in Figure 6–7. The report may not be very fancy, but it does give you what you need to know immediately. In other words, you can ask questions of your files and get timely answers.

The part of the file management software that prepares reports is usually called a **report writer.** Some report writers provide elementary arithmetic functions, such as finding sums, counting, finding averages, finding the lowest amount, and finding the highest amount. Some report writers also provide some statistical functions, such as cross tabs and regression.

The file management software may also contain a graphics program to let you produce a line, bar, pie, or other graph of your data. For example, you may use the software to produce a three-dimensional pie graph showing the percentage of total facsimile machine expenditures by vendor (see Figure 6–8).

Searching the Files

Commercial file management software is available for all computer platforms. Many of these packages use an indexed sequential access method for their file structure. That is, they store records sequentially by the primary key, but allow direct access to any record

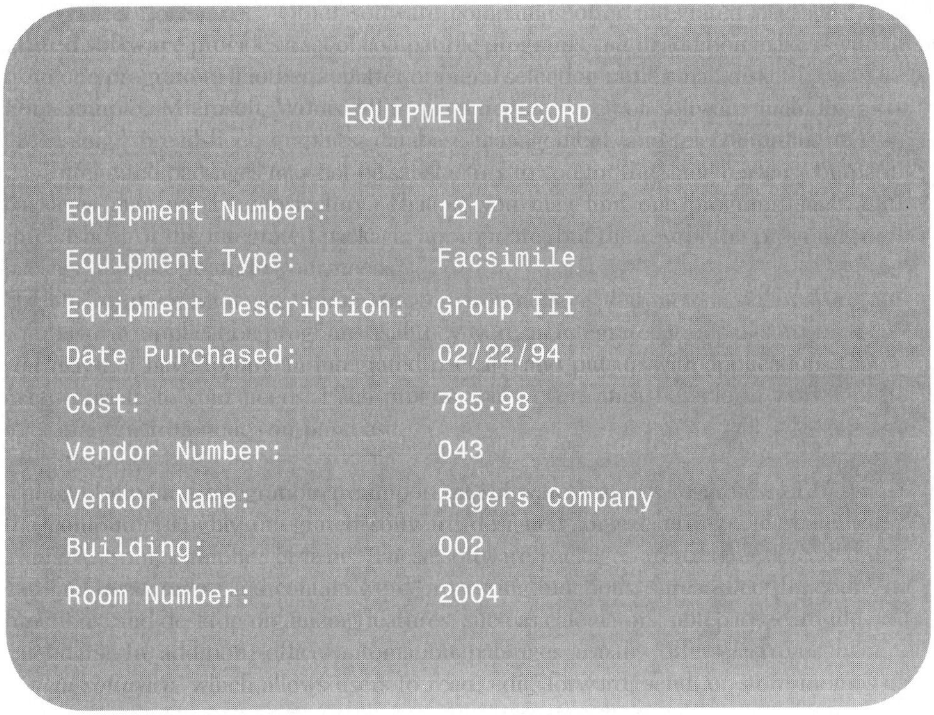

```
EQUIPMENT RECORD

Equipment Number:        1217
Equipment Type:          Facsimile
Equipment Description:   Group III
Date Purchased:          02/22/94
Cost:                    785.98
Vendor Number:           043
Vendor Name:             Rogers Company
Building:                002
Room Number:             2004
```

Figure 6–6
Equipment record

because they maintain an index of the location of each record. The primary key for the equipment record shown in Figure 6–6 would probably be the field *equipment number*, because this value would be unique to each equipment item. The equipment records would probably be stored sequentially using the primary key. However, you are not often likely to ask for information based on equipment number. So you would probably choose several other fields as secondary keys. **Secondary keys** are used for those fields on which you wish to search or sort the records. For example, you may wish to select the location fields *building* and *room number* as secondary keys so that you can list all equipment located in a given room or building.

When you select a field as a secondary key, the file management program constructs an index for the values in that field. If you choose the field *building* as a secondary key, the program develops a table listing the buildings in numerical order. Next to each building, it lists the disk addresses of each piece of equipment in that building. When you ask the software to produce a list of equipment in a given building, it reads the index to locate the building. It will then be able to find each item of equipment on disk without having to read each equipment record sequentially. Searching for records or printing reports is much faster when records can be found by using the index rather than by searching every record in a file.

File management software usually gives you the ability to search and find one or more records in the file. In our example, if you wished to find a particular record or group of records and display them on a screen, you would select the word, SEARCH, from the menu bar (see Figure 6–5). The software would then display the equipment form again. You would direct the software to find those records that fit your search parameters. **Search parameters** are those values or value ranges in one or more fields that you wish to use to select records. You could enter in the equipment number field a specific number or a range of numbers, and the software would then display that record or the first record in the group of records. For example, you could ask the

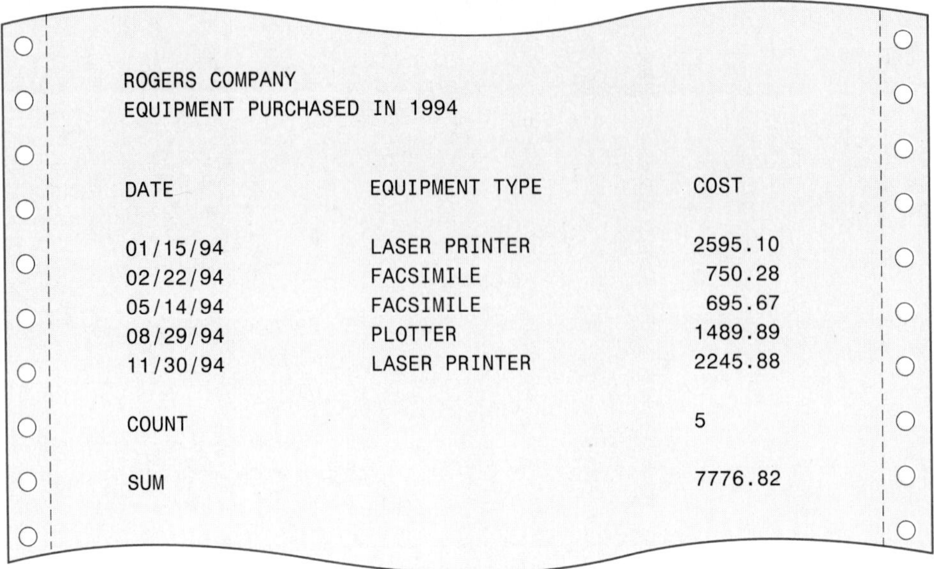

ROGERS COMPANY
EQUIPMENT PURCHASED IN 1994

DATE	EQUIPMENT TYPE	COST
01/15/94	LASER PRINTER	2595.10
02/22/94	FACSIMILE	750.28
05/14/94	FACSIMILE	695.67
08/29/94	PLOTTER	1489.89
11/30/94	LASER PRINTER	2245.88
COUNT		5
SUM		7776.82

Figure 6–7
A report created by a report writer of a file management software package

program to find the record for item 1217, and the record in Figure 6–5 would be displayed. You would do this by merely typing "1217" in the equipment number field.

You might also ask the program to find all those equipment items with numbers between 1000 and 2000 by entering "1000 > < 2000" in the equipment number field. You also might ask for only those equipment items that are facsimile machines purchased after February 1, 1994, by typing in "facsimile" in the description field and "02/01/94> " in the date purchased field. Most file programs allow you to select several search parameters, including the use of wild cards, in a single search of the file.

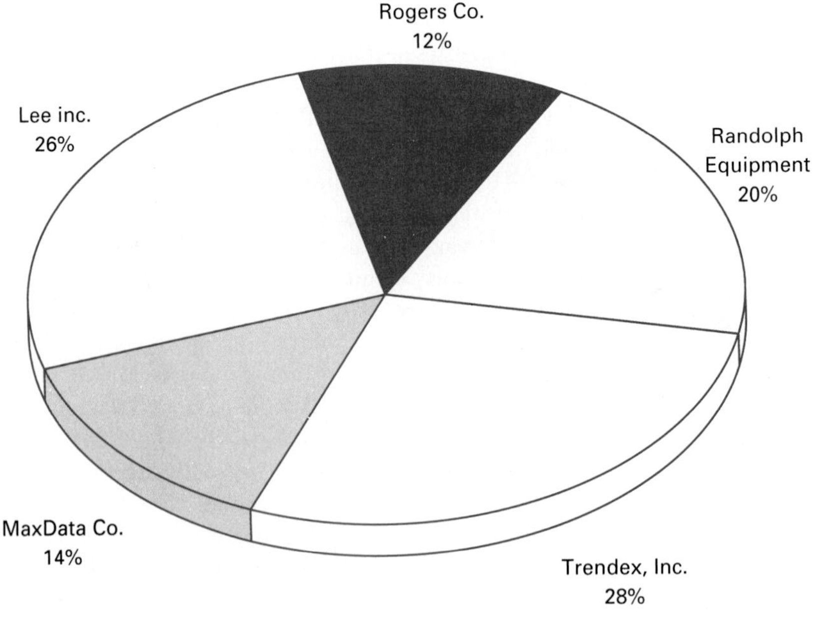

Figure 6–8
A three-dimensional pie chart prepared by the graphics program of a file management software package

File Management Programs Developed In-House

Commercially developed file management programs are usually acquired for standard applications commonly found in organizations. However, sometimes your application is not exactly standard and you may not be able to find a commercial package that will fully satisfy your needs. If you want a program developed in-house to meet specific needs, a series of steps typically follows (these steps are described in detail in Chapters 16, 17, and 18). You'll contact the management information systems (MIS) department, where an analyst will determine the exact nature of the reports you want and the data required for them. The MIS department will write a program to produce the reports, debug it, and then implement it. Because of the backlog of work facing most management information systems departments, this process may take many months. Commercial software, on the other hand, can often be acquired and implemented in a very short period of time. A second advantage is that the software may cost less to acquire than to develop in-house because the costs of developing the software are spread across many buyers. Another advantage is that the software has usually undergone extensive testing and use in the market place and is less likely to contain errors.

In some cases, the MIS department may wish to modify a commercial software package to fit your needs. This approach can save lots of time and money and still provide you with a program that fits your needs.

DATABASE CONCEPTS

Whereas a file is a collection of related records, a **database** is a collection of related files (see Figure 6–9). To understand why database software was developed requires an understanding of the limitations of file management software. The business world

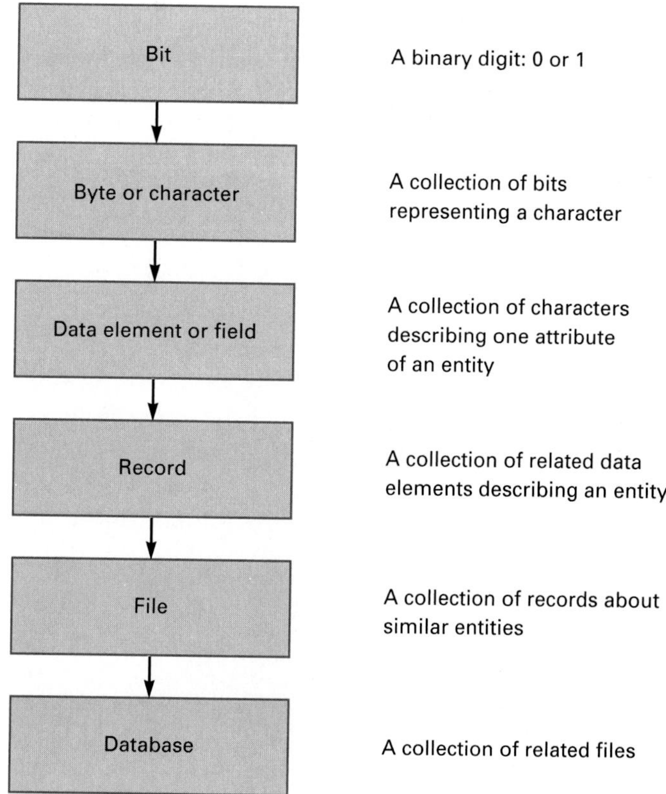
Bit
A binary digit: 0 or 1
Byte or character
A collection of bits representing a character
Data element or field
A collection of characters describing one attribute of an entity
Record
A collection of related data elements describing an entity
File
A collection of records about similar entities
Database
A collection of related files

Figure 6–9
Building blocks of a computer-based electronic database

turned to data processing in a big way in the 1960s. Often firms computerized their operations on an application-by-application basis. For example, they may have computerized their payroll activities first. Once that was completed, they may have computerized order processing and so on through the applications they felt should be computerized.

Converting a firm's manual applications one by one took time; the process was usually spread out over several years. Furthermore, the programs for each application were usually written specifically for that application. As a result, each program may have been written by different programmers, perhaps even in a different programming language. Thus, the records in each file were designed specifically for each application and might not have been appropriate for the other application software the firm had developed (see Figure 6–10).

For example, the equipment inventory application program discussed earlier in this chapter was designed to read from and write to a record with the exact fields, arranged in the exact order, with the exact field lengths that the equipment record contained. Other programs would be unable to read that record unless those programs were redesigned to that record's specifications.

Data Independence

Thus, many file programs developed in-house were *dependent* on the data files created for them. Or, in the language of information systems people, the file programs lacked **data independence.** The lack of data independence meant that any time the record format of a file was changed (e.g., a field was dropped, added, or changed), every program that accessed that file had to be changed. You can imagine the work that was created when the five-digit ZIP code was replaced by a nine-digit ZIP code. All the application programs that accessed files with ZIP codes had to be changed so that they would be able to read and process the changed records!

Data Redundancy

Let's look at another problem associated with file management software. Consider how many college or university offices maintain files on you as a student. You may have a file in the enrollment office, a file in the placement office, a file in the bursar's office, and a file in the office of your major field of study. Every file includes a record containing

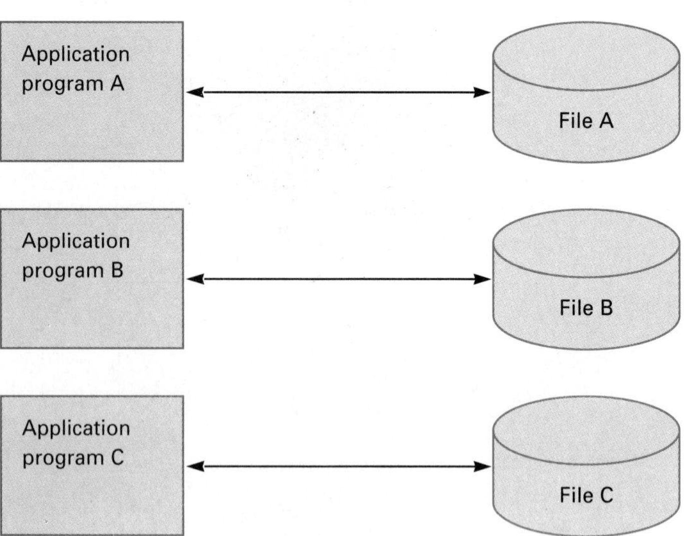

Figure 6–10 Dependence of application programs on files specifically designed for these programs

your first name, last name, middle initial, student ID number, home address, and college address. In other words, the files have considerable **data redundancy.**

Data Integrity

As is often the case during your college days, you may decide to change your address. You would notify the placement office about your address change to ensure that they send job notices to the right location. The placement office would then bring up your record on a screen and update your college address. However, it is still incorrect in all the other files at the college (see Figure 6–11). You can see that data redundancy usually leads to data inconsistency. When many files contain records with the same or similar data fields, updating one record in one file will lead to inconsistency in those data in the other files. Inaccuracies in your data files, such as inconsistencies, mean that your files lack **data integrity.**

Furthermore, each of these offices might run separate programs to process their files. The enrollment office might run a COBOL program to access its record on you to produce a transcript. The placement office might run an assembler-language program to access its record on you to produce a list of job openings appropriate to your stated needs and qualifications. The bursar's office might run an RPG (report program generator) program to access their record on you to produce a tuition invoice. Because of the differences in the records and the programs that use them, there may be no easy

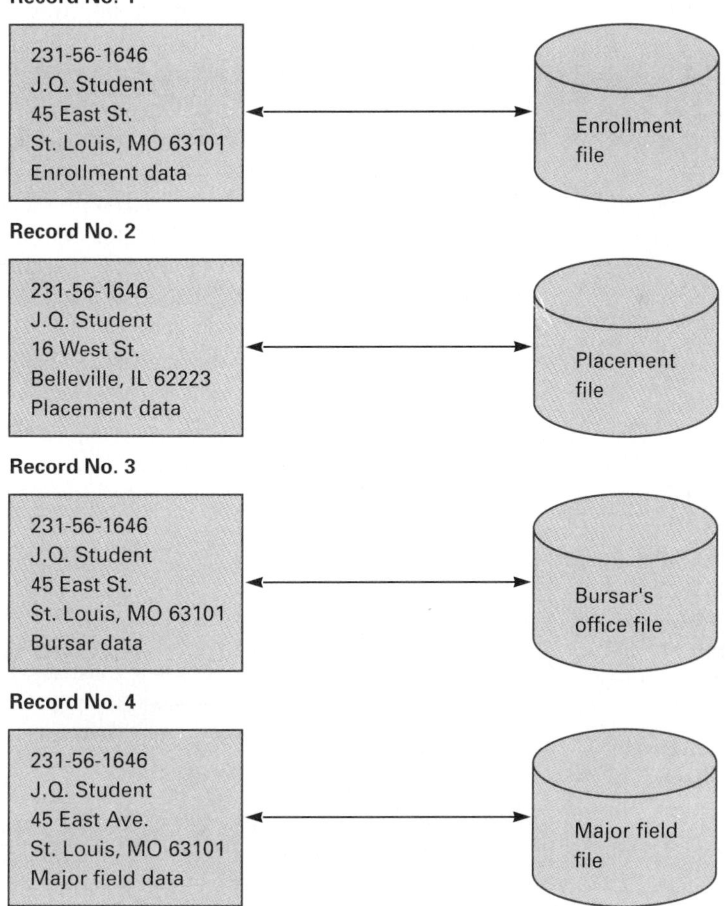

Figure 6–11
Multiple files lead to data redundancy and inconsistency

way for a college administrator to produce a report showing how many students who have found positions through the placement office also owe tuition.

Thus, with file management software, it was at best difficult and usually impossible for managers to obtain information useful for analysis and planning from the files of the entire organization. What they needed was a system that would eliminate data redundancy and provide data consistency—or make sure that data are accurate wherever they are stored. They also needed a system to provide data independence so a user could access data regardless of the file or record in which it resided. To meet these needs, database management systems were developed.

DATABASE MANAGEMENT SYSTEMS

A **database management system,** or **DBMS,** is a collection of software programs that

1. Stores data in a uniform way.
2. Organizes the data into records in a uniform way.
3. Allows access to the data in a uniform way.

In a database management system, application programs do not obtain the data they need directly from the storage media. They must first request the data from the DBMS. The DBMS then retrieves the data from the storage media and provides them to the application programs. Thus, a database management system operates *between* application programs and the data (see Figure 6–12).

COMPONENTS OF A DATABASE MANAGEMENT SYSTEM

Database management system software is usually developed by commercial vendors and purchased by your organization. The components of a particular DBMS will vary somewhat from one vendor to another. The DBMS components found in many commercial products available on the market today are described next. Some of these components are typically used by specialists in information systems. For example, information systems specialists typically use the data dictionary/directory, data languages, teleprocessing monitor, application development systems, security software, and archiving and recovery system components of database management systems. Other components, such as report writers and query languages, may be used both by programmers and by managers and other nonspecialists.

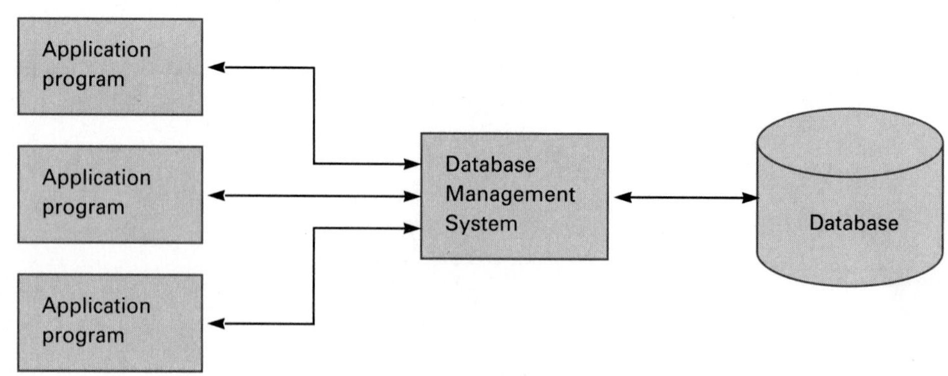

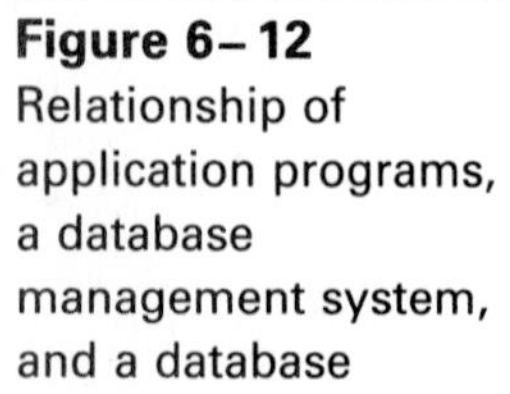
Figure 6–12
Relationship of application programs, a database management system, and a database

Data Dictionary/Directory

A **data dictionary/directory** contains the names and descriptions of every data element in the database. It also contains a description of how data elements relate to one another. Through the use of its data dictionary, a DBMS stores data in a consistent manner, thus reducing redundancy. For example, the data dictionary ensures that the data element representing the number of an inventory item (named STOCKNUM) will be of uniform length and have other uniform characteristics regardless of the application program that uses it. The data dictionary also enforces consistency among users and application developers. For example, the data dictionary prevents users or application developers from adding data elements that have the same name but different characteristics to the database. Thus, a developer would be prevented from creating a second inventory record and calling the data element for stock number INVNUM. Application developers use the data dictionary to create the records they need for the programs they are developing. The data dictionary checks records that are being developed against the records that already exist in the database and prevents inconsistencies in data element names and characteristics from occurring.

Because of the data dictionary, an application program does not have to specify the characteristics of the data it wants from the database. It merely requests the data from the DBMS. This may permit you to change the characteristics of a data element in the data dictionary without having to change all the application programs that use the data element.

Data Languages

To place a data element in the dictionary, special language is used to describe the characteristics of the data element. This language is called the *data description language,* or *DDL.*

To ensure uniformity in accessing data from the database, a DBMS will require that standardized commands be used in application programs. These commands are part of a specialized language used by programmers to retrieve and process data from the database. This language is called the *data manipulation language,* or *DML.*

A data manipulation language usually consists of a series of commands, such as FIND, GET, and INSERT. These commands are placed in an application program to instruct the database management system to get the data the application program needs at the right time.

Teleprocessing Monitor

A *teleprocessing monitor* is a communications software package that manages communications between the database and remote terminals. Teleprocessing monitors often handle order entry systems that have terminals located at remote sales locations. Teleprocessing monitors may be developed by database management systems software firms and offered as companion packages to their database products.

Application Development System

An *application development system* is a set of programs designed to help programmers develop application programs that use the database.

Security Software

A *security software* package provides a variety of tools to shield the database from unauthorized access. The security of data will be discussed in greater detail in Chapter 20, "Security and Ethical Issues of Information Systems."

Archiving and Recovery Systems

Archiving programs provide the database manager with tools to make copies of the database, which can be used in case original database records are damaged. *Restart/recovery systems* are tools used to restart the database and to recover lost data in the event of a failure.

Report Writers

A report writer allows programmers, managers, and other users to design output reports without writing an application program in a programming language, such as COBOL.

SQL and Other Query Languages

A **query language** is a set of commands for creating, updating, and accessing data from a database. Query languages allow programmers, managers and other users to ask ad hoc questions of the database interactively without the aid of programmers. One form of query language is **SQL, or Structured Query Language.** SQL is a set of about 30 English-like commands that has become a standard in the database industry. Many vendors of DBMS software now provide SQL for their database software.

Because SQL is used in many database management systems, managers who understand SQL syntax are able to use the same set of commands regardless of the database management system software that they must use. Thus, learning SQL provides the manager with access to data in many database management systems.

The basic form of an SQL command is SELECT . . . FROM . . . WHERE . . . After SELECT you list the fields you want. After FROM you list the name of the file or group of records that contains those fields. After WHERE you list any conditions for the search of the records. For example, you might wish to SELECT all customer names FROM customer records WHERE the state in which the customer lives is Michigan. So you would enter this:

```
SELECT     NAME, ADDRESS, CITY, STATE, ZIP
FROM       CUSTOMER
WHERE      STATE = 'MI'
```

The result would be a list of the names and addresses of all customers located in Michigan. Additional information about SQL (specifically SQL servers) will be presented in Chapter 7, "Communications and Distributed Systems."

Some query languages use a *natural-language* set of commands. These query languages are structured so that the commands used are as close to standard English as possible. For example, the following statement might be used:

```
PRINT THE NAMES AND ADDRESSES OF ALL CUSTOMERS WHO
LIVE IN MICHIGAN
```

Query languages allow users to retrieve data from databases without having detailed information about the structure of the records and without being concerned about the processes the DBMS uses to retrieve the data. Furthermore, managers do not have to learn COBOL, BASIC, or other standard programming languages to access the database. The downside is that seemingly simple queries generated by naive users can take hours to execute. Knowing query shortcuts and strategies and the types of data in the database can improve the efficiency of retrieving data. Training managers and other users to use query languages efficiently for database retrieval is important.

Microcomputer and Minicomputer Versions of Mainframe Databases

Some vendors of DBMS software also provide microcomputer and minicomputer versions or counterparts to their mainframe products, including versions that run under many different operating systems. Though not usually sold as a component of a mainframe database management system, these other versions of the mainframe DBMS software can be helpful. The versions often simplify downloading data from the mainframe database into the microcomputer or minicomputer database for local processing. For example, the makers of Oracle provide both microcomputer and minicomputer versions of their mainframe product that makes downloading and uploading data between these platforms more convenient. Some microcomputer and minicomputer versions even contain a communications program for transferring files between the mainframe and the microcomputer. By having versions for several platforms and operating systems, developers can create applications on one platform and use them on others.

The Database Administrator

The development of database management systems has created a need for organizational changes within firms. The focal point of these changes is the position of database administrator, or **DBA**. The **database administrator** is charged with managing the organization's data resources, a job that often includes database planning, design, operation, training, user support, security, and maintenance. The role of the DBA requires a person who can relate to top management, systems analysts, application programmers, users, and systems programmers. Such a person needs not only effective management skills but also a fair amount of technical ability. Selection of the DBA and the organization of this important function are critical to the success of a database management system.

The deployment of a database management system in a firm generates a number of changes in the way records and files are administered. The most prominent change is that data are now shared by many users instead of being "owned" by one or more users. Thus, payroll records are no longer the property of the payroll department; they are part of the company's database. Giving up data ownership can be very painful for some units within an organization. The DBA must get users who are accustomed to such ownership to give up "their" data to a common database, and this may not be an easy task.

Another change occurs when data are added to a database. Pooling data in a common database requires consensus concerning the structure of the data elements. The users of the database must agree on the nature of each data element and its characteristics, such as length, type of data, and the like. Though this sounds like a trivial matter, previous ownership of the data element may cause considerable problems for the DBA when seeking agreement on their definitions. However, uniform definitions of the data elements must be achieved before the elements are recorded in the data dictionary. In a very real sense, the data dictionary serves as a common discipline for all database users by requiring agreement on the data elements to be stored in the database. Thus, the DBA should be involved to some extent in all applications under development because the DBA is the final authority on the structure of the database.

Another change pertains to data access. Maintaining data integrity and security is an important role of the DBA. Thus access to data stored in the database must not only be approved, it also must be made using standard procedures approved by the DBA. Because the data are shared, it is important to permit only those who need the data to have access to them. The ability to add, delete, or modify existing data must be tightly controlled.

Consider the college file problem discussed earlier. If the placement file, enrollment file, bursar's office file, and major field file were reorganized under a DBMS, only one master record for each student would be necessary. This master record would contain the student's number, name and address, and other relatively permanent data. It also would include separate records for enrollment, placement, bursar, and major field data, but these records would not contain the data in the master record. They would contain only the student's number and the data pertinent to the department or unit. Thus the only connection between the various data elements pertaining to enrollment, placement, bursar, or major field and the student master record is the student number (see Figure 6–13).

Though such a scheme reduces redundancy and thereby reduces the threat to data integrity, consider what would happen if the student decided to drop the major field and

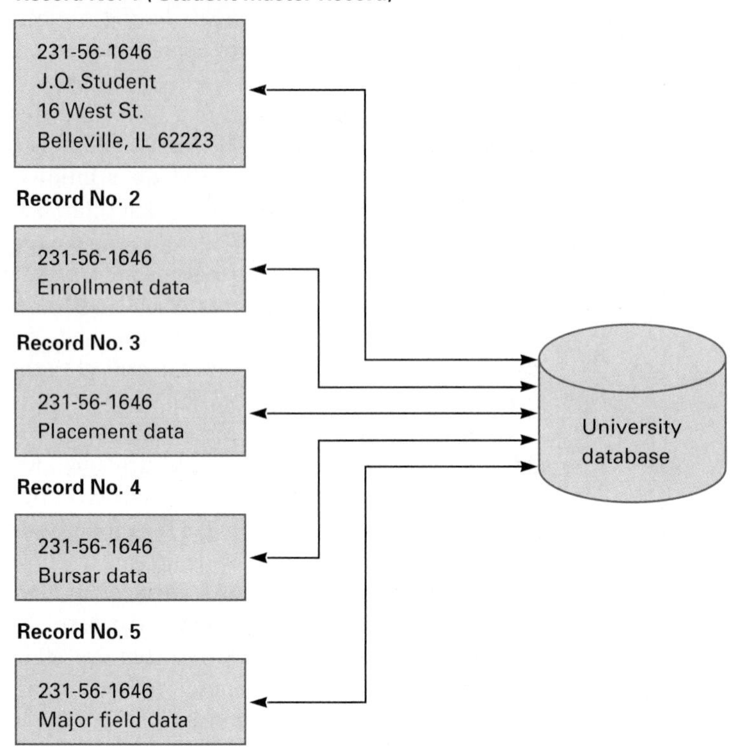

Figure 6–13 Reduction of redundancy in a database

the clerk in that department eliminated the student master record. That would mean that the college would have enrollment data, placement data, even bills payable to the bursar's office with no student name and address to match.

You can see now why the DBA must tightly control the ability of users to add, delete, or modify information in the records. Also, because so much of the organization's data are in one resource, the organization is more vulnerable than before. This vulnerability must be protected by the DBA. Achieving this protection is complicated by the fact that many people within the organization view access to data as essential for success. Others view data access as a symbol of status. Restricting access to data then becomes a political problem for the DBA.

Another facet of database security is ensuring that adequate precautions have been taken for regular *backup* of the database. Backing up the database may take several forms. One of the most common is *archiving*, or making a complete backup copy of the database at regular intervals, usually on tape. Providing backup security for a database is essential to avoid total loss of data in the event of an equipment failure.

Additional information about security is presented in Chapter 20, "Security and Ethical Issues of Information Systems."

VIEWS OF THE DATABASE

Any database contains two types of data: the actual data, such as employee names, hourly wage rates, and hours worked, and information about the data. That is, it contains (1) the definitions of each data element and (2) how each data element relates to other data elements. The data kept about data are called *metadata*.

The data in a database are also organized both logically and physically. Logical organization of data in a database takes place when you conceptually arrange data elements into a record. For example, these data elements can be logically organized into a payroll record:

1. Employee number (primary key).
2. Employee last or family name.
3. Employee first or given name.
4. Employee middle initial.
5. Employee street address.
6. Employee city.
7. Employee state.
8. Employee ZIP code.

We may also logically organize all employee records into a file called the employee master file. However, there is no assurance that the employee records in the file will be physically stored contiguously on the storage media used. As you have learned, storing data randomly with a hashing algorithm may scatter records and parts of records that logically belong together all over a hard disk. Thus, the data elements of a *logical record* may be stored in many different actual locations on disk. A *physical record* is a collection of data elements grouped together on a disk. A physical record may contain the data elements of more than one logical record. In the same way, records in a *logical file* may be stored in many different actual locations on disk. A *physical file* is a collection of records actually grouped together on a disk track.

In other words, the logical organization of records and files is the way these items appear to the user. The physical organization of records and files is the way these items are actually stored on disk or tape.

The Conceptual View

The database itself may be viewed from at least three perspectives. The **conceptual view** of the database is a logical view: It is how the database appears to be organized to the people who designed it. The conceptual view, also called the *schema* is a global view of the entire database and this is the view usually used by the DBA. The conceptual view includes all the data elements in the database and how these data elements logically relate to each other. The DBA is concerned with the selection of data elements to be included in the database, the definition of those data elements, and the relationship of each data element to the others.

The External View

Another, less comprehensive view is the external or user view of the database. This view is also called a *subschema* and is usually used by an application programmer, an application program, or a user. The **external view** encompasses only a subset of the data elements in the entire database, those data elements needed by one application program or user. Thus each application program holds an external view of the database.

Both the conceptual and external views are logical views of the database; that is, these views are not concerned with how data are physically organized on cylinders, tracks, and sectors. The conceptual and external views both describe the logical organization of the data elements and how each data element relates to another. Their differences can be found in that the conceptual view includes all the data elements and their relationships whereas an external view includes only those data elements and relationships needed by an application program (see Figure 6–14).

External views of data provide one means of making the system secure. Users of one application program, for example, may be restricted to their own views of the

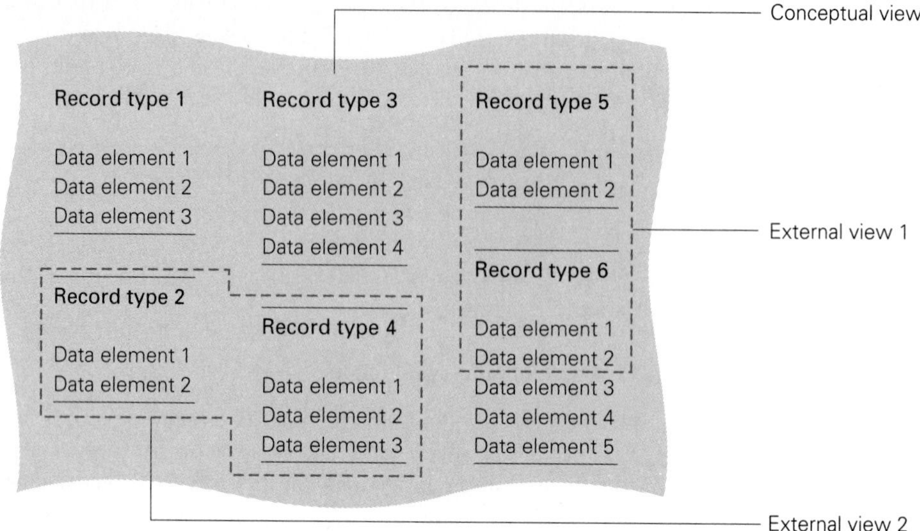

Figure 6–14 Conceptual and external database views

database. The DBMS may not allow users of an application program to use data beyond their views.

The Internal View

A third view of the database is the **internal,** or **physical, view.** This view is usually the one taken by the systems programmer. The system programmer is concerned with the actual physical organization and placement of the data elements in the database. The internal view is a physical, or hardware, view of the database. The systems programmer designs and implements this view by allocating cylinders, tracks, and sectors for the various segments of the database so various programs run as smoothly and efficiently as possible.

In summary, the DBA is responsible for the logical structure of the entire database. An application programmer or user has authority to view only a small portion of that logical database. Both the programmer and the user take logical or conceptual views of the database. The systems programmer, however, is responsible for placing the data physically on actual media and hence takes a physical view (see Table 6–1).

Table 6–1 Three views of a database

1. **Conceptual view**
   a. Held by the database administrator
   b. Involves the identification and description of all data elements and their relationships to other data elements
   c. Reflects a logical view of the entire database
2. **External or user view**
   a. Held by the application programmer, application program, or user
   b. Consists of the identification and description of each data element needed for a given application
   c. Constitutes a logical view of one part of the database
3. **Internal view**
   a. Held by the systems programmer
   b. Involves the organization and placement of the actual data on the physical storage media
   c. Represents a physical view of the database

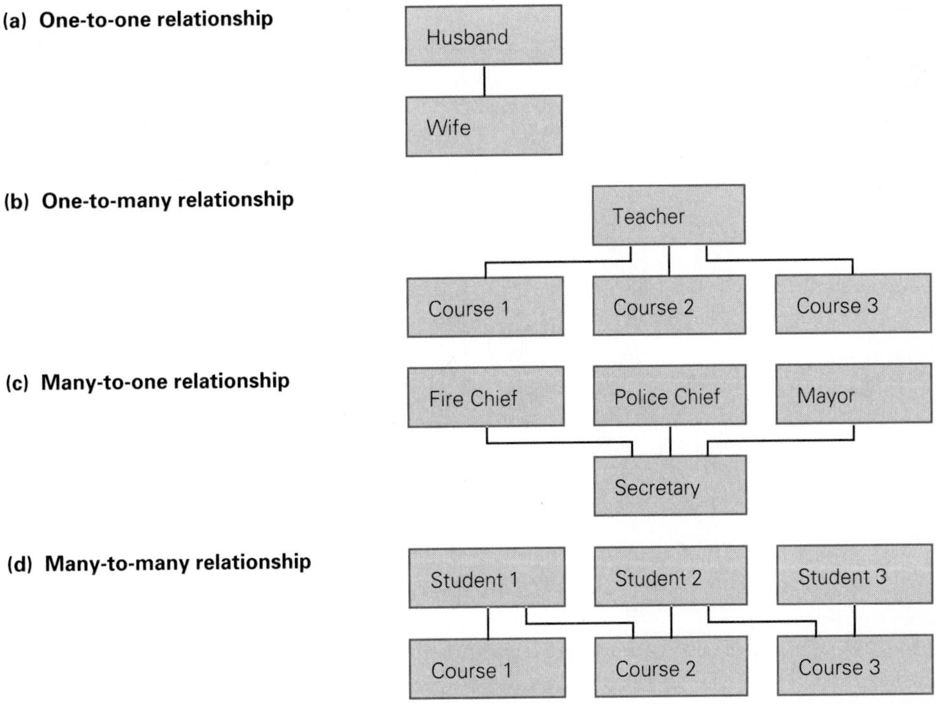

(a) **One-to-one relationship**

Husband
Wife

(b) **One-to-many relationship**

Teacher
Course 1 Course 2 Course 3

(c) **Many-to-one relationship**

Fire Chief Police Chief Mayor
Secretary

(d) **Many-to-many relationship**

Student 1 Student 2 Student 3
Course 1 Course 2 Course 3

Figure 6–15
Record relationships: **(a)** one to one, **(b)** one to many, **(c)** many to one, and **(d)** many to many

DATABASE STRUCTURES

Organizing a large database logically into records and identifying the relationships among those records are complex and time-consuming tasks. Just consider the large number of different records that are likely to be part of a corporate database and the numerous data elements constituting those records. Even a small business is likely to have many different record types, each of which possesses several distinct data elements. Then consider the many relationships records may have with one another. For example, an invoice can be related to the customer who purchased the merchandise, the salesperson who sold the customer the merchandise, the products included on the invoice, and the warehouse from which the merchandise was picked.

Several general types of record relationships can be represented in a database:

1. One-to-one relationships, as in a single parent record to a single child record or as in a husband record and wife record in a monogamous society (see Figure 6–15a).
2. One-to-many relationships, as in a single parent record to two or more child records—for example, a teacher who teaches three single-section courses (see Figure 6–15b).
3. Many-to-one relationships, as in two or more parent records to a single child record—for example, when three administrators in a small town share one secretary (see Figure 6–15c).
4. Many-to-many relationships, as in two or more parent records to two or more child records—for example, when two or more students are enrolled in two or more courses (see Figure 6–15d).

Three traditional approaches have been implemented commercially to organize records and their relationships logically. These logical organizational approaches are known as **database structures.** The three traditional database structures are the

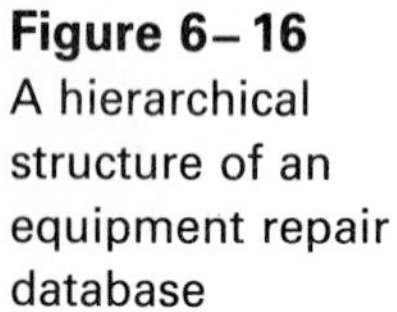

Figure 6–16
A hierarchical structure of an equipment repair database

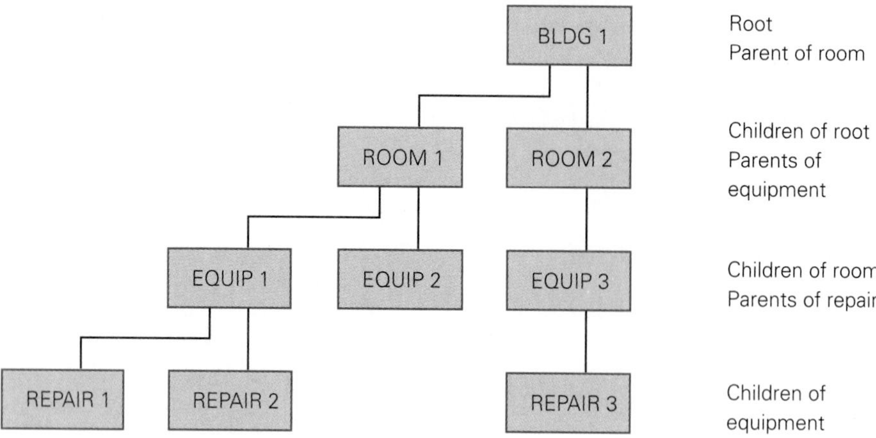

1. Hierarchical database structure
2. Network database structure
3. Relational database structure

Hierarchical Database Structure

In a **hierarchical database,** records are logically organized into a hierarchy of relationships. A hierarchically structured database is arranged logically in an inverted tree pattern. For example, an equipment database, diagrammed in Figure 6–16, may have building records, room records, equipment records, and repair records. The database structure reflects the fact that repairs are made to equipment located in rooms that are part of buildings.

All records in a hierarchy are called *nodes.* Each node is related to the others in a parent-child relationship. Each parent record may have one or more child records, but no child record may have more than one parent record. Thus, the hierarchical data structure implements one-to-one and one-to-many relationships.

The top parent record in the hierarchy is called the *root* record. In this example, building records are the root to any sequence of room, equipment, and repair records. Entrance to this hierarchy by the database management system is made through the root record, building. Records that "own" other records are called *parent* records. For example, room records are the parents of equipment records. Room records are also the *children* of the parent record, building. There can be many levels of node records in a database.

Hierarchically structured databases are less flexible than other database structures because the hierarchy of records must be determined and implemented before a search can be conducted. In other words, the relationships between records are relatively fixed by the structure. Ad hoc queries made by managers that require different relationships than are already implemented in the database may be difficult or time consuming to accomplish. For example, a manager may wish to identify vendors of equipment with a high frequency of repair. If the equipment record contains the name of the original vendor, such a query could be performed fairly directly. However, data describing the original vendor may be contained in a record that is part of another hierarchy. As a result, there may not be any established relationship between vendor records and repair records. Providing reports based on this relationship in a large database is not a minor task and is not likely to be undertaken by the data processing staff for a one-time management query. Managerial use of a query language to solve the problem may require multiple searches and prove to be very time-consuming. Thus, analysis and planning activities, which frequently involve ad hoc management queries of the database, may not be supported as effectively by a hierarchical DBMS as they are by other database structures.

On the plus side, a hierarchical database management system usually processes structured, day-to-day operational data rapidly. In fact, the hierarchy of records is usually specifically organized to maximize the speed with which large batch operations such as payroll or sales invoices are processed.

Any group of records with a natural, hierarchical relationship to one another fits nicely within this structure. However, many records have relationships that are not hierarchical. For example, many record relationships require that the logical data structure permit a child record to have more than one parent record. The query to isolate vendors of equipment with extensive repairs might be completed more easily if the equipment records were the children of both the room records and the vendor records. Though a hierarchical data structure does not permit such a structure conceptually, a commercial hierarchical database management system must have ways to cope with these relationships. Unfortunately, they may not always be easy to implement.

One major commercial hierarchical database management system is Information Management System, or IMS, an IBM product. This commercial database management system, designed for mainframes, was introduced in the 1970s.

Network Database Structure

Another database structure is a *network*. A **network database** structure views all records in sets. Each *set* is composed of an *owner* record and one or more *member* records. This is analogous to the hierarchy's parent-children relationship. Thus, the network model implements the one-to-one and the one-to-many record structures. However, unlike the hierarchical model, the network model also permits a record to be a member of more than one set at one time. The network model would permit the equipment records to be the children of both the room records and the vendor records. This feature allows the network model to implement the many-to-one and the many-to-many relationship types.

For example, suppose that in our database we decided to have the following records: repair vendor records for the companies that repair the equipment, equipment records for the various machines we have, and repair invoice records for the repair bills for the equipment. Suppose further that recently four repair vendors have completed repairs on equipment items 1, 2, 3, 4, 5, 7, and 8. These records might be logically organized into the sets shown in Figure 6–17.

Notice these relationships in our example:

1. Repair Vendor 1 record is the owner of the Repair Invoice 1 record. This is a one-to-one relationship.
2. Repair Vendor 2 record is the owner of the Repair Invoice 2 and 3 records. This is a one-to-many relationship.
3. Repair Vendor 3 record is the owner of Repair Invoice 4 and 5 records, and the Equipment 7 record owns both the Repair Invoice 5 and 6 records because it was fixed twice by different vendors. Because many equipment records can own many Repair Invoice records, these database records represent a many-to-many relationship.
4. Equipment 6 record does not own any records at this time because it has not needed to be fixed yet.
5. Equipment 7 and 8 own Repair Invoice 6 because the repairs to both machines were listed on the same invoice by Repair Vendor 4. This illustrates the many-to-one relationship.

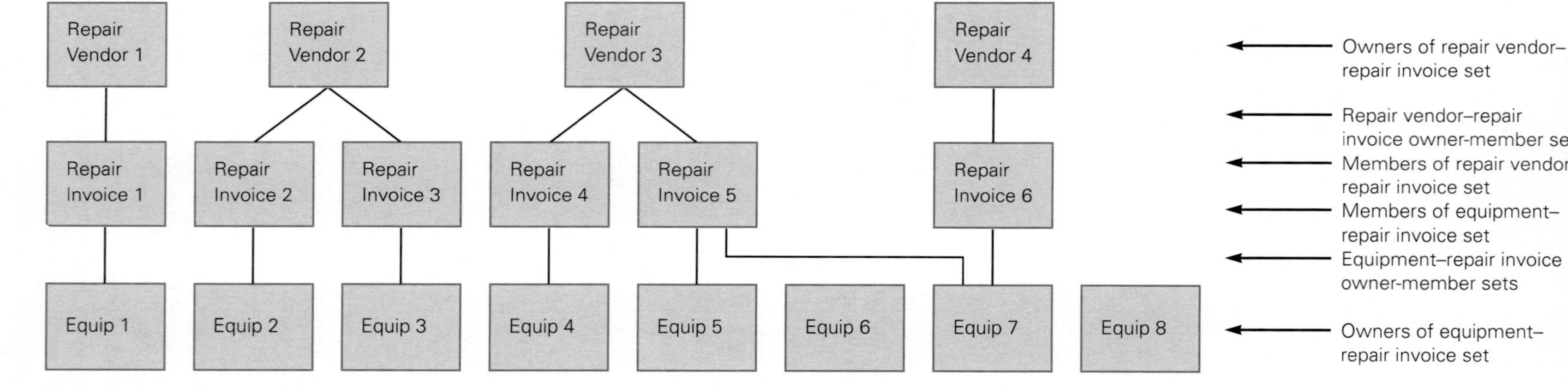

Figure 6–17
Network structure showing one-to-one, one-to-many, many-to-many, and many-to-one relationships

	Repair Vendors Records	
Column 1	Column 2	Column 3
Repair Vendor Number	Repair Vendor Name	Repair Vendor Address
43623	Telo, Inc.	15 Troy Street
43890	A-Repair Company	25 Vine Street
43118	Beeline, Ltd.	498 Olde Street
43079	Aspen, Inc.	12 Dome Avenue
43920	Calso, Inc.	5 Estes Street

Figure 6–18
Repair vendor table in a relational database system

Thus, all the repair records are members of more than one owner-member set: the repair vendor-repair invoice set and the equipment-repair invoice set. The network model allows us to represent one-to-one, one-to-many, and many-to-many relationships. The network model also allows us to create owner records without member records. Thus, we can create and store a record about a new piece of equipment even though no repairs have been made on the equipment yet.

Unlike hierarchical data structures that require specific entrance points to find records in a hierarchy, network data structures can be entered and traversed more flexibly. Access to repair records, for example, may be made through either the equipment record or the repair vendor record. However, like the hierarchical data model, the network model requires that record relationships be established in advance because these relationships are physically implemented by the DBMS when allocating storage space on disk. The requirement of established sets means that record processing for regular reports is likely to be swift. Record relationships are usually structured to fit the processing needs of large batch reports. However, ad hoc requests for data, requiring record relationships not established in the data model, may not be very swift at all, and in some cases, they may not be possible.

An example of a well-established commercial network data model is Cullinet Corporation's Integrated Data Management System, which has been implemented in many organizations.

Relational Database Structure

A third database structure is the relational database model. Both the hierarchical and network data structures require explicit relationships, or links, between records in the database. Both structures also require that data be processed one record at a time. The relational database structure departs from both these requirements.

A **relational database** is structured into a series of two-dimensional tables. Because many managers often work with tabular financial data, it is easy for most of them to understand the structure used in a relational database. For example, our repair vendor records might be structured as in Figure 6–18.

The repair vendor table consists of the repair vendor master records, which contain the repair vendor number, name, and address. The table itself is really a file. Each row in the table is really a record and each column represents one type of data element.

A similar table for equipment could look like the one in Figure 6–19. The table contains the records for each piece of equipment in the firm. Each record also contains the number of the repair vendor who has a contract to repair that piece of equipment.

If the manager wished to create a report showing the names of each repair vendor and the pieces of equipment that each vendor repairs, he or she could combine both tables into a third table. The manager might join the two tables with a query statement such as this: JOIN REPAIR VENDOR AND EQUIPMENT ON REPAIR VENDOR NUMBER. This would create a new table with six columns: Repair Vendor Number, Repair Vendor Name, Repair Vendor Address, Equipment Number, Equipment Name, and Date Purchased. Now the manager could print out only the columns for vendor name and equipment name. Such a report might look like the one shown in Figure 6–20.

The manager might also produce a report by selecting from both tables only the rows for specific equipment types or for equipment purchased in specific years. The important things to notice are that the relationships, or links, do not need to be specified in advance and that you manipulate whole tables, or files.

Relational databases allow the manager flexibility in conducting database queries and creating reports. Queries can be made and new tables created using all or part of the data from one or more tables. The links between data elements in a relational database do not need to be made explicit at the time the database is created—new links can be structured at any time. Thus, the relational database structure is more flexible than hierarchical or network database structures and provides the manager with a rich opportunity for ad hoc reports and queries. However, because they do not specify the relationships among data elements in advance, relational databases do not process large batch applications with the speed of hierarchical or network databases.

Many relational database management system products are available. For example, Oracle and IBM offer commercial relational database management systems, Oracle and DB2 respectively.

Object-Oriented Databases

Generations of new file and database structures have evolved as the old structures became less suitable to current applications (see Figure 6–21). When applications were built one by one over time, simple file structures were satisfactory. When a need arose

Figure 6–19 Equipment table in a relational database system

Equipment Records			
Column 1	Column 2	Column 3	Column 4
Equipment Number	Equipment Name	Date Purchased	Repair Vendor Number
10893	Typewriter	12/02/94	43623
49178	Microcomputer	01/31/87	43920
10719	Telephone	03/12/94	43079
18572	Copier	11/06/93	43890
60875	Calculator	08/01/94	43118

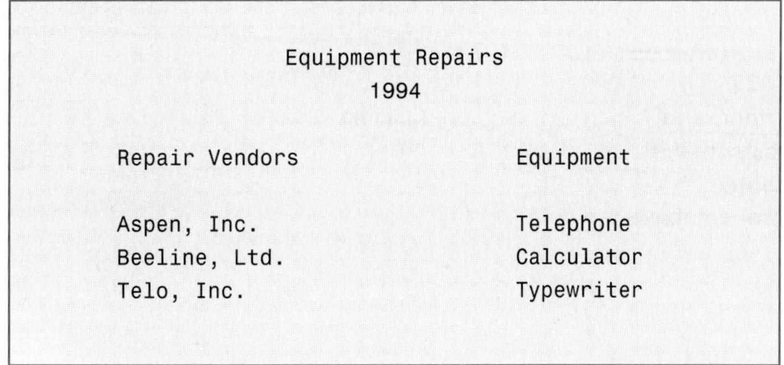

Equipment Repairs
1994

Repair Vendors	Equipment
Aspen, Inc.	Telephone
Beeline, Ltd.	Calculator
Telo, Inc.	Typewriter

Figure 6–20
Report created from two tables

for integrated databases, hierarchical, network, and finally relational structures were developed. However, as flexible as the relational structure is, it is not particularly well suited for many business and engineering applications today. The relational structure still is based on data elements that describe records, and the nature of the data entered into a relational database is strictly constrained by the data dictionary.

Much of the information managers use is stored in organization files and represents the results of the organization's transactions, such as sales invoices, payments to vendors, and payments to workers. However, a great deal of information managers use cannot be stored in the organization's database, such as images, drawings, videos, and other nontext data. A new structure is needed to handle the needs of such applications as expert systems, multimedia systems, computer-aided systems engineering (CASE), computer-aided design (CAD), and many other engineering, design, and manufacturing systems. These applications produce information useful to the organization, but rather than being kept in the organization's database it is scattered among letters, reports, memoranda, magazine articles, engineering drawings, charts, graphs, or other "objects." The data in these objects differ fundamentally from the data in a typical transaction-

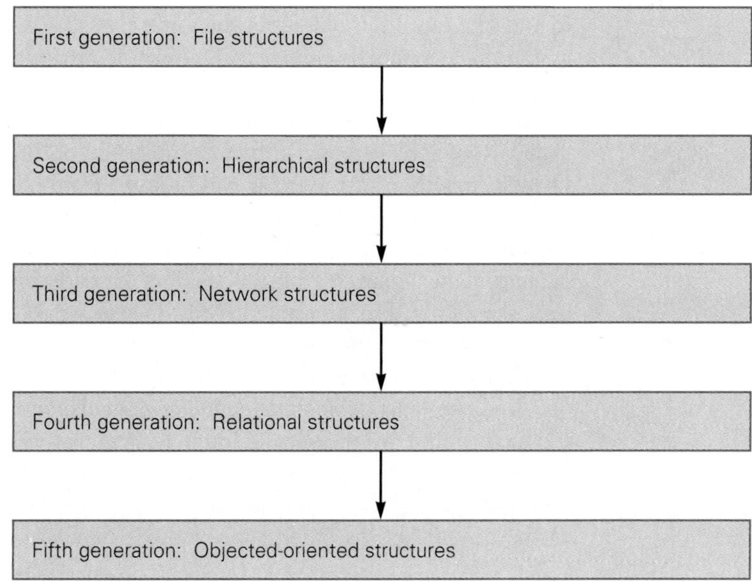

Figure 6–21
The evolution of database structures

Source: Adapted from Won Kim, "A New Database for New Times," *Datamation* 36, no. 2 (January 15, 1990), pp. 35–42)

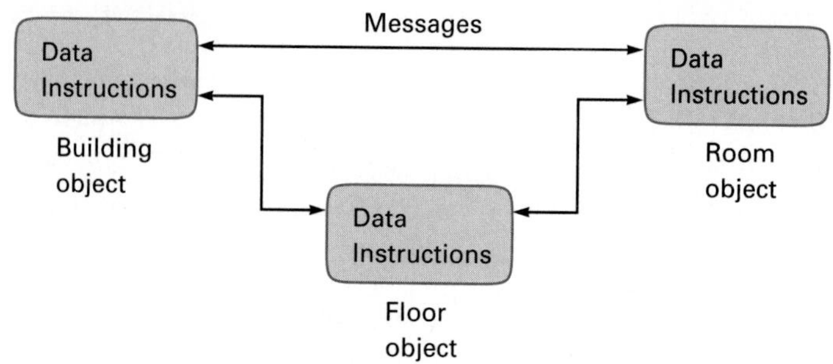

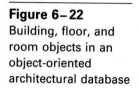

Figure 6–22
Building, floor, and room objects in an object-oriented architectural database

oriented database system. In the latter, specific information is entered in a very restricted manner and the manager typically wishes to summarize, total, or list selected data from the records. In the former, the data are not transactions but instead include many complex data types, such as drawings, charts, multimedia documents, and other documents. These data types may vary substantially in type, length, content, and form. At present, object-oriented database technology appears best suited to manage the latter data types.

Object-oriented databases (OODB) are built with *object-oriented programming,* which was briefly described in the previous chapter. Each object in the database is bound together with its own data and a set of instructions that describes the behavior and attributes of the object. Objects use *messages* to interact with one another. In an object-oriented database, every object is described by a set of *attributes.* For example, the object *building* in a database of architectural drawings may have the attributes type, size, and color, just as in any other database. Every object must also have a set of *methods,* or routines and procedures. For example, methods stored with an architectural drawing of a maintenance building might include instructions to display, rotate, shrink, or explode the drawing on a screen (see Figure 6–22).

Objects that have the same set of attributes and methods are grouped into a *class.* For example, building, floor, and room might be three classes of objects in the database of architectural drawings. Furthermore, the attributes and behaviors of one object can be *inherited* by other objects in the same class. Thus, another building in the same class as the maintenance building may inherit its attributes and behaviors. This speeds application development time by reducing the amount of programming code needed. What results is large libraries of *reusable objects,* which can be employed over and over again. New applications can be assembled by putting off-the-shelf objects from these libraries together, just as a car can be built from component parts.

Object-oriented database technology has only recently been given widespread attention. Standards in the field are not firm but are under development by the Object Management Group, a group of vendors. In addition, other vendors have offered their own standards. For example, IBM, Hewlett-Packard, and Sun Microsystems have formed an alliance and agreed on a common object-oriented interface that will permit developers to create applications that will be able to run on several platforms.

Because object-oriented technology is substantially different from other database technology, it requires a considerable learning curve for practitioners. Although a number of commercial object-oriented databases are now available, some industry observers feel that many of the companies that have created these products will be swallowed up in the near future by older, more mature database management system vendors who

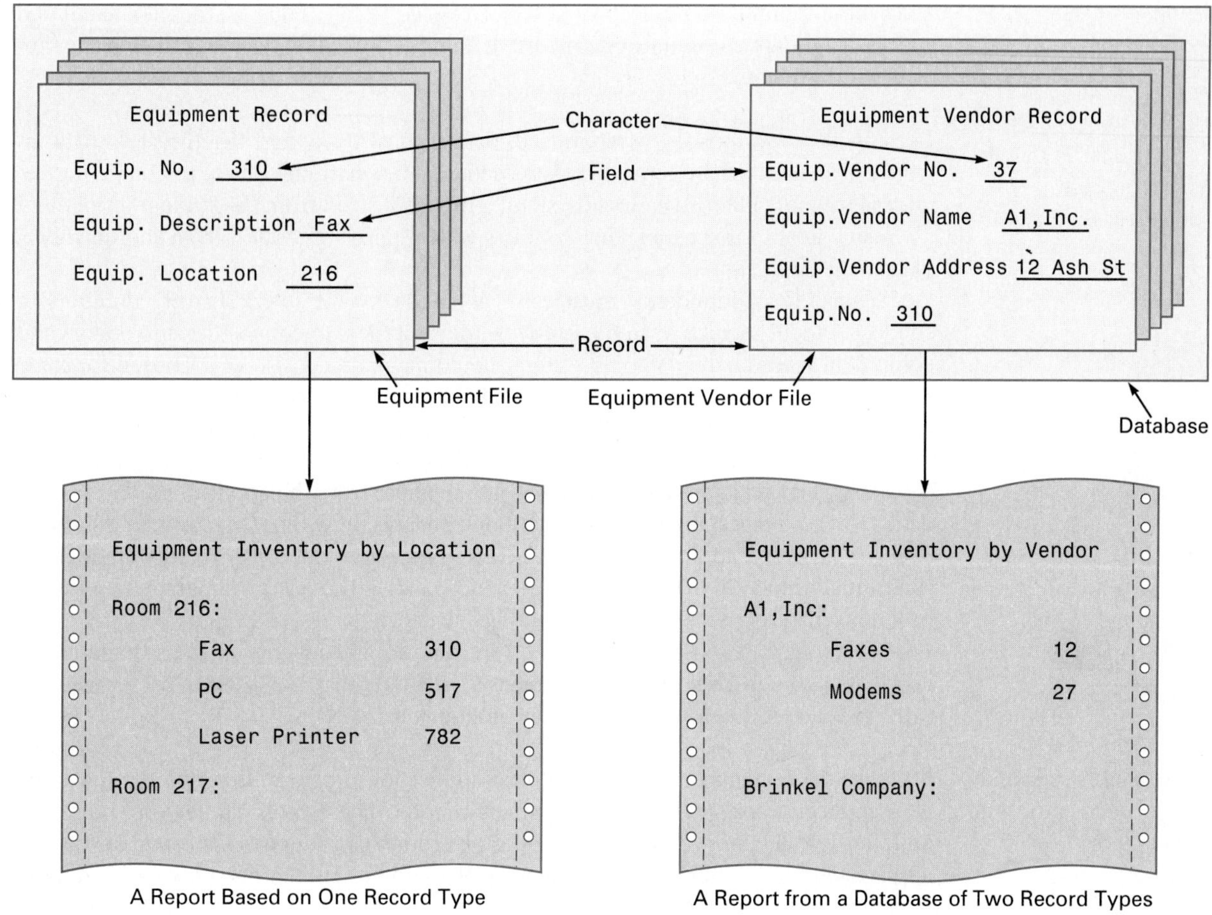

A Report Based on One Record Type

A Report from a Database of Two Record Types

Figure 6–23
Reports produced from one record type (file) and two record types in a database

will use the object-oriented database systems as extensions to their own database management software.[1]

ADVANTAGES OF DATABASE MANAGEMENT SYSTEMS

Companies find a number of advantages in using a database management system instead of a series of separate files controlled by file management software.

Data Sharing

The data from the entire company are at the disposal of users who need them. Managers may analyze a much more extensive store of information than is available in the typical file management, or single record type, environment (see Figure 6–23).

[1]Laura Smith. "Developers Eye Object Databases," *Development Tools*, a special supplement to *PC Week*, February 15, 1993, p. S8.

Reduced Data Redundancy

A database minimizes duplication of data from file to file. Thus, a student's name and address might appear in only one record in a university database rather than in the files of many departments.

Improved Data Integrity

Because data redundancy is minimized, data inconsistency and the threat to data integrity are substantially reduced. Data inconsistency naturally leads to conflicting reports. Thus, in a file management system, a report derived from the student enrollment file may contain information that conflicts with reports generated from the university placement file.

Where data redundancy must exist, as in the use of social security numbers to connect student records or in the use of vendor numbers to connect repair vendors and equipment records, the database system should maintain consistency. Thus, if for some reason a vendor's number were changed, the database system should change that number everywhere it exists in the database.

Data Independence

A database system keeps descriptions of data separate from the applications that use the data. Thus, changes in the data definitions can occur without necessarily requiring changes in every application program that uses those data. The result could be a substantial reduction in program maintenance costs—the costs to upgrade application programs in response to changes in the file structure.

Some databases also store data in ways that do not depend on the storage media used. Thus, if new disk drives are purchased, the data may not need to be reorganized to remain accessible to the application programs using them.

Increased Application Programmer and User Productivity

Most database management systems offer application program development tools that help application programmers write program code. These tools can be very powerful, and they usually improve an application programmer's productivity substantially. Some application development tools may increase the number of lines of code produced by an application programmer as much as 5 to 10 times within a given period of time. Object-oriented databases provide developers with libraries of reusable code to speed development of applications.

Users also increase their productivity when query languages and report generators allow them to produce reports from the database with little technical knowledge and without any help from data processing, thus avoiding the long time periods that management information systems departments typically require to develop new applications. The result is greater use of the corporate database for ad hoc queries and managerial decision making.

Users also increase their productivity when they use microcomputer software designed to work with the mainframe database. This allows them to acquire and manipulate data with ease without requiring the assistance of programmers.

When users can obtain many of their reports and data without intervention by systems analysts or application programmers, demand on the services of these professionals for routine application requests decreases. Systems analysts and application programmers are thus freed to focus their attention on applications that require their talents, which increases their productivity to the organization.

Improved Data Administration and Control

Placing responsibility for the database in the hands of one person or department provides a number of advantages. It permits better enforcement of standards for defining data elements and data relationships. In this way, the discipline of the data dictionary becomes easier to enforce and control. Access to data, the privacy of data, and updates and deletions of data are also easier to control. In addition, a department devoted to the supervision of data is more likely to archive the database and take other security measures than a department preoccupied with its own problems.

Increased Emphasis on Data as a Resource

Establishing database administration and deploying a database management system emphasize throughout an organization the importance of information to the management function. The DBA acts as an advocate for the concept of information as a corporate resource. The result is likely to be greater corporate attention to information systems as an aid to managerial decision making and long-range planning using the database as the basic information resource.

PROBLEMS OF DATABASES

Database management systems provide many opportunities and advantages, but these advantages may come at a price. Database management systems also pose problems.

Concurrency Problems

When more than one user utilizes a database management system, problems can occur if the system is not designed for multiple users. One of these problems is concurrent access to records, or **concurrency.** Suppose that two of your salespeople are using terminals at two different company sites. Salesperson A is selling blue widgets to customer A, who wants to buy 200 of them. The salesperson retrieves the inventory record for blue widgets on the screen to see if there is enough stock on hand to make the sale. The blue widget inventory record shows a balance of 300 widgets.

At the same time, salesperson B is selling blue widgets to customer B at another location. Customer B wants to buy 150 of them (blue widgets are a popular item). This salesperson also retrieves the blue widget record. In other words, both salespeople have retrieved and are viewing the blue widget record that shows 300 items on hand. Now salesperson B, being a fast talker, closes the sale first. The right keys are pushed on the terminal, and the blue widget file showing a balance of 150 is copied back to the database. Unfortunately, no change is made in the screen being viewed by salesperson A. Salesperson A, you will remember, is looking at the original blue widget record, which still shows a balance of 300 items. So, salesperson A closes and records the sale of 200 widgets from the terminal, and that record shows a balance of 100 widgets. What happens next is that the record viewed by salesperson A, showing an old balance of 300, less a sale of 200, is now copied to disk. The sale by salesperson A overwrites the sale of salesperson B, and the blue widget record shows a balance of 100. But there is actually a shortage of 50 items in inventory.

The problem of concurrent access can be solved in a number of ways. Some simple database systems merely lock a file when one user is using it. If salesperson A was using the inventory file, salesperson B would not be able to either view or write to that file. *File locking* is likely to be a poor choice to avoid the problem of concurrency, however. In our example, it would mean that only one of your salespeople could sell a product at any time.

Another way to avoid concurrency problems is to lock only the record being used. Thus, salesperson B may view and write to any inventory item *except* the blue widget record because salesperson A is already using that record. *Record locking* still presents problems, though. Popular inventory items would frequently be locked and unavailable for use by other salespeople.

Still another way to avoid concurrency is to lock a data element, or field, when it is being used. *Field locking* would permit more than one person to use a popular record but would only allow one person to make a change in a particular data element.

A more sophisticated means of handling concurrency problems is to use a database management system that permits every user to view a record and make updates in that record. However, before any record update is actually saved, the system checks to see if the record has changed. Before salesperson A would be able to close the sale, the system would recheck the blue widget record to see if any updates have been made in the record. The system would notify salesperson A that there has been a change and update the screen being viewed to reflect that change. Salesperson A would then have to tell customer A that there are not enough blue widgets on hand. No doubt that would lead to a discussion of how nifty yellow widgets are.

A database management system designed for a mainframe or minicomputer is usually designed to handle multiple users simultaneously; that is, it is a multiuser system. This means that the database management system will usually provide for some form of concurrency protection. Many microcomputer database management systems, on the other hand, are designed for one user. Therefore, the single-user versions of microcomputer database systems will not have concurrency protection. If you connect several microcomputers together in order to share data files on a hard disk, you should upgrade your version of the database management system to a multiuser version with concurrency protection.

Ownership Problems

In file-based systems, employees who run application programs on application-specific files frequently feel that the data in those files are theirs and theirs alone. Users, such as payroll department personnel, develop ownership of the files in the system. When a database of such files is created, however, the data are no longer the specific property of application users, but instead are owned by the entire company. Any user with a need should be able to obtain the authority to read or otherwise access the data. Giving up ownership of data may be traumatic for many company employees and managers. It is difficult for company database administrators to get file users to give up their feelings that data are exclusively "theirs" and to share data with others in a database. However, for a database to be successful, the data must be viewed and treated as a corporate resource, not as an individual's property.

Resource Problems

A database management system usually requires extra computing resources. After all, the new database management systems programs must be run. Much more data must be stored on-line to answer queries, which we hope will increase. As a result, more terminals may be needed to put managers and other users on-line to the database. Additional hard disk systems may be needed to put more data on-line and make it available to managers. Communication devices may be needed to connect the extra terminals to the database. It may even be necessary to increase the size or number of CPUs to run the extra software required by the DBMS.

Security Problems

A database must have sufficient controls to ensure that data are made available only to authorized personnel and that adding, deleting, and updating data in the database are accomplished only by these personnel. The manager must realize that access security means more than merely providing log-on codes, account codes, and passwords. Security considerations should include means of controlling physical access to terminals, tapes, and other devices. Security considerations should also include the noncomputerized procedures associated with the database, such as forms to control the updating or deletion of records or files and procedures for storing source documents.

In addition, access to employee, vendor, and customer data should conform to various federal and state regulations, such as the 1971 Fair Credit Reporting Act, the 1974 Privacy Act, and the 1978 Right to Financial Privacy Act.

Certainly the DBMS should contain an archiving feature to copy all important files and programs, and there should be procedures for regular update and storage of these archival copies. Also the DBMS should provide software to assist in recovering data lost when the system fails and in restarting the DBMS after the failure.

Additional information pertaining to database backup, archiving, and other security matters are presented in Chapter 20, "Security and Ethical Issues of Information Systems."

Distributed Databases

The discussion so far has considered only one organization of the database management system: a centralized system. In a centralized system, the computer system and the database of an organization are both found at one location under the management of one group. Databases in this setting are called **centralized databases.** Organizations that need to decentralize their computer processing will also need to decentralize their databases. When computing resources and databases are scattered rather than centralized, they are called **distributed data processing** and **distributed database systems.**

Distributed data processing refers to a system in which computer intelligence is located at more than one site and the actual running of application programs and processing of data are completed at more than one site. Distributed data processing may save a lot of time and money for an organization. For example, an organization may find it less expensive and time-consuming to have payroll information processed at each of its locations, including having the checks printed and distributed locally, than to have all that information sent back to a centralized computer system, processed, and the output returned to each location. Chapter 7 discusses distributed data processing in more detail.

When processing is distributed, the data to be processed usually must be located at the processing site. This means that the database, or parts of the database, must be distributed. There are basically two ways to distribute a database. The first is to provide duplicates of all data at all sites. This approach is called a **replicated database.** If it is necessary for every location to have frequent access to the same data, replication of the database may be recommended. However, replication of a database is very expensive in terms of computer system resources, and it is difficult to maintain consistency for each data element. On the other hand, replication does provide some measure of security by providing duplicates of the database in case of failure at one location.

Another means of distributing the database is to partition it. The database may be divided into segments that are appropriate for certain locations and those segments distributed only to those locations. This approach is called a **partitioned database.** The database may be partitioned along functional lines; for example, financial, marketing, and administrative data may be kept at corporate headquarters and relevant production and personnel data at each manufacturing plant and office site.

Partitioning may also be achieved along geographical lines. That is, all information—financial, marketing, administrative, production, and personnel—may be kept at each of the separate locations of an organization. If an organization is composed of four companies, each quite different in purpose and each located at a different site, partitioning on a geographical basis may make a lot of sense. If a distributor maintains seven warehouses for storing merchandise at seven different locations, partitioning the inventory database on a geographical basis also may make sense.

Many organizations with many locations partition the database hierarchically. Detailed data, such as payroll and sales data, are kept close to their source—the local site. Regional and national locations receive increasingly less detailed summaries of the detailed data as these data are transmitted up through the organization's hierarchy. For example, the detailed information on customer orders, salesperson commissions, and product inventory status may be kept at each store location for a national department store chain. Only summary data on total sales, total commissions, and total inventory may be kept at the home office.

Distributed database systems usually reduce costs for an organization because they reduce transfer of data between remote sites and the organization's headquarters. Distributed database systems may also provide organizations with faster response times for filling orders, answering customer requests, or providing managers with information. However, distributed database systems also magnify the problems of databases. They compound the problems of control over the database, increase problems of security for the database, increase data redundancy and the resulting danger to data integrity, and increase the need for more computer resources. Unless the distribution of a database is done very carefully, many of the advantages of having a database in the first place can be lost.

The increased power and use of microcomputers by managers and professionals have created additional problems for database administrators. When managers download data from a centralized database to their microcomputers, there is no longer a truly centralized database. Parts of the database are segmented and distributed to these microcomputers.

Because of the backlog of requests to be filled at many management information systems departments, other departments may become so frustrated that they decide to acquire their own minicomputers or microcomputers to provide their own information services. When this happens, additional files and databases are established throughout an organization, creating much of the same redundancy, inconsistency, and incompatibility that characterized corporate data in the 1960s and 1970s.

An important type of distributed database system, called client/server systems, will be presented in Chapter 7, "Communications and Distributed Systems."

ON-LINE DATABASES AND INFORMATION UTILITIES

A great deal of information is available to managers through computerized databases provided by information utilities, such as CompuServe, America Online, and Prodigy (see Box 6–1). **Information utilities** are companies that provide a variety of information services to organizations or individuals who subscribe to their services. These services are also called *on-line information services* and might include providing programs to process your data, such as a payroll program for a small subscribing organization or an investment portfolio management program to help a financial manager analyze and manage organization investments. These services might also include providing a network over which your computers may communicate with one another, such as a long-distance communications network that each of your branch managers might use to communicate data to headquarters (see Box 6–2).

One of the services offered by information utilities is **on-line databases** that make it possible for managers to access large quantities of information external to their organizations. Access includes searching the databases for information on key words or phrases, generating reports from information downloaded from the databases to the managers' computer systems, manipulating data downloaded from the databases to the

Box 6–1 Popular Information Utilities

America OnLine does not offer a flat rate service. They charge a rate of $9.95 a month for the first 5 hours and $3.50 per hour for each added hour.

CompuServe is the dean of information utilities. CompuServe charges a flat monthly rate of $9.95 for basic services, which do not include most of the on-line databases but do include encyclopedias, shopping, market quotes, games, movie reviews, travel reservations, weather, and some news services. These extended services will cost you $4.80 or $9.60 an hour, depending on the speed of your modem. You also get a $9 monthly E-mail credit.

GEnie is General Electric's information utility. GEnie charges a flat monthly rate of $8.95 for its basic services, which include E-mail and bulletin boards. Extended services cost $3 or $18 per hour, depending on the time of day.

Prodigy charges $7.95 for two hours a month or $14.95 for 5 hours for all services except bill paying and investor services. You also get 30 monthly E-mail messages free. Use beyond 5 hours per month is billed at $3.60 an hour and 25 cents per E-mail message.

Source: David Coursey, "CompuServe Will Offer Basic Services for Flat Rate," *InfoWorld* 14, no. 2, (January 13, 1992), p. 37.

managers' spreadsheets or database programs, and printing summaries of information selected from the databases.

On-line databases are essentially electronic libraries. They can offer managers a large variety of different types of information literally at their fingertips. These information sources help managers stay current on topics of importance to their organizations and provide them with a competitive edge over others who do not have such information immediately available at their desks. Some typical types of information available through these databases follow.

Market Quotations

Some on-line databases provide you with price quotations for stocks, bonds, mutual funds, options, and commodities. These price quotations may include real-time price quotations, quotations that are less than an hour old, and historical price quotations that allow you to define the history of an organization or commodity and perform projections and forecasts for specific companies or industries. For example, the Dow Jones Quotes component of the Dow Jones News/Retrieval Service offers current and historical quotes on stocks, bonds, mutual funds, options, and commodities.

Market Information

Some on-line databases provide you with information on market indexes, market commentaries and news, industry statistics, investment advisories, and even information relating to an organization's earnings forecasts, financial statements, and other financial data. Organization information might also include such details as cash flows, advertising budget, levels of profits, and growth during a selected period of time. Furthermore, a database may provide information on insider trading, Securities and Exchange Commission filings, and research reports on an industry or organization. Such information is very helpful to a financial manager who is managing organization investments, and it is also useful for obtaining industry averages for use as benchmarks of organization success or failure. Moreover, knowledge of competitor finances might influence decisions by your organization to pursue or not pursue new markets, new products, or new capital investment. Knowledge of your competitors' financial weaknesses may spell the difference between a successful or unsuccessful attempt by your organization to obtain a larger percent of market share.

Box 6–2 Some Services Offered by CompuServe—An Information Utility

CompuServe is one of the oldest and largest information utilities available today with close to 1 million subscribers. It offers hundreds of services and access to over 1,700 on-line databases, libraries, and forums. Some of these features are included in their basic monthly service fee. Others are accessed at additional costs. These costs may be on an hourly basis or on a different usage basis. For example, if you download articles from a newspaper database, you may be charged on an article-by-article basis.

The number of services and on-line databases offered through CompuServe are too numerous to identify here. However, the services CompuServe offers subscribers to its services include these:

- **Electronic mail**
  CompuServe offers electronic mail access to users of a variety of mail services, such as AT&T Easylink, MCI Mail, and Internet. It also offers its own CompuServe Mail services.
- **Fax**
  CompuServe allows you to transfer memos, letters, and the like that you have on disk or that you type directly to fax machines around the world.
- **Teletype**
  CompuServe lets you send and receive Telex and TWX messages.
- **Forums**
  CompuServe offers more than 200 forums, each of which is managed by a Sysop, or system operator. This is the person who runs the forum and is usually an expert on the subject matter of the forum. Included are hardware and software forums that are usually run by expert technicians from specific hardware and software vendors. For example, Gateway 2000, a computer manufacturer, provides a forum for its users. The forums offer you a chance to ask questions or discuss solutions to issues and problems with expert technicians and users. You can communicate with others by sending and receiving messages or by entering into a conference on a special topic with others.
- **Libraries**
  Libraries offer you the opportunity to download program updates to your software, program fixes to your software problems, and program utilities. The programs may be developed by the vendor for the library or by others. Libraries are usually part of a forum. Thus, in a forum on Microsoft Windows, you will find libraries of software programs, including updates, fixes, and utilities. CompuServe offers access to hundreds of software libraries.
- **On-line databases on investing and finance**
  CompuServe offers a wealth of information about investing and finance including stock, option, and commodity market quotations, brokerage services, magazine and journal articles, a variety of sources of information about specific companies, company directories, stock market games, stock issue analysis, investment analysis, portfolio valuation, and investment forums.
- **News, weather, sports**
  The service provides about 25 different news services, sports forums, and even gossip. For example, the Business Wire contains articles and press releases about companies around the world and Newspaper Library contains full-text articles from more than 50 newspapers in the United States. You can also access Roger Ebert's Movie Reviews and aviation weather forecasts.
- **Electronic shopping**
  Subscribers may purchase or shop in more than a hundred different stores, catalog stores, and other electronic shopping firms. For example, subscribers may buy from pharmacies, bookstores, pet supplies stores, and many different discount stores. You can even enroll in business degree programs on-line.
- **Travel**
  Fifteen different travel services provide information on hotels, airline schedules, restaurants, and government travel advisories, and allow you to reserve airline seats.
- **Other on-line databases and services**
  CompuServe is filled with other services, including Consumer Reports, electronic encyclopedias, the Associated Press Online, electronic classified ads, games, programs, numerous on-line databases, forums, conferences, libraries for personal and professional interests, and a reference library of on-line databases, forums, and conferences on nearly every conceivable topic.

General News and Information

Many on-line databases provide news and information on general topics, such as the economy, politics, the courts, medicine, and sports. These services may provide complete newspapers and magazines on-line, allowing the subscriber to view current issues and articles and search previous issues using key words. Such services are invaluable for developing background reports about the economy, government, fashion, medicine, and the like.

For example, you might be considering investing corporate dollars in organizations that develop artificial intelligence computer systems and software. You can quickly search through a mass of articles on the topic of artificial intelligence by requesting references using such key words as *artificial intelligence, expert systems,* and *AI.* The output you would receive might be a list of articles that contained those words in the title or in the text. Your next step might be to examine the titles in the list of references and request that abstracts of selected titles be downloaded to your computer so that you could print them out and read them carefully. You may finally request the full text of those articles you found most helpful.

A search of an entire library's journals, magazines, and newspapers would take you days, if not weeks, to complete manually. For decisions that must be made quickly, the time required to perform a manual library search usually makes a systematic search of current information impossible.

Examples of information utilities that provide large numbers of databases of general interest include Dialog Information Services, Inc.; Dow Jones News/Retrieval; Compuserve, Inc.; IQuest Service; CORIS (Company Research and Information Service); Data-Star; and GEnie (which offers RoundTable, a forum on Canadian politics, news, culture, and other topics).

Specific News and Information

Some on-line services provide news for particular industries or segments of our culture. These services can be of inestimable help to managers. For instance, Chase Econometrics provides financial and economic databases. Donnelley Demographics provides databases describing national demographics. Lexis provides legal databases, which include court case outcomes and legal precedents. NewsNet provides a business news database of over 500 business newsletters, 20 worldwide news wire services, the *Official Airlines Guide,* and two credit bureaus.

Some information services even allow you to tailor the service so it provides you with automatic updates whenever anything new is published on topics of interest to you. Using the search software provided with the database service, you can develop *selective dissemination of information* (SDI) services on special topics. The information service searches the appropriate databases whenever they are updated and sends you the results of the search. For example, you might set up an SDI for artificial intelligence with several information services to which you subscribe. Whenever anything new on artificial intelligence appears in sources monitored by these information utilities, it will automatically be identified and the reference, abstract, or even the full text will be mailed to you or telecommunicated to your computer system.

You may not wish to learn how to use, search, and manipulate these database services yourself. Though most on-line services are menu-driven, you may still have to learn quite a bit if you subscribe to many of them because each has a slightly different set of software commands, key-word structures, and other procedures that you must know to use the service. Instead, you may wish to delegate the job of searching to a subordinate. In fact, many large organizations have search specialists to keep organization managers abreast of their areas of interest and their competitors. Smaller organizations may hire the services of an information service search consultant. However,

Box 6–3 Specialized File Management and Database Software

Through the years, a number of software packages have been developed to meet the special needs of people or applications. Some of these special software types are listed here. You have already learned about some of them. You will learn about others in later chapters.

HYPERTEXT

Software that allows you to link nearly any kind of information that can be stored magnetically, including sounds, images, text, and data. The information is usually stored in "cards," "pages," or "books" so that it can be accessed in a nonsequential fashion. The length and content of the cards can vary. The software can also link data, images, sound, and text from multiple sources.

PERSONAL INFORMATION MANAGERS

A diverse set of software designed to help you work and think. PIMs let you organize the information you work with every day so that you can find it easily. PIMs may provide several of the following features: telephone and address files, to-do lists, individual scheduling and group scheduling, project planning, calendars, notepads, simple word processors, report writers that combine data from multiple files and even mainframe databases, telephone logging and time billing programs, and menu builders, among others.

CONTACT MANAGERS

A specialized file manager or database manager that allows sales personnel to keep track of their customers and prospective customers. Contact managers often are combined with other utilities into a PIM (see previous entry). Contact managers will be described in greater detail in Chapter 11, "Marketing Information Systems."

IMAGE DATABASES

Multimedia, CAD/CAM, presentation graphics, drawing programs, and a host of other software that produces images of one kind or another have created an avalanche of images that can be used by employees throughout an organization—provided they can be found and translated into the format that the employee needs. The job of an image database is to store images in such a way that they can be quickly found, easily accessed, and if needed, easily converted to the format needed.

Some image storage system databases are far more modest in their aims. Some file management software merely provides the ability to store images along with text.

really creative searches of databases are best done by someone who is very knowledgeable and experienced in the specific field in which information is required. The synergistic effects of poking through references and abstracts inevitably lead to new key-word choices or whole new topics of interest for managers who take the time to do this work themselves.

DATA REPOSITORIES

Large companies often have many computer applications that have been developed and are being used to solve business problems. Each of these applications is usually documented in detail, including the business activities the application supports, the flow of information in the application, what data are needed for the application, and the processes the application handles. In addition, each application is composed of program modules used to process the application's data.

Until recently, these applications were not managed as well as they could be. The database of information pertaining to an organization's applications—descriptions of the business functions they support, the data they require, and the processes they use—has been kept largely in paper files, which meant that it was often managed

For example, some companies produce packages that let you store a picture taken by a VCR camera in a record. Thus, employee records managed by that software could contain pictures of employees as well as traditional alphabetic and numeric employee data. Storing data and images pertaining to auto insurance claims is another useful application. Consider how helpful photos of stock items might be to stock clerks taking inventory. You might expect fewer errors in taking inventory if you could be sure that the inventory clerks knew what they were looking at on the warehouse shelves. Consider how helpful photos of employees might be to members of the personnel department of a large company. After all, it's nice to be able to greet people by their names.

DOCUMENT MANAGERS

The data in letters, memos, reports, and other documents in an organization may easily rival in quantity and sometimes in importance the financial data of that organization. However, an organization's stored documents are usually scattered across the filing cabinets, hard drives, and other storage media found in the departments and divisions of that organization. Finding what you want can be the equivalent of looking for the needle in the haystack. Document management software allows you to search, select, view, and otherwise manipulate these documents no matter where they are located. Search and select functions are usually completed through the use of key words. Chapter 8, "Office Automation," describes document managers in greater detail.

DISTRIBUTED DATABASES

Database management systems that allow data to be stored in more than one computer system, but control and offer the data to users as if all the data were centralized in one location. In other words, although the data is scattered among different locations, it appears as a single database to users. Chapter 7, "Communications and Distributed Systems," discusses distributed databases in greater detail.

CLIENT/SERVER DATABASES

A specialized form of distributed database software. A client is usually a PC or other terminal, which is connected to a server, or larger computer platform, such as a supermicro, minicomputer, or mainframe computer. In a client/server system, the database data and database tasks can be shared by the client and the server. Chapter 7, "Communications and Distributed Systems," discusses client/server systems in greater detail.

inefficiently. For example, code used in one application program that might also be useful in other application programs was not reused because it was too time-consuming to identify that the code existed and then locate it. Changes in the environment of the organization could affect many application programs, but identifying them in a very large portfolio of applications could be time-consuming and some applications that needed to be updated might be overlooked. For example, when the ZIP code was changed from five digits to nine digits, many application programs were affected. But which ones? Sorting through the paper documentation to determine which applications had fields for ZIP codes was clearly an inefficient means of solving the problem.

So along comes the concept of a *data repository,* basically, an enhanced data dictionary. You now know that a data dictionary defines the data elements in a database system and the relationship among those data elements. A data repository, however, extends its reach to many more types of data about data, or metadata, including information about application programs, business processes, data flows, business controls, program modules, application program screens, computer jobs, and business procedures. Thus, a data repository not only includes metadata about the operational data used by an organization, it also documents, defines, and provides a directory to the many other component parts of an organization's information resource. Thus, the data repository may prove to be the means to unify disparate corporate information resources running on a variety of computer system platforms. These resources include multiple databases using different database models and the diverse application programs that use these databases.

To manage the data repository, a number of firms have developed repository management software, or *repository managers*. An immediate use for repository management software is to allow information systems personnel to manage their application portfolios much more efficiently than they have in the past. Repository managers allow them to develop reusable program code and store data about the code in the data repository for future use. Repository managers also allow information systems specialists to ascertain quickly the impact of changes in an organization's environment on its application programs so that updates in these programs can be made as quickly as possible.

Another important use of a data repository is with application development tools, such as computer-aided systems engineering or CASE tools (see Chapter 17). The hope is that information systems specialists will be able to specify the requirements for an application and store these specifications in the repository. Application development and database generation tools would then convert these requirements into a finished application. Thus, application programs may be "manufactured" in the future from specifications for the applications housed in the data repository.

Management Summary

To make decisions and plan for the future, managers need information. Much of the information they need is in the records kept by their organizations. In the past, these records have been kept in paper and computer files. More recently, organizations have used database management systems to increase the accuracy, timeliness, and quality of information available to their executives.

A database is a collection of related files. A file is a collection of one type of record. A record is a logical collection of related data elements. Data elements are attributes that describe an entity for which the business needs to keep records. Data may be stored by computers using file management systems or database management systems. File management systems are usually organized so that they can be accessed sequentially, directly, or through an indexed sequential access method. Database management systems are usually organized into a hierarchy, a network, relations or tables, or objects.

File management systems allow users to create records, manipulate data, search files, and create reports easily and rapidly without the aid of information systems personnel. Many commercial file management programs also allow you to create graphs and charts from the data in the files. However, file management software does not usually permit you to search data contained in files other than the file for which the software was specifically developed. Another problem is that users of the software may not allow the data to be used by others in the company. In addition, files usually contain data found in other files, which leads to data integrity problems among the files of the organization.

Database management systems provide a means of storing corporate data, formerly stored in numerous individual files, in one system. This reduces data redundancy and the threat to data integrity, and permits managers to search larger and more diverse amounts of data. Database management systems, however, may cause political problems within organizations, may require additional computing resources, and must be carefully managed to ensure data integrity and security.

Like file management systems, database management systems usually provide executives with a relatively easy-to-use query language to search for data, a report writer for reports, and microcomputer-to-mainframe support for downloading information from the database to their microcomputers.

Many organizations process data at more than one site. These organizations must wrestle with the problem of distributing their data to make distributed processing possible. At the same time they must maintain management control over their databases. Databases may be replicated at each processing site or partitioned and parts distributed selectively to appropriate sites. Distributed database systems offer the opportunity for lower costs and faster response time but carry the burden of increasing security, redundancy, consistency, and compatibility problems for an organization.

Managers may also wish to access data located outside their organizations, especially those managers making planning decisions. Information utilities provide subscribers with a diversity of on-line services, including access to a variety of on-line databases. On-line databases include diverse data, such as financial, market, census, newspaper, magazine, legal, and medical data, and data for a particular industry.

Files and databases store information that many people want to access, whether they are in the next room, floor, building, state, or even the next country. You will learn how computer systems allow people to communicate with remote files, databases, and other users in the next chapter.

Key Terms for Managers

archiving programs, **197**
centralized databases, **215**
conceptual view, **201**
concurrency, **213**
data dictionary/directory, **197**
data element, **184**
data independence, **194**
data integrity, **195**
data redundancy, **195**
database, **193**
database administrator (DBA), **199**
database management system (DBMS), **196**
database structures, **203**
direct access, **186**
distributed data processing, **215**
distributed database systems, **215**
external view, **201**
field, **184**
file, **184**
file management software, **189**
hierarchical database, **204**
index, **187**
indexed sequential access (ISAM), **187**
information utilities, **216**
interactive processing, **188**
internal view, **202**
network database, **205**
object-oriented databases (OODB), **210**
on-line databases, **216**
partitioned database, **215**
physical view, **202**
primary key, **186**
query language, **198**
record, **184**
relational database, **207**
replicated database, **215**
report writer, **190**
search parameters, **191**
secondary keys, **191**
sequential access, **186**
structured query language (SQL), **198**

Review Questions

1. What are the building blocks of a computer-based electronic file system?
2. Explain the three types of file structures and describe one application appropriate for each type.
3. List and describe the three traditional database structures or models.
4. List five typical reasons why you might wish to access records in a file.

5. What is the role of the database administrator?

6. What are three views of a database? List the job title of each person who is usually responsible for each view.

7. What is the difference between a logical file and a physical file?

8. List and briefly describe the components that might be included in a database management software package.

9. List and briefly describe the disadvantages to an organization that employs a database management system.

10. What is the difference between interactive processing and batch processing?

11. What is meant by concurrency protection? Describe three levels of concurrency protection that might be provided in a database.

12. What is the difference between data and metadata?

13. Explain what is meant by data independence in a database management system.

14. What is the difference between a primary key and a secondary key?

15. Why are employee number and stock number often chosen for primary keys to employee and stock records rather than employee name or stock description?

16. Why is it important that files and databases be archived?

17. Explain the term *distributed processing*. How does distributed processing differ from a distributed database?

18. Explain the term *search parameters* and describe how they are used in a file or database management system. How might a manager use wild cards to advantage in searching a file or database?

19. How might a microcomputer version of a mainframe database management system help the manager?

20. Describe the possible services offered to a subscriber by an information utility organization, such as CompuServe.

21. Describe the types of information commonly available to subscribers of on-line databases.

22. Explain how an on-line database might help a manager improve the quality of management planning. Provide one example of a decision in which the data from an on-line database might provide support for management planning.

23. List the generations in the evolution of database structures.

24. What is a report writer? How might report writers shorten the time it takes for a manager to receive a report?

25. What is a query language? What do query languages provide for managers?

26. What two items does each object in an object-oriented database contain?

27. Which of the three database structures permits you to link data elements together to create a report even though these linkages have not been specified previously?

Questions for Discussion

1. Which of the three database structures is best suited for ad hoc queries and reports and which is best suited for large, batch operations? Explain your choices.
2. What are the differences between a file management system and a database management system?
3. What problems have been associated with file management systems in the past?
4. Select three components of a database management system that you consider important to the decision-making capabilities of a manager. Explain why you think these components are more important than others.
5. What are the advantages to an organization of using a database management system rather than a file management system?
6. What is meant by the "ownership of data"? How does the ownership of data change when an organization changes from a file management system to a database management system?
7. What are the dangers of having many file management systems that contain data common to each other?
8. What may be the consequences to managers who do not back up their records regularly?
9. Why might an organization want to have a distributed database system? What problems might a distributed database system generate for the organization?
10. How might an on-line database help a manager to improve the quality of decision making? Provide one example of a decision in which the data from an on-line database might provide decision support.
11. Why might a loan manager at a bank want loan accounts for customers stored in an indexed sequential or direct access fashion rather than only sequentially?
12. What is SQL? What is the advantage to the manager of learning SQL as opposed to other query languages?
13. What is an object-oriented database? How does it differ from the traditional database structures?

Problems

1. **Aztec Promotions, Inc.** You run a video store and wish to develop screen reports that would help your sales clerks help customers choose videotapes for viewing. You have noticed that people tend to ask for tapes based on several features. Some ask for the latest tapes received by the store. Others ask for tapes based on the actors that star in them. Still others ask for tapes by type; for example, westerns, horror, science fiction, drama, and comedy. Many ask for tapes based on combinations of these features. For example, a customer may ask if the store has a western starring John Wayne or a recent comedy starring Dan Aykroyd.

   a. Outline four reports as they might look on a computer screen to allow your salesclerks to respond to each of the typical requests your customers make. The screen report should contain the report title, the column headings, and possible data.

   b. Create a record that could be used to provide the reports you outline in (a) above. The record should contain all the data elements that are needed to complete the reports you outlined. Name each data element and indicate a recommended field length and data type (alphabetic, numeric, date). Finally, identify or create a primary field that will be used to distinguish one record from another.

c. (Optional) If you have a PC database management system available, create the record you developed in (b) above, populate 20 records with fictitious values, and print out the reports you developed in (a) above.

2. **Velor Sporting Goods, Inc.** You are the sales manager for Velor Sporting Goods, Inc., a sporting goods wholesaler. You wish to use a database management software package to maintain vendor and customer records. The records do not contain financial data, but rather the names, addresses, past buying preferences, past product portfolios, and other important data about vendors and clients. Your current manual files include these records:

   a. 350 vendor records, each of which may contain a maximum of 225 characters of information.

   b. 735 customer records, each of which may contain a maximum of 430 characters of information.

   Further, suppose you estimate that the data about the data in your database (the metadata) will take 20 percent of the space occupied by the records themselves and that you are not using any compression storage methods.

   c. What is the minimum storage capacity, stated in kilobytes, that the database management software package you buy must be able to handle to meet the maximum of your current record needs?

   d. If you estimate that your files will increase by 5 percent each year, what will be the estimated maximum capacity in kilobytes of your database system in five years?

3. **Talbot Company (A).** The Talbot Company uses a file of manually prepared stock record cards to manage its inventory. Each record contains the following data elements: the name of the stock, a description of the stock, the stock number, the unit of purchase (e.g., dozen, gross, crate), the minimum amount required that should be on hand, the maximum amount to have on hand, the warehouse section number, and the aisle location number. The firm now wishes to computerize these records to improve the management of its inventory.

   a. Which data element(s) should be used as the primary key for the record? Why?

   b. Which data elements might be used as secondary keys for the record? Why?

   c. Which of the three file structures discussed in this chapter would you recommend for these records? Why?

   d. Do you recommend that in-house programmers develop the inventory system or that a commercial file management software package be selected? Why?

4. **Talbot Company (B).** After the inventory system was developed and implemented, the Talbot Company (see Problem 3) considered computerizing two of its other files: the stock vendor file and the stock quotation file. The records in the vendor file contain the following data elements: vendor number, vendor name, vendor address, and vendor product using Talbot stock name and number. The stock quotation file contains these data elements: stock number; stock name; stock description; vendor name; vendor number; vendor address; and the date, quantity, and price of each quotation obtained from the vendor.

a. If the inventory, vendor, and stock quotation files are developed into computerized files using file management software, what problems are likely to occur?
b. What do you recommend that the firm do before developing two more computerized files?

5. **Talbot Company (C).** Using a microcomputer database management system, develop a simple database containing the stock record and stock vendor record described in Problems 3 and 4. Then create 10 actual records for each record type using fictitious data. Once the 20 records are completed, prepare the following:

   a. A report listing stock numerically by stock number.
   b. A report listing each vendor alphabetically by name.
   c. A report listing each vendor with the number and name of each stock item purchased from the vendor.

6. **Daniel Distributors, Inc.** Daniel Distributors, a wholesaler, has a home office in Los Angeles and 95 field representatives and seven warehouses scattered in three western states. The bulk of the administrative and clerical staff is located in the home office. The field reps work out of offices in the warehouses. How do you recommend that the organization distribute

   a. Payroll and personnel data?
   b. Inventory data?
   c. Sales data?

7. **Landcrest Realtors, Inc.** Landcrest Realtors, Inc., a national real estate chain, has offices across the United States and headquarters in St. Louis, Missouri. The home office provides corporate-level services. Each of the chain locations has a manager, several real estate agents, and the necessary supporting staff. How do you recommend that the organization distribute

   a. Commercial property listing data?
   b. Home or family property listing data?
   c. Sales data?
   d. Payroll data?

8. **Software Comparison Project (A).** Prepare a report comparing a file management software package for a microcomputer with a database management software package for a microcomputer. The report should contain (a) the costs of each package, (b) the features of each package, (c) some evaluation of the ease with which a manager might learn and use each package, and (d) measures of each package's capacity, such as the number of records the package will store, the number of fields permitted per record, the number of characters allowed per field, and the number of secondary keys permitted. Refer to the "General Features of Software" in Chapter 5 for additional help in preparing your report.

9. **Software Comparison Project (B).** Prepare a report on one of the following types of microcomputer file management packages or databases: a personal information manager; or an image file management package or database. The report should contain (a) the costs of the package, (b) the features of the package, and (c) some evaluation of the ease with which a manager might learn and use the package. Refer to the "General Features of Software" in Chapter 5 for additional help in preparing your report.

10. **Information Utility Identification Project.** Identify and describe three general-purpose information utilities. Prepare a report listing the three information utilities along with a brief overall description of each information utility. Also, identify the major categories of services each utility provides.

Cases

1. **Jay Stuart, Inc.** Jay Stuart, Inc., was a small retail furniture firm located in the city of Barrett. Jay Stuart, Sr., the founder, started the store in 1968. At that time, the furniture warehouse was simply the back end of the original store. In 1984, the firm decided to automate some of its operations. Jay Stuart, Jr., who had recently taken over management of the store, contracted with Data Advisors, Inc., a computer consulting firm, to develop a database application that maintained data on, among other things, sales orders, purchase orders, and inventory levels. The automation decision paid off for the Stuarts. The store grew in sales consistently throughout the rest of the 1980s and early '90s. The automation reduced the firm's costs and allowed it to offer quality merchandise cheaper than many stores in the city and surrounding towns.

   As the firm grew in sales volume, it also decided to add a small MIS department to handle its automation needs rather than depend on the computer consulting firm. So, in 1991, Jay Jr. hired Vicky Penn as head of the department. She promptly hired a small staff to handle the maintenance of existing programs and to operate what now was being called the Data Center.

   By 1995, however, Jay Jr. and his management staff recognized that they had saturated the firm's local market. If revenues were to increase, they would have to add other product lines, other services, or other locations. After considerable analysis of marketing data, some of which were obtained from on-line databases, Jay Jr. decided to grow geographically by adding additional stores beyond the reach of their present location. He decided to add three stores, each located in a city to the north of the original store and just over the line to another state. He also decided to add one warehouse that was centrally located to serve as an inventory hub for the three stores. Suddenly, the firm had decided to grow from one store and one warehouse to four stores and two warehouses. It had also shifted from a store serving a local area to a regional store serving customers in a two-state geographical area.

   As these decisions were made, Vicky Penn began to consider the implications of them for the Data Center. She began to realize that she would have to make decisions about how she would handle the data processing and data storage needs of the new store and warehouse locations. To help her formulate a well-founded decision, she has asked Arif Buhkta, a member of her staff, to prepare a report on her options.

   Assume the role of Arif Buhkta and prepare a report of Vicky Penn's options for organizing the firm's database. Your report should include a list and brief description of her options and a brief analysis of the advantages of each.

2. **Urban Advantages, Inc.** After a successful career as an advertising executive in a large corporation, Jill Roncine left that world to start her own consulting firm. The firm, Urban Advantages, Inc., advises communities and states on attracting and holding new businesses. At the start, Roncine ran her firm from her home. She purchased a microcomputer and a presentation graphics package, a desktop publishing package, and Busio, a software package her husband, Fred, who helped her

as a part-time bookkeeper, used to record the firm's transactions into a financial database and prepare its financial statements.

Over the next two years, the firm grew rapidly. Roncine hired five professionals in marketing, management, public planning, and other specialties to help her serve her clients. She also hired a full-time bookkeeper and two full-time secretaries. The firm's workload has grown so much, however, that she is now considering adding two more office personnel: a part-time bookkeeper/secretary, and a general office clerk.

Because of the increased staff, she is considering buying more personal computers and connecting them to allow both bookkeepers, the general office clerk, and her husband to enter transactions into the financial database using the Busio software at the same time. She plans to place the personal computers for these personnel in the open office area that separates her office and those of the professional staff from the client waiting and meeting room area. Because she knows little about personal computers and financial software, she has asked Lammert and Associates, a computer consulting firm, to advise her about her plans.

If you were assigned as the computer consultant by Lammert to advise Roncine, what problems would you suggest she is likely to encounter with her plan?

3. **Roget College Affirmative Action Office.** Ms. Martha Radcliff is the director of Roget College's Affirmative Action Office. Radcliff's office is responsible for identifying the organization's affirmative action goals, assisting the organization in carrying out the goals, and reporting on the goals to various organization units and state and federal agencies. The reporting requirements have increased considerably in the last few years. Numerous federal and state agencies and college units require information about minority status, affirmative action goals, compliance with state and federal regulations, and similar matters for the college's clerical, professional, and teaching personnel. Each agency seems to want similar information in different formats at different times during the year. Providing these agencies with the information required has become a clerical headache.

Currently, the college maintains information about employees in payroll files and some personnel files on its mainframe. The management information systems department developed these files at the request of payroll and the personnel departments using a mainframe database management system. Radcliff and her employees use the mainframe system for a variety of applications. However, although the current mainframe database management files contain some of the data Radcliff needs for the affirmative action reports, they do not contain all the necessary data. Radcliff and her employees have been using the mainframe system to obtain what data they could, but these data were insufficient to prepare the reports needed. So Radcliff approached the management information systems department about the problem last year and was told that they were completely overwhelmed by the development of a student information system, which was already behind schedule. The administration was breathing down their necks over the student information system, and they simply would not be able to devote any resources to her project—although they would like to very much.

As a result, Radcliff contacted an information systems consultant, Robert Ahmed. Ahmed suggested that he could develop a system for her quickly and inexpensively, although it would involve recreating some of the files that already exist on the mainframe. He proposed purchasing a microcomputer with hard disk drive and dBASE IV, a microcomputer database management software package.

He felt that he could develop a database of personnel files that would provide her with all the reports that she needed with this package. He estimated that the costs would include $2,900 for the microcomputer, $1,500 for a laser printer, $500 for the software, and $3,000 for development of the applications she required. He estimated that it would take him about one month to complete the programming for the project.

Radcliff has the $8,000 in her budget to fund Ahmed's plan. Since neither Radcliff nor any member of her staff has had any experience with microcomputers, she has asked you to evaluate Ahmed's plan and advise her about it. Prepare a report identifying the concerns you have with Ahmed's plan and how those concerns might be reduced or eliminated.

4. **Pelegrin Industries.** Pelegrin Industries has been in business for over 70 years. The company manufactures sports equipment, and its specialty is hunting and fishing equipment. The firm has its headquarters and manufacturing plants in Dayton, Ohio. It ships directly to sporting goods wholesalers and a number of large retailers located throughout North America.

   Pelegrin has grown rapidly during the last few years as a result of close attention to quality products and customer satisfaction. As the company has grown, it has become increasingly difficult for the production department to assess the market success of its increasingly larger product line. As a result, production has not always matched demand, resulting in crisis production runs or large overruns of unpopular products. A major contributor to this situation is that sales data are buried in paper invoices that are not analyzed easily.

   To support its information needs, the company has a large number of paper file systems for its financial, personnel, marketing, and production records. Recently, the slowness of processing paper files has become painful to the company. Some customers have canceled orders because they were taking too long to fill. In addition, the managers have been finding it difficult to make decisions or develop long-range plans simply because the paper files do not permit the timely construction of reports useful for decisions. At a recent executive meeting, the problems with the paper recording system were discussed.

   Alice Noel, the production officer, felt that developing computerized files for the company's various paper records was long overdue. She stated that computerizing the files would speed up order processing and shipping and allow for many timely reports. She felt that a great deal of commercial file management software was available from which the company could choose. She also felt that the company was not so unique that it had to develop its own programs in-house. She felt that it should hire some consultants, buy the programs, and get the computerized files implemented as soon as possible.

   Clyde Morehouse, the personnel officer, felt that it was silly to go to the expense of purchasing commercial software and hiring "a bunch of consultants." He felt that the firm should hire its own programmers on a full-time basis to develop the software in-house. That way, the company would also have the programmers available to develop additional programs in the future. He felt it was high time that Pelegrin had its own management information systems department.

   John Akers, the financial officer, suggested that there was really nothing seriously wrong with Pelegrin information systems that a few more people wouldn't cure. He recommended that additional order entry and shipping clerks be hired to move the products out the door faster. He argued that computerizing the files would take a lot of money and a lot of time, and during the developmental stages of the project, the company would still require additional help to meet its immediate needs for speedier order processing.

You are the new assistant to the chief executive for the firm, and you have just completed a number of seminars on the use of computers to support managerial decision making. Your boss, Claire Williams, has asked you to prepare a report on the filing systems at Pelegrin for the next meeting. She would like to know what you think about each of the other officer's views and what you would recommend that they do to solve their paper problems.

Prepare a memo to Claire Williams (a) analyzing each of the other officer's ideas and (b) detailing the approach you would recommend to solve the problem. Make certain that you justify each of your recommendations.

5. **Babcock Valve Corporation.** Janice Kalimeyer is the personnel manager of the Babcock Valve Corporation. She has spent a number of years developing a series of files to help her manage the personnel function within Babcock. Among the files developed are an employee skills inventory file, a personnel history file, and an employee placement file. Last year, however, Betty Fuller was hired by the corporation with the title of database administrator. Janice wants the management information systems department to develop a new file to help her manage her recruiting activities and to maintain data for reports to various federal agencies. When Janice requested the help from the department, however, Jason Culver, the MIS director, told her that her plans for the file would have to be cleared with Betty Fuller. Janice was at first surprised, then outraged. She said to the director, "What right has Fuller to tell me what my files should look like? I've been working on these information systems for years. Who is she to tell me what to do with my files?" However, Culver said that it was the new policy that all file structures be cleared with the new database administrator and that he had no choice.

   When she returned to her office, Janice had cooled down only slightly but made an appointment with Betty Fuller for the afternoon to talk about the new file she wanted to develop for her needs. When she arrived at Fuller's office, she described the history of the development of her files and the need she had for the new file. She next told Fuller that she felt that she could handle the new file herself, with the help of the management information systems department. She asked Fuller why she had to have anything to do with her files, and why she couldn't just proceed as usual.

   a. What reasons justify Betty Fuller's involvement in Janice Kalimeyer's new files?

   b. If you were Betty Fuller, how would you approach Janice Kalimeyer?

Selected References and Readings

Anderson, Ron. "SQL Databases: High-Powered, High-Priced." *PC Magazine* 11, no. 15 (September 15, 1992), pp. 369–372 ff. A discussion of how to choose PC-based client/server databases.

Cashin, Jerry. "Data Model Standards in Competitive Stage." *Software Magazine* 9, no. 15 (December 1989), pp. 78–81. Compares IBM's, DEC's, and ANSI's models for data repositories.

Coad, Peter, and Edward Yourdon. *Object-Oriented Analysis.* 2nd ed. Englewood Cliffs, NJ: Yourdon Press, 1991, A popular text on object-oriented systems development.

Cummings, Stephen. "Completing the Circle from Mainframe to Desktop." *Corporate Computing* 1, no. 3 (September 1992), pp. 190–193. A description and comparison of client/server application development software.

Duncan, Ray. "Managing Random Access Files." *PC Magazine* 8, no. 6 (March 28, 1989), pp. 291–302. A discussion of nonindexed, direct access files and binary search routines.

Kim, Won. "A New Database for New Times." *Datamation* 36, no. 2 (January 15, 1990), pp. 35–42. A discussion of object-oriented and extended relational database structures.

Kroenke, David M. *Database Processing: Fundamentals, Design, Implementation.* 4th ed. New York: Macmillan, 1992. A basic text on database management systems.

McFadden, Fred R., and Jeffrey A. Hoffer. *Database Management.* 3rd ed. Redwood City, CA: Benjamin/Cummings, 1991. A basic text on database management systems.

Moriarty, Terry. "Are You Ready for a Repository?" *Database Programming & Design* 3, no. 3 (March 1990), pp. 61–71. Describes the features and advantages of a data repository.

Moser, Karen. "Natural Language Tool to Support Windows." *PC Week* 9, no. 3 (January 20, 1992), pp. 45 and 48. Discusses Natural Language, a multiplatform natural language access tool for database queries.

Oz, Effy. "Toward a Document Base Management System." *Information Executive* 3, no. 1 (Winter 1990), pp. 19–23. Describes object-oriented databases.

Petreley, Nicholas. "How to Pick a Winning DBMS Platform." *Enterprise Computing,* an editorial supplement to *InfoWorld,* March, 23, 1992. An analysis of key features in PC-based database servers.

Pratt, Philip J. *A Guide to SQL.* Boston: Boyd and Fraser, 1990. An introductory text providing descriptions, cases, and problems about structured query language (SQL).

Ricciuti, Mike. "Distributed DBMSs Move into the Trenches." *Datamation* 39, no. 8 (April 15, 1993), pp. 59–62. A discussion of the major distributed DBMSs, with attention to maintaining currency.

Smith, Laura. "Developers Eye Object Databases," *Development Tools,* a special supplement to *PC Week,* February 15, 1993, p. S8. A comparison of relational to object-oriented database systems. Also provides reasons why relational database developers will resist object-oriented databases.

Communications and Distributed Systems

Chapter Outline

MANAGER'S VIEW

At one time communications technology was the purview of telephone companies and small groups of technical people located in very large firms. This state of affairs no longer exists. The communication of voice, data, text, and images pervades computer information systems regardless of the size of a manager's computer resources. Consider the diversity of tasks that now utilize some form of communications system.

Branch Sales. A company wishes to speed up its order entry system by developing a network of order entry terminals at each of its branch sales offices in several major cities. Each sales office is to have terminals that permit salespeople to be on-line directly with the mainframe computer at the home office. Salespeople will be able to enter an order at a remote terminal, immediately determine the customer's credit status and the availability of the stock the customer wants, and provide both a hard copy invoice to the customer at the remote site and a hard copy shipping order to the shipping department at the warehouse within seconds.

Field Sales. A company wishes to have on-the-road salespeople equipped with laptop microcomputers to implement an order entry system like the one previously described. However, the salespeople will complete orders via the laptops on the customer's premises, in their hotel rooms, or in their cars, using whatever phone is available at any of these locations.

Assembly Line. A company wishes to have data about production on an assembly line input directly from the assembly line. It wants terminals placed on the factory floor at key locations so that workers can enter data easily about the raw materials they use, the products they are working on, and the products they have finished making. Management hopes to use the system to control inventory and materials costs better.

Desktop Publishing. A department in a large corporation wishes to develop an in-house publication capacity so several secretaries, using inexpensive desktop publishing software, can create documents on microcomputers connected to each other. Also connected is a special laser printer used to produce hard copy containing text, charts, and drawings.

Executive Decision Making. A number of executives wish to access the mainframe database using the microcomputers they have in their offices and homes. Sometimes they want to view information in the database. At other times they want to transfer information from the database to programs they are running on their microcomputers. They hope that the increased quantity and quality of data available to them will improve their decision making.

Working at Home. Some employees wish to work at home on projects and send reports of these projects over communications lines to their offices for hard copy printout and distribution. This will allow parents with sick children, workers who live a long commuting distance from the office, and others who may have to stay home for a time to continue working. Working at home but staying in touch with the office using communications systems is called *telecommuting*.

On-Line Databases. Some managers wish to use the information found in on-line databases for planning. Sometimes they only want to view the information. At other times, they want to transfer the information they find to the programs they are running on their microcomputers. They hope to use the on-line databases to bring increased knowledge of the competition, the market, and the customer to their decision making.

Messaging. The field representatives of one company are concerned because they spend too much time dialing and redialing the home office to leave routine phone messages. At the same time, home office personnel are frustrated because they have difficulty getting messages to the field reps. The company wants to install a voice mail system so voice messages can be delivered where and when they are needed.

Employee Training. An organization wishes to provide a three-hour seminar for its production engineers with opportunities for the engineers to ask questions of an expert in the field. However, the engineers are scattered across the country. The organization feels that the travel expenses and costs associated with time away from work for the engineers would make the seminar prohibitive. The organization is considering using the videoconferencing facilities of a hotel chain to reduce these costs. The engineers could gather at locations of the hotel chain near them and take part in a *teleconference* conducted at a hotel location near the home office. The conference system would allow them to see, hear, and communicate with the expert and each other without having to travel far.

Tracking Shipments. An express package delivery firm wants to get immediate data on the location of every delivery truck in its fleet. Managers place microwave transmitters/receivers on each vehicle and give each driver a handheld computer with a wand that can scan the bar codes on packages. They use the system to track every shipment. Later, they provide major customers with on-line access to their tracking data so customers can track their own shipments.

These examples demonstrate that communications systems are likely to have an impact on every possible information system the manager uses. The ability to create, send, and receive voice, data, text, and images electronically has become as important today as the ability to create, send, and receive paper documents was in the recent past. Information is the lifeblood of the effective manager. Accurate, timely, and appropriate information is necessary for managers to make effective decisions. Communications equipment and software play an important part in delivering the information managers need when they need it. Thus, managers must understand the basics of communications so they can use communications resources for their operations and their planning needs.

The goal of this chapter is to provide you with a basic understanding of communications systems, communications modes and codes, communications channels, wide area networks, private telephone networks, local area networks, and microcomputer communications. Additional information pertaining to electronic communications is presented in Chapter 8 which covers such topics as facsimile, communicating copiers, electronic mail, voice mail, and teleconferencing systems.

COMMUNICATIONS SYSTEMS

Communications systems are often defined as systems for creating, delivering, and receiving electronic messages. To accomplish these tasks, every communications system comprises at least three elements (see Figure 7–1): (1) a device to send the message, (2) a **channel,** or communications medium, over which the message is sent, and (3) a device to receive the message.

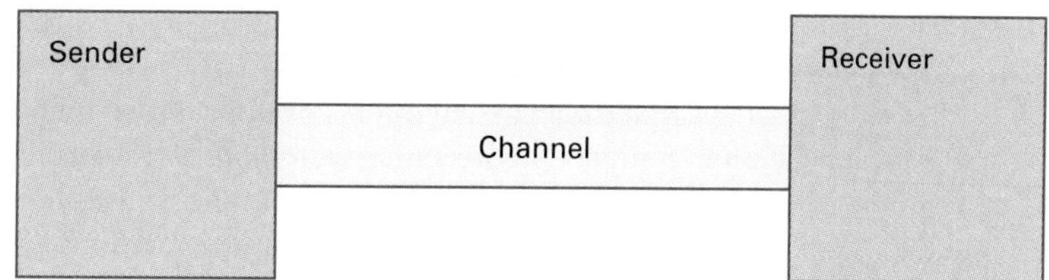

Figure 7–1
Basic elements in a communications system

Communications systems are also referred to as **telecommunications systems,** or networks. Very simply, a **communications network** is a group of devices connected to one or more communications channels. The devices could be those that send signals, or receive signals, or do both such as telephones, terminals, printers, mainframe computers, or microcomputers. The devices also could be those that encode, decode, relay, or otherwise manipulate signals so that they may be transmitted and received.

Communications Modes and Codes

You may select from a number of transmission modes and data codes for transmitting signals from a sending device to a receiving device. In fact, many networks use a variety of transmission modes and data codes for signaling.

Analog and Digital Transmission. The majority of computers communicate with digital signals. Digital signals are discrete "on" and "off" pulses of electricity that most computer systems use to create the bits that make up bytes, or characters (see Chapter 4). For example, a computer may create an "on" bit by placing a short positive signal of five volts on a channel. Conversely, it may create an "off" bit by placing a short negative signal of five volts on the channel (see Figure 7–2a). Sending data with digital signals is called **digital transmission.**

Sound, including the human voice, travels over analog signals. Analog signals are continuous sine waves. In a communications system, an analog signal may send a continuous five-volt signal on a channel, but the signal will vary continuously from +5 volts to −5 volts (see Figure 7–2b). Compare, for example, using the loudness dial on your radio versus the on/off button. If you continuously moved the loudness dial from maximum to minimum loudness, you would be simulating the action of an analog signal. If you turned the radio on and off, however, you would receive discrete bursts of radio sound waves and be simulating the action of a digital signal.

Many voice telephone lines still use **analog transmission** because the telephone system was originally designed to carry the human voice. Radio signals also are analog transmissions. Many data channels use digital signaling because computers use digital signals. However, today's technology allows both voice and data to be transmitted by

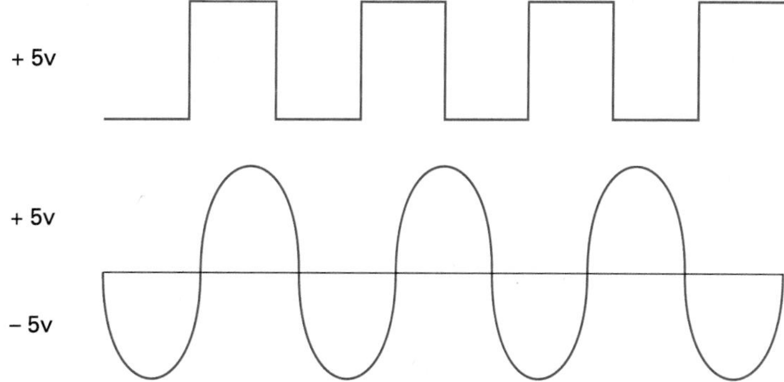

Figure 7–2
(a) Digital signal and **(b)** analog signal

either analog or digital signaling. Also, any new telephone lines that are installed are almost always digital.

Digital transmission offers advantages over analog transmission because it is usually easier to reduce and clean up noise and errors in digital transmission, especially when messages must be sent over long distances. Another advantage is that digital transmission is compatible with digital computer systems. Thus, it is not necessary to convert data messages to and from analog to digital when computer systems use digital transmission channels.

Data Codes. You know that computers use codes to represent data, which can be alphabetic, numeric, or special characters. Two frequently used data codes for communications systems are ASCII and EBCDIC (see Chapter 4). In fact, many communications networks have devices that use both codes.

Asynchronous Transmission. Still another choice is whether your messages will be sent as a series of single characters or as a block of characters. In *asynchronous transmission,* each character is sent down a channel separately; that is, each transmission unit is only one character in length. The character is headed with a start bit and ended with one or more stop bits. The start and stop bits tell the receiving device that a character is coming and that the character has been sent. The character usually contains a *parity bit,* which is used by the receiving device to verify that the transmission was received correctly. In a system using even parity, the number of 1 bits in all characters sent must equal an even amount. So, the sending device will place a 1 bit in the parity slot whenever it sends a character whose 1 bits don't add up to an even number. The receiving device checks each character it receives by summing the 1 bits. If the character arrives with an even number of 1 bits, the device assumes that it has received a correct character. If the number of 1 bits is odd, the device assumes that an error in transmission has occurred. Some systems verify transmissions using an odd-parity procedure.

Many terminals send messages asynchronously in ASCII code (see Figure 7–3a); that is, they send messages by transmitting a series of separate, single characters composed of these elements:

1. A start bit.
2. Seven bits that represent an ASCII-coded character.
3. A parity bit.
4. A stop bit.

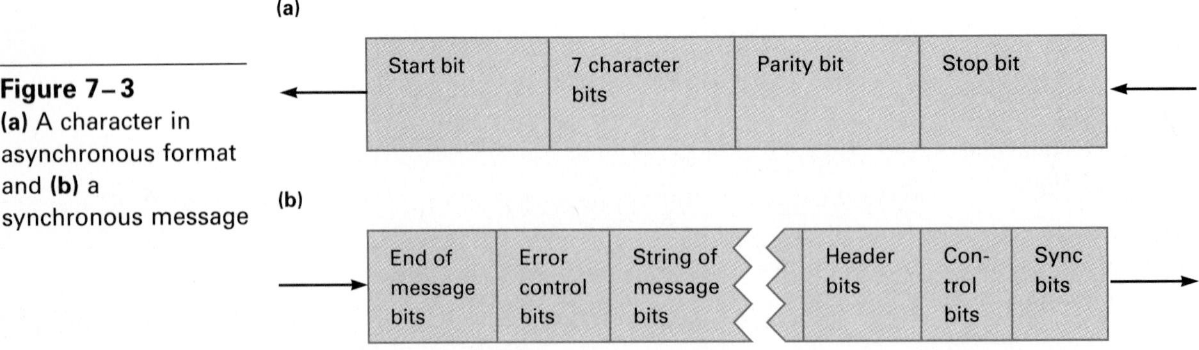

Figure 7–3
(a) A character in asynchronous format and **(b)** a synchronous message

That means that to send one character, the terminal actually must send a total of 10 bits. Thus, the overhead to send a character is 30 percent of the total bits sent or 3 bits out of 10. For the manager, this means that 30 percent of the transmission costs paid to the common carrier are for nonmessage bits. That's a pretty hefty percentage of your costs for sending nothing but start, stop, and parity bits. If the terminal uses EBCDIC code—an 8-bit code—11 bits are sent for each character: 8 character bits plus 1 start bit plus 1 stop bit plus 1 parity bit.

Synchronous Transmission. To reduce the overhead costs of data transmission, some networks send messages using *synchronous transmission.* Synchronous transmission blocks many characters together for transmission (see Figure 7–3b). The message block is preceded by several bits so the receiving device knows what is coming and can prepare for the message. The block also is followed by several bits so the receiving device can verify what it received. However, the beginning and ending bits are a small percentage of the total number of message bits sent. Thus, synchronous transmission reduces the overhead costs of communications. It should be noted, however, that the cost of synchronous equipment is usually higher than the cost of asynchronous equipment. Thus, the manager must be sure that the higher investment in the synchronous equipment will be justified by the reduced overhead costs of using synchronous transmission.

Simplex, Half-Duplex, and Full-Duplex Transmission. Some networks have communications channels that send messages only one way—this is called *simplex transmission* (see Figure 7–4a). Commercial radio networks are simplex networks. You can listen to your favorite station, but you cannot communicate back to the station on the same radio frequency. Simplex channels are often used to connect fire and smoke alarm devices in offices and factories to nearby fire stations. Simplex transmission is also used for airport monitors.

Many networks use transmission channels that permit messages to be sent both ways, but only one way at a time—like a CB radio. This is known as *half-duplex transmission* (see Figure 7–4b). Other networks use transmission channels that permit simultaneous transmission of messages in both directions, or *full-duplex transmission* (see Figure 7–4c). The public voice telephone network uses many full-duplex channels. Many companies have networks that include all three types of channels.

Circuit Switching. Many voice telephone networks link a sender and receiver over a channel that is dedicated to their communications for the length of their session. It does not matter if the sender and receiver remain silent for long periods of time; the

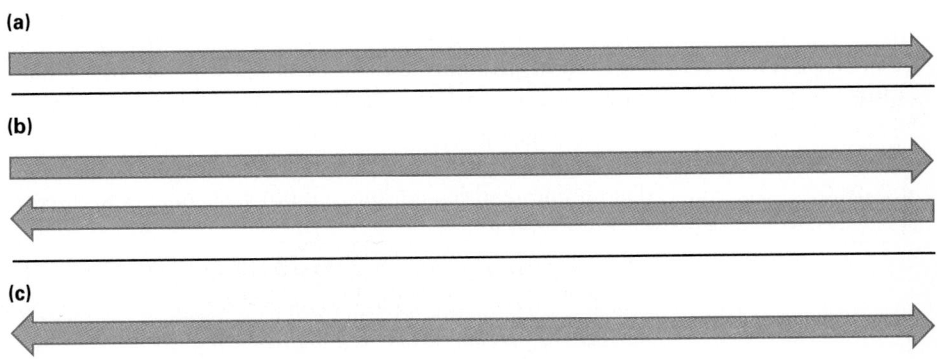

Figure 7–4
(a) Simplex, or one-way transmission, **(b)** half-duplex, or transmission in two directions but not at the same time, and **(c)** full-duplex transmission, or transmission in both directions at the same time

channel is still theirs until they hang up. That type of channel mode is called *circuit switching.* A circuit switching network may use a different route to make the connection between sender and receiver each time they call each other. However, once the connection is made, the parties may use the channel as they wish.

Message Switching. *Message-switching* networks differ from circuit switching in that the connection from sender and receiver is not kept open unless there are messages to send. They also differ in that in circuit switching, if a route from the sender to the receiver is not available, the sender gets a busy signal.

In message switching, each message from the sender may be sent immediately to the receiver if a route to the receiver is available. If a route is not available, the message will be *stored and forwarded* later when a route does become available or when the receiver demands its stored messages.

Packet Switching. *Packet-switching* networks are also store-and-forward networks. Packet-switching networks transmit messages in one or more fixed-size packets, or message blocks. Packet-switching networks consist of a series of channels that are connected to *nodes,* or computer-controlled switching centers. A voice, data, text, or image transmission is first broken up into small packets, then each of the packets is sent to the destination via the fastest route. This may mean that many of the packets will travel different routes to the destination. At the destination, the packets are put in sequential order and delivered to the receiver (see Figure 7–5).

Packet switching is used because it provides better use of the network than circuit switching. If the packets are kept small in size and if there are enough alternative routes in the network, the packet-switching system can even the traffic loads on the channels by routing packets appropriately.

Many public networks, for example, both the Tymnet and Sprintnet networks, use packet switching.

Communications Channel Sources

Communications channels may be obtained from many sources. For example, you can purchase both analog and digital channels from a **common carrier,** which may be the local telephone company or a long-distance carrier such as AT&T, Sprint, or MCI. You may also purchase channels from **value-added networks (VANs),** such as Telenet from GTE or Tymnet from British Telecom. Value-added networks often lease channels from other common carriers and then re-lease the channels to others. They usually add value to those channels by providing special features for their customers, such as packet-switching services, electronic mail, data code conversion, protocol conversion, matching the speed of transmissions to the receiving equipment, or the use of their host computers. Many on-line database and information utility companies, for example, Dow-Jones News Retrieval Service, CompuServe, The Source, and Dialog, connect their computer systems to packet-switching, value-added networks.

If your channels will be confined to your own building or campus, you could purchase and install the channels yourself, which usually saves a considerable amount in leasing fees over the long haul.

Common carriers offer many types of channels. Two of the most common are dial-up lines and leased lines. Another channel type growing in popularity is wireless network service.

Dial-Up Telephone Lines. **Dial-up telephone lines** are telephone lines that you rent from the local telephone company and pay for largely on a usage basis. Dial-up lines are often called *switched* lines because the route used to connect your phone and

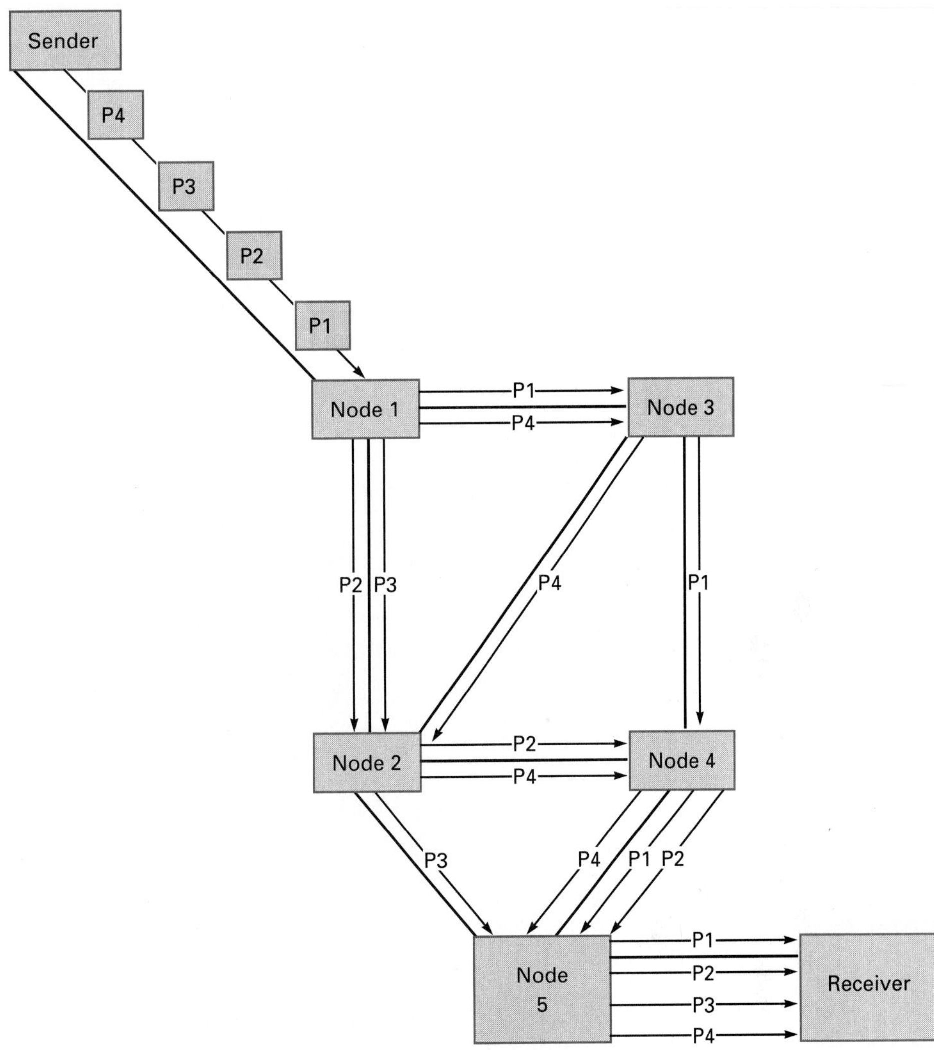

Figure 7–5
Delivery of packets on a packet-switching network

the party called may be different each time you call; that is, your call may be routed through different telephone switching centers each time.

Dial-up lines represent the telephone service you typically have in your home. Although you pay for installation of the lines and a small flat monthly fee to keep them in service, your telephone bill largely depends on how much you use them. That is, the cost of the lines is usage sensitive. For example, suppose that you need to make a long-distance connection between a remote terminal and a host computer. Suppose further that the terminal needs to be connected to the host only occasionally during the day. Rather than lease a line that is dedicated to communications between the terminal and the host for the entire day, you would probably simply dial up the host on the ordinary public switched telephone network when communications needed to occur. You would then pay for the line only for the time you actually used it.

Dial-up lines thus use the public telephone switched network—a very large network indeed. Dial-up lines often use analog signaling and are not usually employed when a user needs frequent or high-speed data communications. Typical data commu-

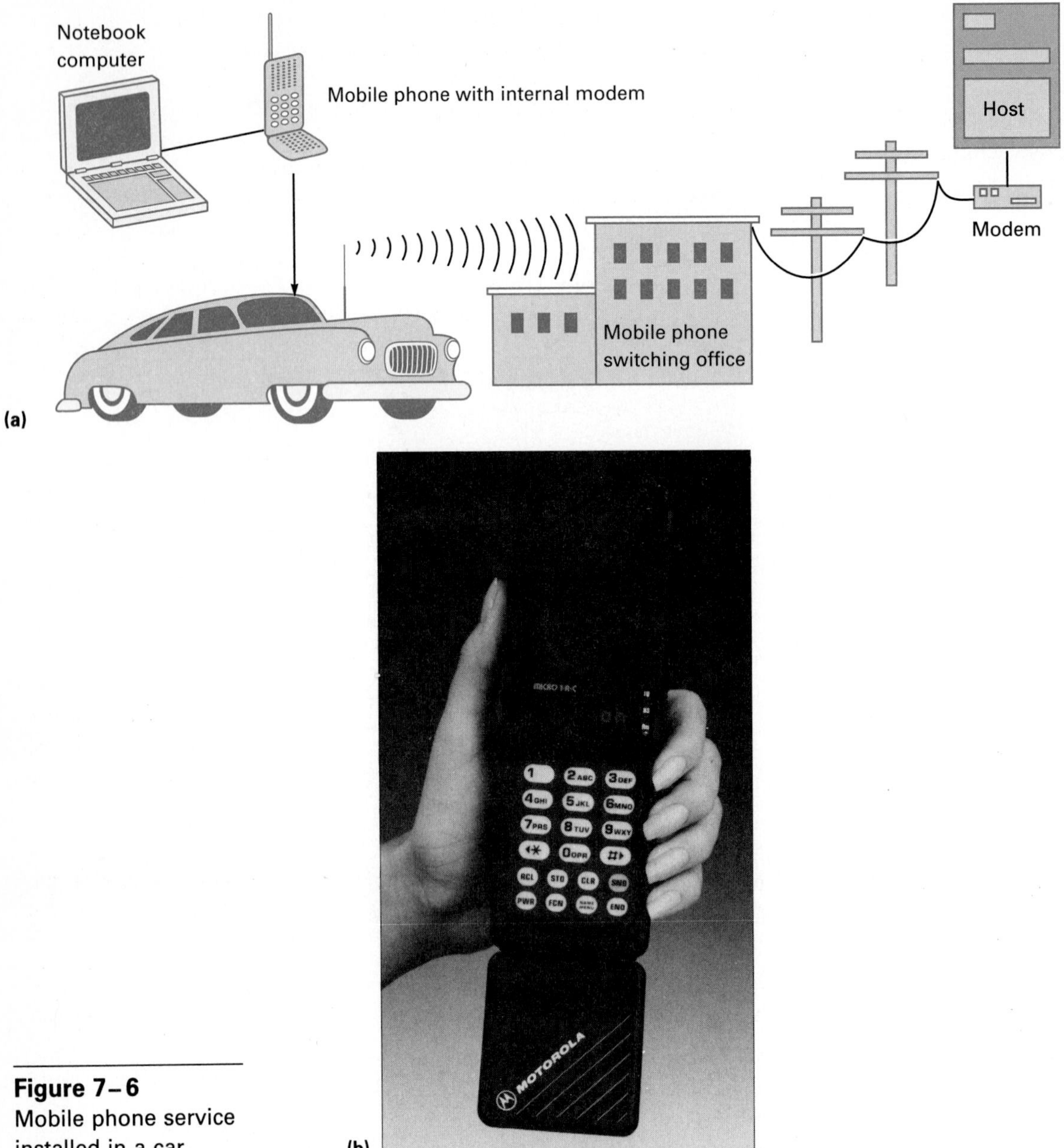

Figure 7–6
Mobile phone service installed in a car

nications speeds on dial-up analog lines include 1,200 **bits per second (bps),** 2,400 bps, 9.6 kilobits per second (kbps), 14.4 kbps, and 19.2 kbps.

Leased Telephone Lines. When you need high-speed data communications or frequent data communications between a sender and receiver, you usually lease the use of a telephone line. You then receive from the carrier use of a dedicated circuit. **Leased telephone lines** typically provide more error-free communications and much higher transmission speeds than dial-up lines. Speeds on a leased line may range from 9.6 kbps to multiples of 1.544 mbps (millions of bits per second).

Wireless Networks. A **wireless network** is just that: a network that uses a medium other than wire or fiber cable. That medium may be radio waves or infrared light waves. A number of communications firms provide radio-based voice and data networks. One type of wireless network is a **cellular telephone system** that provides mobile telephone service, typically to persons in vehicles (see Figure 7–6a). Cellular telephone service is often used by employees who must spend a great deal of time in their cars and away from their offices. For example, salespeople using mobile telephones in their cars can maintain contact with clients even when they are driving. They can also communicate with the computer systems in their home offices.

However, wireless networks are not limited to voice communications. A number of radio-based and cellular packet data networks permit mobile computer systems to connect to other computers and other networks. For example, IBM and nine cellular companies offer a public packet cellular data network (Celluplan II) that provides communications speeds up to 19.2 kbps.

Communications Media

Communications media represent the types of channels over which messages are transmitted. You may choose from many types of communications media, including, for example, twisted-pair wire, fiber optic cable, coaxial cable, microwaves, and radio waves. Many communications systems, such as telephone systems, use several different media. When you call a friend, for example, your voice may travel over twisted-pair wiring, fiber optic cabling, and microwaves to reach its destination.

A brief description of some of the more common media follows.

Twisted-Pair Wiring. *Twisted-pair wiring* or cabling is the same type of cabling system used for home and office telephone systems (see Figure 7–7a). It is inexpensive and easy to install. Technological improvements over the last few years have increased the capacity of twisted-pair wires so that they can now handle data communications with speeds up to 10 mbps over limited distances.

Coaxial Cable. *Coaxial cable* is a well-established and long-used cabling system for terminals and computers. This cabling comes in a variety of sizes to suit different purposes. Coaxial cable is commonly used to connect computers and terminals in a local area, such as an office, floor, building, or campus (see Figure 7–7b).

Fiber Optic Cables. Many common carriers are replacing older, copper wire cables in their networks with *fiber optic cables.* Fiber optic cables use light as the communi-

Box 7–1 Movies Calling

It seems that the capacity of simple, inexpensive telephone cabling—twisted-pair wiring—continues to increase with technological innovation. It was long a conventional wisdom for industry experts to consider the capacity of twisted-pair wiring too meager to support the large data transmission rates required for video or movie films. Now comes a joint project of AT&T and Compression Labs, Inc., with a system that may deliver video services to homes as early as 1994. At the heart of the system is compression technology that reduces a digital signal of 100 mbps to 1.5 mbps. The system will allow subscribers to choose a wide variety of interactive services, including home entertainment, home shopping, and educational programs.

Source: *St. Louis Post Dispatch,* Tuesday, January 19, 1993, p. 5C.

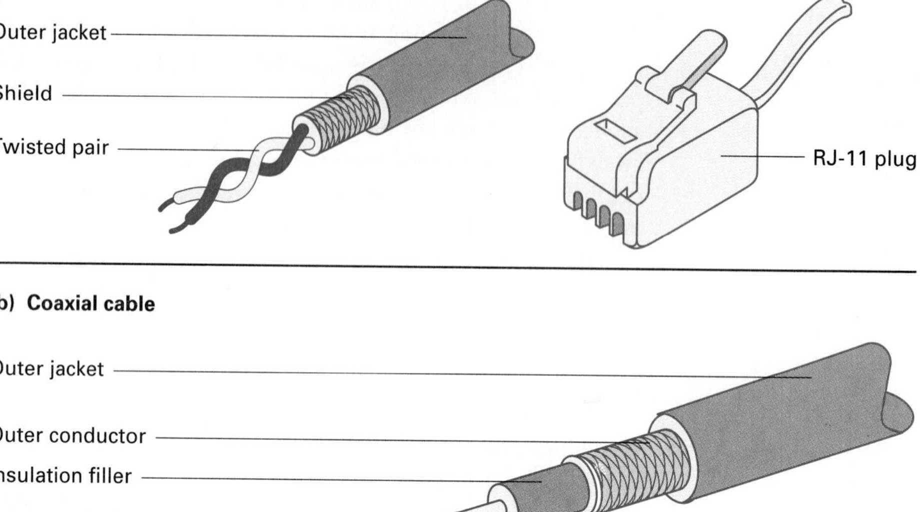

Figure 7–7
(a) Twisted-pair wiring and telephone plug **(b)** coaxial cable

cations medium. To create the on-and-off bit code needed by computers, the light is rapidly turned on and off on the channel. Fiber optic channels are lightweight, can handle many times the telephone conversations or volumes of data handled by copper wire cabling, and can be installed in environments hostile to copper wire, such as wet areas or areas subject to a great deal of electromagnetic interference. They are also less susceptible to spying; that is, conversations or data are more secure in a fiber optic network (see Figure 7–8).

Microwave Transmission Channels. For heavy users, *microwave transmission* channels provide what amounts to bulk-rate service. You can lease long-distance microwave transmission facilities from common carriers or acquire short-haul microwave networks and run them yourself, for example, to transmit large amounts of voice and data between buildings on a large campus. Microwave transmission may involve "dishes" located on top of buildings or on towers, or it may involve transmitting data and voice to and from satellites placed in stationary orbits (see Figure 7–9).

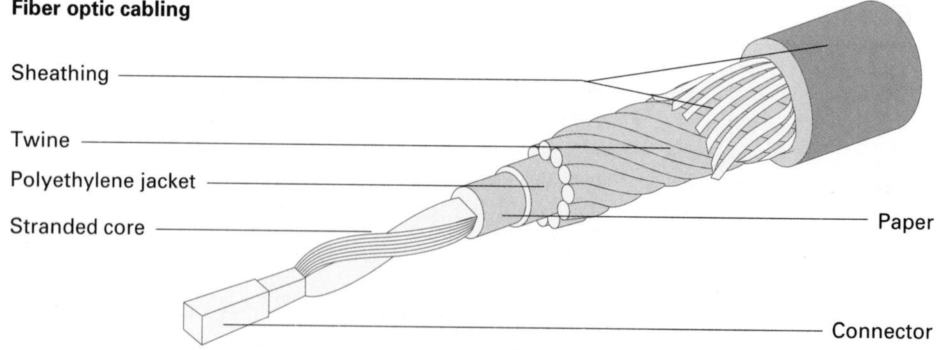

Figure 7–8
Fiber optic cabling

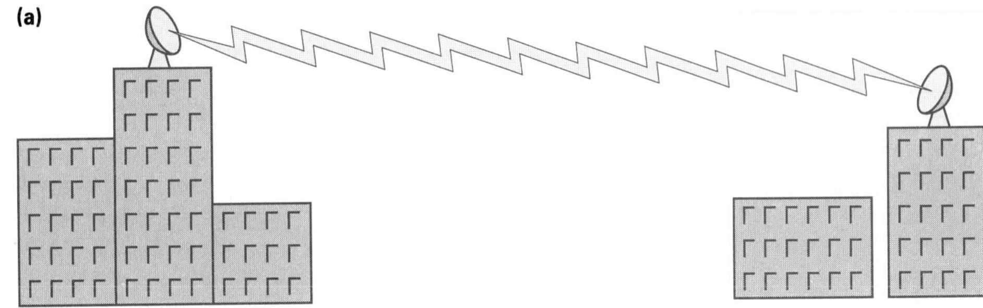

Figure 7–9
(a) A campus-to-campus satellite-based microwave network **(b)** a satellite-based microwave network

Wireless Transmission Channels. radio channels are increasingly used for short-distance voice and data telephone communications (see Box 7–2). Infrared light signals are also used for data transmission. These types of channels are often referred to as *wireless channels.*

Another cellular radio system is called **personal communications network,** or **PCN.** Personal communications networks use high-frequency radio waves to create very short-range networks, often with a broadcast radius of about eight miles, to allow voice and data communications for persons close to each other. These systems use small, easily carried, and relatively inexpensive handheld communication devices. PCN systems, if implemented widely, would permit a user to remain in contact with a global, intelligent voice and data network regardless of location.

Box 7–2 The Wireless Era

Wireless communications systems are expected to grow wildly in the next 10 years because more people are working away from the office, new networking technologies are making connections from anywhere to anywhere at anytime possible, and because convenient, hand-held computing devices are proliferating. Currently, cellular networks allow you to call or transmit data from your car, a taxi, or airport limo, and you can also make calls to the ground while in flight. But many other systems are planned.

- **Global Satellite Network.** Motorola, Inc., plans to offer a satellite network, called the Iridium Network, that will allow you to use a telephone that fits into your shirt pocket to call anywhere in the world. The network will use 77 low earth-orbit satellites so that anyone, anywhere on the planet, will be able to connect to anyone else on the planet using a three-pound handset device that will permit both voice and data transmission. The first satellite is expected to be launched in 1994 and the network will be linked to the public, switched telephone network.
- **Portable Computing.** Notebook computers, personal digital assistants, pen-based computing devices, cellular phones, and cellular modems make remote and portable computing convenient. Motorola even offers wristwatch pagers that receive short messages from anywhere in the United States.
- **Personal Communicators.** AT&T also produces a battery-operated, pen-based, notebook computer system called the Personal Communicator that provides fax, paging, E-mail, and cellular phone features. The system uses a GUI operating system (see Chapter 5) and a RISC microprocessor (see Chapter 4). AT&T suggests that the system can be used to take notes during a meeting or in a library. It will then read your handwriting, translate it into text, and allow you to transmit the notes through the public telephone network.
- **Car/Office Phone.** A new cellular phone will soon be commercially available that you can use in your car or elsewhere that switches from being connected to the cellular network to being connected to your PBX when you enter your office.

WIDE AREA NETWORKS

A **wide area network,** or **WAN,** is simply a network spread out over a wide area. For example, the telephone networks in the United States, Canada, and Mexico are wide area networks. The order entry system described in this chapter's "Manager's View" would probably use one of the telephone networks to provide channels for the system. One or more hosts, or mainframe computers, would be in the home office, which might be in the United States. The terminals would be placed in each of the company's offices, which might be located in a number of major cities throughout the United States, Canada, and Mexico. The mainframe computers are called **hosts** in a WAN because they serve the terminals attached to them much like party hosts serve their guests.

Reasons for Implementing Wide Area Networks

Wide area networks are often very expensive additions to a computer system. Such expenses would not be incurred if an organization did not have important reasons for them. Many of the reasons for wide area networks are implied by the examples described earlier in "Manager's View." A brief discussion of these reasons follows.

Capturing Data at Its Source. A WAN permits the use of remote terminals in sales offices, factory production lines, cars, and even on customer premises. These remote terminals permit employees to enter data into a computer system immediately, eliminating the need to rekey data captured originally by hand or by typewriter. For the manager, source data capture reduces the errors and costs associated with copying data from one form to another several times. Computer system input controls, available to remote users, reduce errors made at the time of original entry.

Increasing Productivity. A salesperson who uses a portable computer terminal at a customer location may find that the merchandise the customer wants to purchase is not in stock at the moment. Knowing that, the salesperson may choose alternate products that are in stock to satisfy the customer's needs. Furthermore, instant distribution of the sales invoice completed by the salesperson to the warehouse, shipping, and accounting departments means the customer order is filled faster and the customer is billed faster. Thus, both merchandise turnover and cash flow increase.

Managers with portable terminals at home or in their cars can use this equipment for planning and decision making whenever they get ideas, not just when they are in the office. Managers with such resources are *always* at the office.

Permitting Expansion. Organizations that expand often do so by purchasing or constructing facilities at other locations. Also, many organizations are so large that they span several buildings. Communications networks allow these remote and dispersed sites to be connected.

Increasing Timely Communications. Wide area networks permit organizations with dispersed personnel to distribute information quickly to the right people, thereby aiding decision making. Using the interoffice mail system and the postal system may delay critical information as much as three to five days. Using the voice telephone system for rapid communications to a large number of people individually would be very labor intensive. Also, the price per character of information sent over a manual mail system or a voice telephone system may far exceed the cost per character of an electronic data communications system. The ability to communicate new prices, stockouts, or changes in organizational policy to dispersed salespeople, managers, other employees, and customers instantly is very important to many organizations.

Increasing Management Control. Instant feedback of data from the assembly line allows supervisors to avoid major problems or to attend to potential problems before they become major. Timely knowledge of salespeople's accomplishments may affect raw materials purchases and production schedules. Communications networks provide managers with early information to permit them to react swiftly to potential problems.

WAN Hardware

A typical WAN might be constructed of a variety of communications hardware devices, software, and communications channels. For example, Figure 7–10 provides a schematic drawing of an order entry system showing the typical hardware that would be needed to serve the home office and two of the branch offices.

Let's examine this communications system in terms of the hardware, software, and communications facilities needed to run it.

Hosts. A host in a WAN is often a large mainframe computer. Some WANs are so large that several mainframe computers or minicomputers are attached to it. The host computers typically provide other users on the WAN with computing power, application programs, and access to database management systems.

The Front-End Processor. One of the most time-consuming tasks for a computer to perform is input and output tasks (I/O). These tasks involve accepting data input from

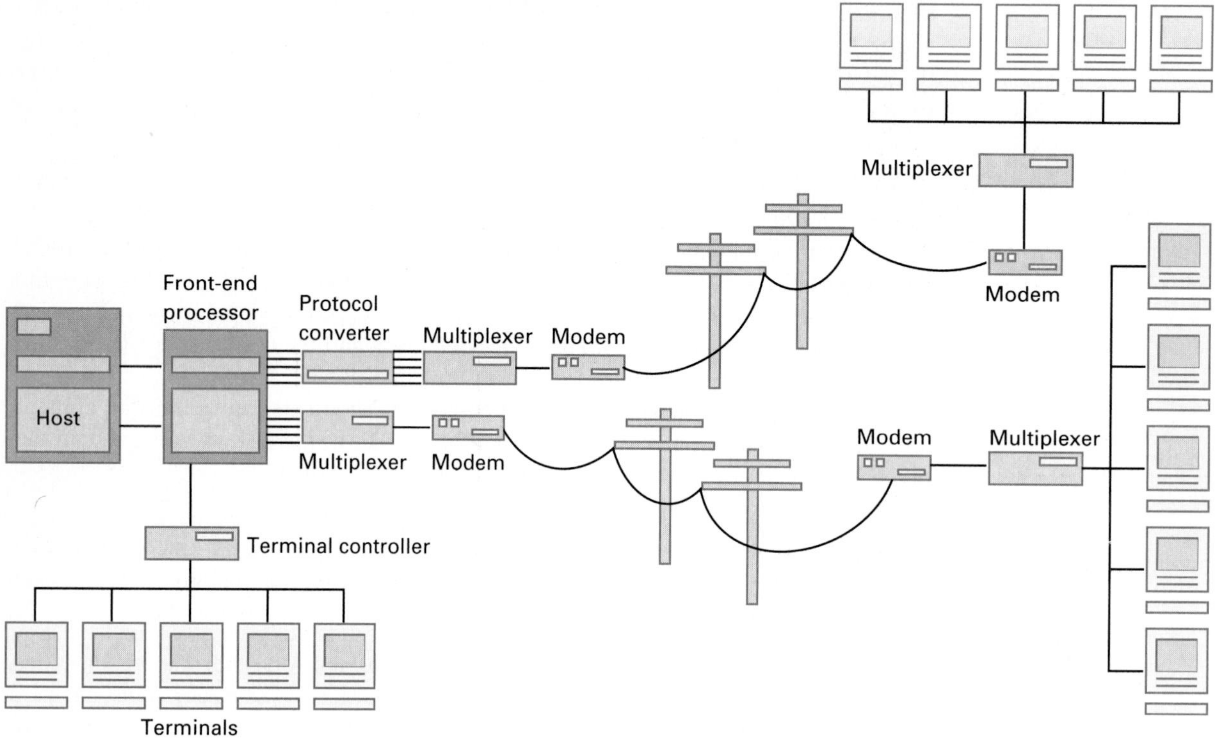

Figure 7–10
A communications system for an order entry system

terminals and providing data output to printers or other terminals. Because these tasks are time-consuming and because a data communications system requires that they be done constantly, communications systems designers often place a minicomputer in front of a mainframe and program it to do as many of these I/O tasks as possible. Minicomputers placed in front of a mainframe, between the remote terminals and a host, are called *front-end processors.* It is their job to take away, or *off-load* as many of the communications tasks from a host as possible, thereby allowing a host to do what it does best: process data.

Modems. Many telephone channels that carry voice communications today are *analog* channels. To send data over these channels requires that the data be in the form of analog signals. However, computers produce *digital* signals, not analog signals. To place host-generated digital signals on a voice, or analog, channel means that the digital signals must first be converted into analog form. At the other end of the communications system, the analog signals must be converted back to digital form so that they are acceptable to the terminals. To provide for the conversion, **modems** *MO*dulate and *DEM*odulate the analog signals to represent digital signals (see Figure 7–11).

Terminals. Many types of terminals can be placed on a WAN. One of the most common is a simple *dumb terminal.* This terminal is called dumb because it is given limited intelligence and memory; that is, it relies on the host computer for its memory and its brains. A dumb terminal usually provides the user with a keyboard and a monitor or screen.

Another type of terminal is the *intelligent terminal.* Such a terminal usually has a keyboard and a screen, but it also has the memory and computing power to process data by itself without host assistance. One type of intelligent terminal is the microcomputer.

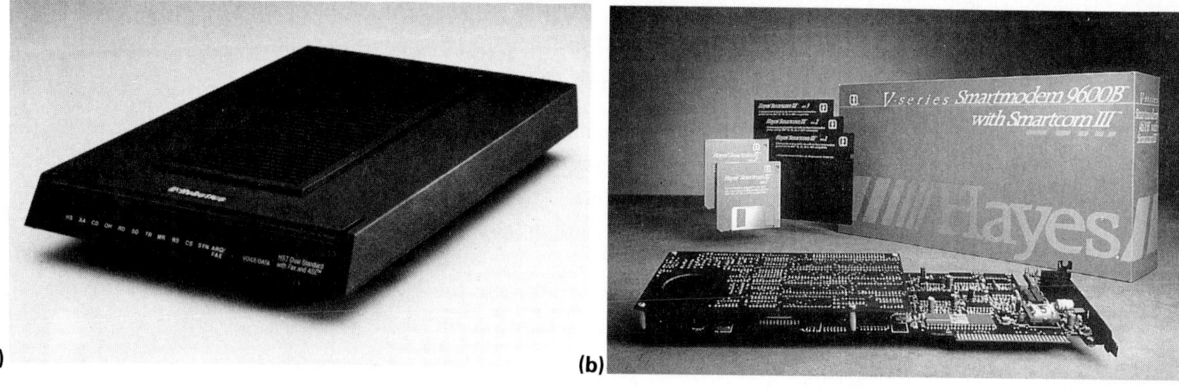

Figure 7–11
(a) A modem in its own housing that connects to a computer system
Courtesy of U.S. Robotics, Inc.
(b) a modem without its own housing that is placed inside a computer system
Courtesy of Hayes Computer Products

Another common device found on a WAN is a printer. This is often a high-speed line printer that provides rapid output of invoices, checks, and other documents.

Multiplexers. When terminals and printers are located at a remote site, telephone lines are usually used to connect the terminals to the hosts. If a separate telephone line were used for each device, the communications system could get very expensive. Not only would the manager have to pay for the installation and rental of one line for each terminal, but also the line would not be kept busy most of the time.

Consider how fast a typical typist is able to enter order entry data on a terminal; with coffee breaks, keystroke corrections, and normal office interruptions, a rate of 20 to 30 words per minute is likely to be a reasonable rate of data entry. If it takes 10 bits to send each character over a telephone line, then one order entry clerk would average about 200 to 300 bits *per minute.* The telephone line attached to the terminal, however, is capable of operating much faster—perhaps in a range of from 300 bits *per second* to millions of bits *per second.* As you can see, one line per terminal is not apt to be cost effective.

Most communications systems take advantage of the difference between the speed of the operator and the speed of the line by placing signals from several of these slow terminals on a fast line. One device that does this is called a *multiplexer.* A multiplexer accepts data from many terminals and places them over one or more communications channels networked to the host (see Figure 7–12) so the company can connect many remote terminals to a host while only paying for a few telephone lines. Because a modem is needed for each incoming or outgoing telephone line, a multiplexer saves more than lines; it saves the cost of additional modems, too.

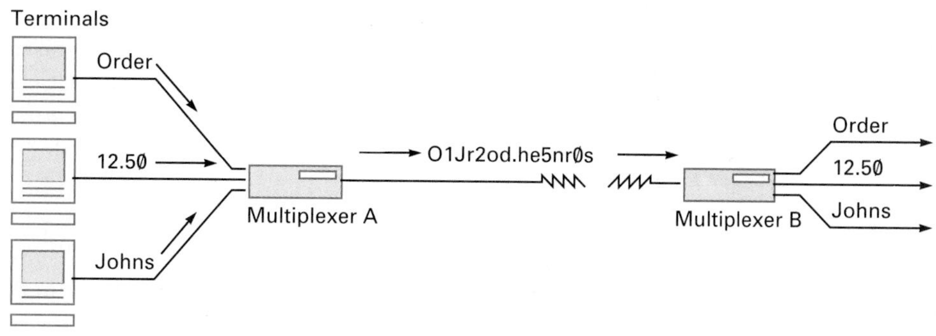

Figure 7–12
A multiplexer combines the signals from many terminals on one line

Like modems, multiplexers are usually used in pairs so that the signals from lines that are combined at one end of the system can be demultiplexed, or sorted back out at the other end of the system.

Terminal Controllers. *Terminal controllers,* or cluster control units, are used in some systems to connect many terminals to a single line. Terminal controllers are basically scaled down versions of front-end processors. Unlike multiplexers, terminal controllers do not need to be used in pairs. Instead, they communicate directly with the front-end processor. Although there are technical differences between the tasks terminal controllers and multiplexers perform, the bottom line is that they both reduce the number of channels you need to connect terminals to hosts.

Protocol Converters. Wide area networks are often eclectic in design because they have grown over a period of years. During those years the organization may have gone through several mergers and acquisitions and experienced many changes in technology. The result is that WANs are often a mixture of many different types of devices, channels, transmission modes, and transmission codes. To permit diverse system devices to talk to one another, *protocol converters* are used to translate the signals from one system to another. For example, a protocol converter commonly is used to permit dumb terminals transmitting ASCII code in asynchronous mode to talk to IBM hosts using EBCDIC code and synchronous transmission mode.

A *communications protocol* is a convention, or a set of rules or procedures for completing a communications systems task. For example, the use of ASCII code is a convention; so is the use of even parity for checking errors or asynchronous transmission for sending characters. Protocol converters are aptly named because they change the protocols used in a message from one convention, rule, or procedure to another.

WAN Software

Any computer system needs system software to make it run. Thus, a host computer in a WAN needs an operating system. A host computer also probably needs a database management system to handle the many records that local and remote terminals wish to access. However, a WAN needs more software than an ordinary computer system, typically telecommunications access programs and teleprocessing monitor programs.

Telecommunications Access Program. A host attached to a network needs software to handle the network channels and equipment. Usually, operating systems are not built to handle network devices and channels. Thus, a host computer on a network needs a software package called a *telecommunications access program.* A telecommunications access program handles the transfer of messages between the host's main memory and the remote devices. It provides an interface between the host's operating system and the telecommunications systems.

On older telecommunications systems, the telecommunications access method was located on the mainframe. On newer ones, the telecommunications access method is located on the front-end processor. On IBM systems, the telecommunications access method is located on *both* the mainframe and the front-end processor. Virtual telecommunications access method (VTAM) is a recent telecommunications access method software product for IBM systems.

Network Control Program. On IBM systems, some functions of the telecommunications access program may be off-loaded to the front-end processor. When this occurs, a separate program, called the *network control program,* is loaded onto the front-end processor. This allows the front-end processor to take some of the burden of running the network off the host. Some of the tasks performed include polling the remote terminals to see if they have any messages to send, routing messages between terminals and the host, logging the traffic over the network, editing incoming messages for accuracy, and translating data codes, if no protocol converter is used.

Teleprocessing Monitor. Often the main reason for a wide area network is to allow remote terminals to interact with the organization's database management system. Thus, much of the interactive "conversation" on the telecommunications system consists of messages between the database management system and the remote terminals. To improve the efficiency with which these tasks are handled, major database management system vendors have developed software packages called *teleprocessing monitors.* For example, IBM markets a teleprocessing monitor called CICS (for Customer Information Control System). Cullinet offers a teleprocessing monitor called IDMS-DC (for Integrated Data Management System–Data Communications).

Network Topologies

All networks are arranged in *topologies,* or configurations. A topology is simply a method or methods by which devices on the network are connected. One basic topology is a *point-to-point network,* in which two devices or points on the network are connected. Often, point-to-point networks connect devices such as terminals, or clusters of terminals connected to a terminal controller, to a host (see Figure 7–13). A point-to-point topology is also called a **star topology.**

One basic advantage of a star topology is that multiple devices on the network do not have to contend for access to the media. Each device has its own channel to the central point or host on a network. A disadvantage is that you have to pay the cost of installing or leasing each channel. Another disadvantage is that if the central point in a star network fails, the entire network fails.

A variation of the star topology is the *hierarchical network* (see Figure 7–14). In a hierarchical network, devices are connected to their host and these hosts are then connected to other hosts. The hierarchical network can provide a number of advantages in certain situations. For example, suppose that your firm owns a series of stores located throughout the country. Having a line from each store computer to the headquarters

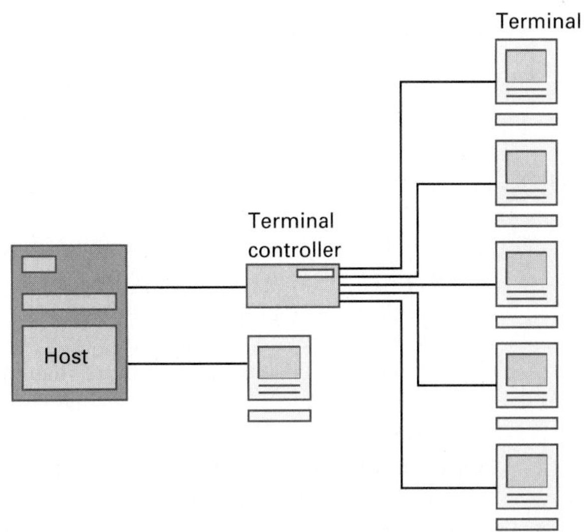

Figure 7–13 A point-to-point, or star network, configuration

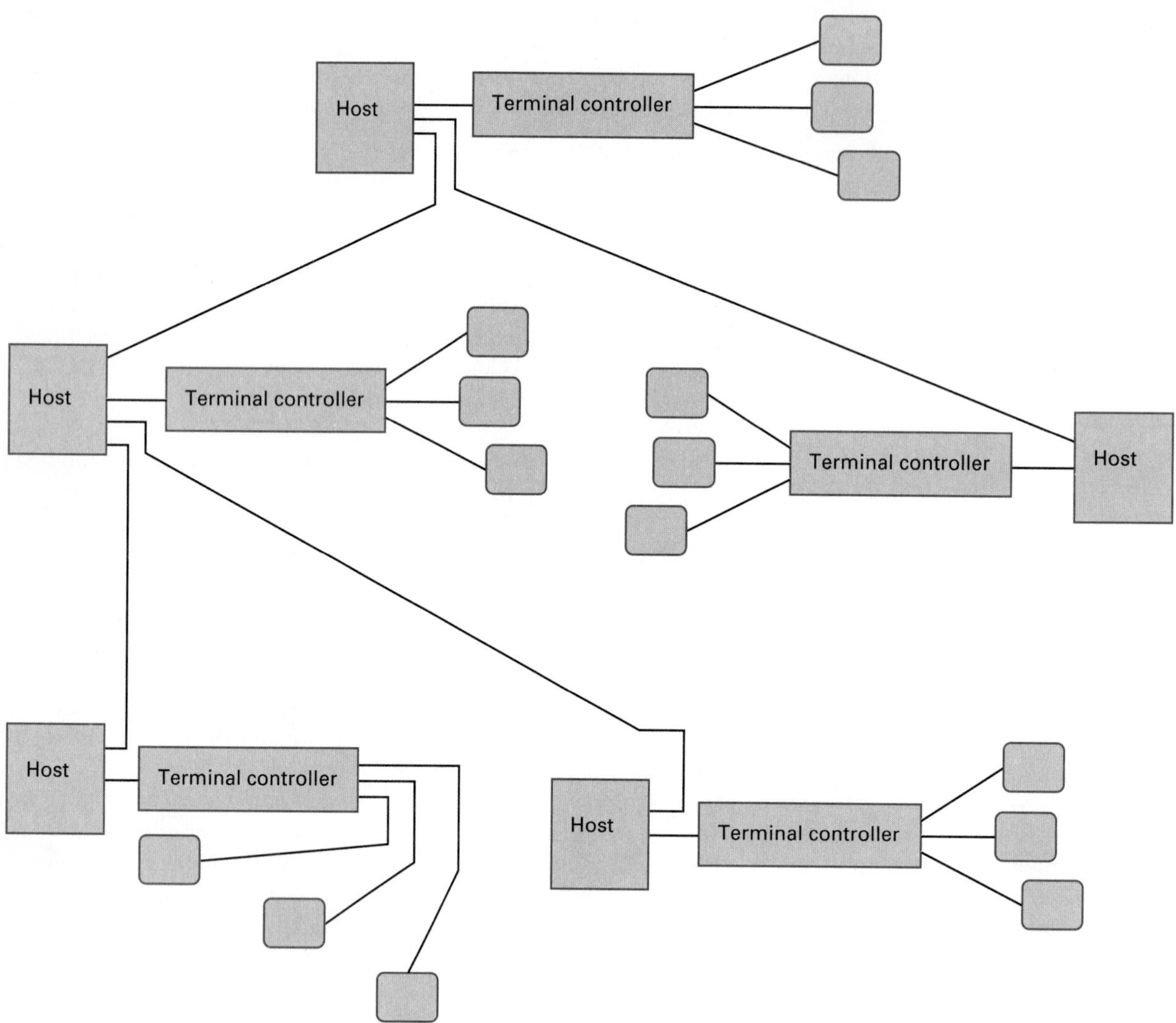

Figure 7–14
A hierarchical network configuration

computer (the host) would be expensive. However, if some store computers act as regional hosts to their surrounding stores, less lengthy channels would be needed to connect to the headquarters computer. Also, the stores may transmit all their data to the regional hosts, but the regional hosts may only transmit summary data to the headquarters computer. Thus, the amount of network traffic may also be reduced.

Another basic topology is a multidrop network, which is similar to a party line. In a *multidrop network,* a number of devices are connected to a single host channel. Multidrop networks may be arranged in the form of a bus or ring (see Figure 7–15). In a **bus topology,** more than one device shares a single channel, but the ends are not connected. In a **ring topology,** more than one device also shares a single channel, but the ends of the channel are connected.

Multidrop networks can offer savings to firms because many devices share one channel, reducing line costs. A disadvantage, however, is if that channel fails, none of the devices can transmit data to or receive data from the host.

A **mesh topology** provide networks that offer more than one path between nodes on the network (see Figure 7–16). Often, mesh topologies are chosen for their reli-

(a) Ring topology

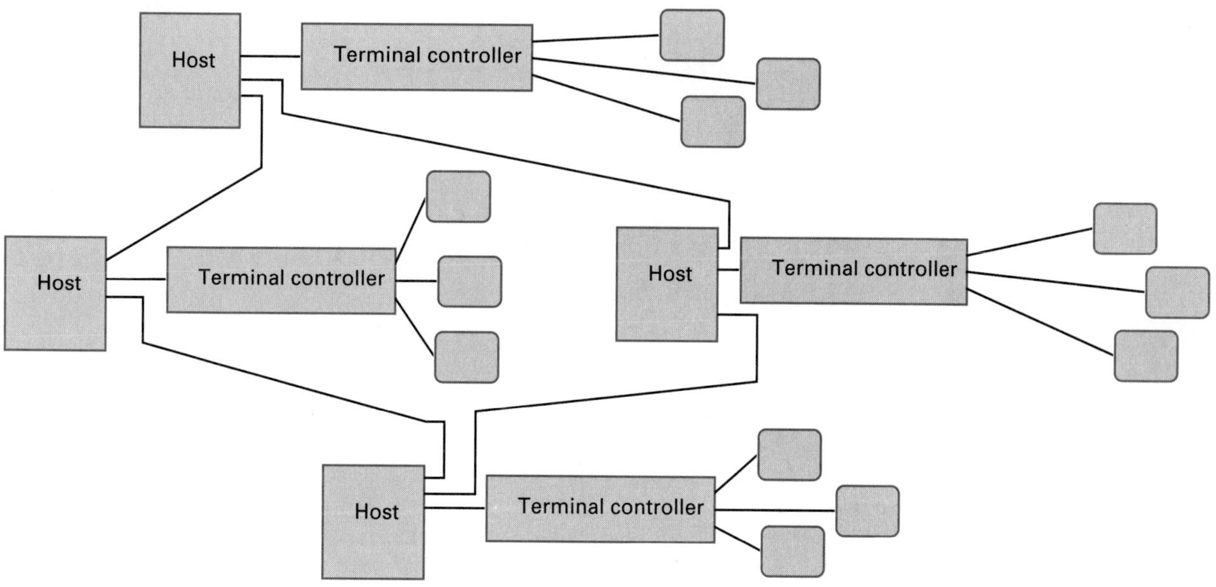

(b) Bus topology

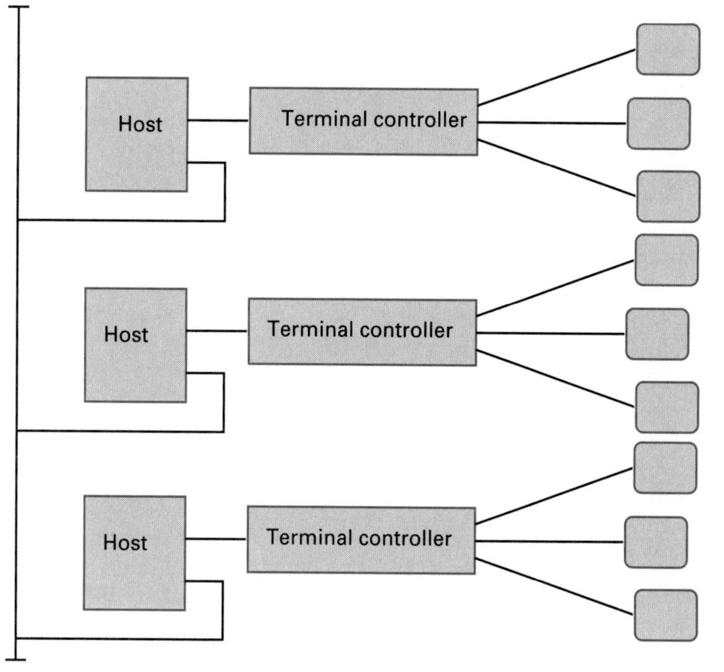

Figure 7–15
Two types of multidrop networks: **(a)** ring and **(b)** bus

ability because they offer alternate paths to workstations if line failures occur. They also are used to increase response time for high-traffic paths.

Most WANs are eclectic, and contain both point-to-point and multidrop channel topologies. The WAN shown in Figure 7–17, for example, includes a point-to-point channel and a multidrop channel.

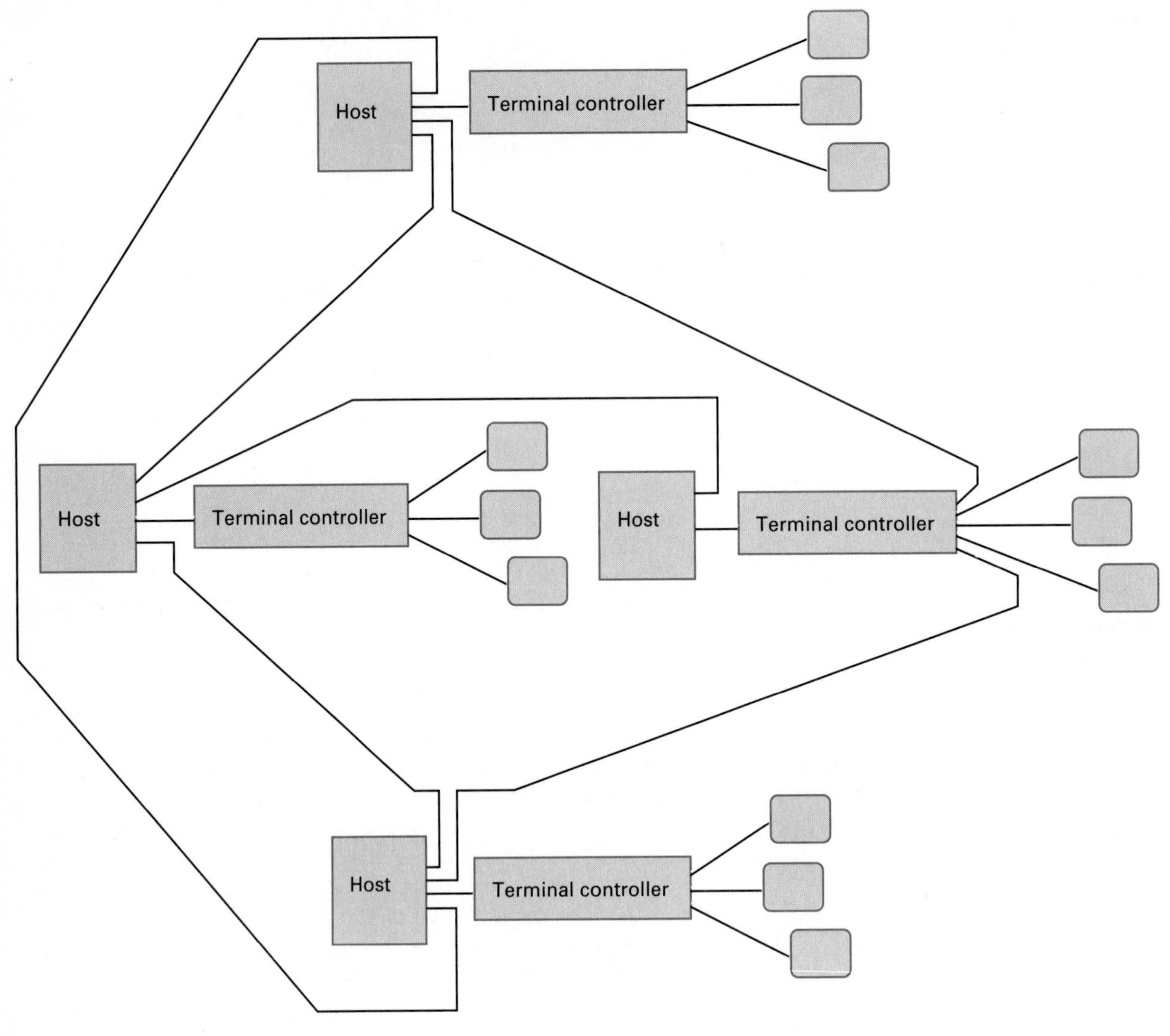

Figure 7–16 A mesh network configuration

Network Concerns for the Manager

A manager should consider a number of concerns about a wide area network. We discuss four of the most important concerns next.

Network Reliability. A network of remote terminals used for order entry that is constantly down loses sales for the organization. How well the network can be relied on to be up and running during work hours is very important. Network reliability is also affected by the rate of errors encountered on the channels during transmissions. High error rates slow down throughput on the network because they usually require that messages be retransmitted, thereby increasing the load on the network and increasing the associated costs of transmitting messages.

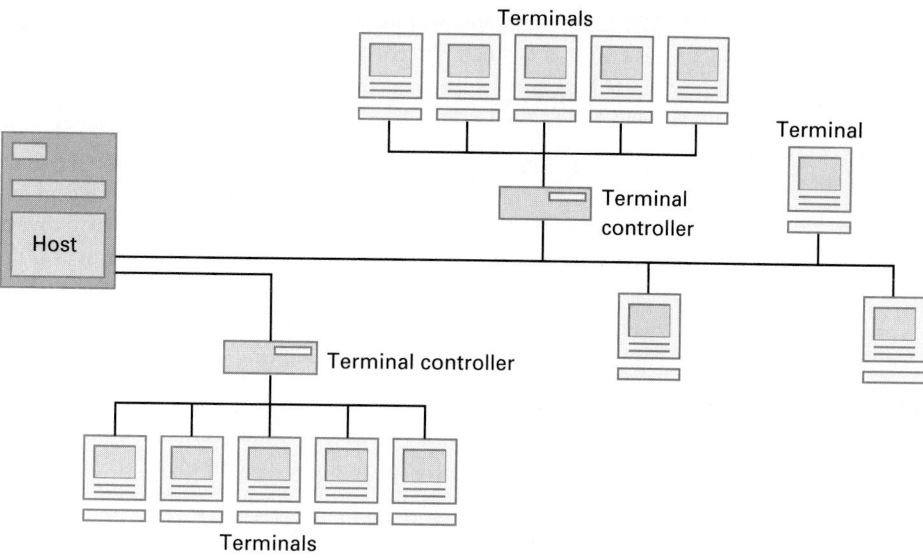

Figure 7–17
Point-to-point and multidrop network configuration

The quality of the channels and devices used on the network contributes greatly to network reliability. The experience, training, and tools given to the organization's network management personnel also contribute significantly to network reliability.

Network Response Time. The time it takes for an order entry clerk to send a request for information to the host and receive a reply is called **response time.** Obviously, the response time of the network is important to the productivity of the manager's staff. When you use a terminal to find out if stock a customer wants is on hand, you must get a response before the customer leaves or falls asleep. Fast response time on wide area networks is affected by many factors, including the distance the signal must travel, the amount of traffic on the network, and the capacity of the network channels. High error rates, of course, slow down response time and increase line traffic because messages must be retransmitted.

When large files—as opposed to a single record, such as a sales order—must be transferred, the capacity of the channel and the capacity of the equipment attached to the channel become very important. Sending a 4-megabyte file over a network with a capacity of 4,800 bits per second will take more than two hours. Sending that same file over a network capable of handling 56 kbps will take only about 12 minutes. High-speed channels and equipment cost more money than low-speed channels and equipment, but slow networks require more transmission time, thus increasing common carrier costs. Slow networks also lower worker productivity and may even lose sales—customers are likely to leave rather than fall asleep.

Network Costs. Networks cost money and wide area networks cost a lot of money. Network costs include the costs of installing and renting the channels, installing and acquiring the equipment, hiring network maintenance and management personnel, training employees to use the network, and repairing and maintaining the equipment and channels. Using multiplexers, transmitting noncritical data during low-cost evening hours, using multidrop channels, reducing transmission errors, and even slowing response time by a fraction may result in large savings.

Configuring networks or comparing various network design alternatives is a complex undertaking. Network design software is available, but basically network design is still an art. That means that the quality of the network management staff available to the manager is critically important to the efficiency of the system.

Compatibility. A major problem with most wide area networks is the incompatibility of the equipment and software used on the system. This incompatibility results from the fact that wide area networks grow over time, with the associated problems of changing technology. Incompatibility also results from lack of central control over equipment and software purchases or from the acquisition of new firms with already established networks or computer systems. Solving incompatibility problems usually means buying equipment that converts the signals from one system to another or developing software to make the conversion. Either way, a lot of money and time can be involved. Furthermore, the conversion software or equipment adds to system processing time and, of course, response time.

Network Access and Security. Many organizations store confidential data, such as long-term company plans, product development and marketing information, employee information, and customer information. Organizations that manufacture products for a nation's defense must secure much of the data they use from unauthorized access. Unfortunately, wide area networks may increase the accessibility of host data to persons who are not authorized to access those data. Thus, careful attention must be paid to the security of the network.

Network security may include these actions:

1. Providing log-on codes to authorized personnel to prevent unauthorized access using a remote computer terminal.
2. Issuing passwords for access to certain files to restrict employees to those data that they are authorized to view.
3. Providing physical access protection to remote terminals, such as locking offices or locking the terminal keyboards.
4. Encrypting, or coding, the information so that if it is stolen it may not be understood.

Probably the most unsettling security issues revolve around the use of microcomputers accessing the host through "dial-up" or switched lines. Frequently, executives and salespeople are allowed to access the mainframe database using their portable or home microcomputers through the use of a simple modem and a telephone line. Security is often maintained through the use of log-on codes and passwords. In addition, the host system may, when called, dial back the calling microcomputer to make certain that the caller is an authorized one. These measures and others have discouraged inexperienced callers from penetrating the system. However, anyone who reads the papers knows that computer hackers have routinely broken the log-on codes, passwords, and other security measures used even in our most tightly controlled defense networks. Thus, when microcomputers have access to host databases through dial-up lines, little real security is available to keep out the persistent computer expert.

PBX NETWORKS

A **private branch exchange,** or **PBX,** is a computer system that provides for switching telephone signals for voice and data on your company's premises rather than at the telephone company's office (see Figure 7–18). A PBX actually takes the place of comparable equipment located in the nearest local telephone office (called the *central office*).

Figure 7–18
PBX versus Centrex

Source: Ken Sherman, *Data Communications: A User's Guide*, 3rd ed., Englewood Cliffs, N.J.: Prentice Hall, 1990, p. 309.

Centrex Services	PBX
Regulated environment	Unregulated
Functions in telephone company central office (CO)	Functions on user premises
Leased only	Lease or buy
Reliability because of redundancy	Reliability when user pays for redundancy
Full maintenace always available	Maintenance not always on site (may require user personnel for service)
Growth practically unlimited	Finite growth limitations
No capital outlay necessary (installation may be amortized)	May require purchase or significant up-front cash outlay
Multiple buildings may be connected to same Centrex through CO	Separate PBXs usually required
Upgrade features can be continuous	Significant upgrade may require new PBX
Simultaneous voice/data available	Simultaneous voice/data available
Relatively limited station message detail recording (SMDR) information	Full SMDR information available
All wiring twisted-pair	Wiring may be twisted-pair or coaxial cable
May have high monthly cost per line	Line cost amortized over time in service
No space or power required	User space and power required
Telephone company personnel provides maintenance	User may need dedicated maintenance personnel
Rate stability plans available	Rate stability not available

Reasons for Implementing a PBX

You might wonder why a manager would acquire a PBX facility for voice telephone service when such service is available from the local telephone company. One reason is to reduce costs. Purchasing a PBX may prove to be more cost effective for a company than leasing telephone service from a telephone company.

Another reason is that PBXs may be used for more than merely voice communications. PBXs have become very powerful—they are sophisticated, programmable computers, even though they are specifically designed for telephone traffic. Because of their power, it is possible to use a PBX to switch not only voice messages for an organization, but also data messages. A third reason is to obtain features that are not available from the local telephone company. In fact, the features of PBXs have broadened their use. Consider the following possibilities.

Using Telephone Keypads as Data Terminals. You may connect an organization's PBX and mainframe computer to allow the telephone keypad to be used as a terminal. Salespeople, customers, managers, and others who have been given authority to do so may address the host computer through the telephone set in their office, home, car, or even airport.

Using the PBX to Network Microcomputers. You may attach a microcomputer to a telephone wall jack and send signals to a mainframe or other microcomputers using

Box 7–3 Using a Personal Computer as a PBX

PCBX Systems makes a PBX adapter card that fits into any AT-class personal computer and turns it into a private branch exchange. The card, called the PCBX 4/12, can support up to four outside lines and 12 extensions. It also can be expanded to support up to 16 outside lines and 48 extensions.

The system provides existing commercial telephone sets with special features, such as call waiting, call forwarding, and conferencing. The PC in which the card is placed can also double as a receptionist console with a headset for the operator, although the system can work automatically without any operators. The system is so efficient that it uses very little of the capacity of the PC. As a result, the PC can also be used for other tasks.

The unit's list price is only $1,800 as compared to PBXs produced by AT&T and other major PBX manufacturers that cost more than three times as much. If the PCBX is successful, it is likely to spark comparable products from a host of telephone systems firms.

Source: *Computer Shopper,* March 1993, p. 85.

your PBX to do the routing or switching. This allows you to use already-installed telephone twisted-pair cabling for your channels.

Offering a Voice Mail System. A **voice mail system** digitizes, stores, routes, and forwards voice messages under the control of the PBX's computer. Telephone users may listen to voice messages that have been digitized and stored in their voice mailboxes. Users may access their voice mailboxes from any telephone handset—anywhere. Thus, a salesperson or field agent can always be in touch with the home office, other salespeople, or even customers. Users may also leave voice messages in other mailboxes or even broadcast messages to many users of the voice mail system. Consider how easy announcing meetings is to a manager with voice mail. Voice mail could also be used by a sales manager to broadcast messages to all or selected groups of salespeople about product price changes or changes in product availability.

Combining Voice and Data Messages. You may combine both voice and data transmissions on your current telephone network using your PBX to do the switching. The result may be better use of the telephone network and reduction in the duplication of switching equipment and channels.

Using the PBX to Connect to Other Systems. You can use the PBX to connect terminals and microcomputers to host computers, remote computers, other networks, and commercial databases. To do so, the PBX is rigged with special hardware and software so that it can route messages and do the necessary protocol conversion between devices attached to it and other networks and computer systems.

PBX Hardware and Software

A PBX has at least one central processor and main memory like any other computer system. Of course, its switching capabilities are extensive and require specialized hardware. The PBX system also includes telephone handsets, central operator consoles, cabling, and distribution boxes for the cabling. The PBX provides software to install, monitor, and control incoming and outgoing telephone lines, telephone handsets, and other devices attached to it.

Some specialized hardware and software that may be added to the PBX system include the following.

Call Directors. A *call director* may be provided to put customers on hold when all incoming lines are busy. A call director would then connect the oldest incoming call to the next available operator. Usually it provides music or information to the caller who is waiting on hold. Sales managers make effective use of call directors to avoid losing customers at busy hours during the day or during busy seasons. You have probably been placed on hold numerous times when you called airlines or stores during rush hours or holiday seasons.

Networking Hardware and Software. The manager may wish to access the organization mainframe from a local microcomputer or to access a different computer system that uses different codes and is located at a remote location. The PBX can be used to provide protocol conversion and routing to other networks for those computer systems attached to the PBX. These systems include the hardware—usually an interface board—and the software to provide communications to another computer, another computer network, or a value-added network (such as Tymnet or Sprintnet).

Voice Mail Software. PBX vendors and other vendors offer *voice mail systems,* like the one described earlier that run on a PBX. Examples of voice mail software for PBXs include Audix from AT&T Information Systems, CINDI (Central Information Dispatch) from Genesis Electronics Corporation, and Phonemail from Rolm Corporation.

Station Message Detail Recording Software. *Station message detail recording (SMDR) software* provides an organization with detailed reports of telephone usage and costs for each department. The software also allows an organization to manipulate the telephone usage data. Thus, the organization can locate high-cost telephone users or identify the amount of time spent talking to clients on the phone. In firms where client billing is done by the hour, the latter capability is very important. Knowledge that every call is being monitored and that a report will show who made what phone calls, when, and for how long usually reduces employee abuse of the phone system for personal phone calls tremendously. Some organizations have found that their long-distance phone bills are reduced by as much as one-third with SMDR. In addition to the costs of personal phone calls, the organization usually saves more money because extra outgoing lines can be eliminated due to reduced traffic.

Data Entry Software. A number of vendors provide software that allows telephone keypads to become data entry terminals. The software uses the PBX to provide switching to a mainframe database. You have already read how such a system might allow salespeople to use any telephone convenient to them to enter an order, or allow students to use their home telephones to register for classes. Some banks have used this type of software to allow customers to access their checking accounts, pay bills, and move money from their checking to their savings accounts.

Management Concerns for PBX Networks

The use of the PBX as a switching device for both data and voice messages holds real promise for increasing productivity. Voice mail and the use of telephone sets as data entry devices for short messages that are sent in bursts seem especially promising. However, the manager should recognize that the typical PBX today is still designed for the type of traffic associated with voice communications. Where data communications are sporadic, short in length, and "bursty" in nature, combining voice messages with data messages through a PBX should be considered. But expecting the current generation of PBXs to process voice communications along with large, batch operation data processing jobs will seriously degrade communications services. Neither the channels nor the switching capacity of the typical PBX system is designed for such activity.

The manager must also be concerned with the resources necessary to operate and maintain the PBX system. Large PBX systems do not run by themselves. They require the attention of skilled technicians, and they require that users be trained in their sophisticated features. This means that the firm must allocate more resources to a PBX system than merely the price of acquisition and installation of the system.

CENTREX

For managers who do not want to entail the initial costs associated with acquiring their own telephone switch, or PBX, and who also do not want the headaches of operating and managing a telephone switch, there is Centrex. *Centrex* provides PBX-like functions and services to the user on a lease basis. Basically, it gives the user dedicated central office (CO) telephone lines and a varying set of features, such as intercom, call forwarding, least cost routing, toll restrictions, and call hold. These features vary with the telephone company and the state in which the service is offered. The local telephone company's central office switch, rather than a switch on the customer's premises, does the switching.

The tradeoffs seem to be that Centrex offers a lower initial cost, lower costs of telephone system management, and the ability to vary the telephone features leased from the telephone company. The PBX offers better usage and management reporting and usually lower costs over the long term (see Figure 7–18).

LOCAL AREA NETWORKS

A **local area network (LAN)** is an interconnected group of microcomputers or other terminals within a small geographic location such as a single room, office suite, floor, building, or campus. Local area networks also differ from wide area networks in that the typical devices attached to the network are intelligent, rather than dumb. In fact, a major reason for the development of LANs was the proliferation of personal computers. Given the continuing drop in microcomputer costs, however, it is likely that more and more micros will serve as terminals on WANs as well as LANs.

Reasons for Implementing a LAN

Managers acquire LANs to connect microcomputers for a number of reasons.

To Share Expensive Peripherals. Laser and line printers and plotters cost more than dot-matrix printers. Large and fast laser printers are especially expensive. Hence providing laser or line printers, plotters, or other specialized printing devices for each microcomputer is usually prohibited by cost. As a result, you may wish to connect a number of micros to a LAN that includes specialized or expensive printers. In that way, the cost of the printing devices is spread over many micros, and it becomes convenient for the micro users to access these devices.

Other peripherals that might be shared are *optical disks,* which provide for mass storage of data; *scanners,* which read and digitize hard copy material for use by computers; modems; and large, fast, hard disks.

To Share Data Files. When you have several order entry clerks entering data affecting sales, inventory, and accounts receivable records, these records have to be available to each worker. When workers using microcomputers must have concurrent access to the same records, as they usually must in accounting and database applications, a LAN is necessary.

To Use Multiuser Software. LANs usually require a computer with a hard disk, called a **file server,** which is shared by everyone on the network. Because both programs and data can be stored on the file server, a manager might conclude that a network would save a great deal of money in software costs. That is, only one copy of each software package would have to be purchased because these copies, if placed on the file server, would be accessible to anyone on the network. However, this conclusion is not valid. Many software companies require that you purchase one copy for each machine on a network, even though you may use only the one version loaded on the file server. Others require that you buy a special LAN version of that software that is priced according to the number of workstations on your network.

Much of the software used on microcomputers is single-user software. This software is not designed for an environment in which many people are accessing the same programs and the same records simultaneously. Problems may result from using single-user software on a network because this software lacks concurrency protection (see Chapter 6).

However, many software programs have been written specifically for LANs; that is, they are written for multiple users. Some examples include groupware packages, electronic mail software, and multiuser database software. LAN versions of common software may also provide more features than the single-user version of the same software. For example, a LAN version of a word processing package may allow multiple users to share and edit a single document on which they are all working simultaneously. A LAN version of accounting software allows many salespeople to enter orders, access the same inventory files, and access the same customer files simultaneously.

The ability to send messages to electronic mailboxes stored on the network file server may prove to be an important productivity tool for managers. **Electronic mail** provides a mailbox for each person on the network and allows users to send messages to individuals or groups of people, or even to broadcast messages to everyone on the network. Users can view the contents of their own mailboxes from a terminal attached to the network locally or from a terminal attached at a remote location.

Local area networks of groups of persons engaged in common work or a common project make a lot of sense—especially when the group is supported by *groupware* software (see Chapter 5) that allows them to share scheduling, document creation and review, electronic mail, and commonly used programs and files. Groupware, or software designed to support groups at work on common projects, requires a network.

To Access a Mainframe, Minicomputer, or Other Network. Connecting to a mainframe or minicomputer through a LAN may save you money because the hardware and software you need to make the connection can be spread over all the workstations on the LAN. Thus, you don't have to buy hardware and software to connect each microcomputer to the mainframe or minicomputer system (see "Communications Servers" and "Transferring Data to and from a Mainframe" later in this chapter).

LAN Hardware and Software

Local area networks may include the following components.

Network Workstations. The workstations on a network are usually microcomputers, although other types of workstations can be attached, including dumb terminals and *diskless workstations.* The latter are microcomputers that do not have their own disk drives; they use the disk drives of the file server (see the following description) to which they are attached.

File Servers. A file server is really a computer system attached to a network that controls network functions, including access to the network; one or more hard disks attached to the network to allow workstations to share disk space, programs, and data and document files; and one or more printers to allow workstations to output data. A file server may be a specially designed computer system sold by a network manufacturer, a high-end microcomputer, or just another microcomputer with one or more hard disks. The file server may also provide printing services and communications services. When one file server is dedicated to database tasks, it is called a *database server.* A number of companies provide special software to allow the server to dedicate itself to database tasks on a local area network (see "Client/Server Computing" later in this chapter).

Print Servers. A **print server** is a computer that controls access to and otherwise manages the printer resources attached to it. Printing services may be provided by the file server. However, if the file server becomes overloaded, printing tasks can be off-loaded to another computer system which is then *dedicated,* or used only for the printing function. Usually, the print server is a microcomputer with one or more printers attached to it.

Communications Servers. A **communications server** is a device that manages external communications from the network. These devices may include modems, specialized gateways to other networks, such as the organization's mainframe or other communications devices. As in the case of print servers, a communications server is usually an ordinary microcomputer dedicated to handling the modems or other communications devices attached to it. Communications services may be provided by the file server. Microcomputers dedicated to communications functions are usually used when the file server is already too busy to handle the additional work of supporting communications.

Media. Each network workstation and server is connected to other units through the network cable. The most common cabling systems used for LANs are coaxial cable and twisted-pair wiring. However, network cabling also includes fiber optic cable.

Some LANs don't use physical cabling. Instead these LANs, called **wireless LANs,** transmit messages through radio waves or infrared waves. Infrared systems, such as Hewlett-Packard's Serial Infrared Communications systems, use infrared light for transmission and reception. Infrared light is a line-of-sight technology and cannot pass through dense obstacles, including walls or people who pass in front of a transmitter. Hewlett-Packard uses their technology with some of their palmtop computers and, more recently, desktop PCs.

Radio systems do not require line-of-sight capability, and they can penetrate many obstacles except thick concrete and steel walls. In addition, these systems can transmit and receive both voice and data messages. Proxim, Inc., uses radio transmission technology in its RangeLAN system, which includes a PCMCIA card and transmitter/receiver for a notebook or handheld computer and adapter cards and transmitters/receivers for desktop machines and the server. The Altair Vista Point system produced by Motorola offers wireless networking in a building or between buildings.

At present, the speed of wireless LAN technology causes a noticeable drop in response time for users accustomed to cabled media. However, the use of wireless LANs and other wireless communications systems appears to be growing substantially (see Box 7–2), and the speed of these systems will increase as the technology matures. Current transmission speeds can vary between 1 mbps to 5 mbps, and the distance between devices connected by a LAN can vary from 20 feet to 20 miles.

Network Interface Cards. Each network component, including workstations and servers, is usually attached to the network through the use of a network interface or adapter card placed in the component. This adapter card provides the necessary translation of signals to and from the device and the network. The adapter card is usually called a **network interface card,** or **NIC.** The NIC may be placed in an expansion slot of a desktop microcomputer or in a PCMCIA slot of a notebook or handheld computer system.

Network Operating System. The network is usually controlled by **network operating system,** or **NOS,** software, which is a set of programs that reside partially on the file server and partially on each workstation. The network operating system provides programs that allow you to install each network device, install application software, diagnose network problems, analyze network usage statistics, and manage and route messages on the network. The network operating system may also include programs to manage the file server, print server, and communications server; provide electronic mail services to network users; and allow remote users to connect to the LAN.

LAN Topologies

Like a WAN, a local area network may be assembled or configured in several ways. The three most common LAN topologies are the star, bus, and ring topologies.

The Star Topology. In the star topology, each component of a LAN has a separate cable that runs from the component to the file server (see Figure 7–19). That means that people using devices on the network do not have to contend for use of the network cable. However, they have to contend for the use of the network resources. Also, installation of the system requires stringing one cable from each machine all the way to the file server. If your workstations are likely to be moved about a lot because of growth or constant shifting of employee responsibilities, star cabling requirements could get expensive.

Remember, the file server runs the network operating system software and may be a specially designed device or (more likely) another microcomputer with one or more hard disks. The device acting as the file server must have sufficient power to handle the requests for print services, file services, and/or communications services from workstations. Of course, if the file server fails, the entire network fails. Employees would then be restricted to using their microcomputers as stand-alone units.

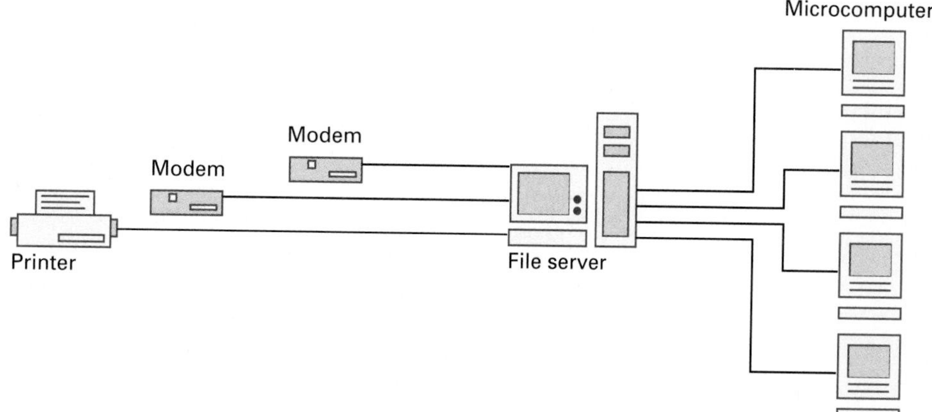

Figure 7–19
A LAN using a star topology

Typically a high-end microcomputer is used as the file server in a star topology LAN, although sometimes a minicomputer may be used.

The Bus Topology. In a bus topology, each LAN component is attached to a single cable, or bus (see Figure 7–20). The components must contend for access to the network cable as well as network resources, such as printers, hard disks, and modems.

The capacity of any network to handle the volume of messages on the LAN is important to its success. A bus LAN with a low capacity may create problems for users; they may have difficulty getting access to the network resources because of high traffic on the network. However, connecting a workstation to the cable is relatively simple. All that is typically needed is a short cable from the workstation to the network cable. The two cables are attached with a *tap,* usually a simple device easily attached to the network cable. Thus, installing new workstations or changing the locations of workstations is relatively simple as long as the network cable comes within reach of the workstation.

Failure of the file server on a bus topology LAN will not bring down individual workstations. However, if the file server controls printers and modems as well as hard disks, the network user will be in the same situation as if the file server failed in a star topology. That is, the user could still operate the microcomputer workstation but couldn't get any network services.

The Ring Topology. A LAN that uses a ring topology runs its cabling between all the devices on the network (see Figure 7–21). Each device passes along to the next device on the ring any message not addressed to itself. In early LAN design, ring networks were used to ensure a working channel in case of the failure of one device. That is, if

Figure 7–20
A bus topology LAN

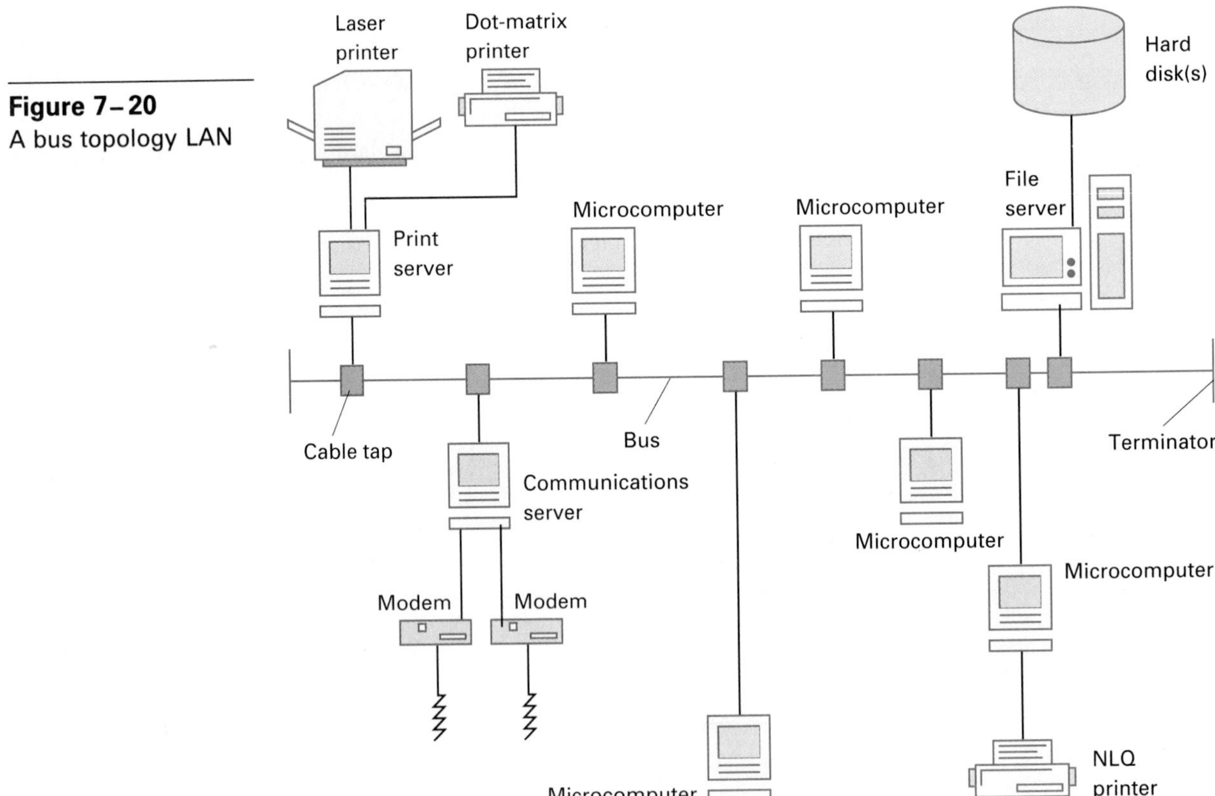

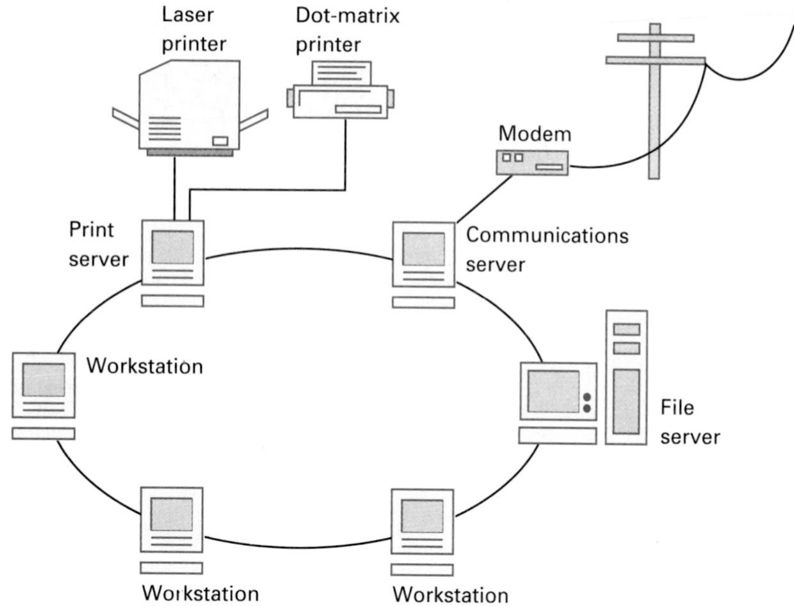

Figure 7–21
A LAN using a ring topology

a device on the network failed, the other devices on either side of it could send messages in another direction. However, later ring designs used bypass technology designed to pass messages through failed workstations. Thus, failure of one workstation on the ring does not prevent messages from reaching their destination on the network.

Wireless Topology. When wireless LAN systems are used, the initial cost of the hardware is typically higher than for other media. However, the costs of installing a wireless system, especially in older buildings, may save far more than the initial hardware cost differential. Wireless LANs can be especially useful when network workstations are moved about frequently. For example, wireless LANs have proven helpful in retail stores, allowing managers to place workstations, including check-out workstations, on the showroom floor. When displays, counters, and other store furniture are changed for a new line or a new season, the workstations are moved easily. Kmart, for example, has purchased thousands of wireless systems for their stores.

Mixed Topologies. In practice, LAN topologies may be mixed—that is, a bus topology may be connected to a star topology, a wireless network may be connected to a bus network, or a ring topology may also include a bus topology. For example, to provide for rows of workstations in a classroom, you may run cables from the file server to a multiport *hub,* which is a box that permits many cables to be attached to it. From the hub, you may run individual cables to several workstations for a star pattern. However, you may use a bus cable to daisy chain several workstations in a row (see Figure 7–22).

LAN Backbone Networks

Because LANs have proliferated in organizations, some means has become necessary to connect LANs to each other and to other networks, such as the organization's wide area network. To connect LANs, organizations frequently use fiber optic cabling within buildings or between buildings as a *backbone network.* Each LAN is connected to the backbone, and the backbone is then connected to one or more of the organization's WANs (see Figure 7–23).

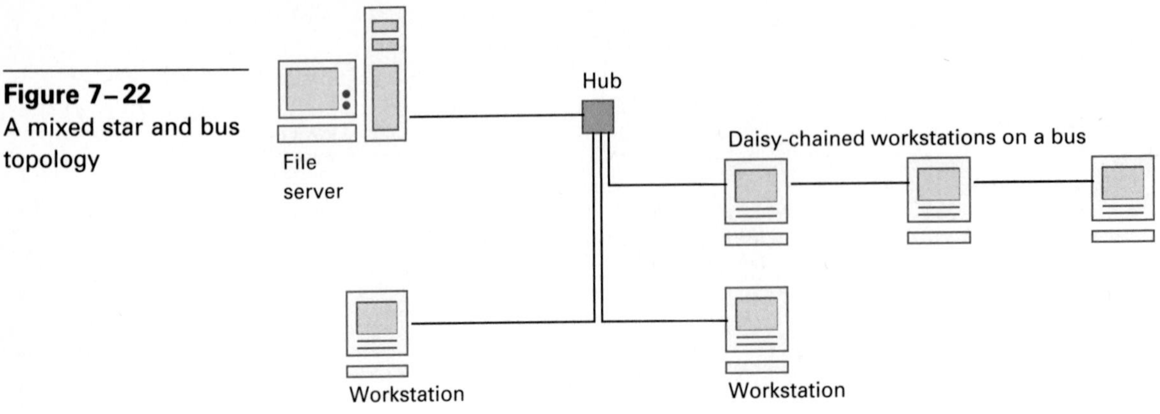

Figure 7–22
A mixed star and bus topology

Hub
File
server
Daisy-chained workstations on a bus
Workstation
Workstation

Figure 7–23
A backbone network connecting LANs and a WAN

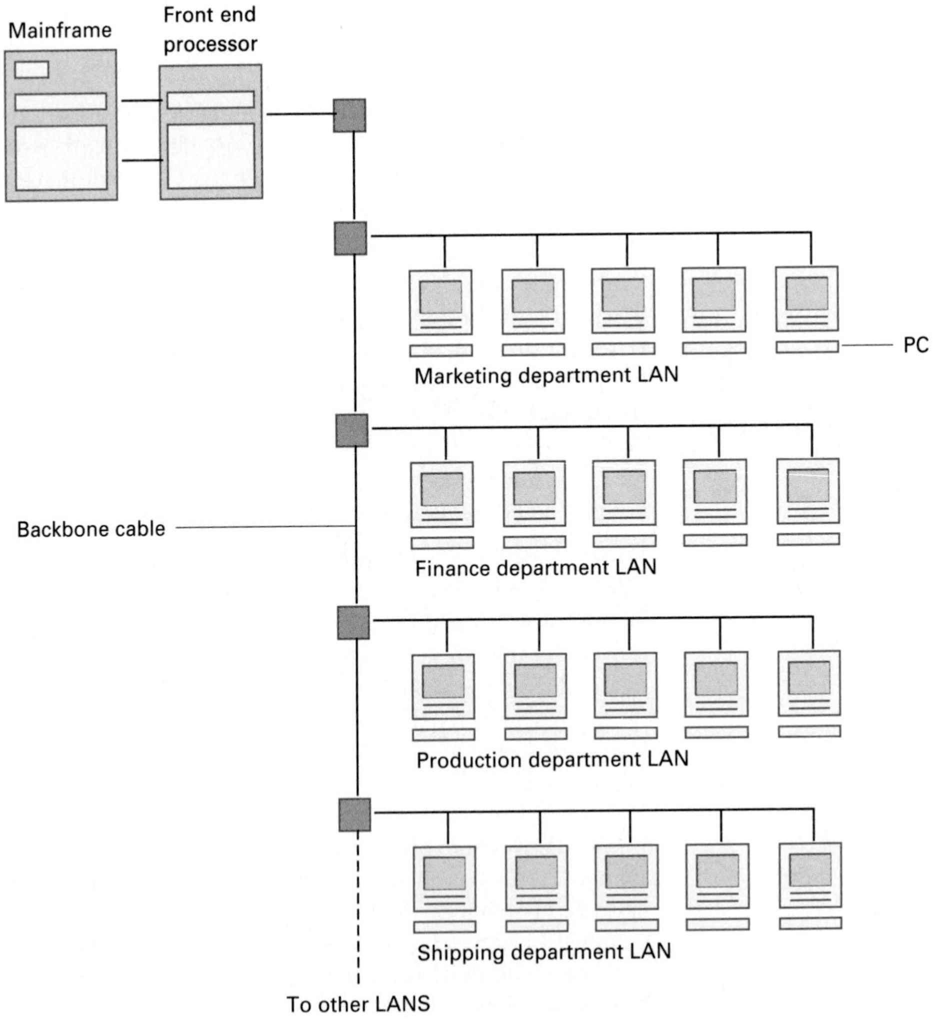

Mainframe
Front end
processor
PC
Marketing department LAN
Backbone cable
Finance department LAN
Production department LAN
Shipping department LAN
To other LANS

Fiber optic cabling is often chosen for backbone networks because it has a very large capacity and is usually capable of handling the traffic of many LANs in a building or on a campus. For example, fiber backbone networks conforming to the industry Fiber Distributed Data Interface (FDDI) standard can handle traffic at 100 million bits per second.

LAN Concerns for the Manager

After many years of unfulfilled expectations of growth, local area networks have finally begun to proliferate in organizations. However, managers should be cautious about implementing LANs for many reasons, including the following.

High Connectivity Cost. One of the most compelling drawbacks to implementing LANs is the high cost of connecting a workstation to a LAN. These costs include the cost of the adapter card and the cabling, the cost of providing the file server, print server, and communications server, the cost of the network operating system, the cost of special LAN application software, and the cost of installing these items. It is not uncommon in a 10-workstation network to pay about $1,000 to $2,500 to connect each workstation to the LAN.

High Cost of Installing Cabling. Often, one of the highest costs of a LAN is the purchase and installation of the network cabling that connects the devices, microcomputers, or terminals attached to a LAN. This is especially true when a LAN is installed in an old building. Pulling cabling through ducts or through walls without ducts can be very expensive because of labor costs. If the twisted-pair phone wire that is already installed in the walls can be used, the costs of the cabling can be reduced tremendously.

Cost of LAN Management and Maintenance. A frequently overlooked cost of a LAN is the time it takes to learn how to run it and then to manage the LAN and its resources. Those who use LANs agree that someone, even in a small LAN, must be appointed as a network manager. It is that person's responsibility to install new workstations, handle archiving of important network programs and documents, winnow out old or unused programs and data files on the file server, diagnose and remedy simple network problems, and otherwise manage the network. That means that someone must be appointed, trained, and then given the time to manage the network. All of these personnel tasks cost money (see Figure 7–24).

Software Problems. A major problem for some managers is the acquisition of software for the LAN. Usually, special LAN versions of the software must be purchased for the network file server. Also, it is likely that most of the software that employees have learned to use is single-user software—that is, software designed to be used by one person on one machine. When employees migrate to a network, they may have to change to multiuser software to avoid concurrency and other problems. Hopefully, all that means is that a multiuser version of the old software must be purchased and installed. However, multiuser versions may not be available for some of the older software. So you will have to acquire new software and train your staff in its use. Even so, it may be difficult or impossible to access the many data files you have accumulated over the years using the old software.

Equipment and Software Compatibility Problems. Another problem for many managers is that they have acquired microcomputers over several years, and they may have several different brands of incompatible microcomputers. These disparate devices may be able to share peripherals, programs, or data files when connected to a network, but you may have to upgrade your network operating system software to a version that provides such connectivity.

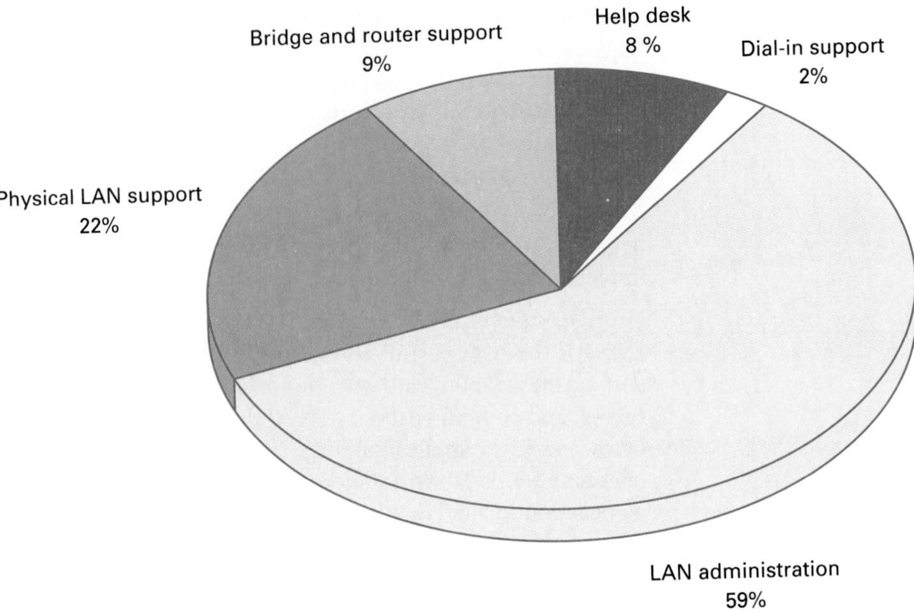

Figure 7–24
The costs of Local Area Networks

Sources: Deborah Asbrand, "Who Pays for the Corporate LAN?" *InfoWorld* 15, no. 33 (August 18, 1993), p. 53; Alan Radding, "The Heavy Burden of LAN Costs," *Datamation* 39, no. 11 (June 1, 1993), pp. 60–64.

The costs of acquiring and installing LAN equipment and software are pretty steep, sometimes amounting to more than the computer system iteslf. However, it is in the maintenance and management of LAN resources where the bill really achieves heights. One of the reasons for the high management and network support costs of local area networks is that many companies do not have a charge back system for these costs to the users, even though many network operating systems have the capacity to track usage. According to Forrester Research, the cost of supporting a LAN PC averages about $1,270 annually. This must be compared to $460 to maintain a mainframe terminal on an IBM system.

Of the $1,270, about $750 are the costs associated with LAN administration.

Employees who should be connected to the network may also be using different software or different versions of the same software acquired over the years. Problems will occur when one word processor tries to use a document prepared by another word processor—the chances are very great that it will not be able to do so without translating it into its own format first. Hence many documents will have to be converted to the formats of other word processors. To allow each person to share document files on this network without constant conversion of documents, some people will have to abandon their old word processors and adopt new word processing software. The old document files must either be rekeyed using the new word processor or converted to the format of the new word processor. All this activity can be disruptive.

OTHER MICROCOMPUTER COMMUNICATIONS

In addition to connecting microcomputers to local area networks or using them as smart terminals in a wide area network, many people who use microcomputers at home and at work need to connect to distant microcomputers, other computers, and other local area networks and wide area networks.

Reasons for Other Microcomputer Communications

Many people who use laptop microcomputers away from their offices need to connect them to their office LANs, their office microcomputers, or their office mainframe computer systems. Managers who are working at home in the evening or on the weekend and need to obtain information on other computer systems, salespeople who need to communicate with the host computer system to complete sales orders, and technicians, drivers, and repair persons who are working away from the office and must report their activities to the home office or who need data from the home office computer systems to complete their assignments are all in this situation.

Other Types of Microcomputer Communications

There are many different types of other microcomputer communications. Some types commonly found in organizations include the following.

Transferring Data Files Between Microcomputers. One of the simplest forms of communications is micro-to-micro communications. When the two microcomputers are distant, communication usually requires that each microcomputer be equipped with a modem and appropriate software to run it (see Figure 7–25).

Typical modems for microcomputers run at speeds of from 300 to 9,600 bps. Some microcomputer modems are placed in separate boxes and attached to the serial port of the microcomputer. These modems are called *external modems* (see Figure 7–11a). Others are placed on a board that fits inside the microcomputer. These modems are called *internal modems* (see Figure 7–11b). Internal modem boards are inserted into one of the slots on the microcomputer's motherboard. Most microcomputer software is capable of transferring ASCII code in asynchronous format, which is the common mode of communications by micros.

Another type of microcomputer modem is the wireless modem. These modems are designed to allow mobile people to connect to other networks and systems. The modems connect to personal computers in the same way that external modems do. However, they use radio signals to communicate with other computer systems over radio-based data networks instead of the public telephone network. For example, Intel Corporation provides a wireless modem that transmits at 8,000 bps and communicates over the RAM Mobile Data network, which is a radio-based data network.

When transferring data between microcomputers that are close together, you usually don't use a modem. Instead you attach a special cable to the serial ports of each computer system and use appropriate software to transfer files. The special cable is called, appropriately enough, a *null modem* because a modem is not needed. This situation often occurs when you wish to transfer data from your laptop to your office microcomputer and the machines use floppy drives of different sizes. Kits containing the null modem and software are bundled with some laptop computer systems.

You should remember that transferring data from one microcomputer to another is one thing; having both microcomputers understand the communications is another. A person who transfers a document prepared with one word processing software package

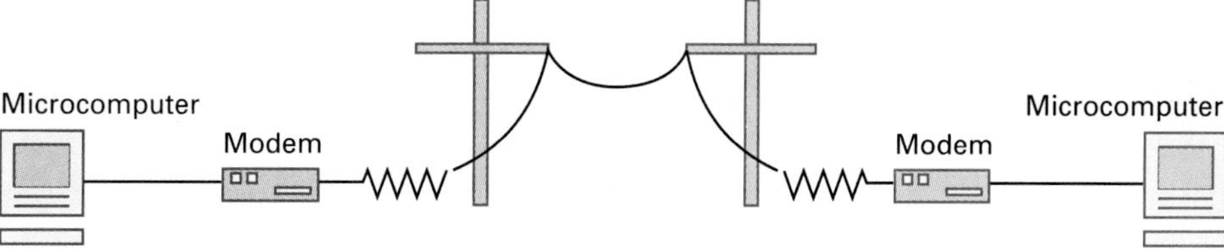

Figure 7–25
Micro-to-micro communications using modems

to a microcomputer equipped with another word processing package may encounter problems. That is, one word processing package may not be able to read the document prepared with the other unless the document is converted to a different format. Often the conversion does not include special features of the original software, such as tab setting, column settings, and special print features, such as bold-faced letters. A secretary may have to go through the converted document and reformat it. For long documents with many special tabs, columns, and other format features, reformatting is a tedious and potentially expensive task.

Box 7–4 The Internet

There has been a great deal of talk about creating an "information highway" akin to the vehicle superhighway system that was begun in the 1950s in the United States. The idea is to construct a network of cables and wireless channels that will let people and organizations communicate faster and better. *The Internet* has become a prototype of this proposed information highway, and has become a hot topic on talk shows and print media. In fact, it has been difficult recently to find a popular or technical magazine that does not include an article on the Internet.[1] Many books have also been published to help newcomers navigate the Internet.[2]

So, what is the Internet? Many people describe the Internet as a network of networks, or an ungoverned aggregation of millions of computers and computer networks located throughout the world. The Internet began in the 1960s as a means to connect research institutions and laboratories with military and government agencies. Originally called ARPANET, for the Advanced Research Projects Agency that managed it in the beginning, the network has joined with other public and private networks over the years to create a vast, worldwide connection of computer systems. Internet now has over 15 million subscribers, including individuals, government agencies, military agencies, educational institutions, small businesses, corporations, and individuals and connects more than 10,000 networks. About 150 thousand new subscribers join the Internet each year, and membership is expected to reach 100 million by 1998.

[1]See *The Internet Business Journal* as an example of a journal devoted wholely to the business use of the Internet.

[2]See, for example, John R. Levine and Carol Baroudi, *The Internet for Dummies* (IDG Books, 1994); Mary J. Cronin, *Doing Business on the Internet*; and Daniel P. Dern, *The Internet Guide for New Users* (New York: McGraw-Hill, 1994).

Access to the Internet can be gained easily if your organization already is a member. All you need do is gain an ID and password from your organization. Technically, access can be achieved in many ways including a modem, using a local area network with Internet access, or using a mainframe computer system with Internet access. Private companies and individuals can also gain access to the Internet by subscribing to organizations that provide access and special software for the user, such as Delphi Internet Services Corp. and The Pipeline.

What can you find on the Internet? Just about anything. For example, there are databases, bulletin boards, forums or discussion groups, news wires, mailing lists, and electronic mail. Internet allows you to get technical support for computer system products directly from vendors and from user groups, to upload and download shareware, to transfer files between Internet users, to take part in discussions of topics from Zen to world trade, and to receive and send E-mail messages to people on the Internet or on other E-mail networks, such as CompuServe and MCIMail.

Internet even allows you to connect to computers at sites around the world to use their services and download documents, data files, and programs. However, the features of Internet are growing as fast as it adds subscribers. For example, the Commercial Internet Exchange, a nonprofit trade group of Internet providers, lets organizations advertise their products and services and will soon let you search for products on-line.

Sources: Andrew Kantor, "Internet: The Undiscovered Country," *PC Magazine* 13, no. 5 (March 15, 1994), pp. 116–18; Paul Strauss, "TO: mis@corporate.com RE: Internet E-Mail," *Datamation* 40, no. 3 (February 1, 1994), pp. 39, 40, 42; Jayne Levin, "Businesses Are Making the Internet Connection," *InfoWorld* 15, no. 21 (May 24, 1993), p. 71.

Remote Communications. Another type of micro-to-micro communications involves communicating remotely from your home or laptop computer to your office microcomputer. There are a number of software packages, for example, Carbon Copy Plus, that allow you to do just that. These remote communications software packages let you connect to your office microcomputer, and all of its on-line data files and programs, from your other microcomputer system. It's as if you were sitting at your microcomputer at the office, even though you may be at home or on the road.

Connecting to On-line Databases, Information Utilities, and Bulletin Boards. Some managers need to access information utilities or the information provided by commercial, on-line databases (see Chapter 6). In addition, thousands of electronic *bulletin board systems (BBS)* allow users to ask questions of other users over the bulletin board network and to share information about their special areas of interest. An example of a bulletin board system is the Health Information Network, offered by US Telecom, which provides 24-hour access to information on drugs, physical fitness, exercise, and other health-related topics to physicians and dentists. It includes specialized databases and bulletin board systems from such agencies as the Center for Disease Control and the Food and Drug Administration. Conversely, many firms provide bulletin boards for their customers. These systems allow customers to ask questions of salespeople or technicians and receive prompt answers without having to be connected on a real-time basis. Thus, a customer who might need information about a product can drop a note to the firm at any time of day and then read the answer anytime that is convenient.

A manager also may want access to *users' groups* that provide bulletin board services for members about different software packages and computer systems. Members can send questions or problems to the group's bulletin board and receive answers or solutions through the same bulletin board. User groups provide tips and problem-solving assistance from experienced users of the hardware or software. To use an on-line database or a bulletin board system usually requires a modem, modem software, and a paid subscription to the database service or membership in a user group.

Transferring Data to and from a Remote Local Area Network. Some people need to transfer data between a remote LAN and a microcomputer that might be at home, in a hotel, or in a car. In any case the connection can be made easily with a modem and software for the microcomputer. At the LAN end of the network, you will usually find a *dial-in server,* which is another microcomputer equipped with a network interface card, one or more modems, and software to manage the dial-in communications system (see Figure 7–26).

Transferring Data to and from a Minicomputer or Mainframe. Managers commonly need to connect an office or home microcomputer to the company minicomputer or mainframe, for example, to use data from the company database in a spreadsheet. Making the connection is relatively easy in terms of the technology. However, the database administrator is not likely to welcome many naive users rummaging around the company database on weekends. Procedures for protecting the integrity of the database must be developed to ensure that the zeal of executives to play "what if" games using data from the mainframe database does not become a disaster.

Connecting a microcomputer to a minicomputer or mainframe computer usually involves making the microcomputer *emulate,* or look like, an ordinary terminal on the mainframe network. For example, if a mainframe computer network uses IBM 3270

Figure 7–26
Connecting a remote microcomputer to a LAN with a dial-in server

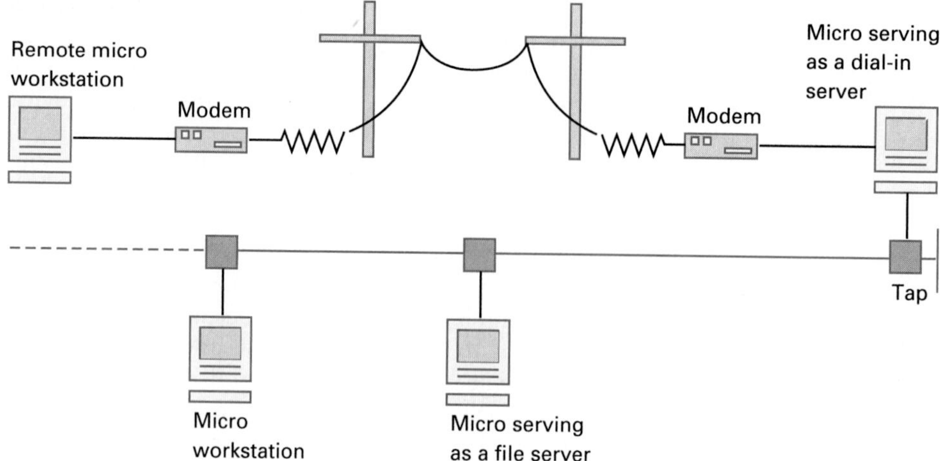

terminals, then one way to connect the microcomputer to the network is to install 3270 emulation hardware and software in the micro. This usually means buying an **emulation board** and an **emulation software** package for the micro (see Figure 7–27).

Some emulation packages only allow the microcomputer to act as if it is a dumb terminal. That means that the micro can read and update data on the minicomputer or mainframe, but cannot *upload* data to the larger computer system or *download* data from the larger computer system to the microcomputer's disk drives. Thus, the manager who needed data for a spreadsheet application could see the data on the screen but would have to rekey it into the microcomputer spreadsheet separately.

Other emulation packages allow the microcomputer to upload and download data to and from the minicomputer or mainframe and store it on the microcomputer's disk

Figure 7–27
Connecting a micro to a mainframe computer system

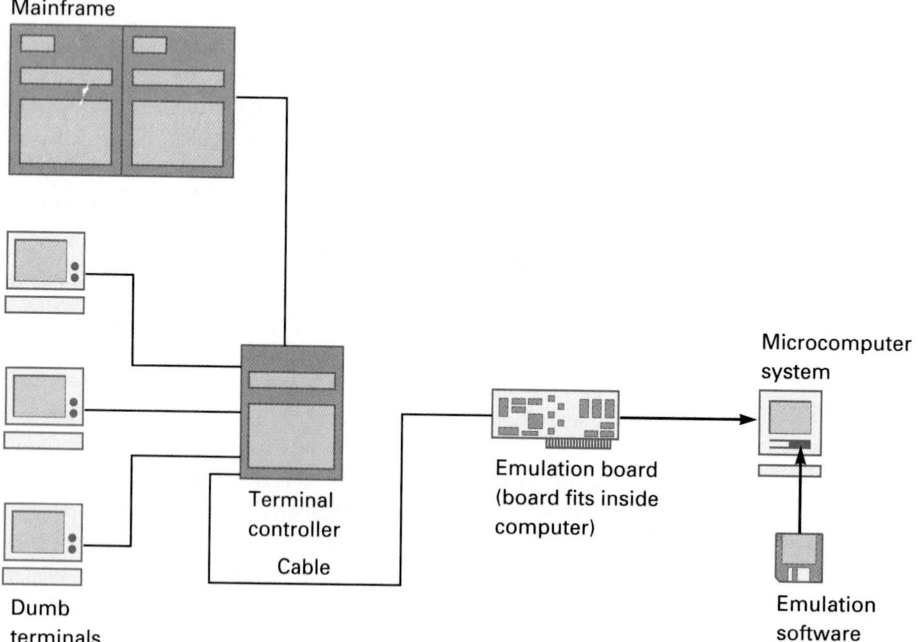

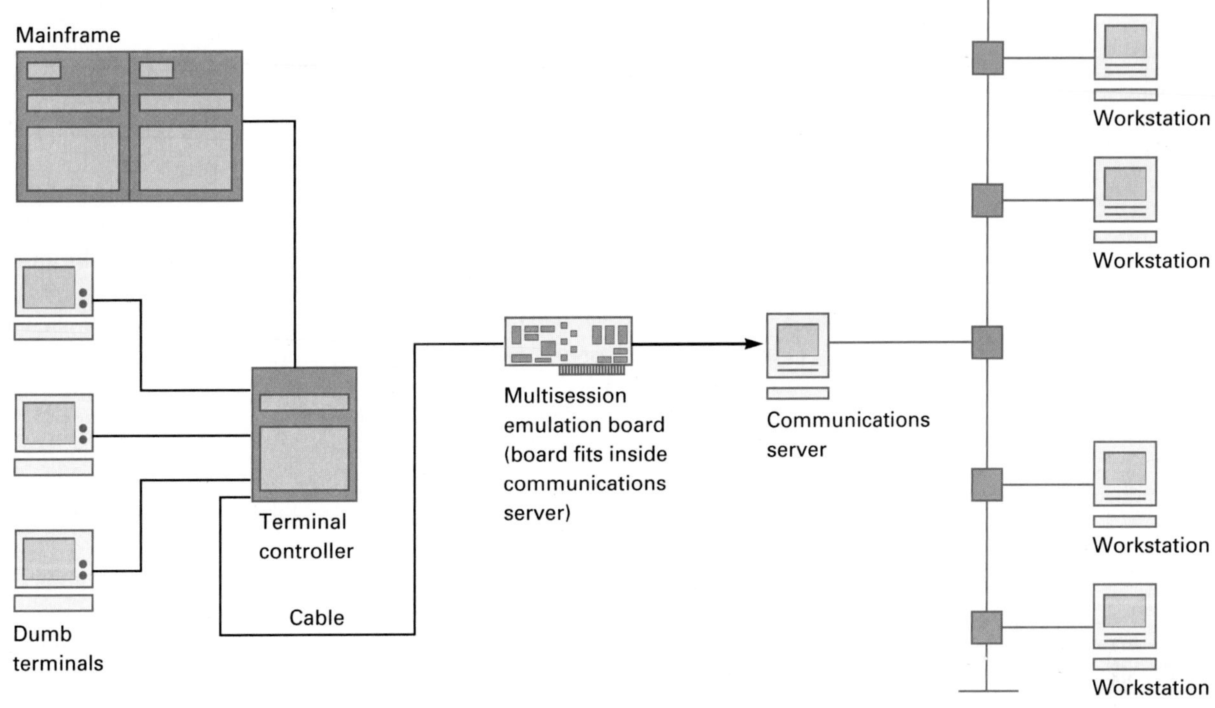

Figure 7–28 Connecting microcomputers on a LAN to a mainframe computer system

drives. Once there, the spreadsheet software may then read the data, eliminating the need to rekey the data into the microcomputer.

Some emulation boards are designed for LANs and provide for multiple users and multiple minicomputer or mainframe *sessions*, or connections. These boards are placed in communications servers to allow access by stations on the LAN. A user may have one session open with the sales order file on the minicomputer or mainframe database and another session open with the inventory file on the same database. Both sessions might appear as windows on the computer screen and allow the user to compare data in them. Some LAN emulation boards allow up to 64 sessions with the minicomputer or mainframe database. These 64 sessions may be divided among users many ways. For example, 64 microcomputer users on the LAN may each have one mainframe session open concurrently, or 16 users may each have four sessions or windows open with a mainframe at the same time (see Figure 7–28).

Many companies provide emulation hardware and software for microcomputer-to-microcomputer or mainframe connections. Digital Communications Associates, Inc., makes a product line called *IRMA boards* for 3270 emulation that has become an industry standard.

INTERORGANIZATIONAL INFORMATION SYSTEMS

Information systems in the past have been largely confined to organization boundaries. For example, an accounting information system was typically confined to accepting data from employees of the organization, processing the data, and then providing reports about the data to employees. Although accounting reports might be shared beyond the company (for example, with the IRS and the Securities and Exchange Commission), the initiation and distribution of reports were in the hands of organization staff. Information system boundaries today, however, increasingly span more than one organization. Such systems are called interorganizational information systems.

Interorganizational information systems can be defined as information systems that permit an employee of one organization to allocate resources and initiate business processes in another organization directly. There are two broad types of interorganizational information systems: electronic data interchange and electronic market systems.

Electronic Data Interchange

Electronic data interchange (EDI) systems are primarily bilateral information systems that allow two organizations to exchange information electronically. Typically, an EDI is an information system that links an organization to its customers or suppliers. For example, a buyer and a seller might create links between the databases of each organization to exchange purchase and sales information electronically, thereby eliminating many paper forms and procedures, such as purchase orders and sales receipts. In such a system, the supplier's computer system monitors the buyer's computerized database to determine when inventory levels of a product need replenishing. When this level occurs, the seller's computer system initiates a purchase order process within the buyer's computer system. EDI handles purchase orders, payments, and inventory and account updates automatically between the two computer systems.

In fact, an important application of communications technology by organizations has been the reduction of costs pertaining to the management of inventory and purchasing. Many large firms have required their smaller suppliers to use EDI to monitor the large company's inventory levels and deliver inventory only when it is needed (see the discussion of just-in-time systems in Chapter 12, "Manufacturing and Production Information Systems"). EDI used in this way passes the burden of large inventories with their accompanying maintenance, interest, insurance, and tax costs to the supplier. The buyer's inventories become lean. In addition, it substantially reduces all the procedures and paper forms that were printed out, examined, mailed, stored, and otherwise managed. Thus, paper purchase orders and sales orders and other forms become relics of the past, and business processes become faster, more efficient, and less costly. The cost savings are shared by the sellers, too.

EDI systems may be classified into supplier-focused systems and customer-focused systems. For example, Wal-Mart has created a supplier-focused EDI system that requires suppliers to query Wal-Mart inventory databases and deliver the appropriate inventory in amounts and within delivery times set by prior agreements. Suppliers are fined for not meeting their agreements and can, if failures occur more than a certain number of times, lose the right to sell to Wal-Mart. There are obvious advantages to the suppliers in these systems, though, too; at the very least, they gain increased sales and a more efficient sales order system.

You have seen how EDI can be used to reduce inventories and costs to an organization through supplier-focused EDI systems. EDI, however, can also be used to increase sales through customer-focused systems. Levi-Strauss, for example, hoped to use EDI as a means of turning around declining sales patterns. They developed Levilink, an EDI system that processes orders and deliveries. The system allows customers to order products in small amounts, as they are needed, instead of in large orders. The orders are then delivered by UPS within two days. The system allowed Design, Inc., a Levi-Strauss customer with a chain of 60 stores, to eliminate its entire warehouse system.

Thus, a firm can use EDI to gain a competitive advantage. In other cases, where most of an organization's competitors already possess EDI systems, developing an EDI system with a customer or a supplier may be a competitive necessity. For example,

R. J. Reynolds Tobacco Co. (RJR) sent letters to 1,500 vendors in December 1992, informing them that unless they had EDI capabilities within about a month they would get no new business from RJR. The company took this drastic step because each purchase order costs about $75 to process, whereas processing EDI purchase orders costs only 93 cents. The 1,500 companies produce 11,000 orders a year, which at a savings of about $74 each, should yield RJR a savings of almost $815,000.[1]

Electronic Market Systems

Electronic market systems are multilateral information systems that allow two or more organizations to share data about products, services, and prices. An example of an electronic market system is the electronic version of the Official Airlines Guide, which allows sellers (the airlines) to share flight information and prices with buyers.

Electronic market systems usually reduce the power of sellers by providing market data to buyers in a convenient form. However, sellers do get the opportunity to present information about promotions, prices, products, and services. If the electronic market system is popular, such as an airline reservation system, it is imperative for an organization to participate; failure to do so reduces the availability of its products or services to potential buyers and could so disable the company that it becomes unable to compete effectively.

For the buyer, however, electronic market systems hold many advantages. The systems inherently put price and feature pressures on sellers and generate better, less expensive products and services for buyers. The systems also reduce the costs of purchasing because they reduce the costs of searching for products and comparing features, prices, delivery methods, and terms.

DISTRIBUTED PROCESSING

Distributed processing was defined in the last chapter as a system in which processing occurs at more than one site. In distributed processing both computer power and data are distributed, and application programs must be run at more than one site. Using that definition, distributed processing is associated with all types of networks, including WANs, PBXs, and LANs. For example, when users of mainframes, minicomputers, microcomputers, or smart terminals located over a large geographical region are connected to a WAN but process data locally, the network provides distributed processing. When users of microcomputers located in different buildings on a campus are attached to a minicomputer system but still use their microcomputers to run application programs, the network is a distributed processing system. When microcomputer users on different floors of a building are connected to a LAN and run application software such as word processors, spreadsheets, or databases, the LAN is a distributed processing network. A network doesn't have to be large or widely scattered geographically to be distributed.

Reasons for Implementing Distributed Processing

Distributed processing systems once were considered uneconomical because of the economies of scale associated with large, centralized computer systems. In recent years, however, distributed processing systems are becoming commonplace for a number of solid reasons.

Improved Response Time. When data and processing power are located close to users, response time improves. Many of the delays associated with centralized systems

[1] "EDI or Else," *Datamation* 39, no. 4 (February 15, 1993), p. 15.

are reduced, including the delays that occur when users contend for the use of an overloaded central host or when slow communications channels are used. Distributed processing may also reduce the variability of response time caused by high requests for services at certain times, for example, when the system is fast at 8 A.M. but slows down considerably at 11 A.M.

Reduced Costs. It costs money to transmit data across distances, and transmission costs (leased lines, dial-up services, and so on) have been declining at a much slower rate than the cost of computer power. When much of the data can be keyed in, edited, and processed locally, those transmission costs are substantially reduced. When data needed only by one department or user are kept by that department or user, no transmission costs are incurred at all. Such a system requires a large centralized host only when there are large data storage or processing needs.

Improved Accuracy and Currency. Giving control of data entry and data storage to local users frequently results in higher degrees of data accuracy and currency. A branch department clerk entering branch data is likely to know more about the data and therefore to spot errors more frequently. For example, the branch clerk is more likely than a clerk at a remote site to know how to spell a branch customer's name, who should be included in the branch payroll, or whether the stock number of a branch product is correct.

Reduced Mainframe Costs. Many local processors reduce the burden on a centralized host by distributing the work to local sites. This means that a larger computer system may not have to be added to the system to meet increased computing demands. A computer system that is nearing maximum load can provide a great incentive for distributed processing. Reducing the burden on the central host also improves the response time for those users who must use it.

Smoother Growth. When a large computer system is acquired, the operational dislocation that results can be enormous. The system has to be installed, programs converted or developed and debugged, data converted or reentered, and new commands and procedures learned by everyone in the organization. The installation of a new system that uses a new operating system can be especially disruptive. On the other hand, if a new, small system is added at a remote site, only the remote site is affected. In this way, growth and change in computing resources can be incremental and easier to manage, rather than all-pervasive and disruptive of the entire organization. The addition of distributed power may eliminate the necessity of a new central system entirely.

Increased Reliability. In a centralized system, if the host fails, the entire system fails. In a distributed system, failure of one processor disrupts only the operations dependent on that processor. Furthermore, because other processors are available on the network, the disruption may not last long because users may be able to switch processing to other sites via the network.

Resource Sharing. It is possible in a distributed system to share the computing resources located anywhere on the network, including expensive printers, large or fast data storage devices, other processors, or other peripherals. Thus, a manager who is unable to use a local processor because it is overtaxed may use a processor at another location that isn't. For example, a branch office on the West Coast might use the processor of a branch office on the East Coast because at 4 P.M. the West Coast processor is very busy and the East Coast processor (where it is 7 P.M.) is relatively idle.

Increased User Satisfaction. Because of the large backlog of application development tasks faced by a centralized application program development staff, users may be dissatisfied with its responsiveness. They may welcome more control over computing power to reduce their program development time.

Management Concerns About Distributed Processing

Although distributed processing has become a welcome necessity for many organizations, it is not without problems. Some of the problems with a distributed processing system include the following.

Lack of Professional MIS Staff. Small branch sites on the distributed network may be run by personnel with little or no training or experience with computing systems. They may lack the knowledge or skills to manage their computing resources with the same care that trained professional computing personnel normally associated with a centralized computing facility can provide.

Standardization. When computing power is distributed, it is essential to maintain some form of organizationwide control over the acquisition of computer resources. Without control, it is very likely that local units will acquire incompatible equipment and software, and the system will be unable to provide integrated computing resources to everyone on the network. For example, compatibility problems occur when a network uses multiple operating systems and application software for the same level of computing power. Compatibility problems also occur when different communication protocols exist because of differing standards used in equipment acquisition. Solving conversion problems is almost never easy or inexpensive.

Given that some or all of the branch sites may not be run by computing professionals, it is also likely that local purchasers may be naive about costs and the appropriateness of the computing resources they are acquiring.

Documentation. Application program development at remote sites increases the risk that these programs may not be fully documented. The result may be that these programs could be difficult to update or maintain, especially if the original program developer has moved on to a new position with another firm. Centralized application development departments are likely to enforce minimum program documentation standards; the single application developer at a remote site may not.

Data Loss. Archiving or backing up computer files is a tedious but necessary activity. In centralized computing departments, archiving activities are an established routine, and someone in these departments has the responsibility to see that the routine is carried out systematically and regularly. Without some form of central control or enforcement of archiving procedures, inexperienced users of minicomputers and microcomputers at remote sites may treat the archiving of data too casually, and data loss is likely to result.

Also, restarting a computer system and recovering data lost from a system failure is not an easy task. Professional MIS personnel, trained in restart and recovery procedures and equipped with the appropriate software tools can handle system failure much easier and with much greater success than inexperienced and untrained personnel.

Security. Most organizations keep data that are sensitive in one way or another. For example, all organizations keep confidential data on employees, customers, and vendors. Many organizations store data about new products, new production techniques, product and customer research, or marketing plans that they do not wish their competitors to obtain. Some organizations store data about national security matters or military equipment specifications.

Centralized computing departments normally establish procedures for security, including the use of physical and electronic security procedures and devices, to keep confidential data confidential. Without some form of organizationwide control, security procedures for confidential data at small remote computing sites may easily become lax, or they may not exist at all. Because distributing power usually means that local sites may view or download information from other sites, very confidential data could be written to a 5¼-inch diskette and carried out the door of a branch office. In these locations the data may have been transferred to diskettes that are casually stored in an unlocked diskette caddy in an open office area.

Data Integrity. Distributed data processing usually means that both data and computing power are distributed. Without careful planning, monitoring, and controls, this situation invites increased risks of data redundancy and therefore data inconsistency, resulting in turn in inconsistencies in the reports prepared by various units on the system.

System Maintenance. Large, centralized data centers have trained professionals who are experienced in program and system maintenance. They also usually have contracts with equipment and software vendors for maintenance of computer hardware and software. When computing power is distributed to small, remote sites, such on-site talent is less likely to be available. It may be very difficult to provide system maintenance swiftly or at all at every distributed site.

An Effective Distributed Processing System

Distributed processing systems must be managed very carefully to be effective. Usually some form of organizationwide monitoring, supervision, training, and control is necessary to ensure that the system does not get out of hand.

An effective system should also be easy to use. Thus, users should not have to be concerned with where the data are or where the processing is occurring when they make a request of the system. To produce a report, for example, a manager should not have to know where the system will find the necessary data or which processors and communications systems it needs to use. This feature of a distributed system is usually referred to as *location transparency*.

An effective system should also guard against loss of data integrity. The software and procedures used should provide for automatic systemwide updates. A user who updates a record in a file should not have to be concerned with whether or not the system updates the data wherever those data exist in the system; the system itself should provide for automatic updates. This feature of a distributed system is usually called *update transparency*.

A major concern of computer system professionals is in the explosion of computing power resulting from the availability of inexpensive computing systems such as minicomputers, microcomputers, and supermicros. Many departments or individuals within organizations, dissatisfied with the responsiveness of the centralized computing department, are going it alone with their own equipment. Though this provides short-term solutions, it often creates major long-term problems for the organization. As a manager, it is important that you understand not only the advantages of local computing power, but also the need for professional organizationwide help in managing that computing power.

When considering distributed processing, it is also helpful to consider the nature of the organziation. Organizing information systems in a distributed processing fashion is often likely to be effective in organizations that are decentralized in other ways. For example, a large firm may acquire a number of other firms as subsidiaries that produce different, though related, products. The large firm may choose not to meddle in the way that the subsidiaries function, delegating to each a lot of decision-making authority. These subsidiaries may further use many different types of computer systems to support their functions. In such an environment, distributed processing is likely to make a great deal of sense because it fits the way the total organization is structured and operates.

CLIENT/SERVER COMPUTING

Recently, many organizations have been adopting a form of distributed processing called **client/server computing**, which can be defined as

> A form of shared, or distributed, computing in which tasks and computing power are split between servers . . . and clients (usually workstations or personal computers). Servers store and process data common to users across the enterprise; these data can then be accessed by client systems.[2]

The basic notion of a client/server computing system is that application processing is divided between a *client*, which is typically a personal computer, and a *server*, which may be a file server on a local area network, a minicomputer, or a mainframe. The client processes run on the personal computer and make requests of the server processes, which, as noted, may run on several platforms. Typical components of client/server computing are a relational database, a powerful server or servers, personal computer workstations, a local area network, and client software for the workstations.

A common application of client/server computing is the use of special relational database software called a SQL server. A *SQL server* is a software package that usually runs on a dedicated computer on a LAN that is also called a SQL server. The SQL server computer usually devotes all its energies to managing the database software and does not handle other network tasks. SQL server software performs database applications faster and more reliably than typical LAN-based database management software. A major reason for this efficiency is that SQL servers process client workstation requests for data differently than other types of LAN database management systems. For example, when you request a record for a LAN database that is on a file server, the typical LAN database management system sends a large block of records from the server over the network to your workstation. Your workstation then must sort through the block of records to find the one you wanted. Furthermore, you won't use much of the traffic placed on the network—only one of the records in the block. In other words, typical LAN database management systems treat file servers as not much more than remote hard disk drives for the workstation. Its equivalent to asking a bat boy to get you your favorite bat and then having him drag the whole bat rack to the on-deck circle so that you can pick the one you want.

In contrast, a client workstation might ask SQL server software to send all records that match certain selection parameters; for example, all employees who earn an hourly rate of more than $15. The SQL server software processes the request *at the SQL server* and sends only those records that meet the selection parameters. The client workstation then displays the records for the user. Thus, the SQL server not only stores the records, but also processes the records. This feature reduces traffic on the network and also might improve processing performance because the workstation may be a less expensive, slower microcomputer than the file server where the processing occurs.

Because SQL servers perform the bulk of the processing, the machines they are placed on are usually fast and powerful microcomputers. To insure fast performance on

---

[2]Harry Newton. *Newton's Telecom Dictionary*, New York: Telecom Library, Inc. 1991.

LANs that make heavy use of a database, many SQL servers are loaded on multiprocessor microcomputers. Thus, a LAN might contain client workstations, a SQL server computer, a printer server, a communications server, and a file server for network control and management and the remaining applications (see Figure 7–29).

In a SQL server environment, records may be sorted on the server running the SQL server database software and sent to a workstation, or client, running a different version of the same database software or another application program for additional processing. For example, a dedicated SQL file server (also called the *back-end processor*) running SQL Server from Sybase may sort and send records requested by a workstation (also called the *front-end processor*). The workstation then reads the records and further processes them by placing them into a Lotus 1-2-3 spreadsheet template.

In client/server computing, the back-end processor provides access to the database and a variety of database services, such as remote connectivity, data integrity, and data security. The front-end processor often provides data entry and data validation, and formats and displays the data. Both the back-end and the front-end processors may perform operations on the data, such as sorting and calculating.

Client/server computing, however, is not limited to local area networks. The basic plan of client/server models is to permit workstations to access data wherever they are found and to have many processors perform whatever processing needs to be done according to their availability and capability. Thus, client/server computing may include WANs as well as LANs; mainframes and minicomputers as well as microcomputers. In these systems, mainframes can be used to perform large, repetitive processing operations, such as sorting, while leaving the formatting and display of the results to microcomputers, which typically use the more user-friendly and easier-to-understand GUI software. Thus, you might search a database for specific records using a relational database management system on an IBM mainframe, but the final results of the search might be displayed on a client microcomputer system running a GUI-based, microcomputer spreadsheet package.

The bottom line is that client/server computing can make all data in any databases that exist on an organization's networks available to any end-user who has a microcomputer workstation and the authority to use the data. Furthermore, client/server com-

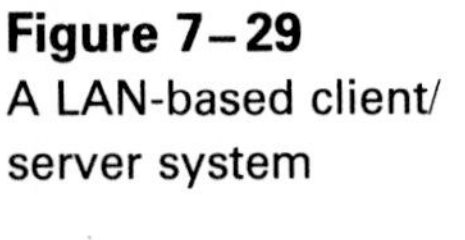

Figure 7–29
A LAN-based client/server system

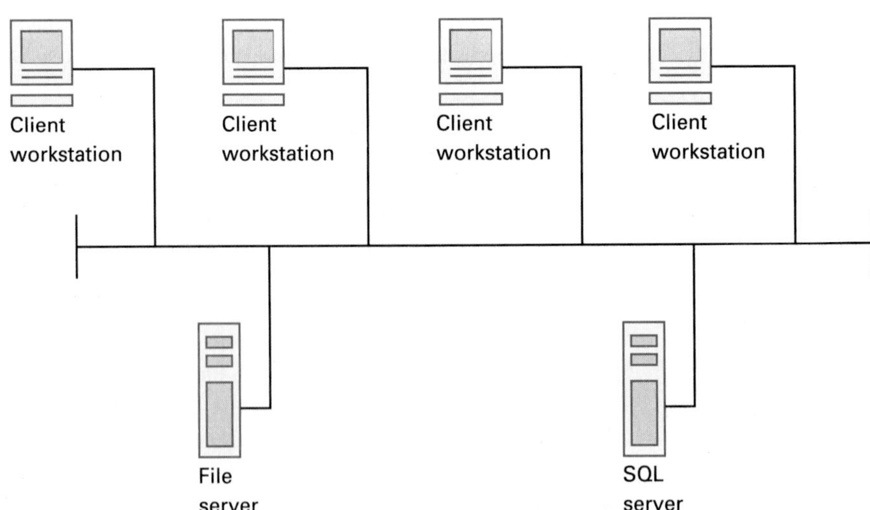

puting promises to let whatever computing resources on the networks can best perform a service do so, using each network computing resource to its best advantage.

Because of the power and efficiency of SQL servers, client/server computing systems running on local area networks have been replacing mainframe-based information systems in many organizations. Organizations faced with high maintenance costs on existing mainframe computer hardware and software or the need to upgrade those systems are increasingly downsizing to LAN-based, client/server computing systems from older, preexisting or "legacy," mainframe-based information systems to reduce costs. Downsizing can provide substantial reductions in systems costs, including equipment costs, software purchase costs, annual hardware and software maintenance costs, and application development costs. The greatest cost reduction is likely to occur when an organization proposes to downsize applications to equipment already in place, such as microcomputers, local area networks, and the supporting operating systems and applications software. By using current equipment, the organization manages to partially protect current system investment.

Many organizations now view client/server systems as vehicles for replacing or expanding costly mainframe systems with the less expensive power of personal computers. Most practitioners do not suggest replacing mainframe systems that are operating efficiently and effectively. They do suggest that mainframe systems be migrated down to mini and micro systems when the mainframe becomes inadequate to its tasks or obsolete, or when new application systems are to be developed.

ENTERPRISEWIDE NETWORKING

As LANs proliferate, WANs expand, and other networks grow in an organization, attempts to make these various networks work together occur. That is, there are attempts at *internetworking* or connecting organization networks. Recently, emphasis on internetworking for an entire organization, or **enterprisewide networking**, has grown. For small firms, enterprisewide networking is a relatively easy task. Small firms are likely to have fewer networks and fewer, different types of networks than larger firms. For large firms that have grown over time, developing an enterprisewide network can be daunting because many different networks, many of which do not share the protocols used by the others, are in place.

Enterprisewide networking includes developing the means by which different networks can exchange data. It also includes setting standards for communications for the entire organization so that future internetworking tasks are easier to handle. Developing a backbone network system, not only for LANs, but for all networks, and setting standards for connecting to the backbone cabling system is a major step to enterprisewide networking. Moving to SQL-based database management systems on all platforms of computer systems used in a firm is another step to enterprisewide networking. Choosing a comprehensive set of consistent communications standards is still another step (see "Communications Standards and the Manager," later in this chapter).

INTERNATIONAL NETWORKS

International networks may generate a number of different problems for managers. These problems may range from simply trying to connect to a bewildering array of equipment specifications, manage power differences, and handle time differences to the more complicated handling of different character sets (Kanji in Japan and China, Hongul in Korea, and Farsi in Arabic countries). Problems in codes arise because seven-bit ASCII codes can only accommodate 128 distinct characters whereas the number of Kanji characters, for example, exceeds 30,000.

Problems with international networks may also be politically based. Most countries have governmental agencies that regulate telephones and other communication networks. These agencies usually have regulations that favor, subsidize, or protect certain interests. For example, some governments may restrict equipment attached to the network to equipment made in their countries. Governments may also levy duties on software passed over the network. Other governments may be more concerned about the nature of the information about a country that becomes more accessible over international networks. In fact, some countries are considering legislating the information that may be placed on international networks because they consider these networks a threat to their national security.

Box 7–5 High-Speed Dilemma

Regardless of the information systems technology that is to be acquired, managers *always* seem to face a choice among many existing standards. Apprehension over their acquisition choice is increased because several more promising standards are always under development. For example, suppose a manager would like to connect the local area networks scattered throughout the organization's many locations across the country using the facilities of a common carrier. That manager may choose to standardize using one of many existing communications technologies, such as frame relay service. The manager might also consider waiting for two emerging technologies, such as asynchronous transmission mode and switched multi-megabit data service. Choosing an existing technology will get the job done quickly but will likely mean the acquisition of a system that becomes outmoded very soon. Waiting for emerging technologies will mean lost connectivity immediately and investing in unproven systems later. Choosing frame relay now or waiting for asychronous transfer mode or switched multi-megabit data service later is a decision facing many information systems managers today.

FRAME RELAY

Frame relay is a form of packet switching that uses small packets that can vary in length. It gets its high speed by performing error detection and correction procedures only at the sending and destination nodes rather than at each node on the network. Frame relay is currently offered by many common carriers on a flat rate basis or a usage basis. Offering speeds of 64 kbps to 1.544 mbps, the system is well suited to the bursty nature of inter-LAN traffic.

ATM

ATM, or *asynchronous transfer mode*, uses fixed-length packets and offers speeds of from 45 mbps to 600 mbps. Future speeds are anticipated in the gigabit range. Because of the high speeds it offers, ATM promises the capability to handle multimedia traffic. MCI has announced an ATM trial service during 1993. However, it is not likely that the system will become a commercial reality until 1995 or later.

SMDS

Switched multi-megabit data service (SMDS) is a standard for data transmission that has been around for over a decade but has been offered on only a limited basis by commercial carriers, although every regional Bell operating company is testing a service presently. SMDS uses a fixed-length packet size. This speeds service by eliminating the need for nodes on the network to determine packet size before routing the packet to the next network node. SMDS offers speeds of 1.544 mbps and 45 mbps, and in the future it may offer speeds of 155 mbps and 600 mbps.

COMMUNICATIONS STANDARDS AND THE MANAGER

The field of communications is extremely complex and includes many diverse technologies. It also includes many organizations that set standards, and thus, many sets of often incompatible standards. In fact, the usual quip of communications professionals is that what makes communications standards so nice is that there are so many of them from which to choose. Such a diverse standards environment makes it difficult for the manager to make decisions regarding communications systems, including hardware, software, and media (see Boxes 7–5 and 7–6). Two major sets of communications standards, which are called *communications architectures,* however, should be given a close look as a means of bringing some degree of order out of the current chaos: Systems Network Architecture (SNA) from IBM and Open Systems Interconnect (OSI) from the International Organization for Standardization (ISO) (see Box 7–7). Each of these architectures is really an organized set of specifications for handling communications tasks, allowing software developers and manufacturers who use these specifications to create products that "fit" together. Communications networks built on the foundation of a comprehensive architecture, or set of standards, present fewer problems because they are built within a coherent framework of specifications. That usually means that hardware and software, built according to the architecture's specifications, usually will work together.

Box 7–6 Integrated Services Digital Network (ISDN)

Because of differences in analog and digital transmission and the differing characteristics of voice, data, image, video, and other transmissions, many specialized networks and communications devices have evolved over the years. Specialized analog networks are now available for voice and data, specialized digital networks for voice and data, and specialized digital networks for facsimile transmissions (see Chapter 8). Specialized networks for cable television, videotext, teleconferencing (see Chapter 8), and local area networking are also available. And this is not a complete list of all the specialized networks available.

The specialized networks have evolved over time because the technology to transmit data, text, voice, image, facsimile, and video over a single network did not exist. As the need arose, special networks serving specific transmission types were developed. AT&T and the other major communications organizations in the world have developed an Integrated Services Digital Network (ISDN). ISDN is designed to replace current analog technology with digital technology so that voice, data, facsimile, image, and video communications are all encoded digitally and can be transmitted through a single set of standardized interfaces.

Proponents of ISDN hope that the network will cover the world and allow users to transmit simultaneously the various information types through a single network. Because the effort is international and because of its complexity, it will take many years to implement fully. The final goal, however, is to provide a totally digital communications system that will link public and private networks on a worldwide basis so that users can access any system remotely from anywhere on earth. The intention is to have ISDN network computers handle conversion for incompatible computer systems so that users will be able to share data worldwide without regard to computer system or data differences.

However, ISDN has been slow to catch on, primarily because telephone carriers have failed to make the capability available in many areas. Recently, however, ISDN services have become more available. ISDN is increasingly being used by universities and also by organizations that need to connect remote LANs. At the same time, asychronous transmission mode facilities (see Box 7–5) may simply make ISDN obsolete or at best a bit player in the communications market place.

Box 7–7 The Layered Standards of Open Systems Interconnect Architecture

The OSI network standards group all communications tasks into seven layers. In each of these layers, specifications about how these tasks will be accomplished (the protocols) are described. On an OSI-based network, messages pass from one computer system to another through each of the seven layers.

Layer	Protocols
Application	Provides network services to users and user applications, including file transfer
Presentation	Formats data between different systems
Session	Establishes and terminates links between computers
Transport	Controls data transfer for the complete path, from sending point to receiving point
Network	Controls the routing of data through the channels of a network
Data link	Controls grouping data into blocks and transferring blocks from one network point to another
Physical	Handles voltages, electrical pulses, connectors, and switches

Because of the widespread use of IBM computer systems and the widespread acceptance of the OSI standards, systems built on either of these two architectures provide many options for acquiring communications components that work together and a sound basis for handling future expansion and technological change. That is, future hardware and software products, built according to the specifications of an architecture, are apt to be compatible with an existing network built on the same architecture.

Management Summary

The transfer of voice, data, text, and images through communications networks has become very important to the success of a business. The solutions to numerous business problems can involve a variety of communications systems.

Every communications system consists of at least a sender, a channel over which the message is sent, and a receiver. However, communications systems, or networks, are likely to be a good deal more complex than that. One reason for complexity is the number of differing sources of communications channels, the variety of communications channels available, the diversity of communications equipment, and the variety of communications modes and data codes used.

Four broad categories of communications networks are typically found in businesses: wide area networks; PBX networks; local area networks; and microcomputer networks, including those that connect micros to external databases and mainframe computers.

Wide area networks are often implemented to capture data at their source, to increase productivity, to permit company expansion and acquisitions, to increase the timeliness of communications, and to increase management control. Typical WAN hardware includes the host, a front-end processor, multiplexers, protocol converters, modems, and terminals. Typical WAN software includes telecommunications access programs, network control programs, and teleprocessing monitors. All WAN configurations revolve around variations of two basic configurations: point-to-point networks and multidrop networks. The manager must be concerned with wide area network reliability, response time, network costs, network compatibility, and network security.

PBX networks are designed primarily for voice communications, but increasingly they include some capability to process data and text communications as well. PBXs are often acquired to reduce voice communications costs, to process a limited amount of data and text communications over the voice system, and to secure features that may not be available from the local telephone company. Besides the ability to handle both voice and data communications, PBXs may also provide gateways to other computer networks, allocate calls more efficiently among receivers, provide voice mail systems, furnish call accounting systems, and provide access to company databases using the telephone keypad.

Local area networks typically serve to connect microcomputers located in an office, floor, building, or campus. They are often implemented to allow micros to share peripherals, programs, and data files as well as to provide electronic mail service to users. Typical LAN hardware includes file servers, print servers, communications servers, and microcomputer workstations. LANs may be connected in a ring, bus, or star network. The manager must be concerned about the high cost of connecting devices to the network, the high cost of installing network cabling, the costs of LAN management, and the usability of current software and hardware.

Microcomputers may also be connected to each other, to external databases and bulletin boards providing information about many specialized topics, and to the company mainframe. Connecting micros to each other and to external databases usually involves purchasing a modem and software to run it. Connecting micros to the company mainframe usually involves purchasing a terminal emulation board and the software to run it.

Interorganizational systems are information systems that extend beyond the boundaries of a single organization. Electronic data interchange systems are interorganizational information systems that allow the direct sharing of information between two organization's computer systems, typically between a buyer and a seller. Electronic marketing systems are muiltilateral information systems that permit many organizations to share information about products, services, and pricing. These systems permit sellers to inform potential buyers of their offerings and allow buyers to comparison shop efficiently.

Distributed processing requires that more than one site on a network have the computing power and the data to run application programs. Distributed processing networks have increased in recent years because they offer lower communications costs, increased reliability, reduced demands on the host system, greater response time, and increased user control and satisfaction. However, they also may incur increased risk of loss of data, data integrity, and data secrecy. In addition, without some overall management control, there is a good chance for loss of standardization in equipment, software, and procedures. In a distributed processing system, it may be difficult to provide equipment and program maintenance swiftly or at all to every processing site. Local control over computer processing may provide immediate gains in response time and costs but, if uncontrolled, may produce major problems for organizations.

A special form of distributed processing, client/server computing, divides application processing between the client, usually a personal computer, and a server, which may be a file server on a LAN, a minicomputer, or a mainframe. A typical client/server application uses SQL server software, which is special relational database software. Typically, the SQL server software is placed on a high-end microcomputer on a LAN and the microcomputer is dedicated to the SQL functions. Many firms are using LAN-based client/server systems to downsize their organization's computing facilities, abandoning or reducing their reliance on mainframe computers in order to reduce information systems costs.

Developing communications systems based on widely accepted technologies (such as Ethernet local area networks) and comprehensive communications standards architectures (such as OSI) helps an organization to construct communications systems that are capable of working and growing together.

In Part 2, you have learned the fundamentals of computer systems, including hardware, software, information storage, and information communications. In Part 3, you will learn how computer systems can be applied to the major functions of most organizations: finance, marketing, production, and personnel. You will also learn how the office has been changed through the application of computer technology.

Key Terms for Managers

analog transmission, **237**
bits per second (BPS), **242**
bus topology, **252**
cellular telephone system, **243**
channel, **236**
client/server computing, **279**
common carrier, **240**
communications network, **237**
communications server, **262**
dial-up telephone lines, **240**
digital transmission, **237**
distributed processing, **275**
electronic data interchange (EDI), **274**
electronic mail, **261**
electronic market systems, **275**
emulation board, **272**
emulation software, **272**
enterprisewide networking, **281**
file server, **261**
host, **246**
interorganizational information systems, **274**
leased telephone lines, **240**
local area network (LAN), **260**
mesh topology, **252**
modems, **248**
network interface card (NIC), **263**
network operating system (NOS), **263**
private branch exchange (PBX), **256**
personal communications network (PCN), **245**
print server, **262**
response time, **255**
ring topology, **252**
star topology, **251**
telecommunications systems, **237**
value-added networks (VANS), **240**
voice mail system, **258**
wide area network (WAN), **246**
wireless LANs, **262**
wireless network, **243**

Review Questions

1. Identify and describe at least five business applications for which data communications systems are appropriate.
2. List and describe the basic components of any communications system.
3. Explain the difference between asynchronous communications and synchronous communications.
4. Explain the difference between simplex, half-duplex, and full-duplex transmission. Provide an example of each type of transmission.
5. What is a communications network? What is a wide area network?
6. Identify and describe at least five types of communications media.
7. What is a communications protocol?

8. Explain the purpose of a front-end processor.
9. Explain why a manager might want the organization to use multiplexers.
10. Why might an organization need one or more protocol converters?
11. Explain why a modem is usually needed when communications must take place over telephone lines.
12. What are the differences between intelligent and dumb terminals?
13. What is the function of a telecommunications access program?
14. Describe the purpose of a teleprocessing monitor.
15. What is a microcomputer terminal emulation board? What is it used for?
16. List the basic types of network topologies.
17. What does the term *response time* mean on a network?
18. What is a central office?
19. Explain what a voice mail system is. What use could a manager make of a voice mail system?
20. What is data entry software for PBXs? How might a manager apply data entry software?
21. What is distributed processing? How do distributed processing systems differ from distributed database systems?
22. What is SMDR software? What does SMDR offer the manager?
23. Explain ISDN. How might this system be an improvement over current communications systems?
24. Explain the difference between circuit switching and packet switching. What advantage does packet switching offer?
25. What are six concerns a manager should have about a communications network?
26. What is a LAN?
27. What is a file server? What purpose does it serve?
28. What are print servers and communications servers?
29. What is electronic mail and what features does electronic mail provide?
30. List seven basic LAN components.
31. List three LAN topologies and explain how these topologies differ. Are these topologies ever combined?
32. Explain the term *backbone network.*
33. What are internal and external modems? How do they differ?
34. What is a users' group? How can users' groups be of help?
35. What is a SQL server? How do SQL servers differ from ordinary networked database management system software?

36. What is client/server computing? What are the typical components of a client/server computing system?
37. What are interorganizational information systems? What are two types of interorganizational information systems?
38. What is a PBX?
39. What is EDI? What is an electronic market system?

Questions for Discussion

1. Why might an organization send messages using a synchronous transmission mode?
2. Why might an organization use a dial-up telephone line for data communications rather than a leased line?
3. What reasons might make organizations utilize a wide area network?
4. Why might a manager want to connect microcomputers into a local area network?
5. Why might a manager decide not to develop a LAN?
6. Why might managers want to connect their microcomputers to the company mainframe?
7. What is a PBX? Why might a manager consider buying a PBX?
8. Why might an organization consider distributed processing?
9. What concerns do distributed processing systems create?
10. Why are communications standards important to the manager?
11. What advantages might a large buyer gain from developing electronic data interchange systems with its major suppliers?
12. What are some problems that might be encountered in an international network?

Problems

1. **Crestfield Sheeting Company.** Currently, Chester Clark, a manager at Crestfield Sheeting Company, has one employee who enters data about vendors into microcomputer files created using a commercial database management system. The system is used to keep track of details about the vendors who provide goods or services to Crestfield Sheeting, including details about the quality of what the vendors sell or the quality of their service.

   Lately, the employee has had a great deal of difficulty keeping up with the data entry task. The company has been growing rapidly, and the number of vendors has increased dramatically. It is clear to Clark that he must hire several more data entry employees to handle the task.

   After visiting with a friend in another department, Clark has decided to acquire and install a LAN with three workstations so that three data entry employees can use the same database management system at the same time. He plans to use the same database management system software that he is currently using. He is pleased with the idea because the LAN will eliminate the need for him to buy any additional software to get the job done.

   Describe two problems that Clark is likely to run into if he implements his idea.

2. **Bear-Reece, Inc.** Bear-Reece, Inc., is considering placing six remote terminals at a site in another city to be used to enter sales orders on-line. The company wishes to connect the terminals to the host at the home office. Company management is considering having six lines installed at the home office and at the remote site so that each terminal can be directly connected to the host. It will also need 12 modems for the installation—6 at the host end and 6 at the terminal end.

    a. Develop and draw an alternative configuration of communications equipment and channels for the company's remote site to save the company lines and modems.
    b. What concerns should Bear-Reece, Inc., have regarding the communications system it is considering?

3. **Centix, Inc.** Bill Franke is a sales manager with Centix, Inc. He has a desktop computer system that is connected to a LAN in his office. He is on the road quite a bit and would like to connect his notebook computer system to the LAN in his office while he is away.

    a. Describe two methods that he might consider using to connect his notebook computer to the office LAN.
    b. Describe, in general, the hardware and software Bill would need to buy for each method.
    c. List actual brand names and prices of one set of hardware and software for each method you described. To gather these data, use a CD-ROM database, such as *Computer Select.* You may also use *Computer Literature Index,* published by Applied Computer Research, Inc., Phoenix, Arizona, to find PC magazines that have recently featured articles on remote computing.

4. **The Vorhees Company.** Jill Sabol, an executive at the Vorhees Company, wants to connect the microcomputer system on her desk to the company's mainframe. Sabol's office is next to a room full of terminals connected to the mainframe via terminal controllers. The mainframe system is an IBM computer and uses protocols that are different from her microcomputer.

    Describe how Sabol can use the terminal controller to connect to the mainframe. Include in your answer what hardware and software she will need to do the job.

5. **Anastasi Imports, Inc.** Anastasi Imports, Inc., wants to develop a communications system to link its branch office with its home office. At the home office, it has a mainframe computer that uses EBCDIC as a data code.

    a. Assume that the company wants to use six dumb ASCII terminals at the branch office site. Draw a configuration of a network that might connect the dumb terminals at Anastasi's branch office to its home office mainframe computer system using multiplexers to save telephone lines. Make sure that you draw and label each piece of equipment you feel should be placed on the network, including the host mainframe computer and the terminals at the branch office. Use Figure 7–10 as a guide.
    b. Assume that the company wants to use six microcomputers as terminals at the branch office site. Draw a configuration of a network that might connect the microcomputers on the LAN at Anastasi's branch office to its home office mainframe computer system. Make sure that you draw and label each piece of equipment you feel should be placed on the network, including the host main-

frame computer, the servers on the LAN, and the microcomputers at the branch office. Use Figure 7–26 as a guide.

6. **Personal Communications Services.** Prepare a report that reviews one model of a personal digital assistant, such as the EO Personal Communicator from EO, Inc., that is equipped to be used as a personal communicator. The review should include price, features, ease of use, and the availability and usefulness of documentation. As sources for your report, you might use the *Computer Literature Index,* published by Applied Computer Research, Inc., Phoenix, Arizona, the *Guide to Business Periodicals, Computer Select,* the CD-ROM database service, or all three.

7. **Microcomputer Modem Model.** Prepare a report that reviews one model of a microcomputer modem and its associated software. The review should include price, features, ease of use, and the availability and usefulness of documentation. As sources for your report, use the *Computer Literature Index,* published by Applied Computer Research, Inc., Phoenix, Arizona, and the *Guide to Business Periodicals.*

Cases

1. **Advanced Financial Services, Inc.** Advanced Financial Services, Inc. (AFS) is a partnership that provides accounting and financial planning services to small and medium-sized businesses and organizations in Oakland, California. Its home office in Oakland employs 94 people and is supported by a minicomputer system. It is considering opening a second office in San Francisco, which is just across the bay from Oakland.

   Advanced Financial plans to start with an office that will be home to approximately 50 people, including one partner, managers, financial planners, field agents, and office support personnel. The field agents visit firms, collect accounting data, and prepare accounting and tax reports. The financial planners advise firms on financial and tax matters and usually conduct their business in the office.

   a. Identify and describe several communications systems that AFS might consider using in its San Francisco office.

2. **Northern Paper Company.** Oki Sumio, the plant manager of Northern Paper Company, is upset with the cost and performance of her telephone service. There have been many complaints from customers, salespeople, and others that they cannot reach the company between 10 A.M. and 2 P.M. The phone lines are almost always busy during those hours. It is particularly annoying to some people to find that they have to call and recall many times when all they want to do is to leave a message for someone at Northern.

   Ms. Sumio is also upset with the cost of her plant's long-distance charges. She suspects that many employees are using Northern's long-distance lines to telephone friends, relatives, and stores for personal reasons. As a result, Ms. Sumio is considering purchasing a PBX for the company to improve the telephone service and lower costs.

   a. What special equipment and software for PBXs might Ms. Sumio consider for the new system?
   b. How will each piece of equipment and each type of software you list in (a) solve a specific telephone system problem she has identified?
   c. What concerns should she have regarding the acquisition of a PBX for the Northern plant?

3. **Right Way, Inc.** Juan Fica is a manager for Right Way, Inc., and has called you in to serve as a consultant for a project. Juan would like to install a local area network in his office suite. He would like to connect his office microcomputer and the microcomputers of each of his three supervisors, two secretaries, one receptionist, and one clerk to the network.

   Juan has an Apple Macintosh microcomputer. His supervisors, the secretaries, the receptionist, and the clerk all have IBM-PCs. The software that is on the Macintosh includes Microsoft's Word for word processing and Excel for spreadsheets. The others use WordPerfect for word processing, Lotus 1-2-3 for spreadsheets, and dBase IV for database.

   The office staff has two letter-quality printers available to them, and Juan and the supervisors each have a dot-matrix printer. Juan would like to acquire a laser printer and desktop publishing software so the secretaries could produce a company newsletter.

   He would like the network to provide the following services: shared programs for word processing and database, electronic mail accessible by him and all employees, shared data and document files, shared disk space, and shared printers. He would also like to connect his home microcomputer, which is an IBM-PC, to the network so that he might work at night and on weekends.

   a. Identify the potential problems that might be generated on the network if Juan's current hardware and software were used.

   b. Describe additional management concerns that he should explore before any LAN is actually developed and implemented.

4. **Cloris, Inc.** Cloris, Inc., employs 120 field representatives who visit customers by car. They often stay overnight in hotels and motels as they sweep their sales territories. Currently, field reps mail in sales orders at the end of each day. It takes about three days for the orders to reach the home office, and another day for the orders to be processed. Cloris field reps can usually promise the customer that their orders will be shipped within five days. Rush orders are handled over the telephone.

   Problems arise when stock ordered is out or discontinued. Delays with such orders can exceed several weeks because the salesperson does not learn of the problem for several days. The customer then has to be contacted and sold alternative stock.

   It is also difficult to locate salespeople on the road or to keep up with their itineraries. There is no way to contact all salespeople quickly when stockouts occur, when stock is discontinued, or when special pricing policies have been implemented.

   The company would like to implement a communications system that would permit its field representatives to maintain close contact with the home office. There is a need for the field reps to contact the home office daily to pick up and deliver messages, and there is also a need for a way to contact the field reps when customers call or when company personnel have to advise them on the stock and price conditions already discussed.

   a. Identify and describe several communications systems that Cloris might explore to solve its problems. Your description should include how each system solves each problem.

   b. Identify and describe concerns that the Cloris management should be aware of for each of the communications systems you included in your answer to (a) above.

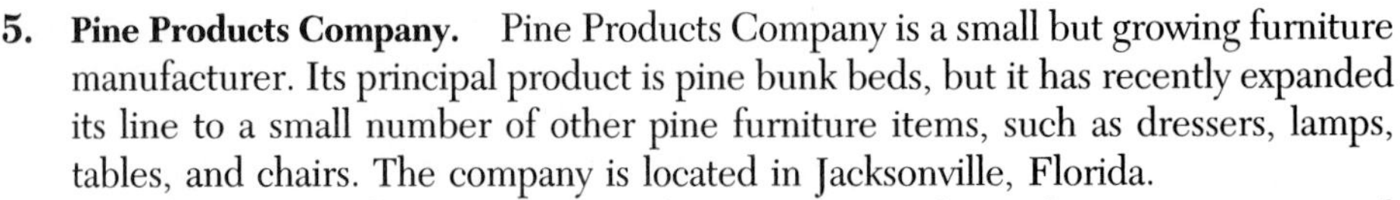

5. **Pine Products Company.** Pine Products Company is a small but growing furniture manufacturer. Its principal product is pine bunk beds, but it has recently expanded its line to a small number of other pine furniture items, such as dressers, lamps, tables, and chairs. The company is located in Jacksonville, Florida.

   The company began operations five years ago with one factory in a converted building and has since spread out into three other buildings within the city and four others in neighboring cities. The home office is located on 10th Street, above the first factory. This office serves as the sales office for the factories in Jacksonville. There are also sales offices and administrative offices in each of the other factory buildings.

   Business has been very good. In the last few years, sales to stores within a three-state area surrounding Atlanta, Georgia, and a three-state area surrounding Lexington, Kentucky, have provided enormous growth for the company. To meet the demand in these two three-state areas, the company has had to operate the four Jacksonville factories on two shifts. Pratt Williams, the founder and president of Pine Products Company, is considering starting factories in two more cities—Atlanta and Lexington—in order to locate production closer to the company's customers in these two areas and to reduce the burden on the Jacksonville operations. He also expects that shipping costs should be reduced for the company to lower the total delivered prices for its products for dealers in the Lexington and Atlanta territories. Based on previous sales, it is estimated that production at each of the new sites will start at nearly 25 percent of the old sites but grow rapidly to 50 percent within three years.

   The company has been using a minicomputer located in the home office to handle its data processing needs. Each of the other factories has several terminals that are connected to the home office through telephone lines. The system provides accounting software for sales orders, invoices, purchase invoices, inventory, payroll, and similar accounting functions.

   Pratt Williams wants to establish two remote data entry and printing stations at each of the new factories. He recommends specifically that three data entry terminals and one printing terminal be placed at the two new sites and that the minicomputer at the Jacksonville office be upgraded to handle the communications and the extra processing from the new sites.

   John Williams, Pratt's son, is in charge of the financial information systems for the firm. John has told Pratt that the current model of minicomputer that the company has is nearly at the limit of its ability to expand, and in fact, that response time on the present system has already begun to slow down. He believes that the current computer system is totally inadequate for the firm and feels that the company should scrap it and purchase a much larger computer system so that it will be in a position to meet planned growth.

   a. Do you believe that Pratt's recommendations are better than John's? Why or why not? Be specific; provide reasons for choosing one plan or the other.

   b. What other options are open to Pine Products? Specifically, how might these options be better than either Pratt's or John's plans?

Selected References and Readings

Anderson, Ron. "SQL Databases: High-Powered, High-Priced." *PC Magazine* 11, no. 15 (September 15, 1992), pp. 369–76 ff. A review of the leading SQL database software.

Bakos, J. Y. "Information Link and Electronic Marketplaces: the Role of Interorganizational Information Systems in Vertical Markets." *Journal of Management Information Systems* 8, no. 2 (Fall 1991), pp. 31–52. An analysis of interorganizational systems.

Braasch, Bill. "Early Adopters Report Architecture Has Pluses." *Software Magazine* 10, no. 5 (April 1990), pp. 63–69. An analysis of the advantages and disadvantages of client/server networks by early users of these systems.

Brown, Ronald. "PBXs: Office Controller Exchanges." *Telecommunications* 23, no. 4, (April 1989), pp. 43–52. Discusses trends and uses of PBXs as an information switch.

Cashin, Jerry. "Choosing a LAN OS: Proceed with Caution." *Software Magazine* 10, no. 3 (March 1990), pp. 59–65. Discusses and compares the major LAN network operating systems.

Cashin, Jerry. "Wireless Links Loom on Horizon." *Software Magazine* 13, no. 6 (April 1993), pp. 99–102 ff. Provides a look into the future of wireless computing.

Chernicoff, David. "Remote Access: Expanding Your Data Horizons." *PC Week Special Report, PC Week* 10, no. 29 (July 26, 1993), pp. 77 ff. This is an editorial introduction to a series of articles about remote access and systems reviews that follow.

Derfler, Frank J., Jr. *Guide to Connectivity.* 2nd ed. Emeryville, Calif.: Ziff-Davis Press, 1992. A detailed description of common PC communications systems, including work-group systems, LANs, multiuser PC systems, and PC modems.

Derfler, Frank J., Jr. *Guide to Linking LANs,* Emeryville, Calif.: Ziff-Davis Press, 1992. A guide to connecting local area networks to create wider networks. You may wish instead to read Derfler's article, "Linking Lans," in *PC Magazine* 12, no. 5 (March 16, 1993), pp. 183–87 ff.

Fitzgerald, Jerry. *Business Data Communications: Basic Concepts, Security, and Design.* 4th ed. New York: John Wiley & Sons, 1993. A comprehensive introductory textbook on communications systems.

Friedman, Rick. "Anywhere, Anytime: the Wireless Office of Today." *The Office* 118, no. 2 (August 1993), pp. 8, 9, and 52. Describes and compares wireless technologies and their recent applications.

Gunn, Angela. "Wireless Communications: Connecting Over the Airwaves." *PC Magazine* 12, no. 14 (August 1993), pp. 359–62 ff. This article describes the types of wireless communications that exist and are on the horizon and discusses network providers, devices, and applications.

Hurwicz, Michael. "FDDI: Not Fastest but Still Fit." *Datamation* 39, no. 7 (April 1, 1993), pp. 31 ff. A companion to Susan Kerr's article below. The pair of articles debate the relative merits of fiber versus asynchronous transfer mode.

Kantor, Andrew. "Internet: The Undiscovered Country." *PC Magazine* 13, no. 5 (March 15, 1994), pp. 116–118. Provides an introduction to Internet features and services including how to sign on and navigate the Internet.

Keen, Peter, and Michael Cummins. *Networks in Action: Business Choices and Telecommunications Decisions.* Belmont, CA: Wadsworth, to be published in 1994. An analysis of the strategic importance of telecommunications for organizations.

Kerr, Susan. "ATM: Ultimate Network or Ultimate Hype?" *Datamation* 39, no. 7 (April 1, 1993), pp. 30 ff. A companion to Michael Hurwicz's article above. The pair of articles debate the relative merits of fiber versus asynchronous transfer mode.

Korzeniowski, Paul. "A Push, However Slow, Is on to Distributed." *Software Magazine* 9, no. 11 (September 1989), pp. 83–87. Discusses the choice of a centralized versus distributed computer system.

Korzeniowski, Paul. "Replication Gains in Distributed DBMS." *Software Magazine* 13, no. 6 (April 1993). Analyzes the increasing use of replicated database information systems to maintain synchronized databases.

Lawton, George. "Worldwide Communications from Motorola." *PC Today* 5, no. 12 (December 1991), pp. 18–19. Describes Motorola's Iridium satellite network.

Lawton, George. "Wireless Computing: Untethering the Network." *PC Today* 7, no. 1 (January 1993), pp. 40–43. Describes wireless LAN technology, its business applications, and major products.

Levin, Jayne. "Businesses Are Making the Internet Connection." *InfoWorld* 15, no. 21 (May 24, 1993), p. 71. Describes several ways in which specific firms are using the Internet to lower cost, increase customer service, and shorten product development time.

McConnell, John. "Internetworking Comes of Age." *Connect* 3, no. 3 (Spring 1990) pp. 27–32. A discussion of the growth and importance of enterprise networking.

Mehta, Suketa. "The Big Switch: Data PBXs Are Viable Alternatives to LANs." *LAN Magazine*, June 1988, pp. 96–111. A description of how PBXs can be used to switch microcomputers and other computing resources.

Nath, Ravinder. "The Impact of Local Area Networks on Users and Their Work: A Field Study." *Journal of Microcomputer Systems Management* 2, no. 2 (Spring 1990), pp. 15–23. Describes the outcome of a research study on the impact of LANs on users.

Salemi, Joe. *Client/Server Databases.* Emeryville, CA: Ziff-Davis Press, 1993. A detailed, practitioner-oriented description of client/server information systems.

Scott, Karyl. "LAN Interconnection Demands on the Rise." *InfoWorld* 14, no. 5 (February 3, 1993), pp. 43 and 46. Presents the advantages and disadvantages of frame relay, asynchronous transmission mode, and switched multimegabit data service.

Strauss, Paul. "TO: mis@corporate.com RE: Internet E-Mail." *Datamation* 40, no. 3 (February 1, 1994), pp. 39, 40, 42. Contains a box of information about Internet service providers, software, and gateway.

Valovic, Thomas. "Metropolitan Area Networks: A Status Report." *Telecommunications* 23, no. 7 (July 1989), pp. 25–32. A description of the developing standards for a metropolitan area range network for voice, video, and data.

Valovic, Thomas. "Will the US Finally See Competition in the Local Exchange? (Part 2)." *Telecommunications* 24, no. 3 (March 1990), pp. 55–58. Presents the potential of personal communications networks in the United States.

Weibel, Robert. "SQL LAN Servers: A Balancing Act." *Connect* 3, no. 3 (Spring 1990), pp. 38–40. A quick, understandable description of SQL server technology.

Office Automation

Chapter Outline

Manager's View

Managers depend on their "offices" to provide support for much of their work. They often spend a great deal of time there, and the office support they receive usually affects their success substantially. Unfortunately they are not likely to spend as much time planning their office support as they should, often because they are preoccupied with concerns about their primary tasks, such as marketing, production, or finance.

Getting the office to work for you depends on what you know about the support an office can provide and what perceptions you have about the office and office work. What is the *office* anyway? What can you expect in the way of support from your office? What kinds of tasks should it be able to perform? What technology can you use to improve office productivity and managerial support? How can office technology best be organized and used? These are the questions this chapter will help you understand and answer.

THE IMPORTANCE OF OFFICE INFORMATION SYSTEMS

To improve the bottom line, organizations have traditionally concentrated on improving their production. Over the years this has resulted in enormous increases in both farm and factory productivity. Improvements in the productivity of American offices, however, have not been either as dramatic or as persistent. Meanwhile, the number of white-collar employees has grown to account for about 75 percent of business payroll expenses (1985).[1] In fact, it has been estimated that every 1 percent of improvement in white-collar productivity will yield more than $10 billion in cost savings for U.S. organizations every year (1987).[2] It is not surprising to find, then, that a major target of corporate downsizers has been white-collar workers, including middle managers.

In the 1960s, financial record keeping was initially automated by implementing electronic data processing systems. Increases in office productivity occurred when sales, inventory, payroll, vendor payments, and other financial transactions were processed first with the aid of electromechanical devices and later by means of electronic devices. Data processing departments were formed in large organizations, and small organizations used data processing service bureaus to handle their high-volume financial records. Later, the minicomputer, and still later, the microcomputer spread the benefits of automation to smaller organizations.

Whereas the number crunching side of the office has been largely automated, the document crunching side has been more resistant to change. As a result, office productivity has lagged behind the productivity of other organizational functions. Because of increasing efficiencies in the factory and on the farm, the costs of office work began to assume a larger proportion of the total costs of doing business. Thus, during the 1970s, many organizations looked to the office for improving their bottom lines. It became apparent that office costs would have to be reduced and office productivity increased to maintain competitiveness. Attention began to be focused on activities other than data processing in the office, and questions about the nature of the office, how the resources employed in the office were organized, and how office work was accomplished were asked with vigor. As this scrutiny has increased, two aspects of the office have received growing attention:

- Reorganizing office tasks and office personnel into systems.
- Computerizing and integrating office tasks through technology, or **office automation.**

THE NATURE OF THE OFFICE

The way that managers view the office and office work is an important determinant of how the office functions and how productive it can become. Three ways in which offices may be viewed by managers are as a place, as a series of functions, and as a system.

The Office as a Place

Many managers view the office simply as a *place.* That is, you may regard a specific location in a building as your office. You associate your job with the place where you have your desk, chair, telephone, and filing cabinet. Managers who hold this view may perceive their status in terms of the lavishness of their office furnishings and measure

---

[1]Casady, Mona J., and Dorothy C. Sandburg. *Word/Information Processing: A System Approach,* Cincinnati: South-Western Publishing Company, 1985.

[2]Forester, Thomas. *High-Tech Society.* Cambridge, Mass.: MIT Press, 1987.

their power in terms of office size. When managers limit their view of the office to a place, they may not be as concerned with the flow of work within the office or how people, equipment, and space are organized to perform work as they are with how many people they supervise and how many desks, chairs, and square feet those employees occupy.

The Office as a Series of Discrete Functions

The office has traditionally performed three major functions:

- Data processing
- Administrative support
- Document processing

The data processing function usually includes the operational tasks associated with creating, processing, and maintaining financial records. This function of the office is described in Chapter 10. The **administrative support function** encompasses a wide variety of activities that provide support for the manager. These support activities typically involve handling the mail, screening callers, scheduling, and many other activities that can be delegated to others to permit the manager to concentrate on decision making (see Box 8–1).

Document processing, or text processing, includes creating, storing, revising, distributing, and duplicating documents. Document processing differs from data processing in that it is primarily concerned with text, or words. Documents include letters, reports, memoranda, proposals, newsletters, and the like.

There are definable steps in document processing and, as in data processing, these steps usually follow a definite cycle. The steps in the data processing cycle consist of input, processing, storage, and output. The steps in the **document processing cycle** are similar but somewhat more elaborate (see Box 8–2).

With the advent of modern telecommunications and laptop computers, it became increasingly obvious that the "office" is wherever you perform your work. Your office may be your home, an airport terminal, a seat on a train, an automobile, or wherever it is that you conduct the activities for which you are responsible. Sales representatives who preview contact files in their hotel rooms on the evening prior to their sales visits are doing office work. Executives who dictate letters and review reports on an airplane

Box 8–1 Administrative Support Functions

Office personnel perform a variety of tasks to support managers. Some typical support functions include these:

1. Calendaring, or maintaining appointments and schedules for administrative personnel.
2. Processing the mail. This may involve merely opening the mail and placing it on the manager's desk for action or reading the mail, gathering pertinent files for the manager, or taking action in lieu of the manager.
3. Handling travel and conference arrangements for administrative personnel and visitors.
4. Filing and finding information in manual and electronic files for administrators.
5. Receiving, making, routing, and screening telephone calls for administrators.
6. Receiving and screening callers, or serving as receptionists for managers.
7. Managing meetings, including preparing minutes and providing logistical support for meetings such as scheduling and preparing agendas.
8. Ordering, maintaining, and controlling office supplies.

Box 8–2 The Document Processing Cycle

The document processing cycle has six steps:

1. Input, or how the document is created. Documents may be created through various means, including handwriting, dictating, keyboarding, or scanning.
2. Processing, or what is done to the input to complete the document. This may include transcribing dictation, editing an existing document, or merging images with text.
3. Storage, or the retention of the document in some form for later use. Storage may include filing the hard copy of a document in a file cabinet, reducing the hard copy to microfilm, or retaining the document electronically on disk.
4. Output, or the production of the document in usable form. This form may involve printing a letter on letterhead paper, displaying a table on a computer screen, or copying a document to magnetic tape.
5. Reproduction, or making more than one copy of the document. This may include using a copy machine, printing more than one copy on a computer printer, or making multiple copies of microforms containing the document.
6. Distribution, or the routing of documents to their destinations. Distribution may include mailing hard copies of documents through the postal system, transmitting magnetic copies of documents over a telecommunications network, or sending copies of documents through the interoffice mail system.

en route to a conference are doing office work. Managers who use home computers to simulate "what if" scenarios with their budgets are doing office work. These people are viewing the office as a series of discrete functions, not a place. Their viewpoint usually makes them more concerned about the tools and information required to perform their work and less concerned with where the office is located or how many people the office holds. In fact, with the advent of inexpensive computers and telecommunications, **telecommuting** has become a reality (see Box 8–3). Telecommuting is the process by which office workers and executives work part time or full time out of their homes and communicate with their offices through their computers using a telecommunications network of some sort.

The Office as a System

Developments in office technology and especially in communications technology have increasingly made it useful to view the office as a system, rather than a place or a series of discrete functions. The systems view seeks not only to automate as many office functions as possible through office automation technology, but also to integrate those automated functions using communications technology. The communications technologies may include mobile voice and mobile data transmission, remote computing, local area networking, wide area networking, and the use of PBXs to transfer information.

From a systems view, each step in the document processing cycle should be automated and integrated with the other steps. Any step not automated is likely to become the weak link in the chain of events needed to produce documents. For example, the automation of the inputting, reproduction, and distribution of text becomes as important to the overall productivity of the system as the processing of text. From a systems view, it makes little sense to acquire word processing equipment and software and to train word processing operators without also paying attention to the input, output, storage, reproduction, and distribution of the documents the word processors produce.

Box 8–3 Telecommuting

White-collar employees may choose telecommuting for several reasons:

- A mother and father in a two-income household want to spend more time with their children and want to switch days going to their offices.
- People want to reduce the number of times they must spend long hours commuting to and from work.
- Organizations want to hold on to capable employees who live long distances from work or who move away from the organization's home office.
- Executives and professionals want to work while they are away from the office, such as on trips to customers or conventions.
- Some professionals, such as writers and programmers, do not always need to be at the office to do their work.
- The Clean Air Act of 1990 requires organizations with more than 100 employees to reduce the number of employees who drive to work alone. Telecommuting provides one means for compliance with the act. Organizations can count telecommuting workers as employees who get to work in zero vehicles.

Some telecommuting data:

- There were 7 million telecommuters in 1994, and experts estimate that number will grow to 25 million in 2000.
- Videoconferencing, desktop conferencing, and other technologies will boost the prevalence of telecommuting.
- The Telecommuting Advisory Council (which can be reached at 619-688-3258) serves as a clearinghouse for information about telecommuting.
- The most frequently used software that telecommuters use at home is word processing.

Source for some of the above: Carol Levin, "Don't Pollute, Telecommute," *PC Magazine* 13, no. 4 (February 22, 1994), p. 32.

The Nature of Office Tasks

Whether the office is treated as a place, a series of functions, or a system, it should be clear from the nature of the tasks described that the work of the office is predominantly at the operational level. That is, office work is primarily task oriented rather than resource or goal oriented. Moreover, in most offices the administrative support function and the document processing function often create a job shop environment. These two functions typically involve one-time activities for a specific event and for a specific person. For example, an annual report may be typed for a supervisor. The report may be prepared, reviewed, and revised on a word processor. Portions of the report may even be copied from the stored text of last year's report. However, once that report is completed, the office workers who prepare it will turn their attention to other document processing activities, which may not even involve typing. Only in a few cases do administrative support functions present the office staff with highly repetitive tasks, as in the preparation of mass mailings. It is much easier to automate the repetitive activities found in financial record keeping than to automate the personal support functions for executives.

THE ORGANIZATION OF THE OFFICE

A major concern about office work has been how office tasks and office personnel are organized. Traditional office workers have typically been generalists. Traditional secretaries answered the telephone, took dictation, typed letters and memos, made travel arrangements, made copies of documents, ordered and maintained supplies, kept a calendar, arranged and supervised appointments, screened visitors, and even made coffee for the boss. These secretaries may have had clerical support. That is, there may have been one or more general office clerks who reported to the secretaries. However, the secretary's primary duty was to serve as administrative assistant to the person or persons to whom the secretary reported. Thus, the traditional office has usually been organized to provide one secretary to serve as an aide to one boss, or *principal.*

In some firms, secretaries and clerks work as a group to support a group of principals. For example, it is common to find a secretary supporting several salespeople or professional and technical staff persons. Larger firms may specialize the administrative support and document processing functions to some extent. There is an extensive body of literature and experience pertaining to the centralization and decentralization of these two functions. It is common in large firms, for example, to find a centralized copy center with a large, fast, and full-featured copy machine under the management of specially trained staff. In like manner, some firms maintain centralized travel services, dictation services, mail services, receptionist services, file or records management services, graphics and printing services, and word processing services (see Figure 8–1).

Though centralized services relieve decentralized office personnel from many duties and responsibilities, they do not remove the administrative support function from these personnel entirely. Office workers still need to transmit files, travel information, mail, and other data to and from the centralized services. For example, they may have to complete a request to obtain a file folder from a centralized records management service, a request for travel arrangements from a centralized travel service, or a request for copies of a document from the centralized copy service.

Centralization

The **centralization** of office services provides many advantages. For example, centralization permits

1. Large-scale, fast, and full-featured hardware to be purchased for the central service instead of small, slow, and limited-featured equipment for use in many offices.
2. Specialization of labor, which usually improves worker quality and productivity.

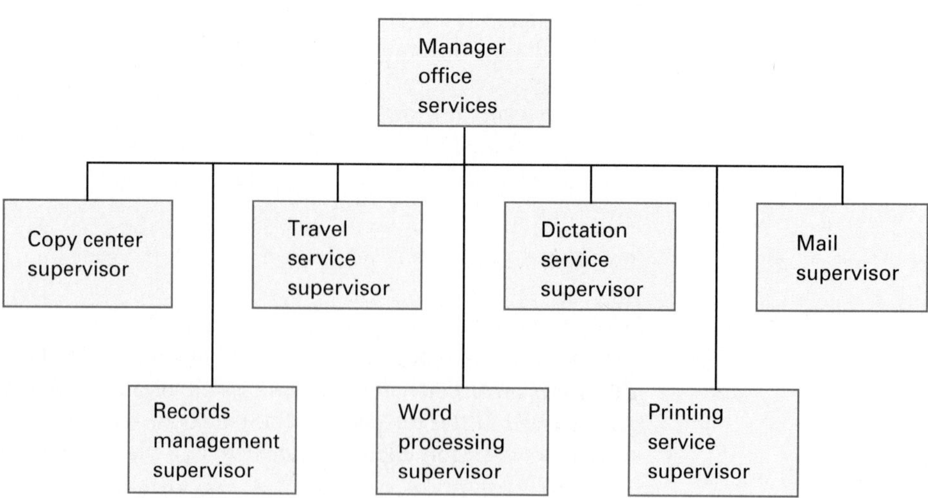

Figure 8–1
A chart showing how centralized office services may be organized

3. Standardization of equipment and supplies with an associated reduction in equipment and supply inventories, reduced training needs, and easier job mobility.
4. The purchase of supplies and equipment in bulk, which leads to financial savings through quantity discounts.

On the other hand, centralization of office services also generates a number of negative side effects. These include

1. Loss of confidentiality when faxed documents, documents stored in files, on disk, or on dictation tapes, or documents in hard copy form must be processed by workers in the centralized services.
2. Loss of continuity of work, which may affect work quality. For example, it is more likely that a secretary who is knowledgeable about an executive's clients will spot errors in amounts, names, and dates in a document than a stenographer in a typing pool.
3. An increase in communications and transportation costs because persons must complete request forms for centralized services and transport documents to and from the centralized service.
4. A possible increase in turnaround time for work because the work has lost its priority. When office services are provided in a decentralized mode, the secretary can complete a task immediately. If a centralized service must be used, the work must be put in queue and wait its turn.
5. A narrowing work focus for employees and possible loss of interest or morale as work becomes routine and repetitive.
6. A possible loss of identification by employees who are placed in centralized work groups.

Decentralization

Decentralization of office services provides advantages and disadvantages as well. These advantages and disadvantages are often the mirror images of those offered by centralization: Decentralization offers the manager immediate attention to the manager's work, greater continuity of work, more confidentiality, less communication and transportation of materials, and greater personal service and support. For example, a secretary who has worked for a manager for some time and who is knowledgeable about the manager's clients might be asked to prepare a response to a client query for the manager's signature. The manager with such a secretary does not have to write down details about travel preferences each time travel must be arranged or details about formatting letters and reports. The secretary knows what the manager wants and does not need these details in writing. The manager also does not need to transport travel requests or correspondence requests to and from a centralized service.

Functional Organization

Some organizations organize office services along functional lines but in a centralized manner. For example, reprographics personnel may be hired and trained by a centralized office services group but assigned to work for specific functional area managers, such as marketing managers or production managers. The centralized services group may also standardize equipment and procedures in each office service arena. By so doing, **functional organization** attempts to blend the best of both centralization and decentralization. Functional organization may provide the employee specialization, specialized training, and standardization of equipment and procedures that ordinarily are associated with centralization, while reducing the problems of continuity, confidentiality, communications, and turnaround time that are associated with decentralization.

Work Groups

Many managers and other office workers work in a group environment for all or part of their day. For example, a group of managers and support personnel may be formed to complete a specific project. Some team project members may be members of more than one team or group. For example, a marketing manager may gather a task force of personnel to review the advertising program of a firm. That same manager may also serve as a member of a computer information systems steering committee.

Because of the widespread use of committees, teams, task forces, and other groups, some offices organize office services around work groups. These work groups may be relatively fixed departmental or committee structures or temporary groups formed to complete projects or ad hoc tasks. The primary emphasis for office services for work groups tends to be document processing and those administrative support functions that require communications. The purpose of such support is to ensure increased sharing of information among work group personnel and greater administrative control over group functions. For example, work groups may wish to

- Share files, reports, other documents, and other data.
- Share calendars.
- Allow group members to work concurrently on files, documents, and reports.
- Coordinate group meetings.
- Share to-do lists and coordinate project management tasks.
- Provide electronic bulletin board, electronic mail, and voice mail communications.
- Provide visual and audio communications via their desktop computers.

Providing group support improves the ability of the group manager to monitor the work of individual group members or subgroups and to communicate to group members. It also allows groups to function even though they work at different times during the day or week or are not physically located together (see Box 8–4). This feature is an additional support for staff who are telecommuting, and it also allows managers to choose group members based on their skills and experience rather than their location.

In many organizations, office services and administrative support are organized in a variety of ways including the traditional, centralized, decentralized, functional, and

Box 8–4 The Virtual Office

Network technologies enable managers from Digital Equipment Corporation (DEC) to supervise employees spread out over many locations worldwide, creating **virtual offices** composed of these employees. This permits DEC to choose staff for projects on the basis of competence and experience rather than convenience. It also allows managers to tap a world pool of talent when needed. For example, about 70 engineers in six offices across the globe are able to work on projects together and to keep in close touch with one another using such technologies as videotex, electronic mail, electronic bulletin boards, audioconferencing, voice mail, distributed slide shows, video workstations, photo phones, and videoconferencing.

Audioconferencing is typically used for meetings of 10 to 15 persons who are reviewing a project or discussing a budget. Electronic bulletin boards are often used for asking all DEC engineers about a particularly difficult technical problem. Personal messages or progress reports are often handled by E-mail or voice mail. Videotex, a two-way interactive communications service for text and graphics, is used to share more static data such as organization charts, project descriptions, and job descriptions.

Source: Wayne Eckerson, "DEC's Net Makes the World One Big Office," *Network World* 7, no. 27 (July 2, 1990), p. 17.

work group organizations. For example, mail and microform services might be centralized in mail and records management departments, desktop publishing services might be decentralized and located in each department, and word processing might be provided by traditional secretaries who support individuals or groups. Even the same type of service may be organized in several ways within an organization. For example, copy services for large, complex jobs may be centralized but convenience copiers for small jobs may be decentralized to each department and work group.

Work groups are also discussed in Chapter 14, "Decision Support Systems."

The Effects of Technology on Office Organization

Because of increasing technological innovation, the traditional office and the role of the traditional secretary are undergoing substantial change. Some foresee a time when the traditional office may disappear entirely in the wake of technological and social changes affecting the activities of both the boss and the secretary. In fact, computer-based technology is increasingly eroding the traditional organization and distribution of office functions because computer systems are changing the way managers and other office personnel work. Managers query databases instead of having secretaries search files. They use spreadsheets instead of having secretaries prepare budgets. They find it more convenient to key in their own memos on their office computer terminals or away-from-home laptops than to dictate those memos to secretaries. They are more comfortable developing reports at a word processor than writing them out for secretaries to key in later. They order their own plane tickets directly using on-line travel services. They schedule their own meetings using the on-line calendaring functions of their computer systems. They often find it more convenient to work at home using a remote terminal or a personal computer with a modem.

In many offices, in short, the traditional work of administrative support staffs is increasingly being performed by executives. Whether this is more or less productive use of their time is a legitimate question. However one answers that question, it is clear that one effect of office automation has been to redistribute office tasks and one effect of communications technology has been to redistribute the physical office.

OFFICE TECHNOLOGY

The amount and variety of technological devices and processes available for use in the office today are bewildering. As the roles of office workers evolve, the tools by which office work is accomplished are changing rapidly and on a wide scale. Nearly every office task is being addressed in some way by computer-based electronic and electromechanical devices. The flow of work in the office is clearly becoming automated to a degree only dreamed of 20 years ago. The major classes of office technology used to automate office work include word processing, reprographics, imaging, electronic conferencing, micrographics, document management, groupware, workflow automation, and a variety of desktop communications including electronic mail, voice mail, and desktop conferencing.

Word Processing Systems

Word processing systems prepare and revise documents that are primarily composed of text, although they may contain data, images, tables, and charts. Word processing in the United States began when IBM developed and marketed its MT/ST, or Magnetic Tape/Selectric Typewriter, in the 1960s. This device employed a magnetic tape on which keystrokes could be recorded so that documents could be stored, edited, and printed out on the Selectric typewriter, which was part of the equipment package.

Because magnetic storage permitted documents to be edited swiftly and easily, the MT/ST forever changed the way memos, reports, and letters were produced.

Word processors today have been reduced to software packages. They are designed to run on general-purpose computers and can use a variety of input and output devices. But word processing software and the computers on which it runs are only one, albeit a major, component of a document processing system. When word processing is viewed as part of a document processing system, systems designers must concern themselves with how data are input to a word processor and how the documents produced by the word processor are stored, reproduced, and distributed.

It is important for organizations to standardize around a limited or compatible set of word processing software and computer hardware to avoid the problem of one system not being able to communicate with another. Remember, the key to office information systems is not only automation of the processes but also communications between processes. Many organizations provide a de facto form of standardization by having their information or end-user computing centers support only a limited number of word processing systems.

Portable Documents. One of the most frustrating tasks in an office or between offices is trying to share documents created by different word processors or spreadsheets. Although most word processors and spreadsheets today provide conversion programs for documents created by other word processing and spreadsheet software, the converted document is almost never free from errors or formatting anomalies. When converted, table formats, paragraphing, font changes, or some other problems occur in the conversion process that usually require the operator to spend tedious time reformatting the document. When you try to view documents from another word processor on your different word processor, you often see strange characters and formatting problems that make the documents difficult to read or use.

To address this problem, several new software packages have been created. These software packages, including Adobe's Acrobat and Farallon's Replica, create what are called **portable documents,** or documents that can be read and printed by another user *exactly* like the original regardless of the software the other person is using. The documents do not lose any of their original styles, fonts, formats, or graphics. For example, Replica is a portable document software package that allows one user to create a document that can be read by a Replica viewer regardless of the computer platform used by another person. If the other person does not have a Replica viewer, the software will either send or store the document and the viewer together. The viewer can be distributed to others free, and its distribution does not violate any license provision.

Creating a portable document is very easy. The software installs itself as another printer within your operating environment. When you print a document, you simply specify Replica as the printer, and then "print" the document. The document is saved as a portable document image in *portable document format,* or PDF, instead of being printed out on your printer. Replica also lets you attach a portable document to an E-mail message for distribution to others on a LAN or to remote LAN users.

Portable document software does not provide much in the way of editing or text manipulation features. The users are largely confined to reading and printing the portable document as it is. However, some products allow the other person to cut text or images from the portable document and paste them into documents produced by other word processors. Some products also allow users to annotate portable documents. Portable documents can also be searched using key word searches.

A more powerful way to exchange documents between different word processors, however, has been available for almost two decades but has not been implemented widely. This technology is **SGML,** or **Standard Generalized Markup Language.** SGML provides standard rules and procedures for describing document formatting features. In other words, it codes documents by structure. For example, it adds a specific tag to indicate the beginning of a paragraph, another tag to indicate a first-level heading, and other tags to describe features such as font styles, type sizes, paragraph indents, and line spacing. Document software that is SGML compliant places appropriate tags to identify each formatting feature of a document as it is being created and can read the SGML tags in documents created by other software.

Additional software now is available that analyzes documents and places appropriate tags for each formatting feature in the appropriate places in the document according to SGML specifications. This software allows users to bring old documents or documents created by systems that are not SGML compliant into conformity. A number of word processing software vendors now offer these products. For example, WordPerfect offers IntelliTAG, a software package that lets users convert its word processing documents into SGML format.

SGML is platform independent; that is, as long as documents are defined with SGML codes the documents can be read, viewed, or otherwise moved from one computer system to another with relative ease. Furthermore, SGML is used on not just text documents, but graphical documents, or those containing images and charts, as well.

Compound Documents. **Compound documents** are documents that contain several data types, such as text, graphics or images, sound or voice annotations, and full-motion video clips. For example, the chapter you are reading would be considered a compound document because it contains text, photographs, and illustrations. Compound word processing documents may be created with graphical word processors or desktop publishing software. However, compound documents may also be created with spreadsheet software, database software, and other common software with compound document capability.

In a compound document, each type of data (text, graphics, voice, video) is linked to the program that created it. Thus, a compound document may be a report that contains text created by a word processor, a Gantt chart showing when key tasks will be completed created by project management software, and a graph showing the costs of each project stage created by a spreadsheet. If text is the base data, you would embed graphics, voice annotations, and video within the document. By clicking on the Gantt chart, you would activate the project management software and be permitted to edit or change the chart. By clicking on the graph, you would activate the spreadsheet and be able to edit the graph. Embedding sound and video in a document usually involves placing voice icons and video icons in it. When you click on the voice icon, you activate the voice program and hear the voice message. When you click on the video icon, you activate the video software and see the video clip.

The reader or editor of a compound document must have all the software needed to be able to take full advantage of the document's contents. The access problem is not a problem if all users are on a LAN that provides access to the needed software.

Desktop Publishing. Very high-end word processing software is called **desktop publishing software (DTP).** When combined with high-resolution printers, such as laser printers, high-resolution computer screens, and optical scanners, DTP forms document processing systems that allow you to originate, input, and mix text, charts, graphs, and drawings on one page of a document using only a microcomputer (see

Figure 8–2). The software frequently provides a screen display of the text very close to what will appear in hardcopy form. This **WYSIWYG,** or **what-you-see-is-what-you-get,** capability reduces the need to print out copies of the text for proofing before high-volume printing can begin.

Desktop publishing software, when combined with scanners, high-resolution computer screens, and laser printers, produces hard copy that challenges the traditional photocomposition systems frequently found in printing houses. Scanners permit you to digitize text, photographs, charts, and drawings and insert them into documents. The high-resolution screens and laser printers allow you to create high-quality output, ready for printing. The software provides you with many of the same features once available only on photocomposition equipment. For example, you may vary type **fonts,** or sets of characters in particular styles and sizes, line height, and character spacing, and produce multicolumned, justified copy. However, desktop publishing usually costs much less than typesetting, especially when changes in the copy must be made.

Once a document has been completed, it may be photographed so an offset printer can use the photographic plates (see Box 8–5). Many organizations use offset printing systems to produce company newsletters, forms, and reports in-house. Alternatively, the document may be produced in quantity directly on a high-speed laser printer connected to the computer system running the desktop publishing software.

Graphical Word Processors. Competition among word processing software vendors has resulted in software packages that acquire more features year after year. Most word processing software packages today contain features that were available in the past only by purchasing separate, additional software. For example, high-end word processors now offer such features as font scaling, footnoting, outlining, drawing, graphics, on-line thesaurus availability, on-line grammar and spell checking, mail-merge capability, modem and FAX communications support, calendaring, electronic mail, and even programs for converting documents produced by other word processors. High-end word processing vendors have added these desktop publishing functions to their products to maintain a competitive position in the market, and they are called **graphical word processors.** Thus, high-end word processing systems are becoming almost indistinguishable from desktop publishing systems; the latter will probably become the standard means of creating and processing text in offices in the near future.

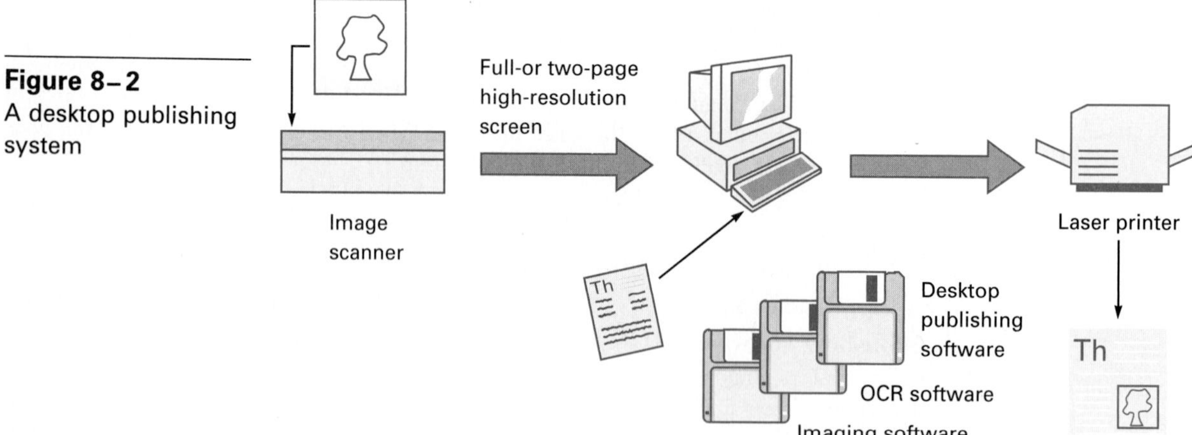

Figure 8–2
A desktop publishing system

Reprographics Systems

A common task of office personnel is to make more than one copy of a memo, letter, report, article, or other document. **Reprographics** is the process of reproducing multiple copies of any document, including output from word processing, imaging, and data processing systems. Reprographics encompasses a variety of devices and processes from simple carbon paper to expensive laser equipment (see Box 8–5). When reprographics is viewed as an office system, however, it must include the associated processes of collating, aligning, folding, and binding documents.

Multiple copies of documents may be produced using many methods. If only a few copies are needed, you may choose to reproduce those extra copies using a character printer attached to your word processor. Sometimes, even if you need a large number of copies, you may choose to use a computer printer. For example, if you are creating a mass mailing using the mail-merge function of your word processor, you will probably add the variable information to each letter and create the letter itself on the printer

Box 8–5 Major Reprographics Processes

There are three basic reprographic processes: duplication, copying, and printing.

Duplication Processes

Spirit duplication is an old process. Documents stored on a word processor are printed out on a carbon-backed spirit or "Ditto" master and used to produce a small number of copies (0–500) quickly and inexpensively.

Stencil duplication uses wax-covered masters. Stencil duplication provides higher resolution copy and longer runs (0–1000).

Offset duplication uses either a metal plate or paper plate as the medium for the master. Metal plates ensure good-quality output even for very long runs and are often used to produce documents that require high volume or that include photographs. Paper plates, or offset paper masters, can be produced by typing, drawing, or writing directly on the plate.

Offset equipment is much more expensive than either spirit or stencil duplication equipment and requires a skilled operator. However, offset duplication provides near-typeset printing quality and is used increasingly by newspapers, magazine publishers, and other printers.

Copying Processes

Copy machines let you make exact duplicates of original material without having to rekey the material onto a special master. They are easy to operate and can be purchased in a variety of sizes, types, and prices. They are also relatively inexpensive to maintain, especially if the copiers use fiber optic technology, which eliminates many of the complex mirrors and lenses needed by older copiers. Copy machines with the ability to reduce or enlarge material let you reduce large computer printouts to a size that may be filed or handled easily.

There are basically two types of copiers: wet copiers and dry copiers. Wet copiers require the use of special chemically treated paper. Dry copiers may use thermal (or heat) processes or electrostatic processes to produce copies. Thermal copiers require special paper that is sensitive to heat. Electrostatic copiers allow you to copy material onto any paper, and are often called *plain paper copiers*. Thus, it is possible to copy material onto letterhead paper or to use any weight and quality of paper you wish. Wet copiers usually prove to be more expensive to run because you must use specially treated paper.

Printing Processes

Photocomposition systems—or more simply, typesetting systems—have been utilized in printing firms and departments for years. Typesetting systems are often used to produce the text you see in books, brochures, business forms, newspapers, and a variety of other professional-looking documents. Typesetting systems offer you a choice of numerous type styles, or fonts, type sizes, line heights, proportional spacing of letters and words, and multicolumn arrangement of text. The systems usually accept input from computers and word processors and allow for the direct creation of text.

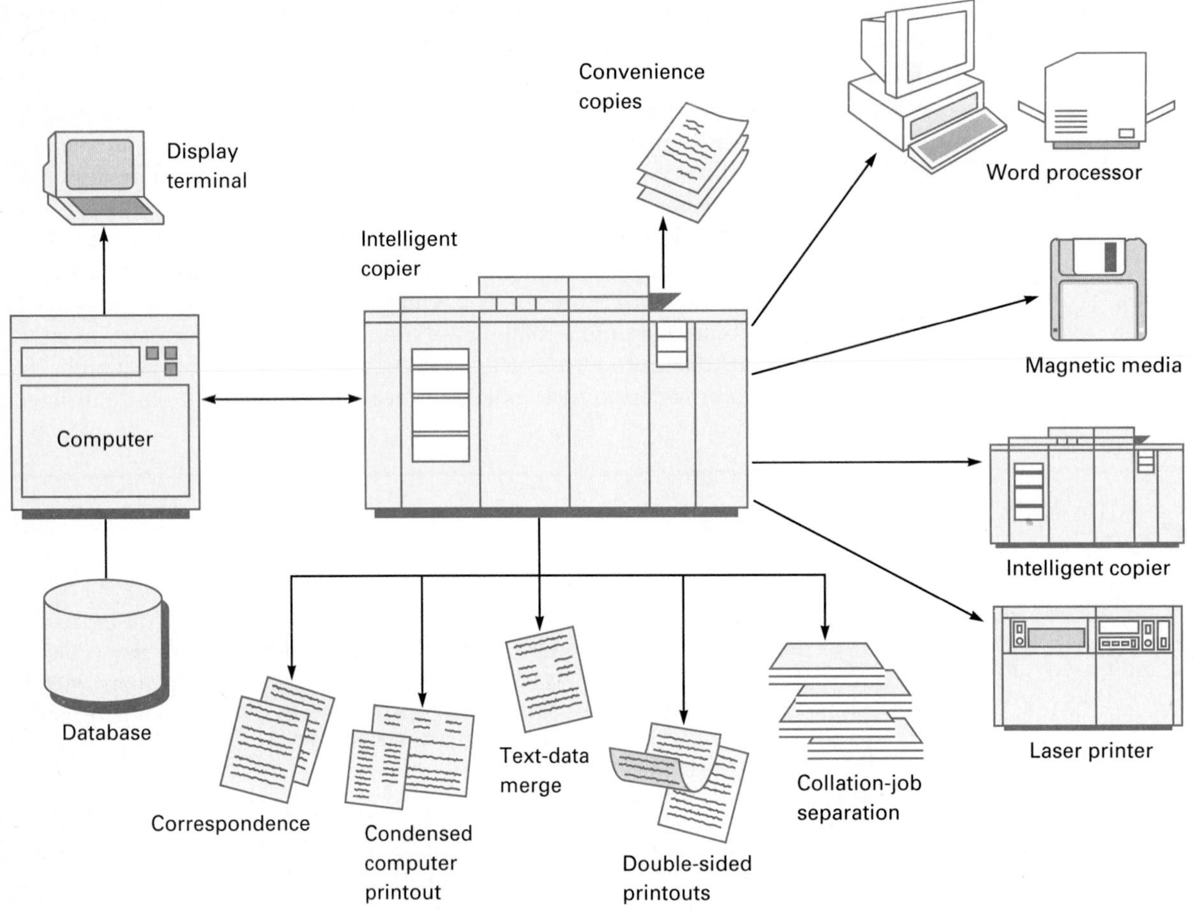

Figure 8–3
An intelligent copier system

attached to the word processor. Although this approach is slower than other reprographic processes, you may choose it so that each letter appears to be personally typed.

At other times, speed is important and the volume of copies to be reproduced is high. In these cases you may choose to use a *copy process*, a *duplication process*, or a *printing process* (see Box 8–5). Which technology you employ depends on many factors: speed; quality of output; volume to be copied; number of pages in the material; cost; and the original nature of the documents you wish to reproduce. The latter refers to the size of the material, whether it is stored on magnetic media, whether it is in color, and whether it includes photographic or halftone images.

The most sophisticated type of copy equipment today is the **intelligent copier,** or *electronic printing system* (see Figure 8–3). These copiers are computer-driven devices capable of communicating with other computers or intelligent copiers. They can store and transmit documents electronically in addition to producing hard copy. A common application for intelligent copiers is to merge a copy of a business form stored in its memory with data obtained from another computer system and then to distribute the completed forms to other computer systems electronically.

Imaging Systems

Imaging systems are of two major types: image digitizers and optical recognition systems. Digitizing devices convert photographs, charts, and other illustrative materials to a series of dots and transfer those dots in magnetic form to disk or main memory. Digitizers do not "understand" what they scan, in contrast to optical recognition systems. They merely digitize images and store the result as digits. Once in magnetic form, graphics software allows the user to enlarge, condense, clip, rotate, and otherwise manipulate the images so captured. Scanners are frequently used today with high-end word processing and desktop publishing systems to input images so they can be merged with text.

Facsimile, or **fax** machines are one type of digitizing equipment that has been available for many years. The facsimile device is an **optical scanner** that reduces text or graphic images recorded on paper to electrical impulses that can be transmitted to compatible facsimile devices over your telephone or other network. Basically, fax systems are an electronic document delivery system that combines scanner technology with modem technology (see Box 8–6).

Facsimile devices may be analog or digital. Analog devices must scan and transmit the entire document, including its unused or white-space portions. Analog devices transmit a copy of a page in about two to six minutes. Digital devices are able to compress the material to be transmitted and are thus much faster. High-speed fax machines are capable of transmitting a page in about 20 seconds (see Figure 8–4). The newest generation of fax machines uses laser technology for speed and high-resolution reproduction. To increase office productivity, fax machines may be equipped with automatic dialers and automatic sheet feeders so that they are able to send and receive transmissions unattended.

Fax machines can easily save organizations money. Typically, organizations use fax equipment to replace same-day or overnight mail services. The telephone line costs of sending a few pages by fax is generally substantially less than sending those same pages by same-day mail. If the fax equipment ships the pages after 11 P.M. in unattended mode, the savings can be greater.

Facsimile devices can be merged with teleconferencing systems to permit sharing of hard-copy materials. Photographs of chalkboards, copies of transparencies, and copies of other documents can be sent quickly to all participating locations, even in color. Combining fax technology with local area networks not only allows any network user to fax documents to others, but also allows fax documents received to be routed directly

Box 8–6 Facts about Facsimile Use

1. Fax volume increased by 41 percent from 1992 to 1993. For a Fortune 500 company, that is an average of 260 pages faxed each day.
2. The average fax machine sends 49 documents per day with an average length of 5.3 pages.
3. The average fax machine receives 62 documents per day with an average length of 7 pages.
4. An average company spends one-third of its phone bill on faxes.
5. About 86 percent of fax users have never been formally trained in the machine's use.
6. About 75 percent of fax users in large and medium-sized organizations do not know how much the fax messages they send cost their organizations.
7. About 65 percent of fax messages sent by users in large and medium-sized organizations are long-distance faxes.
8. Only 3 percent of fax users at large and medium-sized organizations send faxes during the evening hours, which usually offer the lowest rates.

Sources: Tom Smith, "Net Execs Try to Tame Fax Monster, *Network World* 7, no. 18 (April 30, 1990), pp. 1 and 8, and Diana Engeszer, "Put the Brakes on Runaway Fax Costs," *St. Louis Computing* 11, no. 2, p. 15.

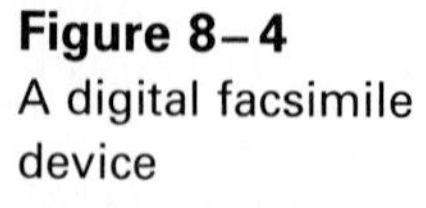

Figure 8–4
A digital facsimile device

Courtesy of CANNON USA, Inc.

to the fax mailbox of the intended recipient, thus avoiding the delay of delivery within a firm.

Fax technology today is commonly added to modem technology to create **fax/modem boards** that are placed in an expansion slot of a microcomputer's mother board or external fax/modem devices that connect to a microcomputer's serial port. These boards or devices, with their associated software, allow your microcomputer to send documents stored on disk to other facsimile devices; to receive and store fax images on disk; and to edit, display, and print the images.

Fax technology is also being combined with other office technologies into multifunction machines. For example, fax technology is being combined with laser-driven electrostatic copying technology to produce machines that provide facsimile transmission, document copying, and document printing—thus merging facsimile, printing, and copying functions in one device.

For those without fax/modems or stand-alone fax machines, faxes can be created and sent by using the services of information utilities. For example, CompuServe, America Online, and GEnie all allow you to send messages and transfer existing files to fax machines using the modem on your computer system. The information utility converts the message or file to a fax format and delivers it to the fax machine. Many common carriers also provide fax services to those with modems but without fax machines. For example, MCI Mail allows users to create and send messages or existing files to fax machines using your computer's modem. These fax services by information utilities and common carriers are often called *on-line faxing.*

It is important to remember, however, that fax systems deliver documents as images—a series of black dots on a white page—rather than as numbers and letters. Images of pages of text cannot be manipulated by word processors unless the images are converted back into number and letter form. That conversion is the job of optical character recognition systems. Optical recognition systems include **optical character recognition (OCR)** technology and **optical mark recognition** technology. OCR technology has been used in offices since the 1950s. The technology may take the form of

OCR software running on a microcomputer that also has a fax device and scanner attached. The technology also may take the form of a dedicated OCR machine that contains a scanner and OCR software. Dedicated OCR machines usually have sheet feeders so that large amounts of hard copy can be scanned and converted quickly.

For companies that have a great deal of text in hard copy form that needs to be revised, OCR technology can provide substantial help by avoiding costly rekeying of hard-copy text. OCR software along with an optical scanner can scan hard-copy text, convert it to digital information, and store it on disk as numbers and letters. Once on disk, word and data processors can edit and otherwise process the information. If the information is an image of text stored in a computer file, like a fax transmission received through an internal fax/modem board, OCR software running on that same microcomputer can convert the image file to a text file so that it can be read and manipulated with word processing software.

OCR equipment can be used to assist firms in converting from manual word processing systems to electronic systems and from one electronic word processing system to another. For organizations that receive a great deal of their text in typewritten or printed form, optical scanners and OCR software can prove very cost beneficial.

The accuracy, speed, and versatility with which OCR software can read text have continually increased during the last decade. OCR software is now able to read images of text in both upper- and lowercase, in different font styles, with paragraph indentation and in columnar form, with varying pitch and line spacing, and even in handwriting.

Optical scanners have become smaller. There are desktop models (see Figure 8–5) and also many handheld models that scan four inches or so of a document at one time. The latter scan a part of a hard-copy document and store the images on disk where drawings, photos, and other images can be cropped, rotated, or otherwise manipulated and words can be converted into text readable by word processors. Some handheld scanners come with software that "stitches" two four-inch images of a page back together.

If the optical scanners are attached to a computer that is also attached to a network, the scanned data can be transmitted to photocomposition systems, word processing systems, and other computer-based office equipment similarly attached to the network (see Box 8–7).

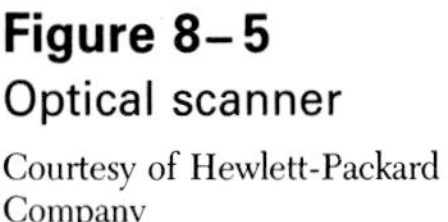

Figure 8–5
Optical scanner

Courtesy of Hewlett-Packard Company

Box 8–7 What Are Scanners Used For?

Input of Typed, Printed, or Handwritten Text or Numbers

Rather than rekeying typed or printed data or text, they can be scanned, converted by optical recognition character software, and then read into a word processor or desktop publishing package. Thus, a brochure that a company had printed by an outside printing firm can be scanned, converted, edited, and then reprinted using desktop publishing software and a high-resolution printer. Likewise the handwritten text and data entered into a paper form by a repair person can also be scanned, converted, and automatically entered into a database application.

Input of Graphic Images and Photographs

Without redrawing line art, company logos, for example, can be read into the PC and edited using graphics software. Photographs also can be scanned and edited. The resulting images may be inserted into desktop publishing documents, entered into image database applications such as a personnel file that contains the photographs of workers, or entered into presentation graphics slides for a sales presentation.

Input of Multimedia

Documents that contain printed text, photos, and graphics can be automatically scanned into a PC and edited with page-composition or graphics software. The images of text may be converted by optical character recognition software, and the images of graphics or photos may be edited by graphics software. The resulting material then may be inserted into newsletters, brochures, presentation graphics shows, and multimedia presentations.

Transmission of Information

With a PC modem card a paper document can be scanned and then electronically transmitted to another PC modem or to a facsimile machine. The receiver of the image may then convert the image into text by optical character recognition software, or crop, rotate, or otherwise edit the image using graphics software.

Storage and Retrieval of Text, Data, Graphics, and Photos

Document management and workflow software uses scanners to input data. Document management systems may then index, print, and store the documents. Workflow systems may then route, store, display, enter into a database, or otherwise process the document.

There are now many other types of imaging systems. For example, digital cameras can break down snapshots into dots or pixels, measure the intensity of the pixels, and record the intensity as a number. Thus, the pictures are stored as files on disk. This type of system includes a digital camera and requires software to manipulate the snapshots. The digital photos can be of products to be inserted in a sales brochure, photos of employees to be inserted in employee records, or photographs of corporate headquarters to be inserted into a presentation graphics presentation.

Desktop video systems allow you to capture video images, convert them to digital data, and store the images on a hard disk or an optical disk. Graphics software is then used to manipulate or display the images. The video images may be captured from VCR tapes or from live television. The software that supports these systems may allow you to capture and manipulate individual frames or full-motion video. Thus, you might capture selected frames from a training videotape to insert in an accompanying training manual. Or, you may insert whole sequences of full-motion video into a multimedia training program.

Document Management Systems

Document management systems allow you to organize text documents, image documents, and documents containing full-motion video and sounds into a document database to assure easy access and use of the many documents that an organization receives and creates. Full-featured document management systems typically provide the means to perform all the following services: scanning, indexing, storing, converting, distributing, searching, viewing, and printing. Indexing may include providing key words to documents, images, sounds, and video. The conversion processes usually include optical character recognition of scanned documents so that they are usable by a word processor. The conversion process may also include converting one form of graphics image format to another. For example, the systems may convert the image of a document received in fax format to the graphics format that can be imported by your desktop publisher. Because graphics files take up large amounts of disk space, document management systems also may provide compression utilities to reduce your storage space requirements.

Document management software lets users search for and retrieve ordinary and compound documents that may be scattered across many files, computer systems, or networks. When documents are created, users complete document profiles that include the names of the authors, the subject matter of the documents, and other data about the documents. The software maintains an index of key information about each document. The system searches documents using the index or by conducting brute searches for text strings. For example, a manager may retrieve numerous documents about one customer located in many files, including account information, reports, and correspondence.

Document management software, such as PageKeeper from Caere Corporation, searches each document and creates indexes of words that are important automatically, screening out words that are considered "noise" as far as indexing is concerned. You can edit the list of noise words that you want PageKeeper to ignore in documents to improve the indexing capabilities of the system. The software search programs even produce a count of the important or key words in each document, displaying the count in a bar chart. You also can instruct the software to use one document as a model to find other documents with similar key words and frequencies of use.

Document management software can accept documents from a variety of sources, such as a scanner or a fax, and documents stored in a variety of text and graphics formats. It also may be able to accept documents directly from an E-mail system and let you annotate text and images. A key to user access for a document management system is the use of portable documents or SGML, described earlier in this chapter. SGML, especially, allows any user to share, view, and edit documents regardless of the hardware platform or software used to create the document.

Electronic Mail Systems

Electronic mail systems may include any system of transmitting messages electronically rather than in hard-copy form. Electronic mail may include transmissions of text by facsimile, teletype, intelligent copier, or any other device that transmits text electronically on a network.

Among the fastest growing segments of electronic mail are computer-based systems that provide for the transmission of short messages between stations on a computer network, whether the computers are micros, minis, or mainframes and whether the network is local, wide area, or PBX. *Computer-based electronic mail systems* generally allow a user to transmit messages to any or all of the other users on the network without the necessity of producing hard copy. You may transmit, view, save, share, edit, or erase memos, letters, and even short reports without ever engaging a printer. These systems let you transmit messages immediately, rather than using the postal service or your organization's interoffice mail service.

When electronic mail systems share existing data transmission networks or local area networks that are operating at less than full capacity, electronic mail provides an extremely inexpensive form of mail service. Adding an electronic mail service to a local area network is likely to cost only the purchase price of the software because the existing network is already in place. Adding electronic mail to a wide area network is likely to increase transmission costs only marginally if the network is composed primarily of leased lines.

A *private electronic mail system* requires a computer-based network, some disk space, and software to manage and control the mail system. Each user also must have a terminal, which may be a dumb terminal connected to a minicomputer or mainframe system, a personal computer connected to a local area network, or a notebook computer or personal digital assistant connected to the network remotely. Each user is allocated so much disk space for a mailbox and is given an identifying number or name so that the user and other people may address the user's mailbox.

If you employ a notebook computer or personal digital assistant with a modem, you can access your mailbox remotely. This means that a salesperson in the field would be able to send and receive mail at any time of the day and at almost any location. To assist in E-mail access from remote sites, you may use *remote E-mail software.* This software creates a mailbox on your remote computing device and enables you to dial the home office E-mail system. Remote E-mail software may offer a number of features. For example, the software may provide security by encrypting IDs, passwords, and actual messages. It also may provide *E-mail filtering* of mail messages. The filtering feature automatically selects E-mail messages according to criteria you have chosen in advance, such as the name of the sender, size of file, message type, or if the message is marked urgent. The filters can also be set to select messages with key words you have chosen. Filtering can be useful to field employees, or "road warriors," because it saves them telephone line charges. Only mail you have indicated is important will be downloaded from the home office to your remote computing device.

Still another feature that some remote E-mail software provides is to synchronize automatically the contents of your home office mailbox with your remote computer's mailbox.

A number of telecommunications and information utility firms provide *public electronic mail systems.* For example, MCI offers MCI mail, AT&T offers AT&T Mail, and CompuServe offers an electronic mail system to subscribers. In addition, Internet provides public E-mail facilities (see specifically Box 7–4, in Chapter 7). Commercial electronic mail systems allow individuals who do not have or cannot afford their own networks to communicate with others. For example, a sales manager may provide MCI mail accounts to all of her sales staff, along with notebook computers with modems. The sales group can then exchange messages and files over the MCI E-mail network. The commercial systems also allow users connected to private E-mail networks to communicate with others outside their private networks, including Internet subscribers.

Electronic mail systems allow you to address messages to a single user, to a group of users, or to all users. A sales manager may, for example, broadcast a price change to all salespeople or a note to only one. Thus, users may construct mailing lists. Many electronic mail systems also allow users to construct bulletin boards on topics of interest to users. For example, an organization might develop an E-mail bulletin board when a desktop publishing software package is introduced. New users of the software could then share ideas, helpful hints, and solutions to problems.

Many electronic mail systems also allow users to attach files to mail messages so that users can transfer document and data files accompanied by a written note. If a scanner is available, text or graphics may be similarly transmitted through the electronic mail system. Also, some of the latest systems allow you to attach voice messages to electronic mail messages. This feature can allow managers to soften or personalize memos to staff.

Filtering software is not only for remote E-mail; it also can be employed at the home office. E-mail packages with filtering features allow you to set up rules for sending and receiving messages. Thus, using *rule-based E-mail software,* messages from some locations, from some people, or about certain topics can be classified as urgent and displayed immediately on your computer screen, routed to others for disposition, or placed in a read-later folder.

One of the major advantages of electronic mail is that it is one way to avoid **telephone tag.** Telephone tag occurs when one person calls another to give a short message and the other person is out or the line is busy. The first person then leaves a message to return the call. When the other person becomes available, the return call is made, but the original caller then may be out or the line could be busy. The two players may end up playing telephone tag for some time before a simple message can be conveyed. Telephone tag is very frustrating, eats up a great deal of time, and is costly to the organization. Many messages, such as price changes, do not really require two-way communications. Simply depositing a note about the price change in the salesperson's mailbox eliminates telephone tag.

Voice Processing Systems

Voice processing systems include voice mail systems, voice messaging systems, and interactive response systems.

Voice mail systems, or **VMS,** usually employ software that runs on PBX equipment rather than the organization's mainframe computer. However, some voice mail systems are PC based (see Figure 8–6). These systems are very similar to electronic

Figure 8–6
PC-based voice mail components

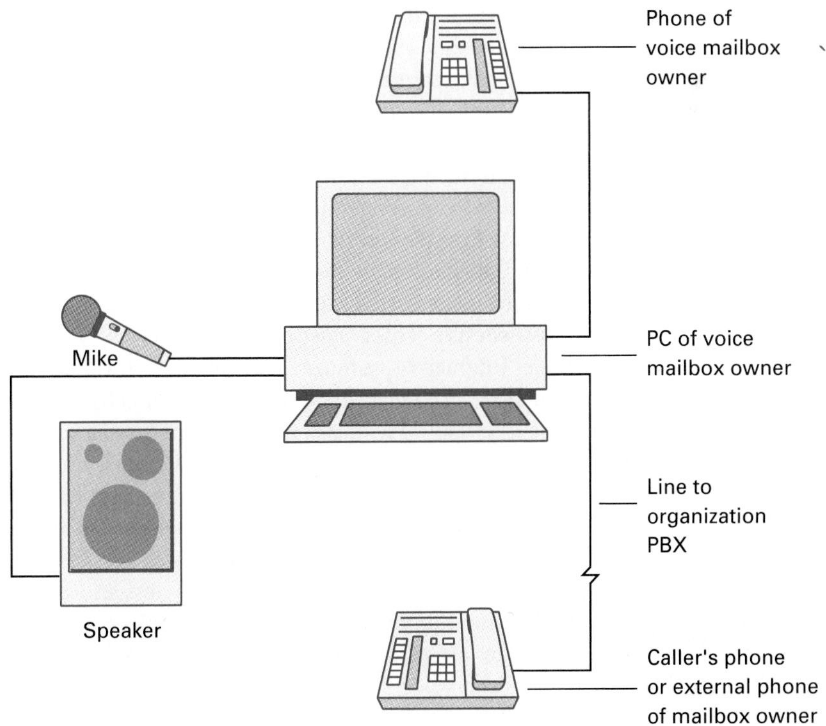

mail systems except that the message stored is a digitized version of the voice message rather than a text message. Still others run on a local area network. Like electronic mail systems, voice mail systems are another means of eliminating the annoying problem of telephone tag.

Voice mail systems require a computer and disk storage space for the software and mailboxes just like electronic mail systems do. The sending and receiving terminal for voice mail, however, is a telephone. The digitized voice message can be played back; sent to one address, a group of addresses, or all addresses; and saved or erased, just like text in the electronic mail system. Users may access their own mailboxes by dialing from any telephone and using the telephone keypad to listen to a list of the messages in the mailbox, "scroll" through the mailbox messages, go directly to a priority message, listen to one or more messages, save a message, or send a message to another person or group of persons. These capabilities permit field representatives or executives who are at a conference to keep up with their messages, to deliver messages, and in general, to maintain contact with the home office (see Figure 8–7). They may not like some of the messages they receive from their bosses, but at least they do receive them in a timely manner.

Voice mail systems can also be interconnected with the mainframe computer, and telephone keypads then can be used to enter data directly into the computer system, permitting salespeople to enter orders directly over the telephone or letting important customers order products directly. Some universities allow students to enroll using their home phones with a voice mail system. The students call the system's special enrollment number, enter their social security numbers, and then enter the section numbers for the classes they wish to attend. The voice system prompts them through the enrollment task and confirms whether the sections are open. If a section is not open, alternate sections are given. Enrolling by voice mail sure beats waiting in long enrollment lines at the beginning of each semester and, especially for commuter institutions, may provide a competitive advantage.

Most people have called an organization and heard, "Good morning. Thank you for calling Detweiler Products, Inc. If you are calling from a touch phone, please press one now . . . " **Voice messaging systems** allow an organization to set up voice menus that route a customer automatically to the correct department, person, or mailbox or provide the correct message without any human operator intervening. They save organizations money by reducing the number of operators needed for routine inbound calls. They also provide service to customers after hours when the customer only needs to leave a message with a person or receive standard information about an organization such as product information or hours. As you can see, voice messaging systems include the features of voice mail systems.

Interactive voice response systems are an enhancement of voice messaging systems. Interactive systems allow callers to respond to voice menu choices and obtain information, products, or services automatically. Such systems are used to automate routine sales calls, such as requests for free demonstration diskettes, free literature, or information about seminars, products, or other company services. They are also used to provide customer service by allowing customers to obtain information about their accounts and order status. Some organizations use them for routine order processing, allowing the customer to order products or services directly, without any intervention by order clerks or salespersons. Other organizations' interactive systems are structured to fax information about products and services directly to customers if they make the appropriate menu selections. The latter systems are usually referred to as *fax-on-demand systems.*

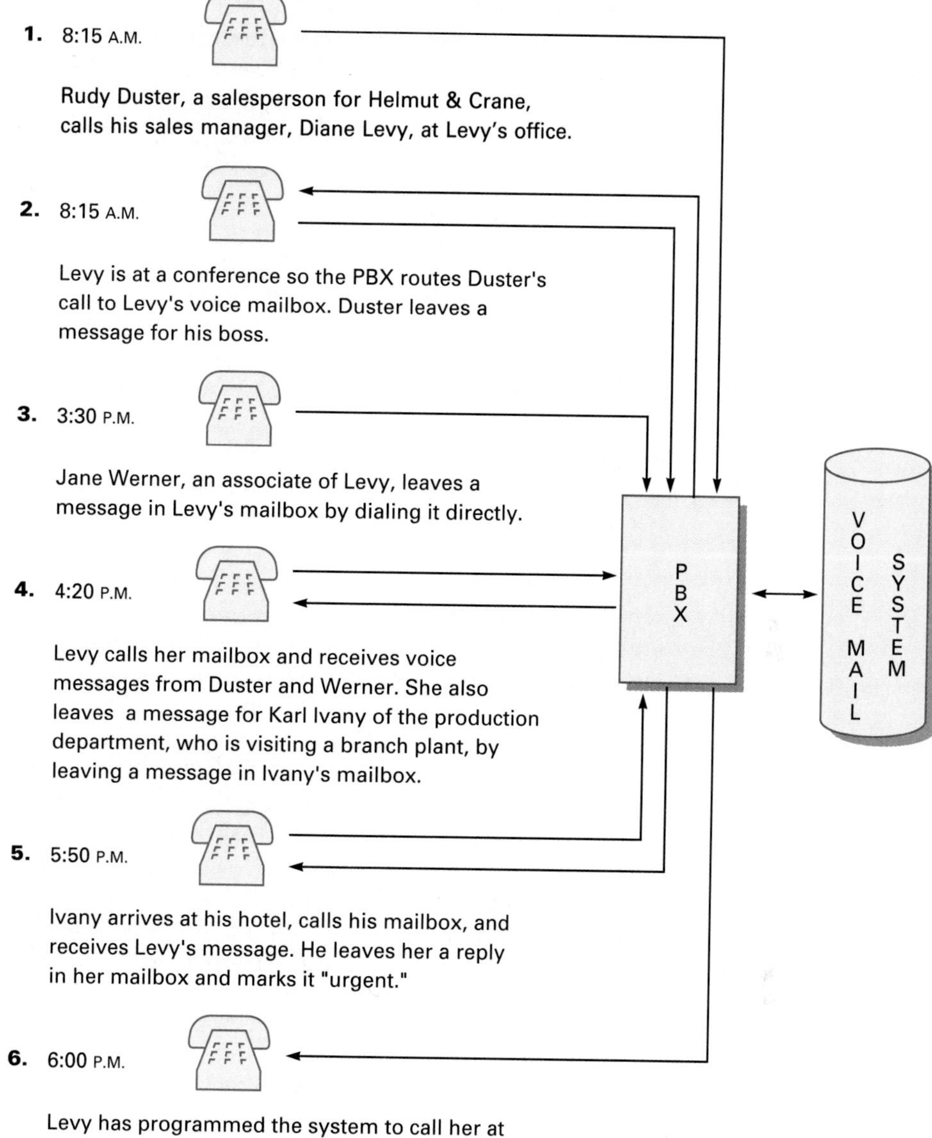

1. 8:15 A.M.
Rudy Duster, a salesperson for Helmut & Crane, calls his sales manager, Diane Levy, at Levy's office.
2. 8:15 A.M.
Levy is at a conference so the PBX routes Duster's call to Levy's voice mailbox. Duster leaves a message for his boss.
3. 3:30 P.M.
Jane Werner, an associate of Levy, leaves a message in Levy's mailbox by dialing it directly.
4. 4:20 P.M.
Levy calls her mailbox and receives voice messages from Duster and Werner. She also leaves a message for Karl Ivany of the production department, who is visiting a branch plant, by leaving a message in Ivany's mailbox.
5. 5:50 P.M.
Ivany arrives at his hotel, calls his mailbox, and receives Levy's message. He leaves her a reply in her mailbox and marks it "urgent."
6. 6:00 P.M.
Levy has programmed the system to call her at her hotel at 6:00 P.M., if there are any "urgent" messages. The system calls her and she listens to Ivany's reply.
PBX
VOICE MAIL SYSTEM

Figure 8–7
A sequence of transactions in a voice mail system

Electronic Conferencing Systems

Electronic conferencing, or **teleconferencing, systems** have been developed to permit many participants to engage in one- and two-way communications without actually having to travel to a common site. The systems are designed to eliminate costly travel expenses and wasted travel time required by ordinary conferences.

Electronic conferencing does not eliminate the need for one-to-one meetings. Such meetings are especially useful when the participants have not met each other or when personal camaraderie or esprit de corps are objectives. Ordinarily, meetings with customers or vendors for price negotiations are better handled face to face. However, teleconferencing is useful when the participants all know each other and when the meeting should last only a short time. For example, when branch managers who are located all over the nation must meet, teleconferencing may prove very cost effective if their meeting is likely to take only an hour or so.

Electronic conferencing has evolved into four types:

1. Audioconferencing.
2. Videoconferencing.
3. Computer conferencing.
4. Desktop conferencing.

Audioconferencing uses the telephone system to provide multiple parties with a chance to meet electronically. The system typically uses a speakerphone at one or more locations and patches together groups of people who are meeting at different sites, such as branch offices. To supplement an audioconference, illustrations, charts, or other graphics may be shared by means of facsimile devices at each location. Another device for supplementing audioconferencing is the **electronic blackboard.** This system captures the writing on a chalkboard in digital form and uses the telephone system to transmit the data to television screens at the remote locations. The system is particularly useful for training sessions.

Videoconferencing combines both voice and television images to provide two-way conferencing between groups (see Figure 8–8). Videoconferencing is especially useful when groups of participants are able to gather at local sites, such as branch factories, warehouses, or offices. Videoconferencing facilities can then be limited to a

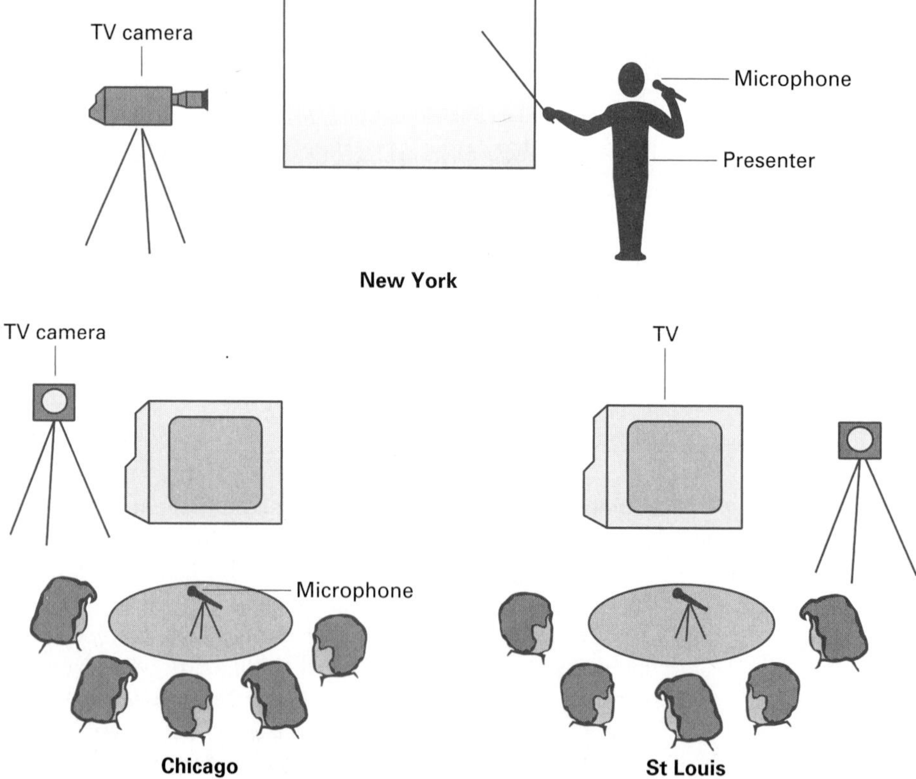

Figure 8–8
A teleconferencing system with presenter in New York and participant groups in Chicago and St. Louis

small number of locations, minimizing travel for the participants. Because videoconferencing systems and facilities are expensive, some hotel chains make videoconferencing services available to organizations at rental fees. Common carriers also make videoconferencing services available to their subscribers. In this way, organizations that do not need to use such facilities often do not need to acquire and maintain videoconferencing systems themselves.

Computer conferencing is similar to electronic mail except that instead of the communications flowing from one participant to one participant, or from one participant to many participants, the sessions allow many participants to communicate with many participants. The "conversations" that are held are all keyed-in messages displayed on computer screens. Basically, participants attend a joint conference through their display screens, sending messages to all participants. Computer conferencing also differs from audio- and videoconferencing in that the latter two approaches are in real time. Computer conferencing is a store-and-forward technology, as is electronic mail. This allows people to participate in conference proceedings at times when it is convenient for them rather than being tied to a specific schedule of events as in most conferences. A number of vendors offer specialized computer conferencing software to manage the communications necessary to bring this form of conferencing about in an orderly fashion.

Desktop conferencing systems are also called electronic meeting systems. These systems typically allow users on a LAN to use their workstations to conduct meetings without physically getting together. The simplest systems allow users to simultaneously view and edit reports, charts, images, and other documents from their LAN workstations. For example, Fujitsu's DeskTop Conferencing system provides real-time, interactive conferencing and tools for annotating documents, including drawing tools so users can circle or underline parts of a screen image. A leader usually runs the conference, preparing the documents or images into folders for sequential viewing, much like a presentation graphics system, and moving the images along when discussion about them is over. DeskTop Conferencing also allows conferees to send written messages to each other using a notepad. Other products also permit users to connect to the conference remotely via a dial-up connection. Thus, key people in a conference do not need to be at the LAN workstation to participate.

More sophisticated forms of desktop conferencing add the capabilities of full-motion video and sound to the conference (See Figure 8–9). These systems are sometimes called multimedia conferencing. For example, IBM Corporation's Person-to-Person/2 software lets conferees use these features:

- A chalkboard for conferees to share reports, images, and other documents.
- A message feature that allows users to broadcast short messages on top of the current display.
- A pointer to highlight parts of a screen display.
- A file transfer capability to allow users to share document, data, image, and other files during the conference.
- A real-time video capability that lets users display images of conferees or other full-motion video material.

US West, a regional Bell operating company, also offers desktop video conferencing. For $8,500 you get a PictureTel live videoconferencing system that includes a video camera, audio system, and the expansion boards for an IBM or IBM clone and the installation costs for a 56 KB telephone line. Users then pay around $40 to $50 a month for the line and $2.40 an hour connect charges during desktop videoconferencing

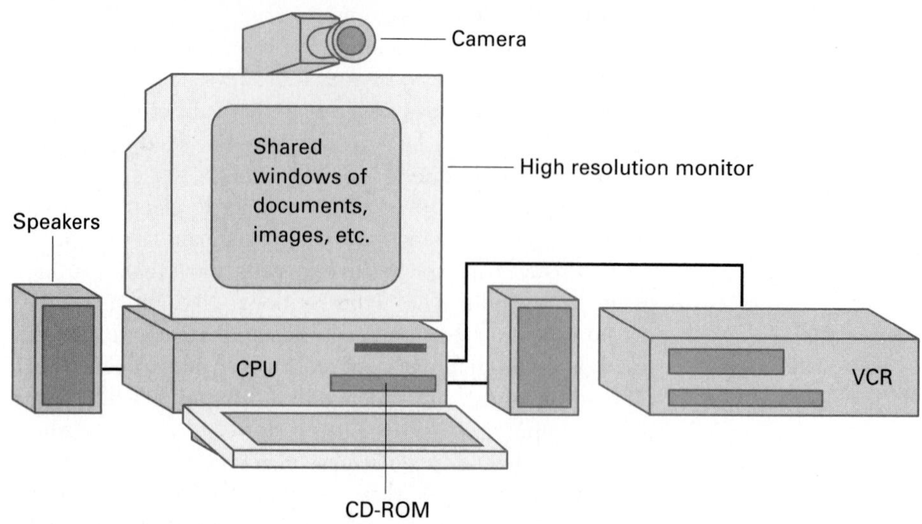

Figure 8–9
A desktop videoconferencing system

Notes: Each PC is connected to a local area network, and each PC contains a videoboard, sound board, and desktop videoconferencing software

sessions. The system allows users to share screens, files, and live TV images. They can also talk to each other and mark up or annotate shared documents or images.

Desktop conferencing systems are inexpensive replacements for full-motion teleconferencing systems. They allow people to collaborate as well as to be relatively passive participants, as at an ordinary conference. As LANs and multimedia systems become commonplace, it is likely that desktop conferencing will become very popular.

Micrographics

Micrographics is the process of reducing the text found on paper documents to a fraction of its size and storing these text images on film. The process dates from the 19th century and has been used in the banking industry to store the images of checks for many decades.

There are five types of *microforms* commonly in use today: roll film, **microfiche,** aperture cards, jackets, and filmstrips (see Figure 8–10).

Micrographics has typically been used to reduce the space consumed by large amounts of paper documents that have low retrieval rates. A firm might microfilm last year's accounting records and store the film off-site in a bank vault. Using **microfilm,** the firm may reduce the documents to 5 percent of their original size.

Another use of micrographics has been to provide archival copies of paper documents in case of fire or other catastrophe or in case duplicates are needed at other locations. Micrographics also allows organizations to convert bulky documents to a series of microfiche. The microfiche can be duplicated and mailed at low cost to users, members, clients, or customers throughout the world. For example, some automobile manufacturers supply their dealerships with parts catalogs in microfiche form.

Documents do not need to be photographed to be placed on microfilm. For many years, many organizations have produced roll film and microfiche directly from documents stored on computer tapes and disks. This process is referred to as **computer output microfilm,** or **COM** (see Figure 8–11). COM permits rapid printout of computer data and is an inexpensive and compact storage medium.

The primary difficulty with microforms in the past was that microform images could not be updated. It was also laborious to find specific images on film. Recent advances in micrographics technology allow microfiche to be updated by removing and adding images to fiche. Also, roll and cartridge film can be indexed by combining micrographics

Figure 8–10
Five types of microforms: fiche, aperture cards, jackets, filmstrips, and rolls

Five Microfilm Types

Microfiche

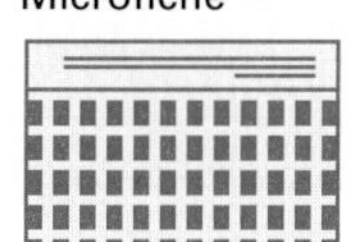

Microfiche
Microfiche is roll film of 105-mm width cut into card size, or 4 by 6-inch size. Microfiche, aperture cards, and microfilm jackets permit you to select a single card, fiche, or jacket, place it on a reader, and find the page or image you wish without sequentially rolling through all the images on a roll of film.

Aperture cards

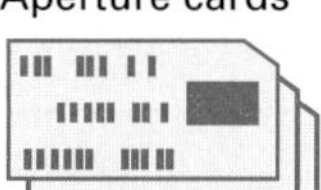

Aperture cards
Aperture cards are strips of roll film mounted on cards that have openings the size of filmstrips. Aperture cards are often used to store large documents such as architectural drawings and blueprints.

Jacketed film

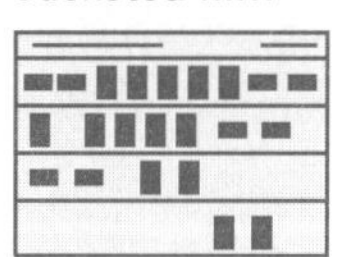

Microfilm jackets
Microfilm jackets are transparent cards with pockets in which strips of roll microfilm can be inserted. The jackets are about the size of a 4- by 6-inch card.

Filmstrips

Filmstrips
Filmstrips are simply sections of microfilm rolls cut into strips.

Roll film

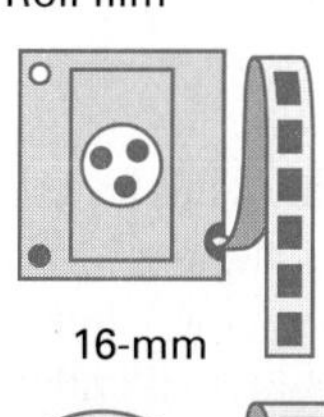

16-mm

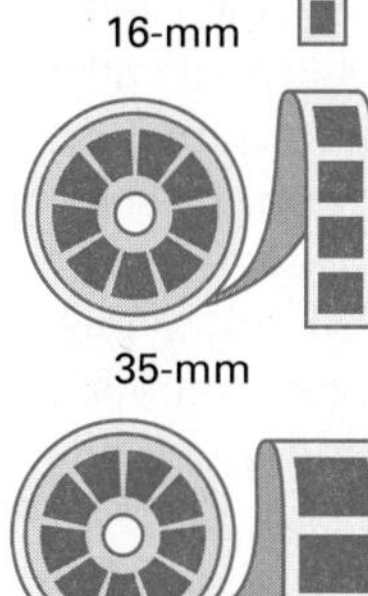

35-mm

105-mm

Roll film
Roll film is commonly used when the document to be reduced and stored is sequential in nature; for example, newspaper and magazine pages may be photographed and placed on roll film. When developed, the film can be placed on a microfilm reader where the images can be enlarged, sequentially scanned, and displayed on the reader's screen. Roll film can be in open reel or cartridge form.

and computer technology. Individual microfilm images are given cartridge and frame addresses that are stored on computer disk. When you wish to view a specific image, the computer micrographics system locates the cartridge and frame numbers, loads the correct cartridge from a motorized storage bin, scans the film until it locates the correct frame number, and displays the image on a reader. A more modestly priced version displays the number of the cartridge on a computer screen and the operator inserts the cartridge into the reader, which scans it, locates the correct frame, and displays it. This technology is called **computer-assisted retrieval (CAR).**

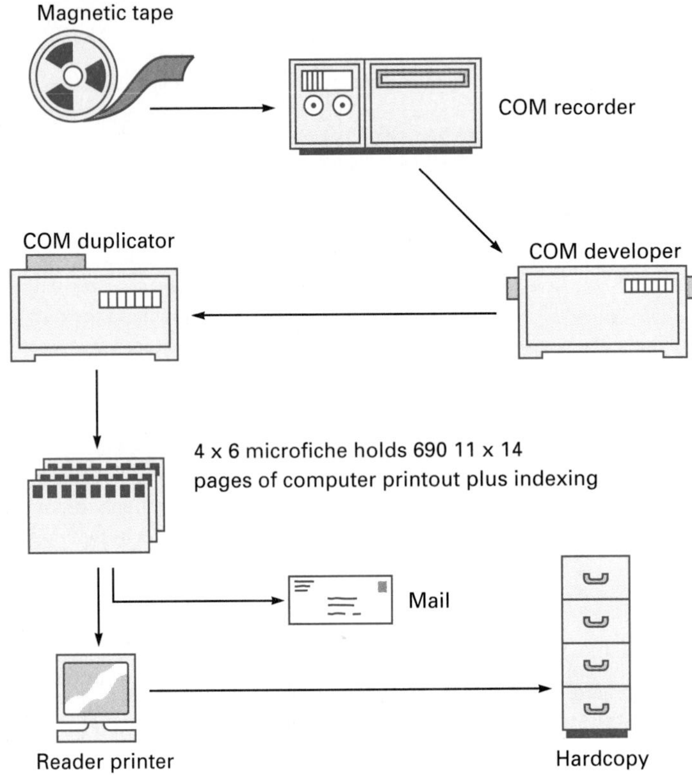

Figure 8–11
Computer output microfilm, or COM, takes images directly from computer memory and stores them on microfilm

Individual Support Software

Numerous software products support individuals in their everyday work tasks. These products have already been discussed in Chapter 5, "Computer Software" under the headings of "Desktop Organizer Software" and "Personal Information Management Software." Desktop organizer software includes calendars and day planners, calculators, memo pads, telephone directories or "electronic rolodexes," address books, to-do lists, index cards, expense logs, and other electronic versions of personal office tools used by nearly every office worker.

Personal information managers, or PIMs, often include many of the personal office tools just described. However, this class of software is usually built around a file management program that allows you to store and search diverse record types, such as notes, customer records, and telephone numbers, or any type of information that managers and other office workers typically want to have on hand.

Groupware

Technology to support work groups has been around for some time. For example, traditional telephone conference calls allowed work groups to communicate together, project management software allowed project leaders to track group project progress, and E-mail systems allowed us to share messages with one or several coworkers. But each of these systems is an independent, narrowly focused system that supports only one type of group activity. In the last few years, integrated software products aimed specifically at improving the productivity of people who are collaborating to achieve common goals have evolved. These packages, called **groupware,** offer integrated support for many of the typical activities needed by work groups, as described earlier in this chapter (see Box 8–8).

Box 8–8 Lotus Notes: An Example of Groupware

Lotus Notes is a comprehensive groupware product. Notes and its companion products consist of a set of software programs built around a flexible document database and local area network E-mail system. The software allows workers to capture, create, store, and distribute unstructured documents, including spreadsheets, memos, reports, and images, over local area networks and other communications technologies. Lotus Notes differs from many other groupware packages because Lotus Notes is not limited to support for a department or small work group. It is designed to provide group support for an entire organization.

Users can build and store forms, search through the document database using key words, view documents, build documents by merging images, text, spreadsheets, and other data, and route documents through E-mail. The documents can be stored for sharing with a work group, they can be faxed to others, or they can be printed. The document creation program contains many of the features of a full-fledged word processor, including spell checker, headers and footers, and dictionary. The E-mail program provides intelligent routing of documents to others within a work group, to other work groups, or to an entire organization.

The document imaging program allows the user to capture, store, manipulate, and annotate text and images. The documents can then be routed or faxed to others. Other programs allow images of text to be converted into actual text via optical character recognition, and allow users to connect to Notes remotely. One effective application is preparing or importing company documents such as personnel manuals, travel regulations, and procedures to the Notes document database. These documents become immediately available to everyone using Notes and can be updated quickly, avoiding the problem of updating and distributing hundreds or thousands of such manuals and booklets throughout a department, division, or organization. Notes also provides a companywide bulletin board for posting notices, new policies, and other announcements.

Source: Randall Kennedy, "Groupware Has Arrived: New Tools for Team Players," *Windows Sources* 1, no. 2 (March 1993), pp. 411–13 ff.

Thus, groupware products may provide many or all of these functions:

- Electronic mail services, including transferring files and voice annotation.
- Voice mail services with the ability to send voice messages to individuals and groups.
- Bulletin board services for broadcasting messages to a group or for group discussion.
- Teleconferencing services, including audio-, video-, computer, and desktop conferencing.
- Fax services, including group faxing and OCR conversion of faxed documents.
- Word processing services, including multiuser document viewing, editing, and annotation.
- Group calendaring and scheduling services, including room scheduling and meeting agendas.
- Shared to-do lists for tracking the status of assignments.
- Shared phone lists.
- Group project management software for optimizing human and other project resources and for monitoring group progress.
- Transparent file, document, and data retrieval services.
- Personal utilities (appointment books, calculators, auto-dialers, notepads, outliners, file managers, personal to-do lists, and expense reporting).

Applications for the bulletin board feature include broadcasting information to all group members, holding group discussions, brainstorming, and posting problems for group solution. Bulletin board, voice mail, electronic mail, and computer conferencing all provide store-and-forward group discussion capabilities. Audio- and videoconferencing provide for real-time group discussion capabilities.

In a groupware system, voice mail may be provided through traditional PBX-based systems, newer PC-based systems, or the voice mail annotation feature of some electronic mail systems.

Multiuser document annotation is a feature of word processors that permits many users to add comments to and revise documents prepared by other users. Furthermore, the feature usually allows users to track and catalog revisions.

Transparency in file, document, and data retrieval services refers to the ability of a user to find, manipulate, and retrieve data wherever it is located on a network without knowing its location and to use the computing power of any public CPU on the network to get the processing done. These features allow group members to share data stored on any member's computer system as well as other storage systems. Thus, full-featured group support software may include the features of a client/server database as described in Chapter 6, "File and Database Management Systems." Transparent file, document, and data retrieval services also may be delivered using document management systems (see "Document Management Systems" in this chapter).

Group project management services may include multiuser project management software, which helps group managers track work assignments by spotting assignments that are overdue, reminding group members when task due dates pass, and even urging members to complete required paperwork. One groupware package, Diamond, a UNIX-based package, handles remote multimedia conferencing by providing users with integrated text, graphics, spreadsheets, charts, and voice annotation. The package also lets users record group sessions for later review.

Groupware and the definition of what groupware represents is still evolving. No package seems to offer all or even most of the features useful to group projects or work tasks. In addition, many vendors of traditional software categories have begun to add group work features to their products. For example, LAN versions of word processors have added group annotation features to their software. The annotation features allow multiple users to view and edit a document but provide a clear trail of the editing and revision process. Thus, edited text is identified by strikeovers, underlines, or some other formatting feature, and the date, time, and name of the reviser is noted right on the document. Some spreadsheets permit versioning so that several people may create different scenarios for an event using the same spreadsheet template. Thus, a team might examine the different outcomes of an event as predicted by each team member using different assumptions. Microsoft will soon release a version of its spreadsheet Excel that will let one member of a team send a range of cells to a colleague for completion using a "delegate" function. Once completed, the colleague will return the range using a "return to sender" function.

It is clear that major software developers are expanding the groupware they offer. It seems safe to say that major software vendors will continue to enhance their groupware products so that they become more comprehensive in terms of the group tasks supported and more integrated in terms of the work flow between these tasks. In fact, a new form of groupware that addresses the need to integrate work group tasks, workflow software, is expanding rapidly (see the following "Workflow Software").

Workflow Software

Recently, a type of groupware software has evolved that lets developers create programs to perform routine tasks at preset time periods. For example, a developer may create a program that automatically collects data from several files located on different networks and then automatically compiles the data and distributes a report each month. This software is called **workflow software** because it allows developers to create a program that automates a series of actions in a flow of work. In short, the software allows the developer to automate a series of tasks that would ordinarily have been completed by the manager and office clerks.

Workflow software has the potential for changing how businesses, especially work groups, are organized because the software directly alters the processes and the flow of work in an organization. If the software is used intelligently, it provides an opportunity for firms to reengineer the business processes to which they apply it.

Workflow software may be built around E-mail systems, word processing software database software, and even fax systems (see Box 8–9). E-mail workflow software allows you to create forms and then automate routing the forms to those who must use them. The E-mail portion of the software provides a rapid transportation medium for the forms. E-mail–based workflow software also provides two types of development tools: a *forms creation tool* that lets users create the forms used in the business processes and a *scripting language* that allows users to create a "script," or the play-by-play procedures through which the forms will be processed. Thus, the user first develops a form, like a purchase order, and then builds a script of who does what with the purchase order and when. The software then follows the script to process each form.

Typical applications for E-mail–based systems are order processing, expense account reporting, and document review and approval. Let's look at a typical example of

Box 8–9 Smart Paper Systems: Another Type of Workflow Automation

Smart paper is paper that appears to file itself, fax itself, transfer its contents to a database itself, and route itself to others automatically. Appropriate applications for smart paper systems are contracts, customer orders, travel expense accounts from field representatives, medical claims processing, and even credit applications. In these systems, fax machines become remote terminals. For example, a firm creates a form using the forms creation programs supplied by the system. The forms might be designed to accept either handwritten entries or marks. The forms are then faxed to clients or customers, who complete them and then fax them back to the firm. The firm receives the faxed forms on an internal fax board in a PC where they are automatically scanned and the data entered into the appropriate customer or client files.

The systems normally come with a number of programs, including form creation programs, fax programs, and optical character and mark recognition programs. The optical character recognition software is capable of distinguishing different types of forms so that these different forms can be processed and routed appropriately, and the data on the completed forms can ordinarily be exported automatically to spreadsheet or database files. The systems also usually come with some utilities, such as a phone book so that documents can be easily and automatically faxed to selected fax machines.

Some systems allow customers or clients to obtain information about the company and its products automatically. These systems, sometimes called *fax on demand systems*, let customers dial in and select information they want from a voice menu. The information is then faxed to them automatically. Other fax on demand systems let customers fax their requests to the firm where they are automatically scanned, entered into a customer database, and the information requested automatically faxed to them.

Source: Kathryn Alesandrini, "Smart Paper Streamlines the Office," *PC Today* 7, no. 4 (April 1993), pp. 44, 46–48.

how, in a manual system, a manager might file an expense report (see Figure 8–12). The manager completes a travel expense form in pencil to report expenses incurred at a recent training seminar. The manager then places the form in the in-basket of an administrative support employee where the form sits until the employee gets to it. At that time the administrative support employee types a copy of the expense report, verifies the accuracy of the arithmetic, and makes certain that the amounts spent are within company guidelines. The assistant then returns the form to the manager's desk to be signed and returned to the administrative support person, who places it in the out-basket to await mail pickup. Eventually, it will be picked up and sent via intracompany mail to the mailbox of the accounting office, where it is opened and placed in the in-basket of a clerk, who once again reviews the expense form for completeness and accuracy and once again checks the amount spent against company guidelines. The accounting clerk also compares the total amount requested against the balance in the

Figure 8–12
Steps in a travel expense reporting system using manual methods and E-mail workflow systems

Steps in Manual System

1. Manager fills out travel expense form in pencil
2. Manager places form in secretary's in-basket
3. Secretary types expense form
4. Secretary verifies arithmetic
5. Secretary checks amounts spent against company guidelines
6. Secretary places form on desk of manager for signature
7. Manager signs form and returns to secretary's in-basket
8. Secretary places signed form in interoffice mailbox
9. Interoffice mail picks up, sorts, and delivers form to accounting
10. Form is placed in in-basket of clerk
11. Clerk verifies arithmetic
12. Clerk checks amounts against company guidelines
13. Clerk checks total amount against manager's budget
14. Clerk places form in interoffice mailbox
15. Interoffice mail picks up, sorts, and delivers to superior
16. Superior's secretary opens and place on desk for review
17. Superior reviews and signs form
18. Superior's secretary places in interoffice mailbox
19. Interoffice mail picks up, sorts, and delivers to accounting
20. Clerk completes check

Steps in E-mail–Based System

1. Manager completes and signs expense form on computer
2. Workflow automation software verifies arithmetic and completeness, checks amounts against company guidelines, checks total against manager's budget, and places form in superior's E-mail box
3. Superior signs form
4. Workflow automation system places signed form in accounting clerk's E-mail box
5. Accounting clerk initiates check

manager's travel budget to ensure that the manager has enough money in the travel line of the budget to pay for the seminar. The form is then placed in an out-basket again, awaits pickup, and is forwarded to the manager's superior for review and a signature of approval, once again by intracompany mail. At the superior's office, it is placed in the in-basket of an administrative support employee until it is opened and placed on the desk of the superior who reviews it. Once signed by the superior, it is picked up by the administrative support employee and placed in another out-basket awaiting mail pickup. After pickup, it is routed back to the accounting department, once again through intracompany mail, where yet another clerk with yet another in-basket and out-basket completes a check to the manager.

Using workflow software, the number of steps and time required to process the same document might be improved dramatically and the life of the same expense form might take quite a different form. The manager completes the travel expense form on an expense report form displayed on a computer screen. The manager signs the form using a light pen. The workflow automation software immediately verifies the completeness of the form, compares the amounts listed to a file of company guidelines for approved expense limits, and using information obtained from another information system, verifies that the manager's travel budget is sufficient to cover the expenses reported. Seconds later, the workflow software places the verified document in the superior's E-mail box for review and signature. Once the superior signs off on the form using a light pen, the workflow software immediately places the form in the E-mail box of an accounting clerk so that the clerk may initiate a check.

In the new process, several redundant steps were eliminated and several routine verification steps completed automatically. In addition, many in-baskets and out-baskets were eliminated, and the intracompany mail delays were reduced from days to seconds. Overall, the time taken for the process is reduced from many days to a matter of minutes.

As you can see from the example, some workflow products allow developers to use scripting tools to extract needed data from existing information systems, such as a budget system, inventory system, or accounts receivable system. Some workflow software also provides libraries of forms and scripts for common business processes that can be modified by users to fit their needs. Still other workflow software adds management and reporting tools that let managers know the status of work in the flow and provides statistics on the number of documents processed, the average time for processing documents, the average time each step in the process takes, and similar information. Management information of this type allows developers to identify bottlenecks in the system, improve productivity, and streamline work flows even further.

INTEGRATING OFFICE TECHNOLOGIES INTO OFFICE INFORMATION SYSTEMS

This chapter has described numerous technologies that are being applied to office work (see Figure 8–13). At the present time, many of these technologies are not being integrated in any significant way. That is, they often are not deployed in an office in such a way that the output of one technology provides input to another. Merging these technologies into an integrated information system to support office work is sometimes referred to as the **paperless office,** or the *office of the future.* Groupware, document management systems, and workflow software applications represent rudimentary forms of the paperless office because they integrate multiple technologies into systems to get office work done. Electronic data interchange is another rudimentary form of the paperless office.

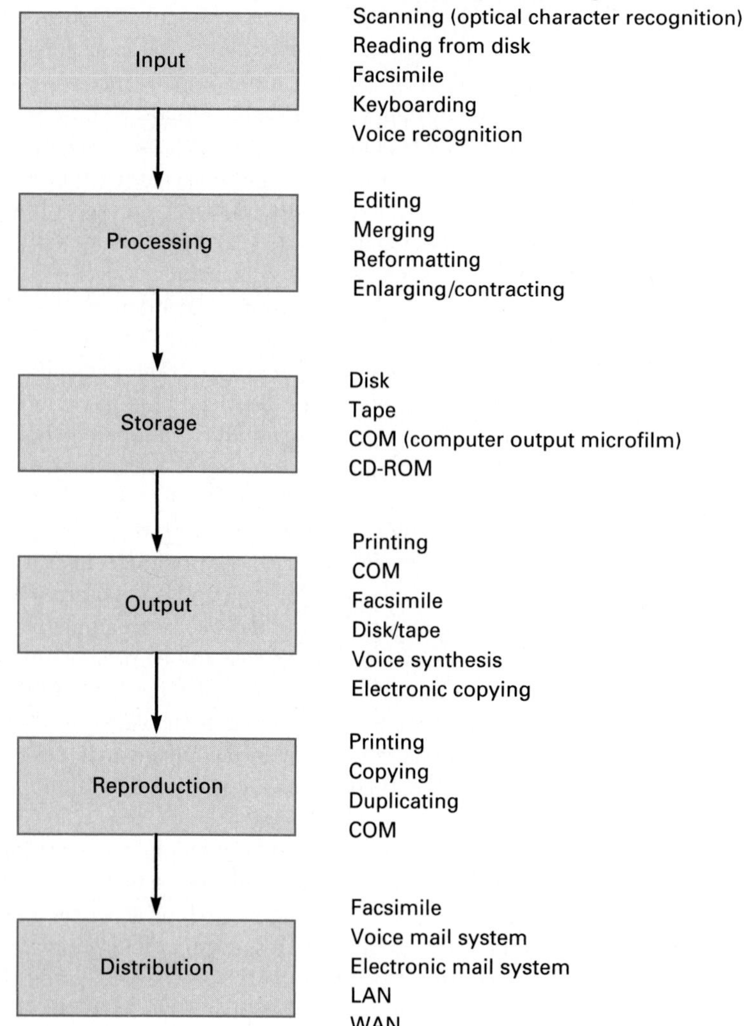

Figure 8–13
The document processing cycle and computer-based office technologies

Many people in the office industry have been predicting a time when office automation makes possible a paperless office—that is, an office in which hard copy is rarely produced or processed (see Box 8–10). The paperless office, or office of the future, will be one in which documents are received in electronic form; processed in electronic form; and stored, replicated, and distributed in electronic form within and between organizations. Keys to the paperless office are a common architecture for application software and telecommunications to insure that the systems adhere to a common set of standards. Providing for the complete electronic processing of information means that a variety of LANs, WANs, and other electronic networks will link various office personnel inside and outside of every organization. This will require that networks become ubiquitous and that the application and communications protocols for creating, editing, storing, and transmitting electronic documents become standardized.

It is expected that the paperless office will use networks to link intelligent copy machines, optical scanners, facsimiles, word processors, computers, printers, optical and hard disk storage facilities, and many other office technologies to each other, to an

Box 8–10 The U.S. Navy's Paperless Ship

The U.S. Navy is a very large organization and, like any large organization, is drowning in paper forms and documents. However, for the Navy, eliminating or replacing mounds of paper documents offers immediate, practical benefits that cannot wait for the "office of the future" to solve.

How will technology help? The Navy plans to exchange thousands of paper manuals with PC- and CD-ROM–based information systems, and expects to save over $1 billion a year using the system. The Navy also knows that ships and aircraft without paper manuals weigh less and maneuver with greater ease. Thus, the ships will gain tactical speed and maneuverability and also burn less fuel. For example, the Ingraham, a guided missile frigate, lost about one ton once it had its manuals converted to digital media.

The Ingraham still depends on paper for many administrative tasks. However, the ship supplanted more than 1,500 technical manuals and architectural drawings with a PC-driven, magnetic library of optical disks. Given that ships usually last for decades, they build up an enormous amount of technical information about them over their lives. Not only is the new system lighter, it is faster and easier for technicians to find the data they need in the manuals. A document management system allows older documents to be scanned into the system.

Source: Dennis Eskow, "U.S. Navy Declares War on Paper," *PC Week* 7, no. 16 (April 23, 1990) pp. 1 and 6.

organization's mainframe, and to the outside world via gateways to external, wide area networks (see Figure 8–14). In such a system, the need to produce hard copy will be almost nonexistent because documents can be displayed, edited, and stored on magnetic media and transmitted anywhere within the system.

The technology to provide a nearly paperless office is available today. LANs, WANs, PBX networks, and other networks could be used to link various kinds of office equipment to provide an electronic path for every document or message, including oral messages. However, given the penchant of most organizations for hard copy, the cost of the technology to make the paperless office, the resistance that some people have to technology, and the plodding speed of the standardization of communications protocols, it seems unlikely that the paperless office will be implemented for some time. Still, office functions are yielding to integration in increasing numbers of firms of all sizes each year, especially through groupware, document management systems, and workflow automation. A reasonable view is that although the office of the future is still clearly that, the rate and extent of technological development in office equipment and the concurrent change in office work seem to make the "paperleast" office a hope for the near future and the paperless office of the future inevitable.

One necessary precursor of this development is the establishment of wide area networks, local area networks, or both as a common feature of almost every office. As WANs and LANs become increasingly commonplace, the most important link for electronic information transfer within offices will be in place.

Short of the paperless office, it is still very important to consider integrating office technology into office information systems wherever possible. It seems clear that technological developments increasingly are leading organizations to widespread, integrated office automation. These developments include communication networks and technologies such as personal digital assistants, personal communicators, E-mail, document management systems, workflow software, integrated groupware packages, and client-server databases. In addition, comprehensive information system architectures, includ-

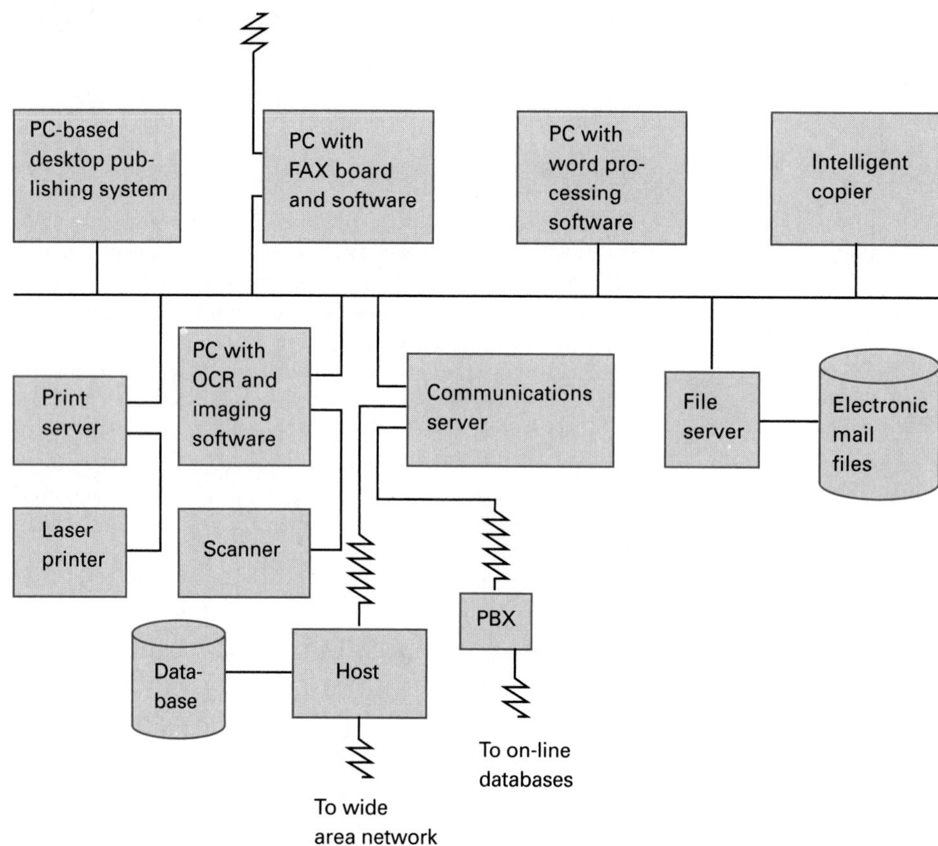

Figure 8–14 Integrating diverse office technologies through communications networks

ing IBM's SAA or Systems Application Architecture, which provides, among other things, a common user interface for applications regardless of the computer platform through which a user encounters the applications, and SGML, which allows for convenient sharing of many types of documents, are important developments supporting the paperless office. To this chorus has been added the voice of Microsoft, Inc., with its plan for Microsoft at Work (MAW), which promises to add a new operating system for office machines, new communications software to link the machines, and common file formats so that the machines can easily exchange and use data. The office machinery that MAW plans to integrate includes faxes, printers, personal digital assistants, scanners, copiers, and PCs.

Management Summary

The office is often viewed in three distinctive ways: as a location in which office work is completed, as a series of discrete functions or tasks, and as an integrated system. The way the office is viewed has implications for the way office work is organized and how the productivity of office workers is measured and improved.

Offices typically perform three functions: administrative support, document processing, and data processing. Although the data processing function has usually been automated, the administrative support and document processing functions may not yet be, and these latter functions offer organizations means of improving productivity and reducing costs. A great variety of office technology has been developed to address the automation of the administrative support and document processing functions. These technologies include word processing, desktop publishing, photocomposition, reprographics, facsimile, OCR, scanning, electronic mail systems, voice mail systems, audioconferencing, videoconferencing, computer conferencing, desktop conferencing, document management systems, groupware, workflow software, and micrographics.

In addition to applying technology to office functions, office productivity may be improved by reorganizing the way office work is performed. This might mean centralizing some office services so that workers can acquire specialized training and develop more productive work procedures and so that better equipment can be acquired.

An important means of improving office work is to integrate the various office technologies into office information systems. When this is done, the computerized output of one technology becomes the input of another. Thus, electronic scanners and graphics software can provide input to desktop publishing systems, the output from which can provide input to computerized databases and electronic mail systems.

Key Terms for Managers

administrative support function, **299**
audioconferencing, **320**
centralization, **302**
compound documents, **307**
computer-assisted retrieval (CAR), **323**
computer conferencing, **321**
computer output microfilm (COM), **322**
decentralization, **303**
desktop conferencing, **321**
desktop publishing software (DTP), **307**
desktop video, **314**
document management systems, **315**
document processing, **299**
document processing cycle, **299**
electronic blackboard, **320**
electronic conferencing, **319**
electronic mail systems, **315**
facsimile (fax), **311**
fax/modem boards, **312**
fonts, **308**
functional organization, **303**
graphical word processors, **308**
groupware, **324**
imaging systems, **310**
intelligent copier, **310**
interactive voice response systems, **318**
microfiche, **322**
microfilm, **322**
micrographics, **322**
office automation, **298**
optical character recognition (OCR), **312**
optical mark recognition, **312**
optical scanner, **311**
paperless office, **329**
portable documents, **306**
reprographics, **309**
standard generalized markup language (SGML), **307**
telecommuting, **300**
teleconferencing systems, **319**
telephone tag, **317**
videoconferencing, **320**
virtual offices, **304**
voice mail systems (VMS), **317**
voice messaging systems, **318**
voice processing systems, **317**
what-you-see-is-what-you-get (WYSIWYG), **308**
word processing systems, **305**
workflow software, **327**

Review Questions

1. What are the major functions of the office? What functions have already largely been automated and what functions are now just beginning to be?
2. What is the document processing cycle? What are the steps in the document processing cycle?
3. Describe how the traditional office was organized. Describe the major differences between the traditional office and an office that has been highly automated.
4. Describe what desktop publishing means.

5. What is reprographics? What are the three major categories of reprographics processes or systems?
6. How does an intelligent copier differ from a desktop copier?
7. What does a fax device do? How does it differ from a copy machine? How does it differ from an intelligent copier?
8. What are four means of providing teleconferencing? Describe an application that might be appropriate for each teleconferencing method.
9. What is an electronic mail system? What are the component parts of an electronic mail system?
10. Explain how users might communicate with each other in an electronic mail system.
11. What is a voice mail system? What are the components of a voice mail system?
12. Explain how users communicate with one another using a voice mail system.
13. Describe an application for which a voice mail system might be appropriate.
14. Describe three microform types. Identify one application that might be appropriate for each form.
15. What are COM and CAR? What is the difference between COM and CAR?
16. Identify the advantages and disadvantages of the centralization of common office services such as document processing, reprographics, mail, and records management.
17. Explain the difference between optical character recognition devices and optical scanning devices.
18. What is groupware? What types of software may be included in a groupware package?
19. What is office automation?
20. Explain telecommuting.
21. What is a portable document? What is Standardized Generalized Markup Language and what is the promise of this technology?
22. What is a compound document?
23. Explain the acronym WYSIWYG. How does it improve the productivity of workers preparing documents?
24. What is graphical word processing software?
25. Explain on-line faxing.
26. What is E-mail filtering?
27. Explain the term *telephone tag*.
28. What is a voice message system? How do interactive voice response systems differ from voice messaging?
29. What is workflow software?

Questions for Discussion

1. What is document processing? How does it differ from data processing?
2. What is the administrative support function of the office? How does it differ from the data processing and document processing functions?
3. Describe three views of the office. How might each view affect how the office is organized? With which view do you agree? How do you justify your decision?
4. What factors have led to the current focus on office productivity? Why did these factors generate this focus?
5. What is there about the traditional office that leads to inefficiency or low productivity?
6. In what ways has technology altered the traditional tasks performed by many secretaries and managers?
7. Explain what is meant by the *paperless office*.
8. What are the essential characteristics of the paperless office?
9. Why is the office of the future likely to be a reality only in the distant future? What new office technologies represent harbingers of the office of the future?
10. Explain what the functional organization of office services refers to and describe why this organization is used in some offices.
11. What are document management systems? Why have these systems become important to organizations?

Problems

1. **Office technology.** For each situation below identify one or more office technologies that might be considered.

   a. Creating multipage text documents without pictures or charts.
   b. Creating multipage text documents containing pictures or charts.
   c. Transmitting text, pictures, or charts in hard-copy form to branch offices in hard-copy form.
   d. Converting text in hard-copy form to a digital storage medium in such a way that the text can be manipulated with word processing or desktop publishing software.
   e. Sending memos and files from one office employee to one or more other office employees.
   f. Communicating by phone to another employee or group of employees who are not at their desks.
   g. Meeting with a group of persons who are located at distant and different locations.
   h. Meeting with a group of persons who are located at distant and different locations but who may not be able to be present at the same time.
   i. Storing large amounts of paper documents in drastically reduced space in a nonmagnetic medium.
   j. Making three duplicates of a single page of hard-copy text.
   k. Making 50 duplicates of a two-page document stored on a magnetic medium.
   l. Capturing, storing, indexing, searching, displaying, and printing documents that contain a variety of data types, such as sound, video, images, text, and data.

2. **Verazano Corporation.** Vincente Mercado is a regional sales manager for the Verazano Corporation. He receives short, two-page field reports from his salespeople on Monday of each week. Since 15 salespersons report to him, 15 reports are submitted each week. He is expected to read these reports and then forward copies of them to the sales manager at the home office as quickly as possible. The reports are typewritten on electric typewriters but may contain charts or graphs, produced using a salesperson's spreadsheet, which have been cut and pasted into the text of the reports. Currently, Vincente has an aide copy the reports on a small copy machine in his office. The aide then collates the pages of each report and mails them by overnight mail to the sales manager. The home office usually receives the copies by the next day.

   Describe two more efficient methods by which the reports could be prepared, duplicated, and distributed using computer-based office technology. Your descriptions should specify the technologies, or pieces of equipment and software, you would recommend for each method. Where possible, your methods should also integrate the technologies you recommend.

3. **Groupware.** Complete a paper about one groupware software package by reading at least three articles or reviews of it. Your report should cover the package's features, shortcomings, and cost. To find reviews, you might examine issues of the following magazines: *Office Systems, Datamation, PC Magazine, Software Magazine, PC World, Byte,* and *Administrative Management.*

4. **Office automation.** Complete a paper about one of the following office automation technologies: desktop publishing, electronic mail, voice mail, facsimile, intelligent copiers, or teleconferencing. The paper should identify the current hardware and software available for the technology and their capabilities. Also identify office applications for the technology, and describe new trends or forecasted changes in the technology. You may wish to examine Applied Computer Research's *Computer Literature Index* for leads, Datapro Corporation's *Datapro Reports* on office automation for technology reviews, and some of the following magazines for product reviews to help you in your task: *Modern Office Technology, Office Systems, Datamation, Telecommunications, PC Magazine, Byte, Today's Office, The Office,* and *Administrative Management.*

5. **Workflow software.** Compare two workflow software packages by reading articles that review the packages. Prepare a report evaluating the two packages on the basis of

   a. Cost
   b. Features
   c. Ease of use.

Cases

1. **Canby, Ltd.** Canby, Ltd., is an accounting firm established in Toronto in the early 1940s. The firm serves clients in several Canadian provinces as well as several midwestern states in the United States. As a result, Canby employees, especially account executives, auditors, tax experts, and general accounting professionals, travel a great deal. They perform work both at the home office and client sites. They also frequently make use of their time while traveling to catch up on memos, draft reports, and contact the office by phone. Many of Canby's clients are large organizations, and Canby often finds it necessary to assign teams of professionals to complete projects for these clients.

Over the last five decades, the company had grown steadily, earning a reputation among its clients for reliability and service. The company recently moved to new office quarters they had purchased in the Toronto suburbs after having outgrown the office space in the city center they had rented for many years. The new office space was designed for them by Worley & Sievers, an office management firm.

Worley developed a plan for the new office space that used an entire floor of a two-floor building. Each major owner of the firm was given a 20-foot square corner office. Each of the accounting professionals was given either a 15-foot by 12-foot office or a 12-foot by 10-foot office, depending on their position in the firm. These offices were all window offices located between the owner offices. The support staff—secretaries, clerks, and aides—were placed in an open office room in the center of the floor. Desks were clustered together in this open area. The entire office space was decorated in bright, cheerful colors.

Each owner, professional, and secretary was given a stand-alone personal computer system with software appropriate to the needs of the individual. Some clerks and aides also received their own computer systems and some, whose work did not involve much in the way of hands-on computer tasks, shared personal computer systems. Each employee had a telephone, and several copiers were spread out in the open office space for the convenience of users.

a. Based on the information in this case, what view of the office do you believe Worley & Sievers hold and how did that view affect the office design?

b. Identify two views of the office other than that identified in (a) above. For each of these views, show how the use of the view might have identified needs not now served.

2. **Casady and Associates.** Casady and Associates is a management consulting firm located in a large city. The firm consists of seven consultants and three associate consultants. The three associate consultants are new members of the firm and are assigned to assist consultants on projects. Each consultant has a secretary, and the three associate consultants share one secretary. Each secretary provides the full range of administrative support and document processing support for the consultant or consultants, including answering the telephone; receiving visitors; preparing expense reports, project reports, and budgets; making copies, maintaining calendars and schedules, making travel arrangements, maintaining files, scheduling and otherwise managing meetings, ordering and maintaining office supplies, and handling the incoming mail for the assigned consultants. The secretaries use electronic typewriters for all their work and share two desktop copiers with a top speed of one copy every three seconds.

The company bookkeeper makes all entries in a manual bookkeeping system; processes all client invoices and payments; prepares weekly salary checks and payroll forms for all employees, associate consultants, and consultants; and processes all vendor invoices and payments. The company pays an accounting firm to prepare monthly statements and to perform other end-of-the-month and end-of-the-year accounting tasks, including preparation of tax forms for the firm.

The firm feels that the current organization of the administrative support personnel is not efficient. There are too many times when secretaries are away from their phones copying documents or delivering materials to others, which forces other secretaries to take their calls. This usually results in a callback because the secretary who knows the consultant's activities is not there to direct or otherwise process the call. To avoid this problem, five of the secretaries have each been given a clerk to assist them in copying, delivering materials, typing, answering the telephone, and otherwise to provide backup to these secretaries. Many of the consultant reports contain boilerplate, or fairly constant information pertaining to the firm and the consultant's experiences. This information is constantly being retyped and duplicated in nearly every consultant report. Furthermore, the firm wishes to add several more associate consultants and does not wish to continue the practice of adding secretaries on nearly a one-on-one basis as the firm grows.

a. How might you reorganize the administrative support, document processing support, and data processing support tasks and personnel to improve the productivity of this firm? Be specific! Identify each member of the administrative support personnel by job title and provide a list of tasks to be performed by that person. Also construct an organization chart showing who reports to whom in the organization. Provide a rationale for the reorganization that will justify your recommendations.

b. How might you improve the productivity of this office through office automation? Be specific! Identify the types of equipment and software you would recommend for each function you wish to automate. Provide a rationale for your recommendations.

3. **Feinstein Publishing Company.** Feinstein Publishing Company produces business textbooks for the collegiate market. The company has a particularly good reputation in the field of quantitative business texts. It markets textbooks throughout the United States, maintaining a large sales force that typically lives in the city, state, or region served. Salespeople visit faculty at various colleges and universities to discuss the firm's texts and to take orders for examination copies of texts that faculty members request. The firm also sets up booths at various business conferences during the year. The booths are filled with the firm's textbooks and are manned by salespeople who live in the area of the conference. Salespeople at these conferences also spend most of their time taking orders from faculty for examination copies. Many faculty members also request examination copies by completing prestamped and preaddressed forms detached from textbook advertising brochures mailed to faculty throughout the United States. If everything goes well, faculty member requests for examination copies will eventually turn into book orders issued from college bookstores.

   Because the sales force is far-flung, the firm holds a sales conference at the home office only once a year. At that time, new products are introduced and explained to the salespeople, and salespeople get a chance to discuss with each other successful sales tactics they have used during the previous year. However, the firm also introduces new products at several other points in the year, and salespeople need written sales documents that explain the new products. The firm has never been happy with this tactic, but it does not wish to spend the money to bring every salesperson back to the home office for several sales conferences each year.

   The marketing director is anxious to improve sales next year and to improve the productivity of her functional area. What office technologies might the marketing director explore to improve productivity in the tasks that have just been described?

4. **Taliana Systems, Inc.** Jill Taliana runs a consulting firm for urban planning. The firm develops proposals for cities, counties, states, and other government units on such topics as urban renewal, zoning patterns, economic analysis, and demographic analysis. The firm generally assigns a team of people with diverse skills and experience to prepare proposals and to manage each project that they subsequently

bring under contract. Some team members must spend substantial amounts of time away from the office working on site or collecting data. Every proposal and project generates a large amount of drawings, charts, photo images, text documents, reports, memos, letters, and sometimes videotapes. Teams often must present their proposals to the government unit to win a contract and to report the progress of contracts they have won.

At a recent staff meeting, Jill Taliana invited members to discuss problems they have experienced operating as teams in the preparation of proposals or the execution of contracts. Tanya Wiggins, a senior staff member, complained that often a team must prepare proposals that are similar to other proposals that have been prepared in the past or that could use photos, images, text, data, or other documents used in the past. However, finding relevant documents in the paper file system used by the firm is a daunting and time-consuming activity. Frequently, team members are so intimidated by the mass of previous documentation that they simply ignore it when they prepare new proposals.

Lamont Wilson, an economist, complains that staff in the field often need to confer with staff at the office. Although he usually creates a conference call through the telephone system, he is unable to share documents, drawings, or other pertinent materials with the home office team.

Louisa Ortiz, a project leader, complains that it is difficult to manage project personnel when some are at the home office and others are in the field. She complains that it is difficult to check on their completion of tasks that she has assigned them and also difficult to leave them messages, including messages about possible meeting times, dates, and places.

Jill has asked you to recommend solutions to the problems her staff has complained about.

Selected References and Readings

Alesandrini, Kathryn. "Automate Your Office with Fax-on-Demand." *PC Today* 6, no. 11 (November 1992), pp. 16–18, 20. Explains fax-on-demand technology, provides example applications, and reviews selected products.

Alesandrini, Kathryn. "Smart Paper Streamlines the Office." *PC Today* 7, no. 4 (April 1993), pp. 44, 46–48. Describes fax-based workflow systems, providing examples of use and details about two products: Teleform 2.0 and Interactive Forms.

Baronas, Jean. "A Guide to Quality Scanning." *Datamation* 36, no. 8 (April 15, 1990), pp. 96–97. Describes the Federal Information Processing Standards (FIPS) scanning guidelines.

Berst, Jesse. "A Paperless Office Is as Likely as a Paperless Bathroom." *Windows Magazine* 4, no. 9 (September 1993), pp. 43–44. A crude title for an interesting article that analyzes the component parts of Microsoft's plan for Windows at Work.

Brandel, William. "SGML Keeps the Flow in Workflow." *LAN Times* 10, no. 4 (February 22, 1993), pp. 1 and 86. A description of SGML, some of its initial applications, and how it fits into document management and workflow automation.

Brunson, Warren. "Imaging and Document Management." *Netware Connection,* September–October 1993, pp. 9–10 ff. Defines document management systems and identifies important features that the buyer should seek.

Burns, Nina. "Ebb and Flow." *LAN Magazine* 8, no. 5 (May 1993), pp. 118 ff. A detailed analysis of workflow software.

Casady, Mona J., and Dorothy C. Sandburg. *Word/Information Processing: A System Approach,* Cincinnati: South-Western Publishing Company, 1985.

Cosgrove, Nancy. "The Paperless Office: Still a Myth in the Nineties." *The Office* 117, no. 4 (April 1993), pp. 25, 27, and 29. Describes the increasing use of paper in the office, the increased availability of recycled paper, and the growth of America's forests.

Crowley, Aileen. "Road Warriors Stay in Loop with Remote Mail" and "E-mail Vendors Play Remote Card to Keep Customers at the Table." *PC Week* 10, no. 41 (October 18, 1993), p. 125. The first article describes the uses of remote E-mail at a bank and the second details features to look for in E-mail packages.

Eckerson, Wayne. "DEC's Net Makes the World One Big Office." *Network World* 7, no. 27 (July 2, 1990), p. 17. Describes the DEC virtual office.

Eskow, Dennis. "U.S. Navy Declares War on Paper." *PC Week* 7, no. 16 (April 23, 1990), pp. 1 and 6. A description of the Navy's plan to move ships and aircraft to paperless information systems.

Forester, Thomas. *High-Tech Society.* Cambridge, MA: MIT Press, 1987. Includes a discussion of white-collar employment and office automation.

Gable, Michael. "Don't Miss Business." *PC Today* 7, no. 6 (June 1993), pp. 49–52. Defines and describes voice processing systems.

Gill, Eric K. "Long Distance Presentations." *Presentation Products* 7, no. 5 (May 1993), pp. 19–20 ff. Explains how lowered costs and increased use of standards for videoconferencing are likely to expand its use in organizations.

Grunin, Lori. "A Window on the Future." *PC Magazine* 12, no. 9 (May 11, 1993), pp. 289–292 ff. The advantages and disadvantages and component parts of desktop video are presented.

Heichler, Elizabeth. "IBM's 'Office Vision': PCs Push Phones Off the Desk." *InfoWorld* 15, no. 8, pp. 1 and 42. Describes IBM's Person-to-Person/2 desktop conferencing software.

Jones, Virginia. "Micrographics: Still a Hit in the Office Market." *The Office* 117, no. 3 (March 1993), pp. 36 and 38. Reviews common uses of microforms. A buyers guide for reader-printers follows the article.

Kennedy, Randall. "Groupware has Arrived: New Tools for Team Players." *Windows Sources* 1, no. 2 (March 1993), pp. 411–413 ff. A detailed look at groupware products including Lotus Notes and Windows for Workgroups.

Kennedy, Randall. "Run a Virtual Meeting on a LAN." *Windows Sources* 1, no. 8 (September 1993), pp. 179 and 182. Reviews Fujitsu's DeskTop Conferencing software.

Korzeniowski, Paul. "'Paperless Office' Deluged with Paper." *Software Magazine* 10, no. 2 (February 1990), pp. 66–69. Discusses the forces behind the movement to a paperless office and the Department of Defense's Computer Aided Logistics Support program.

Levin, Carol. "Don't Pollute, Telecommute." *PC Magazine* 13, no. 4 (February 22, 1994), p. 32. A discussion of the motivations for telecommuting, including a discussion of compliance with the Clean Air Act of 1990.

Mantelman, Lee. "Workflow Application Tools." *InfoWorld* 15, no. 8 (February 22, 1993), pp. 57 and 58. Categorizes workflow applications and describes the development tools appropriate to each category.

Mendelson, Edward, et.al. "Documents Take Center Stage." *PC Magazine* 12, no. 19 (November 9, 1993). The first of a series of articles reviewing nine word processors, which is the focus of the issue.

Mohan, Suruchi. "Fax-Server Market Heats Up." *LAN Times* 10, no. 8 (September 1993), p. 7. An inset in the article identifies the various methods used to route inbound faxes directly to users.

Ores, Pauline. "Can Form Follow Content." *PC Magazine* 12, no. 9 (November 1993), pp. 203–207 ff. Describes three portable document software packages and SGML technology.

Purchase, Alan, and Carol Glover. *Office of the Future: Stanford Research Institute Business Intelligence Program Guidelines.* Menlo Park, CA: SRI International, April 1976.

Rash, Wayne. "Cut Through the Paper Chase." *Windows Sources* 1, no. 2 (March 1993), pp. 441–447 ff. A detailed description of six desktop and network document and image management software products.

Resnick, Rosalind. "Send Faxes Easily, Quickly." *PC Today* 7, no. 7 (July 1993), pp. 38–40. Explains how you can use a modem to send messages and files to fax machines using information utilities and common carrier mail services. The issue contains several other articles on fax technology.

Rosenberg, Sol. "Go with the Flow." *Netware Solutions* 2, no. 5 (February 1993), pp. 36–38. Analyzes and categorizes workflow software and identifies and compares the attributes of workflow between manual and automated.

Sivula, Chris. "The White-Collar Productivity Push." *Datamation* 36, no. 2 (January 15, 1990), pp. 52–56. A discussion of the impact of office automation on office costs and productivity and the integrated office automation offerings of DEC, IBM, and other major players.

Smith, Tom. "Net Execs Try to Tame FAX Monster." *Network World* 7, no. 18 (April 30, 1990), p. 1 and 8. Describes abuses and cost control measures used by companies employing fax technology.

Turban, Efraim. *Decision Support and Expert Systems: Management Support Systems.* New York: Macmillan Publishing Company, 1990. Chapter 4 includes a discussion of group decision support systems.

Williams, Daniel. "New Technologies for Coordinating Work." *Datamation* 36, no. 10 (May 15, 1990), pp. 92–96. A description of the research efforts underway at a number of universities on groupwork and coordination relationships.

CASE 2 UPGRADING OFFICE INFORMATION SYSTEMS AT THE RIVERBEND ELECTRIC COMPANY

INTEGRATED CASES

BACKGROUND

The corporate headquarters offices and main manufacturing facility of the Riverbend Electric Company, Inc. (REC) are located on Riverbend Parkway in North Alton, Illinois, near the Mississippi River only 10 miles from St. Louis, Missouri. REC manufactures a full line of electronic and magnetic products such as electric coils, transformers, voltage regulators, power distribution relays, and battery chargers, among other items (see Integrated Case 1 for additional background on the firm).

REC has a mature corporate management structure organized along traditional, manufacturing, functional lines. The current organization chart is shown in Figure C2–1. The current president is Mr. Joseph Pyszynski, son of the founder, Mr. Stanley Pyszynski, who is still the majority stockholder. Mr. Delbert St. Onge, executive vice president and brother-in-law of the current president, oversees day-to-day operations. Five vice presidents include Mr. Richard Washington, vice president of administration, Mr. Marvin Albert, vice president of operations and manufacturing, Mr. Mike Chen, vice president of engineering and quality assurance, Ms. Susan Thornberry, vice president of marketing and sales, and Ms. Denise Medeiros, vice president of finance.

In addition to administration, which includes some 20 employees, Mr. Washington is the direct supervisor of the director of management information systems, Ms. Karen Rasp. MIS includes six programmer-analysts assigned to two project teams, the project team leaders, one senior systems programmer, two systems programmers, and two computer operators.

Mr. Albert supervises the shop floor manager for manufacturing at the North Alton plant. The directors of plant operations at the West Martin, Tennessee; Calgary, Canada; and Guadalajara, Mexico, manufacturing facilities also report to Mr. Albert.

Mr. Chen supervises some 35 engineers who are responsible for customer product design. There are also 8 quality assurance engineers and technical specialists who inspect and monitor quality assurance and safety operations for the firm.

Ms. Thornberry's marketing and sales functional area is divided into three sales management groups—electronics, magnetics, and special contracts. Altogether, they include approximately 18 full-time sales personnel with four additional clerical support specialists.

The financial area includes accounting and the traditional data processing operations including accounts receivable, accounts payable, and general ledger operations. Ms. Medeiros has a staff of nine full-time personnel.

CURRENT SITUATION

Joe Pyszynski, Delbert St. Onge, and Richard Washington traditionally meet over coffee on Monday mornings to discuss current activities in the firm. Although Joe prides himself on his ability to delegate authority to his executive vice president and the various functional area vice presidents, he actually keeps a very close handle on all aspects of the firm's operations. On this particular morning, Joe is concerned with office productivity.

"I had a really interesting discussion with Sam Simeon, one of my golf partners, on the course over the weekend. You know Sam, the chief executive officer of the Riverbend area news agency," Joe related to Del and Richard. "Sam was telling me how much his firm has improved normal operations and communications among managers and the overall productivity of operations by upgrading their office computing facilities. Do you think we ought to consider upgrading our office computing facilities?"

Del answered first. "I think it's a very timely idea. As we've grown as a firm over the last several years, it has become increasingly difficult to communicate on a timely basis." Richard was quick to add, "Yes, and I've noticed an increasing number of requests for upgrades to existing office computer equipment. I believe Karen Rasp should study the situation and prepare a formal

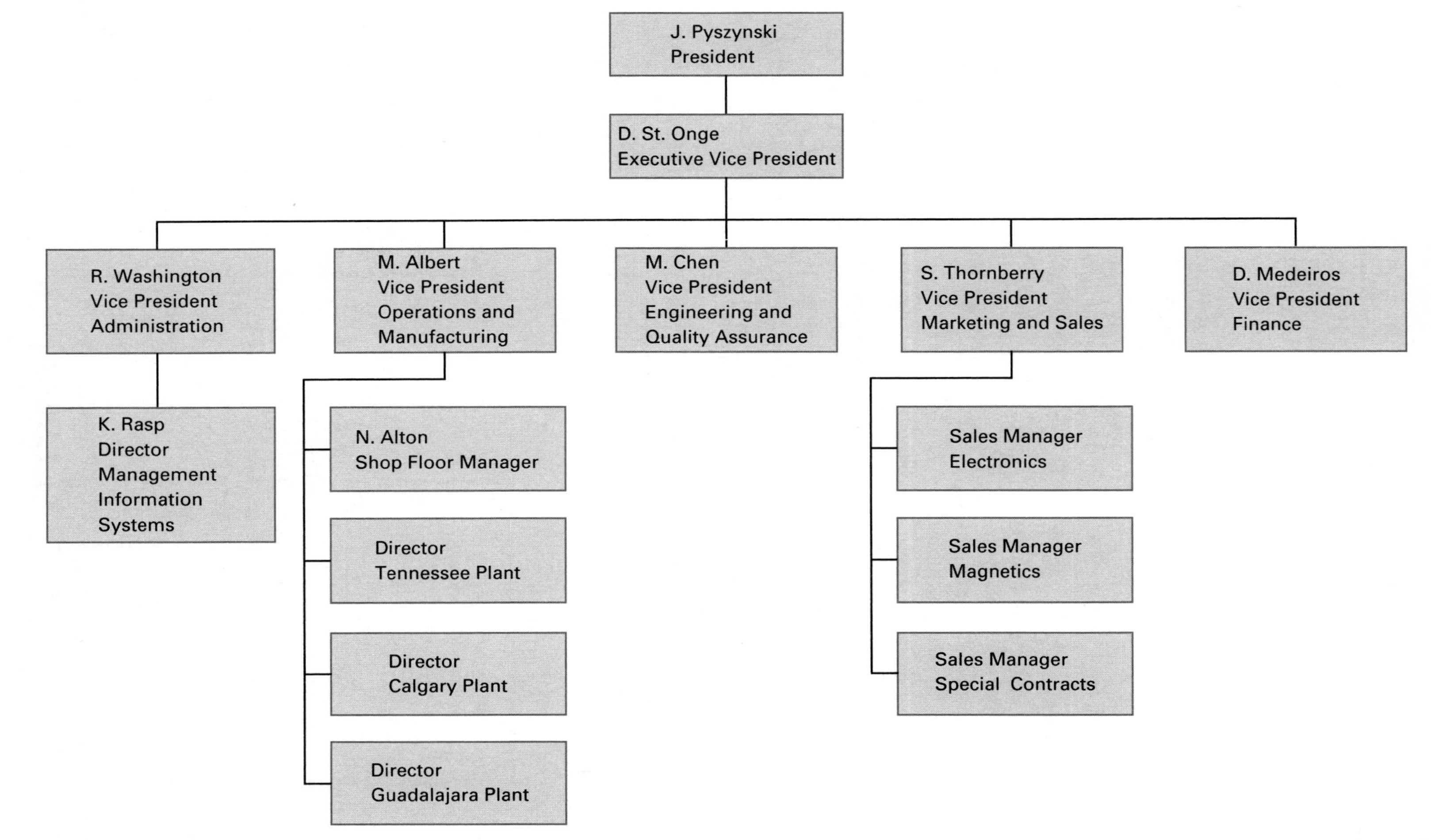

Figure C2–1
Riverbend Electric Company organization chart

recommendation. We want to make certain that our approach to the upgrade is well organized so we don't throw money down the drain buying equipment that we don't really need or that may cause compatibility problems. We've had increasing problems sharing information on the different microcomputers throughout the corporate offices."

"An excellent suggestion," replied Joe. "Del, you and Richard can have Karen prepare a briefing for us—let's say two weeks from today."

The Current Office Environment

Figure C2–2 shows a layout of the corporate offices. The corporate offices occupy two floors of an administrative wing that immediately adjoins the main manufacturing facility. Some shop control offices and engineering offices are located on the manufacturing shop floor.

The MIS Department provides administration, finance, and general data processing support via an IBM AS/400 minicomputer. This computer is about two years old and is located in the MIS Department. Computer terminals are located in all the functional areas. Manufacturing shop floor control and work station scheduling is provided by software located on the AS/400. This support is generally viewed as satisfactory.

The engineering department has a modern, UNIX-based computer network running computer-aided design/computer-aided manufacturing software on SUN workstations. The engineering LAN has a laser printer, flat-bed page scanner, and color plotter that can be shared by the other engineers.

Administrative managers and clerical workers in the other functional areas have a mixture of stand-alone microcomputers, primarily older 80286 and 80386 DOS-based microcomputers that were purchased from several different vendors. None of these microcomputers are networked. Most of them have individual dot-matrix printers, and two clerical workers in the Administration Department have laser printers.

Each functional area has telephone lines dedicated to facsimile machines, but none of the computers have fax-modems. The firm has a voice mail system that is adequate to route incoming telephone calls.

The Desired Office Environment

In completing her analysis of the firm's office technology requirements, Karen determined that each functional area needs to be supported as a work group. Within functional groups, computer-based support should be provided for a number of work group activities, including the ability to

1. Share files, reports, other documents, and other data.
2. Share calendars.

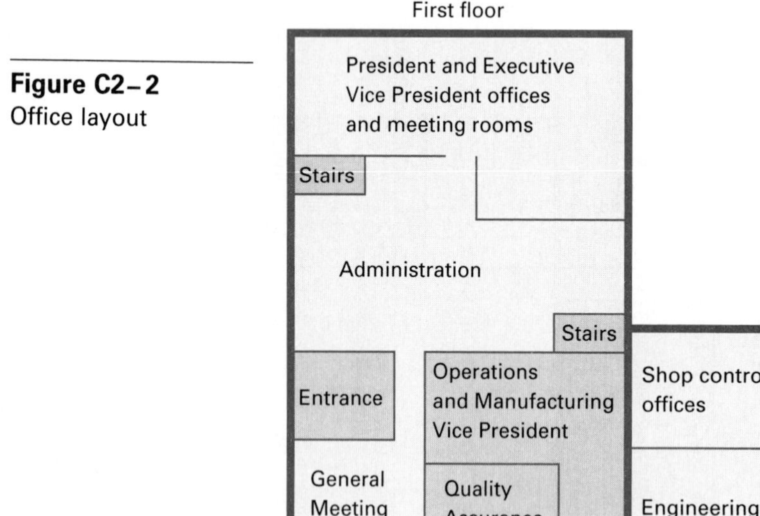

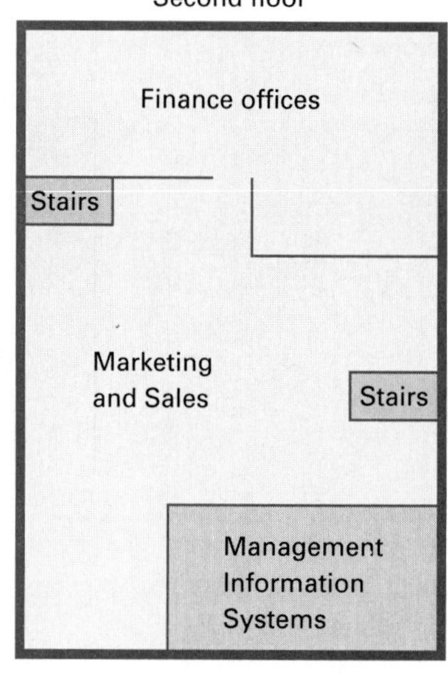

Figure C2–2
Office layout

3. Allow group members to access files, documents, and reports concurrently.
4. Coordinate group meetings.
5. Coordinate project management tasks.
6. Provide electronic mail, bulletin board, and voice mail.

Some work groups have specialized needs. Mike Chen emphasized the need to improve the coordination of engineering efforts by enabling engineers at all four plants to share data files about product engineering specifications. Most clerical workers expressed an interest in learning how to use tools that would provide a "what-you-see-is-what-you-get" approach to word processing. Managers in all areas were interested in the ability to access and share information to obtain ad hoc information needs to support decision-making activities. They also stated that any system acquired should provide for dynamic data exchange between packages to reduce the amount of time currently dedicated to rekeying data that is already available in computer format elsewhere in the firm.

The sales managers went beyond hardware technology requests and emphasized the need for an improved on-line order entry and order monitoring system; however, Karen believed that this particular request was beyond the scope of the assigned analysis task. She did note that individuals in the Marketing Department who prepare advertising materials need either a full-page or hand-held scanner and desktop publishing software. Karen outlined some of the requirements in a table format as shown in Table C2–1. The group size column refers to the number of administrative and clerical workers and managers who need office technology support.

Table C2–1
Draft list of office technology requirements

Work Group	Group Size	Current Computer and Other Equipment	Computer and Other Equipment Needed
Administration	20	8 stand-alone 80286 and 80386 PCs	12 additional PCs
Management Information Systems Department	13	2 stand-alone PCs with terminal emulation hardware/software to link to the AS/400	3 additional PCs
Engineering	43	UNIX network with 30 PCs serving as terminals 3 stand-alone 80486 PCs	8 additional PCs; linkage to other plants
Marketing and Sales	22	6 stand-alone 80286 and 80386 PCs	12 additional PCs; full-page scanner; desktop publishing software
Manufacturing	6	2 stand-alone 80286 PCs	Project management software; 4 additional PCs
Finance	9	8 stand-alone 80286 and 80386 PCs	
All work groups			Work group network; network to link VPs and functional areas; network laser printer for each work group; work group software; graphical user interface software

Case Questions and Exercises

1. Consider the Administration Department as a work group. Mr. Washington wants to acquire 12 additional PCs and to have the MIS Department develop a Novell ethernet network that connects these new PCs with the existing eight 80286 and 80386 PCs. Draw a recommended diagram of the network. List all suggested hardware and software (application package, operating system, and network operating system) components needed for the network.

2. The Engineering and Quality Assurance Department wants to link its existing DOS-based microcomputers and additional microcomputers to a single network with a link to the existing AS/400. Department members also want to link to the Engineering Departments at the three remote plants in Tennessee, Canada, and Mexico. Assume the microcomputer network is similar to that described in question 1 above. Describe the computer hardware and software that would provide linkage to the AS/400 and to the remote plants.

3. Describe the type of office software needed to support work group activities such as calendar sharing, file sharing, electronic mail, bulletin boarding, and the other activities mentioned in the case. Identify specific software packages and the current price of the packages (assume that enough copies would be acquired to support each department and that each department has a work group LAN that is also connected to a central firmwide microcomputer network.)

4. Assume each department will have a work group LAN. Describe the backbone network needed to connect each LAN in order to provide a connection to the AS/400.

5. Identify two alternative full-page scanners the firm could acquire and the associated price of the hardware and software. Identify two different types of laser printers that would serve the firm's needs for the planned work group LANs and the cost of the printers.

PART III COMMON BUSINESS APPLICATION AREAS

So far, you have learned about information systems, the role of systems within organizations, the strategic uses of information systems, and the basic computer resources available to the manager. What you learned generally emphasized the organization as a whole, rather than the major areas of decision making commonly found in organizations. Part 3 focuses on these areas. You will apply what you have learned about information systems and computer system resources to problems in managerial decision making, accounting and finance, marketing, manufacturing and production, and human resources. You will also learn about information tools such as artificial intelligence and expert systems are used to solve managerial problems.

At the end of Part 3, you will understand the nature of the decisions to be made in these areas and the nature of the information systems that are designed to support these decisions.

A Manager's View of Information Systems

Chapter Outline

Manager's View

The process of management involves planning, organizing, directing, and controlling people and activities. At each level of management, the responsibilities for handling these tasks differ. Top-level managers are responsible for establishing organizational objectives. Middle-level managers organize and control the organization's resources to achieve these objectives, whereas lower-level managers supervise day-to-day activities.

Each of these three levels of management has different information systems needs. First-line supervisors require feedback about day-to-day activities. Middle-level managers need information that will enable them to reallocate resources to achieve objectives. Top-level managers use external information to identify new business opportunities and to establish goals for the firm. This chapter helps you understand information systems that support management decision making at the operational, tactical, and strategic planning levels. Knowledge of the nature of operational, tactical, and strategic planning information systems is necessary to understand the application of these information systems to the problem of managing the marketing, finance, accounting, production, and human resource functions.

The development of information systems within organizations has been characterized by a process of evolution involving more than technology alone. This process requires planning, a balanced mix of application development, and leadership on the part of both management information systems (MIS) professionals and user-managers. In this chapter, you'll learn about the roles and responsibilities of user-managers in determining which types of data processing projects support business goals and in working with the MIS function to accomplish these projects.

THE FUNCTIONS OF MANAGEMENT

Management is the process of directing tasks and organizing resources to achieve organizational goals. The main functions of management are planning, organizing, leading, and controlling. **Planning** is deciding what to do. This function entails evaluating the organization's resources and environment and establishing a set of organizational goals. Once these goals are established, the manager must develop tactics to achieve these goals and create a decision-making process that will monitor the results.

Let's return to our earlier case study of the office equipment dealer. During the mid- to late 1970s, the dealership's primary product was copier equipment. Growing competition, brought on by the introduction of Japanese products and an increase in the number of dealers in the market area, made top management realize that it would either have to introduce new products or create more effective advertising and service programs. As a result, a company goal was established: to generate at least 50 percent of the company's revenues from microcomputer and related devices by 1990.

The second managerial function is **organizing.** Organizing is the art of deciding how to achieve goals. This decision requires developing the best organizational structure, acquiring and training personnel, and establishing communications networks. The manager of the office equipment dealership will have to organize resources to achieve the objective. A computer department may be organized and staffed with salespeople, technical support representatives, training personnel, and systems analysts to help support the marketing effort. Communications channels between managers, customers, manufacturers, salespeople, and technical specialists will all have to be established under this new plan.

Leading, the third managerial function, involves directing and motivating employees to achieve the organization's goals. The manager of the office dealership may need to develop incentive programs to motivate salespeople and to organize team-building efforts to maintain good morale. The fourth managerial function, **controlling,** enables the manager to determine if the organization's performance is on target. He or she may develop and use performance standards to assess employee performance. Information systems can also provide feedback on how effectively financial and physical resources are being used to achieve business goals. Reports that summarize sales statistics and compare planned versus actual expenses provide information that can be used to control the use of the organization's resources. The basic managerial functions are summarized in Figure 9–1.

Besides handling the basic managerial functions of planning, organizing, leading, and controlling, managers are also responsible for adapting to changes in the internal and external environment. When a new competitor unexpectedly enters the marketplace or when a key manager suddenly quits, the manager of the office equipment

Figure 9–1
Managerial functions

Planning	Establishing organizational goals Developing strategies to achieve goals
Organizing	Developing the structure of the organization Acquiring human resources
Leading	Motivating and managing employees Forming task groups
Controlling	Evaluating performance Controlling the organization's resources

dealership has to investigate possible alternatives and solutions. These decisions, too, may require access to information on an on-demand or ad hoc basis.

MANAGERIAL ROLES

Successful management also requires performing a variety of managerial roles. Mintzberg (1975) studied three different managerial roles: *interpersonal, informational,* and *decisional*.

The manager's interpersonal roles include the figurehead role, the leader role, and the liaison role. In the figurehead role, the manager performs ceremonial duties such as greeting job candidates and dignitaries. As much as 12 percent of the manager's time is spent in these roles. In the leadership role, the manager must hire, train, and motivate employees. Informal leadership is a good measure of real power. Finally, in the liaison role, the manager makes contacts outside the vertical chain of command. Most studies of managers show that they spend as much time with their peers and with people outside their units as they do with their own subordinates. For example, in a study of foremen, Robert Guest found that managers spent 44 percent of their time with peers, 46 percent of their time with people inside their units, and only 10 percent of their time with their superiors. Chief executives make contact with a wide range of people, including subordinates, clients, business associates, government officials, trade union officers, and suppliers.

The second type of role Mintzberg depicts is the informational role. Managers have formal access to information from virtually every internal staff member as well as extensive external information. In Mintzberg's research, 70 percent of incoming mail was informational. Communications is a large part of the manager's job. In fact, monitoring or scanning the environment for information is one of the most important tasks of managers.

The manager is also a disseminator of information. In this role, the manager may choose to pass certain information along to peers and to subordinates. In the spokesperson role, the manager provides information to the external community: to suppliers, to the press, to lobbying organizations, and to government officials.

The decisional roles of the manager are of primary importance. They include the entrepreneurial role, the disturbance handler role, the resource allocator role, and the negotiator role.

In an entrepreneurial role, the manager is constantly looking for new ideas. An effective chief executive may initiate and keep track of as many as 50 different projects. Some of these may involve new products, others may relate to organizational changes, and still others may attempt to identify new markets. "Like jugglers, chief executives keep a number of projects in the air; periodically, one comes down, is given a new burst of energy, and sent back to orbit." (Mintzberg, 1975.)

Sometimes the manager has to be a disturbance handler. When internal or external disputes affect the company's operations, a senior manager may have to respond to pressures. The manager must act when a strike occurs, when a major advertising account defaults, or when a supplier defaults on a contract.

Another decisional role is the resource allocator role. As a resource allocator, the manager determines who will get what. He or she may decide how much money to spend on recruiting and training new sales personnel and how much time to spend on developing an advertising program. In the role of resource allocator, executives face very complex choices. Yet, one common solution to selecting what projects will be

Box 9–1 The Manager's Job: Folklore and Fact

Henry Mintzberg discussed the role of the manager in his classic article, "The Manager's Job: Folklore and Fact," which appeared in the *Harvard Business Review.* In the classic view, managers are responsible for planning, organizing, coordinating, and controlling. In reality, Mintzberg argues, these words tell us little about what managers actually do. The following four myths are not confirmed by the facts.

Folklore: The manager plans in a careful and systematic way.

Fact: In contrast, managers work at an unrelenting pace, focusing on hundreds of brief and varied activities.

Chief executives encounter a steady stream of callers and mail from morning until night. In one study, Guest found that foremen averaged 583 activities per eight-hour shift, or one every 48 seconds. Rather than planned, 93 percent of the verbal contacts of executives are ad hoc. Managers are constantly interrupted; they try to balance the time they have available for ever-present obligations with the time they need to invest in getting things done. Rather than charting complex strategic plans, most senior executives have intentions that loom in their heads and guide their decisions.

Folklore: The effective manager spends most of the time planning and delegating and less time doing regular duties such as seeing customers and negotiating disputes.

Fact: Managers spend a great deal of their time doing regular tasks, participating in ritual activities, and processing "soft" information about the external environment.

Many senior executives spend a good deal of their time performing ceremonial duties, such as presiding at holiday dinners and giving out gold watches. They also may have access to soft external information (e.g., golf course information) about customers or competitors. Sometimes, they are called upon to greet important incoming visitors, job candidates, and vendors. All of these activities are fairly routine tasks, but they still need to be done.

Folklore: The senior manager uses aggregated and summarized information that a management information system provides.

Fact: Managers prefer information from telephone calls, personal conversations, and meetings.

On the average, according to Mintzberg's data, managers spend about 80 percent of their time in verbal communications. In addition, managers are inundated by mail—even though not much of the mail provides interesting, current information on such things as competitor strategies and customer preferences. In one study, five executives responded to 2 out of 40 routine reports and to 4 items out of 104 periodicals in five weeks.

supported is to pick the person, not the proposal. The manager tends to support the projects that are proposed by people he or she trusts.

The final decisional role is negotiator. The manager is responsible for representing the organization in bargaining with others—with customers, with shipping companies, and with manufacturers. Negotiating with equipment manufacturers for exclusive marketing and service rights for certain lines of equipment is an example of this role.

The interpersonal, informational, and decisional roles of managers are summarized in Figure 9–2. Although the basic tasks of planning, organizing, leading, and controlling are significant activities, most managers are constantly responding to internal and external changes and are responsible for communicating information within the firm and to external groups.

One of the keys to managerial performance is the ability to distinguish between *efficiency* and *effectiveness.* **Efficiency** is "doing things right," whereas **effectiveness**

In contrast to the hard data they receive, managers love soft information, especially hearsay and speculation. Managers use information in two important ways: to identify problems and opportunities and to build mental models of such things as budget forecasts and customer buying patterns. In specific decision situations, managers use small tidbits of data to build models.

Richard Neustadt, who studied the information-collecting habits of Presidents Franklin Roosevelt, Truman, and Eisenhower, commented that "it is not information of a general sort that helps a president see personal stakes; not summaries, not surveys. . . . Rather . . . it is the odds and ends of tangible detail that pieced together in his mind illuminate the underside of issues put to him. To help himself, he must reach out as widely as he can for every scrap of fact, opinion, gossip, bearing on his interests and relationships as president. He must become his own director of his own central intelligence."[1]

Managers cherish hearsay because today's gossip may be tomorrow's fact. Managers rely on verbal information that is stored in people's brains, not in their files. Sometimes it is difficult for managers to delegate tasks because much of the critical detail they expect to be used in making decisions is stored in their memories, not in reports and office records.

Folklore: Management is a science and a profession.

Fact: Management is not a science; managers process information and make decisions using judgment and intuition, not preprogrammed logic.

If management were a science, managers could make decisions using systematic, predetermined programs and procedures. But this is not the case. Managers make hundreds of judgment calls per day, given the hundreds of brief, fragmented issues and problems they must confront. They use verbal communications extensively to get a grasp of critical facts. Because of the nature of managerial work, it is very difficult for science to improve it.

As you can see from Mintzberg's article, managers have a variety of roles. Their performance depends largely on how well they respond to the pressures of their jobs. A large part of their time is spent assimilating and disseminating important information about the organization's people and problems through verbal communications. In general, the pressures of a manager's job encourage constant interruption, the need to respond to many different stimuli, the desire to get tangible detail, and the importance of making small but crucial decisions.

[1]Henry Mintzberg, "The Manager's Job: Folklore and Fact," *Harvard Business Review*, March–April 1990, pp. 163–76. Originally appeared in *Harvard Business Review* in July–August 1975.

is "doing the right things right." In a business context, efficiency means being able to achieve high levels of output with a given base of inputs, or resources. An *efficient* secretary, for example, may be able to type 75 words per minute and to generate hundreds of letters per week. But she or he would only be considered *effective* if these efforts support the goals of the business.

Most managers are responsible for monitoring the performance of people, programs, and other resources that are organized to support the achievement of organizational goals. Managers are responsible for maintaining existing performance as well as for organizing resources to improve performance. They must also develop criteria to measure successful performance. The information they use to make decisions should provide measures of performance that relate to the successful achievement of business goals. If performance is not suitable, information from reports should highlight the discrepancy between planned and actual performance so that the manager can study the situation and reallocate resources effectively.

Figure 9–2
Managerial roles

Interpersonal	Figurehead Leader Liaison
Informational	Monitor Disseminator Spokesperson
Decisional	Entrepreneur Disturbance handler Resource allocator Negotiator

THE LEVELS OF MANAGEMENT

The levels of management consist of top, middle-level, and first-line management. Members of top management are the organization's senior executives. Their most important role is establishing the goals of the organization. They are typically responsible for interacting with representatives of the external environment, such as financial institutions, political figures, and important suppliers and customers.

Middle-level managers are responsible for allocating resources so that the objectives of top management are accomplished. They do so by implementing plans and by supervising lower-level managers under their functional area of responsibility. A sales manager, for example, organizes resources—salespeople's time, training budgets, entertainment budgets—to achieve sales results that are consistent with the growth plans of senior management. If these goals are not being met, then the sales manager needs to study the existing scope and level of sales force activity and reallocate resources accordingly. Other types of middle-level managers are research directors, plant managers, market research directors, and directors of data processing.

First-line supervisors are responsible for supervising day-to-day operations. They typically supervise functions such as order entry, credit checking, inventory control, and preventive maintenance. If problems such as errors in pricing or frequent breakdowns of equipment on the plant floor occur, first-line supervisors work to solve them. They use information such as quality control reports and inventory turnover reports to supervise the activities for which they are responsible and to make sure that performance is suitable.

THE ACTIVITIES OF THE ORGANIZATION

The activities of an organization are of three kinds: operational, tactical, and strategic planning, as shown in Figure 9–3. Operations are the day-to-day activities of the firm that involve acquiring and consuming resources. First-line supervisors must identify, collect, and register all transactions that result in acquiring or expending these resources. When sales are made or goods are shipped, a department manager needs to record these events. These day-to-day transactions produce data that are the basis for *operational systems.*

The tactical function of an organization is the responsibility of its middle-level managers. They review operational activities to make sure that the organization is meeting its goals and not wasting its resources. The time frame for tactical activities may be month to month, quarter to quarter, or year to year. For example, orders for raw materials might be monitored monthly, productivity might be assessed quarterly, and department budgets might be reviewed annually. Managers responsible for control have

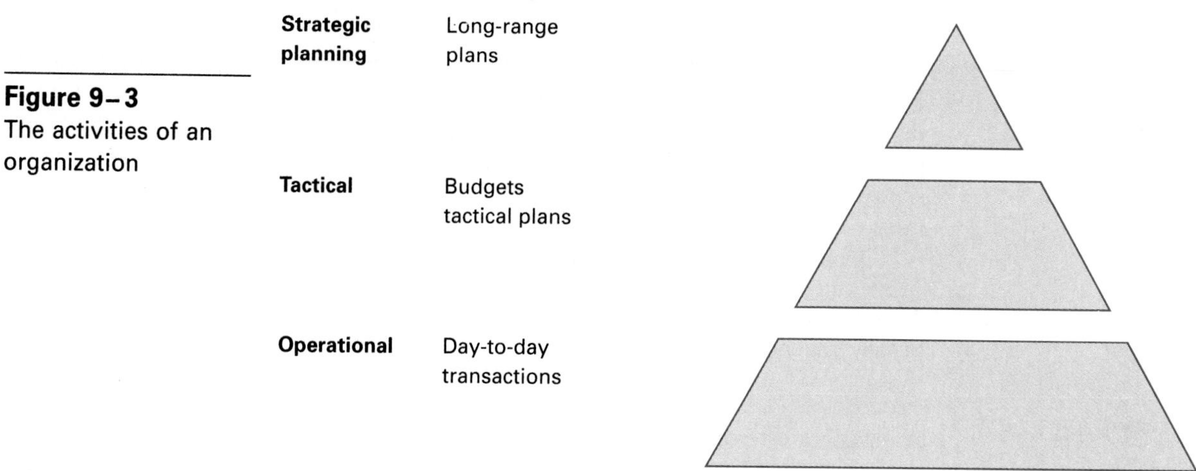

Figure 9–3
The activities of an organization

to decide how to allocate resources to achieve business objectives. Data that can be used to predict future trends can be useful in helping managers make these resource allocation decisions.

Strategic planning is carried out by the top management of the organization. Though managers responsible for operational and tactical decision making are primarily involved in reviewing internal data, the managers responsible for planning are also interested in external information. They need to set the organization's long-range goals, for example, by deciding whether to introduce new products, to build new physical plant facilities, or to invest in technology. In order to make these decisions, they need to know the activities of competing firms, interest rates, and trends in government regulation. Problems addressed by strategic planners involve long-range analysis and prediction and often require months and years to resolve.

A FRAMEWORK FOR INFORMATION SYSTEMS

Each of these levels—operational, tactical, and strategic planning—requires different information systems, as shown in Figure 9–4.

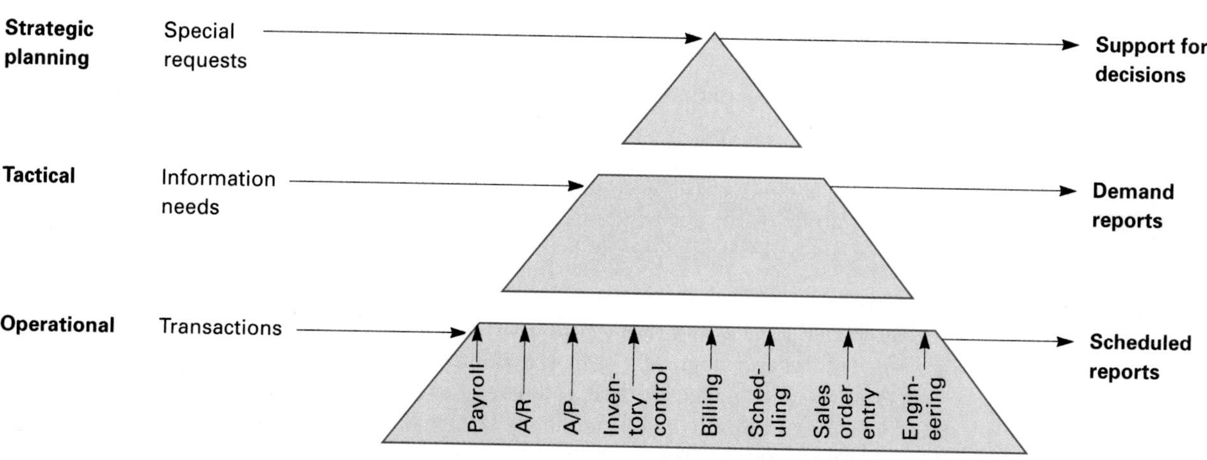

Figure 9–4 A framework for information systems

Operational Systems

At the **operational systems** level the primary concern is to collect, validate, and record transactional data describing the acquisition or disbursement of corporate resources. Financial data on accounts receivable, accounts payable, payroll, and cash receipts must be recorded as they occur. When a sale is transacted, data on the items ordered are recorded, the inventory level for these items is adjusted, a shipping label and packing slip are prepared, and an invoice is generated. The original transaction—the sale of the item—creates numerous transactions in order processing, inventory, and billing.

Operational-level information systems often have the following characteristics.

Repetitiveness. The information operational-level information systems produce is usually generated repetitively at periodic intervals, such as daily, weekly, or monthly.

Predictability. The information they produce usually does not contain any surprises or unexpected results for the manager or other users of the system. That is, people are paid what they were expected to be paid and customers are billed for what they purchased during the month.

Emphasis on the Past. The information produced usually describes past activities of the organization. For example, the output of a payroll system describes employees' past work. The checks to vendors describe past purchases by the organization. Customer invoices describe past sales to them. Stock reports describe past changes in inventory.

Detailed Nature. The information produced is very detailed. That is, paychecks provide detailed information on the work week of each employee and the specifics of each employee's gross and net pay. Customer invoices specify details regarding purchases made during the period, the terms under which the purchases must be repaid, and the total amount, including taxes and other charges, due.

Internal Origin. The data for operational systems usually spring entirely from internal sources. That is, the data for paychecks come from internal documents such as time cards and employee master records. The data for customer invoices come from sales orders and shipping documents.

Structured Form. The form of the data used as input and the form of the information produced by operational-level systems are usually very structured. That is, the data on time cards are carefully formatted in identical fashion on each. Or the data on each customer invoice are carefully formatted in identical fashion. In short, the form and format of the data input and the information output of the systems are highly structured.

Great Accuracy. The accuracy of the data used as input to such systems and of the output produced by such systems is usually very high. The data input and information output are carefully checked in a variety of ways.

Tactical Systems

The second level in the framework consists of **tactical systems**. Tactical systems provide middle-level managers with the information they need to monitor and control operations and to allocate their resources more effectively. In tactical systems, transactions data are summarized, aggregated, or analyzed. Tactical systems are designed to generate a variety of reports, including *summary reports, exception reports,* and *ad hoc reports.*

Summary reports provide management with important totals, averages, key data, and abstracts on the activities of the organization. An example of a summary report might be a list of the total regular and overtime hours earned at each plant for the week by job classification. Another example is a list of total weekly sales, by salesperson, by product, and by sales region.

Exception reports warn managers when results from a particular operation have exceeded or not met the expected standard for the organization. An example of an exception report is a list of all plants that have logged more overtime hours than expected for the week. Another example is a list of those sales personnel whose sales fall in the top and bottom 10 percent of the organization.

Ad hoc reports are reports that managers need, usually quickly, that may never be needed again. Ad hoc reports present information that the manager needs to solve a unique problem. An example of this type of report might be a list of the total number of employees absent during the week arranged by plant and by job title along with the hours or days missed. Another example might be a report that presents the production record of each plant for the week. These reports might be requested only when an exception report shows high overtime earnings at certain plants. The manager may ask for a number of ad hoc reports such as these to identify the nature of the overtime problem.

Tactical information systems differ from operational information systems in their basic purpose: Their purpose is not to support the execution of operational tasks but to help the manager control these operations. As a result, the types of data used as inputs and the information produced as outputs also differ. Tactical information systems often have these characteristics.

Periodic Nature. The information from a tactical system is sometimes produced periodically. For example, a branch credit manager for an organization may receive a weekly report showing the total dollar amount of accounts that are more than 60 days overdue, 90 days overdue, and in the hands of a collection agency. The report might also compare these three dollar amounts with the same data from other branches of the organization and with the same data for last year at this date and last month at this date. Using the data from other branches and from previous periods as standards for comparison, the credit manager can decide whether the overdue account totals are within the normal range for the branch or whether the difference between the amounts warrants special managerial action or decisions. Thus, this information system provides the means by which the credit manager can quickly identify problems and bring them under control.

However, tactical information systems may also produce information when it is needed, on an ad hoc basis. For instance, once the credit manager has identified a problem with overdue accounts, he or she may wish to query the accounting system database to find out what customer data, if any, correlate with those who have credit problems. That is, is there a relationship between family income and credit difficulty? Is there a connection between location or address and credit difficulty? Is there a relationship between age and credit difficulty? Is there a link between the number of years that customers have resided in the same home or apartment and credit difficulty? Is there a connection between home ownership versus renting and credit difficulty?

The answers to these questions, and others that the credit manager pursues by querying the accounting system records, may assist in identifying the problem or proposing new credit limitations or requirements for credit status within the organization.

Unexpected Findings. The information produced by a tactical information system may not be the information that was expected to be produced. For example, in querying the accounting system database, the credit manager may find that the major customer characteristic correlating with credit difficulty is the relationship between type of position and type of employer. Further investigation may reveal that organizations in a particular industry have had to cut their workforces and have laid off selected workers in certain positions. Such findings may lead to a review of all customers who work in that industry in those positions to find ways to solve or ease their credit problems and to prevent them from becoming bad debts to the organization.

Comparative Nature. The information produced is usually comparative in nature rather than merely descriptive. Tactical information systems should provide managers with information that alerts them to variances from accepted standards or results that are not within the normal range so that remedial action can be taken swiftly. This type of tactical information system is analogous to process control systems that monitor output constantly and provide feedback when output parameters are at variance with accepted standards.

An example drawn from the home would be the heating system. As long as the temperature of the air in the house falls within the range specified on the thermostat, no action on the part of the heating system is required. When the air temperature falls below the thermostat setting, however, the thermostat sends a signal to the furnace to turn on. When the air reaches the temperature on the thermostat, it sends a signal to the furnace to turn off.

With comparative overdue account information from other branches and other periods, the credit manager can determine whether the amount overdue is normal or beyond acceptable limits. In some cases, the manager is given the standard by top management. That is, top management may have set a credit goal of no more than 5 percent bad debts. Reports comparing the actual bad debts to this standard help the manager spot credit problems quickly.

Summary Form. The information produced is usually not detailed but in summary form. The credit manager is not interested in a detailed listing of each customer account and its balance. In large organizations, that would be an enormous quantity of data and would not, therefore, be information to the manager. What the manager needs is summary information relating to credit performance or balances of accounts that are overdue or in collection.

Both Internal and External Sources. The data used for input to the system may not be confined to sources internal to the organization. In our example, the credit manager compared the information pertaining to problem customers to other branches, to other periods from the same organization, or to a goal set by top management. The credit manager might also have compared the branch's credit information with the average overdue account experience reported for the whole industry of which the organization is a part. Such a comparison might show that though the branch is experiencing an increase in credit problems, so is the whole industry. Further investigation may reveal that a downturn in the economy is the likely culprit, not any unusual credit policies of the organization.

Thus, tactical information systems differ from operational information systems not only in their intended purpose but also in the regularity with which information is produced, the predictability of the results, the comparative nature of the information, the amount of detail produced, and the rigidity of the structure of the information.

Box 9–2 How Information Technology Supports Tactical Decisions

Information technology—which includes databases, telecommunications networks, personal computers, optical scanners, and a host of other technologies—is rapidly becoming an effective tool for monitoring and tracking critical data. These examples will show you how.

In one food marketing company, data is transmitted via a telecommunications network to inform manufacturing plants to beef up inventories in response to unanticipated sales trends. Timely data helps management reduce the "react time" when actual sales are greater than forecasted sales.

Sometimes shifts in government laws require quick alterations in business strategy. In 1986, a tax law affecting insurance companies was passed. One insurance firm immediately extracted policyholder data from its files in order to inform its clients of the changes, whereas other companies scrambled to obtain lists of customers who would be affected by the change. The first company encouraged its customers to pay back loans against their whole life policies because loan interest was no longer deductible. The net effect of the program was that customers were convinced to repay millions of dollars in loans and to reinvest in single-premium life insurance programs, which were considered liquid and nontaxable under the new law.

Modern tactical systems can also detect deviations in equipment performance in a manufacturing environment. If problems are cited early, preventive maintenance procedures can minimize equipment downtime. Carefully tuned production machinery can also improve the quality of manufactured goods. Sophisticated monitoring devices used by paper companies double-check paper thickness and enable engineers to make modifications in production processes if flaws are detected.

Information systems can also help managers market new products and services. Trust officers at one commercial bank scanned through a database of trust accounts to draw the names of beneficiaries. When the trust initiator died, these beneficiaries were good prospects for banking services. With the use of a tracking system to generate their names when they became the eligible age, the trust officer could establish a banking relationship with inheritors at an opportune time.

Still other information systems enable manufacturers to control their inventories. An automobile manufacturer is linked electronically to the order-entry system of one of its major suppliers, a steel company. By ordering electronically, the manufacturer can rely on timely delivery and reduce its own in-house inventory investment. For decades, Japanese electronics manufacturers have been linked to their suppliers, in some cases ordering inventory at the beginning of each day for that day's manufacturing operations. This strategy, known as just-in-time manufacturing, is rapidly becoming a reality in many U.S. companies because of information systems linking buyers and suppliers.

Another example from the food industry shows how computer systems can aid just-in-time delivery. One national food company uses sales trends for various inventory items to stock the grocery stores it serves. Each store has a different inventory mix because of regional and ethnic differences in various neighborhoods. Truck drivers with inventory items did not always have timely information on previous day's items sold to adjust their deliveries. That changed when the food company put microcomputers in its 1,000 delivery trucks. Each morning, each driver's microcomputer receives data on the recommended stock mix for each store on his or her route. At the end of the day, drivers key in information on deliveries made and stale stock removed from the store shelves. This system helps the drivers respond to local store sales trends and also enables the food company's customers, the grocery stores, to manage their inventories more effectively.

Finally, intelligent information systems can create incentives for customers to buy more. Traditionally, customer discounts are based upon volume purchases. Opticians receive consignment inventory from a contact lens manufacturer, based on their ability to turn it over 13 times a year. In response to this benefit, the opticians attempt to push this manufacturer's line. On-line information about inventory turnover in each of the stores helps the contact lens manufacturer adjust production in response to sales trends and boosts the firm's market share.

In general, tactical systems are becoming more flexible and more closely tied to a firm's competitive strategy. Information systems enable a manufacturer to cut inventories and to troubleshoot equipment downtime problems. They help marketers zero in on the most profitable market targets and financial services companies to identify the most profitable products and services. Throughout this text, you will have an opportunity to learn more about tactical systems and how they enable managers to allocate resources more effectively.

Source: William J. Bruns, Jr., and E. Warren McFarlan, "Information Technology Puts Power in Control Systems," *Harvard Business Review*, September–October 1987, pp. 89–92.

Strategic Planning Systems

The third level in the framework for information systems is **strategic planning.** Strategic planning–level information systems are designed to provide top management with information that assists them in making long-range planning decisions for the organization. The distinction between strategic planning information systems and tactical information systems is not always clear because both types of information systems may use some of the same data. For example, when budgeting information is used to help middle-level managers allocate resources to best meet organizational goals, budgeting becomes a tactical decision activity. When budgeting information is used by top management to plan the long-term activities of an organization, budgeting becomes a strategic planning activity. In either case, accurate budget information delivered in a timely fashion to managers is an important function of the financial information system of the organization. However, the key differences between the systems have to do with who uses the data and what they are using it for.

Strategic planning information systems are ordinarily used by top management for setting long-term organizational goals. Tactical information systems are typically used by middle managers to control their areas of supervision and to allocate resources to meet organizational goals set by top management. Though the data used in tactical and strategic planning information systems sometimes overlap, typically there are differences in the data used by the two information systems. Strategic planning information systems often have these characteristics.

Ad Hoc Basis. The information may be produced either regularly or periodically. For example, top management uses periodic accounting system reports such as the income statement, balance sheet, statement of sources and uses of funds, and capital statement in its planning function. However, strategic planning information is more often produced when it is needed, on an ad hoc basis. For example, marketing analysis information pertaining to a new product or to a new cluster of stores may be requested when organization planners are considering the addition of several new stores in a new region.

Unexpected Information. The information produced by the system may not be the information that was anticipated. For instance, economic forecast information may be requested for the economy as a whole and for the industry in particular. The results of the economic forecast may be a surprise to organization planners. Or, the results of a marketing survey of potential customers to be served by the new stores described above may produce store locations that had not been predicted or expected by planners.

Predictive Nature. The information produced is usually predictive of future events rather than descriptive of past events. Long-range planners try to set a course for an organization through an uncharted future. Their primary task is to choose a route that will improve the organization's level of success. The information that the strategic planning system provides should help these planners reduce the risks involved in their choice of routes.

Because organizational long-range planning groups make decisions that will affect the organization for some time in the future, much of the information used in the system is future oriented and predictive in nature. For example, forecasts of future economic conditions, projections of new product sales, and forecasts of the changing demographic characteristics of target customer groups are all forms of information that may be used in strategic planning information systems to help planners make decisions.

Summary Form. The information produced is usually not detailed but in summary form. Long-range planners are not usually interested in detailed information; they are usually concerned with more global data. For instance, long-range planners are not ordinarily concerned about the details of customer invoices. They are more likely to be interested in the overall buying trends reflected in the summaries of sales by product group. And they are not usually interested in the specific demographic characteristics of a particular customer. They are more likely to be concerned with the overall demographic characteristics of groups of customers.

External Data. A large part of the data used for input to the system may be acquired from sources external to the organization. For example, information pertaining to investment opportunities, rates of borrowed capital, demographic characteristics of a market group, and economic conditions must be obtained from data maintained outside the organization.

To assist long-range planners, MIS personnel may help them select a variety of on-line external databases to provide them with the information they need quickly and in a form that can be manipulated further. Long-range planners may wish to obtain access to databases containing economic data from which forecasts might be made, for example. They may also wish to obtain access to databases that contain census data from which demographic trends and forecasts can be drawn.

Unstructured Format. The data used for input to the system may contain data that are unstructured in format. For instance, forecasts of future market trends may use the opinions of store buyers, salespeople, or market analysts obtained in casual conversations.

Subjectivity. The data used for input to the system may be highly subjective and their accuracy may be suspect. For example, forecasts of future stock market trends may be based partly on rumors reported by brokers. Forecasts of the expected market share of your organization within the industry might use the opinions of industry observers who are basing their information on rumors and on conversations held with a variety of industry personnel.

A summary of the characteristics of information systems at the operational, tactical, and strategic planning levels is shown in Table 9–1. As you can see from this chart,

Table 9–1
A comparison of information systems in operational, tactical, and strategic planning systems

Summary Classification of Information Systems

Characteristic	Operational	Tactical	Strategic Planning
Frequency	Regular, repetitive	Mostly regular	Often ad hoc
Dependability of results	Expected results	Some surprises may occur	Results often contain surprises
Time period covered	The past	Comparative	Predictive of the future
Level of detail	Very detailed	Summaries of data	Summaries of data
Source of data	Internal	Internal and external	Mostly external
Nature of data	Highly structured	Some unstructured data	Highly unstructured
Accuracy	Highly accurate data	Some subjective data used	Highly subjective data
Typical user	First-line supervisors	Middle managers	Top management
Level of decision	Task oriented	Oriented toward control and resource allocation	Goal oriented

first-line supervisors use operational information systems and middle-level managers use tactical information systems. The top executives of the organization use strategic planning systems.

SEQUENCE OF DEVELOPMENT OF MANAGEMENT INFORMATION SYSTEMS

Experience has shown that the base of operational systems has to be in place before tactical systems can be built. This is because the data input into operational systems become the source of data for tactical systems. For example, sales transactions must be captured at the operational level to summarize these data over a six-month or yearly time frame for use in summary reports. However, tactical systems do not necessarily have to be in place for strategic planning systems to be developed. The latter rely heavily on external data sources.

As you learned earlier, data and information differ. Data are the individual elements of a transaction, such as item number, item quantity, and price on a sales order transaction. Information, on the other hand, is data with meaning for decision making. An information system is a set of procedures organized to generate information that enables managers to review operational, tactical, and strategic planning activities. A management information system, in particular, is designed to provide information for effective planning and tactical decision making.

Data are often aggregated to provide the information needed for tactical information systems. Therefore, most management information systems need a foundation of operational-level data systems. In the next section, we'll walk through several information systems within various types of organizations.

CASES IN INFORMATION SYSTEMS

Cases of information systems in an insurance company, a food marketing company, and a county welfare agency illustrate a range of applications that are designed to produce information for operational and tactical decision making. Each of the systems described in these cases supports important business objectives.

General Life Insurance Company

Early in the insurance business, massive amounts of paperwork involved in creating, maintaining, and generating bills for policies made computer systems essential at General Life Insurance Company. On-line systems supporting policy screening, creation, and issuance were designed in the 1970s. Using an on-line system, an operator keys in new application information at a CRT. As new information arrives from physicians to update an application, it is used to update policy information on-line. When all information is compiled, a worksheet is created for an underwriter who evaluates the insurability of potential customers. Policy information is then entered into the system and a policy data sheet is created. On-line access to policy information makes it possible to handle inquiries from policyholders and from agents seeking information about policy status.

During the 1970s an on-line data communications network was set up to link the home office with insurance sales agencies. This system makes it possible for sales agents to inquire on-line about policies and to enter application information at remote sites. It also makes it possible to update policies in the home office.

Many of the newer systems at General Life provide the firm with a competitive advantage in product marketing and customer service. General Life has developed software available through its network that enables local sales agents to analyze alternative product and service options on a timely basis (for example, what if a customer changes to this option after 10 years instead of 5?). This software provides the information needed to close many sales immediately.

One of the major projects at General Life today is developing software for producing new insurance products. With competitors introducing new products all the time, it is important to have new services and product options "on the shelf" for new marketing efforts. Market studies forecasting customer needs can provide senior management with valuable information for new product planning.

Figure 9–5 summarizes the operational, tactical, and strategic planning applications at General Life Insurance Company.

New systems projects are clearly directed at cutting costs, improving productivity, and providing managers with better information for decision making. Increasingly, sales managers are designing applications that will help them analyze product profitability, agent profitability, customer profitability, and the impact of marketing strategies on sales. Information on customer profitability, for example, helps the company concentrate its resources (such as salespeople's time or in-house presentations) on the most profitable customers. This supports the tactical objective of achieving maximum profitability.

Dellco Foods, Inc.

At Dellco Foods, Inc., a company that manufactures, markets, and distributes food products, the information systems at the operational and tactical levels support marketing, physical distribution, production, and administration.

The information systems in physical distribution are operational. Orders are entered at six service centers, and order data are used to update accounts receivable and distribution files. Invoices can be printed out either at the originating location or at a service center nearest the customer's location. As a result, payments can be received earlier, and cash flow improves. An accounts receivable status report provides on-line credit checking so that orders submitted by delinquent accounts will not be filled without prepayment.

Once order data are keyed in, customer service personnel have immediate access to an open order file that can be used to respond to customer inquiries about deliveries

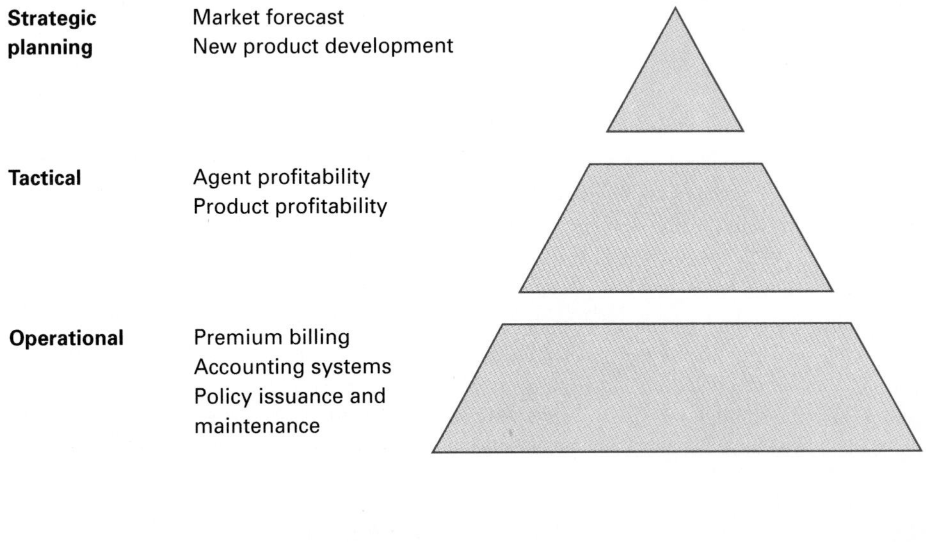

Strategic planning — Market forecast; New product development

Tactical — Agent profitability; Product profitability

Operational — Premium billing; Accounting systems; Policy issuance and maintenance

Figure 9–5
Information systems in an insurance company

and shipments. When cash payments from customers are received, they are applied almost automatically to customers' accounts.

A number of tactical information systems at Dellco Foods, Inc., support the marketing efforts of the company. The basis for much of the sales analysis is a customer product information file with 24 months of order history data on purchases. These data are used to generate reports on monthly sales by product line within each territory. Other reports supporting tactical decisions are an important account report, showing sales activities within major accounts, and a new product report, showing a reorder analysis of newly introduced products.

Other operational systems are in the production area. A bill-of-materials file containing the list of ingredients and fixed batch sizes for each product is computerized. Recipes, or sets of instructions on how to make products, are merged with the bills of material to produce the manufacturing orders for each batch of the product.

The product specifications file, another operational data file, serves as a database of raw materials information for reference and for printing text on purchase orders. After production, finished goods inventory must be transferred to branch warehouses. Forecasting reports guide inventory management personnel in allocating warehouse stock to various field locations, based on anticipated demand.

In finance and administration, an accounts receivable application is updated with customer billings and cash receipts. Aged trial balance reports are generated monthly, producing account collection letters at specified intervals.

Figure 9–6 summarizes the information systems at Dellco Foods, Inc. Without the operational systems at Dellco Foods, Inc., it would not be possible to process orders on a timely basis, to manage inventories, and to organize production. These systems cut costs, increase revenues, and improve service to customers. For example, the order processing system that makes it possible to generate invoices and shipping orders automatically at remote distribution centers cuts down order processing time by days and makes it possible to collect accounts on a timely basis. Tactical information systems make it possible to analyze sales, by product and by territory, so that marketing efforts can be allocated to serve demand. Strategic planning systems provide senior managers with competitive industry data so that they can identify emerging trends in the marketplace.

Figure 9–6
Information systems at Dellco Foods

Strategic planning Competitive industry statistics

Tactical Sales analysis, by customer
Reorder analysis of new products
Sales analysis, by product line
Production forecast

Operational Bill of materials
Manufacturing specifications
Product specifications

Order processing
On-line order inquiry
Finished goods inventory

Accounts receivable
General ledger

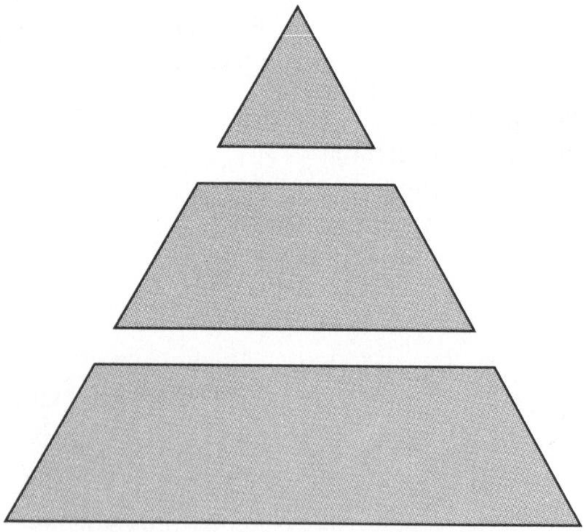

Sea Lake County Welfare Department

The Sea Lake County Welfare Department offers an example of information systems in the public sector. It provides financial assistance to residents, including medical assistance, a food stamp program, social services (for instance, adoptions and foster home placements), and special services (day care, school services, family planning, housing, legal services, and so on). The major information systems are designed to process new applications and to pay welfare recipients.

When a welfare applicant applies and becomes eligible, new on-line records are created for public assistance and for the food stamp program. The system automatically prints an identification card from the welfare payroll master file that entitles the client to services for which the welfare department is charged. On-line inquiry and on-line update of client records are also possible. The welfare payroll master file generates the welfare check and a listing on the payroll register. Public assistance also entitles the welfare recipient to food stamp program participation. Recipients apply for food stamp authorizations, which are mailed out periodically.

Although most of the welfare department data processing applications are operational in nature, several tactical information systems exist. For example, reasons for welfare denial are accumulated and reported for management analysis. Welfare participant data can also be accumulated and analyzed on a long-term basis to detect trends in client needs and to predict needed services. Information about changing government regulations provides senior managers with input into the planning process. A summary of welfare department applications at the operational, tactical, and strategic planning levels is included in Figure 9–7.

These three case studies show that many of the original information systems within organizations are operational systems supporting transactions processing. These systems are a necessary foundation for the development of tactical information systems. In contrast, strategic planning systems often use external data about markets, competitors, and government regulations.

The growth of data processing within organizations involves investments in technology and in application development. Normally, a foundation of operational systems is built before tactical systems are developed. But the evolution of information processing not only involves the construction of application systems; it also entails the organization of a data processing function, user involvement in project selection, and the introduction of planning and control strategies. Nolan's stage theory describes the factors that contribute to the evolution of information processing.

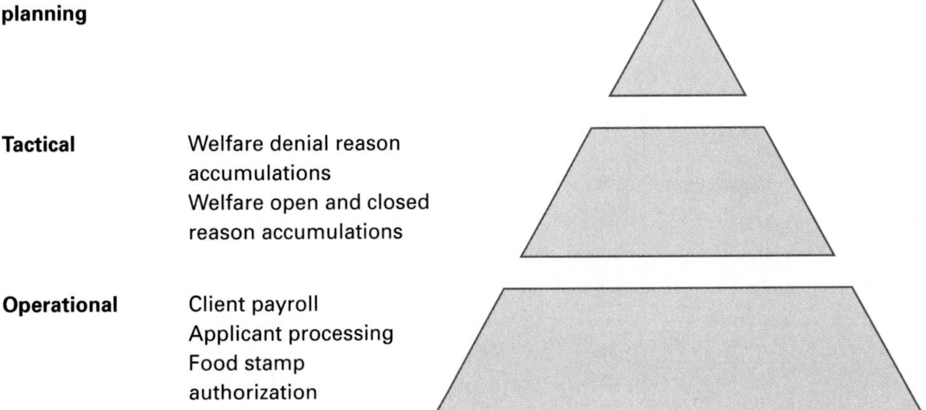

Figure 9–7 Information systems in a welfare agency

THE STAGE EVOLUTION OF DATA PROCESSING

In his article "Managing the Crises in Data Processing" (1979), Nolan argues that the growth of data processing involves growth in technology and application development, changes in planning and control strategies, and changes in user involvement. His six-stage theory of data processing growth describes a learning curve that he argues cannot be overcome. This means that organizations need to experience the growth characteristics associated with each stage of evolution. A stage of growth cannot be skipped over because of the learning process associated with it. Understanding this learning curve can help organizations manage this evolutionary process effectively. (Figure 9–8 depicts the six stages of data processing growth that Nolan outlines.)

The first stage of data processing growth is *initiation,* when cost-effective transactions processing systems like accounts receivable and payroll are introduced. Most of these systems are developed by technical specialists within functional areas such as accounting. At this stage there are few controls over data processing expenditures, and users have a "hands-off" attitude.

This initial success with data processing moves the organization into stage 2, which Nolan calls *contagion.* A proliferation of applications occurs during this stage, and data processing specialists are given the go-ahead to pursue many different kinds of automation opportunities. Because controls are virtually nonexistent, expenditures for computers and data processing personnel skyrocket and cause corporate management to become concerned about the business benefits of investments in information systems.

Figure 9–8
The six stages of data processing growth

Growth Processes	Stage 1 Initiation	Stage 2 Contagion	Stage 3 Control	Stage 4 Integration	Stage 5 Data Administration	Stage 6 Maturity
Applications Portfolio	Cost reduction applications	Proliferation	Upgrade documentation	Existing applications are upgraded using database technology	Common systems use shared data	
DP Organization	DP professionals work in user departments		Formal MIS organization	Transition point X	Data administration function introduced	
DP Planning and Control	Lax	More lax	Planning and control introduced	More formal planning and control systems		Planning for data resource management
User Awareness	Hands-off		Users become accountable			Joint responsibility between DP and users
Level of DP Expenditures						

This concern brings about stage 3, *control.* Motivated by the need to control data processing expenditures, management organizes steering committees with representatives from user areas who become responsible for setting priorities for application development projects. The MIS function becomes a formal department and begins to control its internal activities, using project management plans and systems development methods. Existing applications lacking documentation are upgraded to provide a better foundation for the development of tactical information systems in later stages of growth.

Between stages 3 and 4, Nolan argues, an important transition occurs—from managing the computer to managing data as a resource. Systems developed during stages 1 to 3 were generally created independently of one another. Beginning in stage 4, *integration,* a major effort is made to integrate existing information systems by using database and telecommunications technologies. The introduction of database technology drives the shift from traditional files supporting single applications to the design of logical databases supporting multiple applications during stage 5, *data administration.*

As the organization moves from technology management to data resource management, in stage 6—which Nolan calls *maturity*—a number of changes occur. As upper-middle and senior management recognize that management information systems are a foundation on which the organization relies, formal planning and control systems for data resource planning are put into effect to make sure that MIS plans support business plans. Priority setting by data processing management is replaced by joint priority setting by top management and data processing management.

During this time frame, corporate data processing establishes the capability to manage computer power for the firm, including mainframe-based data systems, telecommunications networks, and links with distributed systems. Application development groups, responsible for the analysis, design, and implementation of information systems, are organized within operating companies. Transition beyond stage 3 is also accompanied by a greatly increased awareness on the part of noninformation systems professionals about the importance of information systems. In particular, users begin to build their own systems using personal computers and mainframe-based data query and reporting tools.

Nolan's framework enables companies to chart a course for managing information systems development and technology. He argues that the evolution of data processing depends on achieving a balance among technology, application development, user involvement, and organizational control. This organizational learning process can be managed. For example, deliberate slack or lack of controls at stage 2, he contends, can accelerate learning about technology and its uses. Without this period of experimentation, many of the most business-effective uses of information technology may not be discovered. Stage 2 is an "out-of-control" situation that forces management to recognize the need to establish effective controls and user accountability in stage 3. In stage 5, however, high control is necessary to move into data resource management.

The Stage Assessment

The objective of the **stage assessment** is to determine the stage to which data processing has evolved within an organization. If an organization can identify its stage, Nolan suggests, it can identify the mix of application development opportunities, data processing management responsibilities, and planning and control strategies needed to move toward the next stage.

In conducting a stage assessment, the manager must determine the application portfolio for the organizational unit being studied by identifying opportunities for using computer technology to support the business functions of the organizational unit. This portfolio represents a stage 6 evolution in which all cost-effective data processing applications have been implemented.

You can see how this works by looking at an example of a large discount department store chain. Discount City, Inc., is a rapidly growing chain of discount stores in the Midwest that carries products ranging from cosmetics and apparel to hardware, sporting goods, toys, and housewares. The stage 6 portfolio of information systems represented in Figure 9–9 shows the coverage of operational, tactical, and strategic planning information systems that would provide total information systems support for the business functions at Discount City, Inc. As you can see, this 100 percent coverage would include inventory control, purchasing, accounts payable, and payroll systems at the operational level. At the tactical level, sales analysis systems providing information on planned versus actual sales by product line and by store location are important for sensing market trends in various regions. An expense analysis system would provide information on planned versus actual expenses for each store, and a vendor analysis system would provide summary information about the performance of vendors. Discount City, Inc., needs to know which vendors are delivering products on a timely basis, if merchandise is damaged in transit, and if products are defective.

At the planning level, the management of Discount City, Inc., is interested in information that could be used for long-range sales and profit planning. Discount City is also planning to expand its stores into the Southwest, and management would like to have information to support store site planning decisions.

After the stage 6 portfolio of applications at the operational, tactical, and planning levels has been identified, management needs to determine how many of these applications have already been designed and implemented. The current coverage of information systems at Discount City, Inc., is depicted in Figure 9–10.

At present, an effective inventory and purchasing system is in place. Sales data entered at the checkout counter in each store are used to update local inventory information. When an item falls below a reorder point, a purchase order for stock replenishment can automatically be generated from the system. Buyers can override the automatic purchase order generation function if they don't feel it's responsive to seasonal trends and unanticipated changes in consumer demand. They can use terminals in the buying department to enter purchase order data, including vendor name, item quantities and descriptions, and store destinations. Once the buyer has issued a purchase order, the order is automatically generated from the computer system and sent to the supplier. As order status information such as planned delivery dates becomes

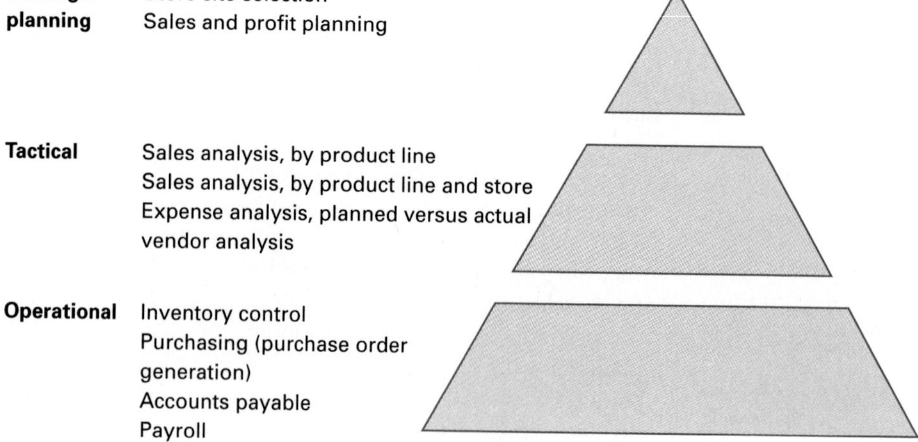

Figure 9–9
Stage 6 portfolio for Discount City, Inc.

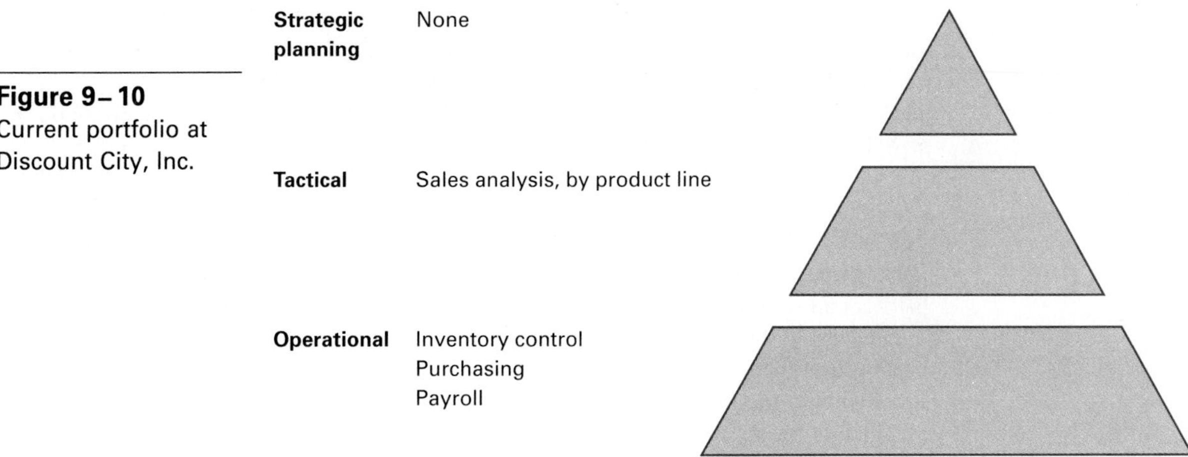

Figure 9–10
Current portfolio at Discount City, Inc.

available, this information is keyed into the purchase order data file so that the buyer always knows the current status of the order.

At the tactical level, a sales analysis system is currently in place. Once a week, the buyers for each department receive a sales summary report that provides information on sales and inventory for each item in their department. They also receive a sales analysis report listing the planned and actual sales for each item on a monthly basis. The planned sales are derived from the same sales period for the previous year. If the sales volumes fluctuate by more or less than 10 percent as compared with the previous year, the product line is highlighted as an exception condition on the report. At the planning level, no current information systems have been developed.

Once the current application portfolio has been described, management can match this current level to a benchmark model. This benchmark model, which is shown in Figure 9–11, illustrates the percentage of coverage of information systems at the

Figure 9–11
Benchmarks for data processing applications

Strategic	Stage 1	0	Economic				
planning	Stage 2	<1%	forecasting				
systems	Stage 3	<1%	Sales and				
	Stage 4	5%	profit planning				
	Stage 5	10%					
	Stage 6	15%					
Tactical	Stage 1	0	Sales	Profitability	Cost		
systems	Stage 2	15%	analysis	analysis	analysis		
	Stage 3	20%	Advertising	Cash	Budgeting		
	Stage 4	30%	and sales	require-	Estimating		
	Stage 5	35%	promotion	ments			
	Stage 6	40%		forecasting			
Opera-	Stage 1	100%	Order	Vehicle	Cash	Billing	Wage and
tional	Stage 2	85%	entry	scheduling	manage-	Accounts	salary
systems	Stage 3	80%	Order	Freight	ment	receivable	admin-
	Stage 4	65%	processing	tracking	Auditing	Accounts	istration
	Stage 5	55%	Order	Distribution	Tax	payable	Govern-
	Stage 6	45%	tracking	center	reporting		ment
				operation			reporting

operational, tactical, and planning levels that supports each of the stages in Nolan's theory. The current level of data processing support at Discount City, Inc., shows an 80 percent coverage of operational systems, a 20 percent coverage of tactical systems, and less than 1 percent coverage of strategic planning systems. According to the benchmark model, these figures reflect a stage 3 level of growth.

Using this method to ascertain the current stage of evolution, management can then identify mismatches between current levels of data processing support and the key functions of the business. This is not the problem with Discount City, Inc., because the applications that have been developed there will serve as a foundation for building tactical and strategic planning information systems. However, if an organization is in the manufacturing business and over 50 percent of its current data processing support goes into accounting systems, management may want to reallocate systems development activities into the manufacturing area.

One of the reasons for conducting the stage assessment is to identify strategies that will be useful in moving the organization from its current stage of growth to the next one. Management may first want to assess current technology. An organization in stage 3 might want to consider introducing database technology and redoing existing applications to use this technology. Old batch systems may need to be converted into on-line systems. In the case of Discount City, Inc., an on-line system could be developed so that local store managers could receive information about fast- and slow-moving product lines in their respective store locations.

Another factor in the stage evolution of data processing is effective planning and control. At earlier stages, controls are purposefully lax to encourage growth. During stage 3, formal systems development methods are introduced to make sure that applications are documented effectively. Users are placed on steering committees and begin to have a voice in identifying and prioritizing application development projects for the firm. At Discount City, Inc., a steering committee should play an active role in planning future systems development projects and making sure that these projects support the needs of the business. As Discount City moves beyond stage 3, MIS management will need to pay more attention to supporting user access to data. In later stages, users can be trained to access data by means of database query and reporting tools.

In summary, Nolan's stage assessment helps organizations evaluate their current stage of data processing evolution and identify strategies to move ahead to the next phase. His method of analysis uses the coverage of operational, tactical, and strategic planning information systems to arrive at its recommendations. These recommendations not only identify what application projects will support business needs; they also explain what kind of planning and control strategies, user involvement, and MIS management will be needed to achieve growth.

AN UPDATE TO THE ORIGINAL THEORY

In an update to his original theory, Nolan presents a new framework for understanding the evolution of information technology within organizations. This framework describes three eras: the Data Processing or DP era, the Information Technology (IT) era, and the Network era (see Figure 9–12).

In the first era, the DP era, organizations were functional hierarchies similar to Mintzberg's machine bureaucratic form described in Chapter 2. Some of these organizations evolved into a divisionalized form of organizational structure, with functional hierarchies within each division. Work methods and procedures were well defined, and control systems were designed to monitor the outputs of functional units.

Figure 9–12
The three eras of information technology

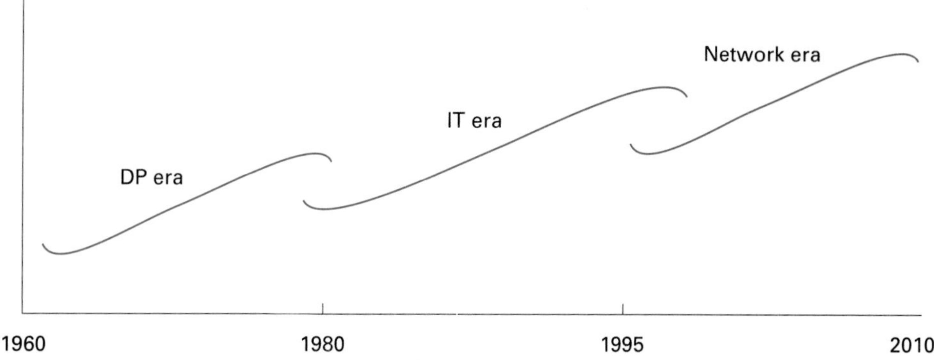

Data processing technology was originally introduced into these forms of organization to automate specific tasks. Transactions processing systems supported paperwork processing, such as generating sales orders and invoices. Tactical-level information systems were designed to provide information for better allocation and control of resources.

The Information Technology era, beginning in the early 1980s, refocused the use of information technology on the knowledge worker. PC workstations were used by financial analysts, stock brokers, and production planners, primarily for "what-if" types of analysis.

In the mid-80s, another major shift occurred. Instead of managing data processing alone, MIS management discovered new application portfolios. You can see these application portfolios depicted in Figure 9–13. Besides the traditional data processing portfolio, application portfolios for office automation, microcomputing, computer-assisted design, and robotics emerged. All these portfolios were characterized by different stages of evolution, with DP at a fairly mature stage of evolution compared with other technologies.

In the Network Era, the move toward using information technology to leverage business results is becoming most pronounced. If major productivity improvements are to occur, Nolan argues, new technology must be introduced along with new forms of organizational structure. Information technology alone will not enable organizations to achieve the business results they seek; but information technology combined with new organizational forms will bring about dramatic productivity improvements.

Figure 9–13
New application portfolios

Source: Richard Nolan, "Managing the Advanced Stages of Computer Technology: Key Research Issues," in *The Information Systems Research Challenge,* ed. F. Warren McFarian (Boston: Harvard Business School Press, 1984), p. 202.

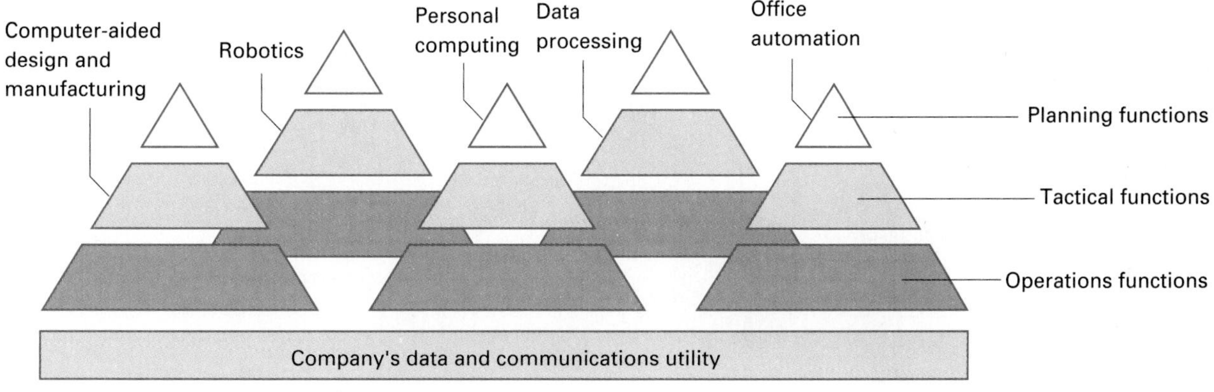

Nolan predicts that information technology, combined with networked forms of organizing people and their work, will create tenfold productivity increases. The networked form of organization, similar to Mintzberg's adhocracy, will create opportunities for multidisciplinary teams to accomplish projects. Traditional departmental barriers will be blurred, and new methods of accomplishing tasks will emerge as work is re-engineered.

STAGES OF NEW INFORMATION TECHNOLOGY GROWTH

Many of the MIS issues you have learned about involve the organization assimilating advanced technologies. Edgar Schein has proposed a framework depicting the evolution of new information technology within organizations that provides a holistic view of the organizational change process. In some ways, his theory is similar to Nolan's stage theory. Schein's phases include (1) *investment or project initiation,* (2) *technology learning and adaptation,* (3) *management control,* and (4) *widespread technology transfer.* These phases are depicted in Figure 9–14.

In the investment phase, the organization makes a decision to invest in a new information technology such as office automation. If this new technology seems to have merit, this initial phase leads to the second phase, technology learning and adaptation. However, if users are not involved in the initial system selection or if vendor-related problems occur, *Stagnation A* may occur. Stagnation A, which may result from significant cost overruns, poor project management, and unanticipated technological problems, delays further evolution of new information technology indefinitely.

In successful projects, the introduction of new technology leads to the second phase—trying the technology—during which users learn how to use the technology for tasks beyond those initially planned. For example, microcomputers may be introduced

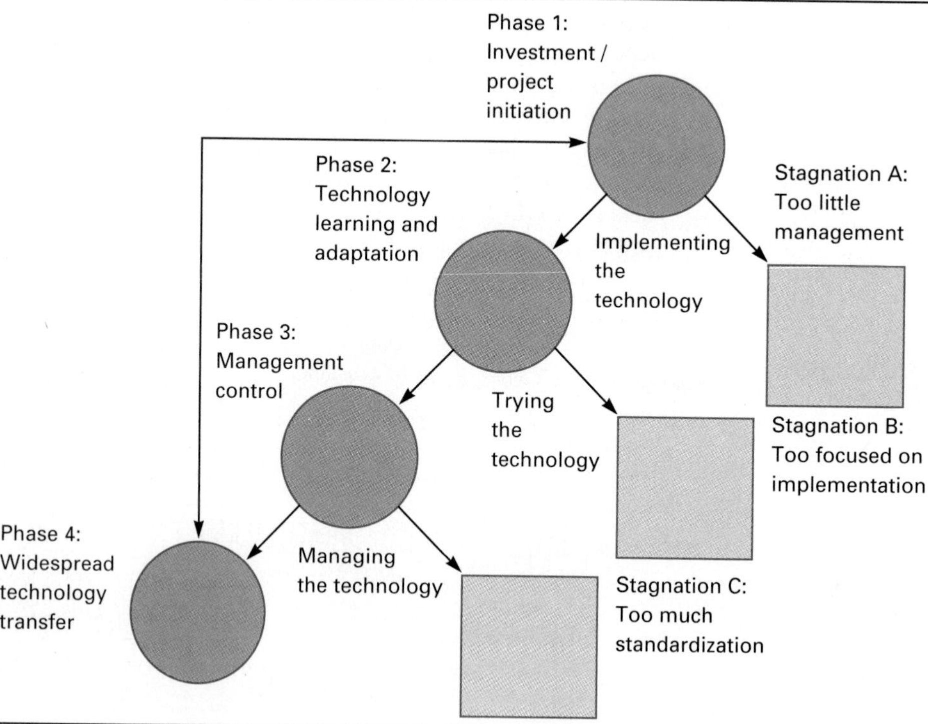

Figure 9–14
Phases of new information technology growth

Source: Adapted from James McKenney and F. Warren McFarlan, "The Information Archipelago—Maps and Bridges," *Harvard Business Review,* September–October 1982, p. 115.

for word processing during project initiation. Experimentation with word processing and database software may lead secretaries to set up mailing list files and office record-keeping systems. Experimentation causes new technology to be used in ways different from those originally planned and brings about unforeseen benefits.

If users have an opportunity to develop a better understanding of new technology and its benefits during phase 2, the organization will move into phase 3. However, premature controls can cause failure to learn how to use new technology and lead to *Stagnation B.* For example, Stagnation B occurred in an organization that introduced word processing to automate mass mailings. This application cut the costs of clerical work, and the organization had no motivation to expand the scope of office automation to new tasks based on its experience with the mailing application. Because of the premature focus on cutting clerical costs, the organization was unable to reap the potential benefits of expanded uses of office automation.

Phase 3—management control—occurs when the organization recognizes the importance of the technology and introduces precise controls over systems development and implementation that help to ensure the cost-effectiveness and success of the applications that result. If this phase is successful, the organization then begins to transfer this application to other groups within the organization.

However, if excessive controls are introduced, *Stagnation C* results. Stagnation C may inhibit further transfer of the technology into other organizational units. For example, in one organization a local area network was established within a research department. To justify the network, its users focused on paperwork reduction and operational efficiency. As a result, the enthusiasm for innovation was lost and the new technology failed to be transferred to other offices throughout the organization. Stagnation C may also lead to surreptitious experimentation with altogether different technologies, causing evolution beginning with phase 1 again.

If technology is successfully implemented, phase 4—widespread technology transfer—should occur. During this phase, a new technology such as local area networking is transferred to other parts of the organization. Technical expertise should be transferred by user analysts and technical support personnel along with the technology itself.

The stage evolution of new technology assimilation creates new challenges for MIS management because organizations may be in different phases of growth for different types of technologies. For example, success with the development of on-line transactions systems may put an organization in phase 4 with regard to data processing technology. Gradual assimilation of word processing may result in a phase 3 evolution in office automation. Finally, the introduction of software supporting the development of expert systems may put the organization in phase 1 in the development of artificial intelligence. Each phase requires different types of management techniques and control strategies. Improper management and premature controls may bring out the various forms of *stagnation* that retard further development.

The stage theory also points out that some of the disorderliness accompanying experimentation with new information technology may be necessary. If managers are unable to experiment, stagnation may occur and the real benefits of new technology may not be found or will be unnecessarily delayed.

Premature controls may also block further learning. Users who construct departmental systems may not be convinced of the importance of data security, documentation, and backup procedures until these applications develop business importance. Eventually, they may take responsibility for developing adequate standards and controls to be sure that local systems are compatible with the organization's information processing network and to ensure that these applications are correctly designed.

Management Summary

In this chapter you have learned about the functions of managers and how information systems support these functions. The activities of an organization include day-to-day operations, effective allocation of resources, and strategic planning. Information systems are designed to support decisions at these three levels. Operational information systems process transactions describing the acquisition and disbursement of corporate resources. First-line supervisors use operational systems to monitor day-to-day activities. Accounts receivable, accounts payable, and payroll systems are examples of operational systems.

Tactical information systems provide middle managers with the information they require to allocate resources needed to achieve organizational goals. Often, these tactical systems summarize or aggregate data generated from operational systems. Strategic planning systems help senior managers identify organizational goals. Information for strategic planning often comes from external sources such as demographic data and competitive industry statistics.

Information systems have evolved within organizations over the past 20 to 25 years. This growth involves the construction of operational, tactical, and strategic planning information systems to support the managers of the business. However, the growth of data processing systems involves more than technology and applications. It requires user involvement in application development, the organization and management of an MIS function, and the development of effective planning and control strategies. In Nolan's stage theory, you learned about the characteristics of various stages of data processing growth, how to make a stage assessment, and how to identify strategies to move from one stage to the next.

Many organizations today are building information systems to achieve a competitive edge. As you learned in Chapter 1, information systems can be used to cut costs, to add value to products and services, and to expand competitive scope. The information systems opportunities selected by the management of a firm may depend on these competitive plans.

Key Terms for Managers

ad hoc report, **359**
controlling, **352**
effectiveness, **354**
efficiency, **354**
exception report, **359**
leading, **352**
operational systems, **358**
organizing, **352**
planning, **352**
stage assessment, **369**
strategic planning, **362**
summary report, **359**
tactical systems, **358**

Review Questions

1. What are the planning functions of the manager?
2. What are the organizing functions of the manager?
3. What are the leading functions of the manager?
4. What are the controlling functions of the manager?
5. What informational roles does the manager have?
6. What interpersonal roles does the manager perform?
7. Give an example of a manager's decisional role.

8. What is the difference between *efficiency* and *effectiveness*?
9. What is the difference between *data* and *information*?
10. What are the characteristics of an operational information system?
11. What types of reports are generated from a tactical information system?
12. What are the characteristics of a strategic planning system?
13. In what stage of Nolan's stage theory are steering committees formed to establish application development priorities?
14. In what stage does a proliferation of applications occur?
15. In what stage are common databases designed to support multiple applications?
16. Between what two stages is there a transition from the management of computer resources to the management of data resources?
17. According to Nolan's stage assessment, what percentage of operational, tactical, and strategic planning systems occurs in stage 3?

Questions for Discussion

1. Why is tactical-level information so important to middle-level managers?
2. What kind of tactical information would be useful to a branch manager of a Coca-Cola or Pepsi distributorship?
3. What kind of strategic information would be useful to the president of a four-year liberal arts college?
4. In Nolan's stage theory, why are slack and the lack of effective planning and control systems useful during early phases of evolution?
5. How can the stage assessment approach help MIS managers chart a course for future evolution?
6. Nolan's stage theory identifies the organizational and management factors influencing the evolution of data processing technology. Explain what types of organizational and management factors influence DP evolution.
7. Mintzberg cites a myth that the manager plans in a careful and systematic way. How does the manager really work, and why?
8. In Mintzberg's analysis, what type of information is most valuable to the manager? Why?

Problems

1. **ABC Industries.** At ABC Industries, managers at various levels need to make the following types of decisions.

   Categorize each of the following decisions by the type of decision it represents. Choose from operational, tactical, and strategic planning.

   a. Rejecting credit for a company with an overdue account.
   b. Analyzing sales by product line within each geographic region, this year to date versus last year to date.

c. Using a simulation model to forecast profitability of a new product, using projected sales data, competitive industry statistics, and economic trends.
d. Comparing planned versus actual expenses for department staff.
e. Allocating salespeople's time to the highest potential market prospects.

2. **Essex Industries, Inc.** The president of Essex Industries, Inc., a $400-million company in the electronics business, is annoyed with the information systems department in her company. She feels that the computer-based information systems are generating too many reports about day-to-day activities and that much of this information is not being used by managers for decision making. Even though the firm is spending over $15 million per year on computers and data processing personnel, she can't see what they are getting for this kind of investment.

   Currently, data processing projects are requested by user-managers and selected by the information systems director. Since there is a two-year backlog of projects, the president is considering bringing in consultants or hiring a service bureau to get some of the work done. However, she isn't sure if all these projects are necessary.

   What steps should the president take to make sure that information systems are more responsive to the needs of the firm?

Cases

1. **Sherwood Stores, Inc.** Sherwood Stores is a retail grocery store chain with a central distribution center and 14 retail stores in a major metropolitan area. Managers at all levels at the headquarters office, at the distribution center, and in the retail stores use reports from various information systems.

   One of the important information systems is the inventory system that keeps track of physical inventory by product line. Sales information gathered at point-of-sale checkout terminals is used to update inventory levels. At the end of each day, the store manager receives a reorder report indicating which items in inventory have reached their reorder point and need to be reordered from the distribution center. The inventory system also includes a report of items on order by product line, prices, and expected delivery dates.

   Each department manager within each store develops a sales plan that indicates the expected sales volume for each item for the subsequent week. Actual sales for each item are compared with the planned sales activity on a weekly basis and a sales analysis summary report is generated that provides information on planned versus actual sales for each item. Department managers in each store use this report to develop a new weekly sales plan. The report is also useful in determining new safety stock levels for each inventory item and for estimating shelf-space allocations.

   All orders from the local stores are filled from the central distribution center. The central distribution center purchases inventory from suppliers and allocates it to the local stores based on a sales forecasting report. If a local store needs to replenish its stock because an item has fallen below a desired inventory level, the store manager can request additional stock from the central distribution center.

   At the central distribution center, a purchasing system is used to generate purchase orders for stock. One by-product of this purchasing system is a purchase order due-in report that indicates when shipments are scheduled to arrive, the shipper, and the warehouse location for the shipped merchandise. Another report helps monitor the performance of various suppliers by providing information on planned versus actual shipment dates and on the quality of the shipped merchandise. For example, if six cases of eggs are damaged in shipment, the damage is indicated on the shipment report. In addition, an accounts payable system keeps track of payment amounts and due dates for Sherwood's suppliers.

Sherwood Stores, Inc., has 24 trucks making deliveries to local stores daily. An information system provides drivers with a computerized schedule of store deliveries. Distribution managers develop standards for truck unloadings based on shipment quantity and weight. Actual delivery data are compared with delivery standards in reports to distribution managers.

Finally, planners on the headquarters staff use external market data and demographic data to forecast sales trends in various regions. They build these data into reports that analyze the sales potential of alternative store sites. Store site selection is an important issue for top managers at Sherwood Stores, Inc., because they would like to expand the number of stores from 14 to 24 within the next three to five years.

The information systems at Sherwood Stores, Inc., are essential to its ability to control inventories, manage the distribution process, and analyze sales trends affecting various product lines and store sites.

a. What information systems are described in the case?
b. What business objectives are supported by each system?
c. What level of decision making (operational, tactical, strategic planning) does each information system support?

2. **Mountain Chemical.** The manager of information systems at Mountain Chemical Company, Bob Gordon, is trying to develop a short- and long-range plan for computers and data processing at the firm, but he is unsure about the steps to take. Some of the questions he is considering are these: Should he revamp old systems? Should he organize a steering committee? Should he encourage user-managers to take on additional responsibilities in systems development projects?

Mountain Chemical is a $500-million company specializing in the manufacturing and distribution of agricultural chemicals. Most of the backbone financial and marketing information systems supporting day-to-day transactions processing activities such as order entry, inventory control, accounts receivable, and general ledger were designed and implemented in the early 1970s. About 95 percent of Mountain Chemical's data processing applications are systems written in COBOL that run on a mainframe computer system.

Because of early problems with a proliferation of application development projects, Bob Gordon, who was brought in as manager of information systems in 1976, asked users to become involved in establishing their own priorities for projects. Users within each department established their own priorities and asked data processing to design and implement them. The number of projects created an overwhelming backlog for the DP department.

In 1986, users had become very frustrated with the three- to five-year backlog of projects. They openly criticized Bob for dragging his feet in introducing new technologies such as microcomputers. Several departments went out and acquired their own software packages on small departmental computers, and others experimented with various types of microcomputers without MIS guidance.

Senior management at Mountain Chemical asked Bob to draft a plan outlining his objectives for MIS for the next year and for the next five years. They asked him to describe the methods to be used in selecting new applications and in identifying new technologies to be introduced.

You have been brought in as a consultant to work with Bob in drafting this plan. You have used Nolan's stage assessment method and have determined that Mountain Chemical has evolved to stage 3. This means that about 80 percent of the operational information systems that are needed are in place. About 20 percent of the tactical information systems needed for sales and inventory analysis also exist.

Using what you know about Nolan's stage assessment, recommend three strategies that Bob should consider in making decisions about applications to be developed, new technologies to be introduced, and control methods to be implemented at Mountain Chemical. You may also describe the role of users in information systems planning and development.

3. **Clark Products Inc.** At Clark Products, Inc., office automation was introduced in the late 1970s when a word processing center was organized. The primary purpose of the word processing center was to efficiently produce thousands of repetitive letters supporting a variety of applications.

While other companies were beginning to experiment with other applications of office automation, such as electronic mail, desktop publishing, and local area networks, Clark Products seemed to be in a rut. Requests for office automation systems within user departments were virtually nonexistent. Secretaries maintained records and filed pretty much as they had in the 1950s. Major production jobs, such as mass mailings of repetitive letters and heavily revised financial reports, were always sent to the word processing center, so secretaries had little or no exposure to office automation.

The president of Clark Products is skeptical about the firm's lack of progress in office automation. Other companies are busily experimenting with new information technology, but little interest in these emerging technologies seems to be surfacing at Clark Products.

As a result, Ralph Mattheus, the president, has called upon Thomas Morris, a consultant specializing in office automation. Assume that you are Thomas Morris and answer the following questions:

a. Using Schein's theory of new information technology growth, at what stage would you place Clark Products in terms of the evolution of office automation?

b. What strategies would you recommend to change the direction of office automation in the future?

Selected References and Readings

Anthony, R. *Planning and Control Systems: A Framework for Analysis.* Boston: Harvard University, Division of Research, Graduate School of Business Administration, 1965.

Mintzberg, Henry. "The Manager's Job: Folklore and Fact." *Harvard Business Review* 53, no. 4, July–August 1975, pp. 49–61.

Nolan, Richard L. "Managing the Crises in Data Processing." *Harvard Business Review*, March–April 1979, pp. 115–126.

ACCOUNTING AND FINANCIAL INFORMATION SYSTEMS

CHAPTER OUTLINE

Manager's View

Whether you are the chief operating officer of a large international organization or merely the supervisor of a small department at one location of that organization, you will find it necessary to make financial decisions. The financial decisions you may encounter as a manager are diverse and could include decisions similar to these:

1. Should you purchase a new piece of equipment or lease the equipment for a three-year period?
2. How much of your department's funds should you allocate to telephone usage rather than travel expenses?
3. How much idle cash does your division have on hand at various times during the year and is it being invested wisely?
4. Is the amount of cash your firm has on hand during each month enough to cover the cash expenditures you expect to incur each month?
5. Should you invest money in new computer equipment or additional merchandise for resale?
6. How will a 15 percent utility rate increase your budget for the coming year?
7. Should you allow a particular customer to make a large purchase on credit?

To make these and similar decisions, you need to understand the basic accounting and financial information systems found in most organizations. These information systems can help you improve the decisions you make about the financial problems within your purview.

You may also work directly in the financial industry, employed as a stock broker, financial analyst, currency trader, or a banker. In these positions, you will find accounting and financial information systems not only helpful but also essential to your decision making.

ACCOUNTING AND FINANCIAL MANAGEMENT FUNCTIONS

The accounting and financial management functions of any organization encompass a number of important responsibilities. These include monitoring and analyzing the organization's financial condition, managing the accounting systems, and preparing financial statements and reports. The accounting and financial management functions are also responsible for the budgeting process; managing customer credit; calculating and paying income, payroll, property, excise, and other taxes; and managing appropriate insurance coverage for the organization's personnel and assets. If you think that's enough, you're wrong. The functions must also provide for an auditing process to ensure the accuracy of the financial information kept and to protect investors' funds.

As you can see, that's quite a bit of responsibility. However, there is still more to consider. The accounting and financial management functions are also responsible for managing the organization's fixed assets, pension funds, and investments in existing plants, equipment, subsidiaries, or other investments. The functions also include evaluating new investments and acquiring borrowed funds or capital to pay for them.

And that's still not the end of it. The accounting and financial management functions must manage the cash flow of the organization to ensure that the necessary funds to operate are available, that extra cash is not left idle, and that the organization has the borrowing power to meet its cash needs when the cash flow is insufficient.

Clearly, accounting and financial management functions are very important to the organization. Because of their importance, accounting and financial management personnel require information systems that provide them with accurate, timely, and appropriate information to carry out their functions.

Like all information systems, accounting and financial information systems may be categorized into those that support operational, tactical, and strategic decisions (see Figure 10–1). As you learned in Chapter 9, operational information systems support decisions concerned with the completion of day-to-day tasks, tactical information sys-

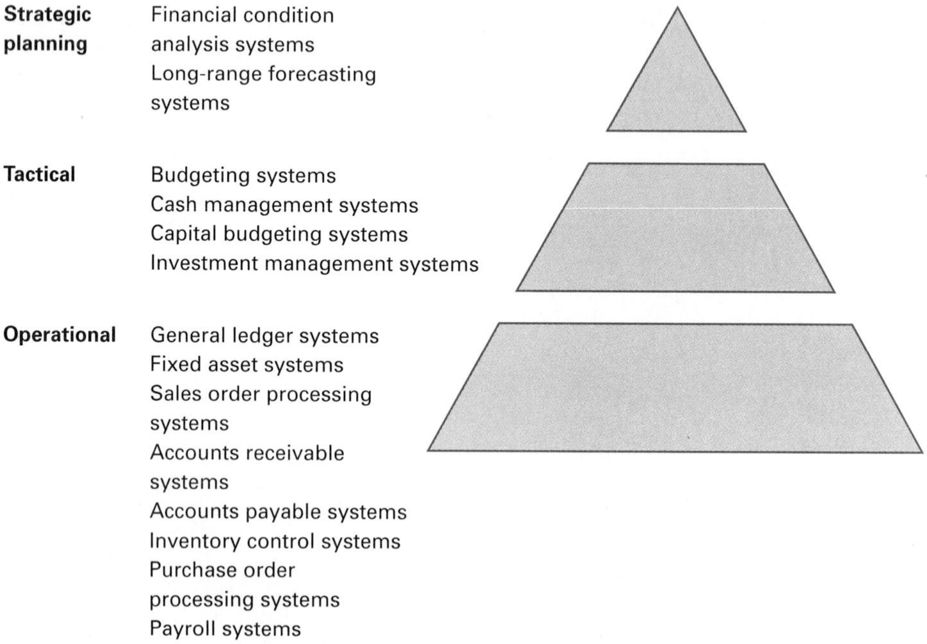

Figure 10–1
The three levels of accounting and financial information systems

Strategic planning	Financial condition analysis systems Long-range forecasting systems
Tactical	Budgeting systems Cash management systems Capital budgeting systems Investment management systems
Operational	General ledger systems Fixed asset systems Sales order processing systems Accounts receivable systems Accounts payable systems Inventory control systems Purchase order processing systems Payroll systems

tems support decisions that are concerned with resource allocation, and strategic information systems support decisions that are concerned with setting long-term goals. You also learned in Chapter 9 that there is no absolute distinction between these three levels of information systems; rather, they represent a continuum of information support that occurs within an organization. Despite this lack of precision, categorizing accounting and financial information systems is helpful to understanding and designing these systems. So let's use these three categories to examine accounting and financial information systems. The operational level information systems that you will examine include the accounting information systems typically found in most firms. The tactical and strategic information systems you will examine include examples drawn from both the accounting and financial areas.

OPERATIONAL-LEVEL ACCOUNTING INFORMATION SYSTEMS

Typically, the applications organizations first computerize are operational-level accounting systems. Computerized accounting and financial information systems for tactical decision making and strategic planning are usually developed after basic operational-level information systems are up and running.

Operational accounting information systems produce the routine, repetitive information outputs that every organization finds necessary, including paychecks, checks to vendors, customer invoices, purchase orders, stock reports, and other regular forms and reports. Operational accounting information systems are typically task oriented—they focus on processing transactions to produce the outputs just described. Because of their focus, operational accounting information systems, like other information systems that emphasize routine, repetitive transactions, are often called financial accounting systems.

The heart of an organization's operational-level accounting information system is the **financial accounting system.** A computerized financial accounting system is composed of a series of software modules or subsystems used separately or in an integrated fashion. The system modules typically include these:

1. General ledger.
2. Fixed assets.
3. Sales order processing.
4. Accounts receivable.
5. Accounts payable.
6. Inventory control.
7. Purchase order processing.
8. Payroll.

When these computerized financial accounting subsystems are integrated, each subsystem receives data as input from other subsystems and provides information as output to other subsystems. The financial accounting subsystems and how they might be integrated are shown in Figure 10–2.

The Importance of Operational Financial Accounting Information Systems

The fact that operational financial accounting information systems are predominantly routine and repetitive in nature does not mean that they do not contribute to decisions that are important to the organization. For example, the accounts receivable subsystem may routinely process credit information about customers. This may include comparing the balance of customer accounts to customer credit limits, which is essential in making

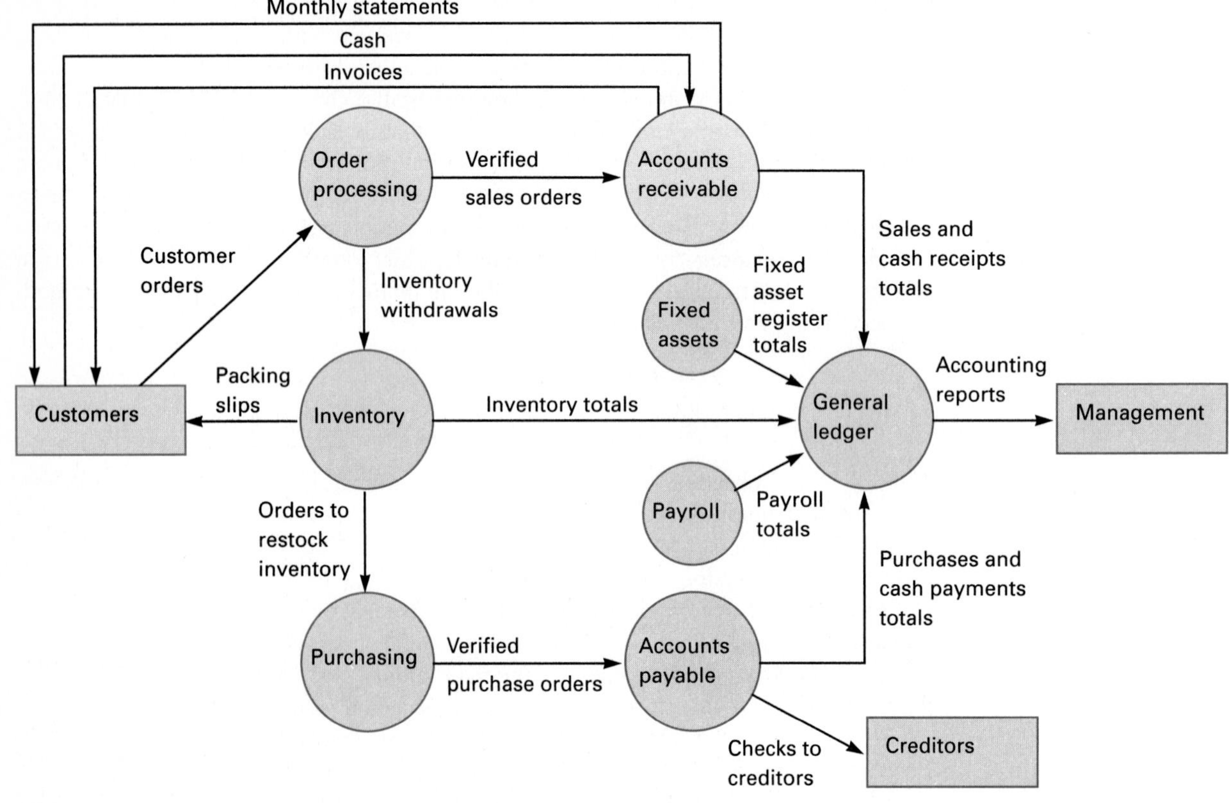

Figure 10–2
An accounting system and its major components

a common operating-level decision faced by the sales force: Should the customer be allowed to make a purchase on credit? Organizations that provide credit information to salespeople on-line reduce the risk of incurring bad debts, which lowers their cost of operations.

Let's briefly examine each of the financial accounting information subsystems.

The General Ledger Subsystem

The *general ledger subsystem* ties all other financial accounting system subsystems together, provides managers with periodic accounting reports and statements, such as an income statement and a balance sheet, and provides support for budgeting. The general ledger subsystem also permits creation of general ledger accounts and definition of the organization's fiscal period, and it produces a list of accounts maintained by the financial accounting system.

Other financial accounting subsystems periodically provide input to the general ledger subsystem. For example, after the payroll subsystem has processed the weekly payroll, it provides the general ledger subsystem with data to update the various payroll accounts.

The Fixed Assets Subsystem

The *fixed assets subsystem* maintains records of equipment, property, and other long-term assets an organization owns. The records include the original cost of the assets, the depreciation rate on each asset or group of assets, the accumulated depreciation to date, and the book value of the asset, which is the original cost less accumulated depreciation to date. The general ledger subsystem uses this information to maintain up-to-date balances in the various long-term asset accounts of the organization. The subsystem also may maintain and process data on the gain or loss on the sale of fixed assets and prepare special income tax forms for fixed assets required by the federal government.

The Sales Order Processing Subsystem

The *sales order processing subsystem,* or order entry subsystem, routinely records sales orders and provides the documents that other subsystems use to fill those orders, that maintain inventory levels, and that bill the customer (sales invoices). The subsystem provides sales tax data to the general ledger subsystem for posting to taxing-agency accounts, stock data to the inventory subsystem for updating inventory balances, and sales invoice data to the accounts receivable subsystem for posting to customer accounts.

A computerized sales order subsystem usually tracks the sales made by each salesperson and provides input to the payroll subsystem so that salespeople's commissions can be calculated. The subsystem should also provide information to the shipping department to ensure that the correct stock is sent to the customer; provide for backorders when there is not enough stock on the shelves; accurately figure prices, totals, discounts, and taxes on the order; and allow a quick and accurate response to customer inquiries about the status of the order.

When the sales order subsystem is on-line, the salesperson can verify customer credit and inventory levels immediately. This provides the salesperson with a competitive advantage over salespeople without on-line order entry systems. Consider, for example, a field sales representative who carries to the client's premises a notebook computer equipped with a modem to connect with the organization's mainframe. Using the microcomputer, the salesperson can verify immediately whether the customer can be granted the credit needed for the sale and if there is enough stock on hand. The sale can be closed at that point and picking and packing slips delivered electronically to the warehouse at the same time. Because the subsystem is on-line, the customer should get the goods much faster than if a manual order entry subsystem were used (see Box 10–1).

The Accounts Receivable Subsystem

The *accounts receivable subsystem* allows you to enter, update, and delete customer information, such as charge sales, credit terms, cash payments received, credit for returned or damaged merchandise, and account balances.

Inputs to the accounts receivable subsystem include sales invoices, credit memoranda, and cash received from customers. Typical outputs are monthly customer statements of account and a schedule of accounts receivable listing each account and its balance (see Figure 10–3).

Many accounts receivable subsystems produce aged accounts receivable reports. These reports classify account balances into several categories, such as more than 30 days, 60 days, and 90 days overdue (see Figure 10–4). An aging report identifies customers with overdue balances to managers, allowing them to use the computer system to prepare collection letters, start collection procedures, and disallow additional credit to poor credit risks. Without aging data, an organization may continue to grant credit to customers already long overdue on their payments.

The accounts receivable subsystem may also provide data to the office automation system of the organization. For example, customer names and addresses may be *imported,* or copied, from the accounts receivable file located on the organization's mainframe to a word processing file located on a local area network of microcomputers used by the marketing department to produce sales promotion letters. This can be especially effective if the customers can be linked with the products or services they have bought. Organizations can often increase sales by targeting sales appeals for add-on products or services to customers who have purchased a basic product.

Box 10–1 How an On-Line Order Entry Subsystem Works

To illustrate how an on-line order entry subsystem works, let's examine how a manufacturing firm might use one to process orders. At this firm, salespeople with notebook computers equipped with modems are responsible for entering customer orders at the customer site. To create an order, salespeople bring up an order entry screen like the one shown.

```
ENTER CUSTOMER ORDER

ACCOUNT NUMBER _
NAME
ADDRESS
CITY
STATE/ZIP
CREDIT TERMS
STOCK NUMBER
STOCK NAME
STOCK DESCRIPTION
QUANTITY ORDERED
```

The salespeople enter the customer's name, and the computer system at the home office supplies the customer's number, address, city, state, ZIP code, and credit terms in the correct places on the screen. The order entry subsystem obtains these data from the accounts receivable subsystem.

The salespeople then enter the stock number of each item ordered by the customer. When they do, the order entry subsystem obtains the stock name, stock description, and price for each item from the inventory subsystem and displays these data on the screen. When the salespeople enter the quantity ordered, the inventory subsystem is queried to determine if there is enough stock on hand to fill the order.

The salespeople continue this sequence of entries and responses until the last item ordered has been entered. Then the order entry subsystem immediately subtotals the order and verifies that the customer's credit is good. It then produces immediately, at the appropriately located printer, a picking slip for warehouse personnel to use to fill the order from inventory shelves, a mailing label for the carton, and a packing slip to be included in the carton with the completed order. The accounts receivable subsystem then uses the completed sales order to bill the customer and create and print the sales invoice.

For example, suppose that a large national retail department store chain wishes to contact all recent charge account purchasers of humidifiers to offer a special savings on annual maintenance contracts. Using a query language like the one discussed in Chapter 6, the manager electronically completes a search of the sales order file for customer numbers on all recent orders that contain humidifiers. Using those numbers, the manager directs the system to search for matches in the customer number field of the

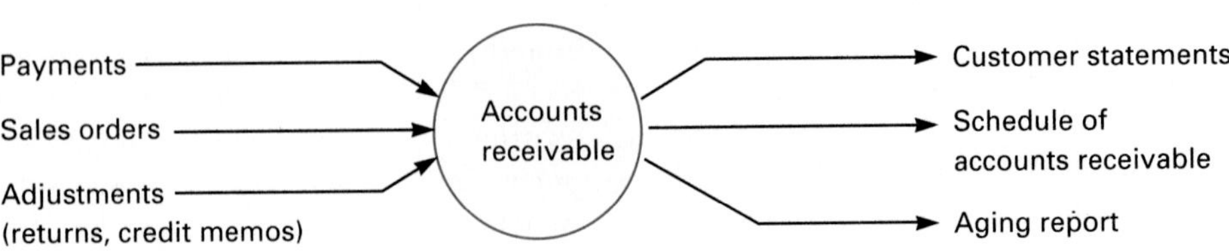

Figure 10–3 Typical inputs and outputs for an accounts receivable system

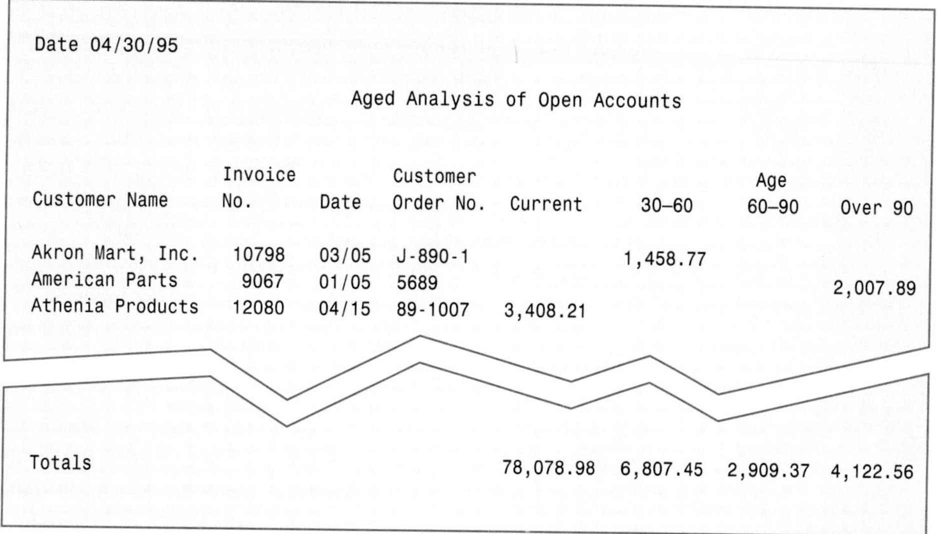

Date 04/30/95

Aged Analysis of Open Accounts

Customer Name	Invoice No.	Date	Customer Order No.	Current	Age 30–60	60–90	Over 90
Akron Mart, Inc.	10798	03/05	J-890-1		1,458.77		
American Parts	9067	01/05	5689				2,007.89
Athenia Products	12080	04/15	89-1007	3,408.21			
Totals				78,078.98	6,807.45	2,909.37	4,122.56

Figure 10–4
An aged accounts receivable report

accounts receivable file. The names and addresses of all the customers whose numbers match are stored in a new file that is sent to the local area network file server used by the word processing department. There, the names and addresses are merged with a sales promotion letter.

The Accounts Payable Subsystem

The *accounts payable subsystem* processes much of the same routine, repetitive information as the accounts receivable subsystem, except that the information is about the organization's creditors rather than customers (see Figure 10–5). For example, the subsystem maintains creditor account information, prepares checks to creditors, and produces the accounts payable schedule. The accounts payable subsystem provides data directly to the general ledger subsystem and receives data from the purchase order subsystem.

The accounts payable subsystem may also find the due dates for purchases on account and the last date on which cash discounts may be taken on those purchases. This subsystem provides important operational-level information that can be used to schedule cash payments to creditors. The effect of such a subsystem is to allow the organization to keep its money working for it as long as possible and yet ensure that all cash discounts are taken.

The Inventory Control Subsystem

The *inventory control subsystem* provides input to the general ledger subsystem and receives input from the purchase order and the sales order subsystems. The basic purpose of the subsystem is to keep track of inventory levels and inventory costs for the organization. The subsystem maintains information about each stock item, such as stock numbers and stock descriptions, receipts and issues of stock, and stock balances. The

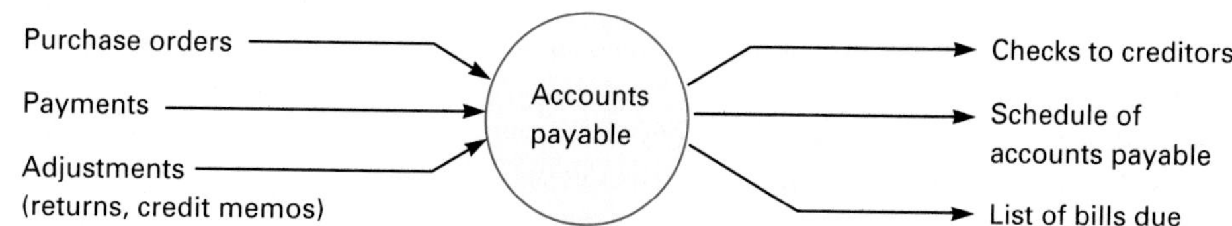

Figure 10–5
The accounts payable subsystem

inventory subsystem may also trigger the purchase of stock when stock levels reach certain points, maintain information about stock item costs, and maintain selling price data on each stock item.

The inventory subsystem maintains stock balance data by obtaining stock receipts from the purchase order system and stock issues from the order entry system. Updates for other stock changes, such as damaged goods, lost stock, shrinkage, or spoilage are usually entered directly into the subsystem by inventory clerks after a physical inventory has been completed.

Manufacturers need specialized inventory subsystems to provide information about the cost of raw materials inventory, goods-in-process inventory, and finished goods inventory. These subsystems are described in more detail in Chapter 12, "Manufacturing and Production Information Systems."

For many organizations, the amount of funds represented by inventory is substantial. Furthermore, many state and local agencies tax inventories. Maintaining as lean an inventory as possible while suffering a minimum of stockouts is an important goal, and computerized inventory subsystems assist managers in achieving this goal. You have already studied how electronic data interchange (EDI) systems can be used to minimize inventory and purchasing costs in Chapter 7, "Communications and Distributed Systems." Lowered inventory costs for an organization may mean that the organization can lower its prices and achieve a competitive advantage over firms without computerized inventory subsystems.

The Purchase Order Processing Subsystem

The *purchase order processing subsystem* processes purchase orders and tracks which purchase orders have been filled, which stock items ordered are on backorder, which stock items have been damaged or do not meet the specifications of the original order, and when orders are expected to be received.

The purchase order subsystem provides information to the accounts payable and inventory subsystems. The subsystem produces a variety of reports, including a backorder report listing all stock items on backorder and an open order report listing all purchase orders not yet received and their expected arrival dates.

The Payroll Subsystem

The *payroll subsystem* processes wage and salary information, such as payments to employees; deductions from employee paychecks; and payments to federal, state, and other taxing agencies for taxes owed. The payroll subsystem produces weekly payroll summary reports; overtime reports; forms for taxing agencies, such as wage and tax statements (Forms W-2); payroll checks; and checks for payroll taxes owed to taxing agencies.

Many financial accounting systems today no longer produce payroll checks. Instead, the payroll data for the checks are stored in electronic files that are sent to various banks for direct deposit in employee accounts. Thus, payroll disbursements are another form of electronic data interchange (see Chapter 7).

As you can see, operational-level financial accounting information systems are transaction-processing systems. They record and report the voluminous, routine, and repetitive transactions that mirror the day-to-day operations of an organization. By computerizing these operational-level systems, organizations often eliminate the drudgery of manually recording the endless detail needed in these systems, usually reduce the costs of processing this work, and frequently provide faster and better service to their customers. They also develop a massive database of information that managers can use to support tactical decisions and strategic planning. Organizations that have computerized their financial accounting systems clearly have a competitive advantage over those that have not.

TACTICAL ACCOUNTING AND FINANCIAL INFORMATION SYSTEMS

The computerization of financial accounting systems was a major event for most large organizations in the 1950s and 1960s. Many large organizations developed data processing departments during those decades to install computer systems and develop computerized versions of financial accounting systems to handle the large amount of transactions they needed to process. Because of the advent of microprocessors and the large drop in the cost of computer systems, computerization of financial accounting systems was a major event for most small organizations in the 1980s.

The computerization of financial accounting systems changed the way managers viewed accounting information. A large database of information became available in computerized form, and it could easily be viewed or manipulated. So managers began to view this information as a resource for tactical planning. Suddenly it became possible for managers to obtain important summaries and comparisons of financial accounting data easily and swiftly. In the past this information would have taken a great deal of time to extract from a manual financial accounting system. The result is that managers now view the financial accounting system as more than merely a transaction-processing system, a producer of checks, invoices, and statements. It has become a repository of important data that assists management in tactical decision making and long-range strategic planning.

The computerization of financial accounting systems helped spawn the development of other corporate databases to support tactical decisions and strategic planning. This led to the development of management information systems, or information systems for tactical decision making and strategic planning.

Applications to Tactical Decision Making

Tactical accounting and financial information systems support management decision making by providing managers with regular summary reports, regular exception reports, ad hoc reports, and other information that helps them (1) control their areas of responsibility and (2) allocate their resources to pursue organization goals. Although the focus of operational information systems is tasks, the focus of tactical information systems is resource allocation.

It is possible to design many computer-supported, tactical-level information systems for the financial decisions that managers must make. Budgeting systems, cash management systems, capital budgeting systems, and investment management systems are common ones. Each will be briefly described to give you an idea of the nature and use of these tactical-level information systems.

Budgeting Systems

The **budgeting system** permits managers to track actual revenues and expenses and compare these amounts to expected revenues and expenses. It also allows managers to compare current budget amounts to those of prior fiscal periods, other divisions, other departments—even industrywide data. Comparisons of budget data against such standards allow managers to assess how they use their resources to achieve their goals. For example, a manager may view the budget to find the amount of money actually spent in the purchasing department on supervisory versus clerical staff. The manager may then compare the actual amounts spent to the actual amounts spent by other purchasing departments in the organization or in the industry.

The general ledger system of computerized financial accounting systems often permits budget amounts to be entered by account number. Periodically (weekly, monthly, quarterly, or annually) these budgeted amounts *(allocations)* and the actual amounts spent or received *(actuals)* for each account are compared and reports are prepared. For example, the general ledger system of a financial accounting system may provide these reports:

1. Current budget allocations by line item.
2. Current budget allocations compared to year-to-date revenues and expenditures.
3. Budget variances by line-item type, or the differences between allocations and actuals.
4. Current budget allocations compared to the previous year's allocations.
5. Current revenues and expenditures compared to the previous year's revenues and expenditures.
6. Current revenues and expenditures compared to the average of the other units or divisions of the organization.

Reports such as these may be prepared for a department, a division, a subsidiary, or the entire organization. An example of a budget variance report prepared by a financial accounting system is shown in Figure 10–6.

Regularly produced tactical-level reports, such as budget reports, often generate managerial questions and concerns. These in turn may lead managers to query the financial accounting database for answers or solutions. Suppose, for example, that you are an accounting manager and supervise several departments, including the billing

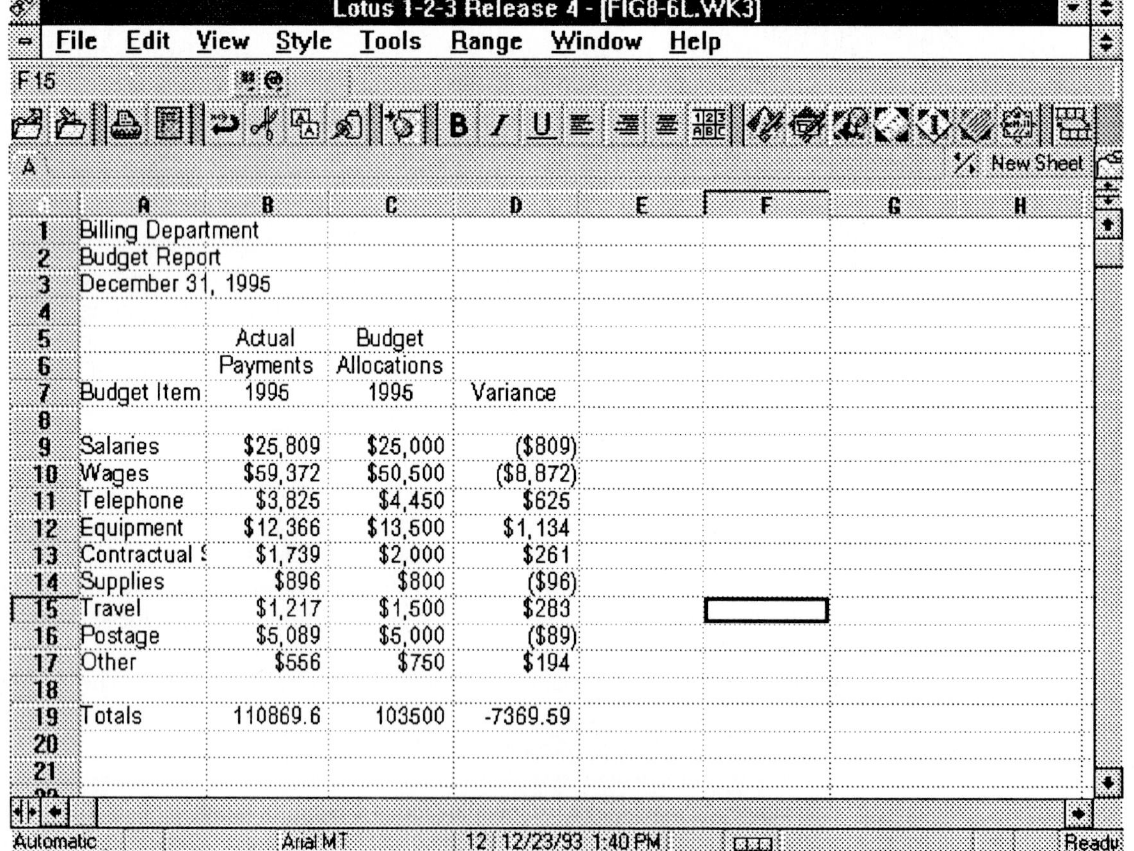

	A	B	C	D
1	Billing Department			
2	Budget Report			
3	December 31, 1995			
4				
5		Actual	Budget	
6		Payments	Allocations	
7	Budget Item	1995	1995	Variance
8				
9	Salaries	$25,809	$25,000	($809)
10	Wages	$59,372	$50,500	($8,872)
11	Telephone	$3,825	$4,450	$625
12	Equipment	$12,366	$13,500	$1,134
13	Contractual S	$1,739	$2,000	$261
14	Supplies	$896	$800	($96)
15	Travel	$1,217	$1,500	$283
16	Postage	$5,089	$5,000	($89)
17	Other	$556	$750	$194
18				
19	Totals	110869.6	103500	-7369.59
20				
21				

Figure 10–6
A budget variance report prepared using a spreadsheet

department. Suppose further that the regular budget report shows that the wages line of the billing department report is much higher than in prior years. To find out why, you might query the financial accounting database for answers. If the database stores the number of statements produced each month, the number of employees in the billing department, and the costs associated with the billing department, you might obtain various measures of the productivity of that department, such as the average number of statements produced per billing department employee and the average cost per statement.

If you found poor productivity results, you might then examine the productivity of each billing supervisor compared to the average for the organization, or each billing clerk as compared to the average for the department. This might lead you to decisions about changing supervisory personnel, providing training for specific billing clerks, acquiring new equipment to produce customer statements, or other possible remedies. Notice that the system does not make the decisions for you; it provides information to help you identify and remedy problems. It is a decision support system, not a decision system.

When the standards against which budgetary data are compared are well known, the manager can generate regular comparative reports using the organization's data processing system. For ad hoc reports, the organization's financial accounting database might be accessed by the manager using a query language or report writer.

Many managers also find it helpful to use spreadsheet software to analyze their departments' budgetary data. Spreadsheet software allows the manager to ask numerous "what if" questions about the budget. For example, top management may have given the manager of the billing department described earlier a goal of not exceeding a 2 percent growth in the department's budget for the year. The manager might then develop a spreadsheet to estimate the budget for the billing department (see Figure 10–7). By entering the estimated changes as percents in the last column of the spreadsheet, the manager can simulate many different budget scenarios. For example, the manager might ask how an increase in hourly pay of 3, 4, or 5 percent for the clerical staff might affect the total department budget. The manager might also estimate how

Figure 10–7
A spreadsheet used to simulate budget situations

	A	B	C	D
1	Billing			
2	Budget Estimate			
3	For 1/1/96 – 12/31/96			
4				
5		Actual	Estimated	Possible
6		Payments	Payments	Percent
7	Budget Item	1995	1996	Change
8				
9	Salaries	25,809	$26,841	4.0%
10	Wages	59,372	$62,341	5.0%
11	Telephone	3,825	$3,902	2.0%
12	Equipment	12,366	$12,613	2.0%
13	Services	4,500	$4,590	2.0%
14	Supplies	3,844	$3,921	2.0%
15	Travel	1,468	$1,497	2.0%
16	Postage	15,783	$16,099	2.0%
17	Other	789	$805	2.0%
18				
19	Totals	127,756	$132,608	
20	Goal		$130,311	
21	Difference		$2,297	

much other budget items must be reduced to accommodate the increases in wages. For example, what percent reductions must be made in telephone, equipment, services, supplies, travel, postage, or other expenses to hold the department budget within the 2 percent growth goal? As you can see from the figure, the manager will have a difficult time meeting the goal if a 5 percent wage increase and a 4 percent salary increase are granted. Many other budget lines will have to be reduced to compensate for these two increases.

To use a microcomputer spreadsheet program, the manager may have to print out data obtained from the corporate database and rekey this information into the spreadsheet. The job will be easier if the manager has the appropriate hardware and software to import or download the data from the corporate database directly into the microcomputer spreadsheet program.

Cash Management Systems

Important functions of financial management include ensuring that the organization has sufficient cash to meet its needs, putting excess funds from any period to use through investments, and providing borrowing power to meet the organization's cash needs in those periods of insufficient cash flow.

An organization needs cash for two major reasons: for working capital (cash needed for day-to-day operations) and for the acquisition of long-term assets. To determine if adequate cash is available for its working capital needs and its long-term asset acquisition plans, the organization must prepare a report of its expected cash flow for the time periods being considered. Typically this report shows the cash flow for each month of the coming year.

A **cash flow report** (see Figure 10–8) shows the estimated amount of cash that will be received and spent each month. The report shows in which months there will be excess funds that might be put to use and in which months there will be insufficient funds, which may require the organization to borrow cash to meet its working capital or fixed asset acquisition needs.

The information supplied by a cash flow report helps the manager make decisions about investing, purchasing, and borrowing money. If this information is placed on an electronic spreadsheet, the manager may simulate a number of possible business conditions, such as (1) increasing or decreasing revenue, (2) increasing or decreasing customer credit problems, (3) deferring the acquisition of an asset, or (4) repairing existing fixed assets instead of replacing them. By simulating many different possible business conditions, the manager is able to make more informed decisions about the use of or need for cash for the short term. In short, the manager can study various reallocations of the resources of a department, division, or other unit.

Cash management systems are more difficult to sustain for smaller organizations that may not be able to afford the resources necessary to track cash balances on a day-to-day basis and invest the excess to maximize organization income. Recognizing that difficulty, Merrill Lynch, a brokerage house, created a product in the 1970s that offered business customers an account combining the attributes of a money market account, a brokerage account, a margin credit account, and a checking account. The product, called the cash management account (CMA) provided business customers with automatic deposits of cash and dividends from other accounts into a money market account. This option gave organizations high interest rates on idle cash resulting from sales of stock, receipts of dividends, or deposits made for the purchase of stock. Organizations could also use a debit card and checks to withdraw money from the money market account. The result was that a small organization could use the

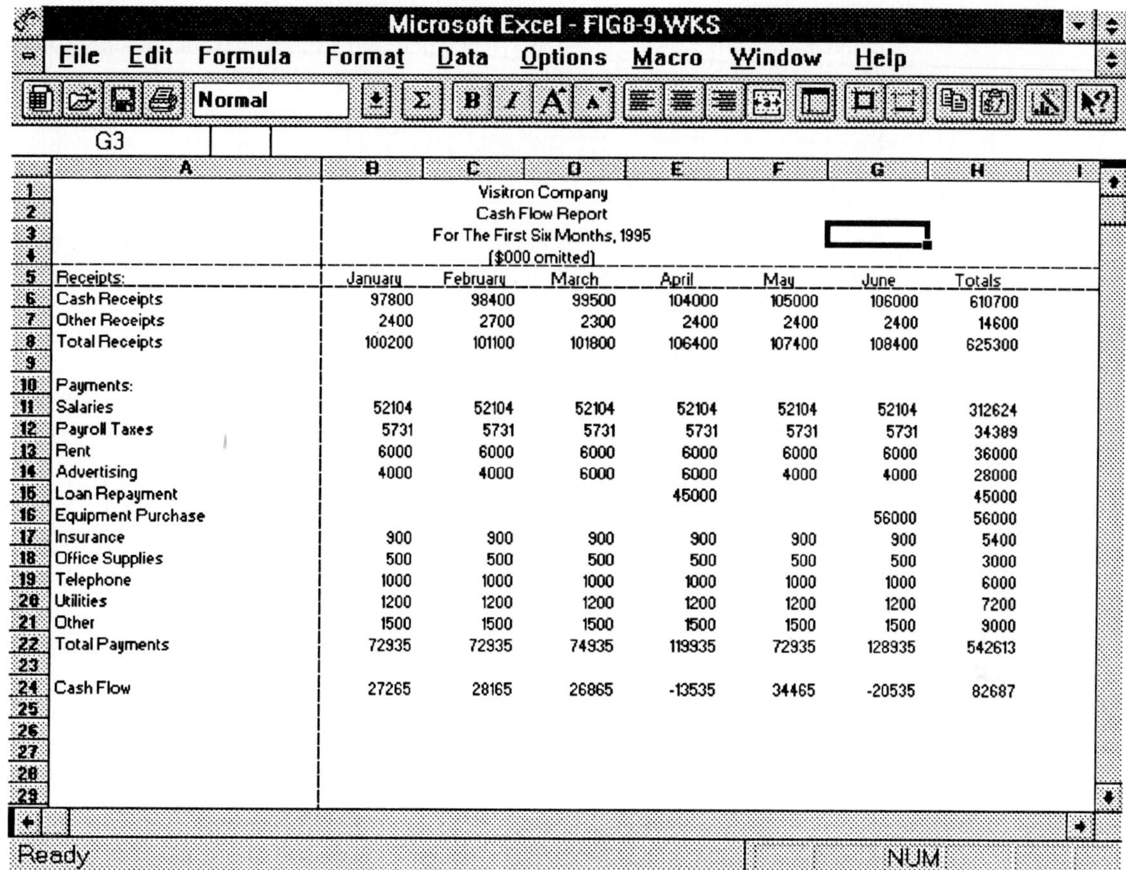

Visitron Company
Cash Flow Report
For The First Six Months, 1995
($000 omitted)

Receipts:	January	February	March	April	May	June	Totals
Cash Receipts	97800	98400	99500	104000	105000	106000	610700
Other Receipts	2400	2700	2300	2400	2400	2400	14600
Total Receipts	100200	101100	101800	106400	107400	108400	625300
Payments:							
Salaries	52104	52104	52104	52104	52104	52104	312624
Payroll Taxes	5731	5731	5731	5731	5731	5731	34389
Rent	6000	6000	6000	6000	6000	6000	36000
Advertising	4000	4000	6000	6000	4000	4000	28000
Loan Repayment				45000			45000
Equipment Purchase						56000	56000
Insurance	900	900	900	900	900	900	5400
Office Supplies	500	500	500	500	500	500	3000
Telephone	1000	1000	1000	1000	1000	1000	6000
Utilities	1200	1200	1200	1200	1200	1200	7200
Other	1500	1500	1500	1500	1500	1500	9000
Total Payments	72935	72935	74935	119935	72935	128935	542613
Cash Flow	27265	28165	26865	-13535	34465	-20535	82687

Figure 10–8
A spreadsheet cash flow report

service to maximize its income from idle cash sometimes available in its normal cash flow.

The cash management account gave Merrill Lynch an enormous competitive advantage and resulted in a large increase in new accounts until other brokerage houses, banks, and financial institutions developed similar products.

Capital Budgeting Systems

A **capital budget** contains information about the planned acquisition or disposal of major plant assets during the current year. The manager may compare the various capital spending plans using three commonly used evaluation tools: net present value, internal rate of return, and payback period. Before the plant asset is acquired, the manager should compare and evaluate various plans for its acquisition using some financial software tool, such as an electronic spreadsheet.

For example, suppose a manager is considering acquiring a large electronic printer and estimates that her firm will keep the machine for five years. The printer may be purchased or leased. Each method requires the manager to spend different amounts of money over different periods of time. The manager can improve the decision to buy or lease by evaluating the present value of the funds each method requires.

Net present value, or **NPV,** is the current value of cash that will be received at some future time. For example, $10,000 spent now is worth more than $10,000 spent one year from now. If you did not spend the money now, you could invest it and earn interest or other income. For example, if the current discount or interest rate is 10 percent, then the present value of $10,000 one year from now would be only $9,090.91. That is, the latter amount, if invested now, would produce $10,000 at the end of one year. Thus the present value of $10,000 to be spent one year from now is only $9,090.91. Using net present value, the manager must first identify all yearly cash inflows and outflows that would result from the lease or purchase of the printer. Cash inflows might include earnings of the asset, expenses saved through the use of the asset, and tax deductions resulting from the lease or purchase of the asset. Tax deductions could include operating expenses, maintenance, and annual lease costs if the equipment is leased, or operating expenses, maintenance, and annual depreciation if the equipment is purchased.

The manager also must determine the current discount or interest rate for money. Then she will be able to compare the discounted value of the net cash flows to the organization from leasing and purchasing the printer. These discounted values represent the net present values of leasing versus buying the equipment.

Many financial analysis software packages and spreadsheet software packages provide for the computation of net present value. A spreadsheet that the manager might use to evaluate the net present value of the cash flows for the lease or purchase of the electronic printer is shown in Figure 10–9.

The **internal rate of return (IRR)** method uses the same types of data as the net present value method. The manager needs to identify the cash inflows and outflows that result from acquiring the asset by the various methods and to identify the present discount or interest rate that the organization can earn on its money. The purpose of the internal rate of return calculation is to find the discount rate that generates a present value of the earnings or savings equal to the present value of the initial investment. The IRR found then can be compared to the rate of return the organization has decided it must make on its investments. Basically, you use IRR to determine whether the organization will make a better return by acquiring the asset than by investing its money in some other venture.

The manager may also wish to estimate the payback period of the investment of her firm's funds in the electronic printer. The **payback period** is how many years or months the increase in revenues or the savings from reduced operating expenses obtained from the asset will take to match the investment in the asset. Suppose that the purchase of the new printer is projected to provide $3,500 annual savings over the old equipment. If the new equipment costs $17,500 to purchase, deliver, and install, then the payback period is estimated to be $17,500/$3,500, or five years. The way the manager calculated the payback period here does not consider the time value of annual savings.

Using payback period, net present value, internal rate of return, and other asset acquisition analysis tools, the financial manager can make informed decisions on the utility of acquiring assets and how these acquisitions may best be funded. Software tools, such as spreadsheets and financial analysis software, assist the manager in accomplishing these tasks quickly. The manager also can see the results when various factors are varied. For example, varying the discount rate, the length of time the asset is held, the amount of down payment, or other variables can help determine the optimum factors for use in negotiating with vendors.

Investment Management Systems

Investment management—overseeing the organization's investments in stocks, bonds, and other securities—is an important part of cash management. Managing investments is also an important part of managing the organization's pension plan.

Figure 10–9
A printout of a spreadsheet showing net present values for two ways to acquire an electronic printer

ASSET ACQUISITION EVALUATION
LEASE VS. PURCHASE

Purchase Price	$17,500
Sales Tax Rate	0.05
Resale/Trade-In	$6,000
Interest Rate	0.1
Mo. Maintenance	$270
Mo. Lease Pay.	$450
Lease Deposit	0
Mar. Tax Rate	0.45
Deprec. Rate	0.2

Purchase Option

Year	0	1	2	3	4	5
Total Cost	$18,375					
Main. Net of Tax		$1,458	$1,458	$1,458	$1,458	$1,458
Total Outgoing	$18,375	$1,458	$1,458	$1,458	$1,458	$1,458
Tax. Sav. Deprec.		$1,571	$1,571	$1,571	$1,571	$1,571
Sale/Trade Amt.						$6,000
Total Incoming		$1,571	$1,571	$1,571	$1,571	$7,571
Net Cash Flow	$18,375	–$113	–$113	–$113	–$113	–$113
NPV	$14,221					

Lease Option

Year	0	1	2	3	4	5
Deposit	0					
Mo. Pay Net Tax		$2,430	$2,430	$2,430	$2,430	$2,430
Main. Net of Tax		$1,458	$1,458	$1,458	$1,458	$1,458
Net Cash Flow	0	$3,888	$3,888	$3,888	$3,888	$3,888
NPV	$14,739					

Whatever their source of investment funds, most organizations invest money in securities of one kind or another. Careful management of these investments is necessary to ensure the achievement of organization goals.

Computer information systems provide unique ways to manage stock and bond portfolios. These ways typically involve the use of on-line databases that furnish immediate updates for stock and bond prices, information about the history of each investment, and various portfolio investment analysis tools to help the manager stay on top of the organization's investments. The system may be a simple one in which the manager has a computer system with a modem and a subscription to an investment service.

For example, companies that provide on-line services, such as Dow Jones and CompuServe, typically provide a host of data about investments, including current and past security prices and company information such as financial statistics, earnings estimates, and brokerage reports, Securities and Exchange Commission filings, and even financial statements and other analyses. Investment databases are also available through other means (see Box 10–2). For example, Value Line is an investment service company that provides investment data on regularly updated disks. The system also allows you to download current stock prices to your microcomputer using a modem. The data

Box 10–2 Some On-Line Financial Services

A wealth of financial information and services is available to financial and other managers on-line today. Below is a list of just a few of these on-line sources of financial data:

Product	Description
Fidelity On-line Xpress	Allows users to trade securities at a discount and to access real-time stock quotes and financial news.
PC Financial Network	On-line discount brokerage service available through Prodigy that allows users to trade stock, certificates of deposit, and mutual funds. Data can be downloaded to a financial management software program.
Strategic Investor	A database of 4,500 stock and 3,000 mutual fund data, including quotes, news, and financial analysis.
Business Database Plus	Provides company profiles and legal and economic analysis.
Company Analyzer	Offers reports on stocks, including earnings and growth forecasts, price histories, analysis, and financial statements.
Dow Jones News/Retrieval	Provides financial news, company financial information, earnings per share estimates, mutual fund and stock quotes, and other financial data.
Market Muse	A weekly stock market newsletter
Disclosure II	A database of more than 10,000 companies containing data on total assets, book value, price/earning ratio, income statements, balance sheets, and many other types of financial information.
Institutional Brokers Estimate System	Contains earnings estimates on more than 3,400 companies for the current year and five years out.
MMS International	Key economic data from a variety of economic reports, including Federal Reserve forecasts. Also provides on-line brokerage services, on-line advice, and an analysis of technical and fundamental factors affecting the markets.
Money Magazine Financial Information Center	A database of more than 1,900 mutual funds.
S & P Online	Standard and Poor's on-line database providing a wide variety of company data including earnings estimates. Also provides stock pick recommendations.
Value Line Corporate Reports	Financial and statistical information about 1,800 companies.

can be analyzed using your own software or with Value/Screen software provided by Value Line. This software provides data on many different variables for about 1,700 stocks (see Figure 10–10). Value/Screen permits the manager to view the data on individual companies or to compare data on companies or groups of companies against the entire database of 1,700 firms. It also permits the manager to analyze and maintain data on the organization's current stock portfolio. When you input the current price of

Current dividend	**Price history**
Current earnings per share	Price stability index
Current price-earnings ratio	Price-to-book value ratio
Current yield	Projected changes in earnings per share
Debt as a percent of capital	Projected growth in book value
Dividend history	Projected growth in dividends
Earnings per share history	Projected growth in earnings per share
Financial strength rating	Projected price appreciation
High price for year	Projected return
Industry ranking	Recent price
Low price for year	Safety ranking
Percent return on net worth	Timeliness
Percent of retained earnings to common equity	Sales

Figure 10–10
Some of the data about stock available from Value Line's Value/Screen software

each stock, it calculates the gain or loss the portfolio would generate if sold now, provides the income and yield of the portfolio, and offers a variety of other measures for each stock owned and the entire portfolio. The data and analyses the software provides allow investment managers to make more informed decisions regarding the sale or acquisition of investments.

Tactical-level information systems focus on the resource allocation problems of the manager. Budgeting systems, cash management systems, capital budgeting systems, investment management systems, and other tactical-level financial information systems give the manager increased control over the financial resources of a department or an organization and provide considerable support for allocating financial resources to meet organizational goals.

STRATEGIC ACCOUNTING AND FINANCIAL INFORMATION SYSTEMS

You have learned that operational-level information systems are task oriented and that tactical-level information systems are resource allocation oriented. In contrast, strategic-level information systems are goal oriented. That is, these systems are designed to support organizational goal and direction setting.

Strategic accounting and financial information systems typically include several types of information flows:

1. Internally generated financial condition analysis data, describing the status of the organization.
2. Externally generated economic, demographic, and social data describing the present and future environments for the organization.
3. Forecasts of the future of that organization in those environments.

Two major outcomes of financial strategic planning are the setting of financial goals and directions for the organization. The former may include setting goals for investments and return on investments. The latter may involve deciding on new investment opportunities or on the mix of capital sources used to fund the organization.

A major source of computerized information about the current and future status of the organization is the organization's own financial accounting database. A promising source of computerized information on the present and future environments in which the organization must operate are on-line databases that contain economic, social, demographic, technological, and political information. Projecting likely scenarios for the organization using these two categories of data is the art of forecasting. A major purpose of strategic decision making is to use long-range forecasts to reduce the risk involved in major organizational decisions.

Financial Condition Analysis Systems

Computerized accounting systems provide the user with many reports to which ratios and analysis tools may be applied. For example, the manager may use a variety of analysis tools, including those shown in Figure 10–11, on the data reported on the income statement and balance sheet. Many computerized accounting systems supply reports that automatically calculate and present the results of these tools and ratios. Along with the data and reports, these tools and ratios make up the organization's **financial condition analysis system.** This system provides management with a variety of measures of the soundness of the organization and makes it possible to explore ways of improving the organization's financial condition.

Financial condition analysis data on competitors, suppliers, buyers, and other organizations is also available through on-line financial databases such as the Dow Jones News/Retrieval Service (see Box 10–2). Information about on-line databases was also presented in Chapter 6 in the section entitled "On-Line Databases and Information Utilities."

Long-Range Forecasting Systems

Strategic planners demand forecasts on a variety of factors that will affect organization performance in the future. Some forecasts may involve the use of internally generated data. For example past sales data may be used to project future sales. Other forecasts may use only external data or both internal and external data. For example, forecasting economic indicators helps planners understand the likely economic environment in which the organization must operate in the future. Forecasting the financial health of the organization through long-range budget estimates—including a variety of possible wage negotiation settlements, actions by competitors, interest rate fluctuations, fuel cost changes, and different inflation rates—provides planners with opportunities to consider actions that will help the organization survive bad times or take advantage of a future environment.

Information used in forecasting the future environment includes descriptions of the past activities of an organization, data on the present economy and forecasts of the future economy, information on the present demographic structure of the region or country and forecasts of the future demographic structure, and descriptions of the

Figure 10–11 Commonly used financial condition ratios

Ratio Name	Ratio Formula
Current ratio	Current assets ÷ current liabilities
Working capital	Current assets − current liabilities
Inventory turnover	Cost of goods sold ÷ average inventory
Debt-to-equity ratio	Stockholder equity ÷ total liabilities
Rate earned on stockholder's equity	Net income ÷ average stockholder's equity
Earnings per share	Net income ÷ number of shares

current social structure and social mores and predictions of the future structure of society and societal mores.

For example, suppose that Juan Aponte is superintendent of a small school district and wishes to predict the economic and demographic conditions in the school district five years from now. He forecasts the school-age population for five years in the future using rather hard data obtained from present census figures adjusted for the life expectancies of the population and the dropout rate of the district. These figures allow him to project the number of classes, teachers, and school facilities the district needs. The data also allow Aponte to project state aid to the district, a major source of its revenue.

Aponte forecasts that part of the district's budget in five years will come from an expanded tax base. This prediction is made using economic projections for the district, including new home construction, new family formations, business additions and failures, and the estimated rate of price increases on real property.

Aponte also uses the current ages of the staff and the district's past retirement experience to project staffing needs five years from now, indicating how many new staff members must be acquired because of retirements and growth or how many present staff members must be let go. Aponte projects the salary increases for the previous five years in the district to the next five years, adjusting those figures for the estimated effects of the projected supply and demand of teachers.

Aponte hopes that these projections will permit him and his staff to identify potential resource problems for the district in time to solve them without needing crisis management. Notice that some of the information he needs can be generated using internal data from the district's computerized database. However, other information critical to strategic planning is external to the organization. Some of this information may be available from an on-line database.

After Aponte acquires the information, he builds a spreadsheet to allow him to forecast the financial condition of the school district. He develops the spreadsheet so he can make changes in assessed values, property tax rates, student enrollment, state aid, interest rates, supplies and expenses, union-negotiated salaries, and the student/teacher ratio (see Figure 10–12). This spreadsheet allows Aponte to simulate how a variety of demographic and economic conditions will impact the financial condition of the school district next year or five years from now.

ACCOUNTING AND FINANCIAL MANAGEMENT SOFTWARE

To provide managers with the capability to handle financial information systems, a number of software products, both general and specialized, have emerged. General software products are not designed specifically for the financial manager and may be used by most people. Specialized software products have been designed especially for the financial manager.

General Software Tools

General software helpful to the financial manager includes spreadsheet software, forecasting and statistical software, and query language and report writer software.

Spreadsheet Software. Spreadsheet software packages provide a versatile tool for financial managers. Spreadsheet software allows the manager to design partially completed tables or forms called **templates** (see Figure 10–13), which contain the headings and names of the items in the spreadsheet. The templates also contain the formulas used to calculate column or row totals, column or row averages, and other statistical

GASPE SCHOOL DISTRICT BUDGET WORKSHEET, 1995		
INCOME:		
Assessed Value: Residential Property	$24,625,000.00	
Assessed Value: Business Property	$5,495,000.00	
Property Tax Rate per $1,000	$65.00	
Residence Property Taxes	$1,600,625.00	
Business Property Taxes	$357,175.00	
Total Income from Taxes		$1,957,800.00
Student Enrollment	823	
State Aid per Pupil	$37.00	
Enrollment State Aid	$30,451.00	
Other State Aid	$6,000.00	
Total State Aid		$36,451.00
Funds Invested	$90,000.00	
Investment Interest Rate	7.00%	
Interest Income	$6,300.00	
Other Income	$4,500.00	
Total Interest and Other Income		$10,800.00
Total Income for District		$2,005,051.00
EXPENSES:		
Student/Teacher Ratio	24	
Number of Teachers Needed	35	
Number of Special Professionals	2	
Number of Administrators	3	
Number of Clerical Staff	3	
Number of Other Staff	2	
Average Teacher Salary	$29,807.00	
Average Professional Salary	$32,867.00	
Average Administrator Salary	$43,082.00	
Average Clerical Salary	$19,253.00	
Average Staff Wages	20,982.00	
Total Salaries and Wages		$1,337,948.00
Instructional Supplies	$210,000.00	
Curriculum Supplies	$440,000.00	
Office Expenses	$26,000.00	
Equipment Expenses	$56,000.00	
Other Expenses	$5,000.00	
Total Non-Salary Expenses		$737,000.00
Total Expenses		$2,074,948.00
SURPLUS/DEFICIT		($69,897.00)

Figure 10–12 A printout of a spreadsheet used to forecast the financial condition of a school district

quantities on the values entered into the template. For example, a budget template might include the table heading, the column headings, the names of the budget line items in the first column, and the formulas for calculating subtotals, totals, and percentages of the total budget. If this template is designed well and saved (see Box 10–3), the manager can use it time after time simply by entering the specific amounts for each

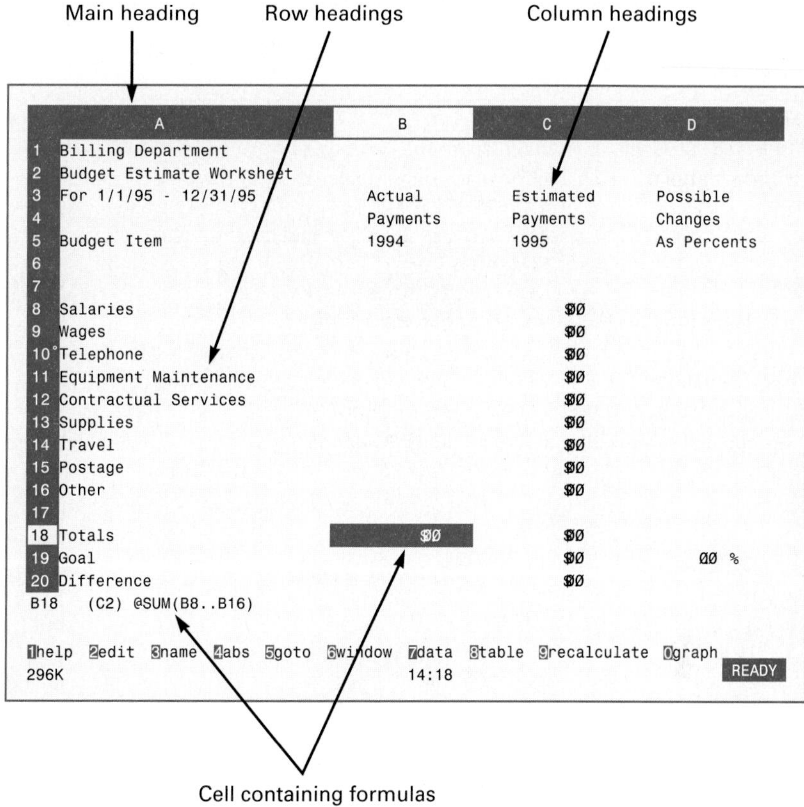

Figure 10–13
A template for a budget spreadsheet

Box 10–3 Evaluating Your Spreadsheet Design

1. Did you include the name of the developer or revisor in the spreadsheet?
2. Did you include the date of construction or revision in the spreadsheet?
3. Did you briefly describe the purpose of the spreadsheet in the spreadsheet?
4. Did you identify the sources of data for the spreadsheet?
5. Did you include a legend in the spreadsheet that defines any special symbols, abbreviations, or terms used?
6. Did you name cells used in formulas where appropriate? For example, in Figure 10–6, you might name the sum of actual payments "actpay" and the sum of budget allocations, "budalloc." Then your variance column total could be created by this formula: actpay – budalloc.
7. Did you use cell references in spreadsheet formulas instead of absolute numbers? For example, you might set up a row that defines the FICA tax rate at 7.51 percent and refer to that cell whenever the FICA rate is needed in a formula. Then, when the FICA rate changes, you only need to change the actual numerical rate in one place.
8. Did you format the worksheet so that it is easy to read and navigate? For example, did you
   a. Round numbers to remove unnecessary detail when appropriate?
   b. Center labels, column titles, or data when useful?
   c. Indent and double space when useful?
   d. Place related columns and rows together?
   e. Divide a long spreadsheet into separate screens so that it can be easily navigated using the page up and page down keys?
9. Did you use any data validation techniques, such as using column widths to control maximum character length or using the protect feature to protect all cells except the input cells?

Box 10–4 Financial Templates for Spreadsheets

The selected products below illustrate the variety of spreadsheet templates available for many different financial tasks.

Product	Vendor	Description
PFS: Business Plan for Windows	Spinnaker Corp.	Tools and templates for financial planning and analysis
Business Valuation	Innovative Professional Software, Inc.	A template for valuing a business in eight different ways
CFO Spreadsheet Applications	Intex Solutions	24 templates for financial tasks, such as cash flow, securities management, taxes, inventories, capital investment, break-even analysis, and firm evaluation
Finance Projection	Software Models	Templates for financial planning and analysis including cash budgeting
Financial Decisions	GenMicronics	Over 100 Excel financial templates including mortgage schedules, mortgage refinancing, bond yields, and APR calculations
Financial Solutions	G F Spreadsheets	100 financial templates for investments, mortgages, annuities, leases, present value, interest, inventory management, depreciation, property analysis, and amortization
Horse Farm Templates	Owens Horse Systems	13 templates for budgets, cash flows, and costs for horse farms
Lotus Small Business Kit	Lotus Development Corp.	Financial templates for companies under 100 employees including cash flow analysis and cost-volume-profit analysis
Lotus Solution for Financial Managers	Lotus Development Corp.	A series of templates including general ledger, depreciation, cash flow, bank reconciliation
MoneyCalc IV	Money Tree Software	50 Lotus templates for financial planners, insurance agents, brokers, and CPAs
Write Up*Plus	UniLink	More than 150 financial templates for use by accounting firms

line item and correcting the dates. Spreadsheet software can be used effectively for many financial functions, not only analyzing the budget, but also comparing various asset acquisition plans; comparing various investment alternatives; estimating the cash flow for an organization, a new product, or a new asset; and simulating the effect of varying demographic and economic conditions on a budget.

It is important to identify the types of financial analyses you wish to perform and to make certain that the spreadsheet software you acquire can perform these analyses quickly and easily. For example, many spreadsheet software products provide a built-in function for calculating net present value. All you have to do is enter the name of the function, the current discount or interest rate available, and the location in the spreadsheet of values for which you wish to calculate the net present value. Other commonly included functions are internal rate of return and return on investment.

If the budget you prepare or work with results from the consolidation of many other budgets, it will be useful for you to have a spreadsheet that allows you to consolidate budgets prepared separately into a single budget automatically. The ability to consolidate department budgets into one divisional budget is a very helpful feature of some spreadsheets.

If your templates require a great deal of input from data already in the organization database, you should select spreadsheet software that can import data from your organization's database. This feature also makes it convenient to update data in your spreadsheet to correspond with current information in your database. For example, if you are using a spreadsheet to help you manage cash, you might need to update information about your organization's cash balances regularly during the day to provide effective management of idle cash flows.

Instead of creating your own spreadsheet templates, you may buy commercially prepared templates. There are many software companies that offer templates, and their products serve nearly every conceivable type of financial analysis (see Box 10–4).

Forecasting and Statistical Software. Many financial analysis tasks involve forecasting future events and require that you use statistical tools. For example, you may wish to forecast the changes in the price of the energy your organization uses to heat, cool, and power its activities. To do that, you may wish to extrapolate the future price of energy using its previous five-year price history. You may also wish to display this information using a line graph.

Selecting **statistical** or **forecasting software** to aid you in tactical-level decisions and long-range planning requires that you carefully analyze what your applications require so that the software you buy has these features (see Box 10–5):

1. It contains the statistical procedures or forecasting methods you wish to use. If the software does not do what you want it to do, no discount given for the software will allow you to paper over the problem.
2. It presents the procedures and methods at a level appropriate to your sophistication with statistics and forecasting techniques. Software designed for statistically unsophisticated users helps users select statistical procedures and enter data.

Query Language and Report Writer Software. If your database management system contains a query language, a report writer, or both, then these tools can be used to poke through the data in the database to find useful information to your ad hoc questions about financial management.

A report writer is a software tool that allows you to identify what data items in a record you wish to list on a report and then allows you to format the report as you would like it. For example, the software might ask you what heading you would like for the report, what data items you wish to list on the report, what column headings you wish to give each data item listed, and what you want to do with the columns of data—find the average for the column, sum the column, and so on. A report writer provides you

Box 10–5 Forecasting Software for Microcomputers

Many financial analysis, statistical, and forecasting programs are available for microcomputers today. Some of these programs are general in nature and may be used for several purposes. A number of software packages are designed specifically for forecasting. Many of these programs are easy to use and provide on-line tutorials to train the user. Some of these programs are listed below.

Product	Vendor	Description
Plan 80	Business Planning Systems, Inc.	Provides sales and cash flow forecasting and many other features
Forecast! for 1-2-3	Intex Solutions	A Lotus template for creating forecasts. Easy to use and menu-driven
Crystal Ball for Windows	Decisioneering, Inc.	An add-on product for Excel spreadsheets that lets you forecast the best, worst, and most likely case scenarios
Encore Plus	Ferox Microsystems, Inc.	A package full of features that includes forecasting as one of many financial analysis tools
RATS (regression analysis of time series)	Estima	A forecasting package with versions for Unix, DOS, and Macintosh systems
Forecast Pro for Windows	Business Forecast Systems	A rule-based expert system that guides the user in selecting and using forecasting techniques
FYPlus for Windows	Pillar Corp.	A corporate financial planning and budgeting system that includes forecasting
SmartForecasts for Windows	Smart Software, Inc.	A forecasting program that uses an expert system to help the novice; includes graphic output

with the ability to extract data from the database and to format it to be useful to you—without the aid of the data processing department. All you do is follow the menus and prompts provided by the report writer software. You could, for example, ask the report writer to list the original cost of each stock that your organization holds for investment purposes in one column, place the annual income generated by the stock in another column, and calculate the annual yield and put this in a third column. The report might look something like the one in Figure 10–14.

General Accounting and Financial Analysis Software

Computerized Accounting Systems. Commercially packaged accounting system software contains the operating-level software used to produce the invoices, checks, monthly financial statements, and other regular, routine output necessary to run an organization. In addition, many computerized accounting systems provide a variety of features (see Box 10–6), including financial analysis tools for the tactical decision maker and strategic planner, such as the various financial statement ratio analyses discussed earlier in this chapter. The manager can produce data automatically simply by selecting reports from a menu displayed by the software.

Figure 10-14
A stock portfolio report produced by a report writer

STOCK PORTFOLIO REPORT
GROUP III STOCKS
03/31/95

STOCK NAME	ORIGINAL COST	CURRENT VALUE	GAIN OR LOSS	CURRENT YIELD
AERODYNE INTERNATIONAL	$89,335.90	$92,410.88	$3,074.98	29.0%
BEEKMAN ENGINEERING	$73,198.00	$71,337.75	($1,860.25)	3.6%
CHESTERFIELD LAMINATING	$29,719.40	$35,098.13	$5,378.72	1.1%
DEERPARK ELEVATOR	$18,067.20	$12,973.63	($5,093.58)	5.6%
DIBBLE FORGINGS	$41,849.80	$40,978.25	($871.55)	4.2%
DYMARK PRODUCTS	$24,579.32	$28,798.25	$4,218.93	4.4%
EAST REFRIGERATION	$32,419.76	$41,089.38	$8,669.62	2.0%
JACKSON MANUFACTURING	$74,078.30	$88,308.63	$14,230.32	3.1%
OAKDALE HYDRAULICS	$22,507.91	$27,861.88	$5,353.97	2.9%
TERRADYNE MECHANICS	$52,919.56	$73,197.50	$20,277.94	1.6%
TOTALS	$458,675.15	$512,054.25	$53,379.10	7.6%

Box 10-6 Selected Features and Specifications of Computerized Accounting Software

Computerized accounting software typically includes a general ledger module and subordinate modules such as payroll, inventory, purchase order, sales order, accounts receivable, accounts payable, job cost, and fixed assets. When buying accounting software, examine the features and specifications of each of the modules to ensure that what is offered matches your organization's needs. Some possible features and specifications of accounting software include these:

FEATURES

1. Handles multiple companies.
2. Processes multicompany consolidated reports.
3. Maintains budgets.
4. Allows entries outside the current period.
5. Allows data export to spreadsheet files.
6. Allows unbalanced entries.
7. Provides billing-cycle functions.
8. Reconciles checking accounts.
9. Provides financial reports at any time for any period.
10. Allows multiuser access.
11. Provides on-line help.

SPECIFICATIONS

1. The maximum number of accounts it handles.
2. The highest account balance it accepts.
3. The maximum number of account number digits it accepts.
4. The maximum number of departments it allows.
5. How it processes purchase discounts.
6. How it processes aging of accounts receivable.
7. What tax form reports it produces.
8. What access security it provides.
9. What auditing features it provides.

Computerized accounting software is also available commercially for specific industries. This software is also called **vertical accounting software,** and it is designed to provide for the unique concerns and problems of firms in specific industries. For example, organizations in the health industry often must collect not only from the patient but also from third parties, such as insurance companies or government agencies. The ability of software to handle accounts receivable from third parties and to provide third-party billing is important to these organizations. This ability is usually a standard feature in accounting software designed for organizations in the health industry.

Computerized Auditing Software. A number of **computerized auditing programs** are available to assist auditors when they evaluate or monitor a computerized accounting system. For example, many software companies and accounting firms have developed *generalized audit software* that can be used by **EDP (electronic data processing) auditors** to help them evaluate electronic accounting system files. Generalized audit software provides access to the computer files; lets EDP auditors create audit files, extract data, and analyze data statistically; sorts, summarizes, and samples data; and generates reports.

For example, generalized auditing software usually allows EDP auditors to develop test decks, or sample files, which can be used to verify how accurately the financial accounting programs process data. Test deck files also contain data that, when entered, measures how well the financial accounting programs control the quality of data that has been input. For example, test decks contain data that test whether alphabetic data can be placed in numeric fields, whether 10 characters can be placed in an 9-character field, whether negative numbers can be entered into fields that should only contain positive data, and so on.

Generalized auditing software also provides EDP auditors with checklists and other prompts for examining the security of the data processing center, including the physical security of the center and the security procedures used by center staff, such as archiving procedures, offsite storage of backup tapes, and documentation.

Financial accounting systems are typically protected by a variety of security software or security procedures. The software and procedures are designed to shield accounting systems from unauthorized access, system failure, viruses, and other threats. A discussion of security software and procedures is provided in Chapter 20.

Specific Accounting and Financial Analysis Software

A variety of commercially prepared software provides the manager with specific financial analysis and planning tools. These financial analysis software products are often quite narrow in scope. For example, some specialized software products assist the financial manager in developing and analyzing the capital budgeting needs of the organization. Other specialized software products assist the investment manager in monitoring and analyzing the organization's investment portfolio (see Figure 10–10). The financial manager can use specialized software products to help manage the cash flow of the organization.

Specialized **financial modeling software** is often more general in nature. For example, Interactive Financial Planning System, or IFPS, is specialized financial modeling software that allows the financial manager to build financial models and manipulate those models to simulate various business scenarios. The product contains many built-in financial, statistical, and mathematical functions to assist the manager in a wide variety of business applications. One of the special strengths of this product is that it allows the manager to optimize. What is more, the product makes it possible to develop models and simulate different scenarios with the models using a language that is close to the natural English of the business world. Also, IFPS allows the manager to set goals for certain factors, such as a budget total, identify to the program which departmental lines can be varied, and then ask the program to "work backwards" to create budgets that meet the goal set.

A number of companies offer microcomputer software packages that help individuals and small companies manage their money. Basically, most **personal financial management software** uses a checkbook as the basic program element. One very popular program is Andrew Tobia$: Managing Your Money (MYM). MYM lets you record your financial transactions in a checkbook, print checks, set up a budget tied to the checkbook, and estimate your taxes. It also offers many other features, including managing investments, paying bills electronically (if you have a modem), planning your retirement, evaluating mortgage refinancing, and tracking your net worth.

For the small business, the package provides a means to manage accounts payable and receivable (with aging); complete budget, cash, and tax forecasting; evaluate buy, lease, or rent options; print invoices, mailing lists, and mailing labels; manage expense accounts; and print financial statements. The package also offers a number of utilities, including a card filer (for mailing lists and labels) and a to-do list.

Management Summary

Financial information systems are essential information systems for any organization. Like other information systems, they can be categorized into operational, tactical, and strategic planning systems. Each category of financial information system uses data of a somewhat different nature, is used principally by persons at different levels within an organization, and supports decisions of a different nature.

Financial information systems include operational accounting information systems, such as general ledger systems, fixed assets systems, order entry systems, accounts receivable systems, accounts payable systems, inventory systems, purchasing systems, and payroll systems. They also include tactical decision making and strategic planning information systems, such as budgeting systems, cash management systems, capital budgeting systems, financial condition analysis systems, investment management systems, and forecasting systems.

A wealth of financial information systems software is available. General software products, which can be used for more than financial applications, include spreadsheets, statistical packages, and database management systems. Also, a variety of specialized financial software products are available to manage specific financial tasks, such as budgeting, cash management, capital budgeting, financial statement analysis, investments, modeling, and forecasting.

Key Terms for Managers

budgeting system, **391**
capital budget, **395**
cash flow report, **394**
cash management systems, **394**
computerized auditing programs, **408**
EDP (electronic data processing) auditors, **408**
financial accounting system, **385**
financial condition analysis system, **400**
financial modeling software, **408**
forecasting software, **405**
internal rate of return (IRR), **396**
investment management, **396**
net present value (NPV), **395**
operational accounting information systems, **385**
payback period, **396**
personal financial management software, **409**
statistical software, **405**
strategic accounting and financial information systems, **399**
tactical accounting and financial information systems, **391**
templates, **401**
vertical accounting software, **408**

1. What is the financial management function? Include in your description at least 10 specific activities of financial management.

Review Questions

2. What program modules are common to an accounting system software package? Describe the major functions of each module.
3. What are transaction-processing information systems?
4. What types of information flows are typically associated with strategic planning systems? What are the sources of those information flows?
5. What are two ways that the accounts receivable system of a computerized accounting system might be useful to the manager?
6. In what ways might a computerized inventory system provide a competitive advantage to an organization?
7. What is an aged accounts receivable report? What level of decision making does this report typically support? What type of report is it, usually—ad hoc, exception, detailed, or summary?
8. What information would a manager need to compute net present value? What types of tactical decisions can net present value information assist the manager in making?
9. Identify the information a manager would need to compute payback period. What kind of tactical decisions can payback period calculations help to support?
10. What types of general-use software can managers use to support financial decisions at the tactical and strategic planning levels?
11. What types of specially designed financial software can managers use to support tactical- and strategic planning-level financial decisions?
12. What is a template? What are commercially prepared templates?
13. What precautions should you take when acquiring forecasting or statistical software?
14. What does the term *import* mean?
15. An advantage of spreadsheet programs is that they can be used to ask "what if" questions. What does "what if" questioning mean when used in this context?
16. What characteristics of spreadsheet software should financial managers consider before purchasing a package?
17. What are two major outcomes of financial strategic planning?

Questions for Discussion

1. How do operational, tactical, and strategic planning information systems for financial management differ in their orientation?
2. How might an accounts payable system provide information that could reduce the costs of payables to the manager?
3. How has the computerization of accounting information changed the views of managers toward that information?

4. Explain what information a cash flow report contains. How might a financial manager use a cash flow report? What tactical decisions might the cash flow report support?

5. Describe one summary report and one exception report that might be useful for these types of managers:

   a. Accounting manager.
   b. Budget officer.
   c. Investment manager.

6. Why are spreadsheet templates useful to managers?

7. How might on-line databases assist a manager responsible for managing a portfolio of stock and bond investments for an organization?

8. What categories of information might be useful for strategic planners concerned about the environment in which the organization may find itself 5 to 10 years from now?

9. Explain how a spreadsheet may prove useful to a manager for financial decision making. That is, what are the characteristics of a spreadsheet that make it helpful for tactical decision making and strategic planning decision support? Provide examples of the use of spreadsheets in financial decision making.

10. Describe how forecasting software, statistical software, or both may be used in the strategic planning process.

PROBLEMS

1. **Financial software problem: investment analysis.** You are a financial officer seeking to invest idle company funds in the stock market. You will use the Value Line Company's Value/Screen III stock selection software demonstration diskette to identify stock investments that meet certain criteria. The demonstration diskette contains data on about 300 stocks. The full-blown version contains statistics on about 1,700 stocks and is used by many individual and business investors. Obtain a copy of the diskette from your instructor. Begin by changing to the A: drive by typing A: at the C:> prompt. Then place the Value/Screen III demonstration diskette in the A drive and type VSDEMO. From the main menu, select S for "Screen Data Base." Now complete a series of investment tasks by identifying the names of stocks that have these characteristics:

   a. A recent price of less than $50 *and* a projected 3 to 5 year appreciation rate of more than 200 percent.
   b. A current yield of greater than 5 percent, a current price/earnings ratio of less than 11 to 1, *and* a price to book value ratio of more than 1.25.
   c. A safety ranking of greater than 3, an historical five-year dividend growth rate of greater than 3 percent, *and* an historical return on net worth of greater than 1 percent.

   Write down the names of the stock for each query or print the screens that display the answers to *a, b,* and *c* by using the print screen feature of your computer system. To do so, make sure your printer is turned on. Then hold down the shift key and press the print screen key on your keyboard. Sometimes even though the contents of your screen is dumped to the printer, the page does not eject from the printer and you may have to use the form feed button on the printer to eject it.

2. **Spreadsheet problem: Accounts receivable department budget estimate.** Using any spreadsheet program that can read or import a Lotus 1-2-3 file, load the file labeled "PROB10-2" on the applications diskette provided by your instructor. The file is a template for estimating the budget expenses for an accounts receivable department. The template contains the column and row headings for estimating the budget. You must enter the goal for the rate of increase or decrease in the total budget amount for next year as a decimal in cell C20. You must also enter the rate of increase or decrease that each budget line amount is estimated to change in cells D8–D16 (for example, enter .03 in cell D8, the Salaries line in the Possible Changes as Percent column).

   a. Enter percentages in columns C and D to reflect these estimates for next year:
   1. The goal is to keep the overall budget to no more than a 5 percent increase over last year.
   2. Salaries will increase by 3 percent.
   3. Wages will increase by 5 percent.
   4. Postage will increase by 12 percent.
   5. All other budget items will increase by 3.5 percent.

   b. After entering the values in *a* above, answer these questions:
   1. What is the total of the estimated budget expenditures for next year?
   2. What is the difference in dollars between the goal for next year and the total estimated payments for next year?

   c. What would be the answers to *b* if both wages and salaries increased by 6 percent?

   d. Using the spreadsheet amounts developed in *c* above, develop a budget estimate that meets the 5 percent overall increase goal stated in *a* and also maintains the 6 percent increases in wages and salaries stated in *c*. The increase or decrease in all other budget items can be varied to achieve the results needed.

3. **Spreadsheet design problem.** Load the spreadsheet file "budget" into your spreadsheet program. Then take these steps:

   a. Identify the errors and problems you find in the spreadsheet.
   b. Redesign the spreadsheet using the suggestions in Box 10–3.

4. **Spreadsheet design problem: budget analysis.** Acquire the current-year budget of an organization such as a town, a school, a university, a department, the business of a relative or friend, or even an extracurricular activity, such as the university newspaper.

   a. Describe the information you would like to have to analyze the budget you acquired.
   b. Identify at least one source for each type of information you described in *a*.
   c. Explain what type of analysis each type of information allows you to make and why such an analysis might prove fruitful.
   d. Develop a spreadsheet template for the budget. Use the design suggestions in Box 10–3. Then, test your template by inputting the data from the actual budget and compare the results.

5. **Budget officer interview.** Identify a budget officer in the university or college you are attending or in the organization for which you are working. Interview the budget officer to determine the following:

a. What types of information the officer uses to compile the budget for each year.
b. What internal types and sources of information the officer uses to analyze the budget.
c. What external types and sources of information the officer uses to analyze the budget.

6. **Financial analysis tools.** Using periodical literature, CD-ROM or on-line databases, or other sources, identify three software packages that provide the manager with financial analysis tools. For example, you might identify software packages that provide support in cash management, capital budgeting, and portfolio analysis.

   a. If they are available, send for a demonstration diskette for each of the packages. You can usually order a demonstration diskette by calling an 800 number. Use the demonstration diskettes to view the features of the packages.
   b. Prepare a report describing each package, including the package's features, cost, ease of use, and hardware requirements.

7. **Spreadsheet design problem: billing department budget report.** Using spreadsheet software, develop a template for the budget report shown in Figure 10–6. Use the design suggestions in Box 10–3. The variance column should contain formulas that subtract the year-to-date actuals from the year-to-date allocated amounts. The total line under the four money columns should contain formulas that sum the columns.

   a. Fill in the template with the data from Figure 10–6 to test the logic of your spreadsheet formulas.
   b. Create a bar graph of the actual payments for June using the graphics portion of the spreadsheet program.

8. **Spreadsheet design problem: cash flow report.** Using spreadsheet software, develop a template for the cash flow report shown in Figure 10–8. You may wish to examine John M. Nevison's 1-2-3 Spreadsheet Design (Brady/Simon & Schuster, 1989), a classic text on spreadsheet design. The most important of Nevison's design rules are presented in Richard O. Mann's article, "Designing Spreadsheets that Make Sense," *PC Today*, October 1990, pp. 22–27. After completing the template, answer the questions below. After answering the first question, return the spreadsheet to its original values.

   a. What would the net amount of the organization's six-month cash flow be if the spreadsheet were adjusted to reflect an unexpected growth of 3 percent in cash receipts for each of the six months?
   b. What would the net amount of the organization's six-month cash flow be if the utility company raised the rates by 12 percent for each of the six months?

9. **Spreadsheet design problem: electronic printer acquisition.** Using spreadsheet software, develop a template for the electronic printer acquisition shown in Figure 10–9. The figure uses an interest rate of 10 percent, a salvage value of $6,000, a corporate tax rate of 45 percent, and a five-year useful life of the copier. It also uses a straight-line depreciation rate of 20 percent, 22 percent, 21 percent, 21 percent, and 21 percent for years 1 through 5, respectively. Maintenance is shown at the net values after taxes have been deducted. Then, answer the questions below. Return the spreadsheet to the original values after answering each question.

   a. What are the comparative NPV amounts if the rate of interest rises to 12 percent? 14 percent?

b. What are the comparative NPV amounts if the salvage value drops to $3,000? If a lease deposit of $1,000 is required?

10. **Spreadsheet design problem: Gaspe School District.** Using spreadsheet software, develop a template for the Gaspe School District forecasting problem shown in Figure 10–12. The following cells should accept data input: B6–B8 (B6 is labeled "Assessed Value: Residential Property."), B12–B13, B15, B17–B18, B20, B25, B27–B35, B37–B41. The remaining cells should be calculated from the data input cells. This includes cell B26, the number of teachers needed. The latter value is a function of student enrollment and the student/teacher ratio. Make sure that your formula in cell B26 rounds the number of teachers needed *up* to the nearest whole integer. Also, use Box 10–3 to help you design the spreadsheet.

    Enter the data shown in Figure 10–12 into your template to test your spreadsheet logic. Then alter one or more of the following factors in the spreadsheet to balance the budget for the year: property tax rate per $1,000, investment interest rate, student/teacher ratio, number of administrators, instructional supplies, curriculum supplies, office expenses, and equipment expenses.

Cases

1. **TICO Press International, Inc.** Eileen Gascon is a financial manager for TICO Press International, Inc. Her main tasks center around managing cash flows for the organization. This means identifying TICO's short-term (one year) cash needs and investing idle funds in short-term investments. Another manager is responsible for identifying and selecting sources of funds to cover short-term cash flow shortfalls.

    Eileen currently uses a calculator to develop cash flow reports daily. She prints out cash reports from the mainframe-based financial accounting system twice a day and enters appropriate information from these reports into her cash flow worksheet. Using her cash flow worksheet, she predicts the amounts and durations of idle cash, which then become targets for short-term investment.

    Depending on the amounts and durations of the idle cash, Eileen calls TICO's commercial banks and brokerage firms and seeks quotes on investment opportunities, such as money market accounts, certificates of deposit, treasury securities, stocks, and bonds.

    Eileen is considering getting a personal computer to help her in her work. What software and hardware peripherals might you recommend to her? Identify each hardware and software item you would recommend and describe how these items might benefit Eileen.

2. **Joslinn Products, Inc.** Alicia Lee is the credit manager for Joslinn Products, Inc., which distributes office equipment such as electronic typewriters, copy machines, and facsimile machines, through five retail stores located in the metropolitan area surrounding El Paso, Texas. Currently, Joslinn is in the process of developing a new computerized accounting system. Charles O'Hara, a systems analyst with Joslinn, has asked Alicia for an interview to determine what her information needs might be. Here are excerpts from that interview:

    Charles: Thanks for taking the time out to answer questions about the new accounting system we are developing. We are really quite excited about it and want to make certain that the system fits the needs of everybody in the organization. That's why I'm here. I would like to find out what kinds of information or reports you need or would like the new system to provide.

Alicia: Well, I appreciate your coming and your desire to serve. It's nice to know that you guys in MIS want to help those of us in the trenches. The trouble is that I know nothing about computers or computer systems. So I don't think that I can help you very much.

Charles: Well, actually, you don't need to know much about computers. What I need from you is what kinds of information or reports you need or would like to have to run your department better.

Alicia: Is this some new way for management to indicate that I could be doing my job better?

Charles: No, no! I'm simply trying to find out what kinds of information or reports you might like to have.

Alicia: Well, if that's all you really need, then why don't you just provide me with the same reports I'm getting now? They seem to be OK!

Charles: I can do that easily. However, would you like information or reports that you are not getting now?

Alicia: I can't think of any. After all, how can I know what reports I would like from a computer system I don't understand? Why don't you let me know the kinds of reports others are getting that I'm not getting? That way, I may be able to find some additional reports that I could use.

a. Do you agree with Alicia that she must understand how the computer system works before she can describe the reports she should have?
b. What questions might Charles ask of her to elicit from her information about current or desired reports?
c. If you were in her place, what are three types of reports that you might find useful in managing credit? Describe these reports in detail by specifying the headings and types of data to be included in each report.

3. Talbert Business College. Goro Okana has just been transferred to the position of purchasing director for Talbert Business College in Trenton, New Jersey. Talbert Business College is a chain of private business schools located in the East. The organization began in 1968 with one college in Baltimore, Maryland. During the 1970s, enrollment in private business schools nationally climbed considerably, and like other business schools, Talbert expanded to a number of new locations. Currently, Talbert consists of 11 colleges, each enrolling from 2,000 to 3,000 full- and part-time students.

Purchasing commodities and equipment at each location of the college is centralized in a purchasing department that usually consists of a director, a secretary, and two or three purchasing clerks.

One of Goro's first tasks as director at the Trenton branch is to review the departmental budget for the coming year.

The budget includes only those expenses needed to perform the purchasing function. It does not include the payments for the various items required. The cost of these items is included in the budgets of the other units of the college.

If you were Goro:

a. What questions do you think you should ask of the financial accounting database that will improve your insight into the budget?
b. What information would you like to obtain from external sources to evaluate the budget better?
c. What are the likely sources for each type of information you described in *b*?

Talbert Business College, Trenton
Purchasing Department Budget Variance Report for 1995

Budget Item	Annual Allocation	Actual for Year	Difference
Salaries	81,500.00	83,569.23	−2,069.23
Services	6,950.00	7,341.99	−391.99
Equipment	8,575.00	9,453.55	−878.55
Travel	8,750.00	6,894.56	1,855.44
Telephone	18,250.00	22,307.98	−4,057.98
Postage	16,600.00	17,978.42	−1,378.42
Supplies	4,575.00	3,060.73	1,514.27
Reprographics	7,550.00	6,895.69	654.31
Totals	152,750.00	157,502.15	−4,752.15

4. **Munson Beverage Corporation.** Munson Beverage Corporation owns 30 warehouses and the distribution equipment necessary to supply a variety of soda products to retailers throughout the Midwest. The headquarters of the corporation are in Muncie, where its largest warehouse is located.

You have just been appointed vice president of finance for the Munson Beverage Corporation. The information system that the corporation currently uses provides you with accounting information gleaned from the typical accounting system database. This system includes modules for accounts receivable, accounts payable, order entry, purchase order, inventory, payroll, fixed assets, and the preparation of statements and reports. At regular intervals, the following periodic statements are sent to your office for your examination:

Aged accounts receivable reports.
Balance sheets.
Current merchandise inventory lists.
Employee earnings records.
Fixed assets and equipment inventories.
Income statements.
Payroll sheets.
Schedules of accounts payable.
Schedules of accounts receivable.
Sources and uses of funds.
Stockout lists.

a. Do you believe that the current reports you receive are appropriate to your tasks? Be specific: Describe which reports are appropriate or inappropriate and why.

b. Outline on separate sheets of paper three new reports that you feel might be helpful to you in tactical-level decision making. On each sheet show the title of the report, the column headings (if any), the nature of the data to be included, and the processing needed on the report (percentages, totals, formula results, and so forth). For each type of data to be included, indicate a possible source.

c. Outline on separate sheets of paper three new reports that you feel might be helpful to you in strategic planning. On each sheet show the title of the report, the column headings (if any), the nature of the data to be included, and the processing needed on the report (percentages, totals, formula results, and so forth). For each type of data to be included, indicate a possible source.

d. Specify any additional types of software you would consider acquiring to assist you in your tactical decisions and strategic planning. Then describe how you would use each type of software you identified to help you in your work.

Selected References and Readings

Falkner, Mike, and Raymond A. August. "Financial Modeling Software." *PC Magazine* 10, no. 1 (February 26, 1991). A review of nonspreadsheet software for building financial models.

Faulkner, Mike, Karen Watterson, and Lee Hendrickson. "Picking the Perfect Spreadsheet." *Windows Sources* 1, no. 2 (March 1993), pp. 351 ff. A review and evaluation of three popular spreadsheets.

Huttig, J. W. "Investing Goes Electric." *PC Today* 6, no. 7 (July 1992), pp. 17–20. Describes some of the on-line investing and trading services available to PC users.

Lake, Matt. "Top Tools for Harder-Working Worksheets." *PC World* 8, no. 4 (April 1990), pp. 180–84. A review of 16 add-on products for spreadsheet software.

Mann, Richard O. "Designing Spreadsheets that Make Sense." *PC Today* 4, no. 10 (October 1990), pp. 22–27. Provides a cogent discussion of the major design recommendations contained in John Nevison's 1-2-3 Spreadsheet Design noted below.

Myers, Edith. "Early DP Implementors Have More Choices Today." *Software Magazine* 9, no. 5 (April 1989), pp. 610–70. Describes how three organizations used financial software to solve problems.

Nevison, John M. "1-2-3 Spreadsheet Design." New York: Brady/Simon & Schuster, 1989. A classic text offering 22 rules of effective spreadsheet design.

Resnick, Rosalind. "Dialing Up Wall Street." *PC Today* 6, no. 7 (July 1992), pp. 22–25. Discusses the various financial databases and services available through information utilities such as CompuServe, Prodigy, and America Online.

Stevens, John M., Anthony G. Cahill, and Josephine M. LaPlante. "The Utilization of Information Systems in State Financial Management: An Empirical Assessment." *Journal of Management Information Systems* 8, no. 1 (Summer 1991) pp. 107–128. A report of the use of information systems in state budgeting offices.

Turban, Efraim. "The Interactive Financial Planning Systems (IFPS),"chap. 7 in *Decision Support and Expert Systems: Management Support Systems.* New York: Macmillan Publishing Company, 1990. A technical description of the features and uses of IFPS.

MARKETING INFORMATION SYSTEMS

CHAPTER OUTLINE

Manager's View

Marketing activities are found in nearly every organization, whether it manufactures products, sells products manufactured by others, or provides services and whether it is profit-seeking or nonprofit. Marketing activities are carried out by retail stores, wholesale distributors, manufacturing firms, service organizations, and a variety of public and private agencies and organizations. For example, if you were a manager in a public community college, your organization may be nonprofit in structure, but it will still sell a variety of products (courses, programs, and degrees) and numerous services (advising, teaching, tutoring, and placement) to your customers (students). Your sales representatives may be called recruiters or admissions counselors, and the marketing bottom line may be the number of students enrolled, the number of degrees granted, or the number of students placed. The fact that your organization is not a manufacturing business or does not show a profit does not preclude the need for marketing activities.

Despite the importance of marketing activities, marketing decision making has often been considered beyond the help of modern computer information systems. In the past, many managers regarded marketing decision making as an art, something not amenable to computer support. However, this attitude has changed. Organizations concerned about developing or maintaining a competitive advantage recognize that computer information systems can be an important tool in achieving that advantage by decreasing costs, improving customer services, improving sales personnel productivity, decreasing risk in product planning, and producing more accurate sales forecasts (see Box 11–1).

This chapter shows how you can use marketing information systems to support marketing decision making and enhance the productivity of marketing personnel.

Box 11–1 How Computer Systems Can Improve the Marketing Bottom Line

Automating your salesforce, typically with laptop microcomputers, can be cost effective in many ways. For example, automated systems may have these advantages:

1. THEY INCREASE SELLING TIME.

Laptop computer systems allow the salesforce to enter and verify orders immediately, on the customer premises. Hence they do not have to spend time calling in orders by phone or delivering them to the office. The more time salespeople spend selling instead of completing office work, the more sales are likely to increase.

2. THEY IMPROVE PLANNING.

Standard reports on sales, prospects, contacts, and competitors, in magnetic form, help tactical and strategic planners at the home office adjust production, inventory levels, and product prices to respond immediately to trends gleaned from the data in these reports.

3. THEY REDUCE COSTS.

When salespeople enter orders directly via laptop computer systems, order entry clerks, paper forms, filing cabinets, and filing clerks are eliminated. When standard reports are completed via laptop computer, all the support needed to create and maintain the manual reporting systems can be eliminated.

Source: Robert L. Scheier, "How to Cost-Justify Sales Force Automation," *PC Week* 7, no. 16 (April 23, 1990), pp. 115–16.

THE MARKETING FUNCTION

The basic goal of the **marketing function** in any organization is to satisfy the needs and wants of existing and potential customers. To plan for effective marketing information systems, however, it is important that you recognize that the marketing function includes a great deal more than merely selling and advertising the organization's products and services. It encompasses a broad range of activities designed to identify who the customers currently are, to decide who they should be, to ascertain what those customers need and want, to plan and develop products or services to meet those needs, to price the products and services, to advertise and promote those products and services, and to deliver those products and services to the customers. The following list (Gross and Peterson, 1987) sums up the components of the marketing function:

- Planning
- Buying
- Merchandising
  - Standardization and grading
  - Pricing
- Selling
  - Advertising
  - Sales promotion
  - Packaging
  - Publicity
  - Personal selling
- Physical distribution
  - Transporting
  - Storing

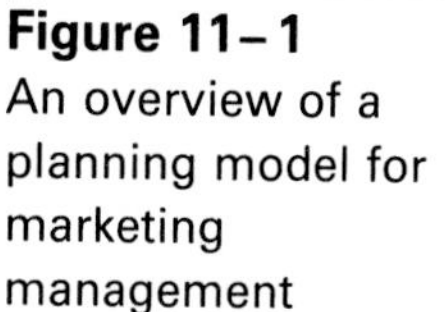

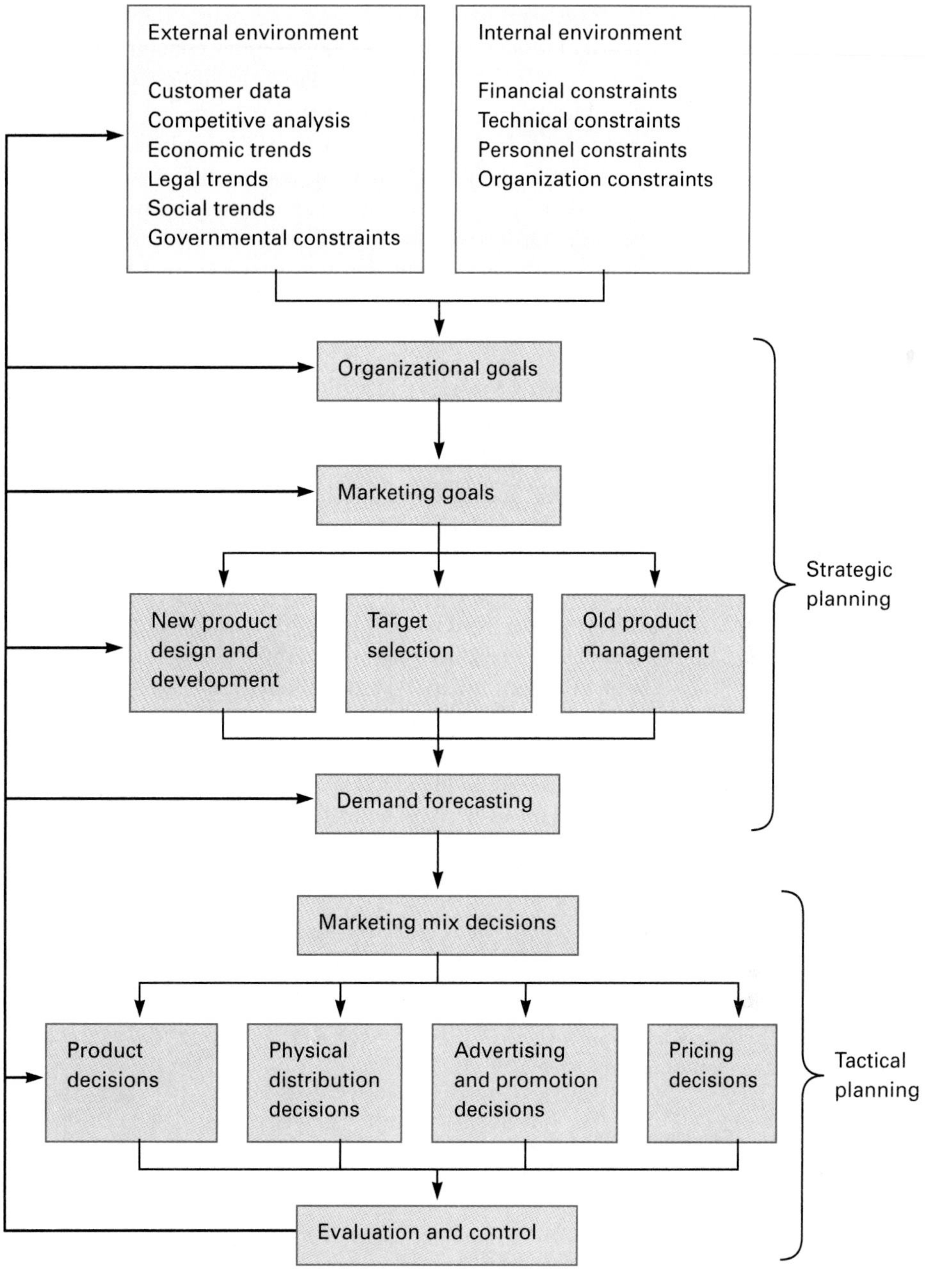

Figure 11–1
An overview of a planning model for marketing management

Facilitating
  Financing
  Risk bearing
  Obtaining information

Marketing managers engage in many planning activities in the pursuit of the marketing function (see Figure 11–1). These planning activities result in a combination of products, services, advertising, promotion, price, and product delivery methods ultimately offered to the organization's customers, which is referred to as the **marketing mix.**

The way management views the marketing function has changed over time. The management of many organizations today concentrates on meeting customer needs and wants in all facets of the business, including planning, developing, producing, and distributing the organization's products and services. An organization that takes this viewpoint is said to have a **marketing orientation** to all its business activities. Such an organization believes that to be successful, it must cater to the needs and wants of customers. This organization had adopted the **marketing concept** as its primary motivation. Ordinarily an organization that adopts the marketing concept elevates the senior marketing executive to a top management position so that marketing views and concerns will be represented in all decisions made by the organization.

MARKETING INFORMATION SYSTEMS

Marketing information systems support the major activities of a marketing organization. The information systems collect data that describe marketing operations, process those data, and make marketing information available to marketing managers to help them make decisions. The information systems also process and report on marketing data found in external databases, such as demographic databases. To be effective, marketing information systems must be coordinated with other organizational information systems, such as purchasing systems, manufacturing systems, inventory systems, accounts receivable systems, credit systems, and order entry systems. The financial accounting information system of an organization provides a great deal of data used by the marketing information system.

Like financial information systems, marketing information systems may be categorized into operational, tactical, and strategic planning information systems (see Figure 11–2). However, it is important to remember that, like other information systems, marketing information systems cannot always be neatly separated into these three

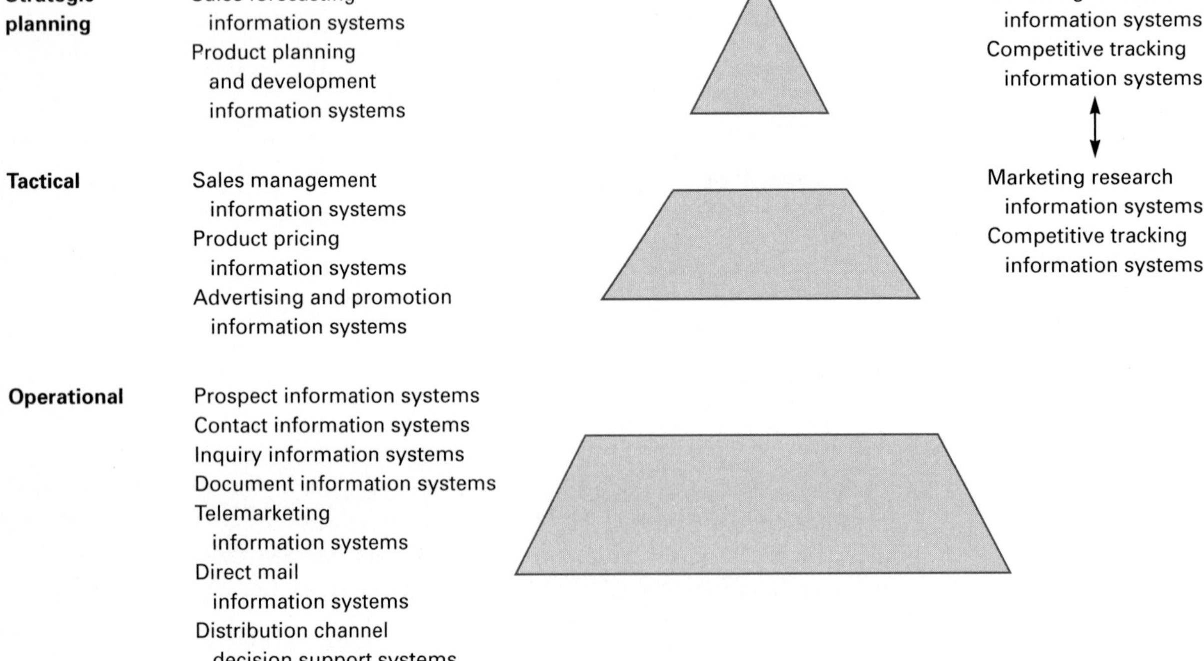

Figure 11–2
A classification of the marketing information systems discussed in this chapter

levels. The information used for operational-level decisions may also be used for tactical decisions, and the information used for tactical decisions may be used for strategic planning decisions. Some marketing information systems, such as marketing research systems and information systems that keep track of competitors, clearly support both tactical and strategic planning decision making.

The decision levels of marketing information systems represent a continuum of complexity rather than discrete boxes. However, this fact does not alter the usefulness of examining marketing information systems using these three levels of decision-making complexity.

OPERATIONAL MARKETING INFORMATION SYSTEMS

Marketing information systems at the operating level are similar to financial information systems at the operational level. They primarily produce routine, repetitive, descriptive, expected, and objective data that describe past marketing activities. The information they produce is usually detailed, highly structured, accurate, derived from internal sources, and produced regularly.

Sales Information Systems

Salespeople are responsible for many sales activities. They must identify potential customers, make contact with customers, call on customers, close sales, and follow up on sales. These are the bread-and-butter sales activities of the salesperson. Many information systems support the salesperson in these activities. Among these information systems are the following.

Contact Information Systems. Customer **contact information systems** provide information to the sales force on customers, their product or service preferences, sales history data, and a historical record of sales calls and visits. One output of these systems may be a call report showing the number of sales calls made by a salesperson categorized by size of organization, previous sales, or some other characteristic, and the number of sales made per customer, per visit, or per category (see Figure 11–3).

Figure 11–3
A call report screen

```
FILE   EDIT   VIEW   INSERT   HELP

                        CALL REPORT

DATE OF CALL: 10/30/94                    CUSTOMER NUMBER: 278

CUSTOMER NAME: Reliance Products, Inc.

TYPE OF CALL: Visit

LOCATION: 21 River Street, St. Louis, MO

PHONE NUMBER: 314-555-3987

SALES PLAN: To sell them stock no. T128 as a companion to
            stock no. T350

RESULTS: Sold 50 units of stock no. T128, Invoice #2978

ACTION OR FOLLOWUP: Call on 11/15 to make sure stock
                    was received

ADDITIONAL COMMENTS:
```

If the information is kept on magnetic media, it is relatively simple for the salesperson to identify all those customers who prefer certain types of products or who may be ready to purchase accessories to previous purchases. Sorting the dates of previous visits allows the salesperson to identify customers who may be running out of a product and need to place another order. When stock has been placed on sale, contact file records permit the salesperson to notify customers who are interested in or who regularly purchase such stock.

Prospect Information Systems. Locating potential customers is often a time-consuming and frustrating part of the salesperson's work. The sources of information for leads on prospective customers are frequently diverse and may include other customers, other vendors who sell supporting or ancillary products, newspaper notices, telephone directories, and direct customer inquiries. Searching hard-copy directories and other paper lists of customers may be very time-consuming and yield few future customers.

Files of sales leads are often called **prospect files.** When these files are stored on magnetic media, they are easier for the salesperson to search or summarize (see Figure 11–4). Outputs of **prospect information systems** may include lists of prospects by location, by product category, by gross revenue, or by other classifications important to the sales force.

On-line or CD-ROM databases also provide prospect information systems (see Box 11–2). On-line and CD-ROM databases may be searched by query software or by mapping software, which maps prospects within geographical areas and provides displays of these maps (see Box 11–4).

Telemarketing Systems. You have probably received many sales calls from salespeople or people soliciting donations. Use of the telephone to sell products and services, or **telemarketing systems,** has become a common and important means by which organizations improve the productivity of their salesforces. The telephone allows salespeople to initiate contacts, offer products and services, or follow up on sales without travel costs or travel time. It also lets salespeople reach many more customers in a given

Figure 11–4
A screen showing one record from a prospect file

```
                         PROSPECTS

COMPANY:   The Bay Company                PROSPECT NO.:  37

ADDRESS:   723 Railroad Avenue

CITY:  Oakland                       STATE:  CA    ZIP:  94621

CONTACT:  Margaret L. Knowlton

CONTACT PHONE:  510-555-1298

DATE FIRST CONTACTED:  10/06/94

DATE LAST CONTACTED:  10/21/94

COMMENTS:  Might be able to use stock no. RG122
```

Box 11–2 Desktop Telemarketing: Using Electronic Directories for Marketing Tasks

A number of large databases have been made available for PC use through CD-ROMs. These databases, once the province of large direct-mail organizations and Fortune 500 companies, are now available to small organizations. The databases consist of telephone directory-type listings of companies, households, or both. The databases are being widely used in marketing for such tasks as creating sales territories, identifying leads for sales visits, identifying leads for telemarketing and direct mail advertising, and even market research and analysis. The CD-ROM databases can be enhanced by applying prospect or contact management software, mapping software, telephone management software, and envelope and label printing software to the database data. Three of these CD-ROM based databases are described briefly below.

MARKETPLACE BUSINESS

MarketPlace Information Corp. offers a CD-ROM–based product that allows managers to use a microcomputer system to perform sophisticated market analyses and sales prospecting for sales to other business firms. The CD-ROM database holds names, addresses, telephone numbers, and marketing data on 7.5 million firms. The software provided with the database allows managers to identify and select customers, analyze markets, and create lists for direct marketing campaigns. For example, you can quickly obtain telephone or mailing lists of firms that meet criteria that you have selected, estimate the size of different market segments, and even pick sites for outlets or warehouses. The system is also useful for generating samples for marketing research. The CD-ROM data are supplied by Dun and Bradstreet Corp.

BUSINESS LISTS-ON-DISC

American Business Information, a provider of many types of CD-ROM databases, offers Business Lists-On-Disc (LOD), which includes information on 9.2 million American business firms taken from over 5,000 Yellow Pages directories. Marketing personnel can search the database by company name, type of business, size, geographic area, headquarters or branch office, and the title of the contact person in the firm. Retrieval software provided with the database allows you to dial any contact automatically if your computer has a modem. You can also generate mailing lists or merge data from the database with letters produced on a word processor.

METROSEARCH DIGITAL DATABASE

This database, a compilation of 3,400 U.S. white-page directories, is available in CD-ROM disks for each region. The full set of disks contains more than 77 million records. You can search the database by individual or business names, telephone number, street address, city, house number, and zip code. You can also direct the system to list homes or businesses on the same street or at the same address as your original search name. Software allows you to direct dial a listing if you have a modem, create mailing labels, and merge records with letters using your word processor.

Sources: "Just Browsing," *PC Today* 6, no. 12 (December 1992), pp. 20–23; and Carol S. Holzberg, "Long Distance Information . . . Give Me Memphis, TN," *PC Today* 7, no. 8 (August 1993), p. 16.

time period than they could have through other means. Some telemarketing systems include computer support for automatic dialing and the delivery of fax or voice messages. The use of electronic telephone directories for telemarketing has become common (see Box 11–2).

Direct-Mail Advertising Systems. Many organizations generate sales by mailing sales brochures and catalogs directly to customers using **direct-mail advertising systems.** To distribute sales documents rapidly to large numbers of potential customers, most marketing departments maintain customer mailing lists for mass mailing. The lists may be drawn from customer files, accounts receivable records, prospect files, or commercial databases of households, businesses, and organizations. They can also be purchased from other firms. Today, electronic directories are often being used in direct mail advertising campaigns (see Box 11–2).

Catalog retailers use direct-mail systems heavily. Many, like Lands' End and L.L. Bean, maintain not only directory listings of potential customers but also information about each customer's response to their mailings. Thus, customers' buying patterns are used to calculate the probability of their buying each of the seller's product lines. Then, only catalogs containing those lines that are likely to be purchased are mailed. In fact, some catalog sellers use customer responses to construct a variety of catalogs to match customer profiles. Robert Blattberg suggests that using computer-driven catalog binding, it is possible for mail-order firms to construct a unique catalog for each customer.[1]

Newspapers and magazines also use database data to customize advertisements for different people and regions. For example, *Time* magazine is one of several magazine publishers that provides special editions for those homes that have recently moved or bought something from a mail-order catalog. Blattberg imagines that possible magazine ads of the future might look like this: "Alan, that pair of loafers you bought three years ago might need replacing. Look at page 46 of the Eddie Bauer catalog you'll be receiving next week."[2]

The capability to target individuals based on a database of information about them undoubtedly raises concerns about privacy. Recently, Lotus Development Corporation canceled plans to sell CD-ROM disks with data on some 80 million US households because of opposition from various groups.

Inquiry Information Systems. When customers inquire about the products and services the organization offers, the inquiries need to be recorded, processed, and stored for management analysis or for sales contact. It is important to compile information about the actual or potential customer who made the inquiry, what products or services the query pertained to, when the inquiry was made, and where the potential customer is located and to record these data on a medium that will allow analysis easily at some future time. This capability lets marketing managers analyze customer requests to identify opportunities for new products, improvements on existing products, and new or improved customer support services.

An **inquiry information system** also should include a method of inquiry response, for example, a series of carefully constructed reply form letters that inform customers about products or services and where they may be obtained or a response delivered by trained telephone operators. An inquiry system usually includes a means of contacting and informing the pertinent salesperson about each inquiry, who made it, and how the potential customer may be contacted.

Computer Kiosks. You learned about electronic market systems in Chapter 7, "Communications and Distributed Systems." One form of an electronic market system that has emerged is the **computer kiosk.** *Kiosks* are small, round or octagonal structures on sidewalks and other public places in Europe where news and advertisements can be posted. Computer kiosks are also small structures, but they usually contain a multimedia microcomputer system with a touch screen. Computer kiosks became popular first in museums, providing patrons with information about exhibits.

Some computer kiosks only allow customers to get information about a company, its products, or its services. However, most of them allow customers to select and purchase products and services interactively. For example, Sears stores use kiosks that provide on-line catalogs from which customers may select Sears products using a touch

---

[1]Robert C. Blattberg, "Interactive Marketing: Exploiting the Age of Addressability," *Business Edge*, May 1992, pp. 12–17.

[2]Op. cit, p. 13

screen and purchase them with a credit card. Baseball fans in Minneapolis can buy tickets to Twins' home games at computer kiosks. What is more, the kiosks show the buyers the view from the seats they have selected before they finalize their purchase. The U.S. Postal Service uses "Postal Buddy" kiosks to sell stamps, let people submit address changes, and produce address labels for packages. Some states are considering kiosks for car registration renewals, copies of birth and death certificates, and other commonly requested documents.[3]

It is clear that technology is making major changes in the way that organizations serve their customers.

Distribution Information Systems

An organization may choose to use existing commercial and public delivery systems for its products and services, such as the U.S. Postal Service, private parcel services, or freight companies. It may also choose to provide its own product delivery systems for its customers. Regardless of the systems chosen, the goods being distributed must be monitored. It is important to track products or services throughout the distribution system to identify and correct delivery errors and reduce delivery time. The speed with which an organization can deliver its products is an important customer service.

If the organization maintains its own distribution system, information about its effectiveness must be collected and reported to management. Information should also be maintained about the acquisition, repair, use, and allocation of equipment.

Previous chapters have described how pen-based computing and a variety of communications systems, such as cellular, mobile data, and satellite systems allow firms to keep on top of their delivery vehicles, personnel, and packages.

Supporting Operational-Level Financial Accounting Systems

Three financial operational information systems—order entry, inventory, and credit information systems—also provide much-needed data to the marketing function.

Sales Order Processing Systems. The financial accounting system of the organization creates a great deal of marketing data. For example, the sales order processing system, or order entry system, provides the marketing manager with the raw data for reports on orders by time period, salesperson, product, and territory (see "The Sales Order Processing Subsystem" in Chapter 10). This information may be used for a variety of marketing decisions at several marketing decision levels. Analysis of sales orders provides the marketing manager with some of the information on which sales forecasts can be based, for instance.

Point-of-sale (POS) systems are another facet of the order entry system. They capture data about orders at the point of sale. POS systems are frequently found in fast-food chain stores, department stores, and grocery chain stores. The information from point-of-sale systems becomes input to the financial accounting system, which then supplies data to marketing information systems (see Figure 11–5). The information from POS systems can also build customer databases, shifting attention from what is being purchased to who is purchasing it. R. H. Macy and Company used about 100 planners to analyze scanned data from their checkout counters. They used the data to select the best products for each of Macy's stores.

Some POS systems are highly specialized. For example, Rocky Rococo pizza restaurants allows the firm's workers not only to take orders from customers over the

---

[3]Evan Ramstad, "Computer Kiosks Move Beyond Information to Sales, Service," *St. Louis Post-Dispatch*, September 15, 1993, p. 5C.

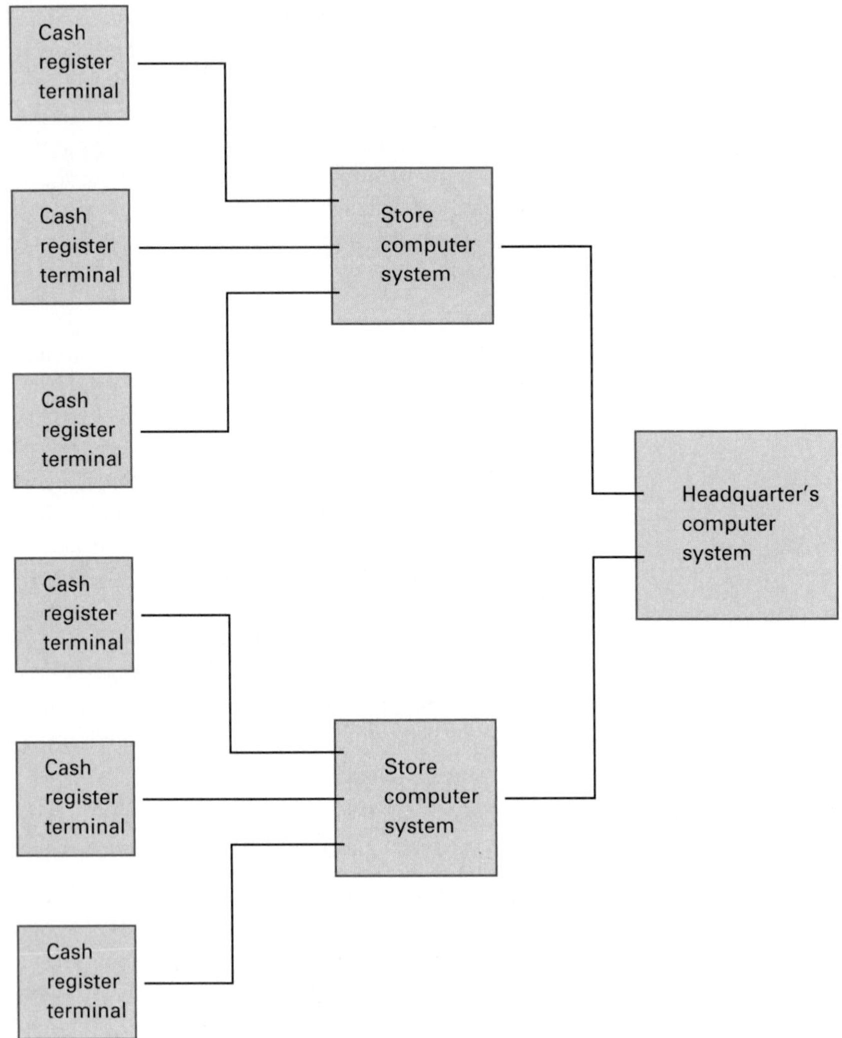

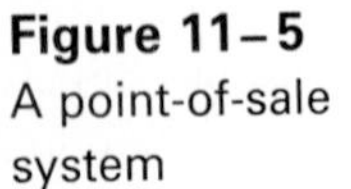
Figure 11–5
A point-of-sale system

phone but also to input the customer's address and directions for drivers. The system has decreased driver errors and allowed them to deliver $650 more orders per week.[4]

Frequently, POS systems are enhanced by the addition of bar code readers and credit card terminals. The POS systems increase efficiency for the firm and the bar code and credit card readers (sometimes called magnetic stripe readers) increase the speed at the checkout counters, making customers happy.

More recently, pen-based data entry systems (see Chapter 4, "Computer Hardware") have taken their place as important POS systems. These systems typically provide an electronic means by which salesclerks, delivery personnel, and others can complete sales order forms. The employees fill out the form, which is displayed on the hand-held computer system, by entering block-printed characters. The software then translates these characters into ASCII characters, which can then be uploaded by cable, disk, or modem to the main computer system that handles the sales orders.

[4] J. W. Huttig, "Point-of-Sale a la Carte," *PC Today* 7, no. 9, (September 1993), pp. 18–21.

Some organizations provide their customers with terminals that have direct access to the organization's sales order system. The idea is to make ordering easy and convenient for the customer. Once customers have learned how to order using the system, they tend to be reluctant to learn a competitor's system. As a result, some firms have achieved an important competitive advantage through their sales order system. A classic example is American Hospital Supply, which provided sales order terminals to its customers so that they could order merchandise directly at any time of the day or night. Not only did the system make it easy for hospital staff to order merchandise for quick delivery, once staff were trained to use the system, they resisted switching to competitor systems.

Inventory Information Systems. **Inventory information systems**—subsystems of the financial accounting system—provide information about inventory levels, stockout conditions, stock receipts, stock issues, stock damage, and the location and distribution of stock within the organization. For example, salespeople should be able to check the amount of available stock in inventory before closing a sale with a customer. Thus, the inventory information system provides important data regarding stock levels to the order entry system. Learning that one version of a product is in low supply may allow a salesperson to offer a different but similar product to the customer. Many operational systems—including such systems as inventory, shipping and receiving, open order, and backorder—are part of the financial accounting system. The data provided by these systems are also very useful for tactical- and strategic-level marketing decision making.

Credit Information Systems. An operational-level credit information system usually provides the salesperson or credit manager with information on the maximum allowable credit that should be granted to a customer. This information is ordinarily integrated with the order entry subsystem of the financial accounting system. The credit information system may manage information on the credit history of customers, including information from external sources such as credit agencies.

The sales and financial operating information systems just described are very important to the sales force and to the organization, especially when these information systems have been computerized. Computerization of these systems allows the salespeople to increase their productivity, increase customer service, and decrease sales costs, any or all of which can provide a competitive advantage to an organization.

TACTICAL MARKETING INFORMATION SYSTEMS

Tactical marketing information systems differ from operational marketing information systems because in addition to producing information on a regular basis, they also generate ad hoc reports, create unexpected as well as expected output, produce comparative as well as descriptive information, provide summary information as opposed to detailed data, include both internal and external data sources, and process subjective as well as objective data.

A great deal of the data that tactical marketing information systems utilize are collected by operational financial information systems. Tactical marketing information systems often combine operational-level financial data with other data to support tactical decision making by marketing managers. Tactical decisions are often made by managers when they prepare and implement marketing plans through which they hope to reach top management's sales and profit goals. For example, tactical decisions regarding market focus for the coming year may be partly based on the sales history of market segments derived from the sales order entry system. This information may then be compared to information about the competition's success with those same market segments gleaned from sources outside the organization.

Examples of tactical marketing information systems that will be discussed in this chapter include systems that support deploying and managing the sales force, managing advertising and promotion campaigns, distributing and delivering products sold, and pricing products.

Sales Management Information Systems

A major objective of sales managers is to reach the sales goals set by top management. To accomplish this objective, sales managers must make many tactical decisions, such as how sales territories should be shaped, how the sales force should be allocated within those territories, and what emphasis should be placed on the products offered and customers served. Sales managers must decide how to reward salespeople to encourage increased sales efforts, which market segments should be emphasized to best reach sales goals, and which products and services will best appeal to each segment. They also must monitor the progress of the sales effort to determine if their decisions were correct or if they need to change their tactical plans (see Box 11–3).

To make these decisions effectively, sales managers should have at their disposal a great deal of data about the sales histories of each salesperson, territory, product, and market segment. Managers can use these data—provided by **sales management information systems**—to develop reports analyzing sales activities that help them make decisions about salespeople, territories, products, and customers. Analysis of past sales efforts might reveal, for instance, that the greatest volume of sales is obtained when certain products are emphasized with certain market segments. This information may be obtained from a report that correlates product or service categories with customer categories. For example, you would expect that such a report produced for an auto-

Box 11–3 Sales Force Automation

Armour Swift-Eckrich of Downers Grove, Illinois, has placed handheld computers in the hands of its field representatives to track information about their food products at grocery stores. The field reps collect data about shelf space, coupon advertisements, special displays, and promotions at the store level.

The computerized system has replaced a manual reporting system in which about 150 merchandise representatives used to spend from four to six hours each week creating reports about shelf space usage and other product information at grocery stores. Now the reps input the data directly while at the stores using the handheld computers. The computers then use a wireless network to allow the reps to upload the data to a sales information system database. Regional and corporate office managers are able to download the sales data into the personal computer spreadsheets and databases with which they are comfortable.

The managers are then able to analyze the store sales data and give instructions or recommendations to the reps quickly. The managers also can analyze and evaluate the performance of the sales representatives, specifically, the impact of the rep on each store that the rep serves. At the same time, the regional managers and corporate staff have become more knowledgeable about the problems field reps face in negotiating shelf space, promotion space, and other product support from grocery store managers.

The system was designed and developed by Fastech, a Pennsylvania systems integration firm that concentrates on sales information technologies. They integrated the handheld personal computers and wireless network and developed the mainframe-based sales information system that Armour uses.

Source: Alice LaPlante, "Armour Deploys Strategic Sales Force Automation," *InfoWorld* 15, no. 48 (November 29, 1993), p. 66.

mobile dealership would show that older, wealthier customers would be the most frequent buyers of the dealership's most expensive four-door sedans. You might also expect that younger, professional customers might be the most frequent buyers of the dealership's sports cars. Additional correlations of the data, using finer classifications of customers, might reveal that younger customers from certain professions do not act like the younger group as a whole. Younger members of some professions may be the most frequent purchasers of traditional family sedans, whereas younger members of other professions are the primary purchasers of sports vehicles. Through the use of these reports, marketing managers may adjust advertising media, promotion schemes, sales calls, and sales approaches to emphasize selected products to very narrowly defined market segments to maximize gross sales.

In addition to planning future campaigns, sales managers need information to control current campaigns. The manager monitoring sales progress may wish to receive daily, weekly, or monthly reports on the sales achievement of each salesperson with averages calculated for the entire sales force. This information might be used to evaluate salesperson effectiveness, the success of the sales reward system, or the appropriateness of the shape of the territories assigned. A report showing the percentage of each salesperson's sales by market segment and by product along with averages for the total sales force would display the current effectiveness of each salesperson in selling the organization's products to each customer group.

The manager can compare sales, product, customer, and territory information from one department against external benchmarks of success, such as the organization as a whole or industry averages. The manager, for example, may wish to compare staff deployment to the deployment of marketing staffs in other marketing departments within the organization or to the industry as a whole. The marketing manager might also view the amount of money spent in the department on salespeople versus support staff and then compare those amounts to the amounts spent by other marketing departments in the organization or to the industry as a whole. If sales data are added to expense data, the marketing manager can compare the productivity of the department to the productivity of the organization and the productivity of the industry. Comparisons that indicate poor productivity might lead the marketing manager to compare the productivity of each salesperson to the average for the department. This comparison, in turn, might lead to decisions changing the configuration of sales territories, training for specific salespeople, product emphasis for certain territories, market segment emphasis for certain sales personnel, or a variety of other remedies.

At the same time, information on the productivity of the present sales force permits managers to estimate annual sales budgets given a set of sales goals from top management. Knowing the sales figures that top management wishes to reach, the manager may use previous productivity information to estimate the number of salespeople or salesperson days needed to achieve success.

These examples should not imply that the marketing manager's job can be performed merely by projecting historical information on current problems. If all marketing decisions could be made merely by referring to the past performance of salespeople with customers and products within territories, marketing managers would not be needed at all. The marketing manager must bring to the table not only historical information, trends, and probabilities, but also considerable knowledge of the current environment. In the end, the marketing manager must make decisions based on less than all of the information desirable. Marketing information systems do not make the decisions for marketing managers, they provide information to support those managers in the decision-making process.

Advertising and Promotion Information Systems

Advertising and promotional tactics also need to be developed by marketing managers to implement strategic sales goals set by top management. Managers must decide which advertising media and promotional devices to use to reach the selected market segments, when these media and devices should be used, and what overall mix of promotional activities should be deployed to achieve sales goals. **Advertising and promotion information systems** assist managers in these tasks.

The order entry system contains the raw data to identify which products or services are selling poorly or well. Reports based on the order entry system data may be used to decide which products and services need the help that advertising and promotion can supply. If marketing managers receive these reports at the right time, they can identify which products and services are falling behind projected sales goals for the year in time to attempt corrections. Managers may then devise tactical advertising and promotional plans to close the gap between actual and projected sales. The reports may also identify products and services selling better than expected that should be pushed. The reports may take the form of summary reports simply listing the sales of each product or service by time period. To be more useful, however, they should compare current sales with sales forecasts for the time period (see Figure 11–6).

Tactical reports based on data from the order entry system also can provide advertising and promotion managers with information about the effectiveness of current advertising campaigns and promotional devices so they can make timely corrections in these marketing systems and in the production and distribution of stock if needed.

To decide what advertising and promotional tactics to use, marketing managers need such information as market segment history, the effectiveness of previous advertising and promotional efforts on each market segment, and the sales history of products by market segment. Historical data on the effectiveness of various advertising and promotional instruments and the sales of products by market segment are not foolproof methods for forecasting future success. Past profiles and trends may not necessarily be projected into the future. The areas of advertising and promotion contain too much managerial art for projection of past data to be perfectly successful. However, the past success of specific advertising and promotion campaigns for specific products and customers is very important information for the manager. For example, a marketing manager may construct a model of the types of advertising media that have been used in the past to advertise certain products. The model may display their success in terms of

Figure 11–6
A tactical marketing report comparing current sales to forecasted sales

Liang Manufacturing Company
Sales for First Quarter (1994)

Stock No.	Current Sales	Projected Sales	Percent on Target
T128	243,891	265,000	92.0%
T129	128,933	129,000	99.9
T218	50,311	54,500	92.3
T219	45,208	45,000	100.5
T251	157,244	152,600	103.0
T310	98,156	95,500	102.8
Totals	723,743	741,600	97.6

dollars of sales generated per dollars spent on each type of media. Using these historical relationships, the manager might decide on the **media mix** (media types used and time or dollars devoted to each) appropriate for this year's sales effort. Another manager may have sufficient historical data to show which advertising instruments within each media type are the most effective for reaching particular market segments. Thus, if the manager wishes to sell a product to newlyweds, he or she will know not only which types of media but also which companies have proved most successful in the past in reaching this market segment.

Product Pricing Information Systems

Product pricing information systems provide information to managers that helps them set prices for their products and services. These information systems are important because the price of a product or service affects the sales volume and profitability of the organization. The marketing manager usually selects a price that will at least recover production costs, but the price chosen is constrained by the prices of competitors for similar products or services and for alternative products or services. To make pricing decisions, the marketing manager should know the expected demand for the product or similar products, the desired profit margin for the organization, the costs of producing the product or providing the service, and the prices of competing products.

The price of a product is also a function of the pricing tactics that the organization assumes. Pricing tactics may merely involve determining the cost of the product and adding a markup to the cost to provide the desired profit, or *cost-plus pricing.*

Other organizations may base the price of their products on the value they believe the customer perceives the product to have, or *demand pricing.* For example, ordinarily automobiles are sold on the basis of the costs of production plus a markup to provide a profit to the dealer. The amount of the dealership's markup depends on the volume of sales for the car model, the inventory of the model on hand, and the prices charged by competitors for similar automobiles. However, some foreign and specialty auto dealers may sell their automobiles at prices in excess of the list or sticker price of their automobiles because many car buyers are willing to pay more than the sticker price for the cars. The demand for the cars exceeds the supply available to dealers.

Price may also depend on other organization objectives. An organization may choose to increase its market penetration by setting much lower prices than competitors for the same or similar products and services. Once the organization has developed a larger market share or a larger customer base, it may then raise prices slowly relative to its competitors, counting on customer satisfaction and customer inertia to retain the market share. Such pricing is known as a *penetration pricing.*

Still other organizations may decide on setting the price of the product above its costs and above its usual markup. Especially for an innovative product—one for which there is no real competition or alternative product—the organization may hope to obtain the maximum profit on the product before other organizations develop a competitive product or service. When competitors or alternative products appear, the organization will then lower prices in an attempt to maintain its market share. Entering the market with a new product priced at a high level is called *market-skimming pricing.*

Pricing decisions also include what types of discounts to give at various levels of the channels of distribution and what promotional devices to use, such as financing options and rebates.

To help the marketing manager price products and services, some organizations develop a pricing model that allows the manager to input data on a variety of forces affecting prices, such as expected competitive prices, expected consumer price indexes, expected consumer disposable income, volume of products produced, costs of labor, costs of raw materials, and the value of expected advertising expenditures. The model then uses arithmetic algorithms that represent the organization's assumptions about the interrelationship of each of these factors. A pricing model makes it possible for the manager to vary the inputs to identify the best price for a product under a variety of possible conditions.

Distribution Channel Decision Support Systems

Deciding how the organization's products and services will be delivered to the ultimate consumer is another important tactical decision. The organization needs to determine if it wishes to sell all or some of its products and services directly to its customers, use middlemen, or do both. If it considers direct sales, then the trade channel or channels within that delivery mode—for example, sales force, direct mail, telemarketing, and so on—must be chosen. If middlemen are chosen to distribute the product or service, the choice of trade channel will be affected by how well the channel distributes the products or services among the targeted market segments.

To support the marketing manager, the marketing information system should provide a **distribution channel decision support system.** This system should provide information on the costs of using the various distribution channels, the time lags caused by the various channels, the reliability of the various channels in delivering the products and services, and the market segment saturation provided by the channels. It should also track the demand and inventory at all levels of the distribution channels so that the manager may anticipate excess inventories or shortfalls.

STRATEGIC MARKETING INFORMATION SYSTEMS

To develop an overall marketing plan, an organization may engage in a variety of tactical and strategic planning activities. The strategic activities include segmenting the market into target groups of potential customers based on common characteristics or needs or wants, selecting those market segments the organization wishes to reach, planning products and services to meet those customers' needs, and forecasting sales for the market segments and products. The tactical activities have already been described and include planning the marketing mix—the best combination of product, price, advertising, promotion, financing, and distribution channels to reach the chosen target groups.

Sales Forecasting Information Systems

Strategic **sales forecasting information systems** usually include several varieties of forecasts: forecasts of sales for the industry as a whole, forecasts of sales for the entire organization, forecasts of sales for each product or service, and forecasts of sales for a new product or service. The results of these sales forecasts are often further categorized by sales territory and sales division. Regardless of type, sales forecasts are usually based on more than historical data; they are not merely projections of past trends. Sales forecasts are also based on assumptions about the activities of the competition, governmental action, shifting customer demand, demographic trends, and a variety of other pertinent factors, including even the weather.

In an organization with a marketing orientation, development of the sales forecast for the entire organization for the coming year is an extremely important undertaking. From that one forecast, tactical decisions regarding the directions of many other organizational functions will flow. For example, based on that sales forecast, management will decide to keep or cast aside products and services in the organization's current marketing mix. Research and development personnel may plan and develop new products and services. Marketing managers will allocate sales personnel, divide territories, plan advertising, and devise promotional campaigns. Production managers will allocate the use of plant facilities, plan the purchase of raw materials, and decide on the size, composition, and allocation of the work force. Finance managers will acquire or reserve the necessary capital to support the expected levels of production and marketing planned by other departments within the organization, project profits for the year, and plan for the use of the organization's cash flows.

Clearly, a lot rides on an organization's sales forecasts. Errors in forecasting sales will have an impact on nearly all facets of the organization. If actual sales are well below expectations, considerable loss may result from excess inventory, excess personnel, and other unnecessary operational expenses associated with gearing up for levels of production and sales that never materialize.

Given that sales forecasts are predictions of the future, there must of necessity be a wide margin for error in any forecast, even when the forecast is made using very sophisticated statistical procedures. Attempting to predict the future is always difficult, and attempting to predict future sales of new products is clearly the most difficult of all sales forecasting activities. Since new products have no prior track record, no data are available from which to project trends. Estimates of sales must be made from the fate of similar products introduced in past years and from customer surveys, market testing of the product, and economic, demographic, and other data external to the organization.

Errors in sales forecasting are compounded by the fact that these forecasts usually attempt to describe sales activity for a three- to five-year period. The further out the forecast is extended, the greater likelihood of error. For that reason, sales forecasts are regularly revised based on data from the financial operating system and from data external to the organization.

Product Planning and Development Information Systems

The major objective of **product planning and development information systems** is to make information about consumer preferences obtained from the marketing research system and the customer inquiry system available for the development of new products. The primary output of planning and development activities is a set of product specifications. In a manufacturing organization, these specifications would be given to the engineering department, which would try to design a product to meet them. Similar activities occur in service organizations. For example, a survey of bank customers may indicate that customers would like a checking account that also acts like a savings account—an account in which they could place all their money, maximize the amount of cash earning interest, avoid multiple statements, and avoid shifting funds between savings and checking accounts. Bank personnel concerned with product development may then identify specifications for such a product that meet current banking laws and regulations. These specifications may require the new account to carry the same rate of interest as a passbook savings account, earn interest on the average balance on deposit during a month, not limit the number of deposits or withdrawals during a month, maintain a minimum balance of $500, and pay interest monthly. The specifications can be tested and refined through additional consumer surveys and focus groups or through testing the product in a subset of the market, such as one branch of the bank.

When new product specifications are developed, it is important that the legal concerns for that new product be addressed. The product development system must provide appropriate organizational personnel with sufficient information to ensure that they accurately and completely address patent and copyright concerns, consumer product safety concerns, and a host of other legal issues pertaining to the new product.

TACTICAL AND STRATEGIC MARKETING INFORMATION SYSTEMS

Two important information gathering systems provide support for both tactical and strategic marketing decisions. These two information systems are **marketing research information systems** and competitive tracking information systems.

Marketing Research Information Systems

In large organizations, research departments conduct and manage marketing research. In smaller companies, marketing research may be completed by outside consultants or by personnel who must wear several hats. Regardless of how the function is completed, the results of marketing research provide important input to tactical and strategic decision making.

Inputs to marketing research are heavily derived from sources external to the organization, including customers, potential customers, census and demographic data, industry or trade data, economic data, social trend data, environmental data, and scientific and technological data. Data may be obtained through such means as direct mail customer surveys, personal and telephone interviews of consumers, library searches of governmental and industry reports, searches of external databases, and reports filed by sales personnel.

Marketing research personnel make heavy use of statistical methodology in analyzing the data collected and in reporting the information to the organization. Obtaining totals, counts, and averages in terms of consumer responses to questions, correlating social and economic characteristics of customers with their buying practices, completing time series analyses of past industrywide sales to determine the projected sales of a product, and testing hypotheses about consumer response to differing product packaging represent only some of the statistical procedures used to analyze information for marketing managers.

These activities are typical of a marketing research department:

1. Conducting trend analyses of industry sales of products and services identical or similar to those offered by the organization to identify products or services that are on the ascent or descent.
2. Analyzing population and target group characteristics, especially for trends or changes in data that could affect the organization.
3. Analyzing and identifying consumer preferences, including testing products and services.
4. Determining and analyzing customer satisfaction with the organization's existing products and services.
5. Estimating market share for all or each product and service offered.

Competitive Tracking Information Systems

To ensure that the marketing mix offered by your organization will continue to satisfy customers, you must keep abreast of major competitors and their marketing activities. In the end, market share is likely to be greatest for the organization that provides the marketing mix most closely matching a given market segment's needs and wants. Thus, *competitive intelligence,* or knowledge of competitor prices, products, sales, advertising, and promotions must be gathered if the organization is to avoid falling behind the competition in the eyes of the customers. Gathering competitive intelligence is carried out through **competitive tracking information systems.**

Information about competitors is readily available through most trade journals and newspapers. *The Wall Street Journal,* for instance, publishes a great deal of information on various industries, product and service types, and organizations that produce the products and services. These publications often provide information about a new product under development by a competitor. Knowledge that a competitor is developing a new product may result in new research into customer preferences. A change in the advertising agency used by a competitor may be a harbinger of new advertising themes. A growing oversupply of products in your competitor's inventory might mean that a price reduction, rebate, or other promotional campaign is likely to occur soon and signal that you should explore promotional campaigns that preempt your competition.

Information about competitor activities is also obtained from informal sources, through such activities as visiting competitor sales outlets and talking to their employees at conventions. Salespeople in most organizations are encouraged to provide feedback about competitor activities by filing field reports. They may obtain information by observing competing salespeople or by asking seemingly casual questions of customers.

Information about the competition may also be gathered more systematically by conducting keyword searches in on-line databases (see Box 11–5). There are general databases, such as business and industry news from the Dialog Information Services database. IQuest is another comprehensive information service that provides access to more than 850 databases of articles and other data about companies, product news, technology, and industry trends within the US and global markets. CompuServe offers access to IQuest as well as Business Database Plus. The latter allows you to track information about companies, trends, industries, technologies, and products found in journals and other publications.

There are also specialized marketing databases. For example, Interactive Market Systems provides on-line access to more than 300 marketing and advertising databases, and C-Systems offers Ad-Line, which provides data on ads placed by more than 20,000 companies in 185 publications. Searching the Ad-Line database can reveal information about such topics as where your competitors are placing their ads, what kind of ads they are running, what the ads cost, and what products are advertised in what magazines.

COMPUTER SOFTWARE FOR MARKETING

You can classify computer software used to support the marketing function into two groups of products: general-purpose software that is applied to marketing problems and software that has been developed to solve specific marketing problems or support specific marketing activities.

APPLICATIONS OF GENERAL-PURPOSE SOFTWARE TO THE MARKETING FUNCTION

Many general-purpose software packages can be applied to marketing information systems. This software includes query-language software, report writer software, graphics software, multimedia software, statistical software, file management software, database management software, mapping software, survey software, word processing software, desktop publishing software, spreadsheet software, and voice and electronic mail software.

Query-Language and Report Writer Software

A major source of data for tactical and strategic marketing information systems is the organization's financial accounting system database. This system collects and maintains data about sales orders, sales invoices, customer credit history, purchases, and inventory levels. It is important that marketing managers be able to access sales, customer, and product information from the financial accounting database on an ad hoc basis. For example, you should be able to ask the database which sales region served by the company had the highest inventory turnover of warehouse stock during the last year and get an answer on the screen.

Software to provide you with the ability to read these data and develop your own reports has been described in previous chapters as *query-language software* and *report writers*. The use of query-language software permits you to ask numerous questions of an accounting database as you pursue an idea.

Report writer software should permit you to identify the data you need and specify how those data will be processed and reported on screen or on paper. This generally means identifying the fields of data you wish shown as columns on the report and indicating the arithmetic operations you wish performed on the columns (for example: sum, count, average). The software should guide you through each step of the process using easy-to-follow menus and prompts.

Graphics Software and Multimedia Systems

Displaying data in the form of line charts, bar charts, or pie charts often allows you to discern trends and relationships faster than you might if you examined the same data in tabular form. Many marketing managers find that the ability to display data in graphic form is not only helpful to them but also is helpful in communicating their conclusions to others. For example, it might be very useful to display the sales of each division of an organization in a line graph or pie chart.

It would be helpful if the graphics software you utilize can read the data that has been extracted from a database and organized by the report writer you use. In that case, you will be able to process accounting data using the report writer and then display the results graphically without additional keystroking.

Presentation graphics software is very helpful to salespeople and marketing managers for making presentations to customers and superiors. Presentation software makes it easy to develop a set of bullet charts that outline your presentation and then to enhance these charts with clip art, photos, and sound. The presentations then can be displayed using a projection panel attached to a notebook computer system.

Multimedia systems can be used to prepare presentations for customers or for conventions. For example, a series of charts, images, and text that describes the features of a product can be placed together into a timed sequence of computer screens for viewing by individual customers or a large audience. Multimedia systems can also be used to train salespeople in the use of products, sales techniques, and putting together sales exhibits.

Statistical Software

Marketing researchers typically require the use of a wide variety of statistical tools. It is essential that appropriate statistical software be available to process the data these tools gather. The statistical software may be applied to data contained in the organization's financial accounting system, obtained from on-line databases, or collected by marketing researchers themselves, such as data obtained through surveys.

It is also helpful for the marketing manager to have statistical software available. Managers may wish to correlate customer data with sales data to determine what customer characteristics are associated with the purchase of certain products. It is important that the statistical software is able to read data organized by the report writer software. In that way, data can be obtained from an accounting system through the use of a report writer and then manipulated further with a statistical package.

Database and File Management Software

In addition to the financial accounting system data, other files or databases may prove useful. For example, salespeople may find it very helpful to maintain files on their customers and sales prospects. Simple file management software enables the salesperson to reduce any file to magnetic media. Magnetic files permit the salesperson to search and analyze large amounts of data easily. With such software, it is easy to identify customers who have recently bought a product for which the company has just begun to offer a service. For instance, a dehumidifier salesperson may identify customers who recently bought a specific model for which the company now offers a low-cost maintenance agreement.

Mapping Software

Mapping software, which is also called *geographic information systems software,* is software that allows you to arrange or place data from a database onto a map of a country, region, state, city, county, or even city street. Some of the software comes with its own prepackaged data. More sophisticated packages offer customizable maps and are bundled with high-end databases. Basically, the software consists of maps and the programs that convert data into map coordinates so that it can be displayed on the maps. The software differs from traditional database report writers or query languages in that instead of merely listing companies or individuals that meet your query, you can also visually present these entities on a map (see Box 11–4).

Mapping software has been used in the past for land-use analysis and geology. Since mapping software has been developed for microcomputers, however, its applications to marketing quickly followed. For example, you might wish to explore a market around a city. You would draw a circle around the city with a light-pen and query the database about all restaurants in that circle that employ more than five workers and have gross sales in excess of $500,000 or about all food processing firms in the circle that use soy beans as raw material.[5] The Democratic National Committee used mapping software to find areas of the country with concentrations of voters who had voted Democratic in

Box 11–4 Using Mapping Software at Bay State Shipping

MapInfo Corporation provides MapInfo, software that searches database files—yours, theirs, or others—to generate maps and provide information to support many business functions. The company offers thousands of database files for use with their software that include data on the population, income, retail activity, television markets, news markets, employment, manufacturing, medical personnel, businesses, and many other categories of data.

In marketing, the system can be used to support such decisions as locating new stores, warehouses, or distribution facilities; finding current and potential customers; creating sales territories; planning delivery routes; analyzing the market potential of cities, towns, and neighborhoods; allocating media expenses; and generating mailing lists.

The software has become critical to a company called Bay State Shipping. Bay State earns its income by picking up and delivering truck, train, and ship cargo containers at water, rail, and other ports, and matching origination and destination ports to its client's needs. An important part of Bay State's job is getting its clients the best shipping rates and shipping speeds possible. When the company started, cargo ramps and shipping services were all identified manually. As it grew, this task became more difficult to complete swiftly and accurately.

Once Bay State found MapInfo, however, they were able to use their data about cargo ramps and shipping services much more efficiently. MapInfo displays the cargo ramps within a selected number of miles of every origin and destination. By clicking on the map symbols for the ramps, Bay State employees quickly get detailed information about each ramp, including the types of shipping services available at the ramp, the name of the ramp supervisor, and the telephone number to use. Thus, they can find the best ramps for loading and transferring cargo containers quickly. The software has cut the time needed to prepare an estimate for clients to less than one hour. It has also allowed Bay State to expand to a national company. Before MapInfo, the company generated only 5 percent of its business out of the New England region. That figure has now grown to 60 percent.

Source: J. W. Huttig, Jr., "The Vision Thing," *PC Today* 6, no. 12 (December 1991), pp. 58–60.

previous congressional elections but who had voted Republican for president. It then targeted these voters with special advertising materials and used the maps to route then-candidate Clinton's bus tours.

Marketing personnel today are using mapping software to carve out sales territories, plan direct-mail promotion campaigns, identify new store and warehouse locations, analyze the market potential of cities, towns, and neighborhoods, allocate advertising funds, generate mailing lists, and plan delivery routes.

Desktop Survey Software

Many companies, especially small companies, often hire marketing research firms to help them assess such topics as customer reactions to a new product or customer desires for product alterations. However, new software for PCs has made conducting market research much easier for any organization. **Desktop survey software** lets you create survey questions and then helps you sum, tabulate, and otherwise treat statistically the answers collected to those questions. Some software allows you to import questions written using your favorite word processor; others provide a text editor for that purpose. Still others let you develop libraries of questions that you can use over and over again. Typical question formats are yes/no and multiple choice, although some packages can also handle completion questions and open-ended comments as well. Once written, the software allows you to print the questionnaires or interview guides in various formats.

The subjects of the surveys or the researchers can enter the answers to the questions. Or the answers can be copied from completed surveys or directly input as subjects answer questions during telephone interviews. Computer-aided telephone interview software (CATI) can select subjects for interviews automatically from an electronic directory using preselected demographic criteria and quotas. Usually CATI software automatically dials subjects, too.

Some software allows subjects to enter the data themselves into computer systems set up at conventions or at stores. Some companies even distribute their surveys on floppy disks, permitting the subjects to enter their answers using their own PCs. The subjects then return the disks by mail. Some programs that allow subjects to enter data using PCs allow skipping; that is, the programs automatically skip certain questions based on the subject's answers to other questions.

Some companies are considering the use of handheld PCs for use in survey research—subjects would complete forms displayed on the handheld PCs using light pens, and the results could be stored on flash-memory cards.

In any case, although the software helps you write, collect, and compile data from surveys, it still requires you to know quite a bit about constructing effective and valid survey questions, how to create an appropriate sample, and how to understand the results.

Word Processing and Desktop Publishing Software

Marketing personnel can use word processing software to improve their written documents, such as letters to customers, vendors, and colleagues and reports to higher management. Marketing researchers can use word processing software to prepare questionnaires, cover letters for surveys forms, and research reports. You should acquire word processing software that can read the output of your statistical, database, and graphics packages so that you can include statistical tables and charts within the reports you prepare with the word processor.

Desktop publishing software allows marketing personnel to prepare simple brochures, advertising fliers, product or service announcements, and even customer news-

[5]Patrick Marshall, "PC Mapping Software Matures," *InfoWorld* 14, no. 49 (December 7, 1992), p. 82.

letters that appear much more professional than those prepared with a simple word processor.

Salespeople frequently prepare quotation documents in response to customer inquiries about products and prices. For large sales, a quotation, or bid, may be prepared in response to a *request for quotation (RFQ)* issued by a potential customer. The bid usually contains not only product descriptions and prices but also a persuasive rationale for why the organization's products or services best meet a customer's needs. The customer's purchasing department may review the bids submitted by vendors in response to an RFQ in a competitive bidding situation. Thus, the bid prepared by a salesperson must represent the organization and the organization's products or services at a competitive meeting.

A certain part of the information in most bids is referred to as *boilerplate* because it contains a description of the organization's key personnel, products, and services that is included repeatedly in nearly all bids. Having boilerplate on hand for salespeople to use when they prepare bids saves them preparation time.

Spreadsheet Software

Marketing managers can use spreadsheet software for all general managerial tasks. For example, spreadsheet software allows the marketing manager to prepare budget estimates and to simulate various budget situations in the hopes of optimizing budget allocations. The manager also can use spreadsheet software to develop cash flows for the manager's department; to prepare salary estimates for the salesforce; to keep track of sales demonstration equipment used by the salesforce; or to analyze sales by salesperson, product, or territory (see Figure 11–7). The data used by spreadsheet software may be entered by keystroking it into a file, downloading it from the organization's mainframe database, or receiving it through a modem from an on-line database.

Voice and Electronic Mail Software

Salespeople are often away from their desks meeting customers or searching for prospective customers, so they find the ability to leave and pick up written or telephone voice messages for and from customers, prospects, managers, or warehouse personnel extremely useful. Voice mail software gives salespeople the ability to listen to telephone

Figure 11–7
A spreadsheet used to analyze salesforce performance

	A	B	C	D	E	F	G	H	I
1	For July, 1994								
2	08/02/94								
3			MONTHLY SALESFORCE PERFORMANCE ANALYSIS						
4									
5									
6		Number	Number	Orders	$ Total	Average	Calls		Percent
7		of	of	per	of	Order	per	Monthly	of
8	Name	Orders	Calls	Call	Orders	per Call	Day	Quota	Quota
9									
10	Andrews	28	58	0 .48	410 4	$70 9	2.5	0400	103%
11	Bali	24	47	0 .51	96256	$2,0 48	20	380	253%
12	Chiang	31	38	0 .82	5 964	$1,341	1.7	0500	102%
13	D'Arcy	17	42	0 .0	520 8	$1,255	1.8	0500	105%
14	Evans	22	59	0 .37	0300	$522	2.6	450	68%
15	Ferino	10	64	0 .16	1875	$293	2.8	0300	63%
16	Garcia	29	44	0 .66	50 13	$1,25	1.9	450	122%
17	Hull	32	41	0 .78	60 88	$1,588	1.8	550	118%
18									
19	Averages	24	49	0 .6	51335	$1,126	2.1	44125	117%
20	Ave/Mo Last Year	23	52	0 .44	47397	$911	2.4	41238	101%
21	No. of Working Days in Current Mo.				23				

messages left by others; to dictate telephone messages for others; and to store, copy, or distribute incoming and outgoing messages from almost any telephone in the world. Voice mail gives each salesperson an electronic "voice" mailbox, which is nothing more than space on a computer disk. Incoming voice messages are digitized and stored for the salespeople in their mailboxes. Salespeople then can access the voice messages from any telephone, respond to the messages, copy them to other mailboxes, store them for later use, or destroy them.

Electronic mail services let salespeople write, receive, store, copy, and forward messages to others much like voice mail systems. The salesperson may use a notebook or handheld device that communicates with others using a modem.

Sales managers can use voice and electronic mail to broadcast messages to sales personnel or to communicate with individual salespeople wherever they may be. For example, a sales manager may provide a new price schedule for the organization's products by broadcasting or copying the schedule to every salesperson's electronic mailbox. (Voice and electronic mail were discussed in Chapter 8.)

SPECIFIC MARKETING SOFTWARE

In the last few years, many specialized software packages have been developed for a variety of marketing activities. According to Horton (1986), specialized marketing software can be classified into five categories: those that (1) help salespeople sell the organization's products and services, (2) help sales managers manage sales personnel, (3) help manage the telemarketing program, (4) help manage customer support, and (5) provide integrated services for many sales and marketing activities.

Sales Personnel Support Software

Sales personnel support software provides document, file, scheduling, and other support for salespeople. Document support features may include a package of form letters that salespeople can use or adapt, the ability to keep customer lists, and the ability to merge letters with customer lists for large mailings.

File support features may include the ability to record and store information about potential and current customers. Customer, prospect, and contact files can be used to schedule or analyze sales calls and for selective or mass mailings. Prospect or current customer files can be searched to identify which customers were visited during a period, to display how often they were visited, to find which customers have not been visited during the last month, to list customers who have requested a follow-up visit by date, and to relate sales calls to other factors, such as total revenues generated by customer, total previous sales, or type of product purchased. Salespeople have adopted sales contact software, which has become known as **contact management software,** in large numbers.

Salesperson support software often includes a calendar module to help salespeople manage their meetings and customer appointments and a tickler file module to ensure that they follow through on their promises to customers at the appointed time. The tickler file may provide an alarm to prompt you to make preplanned calls, even if you are working in another software package at the time. Many vendors provide to-do lists, E-mail, fax capabilities, and autodialers with their products so that the salesperson can automatically dial customers for voice or fax sessions.

Sales Management Software

Sales management software gives the sales manager the ability to assess the productivity of the sales force, the fertileness of sales territories, and the success of products by salesperson, territory, and customer type. Sales management software keeps track of salesperson call activities, sales orders, and customer activity. The software allows the manager to identify weak territories or weak products in a territory; to compare salesperson performance by product and customer type; to compare salesperson performance against salesperson goals; to analyze salesperson calls within territories or by customer type; to identify trends in customer purchases; to identify potential shortages or excess stock in inventory; and to perform other planning, controlling, and organizing tasks with ease and speed.

Sales management software may access data from the financial information system or from the database created by salespeople using sales support software.

Telemarketing Software

Telemarketing software provides computer support for identifying customers and calling them from disk-based telephone directories or from customer files maintained on a database. The software company might provide you with regularly updated telephone directories of major corporations or specialized lists of selected customer types. The packages may allow you to make notes about the telephone calls you make, generate follow-up letters to the customer, and view a customer file while a call to that customer is in progress.

Other software is designed to find, dial, and connect salespeople automatically to people or companies listed in disk-based telephone directories. This software may then provide a digitized message about a product to those who answer the phone, or permit the salesperson to answer the call.

Telemarketing has moved from mainframe systems to microcomputer systems (see Box 11–2). Davis Software Engineering, Inc., has even provided a LAN-based system that permits more than 200 employees to use the system at the same time. The system also provides management features that permit analysis of data pertaining to calls, contacts, sales approaches, and sales transactions.

Telemarketing software has allowed many firms to substantially increase sales while decreasing the costs per sale. These firms have increased market shares over their competitors by using the technology.

Customer Support Software

Customer support software provides information to salespeople about the previous experiences of customers with the organization such as detailed information on purchases, payments, and specific products purchased by each customer, including competitor products. Customer support software allows salespeople to view customer data prior to sales calls, to identify customers who should be called, to analyze customer purchasing trends, to identify customers who have purchased products that require follow-up calls, and to perform many other sales activities pertaining to customer maintenance. For example, some systems tie the PBX into the computer system so that when a customer calls, the computer system identifies the caller and displays the caller's record on the salesperson's screen. Thus, the use of customer support software results not only in improved salesforce productivity, but also improved customer service.

Integrated Marketing Software

Integrated marketing software combines programs that also may be sold as standalone packages for salesperson support, sales management, or customer support. In addition, highly integrated software supports many marketing professionals throughout the organization by drawing on data not only from salespeople but also from the organization's financial database. Thus, integrated software can bring together the islands of unintegrated data contained in, for example, contact files, prospect files, and order entry files to enhance decision support. Because of the wide variety of data available through such software, it is helpful to a large number of marketing personnel, including marketing researchers and those who develop strategic marketing plans.

ON-LINE MARKETING DATABASES

To help gather current demographic, economic, and financial data on the world or a nation, on an industry, or on a specific customer or competitor, you can use a modem to connect to specialized on-line marketing databases (see Box 11–5). The software

Box 11–5 On-Line Marketing Databases

The databases below are only a few of the many databases of use to marketing decision makers. The databases listed show the diversity of resources available.

Database Name	Description
CENDATA	US Census Bureau database
SuperSite	Provides demographic data and data for retail store sales potential
Findex Directory of Market Research	A Dialog database providing summaries of market studies
Donnelley Demographics	A demographic database similar to CENDATA
UK Marketing Library	Market research reports focusing on the United Kingdom
CandiSnacs Marketing Data Base	Candy distributor sales data on over 4,000 products, including gum and snack products
Easy Vet	Sales of animal health care products categorized by veterinarians, drug stores, livestock supply stores, farming coops, poultry owners, feed lots, feed mills, and feed manufacturers
LabNet	Sales data on diagnostic products purchased by about 350 hospitals and 220 private labs, including projected sales, average prices, product shares, and sales trends
Market Share Reporter	Market share data on companies, products, and services
Mercatis	Consumer purchases by product category, total sales by product and market sector, wholesale and retail prices, advertising expenditures by product and medium for French domestic markets
Advertising and Marketing Intelligence	Abstracts of articles on new products, market research, consumer trends, sales promotion, and advertising
Green Markets	Data on chemical and fertilizer industry, including legislation, production, and research
Market Search	Market research reports, surveys, forecasts, market sizes and market shares by industry, commodity, and region for Japan
MediaWatch	Database on broadcast media
Minority Markets Alert	Text of *Minority Markets Alert* newsletters
Marketing to Women	Text of *Marketing to Women* newsletters
Nielsen Station Index	Ratings on local TV stations

provided by the on-line database vendors permits you to analyze large amounts of data for trends, for information useful in forecasting, or for information pertaining to customers and competitors. Usually you need telecommunications software to control the modem and the specific software provided by the on-line database.

Management Summary

The marketing function occurs in all organizations. Because of its importance, many organizations take a marketing orientation to all organization planning. The basic goal of the marketing function is to satisfy the needs and wants of customers. To achieve that goal, marketing personnel engage in activities such as planning and developing new products; advertising and promoting, selling, and storing and distributing goods and services; providing financing and credit to customers; and conducting market research.

Marketing information systems support the marketing function. They may be categorized as operational, tactical, and strategic in nature. Operational marketing information systems include systems that support the sale of the organization's goods and services. Examples of operational marketing information systems include prospect information systems, contact information systems, telemarketing systems, direct mail information systems, product delivery systems, and distribution information systems. Operational level financial information systems that provide important support include order entry information systems, inventory systems, and customer credit systems.

Tactical marketing information systems support marketing managers in the management and control of the sales force, sales campaigns, advertising and promotion campaigns, pricing, and the distribution and delivery of goods and services. Strategic marketing information systems help top management plan and develop new products and forecast sales. Two major information systems that support both tactical and strategic decision making are marketing research systems and competitive tracking information systems.

Marketing managers may use general software to help them in their operations and decision making. This software may include query-language and report writer software, graphics software, multimedia systems, statistical software, database and file management software, mapping software, desktop survey software, word processing and desktop publishing software, voice mail software, and electronic mail software. Five categories of specialty software also have been developed for marketing: software to support salespeople, software to support sales managers, software to support telemarketing, software for customer support, and specialized software that integrates several of these categories.

Key Terms for Managers

advertising and promotion information systems, **432**
competitive tracking information systems, **436**
computer kiosk, **426**
contact information systems, **423**
contact management software, **442**
customer support software, **443**
desktop survey software, **440**
direct-mail advertising systems, **425**
distribution channel decision support system, **434**
inquiry information system, **426**
integrated marketing software, **443**
inventory information systems, **429**
mapping software, **439**
marketing concept, **422**
marketing function, **420**
marketing information systems, **422**
marketing mix, **421**
marketing orientation, **422**
marketing research information systems, **436**
media mix, **433**
point-of-sale (POS) systems, **427**

product planning and development information systems, **435**
product pricing information systems, **433**
prospect files, **424**
prospect information systems, **424**
sales forecasting information systems, **434**
sales management information systems, **430**
sales management software, **443**
telemarketing software, **443**
telemarketing systems, **424**

Review Questions

1. List six operational-level sales information systems that are not part of the financial accounting system.
2. Identify three financial accounting information systems that provide operational-level input to marketing decision making.
3. How might the data from the sales order processing subsystem be used in marketing?
4. What are sales information systems? Are these systems primarily operational, tactical, or strategic planning information systems?
5. What is a prospect information system? What computerized sources of information are available to identify prospects?
6. What types of outputs might a computerized prospect information system generate?
7. What is contact management software? What features might contact management software offer?
8. What is the purpose of an inquiry information system? What are the common features of an inquiry information system?
9. What is boilerplate and how can it be used to respond to a request for quotation?
10. Describe a telemarketing system.
11. What is a direct mail advertising system? From what sources might an organization obtain names and addresses for a direct mail advertising campaign?
12. Identify sources of information that may be used to obtain information about competitors and competitive products.
13. What is competitive intelligence? What tasks do competitive information professionals complete? What information systems support gathering competitive intelligence?
14. What are five major categories of specialized marketing software?
15. In what ways can CD-ROM and on-line databases be useful to the marketing manager?
16. What is integrated marketing software? What advantages does integration provide?
17. Describe ways in which a marketing manager might use a spreadsheet software package for tactical decision making.
18. Describe ways in which a marketing manager might use query languages and report writers for tactical decision making.

19. Describe five activities frequently performed by marketing research departments. How might computer information systems support each of these activities?
20. Identify ways in which marketing research departments can support marketing managers' tactical decision making and strategic planning.
21. What internal and external sources of information might managers use to prepare a sales forecast for a new product? What computer-based information systems and software provide support for this activity?
22. How can a salesforce use electronic and voice mail to enhance its productivity and effectiveness?
23. Why are sales forecasts important? What other organizational personnel or systems use sales forecast reports?
24. What is an electronic directory? How might such a directory by used by marketing personnel?
25. What is a computer kiosk?
26. Describe desktop survey software. What are some of its typical features?
27. What is mapping software? How can mapping software be used in marketing?

Questions for Discussion

1. How does the focus of an operational-level marketing information system differ from a tactical-level marketing information system?
2. Compare operational and tactical marketing information systems in terms of the type of data they process and the types of output they produce.
3. Some people feel that marketing decision making is an art and that computer information systems offer marketing managers little help in their decision-making activities. Do you agree with this attitude? What are four ways that computer information systems might help marketing managers?
4. Describe how computer systems might be helpful to a salesperson who maintains a manual prospect file.
5. Describe how computer systems might be used to support the sales management function of the organization.
6. Explain the differences in focus between sales personnel support software and sales management software.
7. Do you believe that marketing activities are carried on only by firms operating from a profit motive? Why or why not?
8. Compare the characteristics of a competitive tracking information system to a contact information system. In what ways are these information systems different?
9. Are projections of past sales an effective measure of future sales? Why or why not? If not, what other types of information might prove helpful?

Problems

1. **Barrington Distributors, Inc.** You are the sales manager for Barrington Distributors, which distributes more than 100 different outdoor furniture products to discount stores, department stores, and other retail outlets in a 24-state area. You

supervise 42 salespeople who must cover territories as narrow as a large metropolitan area and as wide as an entire state.

Barrington is implementing a computer system, and the systems analysis group is in the process of questioning managers to determine their reporting needs. You have been asked to identify reports that would be helpful to you in making the tactical decisions regarding the allocation and control of your salesforce.

Identify five reports that you would like to have to assist you in making tactical decisions regarding the salesforce. Then develop an outline of each report, showing the main headings, the column headings, and the types of totals, counts, averages, or other statistical results you wish in each report. Finally, indicate the internal or external source for the data you want in each column.

2. **Database problem: Customer call report.** Design a customer call record to be used by the salespeople for Barrington Distributors (see Problem 1) to record calls they make on their customers. To plan the record design, first identify three reports you, as a salesperson, would like to be able to generate from a file of the records. Then plan the fields in the record that will collect the data you need for those reports. If you have access to file management or database management software, implement your record using the software, populate the file with data for 10 records, and then produce one of the three reports you planned.

3. **Spreadsheet problem: Gross sales and sales calls.** Using a spreadsheet program that will read .WKS files, load the file labeled "Prob11–3. LOTUS 1-2-3" on the diskette provided by your instructor. The file is a template for analyzing salesperson performance for the Walsh Distribution Corporation. The template contains the column headings, row headings, and formulas for determining how well the salesforce reached its sales goals and the average amount sold per sales call.

   To use the spreadsheet, you must enter the gross sales and number of sales calls made for each salesperson. These amounts are:

Salesperson Name	Gross Sales ($)	Number of Calls
Akers	128,349	472
Bernstein	187,525	517
Clark	207,009	532
Diangelo	144,366	368
Ennosuke	261,318	701
Figueroa	283,214	742
Grandeis	169,767	521
Holbrook	176,354	489

   After entering the amounts, answer these questions:

   a. What was the total gross sales for the year for the firm?
   b. What was the average gross sales per salesperson?
   c. Who had the highest gross sales for the year?
   d. What was the average number of sales calls made by the salesforce?
   e. What was the average amount of sales per call for the salesforce?

f. What would the answers to *d* and *e* be if Diangelo and Holbrook were replaced by Dresner and Hall, who had gross sales of $173,462 and $185,507 and sales calls of 457 and 483, respectively?

4. Forecasting Problem: Forecasting Sales. You are the sales manager for Media Sources, Inc. The gross annual sales for your firm for the last 10 years are shown below:

Year	Gross Sales
1	$145,340
2	$140,389
3	$142,580
4	$151,190
5	$151,440
6	$157,180
7	$159,210
8	$156,950
9	$162,560
10	$174,810

a. Forecast the sales for years 11, 12, and 13. If you have a DOS- or Windows-based computer system, use the 4KAST forecasting program that is contained on the applications diskette that your instructor should provide you.

1. Make sure that your computer system is turned on and that the DOS operating system has been loaded. Place your diskette in the A drive of your computer system. Make sure that the system prompt shows A:> . Load the forecasting program by entering 4KAST at A:> and pressing the ENTER key. If you are using Windows, from the Program Manager screen, click on FILE and RUN. Then type A:[4]KAST in the Command Line box that appears on the screen. Then click on OK.
2. When the opening screen of 4KAST is displayed, press the ENTER key. At the "Select A Forecasting Technique" menu, enter L for *linear regression.* This tells the program that you wish to complete a linear regression on data.
3. At the "Simple Linear Regression" menu, enter 2 for *data entry-data file.* This tells the program that the data on which you wish to complete a linear regression is already in a data file.
4. Enter the filename, PROB11–4 and press the ENTER key. This will load the annual sales data from a file on your diskette that already contains the data shown under "Annual Sales."
5. At the "Simple Linear Regression" menu, enter 5 to make a forecast. Choose as your begin point the first year of sales by entering 1 and pressing ENTER. Choose the last year of sales as your end point by entering 10 and pressing ENTER.
6. Forecast sales for the years 11, 12, and 13 by entering 11 as the begin point and 13 as the end point.

7. Enter S to display the forecast on the screen or P to print it out. If you decide you want to print the forecast out, make certain that a printer is attached to your computer, that paper is loaded, and that the printer is turned on before you enter P.

If you did your work correctly, your screen should show the following data:

```
                         4KAST OUTPUT
                   Simple Linear Regression
            ACTUAL            4KASTed                % ERROR
11                          171567.4667
12                          174731.5697
13                          177895.6727
```

b. After reviewing the sales for the last 10 years, you decide that the last 6 years are probably more representative of sales than the last 10 years because in the first 4 years the company was just getting off the ground. Forecast the sales for years 11, 12, and 13, using sales data from years 6 through 10.

5. Spreadsheet Design Problem: Salesperson Performance. Design a spreadsheet like the one shown in Figure 11–7 to analyze salesperson performance. Provide cells to input the number of orders, the number of calls, the total dollar amount of orders, the monthly quotas for each salesperson, the number of working days in the month (Mondays through Fridays), and the monthly averages for each column for last year. Then provide cells to calculate the number of orders per call, the average order per call, the number of calls per day, the percent of sales made to quota, and averages for each column for the entire firm for the month. Test the accuracy of your spreadsheet design by entering the values found in Figure 11–7 and comparing the results you get in your calculated cells. Then evaluate your spreadsheet design by reviewing Box 10–3. Adjust your spreadsheet, if necessary.

6. Spreadsheet Design Problem: Sales of Products by Territory. Design a spreadsheet to analyze sales of products by territory. In your spreadsheet, provide the following:

a. Cells to input gross sales for products 1, 2, 3, and 4 in sales territories A, B, C, and D.
b. Cells to calculate the total sales for each product.
c. Cells to enter the sales of each product for last year.
d. Cells to calculate the estimated increase or decrease (in percent) of sales for each product over the previous year.

Evaluate your spreadsheet design by reviewing Box 10–3. Adjust your spreadsheet, if necessary.

7. Marketing Information Systems Software Report. Using computer or marketing publications, prepare a report on one type of marketing information systems software, such as telemarketing software or salesforce management software. In your report, identify two major software vendors and their products and describe the major features of these products.

8. Marketing Database Report. Using computer or marketing magazines or a CD-ROM database such as Computer Select, identify at least five on-line or CD-ROM databases that may be used to support marketing decision making. Briefly describe the content of each database and its application to marketing.

9. Desktop Mapping Software. The problem assumes that a demonstration diskette of MapInfo, desktop mapping software from MapInfo Corporation, is installed on a computer system available to you. To complete the problem, turn on the computer, change to the *mapinfod* directory, enter "mapinfod," and run the demonstration. Then, answer these questions:

a. What are the major features of MapInfo?
b. What are examples of uses to which MapInfo may be put?
c. How might Melinda Kaikati use MapInfo (see Case 2, Ralston Electric Company).

CASES

1. **Dell Competitor Analysis** You are an assistant to the Vice President of Marketing for a large computer company that produces microcomputer hardware, including desktop and notebook PCs. Your boss has asked you to prepare an analysis of Dell Computer Corporation, a major competitor and producer of PCs. Your boss wants your report to analyze the nature of the competitive threats posed by Dell, based on the data collected. It should also recommend specific actions that your company might take to counter or reduce these threats.

   The report should be limited to five pages, not including cover or reference pages. The report may be enhanced with illustrations from a presentation graphics package, including charts on sales trends, margins, market share, revenues, or similar data.

   To gather data for the report, use CD-ROM or on-line databases available to you, such as ABI/Inform, Computer Select, Lexis/Nexis, and Dialog.

   The competitor analysis report might contain the following types of information about Dell, when available:

   Market share
   Financial statistics
   Sales history
   Product lines
   Territories served
   Advertising themes
   Plans for expansion in products or territories
   New products
   Products under development
   Product margins
   Market strategy
   General market outlook for the industry
   Marketing mix
   Competitor strengths
   Competitor weaknesses
   Best and worst selling product lines
   Trends in U.S. and world markets affecting products

2. **Ralston Electric Company.** Melinda Kaikati, a sales manager for Ralston Electric Company, is considering providing computer support for her sales personnel. Her salespeople sell electric motors to manufacturing firms in seven Midwestern states and spend most of their time on the road. Most of them live in the areas they serve.

   At the present time, salespeople telephone orders to order clerks located at the main office who use terminals connected to the firm's mainframe. This allows the salespeople to confirm immediately that there is enough stock on hand to meet each order and that the customer's credit is satisfactory. Ms. Kaikati doesn't want to alter this procedure because it is working very well. What she wants to know is if she can provide additional computer support to her salespeople to help them manage their sales activities so as to improve their productivity and performance. Ms. Kaikati has asked you for help.

   a. Provide a list of potential applications that might help the salespeople manage their everyday sales activities more efficiently and productively. Describe how each application will improve the productivity and performance of the salesforce.

b. Identify types of software that could be used to support each of the applications you listed in *a.*

3. **Merrill's.** Ralph Johnson and Teresa Merrill are partners in Merrill's, a fashion clothing retailing firm. Teresa Merrill has been primarily concerned with the marketing aspects of the firm and Ralph Johnson has concentrated on the accounting and finance functions. The firm has three stores in the Dallas/Fort Worth area, two stores in Houston, and two stores in El Paso, Texas. Merrill's has been very successful, growing from one store three years ago to its current total of seven stores. Its success has been largely due to Teresa's ability to guess what fashions customers will like and to stock these items in the stores. It has also been due to her persistence in identifying stock that is moving too slowly or very fast and adjusting inventories accordingly. Until recently, she did all the buying, and it was relatively easy for her to stay on top of inventory turnover when there were only one or two stores. As the firm became larger, however, Teresa has had to hire professional buyers and increasingly delegate these duties to them.

   The partners are now considering establishing their own data processing department and computerizing the accounting system, including the order entry and inventory subsystems. Ralph recently attended a two-day seminar on the use of computers for decision support. He has become interested in using the computer system to help him manage the financial activities of the firm and to help Teresa manage the marketing functions in some way, especially in helping her forecast product sales. When Ralph discussed this with Teresa, Teresa became agitated. She felt that there was no way that a computer system could help her or her buyers forecast the sales of individual products. After all, they were in the fashion business, and predicting customer acceptance using a computer would be impossible. Teresa feels that the fashion business is simply too erratic for computer support.

   However, Ralph still believes that the use of the computer system in marketing is a real possibility. He simply does not have the background, though, to show Teresa how the computer could help her. As a result, Ralph has asked you to serve as a consultant to the firm to identify how a computer system could be used to assist Teresa in marketing, especially in the area of forecasting product sales and controlling inventory levels.

   Prepare a report for Ralph in which you take these steps:

   a. Identify and describe at least three ways in which a computer system might help Teresa in her tactical decision making.

   b. Develop the layouts for two reports that will help her with her tactical planning. The report layouts should include report, row, and column headings and show totals, averages, or other ways in which column data are to be treated.

   Make certain that your report addresses Teresa's forecasting and inventory control activities.

Selected References and Readings

Bandrowski, Paul. "Using Technology to Increase Sales (Tools of the Trade)." *Corporate Computing* 2, no. 1 (January 1993), p. 166. Describes how the use of pen-based computing systems and cellular modems can increase sales.

Blatberg, Robert C., and John Deighton. "Interactive Marketing: Exploiting the Age of Addressability." *Business Edge,* prototype issue (May 1992), pp. 12–17. A reprint of an article in the

Fall 1991 issue of the *Sloan Management Review*. It describes the changes in marketing underway because of the ability to address or target specific customers easily.

Broughton, Jan. "Why Spy." *American Way* 22, no. 9 (May 1, 1989), pp. 44–50. Discusses competitive intelligence gathering.

Gable, Michael. "Spotlight on Marketing Lists: When Does Direct Marketing Interfere with Consumers' Privacy?" *PC Today* 8, no. 1 (January 1994), pp. 20–22. Discusses the ethical issues surrounding the use of electronic directories. A sidebar describes how American Business Information was formed.

Goldsborough, Reid. "Automated Customer Service Centers." *PC Today* 7, no. 10 (October 1993), pp. 46–48. Describes how computer kiosks can be used to market a firm's products and services.

Gross, Charles W., and Robin T. Peterson. *Marketing Concepts and Decision Making*. St. Paul, Minn.: West Publishing Co., 1987, p. 129. A basic marketing management text.

Henricks, Mark. "Contact Managers Find New Calling in Business." *PC World* 8, no. 5 (May 1990), p. 66. A brief description of sales contact management software.

Holzberg, Carol S. "Long Distance Information . . . Give Me Memphis, TN." *PC Today* 7, no. 8 (August 1993), p. 16. Reviews four electronic directories and their use in the marketing function.

Holzberg, Carol S. "Playing the Numbers: Statistical Programs Can Crunch Your Market Research Data." *PC Today* 7, no. 1 (January 1993), pp. 24–27. A review of popular PC statistical programs and their applications to marketing research problems.

Horton, Len. "Sales Reps Take Computing on the Road." *Software News,* October 1986, pp. 40–54. Describes how salespeople can use laptop computers in their work.

Huttig, J. W. "Point-of-Sale a la Carte." *PC Today* 7, no. 9 (September 1993), pp. 18–21. A discussion of PC point-of-sale systems, including hardware and software.

Huttig, J. W. "This Is Your Survey. This Is Your Survey on PCs. Any Questions?" *PC Today* 7, no. 1 (January 1993), pp. 20–23. Describes PC-based survey software and how it can be applied to marketing research problems.

Huttig, J. W. "The Vision Thing." *PC Today* 6, no. 12 (December 1992), pp. 58–60. Reviews MapInfo Corporation's products.

Huttig, J. W. "'X' Marks the Spot: Geographic Information Systems Turn Databases into Marketing Treasure Maps." *PC Today* 8, no. 1 (January 1994), pp. 16–19. Reviews mapping software and its application to the marketing function.

Johnson, Steven J. "Retail Systems: No Longer Business as Usual." *Journal of Systems Management* 43, no. 8 (August 1992), pp. 8–12. Focuses on how POS systems can cut costs, improve customer service, and gather useful data on customers.

Marshall, Patrick. "PC Mapping Software Matures." *InfoWorld* 14, no. 49 (December 7, 1992), pp. 82 ff. Reviews four geographic information systems software packages.

Pantages, Angeline. "The New Order at Johnson Wax." *Datamation* 36, no. 6 (March 15, 1990) pp. 103–106. Describes the Computer Integration of Customer Service Systems project at Johnson Wax, including its order-processing system and the use of EDI.

Scheier, Robert L. "How to Cost-Justify Sales Force Automation." *PC Week* 7, no. 7 (April 23, 1990), pp. 115–16. A brief description of the major cost factors in automating salespeople's work.

Yakal, Kathy. "Contact Management: Keeping in Touch." *PC Magazine* 12, no. 14 (August 1993), pp. 271–74 ff. A review of 16 contact management software packages and a discussion of their applications in some firms.

Manufacturing and Production Information Systems

Chapter Outline

Manager's View

Manufacturing and production systems are normally associated with organizations that manufacture tangible products. We ordinarily envision a manufacturing firm that purchases raw materials and uses machines and labor to shape those materials into finished products. However, services must also be produced (see Box 12–1). For example, a hospital uses medical supplies (such as medicines), medical machinery and equipment (such as anesthetic equipment), a medical plant (such as an operating room), and medical personnel (such as nurses, orderlies, and surgeons) to produce surgical operations for its patients. Legal firms use secretaries, office clerks, and lawyers; law libraries; office space; typewriters, desks, and other office equipment; and office supplies to provide legal services for their clients.

Box 12–1 Typical Manufacturing and Production Decisions

1. A university dean deciding capacity needs for the school of business, such as courses to be offered next year, number of sections of each course to be offered next year, and the number of instructors needed to staff the schedule.
2. A word processing supervisor deciding how many word processing clerks, word processing editors, and statistical typists will be needed for each shift next week and how these employees will be scheduled.
3. A retail store planner selecting criteria for potential new sites for retail stores and using those criteria to rank potential sites.
4. An inventory manager and a production planner deciding how many units of each item of certain raw materials must be on hand at each production site in an attempt to reduce the quantities of raw materials held without disrupting production.
5. A quality analyst deciding which evaluation techniques to use to test certain raw materials used in the production process.
6. A production process engineer and a product design engineer examining the design of a subassembly to ascertain the cost of producing and assembling it.
7. A plant manager and production scheduler evaluating off-the-shelf software for production scheduling against the needs of their organization.
8. A production scheduler determining how many materials and parts to order and when to release the purchase orders to meet the requirements of the production schedule.
9. A systems analyst examining the process of creating, receiving, entering, processing, and distributing sales orders in order to spot and eliminate bottlenecks in order processing, reduce the time between order receipt and order shipment, and reduce the number of steps in the order entry process.
10. A manufacturing manager deciding the number and types of personnel needed to staff a new plant in another state under consideration by top management.

As these examples suggest, manufacturing and production systems are present in all types of organizations. Furthermore, the importance of productivity for all organizations in these times of intense international competition cannot be overemphasized. Thus, although this chapter focuses primarily on traditional manufacturing and production processes and the information systems that support them, the processes and information systems are important to all managers. Manufacturing and production information systems can provide all managers with the means to improve productivity and gain competitive advantages.

THE PURPOSE OF MANUFACTURING AND PRODUCTION SYSTEMS

Manufacturing systems encompass all the activities necessary to ensure production. These activities may include the evaluation of production sites; the planning, development, and maintenance of production facilities; and the setting of production goals to meet the requirements of the sales forecast generated by the marketing system. Production systems are subsystems of manufacturing systems. They are designed to produce the goods and services that the marketing system plans to sell. **Production systems** typically focus on these aspects of the business:

1. Acquisition, storage, and availability of raw materials and production supplies.
2. Scheduling the necessary equipment, facilities, and workforce to process these raw materials into finished goods ready for the marketing system to sell.
3. Designing and testing the products and services.
4. Producing the correct *quantity* at the required level of *quality* within the projected *cost* parameters of the budget at the *times* required by the production goals.

The nature of manufacturing and production systems reflects the nature of the products or services being produced and how they are produced. The composition of some products—such as spools of copper wire—is relatively simple. Other products, such as radios, may consist of numerous component parts and subassemblies. Some products—socks for example—are produced in relatively stable amounts over long periods of time. Other products are produced in varying quantities as they are needed. Thus, the production of air conditioners depends on the season, of fashion clothing on the whims of the buying public, and so on. Producing products that vary in demand makes the production manager's job much more difficult.

Some products or services are produced continuously, or through *continuous-flow production.* For example, oil refineries continuously produce refined oil from raw oil products. Other products or services, such as television sets or bottled soda, are produced on an assembly-line, or *mass-production,* basis. Frequently, this type of production is scheduled on the basis of sales forecasts that predict certain quantities of certain products will be required by the marketing system at certain times. Still other products are produced in batches when they are requested and according to the specifications in the request, that is, through *job-order production.* For instance, a printing organization may produce 5,000 conference brochures to fill an order made by a professional organization. A final type of production is scheduled for a specific *project,* such as the construction of a bridge or the prosecution of a legal case.

To compound the production process further, subassemblies may be produced in some parts of the world while the final assembly of the finished good occurs in another. Thus, raw materials, component parts, and finished goods may be scattered geographically.

To perform its functions, the manufacturing system must locate production sites, plan the layout of those sites, and produce a production plan. The production system has to acquire the raw materials, parts, and subassemblies needed to produce the products or services described in the plan and to identify how many workers of each type are required. The system must then allocate or acquire workers with the appropriate skills, make certain that sufficient work space and production equipment are available, and schedule an integrated use of these resources to produce the correct quantity of goods at the correct time to meet the marketing system's forecasted needs. While production is under way, the system also must monitor the use and cost of those resources.

MANUFACTURING AND PRODUCTION INFORMATION SYSTEMS

Manufacturing and production information systems provide the data necessary to plan, organize, operate, monitor, control, and otherwise manage production systems (see Figure 12–1). Manufacturing and production information systems may differ from other information systems in the variety of input and output devices used and the nature of data typically included in the system. For example, production information systems may include robotics as well as heat sensors, pressure sensors, and other process control devices that measure the temperature and thickness of steel wire as it is produced in a mill. In general, however, manufacturing and production information systems can be classified into operational, tactical, and strategic planning systems, just as other information systems are (see Figure 12–2). Usually, the nature of the data input into and output from these three levels of information systems parallels the nature of the input and output of the three levels of information systems that serve other functional business areas.

Production information systems usually support operational and tactical decision making. Manufacturing information systems ordinarily support tactical and strategic planning decision making. Typically, operational production information systems collect and report information about the status of production tasks, tactical manufacturing and production information systems collect and report information relevant to the management and control of resources, and strategic planning manufacturing information systems support managers who are setting goals.

OPERATIONAL PRODUCTION INFORMATION SYSTEMS

Numerous operational information systems support the production function. Many are part of the financial accounting system of an organization (see Figure 10–2). For example, purchasing, accounts payable, inventory, order entry, accounts receivable, and payroll subsystems of the accounting system provide information to support manufacturing and production activities. This section briefly describes some of the major operational information systems used in production.

Purchasing Information Systems

To produce goods and services, you must have the right quantity of raw materials and production supplies on hand. Furthermore, you will want to procure these materials and supplies at the lowest cost and have them delivered at the right time. To assist in this function, the purchasing information system has to maintain data on all phases of the acquisition of raw materials and purchased parts used in production. For example, the purchasing information system must maintain vendor files with price quotation infor-

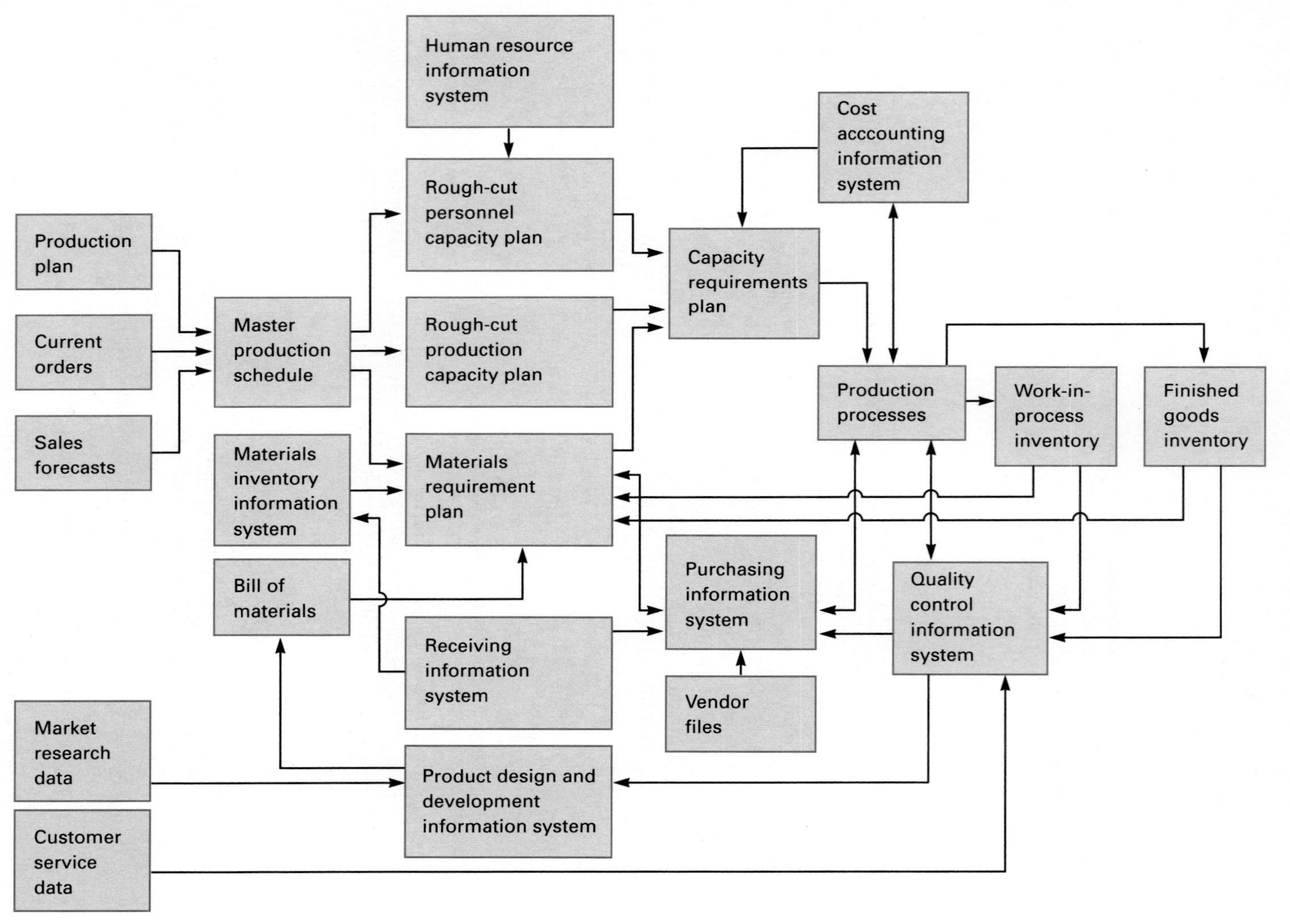

Figure 12–1
Production processes and information systems

Strategic planning

Site planning and selection
Technology planning and assessment
Process positioning
Plant design

Tactical

Materials requirements planning systems
Just-in-time systems
Capacity planning information systems
Production scheduling information systems
Product design and development information systems

Operational

Purchasing information systems
Receiving information systems
Quality control information systems
Shipping information systems
Cost accounting information systems
Inventory management and control information systems

Figure 12–2
Manufacturing and production information systems

mation on all production materials and supplies so that intelligent choices can be made among suppliers (see Figure 12–3). Also, records must be maintained of those goods already on order. Such records, often called an *open order file* (see Figure 12–4), are used to monitor the ordering and delivery of production materials and supplies to keep you from exceeding budget allocations and targeted inventory levels.

Receiving Information Systems

When shipments of purchased goods and supplies are received, they must usually be inspected and verified and the information about their status passed on to the accounts payable, inventory, and production departments (see Figure 12–5). Delivery dates should also be noted so that data on delivery times can be collected. This type of information is supplied by **receiving information systems.**

Figure 12–3
An example of a price quotation screen for a purchased part

FILE EDIT VIEW OPTIONS HELP

ITEM: Casing STOCK NO: C459

PRODUCT: R10 Motor Assembly UNIT OF PURCHASE: Dozen

DATE	VEN. NO.	VENDOR NAME	PRICE	TERMS	REMARKS
03 22 94	1077	Aponte Mfg., Inc.	24.79	30 da.	
03 23 94	893	Banner Corporation	25.69	60 da.	
03 23 94	499	Berne & Sons, Inc.	25.19	30 da.	
03 24 94	501	Crest Products, Inc.	27.28	60 da.	
03 24 94	178	Eastman Corporation	23.77	10 da.	
03 24 94	277	F & S Company	25.99	30 da.	
03 25 94	312	Grand Designs, Inc.	26.50	45 da.	
03 25 94	721	Havre Metals, Inc.	26.49	45 da.	
03 25 94	745	Inacker Molding Co.	24.49	30 da.	
03 25 94	822	J & J Castings, Inc.	25.90	45 da.	

Figure 12–4
A screen from an open order file showing the stock of raw materials and purchased parts on order

OPEN ORDERS

REQUISITION DATE	REQ. NO.	DATE WANTED	RECEIPT DATE	REMARKS
11 05 95	30789	11 21 95		
11 08 95	30790	11 25 95		
11 08 95	30791	11 23 95	11 22 95	
11 09 95	30792	11 27 95		

Quality Control Information Systems

Quality control information systems provide information about the status of production goods as they move from the raw materials state, through goods-in-process, to the finished goods inventory. Quality control systems also ensure that raw materials or parts purchased for use in the production processes meet the standards set for those materials.

Quality control data can be collected with **shop-floor data collection systems,** which can include a rich assortment of input devices—counters, assembly-line data entry terminals, process control sensors, and so on. Workers can use assembly-line data entry terminals to enter data regarding the status of goods in process and the amount of worker time devoted to each phase of the production process. Process control sensors are frequently used to monitor the gauge of metal as it is fabricated into such final products as sheets, bars, or wire.

Shop-floor data collection devices can be connected to a **factory local area network (LAN)** for local data collection (see Figure 12–6). The LAN may in turn be

Figure 12–5
A sample receiving report

ZUMAR-READE
Receiving Report

DATE RECEIVED: 09/04/94

VENDOR NO: 803

VENDOR NAME: Vineta Fabrication, Inc.

OUR PURCHASE ORDER NO: 38097

VENDOR INVOICE NO: 9077

ITEM NO.	DESCRIPTION	QUANTITY ORDERED	QUANTITY RECEIVED	REMARKS
T-345	4" Brace	1000	1000	
T-500	8" Brace	200	100	100 backordered
T-750	Angle brace	500	499	1 damaged

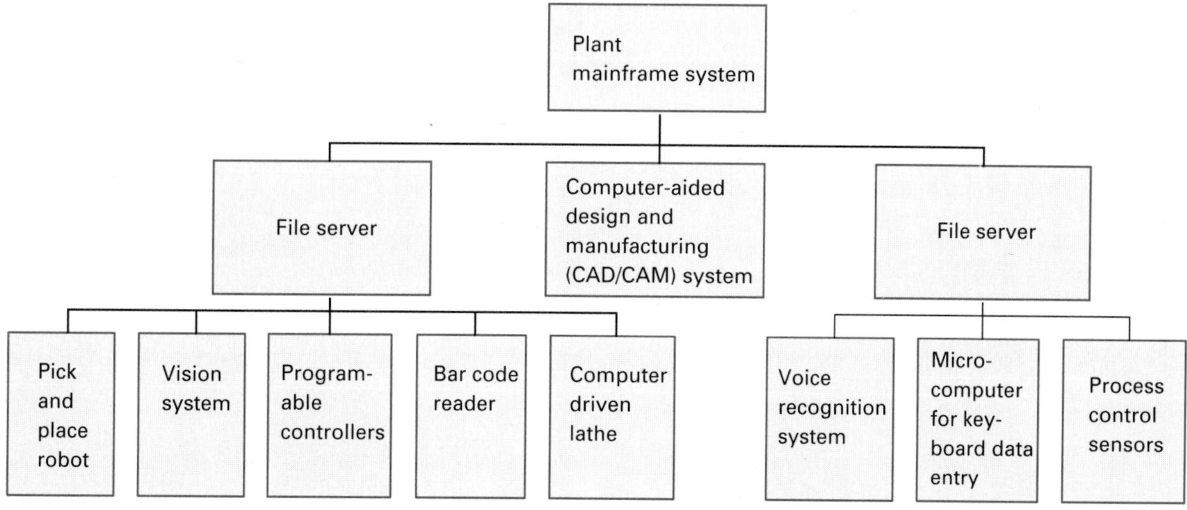

Figure 12–6
A factory LAN may connect many different shop-floor devices

connected to a minicomputer or mainframe computer system. A factory LAN is a communications network that often connects very different devices found on a factory floor, such as robots that handle, load, or weld parts; programmable controllers used to sequence processes; vision systems that inspect or sort parts; bar-code readers that count or sort parts; and microcomputers with keyboards or voice recognition systems that allow factory floor personnel to enter data about the time spent on a job order, piece counts, and the number and types of waste and scrap materials identified.

When inspection, testing, or monitoring identifies items that fail to meet the standards that have been set, a *variance* occurs. If the variance occurs in raw materials or purchased parts, it may be reported on the receiving report. If it occurs during the production processes, the quality control system may shut the production system down, or it may report the variance in some way to employees or supervisory personnel. If the variance occurs in finished goods, the goods must not be placed in inventory and the nature of the variance must be reported to the production manager. For example, the standards for sheets of copper rolling off a mill may demand that the sheet thickness never vary more than 0.01 mm positively or negatively. If, at any time during the production process, failures occur in equipment, raw materials, or human procedures that result in the sheets exceeding this *tolerance*, the quality control mechanisms may activate a warning light or bell, print a report, or shut down the production equipment entirely.

The product development and design system can use quality control information to determine realistic specifications for a product under development. The purchasing system can use it to set effective specifications for raw materials, purchased parts, and production supplies (see Box 12–2). In addition, quality control information systems allow managers to identify vendors that consistently ship poor-quality materials or whose material quality is highly unreliable. These systems can also help managers identify unreliable or faulty production machinery and workers whose training, procedures, or attention are not sufficient for their work. At the same time, quality control information systems should include an information stream from the customer service department to ensure that customer complaints and concerns about quality are directed back to the production system.

Two management approaches that require organizations to improve quality are just-in-time systems and total quality control (TQC). Just-in-time systems will be dis-

Box 12–2 Supplying McDonnell Douglas Corporation

McDonnell Douglas Corporation decided to reduce the number of its suppliers, and improve the quality of its products and delivery in the same process. Starting with about 2,875 suppliers, the aerospace manufacturer wants to cut that list to about 1,000 through a tough supplier certification program. To be certified as a McDonnell Douglas supplier, a firm must meet a set of quality and delivery-time standards and demonstrate a priority for improving performance in these two areas.

McDonnell's major buyer, the Pentagon, has been increasing its own quality management recently, which put pressure on McDonnell Douglas to do likewise. To be certified, a firm must undergo an on-site assessment of management, quality, technology, cost, delivery speed and reliability, and customer support. McDonnell Douglas reviews each firm quarterly for quality, delivery, and customer support. It also offers training classes in statistical process control for suppliers.

Certification is at three levels: bronze, silver, and gold. Each level brings with it increased benefits to the supplier, such as length of contracts and contract rates.

Source: Adam Goodman, "McDonnell's Suppliers Face Quality Challenge," *St. Louis Post-Dispatch*, November 29, 1992, Business Section, pp. 1 and 8.

cussed later in this chapter. Some suggest that TQC is the brainchild of W. Edwards Deming, who, along with other Americans, is credited with helping to improve the quality of Japanese manufacturing.

In a traditional manufacturing environment, quality control tasks and production tasks are separated. In an organization using **total quality control** and committed to the fabrication of quality products, quality control information pervades the production processes—everyone in the production chain is responsible for quality. Furthermore, emphasis is placed on the prevention of defects rather than on measurement and inspection.

Quality control systems embedded in the production processes are typically continuous and automatic and may not require direct management decisions. Those designed for raw materials and finished goods usually consist of routine and repetitive sampling and testing procedures. These procedures are used to sample the raw materials and parts received and the finished goods produced to determine if their specifications fall within the standards that have been previously set.

Shipping Information Systems

At the other end of the production process, finished goods are placed in inventory or shipped to customers. Many records and documents assist and monitor the inventory and shipping processes—for example, shipping reports and packing slips. Packing slips usually include a partial copy of the sales invoice and list the quantity, stock number, and description of the merchandise packed in a shipping carton. The information from the shipping system affects the inventory and accounts receivable systems.

Cost Accounting Information Systems

Many operational information subsystems of the financial accounting system collect and report information about the resources used in the production processes so that accurate production costs can be obtained for products and services. Cost accounting systems monitor the three major resources used in production: personnel, materials, and equipment and facilities.

Workers, supervisors, and managers are among the most important resources available to managers. Payroll information systems collect and report information about the costs of this resource and how much personnel time has been allocated to different products and services. Personnel time and costs are often collected through employee time-card or job-ticket systems. Accurate information about the allocation and costs of direct and indirect labor is required to control existing production processes and to plan and schedule future manufacturing and production activities.

Materials management information systems provide information on current inventory levels of production materials, usage of these materials in the production processes, location of materials, and specifications of how these materials are employed in the products. The latter system is usually referred to as a **bill-of-materials (BOM) system** (see Figure 12–7). A bill-of-materials system lists the raw materials, subassemblies, and component parts needed to complete each product. It provides, in essence, a list of ingredients for the end product.

In addition to getting information about the use of materials and personnel, manufacturing and production managers must get information about the use of equipment and facilities in the production processes. The information systems needed provide operational-level information about what equipment and facilities have been used for what length of time on what products and services and at what costs. Materials usage, personnel usage, and equipment and facilities usage information systems provide input

Vasquez Industries, Inc.
Bill of Materials
Stock No. 1046

Part Number	Description	Quanity	Unit
C120	Shaft assembly	1	Each
1201	1/2-2 bolts	4	Each
1202	1/2" nuts	4	Each
1203	1/2" washers	4	Each
1204	1" shaft	1	Each
1205	Base plate	1	Each
D250	Motor assembly	1	Each
R250	Casing assembly	1	Each
2501	Sides	4	Each
2502	Top/bottom	2	Each
2503	1/4-1 screws	16	Each

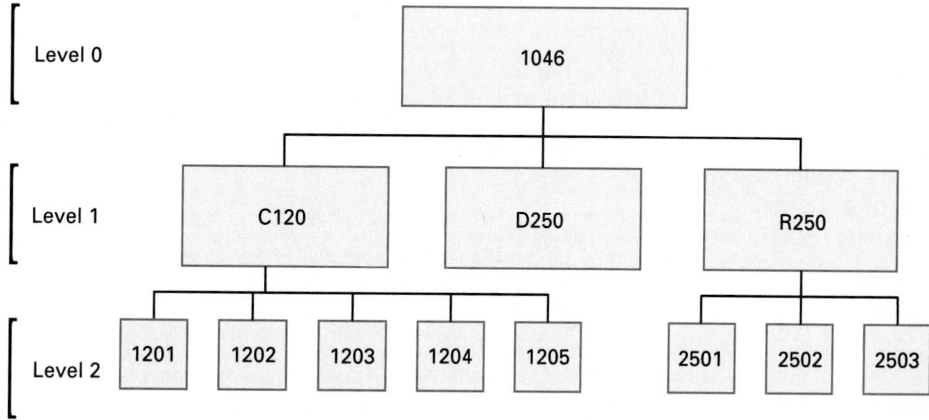

Figure 12–7
A bill of materials needed to produce a product (stock no. 1046) and a diagram of the product (1046), subassemblies (C120, D250, R250), and subassembly parts (1201-1205 and 2501-2503)

to job costing systems. Reports from each of these information systems allow managers to monitor production costs and the allocation of production resources.

Inventory Management and Control Information Systems

The management and control of raw materials, goods-in-process, and finished goods inventories is an important part of the production system. Careful management and control of these inventories usually provide considerable savings to the organization. **Inventory management and control systems** use information from operational information systems, such as the shipping and receiving systems, purchasing systems, and order entry systems (see also "Just-in-Time Systems" later in this chapter).

Maintaining inventories at their proper levels eliminates production shutdowns from lack of raw materials and lost sales from lack of finished goods. However, maintaining inventories also represents a number of costs to the organization, including the costs of procuring and carrying the inventory and stockout costs, those costs that result when the right amount of the right item is not on hand at the right time.

In a conventional production system, two basic information tools are used to manage inventories: a *reorder-point system* and a system for determining the least expensive quantity to order, or **economic order quantity (EOQ)** system. A reorder-point system is used to make certain that production materials are ordered in sufficient lead time to arrive at the plant when they are needed in the production process. The system uses predefined levels of inventory to initiate the purchasing process. The predefined levels of inventory are those levels required to cover the organization while waiting for new orders of the stock to be delivered. Some organizations do not wish to cut their timing this close, however. As a result, they maintain an additional amount of stock, called *safety stock*, on hand in case shipments are delayed, some stock items are defective, or some other foul-up occurs.

The second conventional inventory management tool provides managers with the means to reduce total inventory costs by identifying the most economic order quantity of each item. Ordering in small quantities reduces taxes, insurance, and other *carrying costs* but increases ordering, shipping, receiving, and other procurement, or *ordering costs*. Ordering in large quantities reduces ordering costs but increases carrying costs. Thus, the best or economic order quantity strikes a balance between carrying costs and ordering costs (see Figure 12–8).

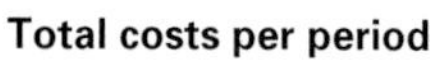

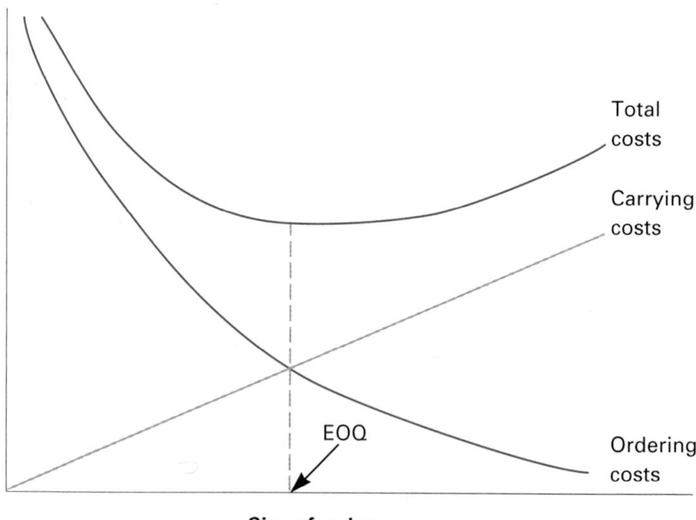

Figure 12–8
Inventory costs graphed to show the balancing of ordering costs and carrying costs, or the economic order quantity (EOQ)

Computing EOQ manually for each item in inventory would be a very large and tedious task. Also, for many inventory items, the managers may wish to ask "what if" questions about the values in the EOQ formulas. Without computers, these tasks would be laborious and may prove too time-consuming to keep the order process fine-tuned to current data.

TACTICAL MANUFACTURING AND PRODUCTION INFORMATION SYSTEMS

Manufacturing and production costs are a major cost component of any organization. It should not be surprising, therefore, to find that many information systems are available to help managers (1) monitor and control manufacturing and production processes and (2) allocate resources to achieve manufacturing and production goals set through the strategic planning process. This section will include a discussion of several tactical information systems: materials requirements planning systems, just-in-time systems, capacity planning systems, production scheduling systems, and product design and development systems.

Materials Requirements Planning Systems

Inventory management can be taken a step further so that the system automatically produces purchase orders for stock that needs to be reordered. The processes of identifying stock that planned production calls for, determining the lead time to get the stock from suppliers, calculating safety stock levels, calculating the most cost-effective order quantities, and then producing purchase orders for those stock items in the right amounts at the right times to ensure that the stock will be on hand when it is needed is known as **materials requirements planning,** or **MRP.**

MRP uses data from the master production schedule, inventory information system, and bill-of-materials information system to manage inventory. Figure 12–9 shows the typical inputs and outputs of an MRP system.

The materials included in the planning system may be raw materials, component parts, or finished goods. The components may be output from other production processes or simply purchases from suppliers. The MRP system must determine what materials are needed for each production period and then match those material needs with materials on hand, with estimated delivery times, and, if appropriate, with the most economic order quantity. An important output of the system is a series of purchase orders and the dates when those purchase orders should be released to meet inventory needs.

An MRP system requires several information inputs, including the **master production schedule,** which identifies what products are needed and when they are needed and is usually based on both sales forecasts and current orders supplied by the marketing information system. Another necessary input is the status of the materials inventory for each production period, which refers not only to the type and amount of stock on hand but also to the type and amount of each item on order. The bill of materials—or list of raw materials and components needed to create each product—is needed as well. Another input to the MRP subsystem is information regarding the lead times and lot sizes of each raw material or part needed.

Just-in-Time Systems

The **just-in-time (JIT) system** is not a tactical information system, but a tactical approach to production. The just-in-time approach was created by the Toyota Motor Company of Japan and has generated many advantages to organizations, especially those that do repetitive manufacturing. The purpose of the approach is to eliminate waste in the use of equipment, parts, space, workers' time, and materials, including the resources devoted to inventories. The basic philosophy of JIT is that operations should

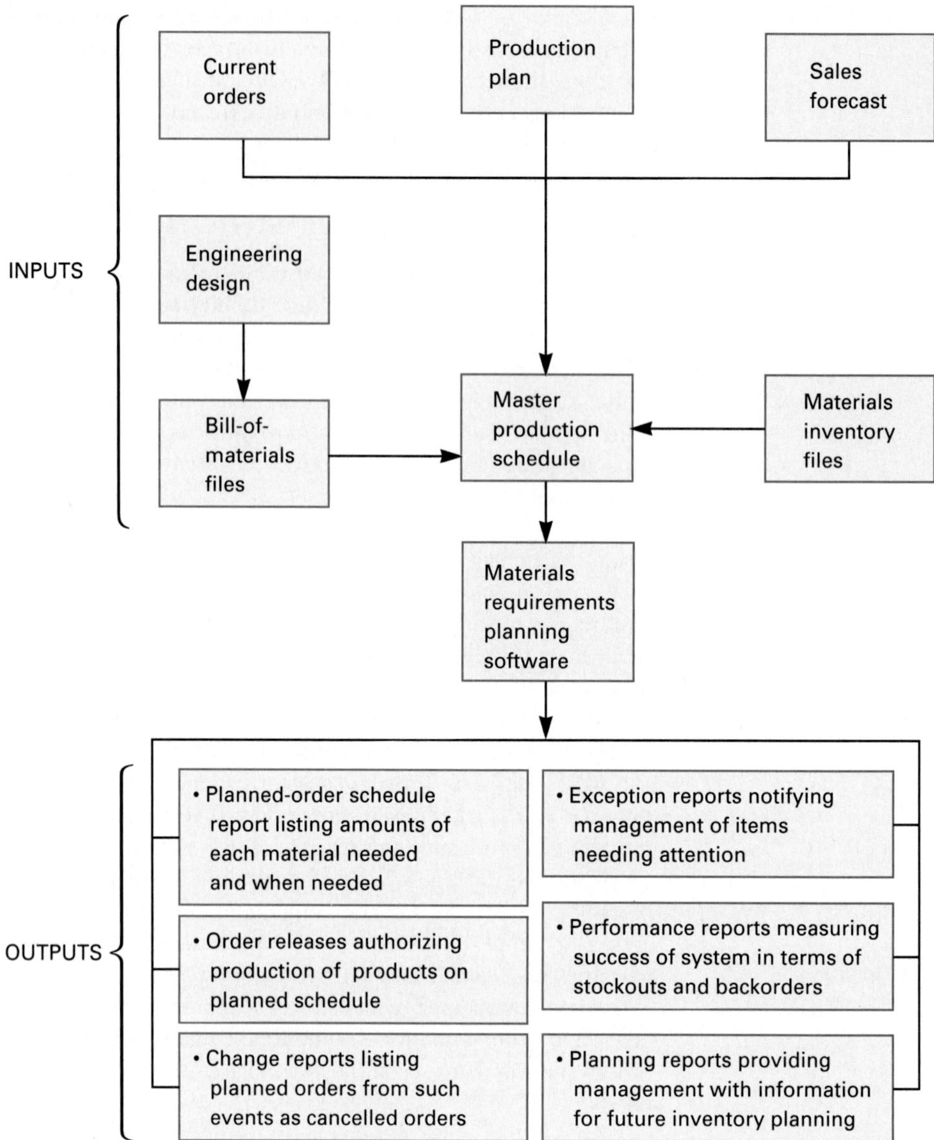

Figure 12–9
A model of a materials requirements planning system showing the system's inputs and outputs

occur just when they are required to maintain the production schedule. To assure a smooth flow of operations in that environment, sources of problems must be eradicated. That means that quality must be emphasized because quality problems interfere with the even flow of work. For inventory management, JIT translates into having just as much inventory on hand as is absolutely needed. This is achieved by developing efficient manufacturing controls. One of these controls is to develop close working relationships with suppliers and require them to deliver just enough acceptable materials to meet the day's or week's production schedule. To assist in this process, manufacturers and their suppliers may use electronic data interchange (EDI). EDI lets suppliers monitor the manufacturer's inventory levels by allowing them to access the manufacturer's inventory files electronically. Suppliers then ship the raw materials or parts to the manufacturer only as needed.

Capacity Planning Information Systems

In addition to ensuring that enough raw materials will be on hand for planned production, the production manager must also see to it that enough production capacity will be available to meet production goals. The purpose of capacity planning is to make certain that sufficient personnel, space, machines, and other production facilities are available at the right time to meet the organization's planned production. Managers also utilize capacity planning to minimize excess production capacity.

Capacity planning decisions are tactical production decisions. They include allocating personnel and production facilities. Selecting sites for constructing plant facilities, acquiring plant facilities, and planning those facilities to meet long-term production goals are usually categorized as strategic planning manufacturing decisions.

One capacity planning technique is called **rough-cut capacity planning.** Rough-cut capacity planning provides an overall estimate of capacity needs using the information provided by the master production schedule as inputs. Rough-cut capacity planning is used to convert the production goals included in the master production schedule into capacity needs by using historical measures of production or shop-floor standards for producing end products. Rough-cut capacity planning produces estimates of the capacity needed, such as the hours of labor and the hours of machine time necessary to meet the production goals. These estimates of labor and machine hours are then allocated to specific work groups and factory locations to determine the feasibility of meeting the production goals with current facilities (see Box 12–3).

The basic purpose of rough-cut capacity planning is to identify whether there is enough, too little, or too much capacity based on the information from the master production schedule. If the rough-cut capacity plan detects too little capacity to meet the needs of the master production schedule, then existing resources must be expanded or resources external to the organization must be used. For example, if you find that you do not have enough equipment or workers to meet the planned production needs of the master production schedule, then you may rent or buy more floor space, rent or buy more equipment, or employ workers from temporary employment agencies. Alternatively, if you find that you will have excess equipment, workers, and facilities, you may choose to reallocate these resources to other production tasks or rent, sell, retire, lay off, or terminate those resources.

You may also choose to meet capacity needs by subcontracting all or some of the production tasks to other organizations. Organizations frequently use external production resources, or *outsourcing,* to meet peak demands. Outsourcing is also used by organizations that wish to reduce costs by subcontracting with firms in third-world countries.

Rough-cut capacity planning allows you to identify your needs in time to adjust capacity to the master production schedule. Alternatively, it allows planners to estimate how realistic the master production schedule is. Where production resources are constrained, such as when few workers with the special skills needed are available, marketing forecasts of demand simply may not be fulfilled; demand may exceed the ability of the production system to supply it.

A more refined tool for capacity planning is capacity requirements planning. **Capacity requirements planning** provides detailed estimates of production capacity availability. This form of capacity planning requires human resources and bill-of-materials information. Capacity requirements planning also necessitates detailed information on the status of raw materials, goods-in-process inventories, finished goods inventories, orders in the plant, lot sizes, lead times for orders, and routing plans for products as they work their way through the production line. The result is a set of detailed, time-phased plans for each product and each production work area. Since cost accounting reports

Box 12–3 Rough-Cut Capacity Planning: An Example

Production goals for a data entry department require that 30,000 sales orders be processed daily at three locations. You know from historical production records kept by the department that you can expect a data entry clerk to type sales orders at a rate of one character per second for an effective day of six hours, given breaks, lunch, interruptions, and delays. You also know that the average sales order requires 300 keystrokes to complete. Thus, you can estimate the number of data entry clerks and terminals to produce the 30,000 sales orders.

1. 30,000 orders × 300 characters per order = 9,000,000 characters per day (CPD) to be produced.
2. 1 character per second × 60 seconds × 60 minutes × 6 hours per day = 21,600 characters produced per data entry clerk (CPDEC) per day.
3. 9,000,000 CPD/21,600 CPDEC = 416,667, or 417 clerks and terminals needed.

If the demand forecast estimates that 20 percent of the orders will be received at location A and 40 percent each will be received at locations B and C, then the data entry clerks and terminals will need to be allocated as follows:

1. 417 clerks and terminals × .20 = 83.4, or 84 clerks and terminals at location A.
2. 417 clerks and terminals × .40 = 166.8, or 167 clerks and terminals each at locations B and C.

Furthermore, your production records may indicate that, on average, 5 percent of the terminals are defective and 2 percent of the clerks are ill or absent on any one day. Thus, you should plan on providing the following:

1. 84 × .05 = 4.2, or 5 extra terminals at location A.
2. 167 × .05 = 8.35, or 9 extra terminals each at locations B and C.
3. 84 × .02 = 1.68, or 2 extra data entry clerks at location A.
4. 167 × .02 = 3.34, or 4 extra data entry clerks each at locations B and C.

The procedures used to estimate production capacity just described assume that direct labor hours, the percentage of sales orders each location receives, and when they are received during the day occur rather evenly and remain relatively constant. When these assumptions are not true, more complicated methods of rough-cut capacity planning must be used. For example, the example assumes that the entry of sales orders can be evenly spread throughout the day because of batch processing of orders. However, if the sales order system were an on-line system, it is likely that there would be busy hours of telephone sales order traffic; that is, customers would telephone most of the orders to the locations during specific hours, such as between 10 and 11 A.M. and 2 and 3 P.M. It might also be true that there are different types of orders, some of which require more time to enter. When the goods to be produced are more complex, more complex rough-cut capacity planning tools must be used.

often provide detailed direct-labor hours for each end product produced, these cost accounting records are often the source of the standards used in capacity estimation.

Personnel capacity planning is that part of rough-cut capacity planning that estimates the numbers and types of workers, supervisors, and managers needed to meet the master production plan. To plan for the allocation of personnel resources, managers need information from the human resource information system maintained by the personnel department. This system provides information about the numbers, skills, and experiences of current employees, applicants, and workers available from other personnel sources, such as temporary employment agencies. Managers also need information on employment constraints imposed by unions and regulatory agencies. (Human resource information systems will be described in Chapter 13.)

Production Scheduling Information Systems

The purpose of the **production schedule** is to allocate the use of specific production facilities for the production of finished goods to meet the master production schedule. To manage the scheduling process, a number of scheduling tools have been developed.

Two of these tools are Gantt and PERT (Program Evaluation and Reporting Technique) charts (see Figure 12–10).

These tools allow managers to control projects and project completion times and also to determine the impact problems will have on project completion dates. For example, top management may ask a manager to complete a project sooner than originally planned. The manager may then consider ways to shorten the duration of the project by completing two tasks at once. However, to complete two tasks concurrently may raise production costs substantially, because two production teams and two production facilities may be needed. To solve the problem, the manager may create "what if" scenarios with the project conditions using the PERT chart tool. However, completing multiple PERT charts manually requires extensive calculations and may prove frustrating to the manager. Computer-generated PERT charts let the manager simulate many scenarios with speed and ease (see Figure 12–11). The use of project management software for this purpose is discussed later in this chapter.

Product Design and Development Information Systems

Many tactical decisions must be made to design and develop a product, especially a new product. The design engineering team usually depends on product specification information derived from customer surveys, target population analysis, or other marketing research information systems. Teams may use other computerized systems for designing new products as well. Software used in the design, testing, and manufacture of products is discussed later in this chapter.

The primary objective of the design engineering team is to develop a product that meets perceived customer needs. However, the team's tactical task is to achieve that objective with the least demand on company resources. Designing products to contain or reduce costs often results in ingenious uses of raw materials, labor, and machinery. Through careful design, an engineering team can often design a product that can be produced at lower costs than competitors can produce it. Careful design may also lead to a simpler product, which leads in turn to fewer maintenance problems, better customer acceptance, fewer product returns, and increased product repeat sales. Through product design, the engineering team may provide the company with important competitive advantages.

Activity name	May 93			June 93				July 93	
	9	16	23	30	6	13	20	27	4	11
Design phase										
Brainstorming										
Marketing										
Engineering										
Design										
Testing phase										
Prototype										
Renderings										
Build										
Final review										
Production phase										
Retooling										
Materials delivery										
Production phase										
Begin shipping										

Figure 12–10
An example of a Gantt chart (from FastTrack Schedule for Windows software, courtesy AEC Software, Inc.)

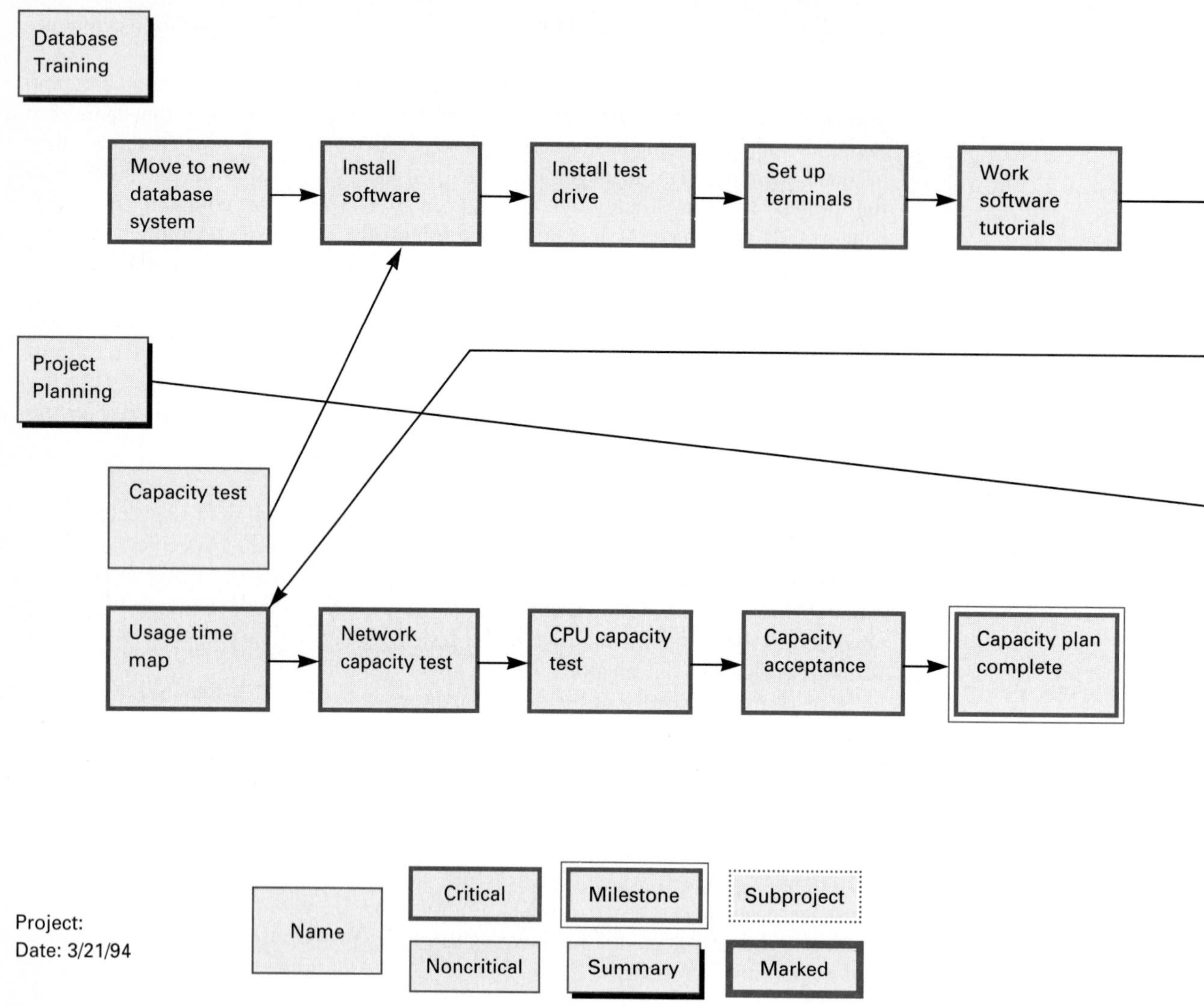

Figure 12–11 An example of a PERT chart prepared using Microsoft Project software (courtesy Microsoft Corporation)

STRATEGIC PLANNING MANUFACTURING INFORMATION SYSTEMS

Production information systems are primarily operational and tactical in nature—they provide information to monitor and control the production of goods and services and to allocate resources to complete production processes. Manufacturing information systems are typically strategic in nature. For example, top-management-level manufacturing decisions that are strategic include these:

1. Selecting a plant site.
2. Constructing a plant addition.
3. Building a new plant.
4. Designing and laying out a production facility.

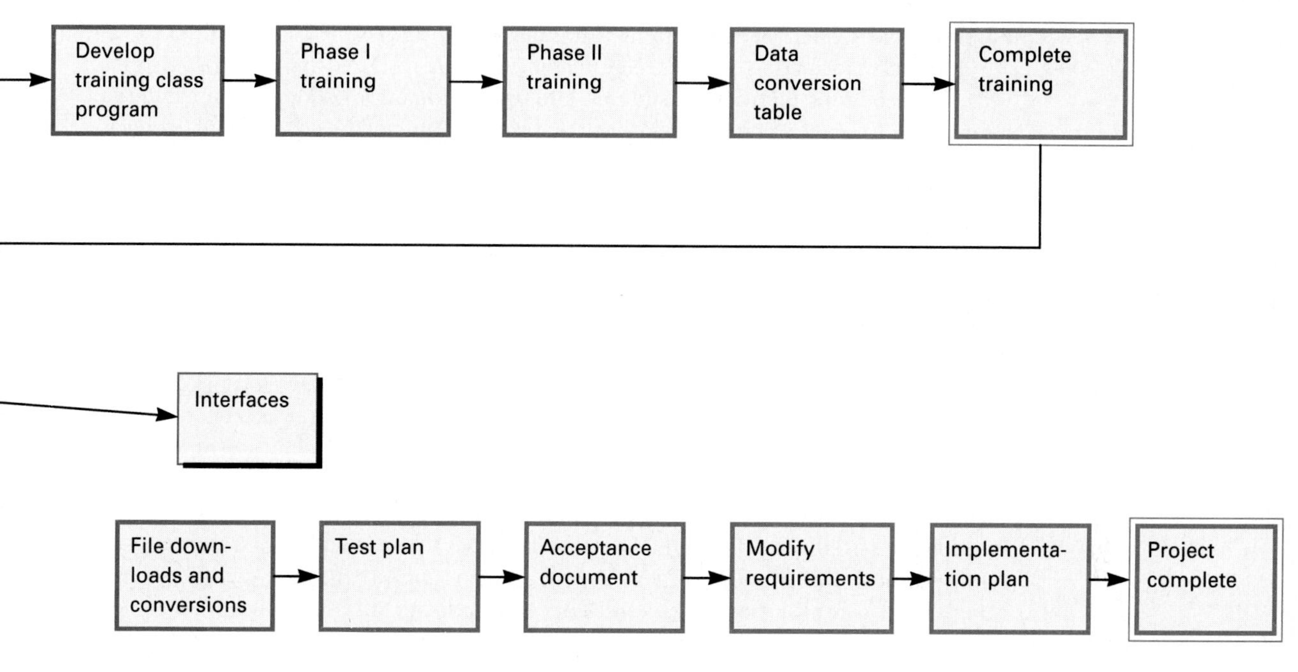

5. Choosing the technologies that will be used in the production processes.
6. Choosing responsibility for production processes—deciding basic policies on vertical integration and outsourcing.

Decisions of this magnitude require the commitment of a large amount of capital and other resources over a long period of time and thus are strategic planning decisions. Clearly, such decisions must not be made lightly.

Site Planning and Selection

Site planning information systems usually rely on a variety of internal and external sources. Some of the external information needed is relatively objective and quantitative, such as the availability and cost of trained or experienced labor and the degree to which it is unionized, the availability and cost of transportation for raw materials and finished goods, the availability of suitable sites, the cost of land, the proximity of raw materials suppliers and finished goods customers, the availability and costs of power, and the rate of property and income taxation.

Other information used in locating a plant may be subjective and qualitative in nature, including community attitudes toward the organization and the quality of community services, such as education and training opportunities.

Internal information sources may include human resource information systems, financial accounting information systems, and production information systems. External information sources may include on-line databases maintained by government agencies, industry groups, private research groups, and consulting organizations. External sources may also include CD-ROM databases and traditional libraries.

The final decision concerning plant location may be made using some form of weighted-average technique, in which factors such as those listed above are ranked and the total scores for several potential sites calculated. Mapping software, similar to that used in marketing, may be used to support site decisions.

Technology Planning and Assessment

Having access to information on new production technologies allows top management to make better and more informed decisions about which production technologies to use for a product or service. **Technology assessment information systems,** which identify new technologies and assess them for their strategic advantage, can help top management in many areas, not merely manufacturing. Like site planning, technology information systems may include CD-ROM databases, traditional library resources, and on-line databases maintained by government agencies, industry groups, private research groups, and consulting organizations. They may also include technology assessment groups within the manufacturing or engineering arms of the organization.

Process Positioning

An important part of any organization's strategic manufacturing plan is the span of production processes it decides to perform for any given product or product line. Decisions of this nature are included in a strategic decision area called **process positioning,** or **vertical integration.** An organization might purchase raw materials, fabricate parts, assemble parts into subassemblies, and then assemble and test the complete product. It may, on the other hand, decide to purchase already constructed subassemblies and parts from others and limit its internal span of production processes to assembling and testing the completed product. Outsourcing subassemblies, for example, to production facilities in third-world countries may allow the organization to gain a competitive advantage by being a low-cost leader for its products.

Deciding on the degree to which the organization vertically integrates—that is, which parts of the material or goods chain it chooses to own, lease, or rely on other organizations to supply—requires a great deal of internal and external information from a variety of information systems. Useful internal information may include the manufacturing skills and experience of the organization's existing personnel, the financial condition of the firm, and the quality of current inventories.

External information useful to the process positioning decision may include information about the skills and experience levels of personnel at the new site, the competitive structure of the organizations within the material or goods chain in the industry, the risks and rewards associated with each link in the production chain, an assessment of future technological developments and their effects on production processes, an assessment of future competitor plans, and the stability of organizations in the chain proposed as suppliers.

The sources of external information for process positioning are similar to those used for site planning and selection and technology assessment.

Plant Design

Designing and laying out a manufacturing plant requires large amounts of diverse information about the proposed plant, including engineering data on the proposed site, proposed production technologies, the number and duties of plant personnel, the expected schedule for the use of the facility, the area transportation system, choices of water and power systems and their costs, the cost and availability of construction materials, the plans for shop-floor information systems, and the need for physical security. Much of this information is available from the site planning, technology assessment, and process positioning decision processes.

GENERAL SOFTWARE FOR MANUFACTURING AND PRODUCTION DECISION MAKING

Production managers often use general-purpose software, such as database software, spreadsheet software, statistical software, and project management software, to support and improve their decision making.

Query-Language and Report Writer Software

An organization's financial accounting information system usually processes a great deal of the data used in the production information systems. For example, invoices, reports, and other output pertaining to purchasing, receiving, encumbrances, open orders, and shipping are typically managed by an organization's database software. The inventory subsystem of the software usually maintains the status of the different inventories and their recommended reorder points. Some accounting information systems software includes the capacity for the purchasing subsystem to identify raw materials or parts that have fallen below present reorder points and to generate purchase orders automatically, which are sent to previously selected suppliers.

Database query-language and report writer software packages let managers access the financial accounting applications of an organization's database to prepare ad hoc reports and to gain information useful for tactical and strategic planning.

Spreadsheet Software

Spreadsheet software also can help the production manager. As a production manager, you may use spreadsheet software to assist you in preparing and revising budgets; evaluating purchase decisions using net present value, internal rate of return, and payback methods; and completing other production management tasks. For example, you may use spreadsheet software to do rough-cut capacity planning. Figure 12–12 shows a spreadsheet that performs rough-cut capacity planning for the data entry situation described in Box 12–3. Using the spreadsheet, you can tweak factors such as hours per day and keystrokes per minute to optimize the data entry operation at each location.

Statistical Software

Quality control personnel often use statistical software packages to complete acceptance sampling reports for raw materials and finished goods. You may also use statistical software to determine production standards from historical data, such as cost control data from the financial accounting database.

Project Management Software

Project management software typically is used to produce Gantt and PERT charts quickly and easily. By generating these charts easily, project management software allows you to simulate several tactical decisions with the data in the charts. Because PERT charts often require numerous, laborious calculations and are time-consuming to draw manually, you are not likely to produce a PERT chart casually. This means you are not as apt to play around with the data in an attempt to optimize scheduling. On the other hand, if you can do these calculations efficiently and draw the chart swiftly, then

Figure 12–12
A printout of a spreadsheet that assists in calculating rough-cut capacity planning values

	A	B	C	D	E
1	CAPACITY PLANNING SPREADSHEET				
2					
3	NO. ORDERS PROCESSED/DAY	30000			
4	CHARACTERS/SECOND:	1			
5	EFFECTIVE WORKDAY:	6			
6	NO. OF CHARACTERS/UNIT	300			
7	PERCENT TERMINALS DEFECTIVE	.05			
8	PERCENT WORKERS ABSENT	.02			
9	PERCENT ORDERS AT A	.20			
10	PERCENT ORDERS AT B	.40			
11	PERCENT ORDERS AT C	.40			
12	TOTAL NO. TERMINALS NEEDED	417			
13					
14			NUMBER OF TERMINALS		
15	LOCATION	GROSS	DOWN	ABSENT	TOTAL
16	A	84	5	2	91
17	B	167	9	4	180
18	C	167	9	4	180
19					
20					

you are very likely to experiment with the data to produce several iterations of the chart in an attempt to improve the project schedule. If conditions change during the project, you can easily alter the PERT chart with the aid of the software.

SPECIFIC SOFTWARE FOR MANUFACTURING AND PRODUCTION DECISION MAKING

Software that addresses the managerial problems in manufacturing and production environments has grown rapidly. Many software packages are available for specific production tasks, such as bill-of-materials software, inventory management software, capacity planning software, production scheduling software, shop-floor scheduling and control software, job costing software—even simulating running a factory (see Box 12–4). However, the industry is clearly moving toward integrated and comprehensive computer hardware and software systems that provide greater control over all or groups of production and manufacturing activities. In the past this software was limited to mainframe systems. Production and manufacturing software today, however, can run on all computer equipment platforms, from micros to mainframes.

This section describes software for quality control, automated material handling, computer-aided design, computer-aided manufacturing, image management, material selection, material requirements planning, manufacturing resource planning, and computer-integrated manufacturing.

Quality Control Software

Quality control software typically includes statistical software tailored to the needs of quality control tasks. For example, quality control software may produce control charts and Pareto diagrams. Control charts are graphical tools that measure the degree to which variances occur in the production of a good or service. The charts let quality control personnel distinguish normal and expected variations in quality from abnormal and unexpected variations. Pareto diagrams display the frequency of modes of failure in a product or service to let quality control personnel identify the quality control problems that should be given priority.

Box 12–4 Refinery Simulation Software

Organizations have used simulation hardware and software for years to reduce the costs of training skilled workers. For example, flight simulation systems have been used to train and maintain the readiness of airline pilots. Military organizations have used simulation systems to train combat officers. However, recently Maxis has developed its simulations as computer games.

Maxis has organized a new division to create simulation games for industry and government. Its first simulation game is SimRefinery, a simulation of a refinery to teach managers how to run one. The managers must choose the oil products to be made, select and control its raw materials, and otherwise make the tactical decisions needed to manage the refinery operation. The company targets the decision making levels at middle and top management.

The prices of simulation games aren't the same as those found on the shelves of your corner computer store, however. The simulations are customized for clients, and this requires considerable custom programming. Chevron recently paid $75,000 for its custom version of SimRefinery.

Maxis also offers SimEnvironment. This package lets managers understand the impact of their decisions on the environment. Several other packages are under development at Maxis for managers in other industries.

Source: Christopher Barr, "Businesses Play War Games," *PC Magazine* 12, no. 11 (June 15, 1993), p. 31.

Automated Materials Handling Software

Automated materials handling (AMH) software tracks, controls, and otherwise supports the movement of raw materials, work-in-process, and finished goods from the receiving docks to the shipping docks. AMH software combines with various materials-handling equipment, including conveyors, pick-and-place robots, and automated guided vehicles, to get this job done.

Computer-Aided Design and Manufacturing Software

A great deal of software has been developed to aid product engineers in the design of new products or the improvement of old products. One type of software that helps product engineers is **CAD/CAM (computer-aided design/computer-aided manufacturing) software.** CAD software normally falls into two categories. One category is designed to help mechanical engineers and architects construct and modify complex drawings, blueprints, diagrams, or illustrations quickly and easily (see Box 12–5). For example, AutoCAD, a software package from Autodesk, Inc., assists engineers and architects in completing their drafting tasks on a computer.

Another category of CAD software includes programs that help electrical engineers produce schematics quickly and easily, alter the schematics, and then produce a final

Box 12–5 Using CAD Software at Marvin Windows & Doors

Marvin Windows & Doors has produced a unique graphical electronic catalog, called MDS, or Marvin Design System. The catalog software is designed to run within AutoCAD, a popular computer-aided design software package. An architect or builder can choose doors or windows from the catalog and then customize them by choosing materials, style, dimensions, and other factors. The end products can be displayed in a variety of ways, including as a three-dimensional image and a detailed plan.

After the windows or doors have been customized, the software analyzes the end products to see if Marvin can build and maintain them. The company offers the software free of charge to professional designers.

Source: Joel N. Orr, "Windows CADD," *Windows Sources* 1, no. 8 (September 1993) p. 84.

draft of the electrical circuits. An example of CAD software for electrical engineering is EE Designer from Visionics Corporation. Of course, both types of CAD software require that your computer system be equipped with terminals and printers capable of graphic output.

Both types of CAD software may provide the engineer with some simulation capabilities—they may be able to simulate the use of the product under many different conditions or various amounts of stress. For example, an engineer might design a handle for a vacuum cleaner and then test the handle's resistance to failure by simulating selected stress conditions. By simulating design faults early in the process, a company can save a great deal of development money, avoid bringing a product to market that will later fail, and ensure that the product will be reliable. Simulation also allows an organization to bring products to market faster. The result is a better product that costs less to develop and reaches the market faster, all of which may provide an organization with a competitive advantage.

CAM software converts CAD drawings into finished products with little human intervention. For example, a bolt may be designed using CAD software. A compatible CAM software packages reads the design and instructs lathe machinery to turn out bolts with the parameters specified in the CAD drawing.

CAD/CAM software has been enhanced by software providing computer-aided engineering (CAE), computer-aided testing (CAT), computer-aided process planning (CAPP), and computer-aided inspection (CAI).

Image Management Software

Engineering and architectural drawings are difficult to store and retrieve in hardcopy form. Parts of one design may be useful in another, if only you can find the design that contained the useful element. **Image management software** is designed to manage the storage and retrieval of engineering and architectural drawings using optical disk storage media. The software also maintains controls over changes made to drawings and distributes the drawings to users with PCs on a LAN.

Materials Selection Software

Many programs are available that aid the engineer in choosing materials for the product under design. These programs are called **materials selection programs,** or **MSP.** Selecting the best materials to account for stress, heat, humidity, and other conditions can be laborious. Sawyer and Pecht (1986) note that in the metals category alone, an engineer might choose from more than 100,000 materials with more than 80 properties.

Materials Requirements Planning Software

Materials requirements planning (MRP) software is basically a set of programs for using data from the master production schedule, item files, work center files, shop floor, inventory files, and bill-of-materials systems to manage production and inventory. MRP systems perform a great deal of calculation and record keeping. When quantities of raw materials and parts are large, the calculations and record keeping become too time-consuming to complete manually, except at high costs. The computer, however, has made such calculations and purchase-order preparation possible for all sizes of organizations, and in recent years, software to implement materials requirements planning has become abundant.

The basic purpose of MRP software is to ensure that the proper amount of the right materials and production capacity are available for the production processes at the right time. The primary objective is to meet the customer's delivery requirements. Ancillary objectives of the system are to ensure that an unnecessary buildup of materials does not occur and that overtime or other extra costs are not incurred to provide the materials on time.

The major output of the software is a series of purchase orders along with information on when these purchase orders should be released to ensure that the right materials are ordered at the right times in the most economical quantities.

Manufacturing Resource Planning Software

More recently, software that provides for **manufacturing resource planning,** or MRP-II, has become available. MRP-II software extends the production information system to finance, marketing, human resource management, and other organizational functions. A fully developed MRP-II system includes modules that provide material requirements planning, shop-floor control, inventory management, and capacity planning. The system also accesses cost accounting data through integration with the financial accounting system. MRP-II software also usually accepts data from a wide range of shop-floor data collection equipment, including voice recognition equipment, factory robots, production-line sensors, process control systems, bar-code readers, and CAD workstations.

MRP-II software can be used in a centralized organizational model where all of its applications run on a centralized mainframe, even though production may be distributed geographically. It can also be used in a decentralized organizational model where MRP-II software runs at each plant location without much communication between plants or between any plant and the organization's headquarters. Finally, MRP-II software can be used in a distributed processing organizational model where appropriate MRP-II software modules run at each plant site and other appropriate modules run at the organization's headquarters. Data are usually shared among all plants and headquarters. Software that permits the distributed processing model is called *distributed MRP-II software.*

MRP-II software uses market projections to generate inventory requirements. During production, design data and output data, including process control, work-in-process, and finished goods inventory data, are fed back to the system.

Many vendors offer MRP-II software for organizations of all types, including mass-production manufacturers, job-order producers, and distributors. Vendors also offer the software for computer platforms of all types and sizes. The software usually consists of many modules, including modules for bill-of-materials, inventory management, purchasing, capacity planning, production scheduling, shop-floor control, and financial planning.

Some MRP-II software is designed so that its modules will work with specific financial accounting software packages. For example, one vendor has developed a series of MRP-II modules that integrate with another vendor's financial accounting modules, thus eliminating the need for the user to make duplicate entries. Other MRP-II software is sold as part of a financial accounting software package.

Computer-Integrated Manufacturing Software

Many production and manufacturing professionals envision a day when factory and product planning, control, design, and operation will be totally integrated and almost totally computerized. Some software and hardware firms that provide MSP, MRP, MRP-II, CAD, CAM, CAE, CAT, CAPP, CAI, robotics, and related information systems are joining forces through mergers, acquisitions, and joint projects to integrate current manufacturing hardware and software products into systems that provide **computer-integrated manufacturing,** or **CIM.** A growing number of manufacturers are utilizing CIM—or at least a great many components of CIM—to run their factories. Implementing CIM can lead to considerable cost savings, improvement in quality, and more flexible responses to customers. For example, benefits from CIM might include these:[1]

1. A decrease in engineering design costs.
2. A decrease in overall lead time.
3. An increase in product quality.
4. An increase in the productivity of engineering design and analysis.
5. An increase in operational productivity.
6. An increase in capital equipment productivity.
7. A decrease in work-in-process inventory.
8. A decrease in personnel costs.

CIM implementations typically include process control sensors and systems, shop-floor terminals, bar-code readers, factory local area networks, CAD workstations, robots, machine tools, automated factory equipment, minicomputers and mainframe computers, the software modules listed previously, and the organization's existing databases. The heart of CIM is usually the MRP-II software and factory local area networks. The key is to integrate all the software and hardware used in manufacturing, to merge numerous manufacturing databases, and to eliminate the paperwork, delays, and errors that occur when systems are operated wholly or in part manually. CIM eliminates the islands of automation created in an organization when each department operates its own system using different hardware, communications protocols, and software.

Although some organizations have developed computer-integrated manufacturing systems, for many, CIM remains an ideal. Organizations with machine-based production that turn out standard products and use repetitive production processes are likely candidates for CIM.[2] Other organizations may find it best to limit their automation to phases of the production process. The tasks involved in both implementing and integrating so many technologies have proven difficult for many organizations or have appeared so daunting to others that they have opted not to consider the concept. A recent study of U.S. manufacturing executives by Peat Marwick Main & Co. revealed the following consensus: Computer-integrated manufacturing still costs too much and is too complex. In fact, 27 percent of the executives reported that they used no automation in their plants. The lack of interest in CIM appeared to stem from lack of cost justification, lack of staff experience, lack of a plan, management and employee resistance, lack of funds, and limited confidence in the technology.[3]

Management Summary

Manufacturing and production systems produce the goods and services that the marketing system predicts the organization will sell. Manufacturing and production information systems support decision making for the operation, allocation, and planning of manufacturing and production resources. Production information systems, which are a subset of manufacturing information systems, primarily support operational and tactical decisions. Manufacturing information systems principally support tactical and strategic planning decisions.

---

[1] Lawrence Gould, "Computer-Integrated Manufacturing: A Shop-Floor Revolution," *PC Week*, April 21, 1987, pp. 129–130.

[2] Joel C. Polakoff, "The Factory Foreman: Alive and Well in the Age of Automation," *The Journal of Manufacturing* 1, no. 4 (Winter 1990), pp. 59–62.

[3] David Hebditch, "Opening Up CIM Opportunities," *Datamation* 36, no. 11 (June 1, 1990), pp. 112–113.

Production systems are diverse and include continuous-flow production, mass production, job-order production, and project production. In addition, production systems include the production of services as well as hard goods. The purpose of the production system is to acquire the raw materials and purchased parts; test the materials for quality; acquire the appropriate personnel, work space, and equipment; schedule the materials, personnel, space, and equipment; fabricate the products or services; test the product or service outputs; and monitor and control the use and costs of the resources involved.

To support the production function, many information systems have been developed to assist in managing inventory; testing the quality of production inputs and outputs; storing and shipping materials; estimating, assigning, and monitoring production capacity; designing products and services; scheduling production facilities; allocating human resources; controlling production projects; assessing production technologies; planning for the development of new plants; deciding on the level of vertical integration; and designing plant facilities.

Many production information systems use data from the organization's financial accounting database, including purchasing, accounts payable, inventory, order entry, accounts receivable, cost accounting, and payroll subsystems. Production managers should be able to use these and other operational information systems, such as shipping, receiving, and quality control information systems, to support their operational and tactical decision-making activities. In addition, many external sources of information, such as on-line government, scientific, and industry databases, provide support for strategic planning.

General software, such as spreadsheets, project management packages, and statistical packages, also provide support for many of the tactical decisions production managers must make.

Software designed especially for the production function has proliferated during the last few years. For example, specialized software has been developed for bill-of-materials, inventory management, capacity planning, production scheduling, shop-floor scheduling and control, job costing, materials requirements planning, manufacturing resource planning, just-in-time inventory management, computer-aided design and manufacturing, and computer-integrated manufacturing. The continued use and refinement of computer support for manufacturing and production operations and decisions is leading organizations to an integrated approach to the management of manufacturing and production systems.

Key Terms for Managers

automated material handling (AMH) software, **475**
bill-of-materials (BOM) system, **463**
capacity requirements planning, **467**
computer-aided design/computer-aided manufacturing (CAD/CAM) software, **475**
computer-integrated manufacturing (CIM), **477**
economic order quantity (EOQ), **464**
factory local area network (LAN), **460**
image management software, **476**
inventory management and control systems, **464**
just-in-time (JIT) system, **465**
manufacturing and production information systems, **457**
manufacturing resource planning (MRP-II) software, **477**
manufacturing systems, **456**
master production schedule, **465**
materials requirements planning (MRP), **465**
materials selection programs (MSP), **476**
process positioning, **472**
production schedule, **468**
production systems, **456**

quality control software, **474**
receiving information systems, **459**
rough-cut capacity planning, **467**
shop-floor data collection systems, **460**
site planning information systems, **471**
technology assessment information systems, **472**
total quality control, **462**
vertical integration, **472**

Review Questions

1. How might you distinguish between operational, tactical, and strategic manufacturing and production decisions?
2. In what way may production information systems differ from other information systems?
3. What financial accounting systems may provide information to operational information systems for production?
4. Describe three operational information systems that are part of the purchasing process that supports the production function.
5. What is a shop-floor data collection system?
6. Explain the function of quality control information systems.
7. What is TQC?
8. What two conventional information tools are used to manage inventories?
9. What are the basic inputs and outputs of an MRP system?
10. What is a bill-of-materials information system? How does this system relate to MRP systems?
11. What information tools does MRP software often use to identify when and in what quantities raw materials should be purchased?
12. What is the purpose of capacity planning?
13. What basic categories of information do managers need for capacity planning decisions?
14. At what decision level are capacity planning decisions?
15. What types of manufacturing decisions may be classified as strategic planning in nature?
16. What is MRP-II software and how does it differ from MRP software?
17. What are the purposes of automated materials handling software? What types of devices might be included in an automated materials handling system?
18. Describe the nature and purpose of materials selection software.
19. What is CIM?
20. What types of software and hardware systems might be included in a CIM system?
21. How does CAD software improve the production function?
22. What does CAM software do?
23. What is outsourcing?
24. What is JIT?

Questions for Discussion

1. Compare and distinguish between production information systems and manufacturing information systems.
2. One of your fellow students plans to be a manager in the insurance industry and another in the banking industry. They both feel that manufacturing and production information systems are interesting to read about but not necessary to know much about because they will not be working in factory environments. Do you agree with their view? Why or why not?
3. How might a manager use the information supplied by a quality control information system?
4. What are the objectives of an MRP system?
5. Compare the approach of JIT and MRP-II systems towards inventory, quality, and workers.
6. How might project management software aid a production manager? What advantages does the software provide that are hard to obtain in a manual planning system?
7. What is process positioning?
8. How can product design information systems contribute to an organization's competitive edge?
9. What are some manufacturing decisions that are strategic planning decisions?
10. What are the advantages of CIM? Why does there seem to be a lack of interest among manufacturing executives in CIM?

Problems

1. **Rollo Furniture Company.** Jane Williams is the purchasing manager for the Rollo Furniture Company, which makes inexpensive beds, dressers, and tables for distribution to furniture outlets in five southern states. Over the years, the company has come to depend on the varnish sold by the Wesley Finishing Products Company. It has found that this product provides a superior finish for its furniture at a reasonable price.

   a. What information does the purchasing manager need in order to know when and how much of the varnish to buy?
   b. What tools might the purchasing manager use to decide how to maintain the varnish inventory at the lowest cost?
   c. What additional information might the company wish to maintain to ensure that the varnish it buys is what it should be buying?

2. **Database problem: price quotation file.** Using file management or database software, create vendor price quotation records for the stock item shown in Figure 12–3. Make one record for each company shown in the figure. Each record should contain at least the following: vendor number, vendor name, item name, product name, stock number, unit of purchase, date of quote, quoted price, terms, and remarks. Make up any data necessary. Then, print a report listing the price quotations for the motor assembly casing, as shown in the figure.

3. **Forecasting problem: Emmet Fabricators, Inc.** You are the plant manager for the Indianapolis plant of Emmet Fabricators, Inc. The plant has been asked to produce the following quantities of stock no. 308 over the last 12 months:

January	10,500	July	12,100
February	10,750	August	12,400
March	10,950	September	12,700
April	11,000	October	13,000
May	11,800	November	13,500
June	11,950	December	13,600

a. Forecast production for the following January and February based on the data for the previous 12 months. If you have a DOS- or Windows-based computer system, use the 4KAST forecasting program contained on the applications diskette that your instructor should provide you.

1. Make sure that your computer system is turned on and that the DOS operating system has been loaded. Place your diskette in the A drive of your computer system. Make sure that the system prompt shows A:>. Load the forecasting program by entering 4KAST at A:> and pressing the ENTER key. If you are using Windows, from the Program Manager screen, click on FILE and RUN. Then type A:[4]KAST in the Command Line box that appears on the screen. Then click on OK.
2. When the opening screen of 4KAST is displayed, press the ENTER key. At the "Select A Forecasting Technique" menu, enter 1 for *linear regression.* This tells the program that you wish to complete a linear regression on data.
3. At the "Simple Linear Regression" menu, enter 2 for *data entry-data file.* This tells the program that the data on which you wish to complete a linear regression is already in a data file.
4. Enter the filename, PROB12–3 and press the ENTER key. This will load the monthly production units from a file on your diskette that already contains the data shown in the table above.
5. At the "Simple Linear Regression" menu, enter 5 to make a forecast. Choose as your begin point the first year of sales by entering 1 and pressing ENTER. Choose the last month of production as your end point by entering 12 and pressing ENTER.
6. Forecast production for January and February by entering 13 as the begin point and 14 as the end point.
7. Enter S to display the forecast on the screen or P to print it out. If you decide you want to print the forecast, make certain that a printer is attached to your computer, that paper is loaded, and that the printer is turned on before you enter P.

b. After reviewing production for the last 12 months, you decide that the last 6 months are probably more representative of production than the last 12 months. Forecast production for months 13 and 14 using production data from months 7 through 12.

4. **Spreadsheet problem: The D. Jackson Manufacturing Company.** The Jackson Company assembles casings and housings from component parts purchased from suppliers. You are the production manager for the firm, and your production records from previous years indicate that an experienced assembly-line worker can assemble 10 casings or 20 housings per day. Your records also show that workers who can assemble casings can also assemble housings. There are no new skills to learn, nor are there any union restrictions on moving personnel from the assembly of one product to another. Using the Lotus 1-2-3 spreadsheet program, a clone of Lotus 1-2-3, or any spreadsheet program able to read Lotus files, load the file labeled "Prob12–4" on the applications diskette provided by your instructor. The file is a template for estimating how many assembly-line workers the company will need to meet sales forecasts. Enter these data in column B:

   Number of weeks vacation: 2
   Number of holidays: 10
   Percent workers ill/absent: .01
   Percent defective products: .02
   Number of casings produced per day per worker: 10
   Number of housings produced per day per worker: 20
   Forecasted production of casings: 200000
   Forecasted production of housings: 600000

   After entering these values, determine the nearest whole number of workers needed for the year to meet the production forecasts under these circumstances:

   a. Rate of illness and absences increased to 5 percent.
   b. Assembly-line workers' union negotiated 16 yearly holidays.
   c. Number of casings forecasted rose from 200,000 to 300,000.

   After answering each question above, return the template cells to their original values.

5. **Spreadsheet design problem: S & I Manufacturing Company.** S & I Manufacturing Company assembles braces and brackets from component parts purchased from suppliers. The company's sales forecast predicts sales of 100,000 braces and 300,000 brackets for the coming year. You are the production manager for the firm, and your production records from previous years indicate that an experienced assembly-line worker can assemble 10 braces or 20 brackets per day. Your records also show that workers who can assemble braces can also assemble brackets. There are no skills to learn, nor are there any union restrictions on moving personnel from the assembly of one product to another.

   You need to know how many assembly-line workers the company will need to meet the sales forecast under these circumstances:

   a. Each worker is given two weeks off for vacation.
   b. Each worker is given eight days off for holidays in the year.
   c. An average of 2 percent of the workers are ill or absent from work each day.
   d. The company estimates that 1 percent of the braces and brackets produced each day are defective.

   Using any spreadsheet software, develop a template for calculating the number of assembly-line workers needed. Design the spreadsheet so that the manager can easily change the number of weeks of employee vacation, the number of holidays, the percent of workers ill or absent, and the percent of defective products. If you don't have spreadsheet software available, construct rows and columns on a sheet of paper. Then, using a pencil, sketch the template, showing the row and column labels you would use, and write in the formulas you would need for the template.

6. **Project management problem: Richard's Painting Company.** Richard's Painting Company's (RPC) major market consists of large business firms and large public sector organizations. Tanya Martin, a project manager for RPC, has been trying to schedule a work crew to complete the painting of a large, two-story, rectangular, wood-sided commercial building. The building's external walls are to be repainted. However, before the final coat of paint is applied, the walls must have all loose paint and dirt removed from them. Next, a primer coat of paint must be applied. Then the primer coat must be left to dry for one full day before the final coat of paint is applied.

   Tanya has visited the site and learned that the building's north and south walls are twice the length of its east and west walls. She has measured the areas to be painted and estimates that it will take a crew of two workers two days to remove loose paint from and clean the east wall, and two workers another two days to do the west wall. Four full days for two workers will be needed to do the north wall and another four days for the south wall. She estimates that four workers will have to spend two full days to paint a primer coat on each of the east and west walls, and four days each for the north and south walls. Then these workers will spend an equal time applying the final coat of paint.

   Tanya would like to start the project on May 5 and has been authorized to use four workers for the project. She is authorized to schedule her work crew for eight-hour days, Monday through Friday. She is not authorized to schedule overtime or weekend work without prior permission of her supervisor. The union contract for her workers does not include any holidays during the first three weeks of May.

   Develop a Gantt chart for the project. Maintain the needed sequence of phases for the project: (1) the preparation phase (remove loose paint and clean walls), (2) the primer phase (apply a primer), (3) the drying phase (allow the primer to dry), and (4) the final coat phase (apply a final coat). However, schedule the tasks to be performed in such way that the project is completed in as short a time as possible given the assigned workers. You may complete the Gantt chart manually or use a project management software package available to you.

   You may also ask your instructor for a demonstration copy of FastTrack Schedule for Windows. The FastTrack demonstration software is a fully functional package except that you cannot save your work. Once you complete the Gantt chart, you must print it out. The demonstration software also contains a step-by-step tutorial to help you learn how to complete Gantt charts. To get to the tutorial, open FastTrack and click on the Help menu in the ribbon bar at the top of the screen. Read the opening paragraph of the first help screen, and then click on the words, "Demo Tutorial" displayed in green in the outline that follows the first paragraph. To move through the tutorial, click on the browse button (>>) to move forward. Use the (<<) button to move backward through the tutorial.

7. **Computer-integrated manufacturing.** Prepare a short paper on the topic of CIM. The paper should include brief descriptions of the hardware and software systems used in CIM implementations. It should also include the advantages and problems

that CIM implementation poses for organizations. As sources for your report, use the *Computer Literature Index*, published by Applied Computer Research, Inc., Phoenix, Arizona; the *Guide to Business Periodicals;* manufacturing periodicals, such as the *Journal of Manufacturing;* and computerized databases, such as Computer Select.

8. **Factory input devices.** Prepare a short paper that identifies and briefly describes common devices used to input data into manufacturing information systems, such as sensors and factory terminals. The paper should include brief descriptions of the hardware and software the devices use and what type of information each device supports. As sources for your report, use the *Computer Literature Index,* published by Applied Computer Research, Inc., Phoenix, Arizona; the *Guide to Business Periodicals,* manufacturing periodicals, such as the *Journal of Manufacturing,* and computerized databases, such as Computer Select.

Cases

1. **Triton Clothing Company.** Triton Clothing Company is headquartered in a city on the West Coast. The firm produces highly stylish models of men's and women's denim and khaki western pants for distribution to clothing wholesalers and retailers throughout the western states. Triton maintains clothing manufacturing plants in three of these western states. Terry Burroughs has just assumed the post of production manager at Triton's Vesta plant. Formerly he had been assistant production manager at Triton's plant at Sterling. Burroughs was moved to the post to see if the Vesta plant productivity and profitability can be revived after several years of decline. Top management is not quite certain what the production problems at Vesta are. However, they know that the plant has not met its production goals for the last two years, and they are hoping that a new broom will sweep clean.

   When Burroughs first arrived at the Vesta plant, he decided to interview some of his plant managerial and supervisory personnel to ask them what they believe are the strengths and weaknesses of Vesta's production operations. In this way, he hoped to gain insight into the nature of Vesta's production operations and to isolate problems that he could prioritize and then attack. Excerpts of some of the meetings Burroughs held follow.

   Darlow Pruitt, the purchasing manager, complained that the purchasing department has been asked to use expediters too often to rush the delivery of raw materials. He feels that his department is not given sufficient warning about the status of raw materials to allow it to obtain the goods on time through regular channels. Pruitt complains that he does not have enough expediters to ensure that purchase orders for raw materials that have been delayed by suppliers are filled on time to meet production schedules.

   Pruitt also feels that production delays have been caused by too many stockouts for raw materials in the past. He thinks that these stockouts have occurred because there has been too much pressure to reduce inventories as a means of decreasing manufacturing costs. The result of the stockouts, as far as he is concerned, is that expediters must deal with raw materials acquisition in a crisis mode.

   Levan Grant, supervisor of quality control, feels that she does not have enough inspectors to ensure that the quality standards for raw materials and finished goods have been met. She notes that there have been too many delays in the production processes because of the variable quality of raw materials and that this variability has also produced a high level of rejections of finished goods.

Bergon Trout, warehouse manager, complains that he lacks enough stock clerks to manage the company's inventory of raw materials, parts, and finished goods. He reports a number of instances in which raw materials that have been reduced to the reorder point were not identified and purchase orders for these materials were not cut. He complains that it is especially annoying when standard raw materials from long-term suppliers are allowed to drop below the reorder point.

Tenlow Fenton, a shop-floor supervisor, charges that there are too many breakdowns in equipment—breakdowns that then delay production schedules. Fenton believes that the workers are reasonably satisfied with their work and are experienced at their jobs. He feels that it's the equipment, not labor, that has caused the problem so frequently.

Ruby Kent, the finance manager, thinks that too much money is being tied up in inventory and that these high inventories generate higher inventory taxes that must be paid to the local community.

a. Given the data obtained in the interviews with the Vesta plant personnel, what production problems seem to be occurring at the plant?
b. How do you think these problems ought to be prioritized?
c. What information systems should be considered to solve the problems?
d. What software do you recommend that Burroughs consider to assist in solving these problems?

2. **Ambrose Technologies, Inc.** I-Chen Yi is the new manager of the product design department of Ambrose Technologies, Inc. She supervises a large staff of design engineers and drafting personnel. During her first month as manager, Yi has noted that operations in the department are entirely manual. Requests for new products are designed according to the specifications received and a preliminary draft of the product is prepared manually. This draft is critically reviewed by numerous company personnel and a second, revised draft drawn. If the second draft is satisfactory, a physical model is put together for testing. This testing usually generates several more drafts of the product and several revised physical models that are tested.

Yi is a strong proponent of rigorous testing and thus fully supports the iterative model building and product drafts that such testing requires. She feels that thoroughly tested products are likely to be received by customers well and to save on warranty costs for the firm. However, Jason Schmidt, the marketing manager, is concerned with the long lead time that the new-product development cycle takes. In several instances recently, the company has taken a very long time to develop new products. As a result, these products entered the market long after those of the competition, allowing the competition to develop a well-established customer base. Schmidt has complained strongly to Yi about the time taken by the new-product development procedures. He feels that the process must be speeded up or the company will continue to lose market share to its competitors.

Yi has asked Clara Wilson from the management information systems department to examine the product development cycle and to recommend changes that can be made to bring products to market faster. As part of her recommendations, Wilson plans to present to Yi some recommendations for computer software that can be used in the development cycle. Wilson has asked you to prepare the software recommendations for the report.

a. Identify the parts of Yi's development cycle that might prove to be suitable applications for computer software.

b. Identify types of software that could be used for each of the applications you listed in *a*.

c. Describe how each software type identified in *b* can be used to improve the applications listed in *a*.

Selected References and Readings

Booker, Ellis. "Manufacturers Turn to Imaging: On-line Engineering Documents Spell Efficiencies for Companies." *ComputerWorld* 26, no. 34 (August 24, 1992), p. 71 ff. A brief discussion of imaging systems that can speed time to market for products by speeding product design and development.

Farish, Michael. "Made to Order: Shop Floor Data Collection Tools have Great Potential for Manufacturers." *Computer Weekly,* March 4, 1993, pp. 30 ff. Describes how shop floor data collection technologies can be used in manufacturing.

Farwell, Robert C., Scott Brady, and Bradley A. Rosencrans. "MRP II in JIT Environment." *The Journal of Manufacturing* 1, no. 4 (Winter 1990), pp. 5–12. Compares JIT and MRP-II systems and shows how they might work together.

Fitzgerald, John M. "Evaluating the Stewart Platform for Manufacturing." *Robotics Today* 6, no. 1 (Spring 1993), pp. 1 ff. Discusses new advances in robotic manipulators.

Haverson, Debra Sheer. "The CIMple Truth," *MIDRange Systems* 6, no. 1 (January 12, 1993), pp. 21 ff. Presents some advice to companies considering CIM.

Hebditch, David. "Opening Up CIM Opportunities." *Datamation* 36, no. 11 (June 1, 1990), pp. 112–13. Discusses the opportunities for CIM in eastern Europe.

Major, Michael. "The Long and Short of It: Developments in Manufacturing Planning and Control Software." *MIDRange Systems* 5, no. 21 (November 10, 1992), pp. 29 ff. A discussion of major trends in manufacturing planning and control software.

Mandel, Dave. "JIT: Strategic Weapon for Aerospace and Defense?" *Industrial Engineering* 25, no. 2 (February 1993), pp. 48 ff. Discusses the problems of applying JIT to airplane manufacturing.

Polakoff, Joel C. "The Factory Foreman: Alive and Well in the Age of Automation." *The Journal of Manufacturing* 1, no. 4 (Winter 1990), pp. 59–62. Describes the information problems presented by CIM and MRP-II systems and the need for the personal intervention of foremen.

Sawyer, Thomas, and Michael Pecht. "A Material Selection Program." *BYTE,* July 1986, pp. 235–248. Describes materials selection software.

Winkler, Connie. "Better Project Management in Uncertain Times." *Datamation* 36, no. 11 (June 1, 1990), pp. 95–98. Describes the use of PM software in large MIS projects.

Young, Jeffrey. "Soft Factories." *Forbes* 151, no. 8 (April 12, 1993), pp. 106–107. Describes the use of software to control and interpret the output of factory sensors used for quality control.

Human Resource Information Systems

Chapter Outline

Manager's View

An organization's personnel, or human resources, often comprise many types of workers. For example, a manufacturing organization may employ assembly-line workers, maintenance workers, security staff, line supervisors and other supervisors, expediters, forklift-truck drivers, stock clerks, clerk typists, data entry clerks, payroll clerks, accounting clerks, office managers, troubleshooters, a plant manager, quality control staff, marketing representatives, purchasing agents, and many other types of employees.

An organization's human resources usually represent its largest operating expenditure, usually between 40 and 60 percent of total operating expenses. However, in service organizations, salaries and wages may account for up to 85 percent of total operating expenses. Cost alone would make human resources a very important element of any firm. However, the skills, knowledge, and attitudes of any organization's employees shape that organization in fundamental ways and represent its human capital. It is important to remember that people are at once the most basic and most important component of any organization. Thus, the management of an organization's human resources is critical to the organization's success.

Managing human resources today is a very different task from what it has been in the past because of changes in the environment within which organizations exist. Today's work force has attended school longer than in the past. A high school education is the norm for most employees, and having some education beyond high school has become common. A bachelor's degree is the norm for most managerial employees and a master's degree is becoming increasingly common. Today's workforce is also more heterogeneous. Women, minorities, and handicapped workers constitute a larger percentage of the labor force now than ever before in our nation's history. The labor pool in this country is also one of the most expensive in the entire world. And the web of federal, state, and local laws governing the workforce has become much more extensive and complex. In addition, because many firms operate in a global environment, work force laws and regulations from many countries must be considered. Recent and widespread employee layoffs, complex early retirement options, and flexible working hour plans further complicate management of the workforce. All these factors make the task of human resource management more difficult now than at probably any other time.

Although human resource management decisions are usually the official province of the human resource department, many human resource decisions must and should be made by functional managers and line supervisors. All managers need information to help them manage the human resources for which they are responsible. The function of **human resource information systems (HRIS)** is to provide managers with enough information in a timely fashion to improve the quality of their human resource decisions.

THE HUMAN RESOURCE MANAGEMENT FUNCTION

The **human resource management** function is concerned with the individuals who constitute the organization. From the standpoint of the organization, the function is responsible for the acquisition and effective use of the individuals within the organization. From the standpoint of the individual, the function is concerned with how the individual's well-being, growth, and development will benefit the organization. To achieve these ends, human resource departments perform a variety of activities. The major activities of the human resource function in an organization include these:

1. Recruiting employees.
2. Evaluating applicants and employees.
3. Selecting, placing, promoting, terminating, and transferring employees.
4. Analyzing and designing jobs.
5. Training and developing employees.
6. Producing required governmental reports.
7. Managing employee wage and benefit plans.
8. Planning for short- and long-term workforce needs.

To perform these human resource management system (HRMS) activities, managers rely on a number of operational, tactical, and strategic planning information systems (see Figure 13–1).

It is important to remember that human resource information systems contain personal information about the employees of an organization. Securing this information against unwanted or unwarranted access, use, or distribution is terribly important to the individuals involved. It is also likely to be illegal under current legislation and subject the organization to serious legal liability. Security issues surrounding databases, such as the human resource information database, and the computer systems that house these databases are discussed in greater detail in Chapter 20.

Figure 13–1
The human resource information systems discussed in this chapter

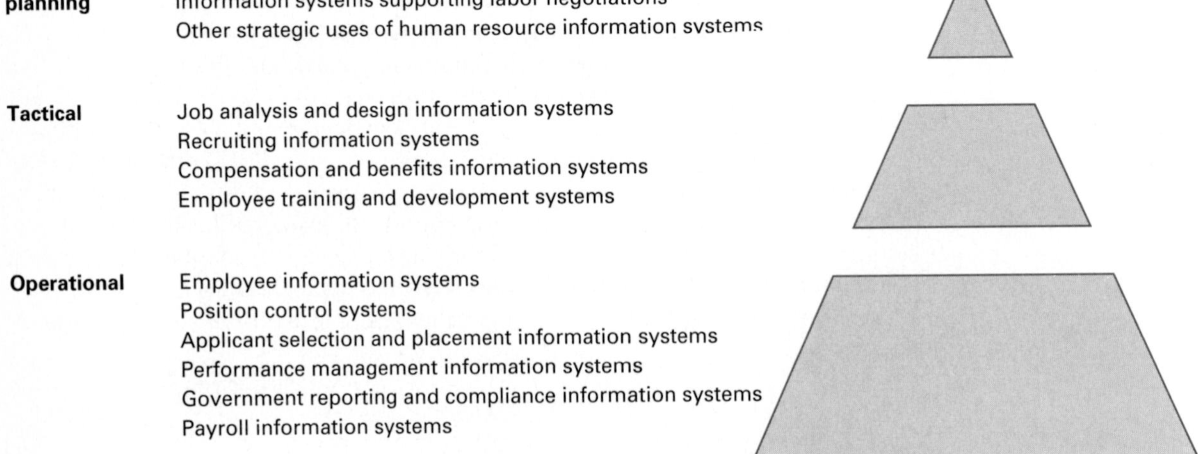

OPERATIONAL HUMAN RESOURCE INFORMATION SYSTEMS

Operational human resource information systems provide the manager with data to support routine and repetitive human resource decisions. Several operational-level information systems collect and report human resource data. These systems include information about the organization's positions and employees and about governmental regulations.

Employee Information Systems

The human resource department must maintain information on each of the organization's employees for a variety of decision and reporting purposes. One part of this **employee information system** is a set of human resource profile records. An **employee profile** usually contains personal and organization-related information, such as name, address, sex, minority status, marital status, citizenship, years of service or seniority data, education and training, previous experience, employment history within the organization, salary rate, salary or wage grade, and retirement and health plan choices (see Figure 13–2). The employee inventory may also contain data about employee preferences for geographical locations and work shifts.

Another part of an employee information system is an employee **skills inventory.** The skills inventory contains information about every employee, such as work experience, work preferences, test scores, interests, and special skills or proficiencies. The skills inventory provides the human resource manager with a valuable resource for completing operational tasks. For example, the skills inventory can be used to identify potential internal applicants for positions in the organization. It may also be used to identify employees for transfer, promotion, or training and development programs. It may even be used to identify employees who are underemployed—those whose skills far exceed their present assignments.

Employee information systems can be used tactically and strategically when the organization is planning to expand, to enter new locations, or to field new products and services. Information about the skills, preferences, and interests of current employees

Figure 13–2
A screen displaying part of an employee record or profile

```
                         EMPLOYEE RECORD

EMPLOYEE NUMBER:  Ø241          SSN:  333-97-376Ø
LAST NAME:  MUNEZ               FIRST:  JUAN              MI:  A
ADDRESS:  17 WYAND STREET       CITY:  ALBANY             STATE:  NY
ZIP CODE:  122Ø8                SEX:  MALE
HPHONE:  738-2978               OPHONE:  438-1556
BIRTH DATE:  Ø3/22/68           EEO CODE:  HISPANIC
DATE OF HIRE:  Ø9/11/87         TERMINATION DATE:
EDUCATION CODE:  3              NUMBER OF DEPENDENTS:  Ø
UNION MEMBERSHIP:  Y            MARRIED:  N
CITIZENSHIP:  USA
JOB TITLE:  INSPECTOR           DEPARTMENT:  RECEIVING
DATE ENTERED JOB:  11/Ø3/9Ø     LAST PROMOTION:  11/Ø3/9Ø
```

is important in deciding whether the organization has the human resources necessary for the changes it wishes to make.

Managers can use employee information systems in numerous other ways. For example, they can identify the percentage of employees who will be of retirement age during selected years and arrange this information by job title, by department within the firm, or by minority category. Such information might lead to tactical decisions regarding pension plan funding, recruiting emphases, or the development of training programs so that younger employees can fill positions vacated by retirements.

Position Control Systems

A *job* is usually defined as a group of identical positions. A *position,* on the other hand, consists of tasks performed by one worker.[1] For example, one job in an organization may be given the title of Data Entry Clerk III. However, there may be 20 Data Entry Clerk III positions in the organization. The purpose of a **position control system** is to identify each position in the organization, the job title within which the position is classified, and the employee currently assigned to the position. Reference to the position control system allows a human resource manager to identify the details about unfilled positions. For instance, routine, repetitive outputs of the position control system might include position inventories or lists of positions by job category, department, task content, or job requirements. Another output of the system might include lists of unfilled positions, which might be organized in a similar manner.

Categorized lists of unfilled positions can be very useful to human resource staff. Such lists allow staff to plan recruiting activities. By listing unfilled positions in terms of their job requirements, for example, recruiting personnel may select appropriate media, such as magazines, newspapers, and journals and plan visits to labor sources, such as educational organizations, that prepare persons for those job requirements.

Position control systems also allow the human resource manager to identify human resource problems. The list of unfilled positions, for instance, may identify vacant positions with the same job title scattered throughout the firm. On investigation, the human resource manager may find that there is a high rate of turnover in the positions with this job title. On further investigation, it may be found that the positions are not compensated highly enough to retain employees, that these positions do not have a clear promotion path within the firm, or that these positions involve duties that employees view as overly tense, boring, frustrating, or difficult. The investigation may lead to tactical decisions regarding the composition of the duties in these positions, the training for employees in these positions, the compensation plans used for these positions, or the skills, knowledge, and abilities of the employees recruited for these positions.

Applicant Selection and Placement Information Systems

After jobs and the employee requirements for those jobs have been identified and after a suitable pool of job candidates has been recruited, the candidates must be screened, evaluated, selected, and placed in the positions that are open. The primary purpose of the **applicant selection and placement information system** is to assist human resource staff in these tasks. Applicant selection and placement information systems also help human resource staff ensure compliance with federal, state, and local employment laws because the procedures followed in screening, evaluating, selecting, and placing employees must be fully documented and carried out in a structured manner. Thus, data from interviews, examinations, and placement decisions should be collected and

---

[1]George T. Milkovich and John W. Boudreau, *Human Resource Management,* Burr Ridge, Il: Irwin, 1994, p. 137.

kept according to the requirements of the various laws and regulations previously described.

If any testing is performed on applicants to improve the selection or placement process, data on the applicants and their test scores should be maintained for later analysis. Follow-up analysis comparing the success of those selected to their test scores should be completed. In this way, test scores can be made more useful to selection and placement staff, or if they are not found to be useful, the tests can be dropped.

Performance Management Information Systems

Many organizations review the work of employees regularly to make decisions regarding merit pay, pay increases, transfer, or promotion. Typically, a new employee is evaluated at the end of the first six months of employment, and other employees are evaluated annually. These reviews are often called **performance appraisals.** The data for performance appraisals are frequently collected by administering employee appraisal forms to each employee's immediate superior. The forms also may be given to peers, the employees themselves, and even customers or clients. An example of an appraisal form is found in Figure 13–3.

Employee appraisals may also be based on performance measures. That is, worker effectiveness may be measured in terms of productivity on the job. Numerous productivity measures have been used in the past. Some are straightforward measures of productivity, such as counting the number of units of work produced in an hour, day, shift, or other time period. For example, purchase order clerks may be measured by the number of purchase orders processed in a day or clerk typists by the number of lines typed during a day. Others are more indirect measures of productivity, such as the number of customer complaints received or the number of products returned.

Performance management information systems include performance appraisal data and productivity information data. Performance management information systems data is frequently used as evidence in employee grievance matters. Careful documentation of employee performance and of how the performance was measured and reported is critical to acceptance of appraisal information in grievance hearings.

Performance management information can lead to a number of decisions beyond merely supporting the operational decision to retain, promote, transfer, or terminate a single employee. For example, the manager may sift through performance management information to identify supervisors who submitted a high number of appraisals on which employees are rated poorly. High numbers of poor appraisals may indicate that these supervisors' ability to work with employees needs to be evaluated. The performance management information may also be sorted to identify those job titles with a high percentage of poor appraisals. High percentages of poor appraisals may mean that the requirements of the job have not been described sufficiently or accurately to permit the selection of applicants with appropriate skills.

Performance management information can also be used to identify labor sources that do not provide acceptable workers. Future recruiting campaigns can then avoid these sources. If the performance management information indicates that there are no reliable sources of acceptable employees, it may be necessary to develop a training program for certain types of workers.

Government Reporting and Compliance Information Systems

Data secured from the position control, employee, performance appraisal, applicant selection and placement, payroll, and other human resource information systems can be used to produce reports required by myriad governmental laws and regulations, including affirmative action and equal employment opportunity regulations (see Figure 13–4). Many federal, state, and local laws, regulations, and executive orders regulate the

Figure 13–3
The first page of an employee appraisal review form used for clerical employees

Time View, Inc.
Clerical Staff Performance Review

Review No. 26 Date of Review 01 / 15 / 94 SNN 335-16-1482

Employee Name Dretsky, Alicia L.
(Last, First, Middle Initial)

Department Data Processing Division Western

Reviewer Name Pallato, Paul R.
(Last, First, Middle Initial)

Directions: Circle the letters that best characterize the employee. If choices are inadequate, use the comments section.

I. Productivity
(A.) Is capable of handling a large volume of work.
B. Is capable of handling a normal volume of work.
C. Is not capable of handling a normal work load.
Comments: Always completes more work than co-workers

II. Quality of Work
(A.) Work produced is of high quality.
B. Work produced is of adequate quality.
C. Work produced is of poor quality.
Comments:

III. Knowledge Required for Job
(A.) Demonstrates a high level of work-related knowledge.
B. Demonstrates knowledge adequate to do satisfactory work.
C. Demonstrates inadequate knowledge to do satisfactory work.
Comments:

IV. Degree of Supervision Required
A. Works well without supervision.
(B.) Works adequately without supervision.
C. Works ineffectively without supervision.
Comments: Needs help in new situations or when learning new tasks

recruitment, selection, placement, promotion, and termination of employees. Many of these laws and regulations are designed to ensure that minorities, women, older workers, veterans, and the handicapped are given a fair shake at getting and retaining jobs and receiving promotions (see Box 13–1).

Furthermore, the growth in number and complexity of federal, state, and local regulations pertaining to employees does not seem to be abating. The Immigration and Naturalization Act was extensively revised in the late 1980s and now requires employers to maintain information that attests to the citizenship of their workers. More recently, the Family Leave and Medical Act was passed guaranteeing unpaid leave to care for

L & M Corporation

		Male					Female				
Job Category	**Total**	**Cauc**	**Black**	**Hisp**	**Asian**	**Indian**	**Cauc**	**Black**	**Hisp**	**Asian**	**Indian**
Clerical	132	15	2	1			91	18	5		
Laborer											
Professional	28	16	1		3		6	1		1	
Sales	59	37	9	3			6	2	2		
Technical	15	7			3		3			2	
Craft											
Operative											
Total	234	75	12	4	6		106	21	7	3	

Source: Katherine Codega, "Compensation Applications," *Handbook of Human Resource Information Systems*, ed. Albert L. Lederer (Boston: Warren, Gorham, & Lamont, 1991).

Figure 13–4
An Equal Employment Opportunity Report

family. Currently, the Occupational Safety and Health Administration (OSHA) is studying repetitive strain injuries, such as carpal tunnel syndrome, that affect workers. It is likely that a series of regulations protecting workers against such injuries will be forthcoming in the near future.

The various regulations not only prescribe how some human resource functions must be carried out, but also require that a variety of records be kept and reports submitted on certain dates to specific governmental agencies demonstrating compliance with the regulations. For example, OSHA requires that information be kept about the health and safety of each employee, including information on each serious accident or illness connected with the workplace.

Though much information is necessary to complete government reports, the same information can be used in other ways to improve the organization. For example, health and safety information kept for OSHA reporting purposes can also be used to calculate the costs of work accidents and work-related illnesses. This information can be an important tool for persuading employees and line managers to emphasize safety procedures and to identify physical and other work factors that contribute to accident and illness.

Managers can also use this information to calculate averages for accidents and illnesses for the organization as a whole and for each unit, shift, project, location, supervisor, and job title. A manager may then identify departments, shifts, projects, locations, job titles, or supervisors associated with a higher-than-average accident or illness rate. A manager can also identify employees who have higher-than-average accident experiences. These employees might require training or retraining in safety practices, or the supervisors of such employees might need retraining in safety procedures.

The manager may also wish to sort the records by accident or illness type. This information may lead to further investigations to identify why there are more accidents or illnesses of certain types. The result may be changes in safety procedures or changes in the work environment.

Thus, **government reporting and compliance information systems** provide information needed both to maintain compliance with government regulations and to improve productivity and reduce costs associated with employees.

Box 13–1 Some Federal Laws, Regulations, and Agencies Regulating Employment

LAWS AND REGULATIONS

Age Discrimination in Employment Act—protects persons age 40 and over from arbitrary discrimination in employment practices, such as mandatory retirement based on age.

Americans with Disabilities Act—prohibits discrimination against disabled persons who can perform the essential tasks of a job.

Davis-Bacon Act—requires certain employers with federal contracts to pay employees the prevailing wage rates of the area.

Equal Pay Act—requires employers to provide equal pay for substantially equal work that requires equal skill, effort, responsibility, and working conditions.

ERISA (Employee Retirement Income Security Act)—regulates pension and benefit plans, including employee transfer of pension funds when switching jobs, and established the Pension Benefit Guarantee Corporation.

Executive Orders 11246 and 11375—prohibit discrimination based on race, color, religion, sex, or national origin by firms with government contracts of $100,000 or more and 100 or more employees.

Fair Labor Standards Act—regulates minimum wages, child labor practices, and overtime compensation.

Family Leave and Medical Act—requires employers with 50 or more employees to offer unpaid leaves of absence for up to 12 weeks to employees to care for newborn children or for ill family members or for the employee's own illness.

Immigration Reform and Control Act—prohibits employers from hiring or employing illegal aliens and from discriminating against employees, legally in the United States who are "foreign looking" or "foreign sounding." Also requires employers to maintain records documenting worker eligibility.

Occupational Safety and Health Act (OSHA)—regulates safety and health standards and working conditions in employment, including providing work environments that are free of known health and safety hazards.

Pregnancy Discrimination Act of 1978 (Amendment to Civil Rights Act)—prohibits discrimination in employment because of pregnancy, childbirth, or related medical conditions and requires medical insurance to cover pregnancy like other long-term medical conditions.

Title VII of the Civil Rights Act of 1964—prohibits employment discrimination because of race, color, religion, sex, or national origin and established the Equal Employment Opportunity Commission.

Vietnam-Era Veterans Readjustment Act—prohibits the federal government and federal contractors from discriminating against disabled veterans and requires them to hire and promote veterans of the Vietnam War era.

Vocational Rehabilitation Act of 1973—prohibits federal contractors from discriminating against physically or mentally disabled persons and requires them to make changes in the work environment to make their sites more open to the disabled.

Walsh-Healey Public Contracts Act—requires employers with federal contracts to pay employees overtime for work beyond eight hours in a day.

AGENCIES

Department of Immigration and Naturalization
EEOC (Equal Employment Opportunity Commission)
Employment Standards Administration
OFCC (Office of Federal Contract Compliance)
OSHA (Occupational Safety and Health Administration)

Other Operational Human Resource Information Systems

Many other operational information systems support the human resource function. For example, **employee relations information systems** assist human resource personnel in helping employees in a variety of ways, such as smoothing employee moves and relocations, assisting troubled employees with counseling, and providing legal assistance and child care services to employees. **Labor relations information systems** assist human resource management in tracking employee grievances and disciplinary actions taken against employees, and **attendance tracking systems** monitor and report on employee leaves, vacations, time off for illness, and absences.

Payroll Information Systems

The financial information system, through its payroll subsystem, collects and reports predominantly operational human resource data. Payroll files contain a great deal of information about employees—employee pay rates, wage classifications, and seniority—that can be useful to managers making human resource decisions. It is important that the data in the payroll subsystem do not duplicate data in the human resource system. As you learned in the database management systems chapter, redundant data often leads to inconsistencies between records and to errors in reports. It is also important that the data in the payroll subsystem be compatible with the data in the human resource system so that tactical reports may be generated from data drawn from both systems. The use of database management systems allows organizations to reduce the redundancy of employee data in payroll and employee information systems. Database management systems also allow managers and others to prepare reports and make inquiries about employees that require data from both payroll and employee information systems records.

Some organizations use external agencies to store and manage employee data about top management, such as payroll, recruitment, performance appraisals, and benefits. Thus, information about top executives may not be included in the organization's HRIS.

TACTICAL HUMAN RESOURCE INFORMATION SYSTEMS

Tactical information systems provide managers with support for decisions that emphasize the allocation of resources. Within the human resource management area, these decisions include recruitment decisions, job analysis and design decisions, training and development decisions, and employee compensation plan decisions.

Job Analysis and Design Information Systems

Job analysis and design includes describing the jobs needed in an organization and the qualities of the workers needed to fill those jobs. These tasks involve the development of *job descriptions* for every type of position in an organization. Each job description specifies the purposes, tasks, duties, and responsibilities of each job and the conditions and performance standards under which those duties and responsibilities must be carried out. (A job description for an office position is shown in Figure 13–5.)

Job analysis and design also includes the development of *job specifications* for each type of job. A job specification describes the skills, knowledge, experience, and other personal characteristics required of workers that are listed in job descriptions. In short, job descriptions describe the jobs, and job specifications describe the workers needed to fill those jobs. (An example of a job specification is shown in Figure 13–6.)

The information inputs to the **job analysis and design information system** include data from interviews with supervisors and workers and affirmative action guidelines. Inputs also include information from sources external to the firm, such as labor unions, competitors, and governmental agencies.

The outputs of the job analysis information system are job descriptions and job specifications. These outputs provide managers with the basis for many tactical human resource decisions. For example, job descriptions and specifications allow managers to set a job's relative worth in relation to similar work performed elsewhere within the organization. This may mean classifying the job into one of the organization's pay

Figure 13-5
A job description for an office position

JOB DESCRIPTION

JOB TITLE: Office Clerk I REVISION DATE: 3/22/93

JOB NO.: 109

PAY GRADE: 6

REPORTS TO: Office Supervisor

SUPERVISES: No one

GENERAL DISCRIPTION:

Performs general office tasks under close supervision.

DUTIES AND RESPONSIBILITIES:

Files, types, answers the telephone, uses calculator, enters data into a terminal, and performs other general office tasks. Checks work, completes forms, requisitions, and memos, and supplies information on request.

Must be able to handle confidential information about employees, customers, and creditors.

JOB CHARACTERISTICS:

Proficiency in use of typewriter and computer terminal keyboards.

Figure 13-6
A job specification for the office position described in Figure 13-5

JOB SPECIFICATION

JOB TITLE: Office Clerk I REVISION DATE: 3/22/93

JOB NO.: 109

PAY GRADE: 6

JOB REQUIREMENTS:

EDUCATION: Minimum, high school education, preferably with emphasis in business subjects

PHYSICAL AND HEALTH: Good health, emotionally stable

APPEARANCE: Neat, well groomed

SPECIAL SKILLS AND ABILITIES: 30 wpm on Keyboard Test, clear and pleasant voice.

WORK EXPERIENCE: None

grades. This process permits a manager to provide, as nearly as possible, equal pay for equal work within an organization. When equal pay for equal work does not exist within an organization, low morale may occur, resulting in poor performance and low productivity.

The information from job analysis and design information systems also can be used to increase the flexibility with which human resources are deployed in the organization. For example, if you were a human resource manager, you might find that a comparison of office jobs with titles such as Records Clerk I, Data Entry Clerk I, and Clerk Typist I reveals identical or nearly identical duties, responsibilities, and requirements. You may decide, therefore, to collapse these three job titles into a single title such as General Office Clerk I. The effect of this act is not only to simplify the job structure of the firm; it also permits managers to move people more easily among positions in this general job title and to simplify recruiting, testing, and placement activities.

Job analysis and design information can also be linked to the position control system. This linking allows position openings, for example, to be listed by job content or by the skills, knowledge, and experience needed for the open positions.

Thus, job analysis and design information helps determine the qualities and types of employees to be recruited, which applicants should be selected, and where new employees should be placed. This information also provides a basis for determining how employees will be paid, evaluated, promoted, or terminated. In fact, the job analysis and design information system provides a legal basis for many human resource management practices. Thus, the information system supports many tactical decisions about the allocation of human resources within the organization.

Nearly every manager can use information from the job analysis and design information system. For example, managers will want to refer to current job descriptions and specifications when they are considering the establishment of new positions within their departments. They also need to be aware of positions to which they can recommend outstanding workers for promotion.

Recruiting Information Systems

The recruiting function should provide the organization with a bank of qualified applicants from which it may fill vacant positions identified through the position control system and described by the job analysis and design information system. The recruiting function should also ensure that the organization is in compliance with various federal, state, and local statutes and contract regulations for affirmative action and equal employment opportunity.

To direct the recruiting function, the organization needs to develop a recruiting plan. The plan specifies the positions to be filled and the skills required of the employees for these positions. To develop the plan and to monitor its success, a **recruiting information system** is necessary to collect and process the many different types of information needed to construct the plan, including a list of unfilled positions; the duties and requirements of these positions; lists of planned employee retirements, transfers, or terminations; information about the skills and preferences of current employees; and summaries of employee appraisals.

Other inputs to the recruiting plan include data about turnover rates and about the success of past placements. For example, if the goal of a recruiting campaign is to improve the quality of the organization's human resources, information about the past success of employee placements is essential. It is also important to identify departments that have had high employee turnover and to determine if this turnover represents poor-quality placements or is a result of other factors. Recruiters need to know whether their past selections have been received well by the supervisors for whom these employees work. Identifying employee factors that have led to past success and failure is essential to improving the recruiting function.

Organizations of a certain size are required to develop affirmative action plans to ensure compliance with various laws. The affirmative action plan requires an analysis of the number of minorities employed in specific job categories and reports the organization's recruiting and hiring goals for meeting deficiencies. The information for this plan is obtained from data in the position control system, the employee information system, and the recruiting information system. The recruiting plan should reflect the organization's affirmative action goals.

A recruiting information system also provides the manager with information that helps to control recruiting activities. Thus, in addition to information about applicants, the system may include information from these sources:

1. Schools and colleges, including placement officers.
2. Federal, state, and local employment offices.
3. Private placement services.
4. Journal, magazine, and newspaper advertisements.
5. Standard job advertisements and recruiting brochures.
6. Prospect files.

Information about the success of recent placements and recruiting drives is essential to evaluate the effectiveness of past recruiting campaign tactics, the media used for advertising positions, and the recruiting sources used. For example, you may wish to know what recruiting sources provided you with the most job applicants who were hired, who were of a minority status, or who are currently rated highly by their supervisors.

Compensation and Benefits Information Systems

The wage and salary systems, or compensation plans, an organization can offer vary widely and include hourly wage plans, piece-rate plans, incentive pay plans, merit pay plans, monthly salary plans, commissions, and profit sharing. Special plans for part-time employees and those in job-sharing programs are also possible. Benefit plans include a wide range of fringe benefits, such as stock options, health insurance, life insurance, dental insurance, medical services, day-care services, tuition for approved courses, and retirement plans.

Although government reporting requirements are an important reason that organizations have implemented computerized human resource information systems, they are not the only reason. The costs of employee benefits have soared in recent years, now averaging 37 percent of wages, and the need to control these costs has become a second major reason for the use of computerized human resource information systems (Stamps, 1990).

In addition, many benefit plans are mandated by governmental units. For example, the federal government mandates coverage for social security, Medicare, disability, unemployment, and other benefit plans for certain workers. These plans may require payments by employees, employers, or both. The social security plan requires that employees and employers split the cost of social security and Medicare. Thus, the total cost of an employee to an employer is the sum of the amounts paid for work and the amounts paid for the various benefits the employee receives, including those benefits that are mandated by governments. The total cost of each worker is an important factor in human resource decision making and should be provided by the HRIS.

To help human resource managers control their compensation and benefit plans, information describing the various pay plans and fringe benefits must be kept and the pay plans and benefits choices of each employee must also be maintained. The **compensation and benefits information systems** may support a variety of tactical human resource decisions, especially when compensation and benefits information is related to information from internal and external sources. For example, you may wish to relate the pay received by employees with the same job duties or job titles to identify employees who are paid more or less than they should be for the skills they have and the duties they must complete.

Some organizations have implemented cafeteria-style, or flexible benefits systems, which allow employees to choose or change their benefits. In some of these systems, employees may also query the benefits system to ask their own "what if" questions. They can alter their benefits package and see the effect it will have on, let's say, their take-home pay. For instance, they can add or remove dependents, change their marital status, redirect payroll deductions to other benefit programs, or find out what happens if they retire at 55 instead of 65. Some human resource professionals feel that cafeteria-style benefits programs provide their organizations with a competitive edge in acquiring and retaining high-demand employees. Flexible or cafeteria-style benefits administration usually requires computer system support. These self-service employee systems may be provided through standard on-line terminals, touch-screen kiosks, and even interactive voice response systems. These systems relieve human resource personnel from answering many routine and repetitive questions employees have about their benefits.

You may also wish to evaluate the effect of various pay plans on retention, promotion, and termination of employees. For example, compensation and benefit plans may be increased to attract or to retain highly marketable or highly skilled employees. In recent years, special retirement benefits have been used by many companies to induce older workers to retire early, thereby lowering payroll costs.

Compensation and benefit plans can play an important part in improving an organization's productivity. Tying employee productivity to pay or encouraging increased productivity with incentive pay plans can often improve an organization's productivity substantially. Thus, these information systems provide important support to managers for tactical decisions.

Employee Training and Development Systems

An important activity of human resource departments in many firms is planning and managing training and career development programs for the improvement of employees. In some firms, the training arm of the human resource department is extensive, comparable in size to a small school or college.

The training offered by the **employee training and development systems** must meet the needs of jobs available in the organization as identified through the position control system and the job analysis and design system. The training should also be directed at those persons interested and capable of benefiting from it, as identified by the skills inventory and human resource files.

To support the management and training function, it is important to keep information about current and potential instructors; current and potential students; the content and scheduling of courses, seminars, and workshops; and the success of past efforts, as measured by tests, student ratings, and supervisor follow-ups. This information system should support tactical decisions regarding the nature of training and development programs. The information system should use data from many sources, including the recruiting information system, the employee information system, the position control system, the job analysis and design information system, and the employee evaluation system. Analysis of information from these sources allows managers to plan training and development activities to improve the quality and quantity of the organization's labor pool and to meet other goals, such as affirmative action goals.

An important role of human resource departments is to make certain that replacements for key organizational personnel are available when the positions key personnel occupy become vacant because of death, injury, retirement, or other reasons. It is important for the human resource department to plan for the succession of these key people. This means identifying replacement employees and providing them with the appropriate training and experience to fill openings. **Succession planning information systems** help human resource personnel with these activities and are increasingly included as part of human resource information systems.

STRATEGIC HUMAN RESOURCE INFORMATION SYSTEMS

Human resource planning ensures that the organization has the right kinds and the right numbers of people at the right places at the right time to achieve its objectives (See Figure 13–7). Several types of human resource planning are strategic in nature, including workforce planning and labor negotiations.

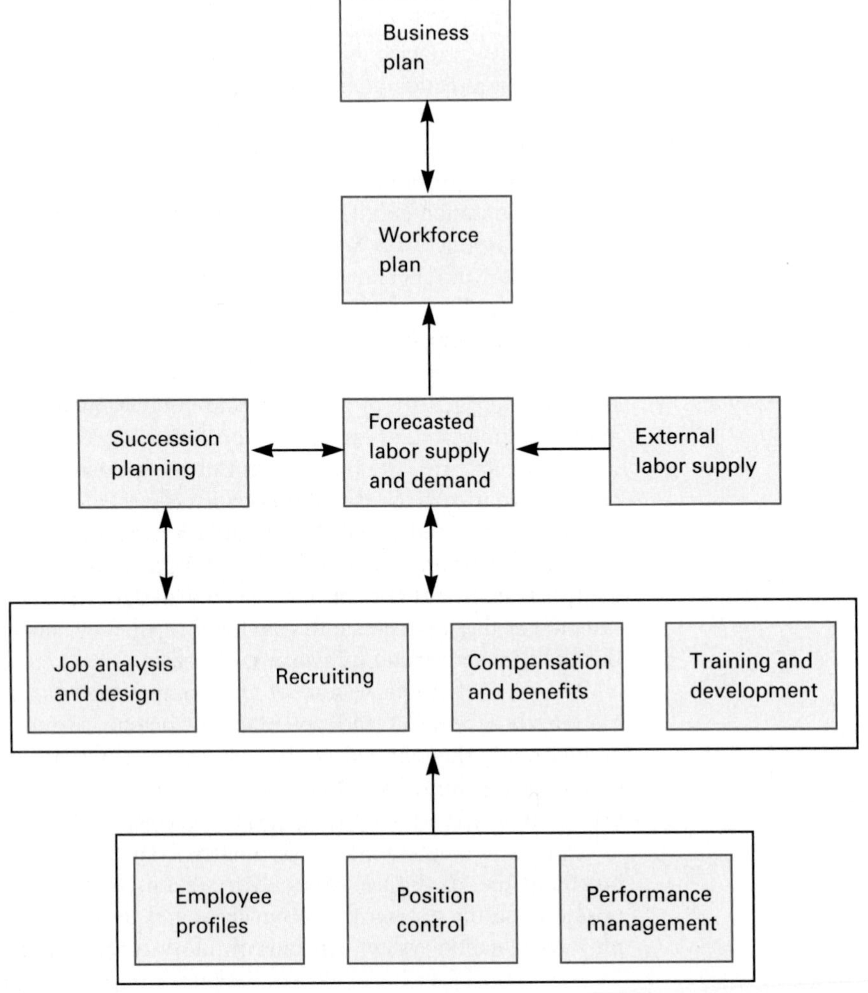

Figure 13–7
A model showing human resource information systems support for a workforce plan

Information Systems Supporting Workforce Planning

Organizations involved in long-term strategic planning, such as those planning to expand into new market areas, construct factories or offices in new locations, or add new products, will need information about the quantity and quality of the available workforce to achieve their goals. Information systems that support **workforce planning** serve this purpose. This type of planning involves identifying the human resources needed to meet the organizational objectives specified in the strategic plan. That means forecasting the supply and demand of the required workforce. These forecasts are estimates of the characteristics, quantity, and pricing of the labor force needed to achieve the long-term plans of the organization.

Forecasting human resource needs requires information to answer a number of planning questions, including the following:

1. What should the labor force of the organization look like to meet the strategic plan? What skills, experiences, knowledge, and other qualities should the organization's human resources possess? In other words, what are the job descriptions and specifications required by the strategic plan?
2. What quantities of human resources with the qualities already identified are needed to carry out the strategic plan? In other words, how many positions for each job title are needed for the strategic plan?
3. What are the current human resources of the organization and how well do they satisfy the organization's strategic needs for human resources?
4. What other human resources are available to achieve the strategic plan?

Identifying the types and quantities of workers needed for the strategic plan is forecasting the demand for human resources. Identifying the human resources available internally and externally is forecasting the supply of those human resources. Forecasting demand and supply can be done on a macroeconomic level or a microeconomic level. Macroeconomic forecasts of supply and demand for workers in various job categories can be obtained for states and regions from a variety of national and state agencies. Microeconomic forecasts involve using data more specific to the organization.

The data for microeconomic human resource forecasts may be obtained from internal and external sources. For example, suppose that a company plans to expand its business by constructing a new factory in an adjacent state. The company's planners examine the economic data relevant to the probable success of this plan and a variety of sites for the new factory. To complete their planning, the planners will need demand data on the types of jobs and the number of positions required to manage and operate the new factory. They will also need supply data about the availability and cost of the workforce with the essential skills and experiences required to fill those positions.

To prepare the forecast, the company planners will have to estimate the demand for each type of job the new factory will require. Demand data may be developed by asking current managers to forecast their workforce needs. Data also may be obtained from industry associations that provide guidelines for estimating worker needs. For instance, industry associations may provide guidelines, based on surveys of its members, for the number of salespeople per square mile of territory or per million dollars of sales, or the number of supervisors per 10 lathe operators, and so on.

Data may also be obtained by using industry or organization performance standards. For example, if the company's production plan for the new factory is 1,000 widgets per day, performance data taken from current workers can be used to estimate the numbers of each type of worker needed to produce that number of widgets each day (see the section on capacity planning in Chapter 12).

To estimate supply, the company's planners may start by examining the current workforce to identify employees with the necessary skills and a preference for the geographical region where the new factory will be located. This information is obtained internally from the skills inventory and the human resource file. A forecast can then be made showing how many of these employees will still be working for the company at the time of the move.

The company can also identify current employees who have a preference for the location but who do not have the skills needed. With additional training, these employees may be able to transfer to the new site. The company must also estimate the pool of workers with the essential skills available near the new location as well as the pool of workers near the present site who must be hired to fill the positions of those who do transfer. This will usually require information about the numbers of each type of worker employed by competitors or other organizations from which the company may recruit.

Information Systems Supporting Labor Negotiations

Negotiating with craft, maintenance, office, and factory unions requires information gathered from many of the human resource information systems already discussed. In addition, negotiators need information from the financial accounting system and from external sources, including competitor wage agreements and appropriate economic data for the industry, employee group, and geographical region. Much of the external information required by a negotiating team can be obtained from the on-line databases discussed in Chapter 6. The human resource team completing the negotiating needs to be able to obtain numerous ad hoc reports that analyze the organization's and union's positions within the framework of both the industry and the current economic situation. It is also important that the negotiating team be able to receive ad hoc reports on a very timely basis because additional questions and tactics will occur to the team while they are conducting **labor negotiations.**

Other Strategic Uses of Human Resource Information Systems

In addition to workforce planning and labor negotiations, human resource information systems data also support other strategic decisions. For example, organizations that are planning to restructure, downsize, sell off divisions, or merge with other organizations need to know what impact these decisions will have on their workforce profiles, the overall cost of their personnel, and the specific costs of benefit plans, such as retirement and health plans. Workforce forecasts can also be used strategically to negotiate for concessions from local governments when making decisions about organization locations.

HUMAN RESOURCE INFORMATION SYSTEMS SOFTWARE

In recent years, considerable commercial software has been developed for use by managers and human resource department staff. Industry experts predict that sales of human resource software will continue to grow from about $500 million in 1991 to $835 million in 1996.[2] In addition to specialized software developed specifically to address human resource needs, general-use software is also available for managers.

General-Use Software

The same types of general computer software used within other business functional areas are useful in human resource management. These software types include database management software, on-line databases, spreadsheets, and statistical software.

Database Management Software. Database management software is probably the most critical and useful of any software for human resource management. A database

[2]Emily Leinfuss, "Employees Empowered by Direct Access HRMS," *Software Magazine* 13, no. 6 (April 1993), p. 83.

management system can be used to construct a variety of files, such as job description files, job specification files, position files, employee skills inventory files, and applicant files. Such files, constructed within a database management system, allow you to ask innumerable "what if" questions for tactical and strategic planning purposes as well as to complete operational tasks swiftly.

For example, if you had the files mentioned stored in a database management system, consider the ease with which you could match a file of applicants to a file of job specifications for open positions in the organization. If you wished to consider current employees for current positions, you could match information from the skills inventory file to information from the job specifications file for open job titles to identify quickly which employees have the minimal interest, experience, and skills for the positions that the organization has open.

Manually maintaining and using the files just described puts the human resource manager at a severe disadvantage. Not only is it much too time-consuming to ask "what if" questions about the information in the files, it is also very time-consuming to complete the routine reports required by many governmental agencies. Consider the immensity of the task of merely classifying new and old employees by minority status in an organization with 1,000 or more employees! Consider how relatively easy the same task is when the employee records are stored on computer media.

Developing a series of integrated files on a mainframe database for use by the human resource department usually requires the expert assistance of the management information systems department. The management information systems department will have to develop the files and the application programs to process the files to serve the human resource department's needs. Although the management information systems department is responsible for the technical development of the system, developing the files on a mainframe will probably require a great deal of effort by human resource management professionals. However, once the files have been planned and constructed, many routine human resource management tasks can be performed in much less time than before and many tactical tasks become possible that were not feasible earlier.

Some human resource departments have chosen to construct their own files using microcomputer database management system software. This approach allows the department to develop the system faster and to control it completely. Some human resource departments have chosen this route because the management information systems department has been too busy to assist them within a reasonable time. However, you must understand that this approach also requires that human resource management staff be proficient in the design and maintenance of database management software. Unfortunately, it also means that a good many files may be developed in such a way that they cannot be used by employees and managers outside of the human resource function. For example, there may be no easy way to integrate microcomputer files developed by the human resource department with the related mainframe files used by the payroll department.

On-Line Databases. On-line databases provide information to human resource planners about economic trends, labor statistics, competitive wage rates, work force skills and experience, and governmental regulations (see Box 13–2). For example, NewsNet offers these databases that may prove useful: U.S. Employment Opportunities, U.S. Census Report, Industrial Health and Hazards Update, Biomedical Safety and Standards, Health Cost Management Weekly, State Regulation Report, and Environmental Compliance Update. CompuServe offers SuperSite Demographic Reports,

Box 13–2 Human Resource Information On-Line Database Service

Executive Telecom Systems, Inc., offers the Human Resource Information Network (HRIN), a rich collection of databases containing information ranging from personnel policies and practices to labor-related news and statistics. HRIN provides immediate access to the latest information from over 100 databases and 65 news services on eight categories of HRMS data:

- Administration, systems, and planning.
- Affirmative action.
- Benefits and compensation.
- Employment and recruiting.
- Labor and legal matters.
- Labor-management relations.
- Safety and health.
- Training and development.

Of special interest, the administration category contains directories and reviews of over 10,000 business, professional, and system software packages for all computer platform levels, reviews of computer hardware and books, and a directory of 400 micro-based HRIS software packages.

Users can retrieve information, automatically track human resource issues, manipulate data, and analyze data on the system. In addition, HRIN provides users with on-line HRMS software to use in their work, electronic mail, bulletin boards, a calendar of professional human resource events, and even flight and hotel reservation services. HRIN can be accessed through any microcomputer or terminal with a modem 24 hours a day.

which provides demographic data by ZIP code or county for any place in the United States. (The use of on-line databases has been described in Chapter 6.)

Spreadsheet Software. Spreadsheet software can be used by human resource managers in much the same way that it can be used by any manager. For example, departmental budgets and special human resource project budgets can be developed using this software. Spreadsheet software can also be used to evaluate data, downloaded from the human resource database, on various human resource problems. For example, a spreadsheet template can be built containing the numbers and percentages of employees in various categories as defined by the Equal Employment Opportunity Commission (EEOC). Expected candidates for openings can be added to the totals to calculate the impact on the organization. Likewise, a template of accidents, injuries, deaths, and illnesses can be constructed to match the definitions of OSHA. As each week or month passes, the new data on these events can be downloaded from the mainframe database to the spreadsheet to calculate the effect on the organization's OSHA profile. A manager might also construct a template containing the numbers and percentages of workers in various age groupings to examine the impact of various early retirement plans the organization is considering.

Statistical Software. Human resource managers can use statistical analysis for a variety of purposes. For example, analysis of the employee composition in divisions and departments can detect low minority participation or high proportions of older workers. These analyses may be used to plan minority recruiting campaigns or to identify worker skills that will soon be in short supply because of retirements. Correlating job groups with accidents or illnesses can identify supervisors or employees who are not emphasizing safety enough, employees in dangerous jobs, or working conditions that need improvement. Costs of employee health insurance and other benefits can be extrapolated for the next five years to forecast future wage and salary expenditures for an organization.

Numerous statistical software packages are available for the microcomputer, minicomputer, and mainframe computer, as you learned in Chapter 5. Because the data to be statistically analyzed probably already exist in the organization's database, it is important to use statistical software capable of reading the database files. Otherwise, you may have to convert the data to the format used by the software, which can be a costly, or at the very least an annoying, step.

Other Software. The productivity of many operators today is measured by the very devices they use. For example, a word processing clerk may find that the word processor counts and keeps the number of lines typed per day. These data are then collected from all word processing clerks, averaged, and compared with standards. Order entry clerks are likely to find that the same computer they use to enter orders collects and maintains the number of orders processed each day. Similar software computes the productivity of service and factory workers. Though production departments typically use this software, the information it provides is important to the human resource function.

Specialized Human Resource Information Systems Software

A great deal of software has been specifically designed for the human resource function. This software is available for all types and sizes of computers, including microcomputers. Software specifically designed for the human resource management function can be divided into two basic categories: comprehensive human resource information systems software and limited-function packages that support one or a few human resource activities.

Comprehensive Human Resource Information Systems Software. In the last few years, the software industry has produced several products that organize the various human resource information systems into integrated software referred to as human resource information system, or HRIS, software.

In general, the computerization of HRIS has resulted in an integrated database of human resource files (see Box 13–3). Position files, employee files, skills inventory files, job analysis and design files, affirmative action files, occupational health and safety files, and many other human resource files are constructed in a coordinated manner using database management systems software so that application programs can produce reports from any or all of the files. Thus, the human resource management director can produce reports listing likely internal candidates for open positions by running an application program that queries position files, job requirements files, and skills inventory files. If the human resource files are part of the organization's total database, they can be shared with other departments, such as payroll and cost accounting.

Box 13–3 Integrated HRIS

Sovran Financial Corporation of Norfolk, Virginia, wanted to provide flexible work schedules for its employees. To accomplish that task, Sovran needed to supplant the batch personnel and payroll information systems it had developed with an integrated human resource management system. With thousands of employees, Sovran required an integrated human resource management system because so much employee data interconnected with data in other company information systems. Simply entering the name of a new employee in every company information system becomes a headache. For example, employee records are related to five separate general ledger applications. The company has 50 incentive plans, 60 payroll deduction plans, and 80 earnings options. Employee records even connect to the information system that monitors the employee parking garage.

Source: David Stamps, "Human Resources: A Strategic Partner or IS Burden?" *Datamation* 36, no. 11 (June 1, 1990), p. 50.

In many organizations the management information systems (MIS) department develops HRIS software in response to a request by the human resource department. In this case, the MIS department may use the organization's current database management systems software to develop files and application programs designed to meet human resource management staff needs. The systems people may, on the other hand, purchase off-the-shelf software designed for the human resource function. Off-the-shelf software reduces the cost of development considerably and allows the human resource department to be up and running relatively quickly (see Box 13–4). However, the files produced by off-the-shelf software may not be capable of being integrated with the other mainframe or minicomputer software. Thus, the payroll department may not be able to access the human resource data files.

The basic motivation for computerizing human resource information should be clear by now: Massive amounts of data on positions and employees must be maintained accurately and searched frequently to produce routine reports for management and numerous governmental agencies in a timely manner. Processing massive amounts of data to produce routine reports is simply too slow and costly using manual methods.

Additional motivation for computerizing human resource information is to allow human resource managers to sift through it on an ad hoc basis to pursue the answers to "what if" questions. This capability supports managers' tactical decision-making and policy-making activities. For example, human resource managers can use information systems to minimize the amounts spent on employee compensation and benefits. They

Box 13–4 Analyzing Your HRIS Needs

Some of the issues to consider when planning an HRIS software purchase include these:

What source documents will be fed into the system?

Document where the data will come from. Include all application, evaluation, or other forms that could provide the data that will be entered into the system. You may need to consider changes to your source documents to provide for your information needs.

What kind of reports (both scheduled and ad hoc) will be produced?

Prepare a layout depicting the information to be included. Be sure that data you want in a report is either stored in the system up front or can be generated later. Once a system is installed, changes or modifications can be expensive or impossible.

What steps need to be completed to get from the input to the output stage?

Examine the entire HR paper trail. Automating manual systems may require changing some procedures, and the HRIS project may provide the opportunity to simplify other processes.

Will the system interface with other systems?

Compatibility with existing systems or hardware can make the difference between a long-term functional system or a short-lived one.

What memory capacity will the system need?

Determine how many employee records the system will have to manage and how large they will be (number and size of fields, historical or current data, etc.); the growth rate of the organization in 5- to 10-year projections, if possible; and how long records will need to be stored on the system.

Who will absolutely need on-line access to the system?

What functions should the HRIS offer?

What should the new system do that the old one didn't?

How might the system be expanded in the future?

Identify functions you might want to implement that you don't need right now. It will be helpful if the software you purchase now will be compatible with additional programs you may need later on.

What are the criteria for success, and what does management expect to gain from this expense?

Source: Reprinted with permission from *HRMagazine* published by the Society for Human Resource Management, Alexandria, VA.

can also use information systems to increase the fairness of an organization's compensation and benefit plans. Forecasting and analyzing trends in accidents, pay rates, and position openings; identifying problems in pay grades, job titles, or supervisory skills; and assessing the impact of various pay increases, benefit plans, or retirement plans for employees are just a few of the many information-seeking activities that a computerized HRIS facilitates.

Limited-Function Human Resource Information Software. Numerous commercial software packages are sold for use on mainframes, minicomputers, and microcomputers that are designed to handle one or a small number of human resource functions (see Box 13–5). Microcomputer versions of these single-function software packages are relatively inexpensive and easy to operate and allow the human resource manager to automate a function quickly and easily.

Take care if you follow the single-function software route, though. The success of the first venture and the ease with which you complete it will likely lead you to add other single-function software packages to automate other human resource activities. If these additional software packages are not compatible with one another, you may be left with a series of data files and software packages that cannot be used in an integrated fashion. Thus, you will not be able to produce reports or ask "what if" questions that require more than one data file for completion.

Training Software. Many **training software** packages are available for all types and sizes of computers to provide on-line training for employees. They include management training software, sales training software, microcomputer training software, word processing training software, and a variety of other software. These software packages can be used in **computer-based training** programs designed by the human resource department for training specific employees in group and independent study programs. Computer-based training aids often simplify the trainer's job and allow the trainer to individualize instruction more easily than in traditional, group-based training classes. Computer-based training also allows employees to work at home or to review previous lessons without special help from human resource staff.

BOX 13–5 SOME TYPES OF LIMITED-FUNCTION HUMAN RESOURCE INFORMATION SOFTWARE

Applicant tracking.
Attendance tracking.
Benefits administration.
Career development.
Compensation administration.
Comprehensive Omnibus Budget Reconciliation Act (COBRA) administration.
Computer-based training.
Employee manual and handbook preparation.
Employee relations.
Equal Employment Opportunity/Affirmative Action.
Flexible benefits administration.
Health and safety management.
Human resources forecasting.
Immigration reform.
Job analysis.
Job description.
Labor relations.
Payroll administration.
Pension and profit-sharing administration.
Performance evaluation.
Relocation management.
Stress management.
Substance abuse management.
Succession planning.
Temporary services management.
Training administration and management.
Turnover analysis.
Workforce planning.

Multimedia hardware and software is also used in training programs as described in Chapter 5.

Management Summary

An organization's employees are its most important and frequently its most expensive resource. Because of our nation's changing social structure, heightened foreign competition, and increasingly numerous governmental regulations, managing human resources has become much more complex than in the past.

Human resource departments are responsible for many facets of human resource management, including recruiting, assessment, selection, placement, training, performance appraisal, compensation and benefit management, promotion, termination, occupational health and safety, employee services, compliance with legal constraints, helping managers with human resource problems, and providing top management with information for strategic planning.

To manage this diverse, expensive, and important resource within a complex environment, human resource departments rely on computer-based information systems. Computer-based information systems can address a variety of human resource functions in an integrated and comprehensive manner. Computer-based information systems also provide support for a single or a small group of human resource activities. Software that helps a human resource department keep the records and produce the reports necessary to comply with federal, state, and local regulatory agencies is one example.

Computer-based information systems not only assist human resource departments in keeping records and producing routine, repetitive reports, they also help staff engage in tactical and strategic planning by providing them with a relatively easy means to simulate, forecast, statistically analyze, query, and otherwise manipulate the human resource data on an ad hoc basis.

Key Terms for Managers

applicant selection and placement information system, **492**
attendance tracking systems, **497**
compensation and benefits information systems, **501**
computer-based training, **509**
employee information system, **491**
employee profile, **491**
employee relations information systems, **496**
employee training and development systems, **501**
government reporting and compliance information systems, **495**
human resource information systems (HRIS), **489**
human resource management, **490**
job analysis and design information system, **497**
labor negotiations, **504**
labor relations information systems, **497**
performance appraisals, **493**
performance management information system, **493**
position control system, **492**
recruiting information system, **499**
skills inventory, **491**
succession planning information systems, **502**
training software, **509**
workforce planning, **503**

Review Questions

1. What is an HRIS? What are the typical components of an HRIS?
2. What operational human resource information systems do organizations commonly maintain?
3. What is a job description? What information does a job description usually contain?

4. What is a job specification? What information does a job specification usually contain?
5. What information does an employee information system typically contain?
6. What is a skills inventory? Identify one report a skills inventory system commonly produces.
7. What is a position inventory?
8. What information does a position control system contain? What is one report a position control system typically produces?
9. Describe one operational and one tactical report that a recruiting information system produces.
10. What information outputs or reports does an affirmative action plan produce?
11. What are the objectives of a recruiting system? How do various human resource information systems support these objectives?
12. How might a compensation and benefits information system be used tactically?
13. Identify five ways that a human resource manager may use spreadsheet software.
14. Differentiate between comprehensive human resource function software and limited-function human resource software.
15. Identify types of limited-function human resource software commercially available in off-the-shelf software.
16. What two types of strategic planning activities do human resource management personnel typically conduct?
17. What are the outputs of a workforce planning forecast? What may be the types and sources of inputs to a workforce forecast?

Questions for Discussion

1. In what ways can human resource managers use information from job descriptions and specifications?
2. How might managers use the information found in the skills inventory?
3. Why is it important that payroll system and human resource system files be compatible and coordinated?
4. How might the information in a position control system be combined with the information found in the job analysis and design information system and the skills inventory?
5. What types of operational decisions might be supported by a performance management information system? How might the performance management information system be used tactically?
6. In what ways can managers use the employee health and safety information collected to meet OSHA regulations?
7. Why is the management of human resources more complex and difficult today than it has been in the past?

8. In what ways do computerized human resource information systems assist managers in reducing the complexity and difficulty of human resource decision making?
9. What are the advantages and disadvantages to the human resource department of developing its own human resource software applications as opposed to having the management information systems department complete this task?
10. What are the advantages of implementing comprehensive human resource software as opposed to limited-function human resource software?

Problems

1. **Averill & Barnes, Inc.** Averill & Barnes, Inc., manufactures lead and colored pencils at one plant in Kansas City, Kansas. Sales have been growing consistently over the last few years to the point that the plant is working three shifts each day. To meet estimated demand three years from now, it is clear that the company will have to expand its manufacturing capacity. Sales growth has been especially strong in the northeastern United States and the company is considering locating a second plant in the area of their growth market. Saratoga and Rochester, New York, are two locations that appear promising after a preliminary survey of data from the standpoint of nearness to wood supplies and customer density.

   Top management also wants to assess the manpower situation in and around those two cities. You are to provide them with this information:

   a. Topics that should be searched in on-line databases to provide information useful to workforce planners.
   b. Two on-line databases that might be included in their search.

2. **Traders National Bank.** Clarice Brown is manager of the West Side branch office of the Traders National Bank. As an assistant human resource manager for the bank, you are in the process of explaining to the other managers how and when your office will be conducting job analysis interviews in order to update and revise the job descriptions and specifications for all bank clerical jobs. Clarice is not particularly happy that she will have to provide time for your staff to interview her employees in order to complete the job analysis project. Obviously frustrated, she asks you why job analysis has to be done anyway, since she hardly ever uses the job descriptions and specifications. Her other comments make it clear that she regards the process as a bureaucratic boondoggle of the human resource department.

   a. What uses could Brown make of the information in job descriptions and specifications? Describe several specific ways that this information might help her in her operational and tactical decision making.
   b. Assume that the job descriptions and job specifications are part of a computerized human resource database. Develop outlines for two reports that Brown might use for tactical planning that are based in whole or in part on data from job descriptions and specifications. The outlines should specify the report titles, the column headings, and any processing of columnar data that the reports should contain.

3. **Database problem: Employee record.** Using a database management software package, create a record similar to the employee record shown in Figure 13–2. Then, complete the record for 20 fictitious employees who work in the following departments: receiving, shipping, accounting. Try to spread the employees as

evenly as you can among the departments. Create the other data needed for the records as you go along. Finally, print out the following lists:

a. The names of all employees who work in the shipping department.
b. The names and phone numbers of employees who work in the accounting department.
c. The names, job titles, and date of last promotion of all married employees who work in the receiving department.

Submit the three lists along with a printout of all records in the database you created to your instructor.

4. **Forecasting problem: Arnold Merchandising, Inc.** You are the human resource manager for the Grand Forks, North Dakota, branch of Arnold Merchandising, Inc. (AMI). You are trying to estimate the costs of fringe benefits for nonsalaried and nonunion employees for the next three years. AMI includes as fringe benefits the employer portion of the social security tax, pension plan payments, and medical plan payments. The cost of fringe benefits for the last seven years is shown in the table below:

Year	Number of Employees	Social Security	Pension	Medical	Total Benefits
1	50	75,200	80,000	72,000	227,200
2	51	79,666	84,864	81,518	246,048
3	52	86,052	89,989	93,091	269,132
4	55	94,657	98,988	110,277	303,922
5	55	98,444	102,948	124,613	326,004
6	55	102,381	107,065	140,812	350,259
7	55	106,477	111,348	159,118	376,943

a. Use linear programming to forecast total fringe benefits for years 8, 9, and 10 based on the data for the previous five months. If you have a DOS- or Windows-based computer system, you can use the 4KAST forecasting program on the applications diskette that your instructor should provide you. Follow these steps:
   1. Make sure that your computer system is turned on and that the DOS operating system has been loaded. Place your diskette in the A drive of your computer system. Make sure that the system prompt shows A:>. Load the forecasting program by entering 4KAST at A:> and pressing the ENTER key. If you are using Windows, from the Program Manager screen, click on FILE and RUN. Then type A:\4KAST in the Command Line box that appears on the screen. Then click on OK.
   2. When the opening screen of 4KAST is displayed, press the ENTER key. At the "Select A Forecasting Technique" menu, enter L for *linear regression.* This tells the program that you wish to complete a linear regression on data.
   3. At the "Simple Linear Regression" menu, enter 2 for *data entry-data file.* This tells the program that the data on which you wish to complete a linear regression is already in a data file.

4. Enter the file name, PROB13–4 and press the ENTER key. This will load the benefit data from a file on your diskette that already contains the total benefits data shown in the table above.
5. At the "Simple Linear Regression" menu, enter 5 to make a forecast. Choose as your begin point the first year of benefits by entering 1 and pressing ENTER. Choose the last year of benefits as your end point by entering 7 and pressing ENTER.
6. Forecast production for years 8, 9, and 10 by entering 8 as the begin point and 10 as the end point.
7. Enter *S* to display the forecast on the screen or *P* to print it out. If you decide you want to print the forecast out, make certain that a printer is attached to your computer, that paper is loaded, and that the printer is turned on before you enter *P*.

b. You decide that years 4–7 would be more representative for forecasting years 8–10. Use the years 4–7 to forecast fringe benefits for years 8–10.

5. **Spreadsheet problem: Wallingford Corporation.** Use microcomputer spreadsheet software to create a template that will allow Joy Breen, the director of human resource management, to consider the impact of various retirement plans on employees who are age 50 or more. The template should have rows for classifying all employees into 21 age categories for ages 50 through 70. It should include columns for numbers of employees in each category, percent of all employees, total wages earned last year, and total fringe benefits earned last year. It also should have a column in which Breen may enter the percentage of employees of any age that she estimates will seek retirement if a plan is offered. The final column should be the amount saved in each age category from earnings and fringe benefits if the estimated percentage of employees do choose to retire. However, note that the total salary and fringe benefits are not saved because Breen estimates that each retired employee costs the organization 15 percent of total wages in retirement benefits. The final row should contain the sums of each column. Use the criteria in Box 10–13 to evaluate their work.

6. **Spreadsheet problem: Lima School District.** Using the Lotus 1-2-3 spreadsheet program or any spreadsheet program able to read .WK1 files, load the file labeled PROB13–6 on the applications diskette provided by your instructor. The file is a template for analyzing the effects of various salary negotiation proposals on the total teaching salary obligation for the Lima School District. The lower part of the template is a seniority table that shows the number of teachers and the number of years of experience they have in the district. Salaries in the district are determined by adding a teacher's base salary to the amount obtained by multiplying the number of years experience for that teacher by the Annual Increase amount.

   The table allows you to enter negotiation data for salary, pension, and health and life insurance. You are to assume that no new teaching personnel will be hired for next year and that after 30 years all teaching personnel must retire.

   After loading the template, enter these data:

   a. In the first row of the contract specifications columns, enter $19,000 under the Old B.S. and $21,000 under the Old M.S. contract columns.

   b. In the second row of the contracts specifications columns, enter $500 as the Annual Increase under the Old B.S. and $750 under the Old M.S. contract columns.

c. In the third row of the contracts specifications columns, enter .08 as the Retirement Contribution Rate under each of the four columns.
d. In the fourth row of the contracts specifications columns, enter $1500 as the Health Plan contribution amount under each of the four columns.
e. In the fifth row of the contracts specifications columns, enter $240 as the Life Insurance contribution amount under each of the four columns.

The spreadsheet now shows the total amount the district would have to pay for teachers' salaries if there were no salary raises or increases in benefits for next year. What would the total district teaching salary obligations be in the following cases:

a. The present raise negotiated was 3 percent? 5 percent? 8 percent?
b. The percentage raise negotiated was 3 percent and the retirement contribution was increased to 9 percent?
c. The percentage raise negotiated was 5 percent, the retirement contribution was increased to 10 percent, and the district paid $1,800 and $250 for every teacher's health and life insurance, respectively?
d. Suppose that the rate for retirement contribution was 8 percent, the amount for health insurance $1,500, and the amount for life insurance $240 next year. Suppose further that the district felt that a maximum of $2,650,000 could be spent on teaching salaries. What would be the maximum percent raise, to the nearest tenth of a percent, that the district could negotiate?

7. **Microcomputer-based human resource information systems.** Develop a report describing microcomputer-based human resource information systems useful to functional managers and line managers. Your report should list the types of software available, the brand name and price of one example for each type, and a description of the typical features of each software type. Some suggested sources of information for this assignment include *HRMagazine,* published by the American Society for Personnel Administration; *Personnel Journal,* published by A. C. Croft, Inc.; and Computer Select, a CD-ROM database of computer-related articles, software specifications, and hardware specifications.

CASES

1. **Southern States Manufacturing Company.** Gilbert Hawthorne is the human resource director for the Southern States Manufacturing Company of Atlanta, Georgia. Southern States is a very traditional, well-established company, having been incorporated in 1888. Hawthorne will be celebrating his 25th year with the company this year, and he has been the human resource director for Southern States for the last 20 years. During that time, the company has grown to 600 employees, and Gilbert now manages the work of several assistant human resource directors. Hawthorne's assistants are charged with the following areas of responsibility: personnel benefits, personnel health and safety, wage and salary administration, and affirmative action.

Though Southern States has had a data processing department to handle the accounting and payroll functions of the company for a number of years, the use of computers has not spread to other departments or functions within the firm. Elizabeth Lucas, current president of Southern States and granddaughter of the firm's founding father, is concerned about making the firm more technologically current and thereby maintaining its competitive edge. As a result, she has asked Wylder

Washington, an information systems consultant, to explore with each of the firm's managers how computerized information systems might be employed to improve the manager's operations.

Hawthorne did not make his scheduled appointment with Washington. When Washington telephoned Hawthorne to ask why, Hawthorne explained that he was tied up because of pressing discussions with his assistant human resource director in charge of personnel benefits. Hawthorne added, however, that "I do not feel an appointment is really necessary. After all, human resource management is a people function and, as such, cannot be computerized. Furthermore, the company's human resource function has been operating very well for the last 20 years without the aid of computers." Hawthorne suggested that Washington pursue the computerization of other functions within the company, as he felt that those functions would be more likely to yield results.

Despite Hawthorne's objections, Washington insisted on setting up another meeting and extracted from Hawthorne the promise that he would attend.

- ***a.*** Hawthorne's opinion about computers is not an uncommon one. What approach might you use to persuade him that the computerization of the human resource information system might be worth exploring?
- ***b.*** What operational, tactical, and strategic planning human resource activities might be plausible applications for computerized information systems in the firm? For each application, spell out how the computerization of these activities might benefit Hawthorne's operation.
- ***c.*** Which application identified in *b* should be given first priority for development? Explain why you chose this application as the first one to develop.

2. **Chase Media, Inc.** The human resource department staff at Chase Media, Inc., serves a labor force of 750 employees, including office workers, factory workers, sales workers, technicians, and professionals. Because the workforce is growing and because of the complexities of governmental reporting, the staff has been considering computerizing its human resource activities. Valerie Epstein, the training director, has been reading articles about full-blown human resource information systems in professional journals and is interested in acquiring a comprehensive commercial HRIS package. Epstein suggests that the department ask the MIS department for help identifying, evaluating, and selecting a commercial package to be used on their mainframe. She feels MIS expertise is needed in this project because none of the human resource staff has much computer training or experience.

   Tyrone Wilson, the benefits administrator for the department, feels that such a move would be too much, too soon. He suggests that it would be easier and faster if the department computerized only one HRIS activity first to see how effective computerization would be and what problems staff would have moving to computer-based systems. Wilson suggests that the department evaluate and acquire commercial benefits management software to see how things go before plowing ahead with a comprehensive package of software. If the benefits software works satisfactorily, the department can proceed to acquire and implement software packages for the other human resource functions one at a time.

   Elicia Watson, the recruiting director for the department, complains that the MIS department may defer the computerization it needs now to manage an increasingly large labor force with some degree of efficiency. Watson points out that the human resource department does not have the highest priority in the firm's pecking order and that its requests for MIS services are likely to be placed behind those of the marketing and production departments. She suggests that the department acquire a microcomputer human resource system so that it can implement the software immediately and not have to worry about the priorities of the MIS department. She also feels that use of the microcomputer software will give greater control over its use and its security. She points out that the microcomputer software is much less expensive than the mainframe software and should be easy for staff members to implement without help from the MIS department.

Marcia Dobbins, director of human resource services for Chase, decides that they need some expert advice and decides to call in a consultant to advise them in their decision making.

If you were the consultant chosen,

a. How would you assess each of the suggestions by Epstein, Wilson, and Watson? What are the strengths and weaknesses of each suggestion?
b. What plan of action would you recommend and why?

3. **Database case: Minitek, Inc.** You work in the training unit of the Human Resource Department of Minitek, Inc., a distributor of computer storage devices located in Glen Carbon, IL. Your job involves using an information system that tracks employees and the seminar programs in which they have enrolled. It is now fall, 1995, and you are using a database that describes employees, seminar programs, instructors, seminar registrations, and seminar schedules. To complete this case, you will query the database. If you are using dBase IV, you may choose to query the database using the command interface, the query-by-example interface, or the SQL interface.

To get started, you will need the following:

a. A copy of a database program that will read and process the dBase files listed below.
b. The following database files stored on the applications diskette provided by your instructor:
1. (*a*) An EMPLOYEE file, which describes the employees.
   (*b*) A SEMINAR file, which describes the seminars which are classified into Professional Development, Management Training, Technical Training, Sales Training, and Specialized Training categories.
2. An INSTRUCT (instructor) file describing the instructors.
3. A REGISTER file describing the employees registered in various seminar programs for the fall semester of 1995.
4. A SCHEDULE file describing the seminars scheduled for the spring and summer semesters of 1996 to be held in certain rooms and their capacities.

Directions:

a. Load dBase IV or your database software on your computer system.
b. Place your data disk in your computer's disk drive. If you are using dBase, get to the "." prompt and key in these commands:
.SET DIRECTORY TO N (where N is the letter of the disk drive in which you inserted your data disk)
.SET CATALOG TO MINITEK
Change to the dBase IV Control Center screen by entering ASSIST at the "." prompt.

c. Scan the contents of records in the database so that you understand the nature of the data in the database. If you are using dBase IV, do this by moving the cursor to each file in the Data panel or column of the Control Center, pressing enter, and selecting Display Data. Move about each file by using the Home, End, Page Up, and Page Down keys.

d. Print the answers to each of the following queries:

Query 1: You are considering offering some seminars off-site in Belleville, IL. Produce two lists: one list of the last names and telephone numbers of all students who live in Belleville, IL, and another list of the last names and telephone numbers of all instructors who live in Belleville, IL.

Query 2: You wish to improve revenues for the training unit by encouraging enrollment in seminars with high fees. Produce a list of all seminars with fees greater than $350.00 that will be offered in spring, 1996. The list should contain the seminar ID, the seminar description, and the seminar fee.

Query 3: Produce a list of all employees registered for PRO108 for fall, 1995. The list should include last name, phone number, and department of each employee in the seminar.

Query 4: Employees who register in seminars have their fees paid by the departments in which they work. Produce a list of all employees enrolled in a fall, 1995, seminar who have not yet paid their fees. The list should contain the employee's last name, the department, the seminar ID, and the fee owed.

Query 5: Produce a schedule of seminars for summer, 1996, showing the Seminar ID, seminar description, building, room number, and instructor's last name.

Hand in each of your lists to your instructor. Add to each list your name and the query number.

To help you understand the records you will work with, the names and characteristics of the fields in each type of record are shown below:

1. EMPLOYEE file (EMPLOYEE.DBF)

Field Name	Type	Width
EID	Character	9
ELNAME	Character	10
EMI	Character	1
EFNAME	Character	10
EDOB	Character	6
ESEX	Character	1
ESTR	Character	15
ECITY	Character	15
ESTATE	Character	2
EZIP	Character	5
EPHONE	Character	10
EDEPT	Character	3
EEOC	Character	3

2. SEMINAR file (SEMINAR.DBF)

Field Name	Type	Width	Dec
SID	Character	6	

SDESC	Character	22	
SPROG	Character	18	
SFEE	Numeric	7	2

3. INSTRUCT file (INSTRUCT.DBF)

Field Name	Type	Width	Dec
IID	Character	9	
ILNAME	Character	10	
IMI	Character	1	
IFNAME	Character	10	
IJOBTITLE	Character	23	
ISTR	Character	15	
ICITY	Character	15	
ISTATE	Character	2	
IZIP	Character	5	
IPHONE	Character	10	

4. REGISTER file (REGISTER.DBF)

Field Name	Type	Width	Dec
RSEM	Character	4	
RSID	Character	6	
REID	Character	9	
RTPAID	Character	1	

5. SCHEDULE file (SCHEDULE.DBF)

Field Name	Type	Width	Dec
SCSEM	Character	4	
SCSID	Character	6	
SCIID	Character	9	
SCBLDG	Character	2	
SCROOM	Character	4	
SCCAP	Numeric	4	

Data Entry Codes:

File: Employee; Field: EDEPT:

ACC	Accounting
MIS	Management Information Systems
PUR	Purchasing
SAL	Sales
SHI	Shipping

File: Employee; Field: EEOC:

CAU	Caucasian
BLA	Black
HIS	Hispanic
ASI	Asian
IND	Indian

Selected References and Readings

Adams, Timothy R. "Buying Software without the Glitches." *HRMagazine* 35, no. 1 (January 1990), p. 41. Describes steps and precautions to take when buying HRIS software.

Allan, Kelley. "Computer Courses Insure Uniform Training." *Personnel Journal* 72, no. 6 (June 1993), pp. 65–66 ff. Describes how the Hudson Bay Company uses computer-based training to improve training outcomes and reduce costs.

Bensu, Janet. "Use Your Data Base in New Ways." *HRMagazine* 35, no. 3 (March 1990), pp. 33–34. Describes the use of computer systems for skill-building training programs.

Frye, Colleen. "HR Looks Toward Future." *Software Magazine* 12, no. 6 (November 1992), pp. 40–42 ff. Explains how several companies have moved their HRIS to a distributed systems platform.

Greengard, Samuel. "How Technology Is Advancing HR." *Personnel Journal* 72, no. 9 (September 1993), pp. 80–86 ff. Identifies and analyzes five technologies and their impact on human resource management.

Herniter, Bruce E., Erran Carmel, and Jay F. Nunamaker, Jr. "Computers Improve Efficiency of the Negotiation Process." *Personnel Journal* 72, no. 4 (April 1993), pp. 93, 95, 97–99. Explains how computer system software can assist negotiators at the bargaining table—and before they reach it.

Holzbert, Carol S. "Position Available, Inquire Within." *PC Today* 7, no. 5 (May 1993), pp. 20–22, 24–26. Describes PC-based comprehensive and limited-function human resource information software packages.

Huttig, J. W., Jr. "Coping with the Family Leave Act: PCs Can Help Small Firms with the Latest Edict from D. C." *PC Today* 7, no. 5 (May 1993), pp. 27–28. Describes how telecommuting, cross training in computer software, and job reengineering can ameliorate the dislocation caused by long-term employee leave policies.

Jacobs, Paula. "Personal Freedom: Advantages of Open Systems and Flexible Client-Server Environments for Human Resource Departments." *HP Professional* 7, no. 1 (January 1993), pp. 25 ff. Describes how distributed processing systems can help national and global firms tailor their HRM systems to the cities, states, regions, and countries in which they operate.

Keary, Deborah. "What Databases Can Do for You." *HRMagazine* 38, no. 3 (March 1993), pp. 44–46. Describes on-line databases helpful to human resource managers.

Kirrane, Dianne E., and Peter R. Kirrane. "Managing by Expert Systems." *HRMagazine* 35, no. 3 (March 1990), pp. 37–39. Describes the use of expert systems in some human resource information systems.

Lederer, Albert L. *Handbook of Human Resource Information Systems.* New York: Warren, Gorham, and Lamont, 1991. Must reading for those developing HRIS software applications.

Leinfuss, Emily. "Employees Empowered by Direct Access HRMS." *Software Magazine* 13, no. 6 (April 1993), pp. 83–84 and 90. Discusses implementation of employee self-service human resource information systems.

Milkovich, George T., and John W. Boudreau. *Human Resource Management,* 7th ed. Burr Ridge, IL: Irwin, 1994. A basic text in human resource management. Chapter 7 is devoted to human resource information systems.

Murphy, Lyn. "Streamline the Application Process." *HRMagazine* 38, no. 7 (July 1993), pp. 35–38. Reviews a software package that automates much of the job applicant recording, selection, and placement process.

Noe, Raymond A., John R. Hollenbeck, and Barry Gerhart. *Human Resource Management: Gaining a Competitive Advantage.* Burr Ridge, IL: Irwin, 1994. A human resource management textbook, a major theme of which is how human resources can contribute to an organization's competitiveness. Chapter 19 is devoted to human resource information systems. In addition, each chapter has a section devoted to "Competing through Technology and Structure."

O'Connell, Sandra E. "Doing More with Less." *HRMagazine* 38, no. 1 (January 1993), pp. 31 and 33. Discusses a survey measuring the affects of automation on the productivity of human resource management.

O'Connell, Sandra E. "Pinpoint Your System Needs," *HRMagazine* 38, no. 4 (April 1993), pp. 33–34. Presents a detailed evaluation scheme for HRIS software selection.

O'Connell, Sandra E. "User-Friendly or User-Hostile." *HRMagazine* 38, no. 3 (March 1993), pp. 33 and 35. Presents the characteristics of HRIS software that make it easy to learn, use, and install.

Stevens, Larry. "Resume Scanning Simplifies Tracking," *Personnel Journal* 72, no. 4 (April 1993), pp. 77–79. Describes how the use of scanner technology for inputting resumes in an HRIS reduces costs and speeds searching applicant files for the right person.

Stamps, David. "Human Resources: A Strategic Partner or IS Burden?" *Datamation* 36, no. 11 (June 1, 1990), pp. 47–52. Describes the relationship between MIS and HRMS and the expected increased role of the HRMS in strategic planning.

Stright, Jay F., Jr. "Strategic Goals Guide HRMS Development." *Personnel Journal* 72, no. 9 (September 1993), pp. 68–71 ff. Describes how Chevron Corp. aligned its HRIS goals with the company's business goals.

Wilson, Susan. "Track Accident Costs with Safety I," *HRMagazine* 38, no. 5 (May 1993), pp. 42, 44–45. Reviews an accident tracking software package.

Decision Support Systems

Chapter Outline

Manager's View

The earliest information systems were transactions processing systems designed to automate payroll, accounts payable, and other accounting operations. In the early 1970s, operational information systems that processed orders, scheduled production, and managed transportation needs were developed. Many of these applications made it possible to reduce clerical effort, to control administrative costs, and to provide better service. Designed by systems development professionals, most of these systems ran on centralized mainframe computers with large databases.

In the 1980s and 1990s a new concept of information systems has evolved because managers increasingly need information to make decisions about how to organize and control resources effectively. These systems, known as decision support systems, are quite different from the information systems of the past. They are designed by managers themselves, sometimes with the help of data processing professionals serving as user-consultants.

This chapter explains the evolution and development of managerial decision support systems. Because decision support systems are designed to support managers' information needs, you should also be familiar with the process of decision making. Decision support systems must constantly evolve, because the decisions that managers need to make change from day to day. Hence this chapter also covers the flexible *design* process that makes it possible to design new systems as information needs change.

MANAGERS' SYSTEMS NEEDS

One reason for the emergence of decision support systems is that many existing information systems do not support the information needs of managers. In a study of managers' systems needs, Alloway and Quillard asked 529 managers in 13 firms to describe how effectively current information systems supported their decision-making needs.[1] Of the information systems in the 13 organizations they studied, Alloway and Quillard learned that 63 percent were operational information systems designed to produce standard reports on a fixed schedule. An additional 16 percent were exception reporting systems designed to support tactical decision making. It will be helpful to review the meaning of the term *exception report.* An exception report produces information about deviations from planned activity, such as identifying all customer accounts doing 25 percent more business this year than last year. Although exception reporting systems can highlight trends affecting the business, the exception conditions are usually fixed. This means that the logic for reporting exceptions is explicitly coded in the computer programs that prepare the exception reports. If a manager wants a report of all customers doing 10 percent less business this year than last year, for example, reprogramming would be required.

Although operational and exception reporting systems were somewhat helpful to the managers Alloway and Quillard surveyed, the managers considered inquiry and analysis systems far more useful in supporting decision-making needs. According to these authors, an inquiry system provides a database that can be used to make ad hoc queries. Using a query language, a manager can ask, "List the names of all customers in the Midwest region who have overdue account balances of more than $500." The next day, the same manager might ask, "List the names and addresses of customers in the Southwest region who have done more than $10,000 worth of business with us in the past year." The types of queries managers want answered change as information needs change.

In their study, Alloway and Quillard learned that only 12 percent of the information systems available to the managers they surveyed were inquiry systems and that the managers considered most of these systems useful. Managers also wanted to use data in existing databases for analysis purposes, and information systems providing data analysis capabilities, using modeling, simulation, and statistical routines, were in great demand with them. Figure 14–1 shows that of the 1,403 information systems used by managers in the Alloway and Quillard study, 70 percent were considered appropriate. The inquiry and analysis systems in particular were considered valuable. For inquiry systems, 81 percent were appropriate, and for analysis systems, 97 percent were appropriate.

In short, the Alloway and Quillard study demonstrates an increase in demand for inquiry and analysis systems relative to the demand for operational and exception reporting systems. In another study of managers' information needs, Rockart and Treacy (1981) also concluded that senior managers want to be able to manipulate and analyze existing databases to obtain the information they need to support important decision-making tasks.

---

[1]Robert Alloway and Judith Quillard, "User Managers Systems Needs," *MIS Quarterly* 7, no. 2 (1983), pp. 27–41.

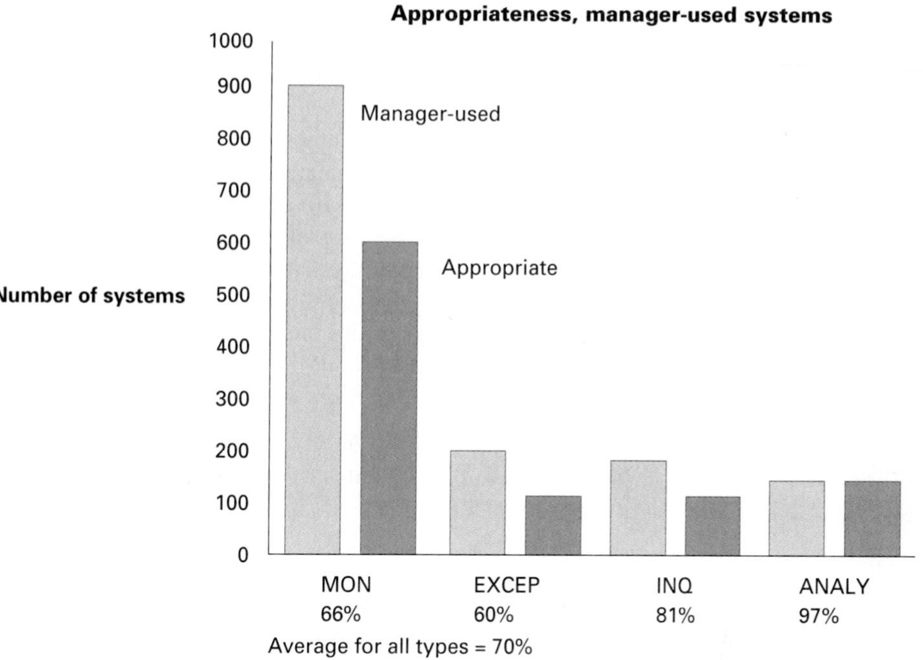

Figure 14–1
Appropriateness of information systems used by managers

Source: Adapted from Robert Alloway and Judith Quillard, "User Managers' Systems Needs," *MIS Quarterly* 7, no. 2 (1983), p. 32.

CHARACTERISTICS OF THE DECISION-MAKING PROCESS

Before learning about the purpose and features of decision support systems, you should become acquainted with the decision-making process, the types of problems addressed in decision making, the attributes of decision makers, and strategies for decision making. All these concepts have implications for the design of decision support systems.

Phases of Decision Making

According to Simon (1960) and Mintzberg, Raisinghani, and Theoret (1976), decision making involves three phases.[2] During the first phase, **intelligence,** the decision maker searches for conditions calling for a decision. The decision maker may be reacting to problems or may recognize opportunities. In either case, a gap between the existing state and a desired state is a necessary condition for the existence of a decision problem.

Design is the second phase of decision making. During design, the decision maker develops and analyzes alternative courses of action by either searching for ready-made alternatives or developing a custom-made solution. The third phase of decision-making is **choice.** During this phase, the decision-maker selects the best alternative.

For a decision situation to occur, the decision maker must be aware of a gap between the existing state and the desired state, must be motivated to solve the problem, and must have the resources to do so.[3] The type of decision problem and the attributes of the decision maker both influence the decision-making strategy.

[2]Herbert A. Simon, *The New Science of Management Decision* (New York: Harper & Row, 1960), pp. 1–8; and

[3]K R MacGrimmon and R N Taylor, "Decision Making and Problem Solving," in *Handbook of Industrial and Organizational Psychology*, ed. M D Dunnette (Chicago: Rand McNally, 1976), pp. 1,397–1,453.

Types of Decision Problems

Problems are structured, semistructured, or unstructured, depending on how familiar the decision maker is with the existing state, the desired state, and the transformation necessary to get from one state to the other. Structured problems are well understood. Pricing customer orders, reordering office supplies, and specifying the wage rate for a new employee are examples of structured decisions because they are routine and can be addressed using standard operating procedures. Standard operating procedures can be in the form of **algorithms** or **heuristics.** Algorithms are sets of standard operations that guarantee a solution to a problem in a finite number of steps. Heuristics are "rules of thumb" that offer procedures or outlines for seeking solutions.

In organizations, managerial decision problems are semistructured or unstructured because the decision environment is uncertain, complex, and unstable. A decision maker may be uncertain about the nature of the problem, about the alternative actions he should take, and about how external events may affect the outcome.

Attributes of the Decision Maker

The attributes of decision makers also affect the types of decision strategies used. These attributes include perceptual ability, information capacity, risk-taking propensity, and aspiration level.[4]

Perceptual ability refers to the way a decision maker perceives a decision problem. If a decision maker has experience dealing with a similar problem, the problem-solving situation will not seem as complex and as uncertain as in a case where her background with a similar situation is limited.

Information capacity is important because all decision making requires an information base. In complex decision-making situations, decision makers who are receptive to new information are better prepared to handle the cognitive demands of information search when they are faced with difficult or uncertain tasks. In contrast, dogmatic decision makers tend to make rapid decisions based on little information. In either case, decision makers resist changing a decision once it has been made.

The other two attributes that account for differences in decision-making behavior are risk-taking propensity and aspiration level. In risky situations, decision makers are more uncertain about outcomes and possible loss of resources. The aspiration level of decision makers also influences their effectiveness in identifying problems, evaluating alternatives, and making *choices.* In general, decision makers attempt to achieve an optimal standard, and prior experiences of success or failure and knowledge of results both influence this standard.

Strategies for Decision Making

The type of decision problem and the attributes of the decision maker influence whether the decision maker will use a **maximizing, satisficing,** or **incrementalizing** strategy (MacGrimmon and Taylor, 1976).

Maximizing. When the outcome of a decision is clear, and the alternatives are well established, the decision maker will make the decision that *maximizes* the desired outcome. Let's say that you are faced with a choice between two alternatives. One of these alternatives offers a 1 percent chance of winning $20,000, and the other alternative offers a 50 percent chance of winning $500. If you multiply the probability of each alternative by its outcome, you will see that the second alternative has a higher expected value.

---

[4]MacGrimmon and Taylor, "Decision Making and Problem Solving."

Probability	×	Outcome	=	Expected Value
.01	×	$20,000	=	200
.50	×	500	=	250

A rational decision maker will select the second alternative to optimize the expected value. The maximizing approach assumes that the decision maker is rational and is aware of the probabilities of each alternative.

Satisficing. Because many decisions are made in situations of uncertainty, decision makers are willing to settle for less than maximum utility. According to Simon,[5] decision makers display rationality only within limits imposed by their experience, background, and awareness of alternatives in a given decision situation. A decision maker will set up a reasonable aspiration level and search for possible alternatives until he finds one that achieves this level. Simon calls this *satisficing* because the decision maker will terminate the search as soon as a satisfactory alternative is found.

Incrementalizing. In the third decision-making strategy, the decision maker attempts to take small steps away from the existing state toward a desired state. This approach may neglect important outcomes because the alternatives considered are generally familiar to the decision maker.

Implications of Decision Making for Decision Support Systems

Decision support systems are designed to support semistructured and unstructured decisions in situations in which information is incomplete and where satisficing is a goal. They are developed to support decisions that are so different each time that it would be hard to develop a standard set of procedures for programming them. Such decisions may be specific and may relate to a one-time-only situation.

A decision support system should enable the decision maker to apply the right decision rules to a problem rather than using standard rules that may not apply because of changing conditions. For example, it would be ineffective to apply an inventory reorder model designed for slow-moving items to a problem situation involving fast-moving items. As you'll see in the next section, a decision support system provides the decision maker with the flexibility to explore alternatives by using appropriate data and models.

IMPORTANT FEATURES OF DECISION SUPPORT SYSTEMS

The design of a decision support system must take into account the characteristics of decision makers and of the decision-making process. An effective decision support system needs to incorporate the following features.

Support of Unstructured Decisions

To begin with, a decision support system must support semistructured and unstructured decisions. Semistructured and unstructured problems involve a decision-making process that can't be defined before actually going through the process or making the decision. In Chapter 9, a framework for information systems describing operational, tactical, and strategic planning systems was discussed. Although traditional data processing applications support structured decision-making requirements at each of these levels, decision support systems need to support less structured decision processes.

[5]Simon, *Management Decision,* pp. 1–8.

Table 14–1 describes the types of decisions and degree of decision structure for both structured and unstructured decisions.

For example, at the operational level an accounts receivable application is a highly structured system with well-defined procedures and outputs. However, cash management, because of the range of money management alternatives and judgmental factors, is a much more complex, unstructured problem.

Another example is the difference between budget analysis and budget preparation, two tactical applications. Budget analysis is a much more structured procedure than budget preparation. Budget analysis requires knowledge of possible cost factors, alternative resource requirements, and future needs. Although budget analysis can be accomplished easily with current or cumulative budget data with a spreadsheet or database program, budget preparation is considerably more challenging. Those responsible for budget preparation tend to be managers with considerable experience in managing projects and with knowledge of the possible cost factors to be considered on a long-term basis.

Support for Database Access and Modeling

Decision support systems (DSS) attempt to combine the use of models or analytic techniques with traditional data access and retrieval functions. A manager can overcome some of the problems associated with traditional information systems by determining what databases can be used, by defining what data analysis techniques are required, and by identifying what outputs are meaningful.

In building a decision support system, you first need to define your information requirements. Ideally, a decision support system should provide a database that serves as a repository of data for easy access and change. Subsets or copies of databases that support transactions information systems are often used in decision support systems. For example, an order history database detailing customer orders over the past 18 months may provide an excellent source of data for a decision support system.

The next step in developing a decision support system is to determine the type of data access or analysis that is needed. **Status access, personal analysis,** and **model-based analysis** are three possible methods of using a database. The characteristics of these types of analysis are summarized in Table 14–2. Status access is read-only access to operational data, usually to generate a set of reports. Personal analysis involves the analysis of data, and model-based analysis uses formal computer-based models of key aspects of a company's performance. When managers first use DSS tools, their access to databases is usually classified as status access or personal analysis. As managers gain insight into the use of database query languages and modeling techniques, their re-

Table 14–1
Types of decisions and decision structure

	Operational	Tactical	Strategic Planning
Structured decisions	Accounts receivable	Budget analysis	New market planning
	Inventory control	Short-term forecasts	Site location
	Production scheduling	Long-term forecasts	Mergers
Unstructured decisions	Cash management	Budget preparation	New product planning

Source: Adapted from G. Anthony Gorry and Michael S. Scott Morton, "A Framework for Management Information Systems," *Sloan Management Review* 13, no. 1 (1971), p. 62.

porting and simple analysis systems can evolve into more sophisticated modeling and analysis systems.

Support for All Phases of the Decision-Making Process

An effective decision support system should support the three phases of the decision-making process: intelligence, design, and choice. As you recall, during the intelligence phase, a situation requiring a decision is visualized. During the design phase, the problem is defined and alternative solutions are considered. During the choice phase, a course of action is selected.

At each phase of the decision-making process, different operations occur. During the intelligence phase, data are collected as a basis for diagnosing a problem or a situation requiring a decision. When alternatives are weighted during the design phase, data may be manipulated or values may be assigned to each alternative. A simulation of the results of the alternatives or statistics describing them may be useful operations for choosing the best option.

An example, making a decision about a new automobile, illustrates some of the activities that take place during the decision-making process. If you were going to buy a new car, you might go through the following steps:

- **Intelligence**— Review automobile maintenance records showing chronic transmission problems. Seek information from dealers and friends about new automobiles.
- **Design**— Establish objectives and criteria for evaluating automobiles. Establish weights illustrating the relative importance of these criteria. Analyze three alternative possibilities.
- **Choice**— Generate summary statistics on the evaluation of each automobile.

Chronic problems with an existing automobile might create a situation in which you need to make a decision about purchasing a new car. During the "design" phase, you may select safety, price, and performance as three important criteria for buying a car. Weights establishing the importance of each of these factors, such as safety (25 percent), price (25 percent), and performance (50 percent), also need to be set. You could get information from consumer reports, dealers, owners, and magazines to help you make comparisons among alternatives and then use summary statistics to provide overall scores for each alternative. These scores should provide evidence supporting a reasonable choice on your part.

Table 14–2
Types of analysis in decision support systems

	Status Access	Personal Analysis	Model-Based Analysis
Database used	Operating data	Operating data	Wide-ranging data
	Mostly internal	Internal and external	Internal and external
Access language	Menu-driven	Very high-level language (English-like)	Programming and modeling languages
Designer	Executive and IS staff	Executive and IS staff	Executive and IS staff
Evolution	More reports	Deeper analyses; more data	Better techniques; bigger models
Principal advantages	Easy to use; quick solution	Increased analytic capability	Increased organizational understanding

Source: Adapted from John Rockart and Michael Treacy, *Executive Information Support Systems,* Sloan Working Paper 1167–80 (Cambridge: MIT Center for Information Systems Research, April 1981), p. 31.

A decision support system, as defined previously, provides data for inquiry and analysis. These data can be used in different ways during each phase of the decision-making process. In making a decision about bad debts, different kinds of data are used at each of the three phases of the decision-making process:

- **Intelligence**—a listing of customers with bad debts; a graph of bad debts over time.
- **Design**—a scatterplot of customers by two attributes associated with bad debts used to partition customers into risk groups.
- **Choice**—a report on simulated bad debt losses for each alternative risk group.

Different types of data and analytical techniques are useful at different phases of the decision-making process. A listing of customers with bad debts might create an awareness of the bad debt expense problem. In an analysis of the bad debt situation, the number of women and the number of men under 25 years old with bad debts can be contrasted to determine the risk of these respective groups. Projecting these bad debt losses over time might provide insight into policies and procedures that could help control losses. For example, if women under 25 comprise a high-risk group and if projections indicate that this risk group will continue to grow, management may take steps to cut policy approvals and to raise premiums to this risk group. Management may also decide to reallocate sales efforts to more profitable buyer groups.

Support for Communications among Decision Makers

Decision support systems must support decision making at all levels of the organization. Because some decisions require communications among decision makers at all levels, decision support systems need to support group decision making. In some cases, decisions are made sequentially, with each decision maker responsible for part of the decision before passing it on to the next decision maker. The process of approving a marketing program might be one example. Senior management may decide to expand an advertising budget by 20 percent for two new product lines. In turn, middle management may seek to develop an advertising program, approving media choices and commercial messages. Operational management may need to make further decisions about timing and frequency of commercials.

Other decisions require pooling knowledge and result from negotiation and interaction among decision makers. An example of this kind of decision might be the choice of a conference site for a professional meeting. Each member of the conference planning committee might have specific preferences based on geographical location and travel-related expenses for conference participants. Negotiations might bring out the advantages and disadvantages of several alternative sites. After these options are evaluated, the decision can be made in everyone's best interest. A decision support system should support interaction among decision makers.

Availability of Memory Aids

In making decisions, managers constantly have to recall information or the results of operations conducted at previous times. Decision makers need **memory aids,** so a decision support system should provide them. Work spaces for displaying data representations or for preserving intermediate results from operations are useful. For example, monthly budget data stored in spreadsheets from prior months could be used for reference. Triggers reminding a decision maker to perform certain operations are also helpful. A trigger, for example, may tell the user that before a cash flow analysis can be completed, the costs of various investment alternatives must be calculated and projected.

Availability of Control Aids for Decision Making

A final important feature of a decision support system is the availability of **control aids** for training and system use. Many managers feel some anxiety about using computer-based systems. Without effective training in the early phases of computer operation, they may give up and turn back to paper-and-pencil methods. Help screens, menus, and prompts are valuable software features that make the training process easier and contribute to the development of language skills.

In summary, a decision support system should support all phases of the decision-making process, have short- and long-term memory aids, provide effective control aids, and support semistructured and unstructured types. It should also support data access and modeling and should facilitate communications among decision makers.

The design of decision support systems creates opportunities for managers to determine their information needs, to select appropriate tools, and to develop outputs they can use. In the next section, you will learn about the tools for decision support systems.

THE TOOLS OF DECISION SUPPORT

The tools of decision support include a variety of software supporting database query, modeling, data analysis, and display. A comprehensive tool kit for DSS would include software supporting these application areas. Examples of software tools falling into these four categories are given in Table 14–3.

Database Languages

Tools supporting database query and report generation use mainframe-, minicomputer-, and microcomputer-based databases. FOCUS, RAMIS, and NOMAD II, for example, are mainframe-based languages supporting database query, report generation, and simple analysis. FOCUS and RAMIS are also available in PC versions. Ingres, Oracle, and Informix are database languages on mainframes, minicomputers, and microcomputers. Managers frequently use microcomputer-based database tools such as dBase IV and R:base 5000.

Using a student database and a database query tool, a college administrator could generate the output shown in Figure 14–2 by asking for a list of courses with tuition greater than $215. This is an example of a simple query requiring a search for records with certain characteristics. Using a database query tool, the user could also generate a report with a title, page headings, column headings, subtotals, and totals.

Model-Based Decision Support Software

Model-based analysis tools such as spreadsheet software enable managers to design models that incorporate business rules and assumptions. Microcomputer-based spreadsheet programs such as Lotus 1-2-3 and Excel all support model building and "what if?"

Table 14–3
Software tools for decision support systems

Data-Based Software	Model-Based Software	Statistical Software	Display-Based Software
DBase IV	Foresight	SAS	ChartMaster
FOCUS	IFPS	SPSS	SASGRAPH
NOMAD II	Lotus 1-2-3	TSAM	TELLAGRAF
RAMIS	Model		
R:base 5000	Multiplan		
SQL	Omnicalc		

Figure 14–2
A database query

```
  DEMO)    .USE COURSE
  DEMO)    .LIST ALL FOR CTUIT > 215
Record#    CID      CDESC                   CDEPT    CTUIT     CLFEE
      3    AC370    AUDITING                AC       250.00    10.00
      7    FIN350   PRIN OF FIN             FIN      250.00     0.00
      9    FIN325   PRIN OF CREDIT          FIN      220.00    15.00
     12    MGT365   BUSINESS ETHICS         MGT      250.00     0.00
     16    MIS350   COBOL PROGRAMMING II    MIS      250.00    25.00
     18    MIS400   DATABASE DESIGN         MIS      250.00     0.00
     19    MIS421   SYS ANALY & DES II      MIS      255.00     0.00
     21    MKT400   PRIN OF MKT MGT         MKT      250.00    17.00
```

types of analysis. Mainframe-based spreadsheets such as Megacalc and Omnicalc fulfill the same purpose. Modeling tools like IFPS and Model are designed to support financial modeling and analysis.

A good example of a spreadsheet application is a cash flow analysis. Figure 14–3 shows a cash flow statement for a small business. The spreadsheet includes formulas that calculate expenses, profits, and cash flow. In developing this spreadsheet, the manager projected that inflation would rise by 10 percent each year. Using this assumption, the free cash flow at the end of five years is $3,351. By building in different assumptions, such as changes in inflation, operating expenses, and revenues, the manager could use the formulas in the spreadsheet to recalculate values such as total expenses, pretax profit, and cash flow. A spreadsheet is a valuable analysis tool because it makes it possible to analyze the impacts of different "what if?" situations.

Tools for Statistics and Data Manipulation

Statistical analysis software such as SAS and SPSS supports market researchers, operations research analysts, and other professionals using statistical analysis functions. Because of the need for increased "number crunching" capabilities, this type of software usually runs on mainframe computers. Microcomputer-based statistical packages are available as well. For example, the micro-based version of SPSS has about the same capabilities as the mainframe version, but it is much slower.

Display-Based Decision Support Software

The final category of decision support software is display-based software. Graphic displays of output generated from Lotus 1-2-3 spreadsheets, for example, are very effective in management presentations. Graphics tools running in a mainframe environment include DISSPLA, TELLAGRAF, and SASGRAPH. Microcomputer-based tools such as Harvard Graphics and Powerpoint display graphics output in the form of pie charts, bar charts, and graphs.

One issue concerning decision support systems is the need for integrated tools. Integrated tools provide the ability to generate, manipulate, and statistically analyze data within a single software package. Individual tools supporting isolated decision support functions such as database query or modeling exist, but these tools are not always integrated with each other.

Figure 14–3
Cash flow analysis using a spreadsheet

Source: Adapted from Arthur Williams, *What IF* (New York: John Wiley & Sons, 1984).

	Year 1	Year 2	Year 3	Year 4	Year 5
REVENUE	50,000	55,000	60,000	66,550	73,205
EXPENSES					
General & Admin.					
Salaries	19,500	21,450	23,595	23,955	28,550
Payroll Taxes	5,000	5,500	6,050	6,655	7,320
Office Expenses	6,500	7,150	7,865	8,652	9,517
Professional Fees	1,000	1,100	1,210	1,331	1,464
Travel	1,500	1,650	1,815	1,997	2,196
Ent. and Promo.	6,000	6,600	7,260	7,986	8,785
Total G & A	39,500	43,450	47,795	52,574	57,832
Total Financing	8,318	8,318	8,318	8,318	8,318
Interest	8,125	8,094	8,057	8,015	7,966
Principal	193	224	261	303	352
Principal Remaining	49,807	49,583	49,322	49,019	48,666
TOTAL EXPENSES	47,625	51,543	55,852	60,589	65,797
PRE-TAX PROFIT	2,375	3,457	4,648	5,961	7,408
Income Tax	1,188	1,728	2,324	2,980	3,704
AFTER-TAX PROFIT	1,188	1,728	2,324	2,980	3,704
Repayment of Debt	193	224	261	303	352
FREE CASH FLOW	995	1,504	2,063	2,677	3,351

An integrated tool can transfer data from a spreadsheet into a graphics program or from a database into a statistics program. For example, you might gather data on the profit percentage contribution of four major customers over the past five years. These data could be stored in a database. Based on these figures, you would like to project the profit percentage and gross income from these customers for the next five years. Using an integrated package like Lotus 1-2-3—which is a microcomputer-based package incorporating spreadsheet, database, and graphics capabilities—you could use data from the database in a spreadsheet and then build a model to generate the desired projections. If you want these projections to be displayed in graphics format, using a line graph or bar chart, you could transfer the data in the spreadsheet into a graphics format for display.

You can get a better understanding of the nature and scope of decision support systems by learning about the experiences of managers who have developed them. The following case studies will give you insight into the reasons why decision support systems are developed.

CASES IN MANAGERIAL DECISION SUPPORT SYSTEMS

The following cases describe decision support applications in a food marketing company, a commercial bank, an insurance company, and a financial services company. All these systems were developed by users serving as computer specialists within various functional areas, including production, finance, and marketing.

A Production Planning System

The first case involves a food marketing company that produces food products in regional plants and distributes them to branch warehouses around the country. Two production planning analysts with considerable computer skills designed a decision support system to determine target inventories in branch warehouses. To build this system, the user-developers used FOCUS, a database query language, to access a sales history database consisting of 3.5 million records. Based on the analysis of sales trends of various food products in certain regions, managers developed a sales forecast depicting how much inventory of each product would be needed in each branch warehouse each month. The sales forecast indicated, for example, the number of boxes of spaghetti sauce needed to accommodate sales orders that would be filled by a branch warehouse in the Northeast region.

An example of the sales forecast is shown in Figure 14–4. This report shows the difference, or variance, between the target inventory level for each product and its actual inventory. In the case of regular spaghetti sauce, for example, the variance shows that actual inventory is 9,000 cases less than target inventory. The target inventory established in this report is used as an input into the production plan, and the production planner may want to increase production of regular spaghetti sauce because she knows that the potential demand for the product is greater during the summer months.

Inventory levels are determined for each branch warehouse not only to serve distribution requirements but also to minimize transportation costs. If demand for

Figure 14–4
Forecast of target inventory levels

SALES FORECAST
NORTHEAST REGION
June 1, 1994

PRODUCT CODE	PRODUCT DESC	SALES FORECAST (IN CASES)	TARGET INVENTORY	ACTUAL INVENTORY	VARIANCE
SS101	SPSAUCE-REG	60,000	22,000	13,000	(9,000)
SS102	SPSAUCE-GARLIC	35,000	18,000	27,000	9,000
SS103	SPSAUCE-MUSH	52,000	25,000	20,000	(5,000)
SS104	SPSAUCE-VEG	22,000	15,000	18,000	3,000

spaghetti sauce increased in the Southeast, for example, management would know that target inventory levels for this product should be redistributed to a branch warehouse in the Southeast region. Continuing to maintain high inventory levels in the Northeast warehouse would require shipping goods much too far to accommodate consumer demand.

After the sales forecast and target inventory levels for each branch warehouse were determined, these data became input into planned production requirements for the various plants serving the warehouses. In this way, the cost of excess inventory being produced and shipped to branch warehouses was greatly minimized. The production planning system also minimized distribution costs and produced overall better service to customers.

A Financial Control System

The second case is a financial decision support system developed at a commercial bank. A cost measurement system, designed to provide unit cost data for each of the bank's services, was designed by a functional specialist within the corporate controller's office. These cost data were originally created and used to determine how to price the bank's products (for example, how much to charge for 2,000 wire transfers).

After several months of using the cost measurement system, its developer recognized that its value was potentially greater than originally anticipated. The availability of cost data for each of the bank's products made it possible to allocate the unit costs of the bank's products to expense centers such as lending areas. Because expense centers were aware of the costs of the products they sold, they were able to determine which products provided the highest profit margins. Figure 14–5 shows a profitability analysis of financial services based on unit cost data. For example, if offering traveler's checks was a much more profitable service than providing money orders, bank personnel could demonstrate greater profitability by focusing their sales efforts on marketing traveler's checks. What was originally designed as a monitoring system to store unit cost data became an effective tactical system for marketing the most profitable services.

An International Loan System

A third case depicts a decision support system designed to monitor existing international loan portfolios. Its developer, a computer specialist in the international loan operations department, set up a database of international loan accounts using a database query and reporting language. This database provided loan information, such as interest income and loan balances, by geographical area and by type of obligor. Using the system, users

Figure 14–5
Profitability analysis of financial services

MIDTOWN BRANCH
PROFITABILITY ANALYSIS
MARCH 16, 1994

SERVICE TYPE	NUMBER OF TRANS	TOTAL CHARGES	UNIT COST	TOTAL COST	PROFIT	GROSS MARGIN AS A % OF SALES
MONEY ORDER	12,000	$ 2,160	.13	$1,560	$ 600	28%
WIRE TRANS	120,000	$ 4,800	.20	$2,400	$2,400	50%
TRAV CHECKS	87,000	$ 7,830	.06	$5,250	$2,580	33%
TOTAL	219,500	$14,790		$9,210	$5,580	38%

could extract the names of all obligors with loan balances over a certain amount or within a certain geographical region. A sample query, shown in Figure 14–6, requests the names of all loan accounts with balances over $250,000 in Central American countries.

Although the original purpose of the international loan system was to create timely access to loan account information, the system fulfilled a much more useful purpose. By analyzing current loan balances by type of obligor and by type of credit rating, the user could determine the riskiness of the current loan portfolio. This information could then be used to monitor future loan decisions. For example, if the current loan portfolio showed large outstanding loan balances for accounts in Latin American countries with credit ratings of "B," then it might be risky to loan additional funds to accounts in this area.

The financial decision support systems designed to determine the unit costs of financial services and to monitor the riskiness of loan portfolios were effective tactical systems. Each of these systems was designed to improve the profitability of banking services and international loan operations by providing information that would enable management to allocate resources effectively. These systems were decision support systems because they supported ad hoc query and reporting requirements. In each case, outputs were generated when they were needed, not according to a fixed schedule. Each of these systems was designed to be flexible and changeable so that different questions could be asked. The characteristics of the decision support systems you have learned about in the production planning, financial control, and international loan functions are summarized in Table 14–4.

These case studies illustrate a number of points about the development of decision support systems. First, in all of these examples, relevant databases were identified and constructed. User-friendly database and spreadsheet tools were used to extract and to manipulate these data as needed.

Second, users were responsible for designing these decision support systems. These projects would not have been accomplished by data processing personnel because of their low priority or because of insufficient resources. However, each of these systems supported important business decisions such as production planning, product marketing, and loan applicant screening.

Third, some of these decision support systems were in constant evolution. Most of these projects were initiated by constructing simple databases for query and reporting purposes, but several of them evolved into important analysis systems. For example, the original purpose of the international loan system was to provide easy access to loan

Figure 14–6
A sample query of an international loan database

INTERNATIONAL LOANS
CENTRAL AMERICA
MARCH 1, 1994

ACCT NO	ACCOUNT NAME	CREDIT RATING	LOAN AMOUNT	LOAN BALANCE	YTD INTEREST	OVERDUE AMOUNT
0311	RF CHEMICAL	B	$2,500,000	$1,450,000	$125,000	$ 25,000
0422	DIAZ CONSTR	AA	$1,780,000	$1,700,000	$ 10,500	0
0673	PANAM HOSPITAL	A	$3,325,000	$2,850,000	$ 68,650	$450,000

Table 14–4
Decision support systems

	Food Marketing Company	Commercial Bank	International Loan Operations
Primary users	Production analysts	Financial analysts	Loan analysts
Databases utilized	Sales history	Unit cost data	International loan accounts
Key tasks	Determining target inventory levels for products	Assessing unit costs of financial products and services	Assessing risk of international loan accounts
Software	FOCUS Mainframe-based	Lotus 1-2-3 Microcomputer-based	dBase IV Microcomputer-based

account records. Eventually, the system evolved into an analytical system providing information about the potential riskiness of future loan decisions.

In this section, you have learned about the nature and scope of a variety of decision support systems. In the next section, you will learn about how decision support systems are developed.

THE DEVELOPMENT OF DECISION SUPPORT SYSTEMS

The development of decision support systems requires an **adaptive design** process that involves the interaction of a user and builder with the information system. DSS development starts when a user identifies a problem area and begins to think of information that would contribute to an understanding of it. A model decision support system is built with close cooperation between a builder and a user. This DSS is designed by a builder, tried out by a user, and continually modified based on the user's evaluation. This continuous or iterative process encourages short-lived ad hoc systems that can be junked when they are no longer needed and refined as the user's needs change.

The dynamic relationship among the user, designer, and system is depicted in Keen and Gambino's adaptive design framework, shown in Figure 14–7.[5] This framework illustrates links among the user, designer, and system. The first link is the cognitive loop between the system and the user. The system-user link shows managerial learning as the DSS stimulates changes in the user's problem-solving process. The user-system link illustrates how the user envisions new approaches to problem solving as she uses the system.

The second link is the implementation loop between the user and the designer. The designer is a facilitator who attempts to understand the user's requirements and to customize the system accordingly, as illustrated in the designer-user link. The user, in turn, provides feedback to the designer on needed adaptations, as shown in the user-designer link.

The third loop is the evolution loop, which refers to the continuing evolution of system functions. As managerial learning occurs and personalized uses of the system

[5]Peter G. W. Keen and Thomas J. Gambino, "Building a Decision Support System: The Mythical Man Month Revisited,"in *Building Effective Decxision Support Systems,* eds. R Sprague and E Carlson (Englewood Cliffs NJ: Prentice Hall, 1982).

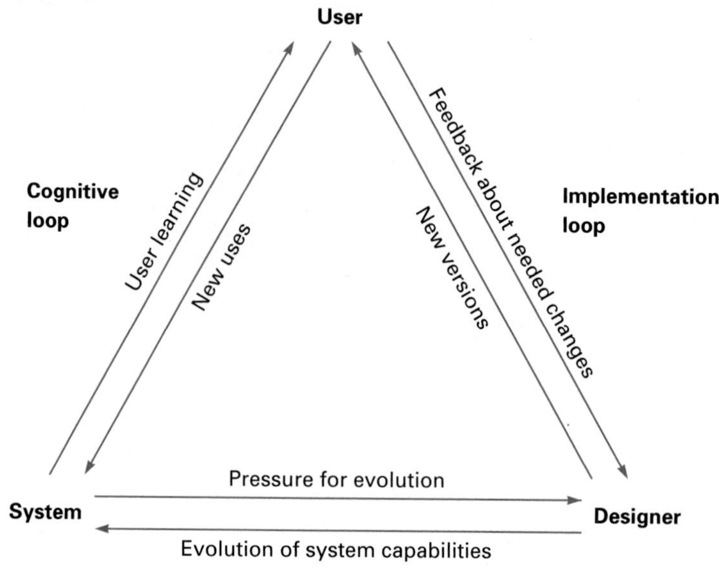

Figure 14–7
Adaptive design framework

Source: Adapted from Peter G. W. Keen and Thomas J. Gambino, "Building a Decision Support System: The Mythical Man Month Revisited," In *Building Effective Decision Support Systems,* eds. R. Sprague and E. Carlson (Englewood Cliffs, N.J.: Prentice Hall, 1982), p. 153.

evolve, pressure for evolution (system-designer link) develops. This pressure results in adding new capabilities to the system, as illustrated by the designer-system loop.

Keen and Gambino's adaptive design framework provides a conceptual view of the DSS development process and the roles involved. The framework illustrates the flexibility of the DSS approach. Users' concepts of the problems they are addressing change as they use their systems. As a result, the actual DSS is likely to differ from the original version. One of the key elements of this process is experimentation because trying new versions provides the learning required for the system to evolve.

The DSS Development Life Cycle

As a user, you will be involved in many phases of the DSS development process. These phases are summarized in Figure 14–8. The first step is *planning,* or diagnosing a problem requiring the development of a decision support system. A user may need information that is not available in weekly or monthly exception reports. Often, users react to concrete, immediate information needs when they recognize a DSS requirement.

Once a need is defined, the user begins to identify relevant approaches to addressing it. This is called *application research.* The user must pay some attention to whether information can be obtained from present information systems, perhaps exploring whether microcomputer-based software or mainframe-based database languages might be possible alternatives to satisfying the need. Vendors and consultants might be considered as well.

During the *analysis* phase, the user considers the overall feasibility of pursuing the project—in technical resources, support requirements, and hardware and software needs. If enough benefits are envisioned to justify developing a prototype or preliminary model of the system, the project moves to the *design* phase, during which system components are specified.

During *system construction,* the technical design is implemented and then *tested* to determine whether the system performs in accordance with its original design. Assuming the system is technically adequate, the designer can determine how well the system satisfies the users' needs during system *evaluation.* The capabilities of the system can be

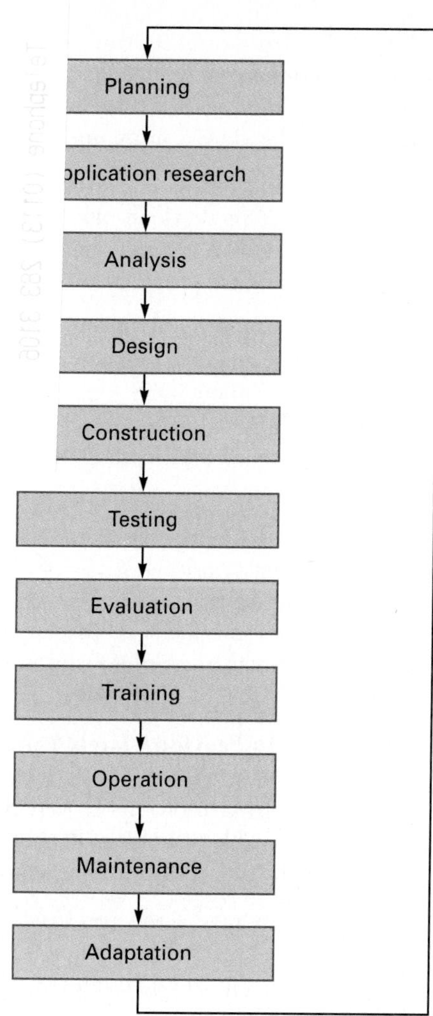

demonstrated to other members of the user community, and top-level managers can be oriented to the system and its features. Actual users of the system must then be *trained* in its structure and operations. Finally, the system is put into operation.

Because decision support systems are constantly modified, *maintenance* is ongoing. Changes are made during *adaptation* that can reinitiate the entire DSS design cycle and the activities already described.

As users are given the tools to develop their own systems, systems designers must respond by providing consulting, training, and ongoing support. Not only must systems analysts be retrained, but also user-developers within functional areas must take on the responsibility of encouraging learning among their peers and maintaining critical departmental systems.

Cost-Justifying Decision Support Systems

Investments in DSS technology, development efforts, and support are growing substantially. Because new versions of decision support systems are constantly evolving, their costs are difficult to quantify. Measuring the benefits of decision support systems also is difficult because many of these benefits are qualitative. Some of these benefits include the following.

The Ability to Examine More Alternatives. Spreadsheet tools make it possible to analyze alternative ways of allocating resources in a business and to visualize the impact of these options on cash flow. Scenarios that would have taken days to construct and analyze can be viewed in minutes.

The Ability to Achieve a Better Understanding of the Business. A DSS can help managers analyze the long-range impact of a new marketing venture or a potential acquisition decision in a reasonable time, making it possible to foresee possible pitfalls and to avoid future problems.

The Ability to Respond Quickly to Unexpected Situations. Confronted with new tax legislation, many companies have to analyze the impact of new requirements on profitability. Without DSS tools, this type of analysis would be time consuming and limited. With DSS, business models can be constructed and quickly adapted to changes in business policy and market share, and new results can be generated in days, not weeks.

The Ability to Carry Out Ad Hoc Types of Reporting and Analysis. Many managers want to ask questions of existing databases and to pull out data relevant to current business operations. For example, a marketing manager can extract data on sales of a new product line to department store customers in the Northeast within minutes rather than waiting for a monthly report that overaggregates these sales data and fails to highlight important market trends.

The Ability to Provide Timely Information for Control of Ongoing Operations. Information from a DSS, for example, can provide a better picture of detailed expenses by company, by division, and by department. A report of energy expenses, broken down by division, enables managers to spot deviations from prior years more quickly and to take remedial action to conserve resources.

The Ability to Save Time and Costs. If a manager takes five hours to make a budget forecast using a spreadsheet when this analysis would have taken 20 hours to complete using a calculator, the time-effectiveness of accomplishing this task improves substantially. The ability to perform "what if?" analyses improves the quality of a budget forecast.

The Ability to Make Better Decisions. DSS systems make it possible to consider issues and alternatives that may not have been explored. Increased depth and sophistication of analysis are possible. Complex issues, such as marketing strategy and personnel productivity, can be explored using relevant data analysis. Access to these data gives managers an opportunity to make better informed decisions and to substantiate the decisions they have made.

In response to the complexity of assessing the benefits of decision support systems, Keen proposes a methodology that addresses the issue of qualitative benefits.[6] **Value analysis,** the methodology he proposes, focuses on the value of decision support systems, not on their costs. Because decision support systems are built in phases, starting with a prototype or model version, the value analysis technique starts with an assessment of the benefits of the prototype system. Working with a prototype keeps the initial investment in a project within a relatively small range.

---

[6]Peter G. W. Keen, "Value Analysis: Justifying Decision Support Systems," *MIS Quarterly* 5, no. 1 (1981), pp. 1–15.

If the benefits of the prototype outweigh its costs, the prototype system is implemented. Then the process of value analysis is applied to the design of the full-blown decision support system. If the perceived benefits of developing a full-blown DSS are greater than the costs of developing the full system, then the full system is built.

Essentially, value analysis permits the user to assess the costs of a system and to determine whether they are outweighed by the value of the perceived benefits. Both the prototype version and the full system are justified in this way. The steps in value analysis are summarized in Table 14–5. The value analysis strategy recognizes DSS development as an investment in business effectiveness with returns that need to be assessed during each phase of development.

THE RISKS OF DECISION SUPPORT SYSTEMS

One of the major motivations behind the development of decision support systems is users' frustration with long systems development cycles, frozen requirements specifications, and unresponsive maintenance procedures. With the availability of fourth-generation languages and microcomputer-based software, managers can design information systems that would not have had high priority because of their departmental scope and limited number of users. One of the major benefits of decision support systems is that users can analyze their own requirements, rather than rely on a systems analyst to understand and to specify these requirements for them.

However, user development has risks. You should be aware of these risks and how to deal with them. The following issues occur when users try to develop their own information systems.

Lack of Quality Assurance

Quality assurance refers to procedures for data validation and testing, documentation, and backup and recovery that are an integral part of a good system. Without adequate validation of input data, output printed on reports may not be correct. Inadequate documentation may result in losing hours spent designing a system. In one organization, for example, a user spent six months developing a system for sales analysis that everyone began to depend on for weekly reports. When the developer suddenly left the firm, the application was lost because no documentation existed. Lack of backup and recovery—

Table 14–5
Summary of value analysis for decision support systems

Stage One: Build Prototype
1. Define operational lists of benefits.
2. Define maximum you would be ready to pay to gain these benefits.
3. Build the prototype version.
Stage Two: Build the Decision Support System
1. Access, revise, and extend the benefits of the prototype version.
2. Establish the full cost of the system.
3. Determine the level of benefits that must be obtained to justify the investment in the full system.
4. Build the full system.
5. Establish its costs and benefits.

Source: Adapted from Peter G. W. Keen, "Value Analysis: Justifying Decision Support Systems," *MIS Quarterly* 5, no. 1 (1981).

another problem—may result in loss of critical data and time-consuming manual rebuilding of these files.

Lack of Data Security

Lack of data security is another issue affecting user-developed decision support systems. Password security for microcomputer-based data management systems may be inadequate or nonexistent, leaving many users to resort to such procedures as key access to hardware or physically locking up diskettes.

Failure to Specify Correct Requirements

Users can visualize their immediate, short-term needs but find it more difficult to understand ongoing or long-term requirements. In one firm, for example, a user failed to keep a log of monthly transactions that was needed for year-end reporting. A systems analyst, serving as a technical expert in systems design, could have recommended that a monthly transaction log be kept and helped the user avoid the problem.

Requirements analysis generally involves validating the logic of a model or calculation used in data analysis. In the design of decision support systems, outputs are constantly modified and the logic used in data analysis often changes. These changes introduce the chance of error, especially if the logic being used is not continually reviewed and documented. If their logic is not validated, computer-based decision support systems may be no better than their paper-and-pencil counterparts of the past.

Failure to Understand Design Alternatives

One of the common problems in user development is a mismatch between software and design requirements. Users in one office, for example, designed a microcomputer database to store information about prospective students without anticipating the growth in file size. After six months, the prospect data file had expanded to close to 100,000 records, and simple operations such as sorting records by zip code were no longer feasible to run on a microcomputer. If a systems analyst had assessed the short- and long-term needs of the users in advance, the feasibility of various design options, including microcomputer, minicomputer, and mainframe approaches, could have been considered.

STRATEGIES FOR BUILDING EFFECTIVE DECISION SUPPORT SYSTEMS

Decision support systems are becoming very important to managers in a variety of organizations so you should understand development practices that will help ensure that decision support systems are designed and used successfully. These practices include the following.

Start with Requirements Analysis

In designing a decision support system, you should work with a systems designer who can assist you in determining your information needs, designing reports, and selecting appropriate methods of analysis. If you don't understand your needs, then all subsequent efforts will be off target.

Select the Best Application Development Approach

During systems design, you should consider the feasibility of several alternatives. You need to decide whether the system should be developed by MIS professionals using traditional methods, by users equipped with fourth-generation tools, or by users with microcomputer-based software. Each of these approaches serves a particular need. You can use microcomputer-based spreadsheet and database packages for many database query and analysis systems. However, if data reside in mainframe-based files, you may need to use mainframe-based database query and reporting languages.

In contrast to personal decision support systems, departmental-level production applications may introduce complex requirements. For these projects you should consider contracting with MIS professionals or with external consultants because rigorous development methods incorporating data validation and testing, controls, and backup and recovery may be needed.

Manage Data Effectively

Data management issues involve data access and integrity. As a user of mainframe-based data, you will probably have access to copies of production data files for making queries and generating reports. MIS professionals are responsible for developing policies governing data access and the downloading of mainframe-based data into local microcomputer-based databases. User consultants may also recommend policies governing the security of data housed in local databases.

Follow Systems Development Guidelines

You should also be aware of practices that will improve the quality of the systems you develop. Experienced systems analysts can review your application and recommend controls, methods of streamlining operations, and appropriate hardware and software. You also need to spend time documenting your design work. At the very least, system documentation should explain the purpose and scope of the system, the database name, the data owner, data definitions, security arrangements, backup and recovery procedures, and program names.

Work with User Computer Analysts

You can obtain valuable assistance from **user computer analysts,** including information center analysts, microcomputer consultants, and office systems analysts. Their primary responsibilities are to train and to provide consulting assistance to users who are developing decision support systems. You can obtain assistance in identifying appropriate hardware and software, in obtaining access to the data you need, and in diagnosing technical problems. You may also want to participate in user groups and to read newsletters that are developed by user support groups.

GROUP DECISION SUPPORT SYSTEMS

Up to now, you have learned about decision support systems that managers use individually to make decisions. However, many decisions occur in groups, and computer-based technology now supports group decision making too. A **group decision support system (GDSS)** is an interactive computer-based system that facilitates the solution of unstructured problems by a set of decision makers working together in a group.

Just like a decision support system, a group decision support system includes a database, a model base, and software supporting group processes. Software might be used to summarize members' ideas, to report votes, to calculate the weights of decision alternatives, and to anonymously record ideas. In the group decision support situation, a group facilitator coordinates the use of the technology in the process of conducting the meeting.

Group decision support can take place in four scenarios: the decision room, the local decision network, teleconferencing, and remote decision making. See Figure 14–9.

The decision room is like a traditional meeting, with the addition of computers. Each member has a computer terminal. Members can interact with each other, both verbally and by computer. A display screen in the front of the room is used to present ideas and to analyze alternatives. Take, for example, a set of executives meeting to make

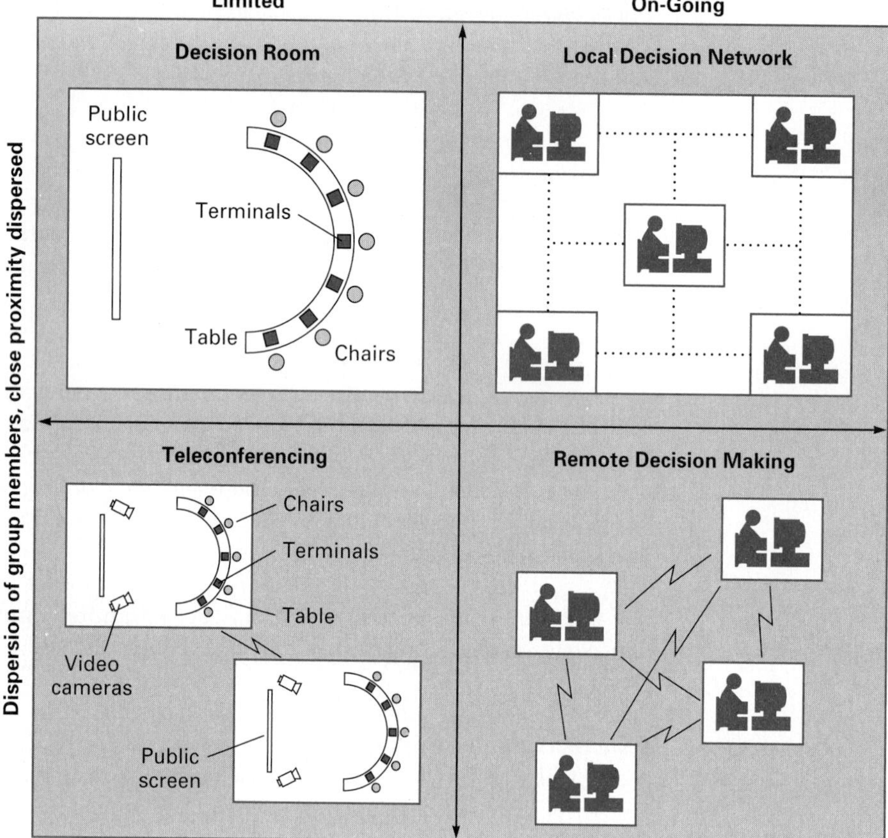

Figure 14–9
Models for group decision support

Source: G. DeSanctis and R.B. Gallupe, "Group Decision Support Systems: A New Frontier," *Database*, Winter–1985, pp. 190–201.

a merger/acquisition decision. Computer-generated information on projected sales, cost constraints, and market statistics may be available while members are discussing personnel and organizational considerations.

The second type of group decision-making scenario is the local decision network. In this situation, the group members are located at workstations in the privacy of their offices. A central processor stores the group decision support software, and the local area network provides intercommunication. At Chemical Bank, one executive used the local decision networking idea to gain insight about fears and anxieties related to the potential merger between Chemical and Manufacturer's Hanover Bank. He instituted "the Rumor Mill," a shared electronic database where employees could express their views. He even took time to answer their questions via the network, thus quieting fears about job loss and circumventing the gossip mill.

The third situation is teleconferencing. Here, decision rooms are located in major cities so that groups can meet with each other. At the University of Minnesota Medical School, for example, scientists meet regularly with their colleagues via videoconferencing. At BASF, a group vice president for carpet products meets with his counterparts at 24 BASF sites via videoconferencing—he and his peers jointly view carpet samples, edit memos, and sign approvals on capital budgeting projects.

In the fourth situation, remote decision-making groups in geographically remote locations are tied together via a long-distance telecommunications network. At Johnson and Higgins, the largest privately held insurance brokerage firm in the world, customized group decision support software is used for electronic problem solving. Electronic forums tie brokers together in remote locations. These electronic forums allow brokers to request help on sticky problems or to volunteer solutions to issues that are troubling other brokers. A request for help goes out to 50 sources and comes back from 50 sources, and everyone benefits from the interaction.

Group Decision Support Software. Group decision support systems are designed to facilitate active participation by all members. The range of software does everything from facilitating the exchange of information among members to providing automated tools for discussion and problem solving. Some of the facilities for group decision support are shown in Table 14–6.

Some of the advanced features that group decision-making software supports are planning, uncertainty reduction, resource allocation, and consensus building. Some systems provide automated tools for meeting management, such as automated parliamentary procedures or automated Roberts' Rules of Order (see Table 14–7).

As you can see, group decision support systems can facilitate planning through the use of electronic brainstorming tools and planning tools such as PERT. Group decision support systems also encourage choice, using tools for weighing preferences, voting, and consensus building. Tools that are used for resolving conflicts include displaying members' opinions and automatic mediation.

Without question, group decision support systems change the nature of meetings. Anonymous input methods encourage people to participate more openly and equally in group discussions. Anonymous communications also reduce the probability that any one member will dominate the discussion and facilitate "democratic" interaction. Members are more willing to suggest controversial views. Because diverse ideas are offered, it is sometimes more difficult to achieve a consensus view in a group decision support environment.

Table 14–6
Basic features of group decision support software (GDSS)

Group Problem	GDSS Feature
Sending and receiving information	Electronic messaging
Display of notes, graphs, and tables	Common viewing screen
Reluctance of some members to speak	Anonymous input
Failure to organize ideas	Summary and display of votes
Failure to quantify preferences	Display of ranking schemes

Table 14–7
Advanced features of GDSS

Group Problem	GDSS Feature
Need for planning and scheduling	Planning models (PERT, CPM)
Decision aids for dealing with uncertainty	Probability assessment models
Decision analytic aids for resource allocation problems	Budget allocation models
Desire to enhance formalized decision procedures	Automated parliamentary procedures

Use of group decision support technology can improve the quality of decisions by encouraging open input of ideas, evaluation of various solutions, and selection of an alternative based upon its merits rather than just a compromise. Participants may sense a more democratic environment in which power and influence are difficult to gain. Overall, the effectiveness of the group's decision making should improve.

ELECTRONIC MEETING SYSTEMS

Another technology that helps groups communicate is the **electronic meeting system.** Electronic meeting systems are designed to help groups organize ideas, draft policies, build consensus, and make effective decisions. Electronic meeting systems also provide an opportunity for individuals to participate equally in discussions. More information is available because more people can participate and because everyone can benefit from access to external information. Another benefit of electronic meeting systems (EMS) is the presence of organizational memory.

A meeting's progress with the use of electronic media depends upon process gains and process losses. Electronic meeting facilities provide process support, process structure, task support, and task structure.

Process support refers to the communications infrastructure that facilitates communications among members. This communications infrastructure enables members to communicate simultaneously and records all electronic comments so that the group has a memory. With the help of anonymity, group members may feel less pressure to conform and may be more likely to challenge others.

Process structure refers to process techniques that affect the timing and content of the communications such as an agenda or a process-oriented methodology such as the Nominal Group Technique. In this strategy, members take turns contributing their ideas, without criticizing the ideas of others. Electronic meeting systems can automate the Nominal Group Technique as well as other strategies.

Task support refers to the information and computation infrastructure for task-related activities, such as external databases and calculators. Task support reduces process losses resulting from incomplete information. An electronic meeting system can provide users with access to information sources and can also create and store an organizational memory.

Task structure refers to the techniques, rules, and models used to analyze task-related information and to gain new insights. Task structure enables the group to analyze task-related information more effectively. Tools for problem modeling and analysis provide automated support for these processes.

Let's take a look at an electronic meeting. Imagine that a group is charged with generating a plan to encourage more European tourists to visit the United States. Sitting in front of a computer terminal, each group member can exchange comments about the issue with other group members. A task support system can provide information about how many European tourists visited last year and the year before. A task structure may provide a framework encouraging group members to consider various regions (e.g., New England) and to identify different markets for tourism (e.g., business versus pleasure travelers). This scenario may produce ideas on the best potential markets for tourism, the regions to highlight, and priorities for each.

In general, electronic meeting systems satisfy some of the same outcomes as group decision support systems. Even though electronic interactions are less rich than face-to-face communications, participants may be more thorough, more objective, and more willing to register their opinions. Results may be more objective, less political, and more likely to contribute to divergence of opinion. In total, the electronic meeting process may offer better solutions because it allows more thorough analysis of alternatives.

Electronic meeting systems have many benefits. Simultaneous communications promote more input into the meeting and reduce the likelihood that a few people will dominate. Anonymity lessens the pressure to conform and encourages members to raise issues more candidly. Meeting "memory" provides a record of what has occurred. Tools for process structure help focus the group on key issues, rather than permitting digressions. Finally, task support systems provide access to external information. With electronic support, meetings can be both more productive and more effective, even though social cues are reduced.

Management Summary

In this chapter you have learned about the purpose and scope of decision support systems. Decision support tools make it possible to construct databases for ad hoc query and reporting of data and to develop models for analyzing these data. Decision support systems must be able to address semistructured and unstructured problems because the decision-making process is usually not known up front and because different managers make decisions in different ways.

One of the most important features of a decision support system is its ability to support the three phases of the decision-making process: intelligence, design, and choice. Intelligence is the awareness that a decision needs to be made. Data on declining sales, increasing bad debt expenses, or rapidly growing student numbers may all support this first phase. Design is the process of identifying and analyzing alternatives. Tools like spreadsheet programs make it possible to evaluate alternative ways of allocating resources and support the design phase. Finally, the selection of an appropriate course of action may be supported by summary statistics or by a graph depicting the preferred alternative.

The DSS design process involves a user, who identifies an information need, and a designer, who develops an initial version of the proposed system and continues to modify it as the user's needs change. According to the adaptive design process, the system continues to evolve as the user gains experience and as the designer continues to incorporate new features into its design.

Cost-justifying decision support systems is difficult because their benefits are often qualitative and because their capabilities continue to evolve. Value analysis is a technique of cost-justifying decision support systems in which the user visualizes the costs and benefits of a prototype version of a decision support system before a full-scale version is attempted. Value analysis is an iterative approach to cost analysis, similar to the design process itself.

As users learn how to develop their own information systems, they need to become concerned with such issues as quality assurance, data validation and testing, backup and recovery, validation of internal logic, and design approach. Greater attention needs to be paid to assessing correct requirements, evaluating alternative design options, and managing data effectively. User support analysts who provide training and support can help users become thoroughly familiar with business requirements and application design techniques.

Key Terms for Managers

adaptive design, **537**
algorithms, **526**
choice, **525**
control aids, **531**
decision support systems (DSS), **528**
design, **525**
electronic meeting systems, **546**
group decision support systems (GDSS), **543**
heuristics, **526**

incrementalizing, **526**
intelligence, **525**
maximizing, **526**
memory aids, **530**
model-based analysis, **528**
personal analysis, **528**
quality assurance, **541**
satisficing, **526**
status access, **528**
user computer analysts, **543**
value analysis, **540**

Review Questions

1. What activities occur during each of the three phases of the decision-making process?
2. Give an example of a semistructured decision and of an unstructured decision.
3. What is an algorithm?
4. What are several attributes of decision makers that influence decision-making strategy?
5. Compare the maximizing and the satisficing strategies for decision making.
6. Which of the following are decision support systems? Explain the reasons for your answers.
   a. A marketing system that provides a weekly sales report, summarized by product line.
   b. A sales prospect database that managers can use to make queries such as "List the names of all prospects in the 63166 zip code."
   c. A personnel information system that provides a listing of all new hires, changes, and terminations at the beginning of each week
   d. A financial system that projects the cash flow impacts of two alternative investment decisions
7. What is a limitation of the exception reporting systems that Alloway and Quillard describe?
8. What is an inquiry system?
9. What are three important features of a decision support system?
10. What information could you use to support the decision-making process involved in selecting a college for potential enrollment? Identify the information that would be helpful in supporting each of these phases of the decision-making process.
    a. Intelligence.
    b. Design.
    c. Choice.
11. Give an example of a memory aid that should be built into a decision support system.
12. Give an example of a control aid that can assist managers in learning how to use decision support software.
13. What is meant by adaptive design?
14. In developing a decision support system, what activities are conducted during the application research phase?
15. What is the role of the systems designer in building a decision support system?

16. Name four types of group decision support systems and describe the characteristics of each.
17. What technologies support electronic meetings?

Questions for Discussion

1. Describe the three phases of decision making with respect to selecting a career.
2. What are three important features of an effective decision support system?
3. Can you think of an application in sales or marketing for the development of a decision support system?
4. Would an information system designed to keep track of maintenance calls on office equipment be an example of a decision support system?
5. Why does the development of a decision support system work best using an adaptive design approach?
6. What are some of the qualitative benefits of decision support systems?
7. What is value analysis?
8. What risks may occur because of lack of quality assurance in building a decision support system?
9. What systems development guidelines should users follow in developing decision support systems?
10. Name several responsibilities of user computer analysts.
11. What are some of the organizational impacts of group decision support systems? How does the decision-making process change when automated tools are used to support groups?
12. How can automated tools make electronic meetings more effective?

Problems

1. **Amalgamated Stores, Inc.** John McDonald is the director of data processing for Amalgamated Stores, Inc., a chain of 35 discount stores with locations in the West and Southwest. Recently he has received a number of complaints from store managers that monthly sales reports do not provide meaningful information. The store managers want to be able to analyze sales trends for various product lines on a timely basis. They receive weekly sales summary reports, but they want a more responsive output.

   John has been exploring some options. Should he hire a consultant? Should he buy microcomputers? Should he hire more programmers to redesign the existing sales summary reporting systems to be more responsive to the needs of managers? Should he acquire tools that would enable managers to extract the information they need themselves?

   Which option would you choose? Explain the reasons for your choice. In your answer, you may want to examine the advantages and disadvantages of some of the options given.

2. **Purcell Industries.** Bob Lobdell, a financial analyst at Purcell Industries, would like to develop a profitability report showing the profit margins on sales for various

product lines on a weekly basis. Current MIS systems show sales by product line this month versus last month, but existing reports do not calculate the profit margin on sales for various products. Bob believes that the profit margins on certain product lines are greater than the profit margins on others. The system he proposes would give sales managers information on product profitability and would enable them to promote the most profitable products.

Bob wants to build a decision support system to examine product profitability. What steps should he take to develop such a system? What kind of assistance will he need?

3. **United National Insurance Company.** In the marketing department of a major insurance company, Joan Phillips, a user-developer, set up a system with information about prospective insurance customers. The system made it possible to query the database to extract information about customers with certain characteristics. It also made it possible to generate mailing labels for various mailings to these customers. Phillips also developed management reports summarizing the number of inquiries about various types of insurance programs.

   Salespeople, clerical employees, and managers used the system extensively. After the system had been in operation for about six months and many users had grown dependent on it, Joan Phillips left to take a position in another firm. Soon after, someone tried to select customers in a certain ZIP code from the database but was unable to do so. Though this capability had been built into the system, no one had been trained to select records with specific characteristics.

   As time went on, the users of the system could not figure out how to perform many of its functions. Eventually, a consultant was brought in to study the system and to develop several new reports that were needed. How could the situation in this case have been avoided?

4. **A job selection decision.** Demonstrate your understanding of the decision-making process by outlining the approach you would take in making a decision about a prospective job as a management trainee. Use your own preferences to establish criteria for making the decision. You have three offers from which to choose. Each is described below.

   The first offer is for the position of management trainee with a large manufacturing firm in a major metropolitan area. The firm has an excellent training program that lasts about six months. The position offers a competitive starting salary and good raises with annual reviews. After two to three years at the corporate office, most junior managers have opportunities to transfer to first-line division-level management positions. The job requires a minimum of travel during the first two to three years and travel mainly between division offices and the home office after that.

   The second offer is for a position as a junior management consultant with a well-established consulting firm in a major metropolitan area. The firm offers a high starting salary and profit sharing. The position requires between 50 percent and 70 percent travel to clients' offices throughout the Midwest. Advancement is based on performance and entrepreneurial skill, and successful consultants have an opportunity to earn six-figure incomes within five to seven years of being employed with the firm. The firm employs between 35 and 40 professionals, and there is no formally established training program.

   The third offer is for a position as a management trainee with a mid-sized organization in the high-technology telecommunications business. The firm is located in a small city of approximately 350,000 people. It offers a good starting salary and a chance for participating in an exciting high-technology sales environment. Training includes on-the-job tutorials and one to two weeks of workshops during the year. Moderate travel is involved to regional clients. The firm is in a very competitive industry, and the job potential depends on its ability to provide state-of-the-art products, effective marketing, and excellent service.

CASES

1. **Universal Widgets, Inc. (A).** Following are extracts from four different reports that are currently produced at Universal Widgets, Inc.

REPORT 11: Sales Report

		Sales by Region					
Product	**Price**	**NE**	**SE**	**Central**	**West**	**Total Units**	**Dollar Totals**
Widgets	80	120	60	130	90	400	32,000

REPORT 44: Production Report

		Quantity			
Product Code	**Description**	**Plan**	**Actual**	**Unit MFG Cost**	**Unit PNT Cost**
303-B-AL	Black alloy widget	100	120	20	4
303-B-FE	Black iron widget	100	100	20	4
303-N-AL	Natural alloy widget	200	240	20	0
303-R-FE	Red iron widget	120	140	20	8

REPORT 77: Materials Purchasing Report

Material Name	Quantity	Unit Cost	Budget	Variance
Iron billets	240	20	6,000	1,500
Aluminum rods	400	30	10,000	2,000
Paint	500	4	2,000	0

REPORT 98: Profitability Report

		Cost				
Product	**Sales ($)**	**MFG($)**	**PNT($)**	**MAT($)**	**Profit(s)**	**PCT of Sales**
Widgets	32,000	12,000	2,000	15,600	2,400	7.5

Notes to the Reports

1. Alloy widgets are made out of aluminum rod, one rod per widget.
2. Iron widgets are made out of iron, one billet per widget.
3. If a widget is to be painted any color at all, it must first be painted black; every coat of paint uses $4 in paint.

Further Notes

1. Actual widget sales by type were

Black iron	0
Black alloy	100
Red iron	60
Natural alloy	240

2. During the last sales period, 550 widgets were sold. Profit as a percent of sales was 9.6 percent.

Instructions: Obviously, Universal Widgets is having problems. As a manager who receives the four reports shown, George Phillips does not have a good idea of how well widgets are doing, what the most profitable lines are, and what the least profitable lines are.

Construct a mock-up of a report (or reports) that will help George better understand widget profitability and make decisions about sales and production. Use your own judgment about what the report should contain. You may use data that is on one or more of the current reports. In creating the mock-up of your report, try to use as much real data in constructing the new report(s) as possible. Explain why you feel the report(s) you propose will be helpful to the manager.

2. **Universal Widgets, Inc. (B).** Use the mock-up of the report you designed in Case 1 to develop a spreadsheet. Using the spreadsheet, develop another version of the profitability report using different sales figures. The new sales figures are:

Black iron	100
Black alloy	50
Red iron	120
Natural alloy	100

What recommendations would you make about the sales and marketing strategy for various lines and for inventory management?

3. **Database project.** In this project, you will use the same database you used in the database project in Chapter 11. You will be using the Employee, Seminar, Instruct, Register, and Schedule files stored on your data disk.

Make the following updates to the instructor (Instruct) file. Please print the file after all the updates have been made.

Update 1: Add the following records to the instructor file.

IID:	453653221	485667890	344213445
ILNAME:	PARSONS	BLAKELY	COLEMAN
IMI:	B	D	M
IFNAME:	MARY	LOIS	WILLIAM
IJOBTITLE:	SALES MANAGER	SALES TRAINER	CONSULTANT
ISTR:	23 BROADVIEW	33 HILLSIDE	21 PARK TERRACE
ICITY:	ST. LOUIS	ST. LOUIS	EDWARDSVILLE
ISTATE:	MO	MO	MO
IZIP:	63105	63121	62026

Update 2: Delete CAROLE MCINTYRE from the instructor file.
Update 3: Make the following changes to the instructor file.
Change the address of PATRICIA JENKINS to 25 AUDUBON.
Change the phone number of GEORGE PHILLIPS to 6184356778.
Change the job title of SUSAN KELLY to PERSONNEL MANAGER.
Print the answers to the following queries:

Query 1: List the names of all instructors with the job title of Training Specialist.
Query 2: List the names and phone numbers of all employees who can speak Spanish and who live in Illinois.
Query 3: List the seminar IDs and room numbers for all seminars to be offered during Fall 1991.
Query 4: List the seminar IDs and seminar descriptions of all Management Training seminars.

Produce a report listing the names and phone numbers of all employees who are in seminars during Winter 1988 and have not yet paid their fees.

4. **Computer-based sales management.** In his article, "Computerized Sales Management,"[7] G. David Hughes describes spreadsheet applications that can enable the sales manager to determine the potential of various accounts and to test different assumptions about account management. In this exercise, you will learn about several spreadsheets and assess the impact of changing assumptions.

Spreadsheet 1: Sales forecast

One of the first questions sales managers must address is "What is the potential of an account?" In Spreadsheet 1, you should enter in the figures shown in brackets, which are the account requirements for the previous period, estimated growth rates per period, sales for the previous period, estimated share points for the next period, and an estimate of the number of calls necessary to achieve these share points.

a. Use the spreadsheet program to estimate the total requirements for the forecast period, the share points for the previous period, company sales, and sales per call. Your output should match the output shown as Spreadsheet 1.

[7]G. David Hughes, "Computerized Sales Management," *Harvard Business Review*, March–April 1983, pp. 102–11.

FOR I PERIOD(S)

ACCOUNTS

	CENTRAL MFG. CO.	WESTERN TOOL INC	NORTHERN ENG. LTD	OTHER ACCTS.	TOTALS
TOTAL REQUIREMENTS LAST PER	[500]	[1230]	[713]	[6245]	8708
ESTIMATED GROWTH/PERIOD	[1.2]	[1.95]	[.95]	[1.00]	1.01
FORCSTD. TOTAL REQRMTS./PER.	600	1312	677	6245	8835
OUR SALES LAST PERIOD	[200]	[125]	[214]	[1249]	1788
OUR SHARE POINTS LAST PER.	40.00	10.00	30.01	20.00	20.24
FORECASTS					
SHARE POINTS	[47.50]	[20.00]	[30.00]	[20.00]	22.63
SALES ($000)	285	262	203	1250	2000
CALLS/PERIOD	[11]	[10]	[20]	[839]	880
SALES/CALL ($000)	25.91	26.25	10.16	1.49	2.27

Note: Planner enters figures in brackets; computer produces in other figures.

Spreadsheet 1: Sales forecast

As you can see from the resulting model, the projections made into the future show that the Central Manufacturing account will generate more sales per call than the other accounts because of its higher growth rate.

Spreadsheet 2: Account Contribution and Product Mix

The sales manager also wants to know which accounts buy the highest-margin products because those accounts may be most profitable. Spreadsheet 2 shows the profit margins on different products, including axles, bars, clutches, and drums. Account profitability also depends upon the product mix an account buys. As you can see, 50 percent of Central Manufacturing's purchases are axles, the lowest-margin product. In contrast, Northern Engineering buys mostly clutches and drums, which have profit margins of .3 and .4 respectively. As a result, Northern Engineering is the most profitable account, based upon its product contribution.

a. Develop Spreadsheet 2, Account Contribution and Product Mix, to generate the output shown below. You will need to enter the data in brackets, including the product margins and the product mix ratios. The other data can be generated by using formulas within the spreadsheet.

FOR I PERIOD(S)

SALES FORCST ($000)		CENTRAL MFG.	285	WESTERN TOOL	262	NORTHERN ENG.	203	OTHER ACCOUNTS	1249	TOTALS	2000
PRODUCT	PRODUCT MARGIN	PRODUCT MIX	CONTRIB ($000)	PRODUCT MIX	CONTRIB ($000)	PRODUCT MIX	CONTRIB ($000)	PRODUCT MIX	CONTRIB ($000)	PRODUCT MIX	CONTRIB ($000)
AXLES	[.1]	[.5]	14.25	[.3]	7.87	[.1]	2.03	[.3]	37.47	0.31	61.63
BARS	[.2]	[.3]	17.10	[.3]	15.75	[.1]	4.06	[.3]	74.94	0.28	111.85
CLUTCHES	[.3]	[.1]	8.55	[.3]	23.62	[.5]	30.48	[.2]	74.94	0.23	137.60
DRUMS	[.4]	[.1]	11.40	[.1]	10.50	[.3]	24.38	[.2]	99.92	0.18	146.20
TOTAL CONTRIBUT		1.00	51.30	1.00	57.75	1.00	60.96	1.00	287.27	1.00	457.28
CONTB.%OF SALES			18.00		22.00		30.00		23.00		22.87
CALLS/PERIOD			11		10		20		839		880
CONTB/CALL ($000)			4.66		5.77		3.05		0.34		0.52

Spreadsheet 2: Account contribution and product mix

b. Modify the product mixes for Central in the spreadsheet:

Axles	.1
Bars	.1
Clutches	.4
Drums	.4

How does this change Central's total contribution?
Which firm now makes the greatest contribution to sales?

Using this spreadsheet, the sales manager can allocate resources to maximize account profitability. For example, he can develop strategies to encourage certain accounts to buy higher-margin products. Because Central Manufacturing has a high growth rate, it should be encouraged to buy higher-margin products.

Spreadsheet 3: Account Costs and Contribution

Different accounts have different costs. The sales manager needs to know which accounts are more costly in terms of freight, inventory, technical services, advertising, and interest on accounts receivable. The net contribution of an account depends upon these costs. Even if an account purchases a high percentage of higher-margin products, high account costs may lower its overall net contribution and diminish its profitability.

Spreadsheet 3, Account Costs and Contribution, shows how account costs can factor into the net contribution of various accounts. As you can see from the spreadsheet, the Western Tool account makes a greater net contribution than Northern Engineering ($33,590 versus $29,420) because Western Tool has lower account costs.

In the lower right portion of the spreadsheet, you will see that 95.34 percent of the sales calls are generating only 58.21 percent of the net contribution. Most of the profits are coming from the three large accounts. Perhaps the sales manager should reallocate these calls to the accounts with greatest potential. Other methods, such as telemarketing and direct mail, might be used to distribute information to many of the other, smaller accounts.

a. Develop spreadsheet 3, Accounts Costs and Contribution. You can enter the data shown in the brackets and develop formulas for the other cells. As you can see, the average cost per sales call is $53. Your output should match the output shown here.

b. Change the spreadsheet to reflect different account costs for Western Tool, as follows:

Freight	13.00
Tech Svc	5.00

How does this change their net contribution? Which firm now makes the greatest net contribution?

As you can see from these spreadsheets, the sales manager can use a number of models to determine the potential profitability of each account. These models can be continually adjusted to reflect market conditions and account characteristics. These spreadsheets are invaluable tools for supporting decisions on how to allocate resources most effectively.

FOR I PERIOD(S)

	CENTRAL MFG.		WESTERN TOOL		NORTHERN ENG.		OTHER ACCOUNTS		T O T A L S	
	ISALES	$(000)	ISALES	$(000)	ISALES	$(000)	ISALES	$(000)	ISALES	$(000)
SALES FCST. ($000)	100.00	285	100.00	262	100.00	203	100.00	1249	100.00	2000
ACCT-PROD CONTRIB.	18.00	51.30	22.00	57.75	30.00	60.96	23.00	287.27	22.87	457
ACCOUNT COSTS										
FREIGHT (DIRECT)	[1.00]	2.85	[3.00]	7.87	[6.00]	12.19	[3.00]	37.47	3.02	60
INVENT. (IMPUTED)	[3.00]	8.55	[4.00]	10.50	[2.00]	4.06	[1.30]	16.24	1.97	39
ACT REC (IMPUTED)	[3.00]	8.55	[2.00]	5.25	[4.00]	8.13	[3.00]	37.47	2.97	59
TEC SVC (DIRECT)	[1.00]	2.85	[0.00]	0.00	[1.00]	2.03	[1.00]	12.49	0.87	17
ADV/PRO (DIRECT)	[0.00]	0.00	[0.00]	0.00	[2.00]	4.06	[1.00]	12.49	0.83	17
TOTAL ACCOUNT COST	8.00	22.80	9.00	23.62	15.00	30.48	9.30	116.16	9.65	193
PERSONAL SELLING										
COST/CALL ($000)		[.053]		[.053]		[.053]		[.053]		
CALLS/ACCOUNT		11		10		20		839		890
SALES COST/ACCT.	0.20	.583	0.20	.53	0.52	1.06	3.56	44.47	2.33	.47
TOTAL MKTG. COSTS	8.20	23.38	9.20	24.15	15.52	31.54	12.86	160.62	11.99	240
NET CONTRIBUTION	9.90	27.92	12.90	33.59	14.48	29.42	10.14	126.65	10.98	218
% OF TOTAL CONTRB.	12.83		15.44		13.52		58.21		100.00	
% OF TOTAL CALLS	1.25		1.14		2.27		95.34		100.00	
NET CONTRB./CALL $000		2.54		3.36		1.47		0.15		0.25

Spreadsheet 3: Account costs and contribution

Selected References and Readings

Alloway, Robert, and Judith Quillard. "User Managers' Systems Needs." *MIS Quarterly* 7, no. 2 (1983), pp. 27–41.

Carlson, Eric D. "An Approach for Designing Decision Support Systems." In *Building Effective Decision Support Systems.* eds. R Sprague and E Carlson. Englewood Cliffs, NJ: Prentice Hall, 1982.

Davis, Gordon. "Caution: User-Developed Systems Can Be Dangerous to Your Organization." MISRC Working Paper 82–04. Minneapolis: Management Information Systems Research Center, University of Minnesota, February 1984.

Dennis, A.; J. George; L. Jessup; J. Nunamaker; and D. Vogel. "Information Technology to Support Electronic Meetings." *MIS Quarterly,* December 1988, pp. 591–624.

DeSanctis, G., and R. B. Gallupe. "A Foundation for the Study of Group Decision Support Systems." *Management Science* 33, no. 5 (May 1987), pp. 589–609.

DeSanctis, G., and R. B. Gallupe. "Group Decision Support Systems: A New Frontier." *Database,* Winter 1985, pp. 190–201.

Gorry, G. Anthony, and Michael S. Scott Morton. "A Framework for Management Information Systems." *Sloan Management Review* 13, no. 1 (1971), pp. 55–70.

Keen, Peter G. W. "Value Analysis: Justifying Decision Support Systems." *MIS Quarterly* 5, no. 1 (1981), pp. 1–15.

Keen, Peter G. W., and Thomas J. Gambino. "Building a Decision Support System: The Mythical Man Month Revisited." *Building Effective Decision Support Systems.* ed. R. Sprague and E. Carlson. Englewood Cliffs, NJ: Prentice Hall, 1982.

LaPlante, Alice. "TeleConfrontationing." *Forbes ASAP,* September 13, 1993, pp. 111–126.

MacGrimmon, K. R., and R. N. Taylor. "Decision Making and Problem Solving." In *Handbook of Industrial and Organizational Psychology,* ed. M. D. Dunnette, pp. 1,397–1,453. Chicago: Rand McNally, 1976.

Meador, C. Lawrence, and Peter G. W. Keen. "Setting Priorities for DSS Development." *MIS Quarterly* 8, no. 2 (1984), pp. 117–129.

Mills, Chester. "The Information Center." *DRS Journal* 1, no. 1 (1983), pp. 1–104.

Mintzberg, H.; D. Raisinghani; and A. Theoret. "The Structure of 'Unstructured' Decision Processes." *Administrative Science Quarterly* 21 (June 1976), pp. 246–75.

Nunamaker, J. F.; A. Dennis; J. Valacich; D. Vogel; and J. George. "Electronic Meeting Systems to Support Group Work." *Communications of the ACM* 34, no. 7 (July 1991), pp. 40–61.

Rockart, John. "The CEO Goes On-Line." *Harvard Business Review,* January–February 1982, pp. 82–88.

Rockart, John; and Michael Treacy. "Executive Information Support Systems." Sloan Working Paper 1167–80. Cambridge: Center for Information Systems Research, Massachusetts Institute of Technology, April 1981.

Simon, Herbert A. *The New Science of Management Decision.* New York: Harper & Row, 1960, pp. 1–8.

Using Artificial Intelligence and Expert Systems

Chapter Outline

MANAGER'S VIEW

New technologies are being introduced daily, and many of these technologies affect the working lives of managers and professional workers. Throughout this book you've learned about the characteristics and uses of information technology. In this chapter, you'll learn about new technology opportunities that will dramatically affect your work and the work of others. These technologies include artificial intelligence and expert systems.

ARTIFICIAL INTELLIGENCE AND EXPERT SYSTEMS

Artificial intelligence (AI) is concerned with the creation of computer programs that do things that require intelligence. In other words, artificial intelligence means programming a computer to perform activities that if done by a person would be thought to require intelligence. The field of artificial intelligence includes the areas of natural-language processing, robotics, machine vision, and expert systems.

Natural-language processing means programming computers to understand language. Using English, for example, a bank customer could ask a computer "What is my bank balance?" and the computer would respond with the proper amount. The problem with natural-language processing systems is that English can be unclear. For example, if a traveler asked a natural-language system "What is the temperature in New York?" the computer would have to know if the traveler meant New York state or New York City. Other English statements, such as "We saw the ship with a telescope," can be interpreted in several ways and cause further natural-language processing problems.

Another application of artificial intelligence is **robotics.** Robots can be programmed to handle specialized tasks such as cutting, drilling, painting, and welding. They are particularly good at performing the same motions, again and again, day after day. They can also be used to perform dangerous or difficult tasks that humans prefer not to do.

In Japanese factories, robots have been put on the assembly line to assemble copiers, automobiles, cameras, and electronic equipment. They are also being introduced into the factories of such American manufacturers as IBM and General Dynamics Corporation. General Dynamics, for example, uses robots to drill holes and to insert rivets in its F-16 aircraft. Other manufacturers view robotics as key to the improvement of manufacturing productivity in the 1990s.

Machine vision, another application of artificial intelligence, has been used to improve the capabilities of robots. For instance, robots with machine vision in an electronics assembly plant can take a snapshot of the circuit board being worked on and then insert components in the proper place. Robots also use machine vision systems to determine where to insert rivets in Ford trucks on the assembly line. The major limitation of machine vision at the present time is that it can handle only very specific tasks.

Expert systems development is the application of artificial intelligence that is having the greatest impact on the business community. In Chapter 14, you learned how managers use decision support systems to analyze information for problem solving. An expert system differs from a decision support system in that it uses rules based on "expert" knowledge to solve problems. An expert system needs to be given a great deal of high-quality, specific knowledge about a problem area. When in use, the expert system acts like an expert consultant, asking for information, applying this information to the rules it has learned, and drawing conclusions.

THE CHARACTERISTICS OF EXPERT SYSTEMS

An expert system is composed of a *knowledge base,* an *inference engine,* a *knowledge acquisition subsystem,* and an *explanation subsystem.* A schematic diagram of the components of an expert system is shown in Figure 15–1.

The Knowledge Base

The **knowledge base** contains the information and the "rules of thumb" that the expert system uses to make decisions. This information should represent high-level expertise gained from top experts in the field. In many expert systems, knowledge is represented

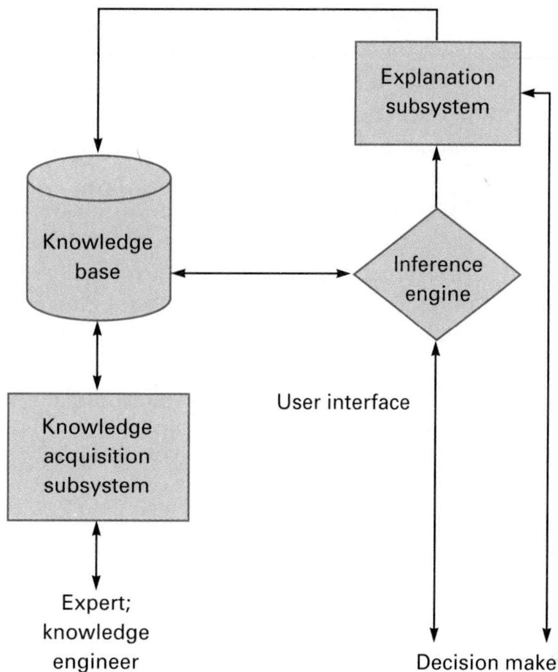

Figure 15–1 The components of an expert system

using rules. An example of a rule is "If Mobil Oil stock drops below $150, then buy 1,000 shares." Most decisions cannot be based on applying a single rule, however. In the case of buying the Mobil Oil stock, other related questions may have to be asked, such as "Do I have enough money?" or "Can the money be obtained from selling another stock?"

Depending on the nature of the decision, the expert system will use different rules. These rules are applied in a different order in different decisions. For example, a simple expert system may include 40 rules. Decision One may use rules 1, 3, 6, and 7 and Decision Two may use rules 6, 3, 12, and 22. Each time a rule is executed, a change in the database is triggered, new questions are asked, and new rules are applied.

An expert system is quite different from a data processing system, even though both may use IF/THEN logic. In a data processing system, the data structures are defined and programmed code is used to express procedures. These procedures are executed in the same way and in the same order on all the data that are processed. In contrast, an expert system does not execute its rules in the same order. When an expert system receives input data, it selects the rules that apply to the problem. As it asks the user additional questions, it learns more about the situation and applies further rules.

For example, a manufacturer has developed an expert system to diagnose potential failures in an automobile's transmission system. The user may key in information about the problem, and the system may respond with a series of questions. If the user asks, "Can it be repaired in two hours?" the system may have to check to see what parts are available and how long it will take to make the repair to recommend a course of action.

The Inference Engine

The **inference engine** is the "central processing unit" of the expert system. The inference engine conducts the dialogue with the user, asking for information and applying it. It uses the knowledge base to draw conclusions for each situation. The structure of the inference engine depends on the nature of the problem and the way knowledge is represented in the expert system.

The inference engine represents both the knowledge base and the procedures to be used for a particular application. The inference engine contains an interpreter that decides how to apply rules to infer new knowledge. It also contains a scheduler that determines the order in which the rules should be applied. An example of an inference engine is Texas Instruments' Personal Consultant.

The Knowledge Acquisition and Explanation Subsystems

Most expert systems continue to evolve over time. New rules can be added to the knowledge base by using the **knowledge acquisition subsystem.** The process of developing an expert system involves building a prototype using a simple problem and continually refining this prototype until the expert system is perfected. As the system matures, new rules may be added and others deleted. The knowledge acquisition subsystem makes this process possible.

The **explanation subsystem** explains the procedures that are being used to reach a decision. In this way, the user can keep track of the methods being used to solve the problem and can understand how the decision is reached.

HOW AN EXPERT SYSTEM WORKS

Knowledge is represented in an expert system in the form of rules or in the form of frames. Rule-based systems consist of sets of rules (IF/THEN) which describe how knowledge is used to reach a conclusion. Frame-based systems are frames, or networks of nodes, that are organized in a hierarchy to represent knowledge.

Rule-Based Systems

As you recall, the knowledge base of a rule-based system consists of rules (for example, IF/THEN) and a database that is continually updated as the problem is being solved. An example of how an ignition-system fault-diagnosis system for an automobile would work will give you an idea of how an expert system operates. Although automobiles today do not have this type of expert system, you may find it to be a feature of future cars.

In our example, the expert system continually cycles through a series of rules to determine if a problem exists. If the temperature in the ignition system is too high, if gas is vaporizing too soon, if the engine is firing too soon, or if the engine is running roughly, the system is alerted. To determine such problems, the system uses data about temperature, air pressure, and voltage to the cylinder.

If the temperature in the ignition system is too high, for instance, the car self-corrects this problem by turning on a fan. If this doesn't work, the ignition data (for example, gas vaporizing, and so on) are reviewed again. The expert system knows that the first corrective action—turning on the fan—did not work, and so it continues through the rules until it flashes on a light to warn the driver about insufficient fluid levels.

The major characteristics of an expert system are summarized in Table 15–1. An expert system is designed to achieve a *goal.* In the case of the ignition-system fault-diagnosis system, the goal is to avoid ignition problems. The *domain* is the mechanics of an automobile ignition system. The *task* is the diagnosis and correction of ignition-system faults. Information about temperature, air pressure, and voltage to the engine's cylinder provides *input* to the system, and procedures or messages that are used to correct the problem are its *output.*

The **paradigm** refers to the problem-solving model that the system applies to diagnose and correct ignition-system faults. The knowledge base includes the rules that consist of data and procedures relevant to the problem. The database is continually updated with new information about the problem. For example, when the fan did not correct the problem, the database was updated to indicate this.

Table 15–1
Characteristics of an expert system

Characteristic	Definition
Goal	Reason for building the system
Domain	General area of application
Task	Specific task the system is to accomplish
Input	Data needed to accomplish the task
Output	Results of the system
Paradigm	Conceptual problem-solving model used to structure the system
Tools	Software environment in which the system is implemented
Methodology	Method used to build the system

The **tools** describe the software that is used to build an expert system. This software includes the knowledge-acquisition subsystem, the explanation subsystem, the knowledge base, and the inference engine. Finally, the **methodology** used to build an expert system, knowledge engineering, uses a **prototyping** approach in which rules are developed, applied, and reviewed. You'll learn more about the knowledge engineering process in a later section.

Frame-Based Systems

A frame-based system represents knowledge using a network of nodes. Each node represents a concept that may be described by attributes and values associated with the node. A frame is a collection of facts and rules about a thing or concept that the computer needs to know. A frame describing the unit *Ozzie Smith* would tell the computer that he is a person, that he is a baseball player, that he belongs to the St. Louis Cardinals, and that he plays in the National League.

A frame might look like a fact sheet. In building a frame, the knowledge engineer decides what kinds of information about a unit might be valuable to the program. These information categories can be typed in as a list, and each category can be filled with a value. For example, a frame for a unit EATING might contain the following values:

EATING:
WHAT HAPPENS WHEN DELAYED: HUNGER
PERFORMED BY: ANIMALS
THINGS CONSUMED: FOOD
MORE GENERAL PROCESS: CONSUMING

Units can also be interrelated. The unit SLEEPING may also be a bodily function. The computer needs to know that both sleeping and eating are part of the unit BODILY FUNCTIONS. This is the same thing as telling the computer that Bob and Paul are neighbors and that Bob's house is in Texas. If the computer knows that Bob's house is in Texas, it will probably know that Paul's house is there too.

How an Expert System Differs from a Conventional Information System

Expert systems differ from conventional information systems in four ways. First, an expert system must demonstrate expertise—it must achieve levels of performance that a human expert can achieve. Second, an expert system must be able to represent knowledge symbolically. A symbol may be a product, a defendent, or a electric motor. The expert system must also be able to depict relationships among symbols, such as "a product is defective."

Box 15–1 CYC: The Intelligent Computer

By the time you are five years old, you have learned how to use a knife and fork, what dogs and cats are, and where the state of Texas is. But teaching a computer these things is a difficult challenge.

Doug Lenat, a computer scientist, plans to teach a computer named CYC, as in en-CYC-lopedia, everything the average adult knows, even though no computer has ever absorbed the knowledge of the average four-year-old. A computer cannot answer simple questions such as "What is a flower?" or "Who is taller—a father or his two-year-old son?"

To accomplish his goal, Lenat must equip CYC with 100 million bits of general information. After CYC's basic knowledge base is in place, Lenat claims that CYC will understand English well enough to teach itself more by reading newspapers and magazines.

The most difficult challenge is finding a way to represent everyday knowledge so that the computer can make use of it. Each piece of information has to be spoon-fed to CYC in just the right form. CYC receives knowledge in the form of frames. As you learned in this chapter, a frame is a collection of facts and rules that tells CYC what it needs to know about a "unit," which is a particular thing or concept. For example, a frame describing the unit *George Washington* would say that it is an example of the unit Person, that he was a U.S. president, and that he belonged to the Federalist Party. A frame looks like a fact sheet containing information about a particular unit.

Sometimes CYC makes decisions using several frames at once. If one of CYC's frames tells it that the Civil War took place between 1861 and 1865, and another frame tells it that the Battle of Vicksburg took place in 1864, then CYC will gather that Vicksburg was a Civil War battle.

CYC uses default logic. For example, CYC may learn that mammals give birth to "live" young. If CYC learns that platypuses are mammals, and that a platypus lays eggs, it must be taught that this is an exception to the birth rule.

In making decisions, CYC has to ignore irrelevant or unrelated information. "When we're deciding whether to lock our car," Lenat notes, "we don't ask ourselves how many humps a camel has or what we had for dinner." CYC has a way of focusing on relevant information. If we ask it a question about freeways, it will search through frames about freeways, roads, and cars long before coming to frames on camels and food.

CYC can try to fill in incomplete information, too. If told that a person has voted and that that person's father is 40 years old, CYC might guess that the voter is 19 or 20. This is because CYC knows that the voting age is 18, and also that if a person is much older than 20, he is not likely to have a 40-year-old parent.

Bringing CYC up to speed in a number of areas is one of the most difficult challenges ever to be addressed by artificial intelligence researchers. Even deciding what to teach CYC is a complex task. Lenat and his team couldn't teach CYC what a truck is, for example, without first teaching it about motion, cars, and wheels.

They started out by picking random sentences and trying to figure out everything the computer needed to know to decipher them. One such sentence was: "Napoleon died in 1821; Wellington was saddened." Explaining this seven-word sentence to CYC required two months of

---

Third, an expert system must be able to handle difficult problems, using complex rules. In other words, it must work in-depth to simulate the reasoning of an expert problem-solver and to produce useful solutions. Fourth, the expert system must demonstrate self-knowledge—it must be able to examine its own reasoning and to estimate the accuracy of its own conclusions. The system uses its explanation facility to explain how it arrived at its answers. Even though an expert system will eventually make mistakes, its developers can work toward correcting these mistakes because the assumptions used in its knowledge-based programs are explicitly stated in code.

The Kinds of Problems an Expert System Can Solve

Expert systems can be designed to solve certain types of problems: problems that have a specific scope, lend themselves to a particular type of analysis, and draw upon available human expertise.

explaining such concepts as life, death, communication, and human emotions. Every bit of knowledge that CYC assimilates makes it easier to teach the next bit of knowledge. For example, if the researchers wanted to teach CYC what a tiger is, they could call up what it knew about lions and cheetahs and make a few changes.

Lenat and his team hope to be able to teach CYC an ontology, or basic worldview, through which it can make sense of reality. Then they plan to pour millions of bits of knowledge into CYC so that it can understand actual activities, objects, and events. As part of its worldview, CYC must be taught abstract representations for such things as time. Time was explained in terms of 50 different relationships between events. Physical objects were broken down into things that were countable, such as marbles, and things that were stuff, like jello or peanut butter.

After teaching CYC lessons, the research team asks CYC questions to see what it has learned. For example, if CYC has been told that someone drove to work in the morning, the researchers may ask how that person will get home in the evening. If CYC says "by boat," then the researchers know that something is wrong.

Sometimes CYC even responds to clarify points. One of CYC's most poignant questions came up when he was told that intelligent things like other intelligent things. CYC was then told that Mary Smith, one of the researchers, liked CYC. To which CYC replied: "Am I a person?" or "Is Mary Smith a computer program?"

What is most amazing about CYC is its capacity to teach itself. During each night, CYC looks through its knowledge base to develop some imaginative associations. On one evening, he concluded that *dad* was analogous to *dictator* and to *head of state*. Although some of CYC's thoughts may be amazing, the real impact of these attempts is that CYC can teach itself.

But CYC will need to learn the English language in order to teach itself. If CYC could read, it could digest everything from Descartes to *Time* magazine, Lenat argues. But natural language processing is a tricky science. What is a red conductor? A piece of red copper wire? Or a Communist orchestra conductor? Imagine CYC's dismay over some typical news headlines, such as "British Left Waffles on Falklands."

Another complex problem is teaching CYC the difference between fact and opinion. CYC may learn that "Jupiter is the largest planet in the solar system" (fact) and that "the New York Yankees are the best team in the American League" (opinion). Even with these challenges, Lenat believes that CYC can be taught to read English in five years.

The CYC project is visionary because it will show us how computers can be taught to learn. The project is also embedding CYC with knowledge that may have practical uses. Who knows? Maybe CYC will be set to the task of tutoring students or to the challenge of designing custom consumer products. Whatever CYC does with its knowledge, the experience of building the smart machine will change the way in which we work and live forever.

Source: David H. Freedman, "Common Sense and the Computer," *Discover*, August 1990, pp. 65–71.

The Scope of Expert Systems. Expert systems are generally developed to address a specific area of expertise. For example, it would be impossible to design an expert system to be an "expert doctor," because the realm of knowledge is much too large. However, an expert system could be designed to diagnose infectious blood diseases, a specific area of expertise.

It is interesting to contrast expert knowledge with general knowledge. We see programs that are expert in diagnosing infectious diseases but know nothing of general medicine. Expert systems have been designed that diagnose faults in atomic power plants but are ignorant of freshman physics. A simple task like answering the telephone is almost impossible for the computer to do because of the vast range of possible responses and topics. But expert systems are routinely designed to attack problems that are difficult for humans. Most people consider diagnosing infectious diseases difficult because it takes years for physicians to be trained in medical diagnosis. However, diagnosing diseases actually takes far less information than answering the telephone.

In general, an expert system should be designed to focus on a rather narrow domain of knowledge. Expert systems may be very smart in very narrow fields of expertise but will be practically ignorant in areas outside their domain of knowledge. One of the most difficult challenges in artificial intelligence is teaching machines to understand simple, everyday language—even though most children understand spoken language at the age of two. You will learn more about teaching machines simple knowledge in the Box 15–1, "CYC: The Intelligent Computer."

Types of Problems. Expert systems are good at problems that require diagnosis, prediction, and planning. One of the best uses of expert systems is diagnosis. Rule-based technology is well-suited to describing many routine diagnostic decisions made by professionals such as doctors and engineers. Their decisions are based upon a large collection of rules of thumb that are well described by situation-action rules.

Some diagnostic systems are designed to detect system malfunctions from facts that are supplied. For example, expert systems have been developed to diagnose faults in electrical systems, gas turbine engines, electronic equipment, and automotive subsystems. An expert system called ACE detects faults in telephone networks and recommends appropriate repair and maintenance work. In the computer field, a system called DART helps diagnose faults in computer hardware systems.

Expert systems have been used extensively in medical diagnosis. For example, MYCIN was developed to assist physicians in diagnosing infectious blood diseases using knowledge of patient history, symptoms, lab test results, and the characteristics of the infecting organisms. MYCIN diagnoses the cause of the infection and recommends appropriate therapy.

The IF/THEN logic of MYCIN might go something like this:

IF (1) the stain of the organism is grampos, and
(2) the morphology of the organism is coccos, and
(3) the growth conformation of the organism is chains,
THEN there is suggestive evidence (0.7) that the identity of the organism is streptococcus.

Another expert system, BLUE BOX, helps diagnose and treat various forms of clinical depression. The system uses data about the patient's symptoms and information about medical, drug, and family histories to suggest a plan that includes hospitalization and drug treatments.

A second area in which expert systems excel is design work. Expert systems can be used to configure computers, circuits, and organic molecules. One of the most successful expert systems is XCON, which Digital Equipment Corporation (DEC) uses to configure its VAX 11/780 computers. XCON uses information on the customer's order to determine necessary computer system components correctly. The system has enabled DEC to cut down on costly configuration errors and has given it a competitive edge in the computer business (See Box 15–2).

A third category of expert systems applications is interpretation. Expert systems are widely used to interpret situations from information provided. Many expert systems in medicine use measurements from patient monitoring (heart rate, blood pressure, and so on) to diagnose and treat illnesses. For instance, an expert system named PUFF interprets data from pulmonary function tests to diagnose lung diseases.

Another application, MUDMAN, helps geologists analyze mud. At drilling sites, mud has to be sampled and analyzed for viscosity, specific gravity, and silt content. If mud contamination is misdiagnosed, drilling operations can be doomed at a particular site. N. L. Baroid, a drilling services firm, used MUDMAN to diagnose a mud contamination problem that had gone undetected by human experts for over 10 years. DIPMETER ADVISOR, another geological interpretation system, uses measures of rock conductivity in and around holes drilled in the earth to determine subsurface geological structure.

A fourth area in which expert systems excel is prediction. Prediction is the ability to infer the likely consequences of given situations. Prediction systems can be designed to estimate global oil demand, to forecast possible areas of international political unrest, and to simulate bad debt losses from faulty credit decisions. Farmers can benefit from an expert system that predicts insect damage to crops. PLANT, an expert system, predicts black cutworm damage to corn crops using a simulation model. A rule that PLANT uses to make its predictions is:

IF (1) the black cutworm versus leafstage table has been computed,
(2) whether there are greater than four weeds per foot of row is known,
(3) the corn variety is known, and
(4) the soil moisture in the field is known,
THEN compute the corn yield without insecticide treatment and assign it the variable YIELD 1.

Not all prediction-type problems can be solved by expert systems, however. One of the best examples of expert system predictive limitations is in oil drilling. In the early 1980s, a team of experts wanted to design an expert system to determine the probable value of oil wells, based upon measurements taken during drilling. The project sounded like an excellent opportunity for the development of an expert system for two reasons: First, millions of dollars rested on these decisions, and second, an elite group of petroleum geologists was responsible for doing these analyses. However, after significant investments had been made in designing an expert system to predict the yield of oil wells, its developers recognized that their system had no more knowledge than a junior geologist. However, the project was not a total waste because it produced a number of intelligent support tools that the expert geologists could use.

Some of the characteristics of expert systems are summarized in Figure 15–2.

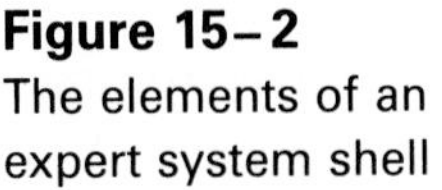

Figure 15–2
The elements of an expert system shell

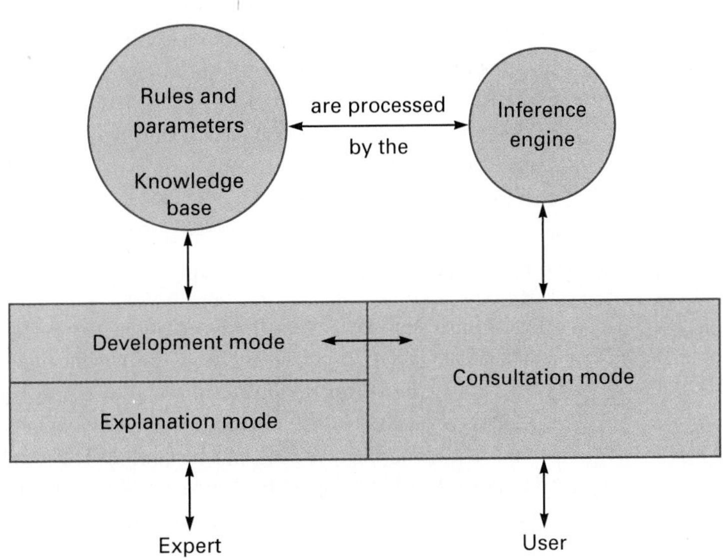

Though many of these systems seem sophisticated, expert systems are currently being developed to address a number of business applications. The cost of expert systems development has decreased with the availability of minicomputer- and microcomputer-based expert systems software. As a result, expert systems development is no longer just applicable to problems in engineering, medicine, and electronics, where the investment and returns are large. Simple, less costly expert systems are being developed to address business problems.

EXPERT SYSTEMS APPLICATIONS IN BUSINESS

American Express Company employs credit authorizers to analyze credit card transactions for clues to determine if charges outside of typical credit patterns are likely to be paid and if they have been incurred by the true cardholder. The "expert" knowledge of credit authorizers was used to develop an expert system for credit authorization. The purpose of this system was to minimize credit losses from incorrect authorizations. Since the rules of credit authorization could be defined, an expert system was feasible. With this system, American Express has been able to make more accurate credit authorizations.

An expert system for personal financial planning named PlanPower is currently available. Using information about its clients' objectives, taxes, prior investments, insurance coverage, and real estate holdings, PlanPower develops financial plans for its clients. To develop these strategies, PlanPower uses its knowledge of interest rates, expected inflation rates, tax laws, and standard investment strategies. Using PlanPower, clients can make "what if?" projections to compare the impacts of alternative financial decisions.

Expert systems also are being used in aircraft design, which requires the development of process plans detailing the steps in manufacturing. The design process involves thousands of parts. If design errors occur, considerable costs result from production delays, the reworking of tools, and the scrapping of parts.

At Northrop Engineering, an expert system has been designed to convert descriptions of parts into process plans. These process plans are permanently stored for future referral, preventing future designers from reinventing the wheel. Before the development of this expert system, much of this aircraft design expertise was in the heads of design engineers. When designers left, their expertise was lost.

Expert systems are also being applied in the financial services business. Expert systems for claim estimation, credit analysis, and underwriting are all being used in the insurance industry. In each of these applications, expertise is available and can be used to develop a knowledge base consisting of rules and data. Other expert systems applications include financial statement analysis, tax advising, conflict-of-interest consulting, and inventory management.

THE KINDS OF OPPORTUNITIES EXPERT SYSTEMS ADDRESS

As you have learned from our description of expert systems in medicine, engineering, business, and other fields, expert systems technology presents an opportunity to capture the knowledge of experts and to share it as a resource throughout an organization.

The initial step in the development of an expert system is the selection of a project in which a recognized expert can be found. This expert should be 10 times better than an amateur problem solver in the particular area. The task involved should be primarily cognitive, such as medical diagnosis, financial planning, or insurance underwriting.

Expert systems do not have common sense and cannot address problems requiring common sense.

The task also must be narrowly defined so that specialized knowledge can be used. It wouldn't be possible to build an expert system to be an "expert lawyer," but one could be developed to provide legal advice in a specialized area like personal tax law. In addition, the task should be one that an expert could accomplish in a relatively short period of time—in a few minutes to a few hours. If a task is too time-consuming, it should probably be broken down into subtasks.

For other reasons, some problems aren't feasible for expert systems development. Simple problems with fewer than 10 rules aren't good candidates because they can be solved by most people. However, problems with thousands of rules may be too complex and time-consuming to develop. Problems that are so complex that there are no experts, or problems involving a great deal of disagreement among the experts, are also not feasible for expert systems development.

Because of the massive investments in time and effort in developing an expert system, managers should realize that only certain projects are justifiable. High-payoff applications such as oil exploration and computer configuration are excellent opportunities for building expert systems. In situations where expert knowledge may be lost because of retirement or job transfer, or in cases where human expertise is very scarce, an expert system can be a good investment.

Even though an expert system may be possible and justifiable, it may not be appropriate unless the task at hand is appropriate. The task must require a heuristic solution; that is, one that requires use of "rules of thumb" to achieve a solution. Second, the task must be sufficiently narrow to make the problem manageable, yet broad enough to be of practical interest. Third, the task must be a serious problem that may take years of study for a human expert to address well.

HOW EXPERT SYSTEMS ARE DEVELOPED

The development of expert systems involves the process of knowledge engineering, which means the creation of a knowledge base. The **knowledge engineer** builds the pieces of the knowledge base. This involves working with an expert who uses her experience to develop rules applying to a problem.

Expert systems development entails the acquisition of knowledge, and several factors related to knowledge acquisition apply to their development. First of all, knowledge is inexact. No one has perfect knowledge, including the expert. An expert auto mechanic, for example, may be able to identify the correct problem with an air-conditioning system only about 75 percent of the time. Making errors can be useful, though, because the expert can learn more about factors involved in diagnosing the problem. An expert system can be no more certain than the expert.

Second, knowledge is incomplete. Knowledge is acquired in pieces, a little at a time and through trial and error. For instance, an expert platform diver learns his skill after hundreds of hours of practice. Gradual learning takes place throughout the college curriculum as well. In the freshman year, an economics major may take a survey course in microeconomics. It isn't until the student takes advanced courses that some of the reasons behind the basic concepts learned in the survey course are conveyed.

Expert systems development is also incremental. In the initial development phase, a preliminary set of rules is defined and applied to a simple problem. However, as experience with the system grows, new rules are incorporated into the knowledge base. An expert system ultimately requires a great deal of knowledge.

The Stages of Building an Expert System

The process of building an expert system involves five stages. The first stage, *identification,* is the stage during which the problem is defined. As you have already learned, the problem must be appropriate in type and scope. At this time, an expert and the required computing resources must be acquired.

The next phase is *formalization.* The knowledge engineer must determine how knowledge will be formally represented. A number of questions must be addressed. Will a rule-based or frame-based approach be used? What key concepts and relationships must be addressed? At what level of detail will the knowledge be represented? During this phase, the knowledge engineer will also select appropriate system building tools.

During the third stage, *implementation,* the knowledge engineer will work with the expert to identify the rules of thumb that make up the formalized knowledge of the expert system. These rules are used to construct a workable computer program using the system building tools or language.

Testing of the system is its final phase. During this phase, the system builder supplies a number of test cases to evaluate whether the prototype system makes decisions that other experts would deem to be appropriate. The system builder must check the rules to see that they are consistent, correct, and complete. She must check to see if the explanations the system provides for reaching its conclusions are sensible and adequate.

The Roles of the Knowledge Engineer and the Expert

The process of expert systems development involves a knowledge engineer and an expert. At first, the expert is presented with a simple problem. Past experience allows him to identify the variables and rules that apply to it. After some of the rules are defined, the expert and knowledge engineer apply the rules to several simple problems.

As new problems are presented, the expert refines the knowledge base by adding more rules and data. After a number of sessions, up to 100 rules may be defined. The knowledge base is continually revised and refined to include the most relevant rules. A final version of the expert system may condense the original 100 rules to 30 or 40 rules. However, producing a final version doesn't mean that the expert system will remain static. As the system is used, its rules continue to be refined. This iterative process is similar to the prototyping approach in systems development.

One of the reasons that expert systems development employs an incremental approach is that the working memory of humans is a surprisingly short six seconds. Working memory consists of knowledge that the person can access immediately. The expert has immediate access to her working memory but needs to refer to long-term memory as well. The simple problems the knowledge engineer uses help the expert extract knowledge from this long-term memory. In general, experts are not very good at describing what they know. The knowledge engineer must be highly trained in order to help the expert identify the rules and test cases that are relevant to the problem.

The Prototyping Approach in Expert Systems Development

As you can see, the expert systems building effort involves exploratory prototyping. The knowledge engineer keeps building the rule base to see if the rules that have been accumulated provide enough information to reduce uncertainty. The expert must constantly review each version of the system to compare it with his own reasoning.

You might want to think of the prototyping approach in terms of a number of stages. The first working prototype of the system might be designed to solve a portion of the problem. Success at this initial phase may suggest that the project is feasible and may lead to the development of a research prototype. The research prototype is designed to address the whole problem, but it may not be of practical value because it has not been thoroughly tested. After continued testing and revision, a field prototype may emerge. The field prototype should display good performance and reliability on practical problems. Prior to commercial use, however, continued testing is needed to create a production version. XCON, Digital Equipment's expert configuration system, is an example of a commercial expert system. XCON, which has over 3,000 rules and is correct over 95 percent of the time, took over six years to develop.

How Knowledge is Acquired from Experts

The process of acquiring knowledge from an expert may take systematic interviews over a period of months. During these interviews, the knowledge engineer presents the expert with a series of realistic problems. Let us say that the knowledge engineer is

Box 15–2 The Impact of XCON

One of the most famous expert systems is XCON, a system developed by Digital Equipment Corporation to configure VAX computers. Many consider XCON to be one of the most successful commercial expert systems in use today.

XCON addressed the knowledge-intensive task of computer configuration, translating a customer's needs into a complete computer configuration. The three basic tasks in configuration include (1) translating customer needs into Digital products; (2) checking the completeness and accuracy of the sales order; and (3) designing the specific placement and connection of all parts in the order. Prior to XCON, technical editors were responsible for the complex task of configuring Digital computers. Equipped with a telephone, a bookshelf of technical manuals, and years of experience, the technical editors ensured that each order was technically complete. Their tasks required knowledge of an enormous amount of technical detail. Even with thorough examination of system requirements, the human configurers were completely correct only 65 percent of the time.

Digital's major method for assuring quality control was at the final assembly and test phase of the project. During final assembly and test, configuration errors were caught by creating and testing the actual system. With rapidly rising sales, Digital was forced to expand its final assembly and test facilities in the late 1970s to include a 13-acre facility in Westminister, Massachusetts, costing between $15 and $20 million to build. Inventory costs approximately $20 million more. With continuing growth, Digital was expecting to quadruple its sales and to need four or five new final assembly and test facilities, thus tying up millions of dollars in plant, equipment, inventory, and assembly operations. All this occurred while the supply of expert technical editors was dwindling.

XCON was developed to configure Digital's computer systems—with XCON, it was easier to apply configuration knowledge consistently and completely. The best configuration knowledge migrated to the software developers responsible for keeping XCON up-to-date. Quality was directly impacted. In comparison to the technical editors' accuracy rate of about 65 percent, XCON's percentage of correct configurations in 1986 approximated 95 to 98 percent on all orders.

The most significant organizational impact of XCON was its impact on the jobs of technical editors, the group of experts who had managed the complex problem of configuration prior to its use. The system had a tendency to reduce their clout and to make their jobs more clerical. As one technical editor noted, "It was more fun before XCON, when you had to figure out each system. You got to keep in touch with many parts of the company—engineering, sales, and marketing—to know what was happening. We still do that now, but not so much."

The business impact of XCON was also clearly felt. XCON was an important part of Digital's ability to move from a final assembly and test manufacturing strategy, in which most systems were assembled prior to shipment, to a strategy in which separate components were assembled at the customer site. Since XCON could configure components more readily, the last stage of the manufacturing process was virtually eliminated and Digital was able to save $15 million in final assembly and test operations.

Digital's experience with XCON makes it clear that organizations that depend on expert decision-making in knowledge-intensive areas such as product configuration and product engineering can benefit from the development and use of an expert system. Without question, XCON has enabled Digital to provide its customers with the value-added feature of correctly designed and configured products.

building a system to assist attorneys in settling product liability cases. In so doing, the knowledge engineer provides the expert with descriptions of actual cases, including statements by witnesses and medical reports. The knowledge engineer then questions the expert in detail about how she would evaluate these cases.

The goal of this effort is to determine how the expert organizes knowledge about each problem. A number of questions arise. What kind of data does the problem require? What kinds of solutions are adequate for the problem? What kind of knowledge is needed to solve the problem? How does the expert handle inconsistent or inaccurate information? What is an adequate explanation for a problem solution?

As the knowledge engineer asks the expert to solve a series of problems, she probes the expert's reasoning and keeps track of the information the expert uses to solve the problems. After an initial prototype of the system is built, the expert attempts to solve sample problems using these rules and makes adjustments in the prototype system's rules to achieve an acceptable level of performance.

Throughout the system building process, the knowledge engineer has to deal with certain obstacles to capturing the expert's knowledge. First, experts tend to state their conclusions in general terms, without providing each step in the reasoning process that was used in reaching these conclusions. An expert may ascribe a judgment to intuition when actually this judgment is the result of a very complex reasoning process based upon a large amount of data and experience.

The more adept an expert becomes, the less able he is to describe the individual steps it takes to solve a problem or to arrive at a conclusion. The role of the knowledge engineer is critical, because the expert needs outside help in clarifying and explicating her expert knowledge. The knowledge engineer must decompile or break down the expert's knowledge into the hundreds of rules that are part of a complex reasoning process. Although the knowledge engineer may be able to gain some insight into this reasoning process by observing the expert's methods of solving problems, the best way to extract knowledge is to present the expert with representative problems and to discuss the strategies used to solve them.

One of the risks of developing an expert system is that it is difficult to estimate the time and effort it will take to complete. At some point, the prototype version must be transported into a production version. But even the production version will have a certain amount of uncertainty and will have to be constantly reviewed and revised. The expert must review each version of the system and compare it with his own thinking. The expert should also validate the system by comparing its performance with the thinking of other experts.

THE ADVANTAGES OF EXPERT SYSTEMS

Expert systems have definite advantages. An expert system can capture the knowledge of an expert and serve as an expert consultant in the absence of a real expert. If the expert system draws on the knowledge of several different experts, it may actually be superior to a single consultant. Once this expertise is acquired, it can be used forever.

Expert systems can provide advice that is more consistent than the advice of consultants, who may be affected by stress and time constraints. An expert system can be trained to process information more efficiently and to provide a recommendation more quickly than its human counterparts. An expert system can also be put to work in a hostile environment (e.g., a nuclear power plant or space station) where you could not afford to keep an expert on hand.

Another advantage of an expert system is that its knowledge can be transferred or reproduced. An expert system can be used for consultation and training in numerous locations simply by duplicating the necessary hardware, software, and data disks. Once the expert system is constructed, it should be documented to prevent losing the valuable expertise of experienced technical experts who may retire. The knowledge of employees who might leave a firm can also be captured. In either case, the expert system prevents system users from having to reinvent the wheel.

Finally, an expert system may be less expensive than an actual expert, particularly if the expertise is needed again and again. Human experts are highly valued and are able to obtain large salaries as consultants. Though an expert system may be costly to develop, its ongoing value should provide benefits that outweigh these initial development costs.

THE LIMITS OF EXPERT SYSTEMS

Although the benefits of expert systems are great, you still need to be acquainted with certain limits to the technology and its uses. First, expert systems cannot truly replace experts. Rather, systems can be used to augment experts' capabilities. In the former example of an expert system to identify the probable value of oil well sites, you learned that the expert system that was developed could not replace the knowledge of an elite group of petroleum engineers. Ultimately, the expert system was used as an expert consultant to the geologists in their work.

You will probably find expert systems used as consultants in a variety of lines of work. You will find financial planners using the expert advice of financial planning systems. You will find physicians using expert systems for medical diagnosis. For example, at Stanford Medical School, ONCOCIN, an expert system, assists physicians in prescribing chemical treatment for cancer patients. In the future, you will find expert systems that become consultants to a number of other professionals.

Finally, expert systems are not truly intelligent. They cannot learn new concepts and rules. They cannot address problems that lack focus and careful definition. They cannot demonstrate common sense. Teaching an expert system the most basic common sense would take thousands of instructions. In a very real sense, expert systems "don't know what they don't know." They will demonstrate unacceptably high levels of uncertainty in situations requiring knowledge outside their very narrow range of expertise.

The practical use of expert systems may be limited by the extent to which humans are willing to let them become accountable for the decisions they make. How to ascribe legal and ethical responsibility to the workings of expert systems is a difficult issue. You have learned that expert systems can excel at medical diagnosis and even bypass human physicians in accuracy. But if a patient dies because of a bad diagnosis by an expert system "doctor," who is responsible? You may be aware of the fact that computers "fly" many airplanes—in simulations, computers actually make fewer mistakes than their human pilot counterparts. Both the real pilots and the computer-pilots make mistakes, however. Somehow, humans are willing to accept, if not tolerate, a plane crash due to pilot error. But if a plane crashes because of a bad computer decision, is that acceptable? The legal implications are enormous.

Because of issues such as these, expert systems are being confined to consulting and assisting roles in such activities as medical diagnosis, computer configuration, and oil exploration. If Digital's XCON makes a mistake, it is not a life or death matter. An occasional mistake can be remedied by an extra shipment of parts. In general, expert systems may be restricted to low-responsibility decision-making applications until legal and ethical responsibilities associated with their use can be resolved.

EXPERT SYSTEM TOOLS

Expert systems can be developed using problem-oriented languages such as LISP or PROLOG. These are symbol-manipulation languages designed for artificial intelligence applications. As you can see from the English and LISP versions of a simple relationship, LISP is an effective language for implementing rule-based logic.

English: If the spill is in a building, call the fire department.
LISP: (IF (LOCATION SPILL BUILDING)
THEN (CALL FIRE DEPARTMENT)

A second type of expert system tool is the expert system shell. An expert system shell includes a knowledge base that specifies the parameters and rules and an inference engine that processes these parameters and rules. A diagram of the components of an expert system shell is shown in Figure 15–2. Expert system shells also include an uncertainty module that conveys information about the certainty of the recommendations being made and an explanation module that keeps track of the rules and procedures that have been accomplished in solving a problem.

Examples of expert system shells are Intellicorp's KEE, IBM's Expert Systems Environment (ESE), and Teknowledge's M.1. Many of these shells run on microcomputer-based systems at a cost that makes it possible for individual users to acquire one. For example, a package called Expert-Ease works on an IBM-PC and only requires 128K of memory.

A Personal Investment Planning System: A Case Study

A case study will give you a better idea of how an expert system is designed. An expert system for personal investment planning makes sense because this is a well-understood task with recognized experts. Furthermore, investment decisions have a high pay-off so the time required in developing such a system will reap good returns.

As you can see from the model shown in Figure 15–3, the personal investment planning decision requires two types of analysis: investor analysis and environmental analysis.

Investor factors include financial factors, such as income, assets, and liabilities, and personal factors, such as the willingness to take risks. As you can see from Table 15–2,

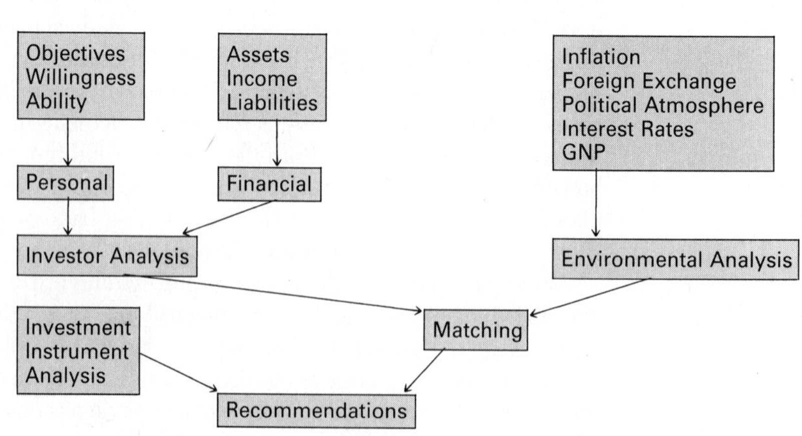

Figure 15–3
An overview of personal investment planning

Adapted from: Robert Mockler, "A Personal Investment Planning System," Chap. 8 in *Knowledge Based Systems for Management Decisions* (Englewood Cliffs, NJ: Prentice Hall, 1989).

each of these factors can be measured by questions designed to reveal different characteristics.

In addition to the investor analysis factors, the expert system must take into account environmental factors, such as foreign exchange, the political atmosphere, inflation, interest rates, and GNP. Inflation, for example, can be caused by expansionary government actions such as government spending and increased taxes. Inflation can also be influenced by a rise in input prices, such as increased wages, and it will increase if the demand for goods increases and prices rise in concentrated industries (e.g., the auto industry). GNP is determined by such factors as consumer spending, business investment, government spending, and net exports.

Each of these factors shown in Table 15–3 affects the investment climate. For example, when foreign exchange rates are stable, foreign investments are more predictable. Investments are more secure when domestic and foreign policies encourage investment. In times of high inflation, equities prove to be poor hedges against inflation.

Table 15–2
Investor analysis factors

Financial factors	Assets Liabilities Income
Personal factors	
Ability	Employment stability Age Health
Willingness	Risk experience Risk tolerance
Investment objectives	Growth Total Return Income

Source: Robert Mockler, "A Personal Investment Planning System," Chap. 8 in *Knowledge Based Systems for Management Decisions* (Englewood Cliffs, NJ: Prentice-Hall, 1989).

Table 15–3
Environmental analysis factors

Factor	**Key Indicator**
Foreign exchange	The dollar
Political atmosphere	Domestic; foreign
Inflation	Expansion forces Rise in input prices Concentrated industries
Interest Rates	Short-term Long-term
GNP	Consumer spending Government spending Business investments Net imports

Source: Robert Mockler, "A Personal Investment Planning System," Chap. 8 in *Knowledge-Based Systems for Management Decisions* (Englewood Cliffs, NJ: Prentice Hall, 1989).

Interest rates are also a factor. As interest rates rise, the value of securities declines. Finally, as GNP increases, financial instruments, especially stocks, become more favorable because the profits rise and companies can then pay interest and dividends more easily.

A combination of investor analysis and environmental analysis variables is used to evaluate different investment portolios. A possible scenario might look like the outline in Table 15–4.

As you can see from Table 15–4, Tom Clark's overall investor analysis profile is moderate because of moderate assets, low tolerance for risk, and overall family stability.

In addition to investor information, information on environmental factors is important for investment planning.

Let us say that the impact of interest rates on inflation is favorable for investment overall because both long- and short-term interest rates are expected to decrease. Also, projections for consumer spending, business investment, and exports and imports are favorable for investment.

Based upon the investor analysis and the overall environmental analysis, a moderate portfolio might be recommended that consists of a mix of 30 percent common stocks, 50 percent Treasury bonds, and a 20 percent investment in a money market fund. This is a moderate investment strategy that allows for both growth and income.

To develop an expert system for personal investment planning, the various factors in investor analysis and environmental analysis are given values using IF/THEN rules. The results confirm an investment portfolio that is consistent with these factors. In a rule-based system, rules such as those listed in Table 15–5 are applied in the analysis of personal investment factors.

Rules in a rule-based system are based upon the types of issues an actual financial planner would take into account in evaluating and recommending financial planning options.

Table 15–4
A summary of personal investor factors

Investor Name: Tom Clark	
Personal factors	
Ability to Invest	Moderate
Employment	Stable
Age	45
Health	Excellent
Family	Married, one child
Willingness to invest	Conservative
Experience	Limited
Risk tolerance	Low
Investment objectives	Growth and income
Financial position	Moderate assets
Overall profile	Moderate

Adapted from: Robert Mockler, "A Personal Investment Planning System," Chap. 8 in *Knowledge-Based Systems for Management Decisions* (Englewood Cliffs, NJ: Prentice Hall, 1989).

Table 15–5
Questions for investment analysis planning

Rule 98:

If in-business = under-1-year and
  layoffs = no or
  layoffs = yes and
  length-service = under-1-year or
  length-service = 1–3 years or
  length-service = over 3 years
Then employment = unstable.

Rule 99:

if in-business = 1-5 years and
  layoffs = no and
  length-service = under-1-year or
  length-service = 1–3 years or
  length-service = over-3-years
Then employment = stable.

Source: Mockler, Robert "A Personal Investment Planning System," chapter 8 in *Knowledge-Based Systems for Management Decisions*. (Englewood Cliffs, NJ: Prentice Hall, 1989).

As you learned earlier in the chapter, rule-based systems can be designed to address a number of business problems. Tax auditing, insurance underwriting, product pricing, and credit authorizing are just a few applications. For a project to be appropriate for expert systems development, the type of reasoning involved in performing the task must be heuristic or symbolic, as opposed to quantitative. Heuristic knowledge is judgmental, which means that the objective is to make a reasonably good decision.

For an expert systems development project to be feasible, expertise must be available. This means that experts must be able to articulate the methods they use to reach conclusions and to make decisions. In addition to expertise, a project must be useful and have a practical business application. A practical system can help repair products, can provide sales assistance to customers, and can help train or retrain employees. If expertise is available and if the project is useful, then the system is a good candidate for expert systems development.

EXPERT SYSTEMS AND DECISION SUPPORT SYSTEMS

As you learned in Chapter 14, managers build decision support systems to obtain the data they need to solve unstructured problems. Decision support systems is an application area. Many of these applications use database query and modeling tools to generate reports and to perform simple data analysis tasks. A decision support system gives control to the decision maker for acquiring and evaluating information and for making the final decision.

In contrast, an expert system provides the intelligence to solve problems within a specific domain. That is, the system makes the decision, not the individual. In Table 15–6 you can see some of the characteristics that distinguish an expert system from a decision support system.

Expert systems tools can be added to a decision support system to extend its capabilities for performing functions that a regular decision support system cannot perform. An expert system can be used to build a knowledge base that the decision maker can use to better understand problems and alternatives. Unlike traditional decision support tools, which are used to invoke a series of procedures in a predetermined manner, expert systems tools can be used to apply different rules depending on the situation and the variables to be considered. Many decision makers deal with incomplete data, and an expert system provides rules of thumb for situations in which some of the factors are uncertain. Table 15–7 summarizes some of the features of decision support systems and expert systems that support decision-making processes.

Managers in sales, finance, and manufacturing are now using expert systems as expert consultants to help them make decisions about how to allocate resources, how to control costs, and how to develop more accurate production plans. Today, for example, staff accountants at Coopers and Lybrand use ExperTAX, an expert system for supporting the corporate tax accrual and planning process. ExperTAX functions like an intelligent questionnaire, guiding the accountant through the information gathering process and providing explanations for why questions are being asked. In this way, the accountant not only gathers the data but also learns about its ramifications. In addition to gathering relevant information, ExperTAX uncovers some of the most important tax accrual and planning issues.

As you can see from this example, an expert system does not replace the manager. Rather, it can be used to augment the manager's capabilities, to accelerate training, and to provide quick analysis of important issues. In the future, expert systems tools are likely to be used in a vast array of environments.

Table 15–6
Differences between expert systems and decision support systems

	Decision Support Systems	Expert Systems
Objective	Assists the human	Replaces the human
Who makes decision	The human	The system
Query type	Human queries the machine	Machine queries the human
Problem area	Complex, wide	Narrow domain
Database	Includes factual knowledge	Includes procedures and data
Evolution	Adapts to the changing environment	Supports a fixed problem domain

Source: Efraim Turban and Paul Watkins, "Integrating Expert Systems and Decision Support Systems." In Ralph H. Sprague Jr and Hugh J. Watson, *Decision Support Systems: Putting Theory into Practice.* (Englewood Cliffs, NJ: Prentice Hall, 1986).

Table 15–7
The connection between expert systems and decision support systems

Processes	Features	
Specify objectives	Modeling syntax	DSS
Retrieve data	Data entry	DSS
Generate alternatives	"What-if" analysis	DSS
Infer consequences of alternatives	Modeling syntax with IF/THEN/ELSE logic	ES
Assimilate numerical and graphical information	Statistical functions	ES
Evaluate sets of consequences	Financial evaluation functions; optimization	ES

Adapted from: Meador, L., et al., "Personal Computer and Distributed Decision Support," *Computerworld,* May 7, 1984.

Management Summary

In this chapter, you have learned about the characteristics and applications of several examples of new information technology. Artificial intelligence has meant the development of intelligent computer systems that can understand language, manage the tasks of robots, and simulate the decision-making behavior of experts. Expert systems have been developed to perform diagnostic and design tasks such as medical diagnosis, computer system configuration, and fault detection in telephone networks. Business-related applications of expert systems, such as financial planning, insurance underwriting, and inventory management, are becoming more common.

Key Terms for Managers

artificial intelligence (AI), **562**
expert systems, **562**
explanation subsystem, **564**
inference engine, **563**
knowledge acquisition subsystem, **564**
knowledge base, **562**
knowledge engineer, **571**
machine vision, **562**
methodology, **565**
natural-language processing, **562**
paradigm, **564**
prototyping, **565**
robotics, **562**
tools, **565**

Review Questions

1. What is the definition of artificial intelligence?
2. Why are natural language processing systems so difficult to develop?
3. What is the function of the inference engine in an expert system?
4. What are the two methods of representing knowledge in an expert system?
5. What is meant by this statement: "Computers can be very stupid."
6. Can expert systems make mistakes?
7. What is an example of an expert system that does diagnosis?
8. What is an expert system shell and how is it used?
9. What are two characteristics of a "good" expert system project?
10. Why is the prototyping approach used in expert systems development?

Questions for Discussion

1. Explain the statement: "The more competent domain experts become, the less able they are to describe the knowledge they use to solve problems." What are the implications of this for the process of knowledge engineering?
2. Describe the phases of building an expert system.
3. Compare the intelligence of an expert system with the intelligence of a two-year-old child.
4. Give two ways in which expert systems programs differ from conventional data processing programs.
5. What are two key skills the effective knowledge engineer should have?
6. What are several characteristics an expert should possess?
7. Could expert systems tools be used to develop a decision support system?
8. Why is knowledge sometimes difficult to extract from experts?

9. What advantages can expert systems provide business?

10. What are some of the limitations of expert systems?

Problems

1. Clark Consulting. John Robertson, a partner in Clark Consulting, Inc., has just been asked by a client about the feasibility of developing several expert systems. Clark Consulting is a firm specializing in the development of managerial information systems, and the area of expert systems development represents a relatively new business opportunity.

Assume that the client has asked about the feasibility of each of the following projects. Do you feel that each of these projects is a good candidate for expert systems development? Why or why not?

a. An expert system to qualify sales leads.
b. An expert system to select potential store sites.
c. An expert system to diagnose problems with plant production equipment.
d. An expert system to develop an effective sales incentive program.
e. An expert system to supply legal advice about corporate taxes.

2. Technology in the year 2000. Read an article in a popular computer publication about new technology in one of the following areas: medical diagnosis, office automation, product design, telecommunications, or artificial intelligence. You may want to search for a recent article in a publication such as *Computerworld, PC Week, PCWorld, Datamation,* or *High Technology.*

Prepare a short summary of the article for presentation to the class. Include the following information in your summary:

a. What is the new technology? What is its purpose?
b. How was it developed?
c. What are the benefits of using this new technology?
d. What effect will it have on existing jobs?
e. What is its potential for development in the year 2000?

Selected References and Readings

Davis, Dwight B. "Artificial Intelligence Goes to Work." *High Technology* 7, no. 4 (April 1987), pp. 16–27.

Keim, Robert, and Sheila Jacobs. "Expert Systems: The DSS of the Future?" *Journal of Systems Management* 37, no. 12 (December 1986), pp. 6–14.

Meador, L., et al., "Personal Computer and Distributed Decision Support," *Computerworld,* May 7, 1984.

Mockler, Robert. "A Personal Investment Planning System." Chap. 8 in *Knowledge-Based Systems for Management Decisions.* Englewood Cliffs, NJ: Prentice Hall, 1989.

Newquist, Harvey P. "American Express and AI: Don't Leave Home Without Them." *AI Expert* 2, no. 4 (April 1987), pp. 63–65.

Nolan, Richard L. "Managing the Advanced Stages of Computer Technology: Key Research Issues." In *The Information Systems Research Challenge: Proceedings,* ed. F Warren McFarlan. Boston: Harvard Business School Press, 1984, pp. 195–210.

Turban, Efraim, and Paul Watkins, "Integrating Expert Systems and Decision-Support Systems." In Ralph H. Sprague, Jr., and Hugh J. Watson, *Decision Support Systems: Putting Theory into Practice* (Englewood Cliffs, NJ: Prentice Hall, 1986).

Waterman, Donald A. *A Guide to Expert Systems.* Reading, Mass.: Addison-Wesley, 1986.

CASE 3 ANALYZING THE EXPEDITING PROBLEM AT THE RIVERBEND ELECTRIC COMPANY

INTEGRATED CASES

BACKGROUND

The Riverbend Electric Company, Inc. (REC) manufactures a full line of electric and magnetic products including electric coils, transformers, voltage regulators, battery chargers, and other electric and magnetic products. Some product orders are very unique, for example, an electric transformer for a large-scale hydroelectric dam. Other product orders are fairly standard and are for products listed in the firm's standard product catalog. Even though these products are considered standard, the customer almost always requires some minor change to the standard specifications; for example, a voltage regulator may require a different type of electrical connector from that described in the standard product catalog or an electrical relay board may require additional holes drilled to mount to a unique chassis.

Because products are manufactured to match specific customer requirements, REC's North Alton manufacturing facility is organized as a job shop with a number of different workstations (see Integrated Case 1, Figure C1–3 for a layout of the manufacturing shop floor). Because the firm manufactures literally hundreds of work orders simultaneously, the control of work in the job shop environment is very complex (see Integrated Case 1 for additional background on job shops).

Recently REC has experienced problems competing with other firms in the electric component manufacturing industry. In particular, a Japanese firm has been promising customers a turnaround time of three to four weeks for completion of an order. Turnaround time is how long it takes to deliver the products a customer orders from the date that the order is first received. REC has been averaging eight weeks for turnaround time. When a customer places an order, the salesperson gives the customer an estimate of the turnaround time. To prevent the loss of orders to competing firms, salespeople have begun to promise shorter turnaround times than those offered by competitors whenever a customer complains about the estimated turnaround time. To meet these promised order delivery dates, the production shop floor manager has to give these rush orders special handling called *expediting* (see Integrated Case 1 for background on the expediting situation). Although expediting can speed up the delivery of an individual order, it can lead to havoc with the general production schedule for the manufacturing facility if the percentage of orders being expedited becomes excessive.

CURRENT SITUATION

Mr. Don Strock is the production shop floor manager of the North Alton manufacturing facility of REC (see Integrated Case 2, Figure C2–1 for REC's organization chart). On this particular Tuesday afternoon, Don is reviewing the previous month's manufacturing work productivity figures. Yesterday Don met with Marv Albert, the VP of Operations and Manufacturing, to discuss the productivity figures. He directed Don to investigate the firm's recent drop in manufacturing productivity. Don recalls the meeting vividly.

"Don, I don't know what is going on with the manufacturing operations on the shop floor, but these latest manufacturing productivity figures are deplorable," complained Marv at the meeting. "The firm can't accept this level of manufacturing productivity. In fact, productivity has been dropping for the past five or six months. Do you have any idea what the problem is?"

"Well, sir, I think the problem is a direct result of the high level of rush order expediting that we're encountering," replied Don. "It seems like every time one of the workers gets his machine set up for a production run and begins work on a work order, one of the expediters shows up and tells the worker to drop everything, tear down the setup and reset the machine to handle a rush order. You know, some of these machines can take over an hour to set up properly. I think this is causing us to incur a lot of unproductive work time because we lose the hours the workers spend setting up the machines for routine work orders twice."

"Don, I don't want you to tell me what you *think* the problem is. I want you to tell me that you *know* what the problem is, and you don't have to lecture me on machine setup time," Marv barked in a loud tone. "I've been in this industry over 20 years and I think I understand machine setup requirements as well as anyone. You know we have to expedite a certain number of orders; otherwise, we won't be able to beat the competition.

"I don't see how we can reduce our level of expediting until we have a new manufacturing shop floor information system in place to improve our ability to schedule rush orders with the routine work orders. Besides, I don't believe expediting is the problem. In fact, I've been thinking about increasing the number of people assigned as expediters. I think our real problem is that the manufacturing workers need more training in how to set up their machines. What I need is some ammunition to take to Mr. Pyszynski (the firm's president) to prove that we need to allocate funds for training. Where's your proof that expediting is interfering with the completion of our other orders? You either get me the evidence I need or get these manufacturing productivity figures up to an acceptable level."

Don was still stewing about the meeting. He knew that most of his workers had years of experience in operating their machinery and were quite adept at setting up the machines for different jobs. Fortunately, he had a plan to prove that expediting was the problem.

THE PLAN

Don knew that if expediting was the key cause of low productivity, then all workstations on the shop floor would be affected in about the same fashion because they all handled about the same amount of expedited work. Hence, he didn't need to examine the productivity problem for every workstation; rather, he could select one workstation and examine it in detail.

Don selected the drilling workstation (see Integrated Case 1, Figure C1–3 for a shop floor layout). The drilling workstation consists of three identical drill presses that can be set up in a variety of fashions. Two of the workers have over 15 years of experience each. The worker on the third drill press is fairly new with 10 months of experience.

Don obtained daily production data for the drill presses for Monday through Friday for each of the last four weeks. The data are given in Table C3–1. Column 1 indicates the work day of the month and column 2 gives the actual day of the week. Column 3 identifies the drill press number. For each drill press, column 4 gives the scheduled production hours for the day, column 5 gives the actual production hours for the day, and column 6 gives the number of hours devoted to setup time for the day. Don was unable to obtain the actual hours required for resetting up a machine whenever expediting occurred; however, he was able to identify whether or not the drill press operator had to set up a drill press over again at some point in the day due to a rush work order. Column 7 gives this information as Y (Yes) or N (No). A value of Y means the operator encountered a rush order at some point that day whereas N means the operator was not required to perform additional setups due to rush orders on that day.

Don decided to analyze the data using two different microcomputer software packages with which he was familiar—a spreadsheet package and a database management system package. He planned to use these tools to analyze the data and to compute averages for days when individual drill press operators were or were not faced with the requirement to reset drill presses due to rush orders. Don believed this would enable him to determine if the problem was related to worker experience or to the amount of expediting the workers faced.

Case Questions and Exercises

For this exercise you will use a microcomputer database management system (DBMS), a microcomputer spreadsheet package, or both. Your instructor will direct you as to the particular DBMS or spreadsheet selected. You will have to create your data files and enter the data into the files in the form of records. Be careful to check your data entry values to insure that you do not make mistakes entering the data.

Microcomputer DBMS Exercises

1. Create a file to store the data given in Table C3–1. The record structure will be as follows. Add the data from Table C3–1 to the file. With three machines for 20 work days in the month you will add a total of 60 records.
2. Use the DBMS query generator feature to create

Table C3–1 Daily production data

Day	Weekday	Drill #	Schedule Hours	Actual Hours	Setup Hours	Expedite Y/N
1	MON	1	8.0	6.6	2.1	Y
1	MON	2	8.0	6.2	1.0	N
1	MON	3	7.8	6.8	0.8	N
2	TUE	1	7.6	6.6	0.9	N
2	TUE	2	7.7	6.4	1.2	N
2	TUE	3	8.0	5.7	2.5	Y
3	WED	1	8.0	6.2	1.8	N
3	WED	2	7.7	5.6	2.2	Y
3	WED	3	7.8	5.1	2.0	N
4	THU	1	7.7	5.1	2.2	N
4	THU	2	8.0	4.4	3.1	Y
4	THU	3	8.0	6.6	1.1	N
5	FRI	1	7.8	6.3	1.7	Y
5	FRI	2	8.0	6.1	0.8	N
5	FRI	3	7.9	5.9	1.9	Y
8	MON	1	6.6	5.0	1.5	N
8	MON	2	7.6	6.7	1.2	N
8	MON	3	8.0	7.1	0.6	N
9	TUE	1	6.6	5.1	1.3	Y
9	TUE	2	7.2	5.3	0.9	Y
9	TUE	3	7.0	6.5	1.1	N
10	WED	1	7.5	5.2	2.2	Y
10	WED	2	8.0	7.0	0.8	N
10	WED	3	7.7	6.3	1.6	Y
11	THU	1	7.7	6.2	1.6	N
11	THU	2	7.7	6.0	1.8	Y
11	THU	3	7.8	6.4	1.1	N
12	FRI	1	7.9	6.6	1.0	N
12	FRI	2	7.8	6.2	1.4	N
12	FRI	3	7.8	6.5	1.2	N
15	MON	1	8.0	4.2	2.4	Y
15	MON	2	8.0	5.8	2.2	N
15	MON	3	8.0	6.1	1.1	N
16	TUE	1	6.8	5.2	1.8	N
16	TUE	2	7.2	4.9	2.8	Y
16	TUE	3	7.5	5.1	2.2	Y
17	WED	1	7.5	6.6	0.8	N
17	WED	2	8.0	5.1	3.3	Y
17	WED	3	7.7	6.8	0.9	N

continued

Table C3–1 *(concluded)*

Day	Weekday	Drill #	Schedule Hours	Actual Hours	Setup Hours	Expedite Y/N
18	THU	1	7.9	6.4	1.4	N
18	THU	2	7.7	6.1	1.5	N
18	THU	3	7.8	6.0	1.9	Y
19	FRI	1	7.9	5.5	2.2	Y
19	FRI	2	7.8	6.4	1.4	N
19	FRI	3	7.8	6.6	1.3	N
22	MON	1	8.0	5.4	1.5	N
22	MON	2	7.9	6.2	1.7	N
22	MON	3	8.0	5.6	3.3	Y
23	TUE	1	7.8	5.5	2.3	N
23	TUE	2	7.8	6.0	1.9	Y
23	TUE	3	7.9	7.0	0.8	N
24	WED	1	7.8	6.8	1.2	Y
24	WED	2	8.0	6.6	1.1	N
24	WED	3	8.0	7.1	1.8	Y
25	THU	1	8.0	7.0	1.0	N
25	THU	2	7.9	6.5	1.5	Y
25	THU	3	7.9	7.0	0.7	N
26	FRI	1	8.0	7.0	0.9	N
26	FRI	2	7.9	6.6	1.1	N
26	FRI	3	7.9	4.8	1.6	Y

Field Name	Field Description	Field Type/Size	Allowable Values
DAY	Day of the Month	Character-2	1 to 30
WEEKDAY	Day of the Week	Character-3	MON, TUE, WED, THU, FRI
DRILL	Drill Press Number	Character-1	1, 2, or 3
SCHEDULE	Scheduled Work Output This Day	Numeric-3.1	0.0 to 8.0
ACTUAL	Actual Work Output This Day	Numeric-3.1	0.0 to 8.0
SETUP	Actual Setup Hours This Day	Numeric-3.1	0.0 to 8.0
EXPEDITE	Rush order required extra setup	Logical-1	Y or N; or T or F

queries that give the following average productivity figures.

a. Compute a separate set of averages for each of the three drill presses: the daily average scheduled hours of production, the daily average actual hours of production, and the daily average setup hours.

b. Compute a separate set of averages for each of the three drill presses using only data for days when there was no expediting: the average figures requested in 2*a* above.

c. Compute a separate set of averages for each of the three drill presses using only data for days when there was expediting: the average figures requested in 2*a* above.

3. Write a short memorandum explaining your results and answering the questions: Does expediting result in increased setup requirements? If yes, how much? Does the experience level of the operators appear to affect work productivity (recall that the operator for drill press 3 is fairly new to the job)? Should Don recommend to Marv that the operators receive additional training on setting up machinery?

Microcomputer Spreadsheet Exercises

4. Create a spreadsheet with the data from Table C3–1. You may elect to either (1) import the data from the microcomputer DBMS file you created for question 1 above, or (2) if you do not import the data, you may desire to restructure the layout for the data in your spreadsheet to facilitate your analysis. A suggested format is to create three separate data sections, one for each drill press. Set up the first data section as follows: Column 1: day; Column 2: weekday; Column 3: scheduled hours for drill press 1; Column 4: actual hours for drill press 1; Column 5: setup hours for drill press 1; Column 6: Expedite Y or N.
Set up the second and third data sections accordingly.

5. Compute the same averages required in question 2 above.

6. If you subtract the setup hours required on any given day from the scheduled production hours for that day, you will arrive at the available hours. One measure of productivity is the ratio of average actual hours worked to average available hours. A ratio close to 1 indicates the worker is very productive in relation to the amount of work for which the workstation was scheduled. Compute this ratio for each drill press. Do the workers appear to be productive?

7. Develop graphs that will support the analysis and memorandum you completed for question 3 above. If you did not complete the microcomputer DBMS portion of this case, complete your analysis and write the memorandum described in question 3 above now.

Part IV

Planning and Development of Information Systems

In this part of the text, you will learn about information systems planning, analysis, and design. Managers need to think about how information technology can be used to support business plans. By learning about planning methods, you will develop a better understanding of how information systems can be used to provide feedback on overall business performance.

In addition, managers must become directly involved in analyzing current business systems, in recommending needed changes in business processes, in evaluating alternative hardware and software options, and in judging the financial and technical feasibility of a project. You will learn about these issues in the chapters on systems analysis, systems design, and implementation.

INFORMATION SYSTEMS PLANNING

CHAPTER OUTLINE

Manager's View

As a manager, you will make decisions on what types of information systems should be developed to support important business plans. The emergence of new technologies, such as office automation, expert systems, personal computers, and robotics, has created new opportunities for improving productivity. To take advantage of these opportunities, you must understand and be able to use appropriate information systems planning methods. Information systems planning methods help managers plan and organize information resources, including data processing systems and new information technology.

INFORMATION SYSTEMS PLANNING STRATEGIES

The major focus of this chapter will be to familiarize you with methods the manager can use to specify information requirements. Today's manager needs information to make decisions on pricing, product development, marketing strategy, and resource allocation. Most managers suffer from "too much information"—they get too many computer-generated printouts. Yet, much of the information they need to make decisions is not available on a timely basis.

Managers need to take a proactive role in defining their requirements for computer-based information systems. But first, they need to determine what information they need. Most managers do not know what information they need, and as a result, they put the systems analyst in the position of producing too much information.

In this chapter you will learn about the major problems involved in determining management information needs. Then you will learn about three methodologies the manager can use to determine these needs more effectively (see Table 16–1): Critical Success Factors, Business Systems Planning, and Ends/Means Analysis. Each of these approaches is fundamental to the establishment of information systems plans that serve the needs of managers.

PROBLEMS WITH DETERMINING INFORMATION REQUIREMENTS

Two important problems with information requirements definition are the failure to understand information needs from a cross-functional perspective and the limited use of joint application design in interviewing and data collection.

In Chapter 1, you learned how business process reengineering is being used as a strategy to define data requirements that must be shared across functional lines. For example, when a consolidated accounts payable, warehousing, and purchasing database was designed at Ford Motor Company, much of the paperwork for reconciling incoming shipments with invoices and purchase orders was eliminated. Instead, when a shipment was received into the warehouse, an individual checked the database to determine if the shipment matched a purchase order. If it did, an accounts payable check was generated to pay for the goods received.

As another example, let us say that a computer manufacturer has hundreds of orders pending. The manager must determine how to allocate existing inventory in the most effective way possible. The decision the warehouse manager needs to make is "Which customer orders will we fill first?" One would think that inventory should be allocated to the "best" customers (e.g., those who do the most business with the company), to the customers who need prompt delivery, to those customers who can provide the greatest profit margin, and to those who are most likely to pay their bills on

Table 16–1
Information planning approaches

Purpose	Method	Developer
To specify problems and decisions	Business Systems Planning (BSP)	IBM
To define critical success factors	Critical Success Factors (CSF)	Rockart
To specify effectiveness criteria for outputs and efficiency criteria for processes	Ends/Means (E/M) Analysis	Wetherbe

time. In order to make the decision on inventory allocation, the warehouse manager will need the following information:

How important is each customer to the business?
Which customer accounts are most profitable?
Which customers need prompt delivery on their orders?
What is the credit status of the customers requiring shipment?

It is evident that the information the warehouse manager needs to allocate the existing inventory to the right customers comes from sources outside the warehouse. For example, information on customer importance and profitability would come from the sales and marketing function. Information on credit history would come from the accounting area, and information on delivery requirements would come from customer service representatives.

In developing information requirements for the warehouse, other functional areas must be taken into account. Perhaps a cross-functional database with information accessible to sales, accounting, customer service, and warehouse personnel will have to be designed. Because information is needed for intelligent decision making within many departments, the old concept of information "ownership" (e.g., sales information being "owned" by sales, etc.) is outmoded and counterproductive. Without shared information, the organization ends up in a situation where the right hand does not know what the left hand is doing.

The concept of shared information also applies to the importance of joint application design as a process for determining the information requirements of managers. Obtaining a cross-functional perspective in defining information needs requires input from managers in a number of departments. It is difficult to achieve an overall organizational perspective if each manager is interviewed individually.

Take, for example, the case of a direct-mail catalog company. Prior to joint application design the credit department viewed its mission as minimizing credit losses and as a result accumulated more and more information about customers—including credit references, credit bureau checks, and internal credit history files. The cost of maintaining credit records was excessive.

After an exercise in joint application design, the company decided it was better off not doing any credit checks. Why? Because it could send catalogs to first-time buyers on a trial basis. Those who made orders and paid for these orders could be maintained as catalog customers; those who didn't pay could be dropped from any future mailings immediately.

Using this logic, the company could use its own credit experience to generate mailings. It quickly learned that its losses from nonpaying customers were actually much less than the former cost of doing all the credit checks themselves. Furthermore, it turned out that people who were often depicted as higher credit risks were generally the best catalog buyers, and people who were better credit risks rarely purchased goods from the company's catalogs. If the company had continued to use creditworthiness as a criterion for making mailings, it would have continued to send out catalogs to people with excellent credit ratings . . . who seldom bought anything. In effect, the company was better off marketing to people who were higher credit risks and then establishing their ability to pay through their own experience with these accounts.

The lesson learned from this case is that if the credit department had been the sole group interviewed, the old system would have remained in place and the company would have continued to send catalogs out to individuals who were least likely to make purchases, while still maintaining expensive credit files. It was the joint work of sales management and the credit department that provided the insight into making a change in the business process and in the information requirements.

MANAGING BY WIRE IN A COMPLEX BUSINESS ENVIRONMENT

In today's business environment, flexibility, responsiveness, and sensitivity to changing customer needs is critical for competitive survival. Stephen Haeckel and Richard Nolan compare today's management challenges to "flying by wire," using computer systems to augment a pilot's ability to assimilate and react to rapidly changing environmental information.[1] When a pilot makes a decision to veer sharply to the left, for example, the pilot's command translates into thousands of detailed orders that orchestrate the plane's behavior in real time.

"Managing by wire" is the same thing. Like a plane at high speeds, a company must be able to respond to a turbulent business environment. The manage-by-wire environment means being able to modify business plans based upon changes in market conditions. It means using information as feedback by sensing environmental conditions, interpreting them, and selecting a plan of action that can be sent out to subsidiary units such as manufacturing and sales.

The Air Force assesses a pilot's ability to learn with the concept of the OODA loop, a model for the mental processes of a fighter pilot. OODA stands for observation, the ability to sense environmental signals; orientation, the ability to interpret these signals; decision, the ability to select from a repertoire of available responses; and action, the ability to execute the response selected. A pilot's ability depends upon this learning loop, which constantly processes information and uses it to take action.

An enterprise must create learning loops that enable it to sense changes in the external environment, to interpret them, to decide what to do to respond to them, and to take action. Feedback from the external environment must provide measures of how well the business is performing. If market needs change, then the information system must provide feedback to trigger changes in the internal mix of activities and in the outputs the system generates.

Let's see how the concept of learning loops can be applied to a business situation. At Mrs. Fields' Cookies, local managers enter projected sales information into a microcomputer each morning. The software analyzes the data and responds with information on how many batches of cookies to make, how to adjust cookie distribution (e.g., chocolate chip versus oatmeal raisin) as the pattern of customer buying unfolds, and how to schedule workers. This decision support system provides a learning loop that is adaptive and changeable as the course of business activity unfolds.

Sometimes the learning loop can generate feedback to suppliers. Wal-Mart, for example, transmits information about sales of jeans to Wrangler, its supplier, each day. This information translates into a distribution plan that sends specific quantities of sizes and colors of jeans to designated stores from certain warehouses. This learning loop lowers logistics and inventory costs and provides customers with the sizes and styles they need.

The concept of a learning loop is basic to identifying the information requirements of managers. Managers need feedback from the external environment that provides data on changing sales and market trends so that they can react on a timely basis. The ability

---

[1]Stephen Haeckel and Richard Nolan, "Managing by Wire," *Harvard Business Review*, September–October 1993, pp. 122–33.

to define these feedback requirements is an essential element in each of the three strategies for information requirements definition that you will learn about in this chapter. Figure 16–1 provides a framework that briefly summarizes the techniques used to gather information requirements in each of the three approaches, CSF, BSP and E/M Analysis.

CRITICAL SUCCESS FACTORS

The **Critical Success Factors (CSF) method,** developed by John Rockart of the Massachusetts Institute of Technology, addresses the information needs of senior management. In particular, it is meant to deal with the frustration of senior managers who receive dozens of computer-generated reports each month, but find little information of value in these reports.

Traditional approaches to helping managers define their information needs are ineffective, Rockart argues.[2] One such method, which he calls the "by-product technique," uses the by-products of transactions processing systems to support managers' needs. However, reports such as sales summaries and monthly budget summaries may not zero in on current business problems.

A more effective way of spotting problems is to develop key indicators of the health of the business and to focus on significant deviations from planned performance. A report comparing the unit margins on various product lines, this March versus last March, is an example of an exception report that may help managers focus on problems and opportunities. One limitation of this type of report is that it may fail to address issues brought on by changes in the business environment and competitive strategy.

As a result of their frustration with current management reporting systems, many managers fail to use computer-generated information to make decisions. They argue that the business environment is so dynamic that no information system could be designed to provide them with the information they need.

Defining Critical Success Factors

The Critical Success Factors approach attempts to overcome the limitations of the by-product technique and other reporting methods by focusing on the individual manager's information needs. The first step in the CSF approach is for the manager to identify her goals. The next question the manager must answer is "What are the critical success factors underlying these goals?" A critical success factor defines "what has to go right" to achieve a business goal. An example of goals and critical success factors for three profit-making organizations is provided in Table 16–2. Even though the business goals of these three organizations are the same, the strategies that must be implemented effectively to achieve these goals vary.

Figure 16–1
Information requirements definition approaches

CSF	⟶			Critical success factors	⟶	Information
BSP	⟶	Problems	⟶	Solutions	⟶	Information
	⟶	Ends	⟶	Effectiveness	⟶	Information
E/M	⟶	Means	⟶	Efficiency	⟶	Information

[2] John Rockart, "Chief Executives Define Their Own Data Needs," *Harvard Business Review,* March–April 1979, pp. 81–93

Some critical success factors are determined by the nature of the industry. For example, succeeding in the paperwork-intensive insurance business requires cost-effective back-office operations and clerical productivity. In the automobile business, manufacturing cost control is an important critical success factor.

Some critical success factors are determined by the competitive strategy of a particular business. For example, two department stores may have similar objectives but different strategies. One, an established department store like Saks Fifth Avenue, may view effective customer service, styling of merchandise, and quality control the key to its competitive success. A discount department store like Kmart would have different CSFs, such as pricing, high turnover of seasonal merchandise, and advertising effectiveness.

Defining Measures

The critical success factors help managers define their information needs. Information that is valuable to the manager should support achievement of these critical success factors by providing measures of how well they are being achieved. As an example, a discount department store's CSFs and the methods of measuring the CSFs are given in Table 16–3. Pricing is important in the discount business because margins are low. A report on the margin percentage for various product lines would enable sales management to make pricing decisions that would ensure an adequate margin on sales. Inventory turnover, another important indicator, could be analyzed by product line so that stockouts could be minimized and year-to-year sales trends evaluated.

Table 16–2
Critical success factors

Goals	Critical Success Factors
Earnings per share	*Seminar Company*
Market share	Mailing list size and quality
New product success	Identification of relevant topics
	Effective speakers
	Life Insurance Company
	Effective training of agency management
	New product development
	Productivity of clerical operations
	Frozen Food Corporation
	Advertising effectiveness
	Effective distribution
	Product innovation

Table 16–3
CSFs and measures

Critical Success Factors	Measures
Pricing	Margin percentage for various product lines
High turnover of seasonal merchandise	Inventory turnover by product line
	Inventory analysis, by item, this year versus last year (for example, March 1989 versus March 1988)
Advertising effectiveness	Change in market share, by product line

Each of these measures can be used to define an information systems requirement. After these needs are established, existing information systems can be analyzed to determine if reports providing the needed information currently exist or if they can be generated from existing databases.

If the reports that are needed cannot be generated from existing information systems, the manager can identify "new" information requirements. If the organization provides access to databases for database query and reporting applications, some of these information needs may be satisfied by user-developed systems. Other projects, however, may require full-scale systems development projects.

Advantages and Limitations

An advantage of the CSF approach is that it enables managers to determine their own CSFs and to develop good measures for these factors. As a manager, you can develop an information system that is meaningful to you. The costly accumulation of unnecessary data is limited. Reports that list data on sales, customers, and inventories, often generated because the data are available and easy to print out, are minimized. The focus of information systems developed to support CSFs is effective control and monitoring of existing operations. If inventory levels are too high or if sales figures of a particular product line are below expected levels, you can use reports that highlight these conditions to take remedial action.

Finally, the CSF approach accommodates changes in competitive strategy, business environment, and organizational structure. In a dynamic business environment, the information needs of managers change. Managers cannot wait six months to a year for an information system to be built that helps them determine how well a particular competitive initiative is doing. By the time the system is built, a completely different strategy may be in effect. The CSF approach enables managers to define information needs that can be supported by flexible inquiry and reporting systems. These systems, which use existing databases to generate a variety of on-demand reports, are commonly known as decision support systems.

The main limitation of the Critical Success Factors approach is that it focuses on manager-specific information needs, rather than on organizationwide information requirements. Its original objective was to help senior executives define the information they needed for effective planning and control. The CSF approach doesn't try to recommend a data architecture planning strategy to accompany the analysis of managerial information needs, and it doesn't address the MIS management responsibilities associated with implementing these systems projects.

BUSINESS SYSTEMS PLANNING

The **Business Systems Planning (BSP) method** is an approach used to assist a business in developing an information systems plan that supports both short- and long-term information needs.[3] The goal of the approach is to provide a formal, objective method for management to establish information systems priorities that support business needs. In the process of participating in a BSP study, top management should improve its relationships with information systems professionals and make a commitment to the development of high-return information systems projects.

---

[3] "IBM Business Systems Planning." In J. Daniel Couger, Mel Colter, and Robert Knapp, *Advanced Systems Development/Feasibility Techniques*. New York: John Wiley & Sons, Inc., 1982.

One of the underlying objectives of BSP is to develop a data architecture that supports information systems development activities. In most organizations, information systems are built one piece at a time. As each system is built, a new database is constructed to store data elements needed to generate reports. After dozens of systems are built, the organization has to grapple with the problem of maintaining dozens of databases. Many of these databases store the same data elements, contributing to problems of data redundancy and data inconsistency.

For example, customer-related data elements may be used in 33 different reports and stored in 18 different databases. When a customer address changes, these data have to be changed 18 times over. The BSP approach attempts to overcome this problem by analyzing data requirements for major business processes and proposing a data architecture that supports multiple applications. In the next section, you'll learn how this is accomplished.

BSP Study Activities

The major activities that are involved in a BSP study are these:

Make a commitment.
Prepare for the study.
Hold a kickoff meeting.
Define business processes.
Define data classes.
Determine executive perspective.
Assess business problems.
Define an information architecture.
Determine priorities.
Review information systems management.
Develop recommendations and action plans.
Report results.

The Study Team

At the outset of the BSP study, a study team is organized to participate in gathering data. The study team consists of managers from different functional areas to do the required interviewing. The first step is to identify the major business processes of the organization. (A business process is an activity needed to manage the resources of the business.)

Methods of Analysis

These business processes become the basis for understanding information systems needs and for identifying key data requirements. The Business Systems Planning methodology utilizes a number of matrixes to establish relationships among the organization, its processes, and data requirements. The process-organization matrix shown in Figure 16–2 relates the activities of the organization to those responsible for these activities.

One of the major objectives of BSP is to identify the data classes that support business processes. These relationships are graphically depicted in the data class-process matrix shown in Figure 16–3. This matrix enables management to determine which data classes support multiple business processes. Identification of shared data creates a basis for developing a data architecture to support multiple applications. You can see borders drawn around clusters of shared data that support multiple business processes in Figure 16–3. The *C* in certain cells of the matrix indicates that a process creates certain data. For example, you can see that the business planning process creates planning data by looking at the upper-left cell. The *U* in some cells indicates that

Figure 16–2
The process/organization matrix

Organization \ Process	Business plan		Order servicing					Sales		
	Plan administration	Plan review	Receipt	Edit	Entry	Processing	Tracking	Territory management	Selling	Administration
General manager	+	+					+	+	+	+
Sales manager		+	+				+	+	+	+
Marketing manager		+		+	+		+	+	+	+
Controller	+	+		+						
Purchasing manager		+								
Service manager		+								
Manufacturing operations manager		+		+	+	+	+			

a process uses certain data. You can see that the business planning process uses financial data.

A BSP study also accomplishes other types of analyses. One of the objectives is to determine how effectively current information systems support major business processes. Another part of the analysis studies the data classes supporting various information systems. If common data support a variety of current information systems, opportunities for designing integrated databases can be defined.

Assessment of Business Problems

Once business/system relationships are established, the BSP study team undertakes in-depth interviews with managers throughout the organization to determine problems and priorities. Managers are asked to identify their problems, possible solutions, value statements, processes impacted, and processes causing the problems. Specific questions that address these issues include these:

What major problem have you encountered that has made your job difficult?
What is needed to solve this problem?
What would be the value to your function or to the overall business if it were solved?
How satisfied are you with the current level of information systems support?
What additional information do you need to help you in doing your job?
What would its value be?

Once interviews are conducted, information is analyzed and consolidated into a summary report. An example of the results of an executive interview is shown in Table 16–4. The interviews conducted during a BSP study are critical in obtaining an exec-

Process \ Data Class	Planning	Financial	Product	Parts master	Bill of material	Vendor	Raw material inventory	Fin. goods inventory	Facilities	Work in process	Machine load	Open requirements	Routings	Customer	Sales territory	Order	Cost	Employee
Business planning	C	U															U	
Organization analysis	U																	
Review and control	U	U																
Financial planning	C	U								U								U
Capital acquisition		C																
Research			U												U			
Forecasting	U		U											U	U			
Design and development			C	C	U									U				
Product specification maintenance			U	C	C	U												
Purchasing						C											U	
Receiving						U	U											
Inventory control							C	C		U								
Work flow layout			U						C				U					
Scheduling			U			U			U	C	U							
Capacity planning						U			U		C	U	U					
Material requirements			U		U	U						C						
Operations										U	U	U	C					
Territory management			U											C		U		
Selling			U											U	C	U		
Sales administration															U	U		
Order servicing			U											U		C		
Shipping			U					U								U		
General accounting		U				U								U				U
Cost planning						U										U	C	
Budget accounting	U	U								U							U	U
Personnel planning		U																C
Recruiting/development																		U
Compensation		U																U

Figure 16–3 Data-class/process matrix

Table 16–4
BSP interview

Major Problem	Problem Solution	Value Statement	Information Needs	Affected Process
Lack of ability to identify qualified people	Better information on personnel resources	Retain good people; improve morale	Skills inventory system	Human resources

utive perspective on information systems needs. The interview process may take months to complete, but the participation of key managers is vital.

Determining Priorities

Defining the information architecture involves analyzing the relationship of data classes to business processes. In Figure 16–3, we noted the clusters of data classes supporting multiple processes. Based on this analysis, a number of systems development projects are identified. These projects need to be prioritized according to their benefit, impact, success, and demand. *Benefit* is measured in terms of the expected financial returns that will occur if the project is implemented. Cost-benefit analysis, using return on investment or net present value, can help to determine the potential benefits of a project.

The *impact* of a project means the number of people affected, its qualitative effect, and its effect on accomplishing overall objectives. *Success* refers to the probability of the project's being implemented successfully, given the risk and the resources available. Finally, *demand* measures the need for and the value of the proposed system.

Each of the proposed information systems projects is rated using these four factors, and an overall ranking of projects is developed. Figure 16–4 shows such a ranking. Projects with the highest ratings become candidates for implementation and become part of the short-term information systems architecture plan.

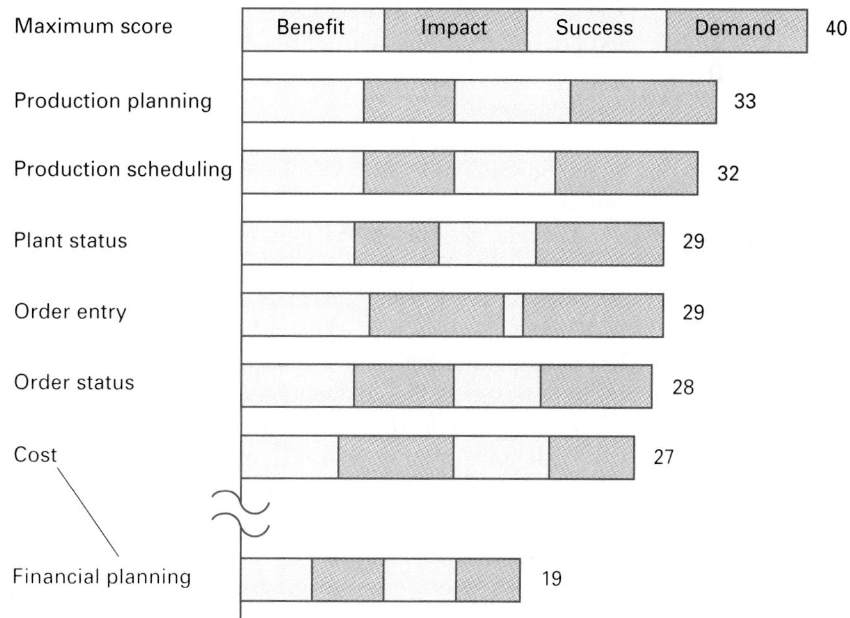

Figure 16–4
Subsystem ranking

Information Systems Management

An important step in planning is to review the capability of the existing information systems organization to develop the proposed information systems. Since the BSP study identifies opportunities for the development of an integrated database environment in which shared data support multiple applications, the information systems group will need to establish plans to move toward this kind of environment. New technology, new personnel, and new procedures may have to be introduced to make this transition.

The Action Plan

The final step of a BSP study is to develop an action plan in which the first subsystem project is scheduled for development, appropriate MIS personnel are assigned, and the project justification is completed. Once this project is underway, longer-range plans for designing the information architecture of the firm can be developed.

Implications of the BSP Approach

The major thrust of BSP is data architecture planning. The method includes identifying business processes, listing information requirements supporting each process, and establishing data element needs. From this analysis it is possible to define data elements that support multiple business processes and to develop an information architecture using a shared database approach. The BSP approach ultimately defines a way of achieving an integrated database architecture by implementing one system at a time. The BSP approach also paves the way for management of data as a resource.

Although the Business Systems Planning methodology is one of the most comprehensive planning techniques, it can be time-consuming and expensive to implement. It is designed to address data architecture planning rather than other issues like information systems organization and project management and control. Some criticisms of BSP include the fact that it does not identify opportunities for the effective use of new information technology and the integration of the technology with traditional data processing systems. Managers who want to use BSP need specialized training in the technique.

ENDS/MEANS (E/M) ANALYSIS

The third technique, **Ends/Means (E/M) Analysis,** has been developed by Wetherbe and Davis at the University of Minnesota.[4] The purpose of E/M Analysis is to determine effectiveness criteria for outputs and to specify efficiency criteria for processes used to generate outputs.

The first question in E/M Analysis is "What is the end or good or service provided by the business process?" As you can see from Table 16–5, the "end" might be to fill customer orders.

The next question is "What makes these goods or services effective to the recipients or customers?" The effectiveness criteria is that these orders be delivered when expected, and, if possible, as soon as or sooner than the competition.

The final question is "What information is needed to evaluate that effectiveness?" In this case, information about customer deliveries and comparative statistics on delivery service versus the competition's will provide the feedback management needs to determine how effectively they have achieved their result.

In the other part of Ends/Means Analysis, the manager needs to specify efficiency criteria for processes used to generate outputs. This analysis asks three questions. First

[4]James Wetherbe, "Executive Information Requirements: Getting It Right," *MIS Quarterly*, March 1991, pp. 51–65.

Table 16–5
Ends-means analysis

Ends	**Effective**	**Information**
Fill customer orders	Customer orders delivered when expected, and as soon as or sooner than the competition's	Summary and exception reports on customer deliveries; comparative statistics on delivery service vs. competition's
Provide customer service	Promptly provide credit to qualified customers	Customer credit status and payment history
	Quick response to and reduction of customer complaints	Report of number and type of complaints by customers and average time to resolve complaint

Source: James Wetherbe, "Executive Information Requirements: Getting It Right," *MIS Quarterly*, March 1991, pp. 51–65.

Table 16–6
Ends/means analysis

Means	**Efficiency**	**Information**
Process orders	Low transaction cost	Cost per transaction with historical trends
Process credit request	Low transaction cost	Cost per transaction with historical trends
Make shipment	Minimize shipment costs	Shipping cost categorized by order, customer, and region

Source: James Wetherbe, "Executive Information Requirements: Getting It Right," *MIS Quarterly*, March 1991, pp. 51–65.

is "What are the key means or processes used to generate or provide good or services?" A key process might be Process Orders, as you can see from Table 16–6. Second, "What constitutes efficiency in providing these goods or services?" Efficiency for processing orders might mean lowering transactions costs for orders and minimizing shipping costs. Third, "What information is needed to evaluate that efficiency?" Information needed to assess efficiency might include cost per transaction, cost per credit transaction, and shipment costs.

As you can see, Ends/Means Analysis seeks to determine information requirements using a simple, straightforward approach.

COMPARISON OF THE THREE APPROACHES

You can see the comparison of the three approaches, CSF, BSP, and E/M Analysis, most effectively by viewing how each of these approaches is used to gather information requirements for the order processing example. In the Critical Success Factors approach, information is used as feedback indicating the extent to which the CSF has been successfully achieved (see Table 16–7).

Table 16–7
Critical success factors for order processing

Critical Success Factors	Information
Adequate inventory to fill customer orders	Percentage of orders filled on time, by customer and by product
Prompt shipment of orders	Delivery time—overall and categorized by customer
High percentage of customer payments	Delinquency report on nonpaying customers
Vendors promptly filling reorders	Exception report of vendor reorders not filled on time

Source: Adapted from James Wetherbe, "Executive Information Requirements: Getting It Right," *MIS Quarterly*, March 1991, pp. 51–65.

Table 16–8
Business systems planning interview for order processing

Problems	Solution	Information
Out of stock too often	Better inventory	Out-of-stock, below-minimum report
Ordering department allocates limited inventory to the least important customers and/or customers with credit problems	Let warehouse know relative importance and credit status of different customers	Customer-importance rating and credit rating

Source: Adapted from James Wetherbe, "Executive Information Requirements: Getting It Right," *MIS Quarterly*, March 1991, pp. 51–65.

The BSP approach starts with a problem statement. The solution to the problem states the business objectives that must be achieved. The information requirements specify the feedback needed to determine how well these business objectives are being accomplished (see Table 16–8).

As you can see, the Ends/Means interview also specifies objectives (ends), factors that are important for success (effectiveness criteria), and measures used to determine whether or not these factors have been achieved successfully (information). Table 16–9 reviews the Ends/Means Analysis for the order processing example.

The Ends/Means Approach seems to be most similar to the CSF Approach. The goals in the CSF approach are similar to the ends in E/M Analysis. The Critical Success Factors are similar to the effectiveness criteria ("what has to go right") in E/M Analysis, and the information requirements in both approaches are designed to provide feedback on the extent to which the CSFs or effectiveness criteria are being achieved. In either case, the information requirements are designed to provide feedback on the responsiveness of the business to the environment.

Although the BSP approach starts with a problem statement, it also specifies business outcomes to be achieved (solutions) and identifies information requirements that are designed to provide feedback on the extent to which these solutions are being achieved. All three approaches use information requirements as a barometer to determine whether or not business outcomes are being successfully accomplished.

Table 16–9
Ends/means analysis for order processing

Ends	Effective	Information
Fill customer orders	Customer orders delivered when expected, and as soon as or sooner than competition	Summary and exception reports on customer deliveries; comparative statistics on delivery service vs. competition's
Provide customer service	Promptly provide credit to qualified customers	Customer credit status and payment history
	Quick response and reduction of customer complaints	Report of number and type of complaints by customers and average time to resolve complaint

Source: James Wetherbe, "Executive Information Requirements: Getting It Right," *MIS Quarterly,* March 1991, pp. 51–65.

Each of the information systems planning methodologies you have learned about so far in this chapter has different objectives, methods, and outcomes. The selection of a planning methodology may determine the outcome of the information systems plan. If the Critical Success Factors methodology is used, the outcome will be a strategy for designing executive information systems for better planning and control. If the Business Systems Planning methodology is used, a data architecture plan will result.

INFORMATION SYSTEMS PLANNING AT THE ORGANIZATIONAL LEVEL

In this chapter you have already learned how managers can use planning approaches such as BSP and CSF to define their information needs. These approaches can also be applied at an organizationwide level. To understand how information systems plans are developed at the organizationwide level, it is important to first understand the connection between information technology plans and business plans.

HOW INFORMATION TECHNOLOGY SUPPORTS BUSINESS STRATEGY

The information planning grid developed by McFarlan and McKenney at Harvard Business School (see Figure 16–5) will help you understand the connection between information technology and business strategy.

The Information Planning Grid

Strategic Quadrant. In the **strategic quadrant** of the information planning grid, you will find companies that are critically dependent on the smooth functioning of information technology for their competitive success. Both existing applications and applications that are under development are closely linked with business plans. Information technology is closely linked with corporate planning.

An example of a firm in the strategic quadrant is a financial services company that uses information processing to manage its loan portfolios, including loan application screening, payment processing, and account management. Without information technology, the firm would literally drown in a sea of paperwork. Financial services that are on the drawing boards cannot be developed and offered to potential customers without a significant information technology infrastructure and management capability.

Figure 16–5
Information planning grid

Adapted from Fig. 2–4: "Categories of Strategic Relevance and Impact," James Cash, F. Warren McFarlan, James L. McKenney, and Lynda M. Applegate, *Corporate Information Systems Management*, (Homewood, Ill: Richard D. Irwin, 1992), p. 39.

Strategic impact of existing systems	Strategic impact of application development portfolio: Low	Strategic impact of application development portfolio: High
Low	Support	Turnaround
High	Factory	Strategic

Turnaround Quadrant. Companies in the **turnaround quadrant** need a substantial information technology planning effort because the impact of applications under development is critical to their ability to achieve strategic business plans. Although information systems plans have not been closely linked with business plans in the past, future uses of information technology are "strategic."

Let's take the example of a four-year comprehensive university. In the past, information systems have been used to handle accounting functions and the management of student information, including registration, grade reporting, transcript generation, and student tuition and fees. These financial and student information systems are critical to the day-to-day operations of the university but they are not necessarily connected with the institution's ability to recruit students, address the needs of new markets, and build new academic programs. Technology has not been critical to the university's ability to implement its strategic plans.

However, this is changing. The university is now designing distance learning classrooms so that it can deliver its courses and programs to remote locations via interactive videoconferencing systems over telecommunications networks. Now, information technology is being used to recruit new students and to address the needs of new markets. Via the distance learning network, for example, the university will be able to develop academic programs with other four-year institutions in the state that would not have been possible before. A graduate program in nursing will be electronically transmitted to distance learning classrooms in remote sites so that nursing students in other locations will be able to get the training they need without driving hundreds of miles. Without question, distance learning is closely linked with the institution's ability to achieve its strategic goals. The change from using technology to support administrative information systems to using technology to achieve strategic objectives places the university in the turnaround quadrant.

Factory Quadrant. The third quadrant of the information systems grid is the **factory quadrant**. Factory firms are in the situation in which existing applications of information systems have a strategic impact, but future applications are not critical to their ability to achieve strategic business plans. In other words, strategic systems have already been built.

An example of a firm in the factory quadrant is a regional commercial bank that has already developed major backbone systems for demand deposit accounting, savings accounting, mortgage accounting, and trust accounting. Now that these information systems are in place, the bank has no current plans for developing other applications that will leverage the use of technology. Although management has considered organizing an at-home banking network, most of their feasibility studies do not indicate that this approach is cost-justified based upon the potential return on investment.

Support Quadrant. In the **support quadrant** are firms in which the uses of information technology are not connected with competitive success. This is true of past systems as well as future information systems plans. A firm in this quadrant is a soft drink distributor. Although the distributor uses information systems to support back-office administrative functions such as inventory control, accounts receivable, and accounts payable, it does not see information technology as strategic. Investments in marketing, advertising, and promotion are more closely linked with its ability to achieve sales goals, as compared with investments in additional uses of information technology.

Management Strategies

In each of the four environments, information systems planning strategies are different. In organizations in the strategic quadrant, it would make sense for the information technology manager to have a higher status and to actively participate in the corporate strategic planning process. For example, if establishing a distance learning network is critical to achieving institutional goals at a university, the manager of information technology should be involved in the strategic planning process. Without input from the IT manager, the university may envision technological capabilities that cannot be successfully implemented without training, specialized personnel, and significant financial resources. The network may involve other costs as well, such as training faculty to teach on a distance learning network and adding administrative staff who can schedule distance learning classes with other colleges and universities on the network.

Table 16–10 shows how management strategies for companies in the support and strategic quadrants vary.

As you can see from this table, the management strategies needed in a strategic environment are much different from those needed in a support environment. Project management, leadership, and effective allocation of resources to high-potential projects are necessary. Firms in the strategic quadrant need to maintain state-of-the-art technology know-how because their competitors do.

Let's take the example of two defense contractors. In both organizations, computer-assisted design and manufacturing (CAD/CAM) systems were brought in during the mid-1970s to provide automated support for manufacturing defense aircraft such as the F-16 fighter. In the 1980s, investments in integrated database management systems made it possible to exchange data with subcontractors so that major defense projects could be completed in a timely manner. In the 1990s, future investments in computer-assisted software engineering tools are forecast as a means of improving application development productivity and guaranteeing an information architecture for the future. Both firms are organized to keep abreast of the latest technologies in networking, software development, and database design so that they are technologically capable of winning future contracts.

Another major difference between organizations in the support and strategic quadrants is the willingness to take risks. Clearly, companies in the support quadrant justify information systems design projects in terms of cost-savings and administrative efficiency. In contrast, firms in the strategic quadrant may pursue projects that cannot be cost-justified up front but that might provide a long-term competitive advantage if they are pursued.

A case in point is the competition between Frontier and United Airlines. Even though these two organizations were both in the airline business, one was in the support

Table 16–10
Managerial strategies for support and strategic companies

Factor	Support Company	Strategic Company
Planning	Less urgent Mistakes in resource allocation not fatal	Critical—must link to corporate strategy
IT management	Can be low	Should be very high
Technical innovation	Conservative posture one to two years behind state-of-art is appropriate	Critical to stay current and fund R and D Competitor can gain advantage
User involvement	Lower priority Less-heated debate	Very high priority Active debate
Expense control	System modernization expenses are postponable in time of crisis	Effectiveness is key Must keep applications up-to-date; save money in other places.
Uneven performance	Time is available to resolve it	Serious and immediate attention needed
Project risk	Avoid high-risk projects because of constrained benefits	Some high-risk, high-potential-benefit projects are appropriate if possibility exists to gain a strategic advantage

Adapted from Table 13–1: Managerial Strategies for "Support" and "Strategic" Companies. James Cash Jr., F. Warren McFarlan, James L McKenney, and Lynda Applegate. *Corporate Information Systems Management*, 3rd ed. (Homewood: IL: Richard D. Irwin, 1992) p. 634.

quadrant and the other in the strategic quadrant. Frontier Airlines used the cost-benefit approach to justify investments in information systems development and focused on developing information systems aimed at cutting costs through operational efficiency. While the company was investing in accounting systems, their competitors in the airline business were developing sophisticated airline reservations systems that eventually put Frontier out of business.

What was happening at United Airlines was quite different. United invested in a computer-based airline reservations system called APOLLO. As United gradually added more and more travel agents to the APOLLO system, it gained a significant strategic advantage because these travel agents had an incentive to book United flights. Without a reservation system of its own, Frontier became a user of the APOLLO system. With information about Frontier's flights on APOLLO, United could cut fares in strategic markets and "accidentally" drop Frontier flights from its system. Inevitably, Frontier lost significant market share to United in the Denver market.

What happened to Frontier Airlines illustrates a mismatch between competitive strategy and information technology. In the 1970s major airlines such as American and United were building reservation systems in order to achieve a strategic advantage. Frontier was making investments that were consistent with a support posture, even though their competitors were in a strategic mode. Using information technology for
United were building reservation systems in order to achieve a strategic advantage. Frontier was making investments that were consistent with a support posture, even though their competitors were in a strategic mode. Using information technology for

support while their competitors were using technology as a strategic weapon was Frontier's mistake.

In the next section, you will learn how important it is to align information technology strategy with the overall competitive posture of the firm.

INFORMATION TECHNOLOGY AND COMPETITIVE STRATEGY

In Chapter 3, you learned about information technology plans that support competitive strategy. In general, competitive uses of information technology must support the strategic goals and objectives of an organization. In Porter's analysis, there are three generic competitive strategies: low-cost leadership, product differentiation, and market specialization.[5] Technology can be used to support each of these strategies. In other words, a firm that is a low-cost leader should use technology to support its low-cost leadership strategy. Similarly, a firm that uses a product differentiation strategy should use technology to reinforce it. Let's review each of the competitive strategies and learn how information technology can be used to support these strategies.

Strategy 1: Low-Cost Producer

One of the basic competitive strategies is **low-cost leadership.** Let's use the computer industry as an example. A company like Gateway 2000 strives to provide quality products at an economical price. How can technology support its objectives? Gateway 2000 relies upon rigorous inventory management practices so that it can avoid the costs of excess inventory. To interact with its customers, Gateway 2000 relies upon an electronic bulletin board system that provides information on service and maintenance. These strategies cut the costs of inventory and administration and support a low-cost strategy.

Strategy 2: Product Differentiation

Another competitive strategy, **product differentiation,** involves adding value to a product or service. In the computer industry, IBM Corporation follows a value-added strategy. IBM provides extensive customer training and support, including specialized workshops, systems consulting services, and publications. Its partnerships and grant programs with business and higher education institutions spur innovative projects. Their value-added strategy clearly costs money.

How can IBM use technology to support its product differentiation strategy? As one example, IBM maintains large customer databases that include industry characteristics, sales forecasts, and equipment purchasing histories. Using these databases, IBM marketing personnel can search for certain customer attributes (e.g., all customers with AS/400s purchased over three years ago and with sales growth of over 5 percent per year) and identify high-potential prospects for hardware upgrades.

Another technology-based service that IBM provides is access to extensive archival repositories of information on microcomputer support issues. These repositories contain information on the combined experience base of microcomputer users who have diagnosed and solved technical problems. A customer with a technical problems can dial-up this archival repository and obtain information to resolve technical problems.

---

[5]Michael Porter, *Competitive Strategy: Techniques for Analyzing Industries and Competitors* (New York: The Free Press, 1980).

Table 16–11
Strategic uses of information technology in the computer industry

Firm	Type of Strategy	Uses of Information Technology
Gateway 2000	Low-cost leadership	Inventory management Bulletin board communications systems
IBM	Product differentiation	Customer information systems Archival repositories of technical documentation for microcomputer support
Digital	Market specialization	Expert system for equipment configuration Market analysis databases

Strategy 3: Market Specialization

Market specialization is a third competitive strategy. An organization with this strategy attempts to serve the needs of a specialized market niche more effectively than any of its competitors. Here too, information technology can be used. Let's take the example of the computer industry again. Digital Equipment Corporation uses a market specialization strategy. Historically, Digital has developed state-of-the-art networked systems in the UNIX operating system environment that support the needs of science and engineering professionals.

How does Digital use technology to support its strategy? In an earlier chapter, you learned about Digital's expert system, XCON. XCON is designed to configure networked computer systems with high levels of accuracy. The market Digital is addressing is particularly interested in doing business with a vendor that can offer advanced expert systems configuration capabilities.

Another application of information technology that supports the market specialization strategy is the use of specialized customer and industry sales databases to identify the buying characteristics of a defined market segment. Using information on the buying behavior of a particular market segment, a vendor can design products and services that meet their needs most effectively.

Summary

As you have seen, a company can use technology to support its competitive strategy. As a result, information systems plans should be coordinated with business plans. It would not make sense for a company pursuing a low-cost leadership strategy to use technology to support the product-differentiation approach. In so doing, the firm might introduce expensive, technology-based value-added services that would make it difficult to offer lower costs to the customer.

For example, Gateway 2000 might decide to offer its customers access to computer-based maintenance histories on its products to give them better information on when to upgrade microcomputer workstations. The creation and maintenance of these computer-based maintenance histories for its customers would represent a major cost of doing business and would ultimately undermine its low-cost leadership strategy. Mismatches between business strategy and the use of information technology can be dangerous.

Mismatches can be avoided if information systems planning is coordinated with strategic planning. Coordination requires the manager of information technology to work closely with business strategic planners so that technology plans are aligned with competitive strategy. In organizations in the strategic and turnaround quadrants, the senior information systems executive should participate in the corporate strategic planning process.

TECHNOLOGY PLANNING IN AN AGE OF UNCERTAINTY

In Nolan's analysis, the current stage evolution of information processing technologies and applications is complicated by the emergence of multiple portfolios.[6] You learned about the stage theory of data processing applications in Chapter 9. In the 1980s and 1990s, however, new portfolios are emerging. One new portfolio consists of microcomputer-based technologies, another is factory automation, and still another consists of office automation technologies (see Figure 16–6). In understanding the management challenges associated with managing multiple information technology portfolios, it is useful to review Schein's theory of technology assimilation.

Schein's Theory of Technology Assimilation[7]

Today, organizations are faced with managing many diverse technologies: videoconferencing, fiber optics, distributed databases, local area networks, mainframe-based administrative information systems, multimedia, and many other new technologies. Some are older, well-understood technologies whereas others are new and unfamiliar. In Schein's view, there are four phases of technology assimilation. Each of these phases creates different management challenges.

Phase 1: Technology Identification and Investment. When an organization invests in a new technology, it must focus on staff development, training, and management of pilot projects. The planning challenge here might mean mobilizing a special team to deal with the new technology implementation and evaluation. Let us say, for example, that a university wishes to introduce a videoconferencing capability. The first step may be to organize a team of professionals, consisting of a telecommunications analyst, a TV-radio specialist, a multimedia development consultant, and a project manager, to undertake a pilot project.

Phase 2: Technological Learning. The focus of planning during this phase is to facilitate learning by encouraging users to examine the technology and its applications. Because phase 2 is an experimentation phase, the major goal is to gain experience. During this phase, the university may encourage faculty to use the videoconferencing center to practice teaching classes to students in remote locations. With the assistance of a consultant, faculty may learn how to use the technology.

Figure 16–6
New application portfolios

Source: Richard Nolan, "Managing the Advanced Stages of Computer Technology: Key Research Issues," in *The Information Systems Research Challenge*, ed. F. Warren McFarlan (Boston: Harvard Business School Press, 1984), p. 202.

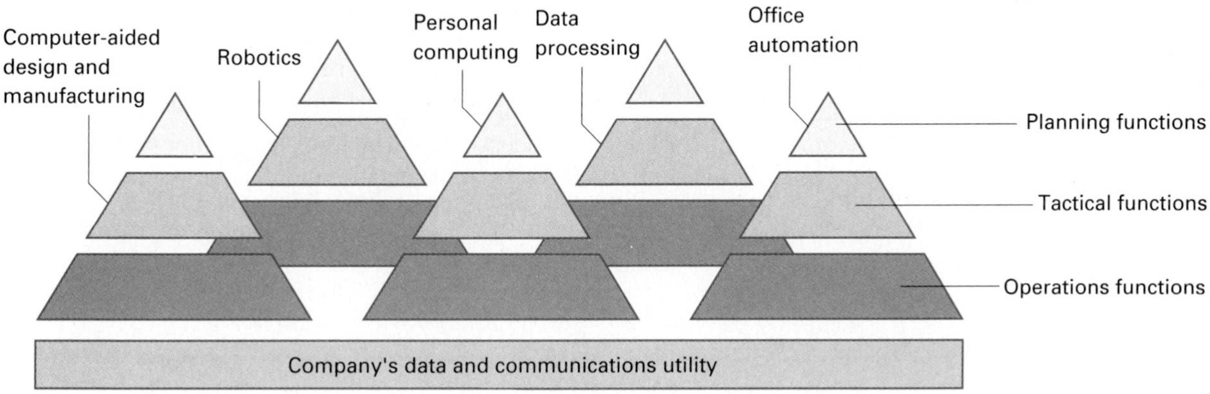

[6]See Richard Nolan, "Managing the Advanced Stages of Computer Technology: Key Research Issues," in *The Information Research Challenge*, ed. F. Warren McFarlan (Boston: Harvard Business School Press, 1984), p. 202.

[7]Edgar Schein "Management Development as a Process of Influence," *Industrial Management Review* 2, 1961, pp. 59–77.

Phase 3: Rationalization/Management Control. At this phase, planning is short-term because the objective is to define uses of the new technology and to implement it in a cost-effective way. Technical support staff for the videoconferencing center may be appointed on a permanent basis, and faculty users may be assigned classes. The major focus is day-to-day implementation of the project.

Phase 4: Maturity/Widespread Technology Transfer. In the final phase of new technology assimilation, a technology such as videoconferencing can be transferred throughout the organization. Now that faculty have learned how to use the system and standards for technology integration have been achieved, it is time to develop longer-term objectives for using the technology. The Dean of the School of Business may foresee using videoconferencing as a way of transmitting courses in the MBA program to conference rooms at local corporations. The School of Nursing may want to transmit courses to two-year colleges in remote locations of the state to enhance educational opportunities for students interested in nursing careers. An entire range of opportunities is possible once the technology is considered workable.

Planning in a Dynamic Environment

In most organizations, planning for the use of information technologies is difficult for two reasons. First, the competitive environment is so dynamic that competitive strategy and technology strategy are constantly changing. Second, the manager of information technology is responsible for managing multiple application portfolios: data processing, microcomputers, office automation systems, and factory automation. Each of these systems is evolving at a different rate and may be at a different stage of automation. The challenge is to use different management strategies to manage multiple application portfolios.

Let's take the university as a case in point. Mainframe-based administrative systems, such as the student information system and the human resource information system, were developed in the 1980s, putting data processing at a Phase 4 level of evolution in 1994. The evolution of microcomputers and local area networks was in its Phase 2 "learning phase" in the mid- to late-1980s and is evolving into a management control phase by the mid-1990s as software, local area networking, and operating systems are being standardized. An electronic mail system, introduced in the early 1990s, is still in its experimentation phase. However, new technologies such as computer-based videoconferencing are just being introduced in the mid-1990s and are clearly at the first phase of evolution.

Table 16–12 depicts these phases.

As already noted, each stage of evolution requires different management planning and control strategies. Because the videoconferencing project is a pilot project, it may require a team approach. In contrast, the administrative information systems that have already been built may need to be accessible to the offices of faculty advisors via a campus network. In the latter case connectivity standards provide a context within

Table 16–12 Technology assimilation at a university

Videoconferencing facilities for distance education	Electronic mail	Microcomputers and local area networks	Administrative information systems
Phase 1: Investment	Phase 2: Learning	Phase 3: Management control	Phase 4: Technology transfer

which technology transfer can occur. In other words, faculty who want access to the network will need to obtain standard network interface cards and communications software.

ORGANIZING THE INFORMATION SYSTEMS PLAN

Rapid changes in technology are creating enormous opportunities, but these opportunities cannot be pursued without effective planning. Without planning, the wrong systems will be developed. Without planning, a proliferation of incompatible hardware, software, operating systems, and database management systems will evolve. Technology is expensive, and mistakes can be costly. For these reasons, an information systems strategic plan must be developed.

The strategic planning process for information systems enables senior management to determine what information technology opportunities will support competitive strategy, what applications will bring about the highest returns, and what patterns of organization are most effective. Once these initiatives are defined, MIS managers must develop tactical plans that organize application development, technology, and organizational resources to achieve these objectives.

Application Development

As you learned in this chapter, one of the major purposes of information systems planning is to define application development projects that support the strategic goals of the organization. MIS management must work with users to set priorities for accomplishing these projects and must also look for methods of improving software development productivity so that critical systems are completed on time. Alternative systems development approaches, such as software packages and prototyping with fourth-generation languages, need to be evaluated. Computer-assisted software engineering tools (CASE), which provide automation support for the systems designer, may also improve productivity.

Moving toward a data-driven application development environment in which shared data support multiple applications is another challenge. MIS management has to determine what applications are appropriate to the data-driven approach, what technologies will support this approach, and how the systems development process needs to be modified. Many new technologies, including database management systems, fourth-generation languages, and code generators, need to be evaluated.

Once systems development projects have been identified, MIS management must organize its resources to make sure that these projects are completed within time and cost constraints. A systems development life cycle methodology organizes projects into phases and identifies the activities and outcomes of each phase. These phases include problem definition, systems analysis, systems design, detailed design, implementation, and maintenance. (You will learn more about the systems development process in Chapter 17.) A life cycle methodology provides review points enabling users to provide systems developers with feedback on changes in their requirements.

Once new systems development approaches have been identified during the planning phase, MIS management must also allocate its resources to make sure that new methods are used successfully. Traditional life cycle methodologies must be reexamined and modified to support data-driven development approaches. Systems analysts and programmers must be retrained to learn how to use new tools such as fourth-generation languages and CASE tools. Both users and systems professionals must be trained to use the prototyping approach to systems development. Some of the issues involving application development that need to be addressed in the information systems planning process are summarized in Table 16–13.

Table 16–13
Application development issues in the MIS planning process

Strategic Issues	Tactical Issues
What applications will bring about the highest return?	Are the phases of the systems development life cycle being successfully accomplished?
What applications will support the strategic goals of the organization?	Are projects being completed within time and cost constraints?
Should we move toward a data-driven application development environment?	Do user-managers have an opportunity to review project activities and outcomes at checkpoints in the systems development process?
Can CASE tools be used to improve productivity?	
Should software packages be used?	
Should fourth-generation languages be used?	

New Technology

The strategic planning process for information management helps senior management identify new technology opportunities that support business plans. These new technologies include office automation, teleconferencing, factory automation, client server, and others. One of the biggest problems MIS managers face today is supporting incompatible hardware and software in decentralized user environments. A technology plan must address strategies for linking mainframe-based operational data systems and decentralized decision support systems. It must address the architecture that will make it possible to design interfaces between data processing and office automation systems, between administrative data processing and manufacturing systems, and between telecommunications networks and local personal computers.

At the tactical level, MIS management must establish an equipment selection strategy and a vendor policy that ensures compatibility between centralized and decentralized systems and enables local computers to share centralized data and network devices. Some of the technology issues that must be addressed in an information systems plan are summarized in Table 16–14.

Organization and Management of Information Processing

One of the major strategy decisions that senior management must make is how to organize information processing to make it responsive to the needs of the organization. In the 1980s, most organizations experienced a shift in processing, database, and application development from centralized groups to distributed organizational levels. This process was driven by the introduction of new, less expensive, more powerful technologies and the growth of workstations, software packages, and user-friendly languages.

Table 16–14
New technology issues in the MIS planning process

Strategic Issues	Tactical Issues
What opportunities does new technology provide?	What equipment selection strategy should be designed?
Do we invest in personal computers? Factory automation? Office automation?	What vendor strategy is needed?
How do we integrate mainframe-based data systems with personal computers?	What controls over equipment acquisition must be introduced?

Table 16–15
Organization and management issues in MIS planning

Strategy Issues	Tactical Issues
How will information processing be organized?	What project management guidelines must be followed by user-managers in accomplishing local projects?
What will be the respective roles of user-managers and information systems professionals?	What training and professional development strategies are needed to prepare information processing professionals for their new roles?
What new skills will be needed by user-managers?	
What new skills will be needed by information processing professionals?	

The centralization of information systems architecture, network management, and database management functions and the decentralization of systems development and operations responsibilities have created some challenges that the MIS planning process must address. The MIS plan must establish central standards and guidelines for managing the organization's database, communications, and computer utilities. It also must identify the new skills needed by information systems professionals to fill consulting and support roles in the end-user environment.

Tactical plans must address training and professional development strategies. The new information systems professional needs communications skills, business understanding, and project management skills. New training and professional development plans must be developed to prepare personnel in the MIS field for new roles as consultants and business systems analysts. With the increasing decentralization of systems development, MIS professionals will also need to provide guidelines for the management and control of local projects. Some of the organizational issues that must be addressed in the information systems plan are described in Table 16–15.

In summary, an information systems planning methodology must establish technology and application development opportunities that support business plans. The MIS plan also must outline tactical plans for developing applications, selecting new technology, and designing organizational structures to meet overall objectives. These tactical plans also must establish the criteria for performance that can be used as a basis for evaluating whether information systems are responsive to the needs of the business.

The Changing Role of the Chief Information Officer

In a study of computing environments in 25 large organizations, Benjamin, Dickinson, and Rockart (1985) found that the development and operation of application systems and the management of hardware and software had become distributed to subsidiary information systems groups and to user-managers. Table 16–16 shows information systems activities that 60 percent of the chief information officers (CIOs) surveyed agreed were either centralized or distributed. As you can see, key systems development activities such as application software selection have been decentralized to local information systems groups or to line managers.

In spite of this decentralization pattern, some key activities remain in the hands of centralized information systems professionals. These activities include responsibilities for designing and managing voice and data communications networks, for creating and maintaining the information utilities, and for providing user consulting and training. MIS professionals are also responsible for technology planning and strategic planning. They will continue to play a major role in determining how information technology can be used to support business strategy.

Table 16–16
Distribution of information systems activities (greater than 60 percent consensus by CIOs)

Centralized Information Systems Activities	Distributed Information Systems Activities
Strategic planning for information systems	Selection and approval of application software
Technology planning	Operation of office systems
Management of voice and data communications	Selection and operation of personal computers
Establishing standards for mainframes and minicomputer systems	Planning what applications to develop
Providing end-user support	Establishing budgets and project plans

Source: Adapted from Robert Benjamin, Charles Dickinson, Jr., and John Rockart, "Changing Role of the Corporate Information Systems Officer," *MIS Quarterly* 9, no. 3 (1985), p. 181.

Management Summary

In this chapter, you have learned about information systems planning methods with different objectives, techniques, and outcomes. The Critical Success Factors approach is a planning method directed at helping senior managers define their information needs. In this approach, executives are asked to define their CSFs (e.g., what has to go right) and to develop measures of how well these CSFs are being achieved. If reports satisfying these needs are not currently available, then new information systems are developed.

IBM's Business Systems Planning methodology helps MIS management develop a data architecture that supports information systems needs. In the BSP approach, a study team identifies the key data classes supporting business processes and recommends a data architecture that supports high-priority applications. In Ends/Means (E/M) Analysis, information systems planners define the ends, effectiveness criteria, and information requirements needed to achieve business objectives.

Defining how to use information technology to gain a competitive edge is a major business planning challenge. Information technology strategy must support business strategy. That means that a firm with an underlying business strategy of product differentiation should use technology as a way to add value to existing products and services. For example, new information technology such as computer-assisted design systems enables shoe manufacturers to capture a competitive edge by offering better-designed products to their customers. Information technology has also made it possible for companies like Merrill Lynch to differentiate their services by providing bundled financial services, making it difficult for competitors to provide comparable offerings.

In a time when the competitive environment is very dynamic and competitive strategy is changing, an organization needs to rely upon planning strategies that are flexible and adaptable. Managers of information technology need to be able to "plan by wire." That is, they need to rely upon the information systems plans to identify the feedback mechanisms they need to survive in a rapidly changing business environment.

Key Terms for Managers

business systems planning (BSP) method, **597**
critical success factors (CSF) method, **595**
ends/means (E/M) analysis, **602**
factory quadrant, **606**
low-cost leadership, **609**
market specialization, **610**
product differentiation, **609**
strategic quadrant, **605**
support quadrant, **607**
turnaround quadrant, **606**

Review Questions

1. What are the objectives of the Business Systems Planning methodology?
2. What factors are used to rank potential BSP projects?
3. Explain what *Critical Success Factor* means.
4. How are Critical Success Factors used to determine information systems opportunities?
5. What questions are asked during an interview using Ends/Means Analysis?
6. How can an automobile manufacturer differentiate its products by using information technology?
7. What are characteristics of organizations in the support quadrant of McFarlan's information planning grid?
8. Identify some differences between the management strategies used in firms in the strategic quadrant as compared with firms in the support quadrant of the information planning grid?
9. What are the characteristics of Phase 2, technological learning, in Schein's model of technology assimilation?
10. What types of decisions does MIS management need to address in developing a tactical-level plan for application development?
11. What types of tactical-level decisions are made with regard to new technology?
12. What types of information systems responsibilities are becoming distributed to line managers and local information systems groups?
13. What new skills are needed by information systems professionals as a result of the distribution of computing activities?

Questions for Discussion

1. What are two Critical Success Factors for an automobile dealership?
2. Why would the Critical Success Factors for an automobile dealership differ from those for a grocery store chain?
3. Could the Critical Success Factors for two different computer hardware manufacturers (for example, IBM and Digital) be different? Explain your answer.
4. Which information systems planning methodology do you feel is more effective? The CSF approach, the BSP approach, or E/M Analysis? Explain why.
5. Why is it important for senior managers to be involved in information systems planning?
6. What are the characteristics of a firm in the turnaround quadrant of the information planning grid?
7. What kind of role should the MIS manager play in an organization in the strategic quadrant of the information planning grid?
8. How can information technology be used to help a computer manufacturer pursue a market specialization strategy?
9. What types of planning issues are relevant to the technology transfer phase of Schein's technology assimilation model?

10. What is the danger of mismatches between competitive strategy and the uses of information technology?

Problems

1. **Sterling Industries.** Sterling Industries is a $200 million company in the textile manufacturing industry. The director of data processing, Malcolm Rogers, has been with the firm for 20 years. Most of the information systems that have been developed use traditional files. Because many of these systems have been developed piecemeal, many of the data elements about customers, products, vendors, and orders are stored in many different databases.

   Managers at Sterling Industries are demanding that new applications be developed in the areas of sales and distribution. Conversion of an old batch order entry and inventory control system to an on-line system is a major need. However, managers in virtually every area have their own "critical needs" and are becoming impatient with the five- to six-year backlog of information systems development projects that currently exists.

   Explain how you would use IBM's Business Systems Planning approach to remedy some of the problems that Sterling Industries is experiencing. In your answer, describe the steps and the outcomes of such a study. What would be the roles and responsibilities of data processing management and user management in conducting the study?

2. **Software Associates, Inc.** Software Associates, Inc., is a vendor that develops custom-designed software for large and small businesses in the St. Louis metropolitan area. The firm has grown very rapidly and now employs over 100 systems analysts and programmers. Almost all the code for application development projects is written in BASIC programming language. Software Associates both develops and maintains its custom software products.

   The president of Software Associates, Edward Rosen, has very little information available for determining how well the firm is doing, whether new marketing efforts are paying off, and whether projects are being completed on time and within budget. Because the firm has grown so rapidly, internal information systems are crude and almost no management reporting systems exist.

   Ed has decided to use the Critical Success Factors approach to determine his information needs for planning new activities for the firm as well as for monitoring existing operations. With the help of a consultant, he has been able to determine the following Critical Success Factors:

   Ease of use of software products.
   Company morale.
   Project completion within budget and time constraints.
   Quality of sales literature.
   Risk recognition in major contracts for software development.

   In the software design business, software products must be easy to use to ensure that information systems will be accepted and used. Company morale is important because Software Associates relies heavily on the technical know-how of its experienced programmers and analysts. One of the major CSFs of the firm is the ability to complete software projects within budgetary and time constraints.

   In addition, Ed is concerned that sales literature provide a high-quality image of the firm. Ed does not want to take on projects with such a high risk that they might not be completed successfully. A significant project cost overrun or a project failure would hurt Software Associates' reputation in a highly competitive marketplace.

Given this situation, recommend measures that Ed can use to determine how well the firm is doing in achieving each of the Critical Success Factors.

3. **The Information Planning Grid.** Indicate which cell of the Information Planning Grid each of these firms would fit into and explain reasons for your answers.

   Firm A: At this uniform manufacturer, operational systems supporting order entry, inventory control, and purchasing have been developed. Most of the work in the Information Systems department is making changes and enhancements to existing systems.

   Firm B: At this financial services company, an on-line telecommunications network linking branch offices and the home office was implemented in the late 1970s. Today, systems projects are underway to analyze buyer and product profitability, to develop a profile of potentially delinquent accounts, and to develop a management control system for cash management.

   Firm C: At this food marketing company, information systems have been designed to support accounting applications such as payroll and general ledger. Today, the firm is designing more effective control systems for sales forecasting, computer-assisted manufacturing, and branch inventory control.

Selected References and Readings

Benjamin, Robert; Charles Dickinson, Jr.; and John Rockart. "Changing Role of the Corporate Information Systems Officer." *MIS Quarterly* 9, no. 3 (1985), pp. 177–88.

Cash, James; F. Warren McFarlan; James L. McKenney; and Lynda M. Applegate. *Corporate Information Systems Management: Text and Cases*, 3rd ed. Homewood, Ill.: Irwin, 1992.

Haeckel, Stephen, and Nolan, Richard. "Managing by Wire." *Harvard Business Review*, September–October 1993, pp. 122–33.

"IBM Business Systems Planning." In J. Daniel Couger, Mel A. Colter, and Robert W. Knapp, *Advanced Systems Development/Feasibility Techniques.* New York: John Wiley & Sons, 1982.

Porter, Michael. *Competitive Strategy: Techniques for Analyzing Industries and Competitors.* New York: The Free Press, 1980.

Rockart, John. "Chief Executives Define Their Own Data Needs." *Harvard Business Review.* March–April 1979, pp. 81–93.

Schein, Edgar. "Management Development as a Process of Influence," *Industrial Management Review,* Second Issue, 1961, pp. 59–77.

Wetherbe, James. "Executive Information Requirements: Getting it Right." *MIS Quarterly*, March 1991, pp. 51–65.

Systems Analysis and Design

Chapter Outline

Manager's View

As a manager, you will be a user of information systems. If you are a sales manager, you probably get printouts detailing sales activity in different regions. If you are a retail store manager, you may receive inventory reports describing the inventory turnover of various items in stock on a weekly basis. If you are a college administrator, you may get a report listing the number of students enrolled in various classes on a semester-to-semester basis. If you are a county welfare department administrator, you may receive a report listing welfare recipients who have been added to the welfare rolls in the past month.

Many users of information systems feel that the systems that have been designed do not meet their needs. One user argues, "The system that was built is technically accurate, but the reports I get don't give me the information I need." Still others argue that systems analysts themselves are out of touch with the business. One user comments that "the systems analyst had good technical training but really didn't understand the marketing business." Another says, "The system that was designed cost over $100,000 and took more than six months to build, but the reports I get don't help me identify business opportunities."

These problems, though they have plagued systems analysts for a long time, have partly been solved by the use of structured systems analysis and design techniques, by increasing user involvement in information systems development, and by better techniques for project management and control. In this chapter, you'll learn about the process of systems development, beginning with **problem definition** and **systems analysis.** You'll also become acquainted with structured analysis and design techniques that allow the systems analyst to communicate more effectively with users and to understand their requirements better. Most important, you'll see that systems must be built to make it possible for management to achieve important business objectives. Without an understanding of these objectives, no information systems design project can succeed in serving the users' needs.

THE SYSTEMS DEVELOPMENT PROCESS

Systems analysis and design is a process that is similar to problem solving. There were systems analysts in business long before the introduction of computers into organizations. They were responsible for analyzing work methods and procedures to simplify work and to improve work flow. You've probably been involved in many systems analysis and design studies without even realizing it. The process of systems analysis involves a number of steps that can be applied to any study. These are the steps in a systems study:

1. Define the problem.
2. Develop an understanding of the system.
3. Identify and evaluate the alternatives that can be used to achieve the organization's objectives.
4. Select and implement one of the alternatives.
5. Evaluate the impact the changes have made.

All these steps were applied to a systems study in Chapter 2. In this chapter, you'll learn how they are applied to an information systems design project.

The Systems Development Life Cycle

The steps followed in designing an information system are known as the **systems development methodology.** A systems development methodology establishes a set of procedures that conform with a life cycle. Without a methodology specifying what events and activities should occur in what order, systems development projects are likely to be out of range in cost and time. When projects are completed, the results may not meet the needs of the business. Adequate documentation may be lacking, making modifications difficult to design and implement. Lack of standardization from project to project may make it necessary to reinvent the wheel again and again.

One reason for introducing a system development methodology is to make sure that users have an opportunity to review and to sign off on system requirements at each phase in the life cycle. These checkpoints make it possible to detect and correct errors at the end of each phase of the project. If errors in analysis are not detected, they may become inputs into errors in systems design and in detailed design. These errors may not even be detected until the system is up and running and a manager points out a missing data element on a report or an erroneous calculation on a financial statement.

Each phase in the systems development life cycle is a checkpoint. Users have an opportunity to review progress and can modify time and cost estimates after each phase of the life cycle. They can choose to cancel the entire project at one of these checkpoints if they believe progress has been unsatisfactory. However, the "sunk cost" syndrome—the emotional resistance to canceling anything on which money has already been spent—is a major deterrent to project cancellation.

The steps and key activities to be accomplished at each phase of the systems development life cycle are shown in Table 17–1. Most organizations use methodologies similar to this one, though some slight variations from one methodology to another may occur.

Problem definition, the process of determining the nature and scope of the problem, is the first step. If the problem is incorrectly or incompletely defined, the entire study could address the wrong issues. The major methods used in problem definition are interviewing and using questionnaires.

Most organizations conduct a **feasibility study** to determine whether a solution to the problem is feasible to prevent wasting many months of effort and many thousands of dollars in cost if the project is too large, too uncontrollable, or simply impossible to

Table 17–1
The systems development life cycle

Step	Systems Development Activities
Problem definition	Examination and evaluation of the problems of the current system
Feasibility study	Development of objectives and a logical model of the proposed system
	Preliminary analysis of alternative design options, including the technical and economic feasibility of each alternative
	Development of recommendations for the systems project, including a projected schedule and proposed costs
Systems analysis	Detailed study of the current system, including its procedures, information flows, and methods of work organization and control
	Development of a logical model of the current system
Systems design	Development of objectives for the proposed system
	Development of a logical model of the proposed system, including process logic definition, logical data dictionary, and logical database design
	Evaluation of alternative design options
	Development of a cost-benefit analysis to evaluate the economic implications of each alternative
Detailed design	Development of specifications for the physical system; including report design, file design, input design, and forms design
	Design of program specifications
	Development of an implementation and test schedule
Implementation	Coding and documentation of programs
	Evaluation and selection of hardware
	Development of security, audit and control, and test procedures
	Development of training programs
Maintenance	Ongoing support, changes, and enhancements for the system

carry out. The feasibility study is a miniature systems analysis and design effort that entails an exploration of alternative design options and an analysis of the costs and benefits of each alternative. If several alternatives seem to be realistic in terms of their potential costs and benefits, the project proceeds to the next phase, systems analysis. However, if no feasible alternatives exist, the project can be terminated.

During the next phase of the project, systems analysis, the current system is studied in detail. Interviews and questionnaires are used to collect information on existing procedures, information requirements, and methods of work organization and control. Interview findings are used to detect inefficiencies in work methods, inequities in work distribution, and inaccuracies in reports and other documents. These findings are used to develop a logical model of the present system by using a **logical data flow diagram.** The logical data flow diagram, a tool that graphically depicts the system, its procedures, and information flows, will be discussed in the next section, which covers structured tools for systems analysis and design.

The analysis of the problems of the current system is used at the beginning of systems design to develop objectives for the proposed system. These objectives must state the business objectives of the information systems design project. If the system doesn't enable management to accomplish important business goals, such as improving profitability, cutting costs, or improving customer service, then it might not be worth the time and cost to design and implement.

Assuming that the system will bring benefits that are measurable in business terms, the next step in systems design is to evaluate alternative design options. This step may mean evaluating **batch** versus **on-line** systems design options, mainframe-based versus minicomputer-based alternatives, or in-house development versus the purchase of a **software package.** The nature and type of design alternatives to be considered depend on the characteristics of the project. The evaluation of alternative design options is a major issue and deserves user management attention.

Systems design also involves the development of a logical model of the proposed system. The proposed logical data flow diagram becomes a model of the new system. By using structured tools and techniques, the logic of major system processes can be defined, a **logical data dictionary** can be developed, and a logical database design of systemwide data requirements can be specified.

Detailed system design is the process of developing specifications for the proposed physical system. This process includes the design of report layouts, screens and input documents, forms, and physical file structures. It also includes detailed data dictionary specifications documenting data names and data definitions for all data elements used in the system. During detailed design, any one of many procedures for program design is used to outline program specifications. Structure charts, Warnier-Orr diagrams, structured flowcharts, and pseudocode are all methods of documenting the design of structured programs. Systems flowcharts depicting the data processing procedures to be implemented are also developed as a part of detailed system design. By the end of detailed design, the blueprints for the proposed system—its programs, reports, screens, and procedures—have been finalized.

Implementation is the process of coding, testing, and documenting programs that are a part of the system. This process may take as much as 60 percent to 70 percent of the overall systems development effort. It involves development of quality assurance procedures, including data security, backup and recovery, and system controls. It also involves testing programs using both artificial and live data and training users and operating personnel.

The development of an information system includes all of the activities that begin with problem definition and end with system implementation. **Maintenance** includes whatever changes and enhancements are necessary after the system is up and running. Systems development activities encompass about 20 percent of the overall lifetime cost of an information system, and maintenance takes up about 80 percent of this overall cost. This breakdown of effort and the percentage breakdown of cost for various phases within the development life cycle are shown in Table 17–2. These data show a great deal more time spent on maintenance than on initial development. This is analogous to a construction engineer building a building and having its owners request continuing modifications costing many times more than its original construction cost.

However, there are reasons why continuing modifications must be made to information systems. Some of these are within the control of information systems designers; some of these are not. In many actual information systems design projects, not enough time is spent in analysis. Errors not caught in analysis and design become a permanent part of the system, and it isn't until the system is in operation that users see the results of these design errors and request changes.

Some of the changes in information systems design are impossible to prevent. Competitive forces may require a company to introduce new products, to reorganize its

Table 17–2
Lifetime cost of an information system

	System Activities (%)	Lifetime Development Cost (%)
Development		
Analysis/design	35	
Coding	15	20
Testing	50	
Maintenance		80
Changes and enhancements		

sales force, or to change reporting relationships. These changes may affect business procedures, data requirements, and reporting requirements. New managers may enter the business requesting different types of reports for planning and control purposes. Government regulations may require reporting new types of information. All of these changes may render existing information systems obsolete or make major modifications necessary. These factors mean that the systems designed today must be flexible and changeable. They must also provide adequate documentation because systems designers who inherit projects must be able to understand these programs and procedures in order to adjust them.

As a user of information systems, you'll have a major role to play in the systems analysis and design process. In fact, lack of user involvement in systems development almost guarantees that an information system will fail because it will not serve the requirements of the business. The major responsibilities of users occur during the phases of problem definition, systems analysis, and systems design.

SYSTEMS ANALYSIS

The major objective of systems analysis is to understand the current system and to determine the importance, complexity, and scope of problems that exist. The scope and boundaries of the system, including its people and procedures, must be defined. Much of this phase involves collecting data about what is being done, why it is being done, how it is being done, who is doing it, and what major problems have developed. The systems analyst cannot presume to understand the system, its procedures and interactions, until existing methods have been thoroughly examined. He needs to avoid the tendency to mistake symptoms of the problems for the real problems.

In manual systems, common problems are job duplication, job overlap, and job inconsistencies. Job duplication is a frequent problem. Two or three people may be checking credit on incoming orders without knowing that this process is being duplicated. Secretaries within different offices may be editing and retyping manuscript copy several times as it makes its way over to the publications office. Poor workload distribution is another common problem. One office worker may be overloaded with work while another one sits idle day after day. Without knowledge of their tasks and reporting relationships, however, it is difficult to suggest alternative patterns of work distribution.

Paperwork bottlenecks, lack of systematic procedures, and inaccuracies are also problems systems analysts frequently run into in manual systems. A purchase order may sit on a supervisor's desk for 10 days before it is signed and passed on to the next office. Time-consuming loan application screening procedures may delay credit approval for weeks. In addition, lack of systematic procedures may mean that different methods are being used by different people within the same organization to apply discounts, to approve credit, and to select authorized vendors for purchasing. Lack of standardized procedures may mean that workers reinvent the wheel, establish their own criteria for making decisions, or simply make mistakes. All these problems lead to errors that cost the organization time and money. They cause a firm to lose customers and business opportunities.

It is important for the systems analyst to collect information about current procedures, controls, and information needs. Interviews, questionnaires, work samples, work distribution analyses, and systems and procedures analyses are all methods of collecting information about the current system. A short case will provide a basis for examining these methods of data collection.

Case Study: A Law School Admissions Office

You are Roger Peterson, a systems analyst. You have been called in by Dr. George Blake, director of admissions for the School of Law. The admissions office is organized into three functions: admissions, financial aid, and student activities.

During an initial interview, George has expressed some of the following concerns. The office is inundated with paperwork, and the current administrative staff, consisting of four secretaries, cannot handle the hundreds of letters—including admissions decision letters, recruiting letters, public relations letters, interview request letters, and financial aid letters—that go out each month. George thinks that much of this correspondence is standardized, but currently it is handled on a piecemeal basis, one letter at a time.

Updating files is another problem. Applicants to the law school change their addresses from two to four times from the point of initial contact to actual entry into the school. Many times, George feels, files are not kept up to date. Although he would like to be able to select applicants with certain characteristics from the files so that he can send them information related to their specific interests, he doesn't feel that the current administrative staff can handle this added responsibility.

Finally, he feels that the work of the office is poorly organized and managed. Some of the secretaries are overwhelmed with work, whereas others are idle much of the time. He is concerned about the poor morale on the part of some of the less experienced secretaries who are overworked.

As the systems analyst, your first task is to collect information relevant to the problems in the office.

The Systems Interview

Although the interview is one of the most important sources of information about the current system and how it operates, it is not always used effectively. Often, people being interviewed feel threatened by the systems analyst or fearful that the changes management is proposing may affect their jobs. As a result, it is important for management to make it clear to everyone that the purpose of the systems study is to improve the current situation. The systems analyst should be introduced to all participants, and they should be aware of the purpose and scope of the study.

Guidelines for successfully conducting an interview are summarized here:

1. Prepare for the interview by learning about the individuals to be interviewed and the overall function of the organization.
2. Introduce yourself and outline the purpose and scope of the study, making sure that any questions are answered.
3. Begin with general questions about the overall function of the office, its organization, and work methods and procedures.

4. Bring up specific questions about procedures that might lead to information about areas of improvement.
5. Follow up on topics and issues raised by the interviewee.
6. Limit the amount of notetaking to avoid distracting the person being interviewed.
7. At the end of the interview, summarize the information gathered during the session and suggest a way of following up.

Even though some of these steps may seem obvious, many systems analysts don't follow them. One of the most common mistakes is to neglect learning about the office and its function. In the law school admissions case, the systems analyst should learn a little about the school, its students, its reputation, and its graduates. If the analyst were interviewing an advertising executive in a major food marketing company, it would help to learn about the products the firm sells and the market share it currently enjoys. Otherwise, the interviewee will think that the systems analyst is ill-prepared or, at worst, uninterested in the organization and its needs.

Another common mistake made by the systems analyst is glossing over key issues and failing to ask for a detailed description of work methods and procedures. Asking yes/no type questions does nothing to reveal hidden issues. For example, if Roger Peterson asked a secretary, "You seem to have an overwhelming volume of letters, don't you?" the likely answer would be "yes." A similar result would occur if he asked a question such as "You seem to have difficulty maintaining up-to-date information in the files of applicants, don't you?" Questions worded this way would not only bring about yes/no answers, but might also be viewed as critical of current practices and be addressed with hesitation or resistance.

The analyst can develop a more comprehensive view of the current system if fact-finding types of questions are asked. These types of questions are far less threatening and encourage people being interviewed to examine existing practices on their own. Fact-finding questions can relate to volume, processes, data, control, and organizational factors. Examples of questions in each of these categories relating to the law school office case are summarized in Table 17–3. The systems analyst can learn a great deal by just pursuing questions about how, why, where, when, and by whom activities are being done. Most users are fully aware of the shortcomings of their current situation and feel more comfortable diagnosing these issues if they are challenged to do so.

Still, some users may rush through an interview, provide irrelevant information, withhold important information, and be generally uncooperative. In this kind of situation, the systems analyst should try to diagnose the reason for their uneasiness and allay any anxieties they may have. Instead of asking direct questions, the interviewer could ask them to describe the current situation in detail, seek other sources of information, and crosscheck answers with other people in the office. The systems analyst can't expect full cooperation in all cases.

Using Questionnaires in Systems Analysis

In many situations, questionnaires can be developed to collect data in a systems study. When detailed information about the nature and volume of work in an office is needed, questionnaires can provide uniform responses to standard questions. Using questionnaires, for example, can save the interviewer the time it would take to gather data about work volumes from over 100 office workers. However, the systems analyst needs to make sure that all respondents answering the questionnaire understand the objectives and scope of the study, or their responses may not be valid.

The design of an effective questionnaire takes careful preparation, pretesting, and evaluation. If the systems analyst does not have training in questionnaire development,

Table 17–3
Questions in a systems interview

Volume	How many repetitive letters are sent out each week?
	How many address changes are made to the admissions master file each week?
Processes	Once a prospective student applies to the law school, what steps are taken to process this application?
	What are the procedures used in making a financial aid decision?
Data	What data do you keep about each applicant?
	What data are needed to make a financial aid decision?
Control	Are there any precautions in place to safeguard against improper access to applicant financial data?
	What procedures are in effect to make sure that transcript data sent in by applicants are accurate?
Organizational factors	Who is currently responsible for supervising office systems and procedures?
	What are the current reporting relationships of the secretarial and clerical employees in this office?

she should work with an experienced researcher to develop questions and appropriate data analysis procedures. Some general guidelines for questionnaire design are the following:

1. Identify the group to be surveyed.
2. Write introductory material clearly so that respondents know the purpose of the study and the use that will be made of the data.
3. Determine what facts need to be collected.
4. State questions with sufficient clarity so that respondents will understand them. Structure the response format so that the amount of time the respondents must spend writing is minimized.
5. Limit the length of the questionnaire so that respondents will be encouraged to take the time to respond.
6. Implement a pilot test of the questionnaire to determine if all questions are clearly understood and if all responses are of the expected type.
7. Design and implement a data collection plan.
8. Determine the method of data analysis that will be used.
9. Distribute the questionnaire, follow up to obtain desired responses, and analyze the results.

As an example, a questionnaire could be designed to collect data on the nature and volume of typing and filing work in the law school admissions office. The resulting data could be used to calculate the percentage of repetitive typing requirements. Using a questionnaire would also make it possible to collect standardized data over a period of time and in this way ensure that actual requirements were reported. Examples of questions that might appear on an office survey are included in Figure 17–1.

Similar questions could be asked to determine the volume and nature of filing requirements, procedures followed in making admissions and financial aid decisions, and information requirements for students and applicants. The specific data gathered from a questionnaire could be used to determine overall typing and filing requirements,

Figure 17–1
Typing questionnaire

A. TYPING REQUIREMENTS

1. What percentage of the documents you type falls into each of the following categories?

 ____% Original
 ____% Light revision (less than 20%)
 ____% Heavy revision (greater than or equal to 20%)
 ____% Repetitive letters

2. Please record the typing work you do over the next ten days using the format below:

Document Name	Document Type*	Revisions? (Y/N)	No. of Pages	Lines/ Page	Urgent? (Y/N)
________	________	________	_____	_____	_____
________	________	________	_____	_____	_____
________	________	________	_____	_____	_____

*CO: Correspondence
SR: Short report (under 10 pages)
LR: Long report (10 pages or over)
FM: Form
ST: Statistical typing
OR: Other (please specify)

to develop patterns of work distribution, to suggest new procedures, and to identify opportunities for automating certain applications, such as database requirements and standardized letters and documents.

For many types of studies, the systems analyst needs to go further than conducting a straightforward data collection effort. Structured tools and techniques, discussed in the next section, can be used to analyze existing work procedures, information requirements, and methods of work organization.

STRUCTURED SYSTEMS ANALYSIS AND DESIGN

The major objective of structured systems analysis and design is to determine the exact system requirements so that the "right" system is designed. The structured approach employs a series of graphic tools and techniques that the user can fully understand. In this way, errors in analysis can be caught in time to prevent their becoming inputs into design and subsequent phases of the systems development process.

If an error is caught during the analysis phase of a project, the cost of correcting it is many times lower than the cost of correcting the same error once the system has been designed and is in operation. For example, if a necessary data element is not identified during the analysis phase, it may be left out of system files during the design phase. Once the system is in operation, a user may notice that certain information is missing from a report. The designer may look into the situation and find out that a data element is missing from a master file. Redesigning the file and the report would take much more time than adding the data element to a data dictionary during the analysis phase of the project. Figure 17–2 summarizes the effect of undetected errors on the cost of systems development.

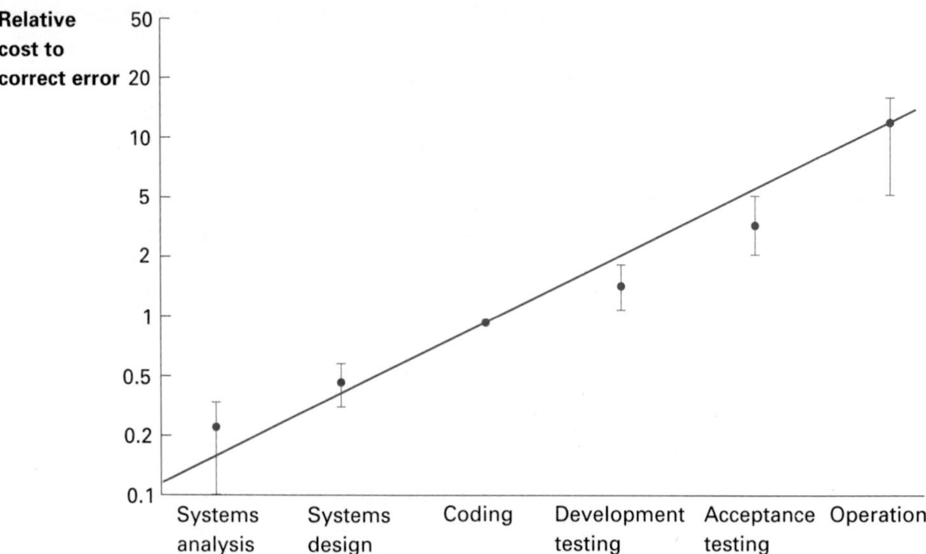

Figure 17–2
Relative costs of correcting systems/analysis errors
Source: McDonnell Douglas Professional Services Company.

The process of structured systems analysis makes it possible to catch errors in analysis during the analysis phase and to catch other design errors as they occur. Instead of giving users pages of system specifications that they cannot understand, the structured systems analysis process uses tools that depict a logical model of the present and of the proposed system that can be clearly understood by the user.

The structured approach to systems development is compared to the traditional approach in Table 17–4. The traditional approach calls for studying the current system, including its data files, reports, procedures, and decisions, and developing an automated version of the system. Although this is an efficient approach, there is a tendency to automate the inefficiencies of the current system. Reports could be produced for no reason in the current situation. Information about applicants could be incomplete, out of date, or simply inaccurate. If the current system is automated, many of these problems could be left undetected.

In contrast, in the structured approach to systems analysis and design, the analyst collects information about current procedures, information flows, decision-making processes, and reports and builds a logical model of the current situation, using a tool called the logical data flow diagram. The data flow diagram is used because it depicts *logical* business processes, information requirements, and information flows—not the *physical*

Table 17–4
Structured approach to systems analysis and design

Traditional Approach	Structured Approach
Study the current physical system	Study the current physical system
Devise a new physical system	Build the current logical model
	Analyze the objectives of the new system
	Derive a new logical model
	Draft alternative designs
	Finalize the new physical system

view of these elements of the system. The user doesn't need to know if personnel records are stored in a tape file, a disk file, or paper files. These are physical types of storage media. The choice of whether to store personnel records in a disk or tape file is a technical design decision that the systems designer should make. The user doesn't need to make technical design decisions. However, the user should have an opportunity to see a logical view of the data. In a logical data flow diagram, personnel records are depicted as a personnel data store, not in their physical representation. The logical data flow diagram provides a graphic model of the current system and can be used to analyze areas of improvement and to develop objectives for the new system. These objectives should be visualized in terms of the business results that need to be achieved in the design of a new system. Major modifications in current procedures, information needs, and decision-making processes, all of which are designed to accomplish desired objectives, are built into the model of the new logical system that is graphically depicted in the proposed logical system data flow diagram.

The logical data flow diagram of the proposed system becomes the basis for developing and evaluating alternative design options for the proposed system. Systems design alternatives could include mainframe-based batch and on-line systems, distributed systems, dedicated minicomputer- and microcomputer-based systems, and a range of software to support these configurations, including software developed in-house, package programs, and software developed using fourth-generation languages.

Once the best design alternative has been selected, the detailed design and implementation of the proposed system can begin. This involves designing output and input specifications, file requirements, and control procedures. These technical tasks are largely the responsibility of information systems professionals. Each of the steps in the structured analysis and design process will be covered in greater detail in the following sections of this chapter.

Developing a Logical Data Flow Diagram of the Present System

The systems analyst uses information collected from interviews and other data collection efforts to develop a logical data flow diagram of the present system. A logical data flow diagram illustrates system processes, information flows, and data requirements using easy-to-understand graphic symbols. These symbols are shown in Figure 17–3.

The "external entity" (square) depicts a source or a destination of data. It is often used to specify the boundary of the system. Processes (rounded rectangle) identify the major activities of a system, such as "verify customer credit" or "send invoice to customer." They are usually best described using action verbs such as *create, produce, compute, determine,* or *verify*. Data stores are the logical repositories of data that are used throughout the system. Data about customers, vendors, shipments, and suppliers may all be housed in data stores. Data flows represent data or information that is being transmitted from process to process, from an external entity to a process, or from a process into a data store.

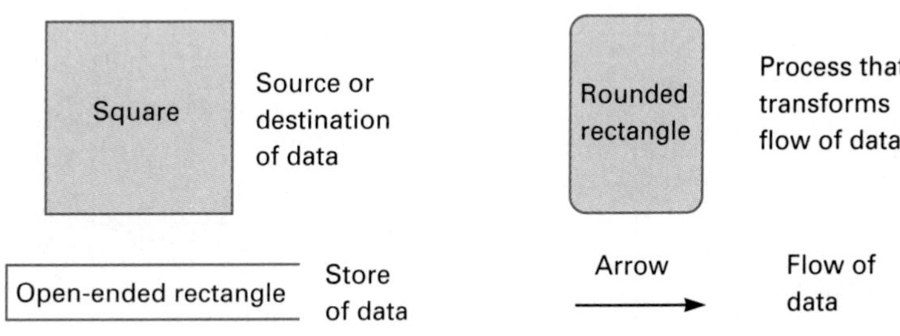

Figure 17–3
Data-flow diagram symbols

The best way to understand how a data flow diagram works is to view one. Figure 17–4 illustrates a simple data flow diagram showing order processing, purchasing, receiving, accounts payable, and accounts receivable activities.

The data flow diagram graphically depicts what happens when a customer sends in an order for a part. The part order goes into a verify-orders-as-valid process, which involves checking customer credit status against a customer data store and checking for the availability of the part being ordered in a part data store. If the order is validated, it is temporarily stored in a pending orders data store. One reason for creating this pending orders data store is to accumulate enough orders to receive a quantity discount from a potential supplier. Batching all the orders to a particular supplier also minimizes the paperwork involved in preparing purchase orders for the supplier.

After the pending orders have been held for a given interval, they are used to prepare purchase orders to suppliers. Two data stores are used in this process. They include a suppliers data store, which is used to obtain the supplier's address, and a purchase orders data store, which is used to file a copy of the purchase order being sent to the supplier.

Figure 17–4
A system data-flow diagram
Source: McDonnell Douglas Professional Services Company.

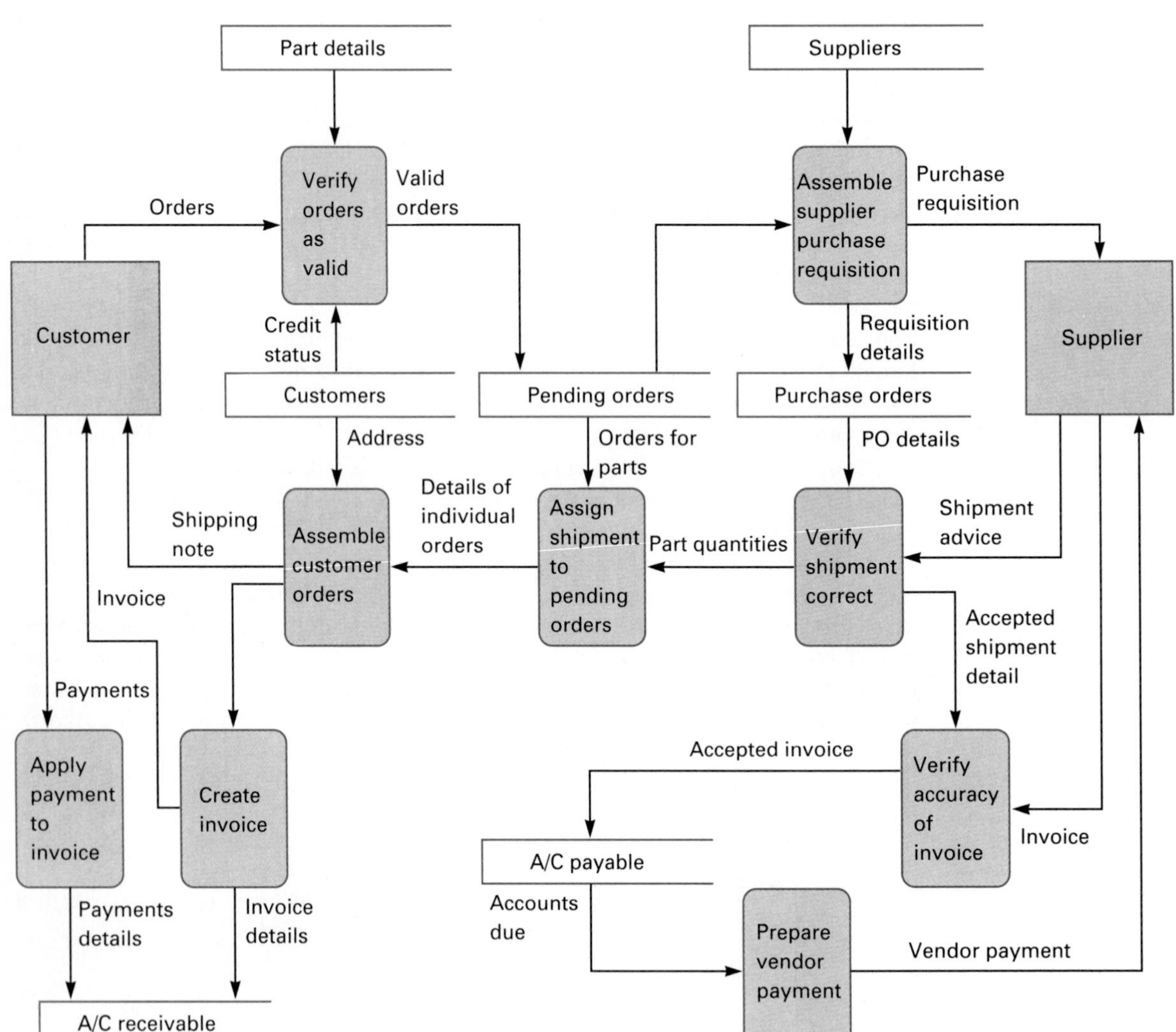

The supplier ships the parts to the company along with shipment advice indicating the contents of the shipment. In the verify-shipment-correct process, the company checks the purchase order data store to make sure that the shipment contains everything that was ordered. If the company has received the correct shipment, it can verify the accuracy of the invoice that has been sent by the supplier, update the accounts payable data store, and prepare a vendor payment to the supplier.

The remaining procedures include filling orders and accounts receivable. When a shipment is received, parts are assigned to specific orders and individual customer orders are assembled. A shipping note and an invoice are sent to the customer, and the invoice amount is used to update an accounts receivable data store for that customer. When the customer receives the invoice, payment is made and applied to the accounts receivable balance.

This system is fairly easy to understand with the graphic techniques of a logical data flow diagram. If procedures or data requirements have been left out, users should be able to detect them. The overall logical data flow diagram includes a number of subsystems, including order processing, purchasing, accounts receivable, and accounts payable. The data flow diagram makes it possible to visualize the relationships among these subsystems. The outputs of some of the subsystems, for example, become inputs into other subsystems. Pending orders, which are outputs of the order processing subsystem, become inputs into both the purchasing and order filling subsystems. The purchasing subsystem produces outputs that become inputs into the accounts payable subsystem. Understanding these relationships is important because data requirements need to be visualized on a systemwide basis.

The data flow diagram in Figure 17–4 shows a system without any particular flaws. A short case study of a mail-order record album and cassette tape concern, Music by Mail, Inc., will give you an idea of how a data flow diagram can be used for analytical purposes.

Case Study: Music by Mail, Inc.

Robert (Bob) Thomas is the owner of a small mail-order music store that features record albums and cassette tapes. He works out of his home and keeps a small inventory of the 50 most popular titles there. He orders other titles from four music distributors he deals with. Orders that cannot be filled from these sources are returned to his customers marked "unavailable item."

All of Bob's business is mail order. He publishes a flier of 200 titles four times a year based on current best-selling titles reported in trade publications. In addition, he sometimes runs spot ads in the local Sunday newspapers.

When an order is received, the payment must be verified before the order is filled. If the payment is a check, Bob holds the order for 14 days or until the check has cleared the bank. Bob deposits checks and money orders every other day at his bank. He also accepts credit cards such as Master Card, Visa, and American Express. In order to verify whether these accounts are good, he looks at a weekly listing of bad accounts provided by the credit card companies. However, on a number of occasions he has accepted a "bad" credit card or a card being used by an unauthorized user because the information in his weekly listing was not 100 percent up-to-date.

Daily orders are separated into two categories: in-stock orders and special orders. In-stock orders are filled and shipped by ZIP code daily. A photocopy of the order form serves as a packing slip. If the item is for a special order, the special order file is updated and the customer's order is placed in a pending orders file.

Every Monday Bob retrieves his special orders from the file and places his weekly purchase orders to obtain sufficient inventory of these titles. He also takes this opportunity to replenish his in-house inventory. Every so often, he reviews the 50 titles he regularly carries in stock, adds new ones, and eliminates slow sellers.

Bob places his orders for inventory over the phone, sends each vendor a follow-up purchase order, and files a copy in his placed-orders file. When he receives these items, he fills the outstanding orders as well as the special orders. After the orders have been filled, he transfers the order form to an orders-filled file.

When an order is filled, the customer's name and address are checked against a customer card file that is used for quarterly mailings. If the customer's address has changed, the customer card file is updated.

At the end of each month, Bob begins to process his accounts payable. He tries to take advantage of vendor discounts by paying bills within the discount period. At the beginning of the next month, Bob's accountant comes in, collects the prior month's records, and provides Bob with a monthly activity report summarizing his profits and losses. At this time, Bob reviews his inventory, adjusts his titles, and updates his flier for mailing purposes.

In studying this case, the systems analyst can identify a number of problems. When customers send in checks, for instance, an order can be delayed for weeks because of Bob's check-clearing policy. Bob is currently limiting his promotion efforts to 50 "best-selling" titles, but he doesn't analyze his own sales history data to determine best-selling and slow-moving items. With further analysis of his market, he could probably expand his inventories. In addition, his direct mail materials are currently being sent to only about 500 customers. This list needs to be greatly expanded. In the direct mail business, it is not unusual to have mailing lists of as many as 50,000 prospective customers.

Bob's accounting procedures could also be improved. He currently hires an accountant to develop monthly profit and loss statements. He sometimes fails to take advantage of vendor discounts, and he has almost no information for customer sales analysis purposes. Information about the most popular titles among certain groups would enable him to direct his marketing and promotional efforts toward customers with particular characteristics.

Based on a thorough discussion of the procedures of the current system, the systems analyst can draw current logical data flow diagrams. Current logical data flow diagrams for Music by Mail, Inc., are shown in Figure 17–5. These logical data flow diagrams depict the current processes, data flows, and data stores in four subsystems, including the order entry, order processing, receiving, and marketing subsystems.

Developing Business and System Objectives

At the end of the analysis phase of the systems study, the user should be able to identify objectives that address the needs of the business. These business objectives should state the business outcomes that need to be achieved. The business outcomes should be measurable so that the user understands the extent of the changes that will be necessary to make them occur. In most cases, a profit-making concern is trying to increase revenues and minimize costs. An example of a measurable business objective is "Increase sales by 25 percent within the next five years."

Sometimes business objectives establish competitive strategies. For example, a manufacturer may want to make it possible for customers to make orders, check on prices and delivery dates, and receive promotional information via personal computers hooked up to the manufacturer's mainframe computer. A business objective might be "Provide on-line order entry and price- and delivery-checking capabilities to 100 customers within the next two years."

Business objectives state the outcomes the business hopes to achieve by designing a new system. System objectives describe the major capabilities of the information

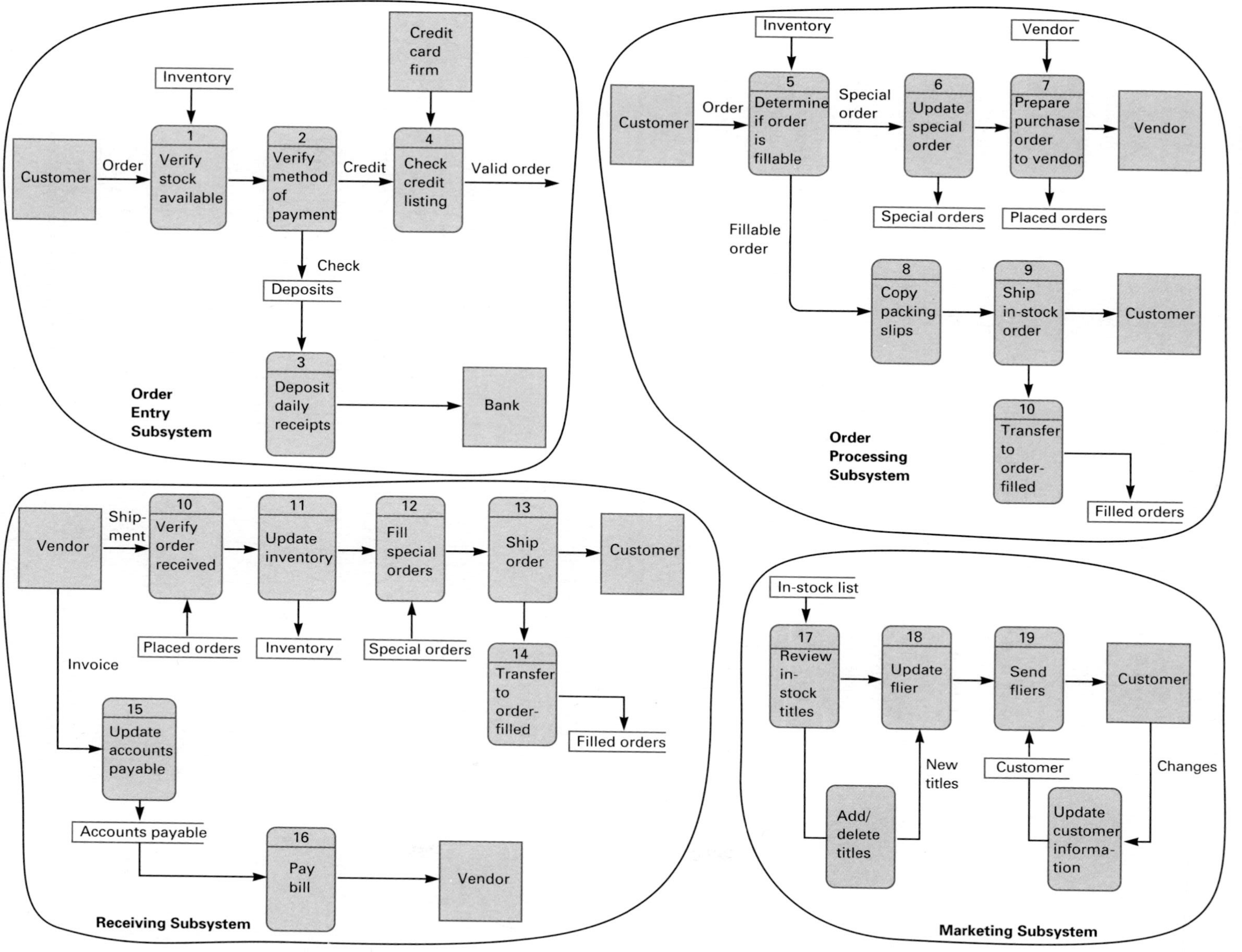

Figure 17–5 Current system data-flow diagrams for Music by Mail

system to be designed. One of the capabilities of computer-based information systems is the ability to process information faster and more accurately than manual systems. For example, a person responsible for manually checking the credit for hundreds of customer orders per day is likely to make an error, but a computer-based system will be almost totally accurate. Information maintained by a computer-based information system is also more likely to be up-to-date. Finally, a computer-based system can introduce new functions for management reporting and analysis purposes. Although it's very difficult to perform many of these analytical functions manually, computer-based procedures can easily be designed to summarize and aggregate sales data, accounts receivable data, and inventory data for analytical purposes.

Business and system objectives developed for Music by Mail, Inc., might include the list shown in Table 17–5. One of the major problems identified during the analysis of the current situation was the excessive delay in filling orders paid by check. One way to handle this bottleneck would be to contract for a telecheck service that would identify bad-check writers. Another method mail-order companies use frequently is to require that all orders be paid by money orders. Bob decides to use the telecheck service.

One of the major obstacles to the expansion of Music by Mail, Inc., is inventory control. Cash is tied up in the inventory of slow-moving items. Sales order history data are not being used to identify poor-selling items, and it seems as if Bob is reordering the same standard list of titles each month. Slow-moving items could be used to make special introductory offers to new customers and also to create sale items for existing

Table 17–5
Objectives for Music by Mail, Inc.

Business Objectives	System Objectives
Improve order processing by filling all orders within three days	Cut check-clearing time by using a check-approval service
Reduce inventories of slow-moving items by 50 percent	Provide introductory specials or sales to get rid of slow-moving items
	Update inventory levels for all items on sales orders
	Establish a reorder point for all inventory items using order history data and reorder titles that have reached their reorder point
Increase revenues by 25 percent within the next year	Expand the mailing list to 30,000
	Use order history data to identify the most profitable titles and slow-moving titles
	Mail promotional fliers to 30,000 prospects monthly instead of quarterly
Reduce order cancellations by 10 percent within the next six months	Expand distributors from 4 to 10
	Expand in-house inventory to 100 items based on sales analysis findings
Cut costs by taking vendor discounts on orders	Implement an accounts payable system to identify payment terms for vendor discounts on orders

customers. Sales analysis data could be used to reduce inventory orders for these slow-moving items.

Bob could manage his inventory more effectively by establishing reorder points for all inventory items. When a customer sends in an order, Bob could update the inventory levels for all items on the order. When a certain item reached its reorder point, Bob would then reorder a sufficient quantity of that inventory item to fill recurring orders. Sales order history data could be used to establish reorder points for inventory items and also to determine reorder quantities.

Bob's major objective should be to increase revenues from sales. He should expand his mailing list, his distributor contacts, and the number of in-stock inventory items he maintains in order to increase sales revenues. These strategies will enable him to provide better customer service, to attract new customers, and to retain current ones. In addition to these strategies, he could cut administrative costs by reducing shipping costs and by taking vendor discounts on orders.

The business and system objectives developed by the user should complement each other. For example, the objective "increase revenues by 25 percent within the next year" could be partly satisfied by setting up an information system to generate a mailing list of 30,000 names and addresses monthly. Although this is a substantially larger list than the one Bob currently maintains, a 25 percent increase in revenues would more than make up the difference in cost of the new system. Each business objective provides some financial projections that are helpful in developing a cost-benefit analysis for the proposed system. The topic of cost-benefit analysis will be covered in Chapter 18.

Preparing the Proposed System Data Flow Diagram

The proposed system data flow diagrams should incorporate changes in procedures that are expressed in the system objectives. The proposed data flow diagrams for Music by Mail, Inc., shown in Figure 17–6, include new functions that were not included on the current data flow diagram. You can find new procedures in the order entry subsystem, in the order processing/inventory subsystem, and in the sales analysis and marketing subsystem. In the order entry subsystem, you will see that "approve check" using a telecheck service has been introduced as process 4. In the order processing subsystem, inventory is verified in process 5. In process 9, inventory is checked to determine if any items have reached their reorder points, and in process 10, orders to distributors are made to replenish the stock of items that need to be reordered.

Another change that has been incorporated into one of the proposed data flow diagrams occurs in the sales analysis and reporting subsystem. An order history data store is used to generate monthly sales analysis reports (process 17) that can be used to identify both popular titles and slow-moving ones. These sales analysis findings are used to determine what in-house inventory should be maintained and which items should be discontinued (process 18). The in-house titles are then used to update the sales promotion flier (process 19), which is sent to customers.

Because the receiving subsystem depicted in the current system data flow diagram does not change in the proposed system, you will not find a new diagram for receiving in Figure 17–6.

Some of the changes in the proposed system do not appear on the proposed data flow diagram. For example, the expansion of the mailing list from 500 to 30,000 prospects is not shown on the diagram. This change in volume would be recorded in the logical data dictionary.

The proposed logical data flow diagram becomes a blueprint for the proposed system, which can be further described by a number of other structured tools and

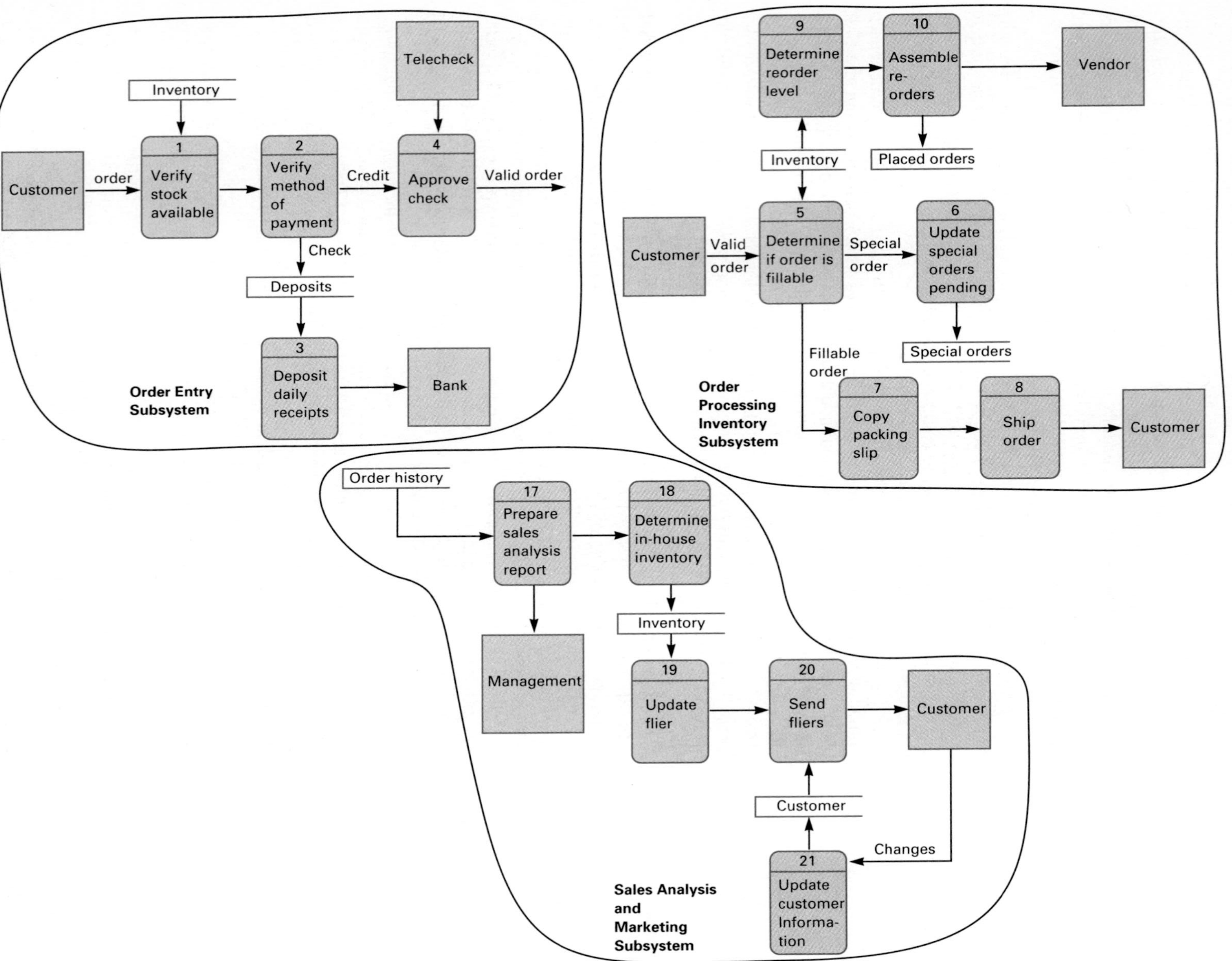

Figure 17–6 Proposed system data-flow diagrams for Music by Mail

techniques. The logic of system processes can be clearly described using **decision tables** and **decision trees.** The data elements that make up the system's data flows and data stores become part of a logical data dictionary. Finally, the data stores become the basis for developing a logical database design supporting systemwide data requirements and ultimately laying the groundwork for file design. The user-manager must review each of these design documents to make sure that system requirements are correct.

Specifying Process Logic Using Decision Trees and Tables

One new procedure Bob might want to introduce is a quantity discount policy for orders. His policy might be as follows:

> The trade discount (to companies, educational institutions, and libraries) is 20 percent. For private customers, a 5 percent discount is given for orders of 10 records/tapes or more, a 10 percent discount for orders of 20 records/tapes or more, and a 20 percent discount for orders of 50 or more. Trade orders for 20 records/tapes or more would receive an additional 10 percent discount over the regular trade discount.

Although this policy may appear straightforward, in its narrative version it could be misinterpreted. A decision table or decision tree is a useful tool for specifying the logic of a process such as this one. The decision tree and decision table for Bob's discount policy are shown in Figure 17–7.

A decision table or tree enables the user to make sure that the systems analyst has interpreted a business policy or procedure correctly. In turn, the systems analyst can use a decision table or tree to explain the logic of a procedure to a programmer.

Describing Data Flows and Data Stores in the Logical Data Dictionary

The data flows and data stores in the logical data flow diagram consist of data elements that the user must identify. The characteristics of these data elements also must be defined—the systemwide data elements and their characteristics are described in a data dictionary.

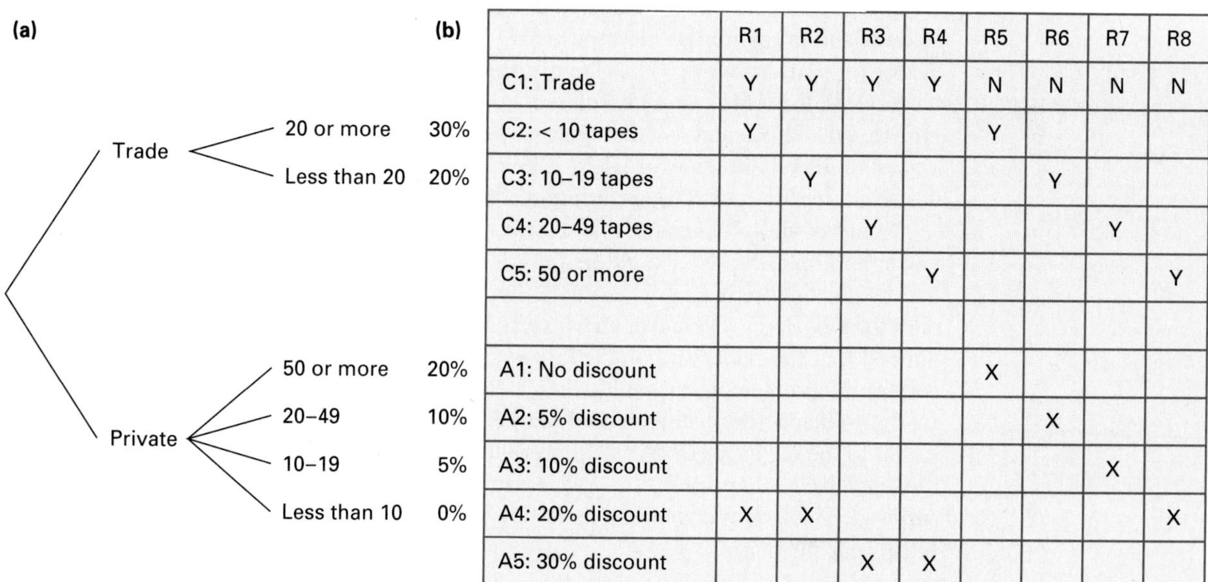

	R1	R2	R3	R4	R5	R6	R7	R8
C1: Trade	Y	Y	Y	Y	N	N	N	N
C2: < 10 tapes	Y				Y			
C3: 10–19 tapes		Y				Y		
C4: 20–49 tapes			Y				Y	
C5: 50 or more				Y				Y
A1: No discount					X			
A2: 5% discount						X		
A3: 10% discount							X	
A4: 20% discount	X	X						X
A5: 30% discount			X	X				

Figure 17–7 **(a)** Decision tree for a discount policy. **(b)** Decision table for a discount policy

Data flows are data in motion. In the Music by Mail, Inc., case, one of the data flows is customer order. This data flow consists of many data elements, each of which needs to be given a unique data name and a standard data definition. Some of the data elements in customer order would be customer name, customer street address, item number, item description, and item quantity. You will learn how to develop a detailed data dictionary describing data elements in Chapter 18.

Once the data elements of the system have been defined, the user must be involved in determining the contents of data stores. Data stores are data at rest. The data stores house the data that become the basis for designing files throughout the system. The most commonly used approach to defining data store contents is to take inventory of the data elements that are used in outgoing data flows. These are typically the data elements that are printed out in some kind of output report. The user must be directly involved in determining these output requirements, particularly the nature of management reports for such functions as sales and inventory analysis. The data stores then become whatever is necessary to support the agreed-upon outputs. They must also include any input data elements that are needed to generate the outputs.

Structured tools for systems analysis and design are created to allow users to identify their systems requirements. The logic of decisions, the definition of data elements, and the description of reports all need to be provided by the user and understood by the systems analyst. These tools enhance communication between the analyst and user and provide logical specifications that become inputs into the next phase of the project, detailed design.

The Organizationwide Data Dictionary

During the systems analysis process, systems analysts collect information about the data elements that make up records and reports. Over the past 20 to 25 years many information systems have been developed, and the data used in these systems has been defined and redefined many times. For example, the data element CUSTOMER-NAME may be called CUST-NAME, C-NAME, CUS-NAM, NAME-OF-CUST, and IN-C-NAME in various programs and records that have been developed by different analysts and programmers over the years. To compound the situation, the characteristics of the data may also be defined differently in different systems. In one system, CUSTOMER-NAME may be defined as a 26-digit alphabetic field, and in another, NAME-OF-CUST may be defined as a 32-digit alphanumeric field. The result is a Tower of Babel situation in which the same element is called different names and described in different ways in different information systems.

Some of the problems of the Tower of Babel situation are illustrated in the following examples. Lawrence Peters describes the experience of a flight instructor who had taught hundreds of private pilots. On one occasion, when he was training a new pilot to land a B-17 that had been converted for use in fighting forest fires, the instructor noticed that the pilot was coming in too low. He waited for the trainee to detect and correct the problem, but when he didn't, the flight instructor shouted, "takeoff power." In the military, the instructor had learned that "takeoff power" meant to apply full power to the engines. However, the student interpreted "takeoff power" to mean to cut the engines further back. The plane crashed, but the instructor and student pilot survived. The lack of a common definition for the phrase "takeoff power" was certainly felt in this incident.[1]

---

[1]Lawrence Peters, *Advanced Structured Analysis and Design* (Englewood Cliffs, N.J.: Prentice-Hall, 1987).

Other problems occur when a data element has many different names. Gordon Davis, a Professor of Management Information Systems at the University of Minnesota, tells of a situation in which a business analyst was asked to assess the feasibility of offering a tuition reimbursement program to the employees of a firm. To determine the number of employees who might use such a program to pay for their children's college education, the analyst queried the employee master file for the number and ages of children. Based on his analysis of children who would be eligible for benefits from the proposed program, he concluded that the program was feasible.

However, the analyst made a serious mistake. In doing his study, he used one data name to extract employee information. But three different data names for the data element EMPLOYEE existed in various files. As a result, there were three times as many employees and potentially three times as many children affected by the program as the number he projected. When the program was implemented, requests for tuition reimbursement tripled the original projection. The president quickly realized that the company could not afford to support the program and withdrew these benefits. Employees were bitter about the outcome because their children's education was a sensitive personal issue. Plant workers went out on strike, demanding that the tuition benefit program be reinstated. In the midst of the turmoil, the president himself resigned.

Scenarios like this one depict the potential dangers of nonstandardized data element names and definitions. Most organizations today are moving toward a centralized database approach and, along with this approach, are implementing organizationwide data dictionaries. These dictionaries enforce standard data names and data definitions for the data elements used in the enterprise. For example, CUST-NAME may be established as a standard data name, and 26 alphabetic digits may be set as the standard data definition for the data element *customer name.* Any other data names used to describe customer name in other programs and records are called *aliases,* or other data names by which customer name is known.

The organizationwide data dictionary concept has many benefits. For one thing, programmers and analysts can use the dictionary to look up the standard data names and definitions for data elements used in information systems under development. This minimizes the Tower of Babel problem. The dictionary also saves time and effort in maintenance. For example, if the data element EMPLOYEE-ZIP, representing ZIP code, has to be changed from a five-digit numeric field (63121) to a nine-digit numeric field (63121–1106), the programmer must be able to search for each occurrence of the ZIP code field in all existing programs and records. If this field is called different names in different programs, the search can be very time-consuming. However, with a data dictionary, the programmer can identify the standard data name (EMPLOYEE-ZIP) as well as aliases (EMP-ZIP, EMP-ZIP-CODE, and so on) for that data element and then make the necessary changes. As you can see, knowing the data element name to look for can greatly reduce the maintenance process.

The organizationwide data dictionary approach also makes it possible for managers throughout the organization to learn the data names and definitions of data they need to generate reports and to make queries from existing databases. It is a critical strategy in moving toward using data as a corporate resource.

Box 17–1 Information Engineering

You have already learned that a structured systems development methodology establishes a set of policies and procedures for accomplishing a systems design project. A methodology attempts to add structure and control to a project so that activities are completed on time and within budgetary constraints. First and foremost, a methodology enables systems designers to create an information system that meets the needs and priorities of the users.

The structured methodologies were introduced in the late 1960s, after years of experience with information systems projects that were out of control in terms of budgets and schedules and that failed to meet users' objectives. The increased complexity of systems and the increased need for maintainability spurred the introduction of structured programming in the 1970s. Structured programming forced the issue of structured design, and the concepts of modularity and stepwise refinement. Programmer teams and structured walkthroughs were introduced as organizational strategies for achieving better quality designs.

During the 1970s and 1980s, two major schools of structured design emerged. The first school, led by such teachers as Yourdon, Constantine, and Gane and Sarson, introduced a process-oriented structured design approach, using the data flow diagram as a principle tool. You learned about a number of tools and techniques using the data flow approach in this chapter. The second school of thought, represented by the Warnier-Orr methodology, used a design approach based upon the structure of the data.

In reality, most systems designers use a variety of tools and techniques to represent both the data flows and data structures within an information system. Depending upon the nature and scope of the design problem, they may mix and match methodologies. Good designers know how to use a variety of methods and how to match the methods they choose to the type of design problem.

In the 1980s, a methodology known as information engineering incorporated both process-oriented and data-driven tools into a single approach. Information engineering includes four phases: information strategy planning, business area analysis, systems design, and construction. These phases are depicted in Figure 17–8.

INFORMATION STRATEGY PLANNING

The purpose of information strategy planning is to investigate how information technology can be used to enable the firm to gain competitive advantage. This means establishing goals and critical success factors that senior management can understand. At the planning stage, the analyst develops an enterprise model depicting what critical business functions exist and how current information systems support these functions. Then, the users identify information systems needs that address important business opportunities. During the information strategy planning phase, information planning matrixes, organization charts, and entity-relationship diagrams are some examples of the types of diagrams used. Figure 17–9 gives an example of an entity-relationship diagram.

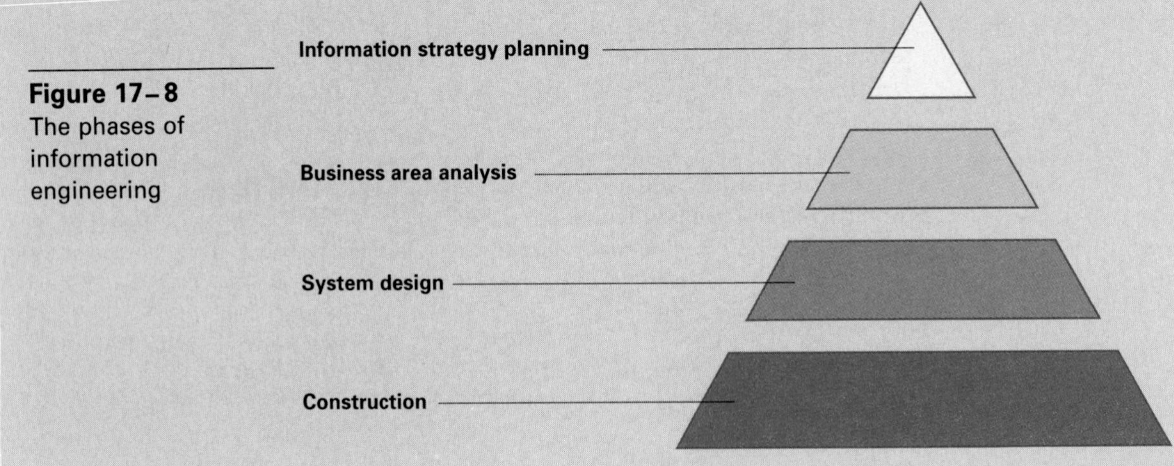

Figure 17–8
The phases of information engineering

Figure 17–9
An entity-relationship diagram

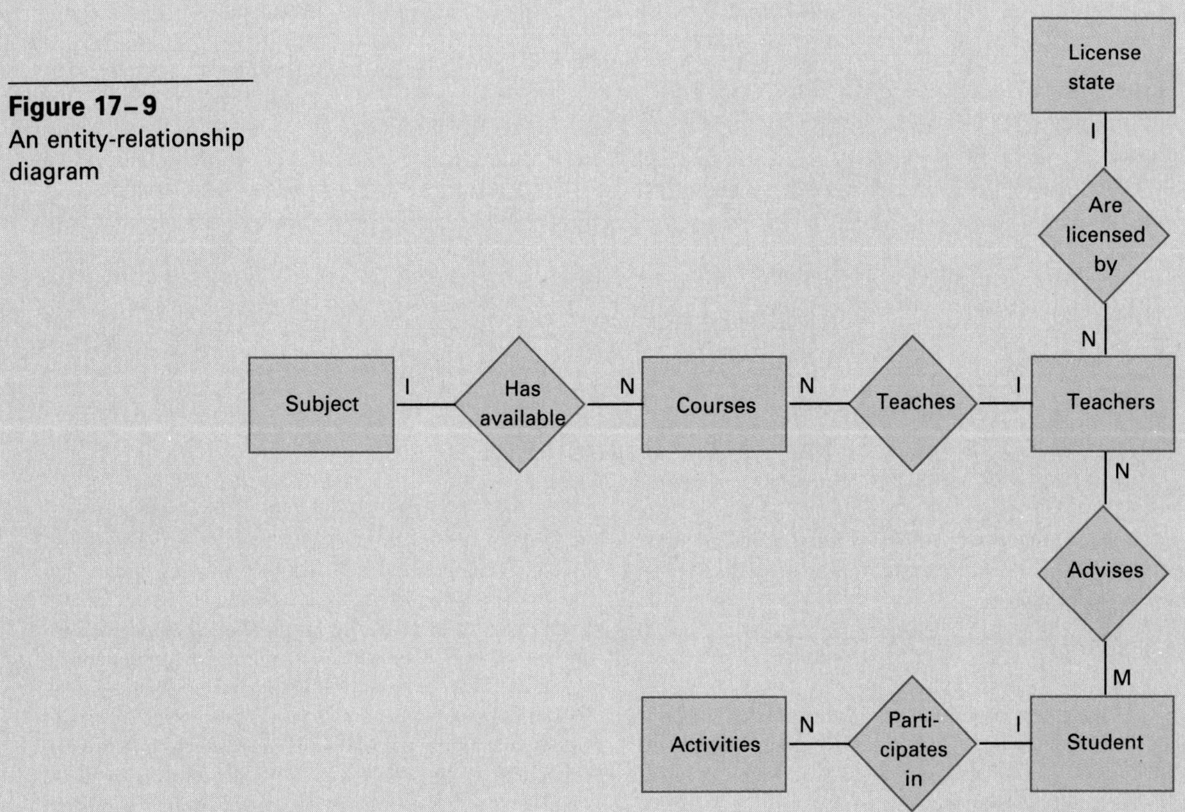

BUSINESS AREA ANALYSIS

During the business area analysis phase, the analyst determines the processes and data needed to support the enterprise. As the analyst and user study each business area, they may rethink existing systems and procedures and identify areas for systems design. The results are recorded in a detailed process model and a detailed data model. At this phase, an entity/process matrix may be used to illustrate which data entities support various business processes. The analyst may decompose the functions described in the planning phase into a detailed process model and may depict the interrelationships among processes using a process dependency diagram. The fully simplified data model illustrating the relationship between data structures is also developed during this phase. You will find an example of such a data model in Figure 17–10.

SYSTEMS DESIGN

After business area analysis, the information systems design process can begin. In the information engineering methodology, systems design uses a prototyping approach in which users work jointly with designers to develop report designs, screen designs, and other specifications. Throughout the process, the users are responsible for establishing system specifications. The analyst works with the user to revise and refine prototypes until the user's needs are met.

During the design phase, design automation tools are used to the greatest extent possible. The data models and process models are stored in a central design repository, or encyclopedia, and are used to generate prototypes. Design automation tools are used to prototype screens and reports and to store design documentation in the encyclopedia.

(continued)

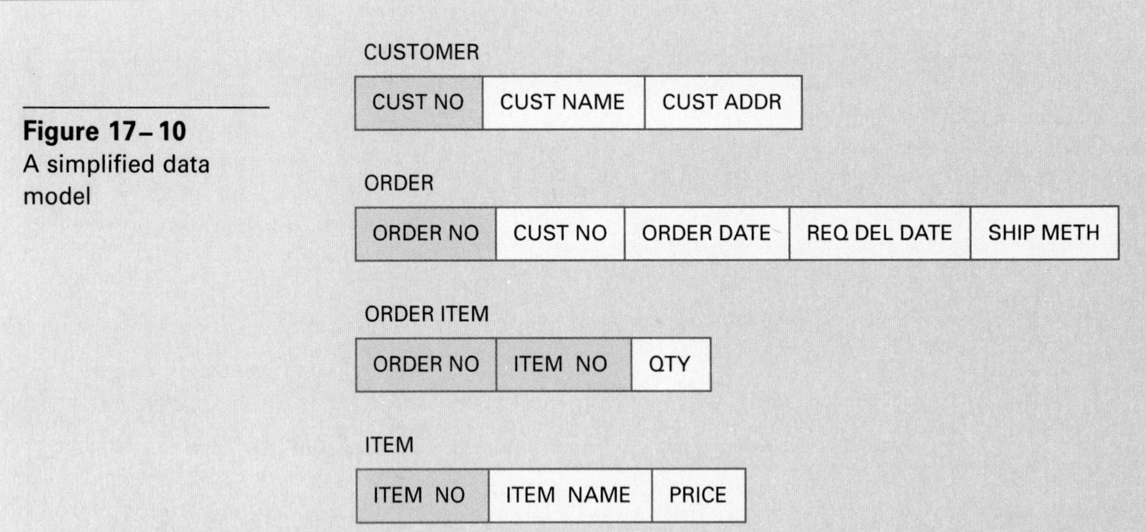

Figure 17–10
A simplified data model

Information engineering advocates using code generators and fourth-generation languages to implement the design wherever possible.

CONSTRUCTION

During the last phase of information engineering, construction, the actual code is generated to implement the system. Report and screen layouts, action diagrams of code, and prototypes are used to implement the design. In some cases, users can access databases and generate reports to meet their needs using high-level languages. If end-users are going to design their own systems, they should be encouraged to use the common data models and standardized data definitions stored in the common repository or encyclopedia. Otherwise, redundant definitions for common data elements will eventually create a Tower of Babel and data management will be almost impossible.

In summary, the information engineering approach combines a variety of tools and techniques to accomplish strategic planning, business analysis, systems design, and construction. One of its main advantages is the linkage between business plans and information systems plans using the Critical Success Factors approach. Another advantage is the focus on establishing design blueprints through the development of data models and process models maintained in a central encyclopedia. Systems designs are implemented using code generators and fourth-generation languages to the extent possible. As a result, systems are easier to build and to modify, and users have an opportunity to be directly involved in systems design from beginning to end. The information engineering approach is supported by a variety of computer-assisted software engineering (CASE) tools, including Knowledgeware's Information Engineering Workbench (IEW) and Texas Instruments' Information Engineering Facility (IEF). Information engineering will continue to be an important information systems development approach throughout the 1990s.

EVALUATING ALTERNATIVE DESIGN OPTIONS

One of the most important elements in systems design is the evaluation of alternative design options. The input of managers who will be using the system is critical at this point. The range of systems design options that should be evaluated includes batch versus on-line systems, mainframe-based versus microcomputer-based systems, and systems developed in-house versus packaged systems. In each systems design project, the alternative design options are slightly different.

Alternative Processing Modes

One range of alternatives to be considered in developing a systems design proposal is the mode of processing that the system will support. Processing modes include batch, on-line, distributed, and decentralized options.

Batch Processing. Batch processing normally uses a central computer system to process all transactions against a central database and to produce reports at fixed intervals in time. Payroll is a good example of a batch processing application because all time cards are used to update a payroll master file, calculate pay amounts, and produce checks and other payroll reports at fixed times.

On-Line Processing. In on-line processing, transactions can be keyed in at remote terminals at remote sites and transferred to the computer system via telecommunications channels. Users at remote sites can also receive outputs that have been processed by the central computer system displayed at their terminals. An on-line order entry system, for example, makes it possible for a local sales clerk to check a customer's credit against an accounts receivable master file at a central office.

In on-line processing, transactions can be edited against a central database or at the local workstation. If transactions are edited by a program running on the central system, error transactions would be printed out on an error report and sent back to the local office that had originated them. However, many local data entry terminals have built-in data validation capabilities so that transactions are edited on-site and only accurate data are transmitted to a central system, where it is used to update a central database.

On-line processing has two types of update procedures: **on-line with batch overnight update** and **on-line immediate update.**

These can be best explained by examples. In batch overnight update, transactions are entered locally at remote terminals, transmitted to the central system, and used to update the central database overnight. A loan company may accept loan payments at branch offices. Payment transactions could be entered and validated at the local branches, transmitted to the central home office, and used to update the central loan file overnight. In this mode of processing, a record of payments made on any given working day would not be available until the next day. However, batch overnight update is an efficient method for most business data processing applications.

Although batched update is normally associated with overnight update, there is no reason that updates cannot be batched more or less frequently than overnight. Updates can be deferred and batched twice a day, once during lunch hour and once overnight. There is no reason why updates couldn't be done once a week if the users of the application found that satisfactory.

In contrast, an on-line system with immediate update makes it possible for transactions to update the central database on a real-time basis or as they occur. Inquiries to the database reflect business that has taken place that same day. Examples of information systems requiring on-line immediate update capabilities are airline and hotel reservations systems.

Distributed Data Processing. In a distributed data processing situation, local transactions can be used to update local files, and summary results can be transmitted to a central system. The point-of-sale processing systems used by stores such as Sears and JC Penney are good examples of this approach. In these systems, sales transactions update local inventory databases, and summary sales and inventory results are sent to the central office for management reporting and analysis purposes.

Decentralized Processing. A dedicated minicomputer or microcomputer with its own database can serve as a decentralized system. When communications with other systems are not necessary and the application is relatively self-contained, decentralized processing is appropriate. A local word processing system in an office and a dedicated production planning system in a plant are good examples of decentralized processing.

Improved Manual Operations. Another alternative that needs to be considered in systems design is improving manual operations. Introducing an automated system into a situation in which work is disorganized, procedures are unclear, and job responsibilities are not equitably allocated may actually worsen the situation. Work procedures must be simplified, methods of work organization and control improved, and work responsibilities distributed equitably before a computer-based information system is introduced.

Each of these alternatives must be evaluated on the basis of user needs, the characteristics of the application, the trade-off between local and central control, and cost-effectiveness. The availability of microcomputer-based workstations has improved the technical and economic feasibility of distributed and decentralized processing approaches.

Computer Design Alternatives

The three major computer design alternatives that should be considered are acquiring an in-house computer system, using a **timesharing** service, or contracting for service with a **service bureau.**

An In-House Computer System. A number of in-house computer options exist, including mainframe-based, minicomputers, and microcomputer alternatives. The improving capabilities of minicomputers and microcomputers make them excellent candidates for distributed, decentralized, and departmental computing options. Frequently, these minis and micros can be linked to mainframe-based databases via telecommunications networks.

Earlier chapters have discussed these computer configurations in greater detail. The choice of computer system depends on processing requirements, including processing mode, the nature and scope of applications, the number of applications, file sizes, number of users, and capacity needs. As discussed in earlier chapters, large mainframe-based systems support multiple users and multiple applications and provide economies of scale in processing and support. In contrast, distributed or dedicated minicomputer and microcomputer options provide opportunities for user control over hardware, software development, operations, and maintenance.

Timesharing Services. Sometimes it is not feasible to purchase an in-house computer system. A few users may want access to statistical analysis software, but their requirements do not justify purchasing the hardware and software to support this system in-house. In a timesharing situation, the user pays only for the computer resources—including processing time and access to computer programs—that are used. Normally, the user has a terminal and a local printer tied to the timesharing computer. He uses the program(s) needed and sends data and receives output on an on-demand basis. The advantage of this approach is that many users can share computer resources and have access to programs and computer capacity that would not otherwise be available to them. The disadvantage of this approach is that the user does not have control over the system and the charges for its use. Timesharing has been largely displaced by powerful desktop workstations and more cost-effective solutions. The only significant use of timesharing today is to access highly specialized, expensive resources such as supercomputers.

Service Bureaus. Many organizations have no experience with selecting and managing a computer system. Service bureaus provide services ranging from full-scale support for applications from accounts receivable and payroll to data entry and distribution of output. The job of application development, processing, maintenance, and support is in the hands of technical professionals working for the service bureau. Some service bureaus rent or sell their customers computers so that some data processing can occur locally.

The biggest advantage of a service bureau is that it allows the use of computer services without incurring the time and expense of organizing and managing an in-house computer operation. A service bureau can be contracted, for example, to maintain a database of 450,000 names and addresses and to generate mailing labels from this database quarterly. Since the computer capacity to handle this application is needed only four times a year, the fund-raising organization would benefit from using the service bureau approach. However, service bureau customers are not totally in control of the processing and maintenance of their application and may have to tolerate poor service levels and lack of responsiveness to their needs.

Some of the advantages and disadvantages of the various computer design alternatives are summarized in Table 17–6.

Software Development Alternatives

A final range of alternatives deals with software development. Today, many software packages on mainframes, minicomputers, and microcomputers provide excellent alternatives to in-house software development. In addition, software vendors or **software houses** offer systems design and programming services that make it unnecessary for an organization to hire in-house programmers.

In-House Software Development. In large organizations with MIS systems development professionals, software for information systems development projects that are

Table 17–6
Computer design alternatives

In-House Computer System	
Advantages	**Disadvantages**
Control over hardware	Cost of systems development
Control over systems development	Cost of hardware operations and maintenance
Control over priorities	Cost of staffing and training computer personnel
Optimum configuration possible; limited to what is needed	
Timesharing System	
Advantages	**Disadvantages**
Variable cost; pay only for what is used	Lack of control over system service levels
Access to computer programs and capacity not otherwise available	Lack of control over charges for system use
Service Bureau Option	
Advantages	**Disadvantages**
Cost-effective	Lack of control over priorities
Use of computer systems without having to bring systems development and operations functions in-house	Data in the hands of an external organization
Availability of specific services	Lack of control over data processing expense

sophisticated, unique to the organization, and maintainable by MIS professionals is usually developed in-house. Unique user requirements can be satisfied more readily with in-house development. However, the time and cost of developing software from scratch argue against using this approach in many projects.

Software Houses. Software houses offer specialized systems design and programming services as well as help with implementation, including conversion and training. In cases where the in-house development staff does not have the time or expertise to support a project, contracting for software development services can be a cost-effective approach. In most cases, software houses also support maintenance and enhancements to the current system. Although contract personnel may have specialized expertise in the application area, they may not be familiar with the business requirements of the user.

Software Packages. The use of software packages can save considerable time and effort in systems development. Software packages must be evaluated in detail to make sure that they support the users' requirements. If modifications are substantial, then in-house development may pay off more effectively in the long run.

Table 17–7 summarizes some of the advantages and disadvantages of various software development approaches.

The selection of an appropriate systems design alternative requires user involvement. A systems design proposal will include an analysis of each alternative, its technical feasibility, its economic feasibility, and its impact on the organization. The development

Table 17–7 Software development alternatives

Advantages	Disadvantages
In-House Software Development	
Can manage and control the program development process	Time and cost greater than other options
Internal professionals can serve unique user requirements	In-house staff may lack specialized expertise needed for the project
Internal systems designers can provide more effective training, evaluation, and follow-up	
Software Houses	
Can contract and pay for specific services that are needed	External project management, including time, cost, and performance considerations
Can obtain experts to do design work	Implementation may be difficult for "outsiders"
Software Packages	
Savings in time and cost of in-house development	Package may not fit users' needs
Availability of detailed documentation and training materials	May incur time and cost necessary to modify the package to meet users' needs

time and cost for each alternative suggest trade-offs that also need to be evaluated. For example, a package software solution may not meet 100 percent of the users' requirements, but it could be implemented within six months, compared with an system developed in-house, which might take two years to design, program, and implement.

Today, information systems are needed to obtain a competitive edge or to provide needed services to customers. These considerations enter into the selection of an appropriate development alternative.

Box 17–2 Take a Look at Outsourcing

Outsourcing of information systems is a trend that is receiving a great deal of attention. Today, firms can contract with external vendors for almost any kind of data processing service, including data center operations, telecommunications, software maintenance, hardware support, or even application development. One of the main reasons for outsourcing is cost reduction. Often, external contractors can offer services at less cost than a company will spend managing its data center internally. However, a firm should be cautious in pursuing an outsourcing arrangement. It should be aware of both the benefits and pitfalls of outsourcing.

One of the major benefits of outsourcing is the ability to redirect MIS staff members away from traditional, maintenance-type projects to application development projects that have strategic value. At Talman Federal Savings and Loan, for example, management decided to outsource data center operations in order to free up Talman's internal information systems staff to develop sophisticated branch banking products and services. These products and services were designed to give them a competitive advantage in the savings and loan market. One of these services was a bank-at-home service that let customers transfer money between their accounts and conduct other banking business at home. Another service enabled customers to do their banking via a touch-tone phone.

As you can see from this example, a firm can outsource nonstrategic activities such as data center management and refocus its attention on projects that have an important business impact. This approach is consistent with an overall business strategy of downsizing operations to essential core business activities while outsourcing the rest.

Outsourcing has its pitfalls, too. Once management has decided to outsource its data center operations, it may be difficult to organize them again. Without careful initial planning, the services provided through an outsourcing arrangement may not be any better than the services provided by an internally managed operation. At Farm Credit Banks of St. Louis, management initiated an outsourcing program in the mid-1980s. The outsourcing contract supported network management, data center operations, computer processing, application development, PC support, systems maintenance, staffing, and database management. However, soon it became apparent that the services provided by the outsourcing arrangement were ineffective.

The major problem was the lack of business systems analysts who had an understanding of the bank's business. To correct the situation, Farm Credit Banks purchased a midsized computer and brought in internal developers who had good knowledge of bank operations. These internal developers focused on key information systems projects. External contractors handled data center management and operations on an outsourcing basis.

Another pitfall to avoid is locking yourself into an inflexible contract. Contracts need to be evolutionary so that new technology and development methods can be pursued. Contracts must also weigh the partnership as a mutually beneficial and cooperative arrangement. If a fixed cost contract is negotiated, the vendor may not be motivated to provide anything other than minimum service. However, if revenues are tied to the success of a project, both the firm and the outsourcing vendor win. In one case, Andersen Consulting, an outsourcing vendor, placed an accounts receivable system in a client company. The new system didn't make any money for Andersen until its clients' revenues grew from better ability to track receivables. When its clients' revenues grew, Andersen's revenues grew as well.

For an outsourcing arrangement to work, the contract should be a two-way street. Without question, outsourcing will pave the way for many companies to refocus their MIS missions toward projects that are critical to achieving business results.

SELECTING A SYSTEMS DESIGN ALTERNATIVE

In a systems design study, a number of alternatives must be considered and evaluated. Typically, the systems analyst presents a menu of alternatives, consisting of a high-cost approach, an intermediate-cost approach, and a low-cost approach. The options that are reviewed depend on the nature and scope of the project. You can obtain some insight into how alternatives are developed by looking at the Music by Mail case.

An Inventory Control System for Music by Mail, Inc.

One of the major problems Bob Thomas, owner of Music by Mail, Inc., had was lack of effective inventory control. Excess quantities of certain records and tapes were drawing on cash flow. Customer orders for merchandise that was not held in stock took a long time to fill. In addition, Bob had very little information about inventory turnover and sales trends.

A menu of alternatives for Music by Mail, Inc., might include a microcomputer-based system with a custom-programmed inventory application, a microcomputer-based system with an inventory software package, and an improved manual system.

A Custom-Programmed Inventory Application. Although a custom-programmed system would take more time to develop, Bob could contract with a local university-trained programmer to develop an inventory system using a microcomputer-based database management program such as dBase IV. Since the program could be menu-driven, Bob would not need to learn the technical aspects of dBase IV himself. However, he would require additional contract work if modifications to the system were necessary.

The inventory system would enable Bob to enter sales information, update inventory data, and generate a reorder report for all items falling below certain stock levels. The system could provide a listing of current on-hand and on-order titles, including vendor contacts. File maintenance, such as adding, changing, and deleting inventory records, could be handled by Bob himself at regular intervals.

According to the systems analyst's estimates, the custom-designed application would cost approximately $12,300. About $6,500 would include hardware and software, including a microcomputer-based system with a 140 MB hard disk, a dot-matrix printer, a tape cartridge backup device, and dBase IV software. Systems design and programming time would include about 120 hours of work at $40 per hour, or $4,800. An additional $1,000 would be required for installation, setup, data entry, and testing.

Although the custom-programmed application would be more time-consuming and expensive to implement, it would provide Bob with exactly what he needs to manage his inventory more effectively. He could be directly involved in designing screens and reports that would help him do his job better. To make the system work effectively, however, he would have to be trained to handle certain operational procedures, such as routine data entry, backup of data files, and report generation.

A Package Software Solution. Instead of contracting for a custom-developed inventory system, Bob could purchase a microcomputer with inventory control software designed for a small business. Several packages could be evaluated with the help of a systems analyst. One major advantage of this approach is that all the documentation, reports, screens, and procedures would be defined. Bob would simply have to be trained to handle the basic operational procedures of the system.

One of the disadvantages of this approach is that a package might provide too many reports that aren't really needed. Simple queries and on-demand reports might not be possible to generate. If modifications were necessary, their cost and feasibility would have to be evaluated. It might not be possible to obtain the source code needed to make the necessary modifications. Source code consists of the listings of actual programs written to implement the information system. If the source code can be obtained, Bob might be able to find a programmer who can make modifications in the programs. However, if the source code cannot be obtained, Bob might not be able to modify the programs, or he might have to contract with the software company for the necessary modifications.

The package solution is slightly less expensive. The microcomputer-based hardware configuration would cost about $5,800, about the same as in the first option. Package evaluation would entail about 10 hours of the systems analyst's time and cost about $400, and the package itself would cost about $400. System implementation and testing would entail hiring a clerical worker for about 10 hours to key in inventory data records, which would cost about $65. In all, the package solution would cost $6,665.

An Improved Manual System. Bob could make improvements in his manual system at very little cost. He could select new titles for his in-house inventory of tapes and records using sales history information from his own records and local trade reports on emerging trends. He could establish reorder points on various types of merchandise (for example, cassette tapes in the country and western category) and also define an economic order quantity based on the monthly inventory turnover of this type of merchandise. He could also keep better records of inventory turnover among various types of merchandise so he could react to sales trends more quickly. Finally, he could put slow-moving items on sale or offer them as introductory specials after one month of sitting in inventory.

Although this alternative would be fairly easy to design and implement, Bob would probably need the help of an experienced systems analyst knowledgeable in inventory control and management procedures. The main disadvantage of this approach is that as inventory grows, it would be more difficult for Bob to keep track of various titles. In addition, it would be almost impossible for him to manually generate various reports on inventory turnover. Based on the time of a systems analyst working with Bob to organize a more effective manual record-keeping system for inventory, the total cost of an improved manual system would be $800.

Some of the advantages and disadvantages of each of these three alternatives are summarized in Table 17–8.

In evaluating these alternatives, Bob would have to assess the technical feasibility, economic feasibility, and business impact of each option. The technical feasibility relates to the technical know-how required to design and implement the proposed system. Bob isn't a technical professional and doesn't plan to hire a programmer or operations technician to run his inventory management system. However, he could be trained to handle simple procedures like data entry, file backup, and report generation if programs were menu-driven.

As it stands, all three alternatives are technically feasible choices. Even though the improved manual system alternative is the least technical in nature, Bob could be trained to use the package or custom-designed programs. In both of these situations, he would have to contract for the services of a programmer or analyst to help with design and implementation of the proposed system.

Assessing the economic feasibility of each design alternative entails developing a cost-benefit analysis. The more expensive design options will require greater benefits. However, if these benefits are important business goals, then the more expensive approaches should be the best choices. Finally, Bob will need to analyze the business

Table 17–8
Menu of alternatives for Music by Mail, Inc.

A Customer-Programmed Inventory Application (Total Cost: $12,300)	
Advantages	**Disadvantages**
System could be designed to meet user's needs	Time-consuming to design and implement
Modifications possible through additional contract work	Most expensive alternative
Possibility of ad hoc query and reporting capabilities using a database management program	Documentation, report layouts, control procedures, and so on would all have to be designed from scratch
A Software Package Solution (total cost: $6,665)	
Advantages	**Disadvantages**
Least time consuming to implement	Package may not meet user's needs
Cost effective	Modifications may not be possible
Documentation of design work would be available	Software solution may dictate hardware choice
May provide training materials and operational procedures to implement	Inflexible
An Improved Manual System (total cost: $800)	
Advantages	**Disadvantages**
Simple to design and implement	Doesn't provide for inventory growth and management reporting
Least expensive	More labor-intensive effort
Enables user to get control of manual procedures	

impact of each option. He needs to go back to his list of business objectives and determine which approach will best allow him to achieve these business objectives. As you recall, Bob was interested in expanding his revenues, his inventories, and his market share. Thus, one of the microcomputer-based options might be important to implement. The time and effort he would spend controlling the manual system could be better expended developing new marketing strategies, identifying new customer market groups, and acquiring new titles that would interest these new markets.

If Bob wishes to acquire a microcomputer-based system, he now has to investigate the feasibility of custom-developed versus packaged software. His choice may depend on whether he is able to identify a package that is well suited to the nature of his business. He might start by looking at packaged software advertised in trade publications he receives. If software has been developed for mail-order bookstores and other types of mail-order businesses, then he would save time and money by using a software package solution. However, if a package is not available that meets his needs, or if current packages include many reports that he really doesn't need, he would be better off contracting with a programmer to develop a custom system.

The selection of a design alternative requires a cost-benefit analysis of the various proposals. The next chapter will cover this topic along with other topics related to the detailed design and implementation of an information system.

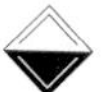

Box 17–3 Computer-Assisted Software Engineering

Computer-assisted software engineering tools are software programs that automate part of the application development process. First introduced in the mid-1980s, these tools range from graphics tools that can be used to depict software designs to systems that can be used to produce code from detailed design specifications. These tools provide the software engineer with support similar to the computer-assisted design and manufacturing (CAD/CAM) workstations that have been used in engineering in the past.

One type of CASE tool enables the systems designer to produce schematic designs of the proposed system producing data flow diagrams, data dictionary specifications, logical data models, and the design of input and output formats. The systemwide data dictionary supported by many CASE tools enables the analyst to create standardized data names and data definitions for data elements used throughout the system. If a data definition is changed in the data dictionary, the change will be made wherever this data element is used.

A logical data flow diagram prepared using a CASE tool is shown in Figure 17–11. One of the main advantages of using a CASE tool is the ability to catch design errors. For example, the tool can be used to check if data elements included in output data flows are present in the data store to be used in generating this output. If a data element has not been created and stored, the system will indicate the error so that it can be corrected.

Some integrated software tools providing similar capabilities for software design include Visible Analyst Workbench from Visible Systems, Inc., the Applications Development Workbench from Knowledgeware, and the Information Engineering Facility from Texas Instruments.

CASE tools that support software design have a number of advantages. Their use forces the systems analyst to design and document algorithms, data flows, data element definitions, and database descriptions. Once these diagrams have been constructed, CASE tools make it possible to make additions, deletions, and changes without completely redrawing them. Most CASE systems provide a standardized set of tools addressing each phase of the systems life cycle. Using these tools, the analyst creates design documentation that people responsible for maintaining the system can understand.

With the use of CASE tools, analysts can generate and analyze alternative design possibilities. Changes in data flow diagrams, data dictionary specifications, and input/output forms can be made and incorporated into the system design. The result may be a better quality design that requires less maintenance.

Using CASE tools to graphically depict system processes and data requirements allows the analyst to involve the user directly and to make modifications based on the user's suggestions. CASE tools support the prototyping approach by allowing the analyst to document the characteristics of various versions of the system and to make revisions until the user's needs are met.

One of the current issues regarding CASE tools is that many different tools exist. Although the majority of the tools focus on schematic design at the front end, some tools generate code from software designs. Examples of code generators are Gamma from Knowledgeware and VAX Cobol Generator from Digital Equipment Corporation.

The ideal CASE tool would provide an integrated set of tools supporting software design and coding. It would include front-end software to pictorially represent data flow diagrams, structure charts, and other design constructs consistent with the methodology being used. The product should also support the prototyping of screens, sample databases, and reports. The central component of a CASE tool is a data dictionary that stores the data names and data definitions of data elements used throughout the system. The tool should also include a code generator that transforms software designs into code. A summary of the key elements of a CASE environment is depicted in Figure 17–12.

Most CASE tools support specific software design methodologies, such as the structured methods developed by Gane-Sarson and Warnier-Orr. If a CASE tool does not support the methodology currently being used within an organization, it may not be used. The organization should select a tool that is consistent with its current systems development methodology.

Because CASE tools can be used to mechanize some of the more repetitive chores of the systems analyst, such as drawing and redrawing data flow diagrams, they provide more time for important tasks such as analysis of alternative design options and checking of accuracy. They also enable the designer to spend more time addressing organizational issues in systems design. This time should result in better-quality designs and more effective use of information systems. Some of the benefits of CASE are summarized in Figure 17–13.

Figure 17–11
Data-flow diagram using a CASE tool

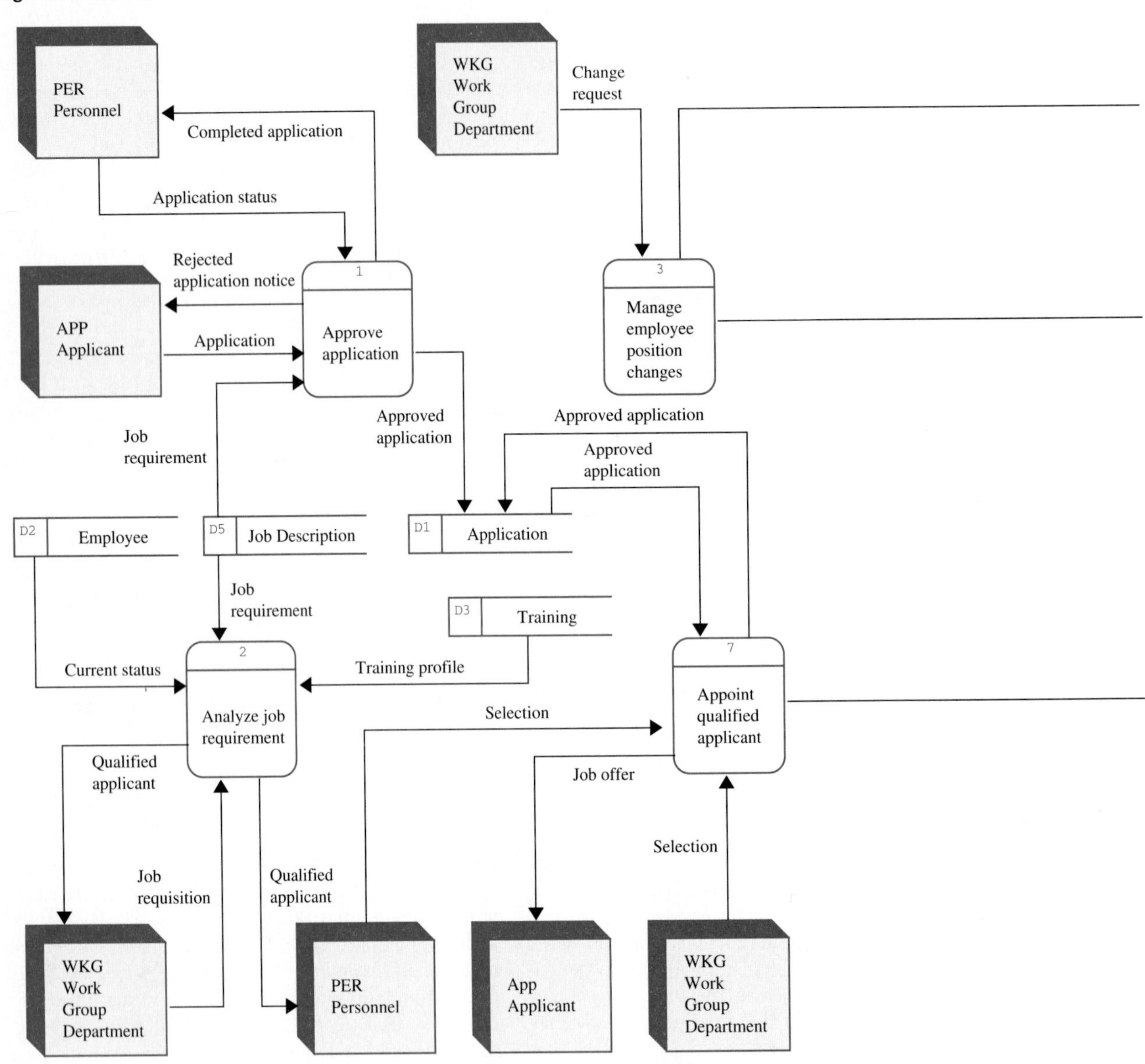

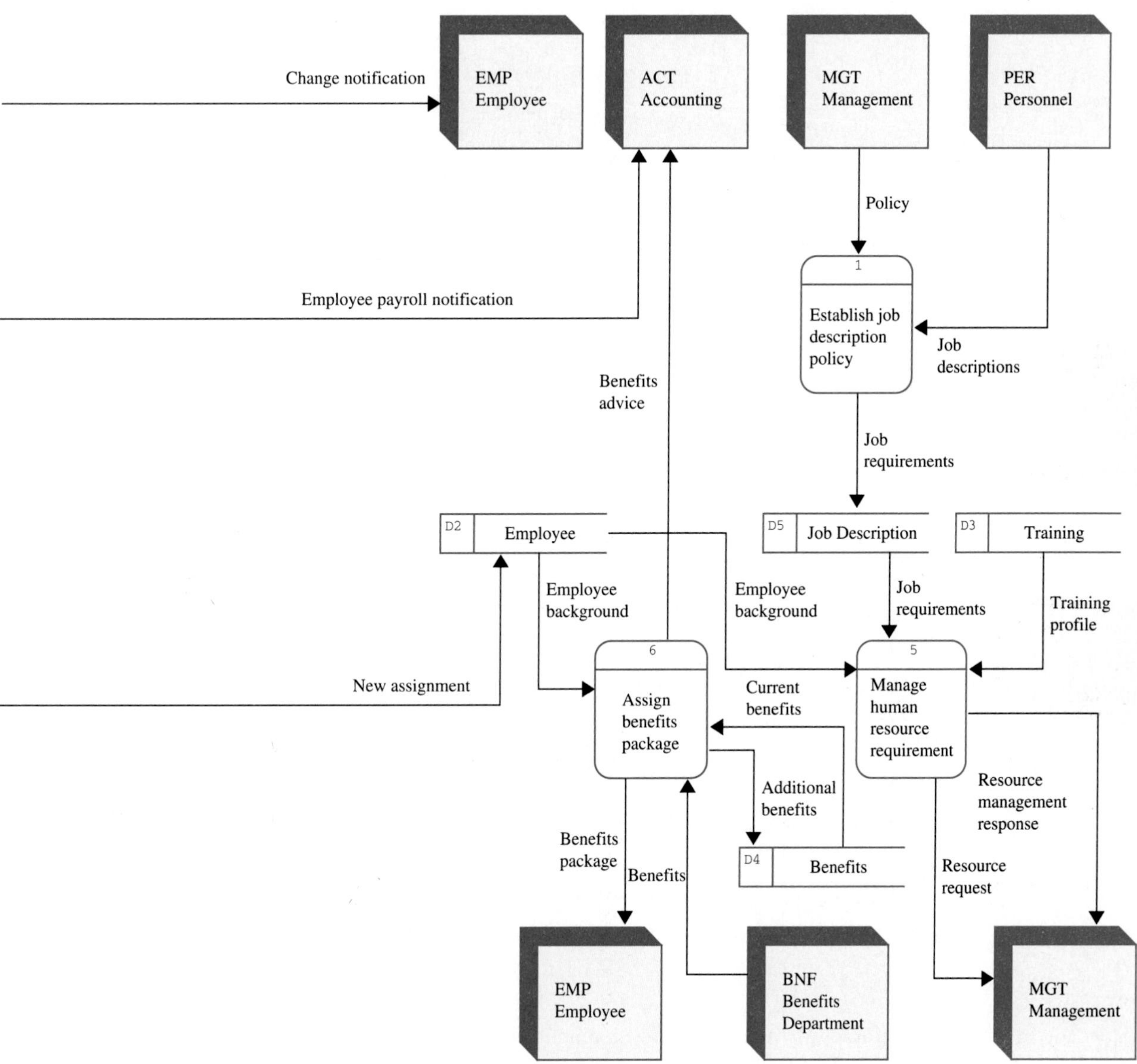

Change notification
EMP
Employee
ACT
Accounting
MGT
Management
PER
Personnel
Policy
1
Establish job description policy
Job descriptions
Employee payroll notification
Benefits advice
Job requirements
D2
Employee
D5
Job Description
D3
Training
Employee background
Employee background
Job requirements
Training profile
New assignment
6
Assign benefits package
5
Manage human resource requirement
Current benefits
Additional benefits
Resource management response
Benefits package
Benefits
D4
Benefits
Resource request
EMP
Employee
BNF
Benefits Department
MGT
Management

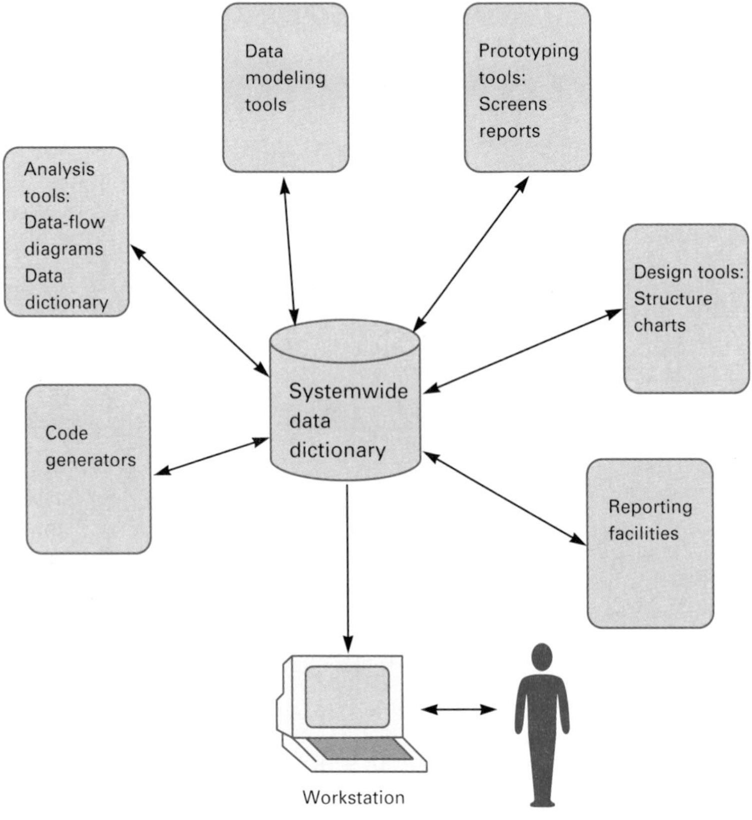

Figure 17–12
Elements of a CASE environment

Figure 17–13
Benefits of CASE

Provides checks on design errors.
Provides a systemwide data dictionary.
Prevents redrawing of diagrams.
Provides opportunities to make design changes.
Ensures conformance with design and documentation standards.
Increases user involvement in systems design.
Creates a repository of systems design documentation.
Improves system reliability and maintainability.
Aids project management and control.

Management Summary

In summary, the systems development process involves a series of steps that must be accomplished if the systems analyst is to be able to develop an information system that meets the users' needs, satisfies business objectives, and can be designed and implemented within time and budgetary constraints. The systems development life cycle provides a methodology for accomplishing these activities. The life cycle begins with problem definition, during which the systems analyst works with the user to identify the nature and scope of current problems. The next step is a feasibility study, intended to determine whether realistic systems design alternatives exist. If the systems project is feasible, the analyst investigates the current system, its procedures, information flows, decisions, and methods of work organization and control during the systems analysis phase.

At the end of the systems analysis phase, the problems of the current situation are identified and the objectives for the new system are proposed. The systems design phase involves the process of determining how the proposed system will be designed and implemented. During this phase, a number of alternative design options, such as batch, on-line, and packaged software alternatives, are studied and evaluated, and the best option is selected. This option creates the framework for detailed design, during which application specifications are established. Reports, screens, files, and procedures all need to be designed. During implementation, programs are coded and tested, training is implemented, and new procedures are introduced to put the new computer-based system into operation.

One of the problems in systems development is that many systems are technically accurate but do not meet the users' needs. Structured methods for systems analysis and design provide logical tools enabling users to participate in systems development activities. According to the structured approach, information about the current system is used to construct a logical data flow diagram. Problems with current procedures are studied and used to develop a set of business and system objectives for the proposed system. The business objectives state what business outcomes must be achieved, and the system objectives define what capabilities the information system must have. Modifications are made to the existing logical data flow diagram, and a proposed logical data flow diagram is developed.

The proposed logical data flow diagram becomes the blueprint for establishing further system requirements. Decision tables and trees are used to specify the logic of business processes. A logical data dictionary is designed to identify the names and definitions of data elements that compose the data flows and data stores of the proposed system. Finally, the contents of the data stores are analyzed and simplified to construct the beginnings of systemwide data files.

The final step in systems design is to evaluate systems design alternatives. A number of different alternatives exist for selecting processing modes, computer configurations, and software development methods. Each of these alternatives must be evaluated in light of proposed system requirements.

At every phase in the systems analysis and design process, user involvement is critically important. The systems development life cycle methodology builds in a number of checkpoints that make it possible for users to review activities that have been accomplished. Structured methods enable users to contribute to the design process. Finally, users are ultimately responsible for identifying and evaluating the feasibility of alternative design options for the proposed system.

Key Terms for Managers

batch, **624**
decision tables, **639**
decision trees, **639**
detailed system design, **624**
feasibility study, **622**
implementation, **624**
logical data dictionary, **624**
logical data-flow diagram, **623**
maintenance, **624**
on-line, **624**
on-line immediate update, **645**
on-line with batch overnight update, **645**
problem definition, **621**
service bureau, **646**
software houses, **647**
software package, **624**
systems analysis, **621**
systems design, **624**
systems development methodology, **622**
timesharing, **646**

Review Questions

1. What are the steps in a systems study?
2. What are the phases of the systems development life cycle?
3. What activities occur during the problem definition phase of the systems development life cycle?
4. What activities occur during the systems design phase of the systems development life cycle?
5. Identify five guidelines for conducting a successful systems interview.
6. What is the purpose of a feasibility study?
7. Why is system maintenance a large percentage of the life span of an information system?
8. What are the major reasons for using structured methods in systems analysis and design?
9. What are the advantages of developing a logical data flow diagram for the proposed system?
10. What are four different processing modes in information systems design?
11. What are the characteristics of an on-line system with batch overnight update?
12. What kind of business data processing application would be supported by on-line with immediate update?
13. What are the major advantages and disadvantages of using a service bureau?
14. What are the main advantages and disadvantages of in-house software development?
15. What are the advantages of using packaged software?

Questions for Discussion

1. What are some of the benefits of using structured tools and techniques in systems analysis and design?
2. What are some of the reasons organizations choose outsourcing as a method of supporting data processing activities?
3. What are some of the methods used in business area analysis as a part of information engineering methodology?
4. Why should organizations have a systems development methodology in place before they introduce computer-assisted software engineering (CASE) tools?
5. What are some of the benefits of CASE tools?

Problems

1. **Southern Oil Company.** Southern Oil Company uses the following credit card procedure: The customer presents a credit card to the service station attendant, who completes the invoice, giving one copy to the customer. Weekly, the station manager batches the accumulated invoices, together with an adding machine tape, and sends them to the company's regional office. The company verifies the amounts, credits the station's account with the amount of the batch, and holds the invoices until the end of the month.

At the end of the month, the company batches the invoices by customer number, microfilms them, adds the invoices to the customer account tape file, prints the monthly statement, and mails it to the customer together with the invoices. On receipt of the payment, the company verifies the amount of the check against the payment stub, batches the daily stubs by customer number, and subtracts the payment from the customer account on the tape file.

Develop a logical data flow diagram for this case.

2. **Processing Modes.** Select the processing mode that would support each of the following applications and give reasons for your answers. You may choose from these alternatives:

   a. Batch.
   b. On-line with batch overnight update.
   c. On-line with immediate update.
   d. Distributed processing.
   e. Decentralized processing.

   The applications are as follows:
   1. An airline reservations system.
   2. A demand deposit accounting system (that is, a system that processes deposits and withdrawals from checking accounts).
   3. A point-of-sale inventory system that updates local inventory files based on sales transactions and transmits summary sales and inventory data to a central office computer system.
   4. A payment processing system for a loan company. Loan payments are made directly to branch offices, where they are entered and validated, and then these loan payments are transmitted to the home office computer, where the central loan files are updated.
   5. A word processing system that is used to generate fund-raising letters from a university development office.

3. **Package Software versus Custom Software Development.** Emily Martin, an owner of an art supply store, is interested in acquiring an accounts receivable system. Her main requirements for accounts receivable are to set up and maintain a customer master file, to update account balances, to generate monthly statements, to apply cash receipts to customer balances, and to generate overdue account notices. Because she doesn't have a computer background, she is considering two alternatives. The first is the purchase of an accounts receivable software package that could run on a microcomputer. The package would provide a variety of extra features, such as sales analysis, customer analysis, and a variety of overdue account notices and reminders.

   The other option Emily is considering is custom software development. Because the system she needs is fairly simple, she feels that software could be developed using dBase IV or another database program on a microcomputer. Although the cost might be greater, the software could be modified.

   Examine the advantages and disadvantages of the software package option versus the custom software development option. Which would you choose? Give reasons for your answer.

4. **Alro Uniform, Inc.** Donald Hudson, the manager of systems and programming for Alro Uniform, Inc., a major manufacturer of uniforms for health care professionals, was preparing for a meeting with user-managers in the production department. The

purpose of the meeting was to enable the users to review systems design specifications for a proposed production planning and scheduling system.

Donald's main concern was that the users had not been involved in the systems design process because they did not have sufficient time and resources to participate in the project. Now, Donald was looking over pages of detailed design specifications that outlined reports, screens, forms, files, and program design requirements. He knew that the users would have a difficult time understanding any of these documents because they were so technical.

Donald was afraid that if he went ahead with the meeting the users would simply sign off on the specifications because they would not understand them. As a result, he would not be able to obtain any input into the design. If mistakes had been made, the users wouldn't be aware of them until after the system was implemented and major costs had been incurred.

Donald would like to develop some documents that the users could understand and approve before moving ahead on the project. Should he involve the users? What approach might he use to describe the proposed system to the user-managers so that they can understand the new system and make their suggestions?

Cases

1. **Movies Unlimited, Inc.** Movies Unlimited, Inc., is a large St. Louis–based company in the videocassette rental business. Currently, it has an inventory of over 15,000 movies in 20 branches. The management of Movies Unlimited, Inc., has described some of the following problems and has asked you to come in to conduct a systems investigation. During your interviews, you have learned about the following checkout, check-in, and inventory procedures.

A customer joins Movies Unlimited, Inc., by paying a $25 membership fee. At the time of joining, customer information is taken, including a driver's license number, major credit card, and home address and phone. This information is recorded in a customer card file. There is no method in place at present to update this information.

After joining Movies Unlimited, Inc., the customer receives a membership card he or she can use to check out movies. The boxes of available movies are arranged in alphabetical order on shelves. The actual videocassettes are kept in boxes in a storage area behind the reception desk. To check out a movie, the customer takes a box to the counter and the clerk looks for the movie on the back shelves. Sometimes a movie is not filed away in correct order and the clerk needs to hunt for it. The customer pays a one- or two-day rental fee at the time of checkout. The clerk is supposed to ask if the customer has changed his or her address and phone, but there is rarely enough time to do this.

When movies are returned, the clerks try to check on whether they have been brought back on time or if a late charge is due. Sometimes a customer drops a movie off in the stack of returned films without informing the clerk whether it is overdue. By the time overdue movies are discovered by the clerk who is responsible for reshelving returned movies, it is often too late to locate the customer. Sometimes a clerk tries to reach a customer by phone, but there is very little that can be done to force payment on overdue returns. Sometimes renters return movies late but are not assessed for late charges because they drop their movies off in an off-hours collection box and there is no way to substantiate the time and date of a movie's return.

Another problem occurs with returns during particularly busy times. Returned movies may stack up because clerks do not have enough time to reshelve them. Sometimes customers want to check out movies they find in the stack of returned films. In most cases, a customer may not be able to locate a movie if it has not been reshelved.

One of the major problems is inventory control. Most of the new releases are out of stock, particularly on weekends when customers are interested in renting them. Management feels that more copies should be made of these videocassettes. However, they currently have no way of keeping track of sales trends in order to reallocate inventory effectively. Also, many of the slow-moving titles are kept in stock when they should be discontinued.

Finally, competition in the movie rental business is great at the current time. Management would like to develop ways of successfully promoting their business and increasing the number of renters without incurring unnecessary costs.

Using the information provided in the preceding case, develop a systems analysis study that includes the following elements:

a. Five questions for a systems interview.
b. A statement of major findings, based on the case.
c. Business and system objectives for the proposed system.
d. Alternative design options for implementing the proposed system (identify two alternatives and describe the advantages and disadvantages of each).

2. **Thinktank University.** After obtaining permission from their advisers, students must prepare a five-part form requesting withdrawal from a course and a refund of money. The adviser has to sign the request form. The student gives the first three copies to him or her and delivers the remaining two copies to the bursar in the business office.

The bursar decides whether a refund is due and prepares a refund check. Copy 5 of the form is returned to the student with the refund check. Copy 4 is marked with the action taken and then filed. If no refund is due, the bursar stamps "no refund" on copy 5 and returns it to the student.

The adviser sends copy 1 to the registrar, files copy 2, and sends copy 3 to the instructor who teaches the course. The registrar cancels the course from the student's schedule and subtracts the hours dropped from the total hours carried on the student's record. The instructor records a grade of "W" for the student on the class roster.

At the end of the semester, the instructor updates the class roster with grades for the remaining active students and sends it to the registrar. The registrar uses this final grade report from the instructors to update student records.

Develop a logical data flow diagram for this case.

Selected References and Readings

Davis, William S. *Systems Analysis and Design.* Reading, Mass.: Addison-Wesley, 1983.

Davis, Gordon. "Caution: User-Developed Systems Can Be Dangerous to Your Organization." Working Paper 82–04. Minneapolis: Management Information Systems Research Center, University of Minnesota, February 1984.

Couger, J. Daniel; Mel A. Colter, and Robert W. Knapp. *Advanced Systems Development/Feasibility Techniques.* New York: John Wiley & Sons, Inc., 1982.

Gane, Chris, and Trish Sarson. *Structured Systems Analysis: Tools and Techniques.* Englewood Cliffs, N.J.: Prentice Hall, 1979.

Peters, Lawrence. *Advanced Structured Analysis and Design.* Englewood Cliffs, N.J.: Prentice-Hall, 1987.

Whitten, Jeffrey L., Lonnie D. Bentley, and Vic Barlow. *Systems Analysis and Design Methods.* 2nd ed. Burr Ridge. Ill.: Richard D. Irwin, 1989.

Detailed Systems Design and Implementation

Chapter Outline

Manager's View

In the last chapter, you learned about the systems analysis and design process. Users participate in the phases of problem definition, analysis of the existing system, development of objectives for the proposed system, and evaluation of alternative design options. After a design option is selected, detailed design begins. During this phase, the user helps the systems analyst design reports, screens, and files. Users and MIS professionals also evaluate hardware and software and establish an implementation schedule.

Today, many companies are experiencing software development backlogs of between two and three years. Over 70 percent of the time spent in information systems development occurs during the detailed design and implementation phases. Coding and **testing** of programs are among the most time-consuming phases of a project. Under pressure from management to complete information systems projects on a more timely basis, MIS management has begun to explore alternative application development approaches, including software packages, user development, and prototyping in systems design. Automated tools for software engineering have also been introduced to speed up the application development life cycle. You'll learn about these alternative development methods in this chapter.

USER INVOLVEMENT IN SYSTEM SELECTION

One of the major responsibilities of users in information systems development is the evaluation of alternative design options. This process may include the development of a **request for proposal (RFP),** followed by the evaluation of software and hardware design options.

Developing an RFP

Many users don't have time to shop around for hardware and software to fit their needs. Developing an RFP can save time and provide valuable information. In an RFP, the user outlines major system requirements, including mandatory features, data requirements, and support needs, and asks vendors to respond to these needs with a proposal. The user also indicates necessary reports, forms, and special interface requirements to existing systems.

Normally, after an RFP is issued, vendors have a deadline within which to respond with their offering, including hardware and software features, cost data, and support features. Vendors provide documentation on technical and systems development support and give the names of contact persons who can provide demonstrations and further information.

Bob Thomas may want to try the RFP approach for gathering information for the inventory control and purchasing application that he needs for Music by Mail, Inc., the example we considered in Chapter 17. (An RFP for Music by Mail, Inc., is shown in Figure 18–1.) The vendors responding to Music by Mail's RFP would probably suggest software packages supporting inventory control and purchasing applications. Then, Bob would need to establish criteria for evaluating these offerings.

Evaluating Software Packages

One of the first steps in evaluating software is to develop a minimum criteria list of important software features. A checklist can be used to assess the features of software packages. Items on a checklist to evaluate an inventory control package might include those in Table 18–1. On the basis of the evaluations of various packages, Bob should be able to narrow his decision down to two or three vendors whose offerings meet these minimum criteria.

Normally, other factors come into consideration in evaluating a vendor. The availability of training and ongoing support is a major consideration. Some software vendors have programmers who can provide software enhancements at a competitive rate. Other vendors provide users with access to source code of the computer programs that their product includes. This source code can then be modified. Some vendors can't support modifications and won't provide source code access. However, others will provide the user with ongoing enhancements to programs for a yearly software **maintenance** fee.

The quality of documentation accompanying software packages is a major consideration. Clear, well-designed user documentation can ease the learning process and provide support for day-to-day operating responsibilities. In Bob's case, clear directions on day-to-day procedures, such as file maintenance, file backup, and system operations, would be very helpful. **Systems design documentation** should include information on input and output documents, file design specifications, and program logic.

The user should also recognize the importance of vendor reputation and financial stability. Some software vendors in the microcomputer field may not be able to provide ongoing, reliable products and support. In Bob's case, the availability of a local software vendor who could provide software development, technical support, and hotline access to answers to day-to-day questions would be very important.

Figure 18–1
A request for proposal (RFP)

Request for Proposal

The Business

MUSIC BY MAIL, INC. is a mail-order company that sells records and tapes to about 1,200 customers in the St. Louis metropolitan area. Current inventory of 300 titles will be expanded to 500 within the next six months and to over 1,000 in the next two years. The system that is needed will handle inventory control, purchasing, and accounts payable. At the current time, these procedures are all manual. In addition, a system must be developed to store a master file of 1,200 current customers and an additional 30,000 prospective customers.

Minimum System Requirements

The proposed system needs to support inventory control and purchasing applications. Optional features include accounts payable and word processing. The software must run in a microcomputer-based operating system environment. A program to generate mailing labels sorted by ZIP code from the customer and prospect master files is also needed.

Data Requirements

At present, inventory data consists of 300 titles, which will be expanded to 500 within the next six months and to 1,000 over the next two years. The customer and prospect databases will consist of over 31,000 records. It is hoped that the customer master file will expand at the rate of 10 to 15 percent per year.

Required Support Features

Bob Thomas prefers to purchase a turnkey system with nontechnical user documentation and the availability of training and support. He would like to learn if source code is available for possible program modifications or if modifications can be made by experienced professionals at the software firm.

Vendor Information

Bob Thomas would like to see a demonstration of the system before making a selection. Information about other customers using the package would be very helpful. The proposal must be submitted on or before July 15, 1994. The implementation schedule would occur between September and December, 1994.

Contact

Please contact Bob Thomas at (314) 555-8776 if you have any questions or need further information.

Table 18–1
Inventory control system checklist

	Yes	No
1. Can the package accommodate 6,000 inventory items?	_____	_____
2. Does the system automatically reorder items when supplies reach a low point?	_____	_____
3. Can the automatic reorder function be overridden for certain inventory items?	_____	_____
4. Does the system have the ability to credit returned items?	_____	_____
5. Does the system provide backorder reporting?	_____	_____
6. Can the system forecast customer buying trends?	_____	_____
7. Can the system determine at what rate a product is being sold?	_____	_____

Finally, Bob should invite the top vendors to give a sales demonstration and to answer questions about software support, training, documentation, and hardware compatibility. He may also wish to talk with other users of the same package to obtain references. In a major software package acquisition ranging between $250,000 and $1 million, a thorough investigation taking several months or longer would be conducted. In Bob's case, phone calls to check out the service and support record of the package's vendor would be very helpful.

If an inventory package exists that serves the needs of Music by Mail, Inc., Bob may make a choice. However, if a suitable package cannot be found, he may want to contract with a systems design consulting firm to develop a system using a database management program. In this case, his major responsibility would be to evaluate several different database programs.

Evaluating a Database Program

The major advantage of using a database management program is that Bob can hire a programmer to develop the system he needs. He would probably want to evaluate three microcomputer-based database packages. A relational database package would enable him to logically interrelate files storing information about customers, inventory items, and purchase orders in order to generate various reports. He would also be interested in a package providing query and report writer features.

In evaluating alternative programs, Bob would want to use an objective method of evaluation. The weighted-factor method is a useful approach. In this approach, the first step is to develop a series of selection parameters, or criteria, to use in determining the value of alternative products. The major parameters in evaluating a database package might include cost, support, software features, and capacity. Table 18–2 provides a list of the parameters, subfactors, and relative weights for each parameter that could be considered in evaluating alternative data management software.

However, just weighting the parameters to be considered in a software decision doesn't determine the outcome. The software packages being considered must be evaluated according to these criteria. In order to assign performance scores to each software product, the user must establish the basis for making performance judgments. Table 18–3 shows a relative performance chart that can be used to make this kind of assessment.

Table 18–2
Weighted factors in a consideration of data management software

Parameters	Weighted Factors
1. COST (30%)	
Price (50%)	.50 × .30 = .150
Implementation (50%)	.50 × .30 = .150
2. SUPPORT (20%)	
Maintenance (30%)	.30 × .20 = .060
Training (30%)	.30 × .20 = .060
Installation (40%)	.40 × .20 = .080
3. SOFTWARE FEATURES (30%)	
Report writer (25%)	.25 × .30 = .075
User-friendliness (30%)	.30 × .30 = .090
Query capability (20%)	.20 × .30 = .060
Documentation (25%)	.25 × .30 = .075
4. CAPACITY (20%)	
Record volume (50%)	.50 × .20 = .100
Number of active files (50%)	.50 × .20 = .100

Table 18–3
Relative performance chart for software products

	Performance Score by Percentage		
Parameter	**0**	**50**	**100**
1. COST			
Price	Greater than $1,000	Greater than $500	Less than $500
Implementation (training and setup)	Greater than $1,000	Greater than $500	Less than $500
2. SUPPORT			
Maintenance	None	Telephone help 9:00 A.M.–5:00 P.M.	24-hour hotline
Training	None	Workshops available at user's expense	Onsite training; tutorial included
Installation	None	Documentation only	Onsite installation help
3. SOFTWARE FEATURES			
Report writer	Command-driven; limited options	Command-driven; broader options	Menu-driven; wide capability of user-defined reports
User-friendliness	Low; command-driven	Moderate; command-driven with help features	High; menus and prompts; help features
Query capability	Command-driven; limited options	Command-driven; broader options	Menu-driven; wide variety of options
Documentation	Limited	Moderate	Extensive
4. CAPACITY			
Record volume	Less than 10,000 records	10,000 to 100,000 records	Over 100,000 records
Number of active files	One at a time	Less than five at a time	More than five at a time

The next step in the software evaluation process is scoring the alternative software products. Given two database management systems (DBMSs), A and B, the scoring might appear as shown in Table 18–4. Based on these scores, the final weighted-factor evaluation would result in a total score of 79.88 for DBMS A and 72.25 for DBMS B, as shown in Table 18–5.

The weighted-score method is one method of evaluating both hardware and software options. The process of establishing weighted parameters and the process of candidate scoring force the user to establish objective criteria for decision making. The candidate software scoring process may require the user to conduct research by consulting software reviews in various trade publications. Microcomputer publications such as *Infoworld, PC Week,* and *Byte* feature buyers' guides comparing popular microcomputer-based software packages. Independent reviews of mainframe and minicomputer-based hardware and software are compiled by research firms such as Datapro in Delran, New Jersey.

The weighted-score method can be somewhat subjective. Initially, the selection of parameters and the percentages allocated to these parameters can be subjective. Further, the scores assigned to the two or more alternatives (e.g., software packages, hardware) also can be subjective. If the systems analyst is careful to guard against a subjective evaluation of parameters and scores, the weighted-score method can be a very useful approach to analyzing alternative design options.

Table 18–4
Software scoring of two database management systems

Parameters	DBMS A	DBMS B
1. COST		
Price	90	80
Implementation	65	70
2. SUPPORT		
Maintenance	85	70
Training	70	55
Installation	95	80
3. SOFTWARE FEATURES		
Report writer	85	90
User-friendliness	90	45
Query capability	75	80
Documentation	90	70
4. CAPACITY		
Record volume	80	80
Active files	60	70

Table 18–5
Weighted-score rating summary

Parameters	Weighted Factors	DBMS A	DBMS B
1. COST			
Price	.150	13.50	12.00
Implementation	.150	9.75	10.50
Subtotal	.300	23.25	22.50
2. SUPPORT			
Maintenance	.060	5.10	4.20
Training	.060	4.20	3.30
Installation	.080	7.60	6.40
Subtotal	.200	16.90	13.90
3. SOFTWARE FEATURES			
Report writer	.075	6.38	6.75
User-friendliness	.090	8.10	4.05
Query capability	.060	4.50	4.80
Documentation	.075	6.75	5.25
Subtotal	.300	25.73	20.85
4. CAPACITY			
Record volume	.100	8.00	8.00
Active files	.100	6.00	7.00
Subtotal	.200	14.00	15.00
Grand Total	100.000	79.88	72.25

Hardware Evaluation

Hardware evaluation and selection take place after software selection because the hardware has to be compatible with software that has been selected. Software packages are generally designed to run in certain operating system environments. A database program like dBase IV may run in several microcomputer-based operating system environments.

Some of the factors to consider in making a hardware choice are memory size, the capacity of hard disk storage, and the type of **peripheral** devices that can be supported. Where growth is anticipated, the user may need to analyze the maximum memory size and maximum capacity of hard disk storage. The cost of installation, training, and

Table 18–6 Hardware and software recommendations

Hardware	**Amount***
486DX2/66 microcomputer system 8MB RAM, 340MB hard drive,	$2,700.00
1.44MB 3½ disk drive, IBM compatible,	
serial port, parallel port,	
enhanced keyboard key lock,	
VGA monitor and graphics card	Included
Laser printer	1,299.00
Tape backup system	1,499.00
Hardware total	$5,498.00
Software	
MS-DOS	Included
dBase IV, Lotus 4.0, Wordperfect 6.0	$995.00
Software total	$995.00
Grand total	$6,493.00

*Prices may not reflect current market prices.

maintenance is also an important factor in decision making. Vendor reputation and financial stability should be taken into consideration because local service and support may be needed.

Once decision-making criteria are established, the user can analyze alternative hardware using the weighted-factor method of evaluation. The hardware choice would be selected and a specific hardware configuration developed. A hardware configuration for a microcomputer-based system with a database management program might look like the one shown in Table 18–6.

The final decision relevant to a hardware choice is whether to purchase training, installation support, and ongoing maintenance from the vendor. In Bob's case, where there is no on-site technical expertise, training and installation support would be useful. However, larger organizations would have technical support personnel to assist users in these areas. The cost of a maintenance contract for the hardware would run about 10 percent to 12 percent of the total hardware cost.

COST-BENEFIT ANALYSIS

The purpose of **cost-benefit analysis** is to determine the economic feasibility of various systems design alternatives. Information systems are investments just like any other business investment, such as building a new warehouse or developing a new marketing program. The benefits of information systems projects must be compared with the benefits of other capital budgeting projects. Cost-benefit analysis is the best way of measuring the financial impact of an information systems design project proposal.

The Benefits of Information Systems

The benefits of an information system have to be measured in terms of their business impact. **Tangible benefits** can be measured in terms of hard dollar savings or profits. Increased revenues and decreased costs are examples of tangible benefits. An on-line order entry system that makes it possible for a company to service more orders on a timely basis may enable that firm to increase revenues. On-line access to credit information about customers may cut down the bad debt expense incurred by filling orders to noncreditworthy customers.

Another tangible benefit is the ability to cut processing errors. If sales clerks at a rental car company manually calculate charges, a much higher error rate may occur as compared with a company using a computerized system. Another benefit of information systems is faster turnaround. A nationwide order processing system can make it possible for order entry clerks to enter order information, update inventory levels, and generate invoices to be printed out at a distribution center nearest the customer location. Orders are filled more efficiently and invoices are generated more rapidly, making it possible to improve cash flow.

Other tangible benefits are reduced inventory cost, reduced administrative expenses, and the reduced cost of paperwork processing. For example, let's consider a university admissions office that processes 6,000 applications a year. In the current manual system, the time it takes secretaries to retype and recompile the same data about applicants amounts to about 30 minutes per application, or about 180,000 minutes a year. If the average secretary makes $12 an hour, the cost of the problem would be $36,000 a year. If a computerized database system were developed to house application data, much of this rekeying would be avoided and at least $36,000 in savings would occur.

Information systems have many **intangible benefits,** too. Intangible benefits cannot be measured in terms of hard dollar savings, but they are important. An on-line order inquiry system, for example, may enable customers to inquire about delivery dates on orders and can increase customer goodwill. Employee morale may also be improved by the ability to provide information to customers. Without access to this type of information, a customer service clerk may have to handle hundreds of complaints per day.

Other intangible benefits of information systems are improved employee job satisfaction and better decision making. If a sales manager uses sales history data to identify the most profitable products and the most profitable buyers, then the marketing strategy she develops can maximize business opportunities more effectively. If a production planner can analyze regional sales trends for various products and recommend target inventory levels in branch warehouses, proper inventory levels are more likely to be available. The benefits of information systems are summarized in Table 18–7.

The Costs of Information Systems

The costs of information systems include development costs, equipment costs, and operations and maintenance costs. Some of these costs are nonrecurring and others are recurring. Development costs are the one-time costs of systems analysis, design, and implementation. Development also includes the costs of training, conversion, testing, and documentation.

Equipment and other start-up costs include the cost of new equipment configuration, packaged software, equipment installation, and materials and supplies. A computer acquisition may also entail the costs of new facilities, air-conditioning, and space. Equipment costs are generally considered nonrecurring costs, although additional costs can be incurred as the original configuration is upgraded, new software is acquired, or new peripheral devices are purchased.

Operations and maintenance costs are recurring costs and start being incurred once the system is installed. Operating costs include the costs of computer usage, overhead costs such as power, insurance, and space, and the cost of supplies. Ongoing personnel costs, such as the salaries of supervisors, clerical staff, and maintenance programmers,

Table 18–7
The benefits of information systems

Tangible Benefits
Fewer processing errors
Increased throughput
Decreased response time
Elimination of job steps
Reduced expenses
Increased sales
Faster turnaround
Better credit
Reduced credit losses
Intangible Benefits
Improved customer goodwill
Improved employee morale
Improved employee job satisfaction
Better service to the community
Better decision making

are included in operating costs. Personnel training costs are additional ongoing costs. Maintenance costs for hardware typically run about 10 percent to 12 percent of the costs of the equipment configuration. Many software companies offer maintenance contracts that enable users to receive copies of enhancements and modifications of software packages and their documentation. The costs of information systems are summarized in Table 18–8.

Cost-Benefit Analysis

Performing a cost-benefit analysis requires the systems analyst and user to estimate the development costs, equipment costs, operating costs, and maintenance costs of the proposed system. The development and equipment costs occur during the systems design and implementation phases of the project, and the operating costs occur over time. Normally, the benefits of the proposed system will be realized over its life span. Although the costs will outweigh the benefits at first during the original system investment, the benefits should eventually overtake the costs.

An example will help you understand how cost-benefit analysis works. Let us say that the one-time development and equipment costs for the new inventory system for Music by Mail, Inc., were $10,000. The proposed inventory system will save the business an estimated $5,000 per year in reduction of excess inventory and avoidance of inventory shortages of needed records and tapes. If these were the only costs and benefits, we could assume that the $10,000 cost would be made up in two years, because the benefits of the new system would be $5,000 per year.

However, this kind of analysis would not take into consideration the time value of money. To understand what is meant by the time value of money, you need to ask yourself how much you would be willing to invest to get $5,000 after one year. The answer would probably not be $5,000. You would expect to invest less than $5,000 because money has a time value and can earn interest. If the interest rate is 12 percent, an investment of $4,468.28 will return $5,000 after one year.

Table 18 – 8
The costs of information systems

Development Costs
Systems analysis (interviewing, etc.)
Systems design (file design, etc.)
Coding, testing, and debugging
Training and conversion
Inspections and walkthroughs
Documentation (systems design and user documentation)
Equipment Costs
New equipment
Packaged software
Equipment installation, test, and debug
File conversion
Materials and supplies
Facilities, light, heat, and space
Operating Costs
Equipment (I/O operations, maintenance)
Personnel costs (supervisory, clerical)
Overhead (power, insurance, space)
Computer program maintenance
Standby facilities
Personnel training
Materials

The present value of a $5,000 benefit five years from now—assuming the same 12 percent interest—could be calculated using the following formula:

$$P = \frac{F}{(1 - i)^n}$$

where F is the future value of the investment
P is the present value of the investment
i is the interest rate
n is the number of compounding periods

In this case, if we invest $2,837.14 at 12 percent interest for five years, we'll have $5,000 after the five years.

Now you can apply this principle to the cost-benefit analysis for Music by Mail, Inc. As you recall from Chapter 17, the original investment cost of the computer-based inventory system was $12,300. This included $6,500 in hardware and software, $4,800 in systems development, and an additional $1,000 for installation setup, data entry, and testing.

The major tangible benefit of the proposed system is elimination of excess inventory and reduction of inventory shortages. During the first year, Bob believes that losses

	Year 0	Year 1	Year 2	Year 3	Year 4	Year 5
Development costs	$ 5,800	$ 0	$ 0	$ 0	$ 0	$ 0
Maintenance	0	0	0	0	0	0
Operations	0	100	100	100	100	100
Equipment	6,500	0	0	0	0	0
Total costs	12,300	100	100	100	100	100
Total savings	0	4,500	4,500	4,500	4,500	4,500
Net balance	−12,300	4,400	4,400	4,400	4,400	4,400
DCF factor*	1.000	.893	.797	.712	.636	.567
Discounted balance	−12,300	3,929	3,507	3,133	2,798	2,495
Cumulative discounted	−12,300	−8,371	−4,864	−1,731	+1,067	+3,562

*The discounted-cash-flow factor assumes an interest rate of 12 percent.

Figure 18–2
Cost-benefit analysis for Music by Mail, Inc.

from excess inventory could be cut by $2,500. Reduction of inventory shortages would mean that more orders could be filled and profits could accrue. Bob estimates that this increased business will bring an additional $1,000 in profits in the first year. He usually hires a part-time assistant 10 hours a week to assist with maintaining and updating his manual inventory records. At a salary of $4 per hour, for 10 hours a week every other week during the year, the total cost of this help is an additional $1,000. This cost, Bob feels, could be eliminated with the computer-based inventory system. In total, the benefits of the proposed system would amount to approximately $4,500 per year.

Figure 18–2 illustrates the cost-benefit analysis for Music by Mail, Inc. The analysis assumes that an interest rate of 12 percent will prevail during the period of the investment. According to this analysis, the breakeven point can be derived by looking at the cumulative discounted balance at the bottom line of the worksheet. Bob will break even by year 4 of his investment. In year 4, his benefits will have accrued to +$1,067. If intangible benefits occur, he may break even sooner.

A cost-benefit analysis is used to study the financial impact of alternative design options. Bob could analyze the impact of the software package alternative and of the improved manual system to determine whether the benefits of these alternatives would be greater. Even though the cost of the improved manual system would be lower, Bob might not be able to achieve his business objective of reducing inventory with this alternative. Without this benefit, the improved manual system would be difficult to justify.

DETAILED DESIGN: TRANSFORMING LOGICAL SPECIFICATIONS INTO PHYSICAL SPECIFICATIONS

Structured Design

Structured design is the process of taking a set of logical specifications for the proposed information system and transforming them into a set of physical specifications. One of the chief objectives of design is changeability. A changeable design is one that allows the system to be changed to meet the users' needs. Changes in management structure, changes in lines of business, and changes in pricing and salary plans may bring about changes in information systems. If the designer can produce a changeable, flexible system, he can reduce the overall lifetime cost of maintaining it dramatically.

A changeable system is one that is built from a set of manageably small modules that are independent of each other in function. If a module is independent in function, it can be taken out of the system, changed, and put back without disrupting the rest of the modules in the system. A *module* is defined as a set of instructions that can be invoked by name and that is designed to perform a specific function within a program.

A structure chart is a set of modules organized into a hierarchy. As you can see from the structure chart depicted in Figure 18–3, the series of modules is organized into a hierarchy with a commander module at the top. The commander module is the "boss." Each module within the structure chart is ultimately controlled by the commander.

Within a system, the commander delegates functions to supervisory modules and to worker modules. Some of the modules are responsible for input functions, some for transforming input into output, and others for output functions. An input supervisor module may delegate work to "read" and "edit" modules. An output supervisor may delegate detailed output functions to "format" and "print" modules.

One of the major characteristics of a good design is cohesion. *Cohesion* refers to the degree to which a module carries out a single, well-defined function within a program. A module designed to "Read a Record" or "Format an Error Message" carries out a specific function. A program that consists of cohesive modules is more changeable and more maintainable. For example, if users want to change a discount policy, the designer could go to the "Compute Discount" module and change its logic without affecting the workings of any other modules. Changing a cohesive module that carries out an independent function has little or no effect on other modules within the program.

In contrast, if a module takes on too many functions or combines many different processes, it will lack cohesion. Large, complex modules are difficult to modify and almost impossible to reuse. If a module takes on too many functions, the chance of triggering errors is much greater.

The degree to which modules are interconnected is called *coupling*. If modules are interconnected with each other, a system will be difficult to maintain. Extensive coupling leads to the "ripple effect," in which a bug in one module generates bugs in other modules. As you can probably imagine, maintaining a program with extensive coupling among modules is troublesome.

One of the major objectives of good structured design is reuseability. In a highly cohesive system, individual modules are reuseable within the same program and within other programs because they execute a single, self-contained function. A module such as "Edit Customer Number" or "Format Print Line" can be reused whenever these

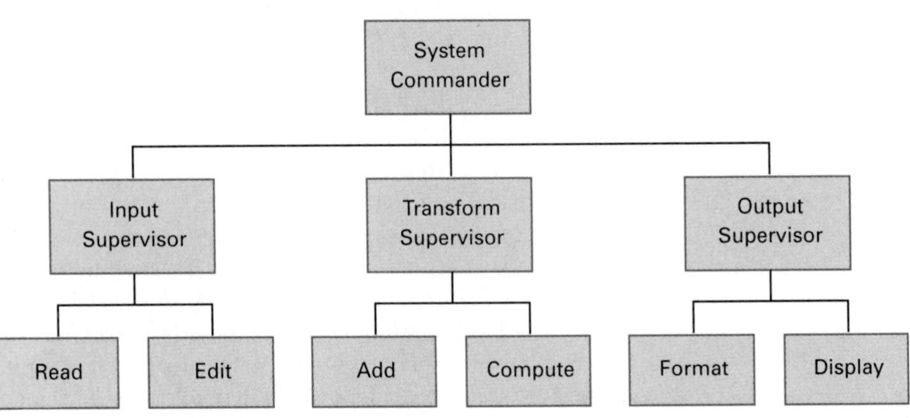

Figure 18–3
A structure chart

functions are needed. Today, a programmer can use "canned" modules with code designed to executive a variety of common functions, such as editing, updating, and reporting. The major job is to design a program structure within which these modules can be used and reused.

In summary, the systems designer is a systems architect. The designer must be able to organize processes into a hierarchy of modules, using the structure chart as a modeling tool. A good structure chart is a blueprint for transforming input data into output data. Within the structure chart, the designer must include processes that take care of data validation, editing, and other functions that assure the correctness and completeness of the system. Specific module-level logic can also be documented using tools such as structured flowcharts, decision tables, and Nassi-Schneidermann charts.

In many cases, the structure chart is sufficient to illustrate the program design specifications for a system. After the structure charts for various programs within a system are documented, the systems designer can work on the physical design specifications for the system, including the design of reports, screens, and forms.

During detailed design, the blueprint of the physical system is laid out. Reports, screens, files, and procedures are designed. Although the systems analyst is primarily responsible for accomplishing these tasks, user input is still important. If the user is not satisfied with the layout of reports or finds it difficult to use the screens that are designed for data input, it's more likely that the system won't be used.

The logical database design developed during the logical design phase of the project should be used to construct physical files during the detailed design phase. The detailed **data dictionary** for the proposed system is also created during this phase. The detailed data dictionary contains the data names and data definitions for all data elements to be maintained in data files, to be generated as output, and to be created as input. The detailed data dictionary is also known as the project dictionary because it includes data elements used in a specific systems design project. If software is to be coded, program design specifications must be written, too.

In the following sections, you will find detailed design specifications for the inventory management system that Bob Thomas of Music by Mail, Inc., is planning to implement. As you recall from Chapter 17, Bob needs to be able to update inventory records, as well as to determine when inventory items have fallen below their reorder points and generate purchase orders to vendors to replenish stock. During the detailed design phase, reports, screens, files, and forms must be designed to meet these needs.

Report Design

Report design is one of the most important aspects of detailed design. Reports must provide managers with the information they need to monitor day-to-day activities, such as the reporting of orders. An open-order, or unfilled orders, listing is an example of an *operational* report. Managers also need information enabling them to control resources more effectively. A sales analysis report depicting sales of a particular item, this year versus last, or this month versus last, may help them identify fast- and slow-moving items. This type of report is an example of a *tactical* report.

In designing these reports, the systems analyst would use a printer spacing chart. A good report has a heading, page number, date, column headings centered over data elements, and subtotal and total lines. The report should be easy to read. A mock-up of a report may be more useful to a manager than the printer spacing chart. One of the reports that Bob Thomas, the owner of Music by Mail, Inc., will need is a report indicating which inventory items have fallen below their reorder points and are being reordered. An example of a mock-up of a Below Minimum Stock report that provides this information is shown in Figure 18–4.

Date 12-07-94		BELOW MINIMUM STOCK REPORT			PAGE 1	
Item Number	Item Description	Stock Condition	On Hand	Reorder Point	Quan on Order	Vendor No.
RC-1345	BILLY JOEL GREAT HIT	BELOW MIN	10	20	40	27
TP-1221	TEMPTATIONS LIVE	OUT	0	40	100	14
RC-0987	BACH FLUTE CONC	BELOW MIN	5	10	25	08

Figure 18–4
Below Minimum Stock Report

Output design, including report design and screen design for terminal output display, is critical to a good system. To the end-user, the output represents the true system. Ideally, the output should be designed by the end-user. In most cases, the output design is a joint effort of the systems analyst and the end-user.

Screen Design

The systems analyst also needs to design screens for data input and for terminal display output. The Below Minimum Stock report could be generated on a terminal display screen instead of a hard-copy report. An effective screen should have a heading and clearly defined fields for data input. Fields that are similar in nature should be grouped.

One of the tasks Bob will perform on a day-to-day basis is updating inventory records in his inventory master file. He will need to add new records, change existing ones, and delete records for items that have been discontinued. A screen for making changes to inventory records is shown in Figure 18–5. In this case, Bob would enter changes in inventory information over current data. A screen for adding inventory records would display field names and instruct Bob to enter inventory information for each new item alongside each field name.

File Design and the Detailed Data Dictionary

As explained earlier, the design of files should result from a systemwide logical database design that was accomplished during the logical design phase of the project. The file design for the inventory file in Bob's inventory control system is shown in Figure 18–6.

Figure 18–5
Edit Inventory screen

```
                    EDIT INVENTORY

ITEM NUMBER              RC-1345
ITEM DESCRIPTION         BILLY JOEL'S GREATEST HITS
ITEM CATEGORY            MVO
QUANTITY ON HAND         10
REORDER POINT            20
QUANTITY ON ORDER        40
SELLING PRICE            7.99
UNIT COST                4.40
PRIMARY VENDOR           26
SECONDARY VENDOR         27

          ENTER CHANGES OVER CURRENT DATA

F1 EDIT DATA    F2 EXIT TO MAIN MENU    F3 STORE CHANGES
```

Figure 18–6
Inventory file design

Field Name	Field Description	Type	Width	Decimals
ITEMNO	Item number	A/N	7	
ITEMDESC	Item description	A	36	
ITEMCAT	Item category	A	3	
QTY-HD	Quantity on hand	N	3	
REORDPT	Reorder point	N	3	
QTY-ORD	Quantity on order	N	3	
SELLPRICE	Selling price	N	2	2
UNCOST	Unit cost	N	2	2
VEN1	Primary vendor	N	2	
VEN2	Secondary vendor	N	2	

The standard data names and data definitions for each of these data elements are recorded in the detailed data dictionary for the proposed system. An example of a complete data dictionary description for one of the fields in the inventory file, the Item Category field, illustrates how coding can be used to minimize the amount of data input. The various codes set up for the item category are explained in the data dictionary in Figure 18–7.

Program Specifications

If the system is to be programmed, then program specifications need to be designed to produce the various outputs from the files and input data. These program specifications can use any one of a number of techniques, including structure charts, Warnier-Orr charts, pseudocode, or Hierarchical Input Processing Output (HIPO) charts. The program specifications would be given to the programmer along with the data dictionary.

Figure 18–7
Data dictionary record for Item Category

```
DATA ELEMENT:       ITEMCAT
DESCRIPTION:        Item category is a unique code
                    assigned to each record or tape.
                    Codes: RNR: Rock n' Roll
                           CLA: Classical
                           COU: Country
                           JAZ: Jazz
                           TEH: Teen Hits
                           MVO: Male Vocalist
                           FVO: Female Vocalist
                           SHO: Sound Tracks of
                                Musical Shows
TYPE:               Alphabetic  LENGTH: 3
ALIASES:            None
RANGE OF VALUES:    Must be a valid code
SOURCE:             Inventory input
WHERE USED:         Inventory file
                    Sales analysis report
                    Member analysis report
MAINTENANCE:        Code is assigned when an inventory record
                    is created; is deleted when the inventory
                    record is deleted.
```

Forms Design

Most systems design projects require forms for such things as source data entry and the generation of output forms such as invoices, purchase orders, and monthly statements to customers. Forms can refer to both screen-based forms and paper forms. Each form should have a heading, including date and company name and address. The format should be clear and concise. Headings should be centered over data elements, and columns should be vertically aligned. Boxed headings and total lines make forms more readable. One of the forms Bob will need for an inventory system is a purchase order to vendors. An example of a purchase order for Music by Mail, Inc., is included in Figure 18–8.

Documentation

Documentation is one of the most critical aspects of an information system. It tells the story of a system, its design and construction, and its objectives. Without documentation, it is difficult to make changes or modifications to the system because no one knows how files, reports, and procedures were designed.

The first type of documentation is *systems design documentation.* Systems design documentation includes the specifications for the new system, including the design of reports, screens, files, programs, and procedures. It should include program design specifications such as structure charts, pseudocode, Warnier diagrams, flowcharts, or decision tables. Systems design documentation specifies the logic used at the module level. In addition, it documents testing methods, test data, and test results. Documentation explains manual procedures, such as data validation and source document data entry. Systems design documentation is essential to those who will ultimately become responsible for enhancing and modifying the system.

User documentation is designed to provide users with the training they need to understand and use the new system. Users need to be familiar with data entry and validation procedures, the interpretation of computer output, methods of dealing with errors, and procedures to follow during testing and conversion activities.

Finally, **operations documentation** includes a systems flowchart identifying programs and the order in which they are executed. The input files, processing requirements, output files, and output reports for the system are identified. The tool used to depict these processing requirements is the systems flow chart. Systems flowcharting symbols depict the physical storage devices and data processing procedures that are implemented as a part of a data processing system.

The systems flowchart symbols and a systems flowchart depicting an inventory control system are shown in Figure 18–9.

Figure 18–8
Purchase order for Music by Mail, Inc.

```
DATE:            May 15, 1994
SHIP TO:         Robert Thomas                 BILL TO:      Robert Thomas
                 MUSIC BY MAIL, INC.                         MUSIC BY MAIL, INC.
                 P. O. Box 1171                              P. O. Box 1171
                 St. Louis, MO 63167                         St. Louis, MO 63167
                      VENDOR:
                      INTERNATIONAL RECORDS, INC.
                      777 SUNRISE HIGHWAY
                      MOUNT VERNON, NY 10803

ITEM QUANTITY    ORDER UNIT   ITEM DESCRIPTION               UNIT COST     AMOUNT
     40              EA       BILLY JOEL'S GREATEST HITS       4.40        176.00
                                                   TOTAL                   176.00
```

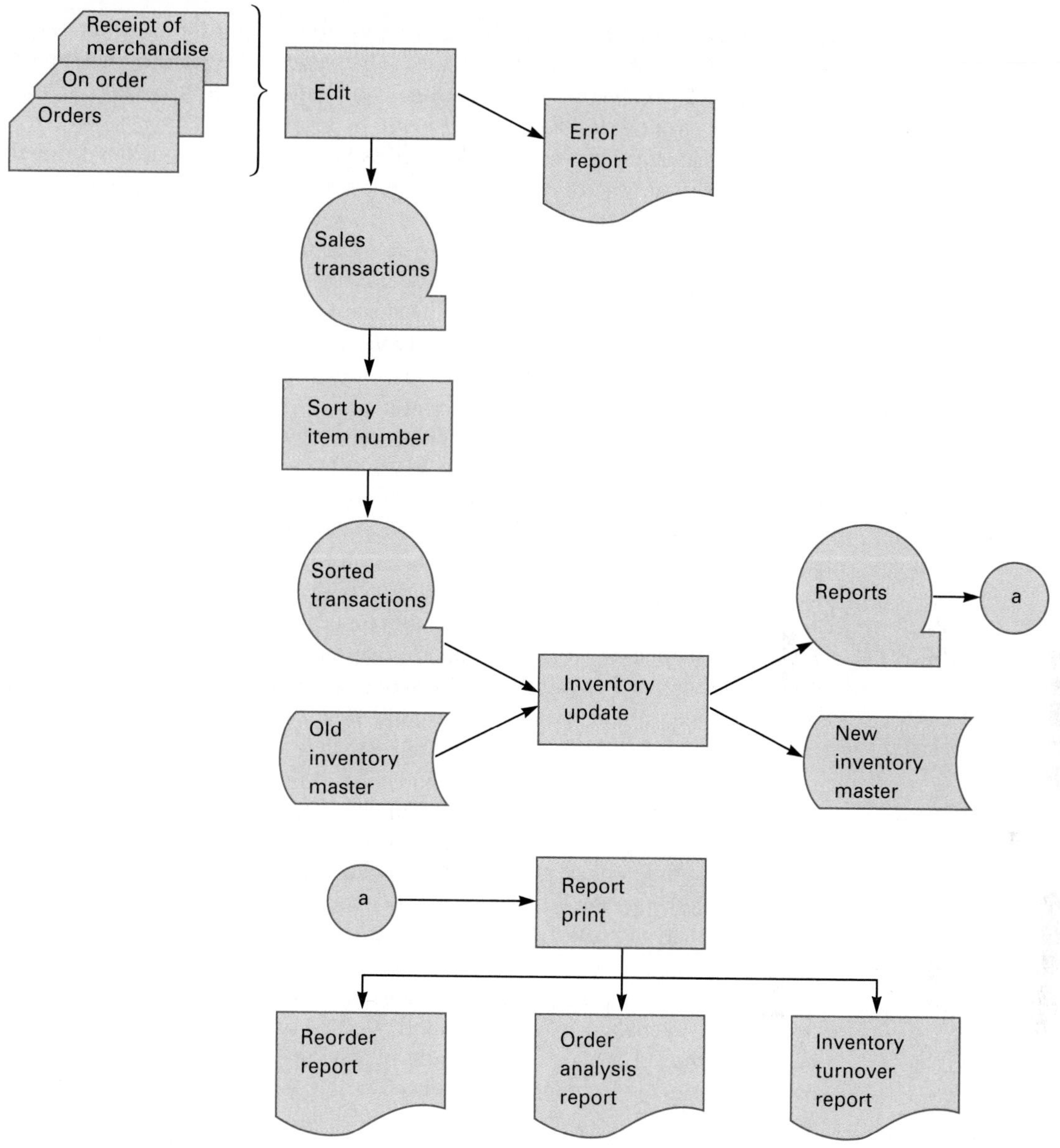

Figure 18–9
Systems flowchart for an inventory control system

In this system, incoming transactions (e.g., receipt of merchandise, on-order items, and order items) are entered as inputs and edited. The outputs of the edit process are valid sales transactions, which are written to a tape file, and error transactions, which are written to an error report. These valid sales transactions are sorted in item number sequence to match the item records in the inventory file and are written to a sorted transactions file. Then the sorted transactions are merged with the old inventory master file in order to update the old inventory records and to generate a new inventory master file. Reports are also generated after the inventory file update. These reports include a reorder report, an order analysis, and an inventory turnover report. The reorder report indicates which inventory items have fallen below their reorder point and their reorder quantities. The order analysis and inventory reports are tactical reports that indicate trends affecting inventory management, such as fast-moving and slow-moving items.

Operations documentation also includes instructions for the distribution of output and for run times and setup requirements. The name of the maintenance programmer responsible for handling problems, changes, and enhancements for the system and the user contact responsible for providing input are also included.

In the case of a single-user system such as Bob's inventory control system, the user documentation and the operations documentation may be the same. In a single-user system, the user and the operator are one.

Documentation is a time-consuming task, and many systems analysts and programmers leave it to the last minute or fail to do it properly. Because of its importance, many MIS organizations hire documentation specialists who are responsible for compiling, maintaining, and updating systems design, user, and operations documentation.

At the end of the detailed systems design phase of the project, the blueprints for the proposed system are in place. The users of the proposed system should have an opportunity to review all design documents, including report mock-ups, input screens, and forms so that their feedback can be used to make improvements before implementation.

An implementation plan is developed during the detailed design phase of the project. If the software is to be written in a procedural or nonprocedural language, the time, cost, and machine resources needed to implement the proposed system have to be determined. If a software package is purchased, provisions for making modifications and enhancements in reports, files, and screens must be determined. During this time, plans for testing and conversion may also be established. Implementation is the most time-consuming aspect of the project and requires careful planning and control of resources.

IMPLEMENTATION

The implementation phase of the project includes programming, testing, training, conversion, and documentation. In this section, you'll learn about implementation procedures that are of interest to the user-manager.

Programming and Testing

Programming and testing software developed in-house are the most time-consuming aspects of a systems development project. Because changes are inevitable, one of the major objectives of program design is developing modular, changeable systems. Structured programming techniques, introduced in the early 1970s, helped to eliminate the problems caused by transfers of control and data among the various procedures in programs. Transfers had caused a "ripple effect": When a programmer attempted to correct a bug in one part of a program, this bug would create a second bug in another part of the program, the second bug would create a third bug, and so on. In structured programming, three control structures governing program logic are implemented through different kinds of procedures. These control structures are *sequence, selection,* and *iteration.* In COBOL, for example, the selection control structure is implemented using the IF THEN ELSE statement and the iteration procedure is implemented using the PERFORM UNTIL statement. The PERFORM UNTIL statement, which makes it possible to execute one module at a time, minimizes the interference of modules with each other.

A program module should be designed to execute a self-contained function within a program. Functions can be reading records, performing edit checks, writing records, and doing calculations. If each module performs a unique function, it is less likely to interfere with the inner workings of other modules. The more functionally independent a module is, the more likely the module can be reused in different parts of the program or in many different programs. The art of designing a program becomes a matter of constructing a hierarchy of self-contained modules that are organized to carry out the major functions of a program.

In the 1970s, many programmers were independent workers. When structured methods were introduced, it was difficult to get them to conform with new procedures for writing programs. As a result, two organizational strategies were introduced into organizations. One of these was the programmer team, consisting of programming specialists and a programming project manager.

The other organizational strategy (which was introduced in the late 1970s) was the **structured walkthrough.** The structured walkthrough provides an opportunity for programmers to have peers review their work. Its objective is to catch errors and to improve work at all phases of systems design and implementation. Participants in walkthroughs provide feedback, not criticism. Structured walkthroughs are used extensively today.

The purpose of program testing is to catch errors in programs. Often, when programmers provide test data for their own programs, they are not testing all the possible conditions that could affect their programs. For example, let us say that a programmer wanted to test a program that would read customer invoice numbers. Because an invoice number is a numeric field, one edit check would be for nonnumeric data. But that would not be enough. Test input data should also include unusual situations such as the existence of symbols, decimal digits, quantities that may be out of range, and blank fields. To get around the problem of inadequate testing, teams are sometimes organized to test programs so that programmers who may be hesitant to develop comprehensive sets of test data can get ideas from other programmers. Users can also provide test data consisting of erroneous transactions.

After programs are tested using artificial data, they should be tested using "live" data. Once individual program modules and programs are tested, subsystem- and system-level tests can begin. Many of the problems are likely to occur because of the interfaces of high-level and lower-level modules and because of the integration of programs into the overall system. Highly modularized system designs make it easier to catch and to fix integration type errors.

Training

All those who will be affected by the new system should have an opportunity to participate in training. Training may make the difference between system acceptance and failure. If people do not understand the new procedures they will be responsible for conducting, or if they are unsure about how the new system will affect their jobs, they will be more likely to sabotage its performance than to make it work.

Managerial, supervisory, and clerical personnel all need some kind of training. Managers may need an orientation on how the system works, how its reports are to be used and interpreted, and how it will affect their business activities. Supervisory personnel need to understand the system, its functions, and its impact on the jobs of the people they supervise in various functional areas, such as order entry and accounts receivable. They should be thoroughly familiar with methods of data input, file maintenance, handling output, and troubleshooting.

Clerical workers may be directly responsible for validating data input, maintaining files, and generating output documents. They need thorough training in these procedures. Procedures manuals must be developed to give workers continuing guidance on how to conduct many day-to-day operations, such as file backup and system security.

Training programs should have definite objectives, relevant, job-related materials, and effective measures of successful performance. Training technologies such as computer-based training can make it possible to train system operators and clerical workers in multiple sites.

Conversion

Conversion from the old to the new system can be accomplished by one of four methods. In the **parallel systems method,** the old and new systems are operated simultaneously until the new system works well. Ideally, the end-users and the systems analyst would have already come to an agreement about the performance measures used to evaluate whether the new system is operating successfully. Conversion to the new system occurs when the new system performs as well as the old system. If the new system does not work, the parallel approach guarantees that ongoing operations won't be disrupted. However, the evaluation of the new system is not based on its running independently.

In a slightly different approach, the phased method, the new system is phased in as the old system is phased out. Phased conversion may call for the use of temporary file conversion modules at the interface between old and new modules. The cost of this approach may be as great as that of the parallel method. In addition, this approach may be confusing to both the user and customers. When a system has multiple modules, such as inventory control, accounts receivable, and accounts payable, one module at a time can be introduced at periodic intervals, such as every six months. This approach may avoid the shock of introducing the entire system at once.

When the cut-over method is used, a complete, one-time conversion from the old to the new system occurs. Although this approach may be risky, it is clear and can be accomplished quickly. A fairly simple microcomputer-based system can normally be introduced by this method.

Finally, the **pilot systems method** entails introducing a new system to a small part of the organization. In this way, the pilot system can be evaluated and modified before being introduced to other users. New technologies like electronic mail are often introduced using the pilot approach because their impact and benefits are not really known. Experiences during a pilot project can help systems designers anticipate the impact of new technology on work methods and procedures.

Human Factors in Systems Implementation

One of the main reasons that information systems fail is that users resist change. Common reasons for resistance to change include uncertainty about new expectations for performance, unfamiliarity with new tasks, and anxiety about potential displacement. When computer-based text processing systems were introduced into many offices in the late 1970s, for example, many secretaries felt that their jobs would be eliminated. Many resisted learning new skills and reorganizing work activities to integrate the new technology into office work.

However, in most cases, word processing did not replace secretaries. Rather than making their jobs less skilled, it mechanized much of the routine, repetitive work that they were responsible for and created opportunities for handling new administrative tasks. Some secretaries were able to provide more effective administrative support for professionals. Others learned technical skills and managed to organize departmental databases and text files to support a variety of applications.

When new technology is introduced into an organization, many people perceive threats to their jobs, their status, and their relationships with others. Feelings of insecurity may cause them to sabotage the success of a system at worst or simply to resume traditional work methods. If new methods of work organization and control are not accepted, then few productivity gains are likely to occur with the introduction of an information system. For example, if a word processing system is introduced into an office, few productivity gains will occur unless clerical and secretarial jobs are redesigned and new procedures for preparing and filing documents are developed. If the system is superimposed on the traditional office, where work is unspecialized and unstandardized, productivity gains will be limited.

One reason for resistance to change is that existing work methods are comfortable. Employees have a **work psychological contract,** which means that they accept the organization's expectations for their performance. When these expectations change, they feel insecure. If the reward system does not change to provide incentives for them to acquire the new skills needed to use new information systems effectively, they may feel frustrated. A good example of this problem occurred in the 1970s when secretaries were expected to become word processing operators. Job classifications for word processing operators were lower than those for secretaries, creating very little incentive to learn the new technical skills needed in the workplace. Word processing operators who were recruited at the clerical level often lacked the educational background and technical know-how to perform well in these jobs. After years of high turnover in the word processing field, many organizations changed the reward system to recruit capable candidates.

To reduce resistance to change brought on by an information system, the systems analyst needs to serve as a change agent. The manager of the department or area into which an information system is being introduced must also fill the role of a change agent. A change agent has to understand the feelings of inadequacy and loss of control that can occur. If new technologies are to succeed, people have to accept them and want to make them work. The systems analyst and the manager should understand strategies for planning, designing, and implementing change.

Planning for Change. Planning for change occurs from the moment that the necessity for change is recognized. This planning should not be put off until the information system is being implemented because by then employees will realize that introducing a computer-based system is a foregone conclusion. They need to become involved in diagnosing problems in work methods, organization, and effectiveness during the problem definition and systems analysis phases of the project. If they recognize a disparity between current and potential methods, they will want to become involved in the design and implementation of a new information system. However, it may be necessary to move slowly and to limit introducing technological advances. Recommended changes should be based on thorough research, including information gathered from questionnaires and interviews. Users should have an opportunity to study this information, to assess alternatives, and to recommend changes.

Designing for Change. During systems design, alternative design options are studied and the blueprints for the new information system are developed. Users should have an opportunity to participate in design, including the evaluation of software packages, the development of reports and screens, and the set-up of new work methods and procedures. In situations where jobs are to be redesigned, workers should help redefine jobs in ways that preserve job satisfaction, skill, and status. Finally, new work procedures and job expectations must be thoroughly documented. If employees do not know what to do or how to do it, the new system will never succeed.

Implementing Change. Implementation must begin with complete communication about the goals and benefits of the new system. Those who will be affected by the change should understand the implementation schedule. Thorough training in technical and operating procedures is absolutely necessary for any system to work effectively.

After the system is in operation, expectations for users' performance should be reasonable. It may even be necessary to designate a period during which performance will not have a negative impact on employee reviews. Finally, if problems occur, systems designers should react quickly so that unfavorable attitudes do not develop.

The role of the systems analyst as a change agent requires an understanding of the impacts of technology on work attitudes and behavior. Even though the systems analyst may be able to put together a technical design, she also has to be able to deal with people-related issues. People who are affected by potential changes should be involved in making design and implementation decisions. The systems analyst may be able to solicit the help of employees who are in favor of innovation and in this way lay the groundwork for leadership after the system is in operation.

Implementation at Music by Mail, Inc.

The implementation of an inventory control system at Music by Mail, Inc., will include preparing documentation, developing a test plan, preparing a training plan, and developing backup procedures. In addition, a physical site for the computer has to be designed.

The programmer-analyst responsible for writing the inventory control system should provide design documentation, including file specifications, report and screen designs, and program flowcharts. A data dictionary identifying the data names and data definitions of all data elements also must be included. Operating procedures governing data validation, file maintenance, and report generation should be carefully outlined in user documentation.

The programmer should test all programs using test data to make sure that all outputs are generated correctly. It would be useful to run the new and old systems in parallel for a few weeks so that manual outputs can be compared with computer-generated ones. Bob could train to use the system by consulting the user documentation. During the testing phase, he can gain some supervised experience handling some of the procedures and have an opportunity to ask the programmer questions.

Once the system is thoroughly tested, Bob will probably need to hire a part-time worker for a few weeks to key in the inventory master file and the customer master file from which the mailing labels will be generated. The accuracy of these data must be verified using a data validation program for data input. Bob should also be taught to back up the master files on a routine basis, and instructions for data backup should be included as a part of the user documentation. At the outset, he will back up data to floppy disks and lock them up in a secure place. Later, he may want to invest in a tape cartridge backup unit. Tape backup units can back up a 70 MB hard drive within minutes to cassette tapes.

Data security is another systems implementation issue. Because Bob and a part-time worker are the only ones who will have access to the data, password security provisions are probably not necessary. Floppy disks with files backed up from the previous day could be checked if Bob feels there may be unauthorized access to item price or other critical information. He could also purchase a key lock system to prevent unauthorized access and use of his microcomputer system.

After the inventory system at Music by Mail, Inc., is operating for several months, Bob may want to evaluate its impact on his business. If changes and modifications are necessary, or if he would like to introduce another application such as accounts payable, he may have to call on a programmer-analyst again. He should have an opportunity to ask questions of the person responsible for designing and implementing the system on an ongoing basis just in case the design documentation and operating procedures aren't clear.

Strategies to Overcome the Systems Development Bottleneck

In this chapter and in Chapter 17, we used a life cycle methodology to show how systems development projects are accomplished: problem definition, systems analysis, systems design, and implementation. Though a life cycle methodology ensures that information systems requirements are carefully studied and that alternative design options are evaluated before detailed design gets underway, these activities are time-consuming. Programming and testing, which may encompass as much as 70 percent of a project, are labor-intensive activities.

A systems development backlog of projects exists in many organizations today. Users, frustrated with the high cost and time commitment involved in traditional development, are anxious to seek alternative development strategies. Many of the information systems design projects in the backlog, they feel, are critical to achieving a competitive advantage by providing better service to customers, by offering new products and services, and by developing better internal information about products, customers, and suppliers.

Requirements documents, the blueprints of the proposed system design, are frozen once a systems proposal has been approved, making changes or modifications difficult and costly. Although these requirements documents are necessary to move to the detailed design phase, users want the opportunity to propose changes.

Three alternative development strategies can substantially decrease the systems development bottleneck. These are the purchase of **software packages,** the use of **prototyping** in systems design, and the creation of **user-developed systems.** Each of these approaches has advantages and disadvantages that you should understand. For certain types of projects, each of these approaches can provide an effective alternative to traditional development.

Software Packages. The purchase of software packages has already been discussed as an alternative design option. Without question, software packages provide economies of scale in development and maintenance. In-house development of a payroll system, for example, would cost more than the purchase of a payroll package. The software package business is a billion-dollar business, and hundreds of payroll programs exist for microcomputer-, minicomputer-, and mainframe-based systems. The main task of the user is to evaluate alternative packages to determine which one best fits his requirements. For a major package, this process of evaluation may take months.

If modifications are needed, most software houses can provide programming support. Sometimes, source code is made available so that in-house development personnel can make modifications. However, if many of the programs need to be modified, in-house development may be more cost effective than purchasing a software package. Another possible disadvantage of a software package is that new hardware may have to be purchased or existing hardware may have to be upgraded. The major advantages and disadvantages of software packages are given in Table 18–9.

Table 18–9
Advantages and disadvantages of software packages

Advantages	Disadvantages
Economies of scale in development	Major modifications may be necessary
Economies of scale in maintenance	May require too much hardware
Large-scale industry with $100 billion in sales	

Prototyping. Prototyping is the process of developing a model of the proposed system design and working with the user to modify it until the user's requirements are met. The availability of fourth-generation languages that can be used to develop on-line screen designs and report mock-ups has made prototyping a practical reality in information systems development. Using prototyping, a systems designer can determine a user's requirements much more efficiently and cost-effectively than with traditional methods. The step-by-step refinement of designs provides opportunities for active user participation and avoids the problem of frozen requirements.

Prototyping may be used in several ways. It can be used to design and implement an information system using a fourth-generation language. This approach works well when system requirements are constantly changing because users can use 4GL tools to make ad hoc queries and to generate reports from existing databases. In some cases, however, 4GL may be inappropriate because of high transaction volumes in a production version of the information system. In these cases, a 4GL may be used to develop a version of the system requirements and a 3GL (e.g., a procedural language like COBOL) to actually implement the system.

The main problem with prototyping is that unending iterations and revisions of the system may be proposed because changes are so easy to make. Fourth-generation languages consume a high level of CPU resources and are generally not efficient for developing high-volume transactions-based systems. A summary of the major advantages and disadvantages of prototyping is included in Table 18–10.

User Development of Information Systems. User-managers today have the opportunity to use microcomputer-based spreadsheet and database software and mainframe-based ad hoc query and reporting languages to develop their own information systems. Many of these systems fall under the general category of decision support systems because they support the decisions managers need to make. Using a mainframe-based order history database and a fourth-generation language like FOCUS, for example, a manager can analyze sales trends by product line, by customer, and by territory. Additional types of analyses can include sales forecasting and production planning. Such user-developed systems usually address specific individual or departmental-level information needs and would not be developed by information systems professionals. However, user-managers feel that these systems are critical to their needs.

User development has been an issue for several years now. Many experts argue that user-developed systems do not decrease the systems development backlog because they consist of one-time-only projects that never become part of the backlog. These projects are not evaluated to see whether a business need exists for them or whether they are cost-justified. In addition, many of these projects, particularly those developed using

Table 18–10
Advantages and disadvantages of prototyping

Advantages	Disadvantages
Rapid development of a working system	Unending iterations may occur
Step-by-step refinement of designs	Fourth-generation-language products require excessive machine resources
Uses new tools (fourth-generation languages, query languages)	Not realistic for high-volume transactions systems
Costs 25 percent of traditional approach	
Allows experimentation	

Table 18–11
Advantages and disadvantages of user-developed systems

Advantages	Disadvantages
Increases user satisfaction	Doesn't attack the backlog problem
Provides users with needed decision support systems	Questionable cost-effectiveness
Allows ad hoc query and reporting	Inferior development methods
Addresses specialized problems	Poor transferability of systems
	Poor quality assurance

microcomputer-based software, are poorly designed and lack quality assurance. Many of these systems lack data validation, testing, documentation, and controls in their design. There is little documentation of the logic of internal algorithms used in making spreadsheet calculations or in generating data into reports.

Another problem with user-developed systems is that procedures for backup and recovery, data security, and system maintenance are seldom laid out. If a user developer leaves a company, the users of the system she developed may not have adequate documentation to use it or to manage it successfully. The advantages and disadvantages of user development are summarized in Table 18–11.

Factors to Consider in Selecting a Development Approach. Each of these development strategies—software packages, prototyping, and user development—has advantages and disadvantages. Each can work to reduce the backlog of systems development projects. The decision to choose one of these methods depends on the nature and scope of the projects to be accomplished.

Gremillion and Pyburn cite three factors to consider in evaluating projects that are candidates for development using one of these approaches: commonality, impact, and structure.[1] *Commonality* means the extent to which other organizations could use the system's solution to the problem. A word processing package would have high commonality because many organizations could benefit from using it.

The second factor to consider in selecting a development approach is *impact.* The more widespread the impact and the more important an information system is, the more information systems professionals must be involved. If a company is planning to develop a national network tying its customers to its order entry system, for example, the major impact of this project on customer service and sales would dictate MIS professional involvement.

The third factor to consider is *structure.* Gremillion and Pyburn define structure as a measure of how well the problem and its solution are understood. An accounts receivable system is a highly structured system because its operations are clearly defined and well understood. However, a decision support system used to make a corporate acquisition decision would be unstructured and complex.

Gremillion and Pyburn suggest that a development approach can be selected on the basis of the commonality, impact, and structure of an information systems design project. Table 18–12 summarizes their recommendations.

---

[1]Lee L. Gremillion and Phillip Pyburn, "Breaking the Systems Development Bottleneck," *Harvard Business Review,* March–April 1983, pp. 130–37.

Table 18–12
Development strategy proposed by Gremillion and Pyburn

Properties of a Project

Commonality	Impact	Structure	Method
Common	Broad	High	Package
Uncommon	Broad	High	Traditional
Uncommon	Broad	Low	Prototype
Common	Limited	High	Package
Uncommon	Limited	High	User-developed
Uncommon	Limited	Low	User-developed

If a project is common to many organizations, is high in structure, and has a broad impact on the organization, a package is a good solution. An example of this type of project is a prospect information system for sales and marketing analysts. Many organizations need a prospect system, and its use would have a substantial impact. Because it is a highly structured system, a package could probably be found to do the job. If a system is common, high in structure, and has limited impact, a package is also a good choice. An example of this is a plant production scheduling system for a single plant.

If a project is not common to many organizations, has a broad impact, and is low in structure, Gremillion and Pyburn argue that prototyping is an effective approach. Prototyping can give the users an opportunity to define their requirements. A decision support system for cash management is a good example of this type of project. Because the impact is broad and the structure is low, prototyping would be a good choice.

If a project is not common to many organizations or to many other users throughout the organization, has a limited impact, and has either high or low structure, user development is appropriate. The limited scope and impact of such projects make them ideal for user development. This category encompasses many of the individual decision support systems in organizations today.

However, if a project is not common, has a broad impact, and has high structure, a traditional approach will be the best alternative. Prototyping is not necessary because the requirements are well defined. In addition, MIS involvement is warranted because of the uniqueness and impact of the project on the overall organization. An example of this type of project is an international order billing system for a chemical company.

In summary, the systems development bottleneck can be attacked by using alternative development methods such as software packages, prototyping, and user development. However, these methods are not the solution for all types of projects. The characteristics of various systems development projects must be studied to determine whether any one of these approaches is realistic.

Project Management and Control

One of the major responsibilities of a project manager in information systems design is project management and control. The project manager assumes responsibility for the completion of systems design and implementation activities within time and budgetary constraints. In major projects, involving dozens of systems designers and programmers, million-dollar budgets, and years of duration, project management is a challenging task. But even in smaller-scale projects, the project manager has to schedule activities, establish completion dates, supervise project team members, monitor progress, and make sure that activities are being completed successfully. When problems occur, he must reallocate resources and reschedule personnel. In addition, the project manager must see that users have an opportunity to review design work and to provide feedback.

At the start, the project manager must define the tasks to be accomplished, the order in which they should be done, and their interdependence. For example, file design must be accomplished before programming can begin. Many project activities will occur simultaneously, whereas some must be completed before others begin. The systems development life cycle methodology will identify major activities, but it will not necessarily show the interdependencies among various tasks.

Once activities and completion dates have been established, the project manager should establish a project management plan showing activities, completion dates, and concurrent tasks. Techniques such as Gantt charts and a project network using the Critical Path Method (CPM) are useful in establishing these goals. Figure 18–10 shows a Gantt chart for a systems development project. The chart shows estimated start and end dates for major tasks. If progress is not on schedule, the project manager can take necessary action. One advantage of the Gantt chart is that both nonsystems personnel and project participants can understand it. The Gantt chart also depicts which systems development tasks overlap. Individual Gantt charts can be developed for project team members, too.

One of the limitations of the Gantt chart is that it does not illustrate how activities depend on each other, however. The project network shows not only start and completion times for project tasks but also how these tasks depend on each other. In addition, the project network identifies slack times, or the amount of time a project can slip from its original schedule without affecting the overall project's completion time. Also, if a major task is not completed on schedule, the project network can detect its impact on the overall project. A project network is shown in Figure 18–11. In this project network, you can see the description of each event, beginning with project initiation. You can also see the description of each project task, including developing a problem definition, conducting a feasibility study, and evaluating alternative design options. Some tasks must be completed before subsequent ones begin; others can occur

Figure 18–10
A Gantt chart

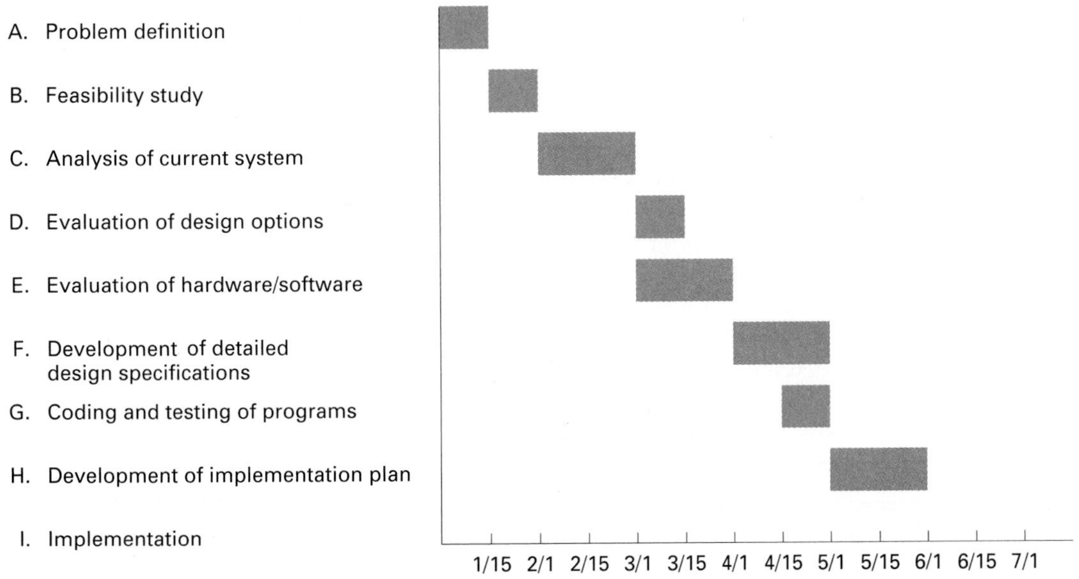

A. Problem definition
B. Feasibility study
C. Analysis of current system
D. Evaluation of design options
E. Evaluation of hardware/software
F. Development of detailed design specifications
G. Coding and testing of programs
H. Development of implementation plan
I. Implementation

1/15 2/1 2/15 3/1 3/15 4/1 4/15 5/1 5/15 6/1 6/15 7/1

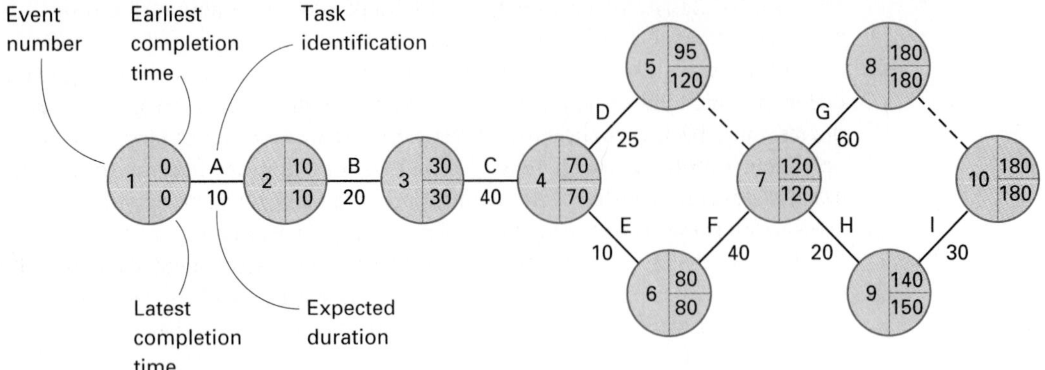

Slack time for event = latest completion time − earliest completion time

Event	Description	Task	Description
1	Project initiated	A	Problem definition
2	Problem statement	B	Conduct feasibility study
3	Feasibility study report	C	Detailed analysis of the current system
4	Systems analysis report	D	Evaluation of alternative design options
5	Design proposal	E	Evaluate hardware/software
6	Hardware/software evaluation	F	Develop detailed design specifications
7	Design specification report	G	Code and test programs
8	Completed programs	H	Design implementation plan
9	Implementation plan	I	Implement the system
10	Post-implementation review		

Figure 18–11
A project network

simultaneously. For example, the feasibility study must be completed before a detailed analysis of the current system can begin. But coding and testing and the development of an implementation plan can occur simultaneously. Using the project network, you can determine the earliest completion time for each event, the latest completion time for each event, and the expected duration of each task. For example, Task A is the problem definition phase of the project. Its duration is 10 hours. The earliest completion time for Event 2, the problem statement, is 10 hours. The latest completion time for this event is also 10 hours, because no other prerequisite tasks are involved in reaching the completion of the problem statement.

As you can see from the diagram in Figure 18–11, the slack time for each event is the latest completion time minus the earliest completion time. For example, the latest completion time for the design proposal (Event 5) is 120 hours and its earliest completion time is 95 hours. The slack time is 25 hours for completion of the design proposal because two other tasks must be completed before Event 7, the design specification report, can be concluded. These tasks are E, evaluate hardware/software, and F, develop detailed design specifications. Tasks E and F can be accomplished in 10 hours and 40 hours respectively. In total, since tasks E and F must be completed prior to Event 7, the design specification report, the tasks leading up to Event 7 entail 120 hours.

The project network approach is a useful approach because it takes into account prerequisite activities and their relationship to accomplishing project events. The network can be used to assess the impact of delayed tasks on the completion of project events. This is important in managing a project in which tasks are dependent upon each other and when project outcomes must be constantly updated as a result of delays, manpower changes, and scheduling difficulties.

Whichever project management method is used, the project manager and users need to use these checkpoints to review progress. During system reviews, people working on various components of the project can communicate with each other and discuss unforeseen problems. User-management must have an opportunity to review interim design documents, to approve changes in schedule, and to suggest changes. Users also must be informed of the impact of desired changes on time and cost estimates. You can gain more insight into what project management strategies should be used in projects with varying degrees of risk by learning about the portfolio approach to project management.

A PORTFOLIO APPROACH TO PROJECT MANAGEMENT

One of the issues in information systems development is how to assess risk. With high-risk projects, hundreds of thousands of dollars can be spent without ever achieving anticipated benefits. McFarlan describes a situation in which a large consumer-products company budgeted $250,000 for a new personnel information system to be ready in nine months. After two years and $2.5 million, the company projected that another $3.6 million would be needed to complete the project.[2] In another case, a sizable financial institution went $1.5 million over budget and lagged 12 months behind schedule on the development of a new financial systems package. When it was installed, the average transactions response times were much longer than expected.

The history of information systems development tells of hundreds of projects that have failed or have suffered severe cost and time overruns. Many of these problems occur, McFarlan suggests, because user managers and MIS professionals take on projects without assessing risk. McFarlan's portfolio approach helps managers identify risk factors and strategies for minimizing risk. Risk may not be all bad. Risky projects, if successful, are often the ones that provide the greatest benefits. Risk must be recognized and managed for these projects to be successful.

Risk Factors

Three major risk factors are (1) project size, (2) experience with the technology, and (3) project structure. The greater the time and expense involved in a project, the greater the risk. If a project team is not familiar with the hardware, operating system, database management system, or telecommunications network, risk increases. Projects with managers who have ill-defined ideas of the outputs and who change their minds throughout design incur greater risk. These are "low-structure" projects.

Strategies for Minimizing Project Risk

Management strategies to minimize project risk include external integration tools, internal integration tools, formal planning tools, and formal control mechanisms (see Table 18–13). External integration tools enable the project team to communicate effectively with users. Internal integration tools are used to manage the internal interactions among project team members. Formal planning tools are designed to estimate the time, cost, and resources needed to complete a project, and formal control mechanisms help managers evaluate progress on completing project activities. Depending on the type of project, one or more of these strategies must be used.

---

[2]F. Warren McFarlan, "A Portfolio Approach to Information Systems Development," *Harvard Business Review*, September–October 1981, pp. 142–50.

Table 18–13
Project management tools

External Integration Tools	Internal Integration Tools
Selection of user as project manager	Selection of experienced DP professional as project manager
Participation of users on steering committee	Regular reviews of project status
Users responsible for approving changes in design	Selection of team members with previous work relationships
Formal Planning Tools	**Formal Control Tools**
Use of network project management tools, such as PERT and critical path	Comparisons of project status with plans
Selection of project phases and activities	Development of strategies for change control
Formal project approval processes	Regular presentations on outcomes

Using Appropriate Strategies to Manage Projects

McFarlan identifies four major types of projects, as shown in Figure 18–12. "High-structure–low-technology" projects have relatively low risk because the outputs are well understood and the technical problems are familiar. An example of this type of project is purchasing an accounts receivable system to run on a minicomputer. Accounts receivable is a highly structured application, and the technology is familiar. Internal integration strategies should be used to manage the project team, and life cycle planning tools should be introduced to ensure that tasks and resources are defined.

"High-structure–high-technology" projects involve new technology and require technical expertise and effective internal integration. The project manager must be able to manage technicians, maintain teamwork, and make sure that all design decisions are well understood. An example of this type of project is converting from one mainframe-based operating system to another. Even though the outputs are clearly defined, users need to be aware that project outcomes may be postponed if technology-related problems occur.

"Low-structure–low-technology" projects require user involvement and direction to reach consensus on project design specifications. If these projects are not managed

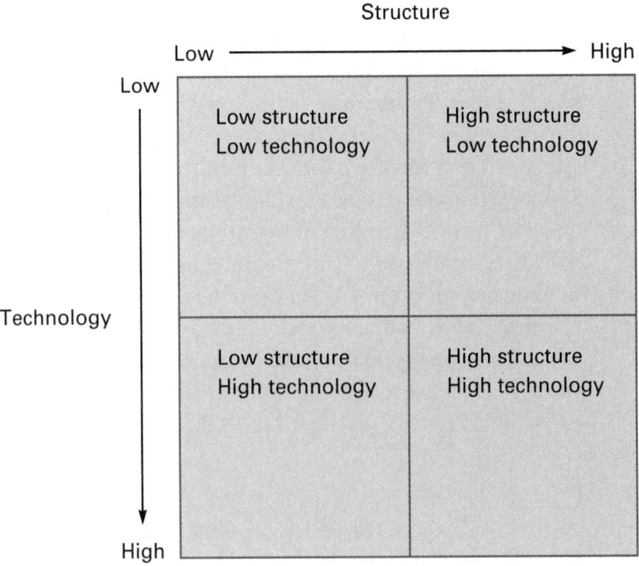

Figure 18–12
Project types

Table 18–14
Tools contributing to project success

Project Type	Strategies
High-structure–low-technology	Formal control Formal planning Moderate internal integration
High-structure–high-technology	High internal integration Moderate formal planning Moderate formal control
Low-structure–low-technology	High external integration High formal control Moderate formal planning
Low-structure–high-technology	High external integration High internal integration

by users, continual change requests will result in time and cost overruns. A good example of this is a personnel information systems project that resulted in millions of dollars of cost overruns because users kept changing their minds about the types of reports they wanted to generate from the database. These projects must enlist a user as a project leader and a user steering committee to evaluate the design at each phase.

"Low-structure–high-technology" projects have the greatest risk. Project managers undertaking these projects must have technical experience and the ability to communicate effectively with users. Internal integration is necessary because teams need to keep abreast of technical issues. Users must also commit to design specifications to keep these projects on track.

Table 18–14 summarizes tools that can be used to ensure project success. Using these recommendations, both information systems professionals and users can work together to successfully manage projects with various levels of risk.

Management Summary

In this chapter, you have learned about the activities that take place during the detailed design and implementation phases of a project. Users are responsible for system selection, which includes developing a request for proposal, evaluating alternative software packages, and evaluating hardware. The weighted-factor method is helpful in evaluating software and hardware options.

Once an alternative design option is selected, a cost-benefit analysis is used to determine the economic feasibility of the proposed system. Benefits of an information system include increased revenues, decreased administrative costs, and better customer service. Costs include development, equipment, and ongoing operations and maintenance. The present value method of cost-benefit analysis considers the time value of money in determining the costs and benefits of a project over a three- to five-year time frame.

During detailed design, the blueprints for the physical design of the new system are established. Reports, screens, files, and forms are designed. The logic of problems is depicted using Warnier diagrams, structured flowcharts, pseudocode, or HIPO charts.

Implementation includes programming, testing, training, documentation, and conversion. Methods such as programmer teams and structured walkthroughs make it possible to catch design errors in programming and testing. The three types of documentation include systems design documentation, user documentation, and operations documentation. Conversion can be accomplished by the parallel systems method, the *dual systems method,* the *inventory method,* or the *pilot systems method.*

Human factors must be taken into account in designing and implementing an information system. New technologies affect work methods and procedures and interpersonal relationships. Anxiety, uncertainty, and resistance need to be anticipated and managed by involving users in planning, designing, and implementing information systems.

Effective project management is one of the major responsibilities of the project manager and user in information systems design. The purpose of project management is to control project activities and personnel so that results are accomplished within time and cost constraints. Gantt charts and project network methods are valuable tools in project management.

Systems development backlogs exist in many organizations today. Strategies to overcome the systems development bottleneck include use of software packages, prototyping, and user development. Depending on the commonality, impact, and structure of information systems design projects under consideration, one of these approaches may be an appropriate development alternative.

Key Terms for Managers

cost-benefit analysis, **669**
data dictionary, **675**
intangible benefits, **670**
maintenance, **664**
operations documentation, **678**
parallel systems method, **682**
peripheral, **668**
pilot systems method, **682**
prototyping, **685**
request for proposal (RFP), **664**
requirements document, **685**
software package, **685**
structured walkthrough, **681**
systems design documentation, **664**
tangible benefits, **669**
testing, **663**
user-developed system, **685**
user documentation, **678**
work psychological contract, **683**

Review Questions

1. What are the advantages of using the weighted-factor method to evaluate alternative hardware and software options?
2. Give some examples of intangible benefits of information systems.
3. Give some examples of development costs in an information systems design project.
4. What is meant by the time value of money? Why should it be considered in conducting a cost-benefit analysis?
5. Describe two guidelines in designing reports.
6. Identify one guideline for designing screens.
7. What is meant by the *ripple effect?*
8. What are the reasons for conducting a structured walkthrough during various phases of an information systems design project?
9. Explain the advantages and disadvantages of the parallel systems method of conversion.
10. In what situations would the pilot systems method of conversion work effectively?
11. What are the components of systems design documentation? Why is it important?
12. What are the components of user documentation? Why is it important?

13. Compare the Gantt chart and project network diagram as tools used in project management.
14. What are several risk factors associated with systems development projects?
15. What are some examples of internal integration tools that can be used to successfully manage projects?
16. What are some strategies that can be used to minimize the risk of low-structure–low-technology projects?
17. What are the advantages of the prototyping approach in systems design?
18. What are some of the disadvantages of user development of information systems?
19. What three factors must be considered in determining if an information system can be created using a software package, prototyping, or user development?
20. What are the characteristics of an information systems project where prototyping could be used effectively?

Questions for Discussion

1. Why is it a good idea for a manager to develop a Request for Proposal for a new information system?
2. What kinds of benefits of an information systems project are most difficult to measure? Should these benefits be included in the justification for a new information system?
3. How can the structure chart be used to create a changeable, flexible system design?
4. Why is systems design documentation so important?
5. What kinds of human factors can cause resistance to systems implementation?
6. What kinds of control mechanisms can be used to minimize the risk of a high-technology–high-structure project?
7. Why are external integration strategies useful in a low-structure project?
8. What are some of the characteristics of an information systems project in which software packages can be used effectively?

Problems

1. **Detailed design for Music by Mail, Inc.** This chapter gave examples of detailed design specifications for Music by Mail's inventory management system. Yet these examples did not show all of Bob's requirements. Imagine that you are Bob Thomas. You would like to have a sales analysis report that indicates which inventory items are most profitable. Design a mock-up of a sales analysis report that compares the profitability of various tapes that Bob currently has in stock. Make up item names, costs, and sales volumes to develop your report.

   Once you develop your report, design a data dictionary describing the data names and data definitions of data elements in your report. You may use the data dictionary example in Figure 18–7 as a guideline.
2. **The MacMillan Manufacturing Company.** The MacMillan Manufacturing Company has a systems development backlog of 52 months. Managers are very anxious to accomplish some information systems development projects and are beginning

to seek the help of consultants. The information systems department, headed by Richard Price, does not want to lose critical projects that should be developed by MIS professionals. Richard also wants to investigate the possibility of using alternative development approaches to accomplish some of the projects that are needed.

Below is a list of some of the projects required by managers at MacMillan. Use Gremillion and Pyburn's framework to determine the best development approach for each of these projects. Traditional development, software packages, user development, and prototyping are possible development alternatives.

a. A manager in the production planning department wants an information system to help branch managers determine target ending inventory levels for their respective branch distribution centers. The production planners need access to a sales history data base for the past 18 months consisting of 3.5 million records. Using these data, they would determine sales trends for various product lines. The sales analysis information would be used to determine the target ending inventory levels.

b. The accounting department needs an information system to maintain records on funded government contracts. The budgets for each contract have to be updated weekly to reflect charges for manpower and equipment, transportation, services, and overhead expense. Reports have to be prepared for the government agencies funding the contracts monthly.

c. The members of the corporate strategic planning department need an information system to enable them to analyze alternative capital budgeting decisions, including investments in real estate, new acquisitions, and new facilities.

d. Senior management proposes developing an international order entry and billing system, making it possible to enter orders and to invoice customers from all 12 district offices.

e. The personnel office wants a computerized job applicant information system. This system would make it possible to query the job applicant database to identify prospective candidates for job openings (for example, "Give me a list of all the job applicants with MBAs in Finance"). In addition, the personnel director would like a database of current job openings so that the criteria for selecting candidates for particular positions could be matched with the applicant data file. In this way, lists of candidates with the qualifications for each job opening could be generated automatically and used to set up interview schedules.

3. **Using McFarlan's portfolio approach.** Use McFarlan's portfolio approach to identify the risk category of each of the following projects. Give reasons for selecting the risk category you choose. Then, recommend strategies that will help minimize the risks and maximize the chances of success for each of these projects.

   Project 1: A major corporation is designing a human resources information system that will enable managers throughout the firm to query personnel files with such questions as, "Give me the names of all employees who have been with the firm for over 15 years and who have degrees in chemical engineering." The system will support over 3,000 users. In addition, the system will enable employees to make queries about employee benefit programs and job openings throughout the firm. The system will be designed using a mainframe-based database management system and a new fourth-generation language, NOMAD II. The fourth-generation language will replace current COBOL programs used to extract personnel reports. Using the 4GL, managers will be able to make queries and to generate reports directly from the database.

Project 2: The chairperson of the Department of Nursing wants to set up a database system storing information about all current nursing students, including their grades in courses, their internship sites, and their areas of specialization. The system will be designed using a centrally located personal computer housing the student information database. A local area network will be used to link the central PC to PCs in faculty offices so faculty members can query the database. The local area network will use a new software package called Netcom, which will enable the PCs on the network to share data and a laser printer. The nursing faculty plans to query the database and to ask questions such as "Give me the names of students who are serving internships at St. Mary's Hospital." The database maintains between 75 and 100 records per semester. It will be updated to reflect changes in addresses, internship locations, and interests.

Project 3: A major insurance company is developing a prospect information system for its sales agents. The sales agents will receive portable PCs with dBase IV for a database management program. Using a custom-designed program, they will be able to store customer prospect information in their databases and to make queries. For example, they will be able to ask questions such as "Give me all the prospects who have not been called on in the past 60 days." They will also be able to generate reports listing customer prospect records in order by ZIP code, age, occupational category, interest category, and socioeconomic group. The database will maintain records on over 20,000 prospects and will be continually updated. The sales agents will also be able to generate reports indicating prospects with the highest sales potential based upon industry growth, product mix, and account service costs. Each sales agent will receive training on the query and reporting language and standardized reports to be generated from the database.

Cases

1. **Sunset Valley Country Club.** Sunset Valley Country Club is considering a proposal to design and implement a point-of-sale system for its shops and restaurants. The proposed system would include electronic cash registers in the club's two shops, the golf shop and the tennis shop, and in its two restaurants, the Thunderbird Room and the Arrowhead Room. Sales transactions would be entered at each of the shops and restaurants, and summary sales data would be transmitted to a central minicomputer system and used to update a central member accounts receivable file. At the end of each month, members would receive their monthly statements. In addition, the system would update inventories for each of the shops and restaurants, making it possible to reorder items on a timely basis. Sales analysis reports, depicting monthly trends, would also be available.

   The total cost of the proposed system, including four electronic cash registers, a central minicomputer, point-of-sale inventory and accounts receivable software packages, a text-quality printer, and a 70 MB hard disk storage device, would be $23,000. The systems development costs, including analysis, evaluation of software packages, testing, and user documentation, will run about $4,500.

   The main benefit of the proposed system is inventory management. With an inventory control program, the golf shop expects to increase its profits by $4,800 per year, and the tennis shop estimates an increase in profits of $2,500 per year. The two restaurants estimate that their profits can be increased by $6,000 each because of more effective sales analysis, more accurate entry of sales transactions, and reduction in excess inventory.

Another benefit of the proposed system is more timely monthly billing and receipt of payments on member accounts. At the current time, some bills are not mailed until 12 days after month-end closings, and checks are not received until a week later. With the proposed system, bills can be mailed out within 24 hours of the month's end, and payments can be recorded much more quickly. Interest charges will be applied to overdue accounts, bringing in an additional $2,800 of revenue per year.

The other savings will come from decreased clerical time, aggregating various bills for each member, and preparing monthly statements. Additional clerical time is spent applying payments to account balances. It is expected that a part-time clerical worker responsible for these tasks could be eliminated for a savings of $8,000 per year.

With the new system, the hardware and software maintenance contracts will run about $2,300 per year. The operating costs, including supplies, part-time clerical help, and ongoing training, will be about $2,000 per year. A part-time data processing supervisor will be paid $13,000 per year.

Other benefits of the proposed system include improved member relations because of faster point-of-sale service and more accurate billing procedures. Employees working in the golf and tennis shops and restaurants should be able to input sales transactions more efficiently and to do their jobs more easily. Managers of the shops and restaurants will be better informed for planning sales and controlling inventory.

Based on the facts of this case, can the proposed point-of-sale inventory and accounts receivable system at Sunset Valley Country Club be cost-justified? Conduct a cost-benefit analysis of the proposed system using the present-value method. Assume an interest rate of 12 percent. Conduct the analysis using a five-year period of time.

2. **A university admissions information system.** A new information system is being developed within the admissions and financial aid offices of a major university. The system will analyze application data, apply criteria for admissions and financial aid decisions, and generate various reports on applicant characteristics. In addition, the system is designed to generate various letters and documents about admissions and financial aid details to applicants and their parents. With the system, it will be possible to recruit applicants more effectively, process their financial aid applications more quickly, and ensure their successful entrance into the university.

   Up to now, all of these procedures have been handled manually. A senior admissions supervisor, Francine Minor, has meticulously handled each application individually. Her personal familiarity with each application, she feels, has enabled her to answer questions more effectively as candidates call. To some extent, she believes, good judgment needs to be used as well as the standard admissions criteria in making admissions decisions. The new computer system, she feels, will treat each applicant as a "punched card" and fail to make good admissions decisions based on judgment and experience, especially in borderline cases.

   The financial aid decisions are handled by another senior administrative supervisor, Malcolm Blake. Malcolm feels threatened by the proposed system because it will take away some of the autonomy he has had over financial aid decisions. He, too, feels that judgmental factors will be ignored.

   Both Francine and Malcolm plan to circumvent the new system in any way they can. They do not plan to support efforts to train the clerical personnel in both the admissions and financial aid offices who will be responsible for keying in data and generating various reports.

You have been brought in as a consultant to the project by Dean Robert Walters, who suspects that the new system may fail because of user resistance. What factors do you feel are creating the resistance to the proposed system? What strategies could you use to deal with them effectively? If you had been the systems analyst at the very outset of the project, what steps would you have taken to minimize potential resistance to the proposed information system?

3. **A student intern tracking system.** Phillips Agricultural Supplies Company hires interns from many universities every summer. Many of them work in the accounting, marketing, information systems, and personnel departments. To keep track of these interns, Louise Miller, director of personnel, asked one of her assistants to design a database management system maintaining data on various college interns. The system would generate reports on interns, their responsibilities, their qualifications, and their evaluations. The system, she hoped, would provide summary reports by functional area and by university program.

   Her assistant, David Conklin, had taken a course in dBase IV and was able to develop the student intern tracking system by the end of the summer. Then David left the firm to attend graduate school in another state. A few months later, Louise asked one of the secretaries in the personnel office to use the system to obtain a report of all that past summer's interns. The secretary was able to find the disks with the programs and data on them, but she was not able to get any of the reports to work. To everyone's amazement, there was no documentation of the reports anywhere to be found. And no one in the office had the knowledge of dBase IV to reconstruct them. No one could find copies of sample outputs or any evidence of the logic used in their design and implementation. Finally, in frustration, Louise hired a programmer to reprogram the reports.

   What steps could have been taken to prevent this problem from occurring? In your answer, develop a list of useful documentation for the system that would help the user understand its purpose, the logic of programs, and data needs.

Selected References and Readings

Davis, William S. *Systems Analysis and Design.* Reading, MA: Addison-Wesley, 1983.

Gremillion, Lee L., and Phillip Pyburn. "Breaking the Systems Development Bottleneck." *Harvard Business Review,* March–April 1983, pp. 130–37.

Isshiki, Koichiro R. *Small Business Computers: A Guide to Evaluation and Selection.* Englewood Cliffs, NJ: Prentice Hall, 1982.

McFarlan, F. Warren. "A Portfolio Approach to Information Systems Development." *Harvard Business Review,* September–October 1981, pp. 142–50.

Whitten, Jeffrey L., Lonnie D. Bentley, and Vic Barlow. *Systems Analysis and Design Methods,* 2nd ed. Burr Ridge, Ill.: Irwin, 1989.

Case 4 — Systems Development at the Riverbend Electric Company

INTEGRATED CASES

BACKGROUND

Order processing at the Riverbend Electric Company is similar to order processing in most make-to-order manufacturing firms. Customers place orders through the product sales department or by direct contact with salespeople. Products are manufactured according to customer specifications. When an order is finished, it is shipped to the customer along with an invoice requesting payment.

Although one might suspect that order processing is fairly standardized across firms, this is rarely the situation. Different industries have different sets of factors that affect how customer orders are handled—for example, REC, a manufacturing firm, processes orders differently than a service industry firm or retail outlet firm. Additionally, REC is a multinational firm with manufacturing facilities at the home base in North Alton, Illinois, as well as in West Martin, Tennessee; Calgary, Canada; and Guadalajara, Mexico. Orders received at corporate headquarters, where all sales activities take place, are often transferred for actual manufacturing to one of these other facilities. Once manufacturing operations at another facility are complete, the home office again takes responsibility for billing operations. Even within the electronics industry, REC processes orders differently than their major competitors in Japan and Germany due to differences in the size of their product line and due to internal factors that affect management's ability to access information that affects their decision-making activities (see Integrated Case 1 for additional background on the electronics industry).

Order processing is a complex system composed of numerous subsystems. In the manufacturing environment, order processing encompasses all activities from the time an order is received through final product delivery and customer billing. This system cuts across functional areas. At REC, order processing involves activities in several departments including Marketing and Sales, Engineering and Quality Assurance, Operations and Manufacturing, and Finance.

REC is experiencing tremendous problems in managing order processing due to excess turnaround time. All orders are not processed in the same way. Some orders are handled in a routine fashion whereas other orders are expedited in an attempt to reduce turnaround time (see Integrated Case 1 for an explanation of expediting in a job shop environment and Integrated Case 3 for further background on the expediting problem). Unless REC solves the excessive turnaround time problem, the firm will continue to lose market share.

CURRENT SITUATION

"This meeting of the Management Information Systems (MIS) Steering Committee will come to order," announced Delbert St. Onge, Executive Vice President of REC. "Let the record show that all members are present." The members included Susan Thornberry, Vice President of Marketing and Sales; Marvin Albert, V.P. Operations and Manufacturing; Richard Washington, V.P. of Administration; Mike Chen, V.P. of Engineering and Quality Assurance; Denise Medeiros, V.P. of Finance; and Karen Rasp, Director of MIS.

"Our agenda today is restricted to a single item, the problem of delivering customer orders on time and reducing turnaround time for order processing," continued Delbert. "I assume everyone has read Mr. Albert's report recommending an upgrade to our order processing and manufacturing shop floor control systems." Everyone indicated having read the report by nodding his or her head.

"I also want to take this opportunity to congratulate Marv on his fine analysis showing that our current level of order expediting is seriously interfering with our ability to deliver routine orders on time."

Marvin Albert beamed his pride in receiving recognition and praise from his boss, Delbert. "I suspected order expediting was beginning to cause problems," said Marvin with an air of braggadocio. "Although he is not present, I want to give partial credit to my shop floor manager, Don Strock, who conducted part of the analysis in my report. Initially we thought we had a problem in the training level of our manufacturing machine operators, but now we understand that by expediting 20 percent of our work orders, we are creating too much havoc with our daily detailed work schedule. Although we are able to deliver expedited orders by the promised delivery date, this is causing almost all other orders to be delivered later than promised." (See Integrated Case 3 for background on these suspected alternative problems.)

The meeting continued with a discussion of order processing. Each member of the committee discussed how order processing affected his or her functional area and the problems encountered. After about an hour, the committee decided to assign Karen Rasp the task of conducting a detailed analysis of the order processing system.

"Karen, I realize that this question may be premature, but what do you see as our alternatives for improving our order processing system?" asked Susan Thornberry. She was extremely concerned about the loss in market share that the firm was experiencing.

"One usual option is to maintain the status quo," answered Karen. "Clearly that option is not viable here. There are two viable alternatives. Regardless of which one we go with, the current system appears to need reengineering to include a combined new order processing and manufacturing shop floor control system. One alternative is for my MIS staff to analyze, design, and program a new system. The second alternative is to purchase a customized system from a contract computer system vendor. Prior to making a decision, I recommend developing a logical model of our current system in order to understand its weaknesses. This may also help us to define system requirements if we decide to examine customized packages from software vendors."

DETAILS OF THE SYSTEM

In developing a logical model of REC's existing order processing system, Karen interviewed managers at all levels. She also gathered and examined copies of documents, such as sales order forms, work order forms, and shipping documents, so that she could identify the type of information managers used in controlling the subsystems that make up order processing.

Karen developed the high-level context diagram for the system shown in Figure C4–1. This context diagram can be further decomposed into four subsystems: (1) order entry subsystem, (2) engineering subsystem, (3) manufacturing subsystem, and (4) shipping and invoicing subsystem.

Order Entry Subsystem

REC receives orders in two ways. The most common approach is for salespeople to make sales calls on established or new customers. Salespeople transmit the orders either via telephone or facsimile transmission to the order entry section that is part of the Marketing and Sales Department. Orders are recorded on a multipart *sales order form.*

If the customer is established, an order entry clerk will forward one copy (yellow) of the sales order form to an account manager in the credit approval section of the Finance Department to obtain credit approval for the amount of the order (customers typically pay for the order within 30 days of receipt of the products). Approval or disapproval is indicated on the yellow copy and the yellow copy is returned to the order entry section. A photocopy of the sales order form is filed in the credit approval section's actions-completed file. All activities associated with order approval for an established customer take one day, on average.

When the customer is new, the order entry clerk fills out a *new customer form* and forwards this form

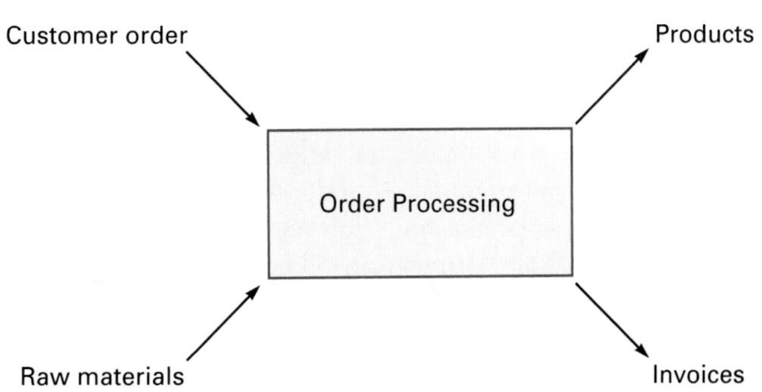

Figure C4–1
System context diagram

and the yellow copy of the sales order form to a credit manager in the credit approval section of the Finance Department, as before. The credit manager establishes a line of credit for the new customer. Approval or disapproval of the order is indicated on the yellow copy and returned to the order entry section. The new customer form is filed in the credit department in the customer-credit file, and a photocopy of the sales order form is filed in the actions-completed file as indicated above. All activities associated with order approval for new customers take two and a half days, on average.

The second way by which orders are received is for customers to call the order entry section directly. An order entry clerk transfers the call to a salesperson in the marketing section of the Marketing and Sales Department, who takes the order. In all cases the salesperson is responsible for negotiating a promised delivery date for the order. The multipart sales order form is then returned to the order entry section for processing as indicated above.

After approval of the order, the yellow copy of the sales order form is filed in the pending-orders file in the order entry section. Two copies (red and green) are forwarded to engineering, and one copy (white) is forwarded to the shop control office. A pink copy is forwarded to the payroll section of the Finance Department for payment of the salesperson's commission.

Engineering Subsystem

An engineer in the Engineering and Quality Assurance Department uses information on the sales order form to establish an *engineering design order.* This form is attached to the sales order form and used to record the manufacturing specifications for the product being ordered. Engineers also refer to the firm's standard product book for guidance in developing the product's manufacturing specifications.

The engineer assigned responsibility for the engineering design order also contacts the customer to verify that the manufacturing specifications are satisfactory. Often the customer will transmit blueprints and other requirement specifications for the product to the engineer. The engineering design order and other documentation is duplicated on a copy machine and attached to the two copies of the sales order form. The red copy of the sales order form and accompanying documentation is filed in the engineering-design file. The green copy of the sales order form and accompanying engineering documentation is forwarded to the shop control office. The activities that comprise this subsystem take two days, on average.

Manufacturing Subsystem

Don Strock, the production shop floor manager, is responsible for coordinating all activities required to manufacture products ordered by customers. This includes procuring raw materials, establishing a detailed daily work schedule for all work stations in the manufacturing area, supervising all work shifts for the North Alton manufacturing facility, and supervising the order shipping section. His staff also coordinates with other manufacturing sites (Tennessee, Canada, and Mexico) to engineer and manufacture selected customer sales orders.

When the white copy of a sales order form is received, a production manager analyzes the order requirements. Using existing manufacturing policy guidelines established by REC's Manufacturing Policy Committee, the production manager determines whether the order should be produced at the North Alton facility or at one of REC's other manufacturing facilities.

When the order is to be completed at one of the other manufacturing sites, the production manager notifies Engineering and copies of all paperwork for the order (green sales order form and any engineering specifications) are transferred via facsimile to the appropriate manufacturing plant. The assigned manufacturing plant is annotated on the white copy of the sales order form, then the white and green copies of the sales order form and accompanying documentation are filed in a subsidiary-production file. This enables Don Strock and Marv Albert to know which manufacturing plant to contact if it is necessary to determine the status of one of these orders. The plant manager and engineers at the other manufacturing sites are then responsible to contact the customer and to complete production of the product on the order.

If the order is manufactured at the North Alton site, a shop control office clerk files the white copy of the sales order form in a pending-production file because nothing can be done until Engineering confirms the actual product specifications. This is a type of suspense file. If someone questions the status of a sales order and the sales order form is in this file, Don knows that the sales order is in the Engineering Department.

When the sales order form green copy and accompanying documentation are received from Engineering, a raw material acquisitions clerk reviews the list of raw materials required to manufacture the product. This raw materials list is attached to the form by Engineering.

If the raw materials needed are not in stock, the clerk completes a *purchase requisition form* and forwards one copy to the purchasing section of the Operations and Manufacturing Department. Managers in the purchasing section acquire the raw materials from a supplier. Karen determined that the purchasing process is not really central to sales order processing and product manufacturing because 98 percent of the time the raw materials needed are already on hand as bulk stock. Thus she does not envision integrating purchasing into the order processing system.

Next a shop floor control clerk initiates a *work order form* (see Figure C1–2 of Integrated Case 1 for a copy of the form). This is a two-part form and one copy (white) is printed on cardboard stock because it accompanies the product from workstation to workstation on the manufacturing shop floor during production and thus must be sturdy.

The work order specifies the actual work in terms of job activities that are necessary to manufacture the product. The work order also specifies the routing of the work order, termed a *job,* throughout the various workstations on the manufacturing shop floor.

A green copy of the work order is attached to the white copy of the sales order form for reference in case it is necessary to locate a work order on the manufacturing shop floor, and to enable cross-referencing the work order to the sales order. The white and green copies of the sales order form, green copy of the work order form, and engineering specifications are filed in a production-in-process file.

The white copy of the work order form and a copy of the engineering specifications are forwarded to the first workstation where the worker assigned to the first job task begins manufacturing the product. The actual manufacturing schedule is provided by the daily detailed work plan for the entire manufacturing facility. As each job task is completed, the work order form, engineering specifications, and work-in-process are forwarded to the next work station until the product is completed. Work station machine operators annotate the work order at each work station as to how much time was required to complete the job task. When manufacture of the product is finished, the work order form, engineering documentation, and finished product are forwarded to the final order assembly section where a shipping clerk notifies the shop control office that the work order is finished.

Actual manufacturing time varies considerably. If the work order is expedited, manufacturing may be completed in as little as one to three weeks. Routine work orders require about five to seven weeks for the manufacturing portion of the process.

Shipping and Invoicing Subsystem

When a clerk in the shop control office learns that a work order is finished, he pulls the white copy of the sales order form and all accompanying documentation from the production-in-process file. The clerk annotates the white copy of the sales order form as complete and forwards it to an accounts receivable clerk in the Finance Department. The other copy of the sales order form and accompanying documentation is filed in a finished-order file.

The accounts receivable clerk prepares an *invoice form.* One copy of the invoice is filed in the accounts-receivable file and one copy is forwarded to the shipping clerk for inclusion with the product being shipped. A separate information copy of the invoice is mailed directly to the customer.

The shipping clerk prepares a *shipping form* that is included with the product being shipped. Finally, the product is packaged with the shipping form and invoice copy and shipped to the customer. The work order white copy and accompanying documentation are returned to the shop control office for filing with the other related documents in the finished-order file.

When manufacturing of a product for an order is finished at another facility site, the shipping clerk at that site faxes a copy of the work order to the shop floor control clerk at the North Alton facility. Three clerks coordinate the paperwork that manages and tracks sales orders assigned to other manufacturing facilities. One of these clerks will pull the white copy of the sales order form from the subsidiary-production file and send it to the accounts receivable clerk to notify the clerk to produce an invoice for the sales order. A copy of the invoice is faxed to the other manufacturing facility where the invoice, shipping form, and product are packaged and shipped to the customer. The invoice copy that is forwarded directly to the customer is mailed from the North Alton accounts receivable section. Other documentation is filed in the finished-order file as indicated above. All billing services are provided by the home corporate offices at the North Alton facility.

Case Questions and Exercises

1. Given the context diagram in Figure C4–1:
   a. Draw a first-level data flow diagram depicting the major subsystems and major data flows between the subsystems that take place in processing.
   b. Draw a detailed data flow diagram depicting the processing for each major subsystem and the internal data flows, data stores, sources and destinations of data, and processes that transform the flow of data.

2. Working individually or as a member of a student team (as assigned by your instructor), brainstorm the different ways that computer technology can be used to track work orders.
   a. Don Strock has reported problems in tracking the status of a work order once it is released to the manufacturing shop floor for production. He cannot determine what percentage of the job activities that comprise the work order are complete or if the work order will be completed by the promised delivery date given on the sales order. Consider, for example, whether a work order might be tracked by using bar-coding technology or whether workstation operators could enter information about the status of a work order by using computer terminals located on the manufacturing shop floor.
   b. If Don Strock has a computer system that can track work orders at the individual job activity level and enable him to determine the status of a work order at any time during the day, what effect might this system have on Don's ability to prioritize work orders? Would Don be able to incorporate the need to expedite certain orders? What would be the effect on his ability to manage work orders that are close to their promised delivery date?

3. Review the chapter material on batch versus on-line information systems. Given your detailed data flow diagrams from question 1, discuss which parts of the subsystems might be based on (1) batch processing, (2) on-line with batch overnight update processing, (3) on-line with immediate update processing, or (4) distributed processing, and why.

4. Assume the firm has decided to evaluate manufacturing shop floor packages available from vendors. Develop a draft request for proposals.

5. Assume the order processing and manufacturing shop floor control system is to be reengineered. Design the following sample screen layouts:
   a. A screen to be used by a worker at a workstation on the manufacturing shop floor to enter information to update the system about completing a particular job activity that is part of a work order.
   b. A screen that gives the status on an individual work order to be used by a clerk in the order entry section when customers call to check the status of their orders.
   c. What fields did you identify on the screens for *a* and *b* that must be stored in data files?

6. Karen Rasp identified two alternatives for acquiring a new combined order processing and manufacturing shop floor control system: (1) build the system in-house by the current MIS staff, or (2) purchase a customized, vendor-supplied package system. Discuss the general relative advantages and disadvantages of these two alternative approaches.

Part V

The Management of Information Systems

In the 1990s and beyond, you will be seeing a gradual decentralization of information systems functions within operating divisions or lines of business. For example, the marketing research department of a major consumer products company may organize an information systems group within their area. Systems analysts in this group may be more responsive to the needs of marketing research personnel.

Strategies for organizing information systems services are constantly being debated. You will find centralized, decentralized, distributed, and recentralized approaches within many organizations. In this chapter you will have an opportunity to learn how information systems activities can be shared by MIS professionals and by line managers.

In the closing chapter of this text, you will learn about new information technology, issues in information management, and strategies for improving productivity. You will learn that changes in work methods, including the reengineering of work, must go hand in hand with efforts to improve productivity by introducing new technology. With this information, you will begin to see that learning how to use technology effectively is an ongoing process.

Organization of Information Systems and End-User Computing

Chapter Outline

Manager's View

Organizations today are facing a tough set of problems related to managing the computing function. Indeed, how to organize data processing is one of the major strategic issues of the 1990s and beyond. In many organizations the tremendous demand for computer-based information systems has created application development backlogs ranging from two to five years. Core business systems need to be replaced, and the shortage of **application programmers** and **systems analysts** continues to be a major constraint.

Accompanying the pressure for application development is the rapid pace of technological change. The related technologies of telecommunications, office automation, and computer-assisted manufacturing pose difficult management problems. These technologies and their organizational effects need to be managed if organizations are to avoid technological obsolescence.

As a manager, you will be confronting the issue of how to organize information resources within a firm. Which information resources should be centralized and which should be decentralized? Which information systems should be managed centrally and which should be managed locally? Today, many managers are becoming responsible for acquiring hardware and software and for developing information systems at the departmental level. Decentralization of these responsibilities has created some new challenges, such as system selection and maintenance.

In this chapter, you will learn about how computing is organized and managed in centralized, decentralized, and distributed environments. You will also learn about the roles and responsibilities of MIS professionals and users for systems development and operations in these different environments. Finally, you will learn how information systems professionals are assuming new functions as consultants and facilitators to support users.

THE ORGANIZATION OF DATA PROCESSING

The Evolution of Computing

Different ways of organizing data processing have evolved over the past 25 years. In the 1960s, data processing was a back-office function, staffed primarily by specialists working directly for departments that were automating various accounting functions, such as accounts receivable and accounts payable. To most users of these systems, data processing was a mystery. "Computer people" spoke their own language and had the technical skills to keep data processing operations running smoothly. The first systems to be developed automated many routine paperwork-intensive operations and were considered very successful.

Success with accounting systems projects led to demands for the development of more data processing systems. Users left the development of these systems up to technical specialists, who didn't always understand the business functions they were attempting to automate. Many users began to question the high cost and disappointing results of these data processing projects. These concerns forced senior management to become directly involved in planning and controlling data processing projects. As a result, MIS departments were formed and MIS professionals were trained to use project management methods to make sure that systems would be developed within budget and on schedule. Functional managers themselves became responsible for selecting the most critical projects and for approving expenses for these projects.

In the 1970s, computing technology became much less expensive. Minicomputers with software packages to handle applications such as accounts receivable and inventory control were aggressively marketed directly to users by vendors who argued that user departments could manage their own computers. Users, motivated by the opportunity to control their own hardware and data, acquired many of these minicomputer systems. The result was an era of decentralized computing.

However, problems such as incompatible hardware, lack of local systems analysts, and lack of capable technical professionals led many of these users to rethink the job of running their own computer systems. By the late 1970s, most organizations had centralized their data center operations. A centralized group of computer professionals managed hardware, computer operations, and technical support for database and communications systems. In many firms, systems development functions were decentralized, with systems analysts working within functional areas of the business. This gave users more control over application development projects.

In the 1990s most organizations have to manage multiple technologies. Computing technology is in the hands of virtually every manager in the form of microcomputers, computer-based telephone systems, CAD/CAM systems, and expert systems. The availability of new technology has created new roles for end-users, as well as for information systems professionals. Many MIS professionals have become involved in training end-users to use new technologies such as fourth-generation languages and microcomputer-based software.

To understand the evolution of data processing and its future development, you need to learn about the characteristics, advantages, and disadvantages of the major approaches for organizing information systems activities. You also need to recognize the factors to consider in selecting an appropriate organization strategy. These questions will be discussed in the next section.

Centralized Data Processing

In the **centralized data processing** environment, a large mainframe computer system supports multiple users and multiple application programs. Users have access to computer resources via hundreds of remote computer devices, including on-line terminals used to input data and printers used to obtain reports.

The types of applications well suited to a centralized system are those with a centralized store of data helpful to many different users. For example, a personnel information system with data about the characteristics and job histories of employees could be used by many different departments. Corporate personnel data may be utilized to generate payroll checks and reports. Users may want to query personnel records to locate employees with certain characteristics. A personnel administrator, for example, may want to locate all employees with secretarial skills and Spanish-speaking ability.

A centralized data processing facility is supported by a staff of highly trained technical specialists, including people responsible for computer operations, systems analysis and design, programming, and telecommunications. These responsibilities will be described in a subsequent section of this chapter.

Computer resources are organized centrally for a number of good reasons. One reason for centralization is that it allows economies of scale. A large computer system can provide large-scale processing capacity for many users. Complex applications such as large linear programming models and statistical analysis programs require the largest available computer capacity. A large computer system supporting many applications can reduce operating and maintenance costs that would result if small processors and operations personnel were dispersed throughout the organization.

Other factors supporting centralization are multiple access to common data and the assurance of data integrity and security. In the airline industry, for example, hundreds of reservations agents need multiple access to centralized databases on seats, fares, and schedules. Organizationwide databases, such as personnel data and financial data, require security and integrity safeguards that can be effectively managed by specialists like database administrators. Problems such as loss of data, access to data by unauthorized personnel, and duplicate data may be minimized in this way.

Decentralized data can create problems of redundancy and inconsistency. An example that you might encounter after graduation concerns alumni information systems, which are developed to maintain records on all graduates of a university. In most universities, central alumni records are used to generate fund-raising letters and to mail various publications. If the particular school of the university that you have attended (such as the business school or the engineering school) decides to set up an alumni information system for its own graduates, you may receive two fund-raising requests—one from the university and one from the individual school. Maintaining correct information in both these files can also be a problem. When you change your address after you graduate, you could inform either the university or your particular school, thus creating lack of consistency between the centralized and decentralized databases.

If alumni data were stored on a central university system, your school could still have access to data on you and your classmates. A procedure could be introduced to enable school personnel to edit and to update their own records and to print out mailing labels and letters locally using the names and addresses of alumni stored in central files. In this way, the central integrity of the alumni database could be maintained, but users could have access to the data they need.

The centralized approach requires the development of a large, specialized MIS staff. Central MIS organizations attract new recruits by offering a chance to work on a variety of challenging projects, to share knowledge with other data processing professionals, and to enjoy richer career paths. Data processing personnel can also find better prospects for training and more diverse career opportunities within a central MIS group. Turnover problems have less impact in a central organization.

A major motivation toward centralization is control of data processing expense. The ability to control the costs of systems development and operations is a strong reason for

Table 19–1
Advantages and disadvantages of centralized data processing

Advantages of Centralized Data Processing	Disadvantages of Centralized Data Processing
Economies of scale	Lack of user control over systems development and operations
Access to large-scale capacity	Limited responsiveness to small development projects
More professional operation and management	Frustration with corporate charges for DP services
Multiple access to common data	
Security, controls, and protection of data	
Better recruitment and training of specialized personnel	
Richer career paths	
Control of data processing expense	

central MIS units. A central operation can be run more cost effectively than multiple smaller operations.

However, centralized data processing has some disadvantages, too. Many central groups have a backlog of application development projects ranging from three to five years. As a result, users find it difficult to get small, locally important projects accomplished within a reasonable time frame or at all. Users, frustrated by central data center charges, lack of responsiveness of central personnel to their needs, and lack of control over their data, may turn to decentralized data processing as an answer to their problems. Although centralized computing has been an effective approach historically, it is rare today. Table 19–1 lists the advantages and disadvantages of centralized data processing.

Decentralized Data Processing

In a **decentralized data processing** environment, minicomputers or microcomputers are used to support local applications. Local systems and operations personnel are responsible for developing and maintaining programs and for managing computer operations. If software packages are used to support application requirements, programming staff may not be necessary. Often, a single application such as plant production scheduling is supported using a local computer and local staff.

The main motivation for decentralized data processing is local control—local control over hardware, software, and data. If a user department wants to develop a management reporting system for sales analysis, for example, management does not have to wait for centralized personnel to get around to its project. Furthermore, local systems analysts may have a better understanding of departmental needs and management preferences for the system.

Decentralization of hardware also makes it possible for users to escape corporate data processing charges for both systems development and operations. Many users feel that they can actually cut their data processing costs by purchasing a single-purpose minicomputer or microcomputer programmed to support a single application. Over the past 10 years, hardware costs have dropped dramatically and have made it possible to justify local operations. Efficiency of hardware operations on a large mainframe is no longer a convincing issue. Decentralized computing also makes it possible to cut telecommunications costs created by on-line access to centralized data files. In addition, users of decentralized systems are shielded by fluctuations in response time on corporatewide computer networks.

Another factor supporting the decentralized data processing approach is better access to local data. If divisions of an organization do not share applications and data, the maintenance of a centralized data center may create more frustration than benefit. Local control and local access to data may be needed. Users may avoid the red tape associated with making sure that data are entered and edited at a central data center by handling these functions themselves. Finally, if each division is relatively autonomous, the various operating units may have no reason for sharing access to data.

One reason for centralization is the development of highly trained technical professionals. In contrast, information systems professionals in a decentralized organization may have excellent opportunities to cross-train themselves in business areas. Better understanding of business functions may improve their ability to define systems requirements and to work with users. MIS professionals in rural divisions, moreover, are isolated from the pressures of urban-based search firms. Thus, user-managers in division settings may be able to reduce the turnover of information systems professionals that commonly affects centralized urban MIS groups.

Today, more user-managers understand their information systems needs and are capable of managing local hardware and data. In companies with relatively autonomous operating divisions, the decentralized approach is consistent with organizational structure. For example, even though airline reservation data must be maintained on a centralized system, much data can be just as effectively managed locally. A network of distributed minicomputers can keep local operations moving and reduce a main corporate computer system's chances of failure.

However, decentralization of computing creates many new responsibilities for user managers who decide to manage their own hardware, software, and data. First of all, they need to manage their own computer operations. Additional staff may have to be hired to handle routine procedures such as backing up data files. Programming personnel also may be needed to develop and to enhance software. These staff members may not be fully utilized. Furthermore, local staff may not have the training to design systems with proper data security, documentation, controls, and backup and recovery procedures.

When users acquire their own data processing systems, they put their local needs above the needs of the organization as a whole. Computer equipment selected by different departments, including hardware, software, and operating systems, may not be compatible. If this situation is allowed to continue, it may become impossible for users to share data and computer network resources, such as hard disk storage devices and high-speed printers.

Some of the main advantages and disadvantages of decentralized data processing are summarized in Table 19–2.

Distributed Data Processing

As you have seen, one of the driving forces behind decentralized data processing is that users want more control over their data processing activities. However, decentralization may lead to inefficient operations and to duplication of data processing expense. One way to solve the problem of organizing data processing is to distribute some data processing activities to users, but to maintain centralized control over other activities. This approach is known as **distributed data processing.** Earlier in the text, you learned that distributed data processing refers to a system in which application programs are run and data are processed at more than one site. This means that both computer power and data can be distributed to local user sites. Distributed data processing can also mean distributing responsibility for other computing activities to the user. Responsibilities for systems development, such as systems design and training, as

Table 19–2 Advantages and disadvantages of decentralized data processing

Advantages of Decentralized Data Processing	Disadvantages of Decentralized Data Processing
Local autonomy and user control	Loss of central MIS management control
Responsiveness to user needs	Incompatible data, hardware, and software
Reduction in telecommunications costs	Failure to follow standard systems development practices
Immediate access to decentralized databases	Duplication of staff and effort
Local systems analysts more attuned to local needs	
Opportunity for career paths within user's functional area	
Consistent with decentralized corporate structure	

well as responsibilities for data processing operations can be distributed to the user. Distributed data processing can take many forms. You will learn about some of these forms in the following case studies of a financial services firm, a retail store chain, and a hospital.

A Financial Services System. One method of distributed data processing is to give the responsibility for data entry and data validation to user departments. A financial services company successfully used this distributed processing approach to process loan payments. Local personnel in over 250 branch offices around the country entered payment transactions at local microcomputers. These microcomputers had storage and processing capabilities. All transactions were edited locally and transmitted once a day to the home office computer, where they were used to perform a batch overnight update of the centralized outstanding loans database.

This division of effort made it possible for local personnel to offload work from the centralized computer system through local data entry and validation. Users in branch offices also had the ability to query customer loan account files and get immediate responses. However, because new payments were not posted to the outstanding loans file until each evening, data accessed by personnel making queries were one day out of date.

To make this system work, centralized MIS personnel set standards for a nationwide telecommunications network linking over 250 terminals to the central computer system. They also provided local personnel with local data entry and validation programs and data transmission procedures. Local personnel had control over and access to the data they needed to service customer accounts and were able to manage local computer operations.

A Retail Point-of-Sale System. In the case of the financial services organization, responsibility for data entry and editing was decentralized. In other forms of distributed data processing, responsibility for computer operations can be decentralized as well. A good example of such decentralization is a retail department store chain with point-of-sale processors in each store. At Sears stores, for example, local sales transactions are entered at local point-of-sale terminals. These transactions are used to update a local minicomputer-based inventory database and to generate local reports on inventory turnover so that buyers can purchase needed merchandise on a timely basis. Summary totals of sales and inventories are transmitted to a host computer system in the central Sears corporate headquarters.

As you can see from this example, all processing of local sales and inventory data is decentralized. It would make no sense to transmit sales transactions to a central computer system because the costs of telecommunications from each store to a central system would be prohibitive. Furthermore, local store management personnel would not have timely access to information on sales trends and inventory levels. In the Sears example, central management personnel also have access to the information they need. A communications network links local store point-of-sale systems to a central host computer, making it possible for company management to receive summary reports periodically.

An Accounts Receivable System. The retail store chain example shows how responsibility for computer operations can be decentralized to user organizations. In many other cases, responsibility for systems development activities is decentralized, whereas computer operations are managed centrally. The visiting nurse division of a major hospital acquired a software package to handle its own accounts receivable. The package made it possible to invoice clients and to generate reports on overdue accounts. Because the central MIS department did not have the time to develop programs for this application, the visiting nurse staff found a package that fit its needs.

However, the manager of the visiting nurse division did not want to acquire a minicomputer system to support the accounts receivable application because she felt that the computer system would not be fully utilized and because she did not want to hire additional staff to handle computer operations. The manager chose to run the application on the centralized data processing system and to pay the MIS department for the time needed to run the program. In this way, central MIS staff was responsible for managing computer operations, but the division was able to identify its information systems needs and to acquire the package best suited to its needs.

Table 19–3 summarizes the division of data processing responsibility in the three organizations you have learned about. In the first two cases, responsibility for systems development was in the hands of MIS professionals. The loan payment processing application was a corporatewide system developed totally by MIS professionals. The complexity of the application, which included on-line edit and batch update procedures as well as a variety of management reports, warranted MIS development. Password security procedures for data entry and coding procedures to protect data being transmitted over telecommunications lines also had to be designed by experienced technical personnel. Database design and administration, including precautions for backup and recovery of both the payment transaction file and the outstanding loans master file, were handled by MIS professionals knowledgeable in these areas.

Systems development activities were also handled centrally in the case of the retail point-of-sale system. A central MIS development team identified the requirements, selected the point-of-sale configuration, and developed the software to support this application. The point-of-sale system that was developed centrally was designed for use in hundreds of retail stores. If each store had designed its own point-of-sale system, users all over the country would have needlessly reinvented the wheel. In addition, each of the decentralized local store systems had to be networked to a central corporate computer system for management reporting purposes. This process required telecommunications planning, network design, and implementation. Technical expertise was provided by telecommunications specialists within the MIS function. In both this case and in the financial services case, it would have been impossible to find local technical

Table 19–3
Case studies in distributed data processing

Case A: Financial Services Company Loan Payment Processing Application

Centralized	Decentralized
Telecommunications planning, design, and implementation	Data entry
Systems development, including requirements analysis and programming	Data validation
Central computer operations	Local computer operations
Technical support	Hiring of local data-entry personnel
Data security and integrity	

Case B: Retail Store Chain Point-of-Sale System

Centralized	Decentralized
Systems development, including requirements analysis, programming, and testing	Computer operations
Telecommunications and network design	Local sales order entry
Technical support	Local inventory update
	Training of store personnel

Case C: Visiting-Nurse Division Accounts Receivable System

Centralized	Decentralized
Computer operations	Requirements analysis
Technical support	Software package evaluation and selection

personnel to handle the technical requirements of designing these systems. Ongoing maintenance and technical support of these applications also were handled by centralized MIS personnel.

Only in the third case were some responsibilities for systems development distributed to the users. In this case, central systems development personnel did not have the time to design and write programs for the system. Visiting nurse personnel were familiar enough with their needs to identify criteria for selecting an appropriate software package. In fact, a package for outpatient nursing services had already been developed by a software vendor and could be utilized effectively by the visiting nurses, saving a great deal of time and expense in potential development.

There are advantages and disadvantages to users being responsible for certain systems development activities. As illustrated by the visiting nurse case study, users are familiar with their needs and are interested in controlling information processing expenditures. They are more likely to invest in training their own personnel to use a system effectively.

However, when users assume responsibility for systems development, they incur some risks. User managers may develop a system, only to discover that they have reinvented the wheel. User-managers may find it more difficult to recruit and retain competent information systems professionals both for application development and for ongoing technical support and maintenance. Data security, backup and recovery, and control procedures may be difficult to develop and maintain in user areas. The next section explains how to determine the best mix of responsibility between users and MIS professionals.

Allocation of Responsibilities in Distributed Data Processing

Much of the motivation for decentralization of data processing stems from users' desire to control certain data processing activities. Increasing exposure to computing technology encourages user managers to set up data processing activities within their own departments. However, distributing responsibility for data processing does not mean that users have to acquire minicomputers and microcomputers. They can take on additional responsibility by sharing systems development and operations functions with MIS professionals.

In some areas, users may take on greater responsibility for data processing activities than in others. The kinds of responsibilities users and MIS professionals can assume are depicted in Figure 19–1. These responsibilities deal with hardware operations, telecommunications, database administration, systems analysis, systems documentation, and user training.

For a particular application, users need to select the level of responsibility they want to have for various data processing activities. A decentralization pattern describing

Figure 19–1 Range of responsibilities involved in information systems activities

Source: Adapted from Jack R. Buchanan and Richard G. Linowes, "Making Distributed Data Processing Work," *Harvard Business Review,* September–October 1980, p. 146.

Data Processing Responsibilities

Low Responsibility	**Increasing User Responsibility** →		**High Responsibility**
Hardware Operations			
Prepare source documents	Manage data entry	Operate a satellite processor with database	Manage an independent facility
Telecommunications			
Specify communications needs	Design network configurations	Implement network	Maintain network
Database Administration			
Control source documents	Carry out logical database design	Carry out physical database design	Manage all databases
Application Development			
Use turnkey system	Communicate needs to programmers	Participate on programming team	Select and develop system-building tools
Systems Analysis			
Conduct preautomation interviews	Define user data and functional specifications	Evaluate system relative to functional specifications	Carry out program-level system design
System Documentation			
Write functional specifications	Write user's manual	Write program design specifications	Write detailed description of data structures
User Training			
Conduct preautomation interviews	Prepare user training materials	Conduct user training	Maintain adequate user competence

user responsibilities for various information systems development and operations activities is shown in Figure 19–2. In this example, users are largely responsible for user training, systems analysis, and systems documentation. Responsibility for such functions as database administration and application programming is shared almost equally by central MIS staff and user staff. However, technical responsibilities such as hardware operations, telecommunications, and systems programming are handled almost entirely by MIS professionals.

Figure 19–2
Decentralization pattern for data processing activities

Hardware operation
The user prepares source documents and manages data entry through terminals to DP center.

Telecommunications
The user specifies the volume and scheduling requirements for communications through his or her configuration of terminals.

Systems programming
The user only uses the DP centers operating system, compilers, and utilities.

Application system maintenance
The user both documents and assists in diagnosing system errors.

Database administration
The user determines his or her data requirements and develops a logical database design.

Applications programming
The user assigns some internal personnel to participate in the programming team

Systems analysis
The user is quite involved in most analysis work including some program-level system design.

System documentation
The user develops his or her own manuals and shares in writing program design specifications.

User training
The user alone is responsible for all internal training activities.

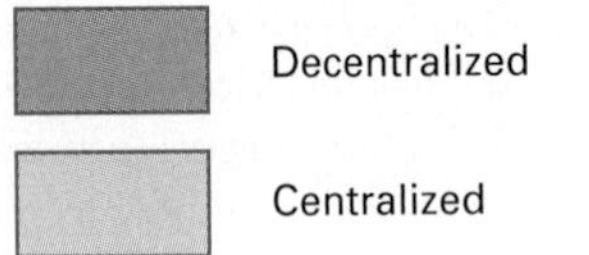

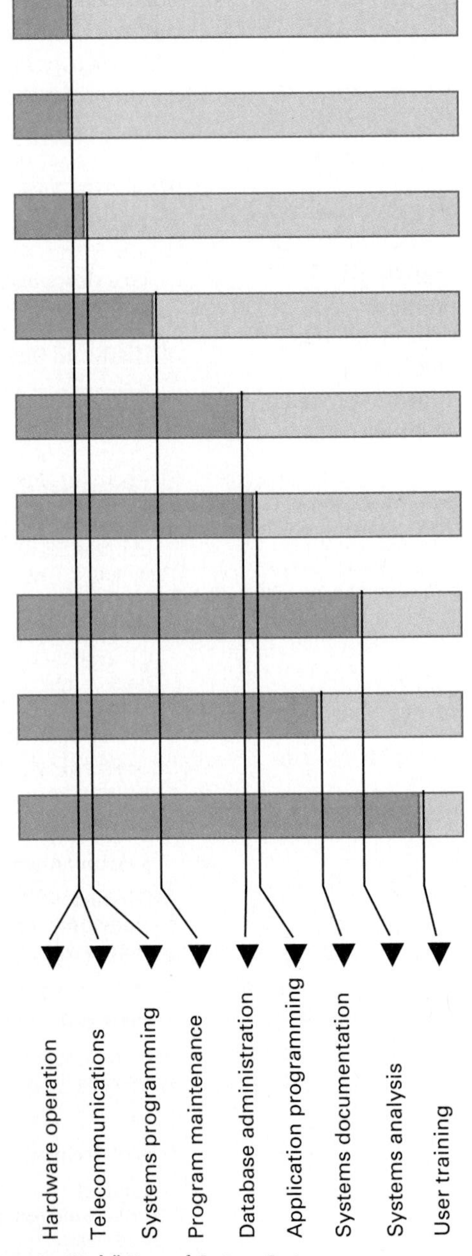

Source: Adapted from Jack R. Buchanan and Richard G. Linowes, "Making Distributed Data Processing Work," *Harvard Business Review*, September–October 1980, p. 151.

The decentralization pattern described in this example builds on the strengths both of users and of MIS specialists. Users are more likely to understand functional requirements and can play an effective role in systems analysis. They have a greater stake in successful training and in the development of adequate documentation and are likely to want to play a major role in these activities. However, they rarely have the technical know-how or interest to play an effective role in hardware operations, telecommunications planning and network design, and systems programming. The strengths of users lie in the systems development area; the strengths of MIS professionals lie in the technical and operations management functions.

However, the distribution of responsibility for systems development and operations management functions may vary depending on the nature of the application. Certain self-contained applications can be run on dedicated minicomputers and managed exclusively by users themselves. For each application, users should select the level of responsibility they want for a variety of data processing functions.

Using the scheme of responsibilities (Figure 19–1) to identify various data processing activities, the user can select appropriate levels of responsibility for each of these activities and depict these responsibilities using the decentralization pattern (Figure 19–2). These tools demonstrate how users can increase their involvement in information processing activities without necessarily acquiring their own hardware or managing computer operations and technical functions. Distributed data processing means distributing certain information processing responsibilities to the user. The best mix is achieved when users assume a greater role for systems development activities, while MIS professionals maintain control over hardware, computer operations, and technical functions.

Effective Organization of Information Processing Activities in the 1990s

In many organizations today, new information technologies, such as office automation, expert systems, microcomputers, and decision support systems, are being introduced. Often, these new technologies are acquired by user departments and are totally out of the control of MIS management. If allowed to proliferate, these technologies may create many of the same problems experienced with decentralized data processing systems in the past. These problems—including incompatibility, lack of data standards, lack of organizationwide planning, and lack control over systems development—have already been discussed.

MIS management must share responsibility with users for managing and controlling systems development activities involving these new technologies. MIS responsibilities include developing hardware standards, providing support and training, and offering technical assistance. In the area of standards, MIS management should establish mandatory standards for hardware, telecommunications, programming languages, and documentation. The systems that users propose to develop must meet corporate communications standards. Systems development projects that users undertake must be reviewed to make sure that they don't conflict with corporate needs. If projects are implemented outside the firm, appropriate professional standards for project control and documentation should also be followed.

With regard to many end-user projects, information systems professionals can serve as consultants, facilitators, and technical specialists. Training programs can be developed to explain the possibilities and pitfalls of new technologies as well as to train users in specific skills.

Users also have important responsibilities when it comes to managing new information technology projects. First, they should define the level of responsibility they want to take in these projects, such as providing guidelines for local network design, implementing filing procedures for word processing systems, or designing programs for user training. Users should work closely with information systems professionals to evaluate and select the best mix of support services, including the use of prepackaged software, the hiring of contract personnel, and the use of centralized MIS personnel. Finally, user-managers should perform periodic audits to ensure that systems are reliable, meet security requirements, and satisfy documentation requirements.

As a user-manager, you'll need to rely on information systems professionals for many systems and technical services. The next section covers the roles and responsibilities of these professionals.

Roles and Responsibilities of Information Systems Professionals

The data processing organization includes three major functions: systems development, operations, and technical support. An organization chart for a data processing group is shown in Figure 19–3.

Systems Development. The systems development group is responsible for analyzing the business system and designing a computer-based information system that will enable users to achieve their objectives. The *systems analyst* is responsible for the analysis of the current business system, its organization, procedures, work flow, information requirements, and problems. As a result of the systems study, the systems analyst develops objectives for a computer-based information system. She evaluates alternative design options, such as batch, on-line, and distributed systems, determines whether software will be purchased or programmed, and develops design specifications for the proposed system, including report layouts, data dictionary requirements, CRT display screen design, and necessary controls and procedures.

Figure 19–3
The functional organization of data processing

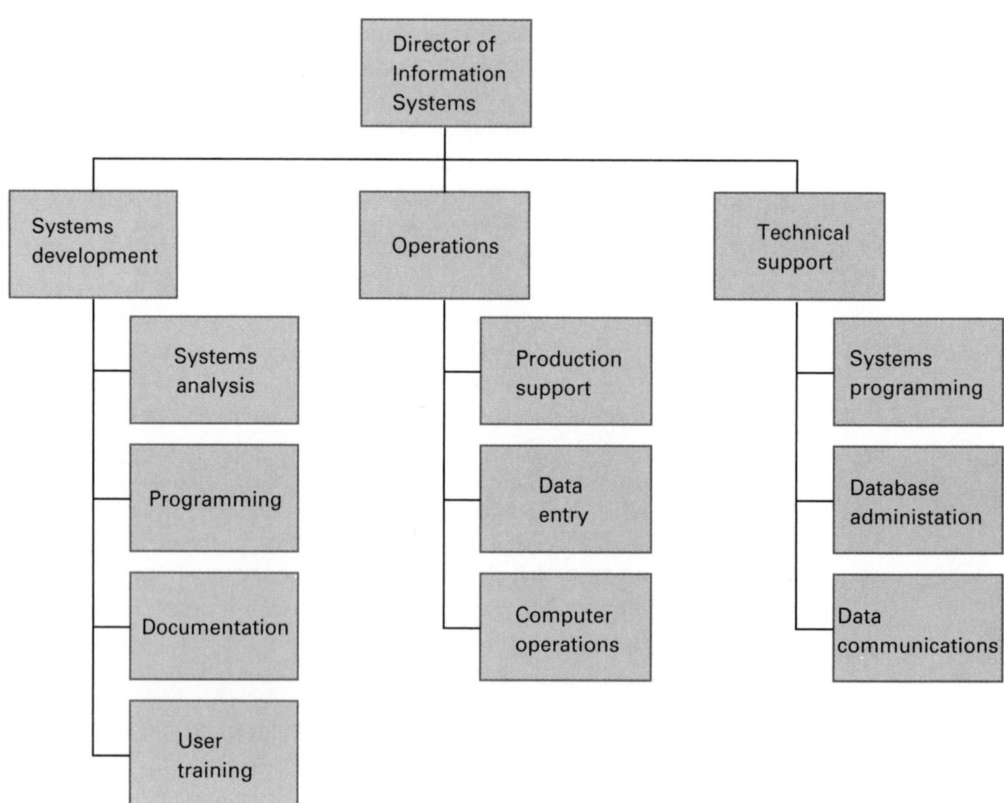

The *application programmer* is responsible for designing, coding, testing, and debugging programs to implement new applications. The application programmer can use both procedural languages, such as COBOL, and nonprocedural tools, such as fourth-generation languages. The **maintenance programmer** works with users to modify or make corrections in existing programs. In many data processing organizations, maintenance programming is about 70 percent of the programming work.

Other roles in systems development include those of the **documentation specialist** and the **user training specialist.** Often, systems analysts and programmers neglect documentation of programs, reports, screens, and procedures. Documentation specialists record systems design specifications, including program specifications, report layouts, screen designs, file descriptions, systems flowcharts, operating procedures, user procedures, and control procedures. The person responsible for training the user how to use a new system is called a user training specialist. A training specialist may instruct users on procedures for entering data, interpreting output, and backing up data files.

Finally, the **project manager** supervises programmers and analysts working on a systems development project. The project manager assigns responsibilities, monitors progress, and makes sure that activities are completed within cost and budget requirements. Sometimes the project manager is from the user department because user leadership in project planning and control decisions is critical for project success.

Systems development groups are organized by type of skill and by type of system. Figure 19–4 shows systems development organized into two skill areas: systems analysis and design, and programming. In this arrangement, the project manager can come from the systems analysis side or from the programming side. This approach makes it possible to recruit specialists and to maintain their competence in each of these areas.

Systems development activities can also be organized by type of system, as shown in Figure 19–5. In this type of organization, systems analysts and programmers are organized into teams responsible for specific types of projects. One team may work on financial information systems and another on marketing information systems. The ad-

Figure 19–4
Systems development organized by skills

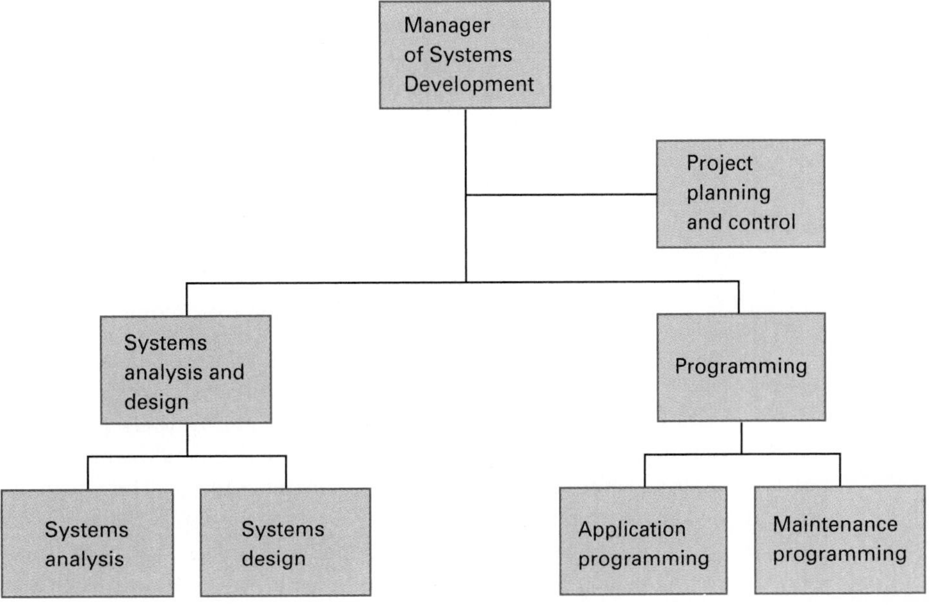

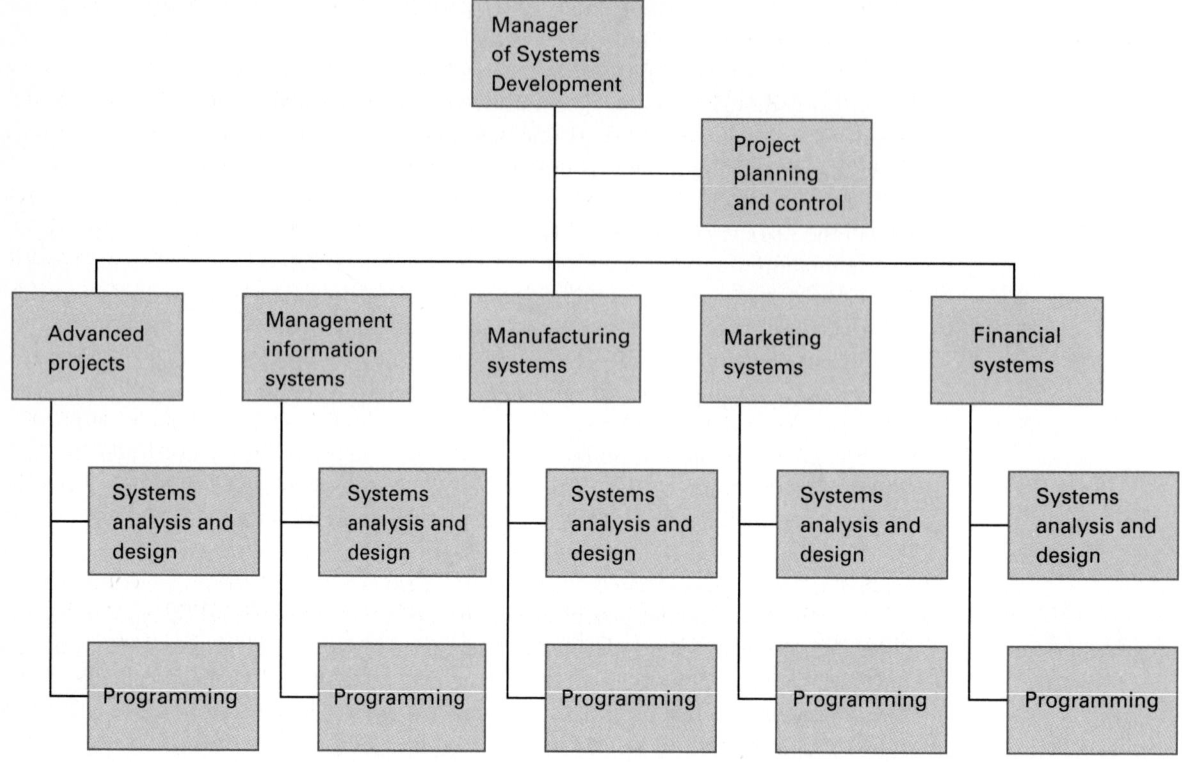

Figure 19–5
Systems development organized by type of system

vantage of this approach is that systems development personnel become very knowledgeable in the functional requirements of the area for which they are responsible.

Operations. Responsibilities for operations relate to the day-to-day operations of the computer system. The **operations manager** is responsible for scheduling the running of programs and for making sure that output is distributed in a timely manner to users. The operations manager also supervises data entry personnel and equipment operators.

Data entry personnel are responsible for keying in data to be input into the computer system, using key-to-tape and key-to-disk devices as well as remote terminals. Today, most data entry is handled by users themselves, and the number of data entry operators has diminished. **Equipment operators** work in the computer room performing such tasks as mounting tapes, reels, and disk packs, putting paper into output devices, and running the computer console. Using the console, operations personnel can determine the data needed by programs that are going to be run and can alert equipment operators to mount necessary tapes or disks. Finally, operations personnel are responsible for production support, including maintaining production schedules and distributing output to users according to schedule.

Technical Support. Technical support personnel are responsible for systems programming, system evaluation, user services, database administration, and communications systems design and maintenance. **Systems programmers** are responsible for maintaining the operating system environment, including the selection, evaluation, and maintenance of operating systems and utilities. They try to optimize the performance of the computer by monitoring hardware and software and by identifying and streamlining inefficient programs. Personnel assigned the task of **system evaluation** examine new technologies and hardware and software alternatives that will improve performance.

Often, they are responsible for identifying preferred vendors for hardware and software based on their assessments.

Two very important positions in the technical support group are the **database administrator (DBA)** and **data communications specialist.** As you saw in an earlier chapter, the database administrator is responsible for analyzing the organization's data requirements, developing a logical database design to support application needs, and maintaining the organizationwide data dictionary. The database administrator is also charged with establishing data security and integrity procedures and providing for database backup and recovery. Because of the increasing emphasis on organizationwide data management, the roles of database administrators and designers have grown in importance.

The increasing need for telecommunications planning and design has created positions for data communications specialists and analysts. Many organizations have centralized mainframes communicating to hundreds of remote terminals via large networks. Applications such as electronic mail, electronic document distribution, and videoconferencing have further increased the need for data communications. Other technologies, such as microwave and satellite communications, may need to be explored.

Data communications specialists are responsible for designing data communications networks, selecting appropriate channels for voice and data communications, and evaluating various communications hardware and software. Standards for network operation must be defined, and security procedures for data being transmitted over communications lines must be established. The need to plan, design, and manage voice communications systems and to integrate voice and data communications has brought new responsibilities to the telecommunications function.

Career Paths and Management of Data Processing

You'll find that there are a variety of career paths in the data processing field today. The traditional progression has been from programmer to programmer/analyst and systems analyst. As an experienced systems analyst, you'd have a chance to move into a project management position where you could exercise organizational and leadership skills. First-line management positions, such as manager of information systems development and manager of computer operations, also require organizational and managerial skills.

The MIS director is responsible for overall MIS planning, for selecting appropriate organizational structures, for working with user managers to determine application development priorities, and for managing equipment and staffing needs. The MIS director is responsible for developing the MIS strategic plan, which identifies application development priorities, the operations needs that support these application requirements, and the implications of these needs for staffing and equipment. A main task of the MIS director is to explain computing to top management and thus to sell top management on its potential for the organization. In large firms, the MIS director may be a Chief Information Officer (CIO) with a vice-presidential level appointment.

New technologies can affect the development of MIS strategy. When the microcomputer was introduced into organizations in the early 1980s, MIS management needed to assess what opportunities this new technology provided, how the technology could be interfaced with existing data processing systems, and how user managers could be trained to use it effectively. The emergence of microcomputers meant that MIS professionals needed to assume roles as trainers and technical support specialists. Applications requiring interfaces between micros and mainframes meant that new technical challenges had to be met.

The MIS director must be able to evaluate alternative organizational arrangements for information systems development and operations, including centralized, decentralized, and distributed approaches. Much of this chapter has been spent examining the advantages and disadvantages of these approaches. The MIS director needs to evaluate these arrangements in terms of their flexibility and responsiveness to user needs, their cost-effectiveness, and their ability to provide adequate service levels. The key issue in organizing data processing is control: central control versus local control. As described earlier, users can gain responsibilities for many data processing functions without necessarily running their own local MIS departments.

The MIS director is ultimately responsible for managing systems development and operations. As a general rule, the director must establish a method for identifying organizationwide application development priorities. One common procedure is to have users and information systems professionals work together on a corporate steering committee. The MIS director is also responsible for making sure that data processing operations meet production schedules, provide adequate response time, and provide effective controls over errors and possible data loss.

In addition, the MIS director must handle equipment and staffing needs. New technologies constantly require recruiting new staff and retraining existing staff in new methods and new skills. Microcomputers, fourth-generation languages, and expert systems development tools are just a few of the new tools that have challenged the resources of the MIS function. The effective use of these new technologies has required the development of new roles for many MIS professionals. MIS professionals responsible for training and supporting users are known as end-user support consultants and analysts. Their roles will be discussed next.

Box 19–1 The New Information Systems Professional

A survey of Fortune 1000 companies indicates that information systems professionals will have to adapt to new roles as information technology becomes increasingly decentralized. As information systems professionals struggle to find new identities, adaptability, the ability to direct one's own career, and solid business skills are emerging as essential survival skills. Technical talent is no longer a key to success.

Herbert McCauley, vice president of information management at Harris Corporation in Melbourne, Florida, notes that some information systems professionals are clinging to technical skills despite increasing pressure. "We don't need MVS experts now," he explains, "because IBM has automated that. Instead, we need security and network experts."

One reason new skills are needed is decentralization. As technology moves out into business functions, central MIS departments are losing budgetary control of computing. Business concerns are becoming more and more important to information systems professionals who are supporting decentralized computing. More than half of the respondents in the survey indicated that they needed professionals with business skills. One MIS director commented, "The emphasis is on communications skills, project management, and business understanding rather than just technical competence."

Increasingly, many information systems professionals will need to understand the marketplace. Acquiring the necessary skills to compete in this new environment will be up to these professionals. Harris's McCauley sums up: "People have to become much more responsible for their own careers. They have to act like individual entrepreneurs, like doctors and lawyers." As competitive pressures and technological developments reshape the information systems profession, adaptability, versatility, and self-reliance will become needed assets.

Excerpted from Curt Hartog and Robert Rouse, "A Blueprint for the New IS Professional," *Datamation,* October 15, 1987, pp. 64–69.

The Organization and Management of End-User Computing

In many organizations, end-user computing has been growing at the rate of 50 percent to 70 percent per year, compared with the growth rate of 10 percent to 20 percent for data processing. Throughout the text, the term *user* is used to describe user-managers who are responsible for planning, developing, and using information systems. To be consistent, the term *user computing* is used in this chapter instead of the term *end-user computing.* Users, frustrated with long systems development cycles, frozen requirements specifications, and irresponsive maintenance procedures, have taken advantage of such tools as report writers and microcomputer-based software to develop their own applications.

MIS organizations have responded to this situation by organizing user support or PC-support centers responsible for facilitating and coordinating user computing. Consultants work with users by providing them with the necessary tools, training, and support services.

The Role of the User Support Center. The major role of the user support center is to provide users with training and consulting services. Consultants are responsible for defining the market for services, providing appropriate hardware and software facilities, offering support for application development, and conducting training programs. Other duties of user support analysts include hardware and software evaluation, technical support, data management, and help desk support. Help desk support means providing technical assistance via telephone from a central desk known as a "help desk."

Most user support centers offer mainframe-based query languages and report generators as well as tools for statistical analysis, graphics, financial modeling, and office automation. They also support microcomputer-based software packages for word processing, spreadsheet, and database applications. In most cases, only approved vendor packages are supported, providing an incentive for users to purchase and use standard software. Hardware and software standards are established primarily to prevent a proliferation of incompatible systems.

A study by Brancheau, Vogel, and Wetherbe surveyed the critical success factors related to effective user support.[1] One of the major CSFs identified by users was that consultants need to provide a technically competent staff available at all times to answer questions and to provide support. Important skills for consultants were technical skills, business understanding, communications skills, and service orientation. These critical success factors are summarized in Figure 19–6.

Users and User-Developed Applications

The market for user support services consists largely of user-managers who have begun to develop their own applications using microcomputer-based software and fourth-generation languages. These users vary in sophistication from novice learners who know a few commands to sophisticated users who build their own systems. In a study of end-users—whom we are simply calling *users*—John Rockart and Lauren Flannery identified six types of users, including nonprogramming users, command-level users, user programmers, functional support personnel, user computing support personnel, and data processing programmers.[2] The characteristics of each of these user groups are described in Table 19–4.

[1] James C. Brancheau, Douglas R. Vogel, and James C. Wetherbe, "An Investigation of the Information Center from the User's Perspective," *Database,* Fall 1985, pp. 4–17.

[2] John Rockart and Lauren Flannery, "The Management of End-User Computing," *Communications of the ACM* 26, no. 10 (1983).

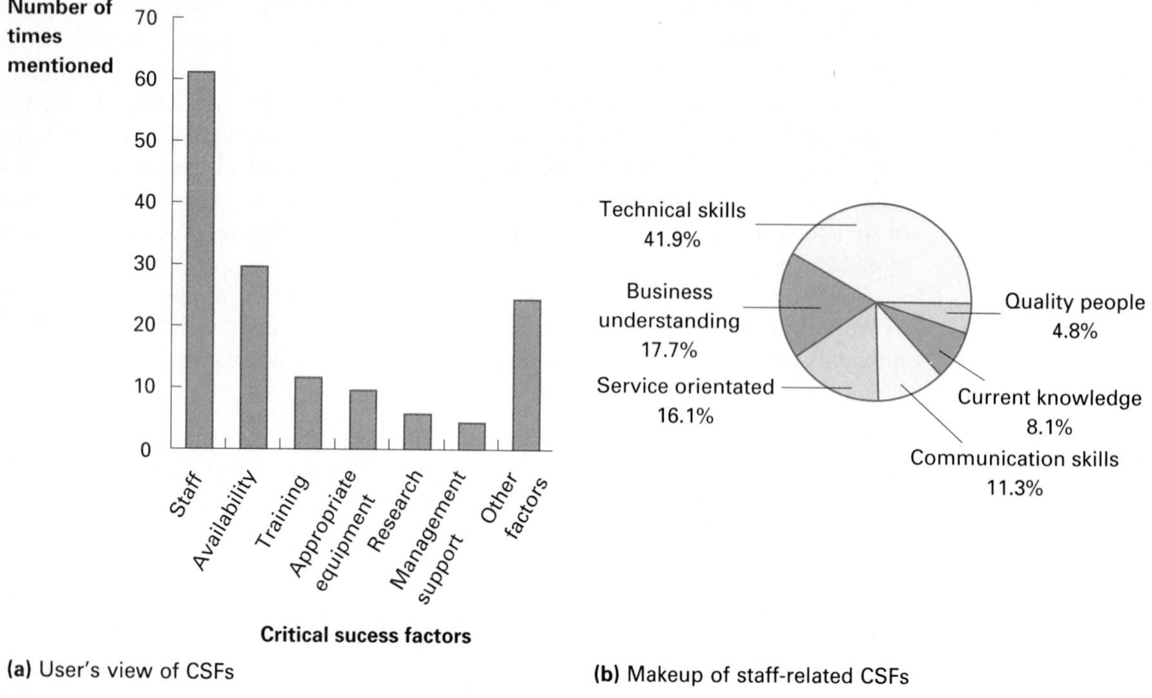

Figure 19–6
Critical success factors for the information center

Source: James C. Brancheau, Douglas R. Vogel, and James C. Wetherbe, "An Investigation of the Information Center from the User's Perspective," *Database*, Fall 1985, p. 11.

The largest percentage of the 140 users studied by Rockart and Flannery were functional support specialists, sophisticated programmers supporting users within functional areas. Even though these specialists spend a good deal of their time developing information systems, they are not DP professionals; they are market researchers, financial analysts, production planners, and so forth.

Most of the applications developed by users in Rockart and Flannery's study and in other studies were designed for inquiry and analysis. This indicates that users were anxious to address the invisible backlog of inquiry and analysis systems demonstrated by Alloway and Quillard's findings. Rockart and Flannery's findings are summarized in Table 19–5. The complex analysis applications, making up 50 percent of the overall

Table 19–4
Types of users

Nonprogramming users	Use software provided by others
Command-level users	Perform simple inquiries and simple calculations
User programmers	Use both command and procedural languages for their own personal information needs
Functional support personnel	Write sophisticated programs and support users within their functional areas
User computing support personnel	Located in a central support organization such as an information center
DP programmers	DP professionals who program in user languages

Source: Adapted from John Rockart and Lauren Flannery, "The Management of End-User Computing," *Communications of the ACM* 26, no. 10 (1983), p. 778.

Table 19 – 5
Types of user-developed applications

Purpose	Number	Percentage
1. Operational systems	24	9
2. Report generation	39	14
3. Inquiry/simple analysis	58	21
4. Complex analysis	135	50
5. Miscellaneous	15	6
Total	271	100

Source: John Rockart and Lauren Flannery, "The Management of End-User Computing," *Communications of the ACM* 26, no. 10 (1983), p. 779.

applications studied, included financial analysis, operations research, engineering calculations, and simulations. The majority of the user-developed applications studied were departmental or personal in scope, indicating that users were building applications that would be considered low priority on an organizationwide basis.

Management and Control Issues

The emergence of user-developed applications creates risks as well as opportunities. The most pressing concern is lack of **quality assurance,** including data validation and testing, documentation, controls, and backup and security procedures. Other specific concerns with systems developed by users are the failure to specify correct requirements, mismatches between hardware and software, and the failure to consider systems design alternatives.

A number of studies indicate that many user-developed applications are developed without proper review and discipline. In a study of 33 user-developed applications, Sumner found that documentation consisted primarily of copies of programs, screens, and reports.[3] Fewer than 20 percent of the users studied had developed controls, backup and recovery, and data security procedures for their applications. Davis[4] and Alavi[5] also point out that lack of documentation, data validation and testing, controls, audit trails, backup and recovery, and data security measures are all concerns with user-developed applications.

In response to these concerns, user support consultants are developing policies and procedures to guide user development. Corporate guidelines for hardware and software acquisition are being established to prevent a proliferation of incompatible systems and to provide links between microcomputers and mainframe-based resources. Many organizations are introducing policies for quality assurance to motivate users to follow procedures for data validation, documentation, and backup and recovery.

Policies are also being formulated for data management. Whereas users cannot update "live" data in production databases, they can request sequential extract files. Using these extract files, which are actually copies of production databases, users can

---

[3]Mary Sumner, "The Impact of User-Developed Applications on Managers' Information Needs," *Proceedings of the Annual Meeting of the American Institute of Decision Sciences,* Las Vegas, Nev., Nov. 12, 1985, pp. 328–30.

[4]Gordon Davis, *Caution: User-Developed Systems Can Be Dangerous to Your Organization.* Working Paper 82–04, Minneapolis: Management Information Systems Research Center, University of Minnesota, February 1984.

[5]Maryam Alavi, "Some Thoughts on Quality Issues of End-User Developed Systems," *Proceedings of the Twenty-First Annual ACM Computer Personnel Research Conference,* Minneapolis: University of Minnesota, May 2, 1985, pp. 200–207.

make queries and generate reports. To gain access to up-to-date data, users can request new extracts on a periodic basis.

In many organizations, PC and user support centers have been successful in introducing policies governing hardware and software acquisition. In many cases, incentives are used to obtain acceptance of these policies. Users adhering to hardware and software guidelines are offered technical support, training, and access to centralized service facilities such as color laser printers.

DEPARTMENTAL COMPUTING

Although many user applications are designed for management reporting and data analysis, departmental-level production projects are growing. Departmental systems projects are occurring for reasons similar to those that led to decentralized data processing in the 1970s. Users are frustrated with application development backlogs and anxious to gain control over their own data, and they feel that MIS departments have not been responsive to departmental-level projects. These projects support multiple users and serve important decision-making needs. These systems require good security, thorough documentation, effective backup and recovery procedures, and validation of data and processing logic.

Assessing the costs and benefits of centralized versus decentralized computing will be one of the major challenges of the era of user computing. User-managers must consider the alternative costs and benefits of developing internal systems development specialists and of relying upon MIS professionals to do systems development work for them. In the future, functional support specialists will oversee the development and maintenance of many departmental systems.

The roles and responsibilities of MIS professionals will also change. MIS professionals will need to specify hardware and software options that are compatible with the corporate data processing network. The network will create the opportunity to develop applications linking microcomputers in decentralized business sites with corporate repositories of data. For example, customers of a commercial bank in St. Louis are already able to use their microcomputers to issue letters of credit that are in turn transmitted to overseas customers via the bank's international communications network.

User computing will require a distribution of responsibility between MIS professionals and users, in much the same way that data processing applications have required a division of responsibility in the past. The same issues that were raised in the 1970s during the era of distributed data processing are reemerging in the 1990s with the era of user and departmental computing. As users begin to assume greater responsibility for requirements analysis and systems development, MIS professionals will provide technical support services, telecommunications planning, central database management, training, and user support.

MANAGEMENT SUMMARY

In this chapter you have learned that the issue of how to organize information systems activities is a major business and MIS strategy question. The evolution of data processing has seen centralized, decentralized, and distributed approaches to organizing both systems development and operations functions. Each of these approaches has advantages and disadvantages. Most projects require a division of responsibility between MIS professionals and users. Users need to determine the level of responsibility they want to take for certain data processing activities, particularly systems development, database design, training, and user documentation. MIS professionals are more likely to assume

Box 19–2 The Future of the Information Systems Organization

In the 1980s, there was a transition to decentralized forms of organization. The evolution of strategic business units, organized around product lines or markets, was a common strategy. In contrast, the bywords of the 1990s are recentralization, networking, and teamwork. The evolving organizational structure recognizes the contribution of multidisciplinary teams consisting of specialists in various disciplines.

In the organizations of the 1990s, management hierarchies will flatten and horizontal networking will come of age. Entrepreneurial teams will work on multidisciplinary projects with a business purpose. Projects will be geared to supporting customer service, introducing innovative new products, or competing effectively on a multinational basis. The networked organization will have many of the characteristics of Mintzberg's adhocracy, which you learned about in Chapter 2.

Where does the MIS organization fit in? In the 1980s, many companies decentralized their MIS organizations within the strategic business units. In the 1990s, MIS functions are becoming recentralized for a variety of reasons. Centralized computing operations, network operations, and software licensing are more cost-effective than multiple decentralized facilities. Centralization also improves the bargaining position with vendors and enables DP management to obtain special terms and extra support that might not otherwise be possible. In addition, centralized operations provide better career paths for DP personnel. Finally, the increasing emphasis on corporatewide information systems that provide value-added services to customers is causing a recentralization of many important systems development projects.

However, the forces behind decentralization are still very real. In the early days of data processing, centralized DP shops were bureaucratic and unresponsive to the needs of user organizations. What resulted were decentralized MIS groups responsible for setting their own priorities and for developing their own computer applications. The recentralization that is occurring in the 1990s is not a return to the entrenched, unresponsive MIS bureaucracies of the 1970s. What is emerging is a hybrid organizational model, based upon power-sharing between information systems professionals and user-managers. In the new model, the central MIS function supports the consolidated data center and communications network—the technological spinal cord of the enterprise. MIS professionals establish and disseminate standards for application development, database design, and networking. They also provide central staff recruitment and training.

Within the decentralized MIS entities, systems analysts and user managers select project priorities and develop information systems in conformance with application development standards. In one Fortune 500 company, a new crop of college graduates is brought into the central MIS organization and trained in the standard systems development methodology and tools. When they move out into the various business units on a series of apprenticeships, these MIS professionals transfer the standards they have learned.

The recentralization of MIS activities has made it possible to "grow" integrated business systems that transcend departmental boundaries in purpose and scope. Three projects are examples of the new integrated systems.

In one firm, a new customer service unit was created to provide customers with a central contact point for tracking shipments, handling service activities, and resolving questions about billing. Because these customer support representatives needed access to integrated databases, MIS had to reintegrate a number of once-separate computer systems.

In an insurance company, the application screening process is being streamlined. Before, an application crossed 20 separate desks and many different computer systems—taking as long as 25 days to process. Streamlining these processes requires the development of computer systems and databases that span departmental boundaries.

In a highly decentralized company, with different products and different markets being addressed by each business unit, a new integrated purchasing database is being designed to pool purchasing information from heretofore isolated purchasing systems. To accomplish this type of project, a strong central MIS organization with a strategic overview of the business must be able to overcome the more parochial objectives of individual business units.

As you can see, the recentralization of MIS organizations is closely connected with building integrated systems that support important business goals. As you have learned throughout this chapter, the ongoing implementation of strategic business information systems will require that MIS be responsible for managing the infrastructure and that user management be responsible for identifying systems priorities that have a business impact. The new hybrid type of organization combines these responsibilities in such a way as to reengineer important business functions.

responsibility for such functions as operating hardware, designing the telecommunications network, and providing technical support.

The emergence of user computing has created new roles for MIS professionals. Users are developing their own applications using fourth-generation languages and microcomputer-based database and spreadsheet software. User support professionals are responsible for "helping users help themselves" by offering training, consulting help, hardware and software evaluation, and purchasing help. In many organizations, they provide guidelines for application design, including quality assurance, documentation, backup and recovery, and security procedures.

MIS professionals establish standards for hardware and software that can be supported by the corporate data processing network so users don't purchase incompatible equipment, database management systems, and operating systems software. MIS professionals are ultimately becoming responsible for managing and maintaining the integrity of centralized organizationwide data respositories—large "file cabinets" of information housed in central mainframe-based computer systems. Users are building local databases supporting departmental functions and also utilizing data housed in central repositories. In almost every application, users and MIS professionals are finding themselves cooperating with each other so that common organizational goals can be achieved.

Key Terms for Managers

application programmer, **709**
centralized data processing, **710**
database administrator (DBA), **723**
data communications specialist, **723**
data entry personnel, **722**
decentralized data processing, **712**
distributed data processing, **713**
documentation specialist, **721**
equipment operator, **722**
maintenance programmer, **721**
operations manager, **722**
project manager, **721**
quality assurance, **727**
system evaluation, **722**
systems analyst, **709**
systems programmer, **722**
user training specialist, **721**

Review Questions

1. What are some of the advantages of centralized data processing?
2. What are some of the disadvantages of centralized data processing?
3. List some of the advantages of decentralized data processing.
4. Give some of the disadvantages of decentralized data processing.
5. What are the characteristics of distributed data processing?
6. What is the difference between the job of application programmer and that of maintenance programmer?
7. Describe the responsibilities of the systems programmer.
8. Briefly discuss the responsibilities of the documentation specialist.
9. What is the career path most likely to be for a programmer?
10. What are some of the major responsibilities of the MIS director for managing systems development activities?

11. Describe some data processing responsibilities that can be distributed to users in each of the following areas:

    a. Hardware operations.
    b. Telecommunications.
    c. Systems documentation.
    d. User training.
    e. Database administration.

12. Why have MIS departments organized PC support centers?
13. What are the major responsibilities of user support consultants?
14. What future challenges does the user support center face?
15. Discuss some of the potential risks of users developing their own applications.
16. What policies have MIS professionals introduced to guide user computing?
17. What are the characteristics of the command-level end-user? Of the functional support specialist?

Questions for Discussion

1. What are some of the motivations for users to set up their own departmental data processing systems?
2. What kinds of data processing responsibilities might a local sales organization assume in planning and organizing a prospect database information system?
3. What kind of central technical expertise might a local insurance agent seek from home office information systems professionals in setting up a sales call reporting system? This information system would monitor each client's current insurance portfolio and keep track of all inquiries and sales calls having to do with new insurance programs.
4. Should a user attempt to design an information system that houses financial records on government contracts that may be subject to audit? Why or why not?
5. What types of skills should an effective PC support analyst have?
6. Should an organization try to encourage end-user computing? Why or why not?
7. Why is the Chief Information Officer (CIO) typically a vice-presidential level position within many large corporations?

Problems

1. **Western National Bank.** A major bank, Western National, centralized all its information processing activities in the 1970s to take advantage of economies of scale in supporting computer resources. It made economic sense to have one large computer system rather than many small processors.

   Recently, some of Western National's managers have attempted to reverse the trend toward complete centralization. In one case, a trust department manager found a trust accounting software package on a minicomputer that could maintain a local database on trust accounts and provide management reports on a timely basis. On-line access to trust account records would be available to all managers in the department. The entire system—including hardware, software, a database management system, and operating system—could be purchased and maintained, he argued, for less cost than the trust department currently was being charged for the trust accounting system running on the central mainframe computer. Furthermore, managers in the trust department would have greater control over their information processing activities with a dedicated minicomputer.

The MIS director of Western National argued that the software and hardware acquisition being proposed by the trust department manager was not compatible with the corporate data processing system and would create many unanticipated operational and personnel problems.

a. Evaluate the advantages and disadvantages of the trust department's proposal to acquire its own hardware and software for trust accounting.
b. What pitfalls may the trust department experience if the manager decides to decentralize its data processing activities?
c. How could the trust department gain more responsibility for its data processing activities without necessarily acquiring its own hardware?

2. **Amalgamated Can Company.** The director of information systems at Amalgamated Can Company is considering how responsibilities for the development and operations of several information systems can be divided between user and MIS professionals. The characteristics of each of these projects are briefly described below.

Given each project, develop a decentralization pattern by identifying which responsibilities in each case could be distributed to users in these functions. Which information processing activities should be in the hands of MIS professionals?

a. *Employee Information Systems.* This system maintains data on all employees, including personnel, job history, and payroll information. The system produces personnel reports required by the government; annual reports on salaries, promotions, and terminations; and payroll-related information, including paychecks and W-2 forms. Users would like to be able to make queries about employees for job placement purposes. They also would like to have access to employee names and addresses in order to generate mailing labels for various internal activities. Which responsibilities for developing, using, and maintaining this system should be handled by MIS professionals and which could be handled by users of the system?
b. *A Word Processing System.* Secretaries throughout the company want to use word processing systems to automate their repetitive and heavily revised documents and letters. Ideally, the system that is selected would be compatible with laser printers for high-speed document printout, particularly for repetitive letters and newsletters. Local printers would also be needed at each secretarial workstation for day-to-day letters and reports. Each secretary could purchase a word processing software package independently, learn how to use it, and purchase upgrades and maintenance according to the department's needs. MIS could also take on a role by planning for and designing a corporatewide word processing system. What do you feel the role and responsibilities of users and MIS professionals should be with regard to this system?
c. *A Sales Order Entry System.* A new system is being developed to enable salespeople to enter sales data more effectively. According to the marketing director who is proposing the system, salespeople would use OCR-scannable

order entry forms to record information about customer orders. This would eliminate the bottleneck created by data entry operators having to transcribe order information from sales order entry forms handwritten by salespeople.

The proposed system would make it possible to receive sales order input information more rapidly. As a result, orders could be processed faster, invoices generated more quickly, and inventory levels updated more efficiently. Salespeople themselves would be able to receive reports from the system describing sales trends within their respective territories.

What do you feel would be the best mix of responsibility between the salespeople and the MIS development staff in the design, operation, and maintenance of this system?

d. *A Sales Forecasting System.* Users in the production planning department would like to design a sales forecasting system to enable them to depict sales trends based on order history data and to use this information to plan target inventory levels in the branch warehouses around the country. The information on target inventory levels would be used to determine plant production requirements in regional plants.

The production planners feel they could develop a forecasting model and an inventory plan using a spreadsheet program on a microcomputer. They would need to have access to order history data stored in a mainframe-based database. These data could be analyzed using a mainframe-based database query language or else downloaded to a microcomputer. Once the target inventory plan was developed, it could be distributed to branch warehouses using the corporate telecommunications network.

What responsibilities should the production planners and MIS department take in the development and implementation of this sales forecasting system?

Cases

1. **Hudson Industries.** Users in the marketing and finance departments acquired microcomputers to use in doing various kinds of sales and financial analyses at Hudson Industries about a year ago. The microcomputer-based software they acquired has made it easier to handle many routine calculations and to produce needed management reports on marketing and financial trends. The initial success of some of the users in these departments has caused other managers throughout the organization to want to acquire microcomputers as well.

Bill Clarke, the director of data processing at Hudson Industries, is concerned about the imminent proliferation of microcomputers within the corporation because he is aware of some of the problems that have resulted. First of all, in the corporate finance department, a user named Carol Carlson spent over six months developing a budget analysis system using a microcomputer-based spreadsheet program. Many of the department's managers began to use the reports from this system. When Carol left the firm for a job with a competitor, the system was "lost" because no documentation existed and no one knew how to reconstruct the system.

In the marketing department, users created a database of 20,000 customer records using a microcomputer-based database package. Simple operations such as sorting the database in ZIP code order took hours because the processing capacity of the microcomputer that had been acquired was not sufficient to handle this kind of data volume. Transferring the data to a larger mainframe-based system could be accomplished by transferring the PC database file into an ASCII sequential file for transmission over an asynchronous communication line. But then the users would need to learn how to use a mainframe-based query language.

Another problem occurred when a secretary using a word processing program on one of the microcomputers in the finance department forgot to back up a data file containing a 50-page financial report. The disk on which the file was stored was accidentally destroyed. As a result, the report had to be completely reconstructed from a rough draft and an important meeting was delayed.

Bill is concerned about some of the problems of users developing their own applications. Inadequate documentation, failure to create backup copies of data files, and lack of sufficient security procedures are just a few of the problems he visualizes. More serious problems could occur if major financial and marketing decisions were made using erroneous data on reports generated from user-developed systems.

a. What steps should Bill take as director of data processing to manage and control user computing more effectively?
b. Should he control the acquisition of microcomputers, including both hardware and software?
c. What kinds of policies and guidelines should be introduced with respect to user computing?

2. **C. F. Industries.** At C. F. Industries, the backlog of systems development projects is two and a half years and the pent-up demand for small projects is probably two to three years beyond that. The MIS department has selected a fourth-generation language tool to enable users to obtain access to mainframe-based data and to generate some of their own reports. However, few users are benefiting from the fourth-generation language program. Most users do not know how to obtain copies of the databases they need or how to use the tools.

You have been asked to organize a user support center to address the needs of users. Develop a plan that includes this information:

a. The objectives of the user support center.
b. The responsibilities of the consultants.
c. The tools to be supported.
d. The policies for managing user computing.

Selected References and Readings

Alavi, Maryam. "Some Thoughts on Quality Issues of End-User Developed Systems." *Proceedings of the Twenty-First Annual ACM Computer Personnel Research Conference.* Minneapolis: University of Minnesota, May 2, 1985, pp. 200–207.

Brancheau, James C., Douglas R. Vogel, and James C. Wetherbe. "An Investigation of the Information Center from the User's Perspective." *Database,* Fall 1985, pp. 4–17.

Buchanan, Jack, and Richard Linowes. "Making Distributed Data Processing Work." *Harvard Business Review,* September–October 1980, pp. 143–61.

Carlyle, Ralph. "The Tomorrow Organization." *Datamation* 36, no. 3 (February 1, 1990), pp. 22–29.

Davis, Gordon. *Caution: User-Developed Systems Can Be Dangerous to Your Organization.* Working Paper 82–04. Minneapolis: Management Information Systems Research Center, University of Minnesota, February 1984.

Rockart, John, and Lauren Flannery. "The Management of End-User Computing." *Communications of the ACM* 26, no. 10 (1983).

Sumner, Mary. "The Impact of User-Developed Applications on Managers' Information Needs." *Proceedings of the Annual Meeting of the American Institute of Decision Sciences,* Las Vegas, Nev., Nov. 12, 1985, pp. 328–30.

Sumner, Mary. "Organization and Management of the Information Center." *Journal of Systems Management* 36, no. 11 (1985), pp. 10–15.

Sumner, Mary, and Robert Klepper. "Information Systems Strategy and End-User Application Development." *Database,* Summer 1987, pp. 19–30.

von Simson, Ernest M. "The Centrally Decentralized IS Organization." *Harvard Business Review* 68, no. 4 (July–August), 1990, pp. 158–62.

Security and Ethical Issues of Information Systems

Chapter Outline

Manager's View

Issues and concerns pertaining to security and ethics typically permeate any manager's job, especially when information systems are involved. For example, consider these situations:

1. A marketing manager is searching the company database to determine what types of customers are buying a product just introduced by the firm two months ago. She is in the process of matching customer location, size, and industry to volume of purchases when her screen clears and displays a strange message. Then she sees that letters on the screen are vanishing. As she reads the disappearing message, she slowly realizes that the database has been invaded by a virus program. What she doesn't realize, however, is that the virus is in the process of destroying the very files she is accessing.

2. A field technician, using a notebook computer, has recorded on his hard disk the fourth customer on-site visit for the day. The data about the visit, which was made to repair a piece of electronic equipment, along with data about all the on-site visits for the week, have been meticulously entered and stored on the notebook's 60 MB hard disk. The data include time and materials data necessary for billing purposes. The data are also used for technician scheduling, product improvements, and marketing campaigns by the various departments of the technician's firm. The technician usually transfers the data to the local area network serving his office when he reports in at the end of the week. When he arrives this time, however, for some reason the hard disk has failed, and he is unable to transfer the critical data. Asked by his superior if he has made a backup to a 3½-inch diskette, the man flushes and admits that he has not made a backup diskette since last week.

3. An angry employee, just fired from her job because she was caught with her hands in the till, decides to get even with her employer. While she is supposed to be packing up her desk and leaving at the end of the day, she turns on her computer terminal and erases hundreds of important customer data files from the company's minicomputer system. She also removes the backup tape from the minicomputer and throws it in a trash container. It is not until the next day that other workers find that important customer files and the backup tape are missing.

4. Several employees of an organization are allowed back into what remains of their building after a blinding rainstorm and a series of tornadoes converged on their town. The storm hit during the peak of their busy season, tore the roof off the building, and broke every window. Descending apprehensively to the basement, they find the computer room filled with two feet of water. One employee cries out in exasperation, "How will we ever get the system working again?" Another says, "Even if we are lucky enough to get it working in a few days, how will we process our work until then?"

5. A student in a finance class has not yet completed his homework assignment as closing time for the computer laboratory draws near. He must have the assignment completed by tomorrow or lose valuable credit toward an already shaky grade in the course. He decides to copy the finance program that he is using to diskettes so that he can take them to his dorm room and work through the night on the assignment. He knows he shouldn't copy licensed software, but decides that it is really OK because he

(Manager's View continued)

promises himself that he won't use the software for anything else but this one assignment.

6. A manager of a data entry department is concerned about the health of her workers from carpal tunnel syndrome, an injury to the wrists that may occur from long-term use of keyboards. To reduce the occurrence of this injury she could spend the money to install wrist rests and adjustable tables and chairs for the operators. However, she is also under intense pressure to reduce the costs of the center and must constantly prepare reports about department costs and worker productivity.

Information systems have become ubiquitous in the organizational world. Through the data they process and store, they control enormous amounts of organizational assets, many employees, numerous procedures, and very valuable data. Because of their development costs and the costs of the hardware and software needed to run them, information systems are valuable assets in and of themselves. However, information systems also contain data about organizational assets with staggering value, critical organizational operations, employees with valuable talents, important customers and vendors, and other information that is vital to the health and welfare of an organization. These same information systems often contain data that are sensitive, personal, and private about people and must be protected from inquiring, unauthorized eyes.

It is no wonder then, that providing security for information systems has become a major concern of managers. Given the value of information systems to organizations and given the people, data, and assets that these information systems control, husbanding these systems to insure their safety and proper use becomes critical. It is not a task that can be taken lightly.

VIEWING INFORMATION SYSTEMS SECURITY

How should a manager view information systems security? When you become a manager, how can you be sure that you have not overlooked a potential security problem? How can you avoid reliving one of the disaster scenarios previously described? One answer to these questions is to approach information systems security with many of the same attitudes and tools that electronic data processing (EDP) auditors bring to the task. *EDP auditors* are charged with the review and analysis of information systems to prevent, discover, and remedy security problems. The approaches and methods used in EDP auditing are an effective resource for managers seeking to remove their information systems from harm's way. In fact, the basic objectives of information systems security are the same as the basic objectives of EDP auditing. These objectives include the following:

1. To control the loss of assets.
2. To insure the integrity and reliability of data.
3. To improve the efficiency/effectiveness of information systems applications.

To accomplish these objectives, the manager must make certain that the risks to information systems are identified and that appropriate security controls are used to eliminate or reduce the risks.

RISKS

The various dangers to information systems and the people, hardware, software, data, and other assets with which they are associated necessitate security controls. These dangers include natural disasters, thieves, industrial spies, disgruntled employees, computer viruses, accidents, and even poorly trained or naive employees.

Risks, Threats, and Vulnerabilities

EDP auditors differentiate among risks, threats, and vulnerabilities. By **risk** they mean potential loss to the firm. Potential risk refers to potential monetary losses, whether those monetary losses are direct or indirect. The monetary losses may result from total loss, partial damage, or even the temporary loss of an information systems asset. For example, monetary loss may result when a computer printer is stolen, when a computer system is damaged as it is moved, when an information systems person is injured in a fire, when a data file is partially destroyed by a virus, or when a line connecting a customer to a sales order entry employee fails.

When EDP auditors use the term **threat,** they refer to people, actions, events, or other situations that could trigger losses. A thief is a threat; so is a sprinkler system placed over a mainframe computer system. Thus, threats are potential causes of loss.

When EDP auditors use the term **vulnerabilities,** they mean flaws, problems, or other conditions that make a system open to threats. Thus, a firm's potential risk of losing all of its microcomputers occurs when the threat of a thief stealing the microcomputers becomes possible, for example, due to inadequate locks and alarm systems in the building in which they are housed.

Assessing Risks

The manager must use common business sense in applying controls to reduce the risks to information systems, and the controls used must be appropriate to the risks faced. It would not do to spend $1 million to control the risk of losing an information system that is valued at $50,000. Thus, the amount of money and time spent on controls should be commensurate with the risks involved. That generally means that there are acceptable risks in any information system. Total freedom from risk is not possible and certainly not affordable. By assessing potential losses, the manager can identify what these acceptable risks are.

EDP auditors estimate potential loss in several ways. These methods usually include not only the amount of the loss that could be sustained but also the probability of the loss actually occurring. For example, suppose that the manager was considering the controls that ought to be used to reduce the risk posed by the theft of 100 microcomputers in locked offices on the 10th floor of an office building. Suppose further that the microcomputers had a book value of $200,000, which included any adapter boards and special peripherals. However, the manager knew that the replacement value of the equipment was $300,000, including not only the boards and peripherals but also the costs of installing the machines and their software and data files. The manager then considered the current location of the building, the fact that the office is on the 10th floor of the building, the current level of security such as locked offices and the required use of keys to use the elevator, and the low incidence of crime experienced in the neighborhood. Given these data, the manager estimated that there was only one chance in 20 that such a theft would occur. Using these data and inferences, the manager computed the potential loss due to theft as $15,000. The prudent manager would consider the potential for loss now at $15,000, rather than $300,000. That assessment would materially affect the manager's level of concern.

Assessing risk means asking two basic questions. First, if a loss occurred, how would the organization respond? Second, what would the cost of the response be? Suppose for example that the microcomputers had been old, unused, and had no scrap value. Suppose further that if they were stolen the organization would not replace them. Then the risk to the firm of their loss is zero and the controls used to reduce or eliminate the threat of theft should be commensurate with the risk.

The manager should similarly assess the potential loss to the organization from the lack of availability or existence of a data file, key information systems people, proprietary software, and other information systems assets. Furthermore, the manager must view potential loss in broader terms than the direct loss of assets. Potential loss also includes such risks as lost sales that occur because an order system is down, wages spent to reconstruct data lost when the data storage devices fail, lost sales from customers who stop buying because an inaccurate inventory system causes too many stockouts, and fines paid for violations of government regulations because an information system failed to deliver the right information to the right agency at the right time.

COMMON CONTROLS

If you examined EDP auditing forms and procedures used by major auditing firms, you are likely to be overwhelmed by the comprehensive lists of potential threats and controls that the auditors should consider. In this chapter, however, you will learn about threats that are commonly posed and controls that are commonly used in an organization's information system environment. Then you will read about the security decisions that were made by personnel at a branch office of a consulting firm. By stepping into the shoes of the decision makers in this branch office, you will see how security decisions can be made.

Controls are countermeasures to threats. Controls are the tools that are used to counter risks from the variety of people, actions, events, or situations that can threaten an information system. Controls range from simple deadbolt locks on office doors that reduce the threat of the theft of information systems equipment to devices that read the palm prints of personnel to prevent the threat of unauthorized access to sensitive data stored on a hard disk. Controls are used to identify risk, prevent risk, reduce risks, and recover from actual losses. These controls can be classified in many ways. One useful classification is by type. Explanations of common types of controls follow.

Physical Controls

Physical controls are controls that use conventional, physical protection measures. Physical controls might include door locks, keyboard locks, fire doors, and sump pumps. Physical controls include controls over the access and use of computer facilities and equipment and controls for the prevention of theft. Physical controls also include controls that reduce, contain, or eliminate the damage from natural disasters, power outages, humidity, dust, high temperatures, and other environmental threats.

Electronic Controls

Electronic controls are controls that use electronic measures to prevent or identify threats. Electronic controls might include motion sensors, heat sensors, and humidity sensors. They may also include intruder detection and biological access controls, such as log-on IDs; passwords; badges; and hand, voice, and retina print access controls. Physical and electronic controls are often used together to counter a threat.

Software controls

Software controls are program code controls used in information systems applications to prevent, identify, or recover from errors, unauthorized access, and other threats. For example, programming code may be placed in a payroll application to prevent a data entry clerk from entering an hourly rate of pay that is too high, or a program may require users to enter a password to use a computer system. Software controls may also include programs that disable computer terminals during certain hours and that monitor who logs on, how long they connect, what files they access, and what type of access they make of those files (e.g., read from or write to).

Management Controls

Management controls often result from setting, implementing, and enforcing policies and procedures. For example, employees may be required to back up or archive their data at regular intervals and to take backup copies of data files to secure, off-site locations for storage. Also, management may enforce policies that require employees to take their vacation time or insure separation of duties to reduce the threat of embezzlement. Required employee training may be used to reduce data entry errors, or background checks may be required for employees who have certain levels of access to information systems.

Some physical, electronic, software, and management controls can be implemented by the manager without any outside assistance. For example, the manager may have employees in every department regularly make backup copies of files and store them in a safe place. Other controls may require specialists in information systems, auditing, or security to effect them. For example, the manager may hire a security firm to provide guards or install a security alarm system in the office area where information systems are housed.

The prevalence of information systems in most organizations usually means that the manager must consider using many controls to identify, reduce, prevent, or recover from potential losses.

COMMON THREATS

A number of threats are common to computer systems and deserve the careful concern of managers. These threats include natural disasters; unauthorized access, such as theft, vandalism, and invasion of privacy; computer crime, software piracy, and computer viruses.

Natural Disasters

In the ordinary course of business, organizations take precautions against the loss of assets from a variety of natural disasters such as fire, floods, water damage, earthquakes, tornadoes, hurricanes, mud slides, and wind and storm damage. Computer systems also are subject to these disasters and should be protected from them (see Figure 20–1). Security planning should consider disaster prevention, disaster containment, and disaster recovery. For example, disaster prevention planning might include the use of backup power supplies or special building materials, locations, drainage systems, or structural modifications to avoid damage during floods, storms, fires, and earthquakes. Disaster containment planning might consider sprinkler systems, halon gas fire suppression systems, or watertight ceilings to contain water damage from fire hoses if fires do occur. Disaster recovery planning should consider how operations can be renewed quickly. Planning for recovery might include developing contingency plans for the use of the computer facilities of vendors or noncompetitors with similar computer systems in the event of disaster. A number of firms specialize in providing computer facilities to organizations in the event of disasters. These firms are called *hot-site recovery firms* because they provide a computer facility for others that can be used almost immediately.

Employee Errors

One of the most common threats is represented by ordinary carelessness or poor employee training. An employee may destroy the contents of a hard disk by accidentally reformatting the hard drive of the computer system instead of formatting the floppy disk in drive A that was the intended formatting target. An employee may enter an incorrect amount in a data entry screen and that amount may then be added, subtracted, multiplied, or otherwise used in many other programs, compounding the error with frightening speed. Consider what would happen if an employee entered the wrong price for a popular product in a file used by the sales order system.

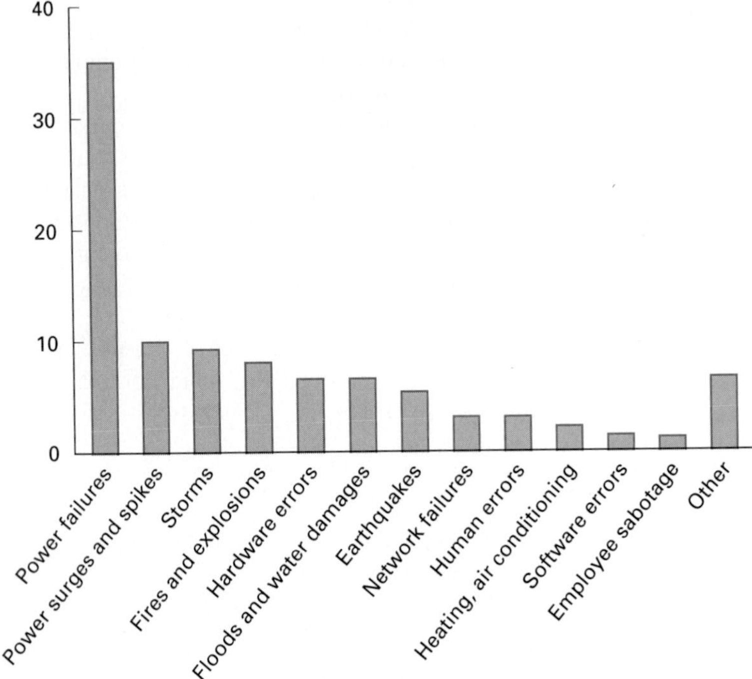

Figure 20–1
Types of disasters that caused data loss in the United States

Source: Contingency Planning Research, Inc., as reported in Kristina B. Sullivan, "LAN Backup Utilities Gain Data Management," *PC Week* 10, no. 29 (July 26, 1993), pp. 119 and 122.

Middle level managers have often created spreadsheets that contain major logic errors, resulting in seriously incorrect decisions. For example, an undetected spreadsheet error in the use of the @SUM spreadsheet function at one construction company caused an erroneous bid on a contract, resulting in an underbid of $254,000. The company won the bid but lost its shirt. In another example, a consultant from an accounting firm discovered over 100 errors in several of his clients' multibillion-dollar spreadsheets. In still another example, a spreadsheet designed to perform market forecasting produced a forecast that was incorrect by $36 million because formulas rounded all amounts to whole numbers. Thus, an inflation rate of 1.04 was eliminated from the calculations.

Computer Crime, Fraud, and Abuse

Computer crime is hard to measure, basically because it has not been very clearly defined. A number of states have attempted to legislate against it (see Figure 20–2), and computer crime, fraud, and abuse have been the subject of numerous pieces of federal legislation (see Figure 20–3). Typical estimates of annual computer crime range from less than $1 billion to more than $15 billion. Some important contributors to those numbers include a Florida stockbroker fraud case of about $50 million, the Volkswagen currency fraud that hit $261 million, and the Equity Funding Insurance fraud that amounted to $4 billion.[1] It is also estimated that as much as 90 percent of computer crime is unreported because organizations do not wish to make known their vulnerability to their customers, suppliers, and stockholders.

[1]Michael J. Major, "Taking the Byte Out of Crime: Computer Crime Statistics Vary as Much as the Types of Offenses Committed," *MIDRANGE Systems* 6, no. 6 (March 23, 1993), pp. 25 ff.

Figure 20–2
The computer crime law in Illinois

Sources: Data Processing and Computing Center, Southern Illinois University at Edwardsville, and George Lawton, "No Copying Allowed: The Software Publishers' Association," *PC Today* 7, no. 3, March 1993, p. 71.

Illinois recently passed legislation designed to prevent certain types of computer crime. The law identifies three categories of computer crime and defines them as misdemeanors or felonies.

Computer Tampering

The crime of computer tampering occurs when a person gains access to a computer system, a program, or a data file without the permission of the owner. The law defines unauthorized access by itself as a misdemeanor. When the tamperer obtains data or services from unauthorized access, the first offense is classified as a misdemeanor. Subsequent offenses are treated as felonies.

If the unauthorized access results in altering, destroying, removing, or damaging a computer, a program, or data, the offense is treated as a felony. Placing or attempting to place a computer virus on a computer system or computer network is included in these offenses as felonies.

Aggravated Computer Tampering

Aggravated computer tampering results when tampering is done with the intention of disrupting or interfering with vital services or operations of state and local governments or public utilities, or when the tampering is likely to cause death or bodily harm to people. Aggravated computer tampering is classified as a felony.

Computer Fraud

When a person gains access to or uses a computer, computer program, or data to deceive or defraud others, that person is guilty of computer fraud. Computer fraud may be perpetrated to gain control of money, services, or property. Property is widely defined to include electronic impulses, electronic data, confidential or copyrighted material, billing information, and software. Computer fraud is treated as a felony.

The federal government has also created legislation pertaining to computer crime. PL 102–561 makes unauthorized copying of copyrighted software a criminal offense. The penalties are substantial and include fines in the hundreds of thousands of dollars.

A major concern for those managing computer systems is the threat of intrusion by employees, competitors, and others. Almost seventy per cent of the companies responding to a recent security survey said that they had experienced a breach in their network security in the past year.[2] The concern is that people might gain access to computer facilities, systems, software, and data to commit a variety of computer crimes, such as stealing data, damaging or vandalizing hardware, software, or data, or using computer software illegally, or committing fraud.

Industrial Espionage. The theft of organizational data by competitors is sometimes called **industrial espionage** or *economic espionage.* Often, this espionage is conducted by foreign countries against US companies. For example, Robert Gates, when Director of the CIA, reported that about 20 countries were so engaged.[3] In fact, the French government has admitted to spying on US firms.

Industrial spies may use a variety of computer systems as tools. For example, using an inexpensive scanner obtainable at such stores as Radio Shack, spies can scan cellular

[2]Didio, Laura. "Security Deteriorates as LAN Usage Grows," *LAN Times* 10, no. 7, April 5, 1993, p. 1 ff.

[3]Patrick Houston, "Easy Prey," *Corporate Computing* 2, no. 5, May 1993, pp. 134–36.

Figure 20–3
Some legislation affecting computer security

U.S. Copyright Law makes it illegal for anyone to make unauthorized copies of copyrighted software or to sell pirated copies.

Software Copyright Protection Act of 1992 is aimed at software piracy on a large scale, not the home user who uses one pirated software package. The law makes selling or distributing more than 50 copies of pirated software a felony, rather than a civil matter between the violator and the software vendor.

Federal Computer Fraud and Abuse Act of 1986 makes it illegal to tamper with computers that are owned by the federal government, government contractors, or interstate organizations. Currently the bill covers access to computer systems with the intent to defraud, damage, alter, or destroy data that results in losses over $1,000. Both the FBI and Secret Service may investigate crimes under this act, depending on the nature of the crime.

Fair Credit Reporting Act of 1970 allows individuals to examine the contents of their own credit records and provides procedures for them to follow to correct errors. The act also restricts credit firms from sharing data on individuals or organizations with anyone else but their clients.

Privacy Act of 1974 restricts federal agencies from collecting, sharing, using, or disclosing personal data that can be identified with a specific person.

Right to Financial Privacy Act of 1978 specifies under what conditions banks can disclose financial information for individuals.

Electronic Communications Privacy Act of 1986 makes it illegal for anyone except the sender or receiver to tap phone and data lines, including reading E-mail messages transmitted over public E-mail systems, such as MCI mail. It also grants exemptions to law enforcement agencies and employers. That means it does not cover private E-mail systems, such as the electronic mail system of a company.

The Crime Control Act, if passed in 1994, will provide stiffer penalties for computer crimes, including intrusion, credit-card fraud, and the theft of computer services. At this writing, the bill is in the House-Senate Conference Committee.

Figure 20–4
E-mail and evidence

Sources: J. W. Huttig, Jr. "News Update," *PC Today* 6, no. 12 (December 1992), p. 8; Shawn Willett, "Eubanks: Borland Would Like to See Me Go to Prison," *InfoWorld* 15, no. 11 (March 15, 1993), p. 110.

It is estimated that in the United States alone more than 19 million users send over 15 billion E-mail messages in a year using their computer systems. Within this torrent of activity, your E-mail messages may have greater import than you think. Two recent cases highlight the use of E-mail as evidence in court cases:

1. Borland International, Inc., a software vendor, accuses Symantec Corporation, another software vendor, of hiring a Borland executive to steal their marketing plans and other trade secrets. Borland's evidence was derived from public E-mail files. Borland says it found the thefts after checking MCI mail files and learning that the executive, Eugene Wang, had sent the plans and secrets to Symantec. Interestingly, Borland International said that it used Norton Utilities, a Symantec software product, to recover data files that were allegedly deleted.

2. The E-mail messages sent by John Poindexter to Colonel Oliver North were used as evidence against Poindexter in the Iran-Contra case. In this case, the E-mail messages used were copies run off on a printer by a Poindexter staffer.

conversations or data transfers. It is also easy for spies to tap into phone lines and snatch important faxed documents. In other cases, copying electronic mail messages may prove fruitful for the spy (see Figure 20–4 on page 744).

Any time a computer system provides dial-in access, that system raises the risk of loss due to unauthorized access and theft of data. When corporate employees use portable or notebook computers, spies can gain important information on the hard disks merely by stealing the computers. Experts usually recommend that dial-in access be limited, that executives avoid toting portables or notebooks with valuable data unless absolutely necessary, and that all data stored on mobile computer systems and sent over communications systems be encrypted.

Hacking. **Hacking,** sometimes called cracking because the person cracks the log-in codes and sequences of a system, is the unauthorized entry by a person into a computer system or network. **Hackers** (also called crackers), or people who illegally gain access to the computer systems of others, may simply be people who enjoy using computer systems to break into other computer systems and intend no harm. However, hackers also can insert viruses onto networks, steal data and software, damage data, or vandalize a system.

Toll Fraud. Defrauding telephone companies out of long-distance toll charges has occurred for many years. Using slugs instead of real coins, letting the phone ring twice to mean you got home OK, and calling person-to-person for yourself with some cute message are all ways that people have swindled common carriers out of toll charges that were rightly theirs.[4]

Today's phone thieves, however, are big time, and they target organizations other than telephone companies. The average **toll fraud** bill to private or public organizations in the United States now is $90,000. In 1992, the national toll fraud bill was estimated at about $4 billion.[5] That's a lot of slugs. Toll fraud thieves now use electronic means to gain free access to an organization's long distance lines. Then they may sell the access codes or the use of the codes to others. For example, when the president of Alexon, a biomedical company located in California, examined the firm's monthly phone bill, he was astonished to find that the normal monthly bill of $1,000 had jumped to $42,000. But, the toll thieves were not yet through with his company. The next monthly bill was for $118,000. When the firm was finally able to deploy some protective measures, it had been defrauded out of over $230,000. Toll thieves even penetrated the Drug Enforcement Agency's phone system and stuck the taxpayers with a bill of about $2 million, some of which paid for calls to Colombia. You can only guess what transpired on those calls.

Brian Quinn warns that long lines of people at phone booths in certain sections of some cities are likely to be people who pay $10 or more to a "call-sell operator." The "operator" in the phone booth places a long-distance call for the "customer" by dialing an access code to some firm's telephone system and then dialing the number the customer wants, which is often an international call.[6]

Toll hackers today are resourceful. They may use maintenance ports, modem pools, voice mail systems, automated attendants, or other facilities of PBXs, the private branch exchanges that are the computerized telephone switches at customer sites. PBX man-

---

[4]Tom Emma. "For Whom the Fraud Tolls," *Telecom Reseller,* April–May, 1993, p. 17.

[5]Ed Simonson, "Reach Out and Rob Someone: A Talk on Tall Fraud," *Telecom Reseller,* April–May, 1993, pp. 17, 18, 20–24.

[6]Brian Quinn, "Dialing for Dollars," *Corporate Computing* 2, no. 5 (May 1993), pp. 124 ff.

ufacturers and common carriers are developing and implementing hardware and software devices that reduce toll fraud theft. In addition, hardware and software protection is available for any organization that reduces the risk of toll fraud substantially. However, preventive measures can never totally secure a communications system. Managers should be on the lookout for these signs of fraud:

1. Numerous short calls.
2. Simultaneous use of one telephone access code.
3. Numerous calls after business hours.
4. Large increases in direct inward system access dialing, or DISA.

DISA allows employees away from the office to dial into an organization and use the organization's telephone system features, including 800 lines and long-distance lines. To reduce toll fraud, managers might consider using access codes that require voice recognition or software that identifies potential indicators of fraud, as listed above.

Data Diddling. *Data diddling* involves the use of a computer system by employees to forge documents or change data in records for personal gain. Alan Krull describes a clerk who promised overdue utility customers to make their bills disappear for sums that were substantially smaller than what they owed. The clerk then changed the accounts of the customers so that they were identified as bankrupt. The clerk eventually changed 10,000 accounts in the system in this manner.[7]

A new twist on data diddling involves the use of high-resolution scanners and laser printers to counterfeit bank checks. Many people are amazed at the high quality of output available from computer systems today. These same scanning and printing tools can be used for forgery and fraud. For example, when financial officials at American Micro Systems, Inc., checked their monthly bank statement recently, they found four fake checks. A criminal had scanned one of their checks into a computer system, altered the scanned image, and reproduced it on a laser printer.

Trojan Horses and Salami Slicing. A *Trojan horse* is a change in code that is made to a program without authorization. The code is called a Trojan horse because it appears to be performing a proper task but may actually perform a variety of mischievous or criminal activities, such as printing paychecks to employees or vendors who don't really exist or who don't work for or sell products to the firm. For example, a Trojan horse program CPro disguises itself as Compact Pro, a shareware disk compression utility program. When the user runs what she thinks is Compact Pro, CPro reformats any diskette in drive 1 and then starts on the hard drive. The virus first appeared on some bulletin boards that allowed users to download shareware programs.

Like a Trojan Horse, *salami slicing* is also unauthorized program code. However, this code is added to a system in order to steal very small amounts from many accounts. The amounts stolen may be the remainders from rounding operations. When you have millions of transactions, partial pennies soon mount.

Trap Doors. Trap doors are procedures or code that allows a person to avoid the usual security procedures for use of or access to a system or data. Originally used for computer maintenance personnel to gain legitimate entrance to information systems, the same type of code can be used for theft of data, vandalism, or malicious mischief by the less scrupulous. Michael Major describes an incident in which a software company that had a disagreement with Revlon used their trap door to disable the software they

[7] Alan Krull, "Computer Rip-Offs and Foul-Ups: Is Management to Blame?" *edpacs (The EDP Audit, Control and Security Newsletter)* 16, no. 11 (May 1989), pp. 10–14.

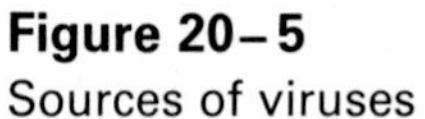

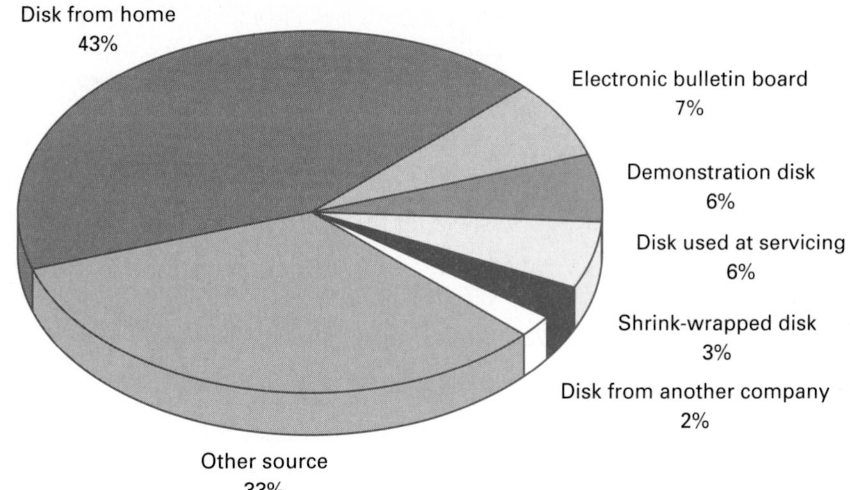

Figure 20–5
Sources of viruses

Source: Christine Sullivan, "Many Users Still Ignore Virus Threat," *PC Week* 9, no. 45, November 9, 1992, p. 141.

had developed. The problem caused a partial shutdown at one of Revlon's major distribution centers for three days.[8]

Computer Viruses. Computer viruses have become a real threat to computer systems. The National Computer Security Association reports that more than 2,000 viruses have been identified and another 75 to 100 are created each month. USA Research of Portland, Oregon, determined through a survey that the average virus attack caused $804.20 in damage. USA Research also found that, on average, 5.8 hours were required to get the infected PC up and running again and another 4.4 hours to restore the lost data.[9]

A **computer virus** is a hidden program that inserts itself into your computer system and forces the system to clone the virus. It can wreak havoc with your computer system. Sometimes, a virus may disguise itself as a utility or other program. With names like April 1st and Black Friday, viruses may simply play pranks by displaying messages on your screen. They also may cause serious damage by modifying your data, erasing files, or formatting disks.

Your computer system may become infected when you download a program from a computer bulletin board, when you log on to a computer network, or when you copy a program or file from a floppy diskette to your system (see Figure 20–5). You may download free public domain software from a bulletin board that ends up costing you a lot of money and time if the viruses it harbors ravage important data files. Because public domain software has been a source of viruses in the past, bulletin board operators who make public domain software available usually take many precautions to be sure that the software they offer is free of viruses. A study by the National Computer Security Association found that more than 60 percent of the computer users in their survey reported having experienced a virus on the system they were using (see Figure 20–6).

A new computer virus, called the cruise virus or stealth virus, is more sophisticated than many of the previous viruses. The cruise virus might lie dormant until it can

[8]Michael J. Major, "Taking the Byte Out of Crime."

[9]As reported in J. W. Huttig, Jr., "Fear of Frying," *PC Today* 7, no. 4, April 1993, pp. 18–21.

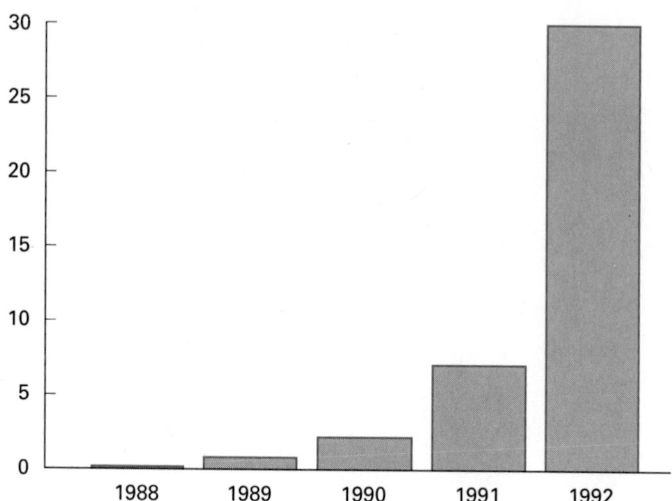

Figure 20–6
Growth of virus infections in 2,500 organizations (the data for 1992 is a projection)

Source: Salvatore Salamone, "Net Managers Focus on Virus Prevention," *Network World*, May 27, 1991.

capture financial information and transmit the data to thieves. A cruise virus might also provide a fake log-on screen in order to capture the IDs and passwords of users, especially of network supervisors who have near total access to the systems. The virus then transmits the log-on data to the criminals.

You can also use vaccination products, or **antivirus programs.** Antivirus programs may help in several ways: preventing the virus program from inserting itself in your system, detecting a virus program so you can take emergency action, and controlling the damage virus programs can do once they have been detected. For example, McAfee Associates produces a suite of antivirus programs and distributes them as shareware. One program is usually run when the system is booted and remains in the PC watching for viruses. Another program can be used to scan floppy disks to identify those that contain viruses. A third program is used to clean the infected disks of viruses (see Figure 20–7).

Most security experts recommend that you use more than one antivirus program because few programs are able to detect all known viruses. It is also suggested that you upgrade your versions of antivirus software frequently to keep up with newly created viruses.

A *worm* is a type of virus program that spreads from computer to computer over a network. Probably the most famous worm incident involved a worm created by Robert Morris, Jr., who was convicted in 1990 of placing a worm on Internet, a major computer network used by universities, research organizations, corporations, and governmental agencies. The purpose of a worm is to overload networks and computer systems as it spreads. Morris's worm shut down over 6,000 computer systems across the country.

Electronic Warfare. Those bent on shutting your organization down can employ microwave "guns" called HERFs, for high energy radio frequency guns. HERFs, if they have sufficient energy, can shut down your computer system temporarily or permanently. Other *electronic warfare* weapons are electronic magnetic pulse/transformer bombs, or EMPTYs. These devices, if they go off near a computer system, can erase the computer's memory.

Figure 20–7
Protecting your computer system against viruses

Only get software, even commercial software, from sources you trust. A group of programmers in one country inserted virus code on diskettes containing illegally copied commercial programs that they sold to buyers in other countries.

Assume that all floppy diskettes, even demonstration and commercial programs, are carrying viruses. Use a virus detection program to scan all floppy diskettes for viruses before you use them or load them. Some vendors of software place software returned by customers in shrink wrapped packages and resell or distribute them without checking them for viruses first. If the seal has been broken on the software you receive, be especially wary.

Avoid booting your system from a floppy drive. Do not borrow floppy diskettes from others. Floppy drives are a major source of computer viruses.

Run and check new programs from a floppy diskette, not your hard drive.

Write-protect your systems and applications program diskettes so that they cannot be altered.

Use only electronic bulletin board systems that check for viruses.

Whenever your PC has been repaired or upgraded at the original vendor or a local PC store, scan your system for viruses.

Buy antivirus software from vendors that update their software at least monthly because the many viruses created each month make antivirus software out of date quickly.

Use more than one antivirus program. Usually, one program does not detect or protect against every virus.

Hardware Theft and Vandalism. Theft of hardware and damage from vandalism represent ever-present threats to organizations, especially when organizations employ easy-to-pilfer notebook computers and personal digital assistants. One estimate is that about 300,000 personal computers are stolen annually and that the cost of the theft is about five times the cost of the hardware because the systems, data, and programs must be replaced, which leads to substantial downtime for employees.[10] Theft of computer systems also presents problems because of the data that reside on the hard drives of the stolen systems. For example, these data may be critical competitively; sensitive because they include data about employees, customers, and vendors; or further damaging because they include IDs, passwords, and communication log-on codes.

Software Piracy. The Software Publishers Association (SPA) holds that "any reproduction of a copyright program is theft." That, of course, would make people who copy programs from their organization for home use or those who copy programs from friends thieves. The "copy cops," or the SPA, believe they are (see Figure 20–8). The SPA estimates that software thieves stole software valued at $2.4 billion in 1992 in the United States alone. That estimate was more than half of the $4 billion in sales for software.

On an international scale, **software piracy** levies a much higher toll. In some countries, piracy is blatantly rampant. Peter Stephenson reports visiting a section of Hong Kong recently where copies of Windows, Lotus 1-2-3, and other software were being sold with mimeographed manuals for a few dollars.[11] An industry watchdog, the

[10]Michael J. Major, "Taking the Byte Out of Crime."

[11]Peter Stephenson, "Negotiating a Cure for Viruses: What the Law Cannot Do," *LAN Times* 10, no. 8, (September 6, 1993), p. 72.

Figure 20–8
Software piracy and the copy cops

Sources: George Lawton, "No Copying Allowed: The Software Publishers Association," *PC Today* 7, no. 3, March 1993, pp. 71–73; and Peter Stephenson, "Negotiating a Cure for Viruses: What the Law Cannot Do," *LAN Times* 10, no. 8 (September 6, 1993), p. 72.

The SPA recommends that organizations take a number of steps to reduce or eliminate the illegal use of software. These steps include:

- Develop a software ethics code and software compliance program.
- Appoint a software manager to implement the ethics code and software policies and monitor software license compliance.
- Store the original disks for software in a locked, secure place.
- Log all purchases and locations for software used in the organization.
- Audit your computer operations for violations of the software ethics code and license compliance program.
- Educate employees about license agreements, piracy, and the legal risks to the organization caused by violations.

To counter software piracy, the SPA advertises regularly in computer journals and newspapers, provides speakers, and distributes leaflets and booklets. It also audits each year hundreds of schools, corporations, small businesses, organizations, electronic bulletin boards, and others. The SPA also maintains an 800 anti-piracy hotline that can be used by employees or others who wish to report suspected illegal use of software.

To help organizations find out if they are violating the license agreements they have with software producers, the SPA created software called SPA Audit. The software permits organizations to inventory their software use and identify where they are in violation of their license agreements.

Business Software Alliance, estimates that more than 80 percent of the software used in China is illegal.[12]

Many people do not realize that when they acquire software they usually do not become the absolute owner of that software. Instead, they may be leasing the software or they may be buying a license to use that software from the software producer. Software is usually licensed to an individual, to the computer on which it is loaded, or to a specified number of concurrent users. The license agreement usually specifies certain conditions under which the software can be used, on how many computers it can be loaded, how many copies may be made, or the maximum number of people permitted to use the software concurrently. Thus, if your division is bought by another company, the software on your computer systems may no longer be yours to use.

Managers must recognize that they jeopardize their organizations and themselves when they permit, either deliberately or by benign neglect, software piracy. Copying a program for use at home or for use on a machine for which it is not authorized is a crime. Discovery of the theft by groups such as the SPA may lead to major legal problems for the organization. It may also lead to the loss of the manager's job. Needless to say, software piracy is also ethically wrong.

Privacy Violations. *Privacy* has been defined as the capacity of individuals or organizations to control information about themselves. Privacy rights usually imply that the

[12] *St. Louis Post-Dispatch*, Thursday, October 21, 1993, p. C1.

types and amounts of data that may be collected about individuals or organizations are limited; that individuals or organizations have the ability to access, examine, and correct the data stored about them; and that the disclosure, use, or dissemination of those data are restricted.

Violations to the privacy of records, especially records about people, may occur accidentally, through carelessness, or intentionally. Many organizations would like very much to secure the data about customers that other firms routinely keep. These data can be used for telemarketing and direct mail marketing. Data kept on customers, employees, and others is usually factual data, such as names, addresses, products purchased, and payments. However, some data may represent the opinions or remarks of others, for example, supervisory comments on employees or a creditor's remarks about a customer's credit capability. Ethical as well as legal questions have been raised about what kinds of information are kept about people, what those data can be used for, and how the data can be distributed.

Privacy also extends to electronic mail messages. It is important for an organization to insure that employee E-mail is secure from the view of others. If certain E-mail is to be viewed by others, such as a supervisor, then the employees should be clearly warned in advance. Epson and Nissan both face lawsuits by former employees over the privacy of their E-mail messages. The employees at Epson claim that the company told them their E-mail messages were private but that superiors in fact viewed them. Several more cases similar to the Epson and Nissan cases are moving through the US courts now.

Even the European Community (EC) has been forced to deal with the privacy issues involved in E-mail. EC members are developing policies that cover the transfer of personal information across the borders of the 12 member nations. Their rules cover not only E-mail, but also EDI, or electronic data interchange, because it often contains personal information pertaining to financial accounts. The EC expects that American firms will implement rigid policies to protect E-mail messages. If that does not occur, it may prohibit US firms from completing electronic business in the EC.

The rules currently under development are very stringent and treat as illegal nearly any transfer or commercial use of data about individuals without their prior consent. One proposed regulation would allow the EC to prohibit a company from transferring any electronic information into or out of the EC if that company does not have policies that meet the EC's standards. Because few companies in the United States have even considered policies surrounding the privacy of E-mail, such a provision would have drastic economic effects.

To insure privacy, hardcopy output of sensitive reporting systems should be shredded and disks should be shredded or demagnetized before they are thrown in the trash. Hard disks should be demagnetized before computer systems are sent out for repair or sold as used equipment. For example, a man bought a used PC hard drive from a computer store in Edmonton, Alberta. After installing the drive, the man found all the personnel records of a provincial agency. The man could view salaries, supervisor evaluations, attendance, and other sensitive matters at his leisure. The government had traded the equipment without erasing the disk's contents. There was quite an uproar when the story hit the papers. The government then ordered, as governments always seem to in these cases, a full investigation of the incident.

It is also important to use automatic screen blanking programs so that sensitive information is not exposed to anyone who happens to pass by a computer system that has been left running.

Meanwhile, the Department of Justice and the FBI have developed a digital telephone proposal that has been poorly received by computer firms and civil libertarians.

The proposal would require these steps from communications systems firms and communications service firms:

1. Ensuring that data and voice systems could be tapped by law enforcement agencies without having to decrypt the data.
2. Permiting the wiretaps to be implemented from remote locations, such as an FBI office.
3. Providing to law enforcement agencies selected transmissions in real time of people who had been named in court orders obtained by the agencies.

Failure to cooperate could result in a $10,000 a day fine to a firm. As you might expect, neither communications firms nor civil rights groups are supporting the proposal.

The proposal results from the fact that recent digital transmission technology and fiber optic systems are not as amenable to tapping as previous communications systems. Law enforcement agencies fear losing the wire tap weapon in the fight against crime. It appears that the proposal will not give any greater rights to law enforcement agencies to conduct electronic surveillance of people than they already have under existing laws. It does give them greater rights in the collection of that information, however.

We can expect a continuing debate on this proposal and similar proposals in the future as our nation continues to consider the complex ethical and legal issues that surround balancing citizens' rights to privacy and the public good in the age of technology.

Program Bugs

A great deal of the commercial software offered today contains **bugs,** or defects, in programming code when the software is first offered for sale. After the software has been on the street for a few months, these bugs are usually discovered by users and the software vendors provide "patches" to their code. These patches are often made available on the software vendors' electronic bulletin boards. Users can log on to the bulletin board and download the patches to their computer systems.

These bugs vary in seriousness from those that crash your system when certain conditions are met to those that process data incorrectly, such as not calculating amounts correctly. To avoid getting buggy software and experiencing the various losses that the bugs can produce, many individuals and organizations make it a point to purchase software only after it has been on sale for some time. Other organizations have extensive testing procedures that they use to test the software before they implement it generally in the organization. In any case, most software licensing agreements stipulate that the vendor is not responsible for any errors, data loss, or other problems that the buyer encounters—so let the buyer beware.

Most commercial software is produced by software specialists with lots of experience in both the programming language and the business area for which the software is designed. It does not take much imagination to visualize the kinds of errors that might occur in the development of an in-house program designed by people who might have to wear many hats. It is important, therefore, that organizations develop quality control procedures to improve the reliability of the programs they develop.

PROTECTING INFORMATION SYSTEMS

As a manager you will need to identify potential risks and consider the use of controls for your information systems, including controls for your information systems facilities, your data, the communications systems you utilize, your applications, and even the applications development process itself.

Securing Information Systems Facilities

Facilities for information systems might include the buildings and rooms in which information systems are housed as well as the furniture, hardware, software, and documentation that comprise the information systems. These facilities may place your organization at risk of potential loss from a number of common threats. When the probability of these threats becomes important to you, you must consider controlling the amount of loss your organization might suffer. Thus, you will want to consider employing controls to prevent, reduce, or eliminate the threats, or to reduce the loss that occurs if disaster actually strikes (see Figure 20–9).

Let's look at the security considerations that might be useful for a typical small business office facility. Sarah Weinstein is the manager of a branch office of the Teliram Corporation that has just opened in Orlando, Florida. The corporation provides consulting services in human resource management to organizations in northern Florida. The office consists of 10 employees: the manager, six consultants, a secretary, and two administrative assistants. Each of the employees has been given his or her own PC. The PCs are loaded with word processing and spreadsheet software. The consultants were given notebook computers so that they could take them on the road and prepare reports, budgets, and other documents easily. The office also has several dot matrix printers and two laser printers.

Sarah is concerned about the security of the PC investment the branch has made. The hardware and software purchased so far has cost $35,000. As a result, she hires Nadeem Syed, an information systems security consultant, to review her computer facilities and recommend measures that she can pursue to reduce the risks. Nadeem spends some time at the branch office talking to employees and gathering data. Nadeem reviews the crime statistics for the part of the city in which the branch office is located, the current levels of fire and police protection offered, and the probabilities of other natural disasters. After the review, he believes that the major threats to the facilities are from fire, water damage, and theft. As a result, Nadeem suggests the following controls: (1) an alarm system for the doors and windows, (2) regular use of the keyboard locks that come with each desktop system during breaks, lunch, and closing hours, (3) password protection software that prevents use of any PC without keying in a password, (4) replacement value insurance coverage for the hardware and software, (5) storage of the original software disks in a locked cabinet, (6) plastic covers for the systems to reduce dust in the machines and to prevent damage to the machines if the water sprinkler system is activated, (7) installation of deadbolt locks on all doors, and (8) installation of tie-down cables to lock the desktop computers to the desks. He recommends the cable system to reduce the number of machines that might be stolen while the police are enroute after a break-in.

For the notebook computers, Nadeem also recommends (1) training the consultants in the care and use of the systems, including not leaving them or data disks in a hot car during on-site visits, keeping them in their waterproof cases to prevent damage from rain, and storing disks properly, and (2) use of a cable locking system to secure the notebooks to the inside door armrests.

Nadeem further recommends training for the entire staff in the use and abuse of software licenses. He believes that all employees should be instructed in the legal and ethical problems caused by software piracy, or the copying and use of business software by employees for home or other use.

In addition, Nadeem recommends that the firm develop a **disaster recovery plan,** which would consider how they would continue business if a disaster occurred and their computer facilities were destroyed or were inoperable for some time. With Nadeem's help, the firm examined some of their choices. They could develop a **hot site** at which they could have identical computer facilities already loaded with their software so that

Figure 20–9
Information systems facilities: common threats and controls

Common Threats

Earthquakes, hurricanes, tornadoes, and other storms

Fire and explosions

Power spikes, static electricity, power outages, power overloads

Water damage from broken pipes, extinction of fires

Dust, smoke, heat, and humidity

Theft

Vandalism

Malicious damage by disgruntled employees

Industrial espionage

Unauthorized or illegal use of computer facilities

Common Controls

Place systems on higher floors

Install water pumps and sump pumps

Arrange for backup facilities at another site

Buy insurance

Use special building construction procedures

Store programs and data off-site

Install fire extinguishing systems, smoke detectors

Use noncombustible building materials

Provide security training for employees

Locate buildings close to fire protection agency or hydrants

Install surge protectors, antistatic mats

Install humidifiers

Install uninterruptible power supplies (batteries)

Develop procedures for orderly shutdowns

Install dedicated power lines for major computer systems

Use waterproof covers for systems

Install air filters and air conditioning

Install window bars and deadbolt locks

Install alarm systems, closed-circuit TV cameras

Bolt equipment to desks

Hire security guards

Bond employees

Screen all job applicants

Develop procedures for identifying disgruntled employees

Use biological access controls

Use IDs, passwords, and PINs

Use a menu system to prevent use of the operating system so that files cannot be copied or deleted or the hard disk formatted

Lockout terminals in open areas and after hours

they could be up and running within a day or two. Or, they could make an agreement with a disaster recovery firm for hot site facilities. They could also develop a **cold site,** which would merely provide space and furniture at another location. The cold site would not be equipped with computers and software ready to go. Instead, the firm would rent the computer systems, install the software from the original diskettes, and load the firm's data files from the archive copies onto the systems. It would take longer to resume business at the cold site, but it would cost little more than rent in the meantime. Because the parent company had unused space on the third floor of a building on the other side of town, Sarah decided to go with a cold site disaster plan.

Figure 20 – 10
Communications systems: common threats and controls

Common Threats

Incorrect or partial data received because of transmission errors or line failures

Loss of business from downed systems or downed lines

Intrusion by unauthorized persons

Incorrect routing and receipt of data by unauthorized person

Signal interception

Poor network performance

Unnecessary lines

Slow lines

Common Controls

Line conditioning, line shielding

Error detection and correction methods

Redundant lines and backup transmission lines

Archived files

Insurance to cover loss of business

Log of hardware and line failures on system

User IDs, passwords, PINs

Modem dial-back

Use of nonradiating media

Access logs of users and terminals, including invalid access logs

Lockout of terminals after hours or after *x* number of failed log-on attempts

Encryption of transmitted passwords

Encrypted data transmission

Restricting access to other networks, file directories, and files

Locating terminals in secure areas

Training communications employees

Use of network management, diagnosis, and planning software

Enforcing information systems compatibility standards

Securing Communications Systems

Communications systems provide users many benefits, such as the ability to share data and printers. They also, however, present additional risks to the security of information systems (see Figure 20–10). For example, the federal Drug Enforcement Agency administration network was cracked by drug dealers.[13] A federal government agency, the Bureau of Public Debt, established an electronic bulletin board system to protect against computer hackers. However, staff members found that hackers had begun to use the bulletin board to share data on how to break into government computer systems. As a result, the bulletin board system had to be shut down.[14]

Protecting computer communications systems assets means insuring your system's confidentiality, integrity, and availability. Thus, you should try to insure that only authorized users can gain access to the data they are permitted to view or use, that programs and data cannot be tampered with, and that the communications system is reliable—it remains up and running. To give you an idea of the planning issues involved, let's look at the concerns of Sarah Weinstein again.

The management information systems group at Teliram has recently cabled together the PCs in Sarah's branch office into a local area network so that files and printers could be shared and an electronic mail system could be installed. In addition, the MIS group equipped the consultants' notebooks with modems and communications software so that they could connect to the office file server and use the electronic mail system while visiting with clients on-site.

After discussing the new systems with Sarah, the MIS group recommended and later installed a number of security measures to reduce the risks posed by the new communications systems. For example, there was concern that the files of one employee stored on the file server of the local area network might be accessed by other employees who were not authorized to access those files. Thus, an administrative assistant who was authorized to work on one client's files should not be able to access the files of other clients. Sarah believed that Teliram's clients had the right to expect that data on their organizations would be kept from the prying eyes of those who had no need to view the data. As a result, the MIS group set up IDs for each user and associated access rights to various subdirectories on the file server with these IDs. They gave each employee exclusive access rights to their own subdirectories so that these employees could store information in their own directories privately. They also created subdirectories for the clients of the branch office and gave rights to these directories to those employees who were involved with those clients' contracts.

Furthermore, any user who wishes to use the services of the local area network must key in a valid password. The password is designed to keep nonemployees off the network, whether the nonemployee attempts to gain access in the branch office or from a remote computer system. Employees are required by the system to change their passwords every month. The MIS group also recommended that employees be warned to choose passwords that would not be obvious to intruders (see Figure 20–11). Finally, the MIS group used the local area network software to restrict log-on attempts to three so that an intruder would have to guess the correct ID and password within three tries or the terminal would be locked out.

For remote users, additional security provisions were considered. For example, one way to increase security for users accessing a computer system through a remote modem is to require the called modem to call the remote modem back. This **dial-back** procedure insures that connections are made only to preauthorized locations. Because

---

[13]Laura Didio. "Managers Flock to Windy City to Discuss Security," *LAN Times* 9, no. 23, December 1992, p. 1.

[14]*PC Today* 7, no. 9, September 1993, p. 10.

Figure 20–11
How to manage your password

1. Passwords, to be effective, should be changed often. Changing your password once a month is effective in many work situations.
2. Use a long password rather than a short one. If your system allows you to choose an eight-character password, create a password of eight digits. Short passwords are easier to uncover.
3. Don't use dictionary words, especially words that can be found in on-line dictionaries, thesauruses, and spell checkers. Intruders can use these programs to uncover your password.
4. Don't use passwords made up of personally traceable characters, such as employee initials, birthdays, spouses's names, and street addresses. An intruder acquainted with you will quickly try these characters.
5. Create passwords composed of random characters with no meaning—for example, 2A0PQ7RT9. Such a password may be harder to remember, but it is also harder to discover. An intruder may simply use Crack, a public shareware program that helps "crack" your password.
6. Keep your password private. Don't share your password with your workmates or keep a note with the password on it in an obvious place, such as in a desk drawer.
7. Do not use old passwords from previous years. Install a password system that logs all the passwords you have used and prevents you from using an old password.

the consultants move from client to client often, however, this call-back security procedure was not implemented. Instead, to insure the safety of private, client information, the MIS group installed **encryption-decryption** software on the file server of the local area network and the notebook computers. In that way, all transmissions are first coded before they are sent. The receiving computer then decodes the messages. To further improve security for remote users, the remote users' IDs and passwords are also encrypted before they are sent to the file server.

The MIS group also used the local area network software to restrict access by users to the local area network by time. That is, they restricted each user to certain time periods in the day and evening. For example, the secretary and administrative assistants were given restricted access to the local area network from 8 A.M. to 5 P.M. Because the manager and consultants frequently work in the evenings and weekends, their access was not restricted to the normal workday.

The MIS group also used the local area network software to create access logs or audit trails and trained the manager to print them out. They recommended that she examine the access logs regularly to detect unauthorized use, inappropriate use, or illegal attempts by others to gain access to the local area network.

Additionally, an antivirus program designed for a network was placed on the local area network. Each workstation was loaded with a virus scanning program and each user was instructed in the importance of virus protection. As policy, users were required to scan any floppy diskettes before they used them or stored their contents on the local area network file server. A software use metering program was placed on the local area network to insure that no more than the maximum number of authorized users used certain software at the same time. The software is designed to prevent violations of software licensing agreements.

Finally, the MIS group recommended that Sarah develop an E-mail privacy policy that would prevent ordinary users and so-called super-users, or those with a password that allows them total access to the network, from reading, copying, or otherwise interfering with the privacy of electronic mail messages.

Securing Database Information Systems

Massive amounts of organizational data are stored today in electronic databases on computer systems. Consider the importance of the financial accounting database information stored on computer systems. Providing security for an organization's database information systems is usually critical to its survival. For example, if an organization's accounts payable information is lost or destroyed, it is unlikely that the organization will be able to forget its debts to others. However, if accounts receivable information is lost or destroyed, a company is likely to lose a substantial amount of the revenue these accounts represent. An Ontario company recently sued a former employee charging him with stealing the firm's entire customer database and using it to start a competing business. The theft, which is not considered a crime in Ontario, was discovered when a mailing label was received by a spouse of another employee who recognized the label by its typographical errors.

Organizational databases also store important information about people: employees, customers, vendors, and creditors. It is both legally necessary and ethically proper to safeguard this information from prying eyes (see Figure 20–12).

Other information about the organization should also be kept secret. For example, financial information must be restricted to authorized personnel to prevent others from gaining information that might give them an unfair advantage in trading the organization's securities. Marketing and product information must be secured so that the tactical and strategic plans of the organization do not fall into the hands of competitors. When database data are restricted to authorized personnel, they are called **trusted systems.**

Figure 20–12
Guidelines for database privacy

Source: Doug Van Kirk, "IS Managers Must Keep Customer Data Secure," *InfoWorld* 15, no. 11 (March 15, 1993), p. 64

In 1973, the U.S. Department of Health, Education, and Welfare, through its Committee on Automated Personal Data Systems, published guidelines for handling information about people called the Code of Fair Information Practices. These guidelines are not law, but they do help the manager who is trying to store and use information about people in an ethical and legal manner. The guidelines suggest the following:

1. No secret files or databases about people should be created or allowed to exist in an organization.

2. Using information about people for other than its original purpose should not be permitted without the consent of the people themselves. Thus, accounts receivable data about customers kept by an organization should not be sold to others to use for direct mail advertising without the prior consent of the customers.

3. The people should have access to their records.

4. A procedure for amending or correcting records should be established and this procedure should be communicated to the people whose records are being kept.

5. Every attempt should be made to insure that the data gathered and stored are accurate.

6. Every attempt should be made to insure that unauthorized access or use of the data be prohibited.

Figure 20–13
Database management systems: common threats and controls

Common Threats

Loss or corruption of data by disgruntled employee

Loss or corruption of data by poorly trained employee

Loss or corruption of data by viruses

Theft of data by competitor, criminal

Malicious vandalism of data

Unauthorized access, loss of confidentiality of sensitive data

Embezzlement

Loss of data consistency from incomplete updates made to redundant or distributed data

Common Controls

Physical facilities controls (see Figure 20–9)

Antivirus software

Restart, recovery systems for disk failure

Backup copies of data and transaction logs

Off-site storage of archived media

Concurrency protection

Appointing a database administrator

Restricting record deletion and update authority

Maintaining deletion and update audit trails

Validating data input

Insurance to cover loss of business, recreation of data

ID and password database, directory, file, and record access controls

Employee screening and bonding

Limiting physical access to database

Enforcing vacations

Encryption

Database access logs, including sensitive file access logs

Disk, file, volume labels

Many client/server database vendors have begun to ship trusted versions of their database systems. These versions permit systems developers to keep unauthorized personnel from sensitive files, typically through log-on procedures, access rights, and audit trails.

Securing data from prying eyes is only one consideration, however, for the protection of databases. Many other security considerations are important, too (see Figure 20–13). Let's look in on Sarah Weinstein again and see how her firm is handling database security.

A number of important files are housed on the file server. Some of these files are sensitive and contain information about clients, employees, and vendors. Some of the files also contain information about the firm's strategic plans for marketing and growth.

So, Sarah is concerned that these files are secure. She knows that IDs and passwords are required to gain access to the files on the server. She also knows that the files are protected against viruses through virus protection software and organization policies. She also knows that any data downloaded to consultant notebooks will be somewhat protected by the encryption system and the antitheft procedures of the organization. She still feels apprehensive, however, and as a result calls in Nadeem Syed again for security advice.

Nadeem suggests that Sarah could take a number of precautions to increase the security of data on the local area network, the PC workstations, and the mobile notebooks. He recommends that Sarah install a tape drive and software on the file server so that the contents of the file server can be regularly archived to tape. He also recommends that one person be charged with this file server task, and that Sarah should store the updated tape each day in a safe deposit box at the local bank, which is on the same block as the office. He also recommends that each workstation upload any workstation-specific files to the server daily for storage. He will write a simple "batch" program that will perform that task automatically daily. In that way, the tape drive system will provide archive copies of important data files stored on workstations as well as those ordinarily stored on the server. Furthermore, the program will remove the need to "bug" employees to back up their drives.

Nadeem is also concerned about disk failure on the file server and the impact on the business when important files are unavailable. As a result, he suggests that a **disk mirroring system** be installed. The mirroring system would require that a second hard disk and hard disk controller be added to the server, and that software be installed that will duplicate all writes to the original hard disk to the second hard disk simultaneously. Thus, the second hard disk will be a mirror image of the original hard disk. The software also switches from one disk drive to another in the event of a disk failure. The mirroring system would allow the business to continue to operate in the event of the failure of one of the hard disks.

Nadeem recommended that an **uninterruptable power supply (UPS)** system be purchased for the file server. The UPS is a battery system that keeps a computer system powered up in the event of a power failure or a brownout or a serious reduction in power. In the event of a power failure, the file server can be shut down carefully so that there will be no loss or corruption of data.

Securing Information Systems Applications

An important method of preventing security problems is to acquire secure applications or to build them from the ground up. Careful attention paid at the software acquisition stage or development stage can reduce or eliminate many security problems that might prove very difficult to find later on.

The Make or Buy Decision. Before software is developed in-house, it is important to consider the design options available. An important design consideration is the **make or buy decision.** For example, is already developed, commercial software that has been tested through extensive market experience available to do the job? How does the cost of the commercial software compare with the expected cost of developing the same software in-house? Does the commercially available software fit the organization's needs? Often, commercial software is cheaper to buy than to develop because the development costs of commercial software are spread over many companies. Commercial software also can be installed and implemented faster than developing the software from scratch. Because a commercial software company may specialize in one or a small number of types of software, its personnel are likely to be more experienced or expert in the software than the information systems personnel at a company.

There are also potential problems with the "buy" decision. What does your firm do if the software vendor goes out of business? If you were dependent on the vendor for software maintenance and upgrades, how will you maintain and upgrade the software? Will the company allow you to purchase the source code (see Chapter 5) for the product so that you can have your MIS department or a consultant maintain and upgrade the software? What happens when your software vendor is purchased by a competitor? Will you feel secure allowing the competitor to maintain and upgrade your software? What happens if a dispute develops between your company and the vendor who developed and is maintaining your software? When a software license payment dispute developed between Revlon and Logisticon, a software vendor, in 1990, the vendor used a trap door to disable the inventory control software it had developed for Revlon. This act caused Revlon to lose full use of a major distribution center for three days.

Testing Software. If the decision is made to consider buying commercially available software, then the available software should be evaluated. Suggestions for evaluating commercial software are presented in Chapter 5. Those commercial products that survive the evaluation process should then be tested in detail. For example, before software is purchased it should be tested for the following aspects.

Appropriateness. The software's appropriateness to the task to be performed should be evaluated. Some people spend inordinate amounts of time creating invoices, payroll registers, and other accounting forms using spreadsheet software. Spreadsheet software, however, was not really designed for transaction-processing financial information systems such as payroll and accounts receivable invoicing. Furthermore, each spreadsheet application is likely to be an island of data. That is, it is not likely that the various spreadsheet applications would be integrated so as to produce reports such as an income statement, sources and uses of funds, and a balance sheet. The appropriate software would be a comprehensive, integrated, financial accounting package that contained software modules pertinent to the task, such as accounts receivable and payroll, and also contained a general ledger module that would produce financial statements.

Stability. The software should be thoroughly tested to make certain at the very least that it is stable and doesn't crash the systems that it runs on. Some software and some hardware may not be compatible. You should test the software on *all* the computing platforms on which you plan to run it. For example, a university academic computing organization upgraded its Lotus spreadsheet program from version 2.2 to version 3.1. It tested the new version on one popular brand of microcomputers it had in some of its laboratories. The software ran fine on this computing platform. However, it found that version 3.1 froze up after students used the software for a certain length of time on another brand of popular microcomputers it had in other labs. The example illustrates that even when highly reputable and popular software and hardware is used problems can arise. Thorough testing is the only way to reduce or avoid these problems.

Security features. The software's security features should be compared to the security features the application needs. For example, does the software provide automatic backup copies of documents, encryption and decryption, password protection, and the like?

When software is developed in-house, it is important to use or implant security measures into applications when they are developed. Thus, an important part of information systems security should be implemented by systems analysts and programmers when they create, test, and debug programs. These developers might be assisted by an EDP auditor from the organization or from the outside who reviews the work of the developers at key stages of the development process. Some security measures might include the review of software code by several people and the use of structured design techniques for analyzing the business problem and designing the software. Another measure might include fully documenting programs so that future programmers can update the code without introducing errors into the software. Still another measure might include using external organizations, such as quality control firms, to complete quality control audits.

Access and Update Security. Other important security measures surround access to and the right to update existing software. It is important to prevent unauthorized access and updates to current programs. Unrestricted access and update capability would allow programmers or others to change programs, permitting fraud or theft. For example, an unscrupulous programmer might add code to a payroll program to send a paycheck to a fictitious person at a drop box.

To insure that access and update controls have been working, it is also important for copies of the current software to be stored in a secure place and that the copies used to run applications be regularly checked for changes in size. Regular comparisons of code and regular executions of the run copies of software using test data should also be conducted to insure that no unwarranted changes are made in the software.

Input Controls. At the home office of Teliram, the MIS department employs a number of development techniques to insure that the applications they create are reliable and accurate. They also test commercial software to see if these programs contain techniques for insuring reliability and accuracy.

The techniques that the MIS department uses include **data validation,** or input controls. **GIGO** is an old information systems term that means **garbage in, garbage out.** The point of the term is that you must insure accurate input if you wish to generate accurate output. **Input controls** are designed to prevent bad data from being entered into a program or a database. They are also used to prevent accurate data from being overlooked and not entered at all. Thus, errors are identified at the source of data entry, and eliminated if possible.

Careful programmers can use many input controls to reduce or prevent the chance of someone keying in inaccurate data, entering data for a record twice, or failing to enter data at all (see Figure 20–14).

Manual procedures and management policies can also be used to prevent or reduce input errors. For example, management might insist personnel rotate jobs, take vacations, and segregate duties to prevent fraud or embezzlement.

Procedures can also be used to prevent input errors. For example, a sales order clerk might count the number of orders entered during a day and compare that sum with the amount the sales order program says the clerk has entered. This procedure is called taking a **record count.** The clerk might also manually total the sales orders entered and verify that sum with the total sales orders the sales order program says have been entered. This procedure is called taking a **batch total.** Both record counts and batch totals are called **batch control** procedures. That is, totals or counts on an entire batch of source documents are compared with totals or counts generated by the application program.

Another batch control is the **hash total.** A hash total is a total that doesn't make any real sense but allows the data entry operator to find out if the operator has omitted a source document, entered one twice, or entered an important number incorrectly. For example, a payroll clerk might sum the employee numbers on the time cards being recorded. This sum will be compared to the sum generated by the payroll program, which also sums the employee numbers. If the amounts are incorrect, the operator may

Figure 20–14
Some input or data validation controls

1. **Field type checks.** Data entered into a field are limited to certain types. For example, data entered into an hourly pay rate field must be numeric. Alphabetic letters or special symbols will not be permitted.
2. **Sign checks.** Data entered into a field are limited to positive or negative numbers. For example, negative pay rates will not be permitted.
3. **Field length checks.** Data entered into a field are limited to a certain number of digits or characters. For example, pay rates beyond five characters (99.99) may not be permitted.
4. **Completeness checks.** Data must be entered into a field. The data entry clerk cannot continue entering data until data are entered in a certain field. For example, hourly pay rates or other data about an employee may not be entered into the employee record until the employee number field is completed.
5. **Logic checks.** Data that are inconsistent with other data in a record are identified and prevented from being entered. For example, the entry of commissions earned into clerical employee records might be prevented, and the date entered into an employee termination date field must be later than the date entered into the employee's date of initial employment field.
6. **File comparison checks.** Data entered must agree with data in certain files. For example, an employee number may not be entered in a payroll program unless that number already exists in an employee number file. This check prevents a person from paying fictitious employees.
7. **Range or limit checks.** Data entered in a field must not be over a certain amount or must fall within a certain range of values. For example, hourly pay rate exceeding $80 an hour may not be accepted by the program. In fact if employees are paid between $5 and $80 an hour, the data entered in a pay rate field must fall within that range or not be accepted.
8. **File label checks.** All data files are labeled and programs that use these files include checks to see if the correct data diskette, data file, or data tape has been loaded.

have entered an employee number incorrectly, left a time card out entirely, or keyed in one twice.

Processing Controls. Processing errors may occur because of faulty logic in a program, incomplete transactions, or other events. For example, an auditor examining the water bills for a small town discovered that almost all of the billed amounts were incorrect by a cent or two. When programmers examined the programming code, they discovered that the program had incorrectly rounded amounts that resulted when water usage amounts were multiplied by water rate amounts. The billing errors caused more than a little embarrassment to the city and the programmers. The auditor insisted on all payments being corrected. So, to correct errors of only a few cents per customer, the city had to spend several dollars per customer generating new bills, mailing them, and updating and correcting accounts.

The Teliram application developers include **process controls** to insure the reliability and accuracy of the programs they develop. They also test commercial software for the presence of process controls. For example, when records entered cannot be processed because they contain errors or missing calculations, or for some other reason, **exception reports** list each transaction that failed to be processed. This insures that bad data or records are identified and allows the firm to correct them. To reduce the possibility that reports are generated before all records are processed, the developers insert **end-of-file checks** into their programs. Thus, processing does not cease until all records are processed. To prevent certain processing from occurring on data out of order, they implant **sequence checks** in their programs.

Teliram developers also insure that any transactions that are incompletely posted, perhaps because of a processing error or perhaps because of a power shortage, are identified. They also prevent processing errors by locking certain fields and records when they are being updated by one person to prevent others from updating the same records concurrently.

To test the programs they develop and the commercial programs they acquire, Teliram developers enter past data and compare the output from the new program with that of the old program or old manual procedure. Thus, entering past payroll data, or a portion of those data, and then comparing new program output to old reports can be used to verify the accuracy of a payroll program.

In some cases, Teliram uses an outside software testing and quality control firm to verify the accuracy of their work.

Output Controls. Attention must be paid to securing the output of computer applications, too. If the printouts of payroll files and other sensitive files are not protected, securing access to the data files or the machines that store the files may be futile. Typical output controls include the use of routing sheets to insure that printouts only go to authorized persons. Shredding sensitive printouts when their useful life is over is another safeguard against the data from falling into the wrong hands. Storing sensitive printouts in locked cabinets or drawers is another.

Outputs stored on disk or paper should be cleaned out regularly. Stored documents should be regularly scanned for destruction or transfer to other media. It is important to note that many businesses must retain records for long periods of time either for operational needs, for legal protection, or to meet statutory requirements. To avoid destroying important documents before their legal or operational time periods are over, most firms establish a document or file **retention schedule.** The retention schedule for documents and files should conform to common practice, laws, and statutes.

ETHICAL ISSUES AND INFORMATION SYSTEMS

Information systems have become ubiquitous. People as well as organizations have come to depend on them not only for success and survival, but also for the conduct of everyday transactions and activities. Computer systems have invaded nearly every aspect of our daily lives. As information technology advances, it creates a continuing stream of new issues pertaining to those parts of our lives that it impacts. In the business arena, information technology has presented ethical issues in four areas. These areas, identified by Richard Mason, are privacy, property, accuracy, and access.[15] In addition, ethical issues surround the impact information technology has on us all.

Ethical and Contractual Behavior

What many people regard as ethical or unethical behavior pertaining to computer systems is often in reality legal or illegal behavior or behavior that is or isn't in violation of a contract. That is, when a person makes a copy of copyrighted software from his firm's computer system for use at home, that is unethical behavior. It is also illegal

[15]See Richard Mason, "Four Ethical Issues of the Information Age," reprinted from *MIS Quarterly*, in Roy Dejoie, George Fowler, and David Paradice, *Ethical Issues in Information Systems*, Boston, Mass.: Boyd and Fraser, 1991.

behavior and a violation of most software contracts. Thus, a good part of behaving ethically is behaving legally and contractually. A good part of the previous discussion in this chapter should be considered a treatment of ethical behavior. However, there are ethical issues that extend beyond the law and that compel individuals to consider what is right, not just what is legal.

Privacy, Access, and Accuracy Issues

It is not illegal to view the electronic mail messages of employees produced and stored on a private, company-owned electronic mail system yet. However, the ethical considerations surrounding the invasion of the privacy of others would surely make most people pause and reflect about doing it. Organizations that do review the electronic mail of their employees may claim they have legitimate reasons for doing it. For example, organizations may have reason to believe that employees are selling trade secrets to competitors. Or, they may suspect that certain managers are engaging in biased behavior toward peers and subordinates. In some cases, organizations may take the position that electronic mail is produced on the organization's time and using the organization's resources and is thus organization property. They might further claim that if the notes, letters, and memos written using electronic means were prepared in the traditional paper-and-pencil manner, these documents would have been stored in the organization's files and would have been subject to review by appropriate organization personnel.

The caller ID feature of modern telephone systems is another example of the mixed blessing of technological advance. Caller ID permits better levels of customer service because it allows computer systems to identify callers and bring up their files on a customer representative's screen as the call is being answered. Caller ID can also severely reduce crank, harassing, and obscene calls. However, with caller ID anonymous calls to the police to provide leads to crimes are impossible. Likewise, people who have unlisted numbers will lose that privacy each time they make a telephone call.

The area of databases abounds with privacy issues. Consider these questions:

1. *What information on individuals and other organizations should any organization have the right to keep?* Although address and billing data seem like pretty safe bets for customers, what about salespeople's personal comments about customers? What about the personal opinions of purchasing agents about vendors when these data may influence credit ratings or bid acceptances? Many marketing organizations today are developing customer databases with an eye to identifying customer needs better, identifying marketing niches for products, and serving customers better. However, the data gathered by such organizations may also intrude on customer privacy. Fingerhut, a large, mail-order firm that targets households of less than $25,000 annual income, maintains a database of about 1,400 items of information on customers, including annual income, home ownership, appliance ownership, purchasing history of products by product types, the name, age, and sex of each occupant, and the credit history of households with the firm. They use the data to identify customers likely to respond to certain promotions, purchase certain merchandise, or use certain credit terms. They then target individual customers for direct mailings and even individualize the catalogs that are mailed to customers. (See Box 20–1).

2. *What rights should these individuals and organizations have about the use to which these data are put?* A major bank may have narrowly avoided tremendous adverse publicity when a marketing department executive asked an IS executive for income and loan data in the bank's mortgage application file. The use of the information was not illegal, but others in the organization felt that it would have violated the privacy of many of the bank's customers and would have led to a loss of confidence in the bank. The

Box 20–1 Computers and Your Privacy

Many daily activities create computer records that are kept by government agencies, nonprofit agencies, and business firms. These records are often sold to others where they may be used for creating new prospect lists, lists for direct mail advertising, or lists for telemarketing campaigns. A brief list of the kinds of data about you and the companies that keep the data follow:

BANK DATA

Telecheck and Chex-Systems keep checking account data on individuals and firms, including the number and amount of checks written with insufficient funds. These data permit their customers—stores, vendors, and others that accept checks for payment—to verify the status of customer checks at the time of approval by entering the driver's license or checking account number.

AUTO DATA

State motor vehicle departments in many states provide data about you, your car, and your driving record to others for a small fee. Carfax, Inc. provides, for a small fee, information about your car's history, including such details as whether it has been "totaled" before and any mileage inconsistencies that have been reported.

PROPERTY DATA

Local government agencies make information about any deeds that you hold available as part of the public record. Any claims on the property made by vendors seeking payment for past due bills are also public information.

MEDICAL DATA

One organization, the Medical Information Bureau (MIB), stores medical information on millions of Americans that is used by medical insurance companies. Data from hospital stays and even your family doctor may find its way into your medical record kept by MIB.

PROFESSIONAL DATA

As a professional, you will often receive free trade publications. To get the free subscriptions, you usually must complete an annual questionnaire that asks for detailed information about your job *and* your company. In the computer field, this data includes how many and what types of computer systems your company has and how much the company spends each year on various computer products. In addition, the professional associations to which you belong ask you to complete membership forms. The professional organizations and trade magazine publishers usually sell these data to others.

CREDIT CARD DATA

If you have a standard credit card from American Express, VISA, or MasterCard, your credit card data is sold to many other companies. That's another reason you probably get more junk mail than you would like.

CREDIT DATA

A number of companies maintain detailed information about your credit history that they sell to other organizations. The information includes bankruptcies, unpaid bills, delinquent accounts, bank, boat, and car loan data, and information about your payment history to department stores, hotels, and many other product or service providers.

OTHER PERSONAL DATA

Birth and death certificate data are available as part of the public record. These data can often lead to telephone calls from salespeople. However, much more data may be available from firms from whom you have bought products or services. Product registration and warranty forms often ask for information about your age, salary, marital status, and where and why you bought the product. Most likely these data will wind up at National Demographics & Lifestyles, an organization that maintains these and other data about you that it sells to other database organizations. If you join some buying groups or get discount memberships at some stores, you provide even more data, including where you work, what products you are interested in, and your buying preferences.

Source for some of the data: Christine Verdi. "Guarding Your Financial Data," *Your Money* 15, no. 4, June–July, 1994, pp. 22, 24, 61, 63.

company subsequently disallowed the use of these data by the marketing department. Lotus Corporation developed Lotus MarketPlace, a CD-ROM database of data on millions of people, to sell at a price acceptable to small and medium-sized organizations. However, Lotus received more than 30,000 telephone calls about the product from people complaining about the invasion of privacy. Lotus subsequently withdrew the product (although it is now offered by another firm).

Sears conducts a booming business selling the customer data they have collected over the years to other firms and organizations. Many retail chains, such as Wal-Mart, Kmart, and Dominick's Finer Foods have been selling the data about customers they have collected with point-of-sale computer systems to manufacturers. Of course, newspaper and magazine publishers have sold their subscription databases for years. However, subscription databases contain far less data than the customer databases that are now kept by many organizations. There is much room for ethical abuse in the use of these databases, especially when there is no control over their use by the purchaser. It is one thing for an organization from whom you have purchased a product to know some of your preferences about the product and its use. It is another for such information to be exploited by other companies and intrude into your life via fax sales messages, mailed catalogs, telephone calls, and sales visits.

When individuals become members of bulletin board systems and on-line databases, purchase goods and services on-line, and pay bills on-line, information about these individuals and their behavior often becomes available to other firms and organizations. More and more information about a person's marriages and divorces, the size and color of the sweater she just bought, the address and value of the person's home, the amount of the mortgage on that home, and the kind and age of the car he drives, has become easily available through on-line databases. Gathering this information from the on-line databases is legal as long as you can afford the search time. The information comes from files on real estate transactions; auto transfers; motor vehicle records; court records on marriage, birth, death, and divorce; business credit files; and bankruptcy files, to name a few sources. However, the ethics of gathering, reading, using, and even selling such data may be questioned by those whose privacy has been invaded. Justifying these activities on the basis of gaining a competitive advantage or because many companies are doing them will hardly quell the typical customer's anguish over loss of privacy.

3. *When an organization is bought by another, what rights should the purchaser have to the data about individuals and organizations that the original firm maintains?* What are the responsibilities of the original firm to protect the privacy of its customers and vendors? There are some legal answers to the latter question, of course. Legislation to protect the privacy of information has been enacted. However, this legislation has not been sufficient to deter organizations from selling data about their customers or vendors to others. Managers are often caught in a crossfire here. On the one hand, managers may be under pressure to produce, and the data about individuals and organizations acquired from the purchased firm can be sold easily for a profit. On the other hand, managers are likely to recognize how they would feel if their data were being used in this manner. As a manager, you must recognize that you may be given access to extensive data about people. You are very likely to confront situations in which the best course for profit conflicts with the privacy of those people.

4. *What is the responsibility of the organizations that maintain data about others for ensuring the data's accuracy?* Keeping inaccurate records about customers may affect their credit ratings, their ability to secure loans, their ability to obtain work. Inaccurate data about the financial well-being of vendors may prevent them from receiving con-

tracts. Although people have some legal rights to review the accuracy of data kept by others on them, they often do not exercise these rights. Most people do not avail themselves of the right to check their credit ratings or their personnel data, for example. Managers can take prudent steps to increase the accuracy of data about employees, customers, and vendors by using many of the security controls mentioned earlier, such as insisting on data validation controls, training employees, and testing programs. Managers can also emphasize the importance of accuracy to employees who create or update records about people and the consequences of errors in those records to the people involved.

Managers, as well as some other organization personnel, often have access to a vast amount of records pertaining to employees, customers, vendors, and other people. It is important that managers understand the ethical responsibilities that accompany that access, including the need to protect the accuracy of data describing people.

5. *What rights do people and organizations have to review the data kept about themselves?* Many records, such as school records and credit records, have by law become open to those whose data are being stored; other types of records have not. As a manager, you must consider how you will deal with peoples' right to know the contents of their files. Managers can use a variety of means, including neglect, to stonewall access to records. On the other hand, they can provide free and open access to those records to insure that they are accurate.

6. *Who in an organization has the right to view the records of others that are stored by the organization?* What should constitute the right to know? What rules should be followed to establish the need to know? It may not be illegal for a manager to access the records of others within an organization, but that does not mean that it is always ethical to do so. For example, a manager in a human resource department may have access to the records of many employees. However, that does not give that manager the right to invade the privacy of employees. Examining the record of an employee for promotion purposes is not the same as examining the record of a rival for a promotion with the aim of identifying weaknesses in that individual's past that can be exploited.

As technology advances, it becomes less expensive and easier for organizations to collect and maintain massive amounts of data on people and other organizations. Many firms are using these databases to identify the buying patterns of their customers and the customers of other organizations. Although this practice may allow organizations to serve their customers more efficiently and effectively, it also allows organizations to invade the privacy of those customers. Furthermore, use of these data has social consequences. For example, a firm may develop profiles of cigarette or liquor buyers and thus find ways to sell these customers more cigarettes or liquor. Although increased sales of these products may benefit the company, they also may lead to higher incidences of lung cancer and traffic deaths.

Property Issues

It is not illegal for a person to use some shareware software without sending in a check to the developer of that software, but it is certainly unethical. Likewise, although it is not illegal in some countries to copy the software developed in another and sell it, it is clearly unethical. Respecting the property rights of the software developers in these cases is simply the right thing to do regardless of the lack of legal recourse available to developers.

Furthermore, the implications of software piracy extend beyond simple crass behavior. The cost of stolen copies usually must be distributed over those who buy their copies legally. Thus, one of the costs of software piracy is to raise the price of software to other organizations, including schools and charities. Widespread piracy also discourages the enormous amounts of time necessary for software development by raising the

Box 20–2 Ten Commandments of Computer Ethics

In an attempt to reduce piracy, privacy invasion, unauthorized access, and inaccuracy in records, the Computer Ethics Institute has formulated a "Ten Commandments of Computer Ethics." These are the ten guidelines for behavior:

1. Thou shalt not use a computer to harm other people.
2. Thou shalt not interfere with other people's computer work.
3. Thou shalt not snoop around in other people's computer files.
4. Thou shalt not use a computer to steal.
5. Thou shalt not use a computer to bear false witness.
6. Thou shalt not copy or use proprietary software for which you have not paid.
7. Thou shalt not use other people's computer resources without authorization or proper compensation.
8. Thou shalt not appropriate other people's intellectual output.
9. Thou shalt think about the social consequences of the program you are writing or the system you are designing.
10. Thou shalt always use a computer in ways that insure consideration and respect for your fellow humans.

risks of a fair return on the expenditure of that time. Thus, some software may not be developed because the authors feel the risks surrounding such ventures are too great.

Protecting the property rights of others, such as the rights of software developers, through ethical behavior as a student and an employee starts with using software at school and at work ethically. That means not copying or using software illegally or without compensating the developers (see Box 20–2).

Information property issues are broader than software piracy, however. Most people understand that taking an object, such as a TV, from another without authorization is theft. However, some people's actions indicate that they fail to understand that making copies of copyrighted material, such as magazine articles or software, without permission from the authors is also theft. So is taking the ideas of someone else without authorization, such as plagiarism. Whether these acts are defined as illegal in a society does not indicate whether or not these acts are unethical. Property rights cover intellectual property as well as tangible property.

Employees who leave their current employers may take with them ideas and trade secrets that have been developed at the expense of the employer. These secrets may be transferred to a new firm or to new enterprises begun by the employees. A recent case involved an executive of Borland International, Inc., who was hired by Symantec Corporation, both software vendors. Borland charged the executive with divulging confidential information and trade secrets to Symantec while he was still working for Borland. They charged Symantec with hiring their employee in order to steal trade secrets and marketing plans. Symantec claimed the charge was an attempt to prevent other firms from hiring Borland personnel (see Figure 20–4).

It is also common today to have a security guard or other employee accompany a fired employee from the termination interview back to the employee's office. At this point, the employee's access keys, badges, and cards are collected, and all IDs and passwords are expunged from the computer system. The employee is then ushered out of the building. These practices, frankly, seem humiliating to employees. However, they are used to prevent not only disgruntled employees from harming the system, but also to prevent key data from being taken.

Ethical behavior regarding intellectual property also extends to maintaining the integrity of that property. Consider the criticism that was leveled at the *St. Louis Post-Dispatch* recently when it ran a staff photographer's Pulitzer Prize–winning photograph on the front page. The paper was criticized because it had removed a soda can from the photograph using digital imaging technology. Understanding that creative work should be protected from theft and unauthorized modification is an important component of ethical behavior.

The Widespread Impact of Information Systems

Information systems have allowed organizations to increase the efficiency and effectiveness with which they produce goods and services. This has allowed some organizations to reduce their workforce and pass these savings on to customers in the form of lower prices. In the world of international competition, reducing costs is critical to survival. The impact of information systems in many organizations has been the elimination of jobs. However, organizations have responsibilities to employees as well as to owners and customers. Employees are also stakeholders in the organization. Thus, it is important for managers to consider means by which adverse impacts of information systems on employees can be reduced. A number of managerial steps can be undertaken to do just that. For example, employees whose jobs will be eliminated can be trained by their firms for different work in the organization or for different work in different organizations. Reductions in the workforce can be accomplished through the normal attrition that occurs from retirements, moves, and resignations instead of by firing employees nearing retirement.

Information systems make it easy and inexpensive to transfer large amounts of data across a room, city, state, or country. They also make it possible to transfer information that is crucial to one nation's defense to others who may deliberately or inadvertently pass it on to the original country's enemies. And they make it possible to transfer pornographic and violent images and text to any computer system with access, including computer systems used in the home by young children.

Dependable and swift information systems make it possible to develop software in third-world countries where programmers are paid a fraction of the cost of those in the original country. The cost to the original country of transferring and testing the programs developed may far overshadow the savings gained by using another country's cheap labor. Furthermore, the third-world country may lack labor laws that are adequate to protect the programmers from such work hazards as carpal tunnel syndrome, repetitive stress injury, or the affects of radiation emitted by cheap computer terminals.

Advances in information technology have made it possible for many people to telecommute. The result has been a reduction in fossil fuel use by telecommuters and the opportunity to work for many people who would otherwise not be able to take jobs. Telecommuting also offers working spouses an opportunity to spend more time at home, reducing the dependence on child care centers or nursing homes. However, it also may offer irresponsible managers, through competitive pressure, opportunities to obtain more work from employees who no longer respond to the traditional plant closing whistle. For these workers, the inability to separate work from nonwork activities may reduce the quality of the time they actually spend with their families.

Information technology, including the inexpensive desktop computer system and the much-talked-about information superhighway are already altering the way children learn. However, information technology costs money that many poor people do not have. It also costs money that many schools in poor areas cannot afford. If distributed widely, information technology can serve as a social leveler in the learning process. If not, it can serve to further distance the underclass from mainstream society.

Computer literacy and information skills not only affect learning, they also affect job success. Many jobs today assume certain levels of computer literacy on the part of job applicants. Students from underfunded schools who have not had the same opportunities as others to develop literacy and information skills are then faced with one more disadvantage in the marketplace.

Management Responsibility

When considering the ethical issues surrounding the impact of information systems, the bottom line is that organizations and their managers should develop and deploy information systems in a socially responsible way. That means that they should consider the impact that information systems will have on employees, customers, vendors, other organizations, and the general public. That impact on people may be widespread and may affect their privacy, jobs, working conditions, health, property, home life, or future. Furthermore, they should attempt to reduce or ameliorate the adverse impact of information systems on human beings whenever possible. That means creating the policies and procedures by which an organization acquires, develops, uses, and implements information systems in a socially responsible manner.

Irresponsible behavior on the part of organizations frequently leads to legislation to correct the problem wrought by the behavior. Often, regulation of business is a direct result of the abuse or neglect of social responsibility by business. Child labor laws, enacted much earlier in this century, are an obvious case in point.

Management Summary

Computer information systems pose numerous security and ethical problems for managers. Managers must assess the risks, or potential losses to their organization, that their information systems represent and apply controls, or countermeasures that are appropriate to those risks. This usually means identifying the threats, or the events, people, actions, or other situations that could trigger a loss, that exist to the information systems and designing controls that reduce the system's vulnerabilities, or the flaws, problems, and conditions that make a system open to threats. The controls used may be physical, electronic, software controlled, or a set of management policies and procedures. The threats posed to the information systems may be from natural disasters, employee errors, crime, fraud, abuse, and software bugs. Computer crime, fraud, and abuse are increasing and now span a wide variety of types, such as industrial espionage, hacking, toll fraud, altering data files for purposes of theft, viruses and worms, theft, vandalism, software piracy, and invasions of privacy.

Managers should consider security measures for a wide range of information system components, including information system facilities, the communications systems used to connect users, the database systems that store organization data, and the application development process.

Many ethical problems involved with computer information systems have been the subject of legislation and court action. The result is that much unethical behavior surrounding the use or abuse of information systems is also illegal behavior or behavior that does not conform to contractual agreements. Ethical issues still surround computer information systems, however, especially in the areas of software piracy, the privacy of individuals and organizations, the accuracy of information kept about individuals and organizations, and the right to access those data and why and when the data should be accessed. Information systems also have adverse impacts on people through job reduction, changes in working conditions, and invasion of privacy. Managers must implement information systems in a socially responsible manner so that the adverse impact information systems may have on human beings is reduced or ameliorated when possible.

The manager can expect that new technology will beget new ethical issues as well as new security concerns. Given the persistent change in technology, security and ethical concerns are likely to maintain a high profile for some time to come.

Key Terms for Managers

antivirus programs, **748**
batch control, **762**
batch total, **762**
bugs, **752**
cold site, **555**
computer virus, **747**
controls, **740**
data validation, **762**
decryption, **756**
dial-back, **756**
disaster recovery plan, **753**
disk mirroring system, **760**
electronic controls, **740**
encryption, **757**
end-of-file checks, **764**
exception reports, **763**
garbage in, garbage out (GIGO), **762**
hackers, **745**
hacking, **745**
hash total, **762**
hot site, **753**
industrial espionage, **743**
input controls, **762**
make or buy decision, **760**
management controls, **740**
physical controls, **740**
process controls, **763**
record count, **762**
retention schedule, **764**
risk, **739**
sequence checks, **764**
software controls, **740**
software piracy, **749**
threat, **739**
toll fraud, **745**
trusted systems, **758**
uninterruptable power supply (UPS), **760**
vulnerabilities, **739**

Review Questions

1. What is a *risk?* Provide two examples of potential losses to information systems.
2. What are the objectives of EDP auditors?
3. What is a *threat?*
4. What is a *vulnerability?* Provide an example of how an information system might become vulnerable.
5. Explain what a *control* is. How can controls be used?
6. List four types or categories of controls.
7. What are *electronic controls?* List four examples of electronic controls.
8. What are *management controls?* List three examples of management controls.
9. List four common types of threats to computer systems.
10. How might encryption be used to reduce threats for a communications system? For a database?
11. What does the term *GIGO* mean? How can you reduce or eliminate the problems that GIGO represents?
12. List and describe five types of data validation controls.
13. What is an *exception report?*

14. What does an end-of-file check attempt to prevent?
15. Describe five types of computer crime, fraud, or abuse.
16. What is toll fraud?
17. What are batch controls? Describe three types of batch controls.
18. Explain what a *trusted system* is.
19. What does a hacker do? How does this threaten information systems?
20. What does the term *economic espionage* mean?
21. What is *salami slicing?*

Questions for Discussion

1. How do threats differ from risks?
2. How do threats differ from vulnerabilities?
3. What is a hot site? A cold site? How may a hot site be used to provide security for an organization's information systems?
4. What are two important questions a manager must ask when assessing risks to information systems?
5. Explain why in some situations software piracy is illegal, in others a violation of a contractual agreement, and in all cases unethical.
6. What are some reasons a firm might buy commercial software rather than make its own?
7. What does *appropriate to task* mean when referring to software testing?
8. What is a computer virus? How can viruses damage a computer information system? What can be done to prevent or recover from them?

Problems

1. **Avondale Shipping.** Avondale Shipping Company is a small owner-operated firm that provides wrapping, shipping, and other services for individuals and businesses that wish to ship packages. The owner, Val Prior, hires part-time help for peak hours during the week and for the holiday seasons. She has two computers. One is an old PC that is no longer used and that has a book value of zero. The other is a new PC that cost $3,500, including the software, installation, and peripherals. Prior stores the old PC in a closet and does not plan to replace it. However, she estimates that the cost of replacing the new PC would be $4,400, including installing the hardware, software, and replacing the data. Prior currently has deadbolt locks on her store doors, uses an alarm system connected to the local police station, has bolted down the microcomputer to a desk in an interior, locked room, and makes archive copies of her data and takes the archive copies to her home each night.

   There have been two robberies in the last year in the strip shopping center in which Avondale is located. Prior estimates that the probability of loss of the computer systems from theft is only 1 in 20. She also estimates that if the computer were stolen, she could carry on business for a day or two without loss until the new system was acquired and installed.

   a. What is your estimate of the potential monetary loss of these PC systems from the threat of theft?

b. What are some additional controls that Prior might consider to reduce the potential risk from the threat of theft?
c. What threats other than theft might Prior consider?

2. **Gordon, Ford, & Little.** Gordon, Ford, and Little (GFL) are partners in a small legal firm in the Midwest. They wish to develop a system that will track the time they spend with clients in the office and on the phone so that they can bill the clients on an hourly basis. Ford wants to buy a commercial time billing software package from Detweiler Software, Inc. Gordon, the senior partner, does not want an off-the-shelf product. He thinks that they should hire a consulting firm to create a program that is specifically designed for their firm. Little has become very adept at a spreadsheet software package that the firm uses for budgeting and other decision support purposes. He feels that they could save a lot of money and time if he just used the spreadsheet software to develop a system for the firm. What are the advantages and disadvantages of the partners' proposals?

3. **Theona U.** You are working on a computer assignment in the TU Computer Laboratory. It is 8 P.M. and the lab closes at 8:30 P.M. You must finish your project report so that you can hand it in to the instructor tomorrow. You have a computer system in your dorm room, but that computer system does not have the word processing program you are using in the lab loaded on it. Your friend, who is using the computer at the next desk, suggests, "Just copy the program to your disk and load it on your dorm machine. Then you can finish the report tonight." You realize that that would be an easy solution but you know the software you are using is copyrighted. It is also not a student edition that can be used by students in your course free of charge. Your friend sees that you are hesitating and says, "Oh, go on! That software company charges big bucks for a disk that costs them a few pennies. They will never miss it."

   You only have a half hour left.

   a. What should you do?
   b. What might the university do to reduce this problem?

4. **Virus protection software.** Prepare a report on virus protection software. Review at least one commercial software package that provides virus protection programs. As sources for your report, you might use the *Computer Literature Index*, published by Applied Computer Research, Inc., Phoenix, Arizona, the *Guide to Business Periodicals*, or *Computer Select*, the CD-ROM database service.

5. **Computer crime.** Prepare a report on computer crime. The report should contain information about dollar estimates of computer crimes and a discussion or explanation of several types of computer crime that have recently been discovered. As sources for your report, you might use the *Computer Literature Index*, published by Applied Computer Research, Inc., Phoenix, Arizona, the *Guide to Business Periodicals*, or *Computer Select*, the CD-ROM database service.

Cases

1. **Babbitt, Inc.** Babbit, Inc., is a wholesale sporting goods firm that serves clients in a two-state area. The sales department of the firm has a local area network that is used by all salespeople, including those who take orders over the phone from customers and those who visit customers in the field. Users of the LAN also are given access to the firm's mainframe computer system. Until recently, field agents used the PCs on their desks to connect to the LAN only when they were at the home office. But the desktop PCs of the field agents have recently been exchanged

for notebook computers, which the agents will use both at the home office and offsite. When at the home office, the agents plug into the LAN using a pocket-sized LAN adapter. In the field, agents use a PCMCIA modem card with software that connects to a dial-in server on the LAN. The agents will use the remote access to the LAN to query the mainframe financial accounting system on availability of stock and customer credit limits. They also will complete sales orders at customer sites by connecting through the LAN to the sales order system on the mainframe. The firm hopes that the system will result in increased sales because salespeople will have timely information about products and customer credit and because they can complete orders on the spot. The system also will allow field agents to send and receive E-mail to the firm through the local area network.

However, the sales manager is concerned about the security of the new system. She has asked you, as a security consultant, to recommend some security procedures that might reduce the risks in the system. The manager is particularly concerned about these issues:

a. What security precautions might be taken to reduce the threat of unauthorized access to the local area network and to the mainframe financial accounting database?

b. What security precautions might be taken to reduce the threat of unauthorized access to the E-mail system?

c. What security precautions might be taken to reduce the risks of theft of the notebook computers and the software and data stored on them?

Prepare a report describing the various options that the sales manager might consider to address her concerns.

2. **Werner Merchandise, Inc.** Werner Merchandise, Inc., is a catalog firm that provides a variety of stock for the home gardener, such as kneeling pads, wind chimes, garden statuary, and garden tools. The company sells directly to the home gardener by taking mail and phone orders.

Werner Merchandise purchases the merchandise it resells from other firms both within the United States and internationally. At present, the company's purchase order system is completely manual and management is considering automating the purchase order system to increase the speed of processing. A copy of the manual purchase order form is shown on the next page.

If the purchase order system is computerized and the fields in the manual purchase order used for the computerized purchase order record,

a. What input controls might be considered for the fields in the purchase order record?

b. What access controls might the firm consider for its purchase order records?

c. What additional controls might the firm consider for its purchase order records?

d. Does automation of the purchasing system pose any ethical issues to the company?

Selected References and Readings

Bowers, Dan M. "Equipment Protection: Lock It or Lose It!" *Modern Office Technology* 38, no. 4 (April 1993), pp. 30 ff. Details how office equipment can be secured through locks, including keyboard locks, cover locks, power locks, and floppy drive locks.

Bessen, Jim. "Riding the Marketing Information Wave." *Harvard Business Review*, September–October 1991, pp. 150–160. Describes the uses of customer databases in advertising, promotion, and sales. Also describes some of the ethical issues raised by these databases.

No. **7923**

Werner Merchandise, Inc.
515 Sagamore Avenue
Cincinnati, Ohio 45227-0515

TO:

DATE:
SHIP VIA:
DATE WANTED:
VENDOR NO.:
TERMS:

QUANTITY	STOCK NO.	DESCRIPTION	UNIT PRICE

Purchasing Agent: ______________________

Werner Merchandise, Inc. case (previous page)

Cheenne, Dominique. "When Software Piracy Strikes Home: A True Story." *PC Today* 7, nos. 8 and 9 (August and September 1993), pp. 41–42 ff and pp. 49–52. A two-part article that describes audits of companies by the Software Publishing Association for software piracy.

Conroy, Cathryn. "Accidents Will Happen: Formulating a Recovery Plan in Case of Disasters, Mishaps and Hard Luck Might Save Business." *Compuserve Magazine* 12, no. 9, pp. 30 ff. Describes procedures to take to reduce or ameliorate the affect of disasters on computer facilities.

Dejoie, Roy, George Fowler, and David Paradice. *Ethical Issues in Information Systems.* Boston, Mass.: Boyd and Fraser, 1991. Readings on ethical issues pertaining to computer systems.

Duffy, Caroline A. "Peace of Mind: LAN Administrators Juggle Long-Distance Data Security." *PC Week* 10, no. 29 (July 28, 1993), p. 98. Describes how several companies secure their LANs by controlling remote access.

Emma, Tom. "For Whom the Fraud Tolls." *Telecom Reseller,* April–May, 1993, pp. 17–18 ff. A detailed discussion of the problems and solutions surrounding telephone fraud.

Haight, Timothy. "Network Security: Seeking Security in the Enterprise-Wide Network." *Network Computing* 2, no. 7 (July 1991), pp. 48–50 ff. Identifies problems and solutions in the ever-widening networks of corporate computing.

Harwell, Jerri A. "Computer Piracy: Is Your Company Breaking the Law?" *NetWare Connection,* March–April, 1993, pp. 6–8 ff. Discusses the Software Publishers Association, software licensing, and methods of protecting a company from violations of licensing agreements.

Huttig, J. W., Jr. "Fear of Frying." *PC Today* 7, no. 4 (April 1993), pp. 18–21. Describes computer viruses and the steps to take to avoid them or reduce their impact on your system.

Keaveney, Claire. "Protecting the Data." *InfoWord* 15, no. 37 (September 13, 1993), p. S61. Describes how many companies are protecting data from unauthorized access on a network and through remote access.

Krull, Alan. "Computer Rip-Offs and Foul-Ups: Is Management to Blame?" *edpacs (The EDP Audit, Control and Security Newsletter)* 16, no. 11 (May 1989), pp. 10–14. Catalogs many types of computer crimes and abuses and suggests preventive measures.

LaPlante, Alice. "Turning Corporate Data into Profitability." *InfoWorld* 15, no. 42 (October 18, 1993), p. 63. Spells out the profits that can be made and the precautions that should be taken by companies considering selling their customer databases to others.

LaPolla, Stephanie. "High Tech's Dark Side: Fraud, Forgery, Check Swindles." *PC Week* 9, no. 29 (July 20, 1992), p. 23. Describes a check forgery incident involving American Micro Systems, Inc., perpetrated with scanners and laser printers.

Lawton, George. "No Copying Allowed: The Software Publishers Association." *PC Today* 7, no. 3 (March 1993), pp. 71–73. Describes the work of the Software Publishers Association in fighting illegal use of software.

Major, Michael J. "Taking the Byte Out of Crime: Computer Crime Statistics Vary as Much as the Types of Offenses Committed." *Midrange Systems* 6, no. 6 (March 23, 1993), pp. 25 ff. A wide-ranging article about all types of computer security problems and computer crime.

McPartlin, John P. "Loose Disks Sink Ships." *Information Week,* no. 437 (August 9, 1993), p. 60. Describes an incident in Alberta in which a government office traded in a hard disk that contained sensitive personnel data.

Oz, Effy. *Ethics for the Information Age.* Dubuque, Iowa: Brown, 1993. A wide-ranging text that covers past, present, and future ethical theories and their social impacts.

Pred, Rachel. "Virus Fever." *PC Today* 1, vol. 4 (January 1990), pp. 32 and 34. A brief article on the dangers of viruses and the means to protect users from them.

Quinn, Brian. "Dialing for Dollars." *Corporate Computing* 2, no. 5 (May 1993), pp. 124 ff. Describes the threat to corporate bottom lines resulting from criminals who sell organizational telephone access.

Resnick, Rosalind. "Anti-Virus Help Online." *PC Today* 7, no. 5 (May 1993), pp. 43–46. Describes on-line help users can obtain from various information utilities and computer bulletin boards.

Ricciuti, Mike. "Spy Proof Your Data!" *Datamation* 39, no. 5 (March 1, 1993), pp. 101–102 ff. Presents the National Computer Security Center's standards for PC security and some of the software products, including database management systems, that meet some of the standards.

Rothfeder, Jeffrey. "E-Mail Snooping." *Corporate Computing* 1, no. 3 (September 1992), pp. 168 ff. Discusses the ethical issues and legal implications of E-mail privacy.

Schultheis, Robert, and Mary Sumner. "The Relationship of Application Risks to Application Controls: A Study of Microcomputer-Based Spreadsheet Applications." *The Journal of End User Computing* 6, no. 2 (Spring 1994), pp. 1–8. Identifies the risks and controls in spreadsheets developed by non-MIS professionals.

Smith, H. Jeff. *Managing Privacy: Information Technology and Corporate America,* University of North Carolina Press, Chapel Hill, 1994, 350 pp. Analysis of and recommendations for policies and practices pertaining to privacy in American business firms.

Stang, David J. "Virus Dangers to NetWare LANs." *NetWare Connection,* January–February, 1993, pp. 10–12 ff. A summary of the findings of the Virus Research Center of the International Computer Security Association.

Sumner, Mary, and Robert Schultheis. "Managing the Risks of User-Developed Database Applications." *The Journal of Manufacturing* 1, no. 4 (Winter 1990), pp. 30–38. Identifies frequent risks found in database applications developed by end users and controls that can be used.

Ubois, Jeff. "Big 10 Legislation." *Midrange Systems* 6, no. 7 (April 13, 1993), pp. 44 ff. Discusses the 10 "most important" issues pertaining to pending legislation (1993) for computer technology.

Key Issues in Information Management

C 21

Chapter Outline

Manager's View

This chapter explains the transformation into "information-based" organizations. Fragmented business processes, nonintegrated data, and information filtering are all problems that interfere with business responsiveness, flexibility, and changeability. Information is essential feedback into business processes.

Business process reengineering is a critical strategy for the future. Its impact on productivity can only occur when business processes are simplified, streamlined, and redesigned. In most cases, business process reengineering entails flattening the organizational structure and decentralizing decision-making responsibility to individuals dealing directly with customers.

As you learned in Chapter 1, information systems support efficiency, effectiveness, and transformation. Ultimately, for business transformation to occur, the use of information will become an integral part of people's work. Information technology is a key factor in facilitating business transformation.

THE CURRENT BUSINESS ENVIRONMENT

In many organizations today, work is fragmented. Accomplishing simple business processes, such as responding to a competitor's price change, involves a large number of people across the organization. Completing these business processes often requires access to databases that are maintained independently in many different departments. In the traditional hierarchical organization, information is filtered as it moves up the hierarchy, causing further delays, possible inconsistency, and misinterpretation.

FORCES MOTIVATING CHANGE

The business environment of the 1990s poses unique challenges. Globalization, consumer sophistication, and technological advances are driving business strategies, including customer focus, quality emphasis, and overall responsiveness. Customers today expect new products and services with consistent levels of quality. Globalization has created a new, diverse workforce and has introduced the challenge of coordinating cross-border project teams. Cross-functional linkages among various departments, such as linkages among marketing, manufacturing, and MIS, are becoming increasingly important in accomplishing many tasks.

In addition to the fast pace and expanding scope of business activity, the rapid rate of technological innovation is spurring the development of new products, creating tools for engaging in global operations and transforming methods of performing work. In the future, an organization's ability to adapt to a volatile and uncertain business environment will be critical to competitive survival. Formulating plans and policies in this dynamic, competitive environment requires continuous assessment. By developing continuous assessment capabilities, the "learning organization" can constantly respond to changing conditions and adapt business tactics (pricing, budgeting, etc.) to compete effectively in the environment.

Tomorrow's manager must be able to anticipate changes in the environment that may require shifts in strategy. Word processing manufacturers such as Wang Laboratories were dominant in the mid-1980s, but their markets virtually disappeared with the emergence of the personal computer. Although a highly visible crisis may stimulate change, it is far better for managers to use sensors to detect changes in the competitive environment, to respond to these changes, and to monitor the results.

THE ROLE OF INFORMATION TECHNOLOGY

Information technology is a critical factor in managing uncertainty. There was a time when information systems were used primarily to process business transactions, such as customer orders, invoices, and purchase orders. Today, every manager uses information as a feedback mechanism to deal with uncertainty. Information technology is also used to facilitate the shift to continuous business processes. In today's organization, project teams are being formed, organized, changed, disbanded, and reconfigured continually. In a volatile organization, management needs immediate access to timely information about employees' skills, experiences, and interests. A central repository of information in a human resources database can facilitate selecting the right candidates for project teams.

Finally, electronic communications systems, another application of information technology, are critical for effective coordination and control of cross-functional teams with members in both centralized and dispersed locations. When information is not available among members of a project team, participants can use electronic mail to consult with external experts. With networked communications systems, team members can share common project schedules and information databases and coordinate their activities effectively.

Electronic networking is facilitating the transition from a bureaucratic organizational structure to a networked form of organization. As Drucker notes, the organization of the 1990s will more closely resemble a networked jazz ensemble than a traditional corporate hierarchy (see Figure 21–1). A case in point is Mrs. Fields' Cookies. Although Mrs. Fields works in Park City, Utah, she maintains personal contact with many of her store managers all over the country via an electronic mail network. This network facilitates coordination, information sharing, and communications in a way that would not be possible otherwise.

As you learned in earlier chapters, the transition to the information-based organization or "networked" organization is occurring. Recall from Chapter 9 that Richard Nolan, of Harvard Business School, has developed a theory of three eras of information technology (IT) that explains the transition to the network era. The theory explains how the changing role of information technology goes hand in hand with changes in organizational structure.

Figure 21–1
The networked organization

THE THREE ERAS OF INFORMATION TECHNOLOGY

Nolan's framework describes three eras: the data processing (DP) era, the information technology (IT) era, and the network era.

In the DP era, mainframe computers automated transactions processing activities, such as processing bank checks, insurance claims, and accounting records. In many cases, MIS professionals provided summary and exception reports from these transactions processing systems to enable managers to monitor business performance.

In the DP era, organizations were functional hierarchies similar to the machine bureaucracy described in Chapter 2. Work methods and procedures were well defined, and management control systems were designed to monitor the performance of business units so that resources could be allocated more effectively.

The IT era, beginning in the early 1980s, refocused the use of information technology on the knowledge worker. PC workstations were used by financial analysts, stockbrokers, and production planners, primarily for "what-if" types of analysis. Whereas traditional data processing systems generated predictable, structured, and repetitive reports, the new microcomputer-based systems were generally unstructured and produced information on demand to support ad hoc queries and requests.

As personal computing expanded, the role of MIS professionals changed from managing large, complex mainframe-based systems to providing end-user training, support, and technology assessment. You have already learned about the role of PC support groups in Chapter 19.

In stage three, known as the network era, the move toward using information technology to leverage business results is most pronounced. In order for major productivity improvements to occur, Nolan argues, new technology must be introduced along with new forms of organizational structure. Nolan predicts that information technology, combined with networked forms of organizing people and their work, will create tenfold productivity increases. In the networked form of organization, cross-functional teams will accomplish projects and traditional departmental barriers will be blurred.

Information technology can facilitate the transition to the networked organization by providing the networked infrastructures that will link people to each other via local area networks and wide area networks. Over half of the PCs in companies today are linked to LANs, and an increasing number of LANs provide access to external communications networks such as Internet. Wide area networks, using fiber optic transmission media, make it possible to do business without geographic constraints. Telecommuting, an increasingly popular work arrangement, is becoming increasingly

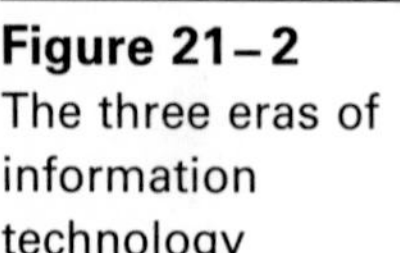
Figure 21–2
The three eras of information technology

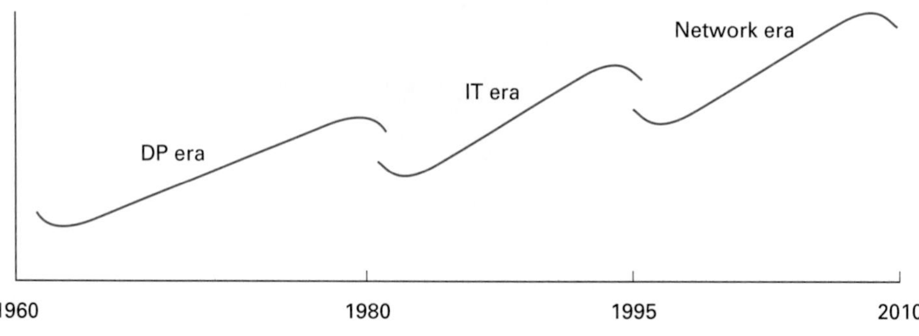

popular because people can gain access to corporate databases and electronic communications networks from almost any remote location.

INFORMATION TECHNOLOGY AND ORGANIZATIONAL STRUCTURE

Information technology affects business processes and organizational structure in four fundamental ways: automating, informating, embedding, and communicating.

Automating refers to the automation of routine work, such as the automation of typing with the use of word processing technology. In contrast, **informating** provides computing support for manipulating, calculating, and analyzing data. Developing a spreadsheet to make budget projections is an example of informating.

Embedding information technology is increasingly common. Automobiles, commercial aircraft, and microwave ovens all have integrated circuits that provide diagnostic and monitoring capabilities. In an automobile, for example, computer chips analyze potential maintenance problems such as insufficient tire pressure or low oil levels.

Communicating is supported by networking technologies such as electronic mail and videoconferencing. Networking technologies are instrumental in increasing the manager's span of control, eliminating the need for a layer of middle management, and improving overall responsiveness. Traditionally, operating-level managers have had the best understanding of local business dynamics—including customers and competitors. Conversely, senior managers chart overall business direction. Middle-level managers

Figure 21–3
The information challenge

Source: James I. Cash, Robert G. Eccles, Nitin Nohria, and Richard L. Nolan, *Building the Information-Age Organization: Structure, Control, and Information Technologies*, Burr Ridge, Ill.: Richard D. Irwin, 1994, p. 266.

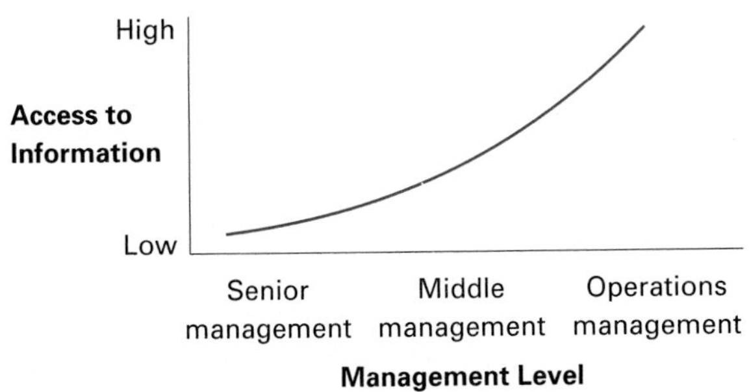

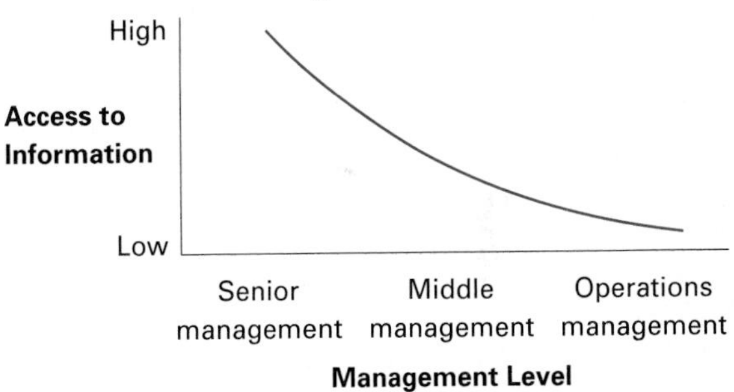

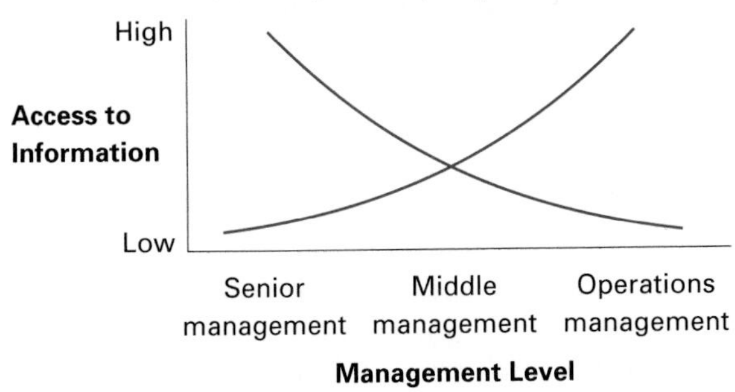

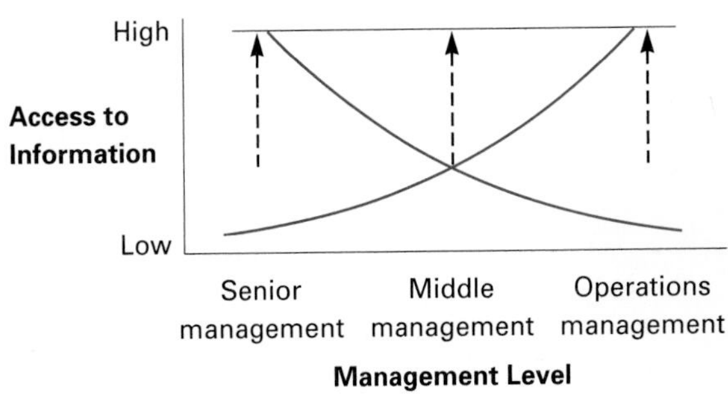

Box 21–1 The Network Manager

The rapid evolution of decentralized computing, brought on by powerful desktop workstations that are easily accessible to managers who want to process their own data, is producing the network manager. Decentralization brings about problems as well as advantages. You can just imagine the problem of hundreds of machines—each with isolated applications—unable to share data with the others. Decentralized data can create substantial risks if left unmanaged.

The network manager won't necessarily impede the process of decentralized computing by taking over the authority of hardware purchasing and software development. Rather, the network manager will seize control over the communications network to provide a conduit for information sharing and distribution. The network manager will also be responsible for establishing connectivity standards so that users can transmit data to and from workstations, mainframes, and file servers.

THE BIG BROTHER APPROACH

In the first stage, the data processing center is regarded as a "big brother." The MIS department in this phase maintains tight control over computing technologies and systems. This stage is characterized by lengthy backlogs of unfinished MIS projects and a lack of responsiveness to users' requests. MIS is faced with the dilemma of whether to expand programming staffs to become more responsive to users' needs or to loosen controls over application development so that users can do it themselves.

THE HELPING HAND APPROACH

Most MIS departments in the 1980s and 1990s have decided to help the users help themselves—a "helping hand" approach. The MIS staff plays a supportive role, offering training, consulting, and technical support. MIS also plays a role in transferring technology throughout the organization so programs developed in one division become available to others, thus preventing the tendency for users to reinvent the wheel.

Although MIS professionals are facilitating and supporting user efforts, they are still setting down standards for operating systems, hardware architecture, programming languages, and development procedures that will maximize connectivity to the network. Standardization often is promoted by offering incentives. MIS can offer training, technical support, and consulting help for end-users who acquire hardware and software that is consistent with corporatewide network standards. In contrast, those who choose not to conform with such standards do not receive support.

One of the toughest sets of standards for MIS to enforce is development discipline. Users, frustrated with backlogs and unable to get project accomplished on time, often hire consultants to develop chunks of programs or even entire applications. Often these systems don't follow MIS guidelines. If these databases are not compatible with existing programs or with network standards, they can create pockets of data that may be difficult to maintain accurately and securely—thus introducing potential inaccuracies into decisions made using these data. Further, if local databases are maintained separately from central corporate databases, they may not be refreshed with "good" data that are byproducts of mainframe-based transactions processing systems.

In one situation, users were frustrated with the backlog and appealed to senior managers to hire consultants to develop much-delayed software. Soon, data began to migrate from the corporate databases to PC programs. These

use their understanding of what is happening at the operating level and their knowledge of overall strategic direction from the top to allocate resources effectively.

The problem with the middle-management layer is that the constant exchange of information hampers the overall speed of operations. Today, most organizations are striving to use communications systems to flatten the organizational structure and to provide top management with timely access to information about activities at the operating core. See Figure 21–3 for a brief synopsis of this transition.

The flattening of organizational structure has another benefit. In dynamic environments, where responsiveness to customer needs is critical, decision making should be "pushed" down to first-line managers. This decentralization of decision making is supported by the use of powerful desktop workstations providing access to internal data

data were sometimes updated locally, but rarely made it back up into the central mainframe-based databases. Eventually, the company could no longer maintain an accurate inventory of its properties because the local data were so incorrect. When management called for an audit of the problematic programs, a corporatewide political struggle ensued. In a more rational environment, the MIS department would have allowed local branches to do their own software modifications as long as the changes met with micro-to-mainframe communications standards so that data could be accurately maintained in both places.

THE WATCHDOG MODEL

Another way of organizing data processing activities combines centralized control with decentralized development. MIS management sets centralized standards for operating systems, programming languages, and database management systems. Within these constraints, local teams can develop software using standard tools and development approaches.

Even though the watchdog approach helps end-user departments overcome the backlog problem, strict central MIS policies are often viewed as harassment. Local programmers try to circumvent these rules. This can lead into trouble if local communications networks that are not compatible with the central network are constructed.

NETWORK MANAGEMENT

The best solution to the debate between local autonomy and central standards is to design a network that allows local flexibility within the context of a standard communications environment. This enables users to control their day-to-day computing activities. It also assures connectivity between applications that run on different platforms—including minis, micros, and mainframes—and makes it possible to transfer data from one platform to another. A standard networking system provides users with access to any application on the network. Obviously, the interfaces that enable different applications to share information on a network require the ability to overcome technical challenges, particularly when it comes to addressing multivendor operating standards, micro-to-mainframe links, and database management systems.

Designing and managing the corporate telecommunications network involves solving connectivity issues involving voice, data, and text transmissions. Today's network manager must build a reliable communications infrastructure and keep it up and running. Much of this infrastructure is transparent to the end-user programmer or analyst who is designing applications within a functional area and who needs to use the network to exchange data. The network manager must have staff who can troubleshoot problems, design complex interfaces between incompatible computers, and provide maintenance.

The network management role is becoming more and more important. In the face of change, more responsibility will fall upon programmers and analysts within functional areas of the business to design information systems. But the infrastructure—including communications and database technology—will be supported by MIS technical professionals.

John J. Donovan, "Beyond Chief Information Officer to Network Manager, *Harvard Business Review*, September–October 1988, pp. 134–40.

resources and communications networks. The empowerment of the decision-maker at the operating level is a fundamental concept of business process reengineering. You will learn about business process reengineering in the next section.

THE REENGINEERING OF WORK

Prior to the network era, computers were used primarily to automate existing business processes. In the 1990s and beyond, existing ways of designing jobs and controlling work are being reanalyzed. This reanalysis of work processes is called business process **reengineering.**

The purpose of reengineering is to achieve quantum leaps in business performance. You already learned how Ford Motor Company reengineered its accounts payable system. In Ford's existing system, the purchasing department sent a copy of each purchase order to accounts payable. When the vendor sent the invoice to accounts payable, accounts payable had to match the purchase order against the receiving document. Mismatches took lots of time to resolve.

In the new system, purchasing enters purchase order information into an on-line database. When goods arrive, the receiving clerk checks the database to see if incoming shipments match the outstanding purchase order. If so, Ford pays. This set-up doesn't require an invoice for payment. Ford doesn't want an invoice—the point of the system is to pay from the purchase order and packing slip. This eliminates one of every three pieces of paper, two of every three comparisons, two of every three people who used to compare pieces of paper, and an entire layer of management.

In most cases, reengineering makes it possible to achieve major breakthroughs in performance because old rules, based upon complex sequences of tasks inherited from former decades, are challenged. Many of these procedures entailed complex control mechanisms designed to control costs. In contrast, the goals of reengineering are quality, innovation, and service—not cost control. Because the conventional process-oriented work structures of the past are fragmented and piecemeal, they lack the integration needed to maintain quality and service. Customers are forced to deal with many different departments to get work accomplished.

At Mutual Benefit Life Insurance Company, for example, insurance application processing entailed 30 steps, five departments, 19 different people, and from 5 to 25 days. When the application screening function was reanalyzed, all these tasks were assigned to a single caseworker—greatly simplifying the process and providing much better customer service. The caseworker could gain access to shared on-line databases and computer networks to make almost all application-related decisions. The underwriting process was accomplished with expert system support.

The Process of Reengineering Work

As you can see, reengineering work requires the ability to rethink traditional work methods and procedures. "Why is this done in this way?" is a critical question. "Why does the division manager need to sign all travel requisitions?" is another. If the answers indicate that some existing procedures can be eliminated, they should be. The process of work reengineering has several principles that you should take into account.

1. **Organize around outcomes, not tasks.** This means assigning one person or a team to accomplishing a task, rather than using the traditional assembly-line approach with many different people conducting many different steps. The case manager at Mutual Benefit Life, for example, was responsible for accomplishing an outcome: processing an insurance application. In an electronics company, a customer service representative is responsible for all order-filling, assembly, delivery, and installation tasks.
2. **Have those who use the output of a process actually perform the process.** If a marketing manager wants to purchase something in most organizations, he has to submit a purchase requisition to the purchasing department. Why does the marketing manager have to be a customer of the purchasing department? In a reengineered system, department managers can make their own purchases using a shared database of approved vendors. This eliminates the costly paperwork of traditional purchasing procedures, yet safeguards the role of purchasing in negotiating the best vendor terms.

3. **Treat geographically dispersed units as if they were centralized.** Some of the greatest inefficiencies occur because decentralized divisions all maintain their own information systems. At Hewlett-Packard, for example, each of the 50 different manufacturing units had its own purchasing department. This was costly and prevented HP from negotiating good vendor agreements. In redesigning the system, HP provided each manufacturing unit with access to a shared database on vendors. Central purchasing officials maintained the database and used purchasing histories to negotiate contracts for the entire corporation.
4. **Link parallel activities during the process, rather than at the end of the process.** In complex manufacturing design and engineering projects, for example, multiple activities can be accomplished by different teams working concurrently with the use of shared databases that make it possible to integrate the final result. Electronic communications systems are also useful in coordinating work groups. At one major defense contractor, a computer-based videoteleconferencing network was implemented to enable work groups in dispersed locations to communicate the progress of various work activities.
5. **Capture information once at the source.** One of the problems with traditional information systems is that the same information may be created, maintained, and used in many different places. In the insurance application screening process at Mutual Benefit Life, for example, the same information was entered into different databases as many as five different times. When the process was reengineered, integrated databases had to be designed. Integrated databases not only eliminated the repetitive data entry, but also assured better data integrity.

The process of reengineering is difficult to accomplish because it challenges traditional work methods, job designs, and departmental functions. However, for drastic changes to occur, executive leadership needs to challenge traditional assumptions. Information technology can provide communications networks, access to shared databases, and access to on-line videoconferencing facilities that can completely change the way in which traditional functions are performed. This is what Michael Hammer meant by *transformation,* described in Chapter 1 of this text. When transformation occurs, drastic changes result. Dramatic productivity improvement increases, such as the ability to cut overhead by 75 percent or the ability to eliminate errors by 80 percent, are the result. In the 1990s, information technology is the means to accomplishing transformation through reengineering business processes.

Organizational Impacts of Reengineering

The transformation that occurs as a result of reengineering has an impact upon jobs, organizational structure, management practices, and training. See Table 21–1 for a brief summary of these impacts.

As you can see, the nature of work in the information-based organization emphasizes adaptability, teamwork, and judgment. Rather than moving step by step up the ranks, individuals will become members of cross-functional teams and will make career shifts across departmental boundaries. Teams will assemble and disassemble as needed to accomplish projects. Instead of relying upon a layer of middle managers to specify work procedures, individuals will have considerably more job autonomy and decision-making capability. They will be free to respond to customer needs in a timely way.

Table 21–1
Transition to the information-based organization

Element	Traditional	Information-Based
Job design	Narrow	Broad
Structure	Layered	Flat
Career path	Vertical	Horizontal
Work standards	Procedures	Judgment
Management style	Supervision	Leadership
People needed	Structured	Adaptive
Training	Hard skills	Education

Table 21–2
Participants in reengineering

Sponsor	Sees the "big picture" Provides the resources—people and money
Steering committee	Represents the affected units Provides guidance, insight
Design teams	Knowledgeable operating managers Represent various functional units Collaborative, creative
Champion	Middle manager with leadership role Direct line to sponsor Coordinates multiple design teams
Implementation team	Focuses on implementation Open to change Able to motivate others to change

Source: Adapted from James I. Cash, Robert G. Eccles, Nitin Nohria, and Richard L. Nolan, *Building the Information-Age Organization: Structure, Control, and Information Technologies*, Burr Ridge Ill.: Irwin, 1994, Figure 8–3, p. 410.

Who Will Reengineer the Corporation?

Some of the roles in business reengineering include the role of the sponsor, the role of the steering committee, the role of design teams, and the role of the champion. You will find some attributes of each of these participants in Table 21–2.

As you can see from Table 21–2, a number of participants play a role in reengineering. The sponsor articulates the overall goals—cutting headcount by one-third, cutting the time it takes to approve credit from 20 days to 2 days—and directs resources to the project. The sponsor recognizes the role that information technology plays in orchestrating these outcomes by providing electronic communications among geographically dispersed workers and by providing operational-level workers with the information they need to make decisions.

A steering committee oversees the reengineering project, reviews its status, and identifies concerns along the way. Although managers on the committee represent various functional areas, they need to see beyond their own functional areas in order to make decisions that will benefit the larger organization. Their participation is needed to make the changes work.

The members of the design teams are the ones who translate the sponsor's goals into new processes. Members must be collaborative, creative, and analytical. The design teams must be able to identify the processes to be redesigned, understand the existing processes, understand how information technology can help, and build working models or prototypes of the new processes.

Table 21–3
Technologies in the 1980s and 1990s

1980s	1990s
Personal computers	Personal digital assistants
MS-DOS	Windows NT
Facsimile machines	Voice-to-text
Local area networks	Client/server computing
Cellular phones	Wireless communications
Relational databases	Hypertext
CASE	Object-oriented programming
CD-ROM	Multimedia/interactive video

Table 21–4
Emerging technologies of greatest interest—CSC/Index survey

	1993	1992	1991
Client/server technology	47%	26%	7%
Imaging systems	29	49	41
CASE	17	19	76
Open systems	14	10	4
Electronic data interchange	14	11	8
Network integration	13	NR	NR
Executive information systems	12	NR	NR
Object-oriented development	10	10	3

Finally, a champion is needed to coordinate the activities of the various design teams and to keep the sponsor informed. In effect, the champion "keeps the ball rolling" and promotes the projects to others throughout the organization. The members of the implementation team implement the work of the design teams and play a critical role in motivating others to cooperate with the changes. Sometimes a pilot test must be conducted to assess the impact of the changes. For example, Wal-Mart and Procter & Gamble pilot-tested their interorganizational system for inventory management with one product line within three stores before disseminating the changes on a widespread basis.

Using New Information Technology for Business Transformation

Throughout this text, you have learned how information technology is critical to improving productivity. As new technologies are introduced, it becomes very important for managers to assess their potential impact. You will find a brief listing of technologies that emerged in the 1980s and 1990s in Table 21–3.

As you can see from this listing, many of the technologies that emerged in the 1980s are taken for granted today. In a survey conducted by CSC/Index in 1991, 1992, and 1993, MIS managers at large corporations were asked to identify the technologies that were of greatest interest to their companies. As you can see from Table 21–4, interest levels have definitely changed.

In the 1990s it is increasingly important for managers to assess the impacts of emerging information technologies. The framework for information technology that was

Table 21–5 The impacts of information technology

	Individual	Functional Unit	Organization
Efficiency	Task mechanization	Process automation	Boundary extension
Effectiveness	Work improvement	Functional enhancement	Service enhancement
Transformation	Role expansion	Functional redefinition	Product innovation

introduced in Chapter 1 provides a useful tool for assessing the potential contribution and changing uses of new technologies (see Table 21–5).

Sometimes a technology that was originally designed to improve efficiency (by automating tasks) can migrate into uses that support effectiveness. When first introduced, the spreadsheet automated basic computations. Soon, spreadsheets were used to forecast consumer demand and to assess budgetary impacts—they improved effectiveness by supporting critical decision-making tasks. As we move into the 1990s, technologies that enable managers to work in new and different ways are having a transformation benefit. New information technology is facilitating the reengineering of work. Through this reengineering process, technology can begin to have the productivity impacts that have been envisioned.

Management Summary

The issues you have learned about in this chapter provide a context for projecting what the role of MIS will be in the 1990s. It is clear that this role will change dramatically. Both users and MIS professionals will be responsible for using and managing new information technology. These responsibilities will involve recognizing new technology opportunities, selecting appropriate systems development strategies, and identifying the best division of responsibility between managers and MIS professionals.

In the 1990s, MIS will play a much more important role in business. MIS professionals will have to understand the strategy of the business they support, its competitive pressures, cost considerations, and regulatory issues. Competitive uses of information technology will have to be found. In some organizations, MIS people are assigned "tours of duty" in functional departments to gain a better understanding of business issues.

In the 1990s, MIS will continue to be responsible for managing large-scale corporate data systems and telecommunications networks. Rather than maintaining their own fiefdom of systems analysts and programmers, however, MIS professionals will be more concerned with helping user-managers construct their own information systems. As a result, MIS professionals will have to understand the technology and the business context in which technologies are being used.

As technology becomes more distributed, the MIS leader in the 1990s will have to manage by establishing incentives and policies for controlling technology and systems development. Users must be convinced that if they adhere to certain communications and technical standards, they will have access to technical support and software facilities that would otherwise be inaccessible. They must also learn that many of the application projects they need to compete successfully in the 1990s will depend on the formation of a disciplined computing environment with necessary standards and controls.

Your Role as a Manager

As a manager in a business function or in an MIS function, you will need to use and to understand information technology in the years ahead. In this book you have learned about the objectives of information systems and the technologies that support these systems, and about your role in dev oping applications of information technology that support business needs. You have also learned that technology will continue to create new opportunities. Some of the technologies and issues described in this text will undoubtedly change by the time you complete your education. Hopefully, the understanding of the manager's role in planning, developing, and using information systems you have gained by studying this book will challenge you to learn about new technologies in the future. As these new technologies emerge, you will be better prepared to determine how they can be used successfully.

Key Terms for Managers

automating, **785**
communicating, **785**
embedding, **785**
informating, **785**
reengineering, **787**

Review Questions

1. What is the difference between using technology in "automating" versus "informating" work?
2. What are the characteristics of the network era?
3. What is the role of the sponsor in business reengineering?
4. Why is reengineering critical to the process of transformation?
5. Give one rule of business reengineering.
6. Identify a new information technology that is emerging in the 1990s.
7. What is the difference between efficiency and effectiveness as impacts of information technology?

Questions for Discussion

1. What are two forces that are forcing organizations to rethink existing work methods and procedures?
2. How did the role of the MIS organization change from the DP era to the IT era?
3. Why is it important to focus on reengineering work processes to achieve true productivity gains?
4. Give an example of how work can be engineered to achieve the following rule: "Have those who use the output of a process actually perform the process."
5. Why is the process of reengineering work so difficult to accomplish?
6. What is the role of the champion in business reengineering?
7. What new information technologies are growing in importance in the 1990?
8. Why do some organizational theoreticians argue that a layer of middle management is no longer needed in many organizations?
9. Why is information technology a critical factor in making the transition to a "networked" organizational structure?
10. How will jobs be affected in the transition to the information-based organization? What skills will be important in the new environment?

Problems

1. **Reengineering case studies.** In this chapter, you learned about reengineering case studies in each of the following organizations. Explain how information technology was a major factor in facilitating the reengineering of each process:

   a. Ford's accounts payable process.
   b. Mutual Benefit Life's application screening process.
   c. Hewlett-Packard's purchasing process.

2. **IT and reengineering.** In this chapter, you also learned how information technology is critical to the reengineering of business processes and the ultimate "transformation" of organizations. How can managers participate in the reengineering effort? How can MIS professionals contribute to business reengineering?

3. **The information-based organization.** Describe some of the key skills and knowledge requirements for a worker in the information-based organization.

Cases

Note: Both these cases are projects that will require you to arrange interviews or to visit companies installing new technology.

1. **MIS manager.** Arrange an interview with an MIS manager in a local business or company. In your interview, ask the following questions about MIS, current issues, and current projects. Summarize your findings in a brief report to the class. These are some questions you may want to ask:

   a. What are the current business goals of your firm?
   b. What MIS systems are designed to support the achievement of these business goals?
   c. What methods are being used to improve systems development productivity? Are software packages being used? Fourth-generation languages?
   d. What kinds of information systems are being developed by users? What kinds of tools are being used? What kind of support is provided by the MIS department?
   e. What are the current issues confronting MIS in your firm?

2. **New technology.** Visit a local firm that has implemented new information technology. Examples might include local area networks, laser printers, computer-assisted manufacturing, desktop publishing, ATMs, electronic mail, or others. Interview someone who has been responsible for planning and designing this new technology. In your interview, ask some of the following questions. Summarize your findings in a brief report to the class.

   a. What new technology has been implemented?
   b. What were the reasons or motivations for selecting this technology?
   c. How is the new technology being used? By whom? For what purpose?
   d. What are the benefits of the new technology?
   e. What pitfalls have you experienced in trying to implement this new technology?

Selected References and Readings

Hammer, Michael. "Reengineering Work: Don't Automate, Obliterate." *Harvard Business Review* 68, no. 4 (July–August 1990), pp. 104–12.

Cash, James I., Robert G. Eccles, Nitin Nohria, and Richard L. Nolan. *Building the Information-Age Organization: Structure, Control, and Information Technologies.* Burr Ridge, Ill.: Richard D. Irwin, 1994.

Case 5 — End-User Computer Systems Support at the Riverbend Electric Company

INTEGRATED CASES

BACKGROUND

REC is a manufacturing firm that produces a broad product line of electronic and magnetic products. This multinational firm has its corporate home offices and original manufacturing facility in North Alton, Illinois. This plant employs 150 corporate office and 650 manufacturing workers. Three other plants are located in West Martin, Tennessee; Guadalajara, Mexico; and Calgary, Canada. They employ a total of 1,400 office and manufacturing workers (for additional firm background, see Integrated Case 1).

Recent efforts to upgrade computer systems technology within the Riverbend Electric Company (REC) have resulted in an increase in the use of computer technology (see Integrated Case 2 for background information about upgrading office information systems at REC). The demand for improved computer applications that support ad hoc decision-making by middle-level managers is extremely high, and the MIS Department is unable to meet this demand.

Centralized, mission-critical information systems for the corporate offices are supported on an IBM AS/400. The information systems include a new order processing and manufacturing shop floor control system that was purchased from a contract software vendor and customized to meet REC's manufacturing requirements. The firm's basic data processing systems—accounts payable, accounts receivable, inventory control, purchasing, payroll, and general ledger—are also located on the AS/400. Terminals providing access to these systems are available in each department, as appropriate.

The Engineering Department has a UNIX-based network with 30 high-end personal computer workstations. These workstations are primarily devoted to computer-aided design/computer-aided manufacturing (CAD/CAM) for the firm's engineers who design the product specifications required to meet customer order requirements.

Each functional department, Administration, Marketing and Sales, Manufacturing, and Finance, is supported by a functional area work group network of personal computers. Further, these work group networks are linked to a corporate network backbone in order to enable corporate managers to communicate more easily with one another. These networks operate on PC-based network software and the end-users have access to work group software with a graphical user interface. Because the functional area networks are fairly new, the MIS Department has not yet had time to develop application systems that regularly download data from the centralized databases to departmental databases.

CURRENT SITUATION

Like many firms, REC is experiencing an explosion in end-user development of information systems. This trend has Karen Rasp, the Director of Management Information Systems (MIS), worried.

One cause of concern stems from the fact that REC's MIS Department operates with minimum personnel staffing. Figure C5–1 shows an organizational chart for the MIS Department. Although the MIS Department has grown slightly since the initiation of earlier efforts to upgrade corporatewide computer systems technology, the department still does not appear to have sufficient personnel to support the number of requests that it receives for end-user technical support. The department receives between 10 and 15 requests for support each day. The average request requires 30 to 60 minutes of attention on the part of current MIS staff members.

Karen has also noted an increase in PC-based systems problems that seem to stem from end-user systems development. For example, one year ago, Mary Ellen Goisdzinski, a marketing research analyst in the Marketing and Sales Department, developed a very useful sales forecasting system. Mary Ellen developed this system herself by using microcomputer DBMS and spreadsheet packages that she interfaced with a common set of data files.

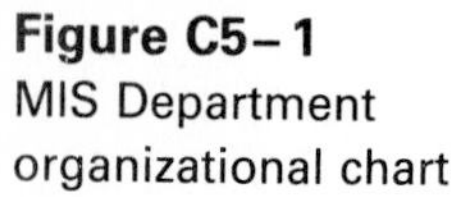

Figure C5–1
MIS Department organizational chart

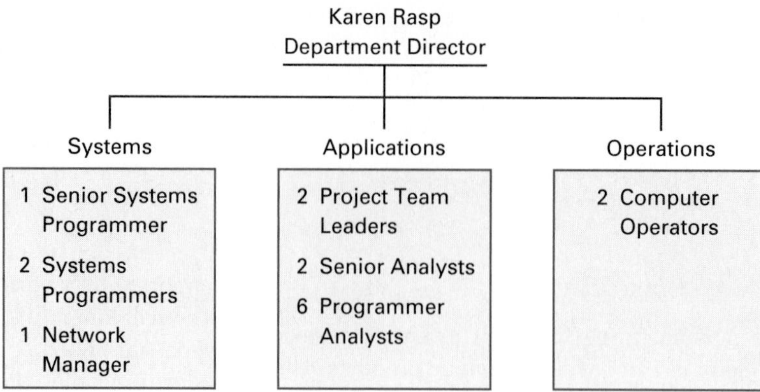

For the first six months, data for this system was obtained from a report produced by the AS/400 and manually rekeyed into the system. About six months ago, Mary Ellen worked with one of the MIS systems programmers to develop a system to download sales data from the AS/400 to the microcomputer data files once a week.

Last month, when Mary Ellen left the firm to move to the West Coast for a new job, the head of marketing research discovered that no one knew how to operate the forecasting system. The system was not documented with the exception of the data downloading component that was developed by the MIS staff. It now appears that the MIS Department will have to devote personnel resources to redeveloping this system because the marketing research director considers it to be critical to the firm's sales forecasting success, and no one in the marketing research area knows anything about developing a forecasting system.

At a recent MIS steering committee meeting, Ms. Denise Medeiros, Vice President of Finance, stated that her department was acquiring its *own* financial analysis software package, even though the AS/400 provided financial analysis software. Denise claimed that the new software had an interface that she liked better and that she could save money in the long run by acquiring the software because she wouldn't need to devote part of her departmental budget to paying the MIS Department for support of the AS/400 financial analysis software. Karen was worried that Denise's new package wouldn't do everything that the current software would. Further, Denise was talking about *her* department's financial data as if no one else in the firm would need to access it.

Similarly, John McEwen, senior assistant to the Vice President of Administration, complained about problems he was experiencing with a new micro-based human resource management (HRM) system software package that was acquired for use by the personnel staff in the Administration Department. John signed and paid for a three-year software lease and site license, then discovered the package would not operate on the microcomputer hardware platforms. The software was also incompatible with the network software available to their departmental computerized work group. John claimed that he wouldn't have encountered this problem if the MIS Department had allocated sufficient personnel to assist him in researching the HRM system in the first place.

Still other office personnel complained about the lack of support being provided by the MIS Department. These complaints covered a variety of topics. Some managers complained that MIS staff members had inadequate knowledge of personal computer hardware and software. Others managers complained about their inability to access corporate data stored in centralized data files on the AS/400 system. Still others complained that there was insufficient technical support to aid end-users in developing and debugging their own information systems. One user even complained that when he called the MIS Department for help at 2 A.M., no one was available! Did they expect MIS personnel to never sleep?

DEVELOPING THE INFORMATION CENTER

Karen determined that the firm needed to organize an information center. Karen's workload precluded her direct supervision of the project, so she assigned responsibility for organizing the information center to Ms. Sonya Karensky, a recently hired senior systems analyst and project team leader. Karen also obtained initial approval from Richard Washington, Vice President of Administration, to hire up to three individuals to staff the information center. These personnel would be end-user, technical support specialists.

Karen gave Sonya only limited guidance. Specifically, she directed that Sonya take these steps:

- Identify the major roles and responsibilities of the information center.
- Use the Critical Success Factors method to determine those factors that would be critical to the success of the information center.
- Determine whether or not the information center should be involved in setting standards for computer hardware and software acquisition.
- Determine the extent to which the information center should provide technical staff to support end-user technical requirements.
- Determine the characteristics that information center staff members should have in terms of technical competence, specific manufacturing business knowledge, and general business knowledge.
- Identify the issues that are critical to the successful development of end-user systems and ways that the information center can work to help guide end-user systems development efforts.

Case Questions and Exercises

1. What should be the primary role and responsibilities of the new information center at REC?
2. Answer Karen's question about the characteristics of information center staff members.
3. Discuss the issues in end-user systems development with respect to quality assurance. Include a discussion of data validation and testing, documentation, system controls, data backup, systems recovery, and security.
4. Discuss the Critical Success Factors that are likely to determine whether or not the information center is adequate from the end-users' perspective.
5. One manager wants to decentralize information systems processing to the departmental level at REC. Discuss whether or not a decentralized approach to information systems processing will or will not work and justify your answer in terms of the firm's competitive market and the fact that the firm is multinational.

Glossary

Accounts payable system An accounting subsystem that manages information and tasks associated with paying an organization's creditors.

Accounts receivable system An accounting subsystem that manages information and tasks associated with collecting money from an organization's credit customers.

Actuals The amount of money actually spent or received that is used as the basis of comparison in a budgeting system.

Adaptive design A looping design method used in prototyping in which the prototype is developed, the user tests it, and then modifications are made.

Add-on software products Programs that can be purchased to enhance the features of other software packages.

Address Identifies the location of data in memory.

Ad hoc report A one-time-only report that provides a manager with information to help solve a unique problem.

Adhocracy A type of organizational structure that combines groups of specialists into small, market-based project teams.

Administrative support function A wide variety of activities, including handling mail, screening callers, and scheduling resources, that provide support for management.

Advertising and promotion information system A marketing information system that helps marketing managers decide what advertising media and promotion devices to employ to reach target markets.

Affirmative action plan An organization's analysis of the number of minorities employed in specific job categories and its recruiting and hiring goals for meeting deficiencies.

Affirmative action regulations Federal, state, and local laws and regulations pertaining to the recruitment, selection, placement, and promotion of minority employees.

Aged accounts-receivable report A report that classifies customer account balances into categories, such as 30, 60, and 90 days overdue.

AI *See* artificial intelligence.

Algorithm A set of standard operations that guarantees a solution to a problem in a finite number of steps.

Allocations The amount of money budgeted to be spent or to be received, which are compared to actuals in an accounting system. *See also* actuals.

AMH software *See* automated material handling software.

Analog channel A communications medium designed to carry continuous sine waves or voice communications.

Analog transmission Sending information using analog signals, or continuous sine waves.

Antivirus programs Software that identifies the existence of viruses in a computer system and may also eliminate viruses the software recognizes.

Applicant selection and placement information systems Systems that assist human resource staff in screening, evaluating, selecting, and placing applicants in open positions.

Application development system A set of programs designed to help programmers develop application programs.

Application generators Fourth-generation languages that can automatically produce programs without requiring programming code to be written by people.

Application programmers Trained personnel who use a programming language or a software package to create computer programs.

Application programs Programs that perform specific data or text processing functions.

Application software *See* application programs.

Archive copy A second copy of data kept in case the first copy is destroyed or corrupted. *See also* backup copy.

Archiving programs Programs that provide the database manager with tools to make copies of the database, which can be used in case original database records are damaged.

Arithmetic/logic unit The part of the central processing unit that performs calculations and logical comparisons.

Artificial intelligence (AI) A broad term for a category of software that simulates human reasoning and decision-making capabilities.

ASCII American Standard Code for Information Interchange. A common computer code that uses seven bits to form each character.

Assembler A language similar to machine language but that uses abbreviations, called *mnemonics*, to represent machine instructions.

Assembly language Same as Assembler.

Asymmetric multiprocessing A method that permits the simultaneous processing of several application programs by allowing two or more CPUs to work together, sharing memory and peripheral devices. Each of the programs is processed by separate CPUs dedicated to one program.

Asynchronous transmission A type of communications mode in which each communication message consists of only one character.

ATM Automated teller machine.

Attendance tracking systems Information systems that monitor and report on such events as employee leaves, vacations, time off for illness, and absences.

Audioconferencing Using a telephone system to provide multiple parties with a chance to meet electronically.

Automated data processing The processing of data into information with the use of a computer.

Automated material handling (AMH) software A manufacturing and production system that tracks, controls, and supports the movement of raw materials, work-in-process, and finished goods from the receiving docks to the shipping docks.

Automating Refers to the automation of routine work (e.g., using word processing to automate typing).

Auxiliary memory Secondary storage; for example, storage on magnetic tape, hard disk, or optical disk.

Backbone network A communications medium, usually high speed, such as fiber optic cabling, that allows an organization to connect local area networks together.

Back-end processor A dedicated processor that provides access to a database and database services, such as remote connectivity, data integrity, and data security. It also may perform operations on the data, such as sorting and calculating.

Background task A task that the operating system performs while the user is working on another task.

Backup copy *See* archive copy.

Badge reader A scanner that reads magnetic data contained on a badge, such as an employee badge.

Ball A print element; a device containing preformed characters used by printers.

Bar-code reader A scanner that reads bar codes such as the Universal Product Code.

BASIC Beginner's All-Purpose Symbolic Instruction Code. A commonly used high-level programming language.

Batch controls A technique that compares totals or counts on a batch of source documents with totals or counts generated by the application program that processed the documents.

Batch processing When transactions are accumulated into a batch for processing at a later time.

Batch processing with overnight update Transactions are accumulated throughout the day and then processed during the night to update the central database.

Batch total The sum of the values from a field in a group of source documents.

BBS *See* bulletin board system.

Benefit plans A wide range of fringe benefits, including stock options, insurance packages, tuition reimbursement, and retirement plans, that are offered to an organization's employees.

Bill-of-materials (BOM) system A manufacturing and production system that produces listings of the raw materials, subassemblies, and component parts needed to complete each product.

Binary digits (bits) The smallest unit of computer storage; used to store data and programs in primary and secondary storage media.

Bits *Bin*ary dig*its.*

Bits per second (BPS) A measurement of the speed of data communications transmissions.

Boilerplate Standard information about an organization that is often included in proposals.

BOM *See* bill-of-materials system.

Boot To load part of the operating system, called the *kernel,* into main memory.

Boundary The scope of activities to be supported by a system.

BPI Bits per inch; commonly used as a measure of the storage density of magnetic tape.

BPS *See* bits per second.

BSP *See* business system planning.

Budgeting system An accounting subsystem that permits managers to track actual revenues and expenses and to compare these amounts to the revenues and expenses that were expected.

Buffer A small amount of memory dedicated for special purposes. For example, a printer buffer holds data for printing. Buffers are often used to compensate for the differences in speed between devices.

Bugs Defects in a program's code.

Bulletin board system (BBS) A communications service that allows users to share information with other users about areas of special interest.

Bus A set of wires or connectors between elements of a CPU or between a CPU and an add-in or expansion card.

Business information systems Information systems that support the day-to-day operations within functional areas of a business.

Business system planning (BSP) method A business information system planning technique developed by IBM that defines a technology plan.

Bus topology A type of network configuration in which each component is attached to a single cable called a *bus.*

Byte The set of bits that represents a character.

C A widely used, general-purpose programming language originally intended to develop system software.

CAD/CAM *See* computer-aided design/computer-aided manufacturing.

Call director An optional feature of a PBX system that automatically places calls on hold when all incoming lines are busy and then connects the oldest incoming call to the next available operator.

Call report A marketing report that provides information about the sales calls made by the sales staff.

Canned programs Commercially developed application programs available for purchase.

Capabilities-based competition An approach in which competitive success depends upon transforming key business processes into capabilities that provide superior value to the customer.

Capacity requirements planning A planning tool that provides detailed estimates of production capacity availability.

Capital budget An accounting report that contains information about the planned acquisition or disposal of major plant assets during the current year.

CAR *See* computer-assisted retrieval.

Card reader A scanner that reads magnetic data contained on a card, such as an employee card.

CASE *See* computer-aided software engineering.

Cash flow report An accounting report that shows the estimated amount of cash that will be received and spent each month.

Cash management system A system that monitors the flow of cash into and out of an organization.

CD-ROM Compact disk read-only memory; an optical-disk storage method that only lets you read data already stored on the disk.

Cellular telephone system A communications medium that uses radio channels to transmit and receive short-distance voice and data communications to and from mobile telephones.

Centralization An organizational pattern for offices that has secretaries and clerks working as a group to support a number of principals. Often the groups are highly specialized.

Centralized databases The databases of an organization are clustered at one location under the management of one group of people.

Centralized data processing Large mainframe computer systems that support multiple users and multiple application programs from one location.

Central office A local telephone office.

Central processing unit (CPU) The brain of a computer system. It contains the control unit, arithmetic unit, and logic unit.

Centrex A telephone-system management service that provides clients with PBX-like features on a leased basis.

Channel A communications medium over which a message is sent.

Character printers Printers that print one character at a time. Include letter-quality printers using preformed characters and dot matrix printers, which form characters with rods.

Children records Records in a hierarchical database that are owned by parent records.

Choice The third phase in the decision-making process in which an alternative is chosen.

CIM *See* computer-integrated manufacturing.

Circuit switching A type of channel mode in which the connection between the sender and receiver can vary each time a message is sent, but once the connection is established the channel is dedicated for the duration of the message.

Client/server computing A processing environment in which PCs or other workstations cooperate with one or more main processing units to accomplish whatever tasks need to be done.

Clock speed The speed at which the CPU completes its internal processing tasks; measured in megahertz.

Closed system A self-contained system that has little or no feedback from its external environment. Such systems tend to deteriorate rather than evolve.

COBOL COmmon Business Oriented Language. A third-generation language used extensively in the development of business application programs.

Coding The process of writing programming instructions.

Cold site A disaster recovery plan that provides space and furniture at another location for a computer facility that can be used when a disaster occurs that makes the original facility unavailable or unusable.

COM *See* computer output microfilm.

Command-line operating environment An operating system in which the user must type commands to communicate instructions to the operating system.

Commands Instructions that cause the computer to perform a task.

Commercial software. Software that has been developed by a software vendor that can be purchased and used by other organizations; canned programs.

Common carrier A local telephone company or a long-distance carrier, such as AT&T, Sprint, or MCI.

Communicating The process of networking technologies such as electronic mail and videoconferencing.

Communications architecture A set of communication standards. Two communications architectures are Systems Network Architecture (SNA) and Open Systems Interconnect (OSI).

Communications network A group of devices connected to one or more communications channels.

Communications protocol A convention—a set of rules and procedures—for completing a communications systems task.

Communications server A device that manages external communications for a communications network.

Communications software Additional software required to allow a computer to communicate with remote devices or with other computers.

Communications system A system for creating, delivering, and receiving electronic messages.

Compatible A device that is like another; for example, a microcomputer that works like an IBM-PC is called an *IBM-compatible computer system.*

Compensation and benefits information system A human resource system that describes and maintains an organization's various pay plans, fringe benefits, and employee choices.

Compensation plan The wage and salary system offered by an organization.

Competitive tracking information system A marketing system that contains information about a competitor's products, prices, sales, advertising, and promotions.

Compound documents Documents that contain several data types, such as text, graphics, or images, sound or voice annotations, and full-motion video clips. In a compound document, each type of data (text, graphics, voice, video) is linked to the program that created it.

Computer-aided design/computer-aided manufacturing (CAD/CAM) The use of computer systems with advanced graphics hardware and software to support engineering design and to convert CAD drawings into finished products with little human intervention.

Computer-aided software engineering (CASE) A set of tools to help application developers complete the software development process more quickly and more accurately.

Computer-assisted retrieval (CAR) Automatic retrieval of information stored on microfilm or microfiche.

Computer-based training The use of computer systems for instruction. Often, these software packages are used to train employees in specific skills.

Computer conferencing A computer system that allows participants in a group to communicate messages with all of the other participants in the group.

Computer-integrated manufacturing (CIM) A concept that stresses the use of computer hardware and software to simplify, integrate, and automate all facets of production and manufacturing.

Computerized accounting systems A series of software modules or subsystems that may be used separately or in an integrated fashion to automate accounting functions such as general ledger, fixed assets, sales order processing, accounts receivable, accounts payable, inventory control, purchase order processing, and payroll.

Computerized auditing programs Software programs that assist auditors in evaluating and monitoring a company's computerized accounting systems.

Computer kiosk A form of electronic market system, usually small structures that contain a multimedia microcomputer system with a touch screen. Some allow customers to get information about a company, its products, or its services. Others allow customers to select and purchase products and services interactively.

Computer output microfilm (COM) Microfilm produced by devices that transfer computer data directly to microfilm; used for mass storage of data.

Computer program A set of instructions that a computer system uses to process data.

Computer terminal A common input device; often uses an attached keyboard for data entry and a screen to display commands, keystrokes, and system responses.

Computer virus A hidden program that can cause damage to computer system files.

Conceptual view The logical view of a database that includes all of the data elements in the database and how these data elements logically relate to each other. This is the view used by the DBA.

Concurrency When more than one user in a database environment accesses or tries to update the same record at the same time. *See also* field, record, and file locking.

Contact information system A marketing system that provides the sales force with information about customers, their product and service preferences, and sales and visit history data.

Contact management software A type of software used by salespeople to track information about clients, including their product and service preferences, visit information, and sales performance data.

Continuous-flow production A production method that does not stop, producing output constantly.

Control aids Features of a decision support system that allow the user to save intermediate results or that remind the user to perform certain activities.

Controlling A managerial function that involves evaluating performance and controlling the organization's resources.

Controls Tools used to counter risks from the people, actions, events, or situations that can threaten an information system. Controls may be used to identify risk, prevent risk, reduce risks, and recover from actual losses.

Control unit The part of the CPU that interprets instructions and notifies other system components to carry out those instructions.

Co-processors Processors, other than the central processing unit, that help the CPU in its work; for example, an

I/O channel used in a mainframe computer system and a numeric co-processor used in a microcomputer system.

Copy-protected software Software written in such a way that it cannot easily be copied.

Cost-benefit analysis A study that determines the economic feasibility of various system design alternatives and the financial impact of an information system proposal.

Cost-plus pricing A pricing tactic that involves determining the cost of a product and adding a markup to achieve the desired profit.

CPU *See* central processing unit.

Critical Success Factor (CSF) method A business information system planning technique that identifies key business goals and strategies that must be addressed with information technology.

CRT Cathode-ray tube; a type of computer screen. *See* display screen.

Customer support software Software that provides information to salespeople about the previous experiences of customers with the organization, including detailed information on purchases, payments, and specific products purchased by each customer, including competitor products.

Custom-written software Custom-designed software written by consultants or programmers external to an organization.

Cut-over method A method of conversion in which a complete, one-time conversion from the old to the new system occurs.

Cylinder The collection of tracks accessible by a single movement of all the read/write heads of a disk drive.

Cylinder storage method A method of storing data on the tracks of a cylinder to reduce the movement of the read/write heads of a disk drive.

DASD *See* direct access storage devices.

Data Raw facts.

Database A collection of related files.

Database administrator (DBA) An MIS professional responsible for planning, designing, and maintaining an organization's data resources.

Database management software A set of programs that creates and manages databases.

Database management system (DBMS) A collection of software programs that allows users to organize and store data in a uniform way and to access data from more than one file.

Database server A computer system with a hard disk, often run by special software, that permits the system to be dedicated to database tasks on a network.

Database structure The method by which a database management system organizes records.

Data communications specialist A technical support person responsible for managing and maintaining an organization's data communication network.

Data dictionary Contains the data names and definitions for all data elements to be maintained in data files, to be generated as output, and to be created as input.

Data dictionary/directory A database management tool that contains the names and descriptions of all of the data elements within a database and how each data element relates to other elements.

Data element A logical collection of characters that represents a basic unit of information, such as an employee's last name. Also called a *field*.

Data entry personnel MIS professionals responsible for keying data into a computer system.

Data independence Being able to define or describe data separately from an application program.

Data integrity The degree to which the data in a database are accurate.

Data manipulation language A specialized language used by programmers to retrieve and process data from a database.

Data processing department A unit responsible for operating and managing an organization's computer resources.

Data redundancy A situation that occurs when the same data element occurs in more than one file.

Data repository An enhanced data dictionary that includes metadata and that documents, defines, and provides a directory to the many component parts of an organization's information resource.

Data validation Controls that are used to prevent bad data from being entered into a program or a database and to prevent accurate data from not being entered at all.

DBA *See* database administrator.

DBMS *See* database management system.

DDE *See* dynamic data exchange.

Decentralization An organizational pattern in which an information system or an office function is operated and managed by individual departments of an organization.

Decentralized data processing A data processing environment in which microcomputers or minicomputers support local applications, systems, and operations personnel.

Decision support systems (DSS) Information systems that provide managers with ad hoc data on an on-demand basis.

Decision table An analysis tool that uses a tabular structure to specify what action should be taken given a set of conditions.

Decision tree An analysis tool that uses a treelike structure to specify what action should be taken given a set of conditions.

Decryption Decoding data that has been encoded (see encryption).

Dedicated server A computer system that performs one or a limited number of special tasks, such as communications, printing, or file management on a network.

Delphi study A study that gives participants knowledge of group results so that they can reevaluate their own views and move toward the consensus view if they wish.

Demand pricing A pricing tactic that bases the price of a product on the value that the customer perceives the product has.

Demonstration diskettes Limited-feature versions of software provided by vendors so that the user can try a software package before buying it.

Design The second phase of the decision-making process during which the decision maker develops and analyzes alternative courses of action.

Desktop Short for desktop computer system. A microcomputer system that fits on a desktop.

Desktop conferencing A system that allows users on a LAN to use their workstations to conduct meetings without physically getting together.

Desktop organizer software Programs that offer a variety of features designed to clear the desktop of calculators, memo pads, telephone directories, calendars, and so forth.

Desktop publishing software (DTP) Software that allows the user to design professional-looking documents with both text and graphics.

Desktop survey software Software that lets you create survey questions and then helps you sum, tabulate, and otherwise treat statistically the answers collected to those questions.

Desktop video technology Technology that permits you to capture video images from live TV or VCR tape as individual frames, store them on a hard or optical disks, and manipulate the images or sequences of images.

Detailed system design The process in the system development life cycle in which specifications for the proposed physical system are developed.

Development software Easy-to-use software tools that allow programmers and nontechnical users to create programs for whatever jobs must be accomplished.

Dial-back A security procedure that requires a called modem to call the remote modem back; it is used to insure that connections made by remote users are restricted to preauthorized locations.

Dial-up telephone lines Telephone lines rented from a common carrier and paid for on a usage basis.

Digital cameras Devices that look like ordinary cameras but capture images digitally and store them on disk. The images can then be manipulated with graphics software. The technology allows you to insert the pictures you take into data files, documents, or presentations.

Digital multimedia technology Allows the user to combine and sequence data, text, images, video, and sound into a presentation.

Digital signals The discrete electronic pulses produced by a computer system that create the bits that make up a byte or character.

Digital transmission Sending data as digital signals.

Direct access A method of storing data in which each record is given a specific disk address so that it can be found directly without reading every record sequentially from the beginning of a file.

Direct access storage devices (DASD) Storage devices, such as floppy and hard disk drives, that allow data to be stored and retrieved directly as opposed to sequentially.

Direct-mail advertising system A marketing system that utilizes mailing lists to distribute sales brochures and catalogs to a large number of potential customers.

Disaster recovery plan A plan for restoring computer operations quickly when a disaster occurs. The plan might include a contingency plan for the use of alternate computer facilities. *See* hot site and cold site.

Disk drives Direct access storage devices used for auxiliary or secondary storage of data.

Diskless workstation A microcomputer that does not have a disk drive but uses the disk drive of a file server *See also* file server.

Disk mirroring system The use of a second hard disk and hard disk controller in a server along with software that duplicates all writes to the original hard disk to the second hard disk simultaneously. Thus, the second hard disk is a mirror image of the original hard disk. The system also switches from one disk drive to another in the event of a disk failure.

Disk pack A collection of platters on which data can be stored. The disk packs may be removable.

Display screen A visual output device that looks like a TV screen used for displaying computer commands, keystrokes, or the results of computer processing.

Distributed database system Distributing a database to either a functional unit or a geographical location to support local processing requirements.

Distributed data processing When computer processing capabilities for an organization are located at more than one site.

Distributed MRP-II software Application software that allows manufacturing resource planning to be distributed to different plant sites.

Distributed processing A computer system in which computing power, data, and processing are located at more than one site.

Distribution channel decision support system A marketing system that contains information about the costs, demands, delays, and reliability of various distribution channels.

Divisionalized form A type of organizational structure that consists of a group of quasi-autonomous entities coupled together by a central administrative structure.

DML *See* data manipulation language.

Documentation specialist An MIS professional who records the documentation produced during the system development life cycle, including design specifications, flowcharts, file descriptions, operating procedures, user procedures, and control procedures.

Document management software Computer software that lets users search for and retrieve documents from many different computers attached to a communications network.

Document processing Text processing, including creating, storing, revising, distributing, and duplicating documents. Document processing differs from data processing in that it is primarily concerned with text, or words.

Document processing cycle The steps followed in documents processing: input, processing, storage, output, reproduction, and distribution.

Dot-matrix printer A character printer that uses rods to form characters on paper.

Download The process of extracting data from a mainframe and sending it to an attached microcomputer.

Dual systems method *See* parallel systems method.

Dumb terminals Terminals that do not have much intelligence or memory; dumb terminals rely on the intelligence and storage of the computer system to which they are attached.

Duplication process A subset of reprographic processes that includes stencil, spirit, and offset duplication methods.

Dynamic data exchange (DDE) Automatically links data in one document with another so that manual updating is not necessary.

EBCDIC Extended Binary Coded Decimal Interchange Code. An eight-bit computer code commonly used on IBM computer systems.

Economic order quantity (EOQ) An inventory management tool that identifies the most economic amount to order for each item of inventory.

EDI See electronic data interchange.

EDP (electronic data processing) auditors Individuals responsible for auditing an electronic information system.

EEOC *See* Equal Employment Opportunity Commission.

Effectiveness Doing the right things right.

Efficiency Doing things right.

Electronic blackboard A system that captures the writing on a chalkboard in digital form and uses the telephone system to transmit the data to television screens or other electronic blackboards at remote locations.

Electronic conferencing Systems that permit many participants to engage in one- and two-way communications without actually having to travel to a common site. Also called *teleconferencing.*

Electronic controls Controls that use electronic measures to prevent or identify threats, for example motion sensors, heat sensors, and humidity sensors, log-on IDs, and passwords.

Electronic data interchange (EDI) Bilateral information systems that allow two organizations to exchange information electronically. Typically, EDI links an organization to its customers or suppliers.

Electronic mail (E-mail) Allows users to read, edit, forward, send, and store messages using word processing and mailing software on a computer.

Electronic mail system Any system for transmitting messages electronically rather than in hard-copy form. Electronic mail may include transmissions of text by facsimile, teletype, intelligent copier, or any other device that transmits text electronically on a network. A popular form of electronic mail systems is a computer-based system that provides for the transmission of short messages between stations on a computer network.

Electronic market systems Multilateral information systems that allow two or more organizations to share data about products, services, and prices; for example, the electronic version of the Official Airlines Guide that allows sellers (the airlines) to share flight information and prices with buyers and other sellers.

Electronic meeting systems Interactive computer-based communications systems that are designed to help groups organize ideas, build consensus, and make effective decisions in meetings.

E-mail software Electronic mail software packages.

Embedding Using information systems to support basic operations (e.g., using computer chips in microwave ovens and automobiles).

Employee evaluation information system A human resource system that tracks past and current employee performance.

Employee information system A human resource system that maintains information about employees.

Employee profile A part of an employee information system. Usually contains personal and organization-related information.

Employee relations information systems Information systems that help human resource personnel help employees in such ways as smoothing employee moves and relocations, assisting troubled employees with counseling, and providing legal assistance and child care services to employees.

Employee training and development system A human resource system that contains information on the planning and management of training and development programs.

Emulation The process of making a microcomputer look like a terminal on a mainframe or minicomputer network.

Emulation board A special expansion board that is added to a microcomputer to allow it to look like a mainframe or minicomputer terminal.

Emulation software The software required by an emulation board to make a microcomputer look like a mainframe or minicomputer terminal.

Encryption Encoding data so that it cannot be read or used without the decryption key.

End-of-file checks Code inserted in programs that reduces the possibility that reports are generated before all records are processed.

Ends/means (E/M) analysis A method of determining management information requirements. Ends-means analysis uses effectiveness criteria to define outputs and specifies efficiency criteria for processes used to generate outputs.

Enterprisewide information management The process of leadership in planning, organizing, implementing, and controlling information resources to meet organizational goals.

Enterprisewide networking Internetworking an entire organization so that different types of existing networks can exchange data.

Entity A conceptual representation of an object, such as a person, place, or thing.

EOQ *See* economic order quantity.

Equal Employment Opportunity Commission The federal commission that monitors compliance with equal employment opportunity laws.

Equal employment opportunity regulations Laws designed to ensure that minorities, women, older workers, veterans, and the handicapped are treated fairly when it comes to the hiring, retention, and promotion of employees.

Equipment operator An MIS professional who works in the computer room performing tasks such as mounting tapes and disk packs, putting paper into printers, and running the computer console.

Erasable optical disk systems Storage systems that permit users to write, read, and alter the data contained on optical storage media.

Error message A brief message generated by the computer that notifies the user that a mistake has been made.

Exception report A report that provides information to a manager that highlights results from a particular operation that have exceeded or not met the expected standard for the organization.

Expert systems Systems that combine the knowledge of experts on a particular subject into a set of procedures that software can execute when faced with an appropriate problem. *See also* artificial intelligence.

Explanation subsystem A component of an expert system that explains the procedures followed to reach a decision so that a user can understand how the decision was reached.

External modem A separate device that is attached to the serial port of a CPU to handle analog communications.

External view A subset of data elements in a database that is used by an application programmer, an application program, or a user. *See also* subschema.

Facsimile (fax) An optical scanner that reduces text or graphic images recorded on paper to electrical impulses that can be transmitted to compatible facsimile devices over a telephone or communications network.

Factory firm Quadrant of the McFarlan-McKenney Information Systems Grid in which a firm's current portfolio of information systems supports strategic goals but its future plans for information technology are not strategic.

Factory local area network (LAN) A communications network that captures data about the production process by connecting different input devices found on a factory floor.

Fax *See* facsimile.

Fax/modem board A board that can be inserted into the bus of a microcomputer system that provides some of the facsimile functions of a facsimile machine.

Feasibility study The phase in the system development life cycle in which a brief analysis and design is conducted to determine if a feasible solution to the defined problem exists.

Field A logical collection of characters that represents a basic unit of information such as a name. Also called *data element.*

Field locking A data-handling method that permits more than one person to access a field at the same time but only allows one of them to make a change to the field.

File A collection of records all of the same type.

File locking A data-handling method that permits only one person at a time to update a file.

File management software Software that allows a user to create, maintain, and access a single file of information.

File server A dedicated computer system, attached to a network, that controls the network and manages access to one or more disk drives shared by the workstations on the network.

File structure The way in which records are organized and stored on magnetic media.

Financial accounting information systems Information systems that maintain and report information about the numerous financial and accounting systems of an organization, including the traditional accounting system, budgeting, cash management, pensions, investments, plant assets, auditing, taxes, and credit.

Financial accounting system The system that supports the accounting function within an organization.

Financial condition analysis system An accounting system that provides management with a variety of measures on the financial soundness of the organization.

Financial modeling software Specialized software that allows a financial manager to build financial models and manipulate those models to simulate various business scenarios.

Firmware Computer programs stored in the form of electrical circuitry on ROM chips.

First-generation languages The lowest-level machine languages, written in binary representation.

Fixed asset system An accounting subsystem that maintains records of equipment, property, and other long-term assets an organization owns.

Fixed disk *See* Hard drive.

Floppy diskettes A flexible, magnetic storage medium used on floppy drives.

Floppy drives A direct access storage device that reads and stores data on floppy diskettes.

Fonts Sets of printable characters that vary in style, size, and spacing.

Forecasting Using mathematical calculations and statistical models to predict future events.

Forecasting software Software that lets you predict future events using one or more statistical procedures.

Foreground task The task that a user is actively performing on a computer.

Formatted Describes a hard disk or floppy diskette that has been initialized and is ready to store information.

FORTRAN FORmula TRANslator. A third-generation language used extensively in the development of scientific application programs.

4GL *See* fourth-generation languages.

Fourth-generation languages (4GL) Easy-to-use programming languages that allow relatively naive users to retrieve, manipulate, and analyze data.

Freeware Software available free of charge, often through bulletin boards. Also called public domain software.

Front-end processor A dedicated processor that performs specialized tasks, such as handling communications to relieve the main processor of that work. In client/server networks, the term is used to refer to a workstation on the network that provides data entry, validates data, formats and displays data, and performs operations on the data received from the back-end processor, such as sorting and calculating.

Full-duplex transmission A transmission mode that permits the simultaneous transmission of messages in both directions on a communications channel.

Functional organization A means of organizing office tasks that permits the centralization of some management tasks, such as training of office workers and the standardization of equipment, while distributing office personnel to the individual departments.

Gateway The hardware and/or software needed to link one network to a different network.

General ledger system An accounting subsystem that manages an organization's general ledger accounts.

Gigabyte (GB) A billion characters or bytes.

GIGO (garbage in, garbage out) Refers to the importance of ensuring the accuracy of input into computer systems.

Glass plasma screen A black and orange screen used on some terminals.

Government reporting and compliance information systems Systems that maintain records and produce reports required by governmental laws and regulations, including affirmative action and equal employment opportunity regulations.

Graphical user interface (GUI) An operating environment that uses pictures, symbols, or menu selections to represent computer commands.

Graphical word processor Word processing software that also has some desktop publishing functions.

Graphics software A software program that allows a user to manipulate, create, and/or display data in the form of a graph, chart, or image.

Group decision support systems (GDSS) An interactive computer-based system that facilitates the solution of unstructured problems by a set of decision makers working together in a group.

Groupware Software that electronically links people who work together so that they can share group-related information, such as documents, calendars, messages, and schedules.

GUI (pronounced *gooey*) *See* graphical user interface.

Hackers People (also called crackers) who illegally gain access to the computer systems or networks of others.

Hacking Sometimes called cracking because the person cracks the log-in codes and sequences of a system to gain unauthorized entry into a computer system or network. *See* hacker.

Half-duplex transmission A transmission mode that permits the transmission of messages in both directions on a communication channel but only one way at a time.

Hard cards Hard drives on an add-in or expansion card that can be connected to the computer system by inserting the card in an empty slot of a microcomputer's motherboard.

Hard drive A magnetic disk storage device used for secondary storage of data.

Hardware Computer equipment, such as disk drives, screens, keyboards, modems, and scanners.

Hash total A total that doesn't make any real sense but allows the data entry operator to find out if the operator has omitted a source document, entered one twice, or entered an incorrect value.

Hashing algorithm A special calculation performed on a record's primary key to determine its physical location on a disk when a random access file structure is used.

Heuristics Rules of thumb that offer procedures or outlines for seeking solutions.

Hierarchical database A database structure that organizes records into a hierarchy of relationships arranged logically in an inverted tree pattern. Each data element is related only to one element above it in the hierarchy.

Horizontally compatible software A set of compatible software that uses common menus and prompts and can easily share files with the other application programs in the set.

Host A mainframe computer system in a wide area network.

Hot keys Simple combinations of one or two keys that allow the user to suspend the operation of one program and move to another program.

Hotline A phone service that allows a user to talk directly to a technician regarding installation or operation problems that may arise with a computer system.

Hot site A disaster recovery plan that uses an identical computer facility located elsewhere that is already loaded with appropriate software so that an organization can be up and running within a day or two of a disaster.

HRIS software *See* human resource information system software.

Hub A device that connects many workstations to a network.

Human resource information systems Provide managers with information to improve the quality of their human resource decisions and support the human resource management function.

Human resource information system software Computer software that provides the information required to support one or more functions within the human resources department of an organization.

Human resource management The function within an organization responsible for the acquisition and effective use of employees.

Image management software Software designed to manage the storage and retrieval of images, for example, engineering and architectural drawings, using optical disk storage media. The software also maintains controls over changes made to drawings and distributes the drawings to users with PCs on a LAN.

Imaging systems Two major types of systems are image digitizers and optical recognition systems. Image digitizers convert photographs, charts, and other illustrative materials to a series of dots and transfer those dots in magnetic form to disk or main memory. Images of text cannot be manipulated by word processors unless the images are converted back into number and letter form. That conversion is the job of optical character recognition systems.

Impact printer A printer that uses a print element that strikes the page.

Implementation The phase in the system development life cycle in which program coding, testing, and documentation occur.

Import To copy data from one computer file for use in another program.

Incrementalizing A decision-making strategy in which the decision maker takes small steps away from the existing state toward a desired state.

Index A table that shows the storage location of a record.

Indexed sequential access method (ISAM) A method of storing records sequentially on disk that builds an index to show the storage locations so that the records can be retrieved directly.

Industrial espionage The theft of organizational data by competitors.

Industry-specific software Software programs tailored to the problems and needs of a particular industry, such as construction, accounting, and health care.

Inference engine The "central processing unit" of an expert system that conducts a dialogue with a user, asking for information and applying the response.

Informating Providing computing support for decision-making processes; for example, using spreadsheets and analytical tools.

Information Data that have been processed and that have meaning.

Information center An MIS unit that specializes in providing application development consulting, technical support, and training to users.

Information management Managing information as an important organizational resource.

Information system A system that converts data into information.

Information utilities Companies that provide a variety of information services, such as on-line databases, to organizations or individuals that subscribe to their service.

In-house programs Computer programs developed and written by application programmers who are employed in the data processing department of an organization.

Ink-jet printer A printer that forms characters by spraying ink on the paper.

Input Data that are entered into a computer system.

Input-bound When a computer system must stop because its input devices cannot keep up with the rest of the system.

Input controls *See* data validation.

Input device Devices that permit you to enter data into a computer system; for example, a keyboard, mouse, or scanner.

Inquiry information system A system that collects, records, and manages customer inquiries so that they can be analyzed by management and followed up by sales personnel.

Intangible benefit A benefit of an information system that cannot be measured in dollar savings, such as improved customer goodwill or employee morale.

Integrated marketing software Software that combines programs designed for salesperson support, sales management, or customer support. The combined programs may be capable of integrating not only with each other but also with the organization's financial accounting database.

Integrated Services Digital Network (ISDN) A communications service that encodes voice, data, facsimile, image, and video communications digitally so that they can be transmitted through a single set of standardized interfaces.

Integrated software A set of compatible software that allows the user to switch between applications, such as word processing and spreadsheet, with menu selections rather than by changing diskettes.

Intelligence The first phase in the decision-making process in which the decision maker searches for conditions calling for a decision, such as a problem or opportunity.

Intelligent copier Computer-driven devices capable of communicating with computers or with other intelligent copiers to store, transmit, and produce documents electronically.

Intelligent terminal A smart terminal, often a microcomputer, that stores and processes data without host assistance.

Interactive processing A type of real-time processing in which the user interacts with the computer through on-line terminals.

Interactive voice response systems Enhancements to voice messaging systems. Interactive systems allow callers to respond to voice menu choices and obtain information, products, or services automatically.

Interface The link between either a user or a program and the computer. Also a connection between two or more systems or subsystems.

Internal memory Random access memory (RAM) used to store data and programs for processing; also called primary memory and main memory.

Internal modem A device that handles digital/analog signal conversion and is placed on a board that fits inside a microcomputer.

Internal rate of return (IRR) A financial calculation used by management to determine whether the organization will make a better return on its money by acquiring an asset or by investing in something else.

Internal view A view of a database taken by the systems programmer, who is concerned with the actual organization and placement of the data elements on the storage media; a physical, or hardware, view of a database.

Interorganizational information systems (IOS) Information systems that permit an employee of one organization to allocate resources and initiate business processes in another organization directly; for example, electronic data interchange and electronic market systems. These systems provide electronic links between different organizations to streamline business processes.

Inventory information systems Subsystems of the financial accounting system that provide information about inventory levels, stockout conditions, stock receipts, stock issues, stock damage, and the location and distribution of stock within the organization.

Inventory management and control systems Systems that use information from operational inventory information systems, such as the shipping and receiving systems, purchasing systems, and order entry systems, to assist managers in controlling inventory levels, costs, and availability.

Inventory method *See* cut-over method.

Investment The phase in information technological change in which a decision is made to invest in a new information technology such as office automation. Also called project initiation.

Investment management An accounting system that assists management in overseeing an organization's investments in stocks, bonds, and other securities.

I/O-bound When a computer system must wait because its input and/or output devices cannot keep up with its processing.

I/O channels Co-processors that help the CPU handle input and output tasks.

I/O management programs Special operating system programs that assign input and output resources to programs and manage the transfer of data between main memory and devices such as disk drives, tape drives, and printers.

IOS *See* interorganizational information systems.

IOS facilitator Provides the information utility or the network that allows the exchange of information among IOS participants.

IRR *See* internal rate of return.

ISAM *See* indexed sequential access.

ISDN *See* Integrated Services Digital Network.

JIT *See* just-in-time system.

Job A group of identical positions in an organization.

Job analysis and design information systems Systems that describe the jobs needed in an organization and the qualities of the workers needed to fill those jobs. Major outputs of the systems are job descriptions and job specifications.

Job description Specifies the purpose, duties, and responsibilities of each job and the conditions and performance standards under which those duties and responsibilities must be carried out.

Job management programs Programs that select, initiate, terminate, and schedule jobs that need to be processed in a way that maximizes the efficiency of a computer system.

Job-order production A production method in which a product is produced in a batch when it is requested and according to the specifications of the particular request.

Job specification Describes the skills, knowledge, experience, and other personal characteristics required of workers for the positions described in a job description.

Jukebox storage Optical-disk storage devices that permit you to access many optical disks from a stack of disks; used for mass storage of data.

Just-in-time (JIT) system An approach to production that performs operations only as required by the production schedule and sets inventory levels to meet only current production requirements.

KB *See* kilobytes.

Kernel The required and most frequently used part of an operating system which is always available in main memory. *See also* supervisory programs.

Keyed in Entered into a computer system with a keyboard.

Key-to-disk A terminal with a keyboard that allows an operator to enter data onto a magnetic disk.

Key-to-tape A terminal with a keyboard that allows an operator to enter data onto a magnetic tape.

Kilobyte (KB) One thousand characters.

Knowledge acquisition subsystem The component of an expert system that lets new rules be added to or deleted from the knowledge base.

Knowledge base The component of an expert system that contains the information and the rules of thumb that the expert system uses to make decisions.

Knowledge engineer An MIS professional who works with an expert to build the knowledge base of an expert system.

Labor relations information systems Information systems that track employee grievances and disciplinary actions.

LAN *See* local area network.

Language translator Translates application programs written in BASIC, COBOL, and other programming languages into machine language so the computer system can process them.

Laptop Short for laptop computer system; a microcomputer system that is small enough to fit on your lap.

Laser printer A printer that prints a whole page at once and is often used when drawings, photographs, and graphic images need to be reproduced with high quality or in color, when the number of pages to be printed is large, or when quality and speed are important.

LCD *See* liquid crystal display.

Leading A managerial function that involves directing and motivating employees to achieve the organization's goals.

Leased telephone line A dedicated communications circuit leased from a telephone company. Telephone lines are normally leased when high-speed transmissions or frequent data communications are needed.

Line printers Printers that print whole lines of a document at a time.

Liquid crystal display (LCD) A flat, lightweight screen display often used on laptop, notebook, and palmtop computer systems.

Local area network (LAN) An interconnected group of intelligent microcomputers or terminals within a small geographic location.

Location transparency A feature of a distributed system in which users submit a request to the computer system without being concerned with where the data are or where the processing will take place.

Logical data dictionary A document that contains the names and descriptions of all the data elements to be developed in an information system. A logical data dictionary provides a list of data elements. This list is later refined in the development of a detailed data dictionary that records information about the physical characteristics of the data.

Logical data-flow diagram An analysis tool that graphically depicts the system, its procedures, and the flow of information throughout the system.

Logical file A collection of logically grouped records. The records may not be stored contiguously or together on a storage medium.

Logical record A collection of logically grouped data elements. The data elements for any record may not be stored contiguously or together on a storage medium.

Low-cost leadership A competitive strategy that concentrates on reducing costs or improving productivity without incurring additional costs.

Machine bureaucracy A type of organizational structure that has a clearly defined hierarchy of authority, centralized power for decision making, and formal communications throughout the organization.

Machine language Lowest-level programming language, in which instructions are written in binary representation that the electronic circuits in the CPU can interpret and execute.

Machine vision An application of artificial intelligence in robotics that allows the robot to "see" images electronically.

Macroinstruction A single instruction that invokes a group of assembly-language instructions.

Magnetic-ink character recognition (MICR) readers Scanning devices that read characters printed in magnetic ink.

Magnetic storage media Media, such as tapes, diskettes, and hard disks, that store data in magnetic form.

Magnetic tape A magnetic storage medium in the form of plastic tape.

Magnetic tape drive A secondary storage device, used for sequential storage, that uses magnetic tape as its storage medium.

Mainframe computer systems Large computer systems, often occupying a whole room, that are usually larger in size and power than minicomputer and microcomputer systems but smaller in size and power than supercomputers.

Main memory *See* internal memory.

Maintenance The process of changing and enhancing a system once it has been implemented.

Maintenance fee A yearly fee that is paid to receive software updates and upgrades.

Maintenance programmer An MIS professional who modifies or makes corrections to existing programs.

Make-or-buy decision The choice faced by an organization to create an application or to purchase a commercial software package.

Management control The phase in information technological change in which the organization recognizes the importance of technology and introduces precise controls over systems development and implementation. Phase in which transfer of technology to other organizational units begins.

Manufacturing and production information systems Computer systems that provide the data necessary to plan, organize, operate, monitor, control, and otherwise manage production systems for an organization.

Manufacturing resource planning (MRP-II) software Software that extends a production information system to finance, marketing, and other functional areas to provide integrated data for material requirements planning, shop-floor control, inventory management, and capacity planning.

Manufacturing system All the activities necessary to ensure production. Such activities include evaluating sites for production; planning, developing, and maintaining production facilities; and setting production goals.

Mapping software Software, also called *geographic information systems software,* that allows you to arrange or place data from a database onto a map of a country, region, state, city, county, or even city street. Some packages come with their own prepackaged data. More sophisticated packages offer customizable maps and are bundled with high-end databases.

Marketing concept Catering to the needs and wants of customers as a primary organizational motivation. *See also* marketing orientation.

Marketing function A broad range of activities that identify current and potential customers; determine their needs and wants; plan and develop products and services to meet those wants; and price, advertise, promote, and deliver those products and services.

Marketing information system An information system that collects and processes data to support the major activities of the marketing function within an organization.

Marketing mix The combination of products, services, advertising, promotion, price, and product delivery methods offered to an organization's customers.

Marketing orientation An approach in which an organization concentrates on meeting customer needs and wants in all facets of the business, including planning, developing, producing, and distributing the organization's products and services.

Marketing research The process of gathering and analyzing data to identify product and service trends, target markets and customer preferences and satisfaction, and estimate market share.

Marketing research information systems Information systems used by marketing personnel to collect and analyze data about such topics as an organization's market, customers, products, and sales regions.

Market-skimming pricing A pricing tactic by which a firm enters a market with a unique product at a high price until a competing product becomes available.

Market specialization A competitive strategy that concentrates on specializing in a particular market or finding a niche for a product.

Mark-sense readers Scanners that read special optical marks.

Mass production A production method that produces a good or service in a standardized fashion using assembly-line methods.

Master production schedule The schedule of overall production requirements for an organization for a specific period of time.

Material requirements planning (MRP) The process of identifying stock that must be purchased to meet a production schedule and then automatically creating purchase orders with the appropriate order quantities and lead times.

Material selection programs (MSP) Programs that aid the engineer in choosing materials for the product under design.

Maximizing A decision-making strategy in which the decision maker makes the decision that maximizes the desired outcome.

MB *See* megabyte.

Media mix The types of advertising media that are used to promote an organization's products or services.

Megabyte (MB) One million characters.

Megahertz (MHz) A measure of the clock speed of a computer system.

Member record In a network database structure, one of two types of records found in a set. A member record is owned by another record.

Memory aid A feature of a decision support system that allows a decision maker to preserve intermediate results for future use or that reminds the decision maker to take certain actions at a particular time.

Memory board A type of add-in or expansion board that contains additional random-access memory.

Menu List of on-screen programming options from which the user can make a selection.

Mesh topology A network configuration that provides more than one path between nodes on the network.

Message switching A type of channel mode in which the connection between the sender and receiver is not kept open unless there are messages to send.

Metadata Data about data.

Methodology A set of methods, rules, and procedures to be applied.

MICR *See* magnetic-ink character recognition readers.

Microcomputer systems Desktop or personal computing systems that are usually smaller in size and power than minicomputer and mainframe computer systems.

Microfiche A sheet of film that stores reduced images of documents.

Microfilm A roll of film that stores reduced images of documents.

Micrographics The process of reducing text found on paper documents to a fraction of its size and storing these text images on film.

Microprocessor A single chip containing the basic elements of a CPU: the control unit, the arithmetic unit, and the logic unit.

Microwave transmission A mode of transmission that sends large amounts of voice and data messages in microwave form from dish to dish.

Millions of instructions per second (MIPS) The number of instructions that a computer system can process in a given time period; a measure of the power of a computer system.

Minicomputer system A mid-sized computer system that is usually smaller in size and power than mainframe computer systems but larger in size and power than microcomputer systems.

MIPS *See* millions of instructions per second.

Model-based analysis Decision support tools, such as a spreadsheet, that allow a decision maker to design a model that incorporates rules and assumptions about a particular business situation.

Modem MOdulator/DEModulator. A communications device that converts signals from analog to digital and vice versa.

Monitor *See* display screen.

Motherboard The basic board of a computer system; often the board on which the CPU chip is placed or that contains the slots to which expansion boards are connected.

Mouse A handheld input device connected to a computer terminal with a wire that lets you enter data or commands without a keyboard. The mouse may use a roller in its base, and the movement of the roller sends signals to the terminal that are converted into computer commands.

MRP *See* material requirements planning.

MRP-II *See* manufacturing resource planning.

MSP *See* material selection programs.

Multidrop network A network configuration where a number of devices are connected to a single host channel.

Multimedia systems A set of hardware and software tools for presenting information in many forms, such as data, text, images, live or taped video, and live or taped audio. Multimedia systems permit you to merge these information types into a presentation or file that can be accessed by users in any order they choose.

Multiplexer A device on a communications network that accepts data from more than one slow-speed terminal and combines them for transmission across a higher-speed transmission channel.

Multiprocessing A computer system that has more than one central processing unit and uses the CPUs to process more than one program simultaneously.

Multiprocessing operating system An operating system that can run on a multiprocessing computer system.

Multiprogramming An operating system that partitions, or divides, main memory so that more than one program and its data can be available for processing.

Multitasking operating system An operating system that allows a user to perform more than one task, or application, at a time.

Multiuser operating system An operating system that allows more than one user to access a computer system at the same time.

Natural language A query and programming language that has commands that are very similar to ordinary English.

Natural-language processing Programming computers to understand language.

Near–letter-quality printers Dot-matrix printers that simulate letter-quality output by making multiple print passes on each line or by using many rods to form the characters.

Negative entropy The process of providing ongoing maintenance to insure that a system operates effectively.

Net present value (NPV) The current value of cash that will be spent or received at some future time.

Network control program (NCP) The software used in IBM networks to offload telecommunications processing to a front-end processor.

Network database A type of database structure that supports many-to-many relationships and has multiple points of entry because any data element or record can be related to many other data elements.

Network interface card (NIC) An adapter that connects workstations and servers to a local area network.

Network operating system (NOS) A set of programs some of which reside on the file server and some on each workstation. A NOS allows you to install network devices and application software, analyze and diagnose network problems and usage, manage file, print, and other servers, and manage and route messages on the network.

NIC *See* network interface card.

Node A record in a hierarchical database structure. In communications, a node is a computer-controlled switching center.

Nonprocedural language A programming language that allows the user or programmer to identify what task is to be accomplished without concentrating on how to accomplish the task. *See also* fourth-generation languages.

NOS *See* network operating system.

Notebook Short for notebook microcomputer system.

Notebook computer A computer system that is approximately the size and shape of a notebook.

NPV *See* net present value.

Object An element that includes both data and the methods or processes that act on those data.

Object code A compiled or assembled program of executable machine instructions.

Object-oriented database (OODB) A database that stores and manages objects.

Object-oriented programming (OOP) Using an object-oriented language to develop programs that create and use objects to perform information processing tasks.

Occupational Safety and Health Administration (OSHA) A federal agency that monitors compliance with laws that pertain to the health and safety of employees in the workplace.

OCR *See* optical character recognition.

Office automation Automating and integrating office tasks through technology.

Office automation software Software that combines word processing, spreadsheet, file management, electronic mail, and desktop organization functions into integrated packages for use by secretaries and executives.

Office of the future The merging of technologies into an integrated information system to support office work; the paperless office.

Offload The process of removing responsibility for processing certain tasks, such as communications, from a computer so that it can process more data.

OLTP *See* on-line transaction processing.

On-line database An electronic library that specializes in a topic, such as medical information, legal information, stock market information, and so on.

On-line help feature Onscreen definitions of commands and suggestions for how to use the commands.

On-line immediate update A processing mode in which transactions that are entered locally update the central database on a real-time basis or as they occur.

On-line transaction processing (OLTP) When a computer system immediately processes each transaction entered.

On-line transaction processing with batch update A computer system that immediately processes data at a local level. These local data later update a central database in batch mode.

On-line transaction processing with immediate update *See* on-line transaction processing.

OODB *See* object-oriented database.

OOP *See* object-oriented programming.

Open system A system that operates in an external environment and that needs to receive feedback from that environment to change and to continue to exist.

Operating environment The method by which a user interacts with an operating system. Examples of such methods include entering commands from the keyboard or selecting a screen symbol that is converted to a command.

Operating system A set of programs that manages and controls computer resources, including the CPU, peripherals, main memory and secondary storage.

Operational financial accounting information systems A classification of financial information systems that provide supervisory-level management with the routine, repetitive information required for day-to-day operations.

Operational system An information system that monitors and reports on the day-to-day activities of the firm.

Operations documentation Systems documentation, such as system flowcharts, that documents how the system operates.

Operations manager An MIS professional responsible for scheduling programs to run, seeing that output is distributed, and supervising data entry personnel and equipment operators.

Optical character readers Scanning devices that convert characters from hard-copy documents into characters readable by a computer system.

Optical character recognition (OCR) A method by which hand, typed, or printed characters are converted from hard copy into characters readable by a computer system.

Optical disks A direct access storage medium that is written to or read by laser light beams instead of magnetic methods; used as the storage medium for CD-ROM drives.

Optical mark recognition A technology that uses scanning devices to read marks placed in certain locations, such as marks made on a multiple-choice answer sheet.

Optical scanner A device that optically scans characters, images, or marks and generates their digital representations.

Order entry system *See* sales order processing system.

Organizing A managerial function that involves deciding how to use the resources available to achieve the goals of an organization.

OSHA *See* Occupational Safety and Health Administration.

Output Information obtained from a computer system; examples include hard-copy documents and screen displays.

Output-bound When a computer system must stop because its output devices cannot keep up with the rest of the system.

Output devices Devices that permit you to extract data from a computer system; examples include a computer screen and printer.

Outsourcing Contracting with external production resources for phases of the production process.

Overlay area A specially allocated area of main memory where transient programs reside.

Owner record In a network database structure, one of two types of records found in a set. An owner record owns one or more member records.

Packet switching A type of channel mode in which messages are divided into packets, or blocks, that can then be transmitted across several different channels and reassembled at the destination.

Page printers Printers that print whole pages of documents at one time, usually using a laser printing process.

Palmtop Short for palmtop computer systems; computer systems that are small enough to fit in your palm. *See* personal digital assistant.

Paperless office An office in which hard copy is rarely produced or processed.

Paradigm A problem-solving model that an expert system uses to perform a process, such as diagnosis of a medical condition.

Parallel processing A computer system that has more than one central processing unit and uses the CPUs to complete several tasks for a single program simultaneously.

Parallel systems method A method of conversion in which both the old and the new systems are operated simultaneously until the new system works well.

Parent record In a hierarchical database structure, one of two types of records. A parent record owns children records.

Parity bit A bit added to each byte for checking purposes.

Partitioned database A means of distributing a database by dividing it into segments that are then distributed to either a functional unit or a geographical location to support local processing requirements.

Pascal A third-generation programming language.

Payback period The time it takes for an asset to either generate increased revenues or to decrease operating expenses to match the amount of money invested in the asset.

Pay grades A classification of jobs into categories based on pay.

PBX *See* private branch exchange.

PCN *See* personal communications network.

PDA *See* personal digital assistant.

Penetration pricing A pricing tactic that offers lower prices for a product or service than the competition in an effort to gain a larger market share.

Performance appraisal A formal review of an employee that is conducted on a regular basis.

Performance management information systems Systems that provide employee performance appraisal and employee productivity information to human resource managers.

Peripherals Devices located next to or outside of the CPU; examples include keyboards, display screens, printers, disk drives, and mice.

Personal analysis A type of database access that allows the user to access corporate data and to use a high-level language to analyze this information.

Personal communications network (PCN) A cellular system that uses radio waves to create short-range networks for transmitting voice and data messages to inexpensive, handheld communication devices.

Personal digital assistant (PDA) An evolving variety of palmtop computer systems, including pen-based computers, electronic clipboards, pocket organizers, and other special function devices.

Personal financial management software Financial management software for small companies or personal use.

Personal information managers (PIMs) A largely undefined class of software that has a file management core and other desktop organizing functions, such as calendars, phone lists, task lists, and so on.

Personnel capacity planning That part of rough-cut capacity planning that estimates the numbers and types of workers, supervisors, and managers needed to meet the master production plan.

Personnel file A file that contains personal and organizational information about employees.

Phased method A method of conversion in which the new system is phased in as the old system is phased out.

Physical controls Controls that use conventional, physical protection measures, such as door locks, keyboard locks, fire doors, and sump pumps.

Physical file A collection of records actually grouped together or contiguously on a disk track. A physical file may contain the records of more than one logical file.

Physical record A collection of data elements grouped together or contiguously on a disk. A physical record may contain the data elements of more than one logical record.

Physical view *See* internal view.

Pilot systems method A method of conversion in which a new system is introduced into a small part of the organization so that it can be evaluated and modified before being introduced to other users.

PIM *See* personal information managers.

Planning A managerial function that requires evaluating the organization's resources and environment to establish a set of organizational goals.

Platform A level or family of computer hardware. For example, a minicomputer is a platform; so is an 80386 microcomputer system.

Platters The individual, polished metal disks in a disk pack.

Plotters Printers that use ink pens to draw maps, charts, and special graphs.

Point-of-sale (POS) systems Computer systems used by salesclerks and others to record a sale at the counter or wherever the sale is completed; examples include the cash registers used at fast-food stores, department stores, and supermarkets.

Point-to-point network A network configuration with direct connections between the host and each device on the network.

Portable documents Documents that can be read and printed by another user *exactly* like the original regardless of the software the other person is using.

Position The tasks performed by one worker.

Position control systems Systems designed to identify each position in the organization, the job title within which the position is classified, and the employee currently assigned to the position.

Position information systems A system that identifies each position in an organization, the job category in which the position is classified, and the employee currently assigned to the position.

Position inventory A list of positions by job category, by department, by task content, or by job requirements.

Presentation graphics software Graphics software that allows the user to enhance standard graphs and charts with features such as sequencing, colors and shades, special print functions, and transition effects.

Primary key A unique identifier for a record.

Primary storage The main memory of a computer system that stores the data and programs to be processed; *See* internal memory.

Printing terminals Computer terminals that usually do not have screens but include a keyboard and a printer to permit the user to enter data into and gain information from a computer system.

Print server Usually a microcomputer with more than one printer attached to it that controls access to and manages those printing resources on a network.

Private branch exchange (PBX) A computer system that provides for the switching of telephone signals, both voice and data, on a company's premises.

Problem definition The phase in the system development life cycle in which the nature and the scope of the problem is determined.

Procedural languages Third-generation languages that require the programmer to provide detailed instructions about each step, and the exact order in which the steps must occur, in order to accomplish a task.

Process controls Programming code that ensures that computer processes are completed accurately; for example, exception reports and end-of-file checks.

Process positioning The span of production processes an organization decides to perform for any given product or product line. Also called vertical integration.

Product differentation A competitive strategy that concentrates on adding value or unique features to a product to improve its image, quality, or service.

Production schedule A schedule that allocates the use of specific production facilities for the production of finished goods to meet the master production schedule.

Production systems Subsystems of manufacturing systems that focus on acquiring and tracking raw materials, scheduling production resources, designing and testing products, and producing production schedules.

Product planning and development information system A marketing system that processes information about consumer preferences to create a set of specifications for developing a product or service.

Product pricing information systems A marketing system that helps to establish an optimum price for a product or service based upon production costs, competing product prices, and desired profit margins.

Professional bureaucracy A type of organizational structure that consists of specialists who have control over their own work.

Program code Program instructions.

Programmable read-only memory (PROM) A form of ROM that can be programmed with special equipment.

Programming language Instructions that can be interpreted into commands that a computer can process. *See also* BASIC, COBOL, FORTRAN, Pascal, and fourth-generation language.

Project initiation *See* investment.

Project management software Allows users to plan, schedule, track, and manage the resources associated with a project.

Project manager An MIS professional who supervises programmers and analysts working on a systems development project.

PROM *See* programmable read-only memory.

Prompts Helpful hints that appear on the screen and indicate what the user should do next.

Proprietary operating systems Operating systems designed to work only on a particular manufacturer's computer equipment.

Prospect files Files of sales leads used by an organization's sales force.

Prospect information system A marketing system that captures and processes information about potential customers.

Protocol converter A communications device that translates signals from one dissimilar device or network to another.

Prototype A model of an information system created with advanced development tools.

Prototyping An abbreviated system development life cycle that uses advanced development tools to create a prototype system in a very short period of time.

Public domain software *See* freeware.

Purchase order processing system An accounting subsystem that processes purchase orders and tracks information on the delivery status of items ordered.

Quality assurance Procedures, such as validation, testing, documentation, and backup and recovery, that help ensure that data is accurate, consistent, and reliable.

Quality control software Computer software that uses statistical analysis to determine variances in the production of a good or service.

Query language A set of commands through which users can update, ask questions, and retrieve data from computer files.

RAM *See* random access memory.

RAM resident software Programs that are placed in RAM for immediate use.

Random access memory (RAM) A type of memory in which data is stored in addressable locations so that the data can be accessed directly without having to move sequentially through all the data stored; random access memory is volatile.

Read-only memory (ROM) Computer memory that can only be read, not written to or changed. Programs stored in ROM are not lost when power is shut off.

Receiving information systems Computer systems that identify anticipated delivery dates for goods on order and record when they have been received.

Record A collection of logically grouped data elements.

Record count A procedure to help ensure that all source documents have been entered and that no source document has been entered more than once. The procedure involves counting the source documents entered into a computer system by hand and comparing that count with the count obtained from the computer system.

Record locking A data-handling method that allows only one person at a time to update a record.

Record set In a network database structure, the way in which the relationship between an owner record and a member record is determined.

Recruiting information system A system that collects and processes information about unfilled positions, the duties of those positions, and the skills and preferences of employees and candidates who may be interested in the unfilled positions.

Reengineering The reanalysis and streamlining of business processes to achieve productivity improvements.

Relational database A database structure in which all data elements in the database are viewed as simple tables that can be linked together through common data elements.

Reorder-level system A system that uses predefined levels of inventory to make certain that production materials are ordered in time to arrive when needed by the production process.

Replicated database A means of distributing a database by copying it and then sending the copy to either a functional unit or a geographical location to support local processing requirements.

Report generator A tool that allows the user to generate reports from data quickly and easily.

Report writer *See* report generator.

Repository managers System software that manages an organization's data repository.

Reprographics The process of reproducing multiple copies of a document.

Request for proposal (RFP) A document outlining major information system requirements that is distributed to vendors that are then asked to respond with a proposal.

Request for quotation (RFQ) A request for bids or quotations from vendors for information system components.

Requirements document The blueprint or definition of requirements used as a basis for designing a new information system.

Resident Loaded and available in main memory.

Resident programs Programs that have been loaded into main memory and are available for immediate use.

Response time The total time it takes for a command to be sent to a host and to receive a reply.

Restart/recovery systems Tools that restart a system or a database and recover any lost data in the event of a failure.

Retention schedule A schedule for the destruction of documents that is used to avoid destroying important documents before their legal or operational time periods are over.

RFP *See* request for proposal.

RFQ *See* request for quotation.

Ring topology A form of multidrop network configuration that has cabling between all of the devices and is designed to pass messages through failed workstations.

Risk A potential monetary loss to an organization.

Robotics An application of artificial intelligence that builds machines with onboard computers that can be programmed to perform specialized tasks, such as cutting, drilling, painting, and welding.

ROM *See* read-only memory.

Root record The top parent record in a hierarchical database structure.

Rotational delay The time it takes for a location on a disk track to rotate underneath the read/write heads so that data can be written to or read from the location.

Rough-cut capacity planning Provides an overall estimate of capacity needs based on information from the master production schedule.

Safety stock The amount of extra stock maintained in case shipments are delayed, some stock items are defective, or some other foul-up occurs.

Sales forecasting information systems Systems that assist management in predicting future sales of an organization. The forecasts may include sales for the industry as a whole, for the entire organization, for each product or service, or for a new product or service.

Sales management information system A marketing system that can be used to develop reports analyzing sales activities such as sales volume by salesperson and by territory.

Sales management software Software that helps the sales manager manage the sales function. For example, the software may help to assess the productivity of the sales force; the fertileness of sales territories; and the success of products by salesperson, territory, and customer type.

Sales order processing system An accounting subsystem that records sales orders, provides the documents that fill those orders, maintains inventory levels, and bills the customers. Also called *order entry system.*

SASD *See* sequential access storage devices.

Satisficing A decision-making method in which the decision maker will terminate his or her search as soon as a satisfactory alternative is found.

Scanners The general term for those devices that are able to convert text or images for use on computer systems; special scanners read and convert magnetic-ink characters, optical marks, bar codes, text, optical characters, and images.

Schema Also called the conceptual or logical view of a database. Includes all the data elements in the databases and how these elements logically relate to each other. This is the view used by the DBA.

Screen *See* display screen.

SDI *See* selective dissemination of information.

Search parameters A value or range of values in one or more fields that is used to select records.

Secondary keys A field other than the primary key that is used to search and to sort a file.

Secondary storage Auxiliary memory; examples include magnetic tape, magnetic disk, and optical disk.

Second-generation languages Assembler languages. *See also* assembly language.

Sector A subdivision of a track on a floppy or hard disk.

Security software A type of systems software that provides a variety of tools to shield a system or database from unauthorized access.

Seek time The time that it takes for the read/write heads to move to the track to which data is written or from which data is retrieved.

Selective dissemination of information (SDI) The use of search software to tailor an information service to provide the subscriber with automatic updates whenever anything new is published on a particular topic of interest.

Sequence check A processing control used to prevent certain processing from occurring on data out of order.

Sequential access A method of storing records sequentially on a magnetic tape or disk.

Sequential access storage devices (SASD) Devices that only permit the storage and retrieval of data in sequential order; for example, tape drives.

Service bureau A computer service organization that provides information services that range from full-scale support for applications, such as accounts receivable or payroll, to data entry and output distribution.

Shareware Relatively inexpensive software packages that are often produced by individuals and distributed through electronic bulletin boards.

Shop-floor data collection systems Input devices that capture data about the production process as it occurs.

Silicon chip A small electronic element made of silicon used for memory, processing, and other tasks; examples include the CPU chip and memory chips.

SIMM memory board A small board containing random access memory chips; the boards are placed in special slots to connect to the CPU of a computer system.

Simple structure A type of organizational structure that has little or no technology in place, a small support staff and management hierarchy, and unspecialized, interchangeable operating jobs.

Simplex transmission A communications transmission mode that sends a message only one way.

Single-tasking operating system An operating system that allows only one program to run at a time.

Single-user operating system An operating system that allows only one user at a time to access the computer.

Site licensing agreement An agreement that allows an organization to pay a flat fee for a software package that can be used on many workstations.

Site planning information systems These systems use a variety of internal and external sources to gather and analyze both quantitative and qualitative data useful to site planners. For example, the systems may collect information about the availability and cost of trained or experienced labor, the degree to which labor is unionized, the availability and cost of transportation for raw materials and finished goods, the availability of suitable sites, the cost of land, the proximity of raw materials suppliers and finished goods customers, the availability and costs of power, the rate of property and income taxation, community attitudes, and the quality of community services.

Skills inventory A system that contains information about every employee's work experiences and preferences, special skills and proficiencies, test scores, and interests.

Slave processor Another term for co-processor.

Slide-show feature A graphics program feature that permits the timed and sequenced display of graphs or images on a display screen.

Smart terminals *See* intelligent terminal.

SMDR *See* Station Message Detail Recording software.

Software Detailed instructions or programs that make computer hardware apply itself to a particular problem.

Software controls Program code used in information systems to prevent, identify, or recover from errors, unauthorized access, and other threats; for example, data validation and process controls.

Software house A company that specializes in writing software packages that are used by other organizations to support information processing needs.

Software piracy The unauthorized copying of a copyrighted program.

Source code Program instructions that are written in a high-level language that must be converted into machine language.

Spreadsheet software A software package that is frequently used to solve financial problems presented in columns and formerly computed by hand with a calculator.

SQL *See* Structured Query Language.

SQL server A software package used on a LAN to provide faster and more reliable performance of a networked database system. Also called a backend processor.

Stage assessment A process of determining the stage to which data processing has evolved within an organization so that the mix of application development opportunities and data processing management needs required for the next stage can be determined.

Stagnation A slowdown in implementation or underutilization of information systems and resources.

Stagnation A A form of stagnation that results from significant cost overruns, poor project management, and unanticipated technological problems and that indefinitely delays the evolution of new information technology.

Stagnation B A form of stagnation that results from premature controls causing failure to learn how to use new technology.

Stagnation C A form of stagnation that inhibits the transfer of technology into other organizational units.

Standalone packages Software packages that function independently and are not part of a family of related packages.

Standard generalized markup language (SGML) Provides standard rules and procedures for describing document formatting features. In other words, SGML codes documents by structure so that they can be exchanged for use with other software.

Star topology A point-to-point network configuration that has a separate cable running between each component and the file server or host.

Station Message Detail Recording (SMDR) software Software that provides an organization with detailed reports of telephone usage and costs for each department.

Statistical software Software that enables a computer to perform statistical analysis, such as chi-square and regression analysis.

Status access A database access method that allows the user menu-driven, read-only access to corporate data.

Store and forward The ability to store a communications message and release it at a later time when either a channel becomes available or the receiver demands the stored messages.

Strategic accounting and financial information systems Accounting and financial information systems that are used by top-level management to plan and set goals for an organization.

Strategic firm A firm in which both the current and planned applications of information technology support strategic business goals and objectives.

Strategic planning system An information system that is future oriented, predictive, and supports an organization's strategic planning process.

Structured Query Language (SQL) A set of English-like commands that have become standard language for accessing data contained in a database management system.

Structured walkthrough An exercise in which peers review the work of an analyst or programmer in an effort to identify errors and improve the work performed during the systems development life cycle.

Subschema Consists of a subset of data elements in a database that are used by an application programmer, an application program, or a user. Also called the external or local view of a database.

Subsystem A part of a system that performs specialized tasks related to the overall objectives of the total system.

Succession planning information systems Systems designed to assist human resource personnel in planning for the replacements of key organizational personnel, including identifying replacement employees and insuring appropriate training and experience for these employees.

Summary report A report that provides information to a manager on important totals, averages, key data, and abstracts on the activities of the organization.

Supercomputers The largest, most powerful computer systems made; often used by military, scientific, and government agencies to process huge volumes of data quickly.

Supermicrocomputer systems High-end microcomputer systems that often challenge minicomputer systems in size and power.

Superminicomputer systems High-end minicomputer systems that often challenge mainframe computer systems in size and power.

Supervisory programs The portion of the operating system that must be resident in main memory.

Support firm A firm in which current applications of information technology and planned applications are not critical to the achievement of strategic business goals and objectives.

Switched telephone line A method of transmission in which the route over which a telephone message travels between the sender and receiver is established every time a call is placed.

Symmetric multiprocessing Using multiple CPUs; one CPU acts as the controller of the others and assigns any CPU any application task. The main CPU also provides control over I/O tasks.

Synchronous transmission A transmission mode in which many characters are blocked together and sent as a single transmission. The block is preceded and followed by several bits of communications information that ensure that the block is transmitted correctly.

System A collection of people, machines, and methods organized to accomplish a set of specific tasks.

System prompt A character, symbol, or combination of the two that tells the user that the computer system is waiting to receive a command.

Systems analysis The phase in the systems development life cycle in which the current system is studied in order to understand how the system works and to determine the scope of the problems that exist.

Systems analyst An MIS professional responsible for the analysis of the current business system, its organization, procedures, work flow, information requirements, and problems.

Systems design The phase in the systems development life cycle in which the specifications of a new system are developed.

Systems design documentation All of the specifications, including report design, screen design, file layouts, program logic, and operational procedures, that are used to develop the new system.

Systems development The process of identifying an information need and developing an information system to satisfy that need.

Systems development methodology A set of procedures that conform to the systems development life cycle and that identify what events and activities should occur, what order they should occur in, and what tools will be used.

Systems evaluation The process of MIS professionals examining hardware and software alternatives to support specific information systems requirements.

Systems feedback Information about the status of an information system or about the activities performed by an information system.

Systems programmers The programmers who write systems software and maintain the operating systems environment.

Systems software A group of software packages that manage the hardware resources of a computer system.

Systems utility programs Programs that handle repetitive tasks and that operating systems users find useful.

Tactical accounting and financial information systems Accounting and financial information systems that provide information in a summary fashion to help middle-level managers allocate an organization's resources.

Tactical system An information system that provides middle-level managers with information they need to monitor and control the allocation of resources. Designed to generate a variety of reports, including summary reports, exception reports, and ad hoc reports.

Tangible benefits The savings or profits of an information system that can be measured in dollars.

Tap A simple device that attaches the short cable from a terminal to the main network cable.

Tape drives Sequential access storage devices; a type of secondary storage device.

Task switching The process of moving between a background task and a foreground task when more than one application is running on a computer.

Technology assessment information systems Systems that identify new technologies and assess them for their strategic advantage. They may include CD-ROM databases, traditional library resources, and on-line databases.

Technology learning and adaptation The phase in information technological change in which users learn how to use technology for tasks beyond those initially planned.

Telecommunications Electronically transmitting voice and/or data from one computer to another.

Telecommunications access program Special system software on a mainframe communications network that manages the network resources, handles the transfer of messages between the host's main memory and the remote devices, and interfaces the operating system to the network.

Telecommunications system A group of devices connected to a communications channel that can send and receive messages to and from each other.

Telecommuting Using a communications system to transmit and receive information between the office and the home.

Teleconferencing systems Systems that permit many participants to engage in one- and two-way communications without actually having to travel to a single site.

Telemarketing software Provides computer support for identifying customers and calling them from disk-based telephone directories or from customer files maintained on a database.

Telemarketing systems A marketing system that uses the telephone, often coupled with computer support, to sell products or services.

Telephone tag A situation that occurs when two people who wish to contact each other by telephone repeatedly miss each other's phone calls.

Teleprocessing monitor A software package that controls communications between a database and remote terminals.

Template A partially completed spreadsheet table or form that can be reused and completed as required.

Terabyte (TB) A trillion characters or bytes.

Terminal controller A device used in some communication networks to connect many terminals to a single line. Also called cluster control units.

Testing The phase in the system development life cycle in which the system inputs, processes, and outputs are tested to make sure they work correctly.

Third-generation languages High-level, procedural languages, used to develop application programs. *See also* BASIC, COBOL, FORTRAN and Pascal.

Third-party software vendor A firm that develops software that can be used to supplement or replace a similar function performed by another software package.

Threat People, actions, events, or other situations that could trigger losses.

Timesharing Providing computer services to many users simultaneously while providing rapid response to each. The user pays only for the services that are used.

Timeslicing A CPU management method in which each user's application is allocated one or more fixed amounts of CPU time. When a user's time slice has expired, the operating system directs the CPU to work on another user's program instructions and the most recent user moves to the end of the line to await another slice.

Toll fraud The act of defrauding telephone companies out of long-distance toll charges, including using slugs instead of real coins and obtaining illegal access to an organization's telephone lines and selling that access to others.

Tools Hardware and software used during the system development life cycle.

Topologies A method or methods by which devices on the network are connected; how a network is configured.

Total quality control (TQC) A commitment to the fabrication of quality products with an emphasis on preventing defects and placing responsibility for quality control at every point in the production process.

TQC *See* total quality control.

Trackball A type of pointing device; often used with notebook computer systems.

Tracks The concentric circles on a disk or diskette on which data are stored.

Training software Computer-based training packages, including management training software, sales training software, microcomputer training software, and word processing training software.

Transaction-processing information systems Operational-level information systems that process a large volume of transactions in a routine and repetitive manner.

Transfer time The time it takes for the read/write heads to read data from a location on a disk and place that data in main memory.

Transformation Using information technology to change the way in which you do business.

Transient programs The components of the operating system that are kept on a direct access storage device, such as a hard disk, so that they may be transferred to main memory quickly when needed.

Trusted systems Systems in which database data are restricted to authorized personnel.

Turnaround firm A firm in which past applications of information technology are not critical to achieving strategic business goals, but future plans do support the achievement of business strategy.

Tutorial software Software packages that teach a user something, such as the commands and features of another software package.

Uninterruptable power supply (UPS) A battery system that keeps a computer system powered up in the event of a power failure or brownout.

Universal Product Code (UPC) A bar-code standard adopted by the grocery industry.

Update To add, change, or delete information to keep it current and accurate.

Update policy A service offered by software vendors that usually provides users of registered software the opportunity to obtain the most recent version of their software free or at reduced prices.

Update transparency A feature of a distributed system by which users can update data within the system without being concerned with where the data is or where the processing will take place.

Upload The process of sending data from a microcomputer to the host to which it is attached.

UPS *See* uninterruptable power supply.

User computer analyst An information system professional who trains and provides consulting assistance to users who are developing decision support systems.

User-developed systems Information systems that are developed by users, sometimes with the assistance of MIS professionals.

User documentation Documentation that provides users with the training they need to understand and use the new system.

User-friendly When a software package has features that make it easy to use.

User group An affiliation of people who share common interests and problem-solving techniques for specific computer hardware or software.

User training specialist A person responsible for training the user to use a new system.

Value activities The distinct activities a company must perform to do business. Value activities include primary activities and support activities.

Value-added networks (VANs) Communication organizations such as Telenet or Tymnet that may lease channels from other common carriers, add services such as packet switching, electronic mail, and protocol conversion to the leased channels, then re-lease the channels to others.

Value analysis A method of justifying a decision support system that focuses on the benefits of the system rather than on the costs.

Value chain A depiction of the value activities that are linked together to create, distribute, and maintain products and services. The primary activities of the value chain include inbound logistics, operations, outbound logistics, marketing, and service.

Value system The larger system of activities within which the value chain of an industry works. The value system includes the value chains of suppliers, of the firm, of the channels through which the firm distributes its products and services, and of the ultimate buyer.

VANs *See* value-added networks.

VDT *See* video display terminal.

Vertical accounting software Commercial accounting software designed for the unique concerns and problems of firms in specific industries.

Vertical integration The span of production processes an organization decides to perform for any given product or product line. Also called process positioning.

Vertically compatible software Software that has a version for several different levels or platforms of computers.

Videoconferencing Combines both voice and television images to provide two-way conferencing between groups located at different sites.

Video display terminal (VDT) A type of screen used on a computer terminal. Also called monitor or screen. *See also* CRT, display screen.

Virtual storage A way to overcome the size limitations of main memory by swapping data or programs between main memory and a hard disk.

VMS *See* voice mail system.

Voice mail system (VMS) A commercial software package that runs on a PBX and digitizes, stores, routes, and forwards voice messages for retrieval from any telephone handset.

Voice messaging systems Voice menu systems that route a caller automatically to the correct department, person, or mailbox or receive the correct message without any operator intervention.

Voice processing systems Voice mail systems, voice messaging systems, and interactive response systems.

Voice recognition technology Sound board, microphone, and software used to convert the analog waves of sound into digital data so that they can be stored on disk, manipulated, and otherwise processed.

Vulnerabilities The flaws, problems, and conditions that make an information system open to threats.

WAN *See* wide area network.

What you see is what you get (WYSIWYG) A term associated with word processing that allows the user to preview a document on the screen as it will appear when printed.

Wide area network (WAN) A communications network that is spread out over a wide geographical area.

Widespread technology transfer The phase in information technological change in which new technology is transferred into other parts of the organization.

Wild cards Special characters, usually astersisks, that identify values in a field that can be ignored when performing a search.

Winchester drives Hard disks that are sealed in a container with the read/write heads to prevent dust, dirt, or other contaminants from damaging the data.

Window One section of a computer's multiple-section display screen, each of which can display different data or programs.

Windowing Splitting a computer's display into multiple sections with each section being able to run a different program or display different data.

Wireless local area network A local area network that doesn't use physical cabling; for example, a wireless LAN may transmit messages through radio waves or infrared waves.

Word processing software A collection of application programs that permit the user to create, edit, and print text material.

Word processing systems Systems that prepare and revise documents that are primarily composed of text. However, the documents may also contain data, images, tables, and charts.

Word size A measure of the power of a computer system; the number of bits that a system can transfer between the CPU and main memory at one time.

Workflow automation software Software that allows a user to create a program that then automates a series of actions in a work flow.

Workflow software See workflow automation software.

Workforce planning Identifying the human resources needed to meet the organizational objectives specified in the strategic plan, including forecasting the supply and demand of the required work force.

Work psychological contract When employees accept the organization's expectations for their performance.

Workstation A type of supermicrocomputer that is used by technical and professional people because they require fast, powerful computer systems with high-quality, high-resolution screens.

WORM Write once, read many times; a method of storing data permanently on optical disks so that they may be read many times, but may not be altered.

WYSIWYG *See* what you see is what you get.

Name Index

Subject Index

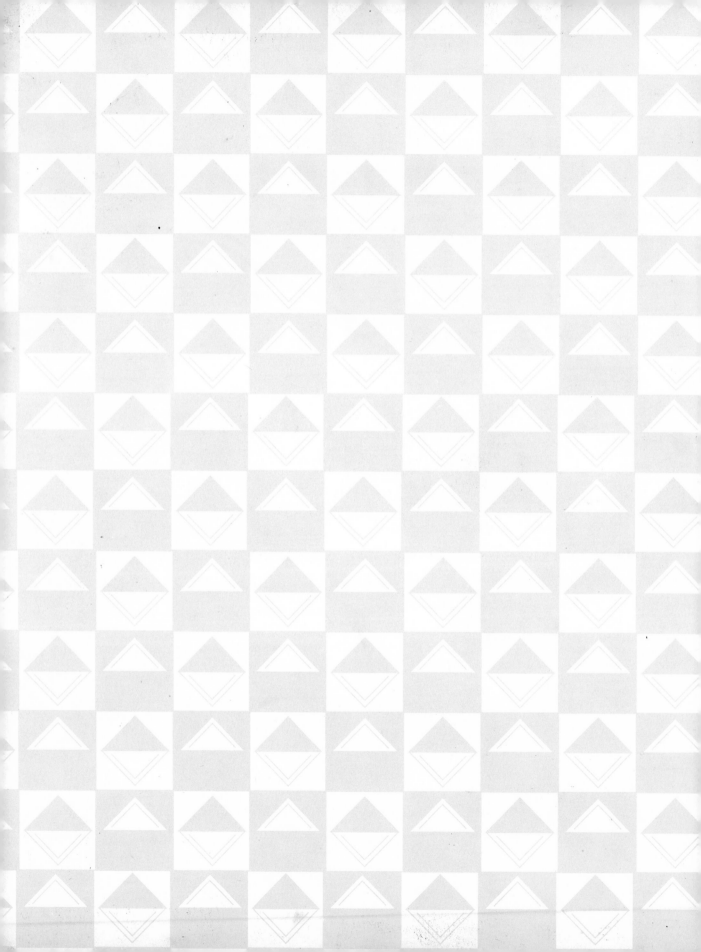